D0006351

Odessa

BLACK SEA

Danube or the
Danube

Constanta
Tulcea
Galati

Bucharest
Fuse

Brașov
Moldoveanu
2544m
FĂGĂRAȘ MTNS

Alba Iulia
Sibiu
ROMANIA
Transylvania
Craiova

Danube

Reșița
Timișoara
Arad

Kecskemét
Szeged

HUNGARY
Drava
Pécs
Balaton Lake

Graz
Klagenfurt
Maribor
Bled
SLOVENIA
Ljubljana
Trieste
Piran
Poreč
Rovinj
Istria
Pula
Krk
Cres

Varaždin
Zagreb
CROATIA
Osijek
Banja Luka

Drava
Sava

Novi Sad
Vojvodina

Belgrade
YUGOSLAVIA

Niš

Shumen
Varna
Nesebâr
Burgas

Veliko Târnovo

BULGARIA
STARA PLANINA
Plovdiv

Sofia
Musala
2925m
RODOPI MTNS
Maritsa

Skopje
MACEDONIA
Vardar

Priština
Kosovo
Bitola
Ohrid
Ohrid Lake
Prespa Lake

Çanakkal

CYCLADES
ISLANDS

AEGEAN
SEA

Lesvos

Limnos I

Xanthi

Thessaloniki

Larisa

GREECE

Athens
Piraeus
Evia

Ioannina

Patras

Tirana
ALBANIA
Durrës
Vlora
Shkodra
Drin
Skadar Lake

Bar

Corfu

IONIAN
ISLANDS

IONIAN SEA

Stretto di Otranto

Brindisi

Bari

Montenegro
Podgorica

BOSNIA-
HERCEGOVINA
Sarajevo
Mostar
Split
Brač
Hvar
Korčula
DINARIC ALPS
Dalmatia
Zadar

Dubrovnik

ADRIATIC SEA

Ancona

Pescara

Naples

TYRRHENIAN
SEA

Sicily

Palermo

Reggio di Calabria

Golfo di
Taranto

Rome
ITALY
Perugia
San Marino
Florence
Bologna
Rimini
Verona
Venice
Adige
Po
Trento
Bolzano

Udine
Rijeka
Klagenfurt
Graz
Lienz
Drau

Eastern Europe
5th edition – January 1999
First published – April 1989

Published by
Lonely Planet Publications Pty Ltd A.C.N. 005 607 983
192 Burwood Rd, Hawthorn, Victoria 3122, Australia

Lonely Planet Offices
Australia PO Box 617, Hawthorn, Victoria 3122
USA 150 Linden St, Oakland, CA 94607
UK 10a Spring Place, London NW5 3BH
France 1 rue du Dahomey, 75011 Paris

Front cover photograph
Simon Bracken, Lonely Planet Images
Images are available for licensing from Lonely Planet Images.
email: lpi@lonelyplanet.com.au

ISBN 0 86442 611 9

Printed by The Bookmaker Pty Ltd
Printed in China

Contents – Text

MACEDONIA 457

POLAND 475

ROMANIA 601

SLOVAKIA 701

4 Contents – Text

Contents – Maps

MAP LEGEND – SEE BACK PAGE

The Authors

Krzysztof Dydyński
Krzysztof updated the Poland chapter. Krzysztof was born and raised in Warsaw, Poland. Though he graduated in electronic engineering and became an assistant professor in the subject, he soon realised there's more to life than microchips. In the mid-1970s he took off to Afghanistan and India and has been back to Asia several times since. In the 1980s a newly discovered passion for Latin America took him to Colombia, where he lived for over four years and travelled throughout the continent. In search of a new incarnation, he has made Australia his home. He is the author of Lonely Planet's guides to Poland, Colombia and Venezuela.

Steve Fallon
Steve worked on the introductory chapters and updated the Slovenia chapter. Born in Boston, Massachusetts, Steve can't remember a time when he was not obsessed with travel, other cultures and languages. As a teenager he worked an assortment of jobs to finance trips to Europe and South America, and he graduated from Georgetown University with a Bachelor of Science in modern languages. The following year he taught English at the University of Silesia near Katowice, Poland. After he had worked for several years for a Gannett newspaper and obtained a master's degree in journalism, his fascination with the 'new' Asia took him to Hong Kong, where he lived and worked for 13 years for a variety of publications and was editor of *Business Traveller* magazine. In 1987, he put journalism on hold when he opened Wanderlust Books, Asia's only travel bookshop. Steve lived in Budapest for 2½ years from where he wrote Lonely Planet's guides to Hungary and Slovenia before moving to London in 1994. He has written or contributed to a number of other Lonely Planet titles.

Kate Galbraith
Kate updated the Bosnia-Hercegovina chapter. Kate fell in love with Bosnia in 1996, when she worked for a local news agency in Sarajevo. She has been astounded by the changes the city has undergone since then, from the development of inter-entity bus lines to the introduction of a Versace gallery in Sarajevo centre. Before settling back into Bosnia for Lonely Planet, she made a grand tour of Eastern Europe as a freelance writer. She suspects that she may forever be a wanderer.

Paul Hellander

Paul updated the Albania, Bulgaria, Macedonia and Yugoslavia chapters. Paul has never really stopped travelling since he was born in England to a Norwegian father and an English mother. He arrived in Australia in 1977, via Greece and 30 other countries, taught Modern Greek and trained interpreters and translators for 13 years and then threw it all away for a life as a travel writer. Paul joined Lonely Planet in 1994 and wrote LP's Greek phrasebook before being assigned to the Greece and Eastern Europe books. Paul also updated the information on Singapore for the *Singapore* city guide, *Malaysia, Singapore & Brunei* and *South-East Asia*. He was last seen heading for Israel, but can always be reached at paul@planetmail.net.

Rosemary Klaskin

Rosemary updated the Romania chapter. Born and raised in St Louis, Missouri, Rosemary also lived in San Francisco before finally settling in New York City. After 10 years as a systems analyst, she hung up her suits, took up photography, and began travelling to Europe. Her first trip to Romania was in 1993 when she went searching for the tiny German village of Banat where her father was born. She found it (though it wasn't on the map and had changed names) and became so captivated with the country she decided she must write about it. She has another book about Romania in the works.

Jon Murray

Jon updated the Hungary chapter. Jon has been writing and updating Lonely Planet guides for some years, but until now he has always travelled to hot countries (Bangladesh, Australia, Papua New Guinea, West Africa and South Africa). This research trip to Hungary was his first time in Eastern Europe, but it won't be his last. Jon lives on a bush block near Daylesford (Australia) which he shares with quite a few marsupials and far too many rabbits.

Richard Nebesky

Richard updated the Czech Republic and Slovakia chapters. Born one snowy evening in the grungy Prague suburb of Žižkov, Richard got his taste for travelling early in life when his parents dragged him away from the 'pretentious socialist paradise' of Czechoslovakia after it was invaded by the 'brotherly' Soviet troops. A stint on a campus was followed by a working trek around the ski resorts of the northern hemisphere and an over- land odyssey across south Asia. He joined Lonely Planet in 1987, and since then has been co-author of LP's *Central Europe* and *Eastern Europe* phrasebooks, the *Prague* city guide and *Czech & Slovak Republics*. Titles he's helped to update include *Central Europe*, *Eastern Europe*, *Australia*, *France*, *Indonesia*, *Russia*, *Ukraine & Belarus*, *South-East Asia* and *Thailand*.

Jeanne Oliver

Jeanne updated the Croatia chapter. Born in New Jersey, she eventually moved to New York City where she got a job at the *Village Voice* newspaper and then earned a law degree. Her legal practice was interrupted by ever more frequent trips to Central and South America, Europe, and the Middle East. Finally she took down her shingle and headed east through Africa, India and Southeast Asia before finally landing in Paris, where she is still based. She now makes her living as a travel writer, covering France and other European destinations. In 1998, Jeanne wrote the 1st edition of Lonely Planet's guide to Croatia. She can be reached in cyberspace at j-oliver@worldnet.fr.

David Stanley

David single-handedly researched and wrote the first three edi- tions of Lonely Planet's *Eastern Europe*. A native of Canada, he has spent much of the past three decades on the road, with visits to around 200 countries and territories, crossing six continents overland. David studied at the universities of Barcelona and Flo- rence, before settling down to get an honours degree in Spanish literature from the University of Guelph, Canada. His travel guidebooks for the South Pacific, Micronesia and Eastern Europe opened those areas to budget travellers for the first time, and in 1996 he wrote the 1st edition of Lonely Planet's *Cuba*.

From the Authors

Steve Fallon
Special thanks to Črtomir Šoba for his assistance in whipping the Slovenia chapter into shape and much, much more. Thanks also to Charlotte Hindle and the staff at the Lonely Planet office in London for throwing me a lifeline (in this case, a desk) when I was adrift at sea. Caroline Birch and Pat Read, who loves paprika, did that too, and it is much appreciated.

Kate Galbraith
In Sarajevo and Banja Luka, thanks to the respective tourist bureaus. In Banja Luka, thanks to Zagatha and her family for the special tour. In Mostar, *sretno* to Michael and Mladi Most, the unofficial bar/hotel/cinema/junk food restaurant. And David B, your support and history wisdom helped enormously. And finally, as always, special thanks to my wonderful family.

Paul Hellander
After an essentially hassle-free trip around a region beset with economic and political woes several persons come to mind whom I would like to thank for their insight and assistance: Graham Witt (Melbourne); Geoff Harvey of DriveAway (Sydney); Mirko Apostolov (Ohrid); Marilyn-Rath Ivanovska, Steven Nicholas, Beti Banovska (Skopje); the Belgrade Tourism Office; Kiril Levterov and Lubomir Popiordanov of Odysseia-In (Sofia); Venera Ćoćolli (Tirana); Alekos and Valentini Papadopoulos (Thessaloniki), and Demetres Dounas (Athens) for providing a home and office away from home. Finally I must thank Stella for putting up with two overseas trips in short succession. My work, as ever, is dedicated to my sons Marcus and Byron in Ioannina, Greece who may one day take inspiration from their father's peripatetic life.

Rosemary Klaskin
Many thanks to Simion Alb of the Romanian National Tourist office in New York for all his help; to Kurt Treptow of the Center for Romanian Studies in Iasi; and to Hannes, Marian, Roberto, Oana and Tim at Villa Helga in Bucharest who kept me laughing.

Richard Nebesky
Richard would like to warmly thank Luděk and Zdena Bartoš as well as Lenka and Jarda Průcha for information and help, and for making his long stay in Prague a pleasant one. Thanks also to his parents for invaluable advice and support, and to the staff at PIS, Martin Měkota, Míša Bartošová and Míťa Kulišová. *Děkuji* to the information office staff in the Czech Republic and Slovakia.

Jeanne Oliver

A special thanks to the indefatigable Mirjana Žilić of the Croatian National Tourism Office for her patient support. Zdravko Kufrin and Damir Foršek of Adriatic Travel worked hard to make sure my trip went smoothly. Marie-Rose Kordić in Rab was exceptionally hospitable and makes a respectable French wine from her Rab vineyard. Thanks to the prizewinning Stanka Kraljević in Korčula for her outstanding dedication and to Aljoša Milat for his invaluable help. Vesna Jovičić in Pula is informative, insightful and went far out of her way to extend a warm welcome. Other tourism workers whose help I appreciate include Majda Šale in Baška, Gordana Perić in Zadar, Zdravko Banović in Split, and Antonjeta-Nives Miloš and Dubravka Vrenko in Dubrovnik. *Hvala* to all.

Acknowledgements

THANKS
Many thanks to the travellers who used the last edition and wrote to us with helpful hints, useful advice and interesting anecdotes:

Damien, Charlie, Dani, Meg & Tracey, Eddie Aerts, Philip Agre, D'Albon Alexandria, Richard & Pauline Allo, R Archer, Jens Arnold, Douglas Balog, Nigel Barnes, Wayne Bartl, Kylie Beer, I Berchier, Peter Van den Berg, Faisal Bhabha, Emma Birks, Peter & Elissa Bishop, Nana Bjerg, William Bliss, Eric Boudin, Liam Branagan, Kevin Brennan, Paul Bryon, Kevin Byrne, Mary Cannon, Karen Carlsen, Richard Carlson, Dan Carteaux, Peter & Wendy Cartwright , Sophia Cathin, RC Chappell, Mark Chernoff, Pauline Clark, Melinda Clarke, Scott Cole, Lydia Conrad, Ben Cook, Alan Cooney, Susan Crandall, Meaghan Crouch, David Curby, Zelko Cvitkovic, Ake Dahllof, Tim Davey, Ashley Davies, Kara Davis, Anthony Dean, Dave Depooter, Ivo Dimitrov, Clare Doube, Aiste Drasutaviviute, Claire Duiker, Scott Eden, Anthony Elgort, John Ellis, Jennifer Escott, Cath Essex, Caroline & Martin Evans, Craig Findlay, Roger Firth, D Ross Fisher, H Fix, Mike Foale, Pietro Fratta, Giles Freeman, Edvin S Fridh, Chad Galloway, Matthias Gamrath, Georgi Georgiev, Sylvia Geosheva, Brendon Gibson, Katie Ginn, Bryan Glendon, Andrew & Julie Godfrey, Jeremy Goldman, Khrisslyn Goodman, Arron & Kirsten Goodwin, Kathryn Grose, Allon Groth, Owen Groves, Massimo Gugnoni, Jan Gunnar, Mark Gunston, Dr Nagy Attila Gyorgy, Alasdair Hamblin, Svein Hanssen, Andrew Jay Harris, Julie Hassenmiller, Estelle & Ron Haylor, Tyrell Heathcote, Andrew Henshaw, Matt Hodges, Roger Hoskens, Petr Hruska, Niamh Humphries, Charles Hunter, Rustom Irani, Poli Ivanova, Patricia Jackson, Jason Jacoby, Derek James, Peter Johnson, Hrvoje Kevic, Andrej Koloja, Roeland Krul, Hitomi Kura, Elizabeth Kuttler, Darren Langley, Gabriel Lau, Robert Lee, Debra Lee, Jeanette Lee, Miranda Legg, Allison Lippey, Malcolm Lloyd, Darren Longley, Matthias Lufkenes, Graham & Sue Lyons, Anne Magusin, Muriel Mathers, Kiyoshi Matsukawa, Claire Mattiner, Joan McAuliffe, Denise & Malcolm McDonough, Matthew Merrall, A Messmer, Melissa Michels, Simon Miller, Natasha Mimms, Dr Fergus Mitchell, Evan Morkel, Angus Morrison, Dragana & Uros Mrda, Michael Murphy, Nicole Myerson, Tara Newcombe, Eric Newman, Chris Newman, George Nicholov, John & Diana Nielsen, N Noordegraaf, Atle Nyhammer, Momo Ohta, Sally Oldham, PA O'Neil, Kathryn Orfini, D Richard Owen, Mike Pain, Alberto Perez, Julian Perry, Mark Pethick, Pat Petronio, Peter Petrov, Maria Pironkova, Marianna Pisano, Jo Ellen Powell, David Power, Mike & Shirley Powley, Chris Pratt, Garrett Prestage, Sophia Pugsley, Nicole Quek, John Reardon, Loran Jane Richardson, Mark Ricketts, Merete Ridley, April K Rinnie, Anthony Roediger, David Roland, Cornelius Rott, Elisa Ruiz, Jay Russian, Sharon Ryder, V Lobo Saar, Gwen Sanderson, Chris Santillo, Frank Schaer, Lars Bisgaard Schmidt, Aaron Schur, Mark Sentor, Frank Shaerf, Nicola Shean, Deborah Sheridan, Penelope Shortland, Mark Sidley, Dragon Simic, Dennis Simmons, Peter Sinclair, Carina Skareby, Greg Slade, Janine Smeets, Phil Smith, Magna Somers, Eve Spence, Jan Stark, Tania Stiglic, Janey Stone, Jan Sturm, Erik Swanson, Toi Chia Tan, Andrew Terlich, James Timmis, Kelic Tomislav, Erik Torch, Julie Toth, Chris Tremann, Mare Trost, Karen Turner, Michal Vallo, Rita Vergano, Kristoffer Vieth, Perry Waddell, Oliver Wagner-Seele, Kevin Wah, Simon Wake, Claire Wallder, Louise Watson, Roghieh & Henk Weijers, Jim Westminister, John Whaite, Lois Wilk, CM Willetts, Jason Williams, Graham Witt, Roger Wyatt, Jeanette Yee, JJ Zanker, Frans JL Zegers, M Ziser

This Book

Many people helped create this 5th edition of *Eastern Europe*. Among the major contributors to past editions was David Stanley who single-handedly researched and wrote the first three editions. Contributors to the 4th edition included Scott McNeely and Dani Valent.

This edition was updated by Krzysztof Dydyński, Steve Fallon, Kate Galbraith, Paul Hellander, Rosemary Klaskin, Jon Murray, Richard Nebesky and Jeanne Oliver. Mark Honan updated the Getting Around chapter.

Eastern Europe is part of Lonely Planet's Europe series, which includes *Mediterranean Europe*, *Central Europe*, *Scandinavian & Baltic Europe* and *Western Europe*. Apart from these titles Lonely Planet also produces *Europe on a shoestring*, which features 40 countries, and phrasebooks to these regions.

From the Publisher

The editing of this edition of *Eastern Europe* was coordinated by Liz Filleul and Chris Wyness, and the cartography was coordinated by Marcel Gaston and Ann Jeffree. They were very ably assisted by Janet Austin, Carolyn Bain, Vicki Beale, Rachel Black, Simon Bracken, Miriam Cannell, Bethune Carmichael, Ada Cheung, Paul Clifton, Katie Cody, Piotr Czajkowski, Tony Fankhauser, Jane Fitzpatrick, Quentin Frayne, Ronald Gallagher, Paul Harding, David Kemp, Chris Lee Ack, Dan Levin, Clay Lucas, Nicholas Lynagh-Banikoff, Craig MacKenzie, Anne Mulvaney, Mary Neighbour, Anthony Phelan, Helen Rowley, Jacqui Saunders, Andrew Tudor, Rebecca Turner, Tim Uden and Tamsin Wilson.

Foreword

ABOUT LONELY PLANET GUIDEBOOKS

The story begins with a classic travel adventure: Tony and Maureen Wheeler's 1972 journey across Europe and Asia to Australia. Useful information about the overland trail did not exist at that time, so Tony and Maureen published the first Lonely Planet guidebook to meet a growing need.

From a kitchen table, then from a tiny office in Melbourne (Australia), Lonely Planet has become the largest independent travel publisher in the world, an international company with offices in Melbourne, Oakland (USA), London (UK) and Paris (France).

Today Lonely Planet guidebooks cover the globe. There is an ever-growing list of books and there's information in a variety of forms and media. Some things haven't changed. The main aim is still to help make it possible for adventurous travellers to get out there – to explore and better understand the world.

At Lonely Planet we believe travellers can make a positive contribution to the countries they visit – if they respect their host communities and spend their money wisely. Since 1986 a percentage of the income from each book has been donated to aid projects and human rights campaigns.

Updates Lonely Planet thoroughly updates each guidebook as often as possible. This usually means there are around two years between editions, although for more unusual or more stable destinations the gap can be longer. Check the imprint page (following the colour map at the beginning of the book) for publication dates.

Between editions up-to-date information is available in two free newsletters – the paper *Planet Talk* and email *Comet* (to subscribe, contact any Lonely Planet office) – and on our Web site at www.lonelyplanet.com. The *Upgrades* section of the Web site covers a number of important and volatile destinations and is regularly updated by Lonely Planet authors. *Scoop* covers news and current affairs relevant to travellers. And, lastly, the *Thorn Tree* bulletin board, and *Postcards* section of the site carry unverified, but fascinating, reports from travellers.

Correspondence The process of creating new editions begins with the letters, postcards and emails received from travellers. This correspondence often includes suggestions, criticisms and comments about the current editions. Interesting excerpts are immediately passed on via newsletters and the Web site, and everything goes to our authors to be verified when they're researching on the road. We're keen to get more feedback from organisations or individuals who represent communities visited by travellers.

Lonely Planet gathers information for everyone who's curious about the planet – and especially for those who explore it first-hand. Through guidebooks, phrasebooks, activity guides, maps, literature, newsletters, image library, TV series and web site we act as an information exchange for a worldwide community of travellers.

Research Authors aim to gather sufficient practical information to enable travellers to make informed choices and to make the mechanics of a journey run smoothly. They also research historical and cultural background to help enrich the travel experience and allow travellers to understand and respond appropriately to cultural and environmental issues.

Authors don't stay in every hotel because that would mean spending a couple of months in each medium-sized city and, no, they don't eat at every restaurant because that would mean stretching belts beyond capacity. They do visit hotels and restaurants to check standards and prices, but feedback based on readers' direct experiences can be very helpful.

Many of our authors work undercover, others aren't so secretive. None of them accept freebies in exchange for positive write-ups. And none of our guidebooks contain any advertising.

Production Authors submit their raw manuscripts and maps to offices in Australia, USA, UK or France. Editors and cartographers – all experienced travellers themselves – then begin the process of assembling the pieces. When the book finally hits the shops some things are already out of date, we start getting feedback from readers, and the process begins again....

WARNING & REQUEST

Things change – prices go up, schedules change, good places go bad and bad places go bankrupt – nothing stays the same. So, if you find things better or worse, recently opened or long since closed, please tell us and help make the next edition even more accurate and useful. We genuinely value all the feedback we receive. Julie Young coordinates a well-travelled team that reads and acknowledges every letter, postcard and email and ensures that every morsel of information finds its way to the appropriate authors, editors and cartographers.

Everyone who writes to us will find their name in the next edition of the appropriate guidebook. They will also receive the latest issue of *Planet Talk*, our quarterly printed newsletter, or *Comet*, our monthly email newsletter. Subscriptions to both newsletters are free. The very best contributions will be rewarded with a free guidebook.

Excerpts from your correspondence may appear in new editions of Lonely Planet guidebooks, the Lonely Planet Web site, *Planet Talk* or *Comet*, so please let us know if you *don't* want your letter published or your name acknowledged.

Send all correspondence to the Lonely Planet office closest to you:

Australia: PO Box 617, Hawthorn, Victoria 3122
UK: 10A Spring Place, London NW5 3BH
USA: 150 Linden St, Oakland CA 94607
France: 1 rue du Dahomey, Paris 75011

Or email us at: talk2us@lonelyplanet.com

For news, views and updates see our web site: www.lonelyplanet.com

HOW TO USE A LONELY PLANET GUIDEBOOK

The best way to use a Lonely Planet guidebook is any way you choose. At Lonely Planet we believe the most memorable travel experiences are often those that are unexpected, and the finest discoveries are those you make yourself. Guidebooks are not intended to be used as if they provide a detailed set of infallible instructions!

Contents All Lonely Planet guidebooks follow the same format. The Facts about the Country chapters or sections give background information ranging from history to weather. Facts for the Visitor gives practical information on issues like visas and health. Getting There & Away gives a brief starting point for researching travel to and from the destination. Getting Around gives an overview of the transport options when you arrive.

The peculiar demands of each destination determine how subsequent chapters are broken up, but some things remain constant. We always start with background, then proceed to sights, places to stay, places to eat, entertainment, getting there and away, and getting around information – in that order.

Heading Hierarchy Lonely Planet headings are used in a strict hierarchical structure that can be visualised as a set of Russian dolls. Each heading (and its following text) is encompassed by any preceding heading that is higher on the hierarchical ladder.

Entry Points We do not assume guidebooks will be read from beginning to end, but that people will dip into them. The traditional entry points are the list of contents and the index. In addition, however, there is a complete list of maps and an index map illustrating map coverage.

There's also a colour map that shows highlights. These highlights are dealt with in greater detail in the Facts for the Visitor chapter, along with planning questions and suggested itineraries. Each chapter covering a geographical region begins with a locator map and another list of highlights. Once you find something of interest in a list of highlights, turn to the index.

Maps Maps play a crucial role in Lonely Planet guidebooks and include a huge amount of information. A legend is printed inside the back cover. We seek to have complete consistency between maps and text, and to have every important place in the text captured on a map. Map key numbers start in the top left corner.

Although inclusion in a guidebook usually implies a recommendation we cannot list every good place. Exclusion does not necessarily imply criticism. In fact there are reasons why we'll exclude an outstanding place – sometimes because it would be inappropriate to encourage an influx of travellers.

Introduction

No region in the world has experienced as much change in the past 10 years as Eastern Europe. When the first edition of this book appeared in April 1989, Eastern Europe was still securely locked behind the Iron Curtain – a destination primarily for the intrepid or politically motivated. Less than one year later the communist regimes of Poland, Czechoslovakia, Hungary and Romania collapsed and in October 1990 East Germany ceased to exist altogether. Bulgaria and little Albania, then one of the most isolationist nations on earth, followed suit and within two years Yugoslavia and Czechoslovakia had broken into a total of seven countries. A 'new world' had been created, one open to all for the most part, with many of the new republics making their own decisions for the first time in centuries (and, in the case of Slovenia, for the first time in history).

The very name of the region is troublesome. During the last century Europe was viewed quite differently to how it has been seen in the 20th. Until as late as 1945 there was the predominantly industrialised west at one end of the spectrum, an undeveloped, almost medieval Balkan region at the other, and in the middle, comprising what are now the nations of Austria, Germany, Switzerland, Poland, the Czech Republic, Slovakia, Hungary and Slovenia, sat the Mitteleuropa (meaning 'Middle Europe' or 'Central Europe') of Prussian rule and the Habsburg Empire. The term 'Eastern Europe' only gained currency during the more than four decades of Soviet domination of much of Central and Balkan Europe following WWII. It was a very convenient epithet for 'us' to call 'them'.

Our problem lies in the fact that about half the book covers the Balkan region, which has never been considered part of Mitteleuropa. And, bad connotations aside, from the traveller's point of view the countries of Eastern Europe still have a lot in common, and basic things like restaurants, accommodation facilities, entertainment and public transportat tend to work in similar ways throughout the region. Several countries also share, to

varying degrees, the same bureaucratic hurdles and occasional hassles.

But Eastern Europe's assets as a region far outweigh the few drawbacks. From the Baltic to the Balkans, a treasure-trove of history and natural beauty awaits you. Eastern Europe has been the source of much of what we know as western culture, especially in literature and music, and this volatile region has shaped world history. In the 20th century alone, both world wars began in Eastern Europe and it was the primary 'battlefield' in the Cold War that had existed between the east and west since 1945 and was brought to an end by the democratic revolutions of 1989.

The region's largest cities – Prague, Warsaw, Budapest – have, at various times, been important centres of European culture, and their museums, theatres, concert halls and historical sites continue to beckon. Apart from cultural legacies, there are vast forests, rugged mountains, pristine lakes, beautiful coastlines and mighty rivers just waiting to be discovered. An added benefit is cost: prices almost everywhere are much lower than those in Western Europe.

The dozen countries covered in this book are fascinating for their diversity, and to gain some understanding of the region you'll need to visit several of them. Don't spend all of your time in the capitals as you'll usually find it's much less crowded and cheaper in provincial towns. Also, the opportunity to meet local people is greater in the countryside. This is not a case of 'authentic' vs 'touristy'; a supermarket counter in, say, Budapest is as much a part of the real Hungary of today as an old village shop on the Great Plain. But life in the provinces is more redolent of times past – simpler, slower, often more friendly.

Be warned that, with inflation and systematic devaluation of the currency in certain Eastern European countries, some of the prices quoted in this book will have gone up by the time you use it. But within individual chapters, the prices of food, transport and accommodation should remain relative to one another, so you'll soon be able to judge how much you'll need to spend.

One thing is certain – travel in Eastern Europe will never be better than it is right now. Prague has been well and truly 'discovered'; the next 'hot' destination is anyone's guess – Kraków, perhaps? What's beyond doubt is that the longer you put off your trip, the larger the crowds will be and the higher prices will go.

There's lots in this region waiting to be discovered and enjoyed, and this newly updated edition of *Eastern Europe* will guide you. All you have to do is go.

Facts about the Region

HISTORY

To put Eastern Europe's incredibly complex history into perspective, it's useful to draw several lines across the map, the most important one representing the Danube River. The Danube formed the northern boundary of the Roman Empire for about 500 years, with an extension into Dacia (Romania) from 106 to 271 AD. When the empire was split into eastern and western halves in 395, another line was drawn from Aquincum (Budapest) in a southerly direction to northern Africa. Even today this line more or less corresponds to the division between the Orthodox and Roman Catholic churches. The western Roman Empire collapsed in 476, but Byzantium survived until Constantinople was taken by the Turks in 1453.

The so-called Great Migrations changed the ethnic character of Eastern Europe. Long before the arrival of the Romans, the Slavs had lived north of the Carpathian Mountains between the Vistula and Dnieper rivers. To the west were the Celts and later the Germans. Beginning in the 6th century, Slavic tribes moved south of the Carpathians and by the 9th century had occupied everything east of an imaginary line running from Berlin south to the Adriatic. In the south they expanded as far as Greece. The Daco-Roman population of present-day Romania was large enough to absorb the newcomers, and the original inhabitants of Albania – the Illyrians – also survived. The Slavs began farming and lived in democratically governed communities.

In 896 the Magyars (Hungarians) swept in from the east and occupied the Carpathian Basin. Hungarian horsemen spread terror throughout Europe with raids as far as the Pyrenees but were defeated by the Germans at Augsburg in 955. The Hungarians carved out a great empire in central Europe extending south to Belgrade and east across Transylvania. In 1018 they annexed Slovakia and in 1102 they acquired Croatia.

Around the turn of the first millennium most of the peoples of Eastern Europe accepted Christianity. Feudal states began to form in Bohemia, Bulgaria, Croatia, Hungary,

Lithuania, Poland and Serbia. After the Mongol invasion of 1241, many cities were fortified.

The German-speaking Saxon communities of Slovakia and Transylvania date from the 13th century when Germans were invited into Hungary and Poland to form a buffer against renewed Mongol attacks from the east. The continual German *Drang nach Osten* – the 'drive to the east' that began at this time – was slowed by the defeat of the Teutonic Knights by a combined Polish-Lithuanian army at Grunwald (near Olsztyn in present-day Poland) in 1410. In 1701 Berlin became the capital of Prussia and a renewed eastward expansion under Frederick the Great (ruled 1740-86) culminated in the complete partition of Poland by 1795.

Turkish expansion into Europe was made easier by rivalry between the Catholic states (Austria, Hungary, Venice) and the Orthodox ones (Bulgaria, Byzantium, Serbia). The defeat of Serbia at the Battle of Kosovo in 1389 opened the Balkans' floodgates. The Hungarians managed to halt the Turkish advance temporarily at Belgrade in 1456, but in 1526 they were defeated at Mohács. The Turks spread as far north as the southern foothills of the Carpathians, drawing another line across the map of Europe. In 1529 they unsuccessfully laid siege to Vienna and in 1532 they were stopped again at Kőszeg in Hungary. Much of Hungary remained under Ottoman rule until the defeat of the second Turkish siege of Vienna in 1683. A combined Christian army liberated Buda in 1686 and by 1699 the Turks had been driven from all of Hungary.

After the fall of Hungary to the Turks, the Austrian Habsburg dynasty assumed the thrones of Hungary, Bohemia and Croatia. In 1620 the Catholic Habsburgs tightened their grip on Bohemia and then expanded into Hungary and the Balkans as the Ottoman Empire declined. From 1703 to 1711 Hungarians led by Transylvanian Duke Ferenc Rákóczi II fought an unsuccessful war of independence against the Habsburgs. During the 18th and 19th centuries the Habsburgs controlled a vast empire stretching from southern Poland to Bosnia-Hercegovina and eastward as far as Transylvania. In 1867 Austria and Hungary agreed to share control of the region through what was known as the Dual Monarchy.

Poland had been erased from the map of Europe by the partitions of 1722, 1793 and 1795. Prussia and Russia took most of Poland for themselves, with Austria receiving a small slice in the south-west. It's not hard to understand why the Poles sided with Napoleon, whose entry into Eastern Europe in 1806 marked the beginning of a transition from autocratic feudalism to modern, bourgeois capitalism. Although Napoleon's defeat at Waterloo in 1815 allowed the Prussians and Habsburgs to reimpose their rule, unsuccessful liberal-democratic revolutions spread throughout central Europe in 1848.

In the Balkans the uprisings and wars against the Ottomans continued into the 20th century. In 1876 the Bulgarians rose against the Turks, leading to the Russo-Turkish War of 1877 and Bulgarian autonomy in 1878. Bulgarian independence followed in 1908. Romania and Serbia declared complete independence from the Turks in 1878, and the Habsburgs occupied Bosnia-Hercegovina in the same year, annexing it outright in 1908. Macedonia and Albania remained under Turkish rule until the First Balkan War (1912). After the Second Balkan War (1913), Serbia and Greece divided Macedonia between themselves. Bulgarian dissatisfaction with this result led to further fighting during both world wars.

The World Wars

In 1914 Habsburg and Russian imperial ambitions clashed in the Balkans, and all of Europe was drawn into a catastrophic war. By November 1918, war weariness led to the collapse of autocracies in Russia, Austria-Hungary, Bulgaria and Germany as sailors mutinied and troops abandoned the fronts. The end of WWI saw the restoration of Poland as a nation and the creation of Czechoslovakia and Yugoslavia.

Although the new borders were supposed to follow ethnic boundaries, northern and western Bohemia went to Czechoslovakia despite those areas' large German populations. Similarly, the Ukrainians of south-east Poland, the Hungarians of Slovakia, Transylvania and Vojvodina, and the Albanians of Kosovo all became minorities in foreign countries bordering their motherlands. In part this situation contributed to the outbreak (and savagery) of WWII.

After 1933 Eastern Europe suffered constant Nazi aggression and violence. In September 1938, Britain and France allowed the dismemberment of Czechoslovakia at the Munich Conference, ending the possibility of any effective military resistance to the Nazis in the east. Bulgaria, Hungary and Romania soon fell in line behind Germany. Uncertain of western backing after Munich, the Soviet Union signed a nonaggression pact with Germany on 23 August 1939 to buy time. When Poland resisted Hitler's demands it was promptly invaded, sparking off WWII. Yugoslavia and the USSR suffered a similar fate in 1941.

Hitler's program of military expansion led to the near destruction of Germany. In February 1943 the German 6th Army capitulated at Stalingrad, and by May 1945 the Soviets had captured Berlin. At the 1943 Teheran Conference, Churchill had proposed another front from the Middle East through the Balkans to forestall a Soviet advance into Europe, but this was rejected, and the Allied landings on D-day (6 June 1944) were in France. At the Yalta Conference in February 1945, Churchill, Roosevelt and Stalin agreed on 'spheres of influence' in Europe. The Potsdam Conference of August 1945 divided Germany and Berlin into four occupied zones. The borders of Poland and the USSR moved westward and those Germans who had not already fled eastern Prussia, Pomerania and Silesia were deported.

The Cold War

With the arrival of Soviet troops in Bulgaria, East Germany, Hungary and Romania, communist-led governments took over from Nazi or monarcho-fascist regimes. Communist partisans took control in Yugoslavia and Albania. Czechoslovakia continued as a democratic coalition until the Communist Party took full control in March 1948. The events in Czechoslovakia set off a chain reaction as the frustrated western allies decided it was time to consolidate the areas under their control against further communist advances. In June 1948, a new currency linked to the US dollar was introduced into the three western sectors of Berlin to facilitate postwar reconstruction.

This created a tremendous problem for East Germany, where nationalisation of the economy had just begun. Fearing an uncontrollable black market, the Soviet army closed the surface transit routes between West Germany and West Berlin a few days later. The air routes remained open and for 11 months what became known as the Berlin Airlift supplied the western zones of the city. This crisis may be seen as the beginning of the Cold War.

The lines were drawn even more precisely when NATO formed in April 1949. The Federal Republic of Germany (West Germany) was created in September, the German Democratic Republic (East Germany) in October. The Council for Mutual Economic Aid (Comecon), the dominant economic planning body in Eastern Europe until 1990, was created in the same year. The Warsaw Pact was signed in May 1955, when West Germany was admitted to NATO. Only after the 1975 Helsinki Conference on Security & Cooperation in Europe (CSCE), at which 35 governments accepted the status quo in Europe, did tensions begin to relax.

Between 1945 and 1989, the communist governments throughout Eastern Europe emphasised heavy industry and central economic planning. Agriculture was forcibly collectivised in all of the countries except Poland and Yugoslavia. In later years, East Germany, Hungary and Slovenia in Yugoslavia (and to a lesser degree Bulgaria and Czechoslovakia) were able to attain relatively respectable levels of development, while the inhabitants of Poland, Romania and the USSR suffered prolonged hardship. Well before the 1989 collapse of communism, there were popular upheavals in East Germany (1953), Hungary (1956), Czechoslovakia (1968), Poland (1956, 1970, 1976, 1981) and Romania (1987), but these were suppressed by brute force.

The Collapse of Communism

By the late 1980s the Soviet Union had fallen far behind the west in economic and technological development and, in practice, had ceased to be a superpower. In effect, Soviet leader Mikhail Gorbachev abandoned the postwar system of 'spheres of influence' and adopted a policy of nonintervention towards Eastern Europe. Thus the communist governments there could no longer count on Soviet military support (or economic bail-outs such as all-but-free oil) to remain in power. The first crack in the eastern bloc appeared in Poland in April 1989, when the communist regime agreed to legalise the independent trade union Solidarity and allow partially free elections. The Solidarity election victory in June 1989 and the appointment of non-communist Tadeusz Mazowiecki as prime minister in August were unprecedented events which were watched all across Eastern Europe.

Changes were also taking place in Hungary, which abandoned border controls with neighbouring Austria in May 1989 and cut away the electrified fence separating the two nations in September. In October the Hungarian communists relinquished their monopoly on power.

Yet the event that really signalled the end of communism in Eastern European was the destruction of the Berlin Wall on 9 November 1989. East Germans had begun flowing to the west through Hungary at the rate of 5000 a week in the summer of 1989. When the Soviet Union failed to order Hungary to halt the flow, antigovernment demonstrations began in Leipzig in September and these flared until hardliner Erich Honecker was forced to resign as East Germany's leader on 9 October. After a demonstration in East Berlin on 5 November attended by one million people, the communists opened the Wall. On 1 July 1990 the two Germanys formed an economic union and on 3 October the country was formally reunited.

The fall of the Wall had sudden repercussions in Czechoslovakia, where student demonstrations began on 17 November 1989 and culminated in the resignation of the communist government 10 days later.

On 10 November 1989 hardliner Todor Zhivkov, who had headed Bulgaria's government for the previous 35 years, was sacked.

Besides the opening of the Berlin Wall, the political event that captured world attention most dramatically was the violent overthrow of the Ceauşescu regime in Romania in December 1989, complete with the execution of Nicolae and Elena Ceauşescu by firing squad.

In the spring of 1991 a general strike in Albania forced the ruling Communist Party to form a coalition with the opposition. Free elections held the following March brought 47 years of totalitarian rule to an end.

The final act was played out in the Soviet Union itself. After an abortive military coup by communist hardliners in August 1991, the three Baltic states quickly declared their independence and in December the USSR was transformed into the 'Commonwealth of Independent States' (CIS) dominated by the Russian Federation.

These events seemed to demonstrate that state socialism had run its course. The booming prosperity of Western Europe made the collapse of uncompetitive Eastern Europe almost inevitable. Eastern European-style communism, with its forced labour, brutal suppression of basic rights and censorship, had rebuilt heavy industry after WWII, but technologically the region was falling far behind and being economically marginalised. Without the two essential ingredients of a modern society – parliamentary democracy and a market economy – further progress would have been impossible.

The fall of communism was also a result of the arms race. With their stable economies, strong national currencies and high rate of economic growth, western countries were able to increase military expenditures and modernise their forces at a rate the communist countries could only match by sacrificing consumer production. In February 1991 the Warsaw Pact was disbanded – though NATO remained intact – and in 1993 it extended its influence eastward by offering the ex-Warsaw Pact countries a cooperative arrangement called 'Partnership for Peace', which included no security guarantees.

Post-Communist Eastern Europe

The crumbling of the totalitarian regimes gave rise to a narrow nationalism right across the region, leading to the break-up of Czechoslovakia and Yugoslavia. In 1986 Serbian ideologues formulated the concept of a 'Greater Serbia', which was to assert its authority in post-Tito Yugoslavia. When Serbia unilaterally scrapped the autonomy of Kosovo Province in 1989, the other republics of Yugoslavia became alarmed and in 1990 non-communist governments were elected in Croatia and Slovenia. These republics declared their independence in 1991, leading to a brief war in Slovenia and, in Croatia, a civil war that only ended with the arrival of United Nations peacekeepers. In 1992 the European Community (now the European Union) bowed to German pressure and recognised Croatia, Slovenia and Bosnia-Hercegovina, thereby contributing to the eruption of a new war as Serbia and later Croatia snatched territory from the elected Bosnian government. In a far more civil separation, Czechoslovakia split peacefully into Slovakia and the Czech Republic at the start of 1993.

Right across Eastern Europe, ethnic intolerance has continued to be exploited by politicians short on economic solutions. Hungary is still haunted by the loss of two-thirds of its territory and half its population after WWI though it has signed a treaty with Romania, where two million ethnic Hungarians still live, renouncing all claims on Romanian territory. The nationalist disease is manifested in the official rehabilitation of prewar or wartime dictators such as Hungary's Miklós Horthy, Ion Antonescu of Romania, Slovakia's Jozef Tiso, Ante Pavelić of Croatia and Poland's Marshall Józef Pilsudski. A clutch of pretenders claim the royal thrones of Albania, Bulgaria, Romania and Serbia but have little popular support.

It's now clear that the crowds that brought about the 1989 revolutions had an unrealistic idea of life in the west. Economic restructuring and the abrupt curtailment of trade within the former Soviet bloc led to big drops in industrial output and gross domestic product, budget deficits, unemployment and declining living standards for large segments of the population. Agricultural productivity declined by 10 to 40% while corruption and crime increased. In countries where the government attempted to solve these problems by printing money, high inflation impoverished millions of people. Social benefits like guaranteed employment, nurseries, free education and medical care were slashed, and the status of national minorities made worse.

The frustration and disillusionment was expressed at the ballot box within just a few years of what became known as 'the change'; former communists were returned to power in free elections in Lithuania (1992) and Poland (1993) as well as in Ukraine, Bulgaria and Hungary (1994). In Romania, Slovakia and Yugoslavia, the old communist establishments retained power by posing as nationalists.

In recent elections, however, voters have tended to install reform-minded governments (Romania in 1996, Bulgaria in 1997, Hungary in 1998).

That Gorbachev's efforts to democratise communism turned into a movement to dismantle it should not have come as such a surprise. For all its rhetoric, the Cold War was mostly a sham that produced profits in the west and stability in the east. Now that this 'phoney war' has finally collapsed, a whole slew of regional conflicts (Bosnia, Albania, Kosovo in Yugoslavia) have erupted and these will be far more difficult to control than the predictable superpower confrontations of yesteryear. For better or worse, Eastern Europe is being remade, and the opportunity to see the process in motion makes it an exciting area to visit.

GEOGRAPHY

The Carpathian Mountains, which swing round from Romania into Slovakia, form the most important range in Central Europe. There's excellent hiking in this range, especially in Romania's Făgăraş Mountains and the Tatra Mountains of Slovakia and Poland. The Balkan Mountains are shared by Albania, Bosnia-Hercegovina, Bulgaria, Croatia, Greece, Macedonia and Yugoslavia. Musala Peak (2925m) in Bulgaria's Rila Massif is the highest in Eastern Europe. North-west of Ljubljana in Slovenia are the Julian Alps and Mt Triglav (2864m).

One of the scenic highlights of Eastern Europe is Croatia's Dalmatian coast. Here the mountains dip into the Adriatic to form a broken coastline with countless idyllic islands. The Black Sea in Bulgaria and Romania also has some excellent beaches. The Baltic coast of Poland has a beauty all of its own. The most popular – and largest – lake in Eastern Europe is Hungary's Lake Balaton.

Another important geographical feature of Eastern Europe is the Danube River, the second-largest river in Europe after the Volga. Called the 'king of European rivers' by Napoleon, the 2858km-long Danube flows through nine countries and past four capitals; some 1075km of it is in Romania and shorter stretches pass through Hungary, Croatia and Yugoslavia. To see the Danube at its best, visit the Danube Bend in Hungary or Romania's Danube Delta. The greatest river north of the Carpathians is Poland's Vistula, which passes through Kraków, Warsaw and Toruń.

Taken together, the 12 countries covered in this book make up an area of 1,166,763 sq km. Poland and Romania are by far the largest countries, while Macedonia, Albania and Slovenia are the smallest.

ECONOMY

The economies of Eastern Europe can bow be divided into two groups: prospective members of the European Union and those that have no prospect of joining that association in the foreseeable future. In the first group are the Czech Republic, Hungary, Poland and Slovenia. In the second group languish Albania, Bulgaria, Romania, Slovakia and most of former Yugoslavia.

In broad terms, those countries that now have a very real chance of joining the EU in the early years of the new millennium took painful measures of restructuring their economies in the early 1990s. Companies that were sold off by state privatisation agencies had to lay off employees in droves as archaic industrial conglomerates and trading monoliths modernised their products and management structures. Unemployment leapt from essentially zero to double-digit percentages, and inflation went almost out of control in certain countries. Worst of all, uncertainty over the future caused new forms of stress for citizens used to 'iron dinner plate' job security and welfare systems.

It was not a simple matter of rationalising out-of-date industries and directing sales away from markets in the former Soviet Union and other Eastern European countries in favour of ones in the west. Accounting principles in Eastern Europe were virtually nonexistent before 1989, ownership laws had to be drafted and banking systems modernised. Until recently something as simple as paying staff salaries meant doling out great wads of cash to thousands of employees who had to queue in front of a single teller at a town's only bank. To buy anything and everything – regardless of its size or price – meant handing over stacks of notes since cheque accounts and credit cards simply did not exist. They still don't for many in the region, though automatic teller machines are the norm nowadays in provincial Hungary and the Czech Republic.

For the more successful countries, dividends for tough decisions made earlier in the decade are finally beginning to pay off. The Czech Republic, Poland, Hungary and Slovenia are now considered 'investment grade' by international rating agencies. This means that foreign bankers and investors feel comfortable about putting their money into companies and government projects there and are willing to charge much lower rates on their loans. However, investors have become less bullish in recent years on the Czech Republic, once the darling of the developing Eastern European economies with an A-grade rating from Standard and Poor's, due to rising unemployment and bankruptcies.

Indeed, foreign investors have favoured this region, attracted by the lower wages (with the possible exception of Slovenia where, at US$10,000, the average annual wage exceeds that of Portugal), the proximity to Western European markets and, in some cases, a decent work ethic. Hungary, which started to reform its economy earlier than any other country in the region, was receiving an annual US$4 billion halfway through the decade in direct foreign investment, with the Czech Republic taking about half that amount. The outlook for Poland, which lagged behind until several years ago, is currently very positive, and foreign investment (US$1.1 billion in 1995) reached almost US$3 billion in 1997. In contrast, Romania

brought in only just over US$1 billion over the same period, Slovakia US$730 million and Bulgaria a mere US$330 million.

The money has been invested in everything from buying stakes in telecommunications firms to establishing joint-venture automobile manufacturing and assembly plants, with Germans by far the largest group of foreign investors. The Czech automobile manufacturer Škoda, for example, a household name throughout Eastern Europe and increasingly so outside the region, is now 70%-owned by Volkswagen.

These factories are producing goods not only for domestic markets but – importantly – for export. It seems ironic that Ikarus in Hungary can supply modern, competitively priced buses to cities across the USA and even Moscow, while vintage buses trundle through the streets of Budapest, Debrecen and Miskolc. Budapest may be a booming tourist destination, but the cost of renovating such a city along with upgrading the infrastructure in the rest of the Hungary is staggering.

The benefits of all this foreign money coming into Eastern Europe have not been uniform even within a single country. Much of Hungary's new production is centred in the Transdanubian region west and south of Budapest, where cities like Győr and Székesfehérvár have state-of-the-art manufacturing plants, low unemployment and a rising standard of living. But a few hours' drive across the country to north-east Hungary is like stepping back in time, with idyllic villages, peasants languidly driving their horse-drawn carriages – and the majority of town dwellers out of work with few benefits.

Travellers with *nostalgie de la boue* – those seeking out scenes and vignettes of life under the former communist regimes of Eastern Europe – will not be disappointed. There are plenty of 'rust-belt' towns with decaying, Orwellian factories in Poland and the Czech Republic, villages where unmechanised farming is common (Romania) and where shops look like something out of a 1950s-vintage black-and-white western propaganda newsreel (Slovakia). Romanian Dacias still rattle along merrily beside Trabants, with their noisy and highly pollutant two-stroke engines. But Hungarian-produced Suzuki Swifts, sleek Škodas, Polish-built Opels and Renaults assembled in Slovenia are speeding along newly opened toll roads, leaving their polluting predecessors back at the starting blocks.

PEOPLE

Eastern Europe is home to over a dozen nationalities. The Slavs – by far the largest ethnic group in Eastern Europe – are divided into three distinct groups: the West Slavs (Czechs, Poles, Slovaks and Sorbs, who live in eastern Germany), the South Slavs (Bulgarians, Croats, Macedonians, Montenegrins, Serbs and Slovenes) and the East Slavs (Belorussians, Russians and Ukrainians). The Albanians, Roma (Gypsies), Hungarians and Romanians are non-Slavic groups.

The Czech Republic, Hungary, Poland and Slovenia have largely homogeneous populations. The largest minority groups are the Albanians of Kosovo in Yugoslavia and of Macedonia; the Greeks of Albania; the Hungarians of Transylvania (Romania), Yugoslavia and Slovakia; the Serbs of Croatia and Bosnia-Hercegovina; and the Turks of Bulgaria.

In the 14th century the Jews were expelled from most of Western Europe and many settled in Poland, Hungary, Romania and Russia where they continued to speak a medieval German dialect called Yiddish. Here they suffered centuries of persecution that was only lessened by the Bolshevik Revolution in Russia and western pressure for minority rights in Poland, Romania and elsewhere after WWI. Before WWII Jews accounted for one third of the population of Warsaw, but the Holocaust and subsequent migration to Israel decimated Jewish communities throughout Europe. Today Hungary's 80,000-strong Jewish community is the largest in Eastern Europe.

Roma

The English term 'Gypsy' reflects an early belief that these people came from Egypt, though it is now known that they originated in northern India. Gypsies refer to themselves as Roma (and that is what they are hereafter called in this book) and their language as Romany. The language shares common features with Sanskrit and later Indian languages. Their westward migration began before the 10th century, and by the 14th century some groups had reached the Balkans and then central Europe. A second wave of westward Roma migration began in 1855, after the Romanian Roma were freed from serfdom by Moldavian Prince Grigore Ghica. Half a million Roma were murdered in Nazi death camps during WWII.

About half of Europe's estimated eight million Roma live in Eastern Europe, including an estimated 1.8 million in Romania, 550,000 in Bulgaria, 250,000 in Hungary, 170,000 in Yugoslavia, 150,000 in Croatia, 115,000 in the Czech Republic, 80,000 in Slovakia, 45,000 in Macedonia, 15,000 in Poland and 10,000 in Albania.

Without a homeland of their own and largely unrepresented in government, the Roma have suffered worsening living conditions, mass unemployment and official harassment since 1989. Statistically, Roma families are twice the size of non-Roma families, and are a form of collective social security common in the developing world. Unfortunately, the Roma are often subjected to extreme racism by people who would be shocked if they heard other racial or religious groups referred to in the same terms.

A 1993 citizenship law in the Czech Republic automatically turned 100,000 Czech Roma into foreigners overnight through its draconian 'Romany Clause'.

RELIGION

Tempered by decades of official disfavour and occasional outright persecution, organised religion in the east has generally been a more influential factor in both public and private life than in the more materialistic west – though that is rapidly changing. Catholicism is the main religion in the Czech Republic, Slovakia, Hungary, Poland, Croatia and Slovenia. There are large Protestant minorities in Hungary and Romania. Muslims constitute a majority in Albania and Bosnia-Hercegovina.

In 1054 the pope excommunicated the Church of Constantinople and all Orthodox churches that refused to accept the Catholic doctrine of papal infallibility. Nowadays the Orthodox faith is prevalent in Bulgaria, Romania, Macedonia and Yugoslavia, with patriarchs in Belgrade, Bucharest and Sofia, and metropolitans (equivalent to archbishops) in Prague and Warsaw. There have been many attempts to unify the Orthodox and Roman Catholic churches. Orthodox churches that have accepted papal supremacy while retaining the Orthodox liturgy are known as Uniates or Greek Catholics.

LANGUAGE

German is probably the most useful language to know in Eastern Europe (though English is definitely preferred by the young). German is widely understood by older people in the Czech Republic and western Hungary. It's also helpful along the Adriatic and Black Sea coasts, where German tourists prevail, and in western Poland. If you know French, Italian or Spanish you won't understand spoken Romanian, but you'll be able to pick up words and the meaning of simple texts.

Russian was taught in schools throughout Eastern Europe after 1945 and is despised, especially among non-Slavic people like the Hungarians and Romanians. Since the changes of 1989, however, English has been far more common, and there's always someone at major hotels and travel agencies who knows it. Many students and young professionals speak English very well and are often happy to have the chance to talk to western visitors. In the past French was widely taught in Bulgaria, Romania and Serbia. French can also be useful in Poland and Italian in Croatia and Slovenia.

Some 12 major languages are spoken in the countries covered in this book. Nine of them – Bulgarian, Croatian, Czech, Macedonian, Polish, Serbian, Slovak, Slovene and Sorbian – are Slavic languages. These languages are closely related in grammatical structure and vocabulary; if you pick up a few words in one language, you'll be surprised how close the corresponding phrases in the others are. The other major languages you'll encounter are Albanian, Hungarian and Romanian.

There are pronunciation guidelines and vocabulary for all of these languages in the Language chapter at the end of the book.

The Cyrillic alphabet used in Bulgaria, Macedonia and Yugoslavia was created in the 9th century by the missionaries Sts Cyril and Methodius of Thessaloniki. It only takes a few hours to learn this alphabet, and it's an absolute must if you're visiting these countries. Without it, you won't even be able to read the destination boards at bus and train stations.

Facts for the Visitor

HIGHLIGHTS
The Top 10
There is so much to see in Eastern Europe that compiling a list of the top 10 highlights is almost impossible. We asked the authors of *Eastern Europe* to list their personal favourites and here they are (in no particular order):

1. Budapest
2. Croatia's Dalmatian coast
3. Dubrovnik's city walls, Croatia
4. Rila Mountains in Bulgaria
5. Kraków's old town, Poland
6. Sighişoara, Romania
7. High Tatra Mountains of Poland and Slovakia
8. Prague
9. Škocjan Caves in Slovenia
10. Painted churches of Bucovina in Romania

The Bottom 10
The writers were also asked to list the 10 worst 'attractions' of the region. The results:

1. Banja Luka, Bosnia-Hercegovina
2. Bucharest
3. Nowa Huta industrial complex near Kraków
4. National Museum of History in Sofia
5. Prague at the height of the tourist season
6. Siófok on Lake Balaton in Hungary
7. U Fleků beer hall in Prague
8. Much of Bulgaria
9. Schmaltzy Hungarian Roma music
10. Service staff at most train and bus stations

PLANNING
When to Go
Any time can be the best time to visit Eastern Europe, depending on what you want to see and do. Spring (from April to mid-June) is an excellent time to visit as the days are long, the weather good, the theatres open, off-season rates apply and the locals are not yet jaded by waves of summertime visitors. The only drawback is that school outings often occur during this period, and being crowded into a hostel or train with a bunch of noisy kids is no fun.

Summer (mid-June to early September) is the ideal time for hiking and camping, the peak season for budget travellers and just about everyone else. September can be an excellent month, with autumn colours on the trees, fruit and vegetables plentiful, shoulder-season tariffs in effect again and the tourist masses home and back at work. You can still swim in the Adriatic in September, but in October most of the camping grounds close down and the days grow shorter.

From October to March it can be rather cold and dark with smog from coal-burning furnaces, though this is the peak theatre and concert season in the cities of Eastern Europe. And if you're keen on winter sports, resorts in the High Tatra Mountains and Julian Alps generally begin operating in early December and move into full swing after the New Year, closing down again when the snows begin to melt in March or even as late as April.

The Climate & When to Go sections in the individual country chapters explain what to expect and when, and the Climate Charts in Appendix I at the back of the book will help you compare different destinations.

What Kind of Trip?
Travelling Companions If you decide to travel with others, keep in mind that travel can put relationships to the test like few other experiences can. Many a long-term friendship has collapsed under the strains of constant negotiations about where to stay and eat, what to see and where to go next. But many friendships have also become closer than ever before. You won't find out until you try, but make sure you agree on itineraries and routines beforehand and try to remain flexible about everything – even in the heat of an August afternoon in Budapest. Travelling with someone else also has financial benefits as single rooms cost more per person than doubles in most countries.

If travel is a good way of testing established friendships, it's also a great way of making new ones. Hostels and camping grounds are good places to meet fellow travellers, so even if you're travelling alone, you need never be lonely.

World Heritage List

UNESCO's list of 'cultural and natural treasures of the world's heritage' includes the following places in Eastern Europe:

Albania
Ancient ruins of Butrint

Bulgaria

Boyana Church near Sofia	Madara horseman relief	Rila Monastery
Ivanovo rock-hewn churches near Ruse	Nesebâr's old city	Srebarna Nature Reserve
Kazanlâk Thracian tomb	Pirin National Park	Thracian Tomb of Svechtari

Croatia

Dubrovnik's old city	Poreč's Euphrasian Basilica	Trogir's old town
Plitvice Lakes National Park	Split's historic centre with Diocletian's Palace	

Czech Republic

Český Krumlov's historic centre	Lednice-Valtice	Pilgrimage Church of St John Nepomuk at Zelena Hora
Kutná Hora medieval silver town & Church of St Barbara	Prague's historic centre	
	Telč's old city	

Hungary

Karst caves at Aggtelek	Hollókő (traditional village)
Banks of the Danube in Budapest and the Castle District	Pannonhalma BenedictineAbbey

The Getting Around chapter has information on organised tours.

Move or Stay? 'If this is Tuesday, it must be Warsaw.' Though often ridiculed, the mad dash that crams six countries into one month does have its merits. If you've never visited Eastern Europe before, you won't know which areas you'll like, and a quick 'scouting' tour will give an overview of the options. In fact, as Eastern Europe is so culturally and physically diverse, this approach to travel can actually be recommended. A rail pass that offers unlimited travel within a set period of time is the best way to do this.

But if you know where you want to go, or find a place you like, the best advice is to stay

put for a while, discover some of the lesser known sights, make a few local friends and settle in. It's also cheaper in the long run.

Maps

Good maps are easy to come by once you're in most parts of Eastern Europe, but you might want to buy a few beforehand to plan and track your route. The maps in this book will help you get an idea of where you might want to go and will be a useful first reference when you arrive in a city. Proper road maps are essential if you're driving or cycling.

The Geocenter *Eastern Europe* map (1:2,000,000; UK£4.99) is very useful for getting an overview of the area. Freytag & Berndt, Kümmerly & Frey and Hallwag all

World Heritage List

Macedonia
Ohrid and its lake

Poland
Auschwitz concentration camp

Kraków's historic centre

Medieval town of Toruń

Castle of the Teutonic Order in Malbork

Warsaw's old city

Wieliczka salt mines near Kraków

Zamość's old city

Romania
Biertan fortified church

Bukovina painted churches

Danube Delta

Horezu Monastery

Slovakia
Aggtelek Caves and Slovakian Karst

Banská Štiavnica medieval mining centre

Spišský Hrad

Vlkolinec folk village near Ružomberok

Slovenia
Škocjan Caves

Yugoslavia
Durmitor National Park

Kotor and its gulf

Stari Ras and Sopoćani Monastery

Studenica Monastery

---

produce meticulously drawn maps to various parts of the region. Some of the best city maps are produced by Falk; RV Verlag's EuroCity series is another good bet. Tourist offices are often another good source for (usually free and fairly basic) maps.

What to Bring

It's relatively easy to find pretty much anything you need in Eastern Europe and, since you'll probably buy things as you go along, it's better to start with too little rather than too much.

A backpack is still the most popular method of carrying gear as it is convenient, especially for walking. On the down side, a backpack doesn't offer too much protection

for your valuables, the straps tend to get caught on things and some airlines may refuse to accept responsibility if the pack is damaged or tampered with.

Travelpacks (combination backpack/ shoulder bags) are very popular. The backpack straps zip away inside the pack when they are not needed, so you almost have the best of both worlds. Some packs have sophisticated shoulder-strap adjustment systems and can be used comfortably even on long hikes. Packs are always much easier to carry than a bag. Backpacks or travelpacks can be made reasonably theft-proof with small padlocks. Another alternative is a large, soft zip bag with a wide shoulder strap so it can be carried with relative ease. Forget suitcases unless you're travelling in style, but if you do take one, make sure it has wheels to allow you to drag it along behind you. Watch out on cobblestone streets, though.

As for clothing, the climate will have a bearing on what you take along. Remember that insulation works on the principle of trapped air, so several layers of thin clothing are warmer than a single thick one (and will be easier to dry). You'll also be much more flexible if the weather suddenly turns warm. Just be prepared for rain at any time of year. Bearing in mind that you can buy virtually anything on the spot, a minimum packing list could include:

* underwear, socks and swimming gear
* a pair of jeans and maybe a pair of shorts or skirt
* a few T-shirts and shirts
* a warm sweater
* a solid pair of walking shoes
* sandals or thongs for showers
* a coat or jacket
* a raincoat, waterproof jacket or umbrella
* a medical kit and sewing kit
* a padlock
* a Swiss Army knife
* soap and towel
* toothpaste, toothbrush and other toiletries

A padlock is useful to lock your bag to a luggage rack in a bus or train; it may also be needed to secure your hostel locker. A Swiss Army knife comes in handy for all sorts of things. Any pocketknife is fine, but make sure it includes such essentials as a bottle opener and strong corkscrew! Soap, toothpaste and toilet paper are readily obtainable almost anywhere, but you'll need your own supply of paper in many public toilets and those at camping grounds. Tampons are available at pharmacies and supermarkets in all but the remotest places. Condoms, both locally made and imported, are widely available in Eastern Europe.

A tent and sleeping bag are vital if you want to save money by camping. Even if you're not camping, a sleeping bag is still very useful. Get one that can be used as a quilt. A sleeping sheet with pillow cover (case) is necessary if you plan to stay in hostels – you may have to hire or purchase one if you don't bring your own. In any case,

a sheet that fits into your sleeping bag is easier to wash than the bag itself. Make one yourself out of old sheets (include a built-in pillow cover) or buy one from your hostel association.

Other optional items include a compass, a torch (flashlight), an alarm clock, a pocket calculator for currency conversions, an adapter plug for electrical appliances (such as a cup or immersion water heater to save on expensive tea and coffee), a universal bath/sink plug (a film canister sometimes works), a portable short-wave radio, sunglasses, a small pair of binoculars for viewing detail on churches and other buildings or when trekking, a few clothes pegs and premoistened towelettes or a large cotton handkerchief that you can soak in fountains and use to cool off while touring cities in the hot summer months. During city sightseeing, a small daypack is better than a shoulder bag at deterring thieves (see Theft in the Dangers & Annoyances section of this chapter).

Also, consider using plastic carry bags or bin liners inside your backpack to keep things separate but also dry if the pack gets soaked.

Appearances & Conduct

Eastern Europeans are tolerant of eccentric fashions and behaviour, especially in big cities like Prague, Warsaw and Budapest, but in general they tend to be more conservative dressers than Western Europeans, North Americans and certainly Australians. You'll usually be admitted to expensive restaurants, opera houses, concert halls, hotel bars and the like in jeans, but you'll feel more comfortable if you dress up a wee bit. 'Smart casual' is the name of the game for these venues.

Ensure sufficient body cover (trousers or knee-length dress) if your sightseeing includes churches, monasteries, synagogues or mosques. Wearing shorts away from the beach, camping ground or back garden is not all that common among men in Eastern Europe. Some clubs and fancy restaurants may refuse entry to people wearing jeans, a tracksuit or sneakers (trainers).

While nude bathing is usually limited to certain beaches and riverside strands, topless sunbathing is common in many parts of

Eastern Europe. Nevertheless, women should be wary of taking off their tops. If nobody else is doing it, don't you do it either.

You'll soon notice that Eastern Europeans are very heavily into shaking hands when they greet one another. Try to get into the habit of doing so with virtually everyone you meet; it's an important ritual. The male tradition of kissing a woman's hand has gone the way of the dodo in most parts of the region, though it can still be seen in Poland. *Csókolom* – 'I kiss it' (your hand) – is a common male-to-female greeting in Hungarian though the actual kissing doesn't usually take place anymore.

It's also customary to greet the proprietor when entering a small shop, café or quiet bar, and to say goodbye when you leave. This is particularly true in Hungary, the Czech Republic and Slovakia.

If you're invited for dinner at a local home take flowers for the hostess (but not red roses, which usually have romantic implications) and a bottle of wine or brandy for the host. As most people get up early to go to work, weekday evening visits usually end by about 11 pm.

VISAS & DOCUMENTS
Passport

Your most important travel document is your passport, which should remain valid until well after you return home. If it's just about to expire, renew it before you go – having this done by your embassy in Prague or Warsaw can be inconvenient. Some countries insist your passport remain valid for a specified period (usually three months beyond the date of your departure from that country).

Applying for or renewing a passport can take anything from an hour to several months, so don't leave it till the last minute. Bureaucratic wheels usually turn faster if you do everything in person rather than relying on the post or agents, but check first what you need to take with you: photos of a certain size, birth certificate, population register extract, signed statements, exact payment in cash etc.

Australian citizens can apply at a post office or the passport office in their state capital; Britons can pick up application forms from major post offices, and the passport is issued by the regional passport office; Canadians can apply at regional passport offices; New Zealanders can apply at any district

Visa Requirements – Country of Origin							
	Aust	Can	Ire	NZ	SA	UK	US
Albania	+	+	+	✓	✓	+	+
Bosnia-Hercegovina	✓	✓	+	✓	✓	✓	–
Bulgaria	✓	✓	+	✓	✓	✓	+
Croatia	–	–	–	–	✓	–	–
Czech Republic	✓	–	–	–	✓	–	+
Hungary	✓	–	–	–	+	–	–
Macedonia	✓	✓	✓	✓	✓	✓	✓
Poland	✓	–	–	✓	✓	–	–
Romania	✓	✓	✓	✓	✓	✓	+
Slovakia	✓	–	–	✓	✓	★	★
Slovenia	–	–	–	–	✓	–	–
Yugoslavia	✓	✓	✓	✓	✓	✓	✓

✓   tourist visa required
+   30-day maximum stay without visa
★   60-day maximum stay without visa

office of the Department of Internal Affairs; US citizens must apply in person (but may usually renew by mail) at a US Passport Agency office or at some courthouses and post offices.

Once you start travelling, carry your passport at all times and guard it carefully. (See the following Photocopies section for advice about carrying copies of your passport and other important documents.) Camping grounds and hotels sometimes insist that you hand over your passport for the duration of your stay, which is very inconvenient, but a driving licence or Camping Card International (see that section) usually solves the problem.

Citizens of many European countries don't always need a valid passport to travel within the region. European Union (EU) and Swiss citizens, for example, can enter Slovenia on just a valid personal identity card for up to 30 days and French and German nationals need only produce an ID to enter Hungary. But if you want to exercise this kind of option, check with your travel agent or the embassies of the countries you plan to visit.

Visas

A visa is a stamp in your passport or a separate piece of paper permitting you to enter the country in question and stay for a specified period of time. Often you can get the visa at the border or at the airport on arrival, but not always, especially if you're travelling by train or bus and the procedure is likely to hold up others. Check first with the embassies or consulates of the countries you plan to visit, otherwise you could be kicked off a train or bus at the border. With a valid passport and visa (if required) you'll be able to visit most Eastern European countries for up to three (sometimes even six) months, provided you have some sort of onward or return ticket and/or 'sufficient means of support' (ie money).

In line with the Schengen Agreement there are no longer passport controls at the borders between most EU countries, but border procedures between EU and non-EU countries can still be fairly thorough (and between nations with less than sterling relations like Hungary and Slovakia even more so). For those who do require visas, it's important to remember that these will have a 'use-by'

date, and you'll be refused entry after that period has elapsed.

Visa requirements can change, so you should always check with the individual embassies or a reputable travel agent before travelling. See the accompanying table and Visas & Embassies under Facts for the Visitor in the individual country chapters for details, but always check this information before setting out. If you plan to get your visas as you go along rather than arranging them all beforehand, carry up to a dozen spare passport photos (you may need from one to four every time you apply for a visa).

Visas are *usually* issued immediately by consulates in Eastern Europe, although Bulgarian and Polish consulates may levy a 50 to 100% surcharge for 'express visa service'. Otherwise Bulgarian consulates could make you wait seven working days for your tourist visa. Bulgarian visas are also available at the border but at about double the usual price. Nationals requiring a Czech Republic, Hungarian, Polish, Slovakian or Yugoslav visa are strongly advised to get it at a consulate beforehand and not to rely on it being available at every border crossing. Croatian and Macedonian visas, on the other hand, are usually easily obtainable at the border. Romanian visas are available at embassies and the border for theoretically the same price, but it's usually better to get your Romanian visa in advance (some travellers have reported being ripped off). Travellers not requiring visas for Bulgaria and Romania have reportedly been charged an 'entry tax' of about US$20 at the borders of both countries.

Consulates are generally open weekday mornings (if there's both an embassy and a consulate, you want the consulate). Consulates in countries not neighbouring the one you want to visit are far less crowded (for example, get your Polish visa in Bucharest, your Hungarian visa in Sofia or Warsaw, your Slovakian visa in Zagreb etc). Take your own pen and be sure to have a good supply of passport photos that actually look like you.

You can also apply for a visa from a consulate in your home country by registered mail, though this takes about two weeks unless you request 'express' service for an additional fee. First you must write for an application form enclosing a stamped, self-addressed envelope.

In the USA you can obtain your visas for an additional fee of around US$45 per visa on top of the consular and mailing fees through Visa Services (☎ 202-387 0300 or 800-222 8472), 1519 Connecticut Ave North West, Suite 300, Washington DC 20036.

Visa fees must be paid in convertible cash. Most countries will issue double-entry visas upon request for double the normal fee. Visas may be used any time within three to six months from the date of issue, and you're usually allowed to spend 30 days or more in a country.

Decide in advance if it's a tourist or transit visa you want. Transit visas, usually valid only for 48 or 72 hours, are often cheaper and issued sooner, but it's usually not possible to extend a transit visa or change it to a tourist visa.

The visa form may instruct you to report to police within 48 hours of arrival. If you're staying at a hotel or other official accommodation (camping ground, hostel, private room arranged by a travel agency etc), this will be taken care of for you by the travel agency, hotel or camping ground. If you're staying with friends, relatives or in a private room arranged on the street or at the train station, you're supposed to register with the police yourself. During the communist days these regulations were strictly enforced, but things are pretty casual in most countries nowadays (though perhaps not in Bulgaria).

If you need a visa extension, ask the tourist office how to go about it. You'll probably have to report to the police in person. Office hours are short and the lines long, so don't leave it till the last minute.

Photocopies

The hassles created by losing your passport can be considerably reduced if you have a record of its number and issue date or, even better, photocopies of the relevant data pages. A photocopy of your birth certificate can also be useful.

Also add the serial numbers of your travellers cheques (cross them off as you cash them) and photocopies of your credit cards, airline ticket and other travel documents. Keep all this emergency material separate from your passport, cheques and cash, and leave extra copies with someone you can rely on back home. Add some emergency money (eg US$50 in cash) to this separate stash as well. If you do lose your passport, notify the police immediately to get a statement, and contact your nearest consulate.

Travel Insurance

A travel insurance policy to cover theft, loss and medical problems is a good idea. The policies handled by STA Travel and other student travel organisations are usually good value. Some policies offer lower and higher medical expense options; the higher ones are chiefly for countries like the USA that have extremely high medical costs. There is a wide variety of policies available so check the fine print.

Some policies specifically exclude 'dangerous activities', which can include scuba diving, motorcycling and even trekking. Some even exclude entire countries (eg Bosnia-Hercegovina and Yugoslavia). A locally acquired motorcycle licence is not valid under some policies.

You may prefer a policy that pays doctors or hospitals directly rather than you having to pay on the spot and claim later. If you have to claim later make sure you keep all documentation. Some policies ask you to call back (reverse charges) to a centre in your home country where an immediate assessment of your problem is made.

Check that the policy covers ambulances or an emergency flight home.

International Driving Permit

Many non-European driving licences are valid in Europe, but it's still a good idea to bring along an International Driving Permit, which can make life much simpler, especially when hiring cars and motorcycles. Basically a multilingual translation of the vehicle class and personal details noted on your local driving licence, an IDP is not valid unless accompanied by your original licence. An IDP can be obtained for a small fee (eg UK£4 in Britain) from your local automobile association – bring along a passport photo and a valid licence.

Camping Card International

The Camping Card International (CCI; formerly the Camping Carnet) is a camping ground ID that can be used instead of a passport when checking in and includes third-party insurance (up to Sfr2.5 million for damage you may cause). As a result, many camping grounds offer a small discount if you sign in with one. CCIs are issued by automobile associations, camping federations and, sometimes, on the spot at camping grounds. In the UK, the AA issues them to its members for UK£4.50.

Hostelling Card

A hostelling card is useful – if not always mandatory – for staying at hostels. Most hostels in Eastern Europe don't require that you be a hostelling association member, but they often charge less if you have a card. Some hostels will issue one on the spot or after a few stays, though this might cost a bit more than getting it in your home country. See Hostels in the Accommodation section for the addresses of hostelling associations in English-speaking countries.

Student & Youth Cards

The most useful of these is the International Student Identity Card (ISIC), a plastic ID-style card with your photograph, which provides discounts on many forms of transport (including airlines and local transport), cheap or free admission to museums and sights, and inexpensive meals in some student cafeterias and restaurants.

If you're aged under 26 but not a student, you can apply for a GO25 card issued by the Federation of International Youth Travel Organisations (FIYTO) or the Euro <26 card, which appear under different names in various countries. Both give much the same discounts and benefits as an ISIC.

All these cards are issued by student unions, hostelling organisations and youth-oriented travel agencies.

Seniors' Cards

Museums and other sights, public swimming pools and spas and transport companies frequently offer discounts to retired people/old age pensioners/those over 60 (slightly younger for women). Make sure you bring proof of age.

European nationals aged over 60 can get a Rail Europe Senior (RES) card. For more information see Cheap Tickets under Train in the Getting Around chapter.

International Health Certificate

You'll need this yellow booklet only if you're coming to the region from certain parts of Asia, Africa and South America, where diseases such as yellow fever are prevalent. See Immunisations in the Health section for more information on jabs.

CUSTOMS

While there's no problem bringing in and taking out the type of personal effects most people travel with, be aware that antiques, books printed before 1945, crystal glass, gemstones, lottery tickets, philatelic stamps, precious metals (gold, silver, platinum), securities and valuable works of art may have to be declared in writing in many countries. Don't carry letters or parcels on behalf of third parties. There may also be restrictions on the import/export of local currency though the amounts nowadays are quite large.

Throughout most of Eastern Europe, the usual allowances on tobacco (eg 200 cigarettes), alcohol (2L of wine, 1L of spirits) and perfume (50g) apply to duty-free goods purchased at the airport or on ferries. Customs checks are pretty cursory and you probably won't even have to open your bags, but don't be lulled into a false sense of security. When you least expect it...

MONEY

Money in Eastern Europe can be a bit tricky. Of the dozen Eastern European currencies in circulation, only some (eg Czech crowns, Hungarian forints, Slovenian tolar) are 100% fully convertible and exchanged abroad. Others are at various stages of convertibility; some can be exchanged relatively easily abroad (especially in neighbouring countries), others not at all. For the time being, the best policy is to spend whatever you have there and export as little as possible. See Money in the individual country chapters for more details.

Costs

This book is written for the independent budget traveller who intends to stay at economy hotels, hostels or in private rooms; take lunch at self-service restaurants and dinner at moderate full-service restaurants; go to a concert or a club a couple of nights a week; see the sights independently on foot or by public transport and travel 2nd class by train or bus. With a little care it should be possible to do all that on US$30 a day in most of these countries (US$40 in Slovenia, US$50 in Macedonia and Yugoslavia). Two people travelling together can save about a third on accommodation costs, and campers will spend even less.

Cash

Nothing beats cash for convenience ... or risk. If you lose it, it's gone forever and very few travel insurers will come to your rescue. Those that will, usually limit the amount to about UK£200/US$300. For tips on carrying your money safely, see Theft in the Dangers & Annoyances section later in this chapter.

In the old days, Eastern Europe worked on a cash-only basis; cheques and credit cards were unheard of, banks kept true bankers' hours and, frankly, the black market rates on the street (especially in Poland and Romania) were so attractive that even the most law-abiding travellers were tempted. That's all changed now with *bureaux de change* everywhere, banks in many countries keeping longer hours and currency exchange machines and automatic teller machines (ATMs) popping up everywhere (with the exception of Bosnia-Hercegovina).

But cash remains more important in Eastern Europe than elsewhere in Europe, and it's a good idea to carry some foreign currency with you (especially US dollars or Deutschmarks). Remember that banks will always accept paper money but very rarely coins in foreign currencies, so you might want to spend (or donate) your local coins before you cross a border. In some countries it's worth having plenty of small denomination banknotes as it's often difficult to make up change in hard currency. However, don't bring banknotes with any writing or rubber stamp marks on them, or that are damaged or badly worn, as these will often be rejected.

Travellers Cheques

The main idea of carrying travellers cheques rather than cash is the protection they offer from theft, though they are losing their popularity as more travellers – including those on tight budgets – deposit their money in their bank at home and withdraw it through ATMs as they go along.

Banks usually charge from 1 to 2% commission to change travellers cheques (from 2 to 5% in Bulgaria and Romania). Their opening hours are sometimes limited. In this book we recommend the most efficient banks of each country in the individual chapters.

Privately owned exchange offices in Poland, Romania, Bulgaria, Slovenia and Albania change cash at excellent rates without commission. Not only are their rates sometimes higher than those offered by the banks for travellers cheques but they stay open much longer hours, occasionally even 24 hours a day. Take care in the Czech Republic, Slovakia and Hungary, however, as some private exchange offices deduct exorbitant commissions. Before signing a travellers cheque or handing over any cash always check the commission and rate.

American Express and Thomas Cook offices cash their own travellers cheques without commission but both give rather poor rates of exchange. If you're changing over US$20, you're often better off going to a bank and paying the standard 1 to 2% commission to change there.

Carrying large amounts of cash on your person is always risky, so you'll have to weigh the advantages of the greater convenience of cash against the greater security of cheques. If you decide to go with cash you'll probably have to bring it with you from home as banks and American Express offices in Eastern Europe charge from 7% commission to convert dollar travellers cheques into dollars cash, if they will do it at all. Only in Poland and Slovenia is it possible to swap cheques for cash without losing a bundle.

Plastic Cards & ATMs

A credit card can be an ideal travelling companion. Though its uses are more limited in Eastern Europe than in the west, that's changing fast. If you're not familiar with the options, ask your bank to explain the workings and relative merits of credit, credit/debit, debit, charge and cash cards.

With a credit card you can put big expenses like airline tickets on your account. Another major advantage is that they allow you to withdraw cash at selected banks or from ATMs that are linked up internationally. However, if an ATM in Europe swallows a card that was issued outside Europe, it can be a major headache. Also, some credit cards aren't hooked up to ATM networks unless you specifically ask your bank to do this.

Cash cards, which you use at home to withdraw money directly from your bank account or savings account, can be used throughout Europe at ATMs linked to international networks like Cirrus and Maestro. They are everywhere in Hungary, Slovakia, the Czech Republic and in increasing use in Slovenia and Romania. Withdrawals may incur a transaction fee.

If you use a credit – not a cash – card to get money from an ATM, you pay interest on the money from the moment you get it. You can get around that by leaving the card in credit when you depart or by having somebody at home pay money into the card account from time to time. On the plus side, you don't pay commission charges to exchange money and the exchange rate is usually at a better interbank rate than that offered for travellers cheques or cash exchanges. Bear in mind that if you use a credit card for purchases, exchange rates may have changed by the time your bill is processed, which can work out to your advantage or disadvantage.

Charge cards like American Express and Diners Club have offices in most countries, and they can generally replace a lost card within 24 hours. That's because they treat you as a customer of the company rather than of the bank that issued the card. In theory, the credit they offer is unlimited and they don't charge interest on outstanding accounts, but they do charge fees for joining and annual membership, and payment is due in full within a few weeks of the account statement date. Their major drawback is that they're not widely accepted off the beaten track of mainstream travel. Charge cards may also be hooked up to ATM networks.

Credit and credit/debit cards like MasterCard and Visa are more widely accepted because they tend to charge merchants lower commissions. Their major drawback is that they have a credit limit based on your regular income, and this limit may not be high enough to cover major expenses like long-term car rental or long-distance airline tickets, especially if you're travelling for an extended period and spending all the while. You can get around this by leaving your card in credit when you leave home. Other drawbacks are that interest is charged on outstanding accounts, either immediately or after a set period (always immediately on cash advances) and that the card can be very difficult to replace if lost abroad.

If you choose to rely on plastic, go for two different cards – a MasterCard or Visa, for instance, with an American Express or Diners Club backup. Better still is a combination of credit card and travellers cheques so you have something to fall back on if an ATM swallows your card or the banks in the area won't accept it (a not uncommon and always inexplicable occurrence).

It has not been all that long since Europe in general embraced credit cards in a major way, and the vast majority of small restaurants and service stations still accept cash only. MasterCard, Visa and Diners Club are the most popular brands. MasterCard (also known as Access in the UK) is linked to Europe's extensive Eurocard system, which makes it widely accepted and thus a convenient card to carry.

A final word of warning: fraudulent shopkeepers have been known to make several charge-slip imprints with customers' credit cards when they're not looking; they then simply copy the signature from the authorised slip. Try not to let your card out of your sight, and always check your statements carefully.

International Transfers

Telegraphic transfers are not very expensive but, despite their name, can be quite slow. Be sure to specify the name of the bank and the name and address of the branch where you'd like to pick it up.

It's quicker and easier to have money wired via an American Express (US$60 for US$1000). Western Union's Money Transfer system (available at post offices in some countries) and Thomas Cook's MoneyGram service are also popular.

Guaranteed Cheques

Guaranteed personal cheques are another way of carrying money or obtaining cash. Eurocheques, available if you have a European bank account, are guaranteed up to a certain limit. When cashing them (eg at post offices), you will be asked to show your Eurocheque card bearing your signature and registration number, and perhaps a passport or ID card. Your Eurocheque card should be kept separately from the cheques. Many hotels and merchants refuse to accept Eurocheques because of the relatively large commissions.

Black Market

The days when you could get five times the official rate for cash on the street in Warsaw and Bucharest are gone for good. A 'black market' exists whenever a government puts restrictions on free currency trading through regulations that prohibit banks and licensed foreign exchange dealers from changing the national currency into western hard currency. A black market is eliminated overnight when a currency is made internally convertible, the way that most Eastern European currencies have gone or are going.

These days the most you'll get on the black market throughout most of Eastern Europe is a couple of percentage points above the official bank rate (though in Romania it's more like 10 to 25%). Changing money on the street is extremely risky not because it is illegal but because many of the people offering to change are professional thieves with years of experience in cheating tourists.

If you decide to use the black market, hang onto your cash until you have the offered money in your hand, then count it one more time before putting it in your pocket. If during an exchange the seller takes the local currency back from you after you've counted it, break off contact immediately as a rip-off is definitely intended. In that circumstance, the money you have counted will disappear in a sleight-of-hand trick and you'll end up with a packet of newsprint, smaller bills or counterfeit bills produced on a colour photocopy machine. You only have to be ripped off once in this way to cancel all your earnings on four or five illegal exchanges.

Never change money when two men appear together. If a second man appears while you're negotiating, take off. Be wary of anyone wearing a jogging suit as they're probably dressed that way to avoid suspicion as they run away. Don't be pressured into changing more than you originally intended. Thieves will always insist that you change a large amount – one way of recognising them. Know what the local currency looks like and don't be in a hurry. Be careful of receiving currency that has been withdrawn from circulation. Black marketeers play on your greed and fear. These days the police are not interested, so if someone starts shouting that the police are coming (as a diversion) it means that you have just been ripped off.

Tipping

Throughout Eastern Europe you tip by rounding up restaurant bills, taxi fares etc to the next even figure as you're paying. In some countries restaurants will already have added a service charge to your bill, so you needn't round it up much (if at all). A tip of 10% is quite sufficient if you feel you have been well attended. The waiters in any establishment catering mostly to foreign tourists will expect such a tip. If you're dissatisfied with the food or service, or feel you have been overcharged, you can convey the message by paying the exact amount with no gratuity included. If 'rounding up' means you're only giving honest waiters a couple of cents, add a few more coins to keep them happy. Never leave tips on restaurant tables as this is not the custom anywhere in Eastern Europe; you tell the waiter how much you're prepared to give him.

Taxes & Refunds

A kind of sales tax called value-added tax (VAT) applies to most goods and services in many Eastern European countries; it can be as high as 25% in Hungary and 20% in Slovenia. In general, visitors can claim back the VAT on purchases that are being taken out of the country. The procedure on making the claim can be fairly straightforward (as in Slovenia) or very complicated (as in Hungary), and there will be minimum-purchase amounts imposed. When making your purchase ask the shop attendant for a VAT refund voucher filled in with the correct amount and the date. This is usually refunded directly at international airports and border crossings, or validated and mailed back by the consumer for a refund.

POST & COMMUNICATIONS
Post
Details of the main post offices are given in the Information section of each city or town. Postage costs vary from country to country and so does post office efficiency – the Polish post office, while improving from the 'dark ages' of a few years ago, is still not very reliable.

If you wish to receive mail you can have it sent care of poste restante (general delivery). Tell your correspondents to put the number 1 after the city name to ensure that the letter goes to the main post office in that city. You should also have them underline your last name, as letters are often misfiled under first names. (The latter is particularly important when sending letters to Hungary where the family name *always* comes first.) Poste restante offices seldom hold letters longer than a month and some charge a small fee for each letter picked up.

You can also have mail sent to you at American Express offices so long as you have an American Express card or are carrying their travellers cheques. When you buy American Express cheques, ask for a booklet listing all its office addresses worldwide. American Express will forward mail for a flat fee of about US$5, but what they won't do is accept parcels, registered letters, notices for registered letters, answer telephone inquiries about mail or hold mail longer than 30 days. In general, they're safer and more efficient than poste restante services.

When deciding on your mail pick-up points, don't choose too many or you'll sacrifice the flexibility of being able to change your plans after arrival. Try to pick a central location you'll be transiting several times during office hours. A good plan is to provide your correspondents with a complete list of all possible addresses before you set out, then inform them which addresses to use as you're going along.

To send a parcel from Eastern Europe you sometimes have to take it (unwrapped) to a main post office. Parcels weighing over 2kg must often be taken to a special customs post office. Have the paper, string and tape ready. They'll usually ask to see your passport and note the number on the form. If you don't have a return address within the country put your name care of any large tourist hotel to satisfy them.

Telephone
Telephone service has improved throughout the region in a very short time. Telephone centres – where they exist – are generally in the same building as the main post office. Here you can often make your call from one of the booths inside an enclosed area, paying the cashier as you leave. Public telephones are almost always found at post offices. Telephone cards, available from post offices, telephone centres, newsstands or retail outlets, are popular everywhere. In fact, in some countries (Hungary, the Czech Republic, Slovenia) they are the norm.

To call abroad you simply dial the international access code for the country you are calling from (most commonly 00 in Europe), the country code for the country you are calling, the local area code (usually dropping the initial zero if there is one) and then the number. If, for example, you are in Hungary (international access code 00) and want to make a call to the UK (country code 44), London (area code 0171), number ☎ 123 4567, then you dial ☎ 00-44-171-123 4567. To call from Bulgaria (international access code: 00) to Australia (61), Sydney (02), number ☎ 1234 5678, you dial ☎ 00-61-2-1234 5678.

To make a domestic call to another city in the same country dial the area code with the initial zero and the number. Area codes for individual cities are provided in the country chapters. For country codes, see Appendix II – Telephones at the end of the book.

Fax & Telegraph
You can send faxes and telegrams from most main post offices in Eastern Europe.

INTERNET RESOURCES
Email & Internet Access
Travelling with a portable computer is a great way to stay in touch with life back home but, unless you know what you're doing, it's fraught with potential problems. A good investment is a universal AC adaptor for your appliance, so you can plug it in anywhere without frying the innards, if the power supply voltage varies. You'll also need a plug adaptor for each country you visit, often easiest bought before you leave home.

Secondly, your PC-card modem may or may not work once you leave your home country – and you won't know for sure until you try. The safest option is to buy a reputable 'global' or 'world' modem before you leave home, or buy a local PC-card modem if you're spending an extended time in any one country. Keep in mind that the telephone socket in each country you visit will probably be different from that at home, so ensure that you have at least a US RJ-11 telephone adaptor that works with your modem. You can almost always find an adaptor that will convert from RJ-11 to the local variety. For more information on travelling with a portable computer, see www.teleadapt.com or www.warrior.com.

Major Internet service providers (ISPs) such as AOL (www.aol.com), CompuServe (www.compuserve.com) and IBM Net (www.ibm.net) have dial-in nodes throughout Europe; it's best to download a list of the dial-in numbers before you leave home. If you access your Internet email account at home through a smaller ISP or your office or school network, your best option is either to open an account with a global ISP, like those mentioned above, or to rely on cybercafes and other public access points to collect your mail.

If you do intend to rely on cybercafes, you'll need to carry three pieces of information with you so you can access your Internet mail account: your incoming (POP or IMAP) mail server name, your account name, and your password. Your ISP or network supervisor will give you these. Armed with this information, you should be able to access your Internet mail account from any net-connected machine in the world, provided it runs some kind of email software (remember that Netscape and Internet Explorer both have mail modules). It pays to become familiar with the process for doing this before you leave home. A final option to collect mail through cybercafes is to open a free Web-based email account like HotMail (www.hotmail.com) or Yahoo! Mail (mail.yahoo.com). You can then access your mail from anywhere in the world from any net-connected machine running a standard Web browser.

You'll find cybercafes throughout Europe: check out the country chapters in this book, and see www.netcafeguide.com for an up-to-date list. You may also find public net access in post offices, libraries, hostels, hotels, universities and so on.

Useful Sites

The World Wide Web is a rich resource for travellers. You can research your trip, hunt down bargain air fares, book hotels, check on weather conditions or chat with locals and other travellers about the best places to visit (or avoid!).

The following Web sites offer useful general information about Mediterranean Europe, its cities, transport systems, currencies etc.

Lonely Planet
    www.lonelyplanet.com – there's no better place to start your Web explorations than the Lonely Planet Web site. Here you'll find succinct summaries on travelling to most places on earth, postcards from other travellers and the Thorn Tree bulletin board, where you can ask questions before you go or dispense advice when you get back. You can also find travel news and updates to many of our guidebooks, and the subWWWay section links you to the most useful travel resources elsewhere on the Web.

Tourist Offices
    www.mbnet.mb.ca/lucas/travel – lists tourist offices at home and around the world for most countries

Rail Information
    www.raileurope.com – train fares and schedules on the most popular routes in Europe, including information on rail and youth passes

Airline Information
    www.travelocity.com – what airlines fly where, when and for how much.
    www.priceline.com – name the price you're willing to pay for an airline seat and if an airline has an empty seat for which it would rather get something than nothing; US-based Priceline lets you know.

Currency Converters
    bin.gnn.com/cgi-bin/gnn/currency; or pacific.commerce.ubc.ca/xr – exchange rates of hundreds of currencies worldwide.

BOOKS
Lonely Planet

Lonely Planet publishes guides to many individual Eastern European countries, including the Czech Republic and Slovakia, Hungary,

Poland, Romania and Slovenia; these provide far greater detail on much wider areas than is possible in an omnibus guide like this. Even if you already have a shoestring (or multi-country) guide, it's still worth picking up the individual country guide if you'll be spending a long time in a particular area.

Travel

Among the most intriguing travel books on Eastern Europe are *A Time of Gifts* and *Between the Woods and the Water* by Patrick Leigh Fermor. In December 1933 Fermor set out on a year-and-a-half walk from Holland to Turkey on a budget of UK£1 a week. The first volume covers the stretch from Rotterdam to the Danube, the second Hungary and Romania. Though the style of travel Fermor describes has long since passed into history, his books make wonderful companions along the way in Eastern Europe.

Balkan Ghosts by Robert D Kaplan offers a contemporary traveller's view of a region torn by ethnic strife and economic upheaval. His book could well be read in tandem with Rebecca West's 1937 classic Balkan travelogue *Black Lamb and Grey Falcon*.

History & Politics

Eastern Europe and Communist Rule by JF Brown is a readable political history of Eastern Europe's four decades of communism with special attention to the 1970s and 1980s. His more recent work is *Surge to Freedom: The End of Communist Rule in Eastern Europe*.

For clear, insightful interpretations of what led to the collapse of communism throughout the region in 1989, read *We the People* by Timothy Garton Ash or Misha Glenny's updated *The Rebirth of History*. For a more scholarly account, see *Revolutions in Eastern Europe* edited by Roger East.

Café Europa: Life after Communism by Slavenka Drakulić is a Croatian journalist's look at Croatia, the Czech Republic, Albania, Bulgaria and Romania since the change. Angus Fraser's *The Gypsies* is a useful history of the Roma up to 1989. *Bury Me Standing* by Isabel Fonseca is a highly readable account of Roma society and culture.

NEWSPAPERS & MAGAZINES

In larger towns and cities you can buy the *International Herald Tribune* on the day of publication, as well as the colourful but superficial *USA Today*. Among other English-language newspapers widely available are the *Guardian*, the *Financial Times* and *The Times*. The *European* weekly newspaper is also readily available, as are *Newsweek*, *Time* and the *Economist*. For a local slant on international coverage and to learn lots more about the country you're in, pick up one of the generally excellent English-language weeklies that have sprouted up in the Eastern Europe like mushrooms after rain (eg the Czech Republic's *Prague Post*, the *Budapest Sun* in Hungary and the *Slovak Spectator* in Slovakia).

Business Central Europe is a monthly magazine put out by *The Economist*. For more detailed coverage of Poland, the Czech Republic, Slovakia, Hungary and the Baltic states, there's the *Eastern European Business Weekly*. It's sold at major newsstands in Eastern Europe. *Transitions*, a monthly published in Prague, has excellent articles on the politics and society of Eastern and Central Europe.

For details on other local newspapers in English, see Newspapers & Magazines in the Facts for the Visitor sections of the individual country chapters.

RADIO & TV
Radio

You can pick up a mixture of the BBC World Service and BBC for Europe on medium wave at 648 kHz AM and on short wave at 6195, 9410, 11955, 12095 (a good daytime frequency) and 15575 kHz, depending on your location and the time of day. BBC Radio 4 broadcasts on long-wave at 198 kHz.

The Voice of America (VOA) can usually be found at various times of the day on 7170, 9535, 9680, 9760, 9770, 11805, 15135, 15205, 15255, 15410 and 15580 kHz. There are also numerous English-language broadcasts (or even BBC World Service and VOA re-broadcasts) on some local AM and FM radio stations.

Radio Canada International's half-hour English-language broadcasts, including relays of domestic CBC programs such as the

World at Six, often come in loud and clear on one or more of these frequencies: 5995, 7235, 11690, 11890, 11935, 13650, 13670, 15150, 15325, 17820 and 17870 kHz.

Although Radio Australia directs most of its broadcasts to the Asia-Pacific region, it can sometimes be picked up in Europe. Frequencies to try include 9500, 11660 and 11880 kHz.

Internet Local and international radio stations from every corner of the globe now 'broadcast' their program via the Internet, to be picked up by Net surfers using software like RealAudio that can be easily downloaded. Station Web sites often include write-ups of the latest news and are an excellent source of short-wave schedules. TRS Consultants' Hot Links (www.trsc.com) has dozens of hypertext links relevant to Internet radio.

Stations with Internet relays include the BBC World Service (www.bbc.co.uk/worldservice), Radio Australia (ww.abc.net.au/ra), Radio Canada International (www.rcinet.ca), CBC Radio (www.radio.cbc.can) and the Voice of America (www.voa.gov).

TV

Cable and satellite TV have spread across Europe with much more gusto than radio. Sky TV can be found in many upmarket hotels throughout Eastern Europe, as can CNN, BBC Prime and other networks. Even a small *panzió* (pension) in rural Hungary will be equipped with a satellite dish nowadays and virtually everyone has cable in Slovenia.

VIDEO SYSTEMS

If you want to record or buy video tapes to play back home, you won't get the picture if the image registration systems are different. Like Australia, Eastern Europe generally uses PAL, which is incompatible with the North American and Japanese NTSC system. The one exception is Poland, which has traditionally had the SECAM system used in France.

PHOTOGRAPHY

Eastern Europe and its people are extremely photogenic, but where you'll be travelling and the weather will dictate what film to take or buy locally. In places such as northern Poland or the Czech Republic, where the sky can often be overcast, photographers should bring high-speed film (eg 200 or 400 ASA). In sunny weather (or when the mountains are under a blanket of snow) slower film is the answer.

Film and camera equipment is available everywhere in Eastern Europe, but obviously shops in the larger cities and towns have a wider selection. Avoid buying film at tourist sites in Europe – eg the Castle District in Budapest or by Charles Bridge in Prague. It may have been stored badly or reached its sell-by date. It certainly will be more expensive than in shops.

In most Eastern European countries (as elsewhere) it's prohibited to take pictures of anything that might be considered of strategic value – from bridges and tunnels to train stations and border crossings. Occasionally you'll see a funny little sign showing a crossed-out camera indicating that there's something of interest in the vicinity. These days local officials are a lot less paranoid about photography than they were, but use common sense when it comes to this issue. And have the courtesy to ask permission before taking close-up photos of people.

TIME

Most of the places covered in this book are on Central European Time (GMT plus one hour), the same time used from Spain to Poland. Romania, Bulgaria and Greece are on East European Time (GMT plus two hours). If it's 6 pm in Warsaw and Madrid, it will be 7 pm in Bucharest and Sofia, 8 pm in Moscow, 5 pm in London, noon in New York, 9 am in Los Angeles and 3 am the next morning in Sydney.

Clocks are advanced for daylight-saving time in most countries on the last Sunday in March and set back one hour on the last Sunday in September. At that time Central European Time is GMT/UTC plus two hours and East European Time (GMT plus two hours).

ELECTRICITY

All the countries of Eastern Europe run on 220V, 50 Hz AC. Check the voltage and cycle (usually 50 Hz) used in your home country. Most appliances that are set up for

220V will handle 240V quite happily without modifications (and vice versa); the same goes for 110V and 125V combinations. It's always preferable to adjust your appliance to the exact voltage if you can (some modern battery chargers and radios will do this automatically). Don't mix 110/125V with 220/240V without a transformer, which will be built in if the appliance can be adjusted.

Several countries outside Europe (the USA and Canada, for instance) have 60 Hz AC, which will affect the speed of electric motors even after the voltage has been adjusted, so CD and tape players (where motor speed is all-important) will be useless. But appliances such as electric razors, hair dryers, irons and radios will work fine.

Plugs in Eastern Europe are the standard round two-pin variety, sometimes called the 'europlug'. If your plugs are of a different design, you'll need an adapter.

HEALTH

Travel health depends on your predeparture preparations, your daily health care while travelling and how you handle any medical problem that does develop.

Predeparture planning

Immunisations No jabs are necessary for Eastern Europe, but they may be an entry requirement if you're coming from an infected area (yellow fever is the most likely requirement). If you're travelling to Eastern Europe with stopovers in Asia, Africa or South America, check with your travel agent or with the embassies of the countries you plan to visit.

There are, however, a few routine vaccinations that are recommended whether you're travelling or not, and this Health section assumes that you've had them: polio (usually administered during childhood), tetanus and diphtheria (usually administered together during childhood, with a booster shot every 10 years), and measles. See your physician or nearest health agency about these. You might also consider having an immunoglobulin or hepatitis A (Havrix, Avaxim or VAQTA) vaccines; a tetanus booster; a vaccine against hepatitis B; or even

a rabies (pre-exposure) vaccination. Some authorities recommend vaccination against typhoid (also spread by food and water), but this would only be necessary if you planned a long stay and really intended to rough it (eg in parts of Romania).

All vaccinations should be recorded on an International Health Certificate (see that section earlier), which is available from your physician or government health department. Don't leave this till the last minute, as the vaccinations may have to be spread out a bit.

Health Insurance Make sure that you have adequate health insurance. See Travel Insurance in the Visas & Documents section for details.

Other Preparations Make sure you're healthy before you start travelling. If you are going on a long trip make sure your teeth are OK. If you wear glasses take a spare pair and your prescription.

If you require a particular medication take an adequate supply, as it may not be available locally. Take part of the packaging showing the generic name, rather than the brand, which will make getting replacements easier. It's a good idea to have a legible prescription or letter from your doctor to show that you legally use the medication to avoid any problems.

Basic Rules

Food Salads and fruit should be safe throughout Eastern Europe though if you're avoiding tap water remember that leafy vegetables served in restaurants will have been washed with it. Take care with raw or undercooked eggs, which can cause intestinal illnesses. Ice cream is usually OK, but be wary if it has melted and been refrozen. Take great care with fish or shellfish (for instance, cooked mussels that haven't opened properly can be dangerous), and avoid undercooked meat.

If a place looks clean and well run and if the vendor also looks clean and healthy, then the food is probably safe. In general, places that are packed with travellers or local people will be fine. Be careful with food that has been cooked and left to go cold, as is often the case in old-style self-service restaurants in Poland, the Czech Republic, Slovakia and Hungary. You could experience some gut problems in Poland where stuffed foods are common and tend to go off quickly; just avoid things like stuffed cabbage and meat *pierogi* (dumplings) in warm weather.

Mushroom-picking is a favourite pastime – some would say a religion – in parts of Eastern Europe, but make sure you don't eat mushrooms that haven't been positively identified as safe. Some countries (eg Hungary and Slovenia) set up free inspection tables at markets or at entrances to national parks to separate the good from the bad or even deadly.

Water Tap water is generally safe to drink in Eastern Europe though it's always best to seek local advice (especially in south-west Poland and Romania). Many Czechs prefer to drink reasonably priced bottled water, and water from the tap doesn't always look so good in Hungary. If you decide not to drink tap water, then you shouldn't use ice cubes either as even luxury hotels often make their ice from unboiled tap water.

Always be wary of natural water. The water in the flowing stream in the High Tatras may look crystal clear and very inviting, but before drinking it you need to be absolutely sure there are no people or cattle upstream. Run-off from fertilised fields is also a concern. If you are planning extended hikes where you have to rely on natural water, it may be useful to know about water purification.

The simplest way of purifying water is to boil it thoroughly. Technically this means boiling for 10 minutes, something that happens very rarely. Remember that at high altitude water boils at a lower temperature, so germs are less likely to be killed. Simple filtering will not remove all dangerous organisms, so if you cannot boil water it should be treated chemically. Chlorine tablets (Puritabs, Steritabs or other brand names) will kill many pathogens, but not some parasites like giardia and amoebic cysts. Iodine is more effective in purifying water and is available in tablet form (such as Potable Aqua). Follow the directions carefully and remember that too much iodine can be harmful.

Medical Kit Check List

Consider taking a basic medical kit including:

☐ **Aspirin** or **paracetamol** (acetaminophen in the USA) – for pain or fever.

☐ **Antihistamine** (such as Benadryl) – a decongestant for colds and allergies, eases the itch from insect bites or stings and helps prevent motion sickness. Antihistamines may cause sedation and interact with alcohol, so care should be taken when using them; take one you know and have used before, if possible.

☐ **Antibiotics** – useful if you're travelling well off the beaten track, but they must be prescribed; carry the prescription with you.

☐ **Lomotil** or **Imodium** – to treat diarrhoea; prochlorperazine (eg Stemetil) or metaclopramide (eg Maxalon) is good for nausea and vomiting.

☐ **Rehydration mixture** – to treat severe diarrhoea; particularly important when travelling with children.

☐ **Antiseptic**, such as povidone-iodine (eg Betadine) – for cuts and grazes.

☐ **Multivitamins** – especially useful for long trips when dietary vitamin intake may be inadequate.

☐ **Calamine lotion** or **aluminium sulphate spray** (eg Stingose) – to ease irritation from bites or stings.

☐ **Bandages** and **Band-aids**

☐ **Scissors, tweezers** and a **thermometer** – (note that mercury thermometers are prohibited by airlines).

☐ **Cold and flu tablets** and **throat lozenges** – Pseudoephedrine hydrochloride (Sudafed) may be useful if flying with a cold to avoid ear damage.

☐ **Insect repellent, sunscreen, Chapstick** and **water purification tablets**

☐ **A couple of syringes** – in case you need injections in a country with medical hygiene problems. Ask your doctor for a note explaining why they have been prescribed.

Medical Problems & Treatment

In emergencies you should resort to the casualty ward of any large general hospital. Finding the right hospital can sometimes take time, so in cases of real urgency you should have someone call an ambulance. (See the Medical & Emergency Services sections of major cities in the country chapters.) Hospital emergency departments in Eastern Europe can cope with most medical problems, and the fees they ask are usually less than in Western Europe. Most hospital doctors are eager to practise their English and will be very helpful, though in many cases the facilities are overcrowded.

Private medical practice is less common in Eastern Europe than it is in the west but with a private doctor you'll receive faster, more personalised attention than you would at a hospital. Embassies, tourist offices and receptionists in luxury hotels can often supply the name of an English-speaking doctor or dentist.

If your problem isn't so serious try asking for advice at a pharmacy (chemist). Locally produced drugs and medicines are inexpensive – Hungary is among the world's leading producers of pharmaceuticals – and there's often someone there who understands a little English, German or at least sign language. Chemists also sell multivitamins, bottled medicinal water and even herbal tea. Western brand names are expensive in Eastern Europe, so bring along any medicines you cannot do without, including something for headaches, common colds and stomach upsets. Prescriptions must be expressed in generic terminology.

Environmental Hazards

Altitude Sickness Lack of oxygen at high altitudes (over 2500m) affects most people to some extent. The affect may be mild or severe and occurs because less oxygen reaches the muscles and the brain at high altitude, requiring the heart and lungs to compensate by working harder. Very few treks or ski runs in the High Tatras or the Julian Alps approach such heights, so it's unlikely to be a major concern.

Mild symptoms include headache, lethargy, dizziness, difficulty sleeping and loss of appetite, confusion, irrational behaviour, vomiting, drowsiness and unconsciousness. Mild altitude problems should abate after a day or so, but if symptoms persist or become worse the only treatment is to descend – even 500m can help.

Fungal Infections Fungal infections occur more commonly in hot weather and are usually found on the scalp, between the toes or fingers, in the groin and on the body (ringworm). You get ringworm (which is a fungal infection, not a worm) from infected animals or other people. Moisture encourages these infections.

To prevent fungal infections wear loose, comfortable clothes, avoid artificial fibres, wash frequently and dry carefully. If you do get an infection, wash the infected area at least daily with a disinfectant or medicated soap and water, and rinse and dry well. Apply an antifungal cream or powder like tolnaftate (Tinaderm). Try to expose the infected area to air or sunlight as much as possible and wash all towels and underwear in hot water, change them often and let them dry in the sun.

Heat Exhaustion Dehydration and salt deficiency can cause heat exhaustion. Take time to acclimatise to high temperatures, drink sufficient liquids and do not do anything too physically demanding.

Salt deficiency is characterised by fatigue, lethargy, headaches, giddiness and muscle cramps; salt tablets may help, but adding extra salt on your food is better.

Heat Stroke This sometimes fatal condition can occur if the body's heat-regulating mechanism breaks down, and the body temperature rises to dangerous levels. Long, continuous periods of exposure to high temperatures can leave you vulnerable to heat stroke. You should avoid excessive alcohol or strenuous activity when you first arrive in a hot climate.

The symptoms are feeling unwell, not sweating very much or at all, and a high body temperature (39° to 41°C). Where sweating has ceased, the skin becomes flushed and red. Severe, throbbing headaches and lack of coordination will also occur, and the sufferer may be confused or aggressive. Eventually the victim will become delirious or begin to convulse. Hospitalisation is essential, but in the meantime get victims out of the sun, remove their clothing, cover them with a wet sheet or towel and then fan them continually.

Hypothermia Too much cold is just as dangerous as too much heat, particularly if it leads to hypothermia. Cold combined with wind and moisture (ie soaking rain) is particularly risky. If you are hiking at high altitudes or in a cool, wet environment, be prepared.

Hypothermia occurs when the body loses heat faster than it can produce it and the core temperature of the body falls. It is surprisingly easy to progress from very cold to dangerously cold through a combination of wind, wet clothing, fatigue and hunger, even if the air temperature is above freezing. It is best to dress in layers – silk, wool and some of the new artificial fibres are all good insulating materials. A hat is important, as a lot of heat is lost through the head. A strong, waterproof outer layer is essential. Carry basic supplies, including food that contains simple sugars to generate heat quickly, and lots of fluid to drink.

Symptoms of hypothermia are exhaustion, numb skin (particularly toes and fingers), shivering, slurred speech, irrational or violent behaviour, lethargy, stumbling, dizzy spells, muscle cramps and violent bursts of energy. Irrationality may take the form of sufferers claiming they are warm and trying to take off their clothes.

To treat hypothermia, first get the person out of the wind and/or rain, remove their clothing if it's wet and replace it with dry, warm clothing. Give them hot, nonalcoholic liquids and some high-kilojoule (high-calorie), easily digestible food. Do not rub victims' skin; place them near a fire or, if possible, in a warm (not hot) bath. This should be enough for the early stages of hypothermia. The early recognition and treatment of mild hypothermia is the only way to prevent severe hypothermia, which is a critical condition.

Jet Lag Jet lag is experienced when a person travels by air across more than three time zones (each time zone usually represents a one-hour time difference). It occurs because many of the functions of the human body (such as temperature, pulse rate and emptying of the bladder and bowels) are regulated by internal 24-hour cycles. When we travel long distances rapidly, our bodies take time to adjust to the 'new time' of our destination, and we may experience fatigue, disorientation,

insomnia, anxiety, impaired concentration and loss of appetite. These effects will usually be gone within three days of arrival, but to minimise the impact of jet lag:

- Rest for a couple of days prior to departure.
- Try to select flight schedules that minimise sleep deprivation; arriving late in the day means you can go to sleep soon after you arrive. For very long flights, try to organise a stopover.
- Avoid excessive eating (which bloats the stomach) and alcohol (which causes dehydration) during the flight. Instead, drink plenty of non-carbonated, non-alcoholic drinks such as fruit juice or water.
- Avoid smoking (if allowed on board).
- Make yourself comfortable by wearing loose-fitting clothes and perhaps bringing an eye mask and ear plugs to help you sleep.
- Try to sleep at the appropriate time for the time zone you are travelling to.

Motion Sickness Eating lightly before and during a trip will reduce the chances of motion sickness. If you are prone to motion sickness try to find a place that minimises movement – near the wing on aircraft, close to midships on boats, near the centre on buses. Fresh air usually helps; reading and cigarette smoke do not. Commercial motion-sickness preparations, which can cause drowsiness, have to be taken *before* the trip commences. Ginger (available in capsule form) and peppermint (including mint-flavoured sweets) are natural preventatives.

Prickly Heat Prickly heat is an itchy rash caused by excessive perspiration trapped under the skin. It usually strikes people who have just arrived to hot weather. Keeping cool, bathing often, using a mild talcum powder or resorting to air-conditioning may help.

Sunburn You can get sunburnt surprisingly quickly, even through cloud. Use a sunscreen, hat, and barrier cream for your nose and lips. Calamine lotion or stingose are good for mild sunburn. Protect your eyes with good quality sunglasses, particularly if you will be near water, sand or snow.

Infectious Diseases
Diarrhoea Simple things like a change of water, food or climate can all cause a mild

bout of diarrhoea, but a few rushed toilet trips with no other symptoms is not indicative of a major problem.

Dehydration is the main danger with any diarrhoea, particularly in children or the elderly as dehydration can occur quite quickly. Under all circumstances fluid replacement (at least equal to the volume being lost) is the most important thing to remember. Weak black tea with a little sugar, soda water, or soft drinks allowed to go flat and diluted 50% with clean water are all good. With severe diarrhoea a rehydrating solution is preferable to replace minerals and salts lost. Commercially available oral rehydration salts (ORS) are very useful; add them to boiled or bottled water. In an emergency you can make up a solution of six teaspoons of sugar and a half teaspoon of salt to a litre of boiled or bottled water. You need to drink at least the same volume of fluid that you are losing in bowel movements and vomiting. Urine is the best guide to the adequacy of replacement – if you have small amounts of concentrated urine, you need to drink more. Keep drinking small amounts often. Stick to a bland diet as you recover.

Hepatitis Hepatitis is a general term for inflammation of the liver. The symptoms are fever, chills, headache, fatigue, feelings of weakness and aches and pains, followed by loss of appetite, nausea, vomiting, abdominal pain, dark urine, light-coloured faeces, jaundiced (yellow) skin and the whites of the eyes may turn yellow. **Hepatitis A** is transmitted by contaminated food and drinking water. You should seek medical advice, but there is not much you can do apart from resting, drinking lots of fluids, eating lightly and avoiding fatty foods. People who have had hepatitis should avoid alcohol for some time after the illness, as the liver needs time to recover.

There are almost 300 million chronic carriers of **Hepatitis B** in the world. It is spread through contact with infected blood, blood products or body fluids, for example through sexual contact, unsterilised needles and blood transfusions, or contact with blood via small breaks in the skin. Other risk situations include having a shave, tattoo, or having your body pierced with contaminated equipment.

The symptoms of type B may be more severe and may lead to long term problems.

HIV & AIDS HIV, the Human Immunodeficiency Virus, develops into AIDS, Acquired Immune Deficiency Syndrome, which is a fatal disease. HIV is a major problem in many countries. Any exposure to blood, blood products or body fluids may put the individual at risk. The disease is often transmitted through sexual contact or dirty needles – vaccinations, acupuncture, tattooing and body piercing can be potentially as dangerous as intravenous drug use. HIV/AIDS can also be spread through infected blood transfusions; some developing countries cannot afford to screen blood used for transfusions.

If you do need an injection, ask to see the syringe unwrapped in front of you, or take a needle and syringe pack with you.

HIV is on the rise in Eastern Europe: in Romania as a result of blood transfusions; in Poland due to drug abuse; in Hungary among homosexuals; in Croatia mostly among heterosexuals. Though the incidence of AIDS is still relatively low in here compared with Western Europe or North America, its very existence calls for a basic change in human behaviour.

The excitement and euphoria of travel can make it easier to fall in love or have sex with a stranger, so travellers must be informed of these dangers. As a tourist you should always practise safe sex. You never know who is infected or even if you yourself have become infected. It's important to bring up the subject *before* you start to have sex. The golden rule is safe sex or no sex. Fear of HIV infection should never preclude treatment for serious medical conditions.

Sexually Transmitted Diseases Gonorrhoea, herpes and syphilis are among these diseases; sores, blisters or rashes around the genitals, discharges or pain when urinating are common symptoms. In some STDs, such as wart virus or chlamydia, symptoms may be less marked or not observed at all especially in women. Syphilis symptoms eventually disappear completely but the disease continues and can cause severe problems in later years. While abstinence from sexual contact is the only 100% effective prevention, using condoms is also effective. The treatment of gonorrhoea and syphilis is with antibiotics. The different sexually transmitted diseases each require specific antibiotics. There is no cure for herpes or AIDS.

STD clinics are widespread in Eastern Europe. Don't be shy about visiting them if you think you may have contracted something; they are there to help and have seen it all before.

Cuts, Bites & Stings
Cuts & Scratches Wash well and treat any cut with an antiseptic such as povidone-iodine. Where possible avoid bandages and Band-aids, which can keep wounds wet.

Bedbugs & Lice Bedbugs live in various places, but particularly in dirty mattresses and bedding, evidenced by spots of blood on bedclothes or on the wall. Bedbugs leave itchy bites in neat rows. Calamine lotion or Stingose spray may help.

All lice cause itching and discomfort. They make themselves at home in your hair (head lice), your clothing (body lice) or in your pubic hair (crabs). You catch lice through direct contact with infected people or by sharing combs, clothing and the like. Powder or shampoo treatment will kill the lice and infected clothing should they be washed in very hot, soapy water and left in the sun to dry.

Insect Bites & Stings Mosquitoes will drive you almost insane during the late spring and summer months in Eastern Europe. If you are without a mosquito net, they also cause sleepless nights in wet areas such as Lake Balaton in Hungary and the Great Masurian Lakes in Poland. Fortunately, mosquito-borne diseases like malaria are pretty much unknown in this part of the world, with the exception of the Danube Delta in Romania. Most people get used to mosquito bites after a few days as their bodies adjust, and the itching and swelling will become less severe. An antihistamine cream may help alleviate the symptoms. For some people, a daily dose of vitamin B seems to keep mosquitos at bay.

Bee and wasp stings are usually more painful than dangerous. However in people who are allergic to them severe breathing difficulties may occur and require urgent medical care. Calamine lotion or Stingose spray will give relief and ice packs will reduce the pain and swelling. There are few spiders with dangerous bites in Eastern Europe, and antivenenes are usually available.

Ticks You should always check all over your body if you have been walking through a potentially tick-infested area as ticks can cause skin infections and other more serious diseases. If a tick is found attached, press down around the tick's head with tweezers, grab the head and gently pull upwards. Avoid pulling the rear of the body as this may squeeze the tick's gut contents through the attached mouth parts into the skin, increasing the risk of infection and disease. Smearing chemicals on the tick will not make it let go and is not recommended.

Lyme disease is a tick-transmitted infection that may be acquired in parts of Eastern Europe. The illness usually begins with a spreading rash at the site of the tick bite and is accompanied by fever, headache, extreme fatigue, aching joints and muscles and mild neck stiffness. If untreated, these symptoms usually resolve over several weeks but over subsequent weeks or months disorders of the nervous system, heart and joints may develop. Treatment works best early in the illness. Medical help should be sought.

Another tick that can bring on more than just an itch is the forest tick, which burrows under the skin, causing inflammation and even encephalitis. It has become a common problem in parts of central and Eastern Europe, especially eastern Austria, Germany, Hungary and the Czech Republic. You might want to consider getting an FSME (meningoencephalitis) vaccination if you plan to do extensive hiking and camping between May and September.

Snakes Snakes tend to keep a very low profile in Eastern Europe, but to minimise your chances of being bitten, try to wear boots, socks and long trousers when walking through undergrowth or rocky areas where snakes may be present. Tramp heavily and they'll usually slither away before you come near. Don't put your hands into holes and crevices, and be careful when collecting firewood.

Snake bites do not cause instantaneous death and antivenenes are usually available. Keep the victim calm and still, wrap the bitten limb tightly, as you would for a sprained ankle, and attach a splint to immobilise it. Then seek medical help, if possible with the dead snake for identification. Don't attempt to catch the snake if there is even a remote possibility of it biting again. Tourniquets and sucking out the poison are now completely discredited.

Rabies Caused by a bite or scratch from an infected mammal, rabies is still found in some parts of Eastern Europe. Dogs are a noted carrier, but cats, foxes and bats can also be infected. Any bite, scratch or even lick from a warm-blooded, furry animal should be cleaned immediately and thoroughly. Scrub with soap and running water, and then clean with an alcohol solution. If there is any possibility that the animal is infected, particularly if it froths at the mouth and behaves strangely, medical help should be sought immediately. Even if it is not rabid, all bites should be treated seriously as they can become infected or can result in tetanus.

A rabies vaccination is available and should be considered if you are in a high-risk category – eg if you intend to explore caves (bat bites can be dangerous), work with animals, or travel so far off the beaten track that medical help is more than two days away.

Women's Health

Antibiotic use, synthetic underwear, sweating and contraceptive pills can lead to fungal vaginal infections when travelling in hot climates. Maintaining good personal hygiene, and loose-fitting clothes and cotton underwear will help to prevent these infections.

Fungal infections, characterised by a rash, itch and discharge, can be treated with a vinegar or lemon-juice douche, or with yoghurt. Nystatin, miconazole or clotrimazole pessaries or vaginal cream are the usual treatment.

Sexually transmitted diseases are a major cause of vaginal problems. Symptoms include a smelly discharge, painful intercourse and sometimes a burning sensation when urinat-ing. Male sexual partners must also be treated. Medical attention should be sought and remember in addition to these diseases HIV or hepatitis B may also be acquired during exposure. Besides abstinence, the best thing is to practise safe sex using condoms.

WOMEN TRAVELLERS

For women travellers, common sense is the best guide to dealing with possibly dangerous situations such as hitchhiking, walking alone at night etc. Women often travel alone or in pairs around Eastern Europe. As a rule this is usually quite safe, but women do tend to attract more unwanted attention than men. Women should refrain from entering working-class bars alone.

To avoid attracting attention, wear slightly conservative dress; dark sunglasses help to avoid unwanted eye contact. A wedding ring (on the left ring finger) sometimes helps.

GAY & LESBIAN TRAVELLERS

Eastern Europe lists contact addresses and gay and lesbian venues in the individual country chapters; look in the Facts for the Visitor and Entertainment sections.

The *Spartacus International Gay Guide* (Bruno Gmünder, Berlin; US$32.95) is a good male-only international directory of gay entertainment venues in Europe and elsewhere. It's best when used in conjunction with listings in local gay papers, usually distributed for free at gay bars and clubs; as elsewhere, gay venues in Eastern Europe change with the speed of summer lightning. For lesbians, *Women's Travel in Your Pocket* (Ferrari Publications, London; UK£8.99) is a good international guide.

DISABLED TRAVELLERS

If you have a physical disability, get in touch with your national support organisation (preferably the travel officer if there is one) and ask about the countries you plan to visit. They often have complete libraries devoted to travel, and they can put you in touch with travel agents who specialise in tours for the disabled.

The British-based Royal Association for Disability & Rehabilitation (RADAR) publishes a useful guide entitled *European Holidays & Travel Abroad: A Guide for Disabled People* (UK£5), which gives a good overview of facilities available to disabled travellers in Europe (published in even-numbered years) and one to places farther afield called *Long-Haul Holidays* (in odd-numbered years).

SENIOR TRAVELLERS
Senior citizens are entitled to many discounts in Eastern Europe on things like public transport, museum admission fees etc, provided they show proof of their age. In some cases they might need a special pass. The minimum qualifying age is generally 60 or 65 for men and slightly younger for women.

In your home country, a lower age may already entitle you to all sorts of interesting travel packages and discounts (on car hire, for instance) through organisations and travel agents that cater for senior travellers. Start hunting at your local senior citizens advice bureau. European residents over 60 are eligible for the Rail Europe Senior (RES) Card; see Cheap Tickets under Train in the Getting There & Away chapter for details.

TRAVEL WITH CHILDREN
Successful travel with young children requires planning and effort. Don't try to overdo things; even for adults, packing too much into the time available can cause problems. And make sure the activities include the kids as well – balance that morning at Budapest's Museum of Fine Arts with an afternoon at the nearby Grand Circus or a performance at the Puppet Theatre.

Include children in the trip planning; if they've helped to work out where you will be going, they will be much more interested when they get there. Lonely Planet's *Travel with Children* by Maureen Wheeler is a good source of information.

In Eastern Europe most car-rental firms have children's safety seats for hire at a nominal cost, but it is essential that you book them in advance. The same goes for highchairs and cots (cribs); they're standard in many restaurants and hotels but numbers are limited. The choice of baby food, infant formulas, soy and cow's milk, disposable nappies (diapers) and the like can be as great

in the supermarkets of many Eastern European countries as it is back home, but the opening hours may be quite different. Don't get caught out at the weekend.

DANGERS & ANNOYANCES
Eastern Europe is as safe – or unsafe – as any other part of the developed world. If you can handle yourself in the big cities of Western Europe, North America or Australia, you'll have little trouble dealing with the less pleasant sides of Eastern Europe. Look purposeful, keep alert and you'll be OK.

Whatever you do, don't leave friends and relatives back home worrying about how to get in touch with you in case of emergency. Work out a list of places where they can contact you. See the previous Post section for where to collect mail. Best of all is to phone home now and then or email from a cybercafé or hostel.

Some local people will regale you with tales of how dangerous their city is and recount cases of muggings, break-ins, kidnappings etc. Mostly they're comparing the present situation with that before 1989 when the crime rate was almost zero or unreported in the press.

Low-level corruption is disappearing fast as the back-scratching system so common during the communist regimes claims its rightful place in the dustbin of history, so do *not* pay bribes to persons in official positions, such as police, border guards, train conductors, ticket inspectors etc. If corrupt cops want to hold you up because some obscure stamp is missing from your documentation or on some other pretext, just let them and consider the experience an integral part of your trip. Don't worry at all if they take you to the police station for interrogation as you'll have a unique opportunity to observe the quality of justice in that country from the inside and more senior officers will eventually let you go (assuming, of course, you haven't committed a real crime). If you do have to pay a fine or supplementary charge, insist on a proper receipt before turning over any money. In all of this, try to maintain your cool as any threats from you will only make matters worse.

Theft

Theft is definitely a problem in Eastern Europe – the threat comes both from local thieves and your fellow travellers. The most important things to guard are your passport, other documents, tickets and money – in that order. It's always best to carry these next to your skin or in a sturdy leather pouch on your belt. Train station lockers or luggage storage counters are useful places to store your luggage (but not valuables) while you get your bearings in a new town. Be very suspicious of people who offer to help you operate your locker. Carry your own padlock for hostel lockers.

You can lessen the risks further by being careful of snatch thieves. Cameras or shoulder bags are great for these people, who sometimes operate from motorcycles or scooters and expertly slash the strap before you have a chance to react. A small daypack is better, but watch your rear. Be very careful at cafés and bars; loop the strap around your leg while seated.

Pickpockets are most active in dense crowds, especially in busy train stations and on buses and metros during peak hours. A common ploy in the Budapest and Prague metros has been for a group of well dressed young people to surround you, chattering away while one of the group zips through your pockets or purse.

Be careful even in hotels; don't leave valuables lying around in your room. Also be wary of sudden friendships.

Parked cars are prime targets for petty criminals in most cities, and cars with foreign number plates and/or rental agency stickers in particular. Cover the company logo with local football club stickers if possible, leave a local newspaper on the seat and generally try to make it look like a local car – provided the car does not have rental plates giving the entire game away! Never, ever leave anything you'd mind losing in a parked vehicle. Regardless of how heavy it is, remove all luggage overnight. In case of theft or loss, always report the incident to police and ask for a statement, or your travel insurance won't pay out.

Violence

Though it's unlikely that travellers will encounter violence in Eastern Europe, skinheads and neo-Nazis have singled out resident blacks and Asians as scapegoats for their own problems, while foreigners have been attacked in Hungary and the Czech Republic. Avoid especially rundown areas in cities and *never* fight back. These people can be extremely dangerous.

Drugs

Always treat drugs with a great deal of caution. There are a lot of drugs available in the region, but that doesn't mean it's legal. Throughout the 1990s, the war in the former Yugoslavia has forced drug traders to seek alternative routes from Asia to Western Europe, sometimes crossing through Hungary, Slovakia, the Czech Republic and Poland. These countries, desperately seeking integration into the 'new' Europe, do not look lightly upon drug abuse. Even a little hashish can cause a great deal of trouble in certain parts of the region.

ACTIVITIES

Skiing

Eastern Europe's premier skiing areas are the High Tatra Mountains of Poland and Slovakia; the Carpathians near Braşov in Romania; Mt Vitosha and Borovets near Sofia in Bulgaria; and Slovenia's Julian Alps. The skiing season generally lasts from early December to late March, though at higher altitudes it may extend an extra month either way. Snow conditions can vary greatly from one year to another and from region to region, but January and February tend to be the best (and busiest) months. Serious skiers with limited time should look into an all-inclusive package tour.

Hiking

There's excellent hiking in Eastern Europe with numerous well-marked trails through forests, mountains and the various national parks. Public transport will often take you to the trailheads, and chalets or mountain 'huts' in Bulgaria, Slovakia, Poland, Romania and Slovenia offer hikers dormitory accommodation and basic meals. In this book we include detailed information on hiking through the High Tatra Mountains of Poland and Slovakia, the Malá Fatra of Slovakia, the Bucegi and Făgăraş ranges in Romania's Carpathian Mountains, the Rila Mountains of Bulgaria and the Julian Alps of Slovenia but there are many other less well known hiking areas like the Bieszczady in Poland, Risnjak and Paklenica national parks in Croatia and the Zemplén hills in Hungary. The best months for hiking are from June to September, especially late in August and early September when the summer crowds will have disappeared.

Cycling

Along with hiking, cycling is the best way to really get close to the scenery and the people, keeping yourself fit in the process. It's also a good way to get around many cities and towns and a way to see remote corners of a country you wouldn't ordinarily get to.

The hills and mountains of Eastern Europe can make for heavy going, but this is offset by the dense concentration of things to see. Physical fitness is *not* a major prerequisite for cycling on the plains of eastern Hungary – they're flatter than pancakes! – but the wind might slow you down. Popular holiday cycling areas in Eastern Europe include the Danube Bend in Hungary, most of eastern Slovakia and the Karst region of Slovenia. Northern Romania is a wonderful place for a cycling tour.

If you are arriving from outside Eastern Europe, you can often bring your own bicycle along on the plane for a surprisingly reasonable fee. The Slovenian flag-carrier Adria, for instance, charges only UK£15 to transport a bicycle from London to Ljubljana. Alternatively, this book lists places where you can hire one (make sure it has plenty of gears if you plan anything serious).

See Bicycle in the Getting Around chapter for more information on bicycle touring, and the individual country chapters and city/town sections for rental agencies and tips on places to go.

Canoeing & Kayaking

Those with folding kayaks will want to launch them on the Krutynia River in Poland's Great Mazurian Lakes district, on the Danube, Rába and Tisza rivers in Hungary or the Soča River in Slovenia. Special kayaking and canoeing tours are offered in these countries, as well as in

Croatia. One of the world's great kayaking adventures is the 2081km Tour International Danubien (TID) on the Danube River in July and August starting in Ingoldstadt in Germany and ending in Silistra in Bulgaria.

White-Water Rafting

This exciting activity is possible in summer on two of Eastern Europe's most scenic rivers: the Tara River in Montenegro and the Soča River in Slovenia. Rafting on the Dunajec River along the border of Poland and Slovakia is fun, but it's not a white-water experience.

Sailing & Yachting

Eastern Europe's most famous yachting area is the passage between the long rugged islands off Croatia's Dalmatian coast. Yacht tours and rentals are available, though you certainly won't be able to do this 'on a shoestring'. If your means are more limited, the Great Mazurian Lakes of north-east Poland are a better choice as small groups can rent sailing boats by the day for very reasonable rates. Hungary's Lake Balaton is also popular among sailing enthusiasts.

Horse Riding

Though horse riding is possible throughout Eastern Europe, the sport is best organised – and cheapest – in Hungary, whose people, they say, 'were created by God to sit on horseback'. The best centres are on the Great Plain though you'll also find schools in Transdanubia and northern Hungary. Horse riding is also very popular (and affordable) in Slovenia and Poland.

Thermal Baths

There are hundreds of thermal baths in Eastern Europe open to the public. The most affordable ones are in Hungary, the Czech Republic, Slovenia and on the Black sea in Romania. Among the best are the thermal lake at Hévíz, the Turkish baths of Budapest and the spa town of Harkány in Hungary; the *fin-de-siécle* spas of Karlovy Vary (Karlsbad) and Mariánské Lázně (Marienbad) in the Czech Republic; and Dolenjske Toplice and Rogaška Slatina in Slovenia.

COURSES

Apart from learning new physical skills by doing something like a skiing course in Slovenia or horse riding in Hungary, you can enrich your mind with a variety of structured courses in Eastern Europe on anything from language to alternative medicine. Language courses are often available to foreigners through universities or private schools, and are justifiably popular since the best way to learn a language is in the country where it's spoken.

The individual country chapters in this book give pointers on where to start looking for language courses. In general, the best sources of information are the cultural institutes maintained by many European countries around the world; failing that, try their national tourist offices or embassies. Student exchange organisations, student travel agencies, and organisations like the YMCA/ YWCA and Hostelling International (HI) can also put you on the right track. Ask about special holiday packages that include a course.

WORK

With their high unemployment, Eastern European countries aren't keen on handing out jobs to foreigners. The paperwork involved in arranging a work permit can be almost impossible, especially for temporary work.

That doesn't prevent enterprising travellers from topping up their funds occasionally, and they don't always have to do this illegally. If you do find a temporary job in Eastern Europe, though, the pay is likely to be abysmally low. Do it for the experience – not to earn your fortune – and you won't be disappointed. Teaching English is the easiest way to make some extra cash, but the market is saturated in places like Prague and Budapest. You'll be much more successful in places like Bulgaria, Romania and Albania.

Work Your Way Around the World by Susan Griffith gives good, practical advice on a wide range of issues. Its publisher, Vacation Work, has many other useful titles, including *Summer Jobs Abroad*, edited by David Woodworth. *Working Holidays*, published by the Central Bureau for Educational Visits & Exchanges in London, is another good source as is *Hiring Now: Jobs in Eastern Europe* (Perpetual Press) by Clarke Caufield.

If you play an instrument or have other artistic talents, you could try working the streets. As every Peruvian pipe player (and his fifth cousin) knows, busking is fairly common in major Eastern European cities like Prague, Budapest and Ljubljana. Some countries may require municipal permits for this sort of thing. Talk to other street artists before you start.

Selling goods on the street is a hard way to make money if you're not selling something special. You could try your luck at the markets in some towns of Hungary, Poland, the Czech Republic and Slovenia, but you'll be competing with fresh arrivals from the east and south – not all of them legal – who know the game a lot better than you do.

ACCOMMODATION

As in the rest of Europe, the cheapest places to stay in Eastern Europe are camping grounds, followed by hostels and student accommodation. Guesthouses, pensions, private rooms and cheap hotels also present good value. Self-catering flats in the city and cottages in the countryside are worth considering if you're in a group, especially if you plan to stay put for a while.

See the Facts for the Visitor sections in the country chapters for an overview of the local accommodation options. During peak holiday periods, accommodation can be hard to find, and unless you're camping, it's advisable to book ahead where possible. Even camping grounds can fill up, particularly popular ones near large towns and cities.

Reservations

Cheap hotels in popular destinations (eg Prague, Budapest etc) – especially the well run ones in desirable or central neighbourhoods – fill up quickly. It's a good idea to make reservations as many weeks ahead as possible – at least for the first night or two. A three-minute international phone call to reserve a room (followed, if necessary, by written confirmation and/or deposit) is a lot cheaper than wasting your first day in a city looking for a place to stay.

If you arrive in a country by air and without a reservation, there is often an airport accommodation-booking desk, although it rarely covers the lower strata of hotels. Tourist offices often have extensive accommodation lists, and the more helpful ones will go out of their way to find you something suitable. In most countries the fee for this service is very low, and if accommodation is tight, it can save you a lot of running around. This is also an easy way to get around any language problems.

Camping

The cheapest way to go is camping, and there are numerous camping grounds throughout the region. Many are large 'auto camps' intended mainly for motorists though they're often easily accessible on public transport and there's almost always space for backpackers with tents. Many camping grounds in Eastern Europe rent small on-site cabins or bungalows for double or triple the regular camping fee. In the most popular resorts all the bungalows may be full in July and August, but try asking.

Quality varies from one country to the next. It's unreliable in Romania and Bulgaria, crowded in Slovenia and Hungary (especially on Lake Balaton) and variable in Poland. Coastal Croatia has nudist camping grounds galore, which are signposted 'FKK' (Freikörperkultur, meaning 'naturist') and excellent places to stay because of their secluded locations. A Camping Card International may get you a discount of between 5 and 10% at some camping grounds and often serves as a guarantee so you don't have to leave your passport at reception.

Camping grounds may be open from April to October, May to September, or perhaps only June to August, depending on the category of the facility and the demand. A few private camping grounds are open year round. In Eastern Europe you are sometimes allowed to build a campfire (though ask first). Freelance camping is usually taboo, so ask local people the situation before you pitch your tent on a beach or in an open field.

Hostels

Hostels offer the cheapest (secure) roof over your head in Eastern Europe, and you don't have to be a youngster to use them. Most hostels are part of the national youth hostel association (YHA), which is affiliated with what was formerly called the IYHF (International Youth Hostel Federation) and has been renamed Hostelling International (HI) in order to attract a wider clientele and move away from the emphasis on 'youth'. The situation remains slightly confused, however. Some countries, such as the USA and Canada, immediately adopted the new name, but many European countries will take a few years to change their logos. In practice it makes no difference: IYHF and HI are the same thing and the domestic YHA almost always belongs to the parent group.

Hostels affiliated with HI can be found in most Eastern European countries. A hostel card is seldom required, though you sometimes get a small discount if you have one. If you don't have a valid HI membership card, you can buy one at some hostels.

HI offices in English-speaking countries include the following:

Australia
    Australian Youth Hostels Association (☎ 02-9565 1699; fax 02-9565 1325; yha@yha.org.au), Level 3, 10 Mallett St, Camperdown, NSW 2050
Canada
    Hostelling International Canada (☎ 613-237 7884; fax 613-237 7868), 205 Catherine St, Suite 400, Ottawa, Ontario K2P 1C3
England & Wales
    Youth Hostels Association (☎ 01727-855215; fax 01727-844126; YHA CustomerServices@compuserve.com), Trevelyan House, 8 St Stephen's Hill, St Albans, Herts AL1 2DY
Ireland
    An Óige (Irish Youth Hostel Association; ☎ 01-830 4555; 01-830 5808; anoige@iol.ie), 61 Mountjoy St, Dublin 7
New Zealand
    Youth Hostels Association of New Zealand (☎ 03-379 9970; fax 03-365 4476; info@yha.org.nz), PO Box 436, Union House, 193 Cashel St, 3rd Floor, Christchurch
Northern Ireland
    Youth Hostel Association of Northern Ireland (☎ 01232-315435; fax 01232-439699), 22-32 Donegall Rd, Belfast BT12 5JN
Scotland
    Scottish Youth Hostels Association (☎ 01786-891400; fax 891333; admin@syha.org.uk), 7 Glebe Crescent, Stirling FK8 2JA

South Africa
Hostelling International South Africa (☎ 021-424 2511; fax 021-424 4119; info@hisa.org.za), PO Box 4402, St George's House, 73 St George's Mall, Cape Town 8001

USA
Hostelling International/American Youth Hostels (☎ 202-783 6161; fax 202-783 6171; hiayhserv@hiayh.org), 733 15th St NW, Suite 840, Washington DC 20005

At a hostel, you get a bed for the night, plus use of communal facilities, which often include a kitchen where you can prepare your own meals. You are sometimes required to have a sleeping sheet – simply using your sleeping bag is often not allowed. If you don't have your own sleeping sheet, you can sometimes hire one for a small fee.

Hostels vary widely in character and quality. The hostels in Poland are similar to those in Western Europe and easy to use. Polish hostels tend to be extremely basic but they're inexpensive and friendly. In the Czech Republic, and Slovakia many hostels are actually fairly luxurious 'junior' hotels with double rooms often fully occupied by groups. Most of the Hungarian hostels are regular student dormitories only open to travellers for six or seven weeks in summer. In Budapest and Prague a large number of privately operated hostels have appeared in recent years, some of which are open year round. The hostels in Bulgaria are usually in rural or mountain areas.

There are many hostel guides with listings available, including the HI's *Europe* (£7). Many hostels accept reservations by phone or fax, but usually not during peak periods; they'll often book the next hostel you're heading to for a small fee. You can also book hostels through national hostel offices. Popular hostels can be heavily booked in summer and limits may even be placed on how many nights you can stay.

University Accommodation
Some universities rent out student accommodation in July and August. This is quite popular in Poland, the Czech Republic, Slovakia, Hungary, Slovenia, Croatia and Macedonia. Accommodation will sometimes be in single rooms (more commonly in doubles or triples), and cooking facilities may be available. Inquire at the college or university, at student information services or at local tourist offices.

Private Rooms
In every Eastern European country, travel agencies arrange accommodation in private rooms in local homes. In Hungary you can get a private room almost anywhere, but in the other countries only the main tourist centres have them. Some 1st-class rooms are like mini-apartments, with cooking facilities and private bathroom for the use of guests alone. Prices are low but there's often a 30 to 50% surcharge if you stay less than four nights. In Hungary, the Czech Republic and Croatia increased taxation has made such rooms less attractive than they were in the past, but they're still good value and cheaper than a hotel.

People will frequently approach you at train or bus stations in Eastern Europe offering a private room or a hostel bed. This can be good or bad – there's no hard-and-fast rule. Just make sure it's not in some cardboard-quality housing project way out in a suburb somewhere and that you negotiate a clear price. As always, be careful when someone offers to carry your luggage: they might just carry it away.

You don't have to go through an agency or an intermediary on the street for a private room. Any house, cottage or farmhouse with 'Zimmer frei', 'sobe', 'szoba kiadó' etc displayed is advertising the availability of private rooms; just knock and ask if any are available. If the price asked is too high, try bargaining.

Pensions, Guesthouses & Farmhouses
Small private pensions have proliferated in Eastern Europe since the changes of 1989. Priced somewhere between hotels and private rooms, pensions usually have less than 10 rooms and the resident proprietors often make a good portion of their income from a small restaurant or bar on the premises. You'll get a lot more personal attention than you would at a hotel at the cost of just a wee bit of your privacy. If you arrive at night or on a weekend when the travel agencies assigning private rooms are closed, pensions are well worth a

try. Call ahead to check prices and ask about reservations – German is almost always spoken, as is, increasingly, English.

'Village tourism', which means staying at a farmhouse, is highly developed in Slovenia and increasingly popular in Hungary. In Slovenia, it's like staying in a private room or pension except that the participating farms are in picturesque rural areas and may offer activities such as horse riding, kayaking, skiing and cycling. It's highly recommended.

Hotels

At the very bottom of the bracket, cheap hotels may be no more expensive than private rooms or guesthouses in Eastern Europe, while at the other extreme they extend to luxury five-star hotels with price tags to match. Although categorisation varies from country to country, the hotels recommended in this book generally range from no stars to one or two stars. You'll often find cheap hotels clustered in the areas around bus and train stations – always good places to start hunting.

Single rooms can be hard to find in Eastern Europe, where you are generally charged by the room not the person and local people refuse to believe that anyone would actually take to the road alone. The cheapest rooms have a washbasin but shared bath, which means you'll have to go down the corridor to use the toilet and shower. In a few hotels the communal showers are kept locked and you're charged extra every time you get the key. Occasionally you can get a reduction on the room rate by asking for a room without breakfast but more often breakfast is extra and mandatory.

FOOD

Sampling the local food is one of the most enjoyable aspects of travel. Eastern European cuisine, though often a heavy and stodgy one of goulash, sausages, dumplings, groats and schnitzel, comes into its own in soups, game, the use of forest products (eg mushrooms and wild berries) and truly extravagant pastries. The Facts for the Visitor sections in the individual country chapters contain details of local cuisine, and there are many suggestions on places to eat in the chapters themselves.

Restaurant types and prices vary enormously in Eastern Europe. The cheapest place for a decent meal is the self-service cafeteria – sometimes called *buffet* or some variation of the word (*büfé*, *bife* etc) – still found in Poland, the Czech Republic, Slovakia and, to a lesser extent, Hungary and Slovenia. Elsewhere, department-store restaurants are a good bet. Official student *mensa* (university restaurants) are dirt cheap, but the food tends to be bland, and it's not always clear whether you'll be allowed in if you're not a local student. Kiosks often sell cheap snacks that can be as much a part of the national cuisine as fancy dishes.

It's worth trying the various folkloric restaurants where regional cuisine is usually on offer. It's called a *csárda* in Hungary, *gostišče* or *gostilna* in Slovenia and *mehana* in Bulgaria. In Slovakia and Hungary there are wine bars/restaurants (*vinárna* or *borozó*) and beer halls (*pivnice* or *söröző*). Czech beer is arguably the best of its type in the world and the wines of Hungary, Slovenia and Bulgaria and Croatia can be quite good. Romanian and Slovakian wine ranges from rot-gut to acceptable.

Self-catering – buying your ingredients at a shop or market and preparing them yourself – is a cheap and wholesome way of eating. Even if you don't cook, a lunch on a park bench with a fresh stick of bread, some local cheese and salami and a tomato or two, washed down with a bottle of local wine, can be one of the recurring highlights of your trip. It also makes a nice change from restaurant food.

If you have dietary restrictions – you're a vegetarian or you keep kosher, for example – tourist organisations may be able to advise you or provide lists of suitable restaurants. Some vegetarian and kosher restaurants are listed in this book.

Vegetarianism is in its infancy in Eastern Europe (a part of the world that has traditionally been *very* big on meat) though vegetarians won't starve. Many restaurants have one or two vegetarian dishes – deep fried mushroom caps, pasta dishes with cheese, vegetable dumplings or Greek-style 'peasant' salads. Others might prepare special dishes on request as long as you approach them about this in advance.

Getting There & Away

AIR

Long-haul air fares to/from Eastern Europe are not the Continent's biggest bargains. Your best bet is to buy the cheapest possible ticket to somewhere in Western or central Europe and proceed by land from there. Look for a ticket to London, Amsterdam, Athens, Istanbul or anywhere in Germany. Vienna is a useful gateway as the Czech Republic, Slovakia, Hungary and Slovenia are all just a few hours away.

Buying Tickets

Your plane ticket will probably be the single most expensive item in your travel budget, and it's worth taking some time to research the current state of the market. Start early: some of the cheapest tickets have to be bought well in advance, and some popular flights sell out early. Talk to recent travellers, look at the ads in newspapers and magazines and watch for special offers. Don't forget to check the press of the ethnic group whose country you plan to visit. These publications often advertise inexpensive flights.

Cheap tickets are available in two distinct categories: official and unofficial. Official ones have a variety of names including advance purchase tickets, advance purchase excursion (Apex) fares, super-Apex and simply budget fares.

Unofficial tickets are simply discounted tickets that the airlines release through selected travel agents (usually not sold by the airline offices themselves). Airlines can, however, supply information on routes and timetables and make bookings; their low season, student and seniors' fares can be quite attractive. Also, normal, full-fare airline tickets sometimes include one or more side trips in Europe free of charge, which can make them good value.

Return (round-trip) tickets usually work out cheaper than two one-way fares – often *much* cheaper. Be aware that immigration officials often ask for return or onward tickets, and if you can't show either you'll have to provide proof of 'sufficient means of support'. This means you have to show a lot of money or, in some cases, valid credit cards.

Round the world (RTW) tickets can also work out to be no more expensive or even cheaper than an ordinary return ticket. The official airline RTW tickets are usually put together by a combination of two or more airlines, and permit you to fly anywhere you want on their route systems so long as you don't backtrack. Other restrictions are that you (usually) must book the first sector in advance and cancellation penalties apply. There may be restrictions on how many stops (or kilometres/miles) you are permitted, and usually the tickets are valid for from 90 days up to a year. Prices start at about UK£800, A$1700 or US$1300, depending on the season and length of validity. An alternative type of RTW ticket is one put together by a travel agent using a combination of discounted tickets. These can be much cheaper than the official ones, but usually carry a lot of restrictions.

Generally, you can find discounted tickets at prices as low as, or lower than, advance purchase or budget tickets. Phone around the travel agencies for bargains. You may discover that those impossibly cheap flights are 'fully booked, but we have another one that costs a bit more...' Or that the flight is on an airline notorious for its poor safety record and will leave you for 14 hours in the world's least-favourite airport, where you'll be confined to the transit lounge unless you get an expensive visa... Or the agent may claim that the last two cheap seats until next autumn will be gone in two hours. Don't panic – keep ringing around.

If you are travelling from the USA or South-East Asia, you will sometimes find that the cheapest flights are being advertised by obscure agencies whose names have yet to reach the telephone directory. Many such firms are honest and solvent, but there are a few rogues who will take your money and run, only to reopen elsewhere a month or two later under a new name. If you feel suspicious about a firm, don't give them all the money at once – leave a deposit of 20% or so and pay the balance when you get the ticket. If they insist on cash in advance, go somewhere else or take a very big risk. Once you have the ticket, ring the airline to confirm that you are booked on the flight.

You may decide to pay more than the rock-bottom fare by opting for the safety of better known travel agents. Firms such as STA Travel (www.sta-travel.com), which has offices worldwide, Council Travel (www.counciltravel.com) in the USA and elsewhere or Travel CUTS (www.travelcuts.com) in Canada offer good prices to most destinations, and won't disappear overnight leaving you clutching a receipt for a nonexistent ticket. Use the fares quoted in this book as a guide only. They are approximate and based on the rates advertised by travel agents at the time of research. Most are likely to have changed by the time you read this.

For details of websites containing airline information, see Internet Resources in the Facts for the Visitor chapter.

Travellers with Special Needs

If you have special needs of any sort – you're vegetarian or require a special diet, you're travelling in a wheelchair, taking a baby, terrified of flying etc – let the airline people know as soon as possible so that they can make the necessary arrangements. Remind them when you reconfirm your booking (at least 72 hours before departure) and again when you check in at the airport. It may also be worth ringing around the airlines before you make your booking to find out how they can handle your particular needs.

In general, children under two travel for 10% of the standard fare (or, on some carriers, for free) as long as they don't occupy a seat. They don't get a luggage allowance either. Skycots, baby food, formula, nappies (diapers) etc should be provided by the airline if requested in advance. Children aged between two and 12 can usually occupy a seat for half to two-thirds of the full fare and do get a standard baggage allowance.

The USA

The flight options across the North Atlantic, the world's busiest long-haul air corridor, are bewildering. The *New York Times*, *LA Times*, *Chicago Tribune* and *San Francisco Chroni-*

cle all have weekly travel sections in which you'll find any number of travel agents' ads. Council Travel and STA have offices in major cities nationwide. You should be able to fly from New York to London, where there are many cheap flights to Eastern European cities, and back for US$400 to US$500 in the low season and US$550 to US$700 in the high season. Equivalent fares from the West Coast are US$100 to US$300 higher.

On a standby basis, one-way fares can work out to be remarkably cheap. New York-based Airhitch (☎ 212-864 2000; wwwairhitch.org) specialises in this sort of thing and can get you to/from Europe for US$175/225/255 each way from the East Coast/Midwest/West Coast.

An interesting alternative to the boring New York-London flight is offered by Icelandair (☎ 800-223 5500), which has competitive year-round fares to Luxembourg with a three-night stopover in Iceland's capital, Reykjavík – a great way of spending a few days in an unusual country that's otherwise hard to get to.

Another option is a courier flight. A New York-London return ticket can be had for as little as US$300 in the low season. You may also be able to fly one way. The drawbacks are that your stay in Europe may be limited to one or two weeks; your luggage is usually restricted to hand luggage (the courier company uses your checked luggage allowance to send its parcels); there is unlikely to be more than one courier ticket available for any given flight; and you may have to be a local resident and apply for an interview before they'll take you on.

You can find out more about courier flights from the International Association of Air Travel Couriers (☎ 561-582 8320; fax 561-582 1581; www.courier.org; iaatc@courier.org), As You Like It Travel (☎ 212-679 6949; fax 212-779 9674; www.asulikeit.com) or Now Voyager Travel (☎ 212-431 1616; fax 212-334 5243; www.nowvoyagertravel.com).

Canada

Travel CUTS (☎ 1-888-838 CUTS) has offices in all major cities. You might also scan the budget travel agents' ads in the

Air Travel Glossary

Baggage Allowance This will be written on your ticket and usually includes one 20kg item to go in the hold, plus one item of hand luggage.

Bucket Shops These are unbonded travel agencies specialising in discounted airline tickets.

Bumped Just because you have a confirmed seat doesn't mean you're going to get on the plane (see Overbooking).

Cancellation Penalties If you have to cancel or change a discounted ticket, there are often heavy penalties involved; insurance can sometimes be taken out against these penalties. Some airlines impose penalties on regular tickets as well, particularly against 'no-show' passengers.

Check-In Airlines ask you to check in a certain time ahead of the flight departure (usually one to two hours on international flights). If you fail to check in on time and the flight is overbooked, the airline can cancel your booking and give your seat to somebody else.

Confirmation Having a ticket written out with the flight and date you want doesn't mean you have a seat until the agent has checked with the airline that your status is 'OK' or confirmed. Meanwhile you could just be 'on request'.

Courier Fares Businesses often need to send urgent documents or freight securely and quickly. Courier companies hire people to accompany the package through customs and, in return, offer a discount ticket which is sometimes a phenomenal bargain. In effect, what the companies do is ship their freight as your luggage on regular commercial flights. This is a legitimate operation, but there are two shortcomings – the short turnaround time of the ticket (usually not longer than a month) and the limitation on your luggage allowance. You may have to surrender all your allowance and take only carry-on luggage.

Full Fares Airlines traditionally offer 1st class (coded F), business class (coded J) and economy class (coded Y) tickets. These days there are so many promotional and discounted fares available that few passengers pay full economy fare.

ITX An ITX, or 'independent inclusive tour excursion', is often available on tickets to popular holiday destinations. Officially it's a package deal combined with hotel accommodation, but many agents will sell you one of these for the flight only and give you phoney hotel vouchers in the unlikely event that you're challenged at the airport.

Lost Tickets If you lose your airline ticket an airline will usually treat it like a travellers cheque and, after inquiries, issue you with another one. Legally, however, an airline is entitled to treat it like cash and if you lose it then it's gone forever. Take good care of your tickets.

MCO An MCO, or 'miscellaneous charge order', is a voucher that looks like an airline ticket but carries no destination or date. It can be exchanged through any International Association of Travel Agents (IATA) airline for a ticket on a specific flight. It's a useful alternative to an onward ticket in those countries that demand one, and is more flexible than an ordinary ticket if you're unsure of your route.

No-Shows No-shows are passengers who fail to show up for their flight. Full-fare passengers who fail to turn up are sometimes entitled to travel on a later flight. The rest are penalised (see Cancellation Penalties).

On Request This is an unconfirmed booking for a flight.

Onward Tickets An entry requirement for many countries is that you have a ticket out of the country. If you're unsure of your next move, the easiest solution is to buy the cheapest onward ticket to a neighbouring country or a ticket from a reliable airline which can later be refunded if you do not use it.

Open Jaw Tickets These are return tickets where you fly out to one place but return from another. If available, this can save you backtracking to your arrival point.

Overbooking Airlines hate to fly empty seats and since every flight has some passengers who fail to show up, airlines often book more passengers than they have seats. Usually excess passengers make up for the no-shows, but occasionally somebody gets bumped. Guess who it is most likely to be? The passengers who check in late.

Point-to-Point Tickets These are discount tickets that can be bought on some routes in return for passengers waiving their rights to a stopover.

Promotional Fares These are officially discounted fares, available from travel agencies or direct from the airline.

Reconfirmation At least 72 hours prior to departure time of an onward or return flight, you must contact the airline and 'reconfirm' that you intend to be on the flight. If you don't do this the airline can delete your name from the passenger list and you could lose your seat.

Restrictions Discounted tickets often have various restrictions on them – such as needing to be paid for in advance and incurring a penalty to be altered. Others are restrictions on the minimum and maximum period you must be away, such as a minimum of 14 days or a maximum of one year.

Round-the-World Tickets RTW tickets give you a limited period (usually a year) in which to circumnavigate the globe. You can go anywhere the carrying airlines go, as long as you don't backtrack. The number of stopovers or total number of separate flights is decided before you set off and they usually cost a bit more than a basic return flight.

Stand-by This is a discounted ticket where you only fly if there is a seat free at the last moment. Stand-by fares are usually available only on domestic routes.

Travel Agencies Travel agencies vary widely and you should choose one that suits your needs. Some simply handle tours, while full-services agencies handle everything from tours and tickets to car rental and hotel bookings. If all you want is a ticket at the lowest possible price, then go to an agency specialising in discounted tickets.

Transferred Tickets Airline tickets cannot be transferred from one person to another. Travellers sometimes try to sell the return half of their ticket, but officials can ask you to prove that you are the person named on the ticket. This is less likely to happen on domestic flights, but on an international flight tickets are compared with passports.

Travel Periods Ticket prices vary with the time of year. There is a low (off-peak) season and a high (peak) season, and often a low-shoulder season and a high-shoulder season as well. Usually the fare depends on your outward flight - if you depart in the high season and return in the low season, you pay the high-season fare.

Globe & Mail, Montreal Gazette, Toronto Star and the *Vancouver Sun*.

See the previous USA section for general information on courier flights. Airhitch (see the USA section) has standby fares to/from Toronto, Montreal and Vancouver.

Australia

STA and Flight Centres International are major dealers in cheap air fares. Saturday's travel sections in the *Sydney Morning Herald* and Melbourne's *The Age* have many ads offering cheap fares to Europe, but don't be surprised if they happen to be 'sold out' when you call: they're usually low-season fares on obscure airlines with conditions attached. With Australia's large and well organised ethnic populations, it pays to check special deals in the ethnic press.

Thai, Malaysian, Qantas and Singapore start from about A$1500 (low season) up to A$2500. All have frequent promotional fares so it pays to check daily newspapers. Flights to/from Perth are a couple of hundred dollars cheaper.

Another option for travellers wanting to go to Britain between November and February is to hook up with a Britannia Airlines charter flight returning to Britain. These low-season, one-way fares do have restrictions, but may work out to be considerably cheaper. Ask your travel agent for details.

New Zealand

As in Australia, STA and Flight Centres International are popular travel agents in New Zealand. The cheapest fares to Europe are routed through Asia. Auckland to Frankfurt or Rome costs NZ$1185 one-way, and NZ$2049 return (low season). An RTW ticket is around NZ$2300.

Africa

Nairobi and Johannesburg are probably the best places in Africa to buy tickets to Europe, thanks to the many bucket shops and the lively competition between them. Several West African countries offer cheap charter flights to France. Charter fares from Morocco and Tunisia can be quite cheap if you're lucky enough to find a seat.

From South Africa, Air Namibia has particularly cheap return youth fares to London

from as low as R3840. The big carriers' return fares average about R6820. Student Travel Centre (☎ 011-447 5414) in Johannesburg, and the Africa Travel Centre (☎ 021-235 555) in Cape Town are worth trying for cheap tickets.

Asia

Singapore and Bangkok are the discount air fare capitals of South-East Asia. Shop around and ask the advice of other travellers before handing over any money. STA has branches in Hong Kong (Sincerity Travel is the handler), Tokyo, Singapore, Bangkok, Jakarta and Kuala Lumpur.

Mumbai (Bombay) and Delhi are the main transport hubs in India but tickets may be slightly cheaper from the bucket shops around Connaught Place in Delhi. Check with other travellers about their current trustworthiness.

The UK

If you're looking for a cheap way into or out of Eastern Europe, London is Europe's major centre for discounted fares. Throughout the year you should be able to fly to any of the following cities and back for between UK£100 and UK£200: Berlin, Budapest, Munich, Prague, Vienna and Warsaw.

You can often find air fares from London that either match or beat surface alternatives in terms of cost. A return fare from London to Budapest is available through discount travel agents, for example, for between UK£165 and £191, and to Prague for between UK£167 and £208, depending on the season. By comparison, a two-month advance-purchase return by rail to Budapest costs UK£243/£193 for adults/youths. Getting between airports and city centres is rarely a problem in Eastern Europe thanks to the ever improving tram networks and good bus services.

If you are travelling alone, courier flights are a possibility. You get cheap passage in return for carrying a package or documents through customs and delivering it to a representative at the destination airport. EU integration and electronic communications means there's increasingly less call for couriers, but you might find something. British Airways, for example, offers courier flights through the Travel Shop (☎ 0181-564 7009).

The following are addresses of some of the best agencies to contact for discounted tickets in London:

Trailfinders
(☎ 0171-937 5400 for trans-Atlantic flights, ☎ 0171-938 3939 for long-haul ones; tube High Street Kensington) 194 Kensington High St, London W8 7RG

STA Travel
(☎ 0171-361 6262; www.sta-travel.com; tube High Street Kensington) Priory House, 6 Wrights Lane W8 6TA

Campus Travel
(☎ 0171 730 7285; tube Victoria) 52 Grosvenor Gardens, London SW1W OAG

Council Travel
(☎ 0171-287 3337; www.counciltravel.com; tube Oxford Circus) 28A Poland St, London W1V 3DB

The entertainment listings weekly *Time Out*, the weekend newspapers and the *Evening Standard* carry ads for cheap fares. Also look out for the free magazines and newspapers widely available in London, especially *TNT* and *Southern Cross*. You can often pick them up outside main train and tube stations.

Make sure the agent is a member of some sort of traveller-protection scheme, such as that offered by the Association of British Travel Agents (ABTA). If you have paid for your flight to an ABTA-registered agent who then goes out of business, ABTA will guarantee a refund or an alternative. Unregistered bucket shops are riskier but usually cheaper.

Continental Europe

Though London is the travel discount capital of Europe, there are several other cities in the region where you'll find a wide range of good deals, particularly Amsterdam, Athens and even Paris.

Many travel agents in Europe have ties with STA Travel, where cheap tickets can be purchased and STA tickets can often be altered free of charge the first time around. Outlets in important transport hubs include: NBBS Reizen (☎ 020-624 0989), Rokin 38, Amsterdam; Voyages Wasteels (☎ 01 43 43 46 10), 2 Rue Michel Chasles, 75012 Paris; SRID Reizen (☎ 069-703035), Bockenheimer Landstrasse 133, 60325 Frankfurt; and International Student & Youth Travel Service

(ISYTS; ☎ 01-322 1267), Nikis 11, 2nd floor, 10557 Athens.

LAND
Bus

In general, international bus travel tends to take second place to going by train. The bus has the edge in terms of cost, sometimes quite substantially, but is generally slower and less comfortable. Eurolines UK (☎ 0990-143219), 52 Grosvenor Gardens, London SW1W 0AU is the main international bus company. Sample return/one-way fares from London's Victoria Coach Station in the high season are Budapest UK£129/119, Prague UK£95/85 and Warsaw UK£95/91. Discounts of 10 to 20% are available to people 25 or under or over 60. There are also discount fares available to all on offer from time to time. Return tickets are valid for six months.

Eurolines offices or representatives in Europe include:

Austria
Eurolines Austria (☎ 01-712 0453), Autobusbahnhof Wien-Mitte, Landstrasser Hauptstrasse 1/b, 1030 Vienna
Belgium
Eurolines Belgium (☎ 02-203 0707), Coach Station, CCN North Station, Brussels
Czech Republic
Eurolines Czech Republic (☎ 02-2421 3420), Opletalova 37, Prague 1
France
Eurolines France (☎ 01 43 54 11 99 or ☎ 01 49 72 51 51), 55 Rue Saint Jacques 75005 Paris
Germany
Deutsche Touring (☎ 069-790 350), Am Römerhof 17, 60486 Frankfurt am Main Deutsche Touring (☎ 089-591 824), Hauptbahnhof, 80335 Munich
Hungary
Volánbusz (☎ 1-117 2562), Erzsébet tér, V Budapest
Italy
Lazzi Express (☎ 06-4423 3928), Via Tagliamento 27R, Rome
Netherlands
Amstel Busstation (☎ 020-694 5631), Julianaplein, 1097 DN Amsterdam

These may also be able to advise you on other bus companies and deals.

Eurolines has seven circular explorer routes, always starting and ending in London. The popular London-Budapest-Prague-London route is UK£112. Explorer tickets are also valid for six months. Eurolines also offers passes, but they're neither as extensive nor as flexible as rail passes. They cover 30 European cities as far apart as London, Barcelona, Rome, Budapest and Copenhagen, and cost UK£229 for 30 days (UK£199 for youths and senior citizens) or UK£279 for 60 days (UK£249). The passes are cheaper off-season.

Eurobus operates buses that complete set circuits round Europe, stopping at major cities. You get unlimited travel per sector, and can 'hop on, hop off' at any scheduled stop, then resume with a later bus. Buses are often oversubscribed, so prebook each sector to avoid being stranded. Departures are daily on the northern circuit (including Paris, Amsterdam, Berlin, Prague, Munich etc) and on the central circuit (Paris, Zürich, Venice, Rome), and every two days on the southern circuit (Paris, Nice, Madrid, Lisbon). For each circuit it costs UK£129/149/159 for one/two/four months, or UK£119/129/139 for students. To travel any two circuits costs about 50% extra, and for all three add about the same again (you couldn't make full use of three circuits within a month). Tickets are available in many countries worldwide; in the UK contact Eurobus (☎ 0118-936 2320; info@eurobus.com).

Busabout (☎ 0181-784 2816; busabout .info@virgin.net) is a new London-based competitor to Eurobus. Prices are almost the same as those offered by Eurobus, as are the routes though buses depart every second day on all three circuits. Its Bedabout scheme gives you 10 nights accommodation in tents for UK£70.

See the individual country chapters for more information about long-distance buses.

Other Bus Routes Coming from Western Europe, you can take a bus from Vienna to Brno in the Czech Republic or Bratislava in Slovakia. As well there are also buses travelling from Vienna to Sopron and Budapest in Hungary.

From Greece to Bulgaria a bus will cost less than the train. From Turkey, there are cheap buses from Istanbul to Bucharest.

Train
Before travelling by train or bus, check with the relevant consulates as to whether you'll need transit visas for countries you'll be passing through. Generally, if you need a visa to visit a country, you'll need a transit visa to pass through it.

International Tickets All regular international train tickets are valid for two months and you may stop off as often as you wish. In Eastern Europe keep in mind that international train tickets are often more easily purchased at a travel agency rather than at the railway station.

Railway tickets are expensive in Western Europe, so only buy a ticket as far as your first major stop within Eastern Europe and buy further tickets from there. From London a one-way 2nd-class train ticket will cost UK£177 to Poznań (Poland), UK£212 to Budapest (Hungary), UK£192 to Vienna (from where it's a short hop to Slovakia and the Czech Republic) and UK£161 to Ljubljana in Slovenia. Domestic tickets within a single Eastern European country are much cheaper. Also compare train travel with the price of international buses.

A good deal to know about if you're coming from Belgium, Denmark, France, Luxembourg or the Netherlands is the Sparpreis fare which allows a round trip anywhere in Germany within one month for DM209 (an accompanying person pays just DM105). This ticket can be purchased at any German railway station, allows unlimited stopovers along the direct route and is valid for 30 days, but you are not allowed to complete the return trip within a single Monday-to-Friday period.

Convenient border stations accessible on the Sparpreis ticket are Görlitz (for Poland), Schirnding (for the Czech Republic), Passau or Simbach (for Slovakia and Hungary) and Salzburg (for Slovenia). Of course, you have to get to a German train station to begin, but even with the cost of additional tickets at each end it might still work out cheaper than a through ticket.

Students without a national student ID card usually don't get discounts on domestic train tickets in Eastern Europe, but all travellers aged under 26 can pick up Wasteels 26 (or BIJ for Billet International de Jeunesse) tickets for 2nd-class travel on selected routes with discounts of between 30 and 40%. Unfortunately, you can't always bank on a substantial reduction. London to Paris return is only UK£89 instead of UK£159, whereas London to Munich return is UK£162, a measly UK£2 less than the normal fare! Various agents issue BIJ tickets in Europe, including Wasteels (☎ 0171-834 7066) in London's Victoria Railway Station and Voyages Wasteels (☎ 01 43 43 46 10) at 2 Rue Michel Chasles, 75012 Paris. Rail Europe (☎ 0990-848 848) sells BIJ tickets as well Eurail and Inter-Rail (see Rail Passes). It has London offices at 179 Piccadilly and in Victoria Railway Station.

In much of Eastern Europe, tickets to/from the countries of the former Soviet bloc are still heavily discounted. In Hungary, for example, there are 30% discounts on return fares to Belarus, Czech Republic, Bulgaria, Latvia, Lithuania, Poland and Slovenia; 50% to Croatia, Russia and Ukraine; 40% to Yugoslavia (Belgrade); and a massive 70% to Romania and Slovenia. There are sometimes even better deals to selected cities in the region. See the individual country chapters for details and check with the local student travel office for any updates or changes.

A number of international trains in Eastern Europe require seat reservations, which are a nuisance to make. Then when you get on the train, you find it is almost empty. This is a hangover from the communist era, when paranoid officials tried to make it as difficult as possible for their citizens to travel abroad, and it will probably take a while for Eastern European railways to get rid of all this unnecessary red tape.

Rail Passes Shop around, as pass prices can vary between different outlets. Once purchased, take care of your pass, as it cannot be replaced or refunded if lost or stolen. European passes get reductions on Eurostar through the Channel Tunnel and on ferries on certain routes (eg Eurail pass holders pay 50% of the appropriate fare for ferry cross-

ings between Ireland and France on Irish Ferries).

Eurail These passes can only be bought by residents of non-European countries, and are supposed to be purchased before arriving in Europe. However, Eurail passes can be purchased within Europe, so long as your passport proves you've been there for less than six months, but the outlets where you can do this are limited, and the passes will be more expensive than getting them outside Europe. Rail Europe (☎ 0990-848 848) in London is one such outlet, as is Drifters Travel Centre (☎ 0171-402 9171), 22 Craven Terrace in London, which may have lower prices. If you've lived in Europe for more than six months, you are eligible for an Inter-Rail pass, which is better value.

Eurail passes are valid for unlimited travel on national railways and some private lines in Austria, Belgium, Denmark, Finland, France (including Monaco), Germany, Greece, Hungary, Ireland, Italy, Luxembourg, the Netherlands, Norway, Portugal, Spain, Sweden and Switzerland (including Liechtenstein). Thus, covering only Hungary of the dozen countries in this book, Eurail passes would be useless for touring around Eastern Europe. Still, if you will be travelling in both Western and Eastern Europe and want to use Hungary as your gateway, they might make sense.

Eurail is also valid on some ferries between Italy and Greece and between Sweden and Finland. Reductions are given on some other ferry routes and on river/lake steamer services in various countries.

Eurail passes offer reasonable value to people aged under 26. A Youthpass gives unlimited 2nd-class travel within a choice of five validity periods: 15/22 days (US$376/489) or one/two/three months (US$605/857/1059). The Youth Flexipass, also for 2nd class, is valid for freely chosen days within a two-month period: 10 days for US$444 or 15 days for US$585.

Overnight journeys commencing after 7 pm count as the following day's travel. The traveller must fill out in ink the relevant box in the calendar before starting a day's travel; not validating the pass in this way earns a fine of US$50, plus the full fare. Tampering with the pass (eg using an erasable pen and later rubbing out earlier days) costs the perpetrator the full fare plus US$100, and confiscation of the pass.

For those aged over 26, the equivalent passes provide 1st class travel. The standard Eurail pass costs US$538/698 for 15/22 days or US$864/1224/1512 for one/two/three months. The Flexipass costs US$634/836 for 10/15 days within two months. Two people travelling together can get a 'saver' version of either pass, saving about 15%. Eurail passes for children are also available.

Inter-Rail Inter-Rail passes are available to European residents of six months' standing (passport identification is required). Terms and conditions vary slightly from country to country, but in the country of origin there is a discount of only 50% on normal fares.

The Inter-Rail pass is split into zones. Zone A is Ireland (and Britain if purchased in continental Europe); B is Sweden, Norway and Finland; C is Denmark, Germany, Switzerland and Austria; D is the Czech Republic, Slovakia, Poland, Hungary and Croatia; E is France, Belgium, Netherlands and Luxembourg; F is Spain, Portugal and Morocco; G is Italy, Greece, Turkey, Slovenia and Italy-Greece ferries; H is Bulgaria, Romania, Yugoslavia and Macedonia.

The normal Inter-Rail pass is for people under 26, though travellers over 26 can get the Inter-Rail 26+ version. The price for any one zone is UK£159 (UK£229 for 26+) for 22 days. Multizone passes are valid for one month: two zones is UK£209 (UK£279), three zones is UK£229 (UK£309), and all zones is UK£259 (UK£349). A two-zone pass including zones D and G would allow unlimited travel throughout most of Eastern Europe

Euro Domino There is a Euro Domino pass (called a Freedom pass in Britain) for each of the countries covered in the Inter-Rail pass, except for Macedonia. Adults (travelling 1st or 2nd class) and youths under 26 can choose from three, five, or 10 days validity within one month. Examples of adult/youth prices for 10 days in 2nd class are UK£79/£59 for Poland and UK£89/£59 for the Czech Republic.

Trans-Siberian/Mongolian/Manchurian/Kazakhstan It is possible to get to Eastern Europe by rail from central and eastern Asia, though count on spending at least eight days doing it. You can choose from four different routes to Moscow: the Trans-Siberian (9297km from Vladivostok), the Trans-Mongolian (7860km from Beijing) and the Trans-Manchurian (9001km from Beijing), which all use the same tracks across Siberia but have different routes east of Lake Baikal; and the Trans-Kazakhstan, which runs between Moscow and Urumqi in northwestern China.

Prices vary enormously, depending on where you buy the ticket and what is included – advertised 2nd-class fares include US$490 from Vladivostok and US$282 from Beijing. All of the details are readily available from the Russian National Tourist Office (www.interknowledge.com/russia /trasib.01.htm) as well as from Finnsov (www.finnsov.fi/fs–trsib.html).

There are countless travel options between Moscow and the rest of Europe. Most people will opt for the train, usually to/from Berlin, Helsinki, Munich, Budapest or Vienna.

The *Trans-Siberian Handbook* (Trailblazer) by Bryn Thomas is a comprehensive guide to the route as is *The Trans-Siberian Rail Guide* (Compass Star) by Robert Strauss & Tamsin Turnbull. Lonely Planet's *Russia, Ukraine & Belarus* has a separate chapter on trans-Siberian travel.

Other Train Routes For the Czech Republic or Slovakia, you can take a train from Linzine Austria to České Budějovice, or from Vienna to Bratislava or Břeclav. For Hungary there are trains from Vienna to Sopron and Budapest.

Railway lines converge from Austria and Italy on Ljubljana, from where you can easily reach Croatia and Yugoslavia. The main line from Munich to Athens runs via Budapest and Belgrade.

From Greece, there are a couple of trains per day between the towns of Thessaloniki and Skopje. From Turkey, the main railway line from Istanbul to Belgrade passes through Sofia.

SEA

Poland has a ferry service (year-round for the most part) to/from Scandinavia. Routings include Gdynia-Karlskrona and Gdańsk-Oxelösund in Sweden; and Świnoujście to Copenhagen. See Getting There & Away in the Poland chapter for more details.

There are Baltic ferries (mostly year round) to Świnoujście, Gdynia and Gdańsk in Poland from several Scandinavian cities and towns, including the Danish capital Copenhagen and, in Sweden, Karlskronaand Oxelösund. There are also Adriatic ferries from Corfu (Greece) and Italy to Albania, as well as numerous lines from Italy to Croatia and Slovenia.

The cheapest way to get from Sweden to the Czech Republic or Slovakia is to take the ferry from Trelleborg to Sassnitz on Rügen Island in Germany (up to five sailings a day). In Sassnitz buy a train ticket across eastern Germany to Děčín (Czech Republic), where you'll be able to pick up a domestic ticket across the Czech Republic and Slovakia. Don't buy a through ticket in Sweden itself as this will be much more expensive.

LEAVING EASTERN EUROPE

Some countries in Eastern Europe charge you a fee for the privilege of leaving from their

airports. Some also charge port fees when you're departing by ship. Such fees are often included in the price of your ticket, but it pays to check this when purchasing your ticket. If not, you'll have to have the fee ready when you leave – usually in local currency. Details are given in the relevant country chapters.

WARNING

This chapter is particularly vulnerable to change – prices for international travel are volatile, routes are introduced and cancelled, schedules change, special deals come and go, and rules and visa requirements are amended. Airlines seem to take a perverse pleasure in making price structures and regulations as complicated as possible; you should check directly with the airline or travel agent to make sure you understand how a fare (and ticket you may buy) works. In addition, the travel industry is highly competitive and there are many schemes and bonuses. The upshot of this is that you should get opinions, quotes and advice from as many airlines and travel agents as possible before you part with your hard-earned cash. The details given in this chapter should be regarded as pointers and are not a substitute for your own careful, up-to-date research.

Getting Around

AIR

Since 1997 air travel within the European Union has been deregulated. This 'open skies' policy allows greater flexibility in routing, and potentially greater competition and lower prices. However, such deregulation has had little effect on domestic air travel in the countries of Eastern Europe, none of which is yet an EU member.

Domestic air travel remains a real luxury in Eastern Europe, especially when you consider how cheap local bus and train transport can be. Domestic flights operate within Bulgaria, Croatia, Poland, Slovakia, Romania and Yugoslavia but fares are high, and there may be a two-tier system with foreign tourists paying much more than nationals.

Air-taxi services are taking off in a big way around the region, but these are even more expensive than scheduled flights. For domestic flights and prices see Getting Around in the individual chapters.

BUS

Buses are a viable alternative to the rail network in most Eastern European countries. Generally they tend to complement the rail system rather than duplicate it, though in some countries – notably Hungary, the Czech Republic and Slovakia – you'll almost always have a choice.

In general, buses are slightly more expensive and slower than trains; in Poland, Hungary, the Czech Republic and Slovakia they're almost the same price. Buses tend to be best for shorter hops such as getting around cities and reaching remote rural villages. They are often the only option in mountainous regions. The ticketing system varies in each country, but advance reservations are rarely necessary. It's always safest to buy your ticket in advance at the station, but nowadays on long-distance buses you usually just pay upon boarding.

See the individual country chapters and city sections for more details about long-distance buses.

TRAIN

You'll probably do most of your travelling within Eastern Europe by train. All the countries have well-developed railway networks, and you'll have a choice between local trains, which stop at every station, and express trains, including some EC (EuroCity) or IC (InterCity) trains. Local trains can cost less than express trains and never have supplements or seat reservation requirements. Remember that supplementary and reservation fees are not covered by rail passes, and pass-holders must always carry their passport on the train for identification purposes.

Once you find a seat on a local train it's yours for the trip, and since passengers are constantly coming and going you eventually get a place even on a full train. First-class travel by local train costs about the same as 2nd class on an express and is quite comfortable, so long as you're in no hurry. First-class compartments usually have six padded seats, 2nd-class ones have eight seats.

If you choose an express be sure to get an express ticket and ask if seat reservations are necessary. It's sometimes a hassle getting these tickets, so don't leave it too late. Express trains are often marked in red on posted timetables, local trains in black. The symbol 'R' with a box around it means reservations are mandatory while an 'R' without a box may only mean reservations are possible. The boards listing departures are usually yellow, and those for arrivals are white.

Tickets for express trains are best purchased at the central train ticket office a day before. On overnight trains always try to book a 2nd-class couchette or a 1st-class sleeper a few days in advance. Check your ticket is in order before you board. If you have to arrange a reservation, buy a ticket or upgrade a local ticket to an express one on a moving train, you'll pay a healthy supplement. As a comparison, a 100km 2nd-class ticket for the cheapest category of train will cost you US$1.60 in the Czech Republic, US$2.30 in Hungary and nearly US$4.50 in Slovenia.

It's best to sit in the middle or front carriages of trains as many stations are poorly marked, often with only one sign on the main building. If there's any doubt, write the name of your destination on a piece of paper and show it to the other passengers so they can let you know when to get off.

If you plan to travel extensively by train, it might be worth getting hold of the *Thomas Cook European Timetable*, which gives a complete listing of train schedules and indicates where supplements apply or where reservations are necessary. It is updated monthly and is available from Thomas Cook outlets in the UK and Australia, and in the USA from Rail Europe Inc, c/o Forsyth Travel Inc (☎ 800-367 7984, fax 914 681 7251), 226 Westchester Ave, White Plains NY 10604. If you are planning to do a lot of train travel in one or a handful of countries it might be worthwhile getting hold of the national timetable(s) published by the state railroad(s).

For information on European rail passes and international tickets, turn to the Getting There & Away chapter. For information on websites which include Eastern European rail information, see Internet Resources in the Facts for the Visitor chapter.

Luggage
Almost every train station in Eastern Europe has a luggage room (left-luggage or cloakroom) where you can deposit your luggage as soon as you arrive. In Poland this can be expensive, as you're charged 1% of the declared value of your luggage, but the fee in other countries is generally pretty cheap. You usually pay the fee when you pick up your bag – handy if you're just arriving in a new country with no local currency on you. In main stations the left-luggage office is open around the clock but this isn't always the case. Inquire before handing your bags over.

Some train stations also have complicated coin lockers. You compose a four-digit number on the inside of the door, insert a coin and close the locker. To open it again you arrange the same number on the outside and with luck the door will open. Don't forget the number or the location of your locker!

Security
Stories occasionally surface about train passengers being gassed or drugged and then robbed. In reality, bag-snatching is more of a worry. Sensible security measures include not letting your bags out of your sight (especially when stopping at stations), chaining them to the luggage rack, and locking compartment doors overnight.

TAXI
Taxis in Eastern Europe are much cheaper than in Western Europe. Although they are metered in most countries nowadays, scams and rip-offs (especially in Hungary and the Czech Republic) can make taking a cab an unpleasant, expensive and even dangerous experience. See the individual country chapters for details. Taxis can be found idling near train stations or big hotels or you can hail one on the street.

CAR & MOTORCYCLE
Travelling with your own vehicle is the best way to get to remote places and it gives you the most flexibility. Unfortunately, the independence you enjoy does tend to isolate you from the local people. Also, cars can be inconvenient in many Eastern European city centres, where it is generally worth ditching your vehicle and relying on public transport.

Paperwork & Preparations
Proof of ownership of a private vehicle should always be carried (Vehicle Registration Document for British-registered cars) when touring Europe. An EU driving licence is acceptable for driving throughout most of Eastern Europe as are North American and Australian ones. But to be on the safe side – or if you have any other type of licence – you should obtain an International Driving Permit (IDP) from your motoring organisation (see Visas & Documents in the Facts for the Visitor chapter).

Third-party motor insurance is a minimum requirement in Europe. Most UK motor insurance policies automatically provide this for EU and some other countries. Get your insurer to issue a Green Card (which may cost extra), an internationally recognised proof of insurance, and check that it lists all the countries you intend to visit. You'll need this in the event of an accident outside the country where the vehicle is insured. Also ask your insurer for a European Accident

Statement form. Never sign statements you can't read or understand – insist on a translation and sign that only if it's acceptable. If the Green Card doesn't list one of the countries you're visiting and your insurer cannot (or will not) add it, you will have to take out separate third-party cover at the border of the country in question.

If you want to insure a vehicle you've just purchased and have a good insurance record, you might be eligible for considerable discounts if you can show a letter to this effect from your insurance company back home.

Taking out a European breakdown assistance policy is a good investment, such as the AA Five Star Service or the RAC Eurocover Motoring Assistance. Expect to pay about UK£54 for 14 days cover with a small discount for association members. Non-Europeans might find it cheaper to arrange international coverage with their national motoring organisation before leaving home. Ask your motoring organisation for details about free and reciprocal services offered by affiliated organisations around Europe.

Every vehicle travelling across an international border should display a sticker showing its country of registration (see the International Country Abbreviations appendix). A warning triangle, to be used in the event of breakdown, is compulsory almost everywhere; some countries (eg the Czech Republic and Slovakia) require two triangles. Recommended accessories are a first-aid kit (compulsory in Croatia, Slovenia and Yugoslavia), a spare bulb kit, and a fire extinguisher. Contact the RAC (☎ 0800-550055) or the AA (☎ 0990-500600) in the UK for more information.

Road Rules

The RAC publishes an annual guide called *Motoring in Europe*, which gives the visiting motorist an excellent summary of regulations in each country, including parking rules. It is free for members taking out RAC European insurance coverage or can be bought through the club or at main bookshops for £4.99. Motoring organisations in other countries have similar publications. These guides will help you avoid unexpected pitfalls: in Romania, for example, you are not allowed to drive a dirty car! Many countries require you to carry a first-aid kit and a warning triangle. In Bulgaria you need a fire extinguisher.

According to World Health Organisation statistics, driving in Eastern Europe is five times more dangerous than in Western Europe. Driving at night can be especially hazardous in rural areas as the roads are often narrow and winding, and horse-drawn vehicles, bicycles, pedestrians and domestic animals may be encountered. In an accident you're supposed to notify the police and file an insurance claim. If your car has significant body damage from a previous accident, point this out to customs upon arrival and have it noted somewhere, as damaged vehicles may only be allowed to leave the country with police permission.

The standard international road signs are used throughout Eastern Europe. You drive on the right side of the road throughout the region and overtake on the left. Keep right except when overtaking, and use your indicators for any change of lane and when pulling away from the kerb. You're not allowed to pass a whole line of cars, whether they are moving or stationary. Speed limits are posted, and are generally 110 or 120km/h on motorways (freeways), 100km/h on highways, 80km/h on secondary and tertiary roads and 50 or 60km/h in built-up areas. Motorcycles are usually limited to 90km/h on motorways, and vehicles with trailers to 80km/h. In towns you may only sound the horn to avoid an accident. Everywhere in Eastern Europe, the use of seat belts is mandatory and motorcyclists (and their passengers) must wear a helmet. Children under 12 and intoxicated passengers are not permitted in the front seat. Driving after drinking even the smallest amount of alcohol is a serious offence.

Throughout Europe, when two roads of equal importance intersect, the vehicle coming from the right has right of way unless signs indicate otherwise. In many countries this also applies to cyclists, so take care. On roundabouts (traffic circles) vehicles already in the roundabout have the right of way. Public transport vehicles pulling out from a stop also have right of way. Stay out of lanes marked 'bus' except when you're making a right-hand turn. Pedestrians have the right of way at marked crossings and whenever you're making a turn. In Europe it's prohibited to turn right against a red light even after coming to a stop.

It's usually illegal to stop or park at the top of slopes, in front of pedestrian crossings, at bus or tram stops, on bridges or at level crossings. You must use a red reflector warning triangle when parking on a highway (in an emergency). If you don't use the triangle and another vehicle hits you from behind, you will be held responsible.

Beware of trams (streetcars) as these have priority at crossroads and when turning right (provided they signal the turn). Don't pass a tram which is stopping to let off passengers until everyone is out and the tram doors have closed again (unless, of course, there's a safety island). Never pass a tram on the left or stop within 1m of tram tracks. A police officer who sees you blocking a tram route by waiting to turn left will flag you over. Traffic police administer fines on the spot (always ask for a receipt).

Roads

Conditions and types of roads vary considerably across Eastern Europe, but it is possible to make some generalisations. The fastest routes are four or six-lane dual carriageways, ie two or three lanes either side (motorway, *autópálya*, *avtocesta*, *autostradă* etc), though they are rare and of short length in the region. These tend to skirt cities and plough through the countryside in straight lines, often avoiding the most scenic bits. Some of these roads incur tolls. There's almost always an alternative (though much slower) route you can take if you don't want to pay. Motorways and other primary routes are in good to fair condition depending on the country. Bulgaria, the Czech Republic and Slovakia levy a general tax on vehicles using their motorways.

Road surfaces on minor routes are not so reliable in some countries (eg the Czech Republic, Slovakia, Poland), although normally they will be more than adequate, and as compensation you can expect much better scenery and plenty of interesting villages along the way.

Rental

The big international firms – Hertz, Avis, Budget and Europcar (Europe's largest rental

agency) – are represented in main centres throughout Eastern Europe and will give you reliable service and a good standard of vehicle. Unfortunately you'll be paying dearly: from US$25 to US$50 a day plus US$0.25 to US$0.40 a kilometre for the cheapest model. On a weekly basis, you'll pay anywhere from US$400 to US$650 with unlimited kilometres. Collision Damage Waiver (CDW) insurance will be around US$10 per day and another US$12 a day may be charged for Loss Damage Waiver (LDW) insurance against car theft. A surcharge is often payable if you rent the car at airport branches and at luxury hotels. Additional drivers are about US$8 per day extra and taxes of up to 25% may not be included in the quoted prices. The most expensive countries in which to rent are Poland and Hungary, though foreigners staying less than 180 days in the latter are now exempt from the 25% ÁFA (VAT-like tax).

Local companies not connected with any chain usually offer lower prices but when comparing rates beware of printed tariffs intended only for local residents, which may be lower than the prices foreigners are charged. If in doubt, ask. The chain companies sometimes offer the flexibility of allowing you to drop off the car at their locations in other cities at no additional charge.

If you're coming from North America, Australia or New Zealand, ask your airline if it has any special deals for rental cars in Europe, or check the ads in the weekend travel sections of major newspapers. You can often arrange something in advance for much less than you'd pay on the spot in Europe.

If renting from abroad, you must tell the agency exactly which countries you plan to visit so it can make sure the insurance is in order. Many German agencies, for example, refuse to allow their cars to be taken to some parts of Eastern Europe because of an increasing incidence of car theft.

Car Purchase

Don't even consider buying a used car in Eastern Europe, where the paperwork is a nightmare and most used cars seem to be held together with rubber bands, glue and paper clips!

Fuel

The problems associated with finding the right kind of petrol (or petrol of any kind without special coupons) are all but over in Eastern Europe. Fuel prices still vary considerably from country to country and may bear little relation to the general cost of living; relatively affluent Slovenia, for example, has very cheap fuel while the opposite is true in inexpensive Hungary. Savings can be made if you fill up in the right place, especially when travelling east to west (from Poland to Germany or Slovenia to Italy). Motoring organisations such as the RAC can give more details.

Unleaded petrol of 95 octane is now widely available throughout Eastern Europe (though not always at stations on back roads or in Romania, Albania, Slovakia and Yugoslavia). To be on the safe side, bring a 20L can in which to carry an extra supply, especially if your car is fitted with a catalytic converter, as this expensive component can be ruined by leaded fuel. Unleaded fuel is usually slightly cheaper than super (premium grade). Look for the pump with green markings and the word *Bleifrei*, German for 'unleaded'. Diesel is usually significantly cheaper in Eastern Europe.

Modern motorcycles are all set up for unleaded fuel but, with one or two exceptions, they don't have catalytic converters, which means they'll have no trouble with 92/94 octane leaded; however, stick to 98 octane super on older models.

BICYCLE

A tour of Europe by bike may seem a daunting prospect, but one organisation that can help in the UK is the Cyclists' Touring Club (CTC; ☎ 01483-417 217; cycling@ctc .org.uk), Cotterell House, 69 Meadrow, Godalming, Surrey GU7 3HS. It can supply information to members on cycling conditions in Europe as well as detailed routes, itineraries, maps and cheap specialised insurance. Membership costs UK£25 per annum, UK£12.50 for students and people under 18, or UK£16.50 for senior citizens.

A primary consideration on a cycling tour is to travel light, but you should take tools and spare parts (extra brake, derailleur cables etc) as well as a puncture repair kit and an extra inner tube. Panniers are essential to balance your possessions on either side of the bike frame. A bike helmet is also a very good idea. Take a good lock and always use it when you leave your bike unattended.

Seasoned cyclists can average 80km a day, but there's no point in overdoing it. The slower you travel, the more local people you are likely to meet. If you get weary of pedalling or simply want to skip a boring section (like Hungary's Great Plain), you can put your feet up on the train. On slower trains, bikes can usually be transported as luggage, subject to a small supplementary fee. Fast trains rarely accommodate bikes: they need to be sent as registered luggage and may end up on a different train from the one you take. To avoid this separation, travel to border towns by train, cross the border by bike, then catch another train on the other side. Another possibility is to semi-dismantle your bike, shove it in a bag or sack and take it on a train as hand-luggage.

One major drawback to cycling in Eastern Europe is the disgusting exhaust put out by Eastern European vehicles, especially buses and trucks. You'll often find yourself gasping in a cloud of blue or black smoke as these vehicles lumber along quiet country roads.

For more information on cycling, see Activities in the earlier Facts for the Visitor chapter and in the individual country chapters.

Rental

It can be very difficult to rent bikes (and almost anything else) in countries like Hungary, Poland, the Czech Republic, Slovakia and Slovenia; the best hunting grounds are always camp sites and resort hotels in season. See the country chapters for more details.

Purchase

For major cycling tours, it's best to have a bike you're familiar with, so consider bringing your own (see following section) rather than buying on arrival. There are plenty of places to *buy* in Eastern Europe (shops sell both new and second-hand bicycles), but you'll need a specialist bicycle shop for a machine capable of withstanding European touring. CTC can provide a leaflet on purchasing. According to one reader, the Czech Republic has the highest-quality bicycles, followed by Slovakia, Poland and Hungary. Bulgaria and especially Romania don't have as much yet, but mountain bikes are becoming popular there too.

Bringing Your Own

If you want to bring your own bicycle to Europe, you should be able to take it on the plane. You can either take it apart and pack everything in a bike bag or box, or simply wheel it to the check-in desk, where it should be treated as a piece of luggage. You may have to remove the pedals and turn the handlebars sideways so that it takes up less space in the aircraft's hold; check all this with the airline well in advance, preferably before you pay for your ticket. If your bicycle and other luggage exceed your weight allowance, ask about alternatives or you may suddenly find yourself being charged a fortune for excess baggage.

HITCHING

Hitching is never entirely safe in *any* country, and we don't recommend it. Travellers who decide to hitch should understand that they are taking a small but potentially serious risk. People who do choose to hitch will be safer if they travel in pairs and let someone know where they plan to go.

Also, as long as public transport remains cheap in Eastern Europe, hitchhiking is more for the adventure than the transport, and in Albania, Romania, and sometimes Poland, drivers expect riders to pay the equivalent of a bus fare. In Romania traffic is light, motorists are probably not going far, and almost everywhere you'll face small vehicles overloaded with passengers. If you want to give it a try, though, make yourself a small, clearly written cardboard destination sign, remembering to use the local name for the town or city ('Praha' not 'Prague'; 'Warszawa' not 'Warsaw'). City buses will usually take you to the edge of town. Hitchhiking on a motorway (freeway) is usually prohibited; you must stand near an entrance ramp. If you look like a westerner your chances of getting a ride might improve.

Women will find hitchhiking safer than in Western Europe, but the standard precautions should be taken: never accept a ride with two men, don't let your pack be put in the boot (trunk), only sit next to a door you can open, ask drivers where they are going before you say where you're going etc. Don't hesitate to refuse a ride if you feel at all uncomfortable, and insist on being let out at the first sign of trouble. Best of all, try to find a travelling companion (although three people will have a very hard time getting a lift).

BOAT

Croatia is the one country in Eastern Europe with significant (and affordable) sea routes. A boat trip along Croatia's heavily indented coast is one of the scenic highlights of Eastern Europe.

Some of Eastern Europe's lakes and rivers are serviced by steamers and ferries; not surprisingly, schedules are more extensive in the summer months. In most cases, extended boat trips should be considered as relaxing and scenic excursions; as a means of transport, they can be grotesquely expensive. The hydrofoil between Vienna and Budapest, for example, costs US$61/$89 one way/return. The comparable bus fares are US$25/$36.

But getting out on the water for the day in countries like Hungary can be cheap and easy: local river ferries link Budapest with the picturesque towns of the Danube Bend to the north, and ferries serve all of the built-up areas on Lake Balaton. In Poland some cities on the Vistula offer river trips in their vicinity, and excursion boats ply the Great Mazurian Lakes in north-east Poland. See the relevant country chapters for details.

PUBLIC TRANSPORT

Though ticket prices have increased substantially in recent years, public transport in Eastern Europe is still inexpensive and the low price is not at all indicative of the service, which is generally very good. In most cities, buses and trams begin moving at 5 am or earlier and continue until around 10.30 or 11.30 pm. There are metro (subway or underground) lines in Bucharest, Budapest and Prague. The Warsaw metro has been under construction for years and the first line was due to open in 1995.

For most forms of public transport you buy tickets in advance at a kiosk or from a machine. Information windows in bus and train stations sometimes have tickets for local transport. Once aboard you validate your own ticket by using a cancelling machine positioned near the door. Watch how the locals do it but don't be surprised if you only see one or two in a carload punching their tickets; most commuters buy much cheaper weekly or monthly passes. Different tickets are sometimes required for buses, trolley buses, trams and the metro, but in most cases they're all the same. If all the kiosks selling tickets are closed, ask another passenger to sell you a ticket. It's also now possible to buy tickets from the driver or a conductor on some services.

Travelling 'black' (ticketless) is riskier than ever in Eastern Europe as public transport systems try to break even or turn a profit. With increased surveillance, there's a good chance you'll get caught, which can be both costly and embarrassing.

ORGANISED TOURS

A package tour is worth considering only if your time is very limited or you have a special interest such as skiing, canoeing, sailing, horse riding, cycling, spa treatment etc. Cruises on the Danube River are available but they're very expensive. Most tour prices are for double occupancy, which means singles have to share a double room with a stranger of the same sex or pay a single supplement for a single room.

New Millennium Holidays (☎ 0121-711 2232), 20 High St, Solihull, West Midlands B91 3TB, England, runs inexpensive bus tours year-round from the UK to Poland, Hungary, the Czech Republic and other European destinations. Packages vary from 10 to 17 days, some combining two or three countries, with return travel from Dover, and half-board or B&B accommodation. Another British company highly experienced in booking travel to Eastern Europe is Regent Holidays (☎ 0117-921 1711, fax 925 4866;

regent@regent-holiday.co.uk), 15 John St, Bristol BS1 2HR. In Australia you can obtain a detailed brochure outlining dozens of up-market tours from the Eastern Europe Travel Bureau (☎ 02-9262 1144), Level 5, 75 King St, Sydney, NSW 2000. The office in Victoria (☎ 03-9600 0299) is at Suite 313, Level 3, 343 Little Collins St, Melbourne, Vic 3000.

Young revellers can party on Europewide bus tours. An outfit called Acacia offers budget coach/camping tours for under US$40 per day, plus food fund. It has a London office (☎ 0171-937 3028; acacia@afrika. demon.co.uk) and is represented in Australia and New Zealand by Adventure World; in North America, call ☎ 800-233 6046. Contiki (☎ 0181-290 6422; travel@contiki.co.uk) and Top Deck (☎ 0171-370 4555; s+m .topdeck@dial.pipex.com) offer camping and hotel-based bus tours, also for the 18 to 35 age group. The latter's 18-day 'Eastern Europe Escape' tour costs from UK£489 plus UK£125 food fund. Both have offices or representatives in North America, Australasia and South Africa.

For people over 50, Saga Holidays (☎ 0800-300500), Saga Building, Middelburg Square, Folkestone, Kent CT20 1AZ, offers holidays ranging from cheap coach tours to luxury cruises (and has cheap travel insurance). Saga operates in the USA as Saga International Holidays (☎ 800-343 0273), 222 Berkeley St, Boston, MA 02116, and in Australia as Saga Holidays Australasia (☎ 02-9957 4266), Level One, 110 Pacific Highway, North Sydney.

National tourist offices in most countries offer organised trips to points of interest. These may range from one-hour city tours to several-day circular excursions. They often work out more expensive than going it alone, but are sometimes worth it if you are pressed for time. A short city tour will give you a quick overview of the place and can be a good way to begin your visit.

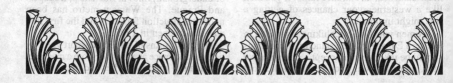

Albania

Until 1990 a closed communist country, Albania caught world attention in November of that year as the last domino to tumble in Eastern Europe's sudden series of democratic revolutions. Yet the changes date back to 1985 and the death of Enver Hoxha, Albania's Stalinist leader since 1944. The statues of Stalin and Hoxha toppled, and the non-communist opposition was elevated to power in March 1992, putting Albania at a crossroads. Its first years of attempted democracy have been troubled by economic chaos, shady elections and outright social anarchy.

Long considered fair prey by every imperialist power, Albania chose a curious form of isolation. Blood vendettas and illiteracy were replaced by what some claimed was the purest form of communism. Right up until December 1990, monuments, factories, boulevards and towns were dedicated to the memory of Joseph Stalin. Although Hoxha's iron-fisted rule did save Albania from annexation by Yugoslavia after WWII, it's unlikely that you'll find many in Albania with much good to say about him. On the contrary, most blame him for the country's present problems.

Politics aside, few European countries have the allure of the mysterious Republika e Shqipërisë. Albanians call their country the 'Land of the Eagle'. Albania is Europe's last unknown, with enchanting classical ruins at Apollonia, Butrint and Durrës, the charming 'museum towns' of Gjirokastra and Berat, vibrant cities like Tirana, Shkodra, Korça and Durrës, colourful folklore and majestic landscapes of mountains, forests, lakes and sea. You can see a great number of things in a pocket-sized area and the Albanians are extremely friendly and curious about their handful of visitors.

In the capital, Tirana, and the port of Durrës people are already quite used to seeing foreigners, but almost everywhere else you'll be an object of curiosity. Things have greatly improved since the collapse of the old system in 1992 – trains are back on the rails, increasing numbers of private buses are plying the roads, private rooms are becoming

AT A GLANCE

Capital	Tirana
Population	3.3 million
Area	28,750 sq km
Official Language	Albanian (Tosk)
Currency	1 lekë (L) = 100 qintars
GDP	US$4.4 billion (1996)
Time	GMT/UTC+0100

more readily available in the towns, fine restaurants have opened up, travel agencies are in operation and all areas of the country are now accessible to travellers. As Albania slowly opens up to the world, visitors have the chance to meet the people in a way that's almost impossible elsewhere in Europe.

Facts about Albania

HISTORY

In the 2nd millennium BC, the Illyrians, ancestors of today's Albanians, occupied the western Balkans. The Greeks arrived in the

73

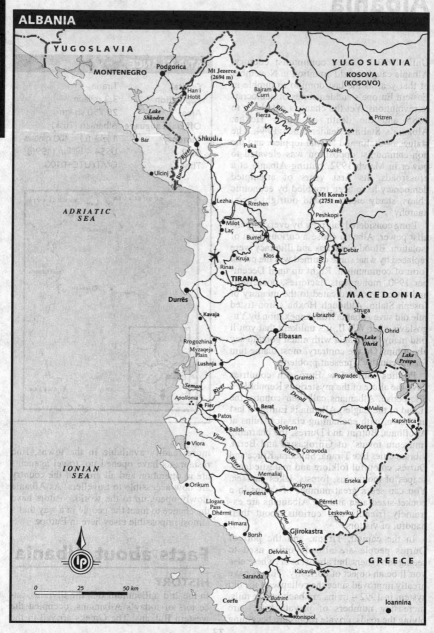

ALBANIA

YUGOSLAVIA

MONTENEGRO

Podgorica

Mt Jezerce
(2694 m)

Bajram
Curri

YUGOSLAVIA

KOSOVA
(KOSOVO)

Han i
Hotit

Drin

River

Fierza

Prizren

Lake
Shkodra

Bar

Shkodra

Puka

Kukës

Bune

River

Ulcinj

Lezha

Rreshen

Mt Korab
(2751 m)

Peshkopi

ADRIATIC
SEA

Milot

Laç

Burrel

Klos

Drin

River

Debar

Kruja

Rinas

TIRANA

Durrës

Kavaja

Librazhd

Struga

Ohrid

MACEDONIA

Lake
Ohrid

Rrogozhina

Myzaqeja
Plain

Lushnja

Elbasan

Lake
Prespa

Gramsh

Pogradec

Seman

River

Apollonia

Fier

Patos

Berat

Devoll

River

Maliq

Korça

Kapshtica

Ballsh

Poliçan

Osum

River

Vlora

Vjose

Çorovoda

Erseka

IONIAN
SEA

Memaliaj

Tepelena

Kelçyra

Orikum

Llogara
Pass

Dhërmi

Përmet

Leskoviku

Himara

Drino

River

Borsh

Gjirokastra

GREECE

Delvina

Kakavija

Saranda

0   25   50 km

Corfu

Butrint

Ioannina

Konispol

7th century BC to establish self-governing colonies at Epidamnos (now Durrës), Apollonia and Butrint. They traded peacefully with the Illyrians, who formed tribal states in the 4th century BC. The south became part of Greek Epirus.

In the second half of the 3rd century BC, an expanding Illyrian kingdom based at Shkodra came into conflict with Rome, which sent a fleet of 200 vessels against Queen Teuta (who ruled over the Illyrian Ardian kingdom) in 228 BC. In 214 BC, after a second Roman naval expedition in 219 BC, Philip V of Macedonia came to the aid of his Illyrian allies. This led to a long war which resulted in the extension of Roman control over the entire Balkans by 167 BC.

Like the Greeks, the Illyrians preserved their own language and traditions despite centuries of Roman rule. Under the Romans, Illyria enjoyed peace and prosperity, though the large agricultural estates were worked by slave labour. The main trade route between Rome and Constantinople, the Via Egnatia, ran from Durrës to Thessaloniki. In 285 AD, a provincial reorganisation carried out by the Roman emperor Diocletian (an Illyrian himself) broke Illyria up into four provinces: Epirus Vetus (capital Ioannina), Epirus Nova (capital Durrës), Praevalitana (capital Shkodra) and Dardania (today the Kosova region of Yugoslavia).

When the Roman Empire was divided in 395 AD, Illyria fell within the Eastern Roman Empire, later known as Byzantium. Invasions by migrating peoples – Visigoths, Huns, Ostrogoths and Slavs – continued through the 5th and 6th centuries and only in the south did the ethnic Illyrians survive. Prior to the Roman conquest, Illyria had stretched north to the Danube. In the 11th century, control of this region passed back and forth between the Byzantines, the Bulgarians and the Normans.

The feudal principality of Arbëria was established at Kruja in 1190. Other independent feudal states appeared in the 14th century and towns then developed. In 1344 Albania was annexed by Serbia, but after the defeat of Serbia by the Turks in 1389 the whole region was open to Ottoman attack. The Venetians occupied some coastal towns, and from 1443 to 1468 the national hero Skanderbeg (George Kastrioti) led Albanian resistance to

the Turks from his castle at Kruja. Skanderbeg (Skënderbeg in Albanian) won all 25 battles he fought against the Turks, and even Sultan Mehmet-Fatih, conqueror of Constantinople, could not take Kruja.

Albania was not definitively incorporated into the Ottoman empire until 1479. It remained there until 1912, the most backward corner of Europe. In the 15th and 16th centuries thousands of Albanians fled to southern Italy to escape Turkish rule and over half of those who remained converted to Islam so as to become first-class citizens of the theocratic Ottoman empire. In the late 18th century, the Albanian nobles Karamahmut Pasha Bushatlli of Shkodra and Ali Pasha Tepelena of Ioannina (Janina) established semi-independent pashaliks (military districts), but Ottoman despotism was reimposed in the early 19th century.

In 1878 the Albanian League at Prizren (in present-day Kosova, Yugoslavia) began a struggle for autonomy that was put down by the Turkish army in 1881. Uprisings between 1910 and 1912 culminated in a proclamation of independence and the formation of a provisional government led by Ismail Qemali at Vlora in 1912. These achievements were severely compromised by the London ambassador's conference, which handed Kosova, nearly half of Albania, over to Serbia in 1913. In 1914 the Great Powers (Britain, France, Germany, Italy, Austria-Hungary and Russia) imposed a German aristocrat named Wilhelm von Wied on Albania as head of state but an uprising soon forced his departure. With the outbreak of WWI, Albania was occupied by the armies of Greece, Serbia, France, Italy and Austria-Hungary in succession.

In 1920 the Congress of Lushnja denounced foreign intervention and moved the capital from Durrës to less vulnerable Tirana. Thousands of Albanian volunteers converged on Vlora and forced the occupying Italians to withdraw. In May 1924, Bishop Fan Noli established a fairly liberal government which was overthrown on Christmas Eve that year by Ahmet Zogu, who represented the landed aristocracy of the lowlands and the tribal chieftains of the highlands. Zogu ruled with Italian support, declaring himself King Zog I in 1928, but his close collaboration with Italy backfired in April 1939 when Mussolini ordered an invasion of Albania. Zog fled to Britain and used gold looted from the Albanian treasury to rent a floor at London's Ritz Hotel.

On 8 November 1941 the Albanian Communist Party was founded with Enver Hoxha (pronounced Hodja) as first secretary, a position he held until his death in April 1985. The communists led the resistance against the Italians and, after 1943, against the Germans. A provisional government was formed at Berat in October 1944, and by 29 November the Albanian Army of National Liberation had crushed the 'Balli Kombetar', a grouping of tribal quislings in the north, and pursued the last Nazi troops from the country. Albania was the only Eastern European country where the Soviet army was not involved in these operations. By tying down some 15 combined German-Italian divisions, Albania made an important contribution to the final outcome.

The Rise of Communism

After the fighting died down, the communists consolidated power. In January 1946 the People's Republic of Albania was proclaimed, with Enver Hoxha as president. In February a program of socialist construction was adopted and all large economic enterprises were nationalised. By 1952 seven years of elementary education had become mandatory (this was raised to eight years in 1963) and literacy was increased from just 15% before WWII to 72% in 1995.

In October 1946 two British warships struck mines in the Corfu Channel, causing the loss of 44 lives. The British government blamed Albania and demanded £843,947 compensation. To back their claim they impounded 1574 kg of gold (now worth £10 million) which the fascists had stolen from Albania and which had passed into British hands at the end of WWII. Albania has never accepted responsibility for the incident, nor has it agreed to pay damages. The stubborn British are still holding Albania's gold, despite agreeing in principle in 1992 to return it, less reparations. It is now widely believed that Yugoslavia placed the mines. Good relations with Tito were always important to the British, whereas Albania was expendable.

In September 1948, Albania broke off relations with Yugoslavia, which had hoped to incorporate the country into the Yugoslav Federation. Instead, Albania allied itself with Stalin's USSR and put into effect a series of Soviet-style economic plans, the first a two-year plan, and then five-year plans beginning in 1951. After WWII there were British and US-backed landings in Albania by right-wing émigrés. One British attempt in 1949 was thwarted when Stalin passed to Hoxha a warning he had received from double agent Kim Philby.

Albania collaborated closely with the USSR until 1960, when a heavy-handed Khrushchev demanded a submarine base at Vlora. With the Soviet alliance becoming a liability, Albania broke off diplomatic relations with the USSR in 1961 and reoriented itself towards the People's Republic of China.

From 1966 to 1967 Albania experienced a Chinese-style cultural revolution. Administrative workers were suddenly transferred to remote areas and younger cadres were placed in leading positions. The collectivisation of agriculture was completed and organised religion banned. Western literary works were withdrawn from circulation and a strong national culture firmly rooted in socialist ideals was carefully cultivated.

After the Soviet invasion of Czechoslovakia in 1968, Albania left the Warsaw Pact and embarked on a self-reliant defence policy. Today, some 750,000 igloo-shaped concrete bunkers and pillboxes with narrow gun slits are strung along all borders, both terrestrial and maritime, as well as the approaches to all towns. The highway from Durrës to Tirana is one bunker after another for 35km. The amount of time and materials employed in creating these defences must have been tremendous and the bunkers still occupy much agricultural land today.

With the death of Mao Zedong in 1976 and the changes in China after 1978, Albania's unique relationship with China came to an end. In 1981 there was a power struggle within the Albanian Party of Labour (as the Communist Party had been called since November 1948) and former partisan hero and prime minister Mehmet Shehu 'committed suicide' after being accused of being a 'polyagent' (multiple spy).

Shehu had wanted to expand Albania's foreign contacts, an orientation which brought him into direct conflict with Hoxha. Until 1978 Albania had thrived on massive Yugoslav, Soviet and Chinese aid in succession, but building socialism alone, without foreign loans or credit, proved to be difficult. Because its exports didn't earn sufficient hard currency to pay for the import of essential equipment, the country fell far behind technologically.

Post-Hoxha

Hoxha died after a long illness in April 1985 and his longtime associate Ramiz Alia assumed leadership of the 147,000-member Party of Labour. Aware of the economic decay caused by Albania's isolation, Alia began a liberalisation program in 1986 and broadened Albania's ties with foreign countries. Travellers arriving in Albania at this time no longer had their guidebooks confiscated and their beards and long hair clipped by border barbers, and short skirts were allowed.

By early 1990 the collapse of communism in most of Eastern Europe had created a sense of expectation in Albania and in June some 4500 Albanians took refuge in Western embassies in Tirana. After a brief confrontation with police and the Sigurimi (secret police) these people were allowed to board ships to Brindisi, Italy, where they were granted political asylum.

After student demonstrations in December 1990, the government agreed to allow opposition parties. The Democratic Party, led by heart surgeon Sali Berisha, was formed. Further demonstrations won new concessions, including the promise of free elections and independent trade unions. The government announced a reform program and party hardliners were purged.

In early March 1991, as the election date approached, some 20,000 Albanians fled to Brindisi by ship, creating a crisis for the Italian government, which had begun to view them as economic refugees. Most were eventually allowed to stay. In the run-up to the 31 March 1991 elections, Alia won the support of the peasants by turning over state lands

and granting them the right to sell their produce at markets. This manoeuvre netted the Party of Labour 169 seats in the 250-member People's Assembly, which promptly re-elected Alia president for a five-year term.

In mid-May a general strike forced the renamed Socialist Party (formerly the Party of Labour) to form a coalition with the opposition Democrats in preparation for fresh elections the following year. As central economic planning collapsed, factories ceased production and the food distribution network broke down. In August another 15,000 young male Albanians attempted to take refuge in Italy, but this time they were met by Italian riot police and quickly deported. By late 1991 mass unemployment, rampant inflation and shortages of almost everything were throwing Albania into chaos and in December food riots began. Fearful of another refugee crisis, the European Union stepped up economic aid and the Italian army established a large military base just south of Durrës, ostensibly to supervise EU food shipments.

The March 1992 elections ended 47 years of communist rule as the Democratic Party took 92 of the 140 seats in a revamped parliament. After the resignation of Ramiz Alia, parliament elected Sali Berisha president in April. In their campaign, the Democrats promised that their victory would attract foreign investors and gain Western immigration quotas for Albanian workers. When these failed to materialise, the socialists bounced back to win the municipal elections of July 1992.

In September 1992 Ramiz Alia was placed under house arrest after he wrote articles critical of the Democratic government, and in January 1993 the 73-year-old widow of Enver Hoxha, Nexhmije Hoxha, was sentenced to nine years imprisonment for allegedly misappropriating government funds between 1985 and 1990. In August 1993 the leader of the Socialist Party, Fatos Nano, was also arrested on corruption charges. He was sentenced to 12 years imprisonment in April 1994.

By mid-1992 Albania had signed a military agreement with Turkey, and followed that in December by joining the Islamic Conference Association. This reorientation towards the Islamic world stems from practical security

ALBANIA

considerations. Greek politicians have made territorial claims to southern Albania (which they call Northern Epiros) and the alliance with Turkey was seen as a balance. In mid-1993 relations with Greece hit a new low following the deportation from Albania of a hardline Greek bishop who had attempted to organise the Greek minority in Albania for political ends. In retaliation, Athens ordered the expulsion of 20,000 of the 150,000 Albanian immigrants in Greece.

Meanwhile, private pyramid investment schemes – widely thought to have been supported by the government – collapsed spectacularly in late 1996 leading to nationwide disturbances and violence, and ultimately to the call for new elections which were won by the Socialist Party under Fatos Nano. Since taking power prime minister Nano has restored a large degree of security within the country and a certain amount of investor confidence and foreign business people are once more active in the capital.

Tension over the Albanian-speaking region of Kosova (Kosovo) Yugoslavia's southern province has meant that relations with the Milošević régime in Belgrade were stretched to the limit and by mid-1998 all-out war with Yugoslavia was only just being averted.

GEOGRAPHY & ECOLOGY

Albania's strategic position between Greece, Macedonia, Yugoslavia and Italy has been important throughout its history. Vlora watches over the narrow Strait of Otranto, which links the Adriatic Sea to the Ionian Sea. For decades Albania has acted as a barrier separating Greece from the rest of Europe. The Greek island of Corfu is only a few kilometres from Albania in the Ionian Sea.

Over three-quarters of this 28,748-sq-km country (a bit smaller than Belgium) consists of mountains and hills. There are three zones: a coastal plain, a mountainous region and an interior plain. The coastal plain extends over 200km from north to south and up to 50km inland. The 2000m-high forested mountain spine that stretches along the entire length of Albania culminates at Mt Jezerce (2694m) in the north. Although Mt Jezerce is the highest mountain entirely within the country,

Albania's highest peak is Mt Korab (2751m), on the border with Macedonia. The country is subject to destructive earthquakes, such as the one in 1979 which left 100,000 people homeless.

The longest river is the Drin River (285km), which drains Lake Ohrid. In the north the Drin flows into the Buna, Albania's only navigable river, which connects shallow Lake Shkodra to the sea. Albania shares three large tectonic lakes with Yugoslavia, Macedonia and Greece: Shkodra, Ohrid and Prespa respectively. Ohrid is the deepest lake in the Balkans (294m), while Lake Prespa, at 853m elevation, is one of the highest. The Ionian littoral, especially the 'Riviera of Flowers' from Vlora to Saranda, offers magnificent scenery. Forests cover 40% of the land, and the many olive trees, citrus plantations and vineyards give Albania a true Mediterranean air.

Large parts of the country were subjected to ecological vandalism during the communist years particularly near the Fier oil fields in central Albania and from industrial fallout in the Elbasan valley from the enormous Chinese-built steel mill. This communist quest for higher production was carried out with little or no consideration for the environment and today's industrial wastelands are scenes of utter desolation far beyond anything else in Europe. You'll see ponds covered with a slick of oil leaking from a nearby oil well and large buildings with every window broken and the walls collapsing. Many Albanians treat their country like a giant rubbish dump, the aluminium cans, chocolate wrappers and other debris joining the tens of thousands of broken concrete bunkers and dozens of derelict factories. Albanians are turning their attention to cleaning up their act, but more pressing issues still take precedence such as rebuilding roads and modernising the basic housing infrastructure.

GOVERNMENT & POLITICS

Albania has a parliamentary democracy with a president (currently Rexhap Mejdani) and prime minister, Fatos Nano of the Socialist Party. Opposition parties include the Democratic Party, the Democratic Alliance and the Social Democrats. Elections were last held in 1997 and are due to be held again in 2000.

The Current Situation

In mid-1998 the situation in Albania had quietened down considerably following the widespread civil disturbances of early 1997. The disturbances had broken out after the virtual collapse of the economic and banking system which was brought about after most people in the country had sunk their savings into fradulent pyramid savings schemes.

These ill-conceived schemes subsequently collapsed leaving many people in dire financial straits. Anarchy and violence ensued throughout most of the country, particularly in the south, and travel to any part of Albania during 1997 was extremely dangerous due to armed gangs and rebels.

At the time this book went to print foreigners were once again able to visit Albania. Tirana, Durrës and Kruja were safe to visit and more intrepid travellers could visit other parts of the country with the possible exception of the north. However, accommodation and restaurant infrastructure outside of Tirana may still not be up to scratch given that much was destroyed and looted during the civil disturbances.

For this edition of *Eastern Europe* only Tirana, Durrës and Kruja were visited and conditions described for other parts of the country may differ from what you will find.

ECONOMY

Albania stuck to strict Stalinist central planning and wage and price controls longer than any other Eastern European country. Under communism two-thirds of the national income was directed towards consumption and social benefits, and the rest was used for capital investment. Industrial development was spread out, with factories in all regions. Unfortunately, much of the technology used is now thoroughly outdated and the goods produced are unable to compete on world markets. Between 1990 and 1992 industrial production fell 60%; huge investments, now gradually entering the economy, will be required to turn the situation around.

Albania is rich in natural resources such as crude oil, natural gas, coal, copper, iron, nickel and timber and is the world's third-largest producer of chrome, accounting for about 10% of the world's supply. The Central Mountains yield minerals such as copper (in the north-east around Kukës), chromium (farther south near the Drin River), and iron nickel (closer to Lake Ohrid). There are textiles industries at Berat, Korça and Tirana. Oil was discovered in Albania in 1917 and the country was until recently supplying all its own petroleum requirements. Oil and gas from Fier also enabled the production of chemical fertilisers.

There are several huge hydroelectric dams on the Drin River in the north. Albania obtains 80% of its electricity from such dams and by 1970 electricity had reached every village in the country. From 1972 to 1990 Albania exported hydroelectricity to Yugoslavia and Greece. The dams were built with Chinese technical assistance.

Under communist central planning Albania grew all its own food on collective farms, with surpluses available for export. About 20% of these farms were state farms run directly by the government, and the rest were cooperatives. The main crops were corn, cotton, potatoes, sugar beet, tobacco, vegetables and wheat. Lowland areas were collectivised in the 1950s, mountain areas during the 1967 Cultural Revolution.

Following the breakdown of authority in 1991, peasants seized the cooperatives' lands, livestock and buildings and terminated deliveries to the state distribution network, leading to widespread food shortages. After a period of neglect in the agricultural sector, farmers have begun the long task of rebuilding the rural infrastructure. Land is once more heavily cultivated and farms are once again providing produce for the markets.

Considering the country's small size, self-sufficiency was a real challenge, yet before 1990 Albania was one of the few countries in the world with no foreign debt (in 1976 a provision was included in its constitution forbidding any overseas loans). By 1994, however, the government had accumulated an estimated US$920 million foreign debt and must seek new loans just to cover interest on the existing loans.

After the breaks with the USSR and China, Albania's foreign trade had to be completely redirected. Until 1990 Albania's main trading partners were Bulgaria, Czechoslovakia, Hungary, Italy and Yugoslavia, which purchased Albanian food products, asphalt, bitumen, chromium, crude oil and tobacco. Minerals, fuels and metals accounted for 47% of Albania's exports. Today Albania still trades with its Balkan neighbours, but also with Italy and Greece. A new east-west trading route is slowly taking shape from Turkey, Bulgaria, Macedonia and Albania to Italy called the 8th Corridor – an envisioned new Via Egnatia. Other new highways and railways are on the drawing board and investments of US$2.5 billion are envisioned over the next 10 years. Foreign investors are once back in Albania after the 1997 disturbances and a cautious optimism among the business community is apparent.

POPULATION & PEOPLE

The Albanians are a hardy Mediterranean people, physically different from the more Nordic Slavs. Although the Slavs and Greeks look down on the Albanians, the Albanians themselves have a sense of racial superiority based on their descent from the ancient Illyrians, who inhabited the region before the coming of the Romans. The country's name comes from the Albanoi, an ancient Illyrian tribe.

Approximately 3.3 million Albanians live in Albania and a further two million suffer Serbian oppression in Kosova (regarded by Albanians as part of greater Albania), in Yugoslavia. (While in Albania you'll avoid offence by calling the region Kosova instead of Kosovo.) A further 400,000 are in western Macedonia. Harsh economic conditions in Albania have unleashed successive waves of emigration: to Serbia in the 15th century, to Greece and Italy in the 16th century, to the USA in the 19th and 20th centuries and to Greece, Italy and Switzerland today. The Arbereshi, longtime Albanian residents of 50 scattered villages in southern Italy, fled west in the 16th century to escape the Turks. As many as two million ethnic Albanians live in Turkey, emigrants from Serb-dominated Yugoslavia between 1912 and 1966. Since 1990

some 300,000 Albanians – 10% of the population – have migrated to Western Europe (especially Greece and Italy) to escape the economic hardships at home. Minorities inside Albania include Greeks (3% of the population) and Vlachs, Macedonians and Roma (comprising a further 2% of the population).

Tirana, the capital, is the largest city, with 444,000 inhabitants, followed by Durrës, Shkodra, Elbasan, Vlora, Korça, Fier and Berat. The apartment buildings which house a high percentage of the population may look decrepit on the outside but inside they're quite attractive. If you travel around the country much you'll most likely be invited to visit one.

The Shkumbin River forms a boundary between the Gheg cultural region of the north and the Tosk region in the south. The people in these regions still vary in dialect, musical culture and traditional dress.

ARTS
Music

Polyphony, the blending of several independent vocal or instrumental parts, is a southern Albanian tradition that dates back to ancient Illyrian times. Peasant choirs perform in a variety of styles, and the songs, usually with epic-lyrical or historical themes, may be dramatic to the point of yodelling or slow and sober, with alternate male or female voices combining in harmonies of unexpected beauty. Instrumental polyphonic *kabas* are played by small Roma ensembles usually led by a clarinet. Improvisation gives way to dancing at colourful village weddings. One well-known group which often tours outside Albania is the Lela Family of Përmet.

An outstanding recording of traditional Albanian music is the compact disc *Albania, Vocal and Instrumental Polyphony* (LDX 274 897) in the series 'Le Chant du Monde' (Musée de l'Homme, Paris).

The folk music of the Albanian-speaking villages founded five centuries ago in southern Italy has been popularised by Italian singer Silvana Licursi. Although Licursi sings in the Albanian language, her music bears a strong Italian imprint.

Literature

Prior to the adoption of a standardised orthography in 1909, very little literature was produced in Albania, though Albanians resident elsewhere in the Ottoman empire and in Italy did write works. Among these was the noted poet Naim Frashëri (1846-1900), who lived in Istanbul and wrote in Greek. Around the time of independence (1912), a group of romantic patriotic writers at Shkodra wrote epics and historical novels.

Perhaps the most interesting writer of the interwar period was Fan Noli (1880-1965). Educated as a priest in the USA, Fan Noli returned there to head the Albanian Orthodox Church in America after the Democratic government of Albania, in which he served as premier, was overthrown in 1924. Although many of his books are based on religious subjects, the introductions he wrote to his own translations of Cervantes, Ibsen, Omar Khayyám and Shakespeare established him as Albania's foremost literary critic.

Fan Noli's contemporary, the poet Migjeni (1911-38), focused on social issues until his early death from tuberculosis. In his 1936 poem, *Vargjet e lira* (Free Verse), Migjeni seeks to dispel the magic of the old myths and awaken the reader to present injustices.

Albania's best-known contemporary writer is Ismail Kadare, born in 1935, whose 15 novels have been translated into 40 languages. Unfortunately the English editions are sometimes disappointing as they are translated from the French version rather than the Albanian original. *The Castle* (1970) describes the 15th century Turkish invasion of Albania, while *Chronicle in Stone* (1971) relates wartime experiences in Kadare's birthplace, Gjiro-kastra, as seen through the eyes of a boy. *Broken April* deals with the blood vendettas of the northern highlands before the 1939 Italian invasion. Among Kadare's other novels available in English are *The General of the Dead Army* (1963), *The Palace of Dreams* (1981) and *Doruntina* (1988). Although Kadare lived in Tirana throughout the Hoxha years and even wrote a book, *The Great Winter* (1972), extolling Hoxha's defiance of Moscow, he sought political asylum in Paris in October 1990. His latest book, *Printemps Albanais* (Fayard, Paris, 1990), tells why.

Cinema

A recent film worth checking out is *Lamerica*, a brilliant and stark look at Albanian post-communist culture. Despite its title, it is about Albanians seeking to escape to Bari, Italy, in the immediate post-communist era. The title is a symbol for ordinary Albanians seeking a better and more materially fulfilling life in the west. Woven loosely around a plot concerning a couple of Italian scam artists, the essence of the film is the unquenchable dignity of ordinary Albanians in the face of adversity.

SOCIETY & CONDUCT

Traditional dress is still common in rural areas, especially on Sunday and holidays. Men wear embroidered white shirts and knee trousers, the Ghegs with a white felt skullcap and the Tosks with a flat-topped white fezes. Women's clothing is brighter than that of the men. Along with the standard white blouses with wide sleeves, women from Christian areas wear red vests, while Muslim women wear baggy pants tied at the ankles and coloured headscarves. Older Muslim women wear white scarves around the neck; white scarves may also be a sign of mourning.

The *Kanun* is an ancient social law outlining most aspects of social behaviour including the treatment of guests. This has meant that Albanians can be hospitable in the extreme and will often offer travellers lodging and food free of charge. Travellers must be wary of exploiting this tradition and while payment may well be acceptable in some cases, a small gift of a book or a momento from home will often suffice.

Observe respect when visiting mosques – remove your shoes and avoid visits during prayer times.

RELIGION

From 1967 to 1990 Albania was the only officially atheist state in Europe. Public religious services were banned and many churches were converted into theatres or cinemas. In mid-1990 this situation ended and in December of that year Nobel Prize-winner Mother Teresa of Calcutta, an ethnic Albanian from Macedonia, visited Albania and met President Alia. Traditionally,

Albania has been 70% Sunni Muslim, 20% Albanian Orthodox (mostly in the south) and 10% Roman Catholic (mostly in the north). Albania is the only country in Europe with an Islamic majority. The spiritual vacuum left by the demise of communism is being filled by US evangelical imperialists. New churches and mosques are springing up all over the country as evidence of the revival of traditional spiritual customs.

LANGUAGE

Albanian (Shqipja) is an Indo-European dialect of ancient Illyrian, with many Latin, Slavonic and (modern) Greek words. The two main dialects of Albanian diverged over the past 1000 years. In 1909 a standardised form of the Gheg dialect of Elbasan was adopted as the official language, but since WWII a modified version of the Tosk dialect of southern Albania has been used. Outside the country, Albanians resident in former Yugoslavia speak Gheg, those in Greece speak Tosk, whereas in Italy they speak another dialect called Arberesh. With practice you can sometimes differentiate between the dialects by listening for the nasalised vowels of Gheg. The Congress of Orthography at Tirana in 1972 established a unified written language based on the two dialects which is now universally accepted.

Italian is the most useful foreign language to know in Albania, with English a strong second. Some of the older people will have learnt Italian in school before 1943; others have picked it up by watching Italian TV stations or through recent trips to Italy (as is the case with many of the young men).

An excellent teach yourself course of Albanian called *Colloquial Albanian* by Isa Zymberi is available from Routledge Publications (11 New Fetter Lane, London EC4P 4EE, UK) or ordered from your bookseller. The book-and-cassette-tape package has 24 well-structured language units, easy to follow grammar tables and an English-Albanian-English vocabulary and would have to be the best modern guide to the Albanian language on the market. Lonely Planet's *Mediterranean Europe phrasebook* contains a helpful list of translated Albanian words and phrases.

Many Albanian place names have two

forms because the definite article is a suffix. In this book we use the form most commonly used in English, but Tirana actually means *the* Tiranë. On signs at archaeological sites, *p.e. sonë* means BC, and *e sonë* means AD. Public toilets may be marked *burra* for men and *gra* for women or may simply show a man's or a woman's shoe or the figure of a man or woman. Albanians, like Bulgarians, shake their heads to say yes and nod to say no.

See the Language Guide at the back of the book for pronunciation guidelines and useful words and phrases.

Facts for the Visitor

HIGHLIGHTS

The Onufri Museum in Berat Citadel houses real masterpieces of medieval icon painting. The National Museum of History in Tirana and the historical museum in Kruja Citadel are excellent. The museum town of Gjirokastra is worth a couple of days visit as is the archaeological site of Butrint.

LOWLIGHTS

Broken-down and abandoned factories that litter the countryside. Abysmal roads and chaotic driving conditions. The one million Kalashnikov rifles that have been taken by one in four residents of Albania. Former state-run hotels. The 'Steel of the Party' factory in Elbasan.

SUGGESTED ITINERARIES

Depending on the length of your stay, you might want to see and do the following things in Albania:

Two days
  Visit Gjirokastra, Saranda and Butrint
One week
  Visit Gjirokastra, Fier/Apollonia, Berat, Durrës, Tirana and Pogradec or Korça
Two weeks
  Visit Gjirokastra, Fier/Apollonia, Berat, Durrës, Tirana, Kruja, Lezha, Shkodra and Kukës
One month
  Visit every place included in this chapter

PLANNING
Climate & When to Go
Albania has a warm Mediterranean climate. The summers are hot, clear and dry, and the winters, when 40% of the rain falls, are cool, cloudy and moist. In winter the high interior plateau can be very cold as continental air masses move in. Along the coast the climate is moderated by sea winds. Gjirokastra and Shkodra receive twice as much rain as Korça, with November, December and April being the wettest months. The sun shines longest from May to September and July is the warmest month, but even April and October are quite pleasant. The best month to visit is September, as it's still warm and fruit and vegetables are abundant. Winter is uncomfortable as most rooms are unheated and tap water is ice-cold.

Books & Maps
Previously, one of the best travel guidebooks to Albania was *Nagel's Encyclopedia-Guide Albania* (Nagel Publishers, 5-7, Rue de l'Orangerie, 1211 Geneva 7, Switzerland), published in English and German editions in 1990. It's seldom found in bookshops, however, so consider ordering a copy through mail order. Nagel's provides no practical hotel or restaurant information but it's good on historical background up to 1990.

High Albania by Edith Durham, first published in 1909, is an Englishwoman's account of the tribes of northern Albania based on seven years of travel in the area.

In *Albania, The Search for the Eagle's Song*, June Emerson gives a picture of what it was like to visit Albania just before 1990. Untainted by hindsight, her book is an unwitting snapshot of a time that has vanished forever.

The Artful Albanian: The Memoirs of Enver Hoxha, edited by Jon Halliday, contains selected passages from the 3400 pages of Hoxha's six volumes of memoirs. Chapters like 'Decoding China' and 'Battling Khrushchev' give an insight into the mind of this controversial figure.

Anton Logoreci's political and factual narrative *Albanians* is a well-balanced and readable account of Albanian history up to 1987, while *Albania and the Albanians* by Derek Hall is a comprehensive political history of Albania published in 1994.

Biografi by New Zealand writer Lloyd Jones is a fanciful but very readable tale set in immediate post-communist Albania involving the search for Enver Hoxha's alleged double, Petar Shapallo.

Probably the best overall country map is the *Albania – EuroMap* with maps of five towns and a handy distance chart.

What to Bring
Most essential items found in Western Europe are available in Tirana. If you are planning to spend some time in the country, bring all your personal toiletries and medications. A universal sink plug is about the most practical commodity you can take to Albania.

TOURIST OFFICES
There are no tourist information offices in Albania, but hotel receptionists will sometimes give you directions. The moribund state tourism authority Alburist may eventually be reincarnated in privatised form, but don't count on it just yet. You can buy city maps of Tirana, but in most other towns they're unobtainable. In addition, many streets lack signs and the buildings have no numbers! Some streets don't seem to have any name at all. Most of the towns are small enough for you to do without such things.

The Albania Society of Britain (☎ 0181-540 6824), 7 Nelson Road, London SW19 1HS, England, exists 'to promote contacts between Albania and Britain, to offer factual information concerning Albania and to foster cultural and social bonds between the two peoples'. The Society's quarterly journal *Albanian Life* carries a good range of interesting, readable articles, and membership (£8 in the UK, £12 overseas) includes a subscription.

In Australasia write to FG Clements, The Albania Society, PO Box 14074, Wellington, New Zealand.

In the USA, Jack Shulman (☎ 718-633 0530), PO Box 912, Church Street Station, New York, NY 10008, sells Albanian books, maps, videos and folk-music cassettes by mail order. Jack also carries English translations of Ismail Kadare's best novels.

In Germany you can contact the Deutsch-Albanische Freundschaftsgesellschaft (☎/fax 040-511 1320), Bilser Strasse 9, D-22297 Hamburg, Germany, which publishes the quarterly magazine *Albanische Hefte*.

An excellent source of rare and out-of-print books on Albania is Eastern Books (☎/fax 0181-871 0880; info@easternbooks .com), 125a Astonville St, Southfields, London SW18 5AQ, England, UK. Write for its 24-page catalogue of books about Albania, or check its Web page (www.easternbooks .com). Also try Oxus Books (☎/fax 0181-870 3854), 121 Astonville St, London SW18 5AQ, England, UK.

VISAS & EMBASSIES

No visa is required from citizens of Australia, Bulgaria, Canada, Iceland, New Zealand, Norway, Switzerland, Turkey, the USA and EU countries. Travellers from other countries can obtain their Albanian visa at the border for a price equivalent to what an Albanian would pay for a tourist visa in those countries. Those who don't need a visa must still pay an 'entry tax' of US$5. Citizens of the USA do not have to pay the US$5 entry tax. Land border authorities may try to take anything up to US$20 from you. Insist on $5 and ask for a receipt.

Upon arrival you will fill in an arrival and departure card. Keep the departure card with your passport and present it when you leave.

Albanian Embassies Abroad

Albanian embassies are found in the following cities: Ankara, Athens, Beijing, Belgrade, Bonn, Brussels, Bucharest, Budapest, Cairo, Geneva, Havana, Istanbul, London, New York, Paris, Prague, Rome, Skopje, Sofia, Stockholm, Vienna, Warsaw and Washington. Listed below are some of the main addresses. For other Eastern Europe embassies, see under the relevant country.

France
(☎ 01-45 53 51 32) 13 rue de la Pompe, Paris 75016
Greece
(☎ 01-723 4412; fax 723 1972) Karahristou 1, 115 21 Athens
Netherlands
(☎ 070-427 2101) Koninginnegracht 12, 2514 AA, The Hague

UK
(☎ 0171-730 5709; fax 730 5747) 38 Grosvenor Gardens, London SW1 0EB
USA
(☎ 202-223 4942; fax 628 7342) 1511 K Street NW, Washington, DC 20005

Foreign Embassies in Albania

Bulgaria
(☎ 33 155; fax 38 937) Rruga Skënderbeg 12; Monday, Wednesday & Friday 10.30 am to noon
Hungary
(☎ 32 238; fax 33 211) Rruga Skënderbeg; Monday and Wednesday 9 to 11 am
Macedonia
(☎ 30 909; fax 32 514) Lekë Dukagjini 2; Monday to Friday, 10 am to noon
UK
(☎/fax 34 973) Rruga Skënderbeg; Tuesday to Friday, 9 am to noon
USA
(☎ 32 875; fax 32 222) Rruga Elbasanit 103; Monday to Friday, 8.30 am to 4.30 pm
Yugoslavia
(☎ 32 089; fax 23 042) Rruga Durrësit 192-196; Monday to Friday, 10 am to noon

MONEY

Albanian banknotes come in denominations of 100, 200, 500 and 1000 lekë. There are 5, 10, 20 and 50 lekë coins. Notes issued after 1997 are smaller and contain a sophisticated watermark to prevent forgery. In 1964 the currency was revalued 10 times and prices are often still quoted at the old rate. Thus if people tell you that a ticket costs 1000 lekë, they may really mean 100 lekë, so take care not to pay 10 times more! Conversely, a taxi driver who quotes a fare of 1000 lekë may actually mean 1000 new lekë, so watch out. This situation can be very confusing.

In mid-1998, US$1 got you about 155 lekë. Everything can be paid for with lekë; hotel and transport prices in this book are usually quoted in dollars or Deutschmarks, but you can pay in lekë at the current rate. Although Albania is an inexpensive country for foreigners, for Albanians it's different as the average monthly wage is less than US$100, though this is changing quickly.

The private Banka e Kursimeve is usually the most efficient when it comes to changing travellers cheques and they keep longer hours than the National Bank. Some banks will change US dollar travellers cheques into US dollars cash without commission. Travellers cheques in small denominations may be used when paying bills at major hotels but cash is preferred everywhere. Credit cards are only accepted in larger hotels and travel agencies. There are no ATMs in Albania yet.

Every town has its free currency market which usually operates on the street in front of the main post office or state bank. Look for the men standing with pocket calculators in hand. Such transactions are not dangerous and it all takes place quite openly, but make sure you count their money twice before tendering yours. The rate will be about the same as at a bank. The advantages with changing money on the street are that you avoid the 1% commission, save time and don't have to worry about banking hours. Unlike the banks, private moneychangers never run out of currency notes.

Deutschmarks are preferred in Yugoslavia but in Albania US dollars are the favourite foreign currency; you should bring along a supply of dollars in small bills as they can be used to bargain for everything from hotel rooms to curios and taxi rides. Greek drachmas are often quite acceptable. The import and export of Albanian currency is prohibited, but there's no reason to do either. Conversion rates for major currencies in mid-1998 are listed below:

Exchange Rates

Australia	A$1	=	95 lekë
Canada	C$1	=	103.8 lekë
euro	€1	=	172.9 lekë
France	1FF	=	26 lekë
Germany	DM1	=	87.5 lekë
Japan	¥100	=	109.6 lekë
United Kingdom	UK£1	=	258 lekë
United States	US$1	=	156 lekë

For the most recent currency rates of the Albanian lek, point your Web browser at: www.gopher://gopher.undp.org:70/00/uncurr /exchrates.

Tipping
Albania is a tip-conscious society. You should round up the bill in restaurants. However, with taxi drivers you will normally agree on a fare beforehand so an extra tip will not be considered necessary.

POST & COMMUNICATIONS
Post
Sending Mail Postage is inexpensive and the service surprisingly reliable, but always use air mail. There are no public mailboxes in Albania; you must hand in your letters at a post office in person. Leaving letters at hotel reception for mailing is unwise, although the Rogner Hotel in Tirana has a reliable postal service. Mail your parcels from the main post office in Tirana to reduce the amount of handling. Letters to the USA, Australia and Canada cost 100 lekë and within Europe 50 lekë.

Receiving Mail Mail sent to Poste Restante, Tirana, Albania should reach you OK. However, Albania is not a good country for receiving mail as letters to Albania may be opened.

Telephone
Long-distance telephone calls made from main post offices are cheap, costing about 150 lekë a minute to Western Europe. The cost of a three-minute call to the USA is 840 lekë. In 1997 Albania introduced public cardphones which makes calling home a lot easier. Cards are available from the post office and street kiosks in versions of 50 units (520 lekë), 100 units (910 lekë) and 200 units (1700 lekë).

Getting through to Albania (country code ☎ 355) may require some persistence. Currently 16 towns have direct-dial access and the relevant codes are listed under each town. For other towns call ☎ 10 for the operator.

Albania also has a mobile phone network covering at present the central plains from Shkodra in the North to Vlora in the South. Check with your home provider for possible roaming agreements. Local mobile phone numbers are in the format 038 123 4567.

Albania's international access code is ☎ 00.

Fax
Faxing can be done fairly easily from the main post office in Tirana, or from major hotels, though they will charge more. Sending a one-page fax from the post office to the USA should cost around 390 lekë.

INTERNET RESOURCES
Albania is linked to the Internet, but there is currently only one Internet Centre providing public access. (See Cybercafés in the Tirana section). Useful Web sites to point your browser at are: www.albanian.com (the Albanian WWW Home Page) or www.tirana.al which was the first Web site established in Albania and set up by the United Nations Development Project.

NEWSPAPERS & MAGAZINES
Some 18 newspapers are published in Tirana, up from seven in 1989. Many are sponsored by political parties, such as *Zëri i Popullit* (The People's Voice), organ of the Socialist Party; *RD* (Democratic Renaissance), the Democratic Party's paper; *Alternativa*, the Social Democratic Party's paper; and *Republika*, the Republican Party's paper. *Koha Jonë* is the paper with the widest readership.

The *Albanian Daily News* (adn@icc.al .eu.org) is a fairly dry English-language publication with nonetheless useful insights into events in the country including a press review of the major Albanian-language papers. It is available from major hotels, or you can read it online – www.AlbanianNews.com.

RADIO & TV
There are many TV channels available in Albania including the state TV service TVSH, the private station TVA and, among others, BBC, CNN, Euronews, Eurosport, several Italian channels and a couple of French ones to boot.

The BBC World Service can be picked up in and around Tirana on 103.9 FM.

PHOTOGRAPHY & VIDEO
Tirana has several good one-hour developing and printing services. In the country it's considered rude to take pictures of people without asking permission, but this will almost never be refused. If you promise to send prints to local people, be sure to honour those promises. As a photographer you'll arouse a lot of friendly curiosity. Do not take photographs of any military or government establishments. Bring your own video paraphernalia – batteries and tapes etc – even though these are now available in Tirana.

TIME
Albania is one hour ahead of GMT/UTC, the same as Yugoslavia, Macedonia and Italy, but one hour behind Greece. Albania goes on summer time at the end of March, when clocks are turned forward an hour. At the end of September, they're turned back an hour.

ELECTRICITY
The electric current is 220V, 50Hz, and plugs have two round pins.

WEIGHTS & MEASURES
Albania uses the metric system.

TOILETS
Public toilets should be used in dire circumstances only! There are only three in the whole of Tirana. Use hotel or restaurant toilets whenever you can. The ones in the main hotels in Tirana are very clean and modern. Plan your 'rest' stops carefully when travelling in the country.

HEALTH
Health services are available to tourists for a small fee at state-run hospitals, but service and standards are not crash hot. You are better off taking out health insurance and using the private clinics where available.

WOMEN TRAVELLERS
While women are not likely to encounter any predictable dangers, it is recommended that you travel in pairs or with male companions, in order to avoid unwanted attention – particularly outside Tirana. Bear in mind that Albania is a predominantly Muslim country. Dress should be conservative.

GAY & LESBIAN TRAVELLERS

Gay sex became legal in Albania early in 1995, however attitudes towards homosexuality are still highly conservative. The Gay Albania Society (Shoqata Gay Albania) is at PO Box 104, Tirana, Albania.

DISABLED TRAVELLERS

Getting around Tirana and Albania in general will be problematic for travellers in wheelchairs since few special facilities exist. There are toilets for disabled people in the Tirana International and the Europapark (Rogner) Hotel in Tirana.

DANGERS & ANNOYANCES

Beware of pickpockets on crowded city buses and don't flash money around! Walking around the towns is safe during the day, even in small streets and among desolate apartment blocks, but at night you must beware of falling into deep potholes in the unlit streets, and occasional gangs of youths. Be aware of theft generally, but don't believe the horror stories you hear about Albania in Greece and elsewhere.

Take special care if accosted by Roma women and children begging, as they target foreigners and are very pushy. If you give them money once, they'll stick to you like glue. When accosted, do not respond and avoid eye contact. Just keep walking and they will soon give up. Head for the nearest hotel if they haven't given up in five minutes. They will soon scarper.

Corrupt police may attempt to extort money from you by claiming that something is wrong with your documentation, or on another pretext. Strongly resist paying them anything without an official receipt. If they threaten to take you to the police station, just go along for the experience and see things through to the end. Always have your passport with you.

Hepatitis B is prevalent in Albania. Get a vaccination before arriving and take care swimming near built-up areas and drinking tap water.

BUSINESS HOURS

Most shops open at 7 am and close for a siesta from noon to 4 pm. They open again until 7 pm and some also open on Sunday. In summer the main shops stay open one hour later but private shops keep whatever hours they like. State banks will change travellers cheques from 7.30 to 11 am only.

Albanian museums don't follow any pattern as far as opening hours go. Museums in small towns may only open for a couple of hours a week. You may find them inexplicably closed during the posted hours or simply closed with no hours posted. Since state subsidies have been slashed, foreigners must pay 100 to 300 lekë admission to major museums.

PUBLIC HOLIDAYS & SPECIAL EVENTS

Public holidays in Albania include New Year's Day (1 January), Easter Monday (March/April), Labour Day (1 May), Independence & Liberation Day (28 November) and Christmas Day (25 December).

Ramadan and Bajram, variable Muslim holidays, are also celebrated.

ACCOMMODATION

Many of the large tourist hotels are still owned by the State Bureau for Tourism, Albturist, though many are being privatised. Most Albturist hotels are in pretty bad shape, so it's always a good idea to check your room first. Albturist itself is barely hanging on in the changing tourist market, so don't depend on it for too much advice on places to stay.

Accommodation is undergoing a rapid transformation in Albania with the opening up of new custom-built private hotels, and the conversion of homes or villas into so-called private hotels. For budget travellers, these are without doubt the best way to go.

New custom-built hotels tend to have Western European prices, ie US$40 to $50 per person per night and upwards, but these are modern, well-appointed establishments – a far cry from the state-run hotels of old – and they usually include breakfast.

In this book we have tended to provide advice on private accommodation and on state accommodation when that is the only option. You can often find unofficial accommodation in private homes by asking around. You may even get a meal or two thrown in as well.

There are no camping grounds but free camping is possible in emergencies. For security, camp out of sight of the road and never leave your tent unattended. Don't camp in the same area more than one night, unless you have permission to camp next to someone's house (even then you risk losing things). Expect to arouse considerable curiosity.

FOOD

Lunch is the main meal of the day though eating out in the evening is very common in Tirana. The quality of restaurants in the capital has improved greatly. In the country and other towns things are also getting much better, so you should have no problem getting a decent meal.

State-owned hotel restaurants are cheaper but the standards are low and they're also poor value. Everywhere beware of waiters who refuse to bring the menu, pad your bill with extras and 'forget' to bring your change. The many hamburger stands in the towns are a much better deal, but choose one that is patronised by a lot of people.

Albanian cuisine, like that of Serbia, has been strongly influenced by Turkey. Grilled meats like *shishqebap* (shish kebab), *romstek* (minced meat patties) and *qofte* (meat balls) are served all across the Balkans. Some local dishes include *çomlek* (meat and onion stew), *fërges* (a rich beef stew), *rosto me salcë kosi* (roast beef with sour cream) and *tavë kosi* (mutton with yoghurt). Lake Shkodra carp and Lake Ohrid trout are the most common fish dishes. Try the ice cream (*akullore*), which is very popular everywhere.

DRINKS

Albanians take their coffee both as *kafe turke* (Turkish coffee) and *kafe ekspres* (espresso). If you ask for *kafe surogato* you will get what is the closest to filter coffee. Any tourist or resident expatriate will tell you not to drink the water, but Albanians do so all the time with no consequences. It all depends on what your stomach is acclimatised to. Avoid unbottled, ungassed drinks as they may be questionable.

Albanian white wine is better than the vinegary red. However the red *Shesi e Zi* from either Librazhd or Berat is an excellent drop. Most of the beer consumed in Albania is imported from Macedonia or Greece, but draught Austrian or Italian beer is available in the posher joints in Tirana. *Raki* (a clear brandy distilled from grapes) is taken as an apéritif. There's also *konjak* (cognac), *uzo* (a colourless aniseed-flavoured liqueur like Greek ouzo) and various fruit liqueurs. *Fërnet* is a medicinal apéritif containing herbal essences, made at Korça.

Public bars and cafés patronised mostly by local men are very sociable and if you enter one for a drink with an Albanian always try to pay. Nine times out of 10 your money will be refused and by having the opportunity to insist on paying your host will gain face in front of those present. The favourite Albanian drinking toast is *gëzuar!*

ENTERTAINMENT

Check the local theatre for performances. These are usually advertised on painted boards either in front of the theatre or on main streets. Ask someone to direct you to the venue if it's not clear. Football is played at local stadiums on Saturday and Sunday afternoons. As a foreigner, you may need someone to help you obtain tickets.

THINGS TO BUY

Most hotels have tourist shops where you can buy Albanian handicrafts such as carpets, silk, ornaments (made from silver, copper and wood), embroidery, handmade shoes, shoulder bags, picture books, musical instruments, and records and cassettes of folk music.

Getting There & Away

AIR

Rinas airport is 26km north-west of Tirana. Taxis and a bus ply the route to Tirana. The airport phone number is ☎ 042-62 620

Ada Air arrives from Bari, Athens and Skopje; Adria Airways from Ljubljana; Albanian Airlines from Rome, Zürich, Munich and Vienna; Alitalia from Rome; Arbëria

Airlines from New York; Hemus Air from Sofia; Lufthansa from Frankfurt and Munich; Malév Hungarian Airlines from Budapest; Olympic Airlines from Athens via Ioannina or Thessaloniki and Swissair from Zürich.

These expensive flights are used mostly by business people or Albanians resident abroad and are of little interest to budget travellers, who can come more cheaply by land or sea. An exception is Malév Hungarian Airlines' service three times a week from Budapest to Tirana, which is usually good value and saves you from having to transit Yugoslavia.

Unfortunately, the Italian government requires its state airline flying between Italy and Albania to charge business class fares for one-way tickets, which makes Italy a poor gateway. For example, with Alitalia, Tirana-Bari is US$318 one way, Tirana-Rome US$462 one way. However, Alitalia does do weekend return specials to/from Rome for US$339. In comparison to flying to Rome, it is cheaper to fly further on Albanian Airlines (☎/fax 42 857), a joint venture with a Kuwaiti concern, which has flights to Zürich (twice weekly, US$388 one way), Munich (three times a week, US$395 one way) and Vienna (three times a week, US$370 one way). Return flights to/from Rome or Bologna with Albanian Airlines cost US$296.

Before investing in any of the above fares, compare them with the price of a cheap flight to Athens or Thessaloniki, from where Albania is easily accessible by local bus with a change of bus at the border; you could also look at the cost of a charter flight to Corfu, from where you can take a ferry to Saranda in southern Albania. Flying to Tirana from Thessaloniki will cost around 23,500 drachmas (US$78) one way.

LAND
Bus
The simplest way to get into Albania by bus is from Greece. For Tirana or Gjirokastra there is a bus from Athens via Ioannina. This bus leaves Athens at 9 pm daily (except Friday) and passes through Ioannina at about 7 am the following day on its way to Tirana. This bus leaves Tirana for Athens (732km, 6000 lekë) daily at 6 am from the Axhensi

bus office on a side street near the art gallery in Tirana. Alternatively, nine local buses a day run from Ioannina, Greece, to the Albanian border at Kakavija (one hour, 1100 dr). You must arrive at the border before 11 am to connect with a local bus on to Gjirokastra (26km) or Tirana (263km).

Alternatively, it's fairly easy to cover the 93km from Korça to Florina, Greece, via Kapshtica (see the Korça section in this chapter for details). There are two buses a day from the Greek border to Florina (1½ hours, 1000 dr), otherwise you will need to take a taxi (6000 dr). Unscheduled local buses from Tirana to Kakavija and Korça to Kapshtica leave throughout the day. There is also a direct bus from Korça to Thessaloniki six times a week. To/from Athens you're better off going via Kakavija, to/from Thessaloniki via Kapshtica.

If you're Macedonia-bound, take the daily bus at 6 am to either Ohrid (15 DM) or Tetovo (20 DM) from the Axhensi bus office. From Tetovo you can take a frequent local bus to Skopje. Tickets can also be bought from Esterida Bus Services behind the Palace of Culture.

Buses for Sofia (505km, US$30 – payable only in US dollars) depart on Tuesday and Wednesday at 10 am from Albtransport on Rruga Mine Peza in Tirana.

Although Shkodra is linked to Podgorica, Yugoslavia, by rail there's no passenger service.

Car & Motorcycle
In the recent past, bringing a car to Albania was a risky business. Today there is no real reason why you should not travel by car through Albania – if we ignore the security problems in the North still prevailing by mid-1998.

Travel is slow because of the poor condition of the roads and the arterial infrastructure cannot yet properly support the marked increase in vehicular traffic that Albania has recently experienced. Apart from an 8km stretch of 'freeway' between Tirana and Durrës there has been no visible improvement in the roads since the days of communism. See the following Getting Around section for further information on local driving conditions.

It should be possible to transit the country from Hani i Hotit on the Montenegran border to the Kakavija border with Greece (or vice versa) in about eight or nine hours, though Tirana makes for a convenient overnight stop. The following highway border crossings are open to both motorists and persons on foot or bicycle.

Yugoslavia Crossing from Yugoslavia may now be extremely difficult if not impossible due to the 1998 border tensions with Kosova (Kosovo). You can in theory cross at Han i Hotit (between Podgorica and Shkodra) and at Morina (between Prizren and Kukës). For information about crossing at Morina, see the Kukës section in this chapter and Prizren in the Yugoslavia chapter. A new border crossing was planned at Muriqan, between Shkodra and Ulcinj in Montenegro, but to date no opening date has been announced.

Macedonia Cross at Tushemisht (near Sveti Naum, 29km south of Ohrid), Qafa e Thanës (between Struga and Pogradec) and Maqellare (between Debar and Peshkopi). See the Pogradec section of this chapter for information about crossing at Tushemisht.

Greece The border crossings are Kapshtica (between Florina and Korça) and Kakavija (between Ioannina and Gjirokastra). A new EU-funded border crossing between Sagiada and Konispol, south of Saranda, is planned but no opening date has yet been announced.

Warning Travel conditions in mid-1998 for private cars are still not favourable or even possible given the threat of banditry in the North and the likelihood of the Albanian/Yugoslav border posts being closed.

SEA

The Italian company Adriatica di Navigazione offers ferry services to Durrës from Bari (220km, nine hours), Ancona (550km, 20 hours) and Trieste (750km, 25 hours) several times a week. The routes are served by 272-vehicle, 1088-passenger ships of the *Palladio* class. The food aboard ship is good.

Deck fares are US$70 Bari-Durrës,

US$100 Ancona-Durrës and US$120 Trieste-Durrës. Pullman (airline-style) seats cost US$80 Bari-Durrës, US$110 Ancona-Durrës, and US$135 Trieste-Durrës. Cabins for the Trieste-Durrës trip vary in price from US$155 for a bed in a four-bed C-class cabin to US$195 for an A-class cabin.

These are high-season fares, applicable eastbound from 4 July to 15 August, westbound from 2 August to 2 September. During other months it's about 25% cheaper. The cost of a return fare is double the one-way fare. Meals are not included and a port tax of 5000 lire is charged on departures from Italy and US$4 from Albania. Bicycles are carried free.

In Trieste ferry tickets are available from Agenzia Marittima 'Agemar' (☎ 040-363 737), Via Rossini 2, right on the old harbour five blocks from Trieste railway station. The booking office is closed from noon to 3 pm and on weekends. In Bari the agent is 'Agestea' (☎ 080-331 555), Via Liside 4. In Ancona it's Maritime Agency Srl (☎ 071-204 915), Via XXIX Settembre 2/0. In Albania tickets are sold at the harbour in Durrës or from Albania Travel & Tours (☎ 042-32 983; fax 33 981) in Tirana.

Transeuropa Lines runs a service twice a week between Bari in Italy and Durrës. One-way deck prices are quoted at 90,000 lire with a 25% discount on the return ticket. In Durrës contact Shpresa Agency (☎/fax 052-22 423) and in Bari contact Morfimare (☎/fax 080-524 0139).

Illyria Lines SA in Durrës (☎/fax 052-23 723), in Vlora (☎/fax 063-25 533) and in Brindisi (☎ 0831-562 043; fax 562 005) runs two ferries between these three ports. Prices are US$69 for a deck ticket or US$83 for an aircraft-type seat.

The fastest ferry connection between Bari and Durrës is the 315-passenger catamaran *La Vikinga* (3½ hours, US$112, VIP class US$125). This high-speed vessel departs Durrës daily at 9.30 am and Bari at 4 pm and travels at speeds of up to 90km/h. The Bari agent is Morfimare (☎/fax 080-524 0139), Corso de Tullio 36/40.

The shortest and least expensive ferry trip to/from Italy is the Otranto-Vlora link (100km, three times a week, US$45). Tickets are available from Biglietteria Linee Lauro

(☎ 0836-806 061; fax 806 062), at the port in Otranto, or Albania Travel & Tours (☎ 042-32 983) in Tirana.

Travellers from Corfu are advised to look for the ticket vendors (from any of the three ferry companies) who hang around the New Harbour before the ferries depart. The *Kamelia* departs Corfu at 10 am, the *Oleg Volvač* at 10.30 am and the *Harikla* at 3 pm. Tickets prices at last count were around US$10, one way. (These times and services may have changed, so check before making concrete plans.)

ORGANISED TOURS

Several companies offer package tours to Albania which include transport, accommodation, meals, admission fees and guides, but not visa fees, airport taxes, or alcohol with the meals. Single hotel rooms also cost extra. As always, group travel involves a trade-off: lack of control over the itinerary and the obligation to wait around for slower group members. Tours also tend to isolate you from the everyday life of Albania, though the trekking tours bring you more into contact with people and places.

The companies to contact are:

Alumni Travel
 (☎ 02-9290 3856; fax 9290 3857) 100 Clarence St, Sydney, NSW 2001, Australia
Exodus
 (☎ 0181-675 5550; fax 673 0779; sales@exodustravels.co.uk) 9 Weir Rd London SW12 0LT, UK
ITS
 (☎ 0161-839 2222; fax 839 0000; all@its-travel.u-net.co.uk) 546-550 Royal Exchange, Old Bank Street, Manchester M2 7EN, UK
Regent Holidays
 (☎ 0117-921 1711; fax 925 4866; 106041.1470@compuserve.com) 15 John St, Bristol BS1 2HR, UK
Kutrubes Travel
 (☎ 617-426 5668; fax 426 3196) 328 Tremont St, Boston, MA 02116 USA
Intertrek BV
 (☎ 070-363 6416) Postbus 18760, NL-2502 ET Den Haag, Netherlands
Scope Reizen
 (☎ 077-735 533) Spoorstraat 41, NL-5931 PS Tegelen, Netherlands

Skënderbeg-Reisen GmbH
 (☎ 0234-308 686) Postfach 102204, D-44722 Bochum, Germany
Egnatia Tours
 (☎ 0222-406 97 32) Piaristengasse 60, A-1082 Vienna, Austria

Regent Holidays has a five-day bus tour of central Albania four times a year at £508, return flight from London included. ITS offers eight-day tours of 'Classical Albania' for £799, covering most of the major sights. Kutrubes Travel offers a 10-day bus tour of southern Albania every two weeks from May to October at US$2260, including return air fare from Boston. Northern Albania is offered once in July and again in August (US$2367).

Exodus offers 15-day hiking and discovery tours between May and September. Its free brochure is quite informative.

LEAVING ALBANIA

Airport departure tax is US$10, which is payable in dollars or lekë. Departure tax from Albanian ports is US$2. Private cars departing from Albania pay US$5 road tax per day for each day spent in the country.

Getting Around

BUS

Most Albanians travel around their country in private minibuses or state-owned buses. These run fairly frequently throughout the day between Tirana and Durrës (38km) and other towns north and south. Buses to Tirana depart from towns all around Albania at the crack of dawn. Tickets are sold by a conductor on board, and for foreigners the fares are low. Although old, the buses are usually comfortable enough, as the number of passengers is controlled by police.

TRAIN

Before 1948, Albania had no railways, but the communists built up a limited north-south rail network based at the port of Durrës, with daily passenger trains leaving Tirana for Shkodra (98km, 3½ hours), Fier (4¼ hours), Ballsh (five hours), Vlora (5½ hours) and

Pogradec (seven hours). Seven trains a day make the 1½-hour trip between Tirana and Durrës. In August 1986 a railway was completed from Shkodra to Podgorica, Yugoslavia, but this is for freight only.

Albanian railways use mostly old Italian rolling stock seconded as a form of aid. There's still only one type of train ticket, so you can sit in 1st or 2nd class for the same price. Train fares are about a third cheaper than bus fares, but both are very cheap by European standards.

Train travel is really only useful between Tirana and Durrës. All trains to southern Albania call at Durrës, a roundabout route that makes them much slower than bus. The bus to Shkodra in the north is also much faster. Still, travelling by train is an interesting way to see the country and meet the people. But be warned: many trains don't have toilets and the carriages can be very decrepit, with broken windows.

CAR & MOTORCYCLE

Albania has only just acquired an official road traffic code and most motorists have only learned to drive in the last few years. The road infrastructure is poor and the roads badly maintained, but the number of cars on the road is growing daily. There are petrol stations in the cities, but they are few and far between in the country. Very few Albanians ride motorcycles and the poor road conditions are a concern for foreign motorcyclists. You can hire a car, but timid drivers might prefer hiring a car and a driver.

Hazards include pedestrians who use the roads as an extension of the footpaths; animals being herded along country roads; gaping potholes; a lack of road warnings and signs and occasionally reckless drivers. Security is also an issue. Park your vehicle in a secure location, such as hotel grounds, or in a guarded parking lot. Store removables like hubcaps inside the car when parked. An immobiliser alarm is a good idea.

Modern petrol stations are opening up all over the country so fuel is no longer a problem. Unleaded fuel may only be available closer to Tirana, so fill up when you can. A litre of unleaded petrol costs 145 lekë.

BICYCLE

Cycling around Albania, while not unheard of, is still a novelty. A number of foreign cyclists, including solo riders, have written of interesting and hassle-free trips through the country, though some caution should still be exercised. If you are planning to cycle into the country, it is preferable to do so in groups of two or more for security – primarily for your belongings on the bike. Facilities outside Tirana, while improving, are not very sophisticated. You will need to be as self-sufficient as possible. Car drivers may not show much respect for cyclists, so ride defensively. Keep a look out for potholes. Mountain bikes are hardier than road bikes.

HITCHING

With buses so cheap, hitching will probably only be an emergency means of transport. You can afford to be selective about the rides you accept as everyone will take you if they possibly can. Truck drivers usually refuse payment from foreigners for lifts (even if Albanian passengers must pay). Never accept rides in cars containing three or more excited young men as they will drive wildly and possibly crash the car.

You can get an indication of where a vehicle might be going from the letters on the licence plate: Berat (BR), Durrës (DR), Elbasan (EL), Fier (FR), Gjirokastra (GJ), Korça (KO), Kruja (KR), Lezha (LE), Pogradec (PG), Saranda (SR), Shkodra (SH), Tirana (TR), Vlora (VL).

LOCAL TRANSPORT

Shared minibuses run between cities. They usually cost about five times the bus fare but for foreigners they're still relatively cheap. Ask locals what they think the fare should be and then bargain for something approaching that.

City buses operate in Tirana, Durrës and Shkodra (pay the conductor). Watch your possessions on crowded city buses.

There are two types of taxis: the older private taxis, which are usually found around the market or at bus and train stations, and the shiny Mercedes tourist taxis parked outside the Rogner and Tirana International hotels (which quote fares in US dollars but also take lekë). Taxi fares are set at approximately 60 lekë per kilometre. Work out the price in your head before getting in and make sure you reach an agreement with the driver before setting off. Car rentals with or without a company driver are available in Tirana.

Don't trust truck drivers who enthusiastically offer to give you a lift somewhere the following day as their plans could change and all the morning buses may have left before you find out about it.

Tirana

☎ 042

Tirana (Tiranë), a pleasant city of 444,000 people (compared with 30,000 before WWII, but now unofficially 650,000), lies almost exactly midway between Rome and Istanbul. Mt Dajti (1612m) rises to the east. Founded by a Turkish pasha (military governor) in 1614, Tirana developed into a craft centre with a lively bazar.

In 1920 the city was made capital of Albania and the bulky Italianate government buildings went up in the 1930s. In the communist era, larger-than-life 'palaces of the people' blossomed around Skënderbeg Square and along Bulevardi Dëshmorët e Kombit (Martyrs of the Nation Blvd). You'll see Italian parks and a Turkish mosque, but the market area on the east side of Tirana is also worth exploring. The city is compact and can be explored on foot.

Orientation

Orientation is easy in Tirana since the whole city revolves around central Skenderbeg Square. Running south from the square is Bulevardi Dëshmorët e Kombit which leads to the three-arched university building. Running north the same street leads to the train station. Coming from the airport (26km) you will enter the city along Rruga Durrësit. Buses from neighbouring countries will drop you off close to Skënderbeg Square. Most major services and hotels are within a few minutes walk of Skënderbeg Square.

Information

Money The State Bank of Albania (Banka e

Shtetit Shqiptar) on Skënderbeg Square (open weekdays from 8.30 am to noon) changes travellers cheques for 1% commission.

A free currency market operates directly behind the State Bank near the post office. One of the men with a pocket calculator in hand will take you aside. A number of small kiosks here will also change your cash for a similar rate.

The Unioni Financiar Tiranë Exchange just south of the post office is a good place to send and receive money electronically and to cash your money as well.

Post & Communications The telephone centre (Telekomi Shqiptar) is on Bulevardi Dëshmorët e Kombit, diagonally opposite Hotel Arbëria and a little towards Skënderbeg Square. It's open 21 hours a day and calls go straight through. This is also the cheapest place to send a fax.

Cybercafés Though not quite an Internet Café (yet) the Open Internet Center (ilirz@ soros.al), Rruga Themistokli Germenji 3/1, is a great place to check mail and surf for free. It's open from 2 pm to 5 pm on weekdays. Visit its Web page: www.soros.al/oic.

Travel Agencies The American Express representative is World Travel (☎/fax 27 908), Mine Peza 2. It can cash and supply travellers cheques, provide air and ferry tickets and arrange private or group tours around Albania.

Albania Travel & Tours (☎ 32 983; fax 33 981), Rruga Durrësit 102, sells tickets for the ferry from Vlora to Otranto, Italy (three a week, US$45), perhaps the cheapest way across the Adriatic. Skanderbeg Travel, a few blocks north-west up the same street, is good about providing general information.

Newspapers & Magazines Foreign newspapers and magazines are sold at all major hotels and at many street kiosks. The UK *Guardian* arrives in Tirana at about 6 pm on the day it is published. Major Sunday papers arrive on Wednesday.

Medical & Emergency Services Hospital services at the Policlinic will cost you a minimum fee of about 1000 lekë, but if you

ALBANIA

TIRANA

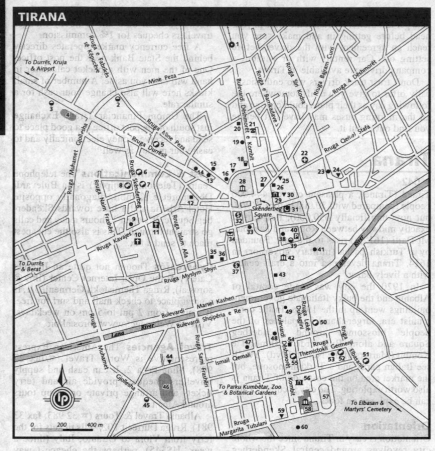

To Durrës, Kruja & Airport

Mine Peza

Rruga e Fabrikës se Këpucës

Rruga e Barrikadave

Rruga Sami Koda

Rruga Balgam Curri

Rruga 4 Dëshmorët

Rruga Qefial Stafa

Rruga Myslym Shyri

Rruga Durrësit

Rruga Aline Peza

Rruga Muhamet Gjollesha

Rruga Naim Frashëri

Rruga Skënderbeg

Rruga Islam Alla

Rruga Kavajes

Bulevardi Dëshmorët e Kombit

Skënderbeg Square

To Durrës & Berat

Bulevardi Shqipëria e Re

Marsel Kashen

Lana River

Bulevardi Leke Dukagjini

Rruga Ismail Qemali

Rruga Sami Frashëri

Rruga Muhamet Gjollesha

Rruga Themistokli Germenji

Rruga Elbasanit

Bulevardi Dëshmorët e Kombit

To Parku Kumbëtar, Zoo & Botanical Gardens

To Elbasan & Martyrs' Cemetery

Rruga Margarita Tutulani

0   200   400 m

---

have travel insurance you would probably be better off heading for the new and private Poliklinika at Luigji Monti on Rruga Kavajes. The phone number for the public Hospital No 1 in Tirana is ☎ 62 620 and for Hospital No 2 it is ☎ 62 641.

The emergency phone number for an ambulance is ☎ 17 and for the police ☎ 19.

Things to See & Do

Most visits to Tirana begin at **Skënderbeg Square**, a great open space in the heart of the city.

Beside the 15-storey Tirana International hotel (the tallest building in Albania), on the north side of the square, is the **National Museum of History** (1981), the largest and finest museum in Albania (open Thursday to Saturday only from 9 am to 3 pm, admission 300 lekë). A huge mosaic mural entitled *Albania* covers the façade of the museum building (the rooms describing the communist era are closed). Temporary exhibits are shown in the gallery on the side of the building facing the Tirana International Hotel (admission free).

TIRANA

To the east is another massive building, the **Palace of Culture**, which has a theatre, restaurant, cafés and art galleries. Construction of the palace began as a gift from the Soviet people in 1960 and was completed in 1966, after the 1961 Soviet-Albanian split. The entrance to the **National Library** is on the south side of the building. Opposite this is the cupola and minaret of the **Mosque of Ethem Bey** (1793), one of the most distinctive buildings in the city. Enter to see the beautifully painted dome. Tirana's **clock tower** (1830) stands beside the mosque.

On the west side of Skënderbeg Square is the State Bank of Albania, with the main post office behind it. The south side of the square is taken up by the massive ochre-coloured buildings of various government ministries. In the middle of the square is an equestrian statue (1968) of Skënderbeg himself looking straight up Bulevardi Dëshmorët e Kombit (formerly Bulevardi Stalin and before that, Bulevardi Zog I), north towards the train station.

A massive statue of Enver Hoxha used to stand on the high marble plinth between the National Museum of History and the State Bank but it was unceremoniously toppled after the return to democracy. A small fairground now occupies the central part of the square.

Behind Skënderbeg's statue extends Bulevardi Dëshmorët e Kombit, leading directly south to the three arches of **Tirana University** (1957). As you stroll down this tree-lined boulevard, you'll see Tirana's **art gallery** (closed Monday), a one-time stronghold of socialist realism, with a significant permanent collection that has been exhibited here since 1976.

Continue south on Bulevardi Dëshmorët e Kombit to the bridge over the Lana River. On the left just across the river are the sloping white-marble walls of the **former Enver Hoxha Museum** (1988), used as a disco and on weekends as a giant slide for hoards of children. The museum closed down at the start of 1991 and the brilliant red star was removed from the pyramid-shaped building's tip. Just beyond, on the right, is the four-storey former **Central Committee building** (1955) of the Party of Labour, which now houses various ministries.

Follow Rruga Ismail Qemali, the street on the south side of the Central Committee building, a long block west to the **former** residence of **Enver Hoxha** (on the north-west corner of the intersection). Formerly it was forbidden to walk along these streets, since many other party leaders lived in the surrounding mansions. When the area was first opened to the general public in 1991, great crowds of Albanians flocked to see the style in which their 'proletarian' leaders lived.

On the left, farther south on Bulevardi Dëshmorët e Kombit, is the ultramodern **Palace of Congresses** (1986), next to which is the **Archaeological Museum** (closed while this book was being researched). There are no captions but a tour in English is usually included in the 300 lekë admission price.

Some 1800 selected objects from prehistoric times to the Middle Ages are on display and it's interesting to note how the simple artefacts of the Palaeolithic and Neolithic periods give way to the weapons and jewellery of the Copper and Bronze ages, with evidence of social differentiation. Although Greek and Roman relics are well represented, evidence of the parallel Illyrian culture is present throughout, illustrating that the ancestors of the present Albanians inhabited these lands since time immemorial.

Behind the museum is the **Qemal Stafa Stadium** (1946) where football matches are held every Saturday and Sunday afternoon, except during July and August. The boulevard terminates at the university, with the Faculty of Music on the right.

Beyond the university is **Parku Kombëtar** (National Park), a large park with an open-air theatre (Teatri Veror) and an artificial lake. There's a superb view across the lake to the olive-coloured hills. Cross the dam retaining the lake to **Tirana Zoo**. Ask directions to the excellent **botanical gardens** just west of the zoo. If you're keen, you can hire a rowing boat and paddle on the lake.

About 5km south-east on Rruga Elbasanit is the **Martyrs' Cemetery** (Varrezat e Dëshmorëve), where some 900 partisans who died during WWII are buried. Large crowds once gathered here each year on 16 October, Enver Hoxha's birthday, since this is where he and other leading revolutionaries such as Gog Nushi, Qemal Stafa and Hysni Kapo were formerly interred. (In May 1992 Hoxha's lead coffin was dug up and reburied in a common grave in a public cemetery on the other side

of town.) The hilltop setting with a beautiful view over the city and mountains is subdued, and a great white figure of Mother Albania (1972) stands watch. Nearby, on the opposite side of the highway, is the **former palace of King Zog**, now a government guesthouse.

West of Tirana's centre on Rruga Kavajes is the Catholic **Cathedral of St Anthony**, which served as the Rinia Cinema from 1967 to 1990. Many foreign embassies are situated along Rruga Skënderbeg just beyond the cathedral. Since the rush of refugees into these in 1991, access for Albanians is restricted.

Organised Tours
World Travel on Mine Peza 2 can arrange individual or group tours around Albania, depending on demand and requirements.

Places to Stay
Private Rooms Staying in private rented apartments or with local families is the best budget accommodation in Tirana. The formerly cheap (and often dire) state-owned hotels have either closed or been renovated, with accordingly higher prices. Newer private hotels are similarly high priced.

Albania Travel & Tours, Rruga Durrësit 102 (weekdays 8 am to 7 pm), has private rooms at around 2500 lekë per person. It can also organise private rooms or hotels in Gjirokastra, Korça, Vlora and Durrës.

Skanderbeg Travel (☎/fax 23 946), Rruga Durrësit 5/11, a couple of blocks west of Albania Travel & Tours (weekdays 8.30 am to 1.30 pm and 4.30 to 7.30 pm), arranges private apartments with TV and fridge for between 4000 and 4500 lekë.

Hotels The 96 rooms at the state-run, six-storey *Hotel Arbëria* (☎ 60 813) on Bulevardi Dëshmorët e Kombit, to the north of Skënderbeg Square, cost 2500/3500 lekë for a single/double with bath. Check your room as some have broken windows and no running water, and the hotel is unheated in winter.

The *Hotel Klodiana* (☎ 27 403) has just a few private rooms but is OK. A single/double costs 3000/4000 lekë. It is just back from Rruga Myslym Shyri and shares the same phone number as the Europa International Hotel.

The ageing and somewhat old-fashioned *Hotel Dajti* (☎ 33 326; fax 31 691) on Bulevardi Dëshmorët e Kombit was erected in the 1930s by the Italians. The 90 rooms with bath are US$55/65 for singles/doubles.

A pleasant private hotel is the *Europa International Hotel* (☎/fax 27 403), which has very modern singles/doubles for US$60/70. Look for the sign on Rruga Myslym Shyri. Just off Rruga Durrësit, at Rruga Mihal Duri 2/7, is the nifty *Hotel California* (☎ 32 228; fax 31 691). Clean rooms with mini-bar and TV cost US$55/65 for singles/doubles.

To the right of the Tirana International is the newer but smaller *Hotel Miniri* (☎ 30 930; fax 33 096) at Rruga e Dibres 3. Singles/doubles with phone and TV are US$60/100.

The high-rise *Tirana International* (☎ 34 185; fax 34 188) on Skënderbeg Square is now Italian-run. Rooms cost US$140/190 for well-appointed singles/doubles. The price includes breakfast.

Finally, the newest and best hotel in Tirana is the *Hotel Europapark* (☎ 35 035; fax 35 050) at Blvd Dëshmorët e Kombit 1, run by the Rogner group. Singles/doubles are a pricey US$200/250 per night.

Places to Eat

There is no shortage of small restaurants and snack bars on and around Skënderbeg Square and Blvd Dëshmorët e Kombit, and small, stylish bars have mushroomed everywhere. Here are some places that you might not easily stumble across.

You can enjoy tasty kebabs, salad and beer at the convenient and economical *Restorant Popullor*, close to Hotel Miniri on Rruga e Dibres.

Check out the *Bar Artisti* cafeteria at the Institute of Art if you want to have a coffee and snack and mingle with Tirana's arty set. If you fancy a cuppa and a sandwich – or even a pizza or nachos – call into *Qendra Stefan*, a friendly, no-smoking American-run place. Lunchtime specials are posted on a blackboard outside. It's near the fruit-and-vegetable market.

The *Berlusconi* bar and restaurant is a trendy Italian-influenced place hidden away behind the Palace of Culture. Pasta and pizza are the main fare and prices are very reasonable.

The *Ujvara* restaurant on the south side of the river near the southern bus station is another alternative spot for an evening meal. Ignore the apparent squalor of the neighbourhood; the restaurant and food is top-notch.

The *Piazza Restaurant* is a tastefully designed and well-appointed establishment just north of Skënderbeg Square. The food and service are excellent and prices, for what you get, are reasonable. The adjoining *Piano Bar* is a relaxing place to unwind with a pre-dinner drink.

Entertainment

As soon as you arrive, check the *Palace of Culture* on Skenderbeg Square for opera or ballet performances. Most events in Tirana are advertised on placards in front of this building. The ticket window opens at 5 pm and most performances begin at 7 pm.

The *Teatri i Kukallave*, beside the State Bank on Skënderbeg Square, presents puppet shows for children on Sunday at 10 and 11 am all year round. During the school year there are also morning shows on certain weekdays (ask when you get there).

Pop concerts and other musical events often take place in the *Qemal Stafa Stadium* next to the university. Look out for street banners bearing details of upcoming events.

The *London Bar* at Blvd Dëshmorët e Kombit 51 (near the Hotel Tirana International) is a mixed gay and straight bar.

Things to Buy

Tirana's public market, just north of the Sheshi Avni Rustemi roundabout several blocks east of the clock tower, is at its largest on Thursday and Sunday. A few shops here sell folkloric objects such as carved wooden trays, small boxes, wall hangings and bone necklaces.

The Philatelic Bureau (Filatelia), on Bulevardi Dëshmorët e Kombit, north-west of Hotel Tirana International, charges 40 times the face value of the stamps but they're still not too expensive by western standards and there is a good selection.

Getting There & Away

Air For information about routes and fares of flights to/from Rinas airport see the Getting There & Away section earlier in this chapter.

Many of the airline offices are on Rruga Durrësit, just off Skënderbeg Square. Here you'll find Ada Air, Adria Airways, Arbëria Airlines, Albanian Airlines, Croatia Airlines, Hemus Air and Malév Hungarian Airlines. Alitalia (☎ 30 023) has an office on Skënderbeg Square behind the National Museum of History and Swissair (☎ 32 011) is at Hotel Europapark. Olympic Airways (☎ 28 960), is in the Ve-Ve Business Centre on Deshmorët e Kombit behind the Tirana International Hotel.

Bus Both private and state-owned buses operate between Tirana and most towns. There's no one central bus station in Tirana and pick-up venues may change, so check for the latest departure points. Service to/from Durrës (38km, 40 lekë) is fairly frequent, leaving from the block adjacent to the train station.

Buses to Berat (122km), Elbasan (54km), Fier (113km), Gjirokastra (232km), Kakavija (263km), Korça (181km), Lushnja (83km), Pogradec (140km), Saranda (284km) and Vlora (147km) leave from southern bus station, on the west side of Selman Stërmasi Stadium. From about 6 am every day you can get buses to almost anywhere south and east from here: they leave when full throughout the day. As late as 5 pm you'll still find some to Berat, Elbasan, Fier and perhaps further.

Buses to Kruja (32km) leave from Rruga Mine Peza, at the beginning of the highway to Durrës.

North-bound buses to Lezha (69km), Shkodra (116km), Kukës (208km) and other places leave from a station out on the Durrës highway just beyond the Asllan Rusi Stadium. Buses to Shkodra leave throughout the day but those to Kukës leave at 4 and 5 am only.

Information on all bus services out of Tirana can be obtained by calling ☎ 26 818.

Train The train station is at the north end of Bulevardi Dëshmorët e Kombit. Seven trains a day go to Durrës, a one-hour journey (36km). Trains also depart for Ballsh (four hours, daily), Elbasan (four hours, three daily), Pogradec (seven hours, twice daily), Shkodra (3½ hours, twice daily), Fier (4¼ hours, daily) and Vlora (5½ hours, daily).

Getting Around

To/From the Airport The bus to Rinas airport leaves from in front of the Albtransport office, Rruga Durrësit (26km, 50 lekë; pay the driver). Buses to the airport leave at 6, 8 and 10 am, and 12.30 and 3.05 pm. Buses to Tirana from the airport leave at 2.30, 4 and 5.30 pm. A taxi to/from the airport should cost a flat US$20, 40 DM or 5000 drachmas – depending on what currency you have in your pocket.

Car & Motorcycle There are two guarded parking lots, both charging 300 lekë a night. One is on Rruga Myslym Shyri, around the corner from Hotel Dajti, and the other is behind the Hotel Tirana International.

World Travel, Mine Peza 2, rents out cars at 5500 lekë daily without a driver, 7500 lekë daily with a driver/guide. As you may expect, they feel more comfortable with their own employee behind the wheel.

Taxi Local taxis park on the south side of the roundabout at the market. These are much cheaper for excursions out into the countryside than the Mercedes taxis parked at Hotel Tirana International, but the drivers don't speak English so take along someone to bargain and act as interpreter.

AROUND TIRANA
Durrës
☎ 052

Unlike Tirana, Durrës (Durazzo in Italian) is an ancient city. In 627 BC the Greeks founded Epidamnos (Durrës) whose name the Romans changed to Dyrrhachium. It was the largest port on the eastern Adriatic and the start of the Via Egnatia (an extension of the Via Appia) to Constantinople. The famous Via Appia (Appian Way) to Rome began 150km southwest of Durrës at Brindisi, Italy.

Durrës changed hands frequently before being taken by the Turks in 1501, under whom the port dwindled into insignificance. A slow revival began in the 17th century and from 1914 to 1920 Durrës was the capital of Albania. Landings here by Mussolini's troops on 7 April 1939 met fierce though brief resistance and those who fell are regarded as the first martyrs in the War of National Liberation.

Today, Roman ruins and Byzantine fortifications embellish this major industrial city and commercial port, which lies 38km west of Tirana. Durrës is Albania's second-largest city, with 85,000 inhabitants. On a bay southeast of the city are long, sandy beaches where all the tourist hotels are concentrated. In 1991 the city saw desperate mobs attempting to escape by ship to Italy and there's now a heavy Italian military presence in the area. Car ferries from Italy dock on the east side of the port. The entry/exit point is even further east. Look for road signs to the ferry quay when departing.

Information The National Bank near the port (open weekdays from 8 to 11 am) changes travellers cheques for a commission of 100 lekë per cheque, as does the Banka e Kursimeve up the street, half-way between the port and the large mosque (open Monday to Saturday from 9 am to 2 pm). Unofficial currency exchange is carried out on the street around the main post office in town.

The post office and phone centre are located one block west of the train and bus stations. Look for the big Telekom sign.

Things to See A good place to begin your visit to Durrës is the **Archaeological Museum** (open 9 am to 1 pm, closed Monday, 100 lekë admission), which faces the waterfront promenade near the port. Its two rooms are small but each object here is unique and there's a large sculpture garden outside. Behind the museum are the 6th-century Byzantine **city walls**, built after the Visigoth invasion of 481 and supplemented by round Venetian towers in the 14th century.

The impressive **Roman amphitheatre**, built between the 1st and 2nd centuries AD, is on the hillside just inside the walls. Much of the amphitheatre has now been excavated and you can see a small built-in 10th-century Byzantine church decorated with wall mosaics. Follow the road just inside the walls down towards the port and you'll find the **Sultan Fatih Mosque** (1502) and the **Moisiut Ekspozita e Kulturës Popullore**, with ethnographic displays housed in the former home of actor Alexander Moisiu (1879-1935). It's open in the morning only.

The former **palace of King Ahmet Zog** is on the hill top west of the amphitheatre. The soldiers guarding the palace will expect you to buy a ticket from them to wander around. In front of the palace is a statue of Skënderbeg and huge radar disks set up by the Italian army. The next hill beyond bears a **lighthouse** which affords a splendid view of Albanian coastal defences, Durrës and the entire coast.

As you're exploring the centre of the city, stop to see the **Roman baths** directly behind Aleksandër Moisiu Theatre, on the central square. The large **mosque** on the square was erected with Egyptian aid in 1993, to replace one destroyed during the 1979 earthquake. At the western end of Rruga Dëshmorevë is the **Martyrs' Cemetery**, guarded by half-a-dozen decrepit bunkers.

Places to Stay Durrës offers cheap private rooms and a few hotels.

In Town You may be able to scrounge a room at the rather run-down four-storey *Hotel Durrësi*, next to the main post office in town. Expect to pay about 1000 lekë. The amenities are pretty basic.

The Romeo Harizi family, left along the waterfront from the museum, a block beyond the Archaeological Museum, rents out private rooms very cheaply. There's a sign outside in English.

There is not much choice these days in Durrës town. The best hotel is *Hotel Pameba* (☎/fax 24 149), about 400m up the hill from the port entrance. Singles/doubles with TV are US$50/70, including breakfast.

At the Beach One traveller reported getting a room in a private *villa* near the beach just south-east of Hotel Adriatik for 1500 lekë, so it pays to look around.

The main tourist hotel used to be the Stalin-era *Adriatik* (☎ 23 612 or 23 001), on the sandy beach 5km south-east of Durrës. The 60 rooms in this stark, neo-classical building prior to the troubles were US$43/46 for a single/double, with bath and breakfast included. It closed down in mid-1997 and may or may not have reopened by the time you read this.

Nearby are the *Durrësi*, *Apollonia*, *Butrinti* and *Kruja* hotels, all in some kind of

DURRËS

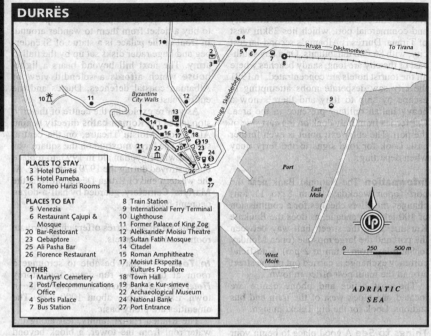

Rruga — Dëshmorevë   To Tirana

Byzantine
City Walls

Rruga Skënderbej

Rruga Durrah

Port

East
Mole

0   250   500 m

West
Mole

ADRIATIC
SEA

PLACES TO STAY
3   Hotel Durrësi
16 Hotel Pameba
21 Romeo Harizi Rooms

PLACES TO EAT
5   Venezia
6   Restaurant Çajupi &
    Mosque
20 Bar-Restorant
23 Qebaptore
25 Ali Pasha Bar
26 Florence Restaurant

OTHER
1   Martyrs' Cemetery
2   Post/Telecommunications
    Office
4   Sports Palace
7   Bus Station

8   Train Station
9   International Ferry Terminal
10 Lighthouse
11 Former Palace of King Zog
12 Alelksandër Moisiu Theatre
13 Sultan Fatih Mosque
14 Citadel
15 Roman Amphitheatre
17 Moisiut Ekspozita
    Kulturës Popullore
18 Town Hall
19 Banka e Kur-simeve
22 Archaeological Museum
24 National Bank
27 Port Entrance

renovation or privatisation process. Prices, once the work is complete, can be expected to be higher than those of the Adriatik.

Places to Eat There's a modern restaurant/bar called *Florence* opposite the port entrance.

On Rruga Durrah, the main street, is a fairly modern and clean nameless kebab place. Look for the *Qebaptore* sign outside. Almost opposite is another decent restaurant simply called *Bar-Restorant*. Look out for the Löwenbräu sign. The *Hotel Pameba* also has a small restaurant.

Restorant Çajupi, west across the square from the train station, is a private restaurant serving rich beef soup. Just behind the Çajupi is the *Venezia*, with good coffee and ice cream. Unfortunately neither place has a menu so get the staff to write down the prices before ordering.

Entertainment Visit the *Aleksandër Moisiu Theatre* in the centre of Durrës and

the *Sports Palace* on Rruga Dëshmorevë to see if anything is on.

There are any number of new bars and cafeterias opening up on and around the main street. There is a disco and even a poker machines joint. Try the pleasant outdoor *Ali Pasha* bar, very close to the port entrance, for a relaxing drink.

Getting There & Away Albania's 720km railway network centres on Durrës. There are seven trains a day to Tirana (1½ hours), two to Shkodra, one to Elbasan, two to Pogradec, one to Vlora and one to Ballsh. The station is beside the Tirana Highway, conveniently close to central Durrës. Tickets are sold at the 'Biletaria Trenit' office below the apartment building nearest the station or at a similar office below the next building. Buses to Tirana and elsewhere leave from in front of the train station and service is fairly frequent.

Ferry Agjencia Detare Shteterore per Adriatica at the entrance to the port sells tickets for car ferries to Trieste, Ancona and Bari. Shpresa Transeuropa (☎ 22 423) in a kiosk nearby handles the ferries between Durrës and a number of destinations.

The ticket office of the fast catamaran *La Vikinga* (☎ 22 555) from Durrës to Bari is on Rruga Durrah, the street from the port to the mosque.

Some of the agencies require payment in Italian lira which you must purchase on the black market. If you have a valid ISIC student card always try for a student discount.

Ferries arrive in Durrës several times a week from Bari, Otranto, Ancona and Trieste in Italy. If boarding a ferry at Durrës allow plenty of time, as it can be a long, complicated process, especially at night.

Getting Around There's a bus service on the main highway from the Adriatik Hotel into Durrës. For the return journey, look for the bus near the main post office in Durrës. Pay the conductor.

Northern Albania

A visit to northern Albania usually takes in only the coastal strip, but a journey into the interior is well worthwhile for the marvellous scenery. Between Puka and Kukës the road winds through 60km of spectacular mountains.

Shkodra, the old Gheg capital near the lake of the same name, is a pleasant introduction to Albania for those arriving from Montenegro. South of here is Lezha and Skënderbeg's tomb. Kruja is 6.5km off the main road but is often visited for its crucial historical importance and striking location 608m up on the side of a mountain.

Other than to Kruja, visits to northern Albania should perhaps be avoided until the security situation has stabilised since there have been reports, up to mid-1998, of sporadic banditry and violence.

KRUJA
☎ 0532

In the 12th century, Kruja was the capital of the Principality of Arberit, but this hilltop town attained its greatest fame between 1443 and 1468 when national hero George Kastrioti (1405-68), also known as Skënderbeg, made Kruja his seat.

At a young age, Kastrioti, son of an Albanian prince, was handed over as a hostage to the Turks, who converted him to Islam and gave him a military education at Edirne. There he became known as Iskënder (after Alexander the Great) and Sultan Murat II promoted him to the rank of bey (governor), thus the name Skënderbeg.

In 1443 the Turks suffered a defeat at the hands of the Hungarians at Niš, giving the nationally minded Skënderbeg the opportunity he had been waiting for to abandon Islam and the Ottoman army and rally his fellow Albanians against the Turks. Among the 13 Turkish invasions he subsequently repulsed was that led by Murat II himself in 1450. Pope Calixtus III named Skënderbeg 'captain general of the Holy See' and Venice formed an alliance with him. The Turks besieged Kruja four times. Though beaten back in 1450, 1466 and 1467, they took control of Kruja in 1478 (after Skënderbeg's death) and Albanian resistance was suppressed.

Things to See & Do

Set below towering mountains, the **citadel** that Skënderbeg defended still stands on an abrupt ridge above the modern town. In 1982 an excellent **historical museum** (open from 9 am to 1 pm and 3 to 6 pm, Thursday 9 am to 1 pm, closed Monday, admission 100 lekë) opened in the citadel. The saga of the Albanian struggle against the Ottoman empire is richly told with models, maps and statuary. The museum was designed by Pranvera Hoxha, Enver's daughter, who attempted to portray Hoxha and Skënderbeg as parallel champions of Albanian independence. Like Hoxha, Skënderbeg was something of a social reformer. He abolished the blood vendetta (*gjakmarrje*) but the feuds began afresh soon after his death.

In an old house opposite the main citadel museum is an **ethnographical museum** (open from 9 am to 3 pm, Thursday 9 am to 1 pm and 3 to 6 pm, closed Wednesday).

Hidden in the lower part of the citadel are the Teqja e Dollmës or **Bektashi Tekke** (1773), place of worship of a mystical Islamic sect, and the 16th-century **Turkish baths** (*hammam*), which are just below the tekke.

Between the citadel and Hotel Skënderbeu is Kruja's 18th-century **Turkish bazar**, which was later destroyed but has now been fully restored and made into a workplace for local artisans and craftspeople.

It's possible to climb to the top of the mountain above Kruja in an hour or so and it's even possible to hike back to Tirana along a path that begins near the citadel entrance.

Places to Stay & Eat

The four-storey *Hotel Skënderbeu* (π 23 29) is next to the equestrian statue of Skënderbeg near the terminus of the buses from Tirana. The 33 rooms are US$20 for a single/double without bath and US$25 with bath. A speciality of the hotel restaurant is a mixed plate with skallop (beef in sauce), kanellane (mince wrapped in pastry) and qofte (a long, mince patty).

The *Pestiqe* restaurant in the main street of the artisans' quarter is very good value for money and does ample meals in comfortable traditional surroundings, with chairs covered in woollen rugs.

The *Karakteristik* restaurant, just up the hill from the museum in the citadel, is also very cosy, but a little more expensive.

Getting There & Away

It's possible to visit Kruja by local bus as a day trip from Tirana (32km). If there's no direct bus to Kruja, get one to Fush-Kruja where you'll find several going to Kruja; for example, the Laç bus stops at Fush-Kruja. In the afternoon it's much easier to get back to Tirana from Kruja than vice versa.

LEZHA
π 10 (operator)

It was at Lezha (Alessio) in March 1444 that Skënderbeg succeeded in convincing the Albanian feudal lords to unite in a League of Lezha to resist the Turks. Skënderbeg died of fever here in 1468 and today his tomb may be visited among the ruins of the Franciscan **Church of St Nicholas**. Reproductions of his helmet and sword grace the gravestone and along the walls are 25 shields bearing the names and dates of battles he fought against the Turks.

Near the tomb, beside the grey apartment blocks, is the **Ethnographical Museum**, and on the hill top above is the medieval **Lezha Citadel**. Much of old Lezha was destroyed by an earthquake on 15 April 1979.

Places to Stay & Eat

The only real option is the state-run but still cosy *Hotel Gjuetisë*, commonly known as the Hunting Lodge – some 5km off the main road at Ishull i Lezhës, a lagoon popular for bird-watching. Doubles here should go for around US$50 including breakfast. There is also a reasonable, folksy-decorated restaurant. The only disadvantage is the surly, state-appointed staff who seem to treat guests as annoyances.

Getting There & Away

There's a bus from Tirana to Lezha.

SHKODRA
π 0224

Shkodra (also Shkodër and, in Italian, Scutari), the traditional centre of the Gheg cultural region, is one of the oldest cities in Europe. In 500 BC an Illyrian fortress already guarded the strategic crossing just west of the city where the Buna and Drin rivers meet and all traffic moving up the coast from Greece to Montenegro must pass. These rivers drain two of the Balkans' largest lakes: Shkodra, just north-west of the city, and Ohrid, far up the Drin River, beyond several massive hydroelectric dams. The route inland to Kosova also begins in Shkodra. North of Shkodra, line after line of cement bunkers point the way to the Han i Hotit border crossing into Montenegro (33km). Tirana is 116km south.

Queen Teuta's Illyrian kingdom was centred here in the 3rd century BC. Despite wars with Rome in 228 and 219 BC, Shkodra was not taken by the Romans until 168 BC. Later the region passed to Byzantium before becoming the capital of the feudal realm of the Balshas in 1350. In 1396 the Venetians occupied Shkodra's Rozafa Fortress, which they held against Suleiman Pasha in 1473 but lost to Mehmet Pasha in 1479. The Turks lost 14,000 men in the first siege and 30,000 in the second.

As the Ottoman empire declined in the late 18th century, Shkodra became the centre of a semi-independent pashalik, which led to a blossoming of commerce and crafts. In 1913, Montenegro attempted to annex Shkodra (it succeeded in taking Ulcinj, but this was not recognised by the international community and the town changed hands often during WWI. Badly damaged by the 1979 earthquake, Shkodra was subsequently repaired and now, with a population of 81,000, is Albania's fourth-largest city.

Even by mid-1998 Shkodra was considered still risky for individual travellers to visit, so it might be better to give the area a miss until the situation clarifies.

Orientation & Information

From the Migjenit Theatre on the Five Heroes Roundabout, Rruga Marin Barleti (formerly Bulevardi Stalin) runs south-east past Hotel Rozafa and the post office. The post office faces north-east up Bulevardi 13 Dhjetori, a delightful old street lit by antique lamps in the evening and lined with harmonious buildings, many of which are now shops selling Albanian handicrafts. The train station is at the far south-east end of Rruga Marin Barleti, 1.5km from the centre of town, whereas buses leave from around Migjenit Theatre.

Money Two adjacent banks on Bulevardi 13 Dhjetori change travellers cheques for 1% commission (open weekdays 7 am to 1 pm). Otherwise look for moneychangers along the street between these banks and the post office.

Post & Communications The post office on Rruga Marin Barleti, across the square from the Rozafa Hotel, is open Monday to Saturday from 7 am to 2 pm, Sunday 8 am to noon. The telephone centre here operates around the clock.

Things to See

Shkodra's skyline is dominated by the brand new and impressive **Sheik Zamil Abdullah Al-Zamil mosque**, completed in 1995. It stands next to the Muzeo Popullor on the corner of Rruga Marin Barleti and Bulevardi 13 Dhjetori. Its pastel façade and silver domes are very striking.

The **Muzeu Popullor**, in the eclectic

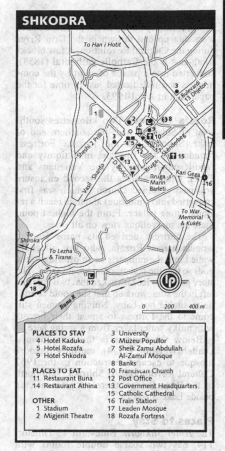

SHKODRA

PLACES TO STAY
4 Hotel Kaduku
5 Hotel Rozafa
9 Hotel Shkodra

PLACES TO EAT
11 Restaurant Buna
14 Restaurant Athina

OTHER
1 Stadium
2 Migjenit Theatre
3 University
6 Muzeu Popullor
7 Sheik Zamu Abdullah
   Al-Zamul Mosque
8 Banks
10 Franciscan Church
12 Post Office
13 Government Headquarters
15 Catholic Cathedral
16 Train Station
17 Leaden Mosque
18 Rozafa Fortress

palace (1860) of an English aristocrat opposite Hotel Rozafa, contains recent paintings and historic photos upstairs, and an excellent archaeological collection downstairs.

Shkodra was the most influential Catholic city of Albania, with a large cathedral and Jesuit and Franciscan monasteries, seminaries and religious libraries. From 1967 to 1990 the **Franciscan Church** on Rruga Ndre Mjeda off Bulevardi 13 Dhjetori was used as an auditorium but now it's a church again. Just inside is a photo exhibit of Shkodra priests who died in communist prisons. Note especially the photos of Catholic poet Gjergj Fishta (1871-1940), formerly buried here but whose bones were dug up and thrown in the Drin River during the Cultural Revolution. A few blocks south-east is the **Catholic cathedral** (1858), converted into a palace of sport by the communists and rededicated just in time for the papal visit in April 1993.

Rozafa Fortress Two kilometres south-west of Shkodra, near the southern end of Lake Shkodra, is the Rozafa Fortress, founded by the Illyrians in antiquity and rebuilt much later by the Venetians and Turks. Upon entering the second enclosure you pass a ruined church (which was first converted into a mosque) and then reach a restored stone palace. From the highest point there's a marvellous view on all sides.

The fortress derived its name from a woman named Rozafa, who was allegedly walled into the ramparts as an offering to the gods so that the construction would stand. The story goes that Rozafa asked that two holes be left in the stonework so that she could continue to suckle her baby. Nursing women still come to the fortress to smear their breasts with milky water taken from a spring here.

Below the fortress is the many-domed **Leaden Mosque** (1774), the only Shkodra mosque to escape destruction in the 1967 Cultural Revolution. At **Shiroka**, 7km north of the Buna Bridge, there's a pleasant café beside Lake Shkodra.

Places to Stay
The *Hotel Shkodra*, Bulevardi 13 Dhjetori 114, has two sparse double rooms with shared bath at 500 lekë per person and three five-bed dormitories at 500 lekë per person. The old people who run this place in their old home are very friendly.

The ramshackle *Hotel Kaduku* (☎ 22 16) can be hard to find but it's adequate and clean enough. It's right next to the Hotel Rozafa; look for the 'Dentist' sign. The owner Hasan Kaduku charges US$15 per person.

The city's main tourist hotel, where all tourists were required to stay until 1991, is the *Hotel Rozafa* (☎ 27 67), a nine-storey building on the Five Heroes Roundabout. Rooms are US$20/40 for singles/doubles with bath, breakfast included.

Places to Eat
Restaurant Buna, close to the big mosque, is an OK kind of choice and a little more convenient to reach if you don't feel like walking.

Shkodra's best restaurant is the *Restaurant Athina*, a little way from the older part of town. The food is nominally Greek and is reasonably good value. The toilet has an electronic soap dispenser!

Around sunset half the population of Shkodra go for a stroll along the lakeside promenade towards the Buna Bridge and there are several small restaurants where you can have fried fish, tomato salad and beer while observing the passing parade.

Getting There & Away
Buses to Tirana (frequent, 116km, 110 lekë) and Durrës (infrequent, 124km, 100 lekë) depart from near Migjenit Theatre, most reliably around 7 am and also at 1 pm.

Two direct daily trains from Shkodra to Tirana depart at 5 am and 1.15 pm (3½ hours, 100 lekë). These trains don't pass Durrës. The train station is on the south-east side of town. Bus travel is more convenient, though perhaps less picturesque.

KUKËS
☎ **10** (operator)
Kukës has perhaps the most beautiful location of any town in Albania, set high above Lake Fierza below the bald summit of Mt Gjalica (2486m). Old Kukës formerly stood at the junction of two important rivers, the White Drin from Kosova and the Black Drin from Lake Ohrid, but from 1962 the town was moved to its present location when it was decided that the 72-sq-km reservoir of the 'Light of the Party' hydroelectric dam would cover the old site. It's a pleasant place to get in tune with Albania if you've just arrived from Kosova, and a good stop on your way around the country.

Information
Cash changes hands among the trees at the market, not far from the bus stop.

Places to Stay & Eat
Cheapest is the *Hotel Gjalica*, an unmarked three-storey building on the nameless main

street in the centre of town, opposite a place with the large yellow sign 'Fruta Perime'. A simple but adequate room with washbasin and lumpy, smelly bed will be US$16 per person.

For a room with private bath the price jumps to 2000 lekë per person at the four-storey *Hotel Drini* overlooking the lake on the same street as the post office.

One of Albania's finest hotels is the *Hotel Turizmi* (☎ 452), a five-storey cubist edifice on a peninsula jutting out into the lake, a five-minute walk from town. Rooms here are 3000 lekë per person – better value than the Drini.

All three hotels have restaurants but forget the wretched one at the Gjalica. The terrace at the Turizmi is great for a drink and their restaurant is the best in town. A few basic places near the market serve lunch.

Getting There & Away
Minibuses to Kukës from Tirana leave from the minibus stand near the guarded parking lot. The fare is 500 lekë per person and the trip takes 6½ hours with meal stops. Look for the KU license plates or ask.

Several buses to Tirana (208km, 300 lekë) leave Kukës around 6 am. Getting to Shkodra (129km, 200 lekë) is problematic; if you can't find a direct bus it's best to take the Tirana bus to Puka (60km) and look for an onward bus from there.

Occasional buses run the 17km from Kukës to the Yugoslav border at Morina. The Albanian and Yugoslav border posts are adjacent but have been closed on occasion since March 1997 and crossing may be problematic if not impossible.

Southern Albania

The south of the country is rich in historical and natural beauty. Apollonia and Butrint are renowned classical ruins, while Berat and Gjirokastra are museum towns and strongholds of Tosk tradition. Korça is the cultural capital of the south, whereas Pogradec and Saranda, on Lake Ohrid and the Ionian Sea respectively, are undeveloped resort towns.

South-east of the vast, agricultural Myzaqeja plain, the land becomes extremely mountainous, with lovely valleys such as those of the Osum and Drino rivers, where Berat and Gjirokastra are situated. The 124km of Ionian coast north from Saranda to Vlora are stunning, with 2000m mountains falling directly to the sea and not a hotel in sight.

The 115km road from Tepelena to Korça is one of the most scenic in Albania. About 60km from Tepelena it takes a sharp turn north at a small village and from here to Erseka there are many switchbacks. There are through buses from Korça to Gjirokastra and Saranda in the early morning. Because of the relatively light traffic this is one road that is in reasonable shape, though winter driving is not advised. You may be stopped by curious police on this section, probably more out of boredom than anything else. Bring your own food supplies since the towns along the way are not used to travellers.

FIER & APOLLONIA
☎ 0642
Fier is a large town by the Gjanica River at a junction of road and rail routes, 89km south of Durrës. Albania's oil industry is centred at Fier, with a fertiliser plant, an oil refinery and a thermal power plant fuelled by natural gas. Fier has a pleasant riverside promenade.

Things to See
Visitors first reach Fier's imposing 13th-century Orthodox **Monastery of St Mary**. The icons in the church, the capitals in the narthex and the Byzantine murals in the adjacent refectory are outstanding. The monastery now houses an extremely rich **archaeological museum** (admission 100 lekë) with a large collection of ceramics and statuary from the ruins of Apollonia. Near the post office is a **historical museum** with well-presented exhibits covering the district's long history.

By far the most interesting sight in the vicinity is the ruins of ancient **Apollonia** (Pojan), 12km west of Fier, set on a hill top surrounded by impressive bunkers. Apollonia was founded by Corinthian Greeks in 588 BC and quickly grew into an important city-state, minting its own currency. Under the Romans the city became a great cultural centre with a famous school of philosophy. Julius Caesar rewarded Apollonia with the title 'free city' for supporting him against Pompey the Great during a civil war in the 1st century BC and sent his nephew Octavius, the future Emperor Augustus, to complete his studies there. After a series of military disasters, the population moved south to present-day Vlora (the ancient Avlon), and by the 5th century only a small village with its own bishop remained at Apollonia.

Only a small part of ancient Apollonia has so far been uncovered. The first ruin to catch the eye is the roughly restored 2nd-century **bouleuterion**, or Hall of the Agonothetes. In front of it is the 2nd-century **odeon** (a small theatre). To the west of this is a long, 3rd-century BC **portico** with niches that once contained statues.

Apollonia's **defensive walls** are nearby. The lower portion of these massive walls, which are 4km long and up to 6.5m high, date back to the 4th century BC.

Places to Stay & Eat

The *Hotel Apollonia* (☎ 21 11), was once a somewhat run-down four-storey hotel in the main square offering basic singles/doubles for 1600 lekë. This place may well have bitten the dust after the disturbances. The six-storey *Hotel Fieri* (☎ 23 94), by the river, has 50 rooms, with prices ranging from US$20/25 to US$50/55 for singles/doubles, depending on the facilities provided.

Hotel Fieri has a clean restaurant. The *Restorant Kosova* on the main square near Hotel Fieri is basic but OK. If you want a pizza or a hamburger, try the *Llapi*, also on the main square.

Getting There & Away

All buses between Tirana and Vlora or Gjirokastra pass this way and other buses run from Fier to Berat (42km). There's also a daily train to/from Tirana (4¼ hours).

Getting Around

There are village buses from Fier direct to Apollonia in the morning. You can also get there on the Seman bus but you'll have to walk 4km from the junction to the ruins. In Fier the Seman bus leaves from a place called Zogu i Zi near the Historical Museum, or from the train station.

VLORA
☎ 063

Vlora (Vlorë), the main port of southern Albania, sits on lovely Vlora Bay just across an 80km strait from Otranto, Italy. Inexpensive ferries run between these towns three times a week, making Vlora a useful gateway to/from southern Italy. This is probably the only real reason to come here as Vlora's own attractions don't warrant a special trip.

Money

Moneychangers hang around the corner between Hotel Sazani and the post office. The Banka e Shtetit Shqiptar is a long block away, if you have travellers cheques and are there on a weekday morning.

Things to See & Do

The **archaeological museum** is across the street from Hotel Sazani, and a house museum dedicated to the Laberia Patriotic Club (1908) is nearby.

In the park behind Hotel Sazani is a large stone **monument** commemorating the proclamation of an independent Albania at Vlora in 1912. A block south of this monument is the well-preserved **Murad Mosque** (1542). In 1480 and 1536 the Turks used Vlora as a base for unsuccessful invasions of Italy.

A **war cemetery** on the hillside directly opposite the 1912 monument overlooks the town and from the cemetery a road winds around to the Liria Café, on a hill top with a sweeping view of the entire vicinity – a good place for a drink at sunset. A stone stairway descends directly back to town from the café.

You can take a bus from the 1912 monument down Vlora's main street to the south end of the **city beach** every half-hour.

Places to Stay & Eat

Accommodation choices in Vlora are limited. The very run-down three-storey *Hotel Sazani* (☎ 23 548), near the post office and market in the centre of town, will start off asking 1000 lekë per person for a basic room with shared bath, but try bargaining. The buffet at the Sazani serves reasonable meals (with beer).

Hotel Meeting on Rruga Jonaq Kilica, opposite the Halim Dhelo school, has been recommended by one traveller who was charged 1200 lekë for a double room without bath.

The best option is the *Kompleksi Turistik VEFA* (☎ 24 179), on the beach about 8km south of Vlora. This modern complex provides motel-style rooms and has a modern restaurant and guarded parking. Prices are US$30 per person including breakfast.

There are a number of very pleasant restaurants in and around the central area near Hotel Sazani, as well as any number of beachside restaurants on the south side of town.

Getting There & Away
There are daily trains to Tirana (5½ hours) and Durrës but buses are more frequent and convenient. Unfortunately, no bus travels the full length of the spectacular 124km Riviera of Flowers – you can only get as far as Himara, from where you will need to take a taxi. The early morning bus to Saranda takes a roundabout 190km route through Fier, Tepelena and Gjirokastra.

If you're interested in taking the Linee Lauro ferry to Otranto, Italy (three times a week, 100km, US$45), pick up tickets beforehand at Albania Travel & Tours in Tirana. The Otranto agent is listed in the introductory Getting There & Away section earlier this chapter. This is probably the cheapest way to cross the Adriatic.

SARANDA
☎ 10 (operator)
Saranda (Sarandë) is an animated town on the Gulf of Saranda, between the mountains and the Ionian Sea, 61km south-west of Gjirokastra. An early Christian monastery dedicated to 40 saints (Santi Quaranta) gave Saranda its name. This southernmost harbour of Albania was once the ancient port of Onchesmos. Saranda's pebble beach is nothing special although the setting of the town is quite appealing. Today, Saranda's main attractions are its sunny climate and the nearby ruins of Butrint. It is also a very convenient entry and exit point for travellers arriving in Albania via Corfu in Greece.

Orientation & Information
Saranda is spread out around a bay. Most tourist accommodation and eating places are on the south side of the bay. The main bus station is right in the centre of town, about 200m back from the waterfront. Taxis congregate on the main square in front of the town hall, which is 200m south of the bus station. The ferry terminal is at the north end of the bay.

Money There are two banks on the main street, but the simplest and best way to change money is to use the money changers behind the town hall on the main square.

Post & Communications The most efficient way to call home from Saranda is to use the informal cellular phone entrepreneurs who congregate around the little boat harbour. A quick and easy-to-make call to the USA or Australia will cost you 300 lekë a minute. Calls are routed via Greece.

Things to See
Saranda's palm-fringed waterfront promenade is attractive and is gradually livening up, with new restaurants and bars opening every month. In the centre of town are some ancient ruins with a large mosaic covered with sand. Ask around town if you are interested in seeing the recently discovered **catacombs** of the Church of the Forty Saints.

The **Blue Eye spring**, 15km east of Saranda, to the left off the Gjirokastra road and before the ascent over the pass to the Drino valley, is definitely worth seeing. Its iridescent blue water gushes from the depths of the earth and feeds the Bistrica River. French divers have descended to 70m, but the spring's actual depth is still unknown.

Places to Stay & Eat
The *Halyl Hyseni* hotel (really just private rooms) on Rruga Ade Sheme has very comfortable singles/doubles for 4000/4500 lekë, with private bathroom and TV. It is about 150m inland from the waterfront. The rooms suffer from some street noise.

The rooms of *Panajot Qyro* (☎ 25 64), also on Rruga Adem Sheme, are basic but clean and have a modern communal bathroom. Single/double rates are 500/1000 lekë. Look for the blue railings of the electricity sub-station. The rooms are right opposite.

About 500m south of Hotel Butrinti is the attractively sited *Hotel Delfini,* with rooms overlooking the water. Rates are 3500 lekë per room. The Delfini also has a very pleasant restaurant. Just 100m north of the Hotel Butrinti is the attractive but pricey *Kaoni Villa.* Single/double rates here are 4500/6000 lekë for spacious rooms with shared bathroom. Look for the big green gates.

The seven-storey, state-run *Hotel Butrinti* (☎ 417), overlooking the harbour just south of town, has singles/doubles for 3000/4500 lekë. Like most state-run hotels, the place is run-down and not all that appealing.

The *Paradise Restaurant* close to Hotel Butrinti has excellent food and the service is top notch. The *Three Roses* restaurant in the middle of Saranda is another good place to eat. It is set back from the waterfront on the 2nd floor of a big building. Look for the prominent sign.

Getting There & Away

Buses to Saranda from both Tirana and Vlora follow an interior route via Gjirokastra; unfortunately, no buses connect Saranda with Himara, north along the coast. A taxi to Himara should cost about 3000 lekë one way or 4000 lekë return. From Himara there is a daily bus to Vlora. Several buses to Gjirokastra (62km) and Tirana (289km) leave Saranda in the morning.

Three daily passenger ferries cross between Corfu and Saranda. One of the ferries takes up to five cars. The *Harikla* leaves Saranda at 10 am; the *Oleg Volvaç* goes at 1 pm; the car-carrying *Kamelia* leaves at 2 pm. The crossing takes 60 to 90 minutes. One-way fares cost 1600 lekë. Taking a car costs 4000 lekë. Check these times before making plans since schedules may have changed since the disturbances.

BUTRINT

The ancient ruins of Butrint, 18km south of Saranda, are surprisingly extensive and interesting. Virgil claimed that the Trojans founded Buthroton (Butrint), but no evidence of this has been found. Although the site had been inhabited long before, Greeks from Corfu settled on the hill in Butrint in the 6th century BC. Within a century Butrint had

become a fortified trading city with an acropolis. The lower town began to develop in the 3rd century BC and many large stone buildings existed when the Romans took over in 167 BC. Butrint's prosperity continued throughout the Roman period and the Byzantines made it an ecclesiastical centre. Then the city declined; it was almost abandoned when Italian archaeologists arrived in 1927 and began carting off any relics of value to Italy until WWII interrupted their work. In recent years the Italian government has returned some important Butrint sculptures to Albania. These are now in Tirana's National Museum of History.

There are two buses daily to Butrint, leaving Saranda at 6.30 am and noon.

Things to See

The site (open daily 7 am to 2 pm, 200 lekë, but check first) lies by a channel connecting salty Lake Butrint to the sea. A triangular **fortress** erected by warlord Ali Pasha Tepelena in the early 19th century watches over the ramshackle vehicular ferry that crosses the narrow channel.

In the forest below the acropolis is Butrint's 3rd-century BC **Greek theatre**, which was also in use during the Roman period. Nearby are the small **public baths**, which have geometrical mosaics. Deeper in the forest is a wall covered with crisp Greek inscriptions, and a 6th-century palaeo-Christian **baptistry** decorated with colourful mosaics of animals and birds. The mosaics are covered by protective sand. Beyond a 6th-century basilica stands a massive **Cyclopean wall** dating from the 4th century BC. Over one gate is a splendid relief of a lion killing a bull, symbolic of a protective force vanquishing assailants.

In a crenellated brick building on top of the acropolis is a **museum** (if it is open) full of statuary from the site. Reports suggest that the contents of the museum may have been looted in the civil disturbances of 1997.

GJIROKASTRA
☎ 0726

This strikingly picturesque museum town, midway between Fier and Ioannina, is like an Albanian eagle perched on the mountainside with a mighty citadel for its head. The fortress surveys the Drino Valley above the three and four-storey tower houses clinging to the slopes. Both buildings and streets are made of the same white-and-black stone. For defence purposes during blood feuds, these unique stone-roofed houses (*kulla*) had no windows on the ground floor, which was used for storage, and the living quarters above were reached by an exterior stairway.

The town's Greek name, Argyrokastro, is said to refer to a Princess Argyro, who chose to throw herself from a tower rather than fall into the hands of enemies, though it's more likely to be derived from the Illyrian Argyres tribe which inhabited these parts.

Gjirokastra was well established by the 13th century, but the arrival of the Turks in 1417 brought on a decline. By the 17th century Gjirokastra was thriving again with a flourishing bazar where embroidery, felt, silk and the still-famous white cheese were traded. Ali Pasha Tepelena took the town in the early 19th century and strengthened the citadel. Today all new buildings must conform to a historical preservation plan.

Gjirokastra really took the brunt of the 1997 troubles and many building were smashed and looted. Things were getting better at last reports.

Things to See

Above the **Bazar Mosque** (1757) in the centre of town is the **Mëmëdheu ABC Monument**, commemorating the renaissance of Albanian education around the turn of the century. The monument, which you may have to ask directions to find, affords an excellent view of the town.

Dominating the town is the 14th-century **citadel**, now a Museum of Armaments (8 am to noon and 4 to 7 pm, closed Monday and Tuesday, 200 lekë), with a collection of old cannons and guns and a two-seater US reconnaissance plane that made a forced landing near Berat in 1957. During the 1920s the fortress was converted into a prison and the Nazis made full use of it during their stay in 1943-44. Definitely visit the prison: the water torture cells are particularly grim.

A National Folk Festival used to be held every five years in the open-air theatre beside the citadel but the last one was in 1988 and

now the festival rotates round various cities in the country.

Enver Hoxha was born in 1908 in his family home, among the narrow cobbled streets of the Palorto quarter, up Rruga Bashkim Kokona beyond the Gjimnazi Asim Zeneli. The original house burned down in 1916, but the building was reconstructed in 1966 as a Museum of the National Liberation War and now houses the **Ethnographic Museum** (100 lekë).

The 17th-century **Turkish baths** are below the Çajupi Hotel in the lower town, near the polyclinic. The remnants of the **Mecate Mosque** are nearby. Gjirokastra has a lively Sunday market. The town was severely effected by the civil disturbances of 1997 and basic facilities may still be struggling to recover.

Places to Stay & Eat

Two cheap hotels are always worth a try. The *Argjiro Hotel* is right next to the Çajupi. A very basic single/double costs 700/1400 lekë with shared, smelly toilets. Across the street is the *Hotel Sapoti* with similarly basic singles/doubles for 600/1200 lekë.

The *Çajupi Hotel* (☎ 23 26) is another run-down former state enterprise. It is located prominently on the main taxi square, just before the old town. Singles/doubles with bath cost 2500/3500 lekë, but the hotel may have been closed because of the civil disturbances.

By far the most accommodating place to stay is the rooms of *Haxhi Kotoni*. Very cosy singles/doubles cost 2000/3000 lekë, including breakfast. The 'Bing Crosby' suite is a sight to behold. To reach the rooms, bear left by the mosque and after 50m take a sharp right turn downwards. You will find a sign on the wall on your left after about another 50m.

Eating places are thin on the ground in Gjirokastra. The *Argjiro Restaurant* next to the hotel of the same name is about as cheap and convenient as you will get. On the hill high above the town is the *Tourist Restaurant* with a great view but higher prices. Follow the road past the Kotoni rooms to walk to it in about 20 minutes.

Getting There & Away

Gjirokastra is on the main bus route from Tirana to Kakavija and Saranda. Most through buses stop on the main highway below Gjirokastra though some buses depart from the Çajupi Hotel below the citadel, including one to Tirana at 5 am.

BERAT
☎ 062

Although not as enchanting as Gjirokastra, Berat deserves its status as Albania's second most important museum town. Berat is sometimes called the 'city of a thousand windows' for the many openings in the white-plastered, red-roofed houses on terraces overlooking the Osum River. Along a ridge high above the gorge is a 14th-century citadel that shelters small Orthodox churches. On the slope below this, all the way down to the river, is Mangalem, the old Muslim quarter. A seven-arched stone bridge (1780) leads to Gorica, the Christian quarter.

In the 3rd century BC an Illyrian fortress called Antipatria was built here on the site of an earlier settlement. The Byzantines strengthened the hill-top fortifications in the 5th and 6th centuries, as did the Bulgarians 400 years later. The Serbs, who occupied the citadel in 1345, renamed it Beligrad, or 'White City', which has become today's Berat. In 1450 the Ottoman Turks took Berat. The town revived in the 18th and 19th centuries as a Turkish crafts centre specialising in woodcarving. For a brief time in 1944, Berat was the capital of liberated Albania. Today, most of Albania's crude oil is extracted from wells just north-west of the city, but Berat itself is a textile town with a mill once known as Mao Zedong.

Things to See
On the square in front of Hotel Tomori is a white hall where the National Liberation Council met from 20 to 23 October 1944 and formed a Provisional government of Albania, with Enver Hoxha as prime minister. It is now a billiard hall. Beyond this is the **Leaden Mosque** (1555), named for the material covering its great dome. Under the communists it was turned into a museum of architecture, but it is now a mosque again.

Follow the busy street north towards the citadel and, after a few blocks, behind the market building, you'll reach the **King's Mosque** (1512), formerly the Archaeological

Museum. Inside is a fine wooden gallery for female worshippers and across the courtyard is the **Alveti Tekke** (1790), a smaller shrine where Islamic sects such as the Dervishes were once based.

By the nearby river is the Margarita Tutulani Palace of Culture, a theatre worth checking for events. Beyond this is the **Bachelor's Mosque** (1827), now a folk-art museum (open Tuesday and Thursday only) A shop downstairs sells cassettes of Albanian folk music.

Continue on towards the old stone bridge (1780) and you'll see the 14th-century **Church of St Michael** high up on the hillside, below the citadel. In Mangalem, behind the Bachelor's Mosque, is the **Muzeu i Luftes** (closed Monday), which is worth seeing as much for its old Berati house as for its exhibits on the partisan struggle during WWII. Beyond the bank on the stone road leading up towards the citadel is the **Muzeu Etnografik** (open Wednesday and Friday only) in another fine old building.

After entering the **citadel** through its massive gate, continue straight ahead on the main street and you will see the sign to the **Muzeu Onufri** (open daily from 9 am to 3 pm, 200 lekë). The Museu Onufri and the **Orthodox Cathedral of Our Lady** (1797) are both within the monastery walls. The wooden iconostasis (1850) and pulpit in the cathedral are splendid. The museum has a large collection of icons, including many by the famous mid-16th century artist after whom the museum is named. Onufri's paintings are more realistic, dramatic and colourful than those of his predecessors.

Other churches in the citadel include the 14th-century **Church of the Holy Trinity** (Shen Triadhes), on the west side near the walls. Its exterior is impressive but the frescoes inside are badly damaged. The 16th-century **Church of the Evangelists** is most easily found by following the eastern citadel wall. At the south end of the citadel is a rustic **tavern** and battlements offering splendid views of Gorica and the modern city.

Places to Stay
The basic *Hotel Dyrmo* has three rooms with bath. They charge 500/1000 lekë for a single/double. It is just back from the west

end of the main street. Ask at the restaurant if no one is around.

The *Hotel Gega* was being renovated but should have reopened by the time you read this. It's a couple of hundred metres east of the Leaden Mosque along the main street.

The five-storey *Hotel Tomori* (☎ 32 462) is named after Mt Tomori (2416m), which towers above Berat to the east. The hotel is by the river on the east side of town. It has no lift but the balcony views of the riverside park compensate for the climb. The 56 rooms are US$32/50 for a single/double with bath and breakfast included. The hotel sign lacks the word 'Tomori'.

Places to Eat

The *Iliri Restorant* alongside the river has good food and an upstairs balcony with a view over the street. The atmosphere, however, can get a little rowdy at times. The cosy little *Onufri Restorant*, very close to the Onufri Museum in the citadel, is very good value for money.

Getting There & Away

The bus station is next to the Leaden Mosque near Hotel Tomori. A bus from Tirana to Berat (122km) takes three hours, a little long for a day trip. Buses to Fier (47km) and Tirana are fairly frequent and some buses run from Berat direct to Gjirokastra (120km). Minibus taxis also run from here to Fier, Tirana and Gjirokastra, and to places south of Berat.

ELBASAN
☎ 0545

Elbasan is on the Shkumbin River, midway between Durrës and Pogradec and 54km south-east of Tirana. It has been prominent since 1974, when the Chinese built the mammoth 'Steel of the Party' steel mill. It also has a cement factory and burgeoning pollution, though the old town retains a certain charm. With 83,000 inhabitants, Elbasan is Albania's third-largest city, having more than doubled in size since 1970.

The Romans founded Skampa (Elbasan) in the 1st century AD as a stopping point on the Via Egnatia. Stout stone walls with 26 towers were added in the 4th century to protect against invading barbarians. The Byzantines

continued this trend, also making Skampa the seat of a bishopric. In 1466, Sultan Mohammed II rebuilt the walls as a check against Skënderbeg at Kruja and renamed the town El Basan ('The Fortress' in Turkish). Elbasan was an important trade and handicrafts centre throughout the Turkish period.

Elbasan can be visited as a day trip from Tirana and the drive across the mountains is spectacular. Look out for the Citadel of Petrela, which stands on a hill top above the Erzen River.

Things to See

The 17th-century **Turkish baths** are in the centre of town, beside Hotel Skampa. Directly across the park on the other side of the hotel is Sejdini House, a typical 19th-century Balkan building, now the **Ethnographical Museum**.

Opposite the hotel are the **city walls**, erected by the Turks and still relatively intact on the south and west sides. Go through the **Bazar Gate** near the clock tower and follow a road directly north past the 15th-century **King's Mosque** to **St Mary's Orthodox Church**, which has a fine stone arcade on each exterior side and a gilded pulpit and iconostasis inside. This church is usually locked to prevent theft but it's worth asking around for the person with the key (who will expect a tip). Visible from behind St Mary's is a large Catholic church (closed). On the west city wall is a museum dedicated to the partisan war.

Places to Stay & Eat

The eight-storey *Hotel Skampa* (☎ 22 40) has 112 rooms at US$21/38 for a single/double with bath. It also has an OK restaurant downstairs.

The *Restaurant Universi*, about 200m west of Hotel Skampa, is another eating option. It is clean and prices are low. Failing that there are any number of snack bars or hamburger stands along or opposite the city walls nearby.

Getting There & Away

All buses to/from Pogradec (86km) pass through here but they arrive full. Getting a bus to Tirana is easier and there are also minibus taxis, departing from the parking lot next to the Skampa Hotel.

The train station is about five blocks from the Skampa Hotel. There are trains to Tirana and Durrës three times a day.

POGRADEC

☎ 10 (operator)

Pogradec is a pleasant beach resort at the southern end of Lake Ohrid, 140km south east of Tirana. The 700m elevation gives the area a brisk, healthy climate and the scenery is beautiful. Pogradec is much less developed than the Macedonian lake towns of Ohrid and Struga. The nearby border crossing at Sveti Naum makes Pogradec a natural gateway to/from Macedonia.

Places to Stay & Eat

The eight-storey *Guri i Kuq Hotel* (☎ 414), opposite the post office, is named after the 'red-stone' mountain on the west side of the lake where nickel and chrome ore are extracted. It was last reported to be gutted and closed down, but it may reopen.

A much cheaper place to stay is the old, privately operated *Hotel Turizmi i Vjetar* on the beach about 180m west of the Guri i Kuq.

The *Hotel Koço Llakmani* is essentially private rooms above a restaurant/bar of the same name. It is on the little square 100m west of the Guri i Kuq Hotel. Just round the corner is the *Greek Taverna* which has very little Greek about it but serves excellent Ohrid trout at one third of the price you'd pay in Ohrid.

Getting There & Away

The train station, with two daily services to Tirana (seven hours) and Durrës, is near the mineral-processing factory, about 4km from the Guri i Kuq Hotel. Buses run to Tirana (140km), Korça (46km) and other towns.

Macedonia It's fairly easy to hitch the 6km east from Pogradec to the Tushemisht border post with Macedonia. Halfway is Drilon, a well-known tourist picnic spot, then the lakeside road goes through Tushemisht village and along the hillside to the border crossing. On the Macedonian side is the monastery of Sveti Naum, where there is a bus to Ohrid (29km), and a boat service in summer.

Tushemisht is a much better crossing for pedestrians and private cars than the Qafa e Thanës border crossing on the west side of the lake, which is used mostly by trucks and other commercial vehicles.

KORÇA

☎ 0824

The main city of the south-eastern interior, Korça sits on a 869m-high plateau west of Florina, Greece, 39km south of Lake Ohrid. Under the Turks, Korça was a major trading post and carpet-making town – it's still Albania's biggest carpet and rug-producing centre. Although it is in the heart of a rich agricultural area, Korça saw hard times in the late 19th and early 20th centuries and became a centre of emigration. Albanians abroad often regard Korça as home and quite a few still come back to retire here. Moneychangers work the street just west of Hotel Iliria.

Things to See

The **Muzeu Historik** is in the old two-storey building on Bulevardi Themistokli Gërmenji behind Hotel Iliria. Further up the boulevard on the left is the **Muzeu i Arsimit Kombëtar**, or Education Museum, housed in the first school to teach in the Albanian language (in 1887). (both museums are apparently closed indefinitely). Nearby at the top of the boulevard is the **statue of the National Warrior** (1932) by Odhise Paskali.

Delve into the small streets behind this statue and veer left to find the former **Muzeu i Artet Mesjetar Shqiptar** (Museum of Albanian Medieval Art), once the most important of Korça's museums, with several icons by Onufri. In a striking reversal of roles, Orthodox Albanians have recently taken over the modern museum building and turned it into a church to replace their original place of worship, which was destroyed by the communists.

Much of the old city centre was gouged out by urban renewal after devastating earthquakes in 1931 and 1960 which toppled the minarets and flattened the churches. Some of the colour of old Korça still remains in the Oriental-style **bazar area** west of Hotel Iliria.

Walk the crumbling cobbled streets lined with quaint old shops and swing south to the **Mirahorit Mosque** (1485), one of the oldest in Albania.

Places to Stay & Eat

Rozetta Qirjako and her husband Niko are a friendly couple and will take people in for about 1000 lekë per person. Their address is Rruga Dhori Lako L1, No 8. Niko is also a mechanic.

Among Korça's hotels catering mostly to Albanians is the friendly *Hotel Pallas*, on Bulevardi Themistokli Gërmenji just up from Hotel Iliria. On the opposite side of the same building is the *Hotel Gramosi* (it has no sign, so just ask). The prices asked of foreigners at these places varies, but for Albanians it's considerably cheaper.

The eight-storey *Hotel Iliria* (☎ 31 68) costs US$16/26 for a single/double without bath, US$30/48 with bath. Breakfast is included.

The *Alfa Restaurant* close to the above hotels is a good place to eat, otherwise Hotel Iliria has a restaurant. *Dolce Vita* on Bulevardi Republike offers fine Italian food and a surreal ambience. It's open until 11 pm.

Getting There & Away

There are buses to/from Tirana (179km) via Elbasan. Korça is a gateway to Albania for anyone arriving from Florina, Greece, via the Kapshtica border crossing 28km east. Buses to Kapshtica leave when full throughout the day from near Skënderbeg Stadium at the east end of Bulevardi Republike. From Krystallopigi on the Greek side of the border it's 65km to Florina (two buses daily, 1000 dr; taxi 7000 dr), a major Greek city with good connections to/from Thessaloniki. There is also a direct bus to Korçca to/from Thessaloniki (5100 drachmas) which leaves from the forecourt of the Thessaloniki train station at 8 am every day except Sunday.

Bosnia-Hercegovina

Sandwiched between Croatia and Yugoslavia, the small mountainous country of Bosnia-Hercegovina has been a meeting point of east and west for nearly two millennia. Here the realm of Orthodox Byzantium mingled with Catholic Rome, and the 15th-century swell of Turkish power settled among the Slavs. This unique history created one of the most fascinating cultures in Europe, with a heterogeneous population of Croats, Serbs and Slavic converts to Islam.

In the 20th century Bosnia-Hercegovina has had more than its share of strife. WWI was sparked in Sarajevo when a Serb nationalist assassinated an Austrian aristocrat, and much of the bitter partisan fighting of WWII took place in this region. Forty-five years of peace ensued, with Bosnia-Hercegovina as the third-largest republic in Yugoslavia. This ended soon after Bosnia declared independence in October 1991. Six months later Bosnian Serb ultranationalists, assisted by Yugoslavia's federal army, began a campaign of ethnic cleansing intended to bring Bosnia-Hercegovina into Belgrade's orbit.

When the three-way war ended in 1995, it left the country physically devastated and ethnically divided. Out of a prewar population of five million, over two million fled their former homes. Peace is currently enforced by 34,000 NATO troops, and a large international civilian presence is working to reintegrate and rebuild the country. Progress since peace has been substantial, but as a destination for visitors Bosnia-Hercegovina itself is unalterably changed.

AT A GLANCE

Capital	Sarajevo
Population	3.2 million
Area	51,233 sq km
Official Language	Croatian/Serbian (Bosnian)
Currency	1 dinar = 100 para; 1 kuna = 100 lipas
GDP	US$1.9 billion (1996)
Time	GMT/UTC+0100

Sarajevo p126

Mostar p131
Medugorje p133

The Two 'Entities' of Bosnia-Hercegovina p118

Facts about Bosnia-Hercegovina

HISTORY

The ancient inhabitants of this region were Illyrians, followed by the Romans who settled around the mineral springs at Ilidža near Sarajevo. When the Roman Empire was divided in 395 AD, the Drina River, today the border between Bosnia-Hercegovina and Yugoslavia, became the line that divided the Western Roman Empire from Byzantium.

The Slavs arrived in the late 6th and early 7th centuries. In 960 the area became independent of Serbia, only to pass through the hands of other conquerors: Croatia, Byzantium, Duklja (modern-day Montenegro), and Hungary. The first Turkish raids came in 1383 and by 1463 Bosnia was a Turkish province with Sarajevo as its capital. Hercegovina is named after Herceg (Duke) Stjepan Vukčić, who ruled the southern portion of the

BOSNIA-HERCEGOVINA

present republic from his mountaintop castle at Blagaj near Mostar until the Turkish conquest in 1468.

During the 400-year Turkish period, Bosnia-Hercegovina was completely assimilated and became the boundary between the Islamic and Christian worlds. Wars with Venice and Austria were frequent. One Christian heretic sect, the Bogomils, converted to Islam, and the region still forms a Muslim enclave deep within Christian Europe.

As the Ottoman Empire weakened in the 16th and 17th centuries, the Turks strength-

ened their hold on Bosnia-Hercegovina as an advance bulwark of their empire. The national revival movements of the mid-19th century led to a reawakening among the South Slavs, and in 1875-76 there were peasant uprisings against the Turks in Bosnia-Hercegovina and Bulgaria. In 1878 Turkey suffered a crushing defeat by Russia in a war over Bulgaria, and it was decided at the Congress of Berlin that same year that Austria-Hungary would occupy Bosnia-Hercegovina. However, the population desired autonomy and had to be brought under Habsburg rule by force.

Resentment against foreign occupation intensified in 1908 when Austria annexed Bosnia-Hercegovina outright. The assassination of the Habsburg heir Archduke Franz Ferdinand by a Bosnian Serb at Sarajevo on 28 June 1914 led Austria to declare war on Serbia one month later. When Russia supported Serbia, and Germany came to the aid of Austria, the world was soon at war.

Following WWI, Bosnia-Hercegovina was taken into the Serb-dominated Kingdom of the Serbs, Croats, and Slovenes (renamed Yugoslavia in 1929). In 1941 the Axis powers annexed Bosnia-Hercegovina to the fascist Croatian state, but the area's mountains quickly became a wartime partisan stronghold. A conference in 1943 in Jajce laid the ground for postwar Yugoslavia, and after the war Bosnia-Hercegovina was granted republic status within Yugoslavia.

In the republic's first free elections in November 1990, the communists were easily defeated by nationalist Serb and Croat parties and by a predominantly Muslim party favouring a multiethnic Bosnia-Hercegovina.

The Croat and Muslim parties united against the Serb nationalists and independence from Yugoslavia was declared on 15 October 1991. Serb parliamentarians withdrew and set up a government of their own at Pale, the village 20km east of Sarajevo where the 1984 Winter Olympics took place. Bosnia-Hercegovina was recognised internationally and admitted to the UN, but this over-hasty recognition caused talks between the parties to break down.

The War

War broke out in April 1992, shortly after Bosnian Serb snipers in the Sarajevo Holiday Inn opened fire on unarmed civilians demonstrating for peace in Sarajevo, killing a dozen people.

The Serbs had inherited almost the entire arms stock of the Yugoslav National Army (JNA). As had been done in Croatia they began seizing territory with the support of some of the 50,000 JNA troops in Bosnia-Hercegovina. Sarajevo came under siege by Serb irregulars on 5 April 1992 and shelling by Serb artillery began soon after. Directed from nearby Pale, the brutal siege was to leave over 10,000 civilians dead and the city ravaged before it ended in summer 1995.

Serb forces began a campaign of 'ethnic cleansing', brutally expelling the Muslim population from northern and eastern Bosnia to create a 300km corridor joining Serb ethnic areas in the west of Bosnia and in Serbia proper. Villages were terrorised and looted, and homes were destroyed to prevent anyone from returning. Crowning their campaign of ethnic cleansing, the Serbs set up concentration camps for Muslims and Croats and initiated the mass atrocities which were a devastating feature of this war.

In August 1992 the UN Security Council authorised the use of force to deliver humanitarian relief supplies and by September 7500 UN troops were in Bosnia-Hercegovina. However, this UN Protection Force (UNPROFOR) was notorious for its impotence, which was dramatically displayed in January 1993 when the vice-premier of Bosnia-Hercegovina, Hakija Turajlić, was pulled out of a UN armoured personnel carrier at a Serb checkpoint and executed in front of French peacekeepers.

By mid-1993, with Serb 'ethnic cleansing' almost complete, the UN proposed setting up 'safe areas' for Muslims around five Bosnian cities, including Sarajevo. The Serbs, confident that the west would not intervene, continued their siege of Sarajevo.

The Vance-Owen peace plan, which would have divided Bosnia-Hercegovina into 10 ethnically based provinces, was rejected by Serb leaders in 1993. Nonetheless, the plan's formulation seemed to confirm to all sides that Bosnia's fate lay in ethnic partition.

The Croats wanted their own slice of Bosnia-Hercegovina. The Croatian Community of Herceg-Bosna was set up in July 1992, and in March 1993 fighting erupted between Muslims and Croats. The Croats instigated a deadly mini-siege of the Muslim quarter of Mostar, which culminated in the destruction of Mostar's historic old bridge in 1993.

In May 1993 Croatian president Franjo Tudjman made a bid for a 'Greater Croatia' by making a separate deal with the Bosnian Serbs to carve up Bosnia-Hercegovina between themselves. This was foiled by the renewed strength of the Bosnian army, and fighting between Muslims and Croats intensified.

NATO finally began taking action against the Bosnian Serbs. After a Serb mortar attack on a Sarajevo market in February 1994 left 68 dead and 200 injured, NATO's threatened air strikes cowed the Bosnian Serbs into withdrawing their guns temporarily from around the city.

US fighters belatedly began enforcing the no-fly zone over Bosnia by shooting down four Serb aircraft in February 1994 (the first actual combat in NATO's 45-year history). Two months later NATO aircraft carried out their first air strikes against Bosnian Serb ground positions after the Serbs advanced into a UN 'protected area'. When a British plane was shot down, the NATO raids quickly ceased.

Meanwhile, at talks held in Washington in March 1994, the US pressured the Bosnian government to join the Bosnian Croats in a federation. Worried about Serb enclaves on its own soil, Croatia went on the offensive in May 1995 and rapidly overran Croatian Serb positions and towns in western Slavonia, within Croatia.

With Croatia now heavily involved, a pan-Balkan war seemed closer than ever. Again, Bosnian Serb tanks and artillery attacked Sarajevo, again UN peacekeepers requested NATO air strikes. When air strikes to protect Bosnian 'safe areas' was finally authorised, the Serbs captured 300 UNPROFOR peacekeepers and chained them to potential targets to keep the planes away.

In July 1995 Bosnian Serbs attacked the safe area of Srebrenica, slaughtering an estimated 6000 Muslim men as they fled through the forest. This was the largest massacre in the war, and highlighted the futility of the UN presence.

Nonetheless, the twilight of Bosnian Serb military dominance was at hand. European leaders called loudly for strong action not just to try once more to defend the Bosnians but to defeat the Bosnian Serbs. Croatia renewed its own internal offensive, expelling Serbs from the Krajina region.

With Bosnian Serbs finally on the defensive and battered by two weeks of NATO air strikes in September 1995, US president Bill Clinton's proposal for new peace talks was accepted.

The Dayton Accord

The peace conference in Dayton, Ohio, USA, began in November 1995 and the final agreement was signed in Paris in December.

The Dayton agreement stated that the country would retain its prewar external boundaries, but would be composed of two parts or 'entities'. The Federation of Bosnia-Hercegovina (the Muslim and Croat portion) would administer 51% of the country, including Sarajevo, and the Serb Republic of Bosnia-Hercegovina 49%. The latter is commonly referred to as the Republika Srpska (RS). Eastern and western portions of the RS would be linked together by the narrow Posavina Corridor in the northeast. The town of Brčko, situated in the narrowest part of the corridor, was so contentious that its final fate was left up to international arbitration, which has subsequently postponed a decision.

The agreement also emphasised the rights of refugees to return to their prewar homes. This was relevant for both the 1.2 million people who sought refuge in other countries (including Yugoslavia and Croatia), and the one million people who were displaced

The Two Entities of Bosnia-Hercegovina

- Muslim-Croat Federation
- Republika Srpska

ZAGREB

Bihać
Prijedor
Posavina Corridor
Sanski Most
Banja Luka
Brčko
Tuzla
Travnik
CROATIA
SARAJEVO
Pale
Split
Goražde
Mostar
Međugorje
ADRIATIC SEA
YUGOSLAVIA
Dubrovnik
ALBANIA
0   50   100 km

within Bosnia-Hercegovina during the ethnic cleansing process.

A NATO-led peace implementation force, IFOR, was installed as the military force behind the accords. IFOR's 60,000 international troops gave way in January 1997 to the 30,000-strong Stabilisation Force (SFOR), whose current mandate has no definite time limit.

The Dayton accords also emphasised the powers of the War Crimes Tribunal in the Hague, which had been established in 1993. NATO was given the authority to arrest indicted war criminals. Thus far, 74 people have been publicly indicted, but only 27 have been brought to the Hague and the most-wanted war criminals, Bosnian Serb leader Radovan Karadžić and his military henchman Ratko Mladić, remain at large.

After Dayton

In early 1996 Bosnian, Serb and Croat forces withdrew to the agreed lines, and NATO-led IFOR took up positions between them. Karadžić stepped down from the RS presidency in July 1996, after the international community threatened to reintroduce sanctions against the Serbs if he did not quit public office. Seemingly unfazed, Karadžić continued to wield behind-the-scenes influence, even as his successor Biljana Plavsić took over as the RS president.

Bosnia-Hercegovina's first post-war national elections in September 1996 essentially shored up the existing leadership. Municipal elections scheduled for the same time were postponed for one year while the international community, which supervised the elections, ironed out the logistics of allowing people to vote in their prewar municipalities. When municipal elections finally took place in September 1997, exile leaders were elected in several towns, notably Muslims in Serb-controlled Srebrenica and Prijedor and Serbs in Croat-controlled Drvar.

Meanwhile Plavsić, wooed by western support and ostensibly concerned about corruption, split from the hardline Karadžić during summer 1997. The RS itself seemed to be splintering along these lines, with the Pale-based eastern RS backing Karadžić and Plavsić's domain in Banja Luka-based western RS becoming more open. Banja Luka emerged

triumphant from the struggle and took over from Pale as the RS capital in January 1998.

Western hopes were given a further boost in January 1998 when a new, relatively liberal Bosnian Serb Prime Minister Milorad Dodik came to power. Dodik quickly pushed several measures through the RS parliament aimed at compliance with Dayton, including a common license plate (that would no longer be entity-specific), common passports and a new common currency called the convertible mark. A new national flag was approved just in time for the 1998 Winter Olympic Games.

Bosnia-Hercegovina today remains deeply divided along ethnic lines. Muslim-Croat tensions have ebbed, but few people dare to cross between the RS and the Federation. Many of the country's towns are physically destroyed, although a US$5.1 billion reconstruction program is underway.

GEOGRAPHY

Bosnia-Hercegovina is a mountainous country of 51,129 sq km on the west side of the Balkan Peninsula, almost cut off from the sea by Croatia. Most of the country's rivers flow north into the Sava; only the Neretva cuts south from Jablanica through the Dinaric Alps to Ploče on the Adriatic Sea. Bosnia-Hercegovina contains over 30 mountain peaks from 1700 to 2386m high.

GOVERNMENT & POLITICS

The Dayton Accords stipulate that the central government be headed by a rotating three-person presidency, with one elected by the Serb Republic and the others, a Muslim and a Croat, by the Federation. The House of Peoples is selected from the legislatures of the two entities and a House of Representatives directly elected by each entity. Two-thirds of each house is from the Federation, one-third from the Serb Republic, and a Council of Ministers is responsible for carrying out government policies and decisions.

Despite ideals of a central government in Sarajevo, each individual division of Bosnia-Hercegovina maintains an essentially separate administration. Few of the ethnically joint institutions called for by the Dayton agreement are functioning, even between Muslims and Croats within the Federation.

In lieu of local cooperation, Bosnia-Hercegovina is essentially ruled by the west, which has taken an increasingly firm hand in forcing the parties to come to decisions together. The international community's High Representative received stronger powers at a conference in Bonn in December 1997 and began dismissing obstructionist officials.

ECONOMY
Bosnia-Hercegovina was one of the poorest regions of Yugoslavia, its economy driven by mining, hydroelectricity and timber. War brought virtually all activity to a halt, but the situation has improved remarkably during peacetime. The unemployment rate has shot down from 50% at the end of 1995 to about 30% in early 1998. And the new figure does not even reflect the country's most popular occupations – working as a translator or driver for the well-paying international organisations.

The Republika Srpska, which until recently received less international assistance, is significantly poorer than the Federation.

POPULATION & PEOPLE
Before the war, Bosnia-Hercegovina's population stood at around four million. In 1991 the largest cities were Sarajevo (525,980), Banja Luka (195,139), Zenica (145,577), Tuzla (131,861) and Mostar (126,067). The massive population shifts have changed the size of many cities, swelling the population of Banja Luka to 220,000 and shrinking Sarajevo (347,901) and Mostar (108,265).

Bosnia-Hercegovina's prewar population was incredibly mixed, but ethnic cleansing has concentrated Croats in Hercegovina (to the south), Muslims in Sarajevo and central Bosnia, and Serbs in areas adjacent to Yugoslavia.

Serbs, Croats and Bosnian Muslims are all South Slavs of the same ethnic stock. Physically the three peoples are indistinguishable.

ARTS
Bosnia's best known writer is Ivo Andrić (1892-1975), winner of the 1961 Nobel Prize for Literature. His novels *Travnik Chronicles* and *Bridge on the Drina*, both written during WWII, are fictional histories which deal with the intermingling of Islamic and Orthodox societies in the small Bosnian towns of Travnik and Višegrad.

SOCIETY & CONDUCT
Removing one's shoes is customary in Muslim households, the host family will provide slippers. The Bosnian people are incredibly friendly, but when the subject turns to politics, the best strategy is listening. People are eager to talk about the war but are generally convinced that their side is right.

RELIGION
Before the war, Bosnia-Hercegovina's population was 43% Muslim Slavs, 31% Orthodox Serbs and 17% Catholic Croats. Of the current population of 2.8 million, approximately 42% are Muslim, 37% Serb, and 15% Croat. The current proportions are roughly the same despite the population shifts. In each part of Bosnia-Hercegovina, churches and mosques are being built (or rebuilt) at lightning speed. This phenomenon is more a symptom of nationalism than of religion, since most people are fairly secular.

LANGUAGE
Dialects notwithstanding, the people of Bosnia-Hercegovina speak the same language. However, that language is referred to as 'Bosnian' in the Muslim part of the Federation, 'Croatian' in Croat-controlled parts, and 'Serbian' in the RS. The Federation uses the Latin alphabet but the RS uses Cyrillic. See the Croatian, Serbian, & Bosnian section of the Language chapter at the back of the book for pronunciation guidelines and useful words and phrases.

Facts for the Visitor

HIGHLIGHTS
Sarajevo is a major historic site, simultaneously vibrant and shockingly destroyed. Beautiful Mostar deserves a visit for its cobbled old town and former Stari Most.

Driving or taking the bus through the ravaged countryside of Bosnia-Hercegovina is an unforgettable experience.

SUGGESTED ITINERARIES

Two days
    Visit Sarajevo
One week
    Visit Sarajevo and Mostar
Two weeks
    Visit Sarajevo, Travnik and Banja Luka

PLANNING
Climate & When to Go
Since Bosnia-Hercegovina is a mountainous country, it gets hot in the summer but quite chilly in the winter, and snowfall can last until April. The best time to visit is spring or summer. Don't worry about a seasonal crush of tourists just yet.

Books & Maps
Noel Malcolm's book *Bosnia: A Short History* is a good country-specific supplement to Rebecca West's mammoth classic *Black Lamb and Grey Falcon*, which exhaustively describes her trip through Yugoslavia in the late 1930s. For a detailed account of the recent war, try *The Death of Yugoslavia* by Laura Silber and Allan Little, or *The Fall of Yugoslavia* by Misha Glenny.

What to Bring
It's a myth that Bosnia suffers from shortages. Shops sell goods imported from the rest of Europe, but bring plenty of Deutschmarks, since you'll be paying in cash.

VISAS & EMBASSIES
No visas are required for citizens of the USA, Canada, Ireland, the UK, and most other EU countries. Citizens of other countries can obtain a tourist visa in advance by sending a personal cheque or money order for US$35, your passport, a copy of a round-trip plane ticket, an invitation letter, and an application to the nearest embassy. According to passport control in the Sarajevo airport, visitors flying into Sarajevo can obtain a visa for DM90 but it may involve some paperwork.

Those entering Bosnia-Hercegovina by land may not need a visa on the border, particularly if you are passing into Hercegovina from Croatia or the RS from Yugoslavia.

RS border officials have been known to charge illegal DM60 'transit visas' to travellers crossing into Yugoslavia.

Tourists in Bosnia are required to register with the local police. A hotel or accommodations agency will do this for you, but foreigners staying in private houses must do this themselves (in Sarajevo, go to Zmaja od Bosne 9, room 3).

Bosnian Embassies Abroad
Bosnia-Hercegovina has embassies and/or consulates in the following countries; check the web page www.bosnianembassy.org/bih/dipoffi.htm for further listings.

Australia
    (☎ (02) 6239 5955; fax (02) 6239 5793) 15 State Circle, Forrest ACT 2603
France
    (☎ 01-426 734 22; fax 01-405 385 22) 174 Rue de Courcelles, 75017 Paris
Croatia
    (☎ 01-276 776 or 425 899; fax 01-455 6177) Torbarova 9, 41000 Zagreb
Slovenia
    (☎ 061-132 2214; fax 061-132 2230) Likozarjeva 6 Ljubljana
UK
    (☎ 0171-255 3758; fax 0171-255 2760) 320 Regent St, London W1R 5AB
US
    (☎ 202-833 3612; fax 202-337 1502) 2109 E St NW, Washington DC 20037
    (☎ 212-751 9015/9016; fax 212-751 9019) (Consulate) 866 UN Plaza, Suite 580, New York NY 10017

Foreign Embassies in Bosnia-Hercegovina
These embassies are in Sarajevo:

Bulgaria
    (☎ 071-668 191; fax 071-668 182) Trampina 12/II
Canada
    (☎ 071-447 900; fax 071-447 901) Logavina 3b
Croatia
    (☎ 071-444 330; fax 071-472 434) 16 Mehmeda Spahe
Czech Republic
    (☎/fax 071-447 525) Potoklinica 6

BOSNIA-HERCEGOVINA

Slovenia
(☎ 071-447 660; fax 071-447 659) Bentbaša 7
UK
(☎ 071-444 429; fax 071-666 131) Tina Ujevića 8
USA
(☎ 071-659 969 or 445 700; fax 071-659 722)
Alipašina 43

MONEY
Currency
The 'convertible mark' has been approved as Bosnia's official common currency, to be tied to the Deutschmark at a rate of KM1 to DM1. However, the KM was not yet introduced at the time of writing, although many menus in Sarajevo already list prices in 'KM.' In theory, the convertible mark will be used throughout Bosnia-Hercegovina. In practice, it may take quite a while.

Bosnia-Hercegovina's currency situation mirrors the country's divisions. Sarajevo and other Muslim parts of the Muslim-Croat Federation use Deutschmarks interchangeably with tattered paper notes called Bosnian dinars, which are fixed at a rate of BHD100 to DM1. In Croat-controlled parts of the Federation, Croatian kuna are widely used, and in the Republika Srpska prices are in Serbian dinars (different from Bosnian dinars!). The good news is that Deutschmarks are accepted everywhere in Bosnia-Hercegovina.

Changing Money
ATMs are unavailable. Travellers cheques can be exchanged at banks in most cities; however, commissions are generally 3% and above, on top of poor exchange rates. Converting to the local currency (Bosnian dinars, Croatian kuna, Serbian dinars) is cheaper than making the extra conversion to Deutschmarks. If you're stuck with large Deutschmark bills, which are difficult to break at markets or shops, go to a bank and ask nicely for smaller bills.

Credit Cards
The Sarajevo offices of some western airlines (Swissair and Austrian Airlines) accept major credit cards, along with a smattering of hotels in Hercegovina. A few banks can give credit card advances, but otherwise the rule is cash cash cash.

Tipping
Tipping is customary at nice restaurants – just leave DM5 or 10 on the table, or round up the bill. Taxi fares can be treated the same way.

POST & COMMUNICATIONS
Post
Bosnia's postal system works, but poste restante is unavailable except at the post office in west Mostar.

Telephone & Fax
To call Bosnia-Hercegovina from abroad, dial the international access code ☎ 387 (the country code for Bosnia-Hercegovina), the area code (without the initial zero) and the number. If you are calling the Republika Srpska, you may have more luck dialing through Yugoslavia (☎ 381, then city code).

To make an international call from Bosnia-Hercegovina, it's cheapest to go to the post office. Dial the international access number (☎ 00 from the Muslim part of the Federation, ☎ 99 from elsewhere), then the country code and number. A three-minute call to the USA costs DM6.

Telephone cards, useful for local or short international calls, can be purchased at post offices. Note however that cards issued in Serb, Croat, and Muslim-controlled areas are not interchangeable.

Some important telephone numbers are ☎ 901 (international operator), ☎ 988 for local directory information, ☎ 92 for police, ☎ 93 for the fire department, and ☎ 94 for emergency assistance.

Faxes can be sent from most post offices, though machines may be slow and prices consequently high.

INTERNET RESOURCES
For general background on the country take a 'Bosnia Virtual Fieldtrip' at (http://geog .gmu.edu/gess/jwc/bosnia/bosnia.html). You can always visit the web site of the Office of the High Representative (http://www.ohr.int) to get detailed news updates.

Although email is so far unavailable publicly in Bosnia-Hercegovina, it can be accessed cheaply and easily from the university in Sarajevo.

NEWSPAPERS & MAGAZINES

All parts of Bosnia-Hercegovina have different papers. Sarajevo's independent daily *Oslobodenje* functioned throughout the war. *Dani*, the popular and outrageous biweekly magazine, keeps the Sarajevo government on its toes with colourful covers and entertaining political satire.

RADIO & TV

Studio 99 is both a television and a radio station; the latter carries some Radio Free Europe broadcasting. Radio Zid has some Voice of America news. Serb Radio Television (SRT) is broadcast out of Banja Luka.

PHOTOGRAPHY & VIDEO

Kodak and Fuji film is available in larger cities for DM10 and up to DM14 a roll. It is quite common to take photographs of war damage, but use prudence and sensitivity.

TIME

Bosnia-Hercegovina is on Central European Time, which is GMT/UTC plus one hour. Daylight savings time in late March sets clocks forward one hour, but in late November clocks are turned back one hour.

ELECTRICITY

Electricity is 220V, 50Hz AC, with the standard three-pronged European plugs.

WEIGHTS & MEASURES

Measurements in Bosnia-Hercegovina fall under the metric system.

HEALTH

Clinics with western doctors serve only international organisations. Visiting a Bosnian doctor costs about DM10 to 30. Make sure that your medical insurance plan does not exclude evacuation from Bosnia-Hercegovina.

WOMEN TRAVELLERS

Women travelling alone should feel no particular anxiety. Indeed, people will be surprised that you are alone and may offer help.

DANGERS & ANNOYANCES

Always look into local political conditions before undertaking a journey. Use particular caution when travelling in the Republika Srpska, where anti-western sentiments are generally higher than in the Federation.

Mines

Over one million land mines are estimated to be in Bosnia-Hercegovina. These were laid mostly in conflict zones. All of Sarajevo's suburbs are heavily mined, as are areas around Travnik and Mostar. The most frightening statistic is that only about half of Bosnia-Hercegovina's minefields are in known locations. The Mine Action Centre in Sarajevo (☎ 071-201 298 or 299; fax 071-667 311) runs valuable 1½-hour mine information briefings which are open to visitors.

Unexploded ordinances (UXOs, mortars, grenades, and shells) also pose a huge danger around former conflict areas.

The golden rule for mines and UXOs is to stick to asphalt surfaces. Abandoned-looking areas are avoided for a reason. Do not drive off the shoulder of roads, do not poke around in abandoned villages or damaged houses, do not get curious about shiny metal objects on the grass, and regard every centimetre of ground as suspicious.

PUBLIC HOLIDAYS

Bosnia-Hercegovina observes Independence Day (1 March), May Day (1 May), Day of the Republic (25 November) and two Muslim religious holidays of Bajram, which will fall in January and March in the years 1999 and 2000.

ACCOMMODATION

The year-round presence of international officials on expense accounts has jump-started Bosnia-Hercegovina's hotel industry. Sarajevo and Mostar have some pleasant new hotels, but in general prices are much higher than the typical socialist-style buildings warrant. Except in a few hotels in west Mostar and Medugorje, payment is in cash only. Deutschmarks are always accepted, and usually US dollars.

Pansions and private accommodation agencies have sprouted in Sarajevo, but elsewhere (except for Medugorje, where every house is a pansion) there are few. The situation is changing quickly, so inquire at the tourist office. Or ask locals at the market or shops.

Private accommodation is usually very pleasant. Likely as not, your host will ply you with coffee, pull out old pictures of Tito (depending on his politics), and regale you with tales of Bosnia-Hercegovina's past glory.

Most accommodations charge tax (DM2 to 5), which is included in the prices listed in this chapter.

FOOD & DRINKS

Bosnia's Turkish heritage is savoured in its grilled meats such as *bosanski lonac* (Bosnian stew of cabbage and meat). When confronted with the ubiquitous *burek* (a layered meat pie sold by weight), vegetarians can opt for *sirnica* (cheese pie) or *zeljanica* (spinach pie). *Čevapčiči*, another favourite, is lamb and beef rolls tucked into a half-loaf of spongy *somun* bread. For sugar-soaked deserts, try baklava or *tufahije*, an apple cake topped with walnuts and whipped cream.

Good wines from Hercegovina include Žilavka (white) and Blatina (red). These are best sampled in the region's wineries. A meal can always be washed down with a shot of *šlivovica* (plum brandy) or *loza* (grape brandy).

Getting There & Away

AIR

Airlines serving Sarajevo include Croatia Airlines, Crossair (the partner of Swissair), Lufthansa, and Austrian Airlines. Air Bosna, a tiny new airline which has leased a few planes from Ukraine, flies to Turkey and Germany.

Yugoslav National Airlines (JAT) has service to Banja Luka from Belgrade. The Mostar airport is not yet open to commercial traffic.

LAND

In the absence of international train lines, buses are an excellent, safe way to enter Bosnia-Hercegovina, and to see the countryside. Stowing luggage costs up to DM5,

depending on the route. Buses usually run on time, although they are slow due to windy roads and occasional stops for drivers and passengers to eat and smoke.

Bus travel between Croatia and the Muslim-Croat Federation of Bosnia-Hercegovina is routine. Two daily buses travel between Sarajevo and Zagreb (417km) and Sarajevo and Split. The Sarajevo-Dubrovnik bus makes one trip each day via Mostar, and buses from Sarajevo go to Germany several times a week. The Republika Srpska is closely connected by bus to Yugoslavia. Buses run every hour between Banja Luka and Belgrade, and a different bus runs from the Serb-held Sarajevo suburb of Lukavica to Belgrade. A daily bus goes between Zagreb and Banja Luka, though you change buses at the border (the other bus will be waiting).

LEAVING BOSNIA-HERCEGOVINA

There is a DM20 departure tax from the Sarajevo airport.

Getting Around

Trains are essentially useless, as they run only from Sarajevo to Zenica and a few other small cities. Trains from Banja Luka have a similarly limited radius within the RS.

Within each entity (the Federation and the RS), Bosnia's bus network is quite comprehensive. Inter-entity travel has become less of a problem since the 1998 introduction of two daily buses between Sarajevo and Banja Luka.

Plenty of rent-a-car places have sprung up, particularly in Sarajevo, Mostar, and Medugorje. However, renting a car does not give you clearance to drive anywhere in Bosnia. License plates are badges of identity. Cars with Sarajevo plates will not be welcome in the Republika Srpska and vice-versa (though the Muslim and Croat-controlled parts of the Federation are compatible). Ask if the rental car agencies use the new common license plates which should facilitate trans-entity travel.

As elsewhere in the Balkans, people drive like maniacs, passing even on sharp curves.

Around the Country

SARAJEVO
☎ 071

Sarajevo, in a valley beside the Miljacka River, is the capital of Bosnia-Hercegovina. Before the war, the city was also an ethnic microcosm of Yugoslavia. For hundreds of years it was where Muslims, Serbs, Croats, Turks, Jews and others peacefully coexisted.

From the mid-15th century until 1878, Turkish governors resided in Sarajevo. The city's name comes from *saraj*, Turkish for 'palace'. Sarajevo is one of the most Oriental cities in Europe, retaining the essence of its rich history in its mosques, markets and the picturesque old Turkish bazaar called Baščaršija. When the Turks finally withdrew, half a century of Austro-Hungarian domination began, culminating in the assassination of Archduke Franz Ferdinand and his wife Sophie by a Serbian nationalist in 1914. In 1984 Sarajevo again attracted world attention by hosting the 14th Winter Olympic Games.

Sarajevo's heritage of six centuries was pounded into rubble by Bosnian Serb artillery during the siege of 1992 to 1995, when Sarajevo's only access to the outside world was via a 1km tunnel under the airport. Over 10,500 Sarajevans died and 50,000 were wounded by Bosnian Serb sniper fire and shelling. The endless new graveyards near Koševo stadium leave a silent record of the terrible years.

Despite the highly visible scars of war, Sarajevo is again bursting with energy. Colourful trams run down the road once called 'Sniper's Alley', innumerable cafés blast pop music into the streets, and locals spend leisurely evenings strolling down the main pedestrian street, Ferhadija. A large international presence made up of government officials and humanitarian aid workers is also altering the face of the city. Large UN jeeps and camouflage SFOR vehicles melt into the rest of the traffic. The energy poured into Bosnia-Hercegovina's recovery has rendered Sarajevo the fastest-changing city in Europe.

Orientation
Surrounded by mountains, Sarajevo is beside the peaceful Miljacka River near the geographic centre of Bosnia-Hercegovina. From the airport 13km to the west, the main road runs through Novo Sarajevo, then past the turn-off to the bus and train stations and into the town centre. Baščaršija is on the east end of town.

Information
The Tourist Information Bureau (☎ 532 606; fax 532 281), ul Zelenih Beretki 22, keeps good tabs on the changes in Sarajevo and can answer most questions about the city. It has a good supply of books and maps and is open weekdays from 8 am to 3 pm and Saturday from 9 am to 2 pm.

Money Most banks will exchange travellers cheques for a hefty commission or poor rates. The Central Profit Banka (☎ 533 582), ul Zelenih Beretki 24 with other branches around town, exchanges travellers cheques for 3% commission (1.5% if you want dinars). Receiving wired money is also possible (1% commission), as are Diner's Club and American Express cash advances (bring personal American Express cheques along). Shed excess kuna at Gospodarska Banka, the Croatian bank on ul Maršala Tita 56.

Post & Communications A post office just behind the eternal flame on Ferhadija sends letters and faxes and sells phonecards. To make a lengthy international call, head to the post office at Obala Kulina Bana 8 (open Monday to Saturday from 8 am to 3 pm; telephones only).

Internet Resources Internet access is available in the University of Sarajevo building on Obala Kulina Bana 7. Go to the top floor and turn right, following the signs to Interlink Computer Centre. The pricing system is odd but thankfully cheap: DM10 for 15 hours. Across the river, the university building on ul Skenderija 70 has computers with free Internet access in room 12.

You can register for an account on the local server (BIHNET) at the post office on Zmaja od Bosne 100, four tram stops past the Holiday Inn. Register between 9 and 10 am at window 16 or 17. It costs DM15 a month plus 1 to 2DM per hour.

Bookshop & Library Šahinpašić, ul Mula Mustafe Bašekije 1 near the eternal flame, sells English-language papers, magazines,

BOSNIA-HERCEGOVINA

SARAJEVO

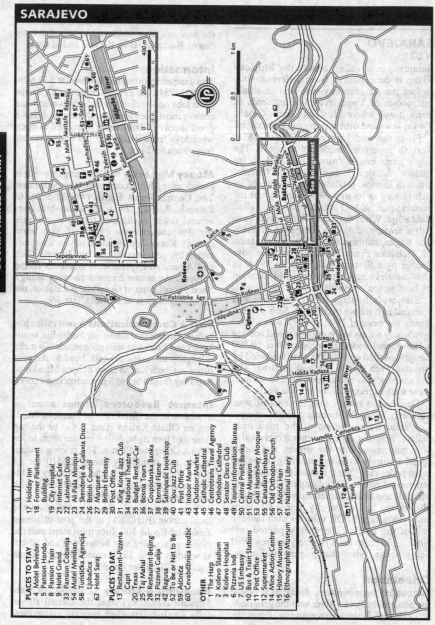

PLACES TO STAY
4 Motel Belveder
5 Pansion Hondo
8 Pansion Train
9 Hotel Grand
33 Pansion Cobanija
54 Motel Meridian
58 Turisticka Agencija Ljubacica
62 Hotel Saraj

PLACES TO EAT
13 Restaurant-Pizzeria Capri
20 Texas
25 Taj Mahal
28 Restaurant Beijing
32 Pizzeria Galija
42 Ragusa
52 To Be or Not to Be
59 Aščinica
60 Čevabdžinica Hodžić

OTHER
1 The Harp
2 Koševo Stadium
3 Koševo Hospital
6 Pizzeria Indi
7 US Embassy
10 Bus & Train Stations
11 Post Office
12 Supermarket
14 Mine Action Centre
15 History Museum
16 Ethnographic Museum
17 Holiday Inn
18 Former Parliament Building
19 City Hospital
21 Internet Cafe
22 Labiwint Disco
23 Ali Paša Mosque
24 Skenderija & Galaxia Disco
26 British Council
27 Marquee
29 British Embassy
30 Post Office
31 King Kong Jazz Club
34 National Theatre
35 Budget Rent-A-Car
36 Bosnia Tours
37 Gospodarska Banka
38 Eternal Flame
39 Šahinpašić bookshop
40 Clou Jazz Club
41 Post Office
43 Indoor Market
44 Outdoor Market
45 Catholic Cathedral
46 Centrotrans Travel Agency
47 Orthodox Cathedral
48 Senator Disco Club
49 Tourist Information Bureau
50 Central Profit Banka
51 City Museum
53 Gazi Husrevbey Mosque
55 Canadian Embassy
56 Old Orthodox Church
57 Morića Han
61 National Library

and cheap Penguin classics. Don't miss the Survival Map (DM10), a striking cartoon-like depiction of wartime Sarajevo, with helpful English-language explanations on the back. The British Council Library (☎ 200 895) is at Obala Kulina Bana 4.

Medical Services Try Koševo Hospital, ul Bolnička 25 (☎ 666 620) or the City Hospital (☎ 664 724), ul Kranjčevića 12. The US embassy can provide a list of private doctors.

Things to See
The cobbled **Baščaršija** (the Turkish Quarter), where bronze artisans ply their trade, is the heart of Sarajevo. This is the only spot in the city where most cafés serve real Turkish coffee in a *džežva*, as opposed to espresso. **Morića Han**, now a café along Sarači, used to be a tavern and stable when Sarajevo was an important crossroads between east and west.

The graceful Austro-Hungarian **National Library** lies on the east end of town along the river at the end of Baščaršija. The building was destroyed by an incendiary shell on 25 August 1992, 100 years after construction began. It has since gotten a new dome courtesy of Austria but is still not open to visitors.

Austrian Archduke Franz Ferdinand and his wife Sophie paused at the National Library (then the town hall) on 28 June, 1914, then rode west along the riverside in an open car to the second bridge. It was here that they were shot, an event which led to WWI. A plaque bearing the footprints of the assassin, Gavrilo Princip, was ripped out of the pavement during the recent war because Princip was a Bosnian Serb. The one-room **City Museum**, where ul Zelenih Beretki meets the river, now stands on 'Princip's corner'.

In the city centre, the **eternal flame** commemorates WWII. Places of worship for four different religions – Catholic, Orthodox, Muslim, and Jewish – lie in close vicinity to one another, as Sarajevans still very proudly point out. These include the large Catholic church on Ferhadija (which has an English-language service on Sunday at noon); the old Orthodox Church on ul Mula Mustafe Bašekija (which predates the yellow and brown Orthodox cathedral); the Gazi-Husrevbey Mosque (1531), built by masons from Dubro-

vnik; and the old Jewish synagogue (now closed) along ul Mula Mustafe Bašekija.

The three-year siege made Sarajevo itself a stunning sight. The road into the city from the airport (now Zmaja od Bosne) was dubbed **'Sniper's Alley'** during the war because Serb snipers in the surrounding hills picked off civilians crossing the road. The bright yellow **Holiday Inn** was the wartime home to international journalists, as the city's only functioning wartime hotel. The side facing Sniper's Alley was heavily damaged, but the hotel has since been given a massive facelift. Across from the Holiday Inn is the **National Museum**, which is closed to the public while it temporarily houses the Bosnia-Hercegovina parliament. A **History Museum** just up the road shows old photographs of Bosnia-Hercegovina and has rotating exhibits, some of which pertain to the recent war.

A **treeline** still rings the city, demarcating the former front line. Residents cut down trees and burned benches for heat during the siege. Watch the pavement for **Sarajevo roses**, which are skeletal hand-like indentations where a shell exploded. Many of these are symbolically filled in with red rubber.

Special Events
In late August, internationally produced films are shown at the annual Sarajevo Film Festival (☎ 668 186; fax 664 547; sff@soros.org.ba). The Winter Festival in February and March features theatre and musical performances.

Places to Stay
Finding a room in Sarajevo is no longer difficult, since hotels and private rooms have sprung up to house visiting international officials. However, prices remain very high, and reservations are wise. Private accommodation is a relative bargain at DM40 to 50 per person, but some rooms may not be near the centre. Wherever you stay, be sure to ask about the water situation, since parts of the city have running water only during certain times of day.

Private Rooms *Bosnia Tours* (☎535 829; fax 202 206/207), ul Maršala Tita 54, near the eternal flame, has plenty of good rooms near the centre for DM40 a person (DM70 for two people). If you don't like the room, they'll gladly show you another. The agency is closed Sunday.

Turistička Agencija Ljubačica (☎/fax 232 109), ul Mula Mustafa Bašekije 65 in Baščaršija, has a handful of rooms near the centre and more rooms further out. Prices are DM30 to 55, depending on location and room quality; you may be able to bargain. If you arrive after 10 pm, call their mobitel (☎ 090 121 813).

Ask at the *Motel Meridian* (☎ 446 177; ☎/fax 446 176), Jaroslava Černija 3 off ul Mula Mustafa Bašekija, about its five private rooms which are pleasanter and much cheaper than the motel itself. The rooms, a 10-minute walk uphill from the cathedral, are all in a spacious, two-storey flat with soft pink walls, a kitchen, and satellite TV (DM63/106 for one or two people).

Pansions The cheapest place in town is the bizarre *Pansion Train* (☎ 200 517), Halida Kajtaza 11, where beds in a stationary train sleeper car cost DM33/40 for a single/double. Besides novelty and price, however, it's a bit cramped, and the showers and toilets are not the cleanest. From the bus station, take the road to Hotel Grand. Turn left at the gas station, and follow the big sign to the pansion.

The cosy *Pansion Hondo*, ul Zaima Šarca 23 (☎ 666 564; ☎/fax 469 375), is a 20-minute walk uphill from the centre. Rooms cost DM80/120 a single/double, with breakfast included. Head straight up ul Pehlivanuša, behind the cathedral. It will turn into ul Zaima Šarca.

Pansion Čobanija (☎ 441 749; ☎/fax 203 937), ul Čobanija 29, just past Pizzeria Galija on the south side of the river, has rooms with nice marbled private baths, cable TV, and a fax machine available for guests' use. Request an upstairs room, and enjoy proximity to the large sitting room. Prices are DM80/120 for a single/double.

Hotels & Motels At DM150 to 300 a night, hotels are not cost-effective. *Hotel Saraj* (☎ 472 691; fax 447 703), ul Nevjestina 5, is the white building visible on the hill behind the National Library. Singles/doubles

begin at DM150/200. Rooms with a view of Sarajevo are more expensive, but all rooms are pleasant, with satellite TV and breakfast included. Another quality option is *Hotel Grand* (☎ 205 444; fax 204 745), on ul Muhameda ef Pandže 7 behind the train station, which has singles/doubles with breakfast for DM182/284.

The aqua-green *Motel Belveder* (☎ 664 877; fax 206 470), on ul Višnjik 2 near Koševo hospital, has plain but comfortable rooms with satellite TV, phone, and shower for DM120/150 a single/double, including breakfast. Call for airport pick-ups.

Places to Eat

Sarajevo's restaurants are the domain of internationals, since Bosnians socialise over coffee and eat at home. Most restaurant menus are in English, and main meals usually cost DM10 to 15.

Ragusa, Ferhadija 10b, serves tasty Bosnian cuisine to diners relaxing at wood tables. Be sure to wash down dinner with a traditional shot of *rakija*. *To Be or Not to Be*, Čizmedžiluk 5 in Baščaršija, has deep, colourful salads in a candlelit setting. Vegetarians can opt for an omelette or spaghetti, while others can enjoy the classic Bosnian steaks. A short way beyond the city centre in Grbavica, the upmarket *Restaurant-Pizzeria Capri*, ul Hamdije Čemerlić 45, has delicious main meals for slightly higher prices (DM20 to 30). Try the salmon, or go for the cheaper pasta and pizza.

Sarajevo's roster of new ethnic restaurants is crowned by *Restaurant Beijing*, ul Maršala Tita 38, a delicious place which actually dares to offer tofu. Main meals are DM13 to 20. Spicy Indian dishes at *Taj Mahal*, ul Hamdije Kreševljakovića 6, are slightly less expensive. Or fill up on hearty burritos at *Texas*, ul Vladmira Perića 4 near the Internet Café.

The most popular pizza spots include *Pizzeria Galija*, ul Čobanija 20 across the river, and *Pizzeria Indi*, at the corner of ul Gabelina and ul Koševo.

For a quick meal, čevapi, burek, and 'Fast Food' joints are ubiquitous, but *Ćevabdžinica Hodžić*, ul Bravadžiluk 34 near the National Library, is a čevapi star. It's just up the street from *Aščinican*, ul Bravadžiluk 28, where you can choose what you want from the array of salads, vegetables and meats.

Self-Catering Sarajevo's only sizeable supermarket is a bright, unmistakable yellow building four tram stops beyond the Holiday Inn along Zmaja od Bosne. A year-round outdoor market, behind the cathedral on ul Mule Mustafa Bašekija, has a good selection of fruits and vegetables. Its indoor counterpart, with dairy products and meats, is across the street in the sandy-coloured building.

Entertainment

Theatre The tourist office keeps a monthly list of concerts, ballets, and performances at the National Theatre on ul Zelenih Beretki, the Sarajevo War Theatre (in the same building as Ragusa restaurant), and Kamerni Theater, upstairs on ul Maršala Tita 56.

Discos The king of Sarajevo's disco world is *Senator*, on ul Strossmayerova near the cathedral (open Thursday to Saturday from 10pm; DM10 cover). Other options are *Labirint*, ul Jezero 1, not far from the US Embassy (closed Monday; DM5 cover), and *Galaxia*, across the river in the Skenderija complex (no cover).

Pubs & Jazz Clubs Sarajevo's best-known bar is unquestionably the *Internet Café*, ul Maršala Tita 5, near the intersection with ul Alipašina. Although Internet access is a myth, the café has live music some weekends and Czech Budweiser on tap, which can be consumed for half-price at happy hour (5 to 7 pm). *The Harp*, on ul Patriotske lige, is an Irish bar with Guinness and other native brews on tap. Head up ul Koševo, which turns into ul Patriotske lige bb. The pub is at the triangular intersection, a 25-minute walk from the centre. The crowded *Marquee*, Obala Kulina Bana 5, plays rock music.

For occasional live jazz, try *Clou*, ul Mula Mustafe Bašekija 5 (open from 6 pm), and *King Kong*, ul Hamdije Kreševljakovića 17.

Cinema Many cinemas play American movies with subtitles. *Oslobođendje,* Sarajevo's daily paper, has daily cinema listings under the 'Kina' column.

Things to Buy

Metalworking craft shops line ul Kazandžiluk, at the end of Baščaršija. Turkish coffee sets and snazzy plates aside, the trendiest souvenirs are engraved shell cases (that's shell as in cartridge). Small ones sell for around DM10. Bargaining is possible, indeed necessary, in these shops.

Getting There & Away

Bus Two buses a day run to Sarajevo from Zagreb, and two from Split and one from Dubrovnik. Two daily buses also go to and from Banja Luka. Buses run from the Serb-controlled Sarajevo suburb of Lukavica to various parts of the RS and Belgrade. Explain to a taxi driver that you want to go to the bus station in Lukavica, and he will take you to a spot on the RS border near the airport, where you can switch cabs or walk 150m to the bus station and buy a ticket.

Getting Around

An efficient but often crowded tram network runs east-west between Baščaršija and Illidža. Tram 4 from Baščaršija peels off at the bus station; tram 1 goes between the bus station to Illidža. Buy tickets (DM1) at kiosks near tram stations. Buses and trolleybuses also cost DM1 (punch your ticket on board); purchase bus tickets from the driver.

To/From the Airport One under-utilised bus goes sporadically to and from the airport, about 13km west of the city centre. Call ☎ 447 955 for departure times or ask at the tourist office. A taxi should cost about DM15.

Taxi Sarajevo's ubiquitous taxis all have meters that begin at DM2 and cost DM1 per kilometre. Call ☎ 970 for Radio Taxi.

Car Budget (☎/fax 206 640), ul Branilaca Sarajeva 21, also has an office at the airport (☎ 463 598); Diner's Club and American Express cards are accepted. ASA Rent has offices at ul Branilaca Sarajeva 20 (☎/fax 445 209/210) and at the airport (☎ 463 598).

AROUND SARAJEVO

Twenty-five kilometres south-east of Sarajevo, the deserted slopes of **Mount Jahorina**, the site of the 1984 Winter Olympics, still offer some of the best skiing in Europe at extremely cheap prices. Unfortunately, Jahorina lies in Bosnian Serb territory just above the politically hardline town of Pale, so getting there can be problematic. The British-based firm Harlequin Leisure (☎ 445 076; in the UK 0044-370-694 069; harlequin–sport@ hotmail.com) knows the ropes and ferries travellers up to Jahorina in sturdy Land Rovers. It can also arrange accommodation (DM30 to 70 per night) and ski rental (DM15 to 25; lift tickets DM10; lessons DM15). Skiing on Jahorina is safe from mines.

MOSTAR
☎ 088

Mostar, the main city in Hercegovina, is a beautiful medieval town set in the valley of the aqua-green Neretva River. Its name derives from the 16th-century Turkish bridge which used to arc over the river; *mostari* means keepers of the bridge. Sadly, the town was the scene of intense Muslim-Croat fighting during the recent war, which left many buildings destroyed or scarred. Even the bridge was destroyed by Croat shelling in November 1993. Once divided only by the Neretva River, Mostar is now segregated into Muslim and Croat sectors. Nonetheless, visitors are slowly drifting back to enjoy the old medieval buildings, cobbled streets, and Turkish souvenir shops that give Mostar its charm.

Orientation
Mostar is a divided city. Though there are no physical barriers, Croats live on the west side of the Neretva River and Muslims on the east (though Muslims also control a small strip on the river's west bank).

Information
Tourist Office Atlas Travel Agency (☎/fax 318 771), in the same building as Hotel Ero, has useful suggestions and a rough map of the west side. The tourist agency on the east side beside the bus station speaks no English and has sparse information.

Money Prices on the east side are in Bosnian dinars or Deutschmarks, and prices on the west side are in kuna (though Deutschmarks

are accepted). Hrvatska Banka, adjacent to Hotel Ero, changes travellers cheques to any currency except dinars for 1.5% commission.

Post & Communications The large, modern post office on the west side, around the corner from Hotel Ero, is the only place in Bosnia for poste restante mail (held for one month; pick-up is at window 12). Address mail to Name, Poste Restante, 88000 Mostar (Zapadni), Bosnia-Hercegovina.

Inquire at the new Training Centre (Centar za Obuku; ☎ 551 127), ul Oneščukova 24 about 60m west of Stari Most, about public Internet access.

Things to See
Stari Most (old bridge) is still the heart of the old town, though it is now replaced by a swinging metal bridge. The small **Crooked Bridge**, built a few years before Stari Most and possibly used as a model, spans a Neretva tributary nearby.

The cobbled old town itself, called **Kujundžiluk**, extends on both sides of Stari Most. It is still pleasantly awash with small shops selling Turkish-style souvenirs. Along the east side, the most famous mosque in Mostar is the **Karadžozbeg Mosque** (1557). The top of its minaret was blown off in the recent war. Not far away, the 350-year-old **Turkish House**, on ul Biščevića, has colourful rugs and furniture in old Turkish style.

The dramatic **front line**, which now essentially divides the town between Muslims and Croats, runs along the street behind Hotel Ero, then jogs one street west to the main boulevard.

Places to Stay
Mostar's three hotels are expensive, but a few pleasant pansions offer relief. All pansion rooms have multiple beds. Reserve a week in advance, because groups occasionally fill the space. The 12-bed *Pansion Zlatni Liljan* (☎ 551 353), ul Sehovina 6, costs DM20, with breakfast DM25. Past the Pavarotti Music Centre, swing left and follow the cobblestone road that starts by the mosque. The 10-bed *Vila Ossa* (☎ 578 322), Gojka Vokovića 40, is on the other side of the river. The price for one/two people is DM30/40, with breakfast DM35/50. *Pansion Ćorić* (☎ 219 560; fax 219 559), ul Matije Gupca

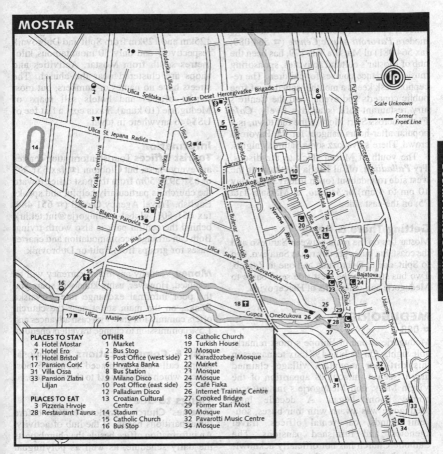

MOSTAR

PLACES TO STAY
4 Hotel Mostar
7 Hotel Ero
11 Hotel Bristol
17 Pansion Corić
31 Villa Ossa
33 Pansion Zlatni
   Liljan

PLACES TO EAT
3 Pizzeria Hrvoje
28 Restaurant Taurus

OTHER
1 Market
2 Bus Stop
5 Post Office (west side)
6 Hrvatska Banka
8 Bus Station
9 Milano Disco
10 Post Office (east side)
12 Palladium Disco
13 Croatian Cultural
   Centre
14 Stadium
15 Catholic Church
16 Bus Stop

18 Catholic Church
19 Turkish House
20 Mosque
21 Karadžozbeg Mosque
22 Market
23 Mosque
24 Mosque
25 Café Fiaka
26 Internet Training Centre
27 Crooked Bridge
29 Former Stari Most
30 Mosque
32 Pavarotti Music Centre
34 Mosque

Scale Unknown

Former
Front Line

125A, is about a 20-minute walk directly west of Stari Most. Beds cost DM50 including breakfast, and the proprietors speak German but not English.

Hotel Ero (☎ 317 166/167; fax 314 394), on ul Ante Starčevića directly across the river from the bus station, has polished rooms with porches for DM72/124 for a single/double (American Express cards accepted). The newly reopened *Hotel Bristol* (☎ 550 082/083/084; fax 550 081), on ul Mostarskog Bataljona on the river's west bank, has singles/doubles for DM81.5/177. *Hotel Mostar*, Kneza Domagoja

bb (☎ 322 679; fax 315 693), has similar prices but is the most cramped of the lot.

Places to Eat

Ćevapi spots are ubiquitous, and restaurants with divine views of the river cluster along the western riverbank near Stari Most. Tables on a covered porch at *Restaurant Taurus* offer a lovely view of Crooked Bridge; the food is hearty and traditional.

For a big salad or good pizza, try *Restaurant-Pizzeria Hrvoje*, Kralja Tomislava (☎ 321 385), in west Mostar.

Entertainment

Since it opened in December 1997, the large modern *Pavarotti Music Centre* (☎ 564 080; fax 564 081) ul Maršala Tita 179, has been the hub of Mostar's cultural activities, sponsoring music and dance courses for children. The reception desk keeps a monthly schedule of free public concerts and events, and the Centre's airy restaurant-café is always lively. *Café Fiaka*, across Stari Most in the old town, is a popular after-hours hangout for the Pavarotti crowd. There's live jazz some Saturday nights.

The youth of Mostar flock to the discos. Try *Palladium*, off ul Kralja Tvrtka near the west side roundabout (open Friday to Sunday 10 pm to 4 am) or *Milano*, ul Maršala Tita 75, on the east side.

Getting There & Away

Mostar lies on the route between Sarajevo and the coast. Six buses per day run to Sarajevo, two to Split, one to Dubrovnik, and one to Zagreb. Two bus stops on the west side send buses to Međugorje and other parts of Hercegovina.

MEĐUGORJE
☎ 088

Međugorje is one of Europe's most remarkable sights. On 24 June 1981 six teenagers in this dirt-poor mountain village claimed they'd seen a miraculous apparition of the Virgin Mary, and Međugorje's instant economic boom began. A decade later Međugorje was awash with tour buses, souvenir stands, car rental offices, travel agencies, and furnished pansions. The Catholic Church has not officially acknowledged the apparitions (the first in Europe since those of Lourdes, France, in 1858 and Fatima, Portugal, in 1917), but 'religious tourism' has been developed as if this were a beach resort.

After a wartime hiatus, the busloads of package pilgrims are returning with renewed fervour. Tourist facilities are fully intact, since the front line did not reach Međugorje – some locals attribute this to divine protection. Crowds are especially heavy around Easter, the anniversary of the first apparition (June 24), the Assumption of the Virgin (15 August) and the Nativity of the Virgin (8 September).

Orientation

Međugorje lies in the heart of Hercegovina, 125km and 129km from Split and Dubrovnik respectively and only 30 mountainous kilometres south from Mostar. Activities and shops are clustered near the church. The streets have no names or numbers, but most tourist offices and hotels sell maps of Međugorje (10 kuna). Taxis cost a flat fee of US$4 to anywhere in town.

Information

Tourist Offices Tourist information centres are everywhere, but Globtour (☎/fax 651 393 or 651 593), 50m from the post office toward the church, is particularly helpful and speaks English. Travel Agency Global (☎ 651 489; fax 651 501; global-medjugorje@int.tel.hr), behind the central park is also worth trying. Both can arrange accommodation and charter buses for groups from Split or Dubrovnik.

Money Virtually any major currency will be accepted. However, using kuna will spare you the poor informal exchange rate. Hrvatska Banka, on the main street near the church, offers commission-free Visa cash advances and 1.5% commission to change travellers cheques.

Post & Communications International phone calls can be placed from the post office, which is right next to the bus stop.

Things to See

St James' Church, completed in 1969 before the apparitions began, is the hub of activity. An information office beside the church posts the daily schedule, as well as polylingual printouts of the Virgin's latest message.

Apparition Hill, where the Virgin was first spotted on 24 June 1981, is near the hamlet Podbrdo south-west of town. A blue cross marks the place where the Virgin was supposedly seen with a cross in the background, conveying a message of peace. It is a place for silence and prayer. To reach Apparition Hill, take the road curving left (east) from the centre of town, and follow the signs to Podbrdo (about 3km).

Cross Mountain (Mt. Križevac) lies about 1.5km south-west of town. The 45-minute hike to the top leads to a white cross planted there in 1934 to commemorate the

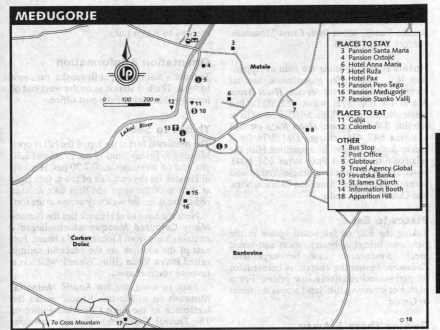

MEĐUGORJE

PLACES TO STAY
3 Pansion Santa Maria
4 Pansion Ostojić
6 Hotel Anna Maria
7 Hotel Ruža
8 Hotel Pax
15 Pansion Pero Šego
16 Pansion Međugorje
17 Pansion Stanko Valilj

PLACES TO EAT
11 Galija
12 Colombo

OTHER
1 Bus Stop
2 Post Office
5 Globtour
9 Travel Agency Global
10 Hrvatska Banka
13 St James Church
14 Information Booth
18 Apparition Hill

1900th anniversary of Christ's death. Pilgrims stop to say the rosary at crosses along the trail. Wear sturdy shoes, as the path is extremely rocky. Candles are forbidden due to fire danger. After the hike, knock on the door of Pansion Stanko Vasilj, 300m from the base of Cross Mountain, and relax with a cool glass (DM1) of the town's best home-made wine.

Places to Stay

With 17,000 rooms, Međugorje has more space than the rest of Bosnia combined. Reduced tourism means that accommodation is easy to find, except around major holidays. Larger pansions and hotels can fill unpredictably with large tour groups, so book in advance. Most pansion rooms look the same, though rooms around the church are the most expensive. Friendly proprietors usually offer the choice of bed and breakfast, half-board, and full-board. Home-made meals are often rounded out with a bottle of *domaći vino*

(home-made wine). Tourist offices can also arrange accommodation, but this is more expensive than contacting the pansion directly. Tour groups can find reduced rates.

The city's few hotels are blander and more expensive than the pansions, and the rooms are not much better.

Pansions The 49-bed *Pansion Ostojić* (☎ 651 562; fax 651 095), not far from the post office, has rooms for DM20/35/45 (breakfast/half-board/full-board). Inquire in the Café Santa Fe, just in front of the pansion.

About 100m behind Ostojić, the white-washed *Pansion Santa Maria* (☎ 651 523; fax 651 723) charges DM26.5/36.5/45.5 for bed and breakfast/half-board/full-board. Reserve early, as it is often filled with groups.

The road to Cross Mountain yields some gems. The *Pansion Pero Šego* costs DM21.5/31.5 for bed and breakfast/half-board. Further on, the homy 25-bed Pansion Međugorje (☎ 651 315; fax 651 452), is a steal at DM15/30/45 a person for bed and breakfast/half-board/full-board. *Pansion Stanko Vasilj*, 300m from Cross Mountain, charges DM25/35/45.

Hotels Hotels lie along the road to Apparition Hill. Most offer group rates, and all include breakfast in the service. *Hotel Anna Maria* (☎ 651 512; ☎/fax 651 023), has singles/doubles for DM66.5/103. Rooms have satellite TV and phone. *Hotel Ruža* (☎ 643 118; fax 647 431) charges DM38/76 for a single/double. Closest to Apparition Hill, the relatively ritzy Hotel Pax (☎/fax 651 604), costs DM61.5/130 for a single/double and accepts MasterCard, American Express, Visa, and Diner's Club cards.

Places to Eat

Taking the half or full-board option at the pansions brings a hearty, meat-and-bread meal. Restaurants can be expensive. *Colombo*, beside the church, is beloved for its pizzas and relatively low prices. For a platter of steaming fish, head across the street to *Galija*.

Getting There & Away

Most visitors come to Međugorje from Croatia. Two buses run daily from Split (3½ hours), one from Dubrovnik (3 hours), and one from Zagreb (9 hours). Buses also go twice a week to and from Germany. Many international bus lines are run by Globtour; ask there for a schedule. A handful of buses run daily between Međugorje and Mostar. There's no posted schedule, so inquire at the post office about times.

TRAVNIK

☎ 072

Tucked into a narrow valley only 90km north-west of Sarajevo, Travnik served as the seat of Turkish viziers who ruled Bosnia from 1699 to 1851. The town grew into a diplomatic crossroads, and earned fame more recently as the birthplace of Bosnia's best-known writer Ivo Andrić.

Though fighting between Muslims and Croats went on in the surrounding hills, it mostly spared the town itself. With its lovely medieval castle and pristine natural springs, the town, in Muslim hands today, is well worth a day trip from Sarajevo or a stop on the way to Banja Luka.

Orientation & Information

Travnik's main street, ul Bosanska, runs east to west. The bus station is on the west end of town, within sight of the post office.

Things to See

The **medieval fort** at the top of the hill is open Monday to Friday from 11 am to around 3.30 pm, and on weekends until 7.30 pm. Head up ul Hendek on the east side of town, turn right at the top of the steps and then take another right; you'll see the walkway across to the fort.

Near the base of ul Hendek lies the famous **Many-Coloured Mosque** which allegedly contains hairs from Mohammed's beard. Just east of the mosque are the peaceful springs called **Plava Voda** (Blue Water), which is a favorite summer spot.

Back in town, the **Ivo Andrić Memorial Museum** on ul Mustafa Kundić marks the birthplace of the famed Bosnian author of *The Travnik Chronicles*. The museum contains Andrić texts in many languages, photographs of the 1961 Nobel Prize ceremonies, and a model 19th-century bedroom. Don't be fooled, though: the museum was reconstructed in 1974 and is not the original birth house. Ask at Restaurant Divan downstairs for someone with the key.

Places to Stay & Eat

The *Hotel Orient* (☎/fax 814 888), ul Bosanska 29, is not far from the bus station. Singles and doubles cost DM82/104. It's best to book in advance.

The much nicer *Hotel Slon* (☎/fax 811 008), ul Fatmić 11, hosted Princess Diana shortly before her death. The spacious, clean rooms have satellite TV. Singles/doubles cost DM90/120. The reception may also have ideas about private rooms.

The best food in town is at *Restaurant Divan*, on ul Mustafa Kundić, directly below the Ivo Andrić museum. Coming from the bus station, turn left on ul Zenjak and go one block. Patio seating is available in summer.

Getting There & Away
Buses go almost hourly to Sarajevo and two per day go to Banja Luka.

BANJA LUKA
☎ 078 (☎ 058 from Sarajevo)
This important crossroads on the Vrbas River in north-western Bosnia is now known to the world as the capital of the Republika Srpska. Banja Luka was never much of a tourist centre and in 1993 local Serbs made sure it never would be by blowing up all 16 of the city's mosques, complementing the damage previously done by WWII bombings and a 1969 earthquake. While not otherwise damaged during the recent war, the city is economically depressed and flooded with Serb refugees from the Bosnian Federation and the Croatian Krajina. Even as the RS leadership in Banja Luka opens slowly to the west, the city's transportation, banking, and communication networks remain closely tied to Belgrade.

Orientation
Banja Luka lies beside the river Vrbas in the north-west Bosnia-Hercegovina, only 184km from Zagreb, 235km from Sarajevo, and 316km from Belgrade. Many of Banja Luka's streets, including the main street Kralja Petra, have been renamed since the war and locals may not recognise the new names.

Information
Tourist Office The surprisingly helpful and well-equipped Turistički Savez (☎/fax 12 323; ☎ 18 022) is at ul Kralja Petra 175. It sells maps of Banja Luka and can give advice; inquire about new accommodation options. Some English is spoken.

Money Commission-free visa cash advances into Serbian dinars are available at Vojvodjanska Banka, ul Kralja Petra 87. Bank Kristal, on Franje Jukića 4 near the town hall, will change travellers cheques to Deutschmarks or dinars (1 to 1.5% commission).

Post & Communications The main post office, ul Kralja Petra 93, has numerous telephone booths and sells phonecards. Getting through to Sarajevo is extremely difficult.

Things to See
The large 16th-century **fort** along the Vrbas river is an interesting place to explore. Note the overgrown amphitheatre, whose benches were burned for fuel during the war.

War is the main theme of Banja Luka's sights. Atop the Šehitluci hill south-east of town stands a huge white stone **WWII memorial**. This solitary and impressive slab affords a great view of the city.

In the city centre is the **presidential palace**, which has been the seat of government since January 1998. It faces the town hall. If you come across a bare patch of land in Banja Luka, most likely it used to be one of the city's 16 destroyed mosques. The most famous of these was **Ferhadija** (1580), built with the ransom money for an Austrian count. Ferhadija used to be across ul Kralja Petra from the tourist office.

Places to Stay
The 200-room *Hotel Bosna* (☎ 41 355 or 31 418; fax 44 536) is situated smack in the centre of town. Functional rooms, all with phone, cable TV, and bath tubs (a novelty in these parts), go for DM120/180 a single/double; breakfast is included. Reserve a week in advance, as this hotel is residually full of international officials. *Hotel Slavija*, ul Kralja Petra 85, has shabby rooms for DM40/50 a single/double.

Places to Eat
Restaurant Tropik Klub is tucked inside the castle walls in the former prison (*kazamat*). It serves excellent traditional food (mains DM11 to 13) and has outdoor seating overlooking the Vrbas river in summer. The best place for fish is *Alas,* Braće Mažar 47, off the transit road between Zagreb and Sarajevo. *Lanaco* is a popular pizza joint, with live bands on weekends. Follow the signs off ul Kralja Petra into Stojanovića Park.

Getting There & Away
Banja Luka airport, 35km north of the city, has flights only to Belgrade on JAT. The train and bus stations lie roughly 3km north of the town centre; a taxi should cost DM3.5. Buses (information ☎ 45 355) run twice a day to Zagreb and Sarajevo, and no less than 23 times to Belgrade (seven hours).

Bulgaria (България)

Bulgaria comes as a pleasant surprise. The landscape is green and lush (not dry and arid as in Greece), and because Bulgaria doesn't get nearly as many Western tourists as it deserves, those who do come are assured of a warm welcome. Bulgarians still manage to be helpful and friendly despite the economic difficulties thrust upon them by a decade of upheaval. Bulgaria is a safe country, there's plenty to see and do, and prices are very reasonable. The Rila, Pirin and Rodopi mountains and the Black Sea coast are great natural attractions. Transport, public services, food, museums, monuments, climate, beaches – everything is good.

Cyrillic script and Turkish mosques are constant reminders that Bulgaria has one foot firmly in the east. Bulgaria has been liberated by Russia twice (in 1878 and 1944) and this close historical relationship made it one of the Soviet Union's most dependable allies.

Politically and socially, Bulgaria has been in more strife than most other Eastern European nations. The United Democratic Forces, a centre-right party under popular president Petâr Stoyanov is back in power and is trying to put an end to the corruption and inertia that marked the short-lived re-emergence of the communists (renamed the Socialist Party) that led the country into virtual financial ruin in late 1996 and early 1997.

Individual tourism is much easier now with visas no longer being required for most Europeans and Americans. A blossoming of private hotels, restaurants and tourism services have meant that travellers have a better choice than before. Bureaucracy may sometimes be frustrating, but most Bulgarians will go out of their way to smooth the path for travellers.

Now is a good time to sample one of Europe's least-known destinations. It is a good choice for budget travellers whether you are seeking pristine hiking trails, historic towns and churches or sunny, sandy beaches.

AT A GLANCE

Capital	Sofia
Population	8.3 million
Area	110,912 sq km
Official Language	Bulgarian
Currency	1 lev (Lv) = 100 stotinki
GDP	US$40 billion (1996)
Time	GMT/UTC+0200

Facts about Bulgaria

HISTORY

In antiquity, Bulgaria, the land of Orpheus and Spartacus, belonged to the Kingdom of Macedonia and the inhabitants were Thracians. By 46 BC, the Romans had conquered the whole peninsula, which they divided into Moesia Inferior, north of the Stara Planina (Balkan Mountains), and Thrace to the south.

Slavic tribes arrived in the mid-6th century and absorbed the Thraco-Illyrian population.

BULGARIA

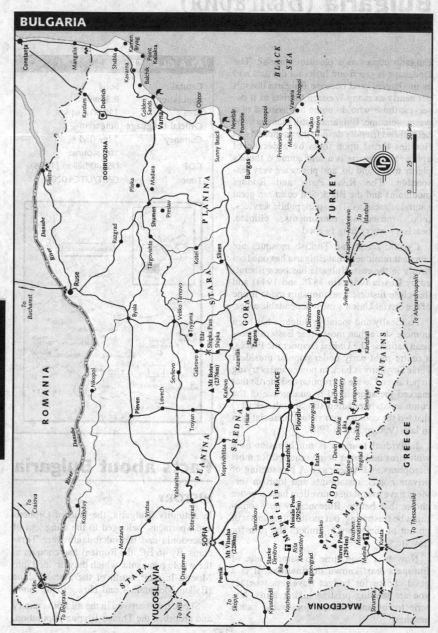

BULGARIA

The Slavs were peaceful farmers organised in democratic local communities.

In 679 the Bulgars or 'Proto-Bulgarians', a fierce Turkic tribe ruled by khans (chiefs) and boyars (nobles), crossed the Danube River after a long migration that had brought them to Europe from their homelands between the Ural Mountains and the Volga. In 681 at Pliska in Moesia, Khan Asparoukh founded the First Bulgarian Empire (681-1018), the first Slavic state in history. In 1981, the 1300th anniversary of this foundation was passionately celebrated. The kingdom expanded south at the expense of Byzantium and in the 9th century extended into Macedonia. The Bulgars were eventually assimilated by the more numerous Slavs and adopted their language and way of life.

In 865 a Byzantine monk frightened Tsar Boris I into accepting Orthodox Christianity by painting a picture of hell on the palace walls, and in 870 the Bulgarian church became independent with its own patriarch. The kingdom attained its greatest power under Tsar Simeon (893-927), who moved the capital to Preslav and extended the empire as far west as the Adriatic. Even the Serbs were brought under his rule.

The literary schools of Preslav and Ohrid were the first in Europe to create a written literature in a language other than Hebrew, Latin or Greek. During this period Kliment of Ohrid, a disciple of Sts Cyril and Methodius (two brothers from Thessaloniki), established the first Slavic university.

However, Simeon's attempts to gain the Byzantine crown for himself weakened the country, as did internal conflicts after his death. Serbia broke away in 933 and Byzantium took back eastern Bulgaria in 972. Tsar Samuel (980-1014) tried to reverse these losses but was defeated in 1014. After the Battle of Belasitsa in 1014, the Byzantine emperor Basil II had the eyes of 15,000 Bulgarian soldiers put out and it is said that Samuel died of a broken heart. Bulgaria passed to Byzantine rule four years later.

In 1185, two brothers named Asen and Peter led a general uprising against Byzantium and the Second Bulgarian Empire (1185-1396) was founded under the Asen dynasty, with Veliko Târnovo as capital. Tsar Ivan Asen II (1218-41) extended his control to all of Thrace, Macedonia and Albania but after Ivan's death in 1241, the power of the monarchy again declined. Tatars struck from the north and the Serbs took Macedonia.

Ottoman Rule

Turkish incursions began in 1340 and by 1371 the Bulgarian tsar Ivan Shishman had become a vassal of the sultan Murad I. In 1389 the Turks defeated the Serbs at the Battle of Kosovo and in 1393 they captured Veliko Târnovo. The last Bulgarian stronghold, Vidin, fell in 1396 and five centuries of Ottoman rule began.

The Turkish governor general resided at Sofia and Turkish colonists settled on the plains, forcing the Bulgarians into the mountains and less favourable areas. Although subjected to heavy taxation, no systematic attempt was made to convert the Bulgarians to Islam or to eradicate their language and customs. Bulgarian Christianity survived in isolated monasteries such as Rila, Troyan and Bachkovo, and folklore served as a bridge between the 14th-century Bulgaro-Byzantine culture and 19th-century romanticism. On a local level, the Bulgarians were self-governing and their economy remained largely agrarian. The towns became centres for Turkish traders and artisans, and during the 16th and 17th centuries Ottoman rule was as enlightened as that of the European dynasties.

As Turkish power weakened in the 18th century, the Bulgarians suffered the burden of unsuccessful Turkish wars against the Austrians and Russians in the form of rising taxes and inflation. English manufactured goods flooded the country, destroying the traditional textile, leather and iron industries. The Crimean War (1853-56), in which Britain and France sided with Turkey against Russia, delayed Bulgarian independence. The Turkish governor Midhat Pasha attempted to use this breathing space to introduce reforms aimed at assimilating the Bulgarians, but it was too late.

In the early 19th century, popular customs and folklore blossomed in the National Revival of Bulgarian culture (vâzrazhdane). Schools were opened and books printed in the Bulgarian language for the first time. A struggle against Phanariote Greek domination of the Orthodox church began in 1860

BULGARIA

when the supremacy of the Constantinople Patriarchate was rejected. Official Turkish recognition of an autonomous church in 1870 was a crucial step towards independence.

Underground leaders such as Hristo Botev, Lyuben Karavelov and Vasil Levski had been preparing a revolution for years when the revolt against the Turks broke out prematurely at Koprivshtitsa in April 1876. The Turks suppressed the uprising with unprecedented brutality, spreading tales of 'Bulgarian atrocities' throughout Europe. About 15,000 Bulgarians were massacred at Plovdiv and 58 villages were destroyed. The story goes that Pazardzhik was saved by a daring clerk who moved one comma in an official order, turning 'burn the town, not spare it' into 'burn the town not, spare it' (which is slightly ungrammatical in English but not so in the original language).

These events led Serbia to declare war on Turkey, and in April 1877 it was joined by Russia and Romania. Decisive battles were fought at Pleven and Shipka. Russia suffered 200,000 casualties in the conflict. With the Russian army advancing to within 50km of Istanbul, Turkey ceded 60% of the Balkan Peninsula to Bulgaria in the Treaty of San Stefano. The modern history of Bulgaria dates from this 1878 liberation.

Fearing the creation of a powerful Russian satellite in the Balkans, the Western powers reversed these gains at the Congress of Berlin, which made southern Bulgaria an 'autonomous province', again nominally subject to the Turkish sultan, while Macedonia was to remain part of the Ottoman Empire. Northern Bulgaria adopted a liberal constitution in 1879, but this was suspended two years later by Prince Aleksander of Battenberg, a German aristocrat whom the Bulgarians had elected as their prince. In 1885, southern Bulgaria (called 'Eastern Roumelia') was annexed to the new state, which had been created in 1878, and complete independence from Turkey was declared on 22 September 1908.

Balkan Wars

All three Balkan states – Bulgaria, Serbia and Greece – coveted Macedonia, which was still in Turkish hands, and the First Balkan War broke out in 1912. Turkey was quickly defeated but the three states could not agree on how

to divide the spoils. On 29 June 1913, the Bulgarian army suddenly attacked its Serbian and Greek allies, probably on orders from the Bulgarian king Ferdinand (who ruled from 1908 to 1918). The Second Balkan War soon resulted in Bulgaria's defeat by these countries together with Romania. Macedonia was divided between Serbia and Greece, and Romania took southern Dobrudzha from Bulgaria.

Bulgarian disenchantment with the loss of Macedonia, and the pro-German sympathies of the king, led Bulgaria to side with the Central Powers (Germany, Austria-Hungary and Turkey) against Serbia and Russia in WWI. There was widespread opposition to this policy within Bulgaria, and in September 1918 a mutiny among the troops led to the abdication of King Ferdinand and an armistice. Bulgaria lost additional territory to Greece and Serbia.

Elections in 1920 brought to office the anti-war leader Aleksander Stamboliyski, whose government passed an agrarian reform bill dividing the large estates. However, there were serious problems with Macedonian refugees in Bulgaria and continuing terrorist activities within Macedonia itself. Stamboliyski was killed during a right-wing coup in June 1923 and an armed uprising by agrarians and communists in September was suppressed. Thousands were killed in the ensuing reactionary terror. Georgi Dimitrov, the communist leader, managed a narrow escape to Russia.

An amnesty in 1926 restored a degree of normality to the country and the League of Nations provided financial aid to resettle the Macedonian refugees. The 1930s world economic crisis led to an authoritarian trend across Eastern Europe and in 1935 Tsar Boris III took personal control of Bulgaria.

WWII

On 24 January 1937, Bulgaria signed a treaty of 'inviolable peace and sincere and perpetual friendship' with Yugoslavia. However, Bulgarian claims to Macedonia again led the country to side with Germany. In September 1940, Romania was forced to return southern Dobrudzha to Bulgaria on orders from Hitler, and in 1941 Bulgaria joined the Nazi invasion of Yugoslavia. Fearing a popular uprising, however, Tsar Boris rejected German demands to declare war on the USSR. In 1942, an underground Fatherland Front made up of all opposition groups, including the communists, was formed to resist the pro-German government. Tsar Boris died mysteriously in August 1943 and a Council of Regency was set up to govern until his six-year-old son, Prince Simeon, came of age. The Front planned an armed uprising for 2 September 1944.

In August 1944, with the Soviet army advancing across Romania, Bulgaria declared itself neutral and disarmed the German troops present. The USSR insisted that Bulgaria declare war on Germany, whereupon Soviet soldiers entered Bulgaria unopposed and Fatherland Front partisans took Sofia on 9 September 1944. The monarchy was overthrown by the communists, led by Todor Zhivkov. After this, the Bulgarian army fought alongside the Soviet army until the war's end.

Post WWII

After a referendum in 1946, Bulgaria was proclaimed a republic and on 27 October 1946, Georgi Dimitrov was elected prime minister. Peace treaties were signed in 1947 and all Soviet troops left the country. In 1954, all outstanding disputes with Greece were settled and in 1955 Bulgaria was admitted to the United Nations (UN). In the 1980s, Bulgaria joined Greece in calls for a Balkan nuclear-free zone, but relations with Turkey remained strained.

Beginning in the late 1940s, industrialisation and the collectivisation of agriculture were carried out. Under Todor Zhivkov, Bulgaria's leader from 1954 to 1989, the country became one of the most prosperous in Eastern Europe. Within the framework of central planning, managers were allowed some flexibility and workers were given incentives to exceed their norms. Private-plot farming was allowed during the workers' spare time.

By late 1989, Gorbachev's *perestroika* was sending shock waves through Eastern Europe and veteran communists looked on uneasily. On 9 November 1989 the Berlin Wall fell, and the next day an internal Communist Party coup put an end to the 35-year reign of the ageing Zhivkov. He was placed under house arrest and, in February 1991, became the first ex-communist leader in

Eastern Europe to stand trial for corruption during his period in office. (Despite being sentenced to seven years imprisonment for misusing state funds, Zhivkov wangled a hasty release and lived comfortably in an affluent suburb of Sofia until his death in August 1998.)

Free elections were planned for June 1990 and the Communist Party agreed to relinquish its monopoly on power and changed its name to the Bulgarian Socialist Party (BSP). A coalition of 16 different opposition groups founded the Union of Democratic Forces (UDF). The BSP won the elections comfortably, supported by rural and older voters. A majority of city dwellers and the young voted for the UDF.

In mid-1990, the Socialist president Petâr Mladenov was forced to resign after a controversy over his advocating the use of force against student demonstrators. On 1 August 1990, the socialist-dominated parliament elected Zhelyu Zhelev of the UDF to replace him in a compromise to quell tensions. During the June 1990 elections, the Socialists had spoken out against 'shock therapy' reforms and advocated an easy transition to capitalism but in October, with the economy collapsing around them, they changed course and introduced a radical reform programme similar to that proposed by the opposition. This sparked nationwide strikes and demonstrations against threatened price hikes, and on 29 November 1990, Andrei Lukanov, the Socialist prime minister, resigned.

Lukanov was replaced by Dimiter Popov, an independent who formed a BSP/UDF coalition government to prepare for fresh elections. The October 1991 parliamentary elections were won by the UDF, and Filip Dimitrov formed Bulgaria's first fully non-communist government. President Zhelev was re-elected in January 1992. In October 1992, the UDF government was defeated in parliament by a coalition of ethnic Turkish members, UDF defectors and Socialists. An administration of technocrats was installed with Lyuben Berov as prime minister. With support for the UDF and Socialists almost equally divided, the small Turkish party held the balance of power in parliament.

Rapid inflation, high unemployment, the lack of a social safety net and the visible wealth

BULGARIA

of legitimised criminal networks subsequently caused widespread disillusionment in a country where hope had burgeoned a decade ago. A culture of disappointment took hold in Bulgaria, and with many of the country's brightest and best hoping to emigrate, there were worrying times in the mid 90s.

Parliamentary elections held in late 1994 saw the BSP, led by Zhan Videnov, win an absolute majority, boosted by staunch support from the elderly and rural voters unsettled by the pace of change. Unfortunately, Videnov's government has repaid the true believers with corruption, short-sightedness and a lack of resolve, cementing mistrust in Bulgaria's fledgling democracy. The current president, Stoyanov, is widely perceived as decisive and effective and is implementing much-needed IMF fiscal remedies and stamping down on once rampant crime and economy-destroying inflation.

GEOGRAPHY & ECOLOGY

Bulgaria lies at the crossroads of Europe and Asia in the heart of the Balkan Peninsula. An amazing variety of landforms are jammed into its relatively small area of 110,912 sq km. From the high banks of the Danube, a windswept plain slopes up to the rounded summits of the Stara Planina. This east-west range runs right across the northern half of the country from the Black Sea to Yugoslavia. The Sredna Gora branch is separated from the main range by a fault that is followed by the railway from Sliven to Sofia. Some 70% of the world's rose oil, used in the manufacture of cosmetics and perfumes, comes from the Valley of Roses near Kazanlâk in this fault.

Southern Bulgaria is even more mountainous. Musala Peak (2925m) in the Rila Mountains south of Sofia is the highest mountain between the Alps and Transcaucasia, and is almost equalled by Vihren Peak (2915m) in the Pirin Massif further south. The Rila Mountains' sharply glaciated massifs with their bare rocky peaks, steep forested valleys and glacial lakes are the geographical core of the Balkans – a paradise for hikers. There's also the Pirin National Park, just south of Bansko. Take a train from Pazardzhik to get there.

The Rodopi Mountains stretch west along the Greek border from Rila and Pirin, separating the Aegean Sea from the Thracian Plain of central Bulgaria. This plain opens onto the Black Sea coast with great bays and coastal lakes at Burgas and Varna. The long sandy beaches that lie all along this coast are among the finest in Europe.

Railways have been constructed along the great rivers of Bulgaria from Sofia: they follow the Iskâr River north-east towards the Danube, the Maritsa River south-east into Turkey and the Struma River south into Greece. About a third of Bulgaria is forested, with deciduous trees in the lowlands and conifers in the mountains.

As in many post-communist countries, the lure of fast cash has outweighed ecologically sustainable development. Logging and animal poaching occurs in protected areas, endangering birds such as the white stork and the black vulture. Bulgaria's bear population, temporarily boosted by 'bear refugees' from war-torn Yugoslavia, is again declining.

The Kozloduy nuclear power plant 200km north of Sofia is rated one of the world's 25 most dangerous nuclear facilities. Since opening in 1974, there have been periodic minor accidents and safety scares forcing partial shutdowns and leading to power cuts across the country. The six reactors at Kozloduy are of the pressurised-water VVER-440 type considered even less safe than the Chernobyl-style RBMK reactor. In 1993, panic-stricken Western governments allocated US$28 million to help improve safety at Kozloduy on the understanding that the reactors would be shut down by the end of the decade, but there has been no move towards closing the facility. In 1990 public protests forced the Bulgarian government to halt construction of a second plant.

GOVERNMENT & POLITICS

Bulgaria is now a parliamentary democracy with Mr Petâr Stoyanov as President and Mr Ivan Kostov as Prime Minister. The ruling party is the United Democratic Forces (UDF) and the opposition is the Socialist Party (BSP) – in essence a remake of the old communist ruling elite. Elections were last held in January 1997.

ECONOMY

During the communist era, five-year plans were prepared and implemented by a Council of Ministers. Half the national budget was devoted to economic development, and industry grew from almost nothing until it contributed over half the gross national product. Growth continued through the 1970s, but the 1980s witnessed a slowdown because of technological shortcomings and economic inefficiencies.

Attempts to introduce Hungarian-style, market-oriented reforms were half-hearted and in its last five years of communist rule Bulgaria rang up a US$12 billion foreign debt just to maintain living standards.

Bulgaria has always been primarily an agricultural country with two-thirds of the land devoted to growing cereals, including wheat, corn, barley, rye, oats and rice. Also important are industrial crops such as sunflowers, cotton and sugar beet. Tobacco and cigarettes make up half of all agricultural exports and wine accounts for another 20%. Prior to WWII, agriculture suffered from the overdivision of land, but by 1965, over one million small holdings had been consolidated into 920 collective and 165 state farms. On average, collective farms in Bulgaria were three times larger than those in Hungary and Romania and, despite a reduction of the agricultural workforce from 82% employment in 1948 to 39% in 1968, production was increased through the use of machinery, fertilisers and irrigation. The farming cooperatives are now being dismantled and the land returned to its former owners, but there is much disruption and confusion because of conflicting claims.

By 1970 the collectivisation of agriculture had led to a doubling of the percentage of Bulgarians living in urban areas, thus providing a basis for industrialisation. There are iron and steelworks at Pernik and Kremikovci, a chemical plant at Dimitrovgrad producing fertilisers, and a large petrochemical plant at Burgas. Textile mills have been established in Plovdiv, Sliven and Sofia. Until recently, about 75% of Bulgaria's foreign trade was conducted with the Warsaw Pact countries, with the USSR alone accounting for over half of the total. The quality of many of the products previously shipped

to the USSR was low and orienting production to Western markets has proved difficult. About two thirds of Bulgaria's exports are delivered to risky ex-Soviet and Arab markets, doing nothing to inspire confidence or fill the coffers, and jeopardising the future of Bulgaria's inefficient heavy industries.

There are oil refineries at Ruse and Burgas, and some oil and gas is produced north-east of Varna, but prior to 1990 Bulgaria obtained over 90% of its oil from the USSR at far below world prices. As deliveries from Russia dwindled, Bulgaria had hoped to switch to oil from Iraq (which owes Bulgaria US$1.2 billion) but the 1991 Gulf War prevented this. UN economic sanctions against Yugoslavia have cost Bulgaria hundreds of millions of dollars and no compensation has been paid by either the European Union or the UN.

Brown coal found near Pernik is used by Bulgaria's iron industry, and lignite from open-pit mines at Dimitrovgrad is burned in dirty thermoelectric plants causing atmospheric pollution. Hydroelectric projects exist in the Rodopi and Rila mountains, but 40% of Bulgaria's electricity comes from the Kozloduy nuclear plant.

Bulgaria's internal political squabbles have retarded economic reform. Tax reform and new banking laws have been enacted, and foreigners are now allowed to own local businesses (agricultural land excluded), but foreign investment remains meagre and privatisation slow. Bulgaria's strategic location, skilled workforce and good infrastructure are big advantages but political instability, the large national debt, vested interests created by the old system and inexperience on the part of the reformers are slowing the way ahead. The International Monetary Fund (IMF) has had to continually prod Bulgarian politicians to take action. Since 1989, the living standards of 90% of the population have been reduced, with inflation hurtling along at about 80%.

IMF prodding was finally heeded in April 1997 when the incoming UDF government pegged the lev to the deutschmark and halted the rampant inflation that had ravaged the economy until that date. The fact that 75% of people own their own residences has helped avert widespread destitution, but with unemployment standing at around 20% (ballooning to 80% in some rural areas where light industry has collapsed) and the average wage more or less static at US$100 per month, the situation for many is still very precarious.

POPULATION & PEOPLE

About 8.3 million people live in Bulgaria, 1,140,000 of them in the capital, Sofia. The other major cities are Plovdiv (400,000), Varna (315,000), Burgas (210,000), Ruse (190,000), Stara Zagora (162,000) and Pleven (140,000). Dimitrovgrad and Pernik are major industrial centres.

The Bulgarians, like the Serbs, are South Slavs. The largest national minorities are Turks (8.5%), Roma (2.6%) and Macedonians (2.5%). Ethnic Macedonians constitute a majority in the Pirin region south of Sofia. For most of this century a controversy has raged over whether the Macedonians are Bulgarians or a distinct ethnic group. Officially, Bulgaria recognises Macedonia as a country but does not recognise the Macedonians as a people. Activists attempting to politically organise the Macedonian minority in Bulgaria continue to suffer harassment by the Bulgarian authorities.

The 800,000 Turks live mostly in the northeast and in the eastern Rodopi foothills. Between 1912 and 1940 some 340,000 ethnic Turks left Bulgaria for Turkey, and after WWII another 200,000 left. In early 1985 the communists mounted a programme to forcibly assimilate the remaining Turkish inhabitants, all of whom were required to take Bulgarian names. The circumcision of male Muslim children was forbidden, separate Muslim cemeteries were abolished, many mosques were closed and Ramadan (the month of fasting) was attacked. Even the wearing of Turkish dress and the speaking of Turkish in public were banned. In early 1989, there were mass protests against these policies and, after a relaxation of passport laws, a further 350,000 Turkish Bulgarians left for Turkey (many have subsequently returned to Bulgaria). With the fall of Todor Zhivkov in late 1989, the mosques reopened and in 1990 legislation was passed allowing the restoration of Muslim names. In 1991 optional instruction in Turkish resumed in public schools.

Some 250,000 Pomaks (Slavs who converted to Islam while Bulgaria was part of the Ottoman Empire) live in the Rodopi region south of Plovdiv. In the past, the Pomaks were subjected to the same assimilatory pressures as the Turks, with a particularly brutal name-changing campaign from 1971-73. Many of the 550,000 Roma live in the Valley of Roses (especially around Sliven) and although the communists improved their living standards, they were denied the right to maintain their separate identity. Three-quarters of the Roma are Muslims.

At the outbreak of WWII, there were 50,000 Jews in Bulgaria and nearly all survived the war, thanks to Bulgarian resistance to Nazi demands that they be deported to death camps in Poland. Though the Bulgarian Jews were assembled in provincial labour camps and forced to wear the Star of David, none were turned over to the Germans. After the war, most left for Israel and only about 5000 Jews live in Bulgaria today.

ARTS

After five centuries of Turkish rule, Bulgarian culture reappeared in the 19th century as writers and artists strove to reawaken national consciousness. Zahari Zograph (1810-53) painted magnificent frescos in monasteries at Bachkovo, Preobrazhenski, Rila and Troyan, with scenes inspired by medieval Bulgarian art, but more human than divine. In Orthodox churches, a high partition, called an iconostasis, separates the public and private areas. Zograph and his contemporaries painted icons on wooden panels to hang on these intricately carved walls.

Literature

It is sadly indicative of the troubled history of the country that Bulgaria's three leading poets met violent deaths around the age of 30. The folk poetry of Hristo Botev (1848-76) features rebels who struggled for independence, or noble outlaws who robbed from the rich and gave to the poor. Borba is a poetic condemnation of injustice, and Mehanata satirises café politicians. In 1876, Botev returned from exile in Romania and was killed in the anti-Ottoman uprising.

The symbolist Dimcho Debelyanov (1887-1916) expressed the purity of human feelings in his melodious lyric poetry. His poem *Orden* (1910) criticises the court of King Ferdinand. Despite this, Debelyanov volunteered for military service in WWI and was killed in action in Macedonia.

Geo Milev (1895-1925), who lost an eye in WWI, wrote poetry dealing with social themes. His epic poem *Septemvri*, about the September 1923 agrarian revolution, is the high point of Bulgarian expressionism. The authorities confiscated the volume in which the poem appeared and Milev was arrested and fined. After the trial he was kidnapped by the police and murdered.

The grand old man of Bulgarian literature is Ivan Vazov (1850-1921), whose novel *Under the Yoke* (1893) describes the 1876 uprising against the Turks. Vazov's *Epic of the Forgotten* is a cycle of poems to the heroes of the Bulgarian National Revival. His plays, written in the early 20th century, bring medieval Bulgarian history to life. Vazov was also a noted travel writer who never tired of writing stories about his country.

In his novel *The Iron Candlestick*, Dimitâr Talev (1898-1966) went beyond socialist realism to portray the complexity of human nature against the background of Macedonia's struggle for liberation from the Ottoman Empire in the 19th century.

Music

An ancient Greek myth ascribed a Thracian origin to Orpheus and the Muses. Bulgarians today are still renowned singers and the country's Orthodox religious chants are the equivalent of classical music in the West. Bulgarian ecclesiastic music dating back to the 9th century played a key role in the 19th-century Bulgarian National Revival. The songs, cantatas and oratorios convey the mysticism of chronicles, fables and legends, and to hear Orthodox chants sung by a choir of up to 100 people is a moving experience. The Bulgarian chants with their Old Church-Slavonic texts are sometimes performed during mass at churches such as Sofia's Aleksander Nevski Church.

Alongside the scholarly Byzantine traditions maintained in Orthodox church music is the Turkish influence evident in the sponta-neous folk songs and dances of the villages. Bulgarians have always striven to maintain their unique cultural identity through folk music, managing to do so during five centuries of Ottoman rule. The most common traditional folk instruments are the *tambura* (a four-stringed long-necked lute akin to the Greek bouzouki), the *gayda* (goatskin bagpipes), the *gadulka* or *rebec* (a small pear-shaped fiddle), the *dayre* (tambourine), the *kaval* (a long, open flute), the *duduk* (a high-pitched flute), the *dvoyanka* (double flute), the *ocarina* (a small ceramic flute), the *zurna* (a small, high-pitched horn), the *tarambuka* (vase drum) and the *tâppan* (a large, cylindrical, double-headed drum). As in most peasant cultures, Bulgarian women were not given access to musical instruments so they performed the vocal parts. Bulgarian female choir singing is polyphonic and sudden upward leaps of the voice are characteristic.

From the 1950s, Bulgarian village music was transformed into a sophisticated art form by the pioneering composer/director Philip Kutev during a remarkable career that ended only with his death in 1982. He composed nearly 500 adapted folk melodies, and directed modern choirs including the National Folk Ensemble 'Philip Kutev'. His vision has been communicated worldwide by groups such as Le Mystère des Voix Bulgares.

International interest has partially offset the decline in popularity of traditional music since the fall of communism. Partly because it was prescribed listening under the old regime and partly because Bulgarians now have access to as much Western schlock-pop as they can handle, the past decade has dealt folk music a telling blow.

Apart from busking Roma, the music you're most likely to encounter in Bulgaria is 'Stambolovo' or wedding music. These six or seven-piece bands are popular at all dances, getting toes tapping by melding traditional music with modern instruments, such as the electric guitar and saxophone.

SOCIETY & CONDUCT

Bulgarians observe a number of traditional customs. Trifon Zarezan on 14 February is the ancient festival of the wine growers. Vines are pruned and sprinkled with wine for a bounteous harvest. On 1 March, Bulgarians give each other *martenitsi*, red and white tasselled threads worn for health and happiness at the coming of spring. When wearers see their first stork of the season, they tie their martenitsa to the nearest tree.

Like in a number of cultures in the region when Bulgarians shake their head it means 'yes' and when they nod their head it means 'no'. This can be possibly confusing. If in doubt, ask *da ili ne* (yes or no)?

RELIGION

About 85% of the population comes from an Orthodox background and 13% are Sunni Muslims. Under communism, religious practice was discouraged, and it was only the elderly who were left unharassed to pursue their worship. Young people are not returning in droves to Orthodox churches, ensuring an erosion of faith in what was once a very religious community.

LANGUAGE

Bulgarian is the first language of most Bulgarians. It is a South Slavonic language, closely related to Macedonian, and is also spoken in parts of Greece, Romania, Ukraine, Moldova and other countries.

The Cyrillic alphabet that it shares with the former USSR, Serbia and Macedonia dates back to the 9th century, when Sts Cyril and Methodius translated the Bible into Old Church Slavonic. As almost everything in Bulgaria is written in Cyrillic, it's essential to learn this alphabet.

For many Bulgarians, Russian is their second language. During the 1950s and 1960s French was the second most-taught foreign language after Russian and many middle-aged Bulgarians in the bureaucracy are tickled to show off their knowledge of it. Young people, tourism workers and business types are more likely to speak English. German tourists have been frequenting the Black Sea coast for years and their language is most widely known in that region.

See the Language Guide at the end of the book for a basic rundown on Bulgarian pronunciation and some useful words and phrases. Lonely Planet's *Eastern Europe*

phrasebook has a much more extensive list of translated Bulgarian words and phrases. It takes a slightly different approach to that followed here by providing an Anglicised phonetic rendering instead of a standard transcription. The original Cyrillic spelling is also given. If you'll be in Bulgaria longer than a few days it's useful to have this book with you.

An excellent teach-yourself course of Bulgarian called *Colloquial Bulgarian* by George D Papantchev is available from Routledge Publications (11 New Fetter Lane, London EC4P 4EE, UK) or ordered from your bookseller. The book and a two-cassette tape package have 18 well-structured language units, easy to follow grammar tables and an English-Bulgarian-English vocabulary and would have to be one of the best modern guides to the Bulgarian language on the market.

Note that in recent years there has been substantial growth, particularly in shop and street signs and advertisements, in the use of a new form of lower-case Cyrillic in which some letters look quite different from the old lower-case forms (which were simply smaller versions of the upper-case letters). This can be confusing if you are not aware of it.

Facts for the Visitor

HIGHLIGHTS

The historic towns of Nesebâr and Veliko Târnovo are survivors from the Middle Ages, while Koprivshtitsa and Plovdiv are representative of the 19th-century Bulgarian National Revival. Melnik is one of many picturesque provincial villages.

Most of Bulgaria's museums and galleries are monolingual, rendering many collections meaningless to foreign visitors. Some exceptions are the National Museum of History in Sofia, which is starting to post English summaries with its rich collection of exhibits, and Sofia's Foreign Art Gallery, which has English labels affixed to its works.

Bulgaria now boasts many high quality private restaurants at prices a half to two-thirds less than their counterparts in Western Europe, making eating out a pleasurable experience.

LOWLIGHTS
Bulgarian lowlights include the string of broken-down abandoned factories that sadly litter the countryside, a legacy of the industrial socialist past.

A classic-hits soundtrack will accompany you wherever you go in Bulgaria, blaring from kiosks, cafés and shops. You can *never* check out of the Hotel California here.

Regional buses are invariably filthy and decked out with soft porn posters. And somebody forgot the shock absorbers!

Stara Zagora has to be the most unattractive, polluted town in Bulgaria.

SUGGESTED ITINERARIES
Depending on the length of your stay, you might want to visit the following places in Bulgaria:

Two days
  Sofia
One week
  Sofia, Veliko Târnovo and Varna
Two weeks
  Sofia, Rila Monastery, Melnik, Koprivshtitsa, Veliko Târnovo, Madara, Varna and Nesebâr
One month
  Most of the places included in this chapter

PLANNING
Climate & When to Go
Bulgaria has a temperate climate with cold, damp winters and hot, dry summers. The Rodopi Mountains form a barrier to the moderating Mediterranean influence of the Aegean, while the Danube Plains are open to the extremes of central Europe. Sofia has average daily temperatures above 15°C from May to September, above 11°C in April and October, above 5°C in March and November, and below freezing in December and January. The Black Sea moderates temperatures in the east of the country. Rainfall is highest in the mountains, and in winter life is sometimes disrupted by heavy snowfalls.

Books & Maps
No serious books about Bulgaria or translations of Bulgarian literature are available in English at Bulgarian bookshops.

The Bulgarians from Pagan Times to the Ottoman Conquest by David Marshall Lang (Thames and Hudson, 1976) brings medieval Bulgaria to life. The maps, illustrations and lucid text make this book well worth reading. *A Short History of Modern Bulgaria* by RJ Crampton (Cambridge University Press, 1987) is also useful if you want to read up before visiting.

The *Baedeker Bulgaria* map is probably the best map you can buy before you leave home. You can find Sofia city maps once you are in Bulgaria.

What to Bring
The availability of consumer goods is Bulgaria's most enthusiastic expression of democracy, so there's no need to fill your pack with batteries, tampons, painkillers or soap ... it's all here (and it's cheap). If you're bringing a car or a bicycle, it's worth carrying some spare parts.

TOURIST OFFICES
Balkantourist, the old government tourism monopoly, arranges accommodation, changes money, books sightseeing tours, and so on. In some towns Balkantourist now operates under a different name, such as Puldin Tours (Plovdiv), Mesembria Tourist (Nesebâr) or Dunav Tours (Ruse). Abroad it uses the name Balkan Holidays.

Staff at Balkan Holidays' offices are often evasive about questions regarding individual tourism and will try to convince you to sign up for one of their package tours. They're a good source of free brochures, but don't believe everything they tell you.

Student travellers are supposedly catered for by the Orbita Youth Travel Agency and by Pirin, the travel bureau of the Bulgarian Tourist Union. However, many Orbita and Pirin offices have closed due to lack of funds and the remaining offices have slumped into a torpor that can be entertaining if you don't actually need any information.

Rila railway ticket offices are found in the city centres. Shipka is the travel agency of the Union of Bulgarian Motorists. Many smaller private travel agencies also exist.

Balkantourist Offices Abroad

Balkantourist (Balkan Holidays) offices outside Bulgaria include:

Netherlands
(☎ 020-620 9400) Leidestraat 43, 1017 NV Amsterdam
UK
(☎ 0171-491 4499) 19 Conduit St, London W1R 9TD
USA
(☎ 212-822 5900; fax 212-338 6830) 20 East 46th St, Suite 1003, New York, NY 10017

VISAS & EMBASSIES

Visa requirements have eased up in recent times so it's not the hassle it once was to get into Bulgaria. Nationals of the USA and the EU are admitted without a visa for stays of less than 30 days.

For visitors to Bulgaria of other nationalities visas are issued based on a sliding fee scale depending on whether the visa is transit, tourist or business. Australian and New Zealand visitors pay AU$75 for a single entry visa, AU$96 for a double entry visa or AU$61 if only in transit. A passport-sized photo is also required. Canadian visitors pay CA$78 for a single entry visa and CA$128 for a double entry visa, US citizens US$53 or US$123 for a multi-entry visa. The on-the-spot visa price is US$68.

Rubber Stamps

Everyone entering Bulgaria is given the 'statistical card' *statisticheska karta* by immigration. This card must remain in your passport until you leave Bulgaria and will be stamped by hotel and room owners at each place you stay. When you leave Bulgaria, immigration will collect the card so don't lose it. If you are staying with friends you must register with the local police within 48 hours. You may also need your host's passport to register, or get your host to register you.

In Sofia the police office is at bul Mariya Luiza 48 (8.45 am to 12.15 pm and 1.30 to 5.15 pm). For further information on registration requirements ring ☎ 02-71 43 28 10.

There is US$23 'border tax' required of all arrivals other than citizens of the EU, Iceland, Norway, Switzerland, the USA and most Eastern European countries. Be sure to have this amount ready in cash when you arrive in the country.

Bulgarian Embassies Abroad

For the addresses and opening hours of Bulgarian embassies in Belgrade, Bratislava, Bucharest, Budapest, Prague, Skopje, Tirana, Warsaw and Zagreb turn to those city sections in this book.

Other Bulgarian embassies include the following:

Australia
(☎ 02-9327 7581; fax 9327 8067) 4 Carlotta Rd, Double Bay, NSW 2028
Canada
(☎ 613-789 3215; fax 613-3524; mailmn@ storm.ca) 325 Stewart St, Ottawa, Ontario K1N 6K5
France
(☎ 01-47 05 36 41; fax 45 51 18 68) 1 Avenue Rapp 7e, Paris
Greece
(☎ 01-647 8105) Str. Kallari 33, Psyhiko, Athens
(☎ 031-829 210) N. Manou 12, Thessaloniki
Netherlands
(☎ 070-350 3051; fax 358 4688) Duinroosweg 9, 2597 KJ The Hague
UK
(☎ 0171-584 9400; fax 584 4948) 187 Queen's Gate, London SW7 5HL
USA
(☎ 202-387 7679; fax 234 7973) 1621 22nd St NW, Washington, DC 20008

Foreign Embassies in Bulgaria

The following embassies are in Sofia:

Albania
(Consulate) (☎ 946 3225) Krakra 10; Monday, Wednesday and Friday from 10 am to noon
Croatia
(Consulate) Krakra 18; weekdays from 10 am to 2 pm
Czech Republic
(Consulate) (☎ 946 1111) bul Yanko Sakazov 9; Monday, Wednesday and Friday from 10 to 11.30 am
Greece
(Consulate) (☎ 946 1027) Evlogi Georgiev 103
Hungary
(Consulate) (☎ 963 0460) 6 Septemvri 57; Monday, Tuesday, Thursday and Friday 9 to 11 am

Poland

(Consulate) (☎ 971 3411) Khan Krum 46; Monday, Tuesday, Wednesday and Friday from 9 am to 1 pm

Romania

(Consulate) (☎ 971 2858) Corner of Sipchenski Prohod and Sitnyakovo (take tram No 20 from bul Janko Sakazov); Tuesday from 3 to 5 pm, Wednesday and Thursday from 10 am to noon

Turkey

(☎ 980 2270) bul Vasil Levski 80

UK

(☎ 980 1220) bul Vasil Levski 65, east of the NDK Palace of Culture; Monday to Thursday from 8.30 am to 7.30 pm, Friday from 8.30 am to noon; serves all Commonwealth nationals

USA

(☎ 980 5241) Kapitan Andreev 1; weekdays from 9 am to 5 pm

Yugoslavia

(Consulate) (☎ 946 1633) Veliko Târnovo 3; weekdays from 9 am to noon

CUSTOMS

Whether or not you are inspected by customs officers depends on how you enter the country. Generally, bona fide tourists are left alone and when exiting the country you're allowed to take out 'gifts up to a reasonable amount', souvenirs and articles for personal use. You could be charged an export tax of 100% or more on works of art.

MONEY
Currency

Bulgarian banknotes come in denominations of 100, 200, 500, 1000, 2000, 10,000 and 50,000 leva. Newer 10,000 and 50,000 leva notes are smaller and can easily be confused or miscounted. Be careful. There are coins of 5, 10, 20 and 50 leva, but they are pretty rare and not much use other than for older-style phones. In early 1991 the lev was allowed to float and price controls were removed, leading to 79% inflation. Devaluation of the lev in the mid-90s was common; during the research period of this book the lev's value was around 1760 leva to US$1, a vast difference to the 140 leva to US$1 two years previously when this chapter was last revised. Since early 1997 it has been pegged to the deutschmark (1 DM = 1000 leva) and inflation had slowed down by mid-1998.

In this chapter hotel room prices and international travel tickets are quoted in US$ or Deutschmarks. All local transport, food and sundry expenses are given in leva.

Currency Exchange

There's no longer any compulsory exchange in Bulgaria and you may pay for almost everything directly in leva. Cash is easily changed in Bulgaria at numerous small exchange offices for no commission. Travellers' cheques, on the other hand, are a bit of a hassle as many banks refuse to change them and those that do deduct up to 5% commission. Hotel exchange counters give low rates and deduct about 5% commission.

Cash advances on credit cards are becoming more common, although you cannot rely on this service outside Sofia and the Black Sea resorts. There is no uniform commission; charges will sometimes be lower than those for travellers' cheques, but you should balance the gains against the interest clocking up on your account. You're well advised to bring a good amount of cash to Bulgaria.

We can't recommend any single bank that consistently offers good service when changing travellers' cheques or advancing cash on cards. For large amounts it pays to compare the varying commission charges at the Bulbank, the First East International Bank and others. It's best to change enough money to tide you over for a week or more rather than waste time searching for a bank every couple of days.

ATMs are a more common sight at least in Sofia and on the Black Sea coast. Cirrus, Maestro, Visa and MC credit cards can be used to draw cash from your credit account.

The lev is now a freely convertible currency and there are no problems changing excess leva back into dollars.

Exchange Rates

Australia	A$1	=	1175 leva
Canada	C$1	=	1242 leva
euro	€1	=	1965 leva
France	1FF	=	292 leva
Germany	DM1	=	990 leva
Switzerland	Sfr1	=	1170 leva
United Kingdom	UK£1	=	2930 leva
United States	US$1	=	1765 leva

BULGARIA

Black Market

There is no black market any more as such, but you may still be approached by hustlers looking for your spare foreign cash to exchange, especially around the train station in Sofia where, if you have just arrived from Greece, you will more than likely be approached for drachmas (even the train conductor is in on the game). You'll be offered up to 10% above the bank rate for cash on the street, but these transactions should be approached with extreme caution. You may be given counterfeit leva, be short-changed or otherwise cheated, and the law won't be on your side.

Costs

In 1996 a 22% value-added tax was introduced but you'll probably still find that all forms of transport (including taxis), souvenirs, admissions, food and drink are cheap. Anything you can get for the same price as a Bulgarian will be cheap, but when there's a higher tourist price (as there is for almost all accommodation) it can get expensive. Students often get half-price on museum admissions.

Note that the average monthly salary of a Bulgarian is not much more than US$100, so bear in mind what the cost of living actually means to them.

Tipping

It is common practice to round restaurant bills up to the nearest convenient figure and waiters may indeed assume that this is what you intend and keep the expected change anyway. The same applies to taxis with meters. With non-metered taxis you can expect to pay what you agree upon beforehand.

POST & COMMUNICATIONS

Postage for postcards is 300 leva and air-mail letters is 600 leva. Stamps and envelopes are available inside all post offices and REP kiosks.

Receiving Mail

Mail addressed c/o poste restante, Sofia 1000, Bulgaria, can be picked up at window No 8 in the main post office at General Gurko 6 (weekdays from 8 am to 8 pm). Mail addressed to Sofia 1 is sent to a branch post office on bul Stamboliyski.

Telephone

It's easy to telephone Western Europe and North America from Bulgaria. International telephones are found in all large post offices and you simply enter a booth, dial ☎ 00 (Bulgaria's international access code), the country code, the city code and the number, and you're immediately connected. If you're calling a number inside Bulgaria itself, dial the city code and the number. You pay the clerk as you leave. Note that Bulgarian phone lines are gradually being digitalised and phone numbers are adding digits, especially in Sofia. Be aware that five or six-digit numbers given in this chapter may have changed by the time you read this.

BulFon and Betcom phonecards are useable all over the country. They come in a 50 unit version (3000 leva) and 200 unit version (9000 leva). These are available from telephone offices, blue kiosks and other locations that advertise their sale. A one-minute call to the USA or Australia costs 2930 leva.

To call Bulgaria from abroad dial the international access code (varies from country to country), ☎ 359 (the country code for Bulgaria), the area code minus the leading zero and the number.

Fax

Faxes can be sent from most post offices, but operator-connected faxes can turn out to be very expensive, if they turn out at all. Incoming faxes can be collected for a nominal fee.

INTERNET RESOURCES

Sofia has a couple of places where you can access the Net. The first and better option is the ICN Internet Agency (☎ 9166 2213; agency@sf.icn.bg) on the lower floor of The Palace of Culture (NDK). There are 11 terminals with fast connections and access time costs 5000 leva per hour. Open 9 am to 7 pm every day. The lesser option is in the business centre in the basement of the Sofia Sheraton Balkan Hotel (US$6 per hour), where the connection is slow and erratic. Internet access is available to guests at Odysseia-In Travel (see the Sofia Places to Stay section).

A good place to start your cybertour is the Lonely Planet page on Bulgaria www.lonely planet.com/dest/eur/bul.htm. *Bulgaria on the Internet,* pisa.rockefeller.edu:8080/Bulgaria/ lists electronic resources within Bulgaria. Check out also the *All about Bulgaria* site at www.cs.columbia.edu/radev/bulginfo.html.

NEWSPAPERS & MAGAZINES

There are at least three English-language publications printed in Bulgaria: the *Sofia Echo* (www.online.bg/sofiaecho) is a newsy and chatty 20-page weekly covering a wide variety of topics. The *Sofia Independent* is a rather staid politically and commercially oriented newspaper, but has a useful colour insert with movie and weekend cable TV listings as well as concerts and other happenings around town. The *Sofia Western News* is a fairly newsy independent magazine. All can be found at major hotels and newsstands around Sofia.

You can pick up major UK papers, *Time* and *Newsweek* in larger towns. The main national dailies are *Trud* and *Standart*. About 50 Bulgarian newspapers cater to soccer fans and a newly awakened taste for the sensational and the skimpy.

RADIO & TV

There is a wide range of radio stations catering to all tastes and local and cable TV stations for those who can afford them. Euro-News, Eurosport and NBC are commonly found in hotel rooms with TVs. The BBC World Service can be heard on 91 FM in Sofia.

PHOTOGRAPHY & VIDEO

Film and video paraphernalia is widely available in Sofia and the Black Sea resorts, less so elsewhere. Bring your own with you. Sofia has some reliable same-day film developing services and prices are generally low. To print and develop a 24-shot print film will cost around 8000 leva.

Be wary of pointing your equipment at anything that looks military. Suspicions still run a little high in these parts.

Bulgarian TVs and VCRs are based on both PAL and SECAM systems, though PAL now dominates the scene.

TIME

The time in Bulgaria is GMT/UTC plus two hours. From the end of March to the end of September, Bulgaria goes on summer time and clocks are turned forward an hour.

ELECTRICITY

The electric current is 220V AC, 50Hz and appliances use the standard two-pronged European plug.

WEIGHTS & MEASURES

All measurements are metric.

LAUNDRY

Coin-operated laundrettes don't exist in Bulgaria but there are many dry cleaners *(himichesko chistene)*. You'll be charged per piece for your laundry. Better hotels often do laundry for guests.

TOILETS

Expect to pay around 100-200 leva. Expect squat toilets at train and bus stations. Expect no toilet paper (carry it!) and put used toilet paper in the bin. Quality of toilets is generally low. Make use of restaurants and hotels whenever possible.

HEALTH

Medical services must be paid for in cash at the time of treatment but the rates are reasonable. Prescribed medicines are quite inexpensive unless they're imported from the West.

There are 530 curative hot springs at 190 locations in Bulgaria, with a total daily output of 1.2 million cubic metres of mineral water. The springs of Bankya, Hisar and Kyustendil have been known since antiquity. Other Bulgarian spas include Sandanski (23km north of Kulata) and Velingrad.

WOMEN TRAVELLERS

Women travelling alone will definitely attract interest from both sexes, but it's unlikely to lead to trouble. In this family-oriented culture, people are simply amazed by solo journeying. Stick close to family groups on trains, especially if travelling overnight. *Omâzhena sâm* means 'I am married' and is a pretty firm message.

GAY & LESBIAN TRAVELLERS

Homosexual sex is legal in Bulgaria (from the age of 21) provided it does not cause 'public scandal or entice others to perversity.' As you might deduce from the wording, the official line in Bulgaria is far from gay-friendly. The local gay organisation is Erotic Center 'Flamingo', at 208 Tsar Simeon, Sofia, 1303. As recently as mid-1996, the Flamingo and other gay venues were subjected to police raids.

DISABLED TRAVELLERS

Disabled travellers will generally have a rough time since few facilities exist to cater for people with special needs. Uneven and broken pavements in the towns and cities will make wheelchair mobility problematic.

SENIOR TRAVELLERS

Senior travellers on tours should face no particular problems other than broken and uneven pavements in towns and cities which can make walking around a bit risky. Good quality restaurants and hotels can be found in most major tourist locations.

DANGERS & ANNOYANCES

The perception that all travellers are wealthy has led to various scams. Taxi drivers, particularly from the airport, have been known to overcharge outrageously. There have been reports of travellers being drugged and robbed by seemingly friendly, English-speaking locals who invited them for a drink. As soon as the drug in your drink knocks you out, your valuables quickly disappear. This can happen in the middle of Sofia in broad daylight, so be on guard.

Official corruption is rampant in Bulgaria and foreigners have been targeted on international trains and while driving. Sometimes all it takes is insistence on an official receipt (*smetka*) to move these hustlers in uniform along.

BUSINESS HOURS

Shops are normally open all day from 9 am to 5 pm except perhaps in smaller villages and towns where they may close for lunch. Offices and public services keep similar times. Money exchange offices are more often than not open until quite late and some of them are 'non-stop' ie 24 hours.

PUBLIC HOLIDAYS & SPECIAL EVENTS

Public holidays include New Year (1 and 2 January), 1878 Liberation Day (3 March), Easter Monday (March/April), Labour Day (1 May), Cyrillic Alphabet Day (24 May) and Christmas (25 and 26 December). The Bulgarian Orthodox Easter falls at a different time to the Catholic Easter.

At the Koprivshtitsa Folk Festival, which is theoretically held every four years (the next in 2000), some 4000 finalists compete for awards in various fields. In Pernik at the National Festival of Sourvakari, held every other year in the second half of January (the next in 1999), thousands of participants perform ancient dances wearing traditional masks and costumes to drive away evil spirits and to ask the good spirits for fertility and a bounteous harvest. Koukeri is another spring festival and it's most avidly celebrated in the Rodopi Mountains.

Annual folk festivals are held at Golden Sands during the second half of July, with Bulgarian groups participating, and at Burgas and Sunny Beach in August, with Bulgarian and foreign groups participating. The Festival of Roses is celebrated with folk songs and dances at Kazanlâk and Karlovo on the first Sunday in June.

The March Musical Days are held annually at Ruse, followed by the two-month Sofia Music Weeks International Festival of Contemporary Music beginning on 24 May. During the first week of June the Golden Orpheus International Pop Song Festival is held at Sunny Beach. Also in June is the International Ballroom Dancing Competition at

Burgas. In July there's the Varna Summer Festival and the International Chamber Music Festival at Plovdiv. A film festival is held in Sofia in November. The New Year Music Festival is held in Sofia's Palace of Culture.

ACTIVITIES
Skiing
Skiing is well developed in Bulgaria with the season running from December to April. Mt Vitosha (2290m), on the southern outskirts of Sofia, is the most accessible of Bulgaria's ski areas. International slalom and giant slalom competitions are held there in March. Bulgaria's largest ski resort is Borovets, 70km south of Sofia, with the highest mountains in the Balkans as a backdrop. The 40km of runs at Borovets are intended for advanced skiers and international competitions are often held there. Skiers on package tours are often sent to Pamporovo, 84km south of Plovdiv, which has 17km of ski runs in all categories serviced by several lifts. The 3800m Snezhanka No 1 run is suitable for beginners and there are steep competition runs and nordic tracks as well. Bansko in the Pirin Mountains is Bulgaria's least commercialised ski resort.

Hiking
Mountain climbing is feasible and you don't have to be Edmund Hillary to scale Musala Peak (2925m) in the Rila Massif, the highest peak between the Alps and the Caucasus. Vihren Peak (2914m) in the Pirin Massif can be climbed from Bansko. The highest peak in the Stara Planina is Mt Botev (2376m), which you can climb via Troyan and Apriltsi. Those who appreciate less strenuous day hikes from the comfort of their lodgings will find possibilities at Koprivshtitsa, Madara, Rila and Veliko Târnovo.

COURSES
Every August since 1977, Sts Cyril & Methodius University (fax 0359-62 28 023), 5003 Veliko Târnovo, has run a one-month 'International Summer Seminar for Students in Bulgarian Language and Slavic Culture'. The US$500 fee includes tuition, accommodation, food and various cultural activities. Beginner-level language classes are available

and the course closes with a five-day group excursion to the Black Sea. Prominent academics and artists participate in the programme and it's a great opportunity to get involved if you're at all interested in Slavic studies. Applications close at the end of May, so write well in advance.

WORK
There is technically nothing to stop you looking for a job and getting a permit, but given the high domestic unemployment rate and the low monthly salaries, it makes the likelihood of success remote. Most foreigners working in Bulgaria are employed by foreign companies. Teaching English may be one avenue, but the pay will not be up to much unless you strike gold with some exclusive private tuition.

ACCOMMODATION
Camping
Less popular camping grounds have struggled since losing government support and the industry is very much in a state of flux. Most camping grounds are open from May to October but you can rely on them only from June to early September. Privatised camping grounds are usually open all year. Campgrounds can be run-down and often unsavoury, so don't have high expectations.

Camping fees are an average of US$4 per person a night. Most camping grounds rent small bungalows for just slightly more than the cost of camping. Camping grounds along the coast tend to be crowded but will usually have tent sites. One of Bulgaria's better camping grounds is at Madara.

Camping outside the set camping grounds is prohibited, although if a camping ground is closed, no-one is likely to stop you pitching a tent.

Student Hotels
If you have a student card, the Orbita Youth Travel Agency, bul Hristo Botev 48, Sofia, can book rooms for you in student hotels around the country. Once the reservations are made, you pay Orbita for the rooms at about US$10 per person a night.

There are Orbita hotels in Rila village (about 22km from the monastery), Batak (in the mountains south-west of Plovdiv), Lovech (between Troyan and Pleven), Veliko Târnovo, Shumen and Varna, as well as in Primorsko resort on the Black Sea. Some student hotels are open only in summer.

Hostels

There are 52 youth hostels in Bulgaria but they're not listed in the Hostelling International handbook. The hostels are of two kinds. A *Turisticheski dom* or a *Turisticheska spalnya* is a fairly comfortable hotel or hostel with double rooms, usually located in or near a town. A *hizha* is a mountain hut offering dormitory beds. Most of the Bulgarian hostels display the standard HI symbol outside.

Show your HI membership card to the hostel clerks as soon as you arrive at a hostel so they'll know you're a member and give you a reduced rate. Hostels in Bulgaria are about US$9 with a HI card, US$11 without, and they're open all day.

Private Rooms

Balkantourist and Tourist Information & Reservations (TIR) and Odysseia-In in Sofia can book rooms for you right around the country, but private agencies are springing up in most towns and will probably be a few dollars cheaper. Along the coast, private rooms are by far the cheapest and easiest way to go but they're only available in the cities and towns, as hotels have a monopoly at the resorts. People travelling alone often have to pay for double rooms, but private rooms are still cheaper than hotels (and more friendly).

Private Hotels

Since November 1989, privately owned hotels have appeared in Bulgaria and are the equivalent of guesthouses or pensions in other countries. All are fairly small with less than a dozen rooms and new ones are opening all the time. Expect to pay anywhere between US$20 and US$70 for a room in a private hotel.

Hotels

Balkantourist used to enforce its monopoly over foreign tourism by preventing Western visitors from staying at cheap hotels that it did not own. As a result, you'd often be told that a hotel or dormitory was reserved for Bulgarians only, or they might just claim they were full. Now you can stay wherever you like, though there are still different prices for Bulgarians and for foreigners.

Hotels are classified from one to five stars. The most expensive are called Interhotels, which can have anything from three to five stars. Many two and three-star Balkantourist hotels are terribly rundown and overpriced.

Very few of the hotels in Bulgaria have air-conditioning.

FOOD

Food is inexpensive in Bulgaria and prices at the cheapest snack bar are only a third of those at a good hotel restaurant, so it's worth splashing out a little. Because the exchange rate is so good it's fairly cheap to dine out, even including a bottle of wine with the meal. McDonalds, KFC, Pizza Hut and Goodys have all made inroads and can now be found all over Sofia and the Black Sea resorts.

Folk-style taverns that serve traditional Bulgarian dishes are known as *mehanas*; these are often located in a basement and offer live music. Ask for the speciality at restaurants. Vegetable side dishes and bread cost extra. Dinner is the main meal of the day for workaday employees.

Some waiters in Bulgaria overcharge foreigners, so insist on seeing a menu with prices listed. They still expect the bill to be rounded up to the next round figure, however, and you can give a bit more if the service was efficient and honest. Tips should be given when you pay and not left on the table.

Bulgarian Specialities

Popular Bulgarian dishes with a Turkish flavour include *kebabcheta* or *kebapche* (grilled meat rolls), *kavarma* (meat and vegetable casserole), *drob sarma* (chopped lamb liver baked with rice and eggs), *sarmi* (stuffed vine or cabbage leaves) and *kebab* (meat on a spit). To try several kinds of meats at one sitting, order a mixed grill (*meshana skara*). *Topcheta supa* is a creamy soup with meatballs. *Plakiya* and *gyuvech* are rich fish and meat stews.

Vegetarians will find several dishes based on cheese (*sirene*). *Sirene po shopski* is cheese, eggs and tomatoes baked in an earthenware pot. *Kashkaval pane* is breaded cheese. *Banitsa* is a baked cheese pastry like Bosnian *burek*, while *mekitsas* is a batter of eggs and yoghurt fried in oil. A *shopska* salad is made of fresh diced tomatoes, cucumbers, onions and peppers covered with grated white sheep's cheese – excellent. Bulgarian yoghurt is famous and *tarator* is a refreshing cold soup of yoghurt, diced cucumber and onions. *Bop*, bean soup, is ubiquitous.

DRINKS
In Bulgaria, the production of wine is an ancient tradition dating back to the Empire of Thrace in the 9th century BC. Bulgaria today is one of the world's five leading exporters of wine, both red (Cabernet, Gamza, Mavrud, Melnik, Merlot, Otel, Pamid and Trakia) and white (Chardonnay, Euksinovgrad, Galatea, Misket, riesling and Tamyanka).

Bulgarians swear by *slivova* or *rakiya* (plum brandy). Beware of their potency! Bulgaria's finest beers are Zagorka from Stara Zagora, Astika from Haskovo and Shumensko pivo from Shumen. All alcoholic drinks are cheap.

Bulgarian fruit juices (apricot, peach, plum) are exported all over Europe. Good quality Turkish and espresso coffee are available everywhere, often served with a sweet drink called *sok* (juice). *Boza* is a thick millet drink sold at bakeries.

Na zdrave! is 'cheers!' in Bulgarian.

ENTERTAINMENT
Go to the theatres, concert halls and ticket offices listed in this chapter to find out about events. If any festivals coincide with your visit, ask staff at the local tourist office if they have a programme. Movies are shown in the original language with Bulgarian subtitles.

SPECTATOR SPORTS
Football (soccer) is the main spectator sport in Bulgaria and teams are followed with partisan zeal. Levski and CSKA are the two top teams in Bulgaria and are based in Sofia. You should be able to catch a match if you are in Bulgaria during the football season which ends in June.

THINGS TO BUY
Typical souvenirs include embroidered dresses and blouses, linen, carpets, Valley of Roses perfume, pottery, leather goods, dolls in national costume, silver-filigree jewellery, CD recordings of folk music and wrought copper and iron.

Getting There & Away

AIR
Balkan Bulgarian Airlines has flights to Sofia from Algiers, Bahrain, Bangkok, Beirut, Cairo, Casablanca, Colombo, Damascus, Doha, Dubai, Harare, İstanbul, Johannesburg, Kuwait, Lagos, Larnaca, Nairobi, Pyongyang, Seoul, Singapore, Tel Aviv, Thessaloniki, Tirana, Tunis and many European and North American cities. Bucket shops in Asia often sell Balkan Bulgarian Airlines tickets at cut rates.

Before buying a return air ticket from Western Europe or North America to Bulgaria, check the price of the cheapest package tour to the Black Sea resorts. This could be cheaper and you can just throw away the hotel vouchers if you don't care to sit on the beach for two weeks. Specifically ask the price of a 'camping flight', which is always the cheapest deal.

Malév Hungarian Airlines, bul Stamboliyski 26, Sofia, has very attractive youth fares for people aged 25 years and under: US$70 one way to Budapest, US$195 to Amsterdam, US$195 to London. Many other destinations are available.

There's a US$8 airport departure tax in Bulgaria.

LAND
Bus
Buses depart from Sofia's international bus station (☎ 52 50 04), Damen Gruev at 20 April, for Niš, Yugoslavia (twice daily, 148km, US$11), and then on to Belgrade (except Sunday, US$22); to Skopje, Macedonia (twice daily, 6½ hours, US$11); to Ohrid, Macedonia (daily except Sunday, 383km, US$19); to Tirana, Albania (Friday

and Sunday, 505km, US$28) and to Istanbul (Tuesday and Sunday, 576km, US$19).

A bus to Athens (US$37) via Thessaloniki (US$17) departs from the Novotel Europa daily at 8.30 am and a bus to Thessaloniki only departs at 1.30 pm. Call Tourist Service (☎ 32 40 32) for reservations. There is also a daily service to Thessaloniki at 10.30 am (US$17) with OSE, the Greek railways bus company. This departs from a small terminal at the northern end of bul Mariya Luiza.

Buses from the parking lot in between Sofia's central train station and the Novotel Europa head daily to destinations such as Frankfurt (DM160), Brussels (DM190), Munich (DM120), Istanbul (US$25), Prague (DM85), Budapest (US$40) and Bratislava (DM80). Some buses also depart from the east side of bul Mariya Luiza.

Unfortunately, no buses operate between Romania and Bulgaria due to long delays at the border. There are lots of buses from Bucharest to Istanbul, however, and as these all pass through Bulgaria you could just get off after clearing Bulgarian customs.

Train

The main railway routes into Bulgaria are from Bucharest (Romania), Niš (Yugoslavia), Thessaloniki (Greece), Alexandroupolis (Greece) and Edirne (Turkey). All these lines are served from one to three times a day with through trains from Istanbul, Athens, Belgrade, Budapest, Kiyïv, Moscow, Vilnius and St Petersburg.

Train travel between Romania and Bulgaria is much simpler than it has been, but you may still encounter occasional difficulties purchasing tickets. Bus travel is cheaper and more comfortable to/from Greece and Turkey. To/from Skopje (Macedonia) all train travel is via Niš, and a Yugoslav visa will most likely be required (take a bus instead). Only to/from Yugoslavia is it as good to take the train.

Romania & Beyond The *Bulgaria Express* originates in Moscow, picks up connections from Ukraine and St Petersburg and runs to/from Bulgaria via Romania. Between Bucharest and Sofia (nine to 10 hours, US$18) there are an additional two trains daily. In the opposite direction, the train from

Sofia to Moscow leaves at 9.25 pm and can get very overcrowded and unless you want to stand jammed in the corridor all night, arrive at the station very early.

A more obscure option is to enter Romania via Vidin/Calafat to Craiova. You will need to cross the Danube by ferry and take a connection on the other side. Currently, only two trains a day in either direction are scheduled to make the ferry connection.

Yugoslavia & Beyond The *Balkan Express* runs daily from Budapest (Keleti) to Sofia (16 hours, US$65) via Belgrade and Niš. Reservations are required if you're going north, but not if you're going south. Between Belgrade and Sofia (nine hours, US$37) the *Balkan Express* travels during the day in both directions. There is an additional afternoon/night service as well as an overnight service in both directions.

Greece There is a morning train (in reality a single carriage that gets passed across the border at Kulata) between Sofia and Thessaloniki (nine hours, US$20) and Athens (18 hours, US$35). If you're travelling from Sofia to Greece, don't take the train! It's better to take one of the relatively hassle-free buses.

There is a very round-about daily service between Plovdiv and Alexandroupolis (eight hours) in eastern Greece via Svilengrad.

Turkey Beginning in 1885, the famous *Orient Express* route passed through Belgrade and Sofia on its way from Paris to Istanbul. Though this classic service sadly no longer operates, the *Balkan Express* from Budapest still rolls through Sofia and Plovdiv on its way south-east to Istanbul (12 hours, US$37). The *Bucureşti Istanbul Express* originates in Romania and traverses Bulgaria on its way to Turkey, via Ruse, Dimitrovgrad and Svilengrad departing at 3.50 pm from Ruse daily.

Westbound, it's cheaper to buy a ticket only as far as the Turkish border town of Kapikule and then pay the additional fare into Bulgaria on the train itself.

Train Tickets International train tickets should be purchased at Rila railway ticket offices. The Sofia Rila offices are crowded, so pick up your open international train ticket at a Rila office in some other Bulgarian city. Do so well ahead, as most Rila offices are open only on weekdays during business hours and such tickets are sold only at larger train stations. Ask about seat reservations when you buy the ticket.

You pay for international train tickets in leva. Theoretically, student-card holders get a 30% discount on international train tickets between Eastern European countries, but don't count on it.

Car & Motorcycle

When you enter Bulgaria by car you must state which border crossing you'll be using to leave the country and pay a road tax accordingly. If your plans change and you leave by a crossing with a higher tax you'll have to pay the difference, but there are no refunds if you leave via a route with a lower tax.

Motorists in transit from Yugoslavia to Turkey can use only the borderposts of Kalotina and Kapitan-Andreevo, and must follow the autoroute between Sofia and Plovdiv. Following is a list of highway border crossings clockwise around Bulgaria, with the Bulgarian port of entry named.

Turkey You can cross at Malko Târnovo (92km south of Burgas) and also at Kapitan-Andreevo (20km west of Edirne).

Greece You can cross at Kulata (127km north of Thessaloniki) and Maritsa Bridge near Svilengrad.

Macedonia You can cross at Zlatarevo (37km west of Kulata), Stanke Lisichkovo (26km west of Blagoevgrad) and Gjueshevo (between Sofia and Skopje).

Yugoslavia There are crossings at Kalotina (between Sofia and Niš) and Vrâshka Chuka (45km south-west of Vidin).

Romania You can cross at Vidin (opposite Calafat), Ruse (opposite Giurgiu), Silistra where the Danube moves into Romania, Kardam (83km north of Varna on the inland route) and Durankulak (between Balchik

and Mangalia). Expect major delays entering/exiting Bulgaria by car to/from Romania at Ruse. The waits are especially long on the Romanian side for southbound vehicles – be prepared to arrive at the Romanian border to find a line of cars a kilometre long waiting to cross.

Walking

You can avoid the hassle of getting an international train ticket by walking out of Bulgaria. One of the easiest ways to travel to/from Romania is on the regular ferry service between Vidin and Calafat, both of which are well connected to the rest of their respective countries by cheap local trains. See the following Ferry section, and the Vidin and Calafat sections in this book for details.

On the Black Sea coast you can catch a bus to the Romanian border 6km north of Durankulak. Another bus covers the last 10km into Mangalia from the Vama Veche border post.

For Turkey take a local train to Svilengrad; if you can't easily get an onward train ticket for the 39km Svilengrad-Edirne hop, take a bus or taxi, or hitchhike the 20km from Svilengrad to Kapitan-Andreevo, the border post, and walk across (the train station is 4km from the centre of Svilengrad and the border is 2km beyond Kapitan-Andreevo village). Moneychangers and Turkish *dolmuş* (minibus taxis) to Edirne (20km, US$0.50) wait on the other side, and there are lots of buses from Edirne to Istanbul (247km, US$4). It's also easy to enter Bulgaria from Turkey this way.

Hitching in Greece and Yugoslavia is pretty bad, so you're probably better off taking a bus (see Bus earlier in this section). If you do decide to hitch to Greece, take a local train to Kulata, walk across and stick out your thumb.

RIVER

A regular car ferry crosses the Danube from Vidin to Calafat, Romania, hourly throughout the year (US$2 per person in hard currency). Bicycles are sometimes another US$2 each, sometimes free.

Getting Around

AIR

Balkan Bulgarian Airlines has five or six flights a day from Sofia to Varna and Burgas (US$129 one way). The expense of a domestic air ticket, however, may convince you that it's better to take the train.

BUS

Long-distance buses serve many points that are not directly connected by train. Take a bus to go from Sofia to Rila Monastery, from Troyan to Plovdiv, from Burgas to Varna etc. Only as many tickets are sold as there are seats, so it's important to arrive at the bus station (*avtogara*) early to make sure you get one. You usually buy the ticket at the office rather than from the driver. At way stations, tickets for long-distance buses can be purchased only after the bus arrives and the

driver tells the ticket clerk how many seats are available. Long-distance buses generally leave in the very early morning.

Private buses now operate regularly on long-distance routes in competition with the railways, especially from Sofia and Plovdiv to the Black Sea resorts. Overnight buses and all buses to the coast must be booked the day before, as they are usually full.

TRAIN

The Bâlgarski Dârzhavni Zheleznitsi (BDŽ), or Bulgarian State Railways, runs trains over 4278km of track. The trains are classified as *ekspresen* (express), *bârz* (fast) or *putnichki* (slow). Trains from Sofia to Burgas go via either Karlovo or Plovdiv. Trains from Sofia to Varna go via either Karlovo or Gorna Oryahovitsa. All trains from Sofia to Ruse go via Pleven and Gorna Oryahovitsa. Service between Sofia and Plovdiv is fairly frequent. Sleepers and couchettes are available

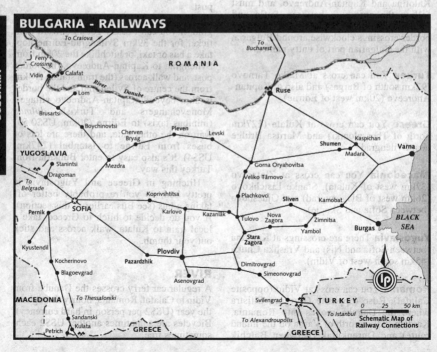

BULGARIA - RAILWAYS

Schematic Map of Railway Connections

between Sofia and Burgas or Varna for a mere 3000 leva on top of the normal fare but you'll need to book well ahead to get one. Seat reservations are recommended on express trains to the Black Sea. Visit Rila offices for these bookings.

Gorna Oryahovitsa is a main railway junction in northern Bulgaria where trains from Sofia, Ruse, Varna and Stara Zagora meet. The branch line south from Gorna Oryahovitsa to Stara Zagora via Veliko Târnovo is the only north-south line across the centre of the country. Another branch line runs from Ruse to Varna, although buses (via Shumen) are faster and more frequent on this route. Bulgaria's most spectacular train ride is up the Iskâr Gorge from Sofia to Mezdra on the line to Vidin or Pleven. For rail buffs, this would be worth doing even as a day trip.

Take care not to miss your station, as stations are poorly marked. Most have a sign in both Cyrillic and Latin script, but it's usually only on the station building itself. It's best to sit in the front half of the train to be able to read the station names. If you have to change at a minor junction or want to get off at a small station, try to find out what time your train should arrive there, then watch carefully and ask the people around you.

A complete timetable of all train services is available at Rila offices at a small cost. However it is only in Cyrillic. Alternatively the Thomas Cook European timetable (published monthly) has the main Bulgarian rail routes in an easy-to-follow format.

CAR & MOTORCYCLE

Travelling around Bulgaria by private car or motorcycle is quite feasible, but not necessarily an easy or relaxing experience. Other than the main motorways, of which there are currently only three sections nationwide, road conditions are generally taxing. Drivers must cope with potholes, roads under reconstruction, poor and sometimes non-existent signposting, slow moving vehicles, horses and carts and sometimes erratic driving. Signs to minor destinations are usually in Cyrillic only.

Vehicle security is another concern, since there has in recent years been a spate of vehicle thefts of and from foreign-registered cars. Take standard precautions against car theft such as locking the car securely and not parking on deserted streets. Use a hotel garage wherever possible. Don't leave any valuables in a parked car overnight and if possible leave a few scattered Bulgarian magazines or newspapers in view.

Renting a low-cost older Bulgarian registered car is a better option and this can work out to as little as US$34 a day inclusive (see Rental section) – a viable option for three or four travellers.

Fuel is available in normal (91 octane), unleaded (95 octane) and super (98 octane). Normal petrol has an octane rating that is too low for Western cars, but unleaded fuel (Euro 95) is now easy to find in major towns. Petrol stations are found along main highways every 30km or less. The price of petrol is based on the Deutschmark and is currently around 1010 leva for a litre of unleaded super. Shell petrol is generally preferred by Bulgarian drivers to the sometimes low quality Bulgarian stuff and you can usually serve yourself just like you do at home.

Shipka, the travel agency of the Union of Bulgarian Motorists, maintains information offices at all major border crossings and can provide current information about insurance, road tolls, traffic regulations etc.

The national road assistance number in Bulgaria is ☎ 12 86.

Road Rules

Car speed limits are either 40 or 50km/h in built-up areas, 90km/h on the open road and 120km/h on autoroutes. Motorcycles are limited to 50km/h in built-up areas, 70km/h on the open road and 100km/h on autoroutes. On highways, cars may stop only at designated places. Beware of overzealous traffic police who levy on-the-spot fines (always ask for a receipt *smetka*). Speeding fines are routine along the autoroute to Turkey. People riding in the front seat of a car must wear seat belts and everyone on a motorcycle must wear a helmet.

Rental

Avis, Hertz and Intercar all have car rental offices in Sofia, Plovdiv and Varna. The age limit at all three is 21 years and all allow free one-way rentals to their other locations in

Bulgaria. All outlets charge about US$57/304 daily/weekly for the smallest car with unlimited distance. Sometimes only the more expensive models are available, for about 75% more. Prices include public liability insurance but a collision damage waiver is about US$10 a day extra. To rent a car you must show your passport and pay a deposit of around US$600, which can be debited against your credit card. Your national driving licence suffices (an international licence is not required).

BICYCLE

Cycling is not popular in Bulgaria, but it is a viable way of getting around. The roads aren't great, but traffic is light off the main routes and generally considerate of cyclists. For 4000 leva or less, long-distance buses and trains will carry your bike. Mountain bikes are available for hire in Pamporovo and Borovets but if touring further afield, it's better to bring your own bicycle. Bring all the spare parts you can carry as you'll only find them in larger towns.

HITCHING

Hitching in rural Bulgaria is often preferable to being restricted by infrequent public transport. It's unusual to wait long for a lift, but travel will tend to be in fits and starts as many cars will be travelling only to the next village. The upsurge in crime over the last few years has turned many Bulgarians off thumbing rides, but you're more likely to be picked up by a worker in a filthy Lada than a thug in a shiny Mercedes.

BOAT

There is a hydrofoil service that operates along the Black Sea coast between Varna, Nesebâr, Pomorie, Burgas and Sozopol, and up the Danube from Ruse to Vidin. These are very popular with foreign visitors. 'Hydrobus' excursion boats also operate between Varna and Balchik, and from Nesebâr to Sozopol.

LOCAL TRANSPORT
Bus & Tram

City bus services are deteriorating despite vastly increased fares, with many irregularities in the schedules. In Sofia, the tram services are still very good.

Bus and tram tickets cost 350 leva a ride or 1000 leva for a day pass. Tickets can be bought at kiosks or from the driver. If you are caught without a ticket you will be hit for a 2500 leva spot fine. Buses and trams run from 5 am to midnight.

Taxi

Taxis are plentiful in Bulgaria and you can flag them down on the street. They are most easily found in front of train stations but beware of those waiting at the luxury hotels. Taxi drivers in Bulgaria charge what the meter says and are not expensive. Always try to take a taxi with a meter that works, otherwise ask beforehand what the fare will be. Drivers don't usually charge you for the return journey, even if it's out of town. Fares are slightly higher between 10 pm and 5 am. Round up the meter fare to the next multiple of five or 10.

To book a taxi in Sofia call ☎ 1280 for an older Lada taxi or ☎ 91119 for a newer car. Call ☎ 0799 42046 (mobile) for an airport taxi.

ORGANISED TOURS

Most travel services in Bulgaria are geared towards organised tours and they will delightedly take your dollars and pack you off to Bulgaria's attractions on luxury coaches. There are numerous fairly cheap all-inclusive tours to the Black Sea resorts (five-day Black Sea packages are available from about US$120 including transport from Sofia) but you're tied to a beach hotel, and outside the peak season (from June to mid-September), facilities are limited. Choose a reputable travel agent as some tourists in recent years have had their holidays ruined by double bookings. There are package ski holidays to Borovets and Pamporovo.

More imaginative than the beach holidays, but three times as expensive, are the tours featuring an eight-country cruise along the Danube from Ruse to Passau, Germany. There are also bus tours around the country, cycle tours, stays at luxury health resorts such as Sandanski, and so on. Balkan Holidays offices will have details.

Hiking and trekking holidays are very well

organised in Sofia and are an excellent way to see the country. Day excursions from Sofia or Plovdiv to Rila Monastery or Koprivshtitsa will set you back about US$35.

Sofia (София)

☎ 02

Sofia sits on a 545m-high plateau in western Bulgaria, at the foot of Mt Vitosha, just west of the Iskâr River and is the highest capital in Europe. Its position at the very centre of the Balkan Peninsula, midway between the Adriatic and Black seas, made it a crossroads of trans-European routes. The present city centre is attractive with large open areas paved with yellow bricks, tastefully rebuilt after WWII bombings. It's a remarkably clean, quiet city considering how much of Bulgaria's industry is concentrated here. If you can find reasonable accommodation, Sofia repays an unhurried stay.

History

Under various names, Sofia has a history that goes back thousands of years. The Thracian Serdi tribe settled here in the 7th century BC. In the 3rd century AD the Romans built strong walls around Serdica (Sofia), their capital of Inner Dacia and an important stopping point on the Roman road from Naisus (present Niš, Yugoslavia) to Constantinople (Istanbul). After the Hun invasion of 441, the town was rebuilt by the Byzantines. The Slavs gave Sredets (Sofia) a key role in the First Bulgarian Empire, then in 1018 the Byzantines re-took Triaditsa (Sofia). At the end of the 12th century, the Bulgarians returned and Sredets became a major trading centre of the Second Bulgarian Empire.

The Turks captured Sofia in 1382 and held it for five centuries. The city declined during the feudal unrest of the 19th century, but with the establishment of the Third Bulgarian Empire in 1879, Sofia again became the capital. Between 1879 and 1939, the population grew from 20,000 to 300,000. Today, 1,140,000 people live in Sofia. The Yugoslav border at Dimitrovgrad is only 55km northwest of Sofia, and the city's off-centre location in Bulgaria is a reminder of the loss of Macedonia to Serbia and Greece in 1913.

Orientation

The central train station is on the northern side of the city centre. On arrival at the station, go down into the underpass and walk right through to just before the far end. From there catch tram No 1 or 7 four stops to the centre of town. You can buy tram tickets in the underpass from sellers or a poorly-marked office on the far right side of the sunken plaza. The left-luggage office downstairs in the train station is open from 5.30 am to midnight and charges 500 leva per piece of luggage. Sofia's bus stations do not have left-luggage offices.

From the station and to your left (look for the Novotel Evropa), bul Mariya Luiza curves around and runs south through ploshtad Sveta Nedelya. Beyond Sveta Nedelya Cathedral this thoroughfare becomes bul Vitosha, the fashionable avenue of modern Sofia. The narrow Graf Ignatiev, Sofia's liveliest shopping precinct, runs south-east from near the beginning of Vitosha (take tram No 2, 12 or 19). Many travel agencies and airline offices are found along bul Stamboliyski, which runs west from Sveta Nedelya Cathedral.

Largo opens east from ploshtad Sveta Nedelya and spills into ploshtad Batenberg. Tsar Osvoboditel continues south-east as far as the Clement of Ohrid University, then runs on and out of the city as bul Tsarigradsko Shose.

Information

Tourist Offices The best place to head for to get independent information on places to stay and things to do is the National Information and Advertising Centre (☎ 987 9778; fax 981 1515) at Sveta Sofia 1. The English and French-speaking staff have are exceedingly helpful and have some excellent printed material for travellers. Equally helpful is Odysseia-In which, apart from being a travel agency (see Adventure Travel) can provide maps and brochures on pretty well any part of the country and make reservations on your behalf if necessary.

Money The First East International Bank, Lege 15, gives the best cash rates. Most private currency exchange offices are clustered along bul Mariya Luiza, Stamboliyski and Vitosha. ATMs taking Visa and MC can be found at the train station, in the main telephone centre and in a growing number of central locations.

The American Express representative is Megatours (☎ 980 8889), corner of Aksakov and Benovsaka.

Post & Communications Sofia's main telephone centre is on General Gurko round the corner from the main post office on Vasil Levski. It's open 24 hours and can be rather chaotic.

The telephone centre in the shopping mall below the NDK Palace of Culture is smaller and only open weekdays from 7 am to 7 pm, and Saturday from 8 am to 1 pm, but it's usually uncrowded and easy to use. There is also a small telephone centre at the train station.

Travel Agencies The main Balkantourist office (☎ 87 72 33) that helps individual tourists is at bul Stamboliyski 27 (open daily from 9 am to 6 pm, to 8 pm in summer). The staff will reserve accommodation, change money and book sightseeing tours. They will also answer questions, if their crosswords are not too engrossing.

The Orbita Youth Travel Agency (☎ 80 01 02), bul Hristo Botev 48, sells ISIC student cards (US$4) and can book beds in student dormitories at US$7 per person for students, US$9 for non-students.

Tourist Information & Reservations (☎ 980 3314), Lavele 22 off bul Stamboliyski (there's also an office at the NDK Palace of Culture), can book rooms at two-star hotels all around Bulgaria for about US$26/40 a single/double with bath and breakfast, which is about 20% off the rate you'd pay if you just walked in and rented a room.

For information on driving conditions in Bulgaria, go to Shipka, the travel agency of the Union of Bulgarian Motorists (☎ 88 38 56), Lavele 18, just off bul Stamboliyski.

The combined transportation ticket office in the lower level arcade at the NDK Palace of Culture sells domestic train tickets and books couchettes or sleepers to Varna and Burgas (only 3000 leva but they are sometimes fully booked well ahead). You can also purchase international tickets at this office. The clerk at the counter marked *'Eisenbahnfahrkarten für Auslandsreisen'* can provide your international ticket and make any required seat or couchette reservations in the one operation. This office is crowded around mid-afternoon, so come early or late.

The main Rila office, General Gurko 5 (open weekdays from 7 am to 7 pm), also sells international tickets. You must queue up for a ticket, queue up to pay, queue up to hand in the slip to get the ticket, then queue up again to make a reservation.

Adventure Travel The Odysseia-In Travel Agency (☎ 989 0535; fax 980 3200; odysseia@omega.bg), behind bul Stamboliyski 20 (enter from Lavele), specialises in adventure travel. This is a terrific place to get information, maps and advice on skiing, cycling or walking your way around Bulgaria. From June to October it runs hiking tours through the Rila and Pirin mountains for Western European groups, and individuals can sign up at the Sofia office. The price is US$210 for one week, including food, transport, accommodation, guides, and horses to carry baggage. Odysseia's English and French-speaking staff also offer short two to three-day mountain treks at US$25 a day half board, horse riding (US$10 per hour), fishing, paragliding and cave exploration. In winter, there are skiing holidays from US$30 per day. If you need mountaineering or camping gear, or even a new backpack, Odysseia sells the best.

It's worth contacting Odysseia before you head to Bulgaria, as the staff can help with everything from visas to airport pick-ups and will happily tailor trips according to individual requirements.

Bookshops The latest foreign newspapers in English can be purchased at the newsstand in the basement of the Sheraton Balkan Hotel. The Bulgarpress bookshop, Graf Ignatiev 33, sells English-language newspapers, magazines and a small selection of novels. Some book stalls in ploshtad Slaveikov sell overpriced English-language novels (you can bargain).

Medical Services Dr Boris Kerezov of 'The Family Doctor' (☎ 712 269; mob 088 700 278) or the Torax Clinic (☎ 988 5259) at Stamboliyski 57 are two services you could contact in emergency. There is a 24-hour pharmacy on ploshtad Sveta Nedelya.

Emergency Emergency numbers are: police ☎ 166; ambulance ☎ 150; fire ☎ 160. These numbers are valid throughout Bulgaria.

Things to See & Do

Sightseeing in Sofia is centred mostly around museums, although there are a number of old churches and mosques to visit. Begin with the largest: the neo-Byzantine **Aleksander Nevski Church** (1912), which is a memorial to the 200,000 Russian soldiers who died for Bulgaria's independence. In the crypt is a museum of icons (closed Tuesday). The 6th-century basilica just west of the church is the **Church of St Sophia**, who gave her name to the city. By the church wall is the **Tomb of the Unknown Soldier**. The large white building behind the Aleksander Nevski Church contains the **Foreign Art Gallery** (closed Tuesday, free Sunday), with an important collection of European paintings as well as African, Japanese and Indian art.

The street that runs south from Aleksander Nevski empties into ploshtad Narodno Sabranie where you'll find the **National Assembly** (1884) and an equestrian statue (1905) of Aleksander II, the Russian tsar who freed Bulgaria from the Turks. Bul Tsar Osvoboditel runs west into ploshtad Batenberg, the heart of official Sofia. On the way, beyond the park, are **St Nicholas Russian Church** (1913) and the **Natural Science Museum**, Tsar Osvoboditel 1, with flora and fauna exhibits on four floors.

Ploshtad Batenberg is dominated by the vacant former **Georgi Dimitrov Mausoleum**. Dimitrov faced Hermann Goering at the Reichstag fire trail in 1933 and after spending the war years in the USSR was elected prime minister of Bulgaria in 1946. From his death in 1949 until mid-1990, when his wax-like body was cremated, the public was allowed to file reverently past the deified figure as an honour guard looked on.

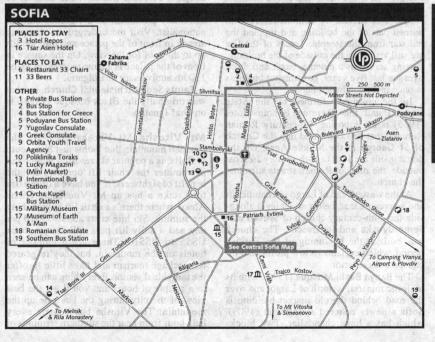

Across the road from the mausoleum are the **National Art Gallery** (10.30 am to 6 pm), with Bulgarian paintings and the **Ethnographical Museum** (10 am to 5 pm), both housed in the former Royal Palace (1887) and both closed on Monday. Before 1878, the residence of the Turkish governor occupied this same site. The park east of the mausoleum is dominated by the neoclassical **Ivan Vazov National Academic Theatre** (1907) designed by the Viennese architects Fellner and Hellmer.

Hidden behind the Bulgarian National Bank, at the eastern end of ploshtad Batenberg, are the nine lead-covered domes of the Buyuk Djami, or the Great Mosque (1496), now the **National Archaeological Museum** (10 am to 4.30 pm, closed Monday). It has an excellent collection of antique sculpture.

Facing Largo, across the street from the Archaeological Museum, is the former **Communist Party Building** (1955), with the former Council of State on the northern side of Largo and the former State Council on the southern side, the most impressive Stalinist ensemble in Bulgaria. In August 1990, Party House was sacked by demonstrators who burned part of the building and toppled the red star from the steeple. Traces of the fire are still visible on the outside of the building. Having served as a cinema, bazar and disco over the last five years, government business is once more conducted here.

In the courtyard formed by the State Council and the Sheraton Balkan Hotel (1955) is an imposing 4th-century Roman Rotunda that was converted into the **Church of St George** in the Middle Ages. On the dome inside are 11th to 14th-century frescos; outside, the ruins of Roman streets surround the church.

At the western end of Largo is a handicraft and souvenir bazar, below street level alongside the 14th-century church of **Sveta Petra Semerdyuska** and its frescos. The church was built at the beginning of the Turkish period, which explains its low profile and inconspicuous exterior.

The **Banya Bashi Mosque** (1576), with its majestic minaret, is north of Largo, and over the road behind the old market building is Sofia's newly restored **synagogue** (1909), which has a huge chandelier. Two blocks beyond the synagogue is the teeming *public market* along bul Stefan Stambolov (watch your wallet).

South of Largo is **Sveta Nedelya Cathedral** (1863), restored after a 1924 bomb attempt on Tsar Boris III in which 124 people (including most of the cabinet) were killed. Beyond it on Vitosha bul is the **National Museum of History** (closed Monday in summer and weekends in winter, US$1) in the building of the former Palace of Justice (1936). This huge museum takes up two floors of an entire city block. On the ground floor there is a multilingual touch-screen introduction to the museum's collection and English labels are displayed for the most important items. Don't miss the 4th century BC Panagyurishte gold treasure in room No 3.

Vitosha, Sofia's most elegant boulevard, runs south from Sveta Nedelya Cathedral to the monstrous **NDK Palace of Culture** (1981), often used for concerts and conferences. This ultramodern building was previously named after Lyudmila Zhivkov, daughter of Todor Zhivkov, and minister of culture until her death in 1981. Lyudmila was extremely prominent as a vigorous cultural nationalist. Visit the underground shopping arcade in front of the palace and take the lift up to the roof for the view. On the square in front of the palace is a huge monument to the 1300th anniversary of Bulgaria.

Saints Sedmotchislenitsi Church, in what was originally the Black Mosque (1528), is on Graf Ignatiev.

Mt Vitosha Mt Vitosha (2290m), the rounded mountain that looms just 8km south of Sofia, is a popular ski resort in winter and in summer the chair lift operates for the benefit of sightseers. If you have a little extra time, take a bus up Mt Vitosha to Hizha Aleko, where there's a chair lift approaching the summit. Ski hire costs about US$10 per day and a daily lift pass will set you back US$5 to US$10. There are a number of hotels on the mountain, but they're geared for package tourism and have little to offer the individual visitor. Everything can be seen in a couple of hours and you'll get the best view of the city during the bus ride up the mountain. The Vitosha bus departs every half-hour from near the southern terminus of tram Nos 9 and 12. Vitosha is also accessible from Ovcha Kupel bus station (tram Nos 4, 5 and 11).

Places to Stay

With the demise of communist-controlled tourism, it has become much easier to find a cheap place to stay in Sofia, although foreigners still pay many times more than Bulgarians at the up-market hotels.

Camping *Camping Vranya* (☎ 78 12 13; open all year) is 9km out of the city on the Plovdiv Highway. From the central train station take bus No 213 out onto bul Tsarigradsko Shose, then change to bus No 5 or 6, both of which pass the site. Alternatively, take tram No 20 south-east, then change to bus No 5 or 6. Camping costs US$4 per person plus US$3 per tent, and bungalows are US$28 for a single or double. There's a restaurant on the premises – don't pitch your tent too close to it if you want to get any sleep.

Hostels There are several hostels on Mt Vitosha. *Hizha Aleko* (☎ 67 11 13) costs US$6 per person in a seven-bed dorm, US$7/9 per person in a single/double. *Hizha Salzitsa* (☎ 67 10 54), 500m off the main road to Mt Vitosha, near the end of the bus line, has rooms for about US$10 per person.

Private Rooms The *exchange and accommodation office* at the western end of the upper level in the train station rents private rooms from US$11 to US$14 per person.

Balkantourist, Stamboliyski 27 (open daily from 9 am to 6 pm, 8 pm in summer), books private rooms. A good room in the city centre is about US$16/18 a single/double.

Odysseia-In Travel (☎ 989 0538; odysseia@omega.bg) on Lavele has a double room for US$10 per person. It's central, handy and has its own bathroom and kitchen and guests have access to email. Call ahead, or email to book.

Sport Tourist (☎ 83 14 73), bul Mariya Luiza 79 (open daily from 11 am to 7 pm), has doubles at US$13 for one or two people.

Markella Company (☎ 81 52 99), bul Mariya Luiza 17, operates out of a red kiosk at the back of the parking lot across the street from the Central Department Store (TsUM). Private room prices are from US$10 to US$14 for one or two people in the centre of town.

Hotels The *Edelweiss Hotel* (☎ 83 54 31), bul Mariya Luiza 79, is an old hotel on a noisy tram route between the train station and the centre of town. It offers only rooms with shared bath at US$10/15 a single/double. It's grungy and really only for hardy low-budget travellers who put price above all else.

Somewhere between bearable and quite pleasant and affordable are two little private hotels run by the same woman. *Hotel Enny* (☎ 83 30 02), Pop Bogomil 46, is the more modern of the two with singles/doubles for US$15/20, while *Hotel Bolid* (☎ 83 43 95), Pop Bogomil 27, is older and offers its rooms for US$10/20. Both are handy for the train and bus stations.

Hotel Maya (☎ 89 46 11), Trapezitsa 4, is a small family-run place right in the centre of town, directly opposite the Central Department Store (TsUM). For US$20/30 a single/double you get a bright room with bathroom, TV and fridge.

The *Tsar Asen Hotel* (☎ 547 801) at Tsar Asen 68, is a fairly central hotel but in a quiet location. It has only four rooms so book ahead if you can. Prices are from US$10 to US$20 per person. It's one street west of the 1300th Anniversary Monument park (just off our map). Take tram 1 or 7 to NDK stop.

Directly opposite the Novotel Evropa, the *Hotel Repos* (☎ 31 48 40; fax 32 21 85; repo@omega.bg) is very convenient for trains and buses. They charge US$40 for a double room without bath and US45 for a double room with bath.

Hotel Baldjieva (☎ 87 29 14), Tsar Asen 23, has singles for US$40 and doubles for US$50, all with shared bath. This pleasant, privately-owned hotel is a good medium-priced choice in an excellent location. Breakfast is included.

Places to Eat

Sofia has a good choice of restaurants, cafés and fresh produce markets. When dining in, keep track of the cost of your order as some waiters have been known to overcharge foreigners.

CENTRAL SOFIA

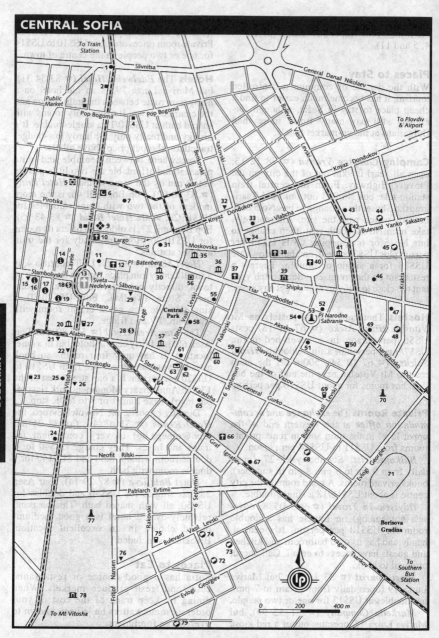

To Train Station

Slivnitsa

General Danail Nikolaev

Public Market

Pop Bogomil

Pop Bogomil

To Plovdiv & Airport

Bulevard Vasil Levski

Knyaz Dondukov

Pirotska

Iskâr

Knyaz Dondukov

Vlabcha

Bulevard Yanko Sakazov

Largo

Moskovska

Pl Batenberg

Pl Sveta Nedelya

Sâborna

Tsar Osvoboditel

Shipka

Central Park

Aksakov

Pl Narodno Sabranie

Slavyanska

Ivan Vazov

Gurko

General

6 Septemvri

Ikaradzha

Graf Ignatiev

Neofit Rilski

Patriarch Evtimii

Bulevard Vasil Levski

6 Septemvri

Borisova Gradina

Dragan Tsankov

To Southern Bus Station

Evlogi Georgiev

To Mt Vitosha

Fritjof Nansen

0   200   400 m

PLACES TO STAY
2 Edelweiss Hotel
3 Hotel Enny
4 Hotel Bolid
8 Hotel Maya
23 Hotel Baldjieva

PLACES TO EAT
15 Vinarna
21 Tai Pan Chinese Restaurant
22 Eddy's Tex Mex Diner
26 Kenar Salad & Sandwich Bar
29 Trops Kushta
32 Bai Gencho Restaurant
34 Luciano Café
64 Restaurant Baalbeck
76 Café Vitosha

OTHER
1 Lions Bridge
5 Synagogue
6 Banya Bashi Mosque
7 Central Mineral Baths (closed)
9 Central Department Store (TsUM)
10 Sveta Petra Semerdyuska Church
11 Sheraton Balkan Hotel
12 Church of St George Rotunda
13 Sveta Nedelya Cathedral
14 Odysseia-In Travel Agency
16 Balkantourist
17 Shipka Travel Agency & Tourist Information & Reservations

18 TS Bank
19 National Information & Advertising Centre
20 National Museum of History
24 Sozopol Mini-market
25 Zadruga Bulgarian Folk Arts Shop
27 Birariya Shveik Pub
28 First East International Bank
30 National Archaeological Museum
31 Former Communist Party Building
33 National Academic Theatre for Opera & Ballet
35 National Art Gallery & Ethnographical Museum
36 Natural Science Museum
37 Sveti Nicholas Russian Church
38 Church of Svela Sophia
39 Patriarch's Palace
40 Aleksander Nevski Church
41 Foreign Art Gallery
42 Vasil Levski Monument
43 Makedonski State Musical Theatre
44 Czech Consulate
45 Albanian Consulate
46 National Library
47 Fine Art Sales Gallery
48 Croatian Consulate
49 Clement of Ohrid University
50 Disco Yalta
51 American Express & Megatours

52 National Assembly
53 Monument to the Liberators
54 Balkan Bulgarian Airlines
55 Zala Bulgaria
56 Former Georgi Dimitrov Mausoleum
57 City Art Gallery
58 Ivan Vazov National Academic Theatre
59 La Strada Jazz Club
60 Ivan Vazov Museum & Luciano Café
61 Rila Railway Ticket Office
62 Puppet Theatre
63 Main Post Office & Telephone Centre
65 Satirical Theatre
66 Sveti Sedmotchislenitsi Church
67 Bulgarpress Bookshop
68 Turkish Embassy
69 Rock Café Luciano
70 Soviet Army Monument
71 Vasil Levski Stadium
72 Hungarian Consulate
73 Polish Consulate
74 British Embassy
75 Underground Nightclub
77 1300th Anniversary Monument
78 NDK Palace of Culture & ICN Internet Centre
79 US Consulate

BULGARIA

Restaurants Very central, modern and cheap is the *Trops Kushta* self-service restaurant, Sâboma 5. They serve tasty Bulgarian dishes and the lunchtime queues bear witness to its popularity with the locals. The *Vinarna* is a cosy little mehana at bul Stamboliyski 29, specialising in Bulgarian *meze* dishes and excellent wine.

Further down bul Stamboliyski on Ploshtad Vâzrazhdane is a good lively pub come restaurant called *33 Beers*. Upstairs the beer is served on a trolley on rails. In the basement at Vitosha 4 *Eddy's Tex Mex Diner* is a funky little restaurant that serves up great Mexican food and top Sofia bands playing ZZ Top and Lynyrd Skynyrd covers. Go before 9 pm to get a table.

Tai Pan, Alabin 46, is a pretty reasonable Chinese restaurant. You're not likely to think you've hit Beijing, but there's a wide selection of dishes and an English menu with English-speaking waiters.

Bai Gencho, Knyaz Dondukov 15, serves traditional Bulgarian food and wines from the owners' vineyard. The atmosphere is pleasant and there's an English version of the menu. *Restaurant 33 Chairs* (☎ 44 29 81), Asen Zlatarov 14, is a charming tavern 10 minutes walk east of the city centre. Reservations are recommended.

Cafés There are many pavement cafés along bul Vitosha and you can tell at a glance which offer the best deals by the number of local people sitting there. A great place for coffee and cakes is *Luciano*, up the top end of Rakovski, on the corner of Moskovska. The pancakes here are yummy. There is another *Luciano* at Rakovski 135.

Café Vitosha, on the corner of Vasil Levski where it meets the NDK plaza, is a ritzy café.

Fast Food *Restaurant Baalbeck*, Vasil Levski 4, right near the corner of Graf Ignatiev, has Lebanese pockets, grills, salads and appetisers. Numerous shops satisfy the inevitable banitsa addiction. KFC, McDonald's and Pizza Hut can't be missed. They are everywhere around Sofia!

Vegetarian Food The modern and breezy *Kenar* salad and sandwich bar on Vitosha is as good a place as any to rustle up a tasty DIY vegetarian meal as well as scrumptious sandwiches with or without meat.

Supermarkets Half way down Vitosha on the right is the *Sozopol* mini-market cum delicatessen; a good place to stock up on picnic items. In similar style is the *Lucky Magazini* on Ploshtad Vâzrazhdane, west along bul Stamboliyski.

Self-Catering The market on bul Stefan Stambolov is the best place for fresh produce and groceries. Salad greens, fruit and mountain tea are available from the stalls near Saints Sedmotchislenitsi church on Graf Ignatiev.

Entertainment

For an unforgettable evening of classical entertainment head for the *National Academic Theatre for Opera & Ballet* on Vrabcha, not far from the Aleksander Nevski Church. Tickets are sold inside.

For lighter fare, it's the *Makedonski State Musical Theatre* on bul Vasil Levski, behind the Aleksander Nevski Church. The operettas here are highly recommended, even if they are in Bulgarian. At both theatres, performances begin at 7 pm, with matinées on weekends.

The *Puppet Theatre*, General Gurko 14, never fails to please. Performances on Saturday and Sunday start at 10.30 am and at noon. Nearby is the *Satirical Theatre*, Stefan

Karadzha 26. You probably won't understand a word of it, but the acting is superb. The *Ivan Vazov National Academic Theatre*, Vasil Levski 5, presents classical theatre in Bulgarian.

Many concerts take place in the *Zala Bâlgaria* at Aksakov 3 and others are performed in the *NDK Palace of Culture*. In July and August, the Palace of Culture maintains a daily programme of events while Sofia's other theatres close for holidays.

The ticket office at the Palace of Culture is accessible from the outside terrace through a separate entrance to the left of the main entrance (closes at 2 pm on Saturday).

A folklore show for tourists begins each summer evening at 9 pm at the *Mehana Vodenitsata* (☎ 67 10 58) in Dragalevtsi, 13km south of central Sofia (bus Nos 66 and 93). Typical Bulgarian food is served before the show from 7 pm.

Bars, Discos & Nightclubs The *Art Club*, Ivan Asen II 6, near Eagles Bridge (go south down Tsar Osvoboditel), sometimes has live music but is always a good place for an evening drink. It's open till midnight. *Underground* is a nightclub in an underpass below Vasil Levski just east of the Palace of Culture.

Rock Café Luciano at the corner of General Gurko and bul Vasil Levski is a trendy, dress-code nightspot owned by the same Luciano of the Luciano Café. Don't turn up in a Trabbie.

The *Birariya Shveik* downstairs off Vitosha directly opposite the National Museum of History is a hip pub with live music, great draft beer and top pub nosh to boot. *La Strada*, Shesti Septemvri 4, is a terrific jazz venue where local and international bands perform. This is Sofia's coolest night spot.

A young crowd keeps *Disco Yalta*, Aksakov 31, rocking.

Things to Buy

If you're in the market for an original painting or sculpture by a Bulgarian artist, go to the Fine Art Sales Gallery, Shipka 6. The Hemus Art Gallery, next to Megatours opposite the mausoleum, sells original Bulgarian iconic and contemporary art. Ask about export regulations before making a major purchase.

For good quality folk art souvenirs visit the Zadruga Bulgarian Folk Arts shop on Vitosha. The shop is a bit on the expensive side, but the range and quality of goods on display makes selecting a souvenir easy.

Getting There & Away

Bus Places that you can reach more easily by bus than by train include Rila Monastery (three hours), Troyan (175km) and Gabrovo (223km).

Direct services to the Rila Monastery and Melnik depart from the Ovcha Kupel bus station (tram No 5 or 11), and buses to Troyan and Gabrovo leave from the Poduyane bus station near the Gerena Stadium, north-east of the centre (trolleybus No 2 or 3). Advance tickets for these buses are available at the ticket office in the arcade below the Palace of Culture, but you must buy them at least one day beforehand.

Private buses chug off to every corner of Bulgaria (as well as many Western European cities) from the parking lot in between the central train station and the Novotel Europa Hotel. Tickets can be booked up to a week in advance at the kiosks here and it's a good idea to do this a day or two before for the popular early morning or overnight buses. Check the bus information in the Getting There & Away section earlier in this chapter.

Train All railway services in Bulgaria focus on Sofia. There are international lines to Belgrade, Athens, Istanbul, Bucharest and beyond. For routes and fares see the Getting There & Away section earlier in this chapter.

Important domestic express trains run to Ruse (via Pleven), to Varna (via Pleven or Karlovo) and to Burgas (via Karlovo or Plovdiv). For Veliko Târnovo change at Gorna Oryahovitsa. Plovdiv is only two hours from Sofia by express train. A local line east to Kazanlâk serves Koprivshtitsa, Karlovo and Kazanlâk (for Shipka). Sleepers and couchettes are available to Burgas and Varna (book well in advance).

Train Station Sofia's central train station can be a little confusing. In addition to the Cyrillic destination signs, the platforms (*peron*) are numbered in Roman numerals and the tracks (*kolovoz*) in Arabic numerals. Allow an extra 10 minutes to find your train, then ask several people to ensure that it really is the right one.

Domestic tickets are sold on the lower level, but same-day tickets to Vidin, Lom, Ruse and Varna are sold at street level. There are two Rila ticket offices downstairs opposite the regular ticket windows. The one closer to the middle of the hall sells sleepers within Bulgaria and international tickets (open daily from 7 am to 11 pm). The one at the end sells advance tickets with seat reservations (reservations cannot be made on Sunday) within Bulgaria (Monday to Saturday from 6 am to 7.30 pm, Sunday from 6.30 am to 2.30 pm). The left-luggage office is also on the lower level (5.30 am to midnight), as is the entrance to most tracks.

At street level are two currency exchanges one of which doubles as an accommodation office, open from 7 am to 10.30 pm. There is an ATM machine that takes Visa cards nearby.

Getting Around

To/From the Airport Vrazdebna airport, 12km east of Sofia, is accessible on city bus Nos 84 and 284 from the stop on bul Tsar Osvoboditel, opposite the university. A taxi between the airport and the city centre should in theory cost no more than 5000 leva. There have been a number of reports of new arrivals being overcharged (US$35!) by taxi drivers at the airport: make sure you take a taxi with a meter and insist that it is turned on, or take the bus.

The main Balkan Bulgarian Airlines office is on ploshtad Narodno Sabranie, off Tsar Osvoboditel, with a branch office in the arcade below the Palace of Culture.

Public Transport Sofia's public transport system is based on trams and is supplemented by buses and trolleybuses. Tickets (350 leva) and passes valid on all vehicles are sold at kiosks but these are poorly marked so get a good supply when you have the chance. Tram drivers also sell tickets. Inspectors often check tickets. On-the-spot fines are 2500 leva.

Public transit passes (*abonamentna karta*) are available for one day (1000 leva) and five days (4500 leva).

BULGARIA

Minibus taxis depart from in front of the train station and from many bus and tram stops. Destinations are posted on the windscreen. The fare is about two and a half times that of buses and trams (pay the driver).

Car For car rentals try Hertz (☎ 980 0461), Gurko 10, Avis (☎ 981 4960), Tsar Kaloyan 8 behind the Sheraton, and Budget (☎ 87 16 82), Vitosha 1. All three big name rental companies start at about US$69 per day for a small car. Avtorent (☎ 43 55 75), Ivan Asen 2, rents out older cars starting from as little as US$28 per day all inclusive. However, all companies require an upfront deposit of US$600 on any rental agreement.

Taxi Almost all taxis have meters these days, but if there's no meter, check the price beforehand. You can flag taxis on the street and the drivers are usually honest, but make sure they understand your destination by naming a major landmark near it. Some drivers will take a roundabout route to justify a higher fare. Beware of taxis parked in front of luxury hotels. A ride around town will cost between 2000 and 3000 leva.

Western Bulgaria

Western Bulgaria merges imperceptibly into Macedonia at the very heart of the Balkan Peninsula. Bulgaria's highest mountains are found in the Rila and Pirin massifs between Sofia and Greece. Medieval Bulgaria was ruled from towns in the north-east, but after independence in 1878, Sofia was chosen as the centrally located capital of 'Greater Bulgaria' (which included Macedonia).

The west has much to offer, from the excitement of Sofia to the history and natural beauty in the area around Rila and the intact folklore in Pirin villages such as Bansko and Melnik. For travellers arriving from Western Europe, the west is the gateway to Bulgaria.

THE RILA MOUNTAINS

The majestic Rila Mountains south of Sofia are *the* place to go hiking. Mountain hostels (*hizhas*) provide basic dormitory accommodation (about US$3 per person) and although

many serve meals, sometimes all they have is soup, so you had best bring food. The larger hostels provide linen, making a sleeping bag unnecessary. For current information on the hostels, inquire at Odysseia-In Travel Agency, behind bul Stamboliyski 20, Sofia.

The classic trip is across the mountains from Complex Malyovitsa to Rila Monastery (Rilski Manastir), which can be done in one day, or in two days if you visit the Seven Lakes. A longer route to Rila Monastery begins at the ski resort of Borovets and includes a climb to the top of Musala Peak (2925m), the highest mountain in the Balkan Peninsula. You could also do both and make the trip there and back in four or five days.

Samokov

Almost everyone on their way to Complex Malyovitsa or Borovets passes through Samokov on the Iskâr River, 62km south-east of Sofia. The town sprang up as an ironmining centre in the 14th century and later devoted itself to trade. The 19th-century Samokov school of icon painting and woodcarving was famous. Just above the bus station is the beautiful **Bairakli Mosque** (1840) with a wooden dome decorated in the National Revival style.

Buses to Samokov leave frequently from the bus station below the overpass beyond Sofia's Park-Hotel Moskva (take tram No 14 or 19).

Complex Malyovitsa

This mountain resort (elevation 1750m) at the foot of the Rila Mountains is the site of the Central School of Alpinism and an ideal starting point for anyone wishing to hike over the mountains to Rila Monastery. The large wooden hotel (make your reservations at Odysseia-In, Sofia) has rooms for US$15 per person including breakfast and there's a good restaurant. In winter the complex functions as a ski resort and the price of a B&B rises to US$25.

From Complex Malyovitsa you get a stunning view straight up the valley to the jagged double peak of Malyovitsa (2729m). You can hike to the peak from the complex in about four hours and a strong climber could make it right through to Rila Monastery in a day.

THE RILA MOUNTAINS

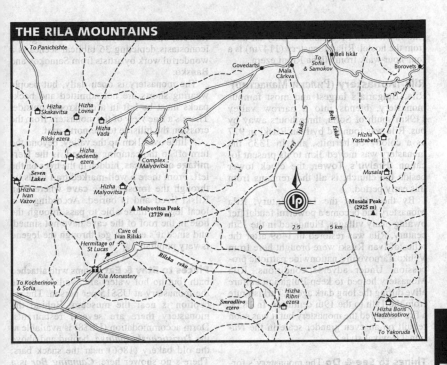

Try to buy the Rila hiking map in Sofia before coming, although maps are sometimes sold at the complex reception.

Take one of the regular buses from the bus station near Sofia's Park-Hotel Moskva to Govedartsi, where you can connect to Complex Malyovitsa.

To Rila via Malyovitsa

About an hour's hike above Complex Malyovitsa is the *Hizha Malyovitsa* (2050m), where a dorm bed and bowl of soup are usually available (open all year). From Hizha Malyovitsa you can hike up to *Hizha Sedemte ezera* (no meals served, bring food) in about six hours. This hizha is right beside one of the legendary Seven Lakes on a mountain plateau at 2200m elevation. A notorious sun-worshipping cult was centred on these lakes before WWII. From Hizha Sedemte ezera you can hike down to Rila Monastery (elevation 1147m) in six hours.

To Rila via Borovets

From Sofia catch the bus to Samokov (see the Samokov section above), where you'll find another bus every 30 minutes to Borovets (elevation 1300m, 72km from Sofia). This popular ski resort founded by Prince Ferdinand in 1897 is up-market, so if your budget's not up to that, arrive early enough to make the stiff four-hour hike up to *Hizha Musala* (2389m) the same day. Check to see if the 4827m cable car (US$2) to *Hizha Yastrebets* (2363m) is operating from Borovets, as it saves you quite a climb. *Hotel Virginia* (☎ 07128-258) in Borovets is US$15 per person, breakfast included.

Musala Peak is only two hours beyond Hizha Musala. Carry on for another four hours to *Hizha Boris Hadzhisotirov* (2185m) beside Granchar Lake. There's a restaurant here and a road south to Yakoruda on the railway to Bansko. The next day it will take you about five hours to reach *Hizha Ribni ezera* (2230m), in between the Fish Lakes.

Smradlivo ezero (Stinking Lake), the largest lake in the Rila Mountains, is only an hour from the hostel. Rila Monastery (1147m) is a four-hour walk from Hizha Ribni ezera.

Rila Monastery (Рилски Манастир)

Rila, Bulgaria's largest and most famous monastery, blends into a narrow valley 119km south of Sofia, three hours away by bus. Rila was founded by Ivan Rilski in 927 as a colony of hermits, and in 1335 the monastery was moved 3km to its present location. **Hrelyu's Tower**, the clock tower beside the church, is all that remains from this early period.

By the end of the 14th century, Rila Monastery had become a powerful feudal fief owning many villages. Plundered in the 15th century, Rila was restored in 1469 after the relics of Ivan Rilski were brought here from Veliko Târnovo in a nationwide patriotic procession. Under adverse conditions, Rila Monastery helped to keep Bulgarian culture alive during the long dark age of Turkish rule from the 15th to the 19th centuries. In 1833, a fire destroyed the monastery but it was soon rebuilt on an even grander scale in the National Revival style.

Things to See & Do The monastery's forbidding exterior contrasts dramatically with the warmth and cosiness of the striped arcades inside. Four levels of balconies surround the large, irregular courtyard and three **museums** occupy some of the 300 rooms. One museum contains the monastery's original charter (1378), signed and stamped by Tsar Ivan Shishman, and Brother Raphael's wooden cross bearing 1500 human figures, each the size of a grain of rice. There are excellent views of the surrounding mountains from the uppermost verandah. Don't miss the **kitchen** (1816) at courtyard level in the northern wing, with a 24m chimney cutting through all storeys by means of 10 rows of arches crowned by a small dome. Food was once prepared in huge cauldrons for the pilgrim masses.

The present magnificent **church** with its three great domes was built between 1834 and 1837. The 1200 frescos painted between 1840 and 1848 depict donors, Old Testament kings, apostles, angels, demons and martyrs, all with an extremely rich ornamentation of flowers, birds and stylised vines. The gilded iconostasis depicting 36 biblical scenes is a wonderful work by artists from Samokov and Bansko.

The monastery is open daily, but people wearing shorts are not admitted and backpacks must be left in a cloakroom outside. There's a fine view of the monastery from the cross on the hillside to the north-east.

A little over 1km up the valley, beyond the turn-off to the camping ground, is the **Hermitage of St Lucas**, hidden in the trees on the left. From there a well-marked trail leads up through the forest to the **cave** where Ivan Rilski lived and is buried. According to a local legend, those able to pass through the hole in the roof of the cave have not sinned, and since it's easy to get through the legend is very popular.

Places to Stay & Eat Rooms with attached bath (but no hot water) are available inside the monastery at US$15 per person. The reception is near the museum. Behind the monastery there are several restaurants. Dorm accommodation (US$8) is available at the *Turisticheski spalnya*, behind and above the old bakery (1866) near the snack bars. There's no shower here. *Camping Bor* is a kilometre further up the valley beyond the monastery (open from June to September). Nearby, *Zodiak Camping* (☎ 22 340) has bungalows for about US$4 per person.

Getting There & Away There's a small bus station on the western side of Rila Monastery. If you catch the early morning bus from Sofia, you can easily visit Rila on a day trip. Three buses a day depart from Sofia's Ovcha Kupel bus station (take tram No 5 or 11). The morning bus operates daily throughout the year. From October to March the afternoon bus does the return trip from Rila to Sofia from Friday to Sunday only. To go from Sofia to Rila get tickets the day before at the booking office in the arcade below the Palace of Culture in Sofia, or try your luck at Ovcha Kupel half an hour before departure.

In summer, on Sunday and holidays, the return afternoon bus from Rila to Sofia may be sold out a day in advance, in which case ask about buses from Rila Monastery to Kocherinovo train station, 29km west on the railway line from Kulata to Sofia, or to Stanke Dimitrov on the road to Sofia.

MELNIK (МЕЛНИК)
☎ 0997437

Melnik, only 20km north of the Greek border, is in the heart of Bulgarian Macedonia and the dramatic sandstone crags rising behind the town make this a distinctly Macedonian landscape. The area was first settled by Thracian tribes but came to prominence in Roman times when it served as an important (and defensible) trading crossroad. From the 18th century local farmers began to specialise in grapes and wine production slowly eclipsed trading as Melnik's foremost industry. The vineyards suffered under communism, mainly because locals didn't get to drink much of their own wine, but tourism has since rejuvenated the town.

Orientation

Melnik's main street runs east-west along both sides of a tributary of the Melnishka River. Lanes and goat tracks wend around the houses and ruins running up both sides of the valley.

Things to See & Do

Wandering the cobblestone paths around Melnik's charming houses will bring you to numerous **wine tasting** cellars – you may end up weaving as much as the paths do. There's a **museum** near the entrance to town (open irregular hours). Climb up to the southeastern corner of the village to **Kordopulov House**, the erstwhile dwelling of one of Melnik's foremost merchant families. Don't miss the huge warren of a wine cellar.

There is a spectacular walk east from Melnik through an arid and rocky reserve to the unassuming **Rozhen Monastery**, 7km away. There's a superb mehana in Rozhen village, 10 minutes walk from the monastery. If you don't fancy walking both ways, hook up with the bus linking Melnik and Rozhen.

Places to Stay & Eat

There are heaps of private rooms available in Melnik: keep an eye out for *chastni kvartiri*.

In summer an *accommodation agency* opens at the western end of the main street.

The *Manchevi Family* rents rooms (US$8 per person) in a congenial home just north of the town centre. There's a mehana downstairs. Nearby, *Mehana Chinarite* is one of Melnik's best restaurants.

Getting There & Away

There is a daily bus from Sofia's Ovcha Kupel bus station at 2.30 pm. It's also possible to leave Sofia on the 6.30 am bus to Rila Monastery and make it to Melnik by evening. From the monastery, take the bus or hitch down to Rila township, and connect with one of the hourly buses to Blagoevgrad, where you can connect with the service to Melnik.

From Melnik, there is a bus every evening at 6.30 pm running express to Sofia. Otherwise, you can take a bus to Sandanski and connect with one of two afternoon trains to Sofia.

Thrace

The Thrace of Greek and Roman antiquity was much larger than modern Thrace, only two-thirds of which lies within Bulgaria. The Maritsa River (which flows through Plovdiv) drains the region and flows south into the Aegean Sea, forming the border between present-day Greek and Turkish Thrace. At Svilengrad, on the Maritsa, the three nations meet. Bulgaria's Thracian Plain is squeezed between the Sredna Gora and Rodopi mountain ranges and opens onto the Black Sea to the east.

Plovdiv is the capital of Bulgarian Thrace and has evocative vestiges of the Roman and Turkish periods. Hisar, north of Plovdiv, has been a major spa since Roman times. Some of the finest monuments of the Bulgarian National Revival are found in the Bachkovo Monastery, Plovdiv and Koprivshtitsa.

KOPRIVSHTITSA (КОПРИВЩИЦА)
☎ 07184

This picturesque village (elevation 1030m) in the Sredna Gora Mountains, 113km east of Sofia, has been carefully preserved as an open-air museum of the Bulgarian National

BULGARIA

KOPRIVSHTITSA

PLACES TO STAY
2   Hotel Astra
4   Mavrudieva House
12 Sapundzhieva House
14 Drelekova House
15 Hotel Koprivshtitsa
16 Shuleva House

PLACES TO EAT
3   Restaurant Bulgaria
6   Hadzhi Gencho Café
8   Lomeva Kăshta
9   April 20 Mehana

OTHER
1   Doganov House
5   Karavelov House
7   Debelyanov House
10 Souvenir Shop
11 Oslekov House
13 April Uprising
    Mausoleum
17 Debelyanov's Grave
18 Assumption Church
19 Kableshkov House
20 Lyutov House
21 Bus Stop
22 Sts Cyril & Methodius
    School
23 Mlatchkov House
24 Post Office
25 Market
26 Biohim Bank
27 Benkovski House
28 Equestrian Statue

Revival. It is laid out across a lush pasture and pine-clad valley, reached after 12km along a winding road from the main highway. Legend tells of a beautiful young Bulgarian woman who obtained a *firman* (decree) from the Ottoman sultan that exempted the Koprivshtitsa villagers from paying tribute and allowed them to ride horses and carry arms. The town was founded at the end of the 14th century by refugees fleeing the Turkish conquerors.

Sacked by brigands in 1793, 1804 and 1809, Koprivshtitsa was rebuilt during the mid-19th century and was as big as Sofia at the time. It was here, on 20 April 1876, that Todor Kableshkov proclaimed the uprising against the Turks that eventually led to the Russo-Turkish War of 1877-78. After independence in 1878, Bulgarian merchants and intellectuals abandoned their mountain retreats for the cities and Koprivshtitsa has survived largely unchanged to this day.

These events are well documented in the various house-museums, but even without its place in history the village would be well worth a visit for its cobblestone streets winding between low-tiled red roofs and its little stone bridges over trickling rivulets. Some 388 registered architectural monuments grace the town. Koprivshtitsa is a joy to wander through, but keep in mind that this is a living village. Try to avoid intruding and say *dobar den* (good day) to those you meet.

Orientation & Information

Many of the house-museums and most of the facilities for visitors are found near the park that contains the April Uprising Mausoleum. Opposite the mausoleum you'll see the modern April 20 Complex, with a mehana downstairs and a restaurant upstairs. A few doors west up the narrowing street is a souvenir shop with a ticket office that sells guidebooks, maps and postcards. It also sells the comprehensive ticket (1500 leva) that will admit you to all the local museums. If this office is closed, you can buy the ticket at Oslekov House. All of the house-museums are open daily, except Monday, from 7.30 am to noon and 1.30 to 5 pm all year.

No left-luggage facilities are available at Koprivshtitsa, but you can ask the clerk at the bus station to mind bags for short periods. There is a Biohim Bank on the south side of the village.

Things to See

The houses of Koprivshtitsa are of two types. The early 19th-century 'wooden house' was characterised by a stone ground floor and a wooden upper floor with two rooms in each. In the second half of the 19th century, this austerity gave way to a more richly decorated house that was strongly influenced by the 'baroque' Plovdiv house. Characteristic of these later houses are the large salons, carved ceilings, sunny verandahs, multicoloured façades and jutting eaves.

Almost next to the souvenir shop is **Oslekov House** (1856), formerly a rich merchant's home. Its spacious interior and stylish furnishings are outstanding. Within the walled enclosure at the top of this street is a cemetery with the grave of the poet **Dimcho Debelyanov** and a statue of his mother anxiously awaiting his return ('I die and am yet born again in light'). Beyond is the **Assumption Church** (1817), which you pass to reach the house of the revolutionary **Todor Kableshkov**, now a museum of the 1876 uprising (all labels are in Bulgarian). Both this house and that of Oslekov are representative of the later Koprivshtitsa style. Continue south to the small stone bridge over the Byala Stream, where the first shot of the 1876 uprising was fired. Right next to the bus station is the **Sts Cyril & Methodius School** (1837), the second primary school to teach in Bulgarian (the first was in Gabrovo).

The other museums on your ticket are **Debelyanov House** (1832), not far from Oslekov House; the **house of Lyuben Karavelov** (1834-79), now a museum portraying the life of this ideologist of the uprising; and **Benkovski House** (1831), which is on the hillside in the south-eastern part of town. The Karavelov and Benkovski houses date from the earlier architectural period. Georgi Benkovski led the insurgent cavalry on legendary exploits through the Sredna Gora and Stara Planina until he fell in a Turkish ambush. The stairway beside his house leads up to a huge **equestrian statue** of the man and a view of the entire valley.

Places to Stay

You can visit Koprivshtitsa on a day trip from Sofia or as a stopover on the way to somewhere else, but it's well worth spending the night here to better capture the atmosphere of the town.

The *Kvartira Bureau* (☎ 25 16) next to the souvenir shop will organise a private room for US$7. The *Hotel Koprivshtitsa* (☎ 21 82), on the hillside just east of the centre didn't seem to be in operation at the time of research. There was talk of privatisation; whether this will be in effect by the time you read this is anyone's guess. *Shuleva House*, where a bed with shared bath is US$10 per person, is next to the stairs leading up to the hotel.

Try also *Drelekova House*, also on the stairs below Hotel Koprivshtitsa; and *Mavrudieva House*, a block behind the Karavelov House. *Sapundzhieva House*, behind the kiosks in the centre of town, has four double rooms and a two-room apartment with its own fireplace.

Hotel Astra (☎ 23 64), on the southern arm of bul Anton Ivanov, is a friendly private hotel. Beds in neat comfortable rooms with shared facilities go for about US$10.

Places to Eat

The *April 20 Mehana* on the main square is a casual place, serving standard Bulgarian fare in a haze of smoke. Keep a careful track of what you eat – the English menu has no prices. *Lomeva Kâshta* is hard to miss with its striking blue exterior. It specialises in national Bulgarian fare.

Hadzhi Gencho Café, one block north, is a good place for salads and light meals. On the other side of the river, *Restaurant Bulgaria* has more variety and higher prices. Watch out for possible overcharging here.

Getting There & Away

The train station is about 10km from town, but connecting buses to Koprivshtitsa are supposed to await every train (ticket from the

BULGARIA

driver). Train service to/from Sofia (1½ hours) is every couple of hours. The morning express train from Sofia to Burgas via Karlovo will drop you here. If you're heading east from Koprivshtitsa, change trains at Karlovo for Hisar, Plovdiv or Burgas, and change at Tulovo for Veliko Târnovo. (Between Koprivshtitsa and Klisura, just east of Koprivshtitsa, is a railway tunnel 6km long.) Going from Koprivshtitsa to Plovdiv is time-consuming as you must return to the railway line and change trains at Karlovo, because it's not possible to connect through Strelcha or Panagyurishte by bus.

PLOVDIV (ПЛОВДИВ)
☎ 032

Plovdiv, on the Upper Thracian Plain, is Bulgaria's second-largest city, occupying both banks of the Maritsa River. Two main communication corridors converge here: the route from Asia Minor to Europe, and the route from Central Asia to Greece via Ukraine.

This strategic position accounts for Plovdiv's pre-eminence, beginning in 341 BC when Philip II of Macedonia conquered Philipoupolis (Plovdiv). The Romans left extensive remains in the city, which they called Trimontium, as did the Turks, who made Philibe (Plovdiv) the seat of the Bey of Roumelia; this was made up of Macedonia, Albania, Thrace and the autonomous province of Eastern Roumelia.

Yet it was the Bulgarian National Revival that gave Plovdiv's old city Three Hills the picturesque aspect that visitors appreciate today. The 19th-century Plovdiv 'baroque' house shares the dynamism and passion of historic baroque but is uniquely Bulgarian. Arranged around the oval or square central salon are the drawing rooms and bedrooms of the family. The carved or painted ceiling and wall decorations are in excellent taste, as are the brightly painted façades. Many of these charming buildings, which were built by prosperous traders, are now open to the public as museums, galleries or restaurants and make a visit to Plovdiv well worthwhile.

Orientation
The train station is south-west of the old town. The left-luggage office (open 24 hours)

faces the parking lot on the right of the station as you come from the city centre. Cross the square in front of the station and take Ivan Vazov straight ahead into Central Square, a 10-minute walk. Knyaz Aleksandre, Plovdiv's pedestrian mall, runs north from this square, and you can reach the old town from here through the narrow streets to the right. The area north of the river is a grey, modern suburb devoid of interest.

Information
Puldin Tours (☎ 55 51 20), formerly Balkantourist, is at bul Bâlgaria 106, near the fairground north of the river.

Money The Bulgarian Foreign Trade Bank, just behind the McDonald's on Knyaz Aleksandre, changes travellers cheques for a 1% commission. There is an ATM in the main post office.

Post & Communications The telephone centre in the main post office on Central Square (at the rear of the building) is open daily from 6.30 am to 11 pm.

Travel Agencies For international train tickets and couchettes, go to the Rila office at Hristo Botev 31. For advance tickets on domestic railway lines, go to Byuro, Nezavisimost 29 (weekdays from 8.30 am to 5 pm).

Walking Tour
Begin your sightseeing with the excavated remains of the **Roman Forum**, behind the post office on Central Square. Knyaz Aleksandre, a bustling pedestrian mall, runs north from this square to 15th-century **Djoumaya Mosque**, also known as Friday Mosque, which is still used for Islamic religious services. Below ploshtad 19 Noemvri, in front of the mosque, is a section of a **Roman amphitheatre** (2nd century AD).

Continue straight ahead on the mall (now Rayko Daskalov) and through an underpass to the **Imaret Mosque** (1445). Plovdiv's **Archaeological Museum** (closed Monday) is nearby on ploshtad Saedinenie. A copy of the 4th century BC gold treasure from Panagyurishte is on display (the original is at the National Museum of History in Sofia). The monument in the square in front of the museum commemorates the 1885 union of Bulgaria with Eastern Roumelia (of which Plovdiv was the capital).

Return to the Djoumaya Mosque and go east on Maksim Gorki into the old city, which was named Trimontium (Three Hills) by the Romans. In recent years the **Church of Constantin & Elena** (1832) has been beautifully restored, and next to it is a very good icon gallery. In the National Revival mansion (1847) of the wealthy merchant Argir Koyumdjioglou, on Doctor Tchomakov, just beyond the end of Maksim Gorki, is the **Ethnographical Museum** (closed Monday), which houses a collection of folk costumes. Up the street from this museum is a hill top with the **ruins of Eumolpias**, a 2nd millennium BC Thracian settlement. There's a good view from the ruins.

The street beside the Ethnographical Museum leads down through **Hisar Kapiya**, the Roman eastern city gate, to Georgiadi House (1848), another fine example of Plovdiv baroque, and now the **National Revival Museum** (closed weekends).

To the south of this museum is a quaint, cobblestone quarter, with colourful 19th-century houses crowding the winding streets, so do a little exploring. At Knyaz Tseretelev 19 is the **Lamartine House** a baroque 1930 residence in which the French poet Alphonse de Lamartine stayed in 1833 during his Voyage en Orient.

Nearby to the west and directly above the southern entrance to a big highway tunnel is the 3000-seat **Roman theatre** (2nd century), now restored and once again in use at festival time. South-west of the theatre is **Sveta Marina Church** (1854) with a photogenic wooden tower and intricate iconostasis. From here it's only five minutes back to the Roman Forum.

Places to Stay

Camping *Camping Trakia* (☎ 55 13 60) is at the Gorski Kat Restaurant, about 4km west of Plovdiv on the Sofia Highway. Take bus No 4 or 44 west on bul Bulgaria, north of the river, to the end of the line, then walk 1km along the highway. Bus No 23 comes directly here hourly from the train station, departing from the station 40 minutes after

the hour and from the camping ground 15 minutes after the hour. Camping costs US$4 per person, bungalow beds US$11. It's open all year.

Private Rooms The privately run *Prima Vista Accommodation Agency* (☎ 27 27 78; fax 27 20 54), General Gurko 6, just off Knyaz Aleksandre, arranges private rooms at US$10/15 for singles/doubles.

Puldin Tours bul Bâlgaria 106, (☎ 55 51 20), can arrange private room accommodation at US$13/16 a single/double. During the Plovdiv Trade Fair (usually the first two weeks in May and September) the price for the rooms offered by both these agencies skyrockets to about US$32/37 a single/double.

Hotels The delightful *Turisticheski dom* (☎ 23 32 11), Slaveikov 5, in the old city, has hostel-style rooms with shared facilities for US$15 per person.

Plovdiv's two-star hotels are the 10-storey *Hotel Leipzig* (☎ 23 22 51), bul Ruski 20, four blocks from the train station (US$35/48 a single/double), and the four-storey *Hotel Bâlgaria* (☎ 22 60 64) in the centre of town (US$30/45 a single/double). Both include bath and breakfast. The *Novotel*, *Trimontium* and *Maritsa* hotels are much more expensive.

Places to Eat

Restaurant Plovdiv, Konstantin Irichik 15, is the best of the restaurants clustered in the area between the Roman amphitheatre and the old town. It's a lively place, popular with resident and visiting artists.

The *Alafrangite Restaurant*, Cyril Nektariev 17, near the National Revival Museum in the old town, offers excellent Bulgarian meals on the outside patio or inside this typical 19th-century edifice.

The *Starata Kushta*, adjacent to Alafrangite, is similar and rather touristy, but pleasant. Folk music is often performed at these two places, usually after 8 pm, so check to see what's twanging before sitting down.

The *Gorski Kat Restaurant* at Camping Trakia is good and there's a popular bar serving grilled meats at lunchtime in the large auto service centre next to the camping ground.

BULGARIA

PLOVDIV

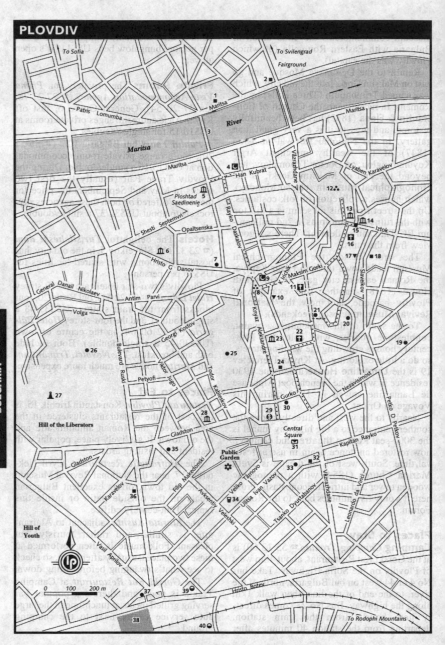

To Sofia

To Svilengrad
Fairground

Patris Lomumba

Maritsa

2

1
Maritsa

3

River

Maritsa

Maritsa

4
Han Kubrat

Vlarazhdane

Lyaben Karavelov

Maritsa

Ploshtad
Saedinenie

5

12

Shesti Septemvri

Opaltsenska

Rayko Daskalov

13

14
Iztok

15

Hristo G. Danov

6

7

Antim Parvi

9

Maksim Gorki

16

17

18

General Danail Nikolaev

8

K. Irechk

11

Slaveykov

Volga

10

Georgi Kostov

Knyaz

Aleksandre

21

20

Bulevard Ruski

26

Viktor Jugo

23

22

19

Petyofi

Todor Kableshkov

24

Nezavisimost

27

Gurko

Petko D Pekov

Hill of the Liberators

28

29

30

Gladston

Central
Square

Kapitan Rayko

35

Public
Garden

31

Filip Makedonski

33

32

Vazrahdane

Gladston

Avksenti Veleshki

Veliko Tàrnovo

Ulitsa Ivan Vazov

Tsanko Dyustabanov

Leonardo da Vinci

Karavelov

36

34

Hill of
Youth

Vasil Aprilov

Hristo Botev

37

39

38

40

To Rodophi Mountains

0   100   200 m

BULGARIA

PLOVDIV

PLACES TO STAY					
1	Hotel Novotel	6	Natural History Museum	26	Open-Air Theatre
2	Hotel Maritsa	7	Puppet Theatre	27	Monument to the
18	Turistichki Dom	8	Roman Amphitheatre		Soviet Army
24	Hotel Bålgaria	9	Djoumaya Mosque	28	Art Gallery
32	Trimontium Hotel	11	Church of the Holy Virgin	29	Bulgarian Foreign Trade Bank
36	Hotel Leipzig	12	Ruins of Eumolpias	30	Prima Vista Accommodation
		13	Ethnographical Museum		Agency
PLACES TO EAT		14	National Revival Museum	31	Post Office & Telephone
10	Restaurant Plovdiv	15	Hisar Kapiya		Centre
17	Alafrangite Restaurant	16	Church of Constantin & Elena	33	State Philharmonic
		19	Byuro Railway Ticket Office	34	Kosmos Bar
OTHER		20	Lamartine House	35	Opera House
3	Clothes Market	21	Roman Theatre	37	Rila Railway Ticket Office
4	Imaret Mosque	22	Sveta Marina Church	38	Railway Station
5	Archaeological Museum	23	Art Gallery	39	Main Bus Station
		25	Clock Tower	40	Rodopi Bus Station

Entertainment

In summer there are folklore programmes in the courtyard of the *Trimontium Hotel* at about 9 pm if a tour group is present (ask at the hotel reception in the late afternoon).

Performances at the restored Roman theatre are a summer highlight. Check posters at the theatre gate for starting times.

Local bands strike out Wednesday to Sunday nights at *Kosmos*, a bar tucked away off Avksentiy Veleshki. Turn left at the shopping arcade just south of Veliko Târnovo.

Getting There & Away

Train All trains between Istanbul and Belgrade pass through Plovdiv, and Sofia is only two hours away by frequent fast train. To get to Burgas takes 4½ hours (there are two overnight trains, as well as trains at three-hour intervals from morning until late afternoon). There are nine trains a day between Plovdiv and Karlovo (1½ hours). For other destinations north, bus connections are more convenient.

For Turkey take a local train to Svilengrad (three hours), a taxi to the border (14km) and walk across. Otherwise, catch the overnight express train to İstanbul (11 hours). For eastern Greece take one of two daily trains to Svilengrad (2½ hours) where you will have to overnight and take the morning train to Alexandroupolis (4½ hours). More conveniently a bus leaves every morning for Thessaloniki from the train station and there is a bus at 8.30 am every Wednesday and Sunday to Alexandroupolis.

Bus Plovdiv has several bus stations. Buses to Troyan (124km) leave from the northern bus station, at the northern end of trolleybus line Nos 2 and 3. Buses to Bachkovo Monastery (30km), Pamporovo (83km) and Smolyan (100km) use the Rodopi bus station, accessible through the tunnel under the tracks at the train station. Buses to Sofia (150km), Burgas (five hours), Nesebâr (307km), Sozopol (303km) and Asenovgrad (19km) depart from the main bus station near the train station. In the high season, bookings for private buses to the Black Sea must be made the day before. There's a bus to İstanbul every night from the Hotel Maritsa (12 hours, US$20). Tickets are available from the kiosk at the bus stop outside the hotel.

Getting Around

City bus tickets are sold by the conductor on board the bus.

Intercar (☎ 26 85 11) and Eurodollar (☎ 55 19 63) have desks at the Hotel Novotel.

Near Plovdiv

The Rodopi Mountains The Rodopi Mountains are home to Bulgaria's most isolated and ethnically diverse communities. The landscape takes in the spectacular gorges

BULGARIA

of Tregrad and Yagodino, and the steep rocky slopes of the Perelik range, and opens out into tiered fields and pine forests, such as the Izvoro and Borovo reservations, which offer wonderful walking. The Eastern Rodopi has diverse plant and animal life, and is especially popular with bird-watchers.

The traditions of Bulgaria's Slavic people are strongest in the Rodopi: wild pagan festivals take place in many villages, and folk music still features in the local culture. Most of Bulgaria's Muslim population lives in the area, both Pomaks whose ancestors converted during the rule of the Ottoman Empire, and ethnic Turks. During the communist era a 20km exclusion zone was enforced along Bulgaria's southern border, ensuring that the villagers in this region were particularly isolated.

Tourist infrastructure dwindles once you leave the resort area incorporating Smolyan and Pamporovo. Buses link all the villages but services are infrequent, so check timetables wherever you go. Hitching is viable as long as you are prepared to be flexible. In many areas, hizhas are the only official accommodation, but the hospitality of the Rodopi folk is renowned and you may well be invited as a guest into someone's home.

Bachkovo Monastery Thirty km south of Plovdiv, beside the highway up the Tschepelarska Valley, is the Bachkovo Monastery (Bachkovski Manastir), which was founded in 1083 by two Byzantine aristocrats, the brothers Gregory and Abasius Bakuriani. This is the largest monastery of its kind in Bulgaria after Rila. Sacked by the Turks in the 15th century, the monastery underwent major reconstruction 200 years later.

In the high courtyard are two churches: the smaller 12th-century **Archangel Church**, painted in 1841 by Zahari Zograph, and the large **Church of the Assumption of Our Lady** (1604). On the northern side of the courtyard is a small **museum**, while one corner of the southern side is occupied by the former **refectory** (1606), with a marvellous painting of the genealogy of Jesus on the ceiling painted between 1623 and 1643.

Through the gate beside the refectory is **St Nicholas Chapel**, with a superb Last Judgment painted on the porch in 1840 by Zahari

Zograph. Note the condemned Turks (without halos) on the right, and Zahari's self-portrait (no beard) in the upper left corner.

Just below the monastery are a *restaurant*, *camping ground* and *bungalows*. To get to Bachkovo, take a bus from outside Plovdiv's main bus station to Asenovgrad (19 km) and then another bus on to Bachkovo. Direct buses to Bachkovo depart from Plovdiv's Rodopi bus station. If you have time, it's worth climbing up to the fortress ruins at Asenovgrad to enjoy the view of the tiny church perched at the edge of the abyss.

The Black Sea Coast

Every summer Bulgaria's Black Sea beaches vie with those of neighbouring Romania to lure masses of sun seekers on holiday. Burgas and Varna take on a carnival atmosphere as camping grounds and hotels fill up, and small towns like Nesebâr and Sozopol become jammed with tourists. Fortunately, the hotel developments are concentrated in a few flashy resorts including Albena, Golden Sands, Sveti Constantin (Druzhba) and Sunny Beach, all absolutely packed with Germans and Brits on package tours, and cash-splashing mafia types. But all along the 378km coast it's fairly easy to escape the crowds and have a stretch of tideless golden beach to yourself.

The climate is warm and mild, and in winter the temperature rarely drops below freezing. Summer is the best time to visit. The average temperature is a warm 23°C but sea breezes keep it cool. Everything will be open, the restaurants will have their tables out on the street, the water will be warm and buses will carry you inexpensively along the coast. In the off season, from mid-September to the end of May, the resorts are dead.

Getting Around

Unfortunately the hydrofoil *(kometa)* service that once shuttled between Varna, Nesebâr, Burgas and Sozopol wasn't able to survive the transition to a market economy and in 1993 it was suspended indefinitely.

Still operating is a regular excursion boat known as a 'hydrobus', which runs from

Varna to Golden Sands and Balchik daily from mid-June to mid-September. Another excursion boat operates between Nesebâr and Sozopol. Private operators are gearing toward taking up the maritime slack – check when you get there.

Though it's convenient to come from Sofia by train, travel up and down the coast is almost exclusively by bus. Hourly buses link Burgas and Varna (1½ hours), and many local buses make shorter trips north and south.

BURGAS (БУРГАС)
☎ 056

In the 17th century, fisher folk from Pomorie and Sozopol founded Burgas on a narrow spit between the *Burgasko ezero* (Burgas Lake) and the Black Sea. An ancient tower known as Pirgos (Greek for 'tower') gave the city its name. The town grew quickly after completion of the railway from Plovdiv in 1890 and the city's port was developed in 1903.

Smaller and less crowded than Varna, Burgas also has less to offer. The northern side of the city is row after row of concrete apartments with a big oil refinery to the west. The old town by the port is still pretty, however, and Burgas makes a convenient base from which to explore the towns along the coast. Once you have a good place to stay, it's a fairly relaxed town with an acceptable beach, good shopping and an abundance of restaurants. It also boasts the most beautiful girls in Bulgaria.

Orientation

The train station and the bus and maritime terminals are all adjacent in the old town. The left-luggage office (6 am to 10.30 pm) is next to the bus station, just outside the train station. Aleksandrovska, the pedestrian mall, runs north to the Soviet soldier monument on ploshtad Troikata. The beach is along the eastern side of the old town.

Information

There's a Balkantourist office (open daily from 8 am to 8 pm) half way north along Aleksandrovska. Orbita Student Travel (☎ 42 380) is at Filip Kutev 2a. The Tourist Office is at the corner of Lermontova and bul Aleko Bogoridi.

Money Balkantourist gives a good rate for cash but charges 2.5% commission to change a travellers cheque.

There are many private exchange offices around the central pedestrian malls and there is an MC and Visa Electron ATM at the Bulbank on Aleksandrovska opposite the Hotel Bâlgaria. The bank also cashes travellers cheques.

Post & Communications The telephone centre in the main post office on Ozvobozdenie is open daily from 7 am to 10 pm.

Travel Agencies For all advance bus or train tickets go to the Rila office, Aleksandrovska 106 (weekdays from 7 am to 7 pm, Saturday from 8 am to 2 pm). If you want to take a bus to Varna be sure to visit the Rila office early, as all buses can be fully booked 24 hours ahead.

Balkantourist has nightly buses to Istanbul (10 hours, US$20) and two early morning buses to Sofia (392km, US$8000 leva).

Things to See

As a commercial port and beach resort, Burgas doesn't lend itself to organised sightseeing. The only specific sights are the **Art Gallery** in the former synagogue at Sterju Vodenicarov 22, which houses a collection of icons and modern Bulgarian paintings, and the **Archaeological Museum**, at Bogoridi 21 just around the block. Both are closed on weekends.

The **Maritime Park** above the beach on the eastern side of Burgas (go east on Bogoridi) is well worth a late afternoon wander. Here you'll find a large open-air theatre and a mausoleum for revolutionary heroes of the period 1923-44.

Places to Stay
Private Rooms *Balkantourist* (☎ 47 2727) has reliable private rooms at US$5 per person. *Feb Tours*, Bogoridi 28, has private rooms for US$6 per person.

Hotels The best private hotel is the *Mirazh Hotel* (no phone), Lermontova 48. It's on a quiet street, it's fairly new and security is good for guests. Room rates are US$15 per person, payable in advance.

There are a couple of good private hotels

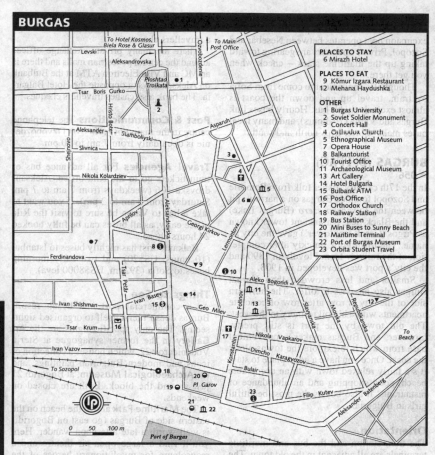

BURGAS

opposite Hotel Kosmos, north of the centre. *Hotel Biela Rosa* (☎ 36 686), Batak 42a, has rooms for one or two people for US$30 with bath and a four-bed apartment for US$45. *Hotel Glasur* (☎ 38 177), Kalover 1, charges US$20 for one or two people, or US$35 for a four-bed appartment.

Places to Eat & Drink

A small but quick Turkish restaurant is *Kömur Izgara Restaurant*, bul Aleko Bogoridi 14. They do great *döner kebab* as well as other popular Turkish dishes.

A relatively new and popular mehana is the *Mehana Haydushka* (☎ 84 37 29), bul Aleko Bogoridi 49. It is decorated inside with tasteful rugs and wall hangings and has a fairly extensive list of menu specialities – in Bulgarian only. German is spoken, if your linguistic skills stretch that far.

McDonald's has now also arrived in Burgas, if you really crave to munch on a Big Mac.

The northern end of bul Aleko Bogaridi is awash in small bars and cafés or you can head down to the beach promenade to gaze at the sea over a beer or coffee.

Entertainment

Sadly, the modern *Opera House* on Hristo Botev in the middle of town has fallen on hard times and part of the main entrance hall has been rented out as an automobile showroom! Check anyway for events.

At Antim I 26, just around the corner from the art gallery, is an *open-air cinema* with screenings nightly at 9 pm in summer.

In summer, countless cafés and bars materialise among the trees of *Maritime Park* as large tents are set up and parasols are erected over tables placed along the walkways. Half of Burgas seems to be here and later there's disco dancing in some of the tents.

Getting There & Away

Balkan Bulgarian Airlines has two flights a day from Sofia to Burgas for about US$129 one way. The Balkan Bulgarian Airlines office is at Hotel Kosmos. The airport is 8km north of town but bus No 15 from the bus station runs directly there every half-hour in the morning, hourly in the afternoon. The bus to Sunny Beach will also drop you at Sarafovo, a five-minute walk from the airport.

Express trains run between Sofia and Burgas nine times a day (470km via Plovdiv or 450km via Karlovo). Couchettes are available on the overnight Sofia trains but you must book well ahead. By express train, Plovdiv is 4½ hours from Burgas. For Veliko Târnovo change trains at Stara Zagora or Tulovo.

Bus service between Burgas and Varna is six times daily (three hours). Frequent local buses run late into the night as far north as Sunny Beach. There are buses south to Sozopol every hour on the hour (tickets from the conductor).

SOZOPOL (СОЗОПОЛ)
☎ 05514

Apollonia (Sozopol) was founded in 610 BC by Greeks from Miletus in Asia Minor. The settlement flourished as an independent trading state until sacked by the Romans in 72 BC, when the town's famous 13m-high bronze statue of Apollo was carted off to Rome as booty. Sozopol (meaning 'town of salvation') never recovered from this calamity and remained a tiny fishing village until a revival in the early 19th century, when 150 houses were rebuilt in the traditional 'Black Sea' style.

In this picturesque little town, sturdy wooden dwellings built on lower floors made of stone choke the narrow cobblestone streets on which women sell lace to visitors. On the western side of the peninsula, a Bulgarian naval base flanks the local fishing port and on the eastern side are two good beaches. A bustling tourist colony is blossoming to the south. Yet the entire Bulgarian coast south of Burgas is much less affected by high-rise resorts than Sunny Beach and Golden Sands are, and the southernmost Black Sea beaches, furthest from the Danube, are cleaner.

Because of all this, Sozopol compares well with historic Nesebâr, its rival coastal town. Although the archaeological remains at Nesebâr are far more significant, Sozopol is more relaxed, with an artistic community that migrates here every summer. It's good to

AROUND BURGAS

come for the arts festival during the first half of September, but Sozopol also rates highly as an unstructured beach resort for the entire summer season from May to early October. It's one of the few coastal resorts that really tries to cater for individual travellers.

Information

The telephone centre is in the post office in the middle of the old town (open daily from 7 am to 8.30 pm).

There are a few private change offices and an ATM at the Bâlgarska Banka.

Things to See & Do

Your best bet is to just wander around the old town, though there's an **Archaeological Museum** (captions in Bulgarian only) in the modern complex between the bus station and the fishing harbour. The tiny 18th-century **Church of Sveta Bogodoritsa** (the Virgin Mary) almost hidden below street level at Anaksimandâr 13, is worth a brief stop to see its wooden iconostasis. Check with the museum, if the church seems closed.

You can hire one of the water taxis serving Zlatna Ribka Camping for an excursion to the **Ropotamo River** south of Sozopol for about US$20 for the boat. The trip takes about an hour each way and since up to 10 people can go for this price, it's worth getting a small group together.

Places to Stay

Camping *Zlatna Ribka Camping* is 5km before Sozopol on the road from Burgas. No bungalows are available but there's plenty of camping space. The camping ground is at the southern end of the long beach you can see from Sozopol's harbour. In summer, small boats shuttle back and forth between Sozopol and Zlatna Ribka, leaving whenever there are 10 passengers waiting to go (400 leva per person or 4500 leva for a special trip). The water at Zlatna Ribka isn't as clear as that lapping the beaches south of Sozopol.

Private Rooms Some of the *kiosks* in the market near the bus station rent private rooms. They're open only from May to September.

Lotos Agency (☎/fax 429 or 282), Apollonia 22 (open all year from 10 am to 5 pm) and

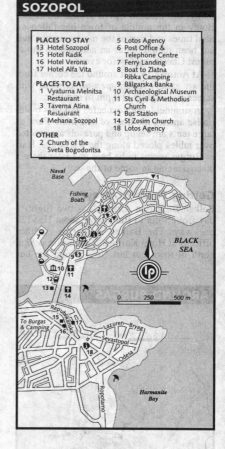

SOZOPOL

PLACES TO STAY	
13	Hotel Sozopol
15	Hotel Radik
16	Hotel Verona
17	Hotel Alfa Vita

PLACES TO EAT	
1	Vyaturna Melnitsa Restaurant
3	Taverna Atina Restaurant
4	Mehana Sozopol

OTHER	
2	Church of the Sveta Bogodoritsa
5	Lotos Agency
6	Post Office & Telephone Centre
7	Ferry Landing
8	Boat to Zlatna Ribka Camping
9	Bâlgarska Banka
10	Archaeological Museum
11	Sts Cyril & Methodius Church
12	Bus Station
14	St Zosim Church
18	Lotos Agency

Ropotamo 1 (open daily from 8 am to 9 pm in summer only), has private rooms at US$10 per person (US$7 out of season) with some singles available. In summer, Lotos runs excursions up and down the coast.

Hotels The three-storey *Hotel Sozopol* (☎ 362), right next to the bus station, is US$12 a double with shower and includes breakfast. It is closed in winter.

There are several small private hotels along Republikanska, the street running south towards the beach. Try the *Hotel Alfa Vita*

(☎ 18 52) at No 9, *Hotel Radik* (☎ 17 06) at No 4 or *Hotel Verona* (☎ 592) at No 8. All charge about US$14 a double with shared bath (no singles). In midsummer and during the September festival all accommodation is tight.

Places to Eat

The *Mehana Sozopol*, a large tavern on the main street leading into the old town, is fairly obvious and touristy but the outdoor terrace is pleasant. Local grilled meats are on offer. Diagonally opposite is the *Taverna Atina* with kerbside tables. Food is cheap and good and is likely to be open when other establishments are closed.

The terrace of the up-market *Vyaturna Melnitsa Restaurant*, below an old wooden lighthouse on Morski Skali at the northern end of the old town, offers a bird's-eye view of a small island just off Sozopol.

Getting There & Away

A crowded local bus travels to/from Burgas (34km) hourly. There's only one bus a day south to Ahtopol (90km) and tickets are sold only after the arrival of the bus from Burgas.

SUNNY BEACH (СЛЬНЧЕВ БРЯГ)
☎ 0554

Sunny Beach, or Sonnenstrand (Slânchev Bryag), is Bulgaria's largest and oldest seaside resort, with over 100 hotels stretching along an excellent 6km sandy beach, 36km north of Burgas. Sunny Beach caters especially to families with small children by providing playgrounds, children's pools, special menus, baby sitters and nurseries, and the gently sloping beach is safe for waders. Other attractions are sailing, windsurfing, tennis and horse riding, although everything along this package-tourist strip is overcrowded in summer and closed all winter.

It's an OK kind of resort destination – in the cement and brick chic socialist mould, looking somewhat jaded and threadbare in places – though efforts are being made to make some of the more obvious eyesores a little more appealing. Others have described it as a 'Stalinist Legoland'. It's not really a destination for individual travellers and you would have to be beach desperado to want to

stay here, but it is possible. Expect to be cheated at the restaurants in Sunny Beach and count your change carefully elsewhere.

Places to Stay

Camping There are two camping grounds at the northern end of the strip, both open from May to mid-October. *Camp Emona* by the beach is US$4 per person and US$4 per tent (no bungalows). It's absolutely jammed with tents.

The *Slanchev Bryag Campground* (☎ 25 92), on the inland side of the main highway a few hundred metres from Emona, has 180 small bungalows with shared bath at US$8 per person. Camping here is US$7 per person. It's crowded and the facilities are only so-so, but there's lots of space. If you're alone this is probably the cheapest place to stay.

Hotels If you want to stay at one of the high-rise hotels in Sunny Beach, you'd do better to come on a package tour, although the people at the Balkantourist office (☎ 22 56), near Hotel Kuban, can arrange hotel rooms ranging from US$20 to US$40 per person. They don't have any private rooms – you must go to Nesebâr for that. Several two-star hotels, such as the *Globus* and *Pelican*, are open all year.

Getting There & Away

Buses to Burgas and Varna leave from the bus station about 250m south of Balkantourist, on the inland side of the main highway. Private minibuses also shuttle between Sunny Beach and Burgas.

The Nesebâr-Sunny Beach bus stops right opposite Balkantourist.

A miniature road train runs from one end of the resort to the other every 15 minutes.

NESEBÂR (НЕСЕБЪР)
☎ 0554

Nesebâr, the ancient Mesembria, was founded in 510 BC by Greek Chalcedonians on the site of an earlier Thracian settlement. Mesembria prospered through trade with the Thracians of the interior but declined after the Roman conquest in the 1st century BC. Under Byzantium, Mesembria regained its former importance and in the 5th and 6th centuries a number of imposing churches were erected, including the Metropolitan Church, the ruin of which can still be seen. Byzantine nobles exiled here built more churches until the town had as many as 40.

Beginning in the 9th century, Nesebâr (the Slavic name now used) passed back and forth between Byzantium and Bulgaria many times, but the town remained unscathed. Even the Turks left Nesebâr alone and allowed it to strengthen its fortifications to defend itself against Cossack pirates. Overshadowed by Varna and later by Burgas, Nesebâr ceased to be an active trading town in the 18th century and today lives mostly from fishing and tourism.

The town sits on a small rocky peninsula connected to the mainland by a narrow isthmus. Remnants of the 2nd-century city walls rise above the bus stop, and along the winding cobblestone streets are picturesque stone and timber houses with wooden stairways and jutting 1st floors. Nesebâr is becoming highly commercialised with lots of twee little shops selling tourist junk at ludicrous prices. You even see restaurants advertising roast beef and Yorkshire pudding! In summer, vendors and tourists from nearby Sunny Beach clog the narrow streets and you have to run a zigzag course to stay out of their way. The crowds do thin out in the eastern part of town, however.

Information

The telephone centre is in the post office in the middle of the old town (open daily from 7.30 am to 10 pm).

Things to See & Do

Scattered through the town are over a dozen medieval churches, most of them now in ruins. Characteristic of the Nesebâr style are the horizontal strips of white stone and red brick offset by striped blind arches resting on

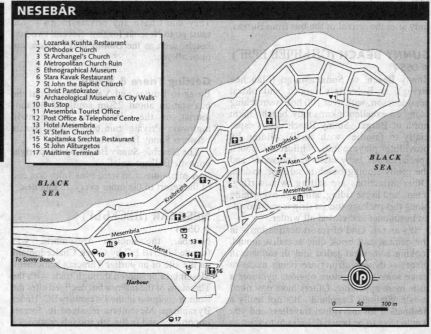

NESEBÂR

1 Lozarska Kushta Restaurant
2 Orthodox Church
3 St Archangel's Church
4 Metropolitan Church Ruin
5 Ethnographical Museum
6 Stara Kavak Restaurant
7 St John the Baptist Church
8 Christ Pantokrator
9 Archaeological Museum & City Walls
10 Bus Stop
11 Mesembria Tourist Office
12 Post Office & Telephone Centre
13 Hotel Mesembria
14 St Stefan Church
15 Kapitanska Srechta Restaurant
16 St John Aliturgetos
17 Maritime Terminal

BULGARIA

BLACK SEA

BLACK SEA

To Sunny Beach

Harbour

Mitropolitska
Ivan Asen II
Mesembria
Kralbrezna
Mesembria
Mena

0 50 100 m

the vertical pilasters, the façades highlighted by ceramic discs and rosettes.

Of special interest is the 11th-century **St Stefan Church** above the maritime terminal, almost completely covered inside with 16th-century frescos. The small but select collection of the **Archaeological Museum** is in the modern building just inside the city walls. Ask about **evening concerts** held in the 6th-century Metropolitan Church ruin.

In summer, another **museum** opens up in the 10th-century church of St John the Baptist.

Places to Stay

The *Mesembria Tourist Office* (☎ 28 55), (open Summer only) between the bus stop and the harbour, has private rooms at US$20 a double (no singles). Many of the rooms are in the new town near the beach, just west across the isthmus.

The *Hotel Mesembria* (☎ 32 55) may be a bit reluctant to deal with independent travellers, but they did quote room prices of US$20/32 for singles doubles.

Places to Eat

You'll find lots of places to eat and drink in Nesebâr. The *Kapitanska Srechta Restaurant*, in an old sea captain's house that overlooks the harbour, has lots of atmosphere. It's rather touristy (the waiters are dressed in sailor suits) but at least you can get seafood here.

Further off the beaten track is the *Lozarska Kushta Restaurant*, near the eastern end of town, a typical Bulgarian tavern with local meat dishes.

Stara Kavak, on a little square next to St John the Baptist Church offers outdoor dining, good food and service under the shade of an oak tree.

Getting There & Away

Jam-packed buses run regularly between Nesebâr and Sunny Beach (10km), where you change buses for Burgas or Varna.

Ask at the Mesembria Tourist Office about private buses direct to Plovdiv and Sofia, and book well ahead. Also ask here about water transport: Nesebâr's hydrofoil service had closed down in recent times, but may have re-emerged if the demand from foreign visitors makes the service financially viable.

VARNA (ВАРНА)
☎ 052

Varna, Bulgaria's largest Black Sea port, has become the country's summer capital. The city's history began in 585 BC when Miletian Greeks founded ancient Odessos. Varna flourished under the Romans and, during the Middle Ages, it alternated between Byzantium and Bulgaria but remained prosperous. The Turks captured Varna in 1393 and made it a northern bastion of their empire. In 1444 the Polish-Hungarian king Vladislav III Jagiello was killed in battle here while leading a crusade against Ottoman expansion. After the Crimean War (1853-56), Turkey allowed its allies Britain and France to sell their products throughout the Ottoman Empire and Varna became a great trading centre. In 1866 the railway arrived from Ruse, providing a direct route from the Danube to the Black Sea. After WWII, much of Bulgaria's trade with the USSR passed through the port of Varna.

In recent years Varna has developed into a kind of urban beach resort with many beaches, extensive parks, museums, historic sites, accommodation, restaurants, theatres and teeming pedestrian malls. The street signs are even in Latin as well as Cyrillic script! It's an atmospheric city on a bay hemmed in by hills that offer scenic views. Industrial installations such as the big chemical plant at Devnya and the Shipbuilding Combine are well west of town. Varna is a good place to base yourself for a few days of beach-bumming and enjoying a spot of urban decadence.

Orientation

The bus and train stations are on opposite sides of the city, but bus Nos 1, 22 and 41 run between them. The maritime terminal is just south of the city centre, within walking distance of the train station. Everything north-east of the maritime terminal is beach and everything west is the commercial port. The left-luggage office at the train station is open daily from 6 am to 10 pm (500 leva). Access to the left-luggage office at the bus station (open daily from 6.30 am to 6.30 pm) is from the platform facing the buses near the men's toilet.

From the train station, walk north up Tsar

Simeoni into Nezavisimost, the centre of town. A broad pedestrian mall, Knyaz Boris-I, runs east from here. North-west of Nezavisimost is a major crossroads, where bul Vladislav Varnenchik runs north-west to the bus station and the airport. The great Asparuh Bridge over the navigable channel between *Varnensko ezero* (Varna Lake) and the Black Sea is just west of ploshtad Varnenska Komuna.

In summer, assorted pickpockets, sleight-of-hand moneychangers and snatch-and-run beggar children work the crowds along Knyaz Boris-I and Nezavisimost. These people are not at all dangerous if you're aware they're there.

Information

Staff at Balkantourist, Musala 3, provide maps, information, rooms and international bus tickets.

CM '92 Tourist Agency, Tsar Simeoni 36b, is a helpful information and bookings office.

The office of the Union of Bulgarian Motorists is at Sofia 28, very near the train station.

Money Varna's oversupply of change bureaus means that you can convert cash at decent rates. The First East International Bank (weekdays from 9 am to 4 pm, Saturday from 9 am to 1 pm), on Knyaz Boris-I opposite Hotel Musala, charges 4% commission to change travellers cheques.

There is an ATM in the forecourt of the Festival & Congress Centre.

Post & Communications You can place long-distance telephone calls at the main post office, Sâborni 36 (open daily from 7 am to 11 pm).

Travel Agencies The Rila office, Preslav 13, sells international train tickets.

Balkantourist, Musala 3, sells tickets for the daily private bus to Sofia (4700 leva), to Veliko Târnovo (3520 leva) and an overnight bus to Istanbul (US$22).

Public Toilet There are public toilets in the park across the street from the Hotel Musala.

Things to See

There are two sets of **Roman baths**. The newer baths are on Primorski, just above the port between the train station and the maritime terminal. The upper floor of the **City Historical Museum** at 8 Noemvri 3, next to these baths, gives an impression of Varna as a prewar seaside resort. Much more interesting are the well-preserved 2nd-century **Roman Thermae** on Khan Krum, north from the City Historical Museum and to the left. The beautiful **St Anastasios Orthodox Church** (built in 1602) is within the compound.

Go east on Graf Ignatiev from the Roman Thermae to **Primorski Park**. This attractive park contains the **Maritime Museum** and, nearby, the **Aquarium** (1911). There's a good beach below Primorski Park, but it's body-to-body in summer.

Walk through the gardens to the Odesa Hotel, then north-west on Slivnitsa to Varna's largest museum, the **Museum of History & Art** at Mariya Luiza 41. The ground floor of this neo-Renaissance former girls' high school is dedicated to archaeology. Unfortunately, most exhibits are captioned only in Bulgarian, but there's an excellent collection of icons.

West of this museum, Mariya Luiza cuts across Nezavisimost, where you'll find the **Assumption Cathedral** (1886), the town hall, the red-coloured Opera House (1921) and other sights.

Between this square and the train station is the **Ethnographic Museum**, Panagyurishte 22, with a large collection of folk art and implements in a National Revival-style house that was erected in 1860.

Many of Varna's museums and archaeological sites are open Tuesday to Sunday from 10 am to 5 pm.

Special Events

If you're in Varna between mid-June and mid-July, be sure to check the programme of the **Varna Summer Festival**, which features outstanding musical events. At this time you can enjoy opera and ballet in the open-air theatre in Seaside Gardens or the Opera House, chamber music in St Anastasios Church, theatre in the Roman Thermae and concerts in the ultramodern Festival &

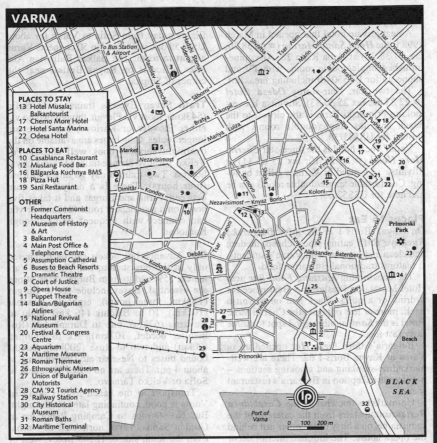

VARNA

PLACES TO STAY
13 Hotel Musala;
    Balkantourist
17 Cherno More Hotel
21 Hotel Santa Marina
22 Odesa Hotel

PLACES TO EAT
10 Casablanca Restaurant
12 Mustang Food Bar
16 Bălgarska Kuchnya BMS
18 Pizza Hut
19 Sani Restaurant

OTHER
1   Former Communist
    Headquarters
2   Museum of History
    & Art
3   Balkantourist
4   Main Post Office &
    Telephone Centre
5   Assumption Cathedral
6   Buses to Beach Resorts
7   Dramatic Theatre
8   Court of Justice
9   Opera House
11 Puppet Theatre
14 Balkan/Bulgarian
    Airlines
15 National Revival
    Museum
20 Festival & Congress
    Centre
23 Aquarium
24 Maritime Museum
25 Roman Thermae
26 Ethnographic Museum
27 Union of Bulgarian
    Motorists
28 CM '92 Tourist Agency
29 Railway Station
30 City Historical
    Museum
31 Roman Baths
32 Maritime Terminal

BULGARIA

Congress Centre (1986) on Slivnitsa, opposite the Odesa Hotel.

Places to Stay

Private Rooms *Tourist Service* (π 60 58 61) in the train station rents private rooms from US$5 to US$10 per person. It's open seven days.

CM '92 Tourist Agency (π/fax 22 74 76; georgesm@revolta.com), Tsar Simeoni 36b, a half-block from the train station (the small exchange office on the left), has private rooms in the old town at US$8/12 for a single/double. Apart from Sunday in winter, the office is open daily from 8 am to 7 pm and the staff speak English. Inquire here about B&B villas outside the city, where you can stay in comfort for US$18.

Balkantourist (π 22 55 24), Musala 3 beside the Musala Hotel, rents private rooms at US$8/12 a single/double.

Hotels The only cheap hotel right in town is the rather seedy *Hotel Musala* (π 22 39 25), Musala 3, off Nezavisimost. The staff were very coy about giving room prices, but if you are asked for more than US$14/20 for single/double, you are probably being ripped off.

A neat private hotel that opened in March 1998 is the *Hotel Santa Marina* (☎ 60 38 26; fax 60 38 25) at Baba Rada 28. Airy, pine-furnished single/double rooms with TV and phone go for US$30/40 including breakfast.

The two-star, four-storey *Odesa Hotel* (☎ 22 83 81; fax 25 30 83), Slivnitsa 1, over-looking Primorski Park, is the closest to the beach and has single/double rooms with shower for US$31/38.

Varna's best hotel is the three-star *Cherno More Hotel* (☎ 23 21 10; fax 23 63 11) at Slivnitsa 33 housed in Varna's tallest building. Comfortable single/double rooms can be had here for US$52/65.

Places to Eat

On Knyaz Boris-I is the nifty *Bâlgarska Kuchnya BMS* eating place, cheap, modern and clean and popular with Varna's students. It features traditional Bulgarian food.

The unassuming *Mustang Food Bar* near Hotel Musala on Preslav is a great place for a drink or a quick snack and on Slivnitsa itself, more or less opposite the Cherno More Hotel is the *Sani*, another good spot for some tasty fast food.

Bulgaria's third *Pizza Hut* opened up in Varna at Knyaz Boris-I 62. There are well-marked no-smoking and smoking sections – a welcome exception in Bulgaria's restaurant scene.

Up-market somewhat is the *Casablanca Restaurant* upstairs from the cafeteria of the same name, on a busy little corner just behind the opera house. The intimate interior décor provides atmosphere for relaxed dining. Note that you are charged extra for 'garnishes' like potatoes and vegetables. The menu is in English.

Entertainment

Both the *Opera House* and the *Dramatic Theatre* are on Nezavisimost. The Varna Opera presents a regular series of operas all summer and the ticket office even has a programme printed in English (tickets 9000 leva).

Otherwise, Varna's main entertainment is its café life and people watching that takes places along Slivnitsa and the beachfront restaurants and cafés.

Getting There & Away

Air Balkan Bulgarian Airlines has three flights a day from Sofia to Varna for about US$159 one way. Bus No 50 connects Varna airport to town. The Balkan Bulgarian Airlines office is on Knyaz Boris-I near the corner of Shipka.

Train Seven Express trains go to Sofia (543km), most via Pleven, though two go via either Plovdiv or Karlovo, but these are longer routes. Couchettes are available on the overnight service (book well ahead). For Veliko Târnovo change trains at Gorna Oryahovitsa. Two trains a day go direct to Ruse (four hours). There is a daily local train between Varna and Burgas and it takes five hours on a roundabout route (218km) or you can connect with frequent trains through Karnobat.

Bus Advance bus tickets can be purchased only at the bus station, bul Vladislav Varnencik 159, and to/from Burgas reservations are essential. Buses include six to Burgas (132km, three hours), eight to Nesebâr (101km), 10 to Balchik (46 km), eight to Kavarna (63km), one to Durankulak (Romanian border, 107km), six to Shumen (90km) and two to Ruse (200km). Southbound buses to Nesebâr etc stop running at about 4 pm. There are no buses from here to Sofia or Veliko Târnovo.

Transport to the beach resorts north of Varna is good, continuing late into the night. Bus No 99 runs to Camping Panorama at Golden Sands, 17km north-east of Varna, from the south side of Hristo Botev, west of Assumption Cathedral. The bus to Albena also leaves from here (the last bus leaves around 6 pm). Purchase tickets in advance at the kiosk (small additional fee for luggage). Private minibuses also leave frequently from this stop, No 9 to Golden Sands and No 8 to Sveti Konstantin (Druzhba). In summer, a 'hydrobus' runs from Varna to Balchik daily, leaving Varna at about 8.30 am and Balchik at 3 pm (US$4).

Getting Around

You will probably find the local bus service only useful for getting to and from the northern beaches (see Golden Sands) since Varna is compact enough to walk around. If you need a car, Avis and Hertz both have offices at the airport.

GOLDEN SANDS (ЗЛАТНИ ПЯСЪЦИ)
☎ 052

Golden Sands, or Goldstrand (Zlatni Pyasâtsi), is theoretically Bulgaria's most chic resort, with green wooded hills rising directly behind the 4km of golden sands. Some 60 hotels are hidden among the trees and, aside from the beach life, Golden Sands offers all kinds of organised sports, such as sailboarding, sailing, diving, water-skiing, archery, tennis and horse riding, with qualified instructors available. However, in recent times it has become decidedly tacky and tired-looking, ill-maintained and generally the spread-out complex lacks soul. It's not the kind or place an adventure-seeking traveller would want to hang out for too long.

Golden Sands was built by the communists to accommodate large tour groups on pre-booked package tours, and they're still not set up to receive individual travellers. Only expensive hotels are available, restaurant prices are high for those without meal vouchers, and you're stuck in the middle of a sterile, tourist-oriented environment, isolated from everyday life, exactly as the socialist central planners intended. In recent years, the inevitable hiccups of privatisation have been exacerbated by the infiltration of organised crime groups fighting for control of business in the resorts.

The beaches are still fine though, and the bus service from Varna is frequent and cheap, so, unless you love places like Waikiki, Miami or Surfers Paradise, the best plan by far is to get a private room in Varna or Balchik and commute to one of the resorts for a day in the sun.

Places to Stay
Camping Panorama is by the highway at the northern end of Golden Sands, about a 10-minute walk from the beach. It's small, run-down and the bungalows here are pretty grungy. Bus Nos 53 and 99 from Varna stop there.

The *Balkantourist* accommodation service

or *'nastanyavane'* (☎ 35 56 81), on the main highway just above Hotel Diana, books hotel rooms. This office is open 24 hours in summer – staff must spend the winter training to be unhelpful. By the time you've extracted a room from this 'service' you'll be assured a good night's sleep.

Getting There & Away
Bus No 9 from Varna stops on the main highway, a 10-minute walk from the beach, though in summer small tourist trains run all around the resort.

ALBENA (АЛБЕНА)
☎ 052

Albena, in contrast to Golden Sands – while still maintaining a sub-veneer of consumer tack – is a much more lively place, has a more identifiable sense of community and at least makes an effort to put on a pretty face for the Summer crowds. It is again another ex-communist holiday resort, but has by and large managed to shed, or at least modify, the socialist-kitsch architecture it inherited. Its profusion of restaurants and bars make it the kind of place preferred by a younger crowd looking for fun and nightlife. The beach is good and is easily accessible to everyone.

The *Tourist Service* office (☎ 27 21), opposite the bus station, rents out hotel rooms beginning at about US$28/35 a single/double with bath and breakfast. In summer, it's open 24 hours a day. There's a *camping ground* near the entrance to the complex, with bungalows for US$20/26 a single/double.

Tourist movement kicks in around mid-May when you'll start finding bars and restaurants open for the start-of-the-season packaged tourists from Germany and the UK.

BALCHIK (БАЛЧИК)
☎ 0579

Balchik is a picturesque old town huddled below weathered white chalk bluffs, 47km north-east of Varna where the brooding and windswept Dobrudzha hinterland drops to meet the sea. The Greek traders who settled here in the 5th century BC called the place 'Krunoi' for its springs, and the Romans changed it to Dionysopolis in honour of the god of wine. From 1913 to 1940 Balchik and

the rest of southern Dobrudzha belonged to
Romania. It was here in 1931 that Queen
Maria of Romania had an Oriental-style
summer residence built overlooking the sea.
The queen is said to have entertained many
lovers in the building, and it's easy to
imagine such affairs in such a place.

Balchik makes a good day trip from Varna,
or you can arrange a stay and patronise the
beach at nearby Albena.

Orientation & Information

Cherno More winds up from the port to the
main bus station in the upper part of town, a
10-minute walk from the ferry wharf. The
bus to Albena leaves from a small bus station
near the port but buses to Varna depart from
the main bus station.

Post & Communications The post office
is on Ivan Vazov, just off Cherno More
behind Hotel Balchik.

Things to See

Up Cherno More, moving from the port to the
upper town, you'll find a **gallery** to the right
above the lurid DSK Bank. There is an **icon
gallery** in the church behind the bank. A
block further up Cherno More is the local
Historical Museum (closed weekends).

Queen Maria's villa is about 2km west of
the ferry wharf (follow the shore) and it's
possible to enter whenever local artists
exhibit their wares inside. This villa and
several other buildings are now included in
Balchik's **botanical gardens**, which allegedly
contain more than 600 varieties of Mediterranean plants and cacti. Unfortunately, they
are poorly maintained, so don't come expecting a lot and you won't be disappointed.

Places to Stay & Eat

The one-star *Dionysopolis Hotel* (☎ 21 75),
on Primorski near the port, charges US$15
per person.

The small *Hotel Esperanza* (☎ 51 48),
Cherno More 16, is US$8 per person. It
usually has room, but if it's full the staff will
find you a private room for a similar price.
Ask at the bar below the hotel. The food in
the Esperanza's restaurant is great.

Restaurant Kavatsi facing the port offers
good seafood.

In summer, when artists congregate at
Queen Maria's villa, this becomes a lively
area with seafood street cafés and sponta-
neous theatre performances.

Getting There & Away

From mid-June to mid-September a 'hydrobus' runs from Varna to Balchik daily,
leaving Varna at about 8.30 am and Balchik
at 3 pm. The boat ride is an enjoyable two-
hour trip with an open deck where you can sit
outside and enjoy the great views of the
coast. This enjoyable Black Sea cruise costs
US$4 from Varna to Balchik. Some services
also call at Golden Sands.

It's fairly easy to make a round trip by returning to Varna on local buses with changes
at Albena and Golden Sands. In summer,
local buses travel from Balchik to Albena
(18km) every 20 minutes, and bus No 2 from
Albena to Golden Sands (16km) is also frequent. From Golden Sands, bus No 9 runs to
Varna frequently.

Travelling further north, buses run direct
only as far as Kavarna (18km), leaving from
the bus station at the top of the town.

Northern Bulgaria

Northern Bulgaria, between the Danube and
the crest of the Stara Planina, corresponds to
the ancient Roman province of Moesia Inferior. To the south was Roman Thrace and to
the north, Dacia. Despite barbarian invasions
in the 3rd century AD, Moesia remained part
of the Eastern Roman Empire until the formation of Bulgaria in 681. Pliska and
Preslav, historic capitals of the First Bulgarian Empire, and Veliko Târnovo, capital of
the Second Bulgarian Empire, are all here.
During the long Turkish period, Ruse and
Vidin served as northern bastions of the
Ottoman Empire. Much later, during the Bulgarian National Revival, the renowned
monasteries at Preo-brazhenski and Troyan
were erected. During the Russo-Turkish War
of 1877-78, the great battles of Pleven and
Shipka decided the fate of modern Bulgaria.

Coming or going from Romania, northern
Bulgaria is the gateway. Many travellers

cross the Friendship Bridge at Ruse, but the Calafat-Vidin ferry is a good alternative. There's also hiking in the Stara Planina. Northern Bulgaria is worth exploring.

MADARA (МАДАРА)

Madara, 18km east of Shumen, is a convenient stopover between Varna and Ruse or Veliko Târnovo. From the train station, a wide stone stairway leads 2km up towards the cliffs. Madara makes a convenient base for exploring the nearby capitals of the First Bulgarian Empire, Preslav and Pliska. There's plenty to see at Madara itself, so you could spend a couple of days here.

Things to See

Archaeological remains dating from the 8th to 14th centuries can be seen below the cliffs of Madara. Higher up are some caves, but more famous is the **Madara horseman**, a relief of a mounted figure spearing a lion, which symbolises victories of Khan Tervel over his enemies. It was carved in the early 8th century 25m up on the rock face, and the adjacent Greek inscriptions date from 705 to 831.

North of the horseman, a regular stairway leads up to the top of 100m cliffs where there are fortifications from the First Bulgarian Empire, part of a defensive ring intended to protect Pliska and Preslav.

Places to Stay & Eat

Camping Madara (☎ 20 62), one of the most pleasant camp sites in Bulgaria, is a few hundred metres from the horseman. Open all year, it has 15 rustic cabins with shared bath (US$6 a double) and tent space (US$2 per person). The camping ground has a good little restaurant. This peaceful site is a good place to come for a rest.

There's a youth hostel at Madara, the *Hizha 'Madarski Konnik'* (☎ 20 91), near the ticket office for the horseman. Beds are US$5 per person and reservations are not required for individuals. It's open all year.

Getting There & Away

Madara is on the main railway line between Sofia and Varna via Pleven but express trains don't stop here (change at Kaspichan). There

are several trains daily to/from Varna (91km, two hours).

Buses run from the archaeological area near the camping ground. There are three afternoon buses to/from Shumen. Trains pass about every three hours and if you don't wish to spend the night it's best to plan a visit between two trains. There's no official left-luggage area at the train station but the staff may agree to keep your bags.

Five buses a day link Madara to the railway junction of Kaspichan (10km), from where there are trains direct to Ruse and Varna. Buses also go to Novi Pasar and Pliska.

PLISKA (ПЛИСКА)

Pliska squats on a level plain 23km north-east of Shumen and 12km north of Madara. Founded by Khan Asparoukh in 681, Pliska was the capital of the First Bulgarian Empire in the 8th and 9th centuries. Though destroyed by the Byzantines in 811, Khan Omourtag rebuilt the town, which remained important even after the court moved to Preslav in 893.

There were three walled circuits at Pliska. The outermost fortification enclosed 23 sq km (including the present village) with an embankment and a ditch. The common people and soldiers lived in this Outer City. The Inner City, 3km north of the village, had a 10m-high stone wall with guard towers. The rebuilt 9th-century Eastern Gate gives access to the foundations of the **Big Palace** with its throne room, the ceremonial centre of the city. Just west was the Court Church, originally a pagan temple. This inner fortress also enclosed the **citadel**, clearly distinguished by its brick walls, where the khan resided. Underground passages led from the citadel to various points in the Inner City.

The **museum** at the site contains a model of the 9th-century, three-naved **Great Basilica**, which has been partly rebuilt a kilometre north of the main archaeological area. This great building, 100m long by 30m wide, is linked to the adoption of Christianity in Bulgaria in 865.

Getting There & Away

Buses from Shumen come every two or three hours but they don't travel all the way to the ruins, which are 3km further north. You can walk, or look for a taxi. Pliska is on the train line between Ruse and Varna, but few through trains stop here. It's best to hook up with one of the three daily trains from Kaspichan.

SHUMEN (ШУМЕН)
☎ 054

Shumen is a large city between Varna, Veliko Târnovo and Ruse, halfway from the Black Sea to the Danube. Both the Thracians and the Romans had settlements here, and during the early Middle Ages, Shumen and nearby Preslav, Madara and Pliska became the birthplaces of medieval Bulgaria. Shumen was captured by the Turks in 1388. For the next five centuries, Chumla (Shumen) was an important market town with the largest mosque in Bulgaria. In the early 19th century, the Turks included Shumen in their strategic quadrangle of fortified towns, along with Ruse, Silistra and Varna, as a defence against Russian advances.

Shumen is a transportation hub that you will pass through once or twice while touring this part of the country, and there are several things to see if you have time. The gigantic hill-top monument that overlooks Shumen was built in 1981 to commemorate the 1300th anniversary of the founding of the First Bulgarian Empire.

Orientation & Information
The adjacent bus and train stations are on the eastern side of town. Follow bulevards Madara and Slavianski west to the centre – a pleasant walk. The old Turkish town is to the west of Hotel Madara. The left-luggage office inside the train station is open 24 hours (except from 1.20 to 2.50 am and from 9.40 to 11.20 pm).

Post & Communications There's a post office across the street from the bus station.

Travel Agencies Balkantourist (☎ 55 313), next to the Hotel Shumen, sells tickets for daily buses to İstanbul (US$18).

Things to See & Do
A half-day visit in Shumen is best organised by taking bus No 10 from in front of the bus

station west to the end of the line at the famous **brewery**. Shumensko pivo, the local beer, dates back to 1882 and the many prizes it has won are listed on the label. It packs a tasty punch.

From Kyoshkovete Park, opposite the brewery, hike, hitch or take a taxi up to the **Shumen Fortress** (Shumenska Krepost), on the hill top directly above. There's a terrific view of Shumen from here.

In the western part of town below the fortress are a few scattered remnants of old Shumen that were not bulldozed to make way for modern buildings. The **Tombul Mosque** (1744), visible from above, is the largest and most beautifully decorated in Bulgaria. The Turks built their mosque with stones torn from the ruins of earlier Bulgarian monuments. Beyond is the 16th-century Turkish **covered market**.

Follow the pedestrian promenade back towards the stations. On the way you'll pass the **District Historical Museum**, bul Slavianski, in the centre of the modern city. It has a large collection but the captions are only in Bulgarian.

Places to Stay & Eat
Balkantourist (☎ 55 313) rents private rooms at US$13 per person, but it's closed on weekends.

The rather run-down *Orbita Hotel* (☎ 56 374) in Kyoshkovete Park, beyond the brewery on the far west side of town, is US$17 for a double.

The three-star, seven-floor *Hotel Madara* (☎ 57 598) is expensive at US$30/50 a single/double with bath and breakfast. The communists began construction of a new shopping mall next to the Madara but the project has been abandoned, leaving a legacy of ugly half-finished buildings.

The old three-storey *Hotel Titcha* (☎ 55 277), on ploshtad Osvobozdanie, below Hotel Madara in a peeling yellow building, is US$9 for a bed in a seedy room with shared bath. *Hotel Stariyagrad* (☎ 55 376) up near the Shumen Fortress is US$11 a double.

The *Popsheitanovata Kushta Restaurant*, halfway between the Madara and Shumen hotels, serves traditional Bulgarian food in a quaint 19th-century building.

Mehana Kristal, south of ploshtad Kristal

down Panayot Volov, is recommended for honest Bulgarian fare.

Getting There & Away

Shumen is on the main line from Sofia to Varna via Pleven. For Veliko Târnovo change at Gorna Oryahovitsa. Madara is accessible by local train on the line to Kaspichan and Varna.

Three buses a day leave Shumen for Ruse (116km) or you can catch a bus to Razgrad (52km, five daily) from where the service to Ruse is more frequent. Other buses leaving Shumen include three to Burgas (178km), five to Varna (90km), five to Pliska (23km), three to Madara (18km) and one every hour or more from platform No 1 to Preslav (20km).

Etar Travel runs private coaches to Sofia and Varna from a kiosk between the bus and train stations.

PRESLAV (ПРЕСЛАВ)
☎ 0538

Preslav, 20km south-west of Shumen, was founded in the year 821 by Khan Omourtag. Khan Simeon moved his seat here from Pliska in 893 and Preslav remained the capital of the First Bulgarian Empire until it was conquered by Byzantium in 971. A notable school of literature existed here and even after the court left for Veliko Târnovo, Preslav remained an important town. The Turks sacked Preslav in 1388 and hauled away its stones to construct mosques elsewhere.

The ruins of Veliki Preslav are 2km south of the present town of Preslav. The 5-sq-km outer city was protected by a high stone wall and contained churches, monasteries and the residences of the nobles. An inner wall encircled the 1.5-sq-km citadel with the royal palace at its centre. The most famous building was the **Round Gold Church**, built by Khan Simeon in 908 and partially restored in recent times. It derived its name from the dome, which was gilded on the outside and covered with mosaics inside.

The **archaeological museum** at the ruins contains architectural fragments and a model of the palace to help you visualise what it must have been like. Prize exhibits are a

10th-century ceramic icon of St Theodore Stratilates from a nearby monastery and the 10th-century silver goblet of Zhoupan Sivin.

The town of Preslav is easily accessible by local bus from Shumen. A good plan on arrival is to take a taxi out to the site museum and walk back. If you want to stay, there's the two-star *Hotel Preslav* (☎ 25 08) in the middle of town with beds for US$10 per person. The hotel also serves meals.

RUSE (РУСЕ)
☎ 082

Ruse, the largest Bulgarian port on the Danube, is a gateway to the country. Russian and Bulgarian riverboats stop here, as does the train to/from Bucharest. The double-decker highway/railway Friendship Bridge (1954), 6km downstream, links Ruse to Giurgiu, Romania. This massive 2.8km-long structure is the largest steel bridge in Europe, and during high water the central section can be raised. The bridge's name is rather ironic as relations between Bulgaria and Romania are far from friendly and a chlorine and sodium plant across the river in Giurgiu delivers massive air pollution to Ruse.

Along the Bulgarian right bank of the Danube at Ruse are parks and promenades full of mementos of the two liberations (1878 and 1944). It's worth a stop if you have the time.

History

A Roman fortress, Sexaginta Prista (60 ships), was established here in 70 AD as part of the defensive Danubian Lines (the Roman defensive line along the southern bank of the Danube). Although strengthened by Emperor Justinian in the 6th century, the fort was finally obliterated during the 'barbarian' invasions of the 7th century.

The Slavs forsook the site and in the 9th century built the town of Cherven 30km south on an easily defensible loop of the Cherni Lom River. Six churches, city walls and a citadel have been excavated at Cherven. The rock-hewn cave churches of Ivanovo, between Cherven and present-day Ruse, are another reminder of this period. After the Ottoman conquest in 1388, Cherven was abandoned.

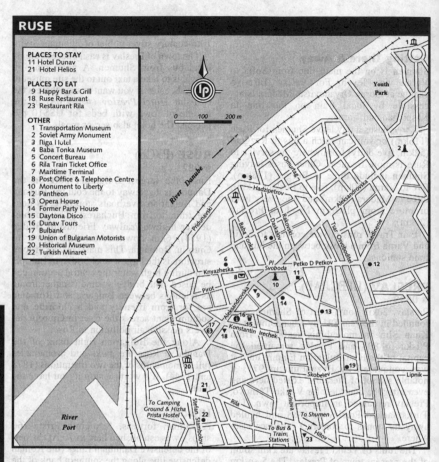

RUSE

PLACES TO STAY
11 Hotel Dunav
21 Hotel Helios

PLACES TO EAT
9 Happy Bar & Grill
18 Ruse Restaurant
23 Restaurant Rila

OTHER
1 Transportation Museum
2 Soviet Army Monument
3 Riga Hotel
4 Baba Tonka Museum
5 Concert Bureau
6 Rila Train Ticket Office
7 Maritime Terminal
8 Post Office & Telephone Centre
10 Monument to Liberty
12 Pantheon
13 Opera House
14 Former Party House
15 Daytona Disco
16 Dunav Tours
17 Bulbank
19 Union of Bulgarian Motorists
20 Historical Museum
22 Turkish Minaret

The Turks rebuilt and strongly fortified Rouschouk (Ruse). The Russians captured the city in 1773 and 1811 but were forced to withdraw because of the Napoleonic attack on Moscow. In 1864, under the reforming Turkish *vali* (district governor) Midhat Pasha (founder of the Young Turks movement), Rouschouk was modernised and became the capital of the Danubian Vilayet (including everything west to Niš, Yugoslavia). In 1866 a railway from Ruse to Varna linked the Danube directly to the Black Sea. The eclectic architecture of the city centre dates from the building boom that followed Ruse's liberation from the Turks by Russian troops in 1878.

Orientation

The adjacent bus and train stations are on the southern side of town. The left-luggage office at the train station is open 24 hours.

From the stations, walk or take a bus a kilometre north up Borisova to ploshtad Svoboda, the centre of town. Among the 18 streets that meet on this square is Aleksandrovska, Ruse's pedestrian mall, which runs in both directions.

Information

Try Dunav Tours, Pristanishtna 22b, just off Aleksandrovska. The Union of Bulgarian Motorists is at General Skobelev 45.

Money Bulbank, Aleksandrovska 11 (weekdays from 8.15 to 11.30 am and 1 to 3.30 pm, Saturday from 8.30 am to 1.30 pm), will change up to US$1000 in travellers cheques for a flat fee of US$7.50. There is an ATM diagonally opposite Bulbank.

Post & Communications The telephone centre in the main post office on ploshtad Svoboda is open daily from 7 am to 10 pm.

Travel Agencies Tickets to Bucharest are sold by Rila, Knyazheska 33 (weekdays from 8 am to noon and 1 to 6 pm, Saturday from 8 am to 1 pm) and at the station. It's only possible to make advance seat reservations at the Rila office, and only for the morning and late afternoon trains.

Things to See

Most of Ruse's monuments and museums are open from 9 am to noon and from 3 to 6 pm, daily except Monday. The **Monument to Liberty**, created by the Italian sculptor Arnoldo Zocchi in 1908, dominates ploshtad Svoboda.

At the end of Petko D Petkov, east of the square, are the graves of Ruse's revolutionary heroes in the gold-domed **Pantheon** (1978). North-east of the Pantheon at the end of Saedinenie is the **Soviet Army Monument** (1949) with **Park na mladezta** (Youth Park) and the Danube beyond.

Proceed upstream along the Danube to the **Riga Hotel**, where there's an attractive terrace and promenade. The Panorama Bar (open from 6 pm to 1 am) on the 20th floor provides a sweeping view. Overlooking the Danube near this hotel is the **Baba Tonka Museum**, Pridunavski 6 (closed for renovations). Seven of Baba (Granny) Tonka's children participated in the 1876 uprising against the Turks and one of them, Bilyana Raicheva, resided in what is now the museum building.

Places to Stay

Camping & Hostels The *Ribarska Koliba Campground* (☎ 22 40 68) is 6km out of Ruse on the road to Sofia. It's US$3 per person to camp, US$7 for a two-person cabin or US$10 for a three-person caravan. There's a small bar by the gate of this pleasant wooded site above the Danube, which is open from May to mid-October. It's best to take a taxi from the train station (4000 leva) as bus Nos 6 and 16 from the centre of town to the camping ground are irregular and stop running at 9 pm.

A kilometre beyond the camping ground is a HI hostel, the *Hizha Prista* (☎ 23 41 67), with dorm beds at US$4 per person with a HI card, US$6 without a card. Reservations are not required and it's open all year round.

Private Rooms *Dunav Tours* (☎ 22 30 88), Pristanishtna 22b, has private rooms at US$12/14 a single/double.

Hotels No really cheap hotels in town, but the concrete *Hotel Helios* (☎ 22 56 61), Nikolaevska 1, is worth seeking out at US$15 per person sharing a bathroom or US$20/35 a single/double with private bathroom.

The *Hotel Dunav* (☎ 22 65 18), ploshtad Svoboda 7, is a mid-range hotel charging around US$35/50 for a single/double.

Places to Eat

If you'd like to experience a genuine proletarian self-service cafeteria go to *Restaurant Rila*, Borisova 49 (Monday to Thursday from 6 am to 8.30 pm, Friday to Sunday from 11 am to 7 pm). The top dish on the menu and a large beer shouldn't set you back more than US$1 – just point. Lots of lusty workers simply sit in there and drink beer, though the bulk of the clientele are pensioners.

The *Happy Bar & Grill* on ploshtad Svoboda spills out onto the square and is good for quick meals and a beer while enjoying the people parade.

For elegant candle-lit dining and soft music try the *Ruse Restaurant*, Aleksandrovska 6. At the fancy *Panorama Restaurant* on the top floor of Hotel Riga (open 6 pm to 1 am) you get a knockout view of the Danube.

BULGARIA

Near the Danube, down the hill from the Ribarska Koliba Campground, is the *Fisherman's Lodge* restaurant. Live music and an outdoor terrace make this a pleasant place on a summer's evening. Take a sunset stroll along the riverside before dinner.

Entertainment

Check the *opera house* just off ploshtad Svoboda. The ticket bureau, Aleksandrovska 61 on the corner of ploshtad Svoboda, will have information on the March Music Days Festival. The flashy *Daytona Disco*, downstairs at Konstantin Irechek 5, is Ruse's top night spot (nightly from 10 pm).

Getting There & Away

Train Two trains a day go from Ruse to Varna (four hours), with others on this line stopping short at Kaspichan (three hours) near Madara. Express trains run to Sofia (seven hours) via Pleven, including one overnight train. For Veliko Târnovo (three hours) change trains at Gorna Oryahovitsa, although some local trains from Ruse go direct to Veliko Târnovo.

Bus Express buses run to Silistra and Varna (each twice daily, 200km) and also to Shumen (three times daily, two hours). The camping ground and youth hostel are in a perfect location if you want to hitchhike to Veliko Târnovo, Pleven or Sofia. Express buses travel to Sofia three times daily from Hotel Dunav.

Romania There are six trains a day to Romania, three of them going through to Bucharest, and three of them terminating in Giurgiu where you can connect with local services.

For backpackers, a viable alternative is to take bus No 12 from Nikolaevska, near the train station, 6km to the Friendship Bridge (Dunav Most) and hitch across the upper level (crossing on foot is prohibited). Cars pay a fairly hefty toll to use the bridge and long delays for southbound vehicles are routine at Romanian customs. The chaos means there's no bus direct from Ruse to Romania.

VELIKO TÂRNOVO (ВЕЛИКО ТЪРНОВО)
☎ 062

Veliko Târnovo (Great Târnovo) is laced with history. The Yantra River winds through a gorge in the centre of this 'city of tsars' and picturesque houses cling to the cliffs. Almost encircled by the river, the ruined Tsarevets Citadel recalls the Second Bulgarian Empire (1185-1393), when Veliko Târnovo was the capital. North-west, across the abyss, is the now overgrown Trapezitsa Hill, residence of the nobles and courtiers, while below in the valley the artisans' and merchants' quarter (Asenova) is marked by medieval churches. Renowned monasteries once stood on Sveta Gora Hill, where the university is today. The narrow streets of old Veliko Târnovo bear the imprint of the Bulgarian National Revival; the modern city spreads west. This is one town you won't want to miss: nowhere is the power of medieval Bulgaria better experienced.

History

Both the Thracians and Romans had settlements here and, in the 5th century AD, a Byzantine fortress was built on Tsarevets Hill by Emperor Justinian. The Slavs captured it in the 7th century, and in 1185 the town was the main centre of the uprising against Byzantium led by the brothers Asen and Peter. With the foundation of the Second Bulgarian Empire in the 12th century, Veliko Târnovo became an imperial city, second only to Constantinople in this region. For the next two centuries, trade and culture flourished. The literary school founded here in 1350 by Theodosius of Târnovo attracted students from as far away as Serbia and Russia.

On 17 July 1393, Târnovgrad (Veliko Târnovo) fell to the Turks after a three-month siege. The fortress was destroyed. In the 19th century, Veliko Târnovo re-emerged as a crafts centre. Bulgarian culture gradually reasserted itself as part of the National Revival movement and in 1877 the Russian general IV Gurko liberated the town. Today there is again a university at Veliko Târnovo.

Orientation

The train station is down by the river, far below the centre of town (catch bus Nos 4 or

13). Hristo Botev ends at a T-intersection with Vasil Levski and the modern city to the left, and Nezavisimost and its continuation Stefan Stambolov, to the right.

The bus station is on Nikola Gabrovski, at the western edge of town (bus Nos 7, 10, 11 or 12). Many buses arriving in Veliko Târnovo stop near the market before going on to the bus station, so ask. Bus No 10 to Gorna Oryahovitsa leaves from the bus station but passes through the middle of town.

The left-luggage office at the bus station is open from 7.30 am to 4.30 pm. At the train station, the left-luggage office is in a small building next to the main station. It's open 24 hours a day.

Information

The receptionist at Hotel Etâr will sell you a map of the town.

The Union of Bulgarian Motorists has a large service centre next to the Bolyarski Stan Camping Ground on the Varna-Sofia highway west of town.

Money Bulgarski Bank, ploshtad Vekhova Zavera 4, across the road from Hotel Yantra, changes travellers cheques for a 1% commission. Amazingly, it gives cash advances on credit cards without taking a slice. The currency exchange counter at the Interhotel Veliko Târnovo changes travellers cheques for a flat US$5 commission.

Post & Communications The telephone centre in the main post office is open daily from 9 am to 10 pm.

Travel Agencies The Rila office, Nikola Gabrovski 42, halfway out to the main bus station (bus No 10), sells advance train tickets and makes seat reservations for express trains.

Walking Tour

Opposite the Hotel Yantra on Stefan Stambolov you'll see a stairway leading up into Varusha, a colourful neighbourhood of picturesque streets. Go up and veer left, then go down stone-surfaced Rakovski, where Bulgarian artisans keep small shops. At number 17 is the **Hadji Nicoli Inn** (1858), one of the best known National Revival buildings in

Bulgaria. The street above Rakovski is lined with quaint old houses and terminates at a church.

Return to the Hotel Yantra and walk east, keeping right on Ivan Vazov, until you reach the **Bulgarian National Revival Museum** (closed Tuesday and from November to March). The museum is in the old Turkish town hall (1872), the large blue building you see straight ahead. Notice the stone building with six arches beside this museum. The **Archaeological Museum** (closed Monday) is in the basement, down the stairway between the two buildings.

Follow the street on the left to the entrance to **Tsarevets Citadel** (open daily 8 am to 7 pm, 2500 leva), which was sacked and burned by the Turks in 1393. This vast fortress offers great views from the rebuilt **Assumption Patriarchal Church** at the top of the hill. Just below, to the north, are the foundations of the extensive **Royal Palace** on three terraces. Twenty-two successive kings ruled Bulgaria from this palace. Continue north to a bluff directly above the large factory. This was **Execution Rock**, from which traitors were pushed into the Yantra River. At the southern end of the citadel is the **Baldwin Tower** (rebuilt in 1932) where Baldwin I of Flanders, the deposed Latin emperor of Byzantium, was imprisoned and finally executed after his defeat in 1205.

From the entrance to Tsarevets Hill walk down the steep incline to the **Holy Forty Martyrs Church**, by the river at the foot of the hill. The church was built by Tsar Ivan Asen II to commemorate his victory over the despot of Epirus, Teodor Komnin, at Klokotnitsa in 1230, as recorded on the Asen Column inside. Originally a royal mausoleum, Holy Forty Martyrs Church was converted into a mosque by the Turks. There are murals to be seen, but the church has been closed for restoration for many years.

Turn right (don't cross the river) and continue two blocks to the 13th-century **Sts Peter & Paul Church**, with frescos. Walk back a little, then cross the big wooden bridge and continue right up through the village till you see a church enclosed by a high stone wall. This is **St Dimitâr of Salonika**, the town's oldest church. During the consecration of this church in 1185, the noblemen brothers Asen

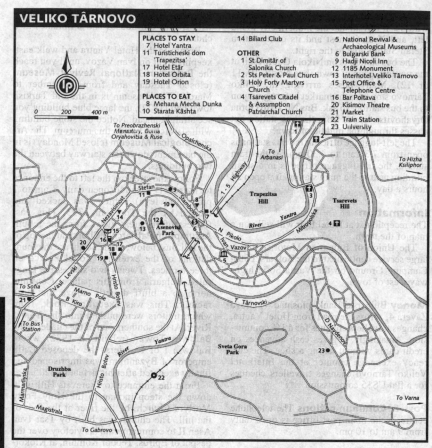

VELIKO TÂRNOVO

PLACES TO STAY
7 Hotel Yantra
11 Turisticheski dom 'Trapezitsa'
17 Hotel Etâr
18 Hotel Orbita
19 Hotel Orion

PLACES TO EAT
8 Mehana Mecha Dunka
10 Starata Kâshta

14 Biliard Club

OTHER
1 St Dimitâr of Salonika Church
2 Sts Peter & Paul Church
3 Holy Forty Martyrs Church
4 Tsarevets Citadel & Assumption Patriarchal Church

5 National Revival & Archaeological Museums
6 Bulgarski Bank
9 Hadji Nicoli Inn
12 1185 Monument
13 Interhotel Veliko Târnovo
15 Post Office & Telephone Centre
16 Bar Poltava
20 Kisimov Theatre
21 Market
22 Train Station
23 University

and Peter proclaimed an uprising against Byzantine rule. Later, the church was used for royal coronations. From here you can return to the city centre on bus No 7 or 11.

To Sveta Gora Another memorable walk begins at the Interhotel Veliko Târnovo. Cross the footbridge behind the hotel to reach **Asenovtsi Park**, which has an art gallery and a great monument to the re-establishment of the Bulgarian Empire by Asen I in 1185. From here you'll get the classic view of the

city's tiers of rustic houses hanging above the Yantra Gorge.

After an eyeful, walk south-east towards **Sveta Gora Park** and climb the stairs to the restaurant (closed) you can see protruding through the trees, from where you'll get a sweeping view of the city and its surroundings. The founders of the Târnovo schools of literature and painting were active in the monasteries of Sveta Gora, which have since disappeared. Return the way you came or ask for directions to the university, where you can get a bus.

Places to Stay

Camping *Bolyarski Stan Camping Ground* (☎ 641 859) on the western edge of town has simple bungalows for US$10 a double and camping space at US$3 per person plus US$3 per tent. There's a good traditional restaurant at the entrance and it's open year-round. Bus Nos 10 and 11 stop near the camping ground on their way from the centre of town to the bus station – get off at the beginning of the Varan-Sofia highway.

Youth Hostels The modern four-storey *Turisticheski dom 'Trapezitsa'* (☎ 622 061) is right in the centre of town at Stefan Stambolov 79, but it's a bit pricey. Dorm rooms are US$9 per person with a HI card, US$14 without a card.

Hostel-style accommodation is available all year at *Turisticheski dom 'Momina Krepost'* (also known as 'Hizha Ksiliphor'), in a lovely woodland setting north-east of Veliko Târnovo. Take bus No 7 or 11 east to the end of the line. Walk straight ahead beside the river for a while until you reach a factory, then turn left up the hill and continue for another 2km to a café, which rents out bungalows (US$22 a double). Alternatively, take a bus bound for Arbanasi to the access road, and then walk down to the hostel.

Hotels *Hotel Orbita* (☎ 622 041), Hristo Botev 15, is US$6 per person – the reception is at the top of the stairs on the fourth floor. Across the street is the *Hotel Orion* (☎ 629 691), Hristo Botev 14, with rooms at US$10 per person. Both options here are pretty well in the grunge category, so be prepared.

The two-star, 14-floor *Hotel Etâr* (☎ 621 838), Ivailo 1, is in the building directly behind the Hotel Orbita. Rooms are US$15/30 a single/double without bath or US$26/52 with private bath.

The three-star *Hotel Yantra* (☎ 620 391), Opalchenska on the corner of Stefan Stambolov, is US$43/64 a single/double with bath and breakfast. The rooms on the main floor are noisy when the band is playing in the restaurant, but the gorge-side rooms have fantastic views, perfect for watching the Tsaravets sound & light show (see Entertainment section).

Places to Eat & Drink

There's a good *market* west on Vasil Levski, on the corner of Nikola Gabrovski. Stock up on fresh vegetables and fruit here.

The *Starata Kâshta* is a friendly little mehana on the cliff side of Stefan Stambolov. The tables by the window have the views, but the food is good and cheap anyway and the menu is in English.

On the back terrace restaurant of the *Hotel Yantra* you can feast on the view of the river as much as the food. The service is fast and reliable, especially if you try to use a few words of Bulgarian. It is, however, a little pricey.

The *Mehana Mecha Dunka*, Mamarchev 12, up the stairs from opposite the Hotel Yantra, serves typical Bulgarian specialities and there's even a menu in English. It's open daily.

For coffee or a beer the *Biliard Club* at Nezavisimost 17 probably has the best view available from any such establishment anywhere in Europe.

Entertainment

Veliko Târnovo's best disco is in the *Bar Poltava* above Cinema Poltava in the large modern complex next to the post office. The *bars* along the cliff side of Nevazisimost are where the local students hang out.

In summer there's an impressive *light-and-sound show* at Tsarevets Citadel at about 10 pm, which lights the whole of Tsarevets Hill in myriad colours. The show's only put on when groups are present, and the receptionist at the Interhotel Veliko Târnovo only knows for sure whether there'll be a show that night two hours in advance, but will sell tickets (US$7 per person) that grant you the honour of watching the show seated in one of the blue plastic chairs in the stand opposite the citadel ticket kiosk. Of course, you can see the show for free from many other parts of town, including the downstairs restaurant at the Hotel Yantra, where you get a more complete view of the show.

Getting There & Away

To get a train to Pleven, Sofia, Ruse or Varna, take bus No 10, which runs frequently, to Gorna Oryahovitsa train station. Some local trains from Dimitrovgrad direct to Ruse

stop at Veliko Târnovo train station. Getting
to Plovdiv is infinitely simpler by bus.

Buses to Plovdiv (197km) run over Shipka
Pass and four a day go to Sofia (247km).
Other buses from Veliko Târnovo include
three to Kazanlâk (96km), nine to Sevlievo
(56km), two to Burgas (223km) and three to
Ruse (103km). To reach Etâr, take the hourly
bus to Gabrovo (49km) and change there.

Several luxury tourist coaches between
Sofia and Varna pick up passengers outside
Hotel Etâr, and you can buy tickets at the
office inside the hotel.

AROUND VELIKO TÂRNOVO
Preobrazhenski Monastery
A recommended side trip is Preobrazhenski
(Transfiguration) Monastery, 7km north of
Veliko Târnovo, on one of the two roads to
Gorna Oryahovitsa. The location on a
wooded hillside below the cliffs of the Yantra
Gorge is lovely. The ruins of the 14th-century
monastery destroyed by the Turks are 500m
south of the present monastery, which was
rebuilt in 1825 with frescos (1851) by Zahari
Zograph and large icons (1864) by Stanislav
Dospevski.

Get there on bus No 10, which runs frequently between Veliko Târnovo and Gorna
Oryahovitsa. From the stop it's a 2km climb
to the monastery. The **Holy Trinity
Monastery** (1847) is below the cliffs on the
opposite side of the gorge from Preobrazhenski and is accessible only on foot (1½ hours).

Arbanasi
☎ 062
In summer, another good side trip from
Veliko Târnovo is to the village of Arbanasi,
10km north-east of Veliko Târnovo. Originally founded by Albanians, Arbanasi grew
rich after Sultan Süleyman I gave it to one of
his sons-in-law in 1538, thus exempting the
town from the Ottoman Empire's ruinous
taxation.

Things to See & Do A comprehensive
ticket (1500 leva) sold at a kiosk near the bus
stop in the centre of Arbanasi admits you to
four buildings in the village.

Hadzhi Ilyeva House is a typical, two-
storey Arbanasi house of the 16th century.

Konstant-salieva House dates from the 17th
century and is built like a fortress. The high
stone walls topped by red tiles surrounding
the property were intended to protect the
womenfolk from prying Turkish eyes (every
house in Arbanasi is surrounded by such
walls). The highlight of this typical Bulgarian village is **Nativity Church**, the interior of
which is completely covered with colourful
frescos painted between 1632 and 1649. Over
3500 figures are depicted in some 2000
scenes. The interior of **Archangel Church**, on
the low hill behind the restaurant in the
middle of the village, is also covered with
marvellous paintings. There's much more to
see along Arbanasi's winding lanes, but on
Monday and from October to March, everything is closed.

Places to Stay If you'd like to spend the
night in the village, contact Daniel Panov
(☎ 34 257) who coordinates pension-style
rooms in typical Arbanasi dwellings for
about US$12 per person including breakfast.

The nine rooms at the five-star *Arbanasi
Palace Hotel* (☎ 30 176) begin at US$120 a
double with breakfast. This building (1975) is
popularly known as the former residence of
communist boss Todor Zhivkov, though in
fact Zhivkov seldom slept here and it was
used mostly for state functions, seminars and
conferences. Even if you're not up to laying
out such big bucks, it's worth visiting the
'palace' for its marvellous view of Veliko
Târnovo.

Getting There & Away Buses arrive from
Veliko Târnovo bus station every couple of
hours, or just take a taxi and catch a bus back.
Most of the private minibuses shuttling
between Gorna Oryahovitsa train station and
Veliko Târnovo use the old road, which
passes within 1km of Arbanasi, and that's the
easiest way to come.

STARA PLANINA
(СТАРА ПЛАНИНА)
A good slice of the Stara Planina (Balkan
Mountains) can be seen on a loop from
Veliko Târnovo to Pleven going via Gabrovo,
Etâr, Shipka, Kazanlâk, Karlovo, Troyan and
Lovech, or vice versa. You'll visit old monas-

teries, war memorials, quaint villages and the forested peaks themselves.

It's not possible to do all this in one day, so you'll have to spend a night or two somewhere. There are several *camping grounds* between Veliko Târnovo and Karlovo, all with bungalows for those without tents, and between Karlovo and Pleven you'll find *youth hostels* and inexpensive *hotels*. The accommodation situation in Kazanlâk is grim, so try to avoid staying there.

It's a bit of an adventure to do this loop on public transport: it calls for a hardy, rough-and-ready traveller willing to put up with occasional difficulties and delays.

ETÂR (ЕТЪР)
☎ 066

This place is one of Bulgaria's most appealing attractions. At the Etâr Ethnographic Village Museum you can see Bulgarian craftspeople (bakers, cartwrights, cobblers, furriers, glass workers, hatters, jewellers, leather workers, millers, potters, smiths, weavers) practising their age-old trades in typical 18th and 19th-century Gabrovo houses that were reconstructed here in the 1960s. Some of the workshops on the right bank of the stream running through the wooded site are powered by water. At the far end of the village is a small tavern where you can sample the local brew. The museum is open from Tuesday to Sunday from 8 am to 5 pm (closed winter). Entry costs 4500 leva.

To get here, take the hourly bus from Veliko Târnovo to Gabrovo (49km), where you connect with the bus to Etâr (9km). The turn-off from the main Gabrovo-Kazanlâk highway is at the *Lyubovo Campground* (☎ 42 281 – open from mid-May to September), 2km west of Etâr. Here you'll find cabins (US$8 a double) as well as tent space, but no restaurant. You can return to Lyubovo on the Gabrovo bus and pick up one of the 12 daily Kazanlâk buses there. These buses are often crowded and it may be better to go back into Gabrovo and board the Kazanlâk bus at its starting point. Check the times of this bus when you're in Gabrovo, before going to Etâr.

SHIPKA (ШИПКА)
☎ 09434

At the top of 1306m Shipka Pass, over the Stara Planina between Gabrovo and Shipka, is a large monument (1934) commemorating the Russian troops and Bulgarian volunteers who, in August 1877, fought back numerous attacks by vastly superior Turkish forces intent on relieving the besieged Turks at Pleven.

Shipka is a quaint little village, 13km beyond the pass. Poking through the trees above the village are the five golden, onion-shaped domes of a huge votive church (1902) built after the Russo-Turkish War (1877-78). The church bells were cast from spent cartridges from the battle and in the crypt lie the remains of the Russian soldiers who perished. You'll get a great view of the Valley of Roses from up there.

The *Stoletov Campground* (bungalows) is up at the pass, but it gets cool at night. A private hotel, *Sveti Nikola* (☎ 27 65) has also opened at the top of the pass. Near a huge circular memorial pavilion, 12km east of the pass along a side road, is *Hizha 'Buzludzha'*, a good base for hikers.

From Shipka village bus No 6 runs hourly into Kazanlâk (12km).

KAZANLÂK (КАЗАНЛЪК)
☎ 0431

Kazanlâk, an important stop on the railway line from Burgas to Sofia, is tucked between the Stara Planina and Sredna Gora mountains in the Valley of Roses. This is not a particularly attractive town, but it is a useful base for visiting nearby attractions. The Festival of Roses, held on the first Sunday in June, features carnivals and parades in Kazanlâk and Karlovo.

Orientation
The bus and train stations in Kazanlâk are adjacent. From the stations, walk about three blocks north on bul Rozova Dolina to the Roza and Kazanlâk hotels.

Things to See & Do
The Archaeological Museum is two blocks north of Hotel Kazanlâk up Iskâra. Many items found in the tombs and other ancient

BULGARIA

sites of this region are kept here, but the captions are only in Bulgarian.

In Tjulbeto Park, 2km north-east of the stations, is a 4th century BC **Thracian tomb** with delicate frescos discovered during the construction of a bomb shelter in 1944. The original brick tomb has been scrupulously protected since then and cannot be visited, but a full-scale replica has been created nearby. Along the vaulted entry corridor, or *dromos*, is a double frieze with battle scenes. The burial chamber itself is 12m in diameter and covered by a beehive dome showing a funeral feast and chariot race.

The Valley of Roses is the source of 70% of the world's supply of rose attar. The roses bloom from late May to early June and must be picked before sunrise when still wet with dew if the fragrance is to be preserved. Two thousand petals are required for a single gram of attar of roses. A **rose museum** is at the edge of town by the road to Shipka.

Places to Stay & Eat
The Shipka bus passes the *Kasanlaschka Rosa Campground* (open from May to mid-October) between Shipka and Kazanlâk.

For a possible private room call Maria Ginyeva (☎ 45 640), Batak 16. She has private rooms for US$8 per person.

The two-star, 80-room *Hotel Roza* (☎ 24 605), at bul Rozova Dolina 1, four blocks up from the train station, charges US$30/50 a single/double with private bath and breakfast.

Hotel Kazanlak (☎/fax 40 029), bul Rozina Dolina 2, opposite the Hotel Roza has fairly pricey single/double rooms for US$42/64.

The *Roza Pizzeria* opposite the Hotel Kazanlak is a convenient and cheap option, though there are a number of more upmarket eateries around town.

Getting There & Away
Kazanlak is on the line from Burgas to Sofia via Karlovo. To/from Veliko Târnovo go by bus via Gabrovo. To go to Shipka (12km) take bus No 6 (hourly) from the stop a block west of the bus station. Other buses from Kazanlâk include 12 to Gabrovo (47km), four to Veliko Târnovo (96km), four to Plovdiv (114km) and two to Hisar (72km).

VIDIN (ВИДИН)
☎ 094
Vidin, the first major Bulgarian town on the Danube River below the chunky Iron Gate, serves as a convenient entry/exit point for Calafat, Romania, opposite. Actually, this is about the only reason to make the long trip up to Vidin.

History
On the site of the 3rd century BC Celtic settlement of Dunonia, the Romans built a fortress they called Bononia to control the Danube crossing here. Medieval Vidin was an important north-western bastion and trading centre of the Second Bulgarian Empire.

In 1371, as Bulgaria wavered before the Ottoman onslaught, the king's son, Ivan Sratsimir, declared this region the independent Kingdom of Vidin with himself as ruler.

The fall of the city to the Turks in 1396 marked the completion of their conquest of Bulgaria. The Turks built an extensive city wall around Vidin, the various gates of which have survived to this day. By the 16th century, Vidin was the largest town in Bulgaria. As Turkish rule in turn weakened, a local pasha, Osman Pazvantoglu, declared his district independent (1792-1807) of the sultan. In 1878, Vidin was returned to Bulgaria by the Romanian army and in 1885 an attempt by Serbia to take the area was resisted.

Orientation
Central Vidin is very convenient, with the train station, bus station and riverboat terminal all a block apart in the middle of town. The car ferry to/from Calafat is 5km north. The left-luggage office in the train station is open 24 hours a day, but the staff take four long breaks, so note the posted schedule carefully.

Information
Tourist Offices Try Balkantourist (☎ 24 976), General Dondukov 4a, or Orbita Student Travel at Tsar Simeon Veliki 6, just around the corner.

Money The National Bank, at the back of the post office building opposite the train station (weekdays 8 to 11 am), charges 2% commission to change travellers cheques.

Post & Communications The telephone centre in the main post office opposite the train station is open daily from 7 am to 9.30 pm.

Things to See

In the riverside park between the town centre and the fortress is the 18th-century **Osman Pazvantoglu Mosque**, with a small religious library alongside. Nearby are the 17th-century **Church of St Petka** and the 12th-century **Church of St Panteleimon**. The former was partially sunk into the ground in deference to the mosque.

Vidin's main sight is the **Baba Vida Fortress** at the northern end of the park, overlooking the river. Baba Vida was built by the Bulgarians from the 10th to 14th centuries on the ruined walls of 3rd-century Roman Bononia. In the 17th century, the Turks rebuilt the fortress and today it's the best preserved medieval stone fortress in Bulgaria.

Places to Stay

Camping Nora (☎ 23 830) is just beyond the fairground, a couple of kilometres west of town along Ekzarh Yosif I. Bungalows are US$6 per person.

The *Turisticheski dom 'Vidin'* (☎ 22 813), Edelweiss 3, just a few minutes walk from the riverboat terminal in the centre of town, is US$9 per person (or US$8 per person with a HI card) in a triple room with shared bath. Singles/doubles are US$25/50.

Balkantourist (☎ 24 976), at General Dondukov 4a between the train station and Hotel Bononia, has private rooms from a ridiculous US$25 per person.

The six-storey, two-star *Hotel Bononia* (☎ 23 031), facing a park near the river in the centre of town, is US$25/45 a single/double with bath. The staff here are helpful.

Getting There & Away

There are direct express trains between Vidin and Sofia (six hours). The overnight train between Sofia and Vidin has only 2nd-class carriages and no couchettes, but it's seldom crowded. When boarding in Sofia be sure to get in a carriage labelled Vidin (and not Lom) as the train splits in half in the middle of the night.

Romania The Vidin-Calafat car ferry operates hourly all year from a landing 5km north of Vidin. The crossing takes half an hour and you buy the ferry ticket on the boat. Only Bulgarians and Romanians may pay in leva or lei – foreigners must pay US$5 in cash per person. Bicycles are either US$2 or free, depending on your luck. Take bus No 1 from beside the train station direct to the ferry. If you're arriving in Bulgaria, the bus stop for Vidin is about 500m down the road from customs. For pedestrians, the Vidin-Calafat crossing is a breeze since you can walk right past the endless line of trucks and shorter line of cars. If using this route, it's best to already have your Romanian or Bulgarian tourist visa and not plan to get it at the border. See the Calafat section in the Romania chapter for more information.

BULGARIA

Croatia

Croatia (Hrvatska) extends in an arc from the Danube River in the east to Istria in the west and south along the Adriatic coast to Dubrovnik. Roman Catholic since the 9th century, and under Hungary since 1102, Croatia only united with Orthodox Serbia in 1918. Croatia's centuries-long resistance to Hungarian and Austrian domination was manifested in 1991 in its determined struggle for nationhood. Yet within Croatia, cultural differences remain between the Habsburg-influenced Central European interior and the formerly Venetian Mediterranean coast.

Croatia's capital, Zagreb, is the country's cultural centre, while coastal towns such as Poreč, Rovinj, Pula, Mali Lošinj, Krk, Rab, Zadar, Šibenik, Trogir, Split, Hvar, Korčula and Dubrovnik all have well-preserved historic centres with lots to see. Before 1991 the strikingly beautiful Mediterranean landscapes of this country attracted nearly 10 million foreign visitors a year.

Traditionally, tourism has been focused along the Adriatic coast, with its unsurpassed combination of history, natural beauty, good climate, clear water and easy access. Seaside resorts are numerous, the swimming is good, and the atmosphere is relaxed – there are few rules about behaviour and few formalities. Since 1960 nudism has been promoted and Croatia is now *the* place to go in Europe to practise naturism.

When Yugoslavia split apart in 1991, no less than 80% of the country's tourist resorts ended up in Croatia. Istria and the lovely Adriatic islands were largely untouched by the fighting and remained peaceful and safe even during the dark days when Osijek, Vukovar and Dubrovnik were world headlines.

The publicity brought tourism almost to a standstill but Croatia is slowly regaining its balance. In July and August, Istria and Krk are filled to capacity and much of Dalmatia is busy as well but outside the peak season all is quiet and, south of Krk in particular, you'll have some beautiful places all to yourself.

AT A GLANCE

Capital	Zagreb
Population	4.7 million
Area	56,538 sq km
Official Language	Serbo-Croatian
Currency	1 Croatian kuna (KN) = 100 lipas
GDP	US$21.4 billion (1996)
Time	GMT/UTC+0100

Facts about Croatia

HISTORY

In 229 BC the Romans began their conquest of the indigenous Illyrians, establishing a colony at Salona (near Split) in Dalmatia. Emperor Augustus extended the empire and created the provinces of Illyricum (Dalmatia and Bosnia) and Pannonia (Croatia). In 285 AD, Emperor Diocletian decided to retire to his palace fortress in Split, today the greatest Roman ruin in Eastern Europe. When the empire was divided in 395, what is now

CROATIA (HRVATSKA)

Slovenia, Croatia and Bosnia-Hercegovina stayed with the Western Roman Empire, while present-day Serbia, Kosovo and Macedonia went to the Eastern Roman Empire, later known as the Byzantine Empire. Visigoth, Hun and Lombard invasions marked the fall of the Western Roman Empire in the 5th century.

Around 625, Slavic tribes migrated from present-day Poland. The Serbian tribe settled in the region that is now south-western Serbia and extended their influence southward and westward. The Croatian tribe moved into

what is now Croatia and occupied two former Roman provinces: Dalmatian Croatia along the Adriatic and Pannonian Croatia to the north.

By the early part of the ninth century, both settlements had accepted Christianity but the northern Croats fell under Frankish domination while Dalmatian Croats came under the nominal control of the Byzantine Empire. The Dalmatian duke Tomislav united the two groups in 925 in a single kingdom which prospered for nearly 200 years.

Late in the 11th century, the throne fell

vacant and a series of ensuing power struggles weakened central authority and split the kingdom. The northern Croats, unable to agree upon a ruler, united with Hungary in 1102 for protection against the Orthodox Byzantine Empire.

In 1242 a Tatar invasion devastated both Hungary and Croatia. In the 14th century the Turks began pushing into the Balkans, defeating the Serbs in 1389 and the Hungarians in 1526. Northern Croatia in 1527 turned to the Habsburgs of Austria for protection against the Turks and remained under their influence until 1918. To form a buffer against the Turks, in the 16th century the Austrians invited Serbs to settle the Vojna Krajina (military frontier) along the Bosnian border. The Serbs in the borderlands had an autonomous administration under Austrian control and these areas were not reincorporated into Croatia until 1881.

The Adriatic coast fell under Venetian influence as early as the 12th century although Hungary continued to struggle for control of the region. Some Dalmatian cities changed hands repeatedly until Venice imposed its rule on the Adriatic coast in the early 15th century and occupied it for nearly four centuries. Only the Republic of Ragusa (Dubrovnik) maintained its independence. The Adriatic coast was threatened, but never conquered, by the Turks and, after the naval Battle of Lepanto in 1571, when Spanish and Venetian forces wiped out the Turkish fleet, this threat receded.

After Venice was shattered by Napoleonic France in 1797, the French occupied southern Croatia, entering Ragusa (Dubrovnik) in 1808. Napoleon's merger of Dalmatia, Istria and Slovenia into the 'Illyrian provinces' in 1809 stimulated the concept of South Slav ('Yugoslav') unity. After Napoleon's defeat at Waterloo in 1815, Austria-Hungary moved in to pick up the pieces along the coast.

A revival of Croatian cultural and political life began in 1835. In 1848 a liberal democratic revolution led by Josip Jelačić was suppressed, but serfdom was abolished. An 1868 reform transferred northern Croatia from Austria to Hungary, united the territory with Hungarian Slavonia and granted a degree of internal autonomy. Dalmatia remained under Austria. In the decade before

the outbreak of WWI, some 50,000 Croats emigrated to the USA.

With the defeat of the Austro-Hungarian empire in WWI, Croatia became part of the Kingdom of Serbs, Croats & Slovenes (called Yugoslavia after 1929), which had a centralised government in Belgrade. This was strongly resisted by Croatian nationalists, who organised the Paris assassination of King Alexander I in 1934. Italy had been promised the Adriatic coast as an incentive to join the war against Austria-Hungary in 1915 and it held much of northern Dalmatia from 1918 to 1943.

After the German invasion of Yugoslavia in March 1941, a puppet government dominated by the fascist Ustaša movement was set up in Croatia and Bosnia-Hercegovina under Ante Pavelić (who fled to Argentina after the war). At first the Ustaša tried to expel all Serbs from Croatia to Serbia. But when the Germans stopped this because of the problems it was causing, the Ustaša launched an extermination campaign which surpassed even that of the Nazis in scale, brutally murdering some 350,000 ethnic Serbs, Jews and Roma (gypsies). The Ustaša program called for 'one-third of Serbs killed, one-third expelled and one-third converted to Catholicism'.

Not all Croats supported these policies, however. Maršal Tito was himself of Croat-Slovene parentage and tens of thousands of Croats fought bravely with his partisans. Massacres of Croats conducted by Serbian Četniks in southern Croatia and Bosnia forced almost all antifascist Croats into the communist ranks, where they joined the numerous Serbs trying to defend themselves from the Ustaša. In all, about a million people died violently in a war which was fought mostly in Croatia and Bosnia-Hercegovina.

Recent History

Postwar Croatia was granted republic status within the Yugoslav Federation. During the 1960s Croatia and Slovenia moved far ahead of the southern republics economically, leading to demands for greater autonomy. The 'Croatian Spring' of 1971 caused a backlash and purge of reformers, and increasing economic inertia due to a cumbersome system of 'self-management' of state enterprises by employees. After Tito died in 1980 the paralysis spread to government; the federal presidency began rotating annually among the republics.

In 1989 severe repression of the Albanian majority in Serbia's Kosovo province sparked renewed fears of Serbian hegemony and heralded the end of the Yugoslav Federation. With political changes sweeping Eastern Europe, many Croats felt the time had come to end more than four decades of communist rule and attain complete autonomy into the bargain. In the free elections of April 1990 Franjo Tudj-man's Croatian Democratic Union (Hrvatska Demokratska Zajednica) easily defeated the old Communist Party. On 22 December 1990 a new Croatian constitution was promulgated, changing the status of Serbs in Croatia from that of a 'constituent nation' to a national minority.

The constitution's failure to guarantee minority rights, and mass dismissals of Serbs from the public service, stimulated the 600,000-strong ethnic Serb community within Croatia to demand autonomy. In early 1991 Serb extremists within Croatia staged provocations designed to force federal military intervention. A May 1991 referendum (boycotted by the Serbs) produced a 93% vote in favour of independence but, when Croatia declared independence on 25 June 1991, the Serbian enclave of Krajina proclaimed its independence from Croatia.

Heavy fighting broke out in Krajina (the area around Knin north of Split), Baranja (the area north of the Drava River opposite Osijek) and Slavonia (the region west of the Danube). The 180,000-member, 2000-tank Yugoslav People's Army, dominated by Serbian communists, began to intervene on its own authority in support of Serbian irregulars under the pretext of halting ethnic violence. After European Community (EC) mediation, Croatia agreed to freeze its independence declaration for three months to avoid bloodshed.

In the three months following 25 June, a quarter of Croatia fell to Serbian militias and the federal army. In September the Croatian government ordered a blockade of 32 federal military installations in the republic, lifting morale and gaining much-needed military equipment. In response, the Yugoslav navy blockaded the Adriatic coast and laid siege to the strategic town of Vukovar on the Danube.

In early October 1991 the federal army and Montenegrin militia moved against Dubrovnik to protest against the ongoing blockade of their garrisons in Croatia. On 7 October the presidential palace in Zagreb was hit by rockets fired by Yugoslav air-force jets in an unsuccessful assassination attempt against President Tudjman. Heroic Vukovar finally fell on 19 November when the army culminated a bloody three-month siege by concentrating 600 tanks and 30,000 soldiers there. During six months of fighting in Croatia 10,000 people died, hundreds of thousands fled and tens of thousands of homes were deliberately destroyed.

In early December the United Nations special envoy, Cyrus Vance, began successful negotiations with Serbia over the deployment of a 14,000-member UN Protection Force (UNPROFOR) in the Serbian-held areas of Croatia. Beginning on 3 January 1992, a 15th cease-fire was generally held. The federal army was allowed to withdraw from its bases inside Croatia without having to shamefully surrender its weapons and thus tensions diminished.

When the three-month moratorium on independence expired on 8 October 1991, Croatia declared full independence. To fulfil a condition for EC recognition, in December the Croatian parliament belatedly amended its constitution to protect minority and human rights. In January 1992 the EC, succumbing to strong pressure from Germany, recognised Croatia. This was followed three months later by US recognition and in May 1992 Croatia was admitted to the United Nations.

The UN peace plan in Krajina was supposed to have led to the disarming of local Serb paramilitary formations, the repatriation of refugees and the return of the region to Croatia. Instead it only froze the existing situation and offered no permanent solution.

In January 1993 the Croatian army suddenly launched an offensive in southern Krajina, pushing the Serbs back as much as 24km in some areas and recapturing strategic points such as the site of the destroyed Maslenica bridge, Zemunik airport near Zadar and the Perućac hydroelectric dam in the hills between Split and Bosnia-Hercegovina. The

Krajina Serbs vowed never to accept rule from Zagreb and in June 1993 they voted overwhelmingly to join the Bosnian Serbs (and eventually Greater Serbia).

The self-proclaimed 'Republic of Serbian Krajina' held elections in December 1993 which no international body recognised as legitimate or fair. Meanwhile continued 'ethnic cleansing' left only about 900 Croats in the Krajina out of an original population of 44,000. Although no further progress was made in implementing the Vance Peace Plan, the Krajina Serbs signed a comprehensive cease-fire on 29 March 1994 which substantially reduced the violence in the region and established demilitarised 'zones of separation' between the parties.

While the world's attention turned to the grim events unfolding in Bosnia-Hercegovina, the Croatian government quietly began procuring arms from abroad. On 1 May 1995, the Croatian army and police entered occupied western Slavonia, east of Zagreb, and seized control of the region within days. The Krajina Serbs responded by shelling Zagreb in an attack that left seven people dead and 130 wounded. As the Croatian military consolidated its hold in western Slavonia, some 15,000 Serbs fled the region despite assurances from the Croatian government that they were safe from retribution.

Belgrade's silence throughout this campaign made it clear that the Krajina Serbs had lost the support of their Serbian sponsors, encouraging the Croats to forge ahead. At dawn on 4 August the military launched a massive assault on the rebel Serb capital of Knin, pummelling it with shells, mortars and bombs. Outnumbered by two to one, the Serb army fled towards northern Bosnia, along with 150,000 civilians whose roots in the Krajina stretched back centuries. The military operation ended in days, but was followed by months of terror. Widespread looting and burning of Serb villages, as well as attacks upon the few remaining elderly Serbs, seemed designed to ensure the permanence of this massive population shift.

The Dayton agreement signed in Paris in December 1995 recognised Croatia's traditional borders and provided for the return of eastern Slavonia, a transition that was completed in January 1998.

Although stability has returned to the country, a key provision of the agreement was the promise by the Croatian government to allow the return of Serbian refugees, a promise that is far from being fulfilled. Housing, local industry and agriculture in Slavonia and the Krajina were devastated by the war, making resettlement both costly and complicated. To the frustration of the international community, the government has clearly manifested more enthusiasm for resettling Croatian refugees while Serbian refugees face a tangle of bureaucratic obstacles and a political environment they fear may be less than welcoming.

Since regional peace depends upon the return of refugees, international pressure upon the Croatian government has been unrelenting. Threats to withdraw the life support of international loans and bar the government from participation in international organisations have been taken seriously by a government that is determined to extract the country from Balkan misery and enter 'civilised' Europe.

GEOGRAPHY & ECOLOGY

Croatia is half the size of present-day Yugoslavia in area (56,538 sq km) and population. The republic swings around like a boomerang from the Pannonian plains of Slavonia between the Sava, Drava and Danube rivers, across hilly central Croatia to the Istrian Peninsula, then south through Dalmatia along the rugged Adriatic coast.

The narrow Croatian coastal belt at the foot of the Dinaric Alps is only about 600km long as the crow flies, but it's so indented that the actual length is 1778km. If the 4012km of coastline around the offshore islands is added to the total, the length becomes 5790km.

Most of the 'beaches' along this jagged coast consist of slabs of rock sprinkled with naturists – don't come expecting to find sand. Beach shoes are worth having along the rocky, urchin-infested shores. Officially there are no private beaches in Croatia, but you must pay to use 'managed' beaches. The waters are sparkling clean, even around large towns.

Croatia's offshore islands are every bit as beautiful as those in Greece. There are 1185 islands and islets along the tectonically submerged Adriatic coastline, 66 of them inhabited. The largest are Cres, Krk, Mali Lošinj, Pag and Rab in the north; Dugi otok in the middle; and Brač, Hvar, Korčula, Mljet and Vis in the south. Most are barren and elongated from north-west to south-east, with high mountains that drop right into the sea.

When the Yugoslav Federation collapsed, seven of its finest national parks ended up in Croatia. Brijuni near Pula is the most carefully cultivated park, with well-preserved Mediterranean holm oak forests. Mountainous Risnjak National Park near Delnice, east of Rijeka, is named after one of its inhabitants – the *ris*, or lynx. Dense forests of beech trees and black pine in Paklenica National Park near Zadar are home for a number of endemic insects, reptiles and birds, as well as the endangered griffon vulture. The abundant plant and animal life, including bears, wolves and deer, in Plitvice National Park between Zagreb and Zadar has put it onto UNESCO's list of world natural heritage sites. Both Plitvice and Krka National Park near Šibenik feature a dramatic series of cascades. The 101 stark and rocky islands of the Kornati Archipelago and National Park make it the largest in the Mediterranean. The island of Mljet near Korčula also contains a forested national park.

GOVERNMENT & POLITICS

Croatia is a parliamentary democracy with a strong presidency. In 1997 Franjo Tudjman was re-elected to a second five-year term as president in an election that foreign observers characterised as free but not fair. State control of the media, especially television, strongly favoured and continues to favour the ruling party, Croatian Democratic Union or HDZ.

Since the election, support for the ruling party may have eroded amid widespread allegations of corruption and cronyism, particularly in the privatisation of state-owned assets. The imposition of the 22% value-added tax is widely perceived as an unfair burden upon an increasingly impoverished population while the ruling elite continues to enrich themselves at taxpayers' expense.

The opposition is too fractured to mount a serious challenge to HDZ leadership but the former communists, refashioned as the Social Democratic Party, may benefit from widespread discontent in the next legislative elections.

ECONOMY

The years since independence have presented the government with some formidable challenges. As a new country, the government must switch from a state-controlled to a privatised economy while rebuilding its infrastructure after a devastating war, rehousing returning refugees and finding new markets for its products after losing markets in the southern regions of former Yugoslavia. Vital transfusions of money from the International Monetary Fund and the World Bank have kept the economy functioning as the government searches for long-term solutions.

The former communist government of Yugoslavia emphasised heavy industry, especially in aluminium, chemicals, petroleum and shipbuilding. The shipyards of Pula, Rijeka and Split made Croatia the world's third-largest shipbuilder. The chemical industry was concentrated at Krk, Rijeka, Split and Zagreb; machine-tool manufacture at Karlovac, Slavonski Brod and Zagreb; heavy electrical engineering at Zagreb; and textiles at Zagreb and in north-western Croatia. Unfortunately, many of these industries have stagnated since the war, their problems compounded by large debts that have inhibited necessary restructuring. Growth in industrial output has been slow, hampered by an overvalued kuna that penalises exports while making imports cheap.

In the past, one-third of Croatia's national income came from tourism, but between 1991 and 1995 tourist numbers fell dramatically. Dalmatia was the hardest hit and has yet to recover while Istria and Krk have begun to rebound with an influx of Germans, Austrians, Italians and Czechs. It may be years before tourism reaches prewar levels, however, and attracting tourism requires capital outlays. Many hotels along the coast require costly renovation after years of sheltering refugees. Investment in air, road and boat connections along the coast are also necessary if tourism is to be the cornerstone of the Croatian economy.

Unlike the trade and industrial sectors, agriculture has been in private hands since the failure of collectivisation just after WWII. Private farmers with small plots continue to work most of the land. The interior plains produce fruit, vegetables and grains (especially corn and wheat), while olives and grapes are cultivated along the coast. The return of fertile eastern Slavonia should eventually give the economy a boost once the war damage is repaired.

Perhaps the most troublesome task facing the government is reform of the banking sector. Too many banks made too many bad loans under circumstances that are cloudy at best. Poor management has made restructuring a lengthy process despite the government's efforts to recapitalise and rehabilitate weaker banks.

For the average Croatian, life is difficult with no gleaming light at the end of the tunnel. The average wage is less than 2500KN (US$400) a month and a high percentage of the population is unemployed (17.6% in 1997). Although inflation is low (3.6% in 1997), the recent imposition of the 22% value-added tax has eroded purchasing power, particularly for pensioners on fixed incomes. There's a widespread perception that the standard of living has fallen since the prewar years and the social safety net has been abruptly snatched away. A middle class faced with growing insecurity could eventually pose a serious threat to further economic reform.

POPULATION & PEOPLE

Before the war, Croatia had a population of nearly five million, of which 78% were Croats and 12% were Serbs. Now it has a population of 4.7 million, but with a constant flow of refugees in both directions, reliable statistics since the war have been difficult to compile. It's estimated that only 5% of the Serbian population remains. Small communities of Slavic Muslims, Hungarians, Slovenes, Italians, Czechs and Albanians complete the mosaic. The largest cities in Croatia are Zagreb (1 million), Split (300,000), Rijeka (225,000), Osijek (175,000) and Zadar (150,000).

ARTS

The work of sculptor Ivan Meštrović (1883-1962) is seen in town squares all around

Croatia. Besides creating public monuments, Meštrović designed imposing buildings such as the circular Croatian Historical Museum in Zagreb. Both his sculpture and architecture display the powerful classical restraint he learnt from Rodin. Meštrović's studio in Zagreb and his retirement home at Split have been made into galleries of his work.

Music

Croatian folk music bears many influences. The *kolo*, a lively Slavic round dance in which men and women alternate in the circle, is accompanied by Roma-style violinists or players of the *tambura*, a three or five-string mandolin popular throughout Croatia. The measured guitar-playing and rhythmic accordions of Dalmatia have a gentle Italian air.

A recommended recording available locally on compact disc (DD-0030) is *Narodne Pjesme i Plesovi Sjeverne Hrvatske* (Northern Croatian Folk Songs and Dances) by the Croatian folkloric ensemble Lado. The 22 tracks on this album represent nine regions, with everything from haunting Balkan voices reminiscent of Bulgaria to lively Mediterranean dance rhythms.

SOCIETY & CONDUCT

Croats take pride in keeping up appearances. Despite a fragile economy money can usually be found to brighten up the town centre with a fresh coat of paint or to repair a historic building. Even as their bank accounts diminish most people will cut out restaurants and movies to afford a shopping trip to Italy for some new clothes. The tidy streets and stylish clothes are rooted in the Croats' image of themselves as Western Europeans, not Yugoslavs, a word that makes Croats wince. Dressing neatly will go a long way towards gaining a traveller acceptance.

Because of the intense propaganda surrounding the recent war, Croats are inclined to see themselves as wholly right and the other side as wholly wrong. Comments questioning this assumption are not particularly appreciated. People who have had their lives disrupted, if not shattered, by war are generally uninterested in the political niceties of their situation.

RELIGION

Croats are overwhelmingly Roman Catholic, while virtually all Serbs belong to the Eastern Orthodox Church. In addition to various doctrinal differences, Orthodox Christians venerate icons, allow priests to marry and do not accept the authority of the Roman Catholic pope. Long suppressed under communism, Catholicism is undergoing a strong resurgence in Croatia; churches have strong attendances every Sunday. Muslims make up 1.2% of the population and Protestants 0.4%, with a tiny Jewish population in Zagreb.

LANGUAGE

As a result of history, tourism and the number of returned 'guest workers' from Germany, German is the most commonly spoken second language in Croatia. Many people in Istria speak Italian and English is popular among young people.

Croatian is a South Slavic language, as are Serbian, Slovene, Macedonian and Bulgarian. Prior to 1991 both Croatian and Serbian were considered dialects of a single language known as Serbo-Croatian. As a result of the civil war in former Yugoslavia, the local languages are being revised, so spellings and idioms may change.

The most obvious difference between Serbian and Croatian is that Serbian is written in Cyrillic script and Croatian in Roman script. There are also a number of variations in vocabulary.

Geographical terms worth knowing are *aleja* (walkway), *cesta* (road), *donji* (lower), *gora* (hill), *grad* (town), *jezero* (lake), *krajina* (frontier), *luka* (harbour), *malo* (little), *novo* (new), *obala* (bank, shore), *otok* (island), *planina* (mountain), *polje* (valley), *prolaz* (strait), *put* (path), *rijeka* (river), *selo* (village), *šetalište* (way), *stanica* (station, stop), *stari* (old), *šuma* (forest), *sveti* (saint), *toplice* (spa), *trg* (square), *ulica* (street), *veliko* (big), *vrata* (pass), *vrh* (peak) and *zaljev* (bay).

Two words everyone should know are *ima* (there is) and *nema* (there isn't). If you make just a small effort to learn a few words, you'll distinguish yourself from the packaged tourists and be greatly appreciated by the local people.

Lonely Planet's *Mediterranean Europe phrasebook* includes a useful chapter on the Serbian and Croatian languages, with translations of key words and phrases from each appearing side by side, providing a clear comparison of the languages. For a basic rundown on travellers' Croatian and Serbian, see the Language Guide at the end of this book.

Facts for the Visitor

HIGHLIGHTS
Museums & Galleries

Art museums and galleries are easier for a foreign visitor to enjoy than historical museums, which are usually captioned in Croatian only. In Zagreb the Museum Mimara contains an outstanding collection of Spanish, Italian and Dutch paintings as well as an archaeological collection, exhibits of ancient art from Asia and collections of glass, textiles, sculpture and furniture. The Strossmayer Gallery, also in Zagreb, is worthwhile for its exhibits of Italian, Flemish, French and Croatian paintings.

The Meštrović Gallery in Split is worth a detour to see and in Zagreb the Meštrović Studio gives a fascinating insight into the life and work of this remarkable sculptor.

Castles

The palace of the Roman emperor Diocletian in Split has been named a world heritage site by UNESCO. Despite a weathered façade, this sprawling imperial residence and fortress is considered the finest intact example of classical defence architecture in Europe.

Just outside Zagreb is an impressive circle of castles. To the north is Veliki Tabor, a fortified medieval castle in the process of restoration but the most impressive is Trakošćan, beside a long lake. Medvedgrad, west of Zagreb, was built by bishops in the 13th century. The square baroque castle of Lukavec lies in the picturesque Turopolje region south-east of Zagreb. The Varaždin Castle in northern Croatia has recently been restored and hosts an annual music festival. Trsat Castle in Rijeka offers a stunning view of the Kvarner Gulf.

Historic Towns

All along the Adriatic coast are white-stone towns with narrow, winding streets enclosed by defensive walls. Each town has its own flavour. Hilly Rovinj looks out over the sea, while the peninsula of Korčula town burrows into it. Zadar retains echoes of its original Roman street plan while Hvar and Trogir are traditional medieval towns. None can match the exquisite harmony of Dubrovnik, with its blend of elements of medieval and Renaissance architecture.

SUGGESTED ITINERARIES

Depending on the length of your stay, you might want to see and do the following things:

Two days
  Visit Dubrovnik.
One week
  Visit Zagreb, Split and Dubrovnik.
Two weeks
  Visit Zagreb and all of Dalmatia.
One month
  Visit all the areas covered in this chapter.

PLANNING
Climate & When to Go

The climate varies from Mediterranean along the Adriatic coast to continental inland. The high coastal mountains help to shield the coast from cold northerly winds, making for an early spring and late autumn. In spring and early summer a sea breeze called the *maestral* keeps the temperature down along the coast. Winter winds include the cold *bura* from the north and humid *široko* from the south.

The sunny coastal areas experience hot, dry summers and mild, rainy winters, while the interior regions are cold in winter and warm in summer. Because of a warm current flowing north up the Adriatic coast, sea temperatures never fall below 10°C in winter and are as high as 26°C in August. You can swim in the sea from mid-June until late September. The resorts south of Split are the warmest.

May is a nice month to travel along the Adriatic coast, with good weather and few tourists. June and September are also good, but in July and August all of Europe arrives and prices soar. September is perhaps the best

month since it's not as hot as summer, though the sea remains warm, the crowds will have thinned out as children return to school, off-season accommodation rates apply and fruit such as figs and grapes will be abundant. In April and October it may be too cool for camping, but the weather should still be fine along the coast and private rooms will be plentiful and inexpensive.

Books & Maps

For a comprehensive account of the personalities and events surrounding the collapse of ex-Yugoslavia it would be hard to surpass *The Death of Yugoslavia* by Laura Silber & Allan Little, based on the 1995 BBC television series of the same name. Richard Holbrooke's *To End a War* is a riveting account of the personalities and events surrounding the Dayton peace agreement. *Café Europa* is a series of essays by a Croatian journalist, Slavenka Drakulić, that provides an inside look at life in the country since independence. Rebecca West's 1937 travel classic, *Black Lamb & Grey Falcon*, contains a long section on Croatia as part of her trip through Yugoslavia. Robert Kaplan's *Balkan Ghosts* touches on Croatia's part in the tangled web of Balkan history.

Kimmerley & Frey's map *Croatia & Slovenia* (1:500,000) is detailed and depicts the latest borders. Most tourist offices in the country have local maps, but make sure the street names are up to date.

TOURIST OFFICES

Municipal tourist offices and any office marked 'Turist Biro' will have free brochures and good information on local events. These offices are found in Dubrovnik, Pula, Rijeka, Split and Zagreb. Most towns also have an office selling theatre and concert tickets.

Tourist information is also dispensed by commercial travel agencies such as Atlas, Croatia Express, Generalturist, Kompas and Kvarner Express, which also arrange private rooms, sightseeing tours etc.

Keep in mind that these are profit-making businesses, so don't be put off if you're asked to pay for a town map etc. The agencies often sell local guidebooks, which are excellent

CROATIA

value if you'll be staying for a while. Ask if they have the schedule for coastal ferries.

Croatian Tour Companies Abroad
The Croatian Ministry of Tourism has few offices abroad, but the tour companies listed here specialise in Croatia and will gladly mail you their brochures containing much information on the country:

Germany
(☎ 069-25 20 45) Kroatische Zentrale für Tourismus, Karlsluher Strasse 18, D-60329 Frankfurt am Main
Netherlands
(☎ 020-405 7066) Kroatische Centrale voor Tourisme, Schipholboulevard 205 WTC, 1118 BH Luchthaven Schiphol
UK
(☎ 0181-563 7979) Phoenix Holidays, 2 The Lanchesters; 162-164 Fulham Palace Rd, London W6 9ER
USA
(☎ 201-428-0707) Croatian National Tourist Office, 300 Lanidex Plaza, Parsippany, NJ 07054

VISAS & EMBASSIES
Visitors from Australia, Canada, New Zealand, the UK and the USA no longer require a visa for stays less than 90 days. For other nationalities, visas are issued free of charge at Croatian consulates. Croatian authorities require foreigners to register with local police when they first arrive in a new area of the country, but this is a routine matter which is normally handled by the hotel, hostel, camp site or agency securing private accommodation.

Croatian Embassies Abroad
Croatian embassies and consulates around the world include the following:

Australia
(☎ 02-6286 6988) 14 Jindalee Crescent, O'Malley, ACT 2601
(☎ 03-9699 2633) 9-24 Albert Rd, South Melbourne, Victoria 3205
(☎ 02-9299 8899) 379 Kent St, Level 4, Sydney, NSW 2000
(☎ 09-321 6044) 68 St George's Terrace, Perth, WA 6832

Canada
(☎ 613-230 7351) 130 Albert St, Suite 1700, Ottawa, Ontario K1P 5G4
(☎ 905-277 9051) 918 Dundas St E, Suite 302, Mississauga, Ontario L4Y 2B8
New Zealand
(☎ 09-836 5581) 131 Lincoln Rd, Henderson, Box 83200, Edmonton, Auckland
UK
(☎ 0171-387 0022) 21 Conway St, London W1P 5HI
USA
(☎ 202-588-5899) 2343 Massachusetts Ave NW, Washington, DC 20008

For the addresses of Croatian embassies in Bucharest, Budapest, Ljubljana, Prague and Sofia, turn to the sections of this book relating to those cities.

Foreign Embassies in Croatia
All the following addresses are in Zagreb unless otherwise noted:

Albania
(☎ 01-48 10 679) Jurišiaeva 2a
Australia
(☎ 01-45 77 433) Mihanovićeva 1
Bosnia-Hercegovina
(☎ 01-46 83 767) Torbarova 9
Bulgaria
(☎ 01-45 52 288) Novi Goljak 25
Canada
(☎ 01-45 77 905) Mihanovićeva 1
Czech Republic
(☎ 01-61 15 914) Savska 41
Hungary
(☎ 01-422 654) Krležin Gvozd 11a
Poland
(☎ 01-278 818) Krležin Gvozd 3
Romania
(☎ 01-23 36 091) Srebrnjak 150a
Slovakia
(☎ 01-48 48 941) Prilaz Gjure Deželića 10
Slovenia
(☎ 01-61 56 945) Savska 41
UK
(☎ 01-45 55 310) Vlaška 121, Zagreb 21000
(☎ 021-341 464) Obala hrvatskog narodnog preporoda 10, Split 21000
(☎ 020-412 916) Pile 1, Dubrovnik 20000
USA
(☎ 01-45 55 500) Andrije Hebranga 2
Yugoslavia
(☎ 01-46 80 553) Mesićeva 19

MONEY

Currency

In May 1994 the Croatian dinar was replaced by the kuna, which takes its name from the marten, a fox-like animal whose pelt was a means of exchange in the Middle Ages. You're allowed to import or export Croatian banknotes up to a value of around 2000KN but there's no reason to do either.

Exchange Rates

Australia	A$1	=	3.90KN
Canada	C$1	=	4.25KN
euro	€1	=	7.13KN
France	1FF	=	1.08KN
Germany	DM1	=	3.6KN
Japan	¥100	=	4.44KN
New Zealand	NZ$1	=	3.29KN
UK	UK£1	=	10.50KN
USA	US$1	=	6.43KN

Changing Money

There are numerous places to change money, all offering similar rates; ask at any travel agency for the location of the nearest exchange. Banks and exchange offices keep long hours. Exchange offices may deduct a commission of 1% to change cash or travellers cheques but some banks do not. Kuna can be converted into hard currency only at a bank and if you submit a receipt of a previous transaction. Hungarian currency is difficult to change in Croatia.

Credit Cards

Visa cards are accepted for cash advances in Croatia only at Splitska Banka. (American Express, MasterCard and Diners Club cards are more easily accepted.) Cirrus cards can be used for cash withdrawals and you get the best rate. Diners Club cards can also be used for cash withdrawals in many places. Major cities have ATM machines but many of the islands are not yet hooked up to the system. Make sure you have a four-digit PIN.

Costs

The government deliberately overvalues the kuna to obtain cheap foreign currency. Hotel prices are set in Deutschmarks and thus are fairly constant, though you pay in kuna calculated at the daily official rate. Accom-modation is more expensive than it should be for a country trying to lure more tourism and real budget accommodation is in short supply. Transport, concert and theatre tickets, and food are reasonably priced for Europe.

Average accommodation prices per person are around 90KN for a private room, 25KN for a meal at a self-service restaurant and 25 to 45KN for an average intercity bus fare. It's not that hard to survive on 200KN daily if you stay in hostels or private rooms and you'll pay less if you camp and self-cater, sticking to things like bread, cheese, tinned fish or meat, yoghurt and wine (cooking facilities are seldom provided).

Your daily expenses will come down a lot if you can find a private room to use as a base for exploring nearby areas. Coastal towns which lend themselves to this include Rovinj, Krk, Rab, Split, Korčula and Dubrovnik. You will also escape the 30 to 50% surcharge on private rooms rented for less than four nights.

Tipping

If you're served fairly and well at a restaurant, you should round up the bill as you're paying. (Don't leave money on the table.) If a service charge has been added to the bill no tip is necessary. Bar bills and taxi fares can also be rounded up. Tour guides on day excursions expect to be tipped.

POST & COMMUNICATIONS

Post

Mail sent to Poste Restante, 10000 Zagreb, Croatia, is held at the post office next to the Zagreb railway station, which is open 24 hours. A good coastal address to use is c/o Poste Restante, Main Post Office, 21000 Split, Croatia.

If you have an American Express card, you can have your mail addressed to Atlas travel agency, Trg Nikole Zrinjskog 17, 10000 Zagreb, Croatia, or Atlas travel agency, Trg Braće Radić, 21000 Split, Croatia.

Telephone

To call Croatia from abroad, dial your international access code, ☎ 385 (the country code for Croatia), the area code (without the initial zero) and the local number.

To make a phone call from Croatia, go to the main post office – phone calls placed from hotel rooms are much more expensive. As there are no coins you'll need tokens or a phonecard to use public telephones.

Phonecards are sold according to units (*impulsa*) and you can buy cards of 50, 100, 200 and 500 units. These can be purchased at any post office and most tobacco shops and newspaper kiosks. Many new phone boxes have button on the upper left with a flag symbol. Press the button and you get instructions in English. A three-minute call from Croatia will cost around 20KN to the UK and 23KN to the USA or Australia. The international access code is ☎ 00. Some other useful numbers are ☎ 92 for the police, ☎ 93 for fire, ☎ 94 for emergency medical assistance and ☎ 901 to place an operator-assisted call.

INTERNET RESOURCES

Croatia has blasted into cyberspace with the speed of the Starship Enterprise. Web sites relating to businesses and organisations are proliferating with a mad pace even as home computers remain out of reach for most Croatians. America Online has access numbers in Zagreb, Split and Rijeka but most Croatians connect through the post office, which offers a connection at 33600bps with unlimited Internet access for 70KN a month plus a 35KN subscription fee. The only cybercafé is in Zagreb but that is bound to change soon.

NEWSPAPERS & MAGAZINES

The most respected daily newspaper in Croatia is *Vjesnik* but the most daring is the satirical newsweekly *Feral Tribune*. Its investigative articles and sly graphics target increasingly unamused political parties, who have responded with taxes, libel suits and general harassment. German and Italian newspapers are widely available and a daily newspaper in Italian, *La Voce del Popolo*, is published in Rijeka. American, British and French newspapers and magazines can be hard to find outside large cities.

RADIO & TV

The three national television stations in Croatia fill a lot of air time with foreign programming, usually American and always in the original language. For local news, residents of Zadar, Split, Vinkovci and Osijek turn to their regional stations. Croatian Radio broadcasts news in English four times daily (8 am, 10 am, 2 pm, 11 pm) on FM frequencies 88.9, 91.3 and 99.3.

TIME

Croatia is on Central European Time (GMT/UTC plus one hour). Daylight saving comes into effect at the end of March, when clocks are turned forward an hour. At the end of September they're turned back an hour.

ELECTRICITY

Electricity is 220V, 50Hz AC. Croatia uses the standard European round-pronged plugs.

WEIGHTS & MEASURES

The metric system is used. Like other Continental Europeans, Croats indicate decimals with commas and thousands with points.

LAUNDRY

Self-service laundrettes are virtually unknown outside of Zagreb. Most camping grounds have laundry facilities, hotels will wash clothes for a (hefty) fee or you could make arrangements with the proprietor if you're staying in private accommodation.

HEALTH

Everyone must pay to see a doctor at a public hospital (*bolnica*) or medical centre (*dom zdravcja*) but the charges are reasonable. Travel insurance is important, especially if you have a serious accident and have to be hospitalised. Medical centres often have dentists on the staff, otherwise you can go to a private dental clinic (*zubna ordinacija*).

WOMEN TRAVELLERS

Women face no special danger in Croatia although women on their own may be harassed and followed in large coastal cities. Some of the local bars and cafés seem like private men's clubs; a woman alone is likely to be greeted with sudden silence and cold stares. Topless sunbathing is considered acceptable;

in fact, judging from the ubiquitous photos of topless women in tourist brochures it seems almost obligatory.

GAY & LESBIAN TRAVELLERS

Homosexuality has been legal in Croatia since 1977 and is generally tolerated, if not welcomed with open arms. Public displays of affection between members of the same sex may meet with hostility, however, especially outside major cities. A small lesbian and gay community is developing in Zagreb but not to the extent of many western European cities. For further information contact LIGMA (Lesbian and Gay Men Action; PO Box 488, 10001 Zagreb).

DANGERS & ANNOYANCES

Land mines left over from the recent war in Croatia pose no threat to the average visitor but it's important to be aware that certain areas of the country are still dangerous. Although the government moved with lightning speed to remove mines from any area even remotely interesting to tourists, the former confrontation line between Croat and federal forces is still undergoing de-mining operations. Eastern Slavonia was heavily mined, outside of the main city of Osijek, de-mining is not yet completed. Main roads from Zagreb to the coast that pass through Karlovac and Knin are completely safe but it would be unwise to stray into fields or abandoned villages. As a general rule, you should avoid any area along this route in which shattered roofs or artillery-pocked walls indicate that rebuilding and, possibly, de-mining has not yet occurred. If a place is abandoned, there may be a reason.

Personal security and theft are not problems in Croatia. The police and military are well disciplined and it's highly unlikely you'll have any problems with them in any of the places covered in this chapter.

See Post & Communications for emergency telephone numbers.

BUSINESS HOURS

Banking hours are from 7.30 am to 7 pm on weekdays and 8 am to noon on Saturday.

Many shops open from 8 am to 7 pm on weekdays and 8 am to 2 pm on Saturday. Along the coast, life is more relaxed; shops and offices frequently close around 1 pm for an afternoon break. Croats are early risers and by 7 am there will be lots of people on the street and many places will already be open.

PUBLIC HOLIDAYS & SPECIAL EVENTS

Public holidays are New Year's Day (1 January), Easter Monday (March/April), Labour Day (1 May), Bleiburg and Way of the Cross Victims Day (15 May), Statehood Day (30 May), Day of Antifascist Struggle (22 June), Homeland Thanksgiving Day (5 August) Feast of the Assumption (15 August), All Saints' Day (1 November) and Christmas (25 and 26 December). Statehood Day marks the anniversary of the declaration of independence in 1991, while Day of Antifascist Struggle commemorates the outbreak of resistance in 1941.

In July and August there are summer festivals in Dubrovnik, Opatija, Split and Zagreb. Mardi Gras celebrations that mark the beginning of Lent have recently been revived in many towns with the attendant parades and festivities. The many traditional annual events held around Croatia are included under Special Events in the city and town sections.

ACTIVITIES
Kayaking

There are countless possibilities for anyone carrying a folding sea kayak, especially among the Elafiti Islands (take the daily ferry from Dubrovnik to Lopud) and the Kornati Islands (take the daily ferry from Zadar to Sali). See Organised Tours in the Getting Around section for information on sailing and kayaking tours.

Hiking

Risnjak National Park at Crni Lug, 12km west of Delnice between Zagreb and Rijeka, is a good hiking area in summer. Buses run from Delnice to Crni Lug near the park entrance about three times daily, and there's a small park-operated hotel (☎ 051-836 133) at Crni Lug, with rooms at around 120KN per person including breakfast. Because of the likelihood of heavy snowfalls, hiking is only advisable from late spring to early autumn. It's a 9km, 2½-hour climb from the park entrance at Bijela Vodica to Veliki Risnjak (1528m).

The steep gorges and beech forests of Paklenica National Park, 40km north-east of Zadar, also offer excellent hiking. Starigrad, the main access town for the park, is well connected by hourly buses from Zadar. Hotels and private accommodation are available in Starigrad, as well as a camping ground, Paklenica (☎ 023-369 236), open May to September.

For a great view of the barren coastal mountains, climb Mt Ilija (961m) above Orebić, opposite Korčula.

Scuba Diving

The clear waters and varied underwater life of the Adriatic have led to a flourishing dive industry along the coast. Most dive shops offer certification courses for about 2124KN and one dive with rented equipment for 227 to 268KN. Cave diving is the real speciality in Croatia; night diving and wreck diving are also offered and there are coral reefs in some places but in rather deep water. You must get a permit to dive but this is easy: go to the harbour captain in any port with your passport, certification card and 70KN. Permission is valid for a year in any dive spot in the country. The fee is slated for the preservation of underwater life. In Hvar, try Divecentre Hvar (☎ 021-761 026) at Hotel Jadran, Jelsa) and Dive and Watersportcentre, (☎ 021-742 490) at Hotel Amphora, Hvar. On Krk, there's Delphin (☎ 051-656 126), Emilia Geistlicha 48, Baška. On Rab, there's Mirko (☎ 051-721 154), Barbat 710, Rab, and Rab-ek-O (☎ 051-6776 272), Kampor, Rab. Diving Center Hidra (☎ 264 474) is in Lumbarda on Korčula Island.

COURSES

The Croatian Heritage Foundation (Hrvatska matica iseljenika; ☎ 01-61 15 116; fax 01-45 50 700; www.matis.hr/odjeli.htm), Trg Stjepana Radića 3, Zagreb, runs a series of programs on Croatian language and culture during July and August (exact dates announced the preceding February). Though designed for people of Croatian descent living abroad, everyone is welcome.

The Faculty of Arts at the University of Zagreb (founded in 1669) organises a more intensive, academically oriented four-week course. Students sit an exam at the end of the course and those who pass receive a certificate of merit.

Contact the Croatian Heritage Foundation in Zagreb for application information. Also ask about regular semester courses offered throughout the academic year.

WORK

The Croatian Heritage Foundation also organises summer 'taskforces' of young people from around the world, often of Croatian descent, to assist in war reconstruction. Often these programs have an ecological or archaeological slant, such as repairing the bridges in Plitvice National Park or restoring a damaged church. For details, contact the foundation.

Suncokret (☎ 01-211 104; fax 01-222 715; suncokret@public.srce.com), Seferova 10, 10000 Zagreb, accepts summer volunteers to do unpaid relief work among women, children and the elderly traumatised by the war in Croatia. Preference is given to teachers, social workers, counsellors and applicants with prior experience in the helping professions.

ACCOMMODATION

Along the coast, accommodation is priced according to three seasons, which vary from place to place. Generally April, May and October are the cheapest months, June and September are mid-priced, but count on paying top price in July and August, especially in the peak period from mid-July to mid-August. Prices quoted in this chapter are for the peak period and do not include 'residence tax' of 7.60KN in peak season, 5KN in June, the beginning of July and September and 4.30KN at other times. Deduct about 20% if you come in June, the beginning of July and September, about 30% for May and October and about 40% for all other times. Prices for rooms in Zagreb are constant all year.

Accommodation is generally cheaper in Dalmatia than in Kvarner or Istria but in July and August you should make arrangements in advance wherever you go.

This chapter provides the phone numbers of most accommodation facilities. Once you know your itinerary it pays to go to a post office, buy a telephone card and start calling around to check prices, availability etc. Most receptionists speak English.

Camping

Nearly 100 camping grounds are scattered along the Croatian coast. Most operate from mid-May to September only, although a few are open in April and October. In May and late September, call ahead to make sure the camping ground is open before beginning the long trek out. The opening and closing dates in travel brochures and this book are only approximate and even local tourist offices can be wrong.

Many camping grounds are expensive for backpackers because the prices are set in dollars or Deutschmarks per person and include the charge per tent, caravan, car, electric hook-up etc. This is fine for people with mobile homes which occupy a large area but bad news for those with only a small tent. If you don't have a vehicle, you're better off at camping grounds which have a much smaller fee per person and charge for the extras.

Germans are the leading users of Croatian camping grounds. Unfortunately, many grounds are gigantic 'autocamps' with restaurants, shops and row upon row of caravans. Nudist camping grounds (marked FKK) are among the best because their secluded locations ensure peace and quiet. Freelance camping is officially prohibited.

Hostels

The Croatian YHA (☎ 01-422 953; fax 01-48 41 269; www.nncomp.com/hfhs/hfhs.html), Dežmanova 9, Zagreb, operates summer youth hostels in Dubrovnik, Šibenik and Zadar and year-round hostels at Zagreb and Pula. Bed and breakfast costs about 65KN for YHA members in May, June, September and October and 75KN in July and August. Non-members pay an additional 12KN per person daily for a welcome card; six stamps on the card then entitles you to a membership. The Zagreb hostel has higher prices.

Private Rooms

The best accommodation in Croatia is private rooms in local homes, the equivalent of small private guesthouses in other countries. Such rooms can be arranged by travel agencies, which add a lot of taxes and commission to your bill, so you'll almost always do better dealing directly with proprietors you meet on the street or by knocking on the doors of houses with 'sobe' or 'zimmer' (meaning 'rooms') signs. This way you avoid the residence tax and four-night minimum stay, but you also forgo the agency's quality control. Hang around coastal bus stations and ferry terminals, luggage in hand, looking lost, and someone may find you. Otherwise, go to town and see if anyone in a local café can help.

If the price asked is too high, bargain. Be sure to clarify whether the price agreed upon is per person or for the room. Tell the proprietor in advance how long you plan to stay or they may try to add a surprise 'supplement' when you leave after a night or two. At the agencies, singles are expensive and scarce but, on the street, sobe prices are usually per person, which favours the single traveller. Showers are always included.

It may be worthwhile to take half-board. Most families on the coast have a garden, a vineyard and access to the sea. You could begin with a home-made aperitif and progress to a garden-fresh salad, home-grown potatoes and grilled fresh fish, washed down with your host's very own wine.

Although renting an unofficial room is common practice along the Adriatic coast, be discreet, as technically you're breaking the law by not registering with the police. Don't brag to travel agencies about the low rate you got, for example.

If you stay less than four nights, the agencies add a 20 to 30% surcharge. Travel agencies have classified rooms as either category I, II or III, which will soon change to a star system. The most expensive rooms will be three-star and include a private bathroom. In a two-star room, the bathroom is shared with one other room; in a one-star room, the bathroom is shared with two other rooms. If you're travelling in a small group, it may be worthwhile to get a small apartment with cooking facilities, which are widely available along the coast.

At the time of writing, accommodation rates were fixed with no variance from agency to agency but that system is changing and, by the time of your trip, it may be worthwhile to compare prices.

Hotels

There are few cheap hotels in Croatia – prices generally average around 350KN a double in the summer along the coast, dropping to around 250KN in late spring or early autumn. Still, if you're only staying one night and the private room agency is going to levy a 50% surcharge, you might consider getting a hotel room. In the off season, when most rooms are empty, you could try bargaining for a more realistic rate.

Hotels are classified as A, B, C and (rarely) D but the country is moving towards a star system which may be in place by the time of your visit. Category A hotels are the most luxurious (satellite TV, direct-dial phones and minibars in rooms that are often air-conditioned); there may be a swimming pool or two, a fitness centre and a nightclub. The vast majority of hotels are category B and equipped with TV, telephones and a hotel restaurant. Category C hotels have a private bathroom but no TV or telephone, while rare category D hotels will have shared bathrooms.

Most hotels along the coast were built to accommodate package tourists and have the sort of blandness that will delight lovers of concrete. Every so often you'll run across faded but elegant older hotels that recall the days when the Austrian aristocracy took holidays on the Adriatic. Unfortunately these solidly built structures were often the ones used to house refugees during the recent war and are now waiting for a Prince Charming to come along with enough money to rescue them from slow decay.

FOOD

A restaurant (*restauracija*) or pub may also be called a *gostionica* and a café is a *kavana*. Self-service cafeterias are quick, easy and inexpensive, though the quality of the food varies. If the samples behind glass look cold

or dried out, ask them to dish out a fresh plate for you. Better restaurants aren't that much more expensive if you choose carefully. In most of them the vegetables, salads and bread cost extra and some deluxe restaurants add a 10% service charge (not mentioned on the menu). Fish dishes are often charged by weight, which makes it difficult to know how much a certain dish will cost. Ice-cream cones are priced by the scoop.

Restaurants in Croatia can be a hassle because they rarely post their menus outside, so to find out what they offer and charge, you have to walk in and ask to see the menu. Then if you don't like what you see, you must walk back out and appear rude. Always check the menu, however, and if the price of the drinks or something else isn't listed, ask, otherwise you'll automatically be charged the 'tourist price'.

Breakfast is difficult in Croatia as all you can get easily is coffee. For eggs, toast and jam you'll have to go somewhere expensive, otherwise you can buy some bread, cheese and milk at a supermarket and picnic somewhere. Throughout ex-Yugoslavia the breakfast of the people is *burek*, a greasy layered pie made with meat (*mesa*) or cheese (*sira*) and cut on a huge metal tray.

A load of fruit and vegetables from the local market can make a healthy, cheap picnic lunch. There are plenty of supermarkets in Croatia – cheese, bread, wine and milk are readily available and fairly cheap. The person behind the meat counter at supermarkets will make a big cheese or bologna sandwich for you upon request and you only pay the regular price of the ingredients.

Regional Dishes

Italian pizza and pasta are a good option in Istria and Dalmatia, costing about half of what you'd pay in Western Europe. The Adriatic coast excels in seafood, including scampi, *prstaci* (shellfish) and Dalmatian *brodet* (mixed fish stewed with rice), all cooked in olive oil and served with boiled vegetables or *tartufe* (mushrooms) in Istria. In the Croatian interior, watch for *manistra od bobića* (beans and fresh maize soup) or *štrukle* (cottage cheese rolls). A Zagreb speciality is *štrukli* (boiled cheesecake).

DRINKS

It's customary to have a small glass of brandy before a meal and to accompany the food with one of Croatia's fine wines. Ask for the local regional wine. Croatia is also famous for its plum brandies (*šljivovica*), herbal brandies (*travarica*), cognacs (*vinjak*) and liqueurs such as maraschino, a cherry liqueur made in Zadar, or herbal *pelinkovac*. Italian-style espresso is popular in Croatia.

Zagreb's Ožujsko beer (*pivo*) is very good but Karlovačko beer from Karlovac is better. You'll have to practise saying *živjeli!* (cheers!).

ENTERTAINMENT

Culture was heavily subsidised by the communists and admission to operas, operettas and concerts is still reasonable. The main theatres offering musical programs are listed in this chapter, so note the location and drop by some time during the day to see what's on and purchase tickets. In the interior cities, winter is the best time to enjoy the theatres and concert halls. The main season at the opera houses of Rijeka, Split and Zagreb runs from October to May. These close for holidays in summer and the cultural scene shifts to the many summer festivals. Ask at municipal tourist offices about cultural events in their area.

Discos operate in summer in the coastal resorts and all year in the interior cities but the best way to mix with the local population is to enjoy a leisurely coffee or ice cream in a café. With the first hint of mild weather, Croatians head for an outdoor terrace to drink, smoke and watch the passing parade.

The cheapest entertainment in Croatia is a movie at a *kino* (cinema). Admission fees are always low and the soundtracks are in the original language. The selection leans towards popular American blockbusters and the last film of the day is usually hard-core pornography. Check the time on your ticket carefully, as admission is not allowed once the film has started.

THINGS TO BUY

Among the traditional handicraft products of Croatia are fine lace from Pag Island, handmade embroidery, woodcarvings, woollen and leather items, carpets, filigree jewellery, ceramics, national costumes and tapestries.

Getting There & Away

AIR

Croatia Airlines (☎ 01-45 51 244), ulica Teslina 5, Zagreb, has flights from Zagreb to Amsterdam, Berlin, Brussels, Copenhagen, Dublin, Düsseldorf, Frankfurt, London, Moscow, Mostar, Munich, Paris, Prague, Rome, Sarajevo, Skopje, Stuttgart, Tirana, Vienna and Zürich. Note that all batteries must be removed from checked luggage for all Croatia Airlines flights.

LAND

Bus

Austria Eurolines (☎ 01-712 0453), Landstrasser Hauptstrasse 1b, A-1030 Vienna, runs two buses a week from Vienna to Rijeka, Split and Zadar (312KN) and a daily bus to Zagreb (157KN).

Benelux Budget Bus/Eurolines (☎ 020-520 8787; Rokin 10, Amsterdam) offers a weekly bus all year to Zagreb (26 hours, 781KN one way, 1218KN return) and another bus to Rijeka and Split with an extra weekly bus to both destinations during summer. All buses change at Frankfurt. Reductions are available for children under 13, but not for students or seniors. Eurolines (☎ 02-203 0707) rue du Progres 80, Brussels, operates a twice-weekly service all year from Brussels to Zagreb, changing in Munich and another twice weekly bus to Rijeka and the Dalmatian coast, changing in Frankfurt. On all Dutch and Belgian services you will be charged DM5 per piece of luggage. An advance reservation (19KN) is recommended.

Germany Because Croatia is a prime destination for Germans, the bus service is good and the buses of the Deutsche Touring GmbH (☎ 069-79 03 50), Am Romerhof 17, Frankfurt, are cheaper than the train. There are buses from Berlin, Cologne, Dortmund, Frankfurt/Main, Mannheim, Munich, Nuremberg, Stuttgart and other cities to Zagreb and three buses a week to Dubrovnik. There's a weekly bus to Istria from Frankfurt and two buses a week from Munich. The Dalmatian

CROATIA

coast is also served by daily buses from German cities and there's a twice weekly bus direct from Berlin to Rijeka and on to Split. Baggage is DM5 extra per piece. Information is available at bus stations in the cities just mentioned.

Hungary Frequent connections between Nagykanizsa (145km, twice daily, 55KN) and Barcs (202km, five daily, 30KN), going on to Pécs. From Barcs there are frequent trains to Pécs (67km) and then less-frequent buses to Szeged (188km), where there are trains and buses to Subotica (47km) in Vojvodina (Yugoslavia). Nagykanizsa is more convenient if you're travelling to/from Budapest.

Yugoslavia Buses leave hourly between 5 am to 1 pm from Zagreb to Belgrade (six hours, 180KN). At Bajakovo on the border, a Yugoslav bus takes you on to Belgrade.

Train
Austria The *Ljubljana* express travels daily from Vienna to Rijeka (eight hours), via Ljubljana, and the EuroCity *Croatia* from Vienna to Zagreb (6½ hours, 304KN); both travel via Maribor.

Germany InterCity 296/297 goes overnight nightly from Munich to Zagreb (nine hours, 443KN) via Salzburg and Ljubljana. Reservations are required southbound but not northbound. The EuroCity *Mimara* between Berlin and Zagreb (1110KN), stopping at Leipzig and Munich, travels by day.

Hungary To go from Budapest to Zagreb (6½ hours, US$28) you have a choice of four trains daily. A daily train links Zagreb to Pécs (four hours, 105KN), leaving Pécs in the early morning and Zagreb in the afternoon, connecting through Osijek. As well as the international express trains, there are unreserved local trains between Gyékényes (Hungary) and Koprivnica (20 minutes) three times daily, with connections in Gyékényes to/from Nagykanizsa, Pécs and Kaposvár. Two unreserved trains daily travel between Varaždin and Nagykanizsa (1½ hours).

Italy Railway fares in Italy are relatively cheap so, if you can get across the Italian border from France or Switzerland, it won't cost an arm and a leg to take a train on to Trieste, where there are frequent bus connections to Croatia via Koper. Between Venice and Zagreb (226KN) there are the *Simplon* and *Venezia* express trains via Trieste and Ljubljana (seven hours). Between Trieste and Zagreb, there's the daily *Kras* via Ljubljana (five hours).

Romania There are no direct trains between Bucharest and Zagreb but there are two daily trains that connect in Budapest with trains to Zagreb (18 to 26 hours).

Yugoslavia Two trains daily connect Zagreb with Belgrade (6½ hours, 220KN).

Car & Motorcycle
The main highway entry/exit points between Croatia and Hungary are Goričan (between Nagykanizsa and Varaždin), Gola (23km east of Koprivnica), Terezino Polje (opposite Barcs) and Donji Miholjac (7km south of Harkány). There are 29 crossing points to/from Slovenia, too many to list here. There are 23 border crossings into Bosnia-Hercegovina and 10 into Yugoslavia, including the main Zagreb to Belgrade highway. Major destinations in Bosnia-Hercegovina, such as Sarajevo, Mostar and Međugorje, are accessible from Zagreb, Split and Dubrovnik.

SEA
Regular boats connect Croatia with both Italy and Greece. The Croatian Jadrolinija line, the Italian Adriatica Navigazione and the Croatian company Lošinjska Plovidba all serve the Adriatic coast. Five or six Jadrolinija ferries run a week year-round between Ancona and Split (10 hours, 249KN), stopping twice a week in July and August at Stari Grad on Hvar Island. Adriatica Navigazione connects Ancona and Split three times a week in summer for the same price and twice a week in winter.

Other Jadrolinija lines in the summer from Ancona stop at Zadar (four times a week, 224KN), Šibenik, Vis Island and Vela Luka on Korčula Island (weekly, 249KN).

From Bari, Adriatica Navigazione runs a ferry to Dubrovnik once a week all year and Jadrolinija connects the two cities twice a week in summer and once a week in winter. The eight-hour trip costs about 249KN.

Both Adriatica Navigazione and Lošinjska Plovidba connect Italy with the Istrian coast in summer. From May to September Adriatica Navigazione runs the *Marconi* between Trieste and Rovinj (3½ hours; L30,000), stopping at the Brijuni Islands six times a week and stopping twice a week in July and August at Poreč. In Trieste, contact Agemar (☎ 040-363 737), Piazza Duca degli Abruzzi, 1a. Lošinjska Plovidba's *Marina* connects Venice with Zadar (14½ hours; L87,000) twice a week from late June to September, stopping at Pula and Mali Lošinj. In Venice, contact Agenzia Favret (☎ 041 257 3511), Via Appia 20. Payment must be made in Italian lire and the prices include departure tax.

From May to September, the Atlas travel agency runs a fast boat between Zadar and Ancona (three hours, 340KN) and there's a new Croatian company, SEM (☎ 021-589 433), that runs a daily boat between Split, Trieste and Ancona; the Split-Ancona trip costs 234KN.

During the summer, Jadrolinija runs a ferry twice a week between Dubrovnik and Igoumenitsa, stopping in Bari (17½ hours, 265KN). Unless the ferry service to Albania resumes, there is no choice but to connect via Ancona or Bari. Both the Jadrolinija line to Bari and the Adriatica Navigazione line to Ancona connect well to other Adriatica Navigazione ferries to Durrës, Albania. From Ancona and Bari it is also possible to catch the Anek Lines boats to Igoumenitsa, Patrasso and Corfu.

Prices given above are for deck passage in the summer season. Prices are about 10% less in the off season and there's a 25% reduction for a return ticket on Jadrolinija ferries. A couchette on an overnight boat costs about an extra 90 to 100KN.

LEAVING CROATIA

The airport departure tax is 37KN. There is no port tax if you leave the country by boat.

Getting Around

AIR

Croatia Airlines has daily flights from Zagreb to Dubrovnik (620KN), Pula (414KN) and Split (556KN). Its twice-weekly flight to Skopje is very expensive at 715KN one way.

BUS

Bus services in Croatia are excellent. Fast express buses go everywhere, often many times a day, and they'll pick up passengers at designated stops anywhere along their route. Prices vary slightly between companies and depend on the route taken but the prices in this book should give you an idea of costs. Because the price is per kilometre it's possible to pay more for a slow local bus than a fast express. Luggage stowed in the baggage compartment under the bus costs extra (5KN a piece, including insurance). If your bag is small you could carry it onto the bus, although the seats are often placed close together, making this impossible on crowded buses.

At large stations, bus tickets must be purchased at the office, not from drivers; try to book ahead to be sure of a seat. Lists of departures over the various windows at the bus stations tell you which one has tickets for your bus. Tickets for buses that arrive from somewhere else are usually purchased from the conductor. On Croatian bus schedules, *vozi svaki dan* means 'every day', *ne vozi nedjeljom ni praznikom* means 'not Sundays and public holidays'.

Some buses travel overnight, saving you having to pay for a room. Don't expect to get much sleep, however, as the inside lights will be on and music will be blasting the whole night. Take care not to be left behind at meal or rest stops and beware of buses leaving 10 minutes early.

TRAIN

Train travel is about 15% cheaper than bus travel and often more comfortable, if slower. Baggage is free. Local trains usually have only unreserved 2nd-class seats but they're rarely crowded. Reservations may be required on express trains. 'Executive' trains have only 1st-class seats and are 40% more expensive than local trains. No couchettes are available on any domestic services. Most train stations have left-luggage offices charging about 10KN apiece (passport required).

There are two daily trains from Zagreb to Zadar and Split stopping at Knin where you can change to Šibenik. Other trains include Zagreb to Osijek (288km, five hours), Koprivnica (92km, 1½ hours, local), Varaždin (110km, three hours, local), Ljubljana (160km, three hours, local), Rijeka (243km, five hours, local) and Pula. There are also trains from Rijeka to Ljubljana (155km, 2½ hours, local).

On posted timetables in Croatia the word for arrivals is *dolazak* and for departures it's *odlazak* or *polazak*. Other terms you may encounter include *poslovni* (executive train), *brzi* or *ubrazni* (fast train), *putnički* (local train), *rezerviranje mjesta obvezatno* (compulsory seat reservation), *presjedanje* (change of trains), *ne vozi nedjeljom i blagdanom* (no service Sundays and holidays) and *svakodnevno* (daily).

CAR & MOTORCYCLE

Motorists require vehicle registration papers and the green insurance card to enter Croatia. Two-way amateur radios built into cars are no problem but must be reported at the border.

Petrol is either leaded super, unleaded (*bezolovni*) or diesel. You have to pay tolls on the motorways around Zagreb, to use the Učka tunnel between Rijeka and Istria, and for the bridge to Krk Island.

Along the coast, the spectacular Adriatic highway from Italy to Albania hugs the steep slopes of the coastal range, with abrupt drops to the sea and a curve a minute. You can drive as far south as Vitaljina, 56km southeast of Dubrovnik.

Motorists can turn to the Hrvatski Autoklub (HAK) or Croatian Auto Club for help or advice. Addresses of local HAK offices are provided throughout this chapter and the nationwide HAK road assistance (*vučna služba*) number is ☎ 987.

Unless otherwise posted, the speed limits for cars and motorcycles are 60km/h in built-up areas, 90km/h on main highways and 130km/h on motorways. Police systematically fine motorists exceeding these limits. On any of Croatia's winding two-lane highways, it's illegal to pass long military convoys or a whole line of cars caught behind a slow-moving truck. Drive defensively, as local motorists lack discipline.

Rental

The large car-rental chains represented in Croatia are Avis, Budget, Europcar and Hertz, with Budget (offices in Opatija, Split and Zagreb) generally the cheapest and Hertz the most expensive. Avis, Budget and Hertz have offices at Zagreb and Split airports. Throughout Croatia, Avis is allied with Autotehna, while Hertz is often represented by Kompas. Independent local companies are often much less expensive than the international chains, but Avis, Budget, Europcar and Hertz have the big advantage of offering one-way rentals which allow you to drop the car off at any one of their many stations in Croatia free of charge. Some local companies offer this service but have fewer stations.

The cheapest cars include the Renault 5, Peugeot 106, Opel Corsa and Fiat Uno. Prices at local companies begin at around 80KN a day plus 0.80KN per kilometre (100km minimum) or 225KN a day with unlimited kilometres. Shop around as deals vary widely and 'special' discounts and weekend rates are often available. Third-party public liability insurance is included by law, but make sure your quoted price includes full collision insurance, called collision damage waiver (CDW). Otherwise your responsibility for damage done to the vehicle is usually determined as a percentage of the car's value beginning at around 1000KN. Full CDW begins at 45KN a day extra (compulsory for those aged under 25), theft insurance at 15KN a day and personal accident insurance is another 10KN a day. Add 22% value-added tax to all charges.

The minimum age to rent a car is 21 and some companies require that you have a licence for at least a year. If you're paying by cash, the amount of the cash deposit is usually based upon the type of car and the length of the rental.

Sometimes you can get a lower car-rental rate by booking the car from abroad. Tour companies in Western Europe often have fly-drive packages which include a flight to Croatia and a car (two-person minimum).

BOAT
Jadrolinija Ferries
Year-round big, white and blue international Jadrolinija car ferries operate along the Rijeka-Dubrovnik coastal route, stopping at Zadar, Split, and the islands Rab, Hvar, Vis Korčula, and Mljet. Service is almost daily to the big cities during the summer but is greatly reduced in the winter. The most scenic section is Split to Dubrovnik, which all Jadrolinija ferries cover during the day. Rijeka to Split (13 hours) is usually an overnight trip in either direction.

Ferries are a lot more comfortable than buses, though considerably more expensive. From Rijeka to Dubrovnik the deck fare is 152KN but is at least 10% cheaper from October to May and there's a 25% reduction if you buy a return ticket. On certain boats there is a surcharge of 10% on weekends to and from Rijeka. With a through ticket, deck passengers can stop at any port for up to a week, provided you notify the purser beforehand and have your ticket validated. This is much cheaper than buying individual sector tickets. Cabins should be booked a week ahead, but deck space is usually available on all sailings.

Deck passage on Jadrolinija is just that: reclining seats (poltrone) are about 26KN extra and four-berth cabins (if available) begin at 329KN (Rijeka to Dubrovnik). Cabins can be arranged at the reservation counter aboard ship, but advance bookings are recommended if you want to be sure of a place. Deck space is fine for passages during daylight hours and when you can stretch out a sleeping bag on the upper deck in good weather, but if it's rainy you could end up sitting in the smoky cafeteria which stays open all night. During the crowded midsummer season, deck class can be unpleasant in wet weather.

Meals in the restaurants aboard Jadrolinija ships are about 80KN for a set menu. All the cafeteria offers is ham-and-cheese sandwiches for 18KN. Coffee is cheap in the cafeteria but wine and spirits tend to be expensive. Breakfast in the restaurant is about 30KN.

It's best to bring some food and drink with you.

Other Ferries
Local ferries connect the bigger offshore islands with each other and the mainland. The most important routes are Baška on Krk Island to Lopar on Rab Island (two daily from May to September), Zadar to Preko on Ugljan Island (nine daily), Split to Stari Grad on Hvar Island (three daily), Split to Vela Luka on Korčula Island via Hvar (daily), Orebić to Korčula Island (10 daily) and Dubrovnik to Sobra on Mljet Island (two daily). On most lines, service is increased from May to September.

Taking a bicycle on these services incurs an extra charge. Some of the ferries operate only a couple of times a day and, once the vehicular capacity is reached, remaining motorists must wait for the next service. In summer the lines of waiting cars can be long, so it's important to arrive early. Foot passengers and cyclists should have no problem getting on.

Travel agencies such as Atlas run fast hydrofoils up and down the coast in the summer, especially between Rijeka and Zadar, with Rab and Hvar also served (Rijeka-Zadar is 3½ hours, 210KN). Stop in any Atlas office and ask for the summer schedule.

HITCHING
Hitchhiking in Croatia is undependable. You'll have better luck on the islands but in the interior you'll notice that cars are small and usually full. Tourists never stop. Unfortunately, the image many Croats have of this activity is based on violent movies like The Hitcher.

LOCAL TRANSPORT
Zagreb has a well-developed tram system as well as local buses but in the rest of the country you'll only find buses. Buses in major cities such as Rijeka, Split, Zadar and Dubrovnik run about every 20 minutes, less often on Sunday. Small medieval towns along the coast are generally closed to traffic and have infrequent links to outlying suburbs.

ORGANISED TOURS

The Atlas travel agency offers 'adventure' tours which feature birdwatching, canoeing, caving, cycling, diving, fishing, hiking, riding, sailing, sea kayaking and white-water rafting in both Croatia and Slovenia. The eight-day tours cost from about US$700 to $900 (all-inclusive) and you join the group in Croatia. These tours allow you to combine the advantages of group and individual travel. Travel agents in North America book through Atlas Ambassador of Dubrovnik (☎ 202-483 8919), 1601 18th St NW, Washington, DC 20009.

The Croatian-owned Dalmatian and Istrian Travel (☎ 081-749 5255; fax 081-740 4432), 21 Sawley Road, London W12 0LG, offers independent packages in accommodation ranging from luxury hotels to camping as well as discounts on boat travel and outdoor activities. A typical package that includes a return London-Dubrovnik air fare and a week's stay in private accommodation costs £320 high season.

An interesting alternative for sailing enthusiasts is Katarina Line (☎ 051-272 110) at the Hotel Admiral, Opatija, which offers week-long cruises from Opatija to Krk, Rab, Pag, Mali Lošinj and Cres. Prices start at 1800KN a week and include half-board.

Zagreb

☎ 01

Zagreb, an attractive city of over a million inhabitants, has been the capital of Croatia since 1557. Spread up from the Sava River, Zagreb sits on the southern slopes of Medvednica, the Zagreb uplands. Medieval Zagreb developed from the 11th to the 13th centuries in the twin towns of Kaptol and Gradec. Kaptol grew around St Stephen's Cathedral and Gradec centred on St Mark's Church. Clerics established themselves in Kaptol as early as 1094, whereas Gradec was the craftspeople's quarter.

Much of medieval Zagreb remains today, although the stately 19th-century city between the old town and the train station is the present commercial centre. There are many fine parks, galleries and museums in both the upper and lower towns. Zagreb is

Croatia's main centre for primitive or naive art. Finding a place to stay at a reasonable price remains the biggest problem for a traveller in this calm and graceful city.

Orientation

As you come out of the train station, you'll see a series of parks and pavilions directly in front of you and the twin neo-Gothic towers of the cathedral in the distance. Trg Jelačića, beyond the northern end of the parks, is the main city square. The bus station is 1km east of the train station. Tram Nos 2, 3 and 6 run from the bus station to the train station, with No 6 continuing to Trg Jelačića.

Information

Tourist Offices The tourist office (☎ 48 14 051), Trg Jelačića 11, is open weekdays from 8.30 am to 8 pm, Saturday from 10 am to 6 pm and Sunday from 10 am to 2 pm. A City Walks leaflet is available free and provides a good introduction to Zagreb's sights.

The Croatian Auto Club (HAK) has two travel offices in Zagreb: a smaller office (☎ 431 142) at Draškovićeva ulica 46 and a main information centre (☎ 46 40 800) six blocks east at Derenčinova 20.

Plitvice National Park maintains an information office (☎ 46 13 586) at Trg Tomislava 19. It also has information on other national parks around Croatia.

Money Exchange offices at the bus and train stations change money at the bank rate with 1% commission. Both the banks in the train station (open 7 am to 9 pm) and the bus station (open 6 am to 8 pm) accept travellers cheques.

The American Express representative is Atlas travel agency (☎ 61 24 389), Trg Zrinjskoga 17. It will hold clients' mail.

Post & Communications Any poste-restante mail is held (for one month) in the post office on the eastern side of the train station which is open 24 hours (except on Sunday morning). Have your letters addressed to Poste Restante, 10000 Zagreb, Croatia.

This same post office is also the best place to make long-distance telephone calls. Public telephones in Zagreb use phonecards.

Cybercafé Zagreb's first and only cybercafé is Sublink (☎ 48 11 329; sublink@sublink.hr) Teslina 12, open Monday to Friday from noon to 10 pm and weekends from 3 to 10 pm. 'Membership' with an email address and 30 minutes of Internet time costs 10KN.

Travel Agencies Dali Travel (☎ 422 953), Dežmanova 9, the travel branch of the Croatian YHA, can provide information on HI hostels throughout Croatia and make advance bookings. It also sells ISIC student cards (40KN), requiring proof of attendance at an educational institution. It's open weekdays from 8 am to 4 pm.

Bookshops Algoritam in the Hotel Dubrovnik on Trg Jelačića has the widest selection of English-language books. Antik- varijat, next to the Atlas travel agency, has some paperbacks in English as well as several excellent (though expensive) maps.

Laundry Predom, across the street from HAK on Draškovićeva 31, is open Saturday morning and weekdays from 7 am to 7 pm. Jeans and shirts cost 6KN each to wash and press. Underwear and socks are washed for 1KN each.

Left Luggage Left-luggage offices in both the bus and train stations are open 24 hours. The price posted at the left-luggage office in the bus station is 1.20KN *per hour*, so be careful. At the train station you pay a fixed price of about 10KN per day.

Medical & Emergency Services If you need to see a doctor, your best bet is the Emergency Centar (☎ 46 00 911), Draskovića 19. It's open all the time and charges 200KN for an examination. The police station for foreigners with visa concerns is at Petrinjska 30.

Things to See

Kaptol Zagreb's colourful **Dolac vegetable market** is just up the steps from Trg Jelačića and continues north along Opatovina. It's open daily, with especially large gatherings on Friday and Saturday. The twin neo-Gothic spires of **St Stephen's Cathedral** (1899), now renamed the Cathedral of the Assump-tion of the Blessed Virgin Mary, are nearby. Elements from the medieval cathedral on this site, destroyed by an earthquake in 1880, can be seen inside, including 13th-century frescoes, Renaissance pews, marble altars and a baroque pulpit. The baroque **Archiepiscopal Palace** surrounds the cathedral, as do 16th-century fortifications constructed when Zagreb was threatened by the Turks.

Gradec From ulica Radićeva 5, off Trg Jelačića, a pedestrian walkway, stube Ivana Zakmardija, leads to the **Lotršćak Tower** and a funicular railway (1888), which connects the lower and upper towns (2KN). The tower has a sweeping 360° view of the city (closed Sunday). To the right is the baroque **St Catherine's Church**, with Jezuitski trg beyond. The **Gallerija Fortezza**, Jezuitski trg 4 (closed Monday), is Zagreb's premier exhibition hall where superb art shows are staged. Farther north and to the right is the 13th-century **Stone Gate**, with a painting of the Virgin which escaped the devastating fire of 1731.

The colourful painted-tile roof of the Gothic **St Mark's Church** on Markov trg marks the centre of Gradec. Inside are works by Ivan Meštrović, Croatia's most famous modern sculptor, but the church is only open for mass twice daily on weekdays and four times on Sunday. On the eastern side of St Mark's is the **Sabor** (1908), Croatia's National Assembly.

To the west of St Mark's is the 18th-century **Banski Dvori Palace**, the presidential palace with guards at the door in red ceremonial uniform. From April to September there is a guard-changing ceremony on weekends at noon.

At Mletačka 8 nearby is the former **Meštrović Studio**, now a museum which is open weekdays from 9 am to 2 pm. Other museums in this area include the **Croatian Historical Museum** (open for temporary exhibitions), Matoševa 9, the **Gallery of Naive Art**, Ćirilometodska 3 (closed Monday), and the **Natural History Museum**, Demetrova 1 (closed Monday). More interesting is the recently renovated **City Museum**, Opatićeka 20 (closed Monday), with a scale model of old Gradec. Summaries in English and German are in each room of the museum, which is in the former Convent of St Claire (1650).

Lower Town Zagreb really is a city of museums. There are four on the parks between the train station and Trg Jelačića. The yellow **exhibition pavilion** (1897) across the park from the station presents changing contemporary art exhibitions. The second building north, also in the park, houses the **Strossmayer Gallery** of the Academy of Arts & Sciences, with old master paintings. It's closed on Monday, but you can enter the interior courtyard to see the Baška Slab (1102) from the island of Krk, one of the oldest inscriptions in the Croatian language.

The **Archaeological Museum** at Trg Nikole Zrinjskog 19 used to display prehistoric to medieval artefacts, as well as Egyptian mummies, but has been closed for several years and plans for its reopening are uncertain. Behind the museum is a garden of Roman sculpture that has been turned into a pleasant open-air café in the summer.

West of the Centre The **Museum Mimara** at Rooseveltov trg 5 (closed Monday) is one of the finest art galleries in Europe. In a neo-Renaissance former school building (1883), this diverse collection shows the loving hand of Ante Topić Mimara, a private collector who donated over 3750 priceless objects to his native Zagreb, even though he spent much of his life in Salzburg, Austria. The Spanish, Italian and Dutch paintings are the highlight, but there are also large sections of glassware, sculpture and Oriental art.

Nearby on Trg Maršala Tita is the neo-baroque **Croatian National Theatre** (1895), with Ivan Meštrović's sculpture *Fountain of Life* (1905) in front. The **Ethnographic Museum** (closed Monday) at Trg Mažuranića 14 has a large collection of Croatian folk costumes with English explanations. South is the Art-Nouveau **National Library** (1907). The **Botanical Garden** on ulica Mihanovićeva (closed Monday; free) is attractive for the plants and landscaping as well as its restful corners.

North of the Centre A 20-minute ride north on bus No 106 from the cathedral takes you to **Mirogoj**, one of the most beautiful cemeteries in Europe. One wag commented that the people here are better housed in death

than they ever were in life. The English-style landscaping is enclosed by a long 19th-century neo-Renaissance arcade.

Organised Tours
Within Zagreb, the tourist office organises walking tours for 45KN per person (minimum four people) and minibus tours every Wednesday morning leaving from the InterContinental and Esplanade hotels for about 80KN.

Special Events
In odd years in April there's the Zagreb Biennial of Contemporary Music, since 1961 Croatia's most important music event. Zagreb also hosts a festival of animated films every other year in June. Croatia's largest international fairs are the Zagreb spring (mid-April) and autumn (mid-September) grand trade fairs. In July and August the Zagreb Summer Festival presents a cycle of concerts and theatre performances on open stages in the upper town.

Places to Stay
Budget accommodation is in short supply in Zagreb. An early arrival is recommended, since private room-finding agencies are an attractive alternative and usually refuse telephone bookings.

Camping There's a camping area outside the Motel Plitvice (☎ 65 30 444) which is not in Plitvice at all but near the town of Lučko on the Obilazinica highway south-west of Zagreb. The motel sometimes runs a minibus from Savski Most. Call to find out if and when their service is operating. Otherwise, take tram 7 or 14 to Savski Most and then the Lučko bus to Lučko village from which the motel/camp site is about a 10-minute walk. The price is 23KN per person and 20KN per tent and there's a lake and a sports centre nearby.

Hostels The noisy 215-bed *Omladinski Hotel*, actually a youth hostel, (☎ 48 41 261; fax 48 41 269), Petrinjska 77, near the train station is open all year and charges 210KN for a double without bath, 280KN with bath, including tax; it has no singles. Some of the six-bed dormitories (73KN per person) may

ZAGREB

PLACES TO STAY
28 Hotel Dubrovnik
32 Hotel Jadran
47 Hotel Sheraton
48 Omladinski Hotel
   (Youth Hostel) &
   Hotel Astoria
55 Intercontinental
   Hotel
59 Hotel Esplanade
60 Central Hotel

PLACES TO EAT
21 Market
22 Delikatese
23 Pizzicato
25 Restaurant Split
31 Mimiće
33 Melong
35 Hard Rock Café
58 Studentski Centar

OTHER
1 Polish Embassy
2 City Museum
3 Natural History Museum
4 Meštrović Studio
5 Historical Museum
  of Croatia
6 Banski Dvori Palace
7 St Mark's Church
8 Sabor (Parliament)
9 Stone Gate
10 Komedija Theatre
11 Gallery of Naive Art
12 Muzejski Prostor
13 Lotršćak Tower
14 St Catherine's Church
15 Dolac Market
16 St Stephen's Cathedral
17 Funicular Railway
18 British Council
19 Nama Department Store
20 Croatian YHA/
   Dali Travel
24 Academy of Music
26 Trg Petra Preradovića
27 Blagasija Oktogon
29 Tourist Office
30 Post Office/
   Telephone Centre
34 Archaeological Museum
36 Sublink
37 Embassy of Slovakia
38 Arts & Crafts Museum
39 Croatian National Theatre
40 Atlas Travel Agency
41 US Embassy
42 Gallery of Modern Art
43 Strossmayer Gallery
44 Emergency Centar
45 Croatian Auto
   Club (HAK)
46 Predom
49 Exhibition Pavilion
50 Puppet Theatre
51 Plitvice National
   Park Office
52 Pivnica Tomaslav
53 Ethnographic Museum
54 Museum Mimara
56 National Library
57 Technical Museum
61 Post Office
62 Train Station
63 City Hall
64 Vatroslav Lisinski
   Concert Hall

still be occupied by war refugees but most rooms remain available. The 5KN YHA discount is only available to people under 27 sleeping in the dormitory. You must check out by 9 am and you can't occupy the room until 2 pm.

The *Studenthotel Cvjetno Naselje* (☎ 61 91 240), off Slavonska avenija in the south of the city, charges 219/287KN for a single/ double, breakfast included. The rooms are good, each with private bath, and the staff are friendly. There's no student discount, although showing your ISIC and pleading

poverty occasionally works. There's a self-service student restaurant here where a filling meal with a Coke will cost 30KN. The Cvjetno Naselje is available to visitors only from mid-July to the end of September – the rest of the year it's a student dormitory. Take tram Nos 4, 5, 14, 16 or 17 south-west on Savska cesta to 'Vjesnik'. Opposite the stop is a tall building marked 'Vjesnik'. The student complex is just behind it.

In July and August head straight for the *Studentski dom Stjepan Radić* (☎ 334 255), Jarunska ulica 3, off Horvaćanska ulica in the

CROATIA

south of the city near the Sava River (tram Nos 5 or 17). Rooms in this huge student complex cost 200/250KN for a single/double and one of Zagreb's more popular discos, The Best, is across the street.

Private Rooms Try not to arrive on Sunday if you intend to stay in a private apartment as most of the agencies are closed. You'll notice that prices are surprisingly high but little of the money actually goes to your host. Taxes bite off a chunk and the agency takes nearly half the money with barely a quarter left for the host.

The Turističko Društvo Novi Zagreb (☎ 65 52 047; fax 65 21 523), Trnsko 15e, has private rooms in apartment buildings in the Novi Zagreb neighbourhood south of the Sava River (tram Nos 7, 14 or 16 to Trnsko) for 200/260KN a single/double, plus tax, with a 30% surcharge for one-night stays. The office is open weekdays from 8 am to 6 pm and Saturday from 9 am to 1 pm.

Lina Gabino (☎ 39 21 27) on Petračićeva, just west of the town centre, rents out both two-bedroom apartments (400/420KN a single/double) and private rooms (265/350KN plus tax). Prices are about 10% cheaper if you stay more than one night. Her office is open weekdays from 9 am to 5 pm and Saturday from 9 am to 2 pm.

Evistas (☎ 429 974 or 48 19 133; fax 431 987), Šenoina 28, between the bus and train station, also rents out apartments, beginning at 350KN for two people and rising to 675KN for five with a minimum stay of three nights. Private rooms are also available in the town centre for 170/230KN a single/double (145/190KN for people under 25). The office is open weekdays from 9 am to 1.30 pm and 5 to 8 pm and Saturday from 9.30 am to 5 pm.

If you're new to Croatia, don't be put off by these high prices. Along the coast, especially from Rab south, private rooms cost less than half as much.

Hotels There aren't any cheap hotels in Zagreb. Most of the older hotels have been renovated and the prices raised to B category.

If you can't arrange a morning arrival and afternoon departure to avoid spending the night in Zagreb, be prepared to bite the bullet

and pay a lot more for a place to sleep than you would elsewhere in Croatia. The only easy escape is to book an overnight bus to Split or Dubrovnik.

The best deal is the brand new and friendly *Hotel Ilica* (☎ 37 77 522; fax 37 77 722), Ilica 102, two stops from Trg Jelačića, which offers 12 quiet, pleasant rooms with bath and breakfast for 251/380KN a single/double and 441KN for a double with two beds.

The 110-room *Central Hotel* (☎ 484 11 22; fax 48 41 304), Branimirova 3 opposite the train station, is blandly modern and charges 308/446KN a single/double, including bath, breakfast and tax.

The six-storey *Hotel Jadran* (☎ 414 600; fax 46 12 151), Vlaška 50 near the city centre, charges 362/432KN with shower and breakfast.

For a memorable splurge, stay at the five-star *Hotel Esplanade* (☎ 45 66 666; fax 45 77 907) next to the train station (890/1200KN a single/double plus tax with a buffet breakfast). There's a 30% discount for weekend stays. This six-storey, 215-room hotel erected in 1924 is truly majestic and has one of the best restaurants in Zagreb.

Places to Eat

One of the most elegant places in town is undoubtedly the *Paviljon* in the yellow exhibition pavilion across the park from the train station. Main courses with an Italian flavour start at 70KN. The fresh fish and local wines at *Restaurant Split*, Ilica 19, also make a delicious treat. For regional dishes and lots of local colour, dine in one of the outdoor restaurants along ulica Tkalčićeva, up from Trg Jelačića, on summer evenings.

Pizza places are everywhere, but it would be hard to do better than the delicious, freshly made pies at *Pizzicarto* Gundilićeva 4 near the Academy of Music. Prices start at 18KN and the menu is translated into English. Vegetarians should head to *Melong*, Petrinjska 9 near Ilica. The menu is in Croatian and the staff speaks limited English but whatever you order is bound to be tasty. *Mimiće*, Jurišićeva 21 has been a local favourite for decades, turning out plates of fried fish that cost from 9KN for 10 sardines and a hunk of bread.

Delikatese, Ilica 39, is a good place to pick up cheese, fruit, bread, yoghurt and cold meat for a picnic. Next door is a *grocery store* that sells whole roasted chicken and an assortment of prepared salads. Further along Ilica at Trg Britanski, there's a daily fruit and vegetable *market* open every day until 3 pm which sells farm fresh produce. Don't hesitate to bargain.

Cafés & Bars The *Rock Forum Café*, Gajeva ulica 13, occupies the rear sculpture garden of the Archaeological Museum (open in summer only) and across the street is the *Hard Rock Café*, full of 1950s and 1960s memorabilia. Farther back in the passageway from the Hard Rock is the *Art Café Thalia* which really tries to live up to its name. A couple of other cafés and music shops share this lively complex at the corner of Teslina and Gajeva streets. Check out the *BP Club* in the complex basement for jazz, blues and rock bands.

Zagreb's most pretentious cafés are *Gradska Kavana* on Trg Jelačića and *Kazališna Kavana* on Trg Maršala Tita opposite the Croatian National Theatre. *Models* café next door to *Kazališna Kavana* is adorned with photos of the superstar models the café is evidently trying (and, so far, failing) to attract.

Entertainment

Zagreb is a happening city. Its theatres and concert halls present a great variety of programs throughout the year. Many (but not all) are listed in the monthly brochure *Zagreb Events & Performances*, which is usually available from the tourist office.

Bars & Clubs The liveliest scene in Zagreb is along Tkalčićeva, north off Trg Jelačića, where crowds spill out of cafés onto the street, drinks in hand. Farther up on Kozarska ulica the city's young people cluster shoulder to shoulder. Trg Petra Preradovića, Zagreb's flower-market square attracts street performers in mild weather and occasional bands. The *Pivnica Tomislav*, Trg Tomislava 18, facing the park in front of the train station, is a good local bar with inexpensive draught beer.

Kulušić, Hrvojeva 6 near the Hotel Sheraton (open Thursday to Sunday from 10 pm to 4 am; entry 30KN) is a casual, funky disco

that offers occasional live bands, fashion shows and record promos as well as standard disco fare.

Sokol klub, across the street from the Ethnographic Museum (open Wednesday to Sunday from 10 pm to 4 am; entry 30KN) is more polished and admits women free before midnight. Live rock concerts are presented every Sunday.

Gay & Lesbian Venues Gays are generally welcome in Zagreb's bars and discos but the city's only exclusively gay bar is *Bacchus* bar on Tomislava near the train station. At the moment the bar attracts mostly men with a sprinkling of women. *Gjuro*, Medveščak 58, in north Kaptol is a disco that attracts a gay and straight crowd.

Cinemas There are 18 cinemas in Zagreb which show foreign movies in their original language with subtitles. Posters around town advertise the programs. Kinoteca, Kordunska 1, shows classic foreign movies on weekdays at 6:30 pm.

Theatre It's worth making the rounds of the theatres in person to check their programs. Tickets are usually available, even for the best shows. A small office marked 'Kazalište Komedija' (look for the posters) in the Blagasija Oktogon, a passage connecting Trg Petra Preradovićeva to Ilica near Trg Jelačića, also sells theatre tickets.

The neobaroque *Croatian National Theatre* (☎ 48 28 532), Trg Maršala Tita 15, was established in 1895. It stages opera and ballet performances and the box office is open weekdays from 10 am to 1 pm and 5 to 7.30 pm and Saturday from 10 am to 1 pm as well as for a half-hour before performances on Sunday. You have a choice of orchestra (parket), lodge (lože) or balcony (balkon) seats.

The *Komedija Theatre* (☎ 433 209), Kaptol 9 near the cathedral, stages operettas and musicals.

The ticket office of the *Vatroslav Lisinski Concert Hall* (☎ 61 21 166) just south of the train station, is open weekdays from 9 am to 8 pm and Saturday from 9 am to 2 pm.

Concerts also take place at the *Croatian Music Institute* (☎ 424 533), Gundulićeva 6a, off Ilica.

There are performances at the ***Puppet
Theatre***, ulica Baruna Trenka 3, on Saturday
at 5 pm and Sunday at noon.

Spectator Sport

Basketball is popular in Zagreb, and from
October to April games take place at the
Cibona Centar, Savska cesta 30 opposite the
Technical Museum, usually on Saturday at
7.30 pm. Tickets are available at the door.

Soccer games are held on Sunday after
noon at the Maksimir Stadium, Maksimirska
128 on the eastern side of Zagreb (tram Nos
4, 7, 11 or 12 to Bukovačka). If you arrive too
early for the game, Zagreb's zoo is just across
the street.

Things to Buy

Ilica is Zagreb's main shopping street. Get in
touch with Croatian consumerism at the Nama
department store on Ilica near Trg Jelačića.

Folk-music compact discs are available
from Fonoteca at Nama. Rokotvorine, Trg
Jelačića 7, sells traditional Croatian handicrafts such as red and white embroidered
tablecloths, dolls and pottery.

The shops, fast food outlets and grocery
stores in the mall under the tracks beside the
train station have long opening hours.

Getting There & Away

Bus Zagreb's big, modern bus station has a
large, enclosed waiting room where you can
stretch out while waiting for your bus (but
there's no heating in winter). Buy most international tickets at window Nos 11 and 12,
and change money (including travellers
cheques) at A Tours open daily from 6 am to
8 pm. The left-luggage office is always open
(take care – the charge is 1.20KN *per hour*).

Buses depart from Zagreb for most of
Croatia, Slovenia and places beyond. Buy an
advance ticket at the station if you're travelling far.

The following domestic buses depart from
Zagreb: Dubrovnik (713km, eight daily,
140KN), Krk (229km, three daily, 95KN),
Ljubljana (135km, five daily, 60KN), Plitvice
(140km, 19 daily), Poreč (264km, six daily),
Pula (283km, 13 daily, 100KN), Rab
(211km, daily), Rijeka (173km, 21 daily
70KN), Rovinj (278km, eight daily, 110KN),
Split (478km, 27 daily, 100KN), Varaždin

(77km, 20 daily, 43KN), Mali Lošinj
(298km, daily, 120KN) and Zadar (320km,
20 daily, 80KN).

Bus services to Yugoslavia have resumed.
From 5 am to 1 pm there are hourly buses to
Belgrade, changing at the border town, Bajakovo, for a local bus. The six-hour trip costs
180KN. There are two buses daily to Sarajevo (417km, 362KN) and four to Međugorje
(420km, 153KN).

There's buses to Nagykanizsa (145km,
twice daily 55KN) and Barcs (202km, five
daily, 90KN) in Hungary. Nagykanizsa is
preferable if you're bound for Budapest or
Balaton Lake, while Barcs is better for Pécs
or Yugoslavia.

Other international buses worth knowing
about are to Vienna (twice daily, 157KN),
Munich (576km, twice daily, 285KN) and
Berlin (twice daily, DM190 – payment in
Deutschmarks only). Luggage is DM5 per
piece.

Train The *Venezia* and *Maestral* express trains
depart from Zagreb for Budapest (seven hours,
181KN) every morning. The *Avas* leaves early
afternoon and the *Kvarner* late afternoon. A
ticket from Zagreb to Nagykanizsa, the first
main junction inside Hungary, costs 72KN. A
useful daily train runs between Zagreb and
Pécs, Hungary (five hours, 105KN).

Zagreb is on both the Munich-Ljubljana
and Vienna-Maribor main lines. There are
trains twice daily between Munich and
Zagreb (nine hours, 443KN) via Salzburg.
Two trains daily arrive from Venice (seven
hours, 226KN).

Four trains daily run from Zagreb to Osijek
(4½ hours, 68KN), six to Koprivnica (two
hours), 13 to Varazdin (three hours, 33KN),
seven to Ljubljana (160km, 62KN), four to
Rijeka (five hours, 58KN), two to Pula (5½
hours, 145KN) and three or four to Split (nine
hours, 91KN). Both daily trains to Zadar (11
hours, 80KN) stop at Knin. Reservations are
required on some trains, so check.

Getting Around

Public transport is based on an efficient but
overcrowded network of trams, although the
city centre is compact enough to make them
unnecessary. Tram Nos 3 and 8 don't run on
weekends.

Buy tickets (4.50KN) at newspaper kiosks. You can use your ticket for transfers within 90 minutes but only in one direction.

A *dnevna karta* (day ticket), valid on all public transport until 4 am the next morning, is available for 12KN at most Vjesnik or Tisak news outlets.

To/From the Airport The Croatia Airlines bus to Pleso airport, 17km south-east of Zagreb, leaves from the bus station every half-hour or hour from about 4 am to 8.30 pm, depending on flights, and returns from the airport on about the same schedule (20KN).

Car Of the major car rental companies, Budget Rent-a-Car (☎ 45 54 936) in the Hotel Sheraton often has the lowest rates (325KN a day with unlimited kilometres). Other companies are Europcar (☎ 65 54 003) at the airport, Avis Autotehna (☎ 48 36 296) at the InterContinental Hotel and Hertz (☎ 48 47 222), Kračićeva 9a near the InterContinental Hotel. Local companies usually have lower rates. Try Niva Rent-a-Car (☎ 61 59 280), Miramarska 22 near the Hotel Esplanade, and, at the airport, Mack (☎ 442 222) and Uni Rent (☎ 65 25 006).

Taxi Zagreb's taxis all have meters which begin at a whopping 15KN and then ring up 6KN a kilometre. On Sunday and nights from 10 pm to 5 am there's a 20% surcharge. Waiting time is 40KN an hour. The baggage surcharge is 2KN per suitcase.

PLITVICE

Plitvice Lakes National Park lies midway between Zagreb and Zadar. The 19.5 hectares of wooded hills enclose 16 turquoise lakes which are linked by a series of waterfalls and cascades. The mineral-rich waters carve new paths through the rock, depositing tufa in continually changing formations. Wooden footbridges follow the lakes and streams over, under and across the rumbling water for an exhilaratingly damp 18km. Swimming is allowed in several lakes. Park admission is 60KN (students 30KN) but is valid for the entire stay.

Places to Stay

Camping *Korana* (☎ 053-751 015) is about 1km north of the entrance along the main road to Zagreb and charges 25KN per person and 18KN per tent.

Hotels *Hotel Bellevue* (☎ 053-751 700; fax 053-751 965) offers rustic accommodation within the park for 252/396KN a single/ double but at the hotels *Plitvice* (☎ 053-751 100) and *Jezero* (☎ 053-751 400) you'll pay about 50% more. Three kilometres north of the entrance along the main road to Zagreb is the *Motel Grabovac* (☎ 053-751 999), which has singles/doubles for 252/366KN.

Check at the Plitvice National Park office in Zagreb for information on private accommodation.

Getting There & Away

Buses run hourly from Zagreb to Plitvice (140km) and then continue to Zadar or Split. It is possible to visit Plitvice for the day on the way to or from the coast but be aware that buses will not pick up passengers at Plitvice if they are full. Luggage can be left at the tourist information centre (open daily from 8 am to 6.30 pm) at the first entrance to the park.

Istria

Istria (Istra to Croatians), the heart-shaped 3600-sq-km peninsula just south of Trieste, Italy, is named after the Illyrian Histri tribe conquered by the Romans in 177 BC.

Istria has been a political basketball. Italy took Istria from Austria-Hungary in 1919, then had to give it to Yugoslavia in 1947. A large Italian community lives in Istria and Italian is widely spoken. Tito wanted Trieste (Trst) as part of Yugoslavia too, but in 1954 the Anglo-American occupiers returned the city to Italy so that it wouldn't fall into the hands of the 'communists'. Today the Koper-Piran strip belongs to Slovenia while the rest is held by Croatia.

The 430km Istrian Riviera basks in the Mediterranean landscapes and climate for which the Adriatic coast is famous. The long summer season from May to October attracts large crowds. Mercifully, Istria was spared the fighting that occurred elsewhere in former Yugoslavia and it's a peaceful place to visit. Industry and heavy shipping are concentrated along the northern side of Istria around Koper and Izola, and Umag is a scattered, characterless resort you could easily skip. Novigrad is nicer, but the farther south you go in Istria the quieter it gets, with cleaner water, fewer visitors and cars and less industry. See Piran quickly, then move south to Rovinj, a perfect base from which to explore Poreč and Pula.

Getting There & Away

Bus Koper and Rijeka are the main entry/exit points, with buses to most towns on Istria's west coast every couple of hours. Train services in Istria are limited, so plan on getting around by bus.

Boat For information on connections between Istria and Italy see the Getting There & Away section at the beginning of this chapter.

In Istria, travel agencies such as Kvarner Express or Atlas should know the departure times and prices of all international boats although tickets may only be available on board. All boats connecting Istria with Italy or the Dalmatian coast depart from the landings marked 'Customs Wharf' on the maps in this book; schedules are sometimes posted there. It's an exciting way to travel.

POREČ
☎ 052

Poreč (Italian: Parenzo), the Roman Parentium, sits on a low, narrow peninsula about halfway down the west coast of Istria. The ancient Dekumanus with its polished stones is still the main street. Even after the fall of Rome, Poreč remained important as a centre of early Christianity, with a bishop and a famous basilica. The town is now the centre of a region packed with tourist resorts but vestiges of earlier times and a quiet, small-town atmosphere make it well worth a stop or at least a day trip from Rovinj. There are many places to swim in the clear water off the rocks north of the old town.

Orientation

The bus station (with a left-luggage office open from 6 am to 8 pm daily, except Sunday, when it closes at 5 pm) is directly opposite the small-boat harbour just outside the old town.

Information

The tourist office (☎ 451 293) is at Zagrebačka 8. The Atlas travel agency (☎ 434 983) at Eufrazijeva 63 represents American Express. There's another office (☎ 432 273) at Boze Milanovića 11.

The Auto-Klub Poreč (☎ 431 665), Partizanska bb (no street number), is in a large white building visible across the field north of the market.

The telephone centre in the main post office, Trg Slobode 14, is open Monday to Saturday from 7 am to 9 pm and Sunday from 9 am to noon.

Things to See

The many historic sites in the old town include the ruins of two **Roman temples**, between Trg Marafor and the western end of the peninsula. Archaeology and history are featured in the four-floor **Regional Museum** (open daily year-round) in an old baroque palace at Dekumanus 9 (captions in German and Italian).

The main reason to visit Poreč, however, is to see the 6th-century **Euphrasian basilica**, a world heritage site which features wonderfully preserved Byzantine gold mosaics. The capitals, sculpture and architecture are remarkable survivors of that distant period. Entry to the church is free and for a small fee you may visit the 4th-century mosaic floor of the adjacent Early Christian basilica.

From May to mid-October there are passenger boats (12KN return) every half-hour to **Sveti Nikola**, the small island opposite Poreč Harbour, departing from the new wharf on Obala Maršala Tita.

Special Events

Annual events include the Folk Festival (June), the Inter Folk Fest (August), the Annual Art Exhibition (June until late August) and the Musical Summer (May to September). Ask about these at the tourist office.

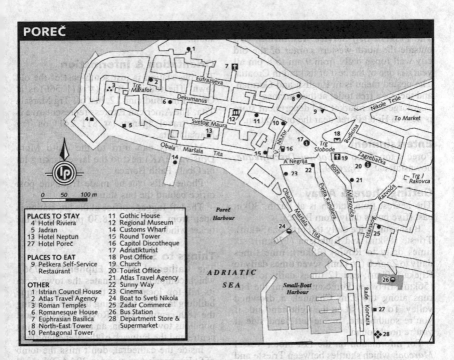

POREČ

PLACES TO STAY
4 Hotel Riviera
5 Jadran
13 Hotel Neptun
27 Hotel Poreč

PLACES TO EAT
9 Peškera Self-Service Restaurant

OTHER
1 Istrian Council House
2 Atlas Travel Agency
3 Roman Temples
6 Romanesque House
7 Euphrasian Basilica
8 North-East Tower
10 Pentagonal Tower
11 Gothic House
12 Regional Museum
14 Customs Wharf
15 Round Tower
16 Capitol Discotheque
17 Adriatikturist
18 Post Office
19 Church
20 Tourist Office
21 Atlas Travel Agency
22 Sunny Way
23 Cinema
24 Boat to Sveti Nikola
25 Zadar Commerce
26 Bus Station
28 Department Store & Supermarket

Places to Stay

Accommodation in Poreč is tight and the camping grounds are far from the town centre, so you might want to stop off only for the day on your way south or north.

Camping There are two camping grounds at Zelena Laguna, 6km south of Poreč. Both *Autocamp Zelena Laguna* (☎ 410 541) and *Autocamp Bijela Uvala* (☎ 410 551) are open from April to mid-October and charge around 24KN per person, 14KN per tent. Take the 'Plava Laguna' bus which runs hourly from the bus station and get off at Zelena Laguna resort. Both camping grounds are a short walk away.

Private Rooms There are very few private rooms available in Poreč and nearly none outside the main season. In the town centre, try Kompas-Istra (☎ 451 200; fax 451 114), Obala Marsala Tita 16 across from the Hotel Neptun. Around Trg Rakovca, there's Kvarner Express (☎ 451 600). Expect to pay about 90/132KN for a single/double with a shared bath in July and August. Make sure to arrive early in the day outside the main May to September tourist season as many agencies close around noon.

Hotels One of the following hotels in the town centre is open year-round but it changes from year to year. Try the modern, five-storey *Hotel Poreč* (☎ 451 811). In July and August a single/double with bath, breakfast and dinner costs 333/556KN. *Hotel Neptun* (☎ 452 711; fax 431 531), Obala M. Tita 15, overlooks the harbour. A single/double with bath and breakfast costs 227/387KN in the peak season. Near the bus station is the *Jadran* (☎ 451 422), Obala Marsala Tita 431-236, which has rooms for 212/366KN.

All prices assume a four-night minimum stay and drop about 50% during May, June, September and October.

CROATIA

Places to Eat

The *Peškera Self-Service Restaurant*, just outside the north-western corner of the old city wall (open daily from 9 am to 8 pm all year), is one of the best of its kind in Croatia. The posted menu is in English and German, and there's a free toilet at the entrance.

A large supermarket and department store is next to Hotel Poreč near the bus station.

Entertainment

Poreč's top disco is *Capitol Discotheque*, downstairs at V Nazor 9.

Getting There & Away

The nearest train station is at Pazin, 30km east (five buses daily from Poreč).

Buses run twice daily to Portorož (54km), Trieste (89km) and Ljubljana (176km); six times daily to Rovinj (38km); nine times daily to Zagreb (264km), seven times daily to Rijeka (80km); and 12 times daily to Pula (56km). Between Poreč and Rovinj the bus runs along the Lim Channel, a drowned valley. To see it, sit on the right-hand side if you're southbound, or the left-hand side if you're northbound.

For information on the fast motor vessel *Marconi,* which shuttles between Trieste and Poreč (2¾ hours; L27,000) inquire at the Sunny Way agency (☎ 452 021), Alda Negrija 1 and see the Getting There & Away section at the beginning of this chapter.

The cheapest price for car rental is at Zadar Commerce (☎ 434 103), Istarskog razvoda 11.

ROVINJ

☎ 052

Relaxed Rovinj (Italian: Rovigno), its high peninsula topped by the great 57m-high tower of massive St Euphemia Cathedral, is perhaps the best place to visit in Istria. Wooded hills punctuated by low-rise luxury hotels surround the town, while the 13 green offshore islands of the Rovinj archipelago make for pleasant, varied views. The cobbled, inclined streets in the old town are charmingly picturesque. Rovinj is still an active fishing port, so you see local people going about their day-to-day business. There's a large Italian community here.

Friendly Rovinj is just the place to rest before your island-hopping journey farther south.

Orientation & Information

The bus station is just south-east of the old town. The tourist office (☎ 811 566) is at Obala Pina Budicina 12, just off Trg Maršala Tita. The American Express representative is Atlas travel agency (☎ 811 241) on Trg Maršala Tita.

Motorists can turn to the Auto Moto Društva (HAK) next to the large parking lot on Obala Palih Boraca.

Phone calls can be made from the post office behind the bus station.

The left-luggage office at the bus station is open from 5.15 am to 8.30 pm (ask at the ticket window).

Things to See

The **Cathedral of St Euphemia** (1736), which completely dominates the town from its hill-top location, is the largest baroque building in Istria, reflecting the period during the 18th century when Rovinj was the most populous town in Istria, an important fishing centre and the bulwark of the Venetian fleet.

Inside the cathedral, don't miss the tomb of St Euphemia (martyred in 304 AD) behind the right-hand altar. The saint's remains were brought from Constantinople in 800. On the anniversary of her martyrdom (16 September) devotees congregate here. A copper statue of her tops the cathedral's mighty tower.

Take a wander along the winding narrow backstreets below the cathedral, such as ulica Grisia, where local artists sell their work. Rovinj has developed into an important art centre and each year in mid-August Rovinj's painters stage a big open-air art show in town.

The **Regional Museum** on Trg Maršala Tita (closed Monday) contains an unexciting collection of paintings and a few Etruscan artefacts found in Istria. These might attract some interest if the captions were in something other than Croatian and Italian. The **Franciscan convent**, up the hill at E de Amicis 36, also has a small museum.

Better than either of these is the **Rovinj Aquarium** (1891) at Obala Giordano Paliaga 5 (open daily but closed mid-October to Easter; 10KN). It exhibits a good collection

ROVINJ

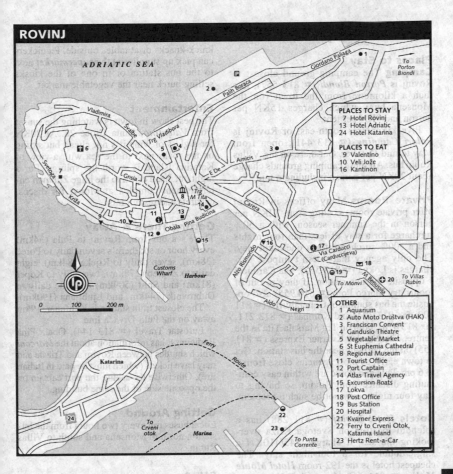

ADRIATIC SEA

Giordano Paliaga

To Porton Biondi

Palih Boraca

Vladimira

Svalbe

Trg Vladibora

Trg M Tita

Grisia

Amicis

E De

Carera

Svetoga

Križa

Obala Pina Budicina

Customs Wharf

Harbour

Via Carducci (Carduccijeva)

Aldo Rismondo

To Monvi

To Villas Rubin

M Benussia

Aldo

Negri

0   100   200 m

PLACES TO STAY
7 Hotel Rovinj
13 Hotel Adriatic
24 Hotel Katarina

PLACES TO EAT
9 Valentino
10 Veli Jože
16 Kantinon

OTHER
1 Aquarium
2 Auto Moto Društva (HAK)
3 Franciscan Convent
4 Gandusio Theatre
5 Vegetable Market
6 St Euphemia Cathedral
8 Regional Museum
11 Tourist Office
12 Port Captain
14 Atlas Travel Agency
15 Excursion Boats
17 Lokva
18 Post Office
19 Bus Station
20 Hospital
21 Kvarner Express
22 Ferry to Crveni Otok, Katarina Island
23 Hertz Rent-a-Car

Katarina

Ferry Route

To Crveni otok

Marina

To Punta Corrente

of local marine life, from poisonous scorpion fish to colourful anemones.

When you've seen enough of the town, follow the waterfront southwards past the Park Hotel to **Punta Corrente Forest Park**, which was afforested in 1890 by Baron Hütterodt, an Austrian admiral who kept a villa on Crveni otok. Here you can swim off the rocks, climb a cliff or just sit and admire the offshore islands.

Organised Tours

Delfin Agency (☎ 813 266), near the ferry

dock for Crveni otok, runs half-day scenic cruises to the **Lim Channel** (70KN) or you can take the hourly ferry to Crveni otok (Red Island; 15KN return). There's a frequent ferry to nearby **Katarina Island** (10KN) from the same landing and you get tickets on the boat. These boats operate from May to mid-October only.

Special Events

The city's annual events include the Rovinj-Pesaro Regata (early May), the 'Rovinj Summer' concert series (July and August),

CROATIA

the Rovinj Fair (August) and the ACI Cup Match Yacht Race (September).

Places to Stay

Camping The camping ground closest to Rovinj is *Porton Biondi* (☎ 813 557), less than a kilometre from the town (on the Monsena bus), which charges 15KN per person and 9KN per tent.

Five kilometres south-east of Rovinj is *Polari Camping* (☎ 813 441), open from May to mid-October. Get there on the Villas Rubin bus. All these camping grounds charge about 20KN per person including a tent.

Private Rooms Many offices in Rovinj offer private rooms costing from 72KN per person in the summer season, with a 50% surcharge for a stay of less than four nights and a 100% surcharge for a one-night stay. The only agency that doesn't impose surcharges is Lokva (☎ 813 365), Via Carducci 4 opposite the bus station. If they're out of rooms, try Marco Polo (☎ 816 955) also opposite the bus station, or Generalturist (☎ 811 402; fax 813 324) and Kompas (☎ 813 211; fax 813 478), both on Trg Maršala Tita in the centre. There's also Kvarner Express (☎ 811 155) on the harbour near the bus station. Get to town early, as most agencies close from 2 to 6 pm. Pula and Poreč are within easy commuting distance from Rovinj, so having to stay four nights may not be such a problem.

Hotels *Hotel Rovinj* (☎ 811 288) has a splendid location on Svetoga Križa overlooking the sea; it charges 245/410KN a single/double for a four-night stay. The cheapest hotel is the 192-room *Hotel Monte Mulin* (☎ 811 512; fax 815 882), on the wooded hillside overlooking the bay just beyond Hotel Park. It's about a 15-minute walk south of the bus station and is open year-round. Bed and breakfast is 198/310KN a single/double (20% lower in spring and autumn).

Places to Eat

Most of the fish and spaghetti places along the harbour cater to well-heeled tourists but *Kantinon*, 18 obala Alzo Rismondo, sells fresh grilled fish beginning at 20KN to a local crowd. *Veli Jože*, Svetoga Križa 1, is some-

what more expensive but is a good place to try Istrian dishes in an interior crammed with knick-knacks or at tables outside. Picnickers can pick up supplies at the *supermarket* next to the bus station or in one of the kiosks selling burek near the vegetable market.

Entertainment

The best show in town is watching the sunset from *Valentino*, Santa Croce 28. At 20KN for a glass of wine it's not cheap but sitting on the rocks next to the sea with a view of Katarina Island is worth the splurge. For a night out, head down to the huge *Zabavni* entertainment complex at Monvi for discos, cabarets and restaurants.

Getting There & Away

There's a bus from Rovinj to Pula (34km) every hour or so; there's seven daily to Poreč (38km), seven daily to Rijeka (84km), eight daily to Zagreb (278km), two daily to Koper (81km) and Split (509km) and one daily to Dubrovnik (744km) and Ljubljana (190km).

The closest train station is Kanfanar, 19km away on the Pula-Divača line.

Eurostar Travel (☎ 813 144), Obala Pina Budicina 1, has information about the *Marconi* which shuttles between Rovinj and Trieste and may have tickets (which must be paid in Italian lire). Otherwise try asking the port captain on the opposite side of the same building.

Getting Around

Local buses run every two hours from the bus station north to Monsena and south to Villas Rubin.

PULA

☎ 052

Pula (the ancient Polensium) is a large regional centre with some industry, a big naval base and a busy commercial harbour. The old town with its museums and well-preserved Roman ruins is certainly worth a visit and nearby are rocky wooded peninsulas overlooking the clear Adriatic waters, which explains the many resort hotels and camping grounds.

Orientation

The bus station is on ulica Carrarina in the centre of town. One block south is Giardini, the central hub, while the harbour is just north of the bus station. The train station is near the water about 1km north of town.

Information

The Tourist Association of Pula at ulica Istarska 11 (open weekdays from 9 am to 1 pm and 5 to 8 pm) will have the latest city map. The American Express representative is Atlas travel agency (☎ 214 172; ulica Starih Statuta 1, Pula 52100).

Long-distance telephone calls may be placed at the main post office at Danteov Trg 4 (open till 8 pm daily).

Jadroagent (☎ 22 568), Riva 14, and the adjacent Kvarner Express office (☎ 22 519) sell ferry tickets.

The bus station has a left-luggage office open daily from 5 am to 10 pm, except for two half-hour breaks. The train station's left-luggage service is open from 9 am to 4 pm but closed on Sunday.

Things to See

Pula's most imposing sight is the 1st-century **Roman amphitheatre** overlooking the harbour and north-east of the old town. At 14KN admission, the visit is expensive, but you can see plenty for free from outside. Around the end of July a Croatian film festival is held in the amphitheatre, but there are cultural events all summer.

The **Archaeological Museum** (10KN; open daily in summer, closed weekends in winter) is on the hill opposite the bus station. Even if you don't get into the museum be sure to visit the large sculpture garden around it, and the **Roman Theatre** behind. The garden is entered through 2nd-century twin gates.

Along the street facing the bus station are **Roman walls** which mark old Pula's eastern boundary. Follow these walls south and continue down Giardini to the **Triumphal Arch of Sergius** (27 BC). The street beyond the arch winds right around old Pula, changing names several times as it goes. Follow it to where you'll find the ancient **Temple of Augustus** and the **old town hall** (1296). Above this square is the **Franciscan church** (1314), with a museum in the cloister (entry from around the other side) containing paintings, medieval frescoes and a Roman mosaic.

The **Museum of History** (open daily) is in the 17th-century Venetian citadel on a high hill in the centre of the old town. The meagre exhibits deal mostly with the maritime history of Pula but the views of Pula from the citadel walls are good.

Places to Stay

Camping The closest camping ground to Pula is *Autocamp Stoja* (☎ 24 144; open mid-April to mid-October), 3km south-west of the centre (take bus No 1 to the terminus at Stoja). There's lots of space on the shady promontory, with swimming possible off the rocks and it's open all year. The two restaurants at the camping ground are good. There are more camping grounds at Medulin and Premantura, coastal resorts south-east of Pula.

Hostels The *Ljetovalište Ferijalnog Saveza Youth Hostel* (☎ 210 002; fax 212 394), is 3km south of central Pula in a great location overlooking a clean pebble beach. Take the No 2 or the No 7 Verudela bus to the 'Piramida' stop and walk back to the first street, turn left and look for the sign. Bed and breakfast is 75KN per person and camping is allowed (56KN including breakfast). The hostel is now heated and open all year. You can sit and sip cold beer on the terrace, where a rock band plays on some summer evenings. Ask about Disco Piramida or the Disco Fort Bourguignon nearby. If the youth hostel is full and you have a tent, it's only a 10-minute walk to *Autocamp Ribarska Koliba* (☎ 22 966), open from June to August.

Private Rooms Arenatours (☎ 34 355), Giardini 4, a block south of the bus station, and Kvarner Express (☎ 22 519; fax 34 961) have private rooms year-round for 54KN per person, with an additional 50% surcharge for one-night stays and 25% surcharge if you stay less than four nights. Brijuni Turist Biro (☎ 22 477), ulica Istarska 3, beside the bus station and Atlas travel agency also have rooms at the same rates.

Hotels There are no cheap hotels but for a little luxury, try the elegant *Hotel Riviera* (☎ 211 166; fax 211 166), Splitska ulica 1, overlooking the harbour. Erected in 1908, it offers large, comfortable rooms for 190/320KN a single/double with shared bath (215/363KN with private bath), breakfast included. From October to May prices are about 25% lower. Compare the price of a room with half and full board when you check in.

Hotel Omir (☎ 22 019), Dobricheva 6, just off Zagrebačka ulica near Giardini, is a private hotel with 11 rooms for 235/375KN single/double with bath and breakfast. If you're willing to pay that, you're better off at the Riviera.

Places to Eat

For grilled meats and local dishes such as goulash, smoked ham and squid risotto, try *Varaždin*, Istarska 30. It's a little expensive, but reasonable if you order carefully. *Delfin*, Kandlerova 17 has a pleasant terrace and an excellent selection of Istrian dishes, especially seafood. Locals rave about the home cooking at *Vodnjanka*, Vitežića 4. It's cheap and casual but open for lunch only. To get there, walk south on Radićeva to Vitežića.

Platak Self-Service, Narodni trg 5 opposite the vegetable market (open from 9.30 am to

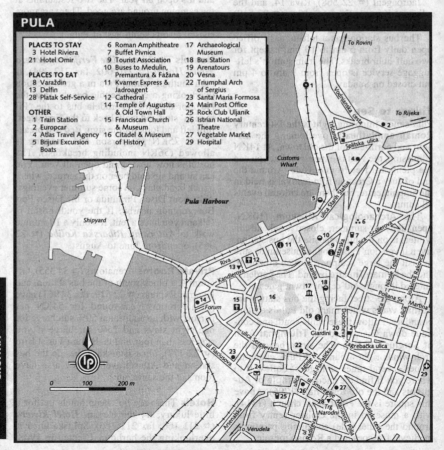

PULA

8.45 pm daily), is easy since you see what you're getting and pay at the end of the line.

The people at the cheese counter in *Vesna*, next to Kino Istra on Giardini, prepare healthy sandwiches while you wait. They're open Monday to Saturday from 6.30 am to 8 pm.

Entertainment

Posters around Pula advertise live performances. *Rock Club Uljanik*, Jurja Dobrile 2, is great whenever something's on. You can dance there.

Buffet Pivnica in the back courtyard at Istarska 34 near the Roman amphitheatre (open daily from 8 am to 4 pm) is one of the least expensive places in Pula to get a draught beer, glass of wine or espresso and all prices are clearly listed. No food is available but there's a convenient free toilet.

Although most of the nightlife is out of town in Verudela, in mild weather the cafés along the pedestrian streets, Flanatička and Sergijevaca are lively people-watching spots.

Two cinemas on Giardini are the *Zagreb* at No 1 and *Pula* at No 12. Quality art films are shown at the *Istrian National Theatre* a couple of times a week.

Getting There & Away

Bus The 20 daily buses to Rijeka (110km, 1½ hours) are sometimes crowded, especially the eight which continue to Zagreb, so reserve a seat a day in advance. Going from Pula to Rijeka, be sure to sit on the right-hand side of the bus for a stunning view of the Gulf of Kvarner.

Other buses from Pula include 18 daily to Rovinj (42km); 12 to Poreč (56km); 11 to Zagreb (292km); three to Zadar (333km); two each to Postojna (161km), Trieste (124km) and Split (514km); and one each to Portorož (90km), Koper (104km), Ljubljana (211km) and Dubrovnik (749km).

Train Ever since Pula was the main port of the Austro-Hungarian empire, the railway line in Istria has run north towards Italy and Austria instead of east into Croatia but there are two daily trains to Ljubljana (four hours, 92KN) and two to Zagreb (6½ hours, 145KN).

Boat The fast boat *Marina* connects Pula and Venice (L57,000) and Zadar (75KN) in the summer. See the Getting There & Away section at the beginning of this chapter. The ferry to Mali Lošinj (28KN) and Zadar (54KN) runs once a week all year. Ask at Jadroagent or Kvarner Express on the harbour.

Getting Around

The only city buses of use to visitors are bus No 1 which runs to the camping ground at Stoja and bus Nos 2 and 7 to Verudela which pass the youth hostel and Pension Ribarska Koliba. Frequency varies from every 15 minutes to every 30 minutes, with service from 5 am to 11.30 pm daily. Tickets are sold at newsstands for 8KN and are good for two trips.

AROUND PULA
Brijuni Islands

The Brijuni (Italian: Brioni) island group consists of two main pine-covered islands and 12 islets off the coast of Istria and just north-west of Pula. Each year from 1949 until his death in 1980, Maršal Tito spent six months at his summer residences on Brijuni in a style any western capitalist would admire. In 1984 Brijuni was proclaimed a national park. Some 680 species of plants grow on the islands, including many exotic subtropical species planted at Tito's request.

You may only visit Brijuni National Park with a group. Instead of booking an excursion with one of the travel agencies in Pula, Rovinj or Poreč, which costs 200KN, you can take a public bus from Pula to Fažana (8km), then sign up for a tour (145KN) at the Brijuni Tourist Service (☎ 525 883) office near the wharf. It's best to book in advance, especially in summer.

Also check along the Pula waterfront for excursion boats to Brijuni. The five-hour boat trips from Pula to Brijuni may not actually visit the islands but only sail around them. Still, it makes a nice day out.

Gulf of Kvarner

The Gulf of Kvarner (Italian: Quarnero) stretches 100km south from Rijeka, between the Istrian Peninsula on the west and the Croatian littoral on the east. The many elongated islands are the peaks of a submerged branch of the Dinaric Alps, the range which follows the coast south all the way to Albania. Krk, Cres and Pag are among the largest islands in Croatia.

Rijeka, a bustling commercial port and communications hub at the northern end of the gulf, is well connected to Italy and Austria by road and rail. The railway built from Budapest to Rijeka in 1845 gave Hungary its first direct outlet to the sea. Big crowds frequent nearby Opatija, a one-time bathing resort of the Habsburg elite, and Krk Island, now linked to the mainland by bridge. Historic Rab, the jewel of the Gulf of Kvarner, is much harder to reach; with some difficulty it can be used as a stepping stone on the way south.

RIJEKA
☎ 051

Rijeka (Italian: Fiume), 126km south of Ljubljana, is such a transportation hub that it's almost impossible to avoid. The network of buses, trains and ferries that connect Istria and Dalmatia with Zagreb and points beyond all seem to pass through Rijeka. As Croatia's largest port, the city is full of boats, cargo, fumes, cranes and the kind of seediness that characterises most port cities.

Although Rijeka is hardly a 'must see' destination, the city does have a few saving graces, such as the pedestrian mall, Korzo, stately 19th century buildings and a tree-lined promenade along the harbour. Because there is so little to interest tourists, accommodation, information and resources for visitors are scarce. The assumption seems to be that everyone will either leave the area as fast as possible or base themselves in Opatija.

Orientation
The bus station is on Trg Žabica below the Capuchin Church in the centre of town. The Jadrolinija ferry wharf (no left-luggage section) is just a few minutes east of the bus station. Korzo runs east through the city centre towards the fast-moving Rječina River.

Information
Tourist Offices Try Kvarner Express (☎ 213 808), Trg Jadranski near the bus

station, or the Turistički Savez Općine Rijeka (☎ 335 882) at Užarska 14. The Auto-Klub Rijeka (☎ 621 824), Preluk 6, assists motorists.

Money You can change money at Croatia Express on platform No 1 at the train station Monday to Friday from 8 am to 9 pm and weekends from 9 am to 1 pm and 5 to 9 pm.

There's an exchange counter in the main post office, opposite the old city tower on Korzo.

The telephone centre in the main post office on Korzo is open from 7 am to 9 pm daily.

Post & Communications Kvarner Express, Trg Jadranski 3, changes money, finds private accommodation and sells excursions.

Jadroagent (☎ 211 276; fax 335 172), at Trg Ivana Koblera 2, is an excellent source of information on all ferry sailings from Croatia.

Left Luggage If the left-luggage office in the bus station (open daily from 5.30 am to 10.30 pm) is full, there's a larger *garderoba* (cloakroom) in the train station (open from 7.30 am to 9 pm), a seven-minute walk west on ulica Krešimirova.

Things to See
The **Modern Art Gallery** (closed Sunday and Monday) is at Dolac 1, upstairs in the scientific library across from Hotel Bonavia. The **Maritime Museum** and the **National Revolution Museum** (both closed Sunday and Monday) are adjacent at Žrtava fašizma 18, above the city centre. Worth a visit if you have time is the 13th-century **Trsat Castle** (closed Monday) on a high ridge overlooking Rijeka and the canyon of the Rječina River.

Places to Stay
The closest camping ground is listed in the Opatija section.

Kvarner Express (☎ 213 808), Trg Jadranski 3, has private rooms for 100/140KN a single/double but only in the summer. Singles are seldom available and frequently all rooms are full.

The A-category *Hotel Bonavia* (☎ 333 744), Dolac 4, is central and has singles/doubles with bath for 348/476KN. The C-category

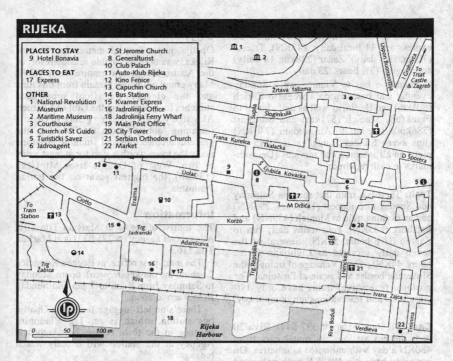

RIJEKA

PLACES TO STAY
9 Hotel Bonavia

PLACES TO EAT
17 Express

OTHER
1 National Revolution Museum
2 Maritime Museum
3 Courthouse
4 Church of St Guido
5 Turistički Savez
6 Jadroagent
7 St Jerome Church
8 Generalturist
10 Club Palach
11 Auto-Klub Rijeka
12 Kino Fenice
13 Capuchin Church
14 Bus Station
15 Kvarner Express
16 Jadrolinija Office
18 Jadrolinija Ferry Wharf
19 Main Post Office
20 City Tower
21 Serbian Orthodox Church
22 Market

Hotel Neboder (☎ 217 355), Strossmayerova 1, and the B-category *Hotel Kontinental* (☎ 216 477), Andrije Kašića Miočaca, are a block apart in an uninspiring neighbourhood north-east of the town centre. Single/double rooms with bath cost 249/311KN at Neboder and 271/333KN at Kontinental. For those prices you might as well pay more and stay in Opatija.

Places to Eat
Restoran Index, at ulica Krešimirova 18 between the bus and train stations, has a good self-service section (samoposluzi). *Express*, 14 Riva, near the Jadrolinija office, is another self-service open daily from 7 am to 9 pm. There's a large *supermarket* between the bus and train station on ulica Krešimirova.

Entertainment
Performances at the *Ivan Zajc National Theatre* (1885) are mostly dramas in Croat-ian, though opera and ballet are sometimes offered. The ticket office is open weekdays.

Club Palach, in the back alley accessible through a small passageway next to the Riječka Banka on Trg Jadranski, opens at 8 pm daily. It's a good, noncommercial place to drink and dance.

Getting There & Away
Bus There are 13 buses daily between Rijeka and Krk (1½ hours, 27KN), using the huge Krk Bridge. Buses to Krk are overcrowded and a seat reservation in no way guarantees you a seat. Don't worry – the bus from Rijeka to Krk empties fairly fast so you won't be standing for long.

Other buses depart from Rijeka for Baška, also on Krk Island (76km, six daily, 39KN), Dubrovnik (639km, three daily, 230KN), Koper (86km), Ljubljana (128km, once daily, 58KN), Mali Lošinj (122km, four daily), Poreč (91km, nine daily), Pula (110km,

CROATIA

17 daily), Rab (115km, two daily), Rovinj (105km, seven daily), Split (404km, seven express and 11 local daily, 145KN), Trieste (70km, five daily), Zadar (228km, 14 daily) and Zagreb (3½ hours, 23 daily).

There's a bus to Vienna every Sunday evening and buses twice a week to Zürich (801km) and Berlin, as well as daily buses to Frankfurt, Munich (571km) and Stuttgart (786km). The bus to Amsterdam (740KN) runs every Sunday. Luggage is DM5 per piece on all international services (Deutschmarks in cash required).

Train There's a train that runs on Saturday and Sunday to Budapest (11 hours, 296KN) and an evening train to Munich (439KN) and Salzburg (283KN). Four trains daily run to Zagreb (five hours, 58KN). Several of the seven daily services to Ljubljana (three hours, 44KN) require a change of trains at the Slovenian border and again at Postojna. The *poslovni* (executive) trains have only 1st-class seats and reservations are compulsory.

Car ATR Rent a Car (☎ 337 544), Riva 20 near the bus station, has rental cars from 480KN a day with unlimited kilometres. On a weekly basis it's 1980KN with unlimited kilometres. Also try Kompas Hertz (☎ 215 425), Zagrebačka 21.

Boat Jadrolinija (☎ 211 444), Riva 16, has tickets for the large coastal ferries that run all year between Rijeka and Dubrovnik. Southbound ferries depart from Rijeka at 6 pm daily.

Fares are 116KN to Split (13 hours), 140KN to Korčula (18 hours) and 152KN to Dubrovnik (17 to 24 hours). Fares are lower in winter. Berths to Dubrovnik are 329KN per person in a four-bed cabin, 399KN in a double or 479KN in a double with private bath.

Since the Jadrolinija ferries travel between Rijeka and Split at night, you don't get to see a lot so it's probably better to go from Rijeka to Split by bus and enjoy excellent views of the Adriatic coast. In contrast, the ferry trip from Split to Dubrovnik is highly recommended.

OPATIJA
☎ 051

Opatija, just a few kilometres due west of Rijeka, was *the* fashionable seaside resort of the Austro-Hungarian empire until WWI. Many grand old hotels remain from this time and the elegant waterfront promenade stretches for 12km along the Gulf of Kvarner. Although you get a passing glance of Opatija (meaning 'abbey') from the Pula bus, the graceful architecture and stunning coastline make the town worth a stop for at least a day or two. West of Opatija rises Mt Učka (1396m), the highest point on the Istrian Peninsula.

Information
The tourist office is at Maršala Tita 101. Atlas travel agency (☎ 271 032) is at Maršala Tita 116.

The main post office, at Eugena Kumičića 2 behind the market (*tržnica*), opens Monday to Saturday from 8 am to 7 pm and Sunday from 9 am to noon.

There's no left-luggage facility at Opatija bus station, which is on Trg Vladimira Gortana in the town centre, but Autotrans Agency at the station will usually watch luggage.

Places to Stay
Preluk Autokamp (☎ 621 913), beside the busy highway between Rijeka and Opatija, is open from May to September. City bus No 32 stops near the camping ground.

For private rooms, try the following places along Maršala Tita: Kvarner Express (☎ 711 070) at No 128, Generalturist (☎ 271 613; fax 271 345) next to the Hotel Paris and GIT (☎/fax 271 967) at No 65. All have rooms for 70KN per person plus a 50% surcharge for single-room occupancy, a 30% surcharge for stays less than four nights and 20KN for breakfast.

There are no cheap hotels in Opatija but the most reasonable are the elegant *Hotel Paris* (☎ 271 911; fax 711 823), 198 Maršala Tita, and the sprawling *Jadran* (☎ 271 700; fax 271 519), Maršala Tita 109 on the sea. Both have rooms for 205/338KN a single/double for a four-night stay in the high season, including bath and breakfast.

Places to Eat

Maršala Tita is lined with decent restaurants offering pizza, grilled meat and fish. There's a *supermarket/deli* at Maršala Tita 80 and a *burek stand* down the stairs next to No 55 on Stubište Tomaševac.

Getting There & Away

Bus No 32 stops in front of the train station in Rijeka (11km, 11KN) and runs right along the Opatija Riviera west from Rijeka to Lovran every 20 minutes until late in the evening.

KRK ISLAND

☎ 051

Croatia's largest island, 409-sq-km Krk (Italian: Veglia) is barren and rocky. In 1980 Krk was joined to the mainland by the massive Krk Bridge, the largest concrete arch bridge in the world, with a span of 390m. Since then, Krk has suffered from too-rapid development – Rijeka airport and some industry at the northern end of Krk, and big tourist hotels in the middle and far south. Still, the main town (also called Krk) is rather picturesque and Baška has an impressive setting. You can easily stop at Krk town for a few hours of sightseeing, then catch a bus to Baška and Krk's longest beach.

Krk Town

From the 12th to the 15th centuries, Krk town and the surrounding region remained semi-independent under the Frankopan Dukes of Krk, an indigenous Croatian dynasty, at a time when much of the Adriatic was controlled by Venice. This history explains the various medieval sights in Krk town, the ducal seat.

Orientation & Information The bus from Baška and Rijeka stops by the harbour, a few minutes walk from the old town of Krk. There's no left-luggage facility at Krk bus station.

Things to See The 14th-century **Frankopan Castle** and lovely 12th-century Romanesque **cathedral** are in the lower town near the harbour. In the upper part of Krk town are three old monastic churches. The narrow streets of Krk are worth exploring.

Places to Stay

There is a range of accommodation options in and around Krk, but many places only open for the summer.

The closest camping ground is *Autocamp Ježevac* (☎ 221 081) on the coast, a 10-minute walk south-west of Krk town. The rocky soil makes it nearly impossible to use tent pegs, but there are lots of stones to anchor your lines. There's good shade and places to swim.

Camping Bor (☎ 221 581) is on a hill inland from Ježevac. *Politin FKK* (☎ 221 351) is a naturist camp south-east of Krk, just beyond the large resort hotels.

From mid-June to September youth hostel accommodation is available at the *Ljetovalište Ferialnog Saveza* (☎ 854 037; fax 434 962) at Punat, between Krk town and Baška. All buses to Baška stop here.

Kvarner Express (☎ 221 403; fax 221 035) on the main square at Krk has private rooms for 90/130KN a single/double plus a 30% surcharge for stays of less than four nights. Similar rooms can be booked from Autotrans (☎ 221 111) at the bus station and Adriatours (☎ 221 666) in the old town. Prices are about 10% cheaper in May and June and about 20% less at other times. Ask for the brochure with pictures of the accommodation.

Getting There & Away About 14 buses a day travel between Rijeka and Krk town (1½ hours), of which six continue on to Baška (one hour). One of the Rijeka buses is to/from Zagreb (229km). To go from Krk to the island of Mali Lošinj, change buses at Malinska for the Lošinj-bound bus that comes from Rijeka but check the times carefully as the connection only works once or twice a day.

Baška

Baška, at the southern end of Krk Island, is a popular resort with a 2km-long pebbly beach set below a high ridge. The swimming and scenery are better than at Krk and the old town has a lot of charm. This is a good base for hiking and you can pick up a map of hiking routes from the tourist office.

Orientation & Information The bus from Krk stops at the top of a hill on the edge of the old town, between the beach and the harbour. The main street is Zvonimirova, which has exchange offices, travel agencies and restaurants.

The tourist office (☎ 856 817) is at Zvonimirova 114, just down the street from the bus stop.

Places to Stay During July and August, it is essential to arrange accommodation well in advance as the town swarms with Austrian, German and Czech tourists. By late spring, hotels are booked solid for the summer season and accommodation is tight in the shoulder season as well.

Camping There are two camping options at Baška. *Camping Zablaće* (☎ 856 909), open from May to September, is on the beach south-west of the bus stop (look for the rows of caravans). In heavy rain you risk getting flooded here.

A better bet is *FKK Camp Bunculuka* (☎ 856 806), open from May to September. A naturist camping ground over the hill east of the harbour (a 15-minute walk), it's quiet, shady and conveniently close to town.

Private Rooms The places to try for private-room bookings are Guliver (☎ 656 004) and Primaturist (☎ 856 132; fax 856 971), both at Zvonimira 98 in the town centre; at the Hotel Corinthia, try Kvarner Express (☎/fax 856 895), Kompas (☎ 856 460) or Ara (☎ 856 298). Expect to pay at least 90/130KN a single/double plus a 30% surcharge for stays of less than four nights.

If you come in July or August, you may find it impossible to rent a room for less than four nights, impossible to rent a single room, impossible to rent a room near town or just plain impossible. Plan ahead.

Hotels The choice of hotels is not outstanding. The cheapest rooms are at the *Hotel Zvonimir* or *Adria*, where you can find singles/doubles for 234/396KN. Next up in price is the *Corinthia II*, which has rooms for 277/486KN. Head of the pack is the *Hotel Corinthia* (☎ 656 111; fax 856 584), with rooms for 366/612KN a single/double. The hotels are all part of the same modern complex on the edge of town right next to the beach. Bookings for these places are made through the Hotel Corinthia.

Getting There & Away The ferry from Baška to Lopar on Rab Island (23KN) operates up to five times daily from June to September but between October and May there's no service and you will be forced to backtrack to Rijeka to get farther south. To reach the Lopar ferry, follow the street closest to the water through the old town, heading south-east for less than 1km.

RAB ISLAND

Rab (Italian: Arbe), near the centre of the Kvarner Island group, is one of the most enticing islands in the Adriatic. The north-eastern side is barren and rocky, whereas the south-west is green with pine forests and dotted with sandy beaches and coves. High mountains protect Rab's interior from cold north and east winds.

Rab Town
☎ 051

Medieval Rab town is built on a narrow peninsula which encloses a sheltered harbour. The old stone buildings climb from the harbour to a cliff overlooking the sea. For hundreds of years Rab was an outpost of Venice until the Austrians took over in the 19th century. Today it is a favourite destination of German tourists, which is not surprising considering the beauty of the town and island. Rab would be the perfect stepping stone between Krk and Zadar if only the transport connections were more convenient.

Orientation The bus station is at the rear of a new commercial centre and around the corner from the Merkur department store, a five-minute walk from the old town. The large Jadrolinija ferries tie up on the south-eastern tip of the peninsula.

Information There are two tourist offices. One is around the corner from the bus station opposite the Merkur department store and the other (☎ 771 111) is on Arba Municipium, across from Café Revelin. There is a post office in the commercial centre and another on Arba Municipium. Both post offices are open Monday to Saturday from 7 am to 8 pm. The Atlas travel agency (☎ 724 585) is on Arba Municipium and opposite the post office. Despite a sign at the bus station advertising a garderoba, the left-luggage service is not operational because the station is only open for limited hours.

Things to See Four tall church towers rise above the red-roofed mass of houses on Rab's high peninsula. If you follow Rade Končara north from the **Monastery of St Anthony** (1175), you soon reach the Romanesque **cathedral**, alongside a pleasant terrace with a view overlooking the sea. Farther along, beyond a tall **Romanesque tower** and another convent, is a second terrace and **St Justine Church**, now a small museum of religious art. Just past the next chapel, look for a small gate giving access to a park with the foundations of Rab's oldest church and the fourth tower (which you can climb).

Rade Končara ends at the north city wall, which affords a splendid view of the town, harbour, sea and hill. The scene is especially beautiful just after sunset. North of the wall is the extensive **city park** with many shady walkways.

Special Events Annual events to ask about include the Rab Fair (25 to 27 July) and the Rab Music Evenings (June to September).

Places to Stay Everything from camping to expensive hotels can be found in and around Rab town.

Camping To sleep cheaply, carry your tent south along the waterfront for about 25 minutes to *Autocamp Padova* (☎ 724 355) at Banjol (14KN per person, 13KN per tent). Farther out of town at Kampor is a small camping ground with a large beach, *Halović* (☎ 776 087).

Private Rooms Several agencies rent out private rooms, including Turist Biro Mila (☎ 725 499) on the south-eastern corner of the bus station and Turist Biro Kristofor (☎ 725 543), on the north-western corner. In town, try Numero Uno (☎ 724 688; fax 724 688) next to Merkantours, Arba Kompas (☎ 724 484; fax 724 284) on Donya ulica 4 and Atlas. Prices are more or less the same, beginning at 54KN per person, 7KN for breakfast and a 30% surcharge for stays less

than three nights. Some agencies forgo the surcharges when things are slow. You could be approached by women at the bus station or at the Lopar ferry offering private rooms.

Hotels The *Hotel International* (☎ 711 266; fax 724 206) on Obala kralja Petra Krešimira IV, facing the harbour, has the cheapest rooms at 241/396KN a single/double with bath and breakfast in peak season. It's a pleasant place if you don't mind the price.

Places to Eat One of the few restaurants in Rab which posts a menu outside is *Alibaba* on ulica Ivana Lole Ribara in the old town. It's not cheap but it does have a good selection of seafood. *Pizza Paradiso*, ulica Radića 2, serves pizza for 40KN in a touristy but attractive enclosed terrace. For fast food, head to *Buffet Buza*, ulica Ugalje near Arba Municipium, where you can eat a plate of fried squid for 20KN. There's a good *supermarket* in the basement at the Merkur department store for picnic supplies.

Getting There & Away All the local travel agencies have bus and ferry schedules posted in their offices.

Bus The most reliable way to travel is on one of the two daily buses between Rab and Rijeka (115km, 62KN). In the tourist season there are two direct buses from Zagreb to Rab (211km, five hours). These services can fill up, so book ahead if possible.

There's no direct bus from Rab to Zadar but there are two daily buses that connect at Senj with Rijeka buses to Zadar (five hours, 94KN). To avoid backtracking from Senj to Jablanac and also save some kuna, you can take the bus to the highway at Jablanac, wait for about an hour and a half and catch the Rijeka bus as it heads to Zadar.

Boat In addition to the summer ferry between Baška on Krk Island and Lopar, there's the weekly Jadrolinija ferry but sometimes it doesn't call at Rab if there's 'fog' (ie not enough passengers to drop off or pick up).

In summer, tourist agencies offer day excursions to Mali Lošinj (130KN return) or Pag Island (70KN return) once or twice a week.

Lopar

The bus from Rab town to Lopar stops in front of Pizzeria Aloha, opposite the small-boat harbour about 300m ahead of the Lopar ferry landing. The stop is unmarked, so ask. There's a bus every hour or two to Rab town (12km). Several houses around here have 'sobe' signs. *Camping San Marino* is about 3km south of the Lopar ferry landing, across the peninsula. It has a long sand beach and the same prices as the *Autocamp Padova* (see above).

Dalmatia

Dalmatia (Dalmacija) occupies the central 375km of Croatia's Adriatic coast, from the Gulf of Kvarner in the north to the Bay of Kotor in the south, including offshore islands. The rugged Dinaric Alps form a 1500m-high barrier separating Dalmatia from Bosnia, with only two breaks: the Krka River canyon at Knin and the Neretva Valley at Mostar, both of which have railway lines.

After the last Ice Age, part of the coastal mountains were flooded, creating the same sort of long, high islands seen in the Gulf of Kvarner. The deep, protected passages that lie between these islands are a paradise for sailors and cruisers.

Historical relics abound in towns like Zadar, Trogir, Split, Hvar, Korčula and Dubrovnik, framed by a striking natural beauty of barren slopes, green valleys and clear water. The ferry trip from Split to Dubrovnik is one of the classic journeys of Eastern Europe. The vineyards of Dalmatia supply half of Croatia's wine. A warm current flowing north up the coast keeps the climate mild – dry in summer, damp in winter. Dalmatia is noticeably warmer than Istria or the Gulf of Kvarner and it's possible to swim in the sea right up until the end of September. This is the Mediterranean at its best.

ZADAR

☎ 023

Zadar (the ancient Zara), the main city of northern Dalmatia, occupies a long peninsula which separates the harbour on the east from the Zadar Channel on the west. The city of Iader was laid out by the Romans,

who left behind considerable ruins. Later the area fell under the Byzantine Empire, which explains the Orthodox churches with their central domes. In 1409 Venice took Zadar from Croatia and held it for four centuries. Dalmatia was part of the Austro-Hungarian empire during most of the 19th century, with Italy exercising control from 1918 to 1943. Badly damaged by Anglo-American bombing raids in 1943-44, much of the city had to be rebuilt. Luckily, the original street plan was respected and an effort was made to harmonise the new with what remained of old Zadar.

In November 1991, Zadar seemed to be re-living history as Yugoslav rockets ploughed into the old city, damaging the cathedral. For the next three months the city's inhabitants were under siege, unable to leave their homes for fear of being hit. Although the Serb gunners were pushed back by the Croatian army during its January 1993 offensive, this experience has embittered many residents and people may be suspicious of you until they know who you are.

Few war wounds are visible, however. Zadar's narrow, traffic-free stone streets are again full of life and the tree-lined promenade along Obala kralja Petra Krešimira IV is perfect for a lazy stroll or a picnic. Tremendous 16th-century fortifications still shield the city on the landward side and high walls run along the harbour. Museums and monuments have recently been repaired and reopened, in an attempt to lure tourists from the beaches and camp sites at nearby Borik. Zadar can be a fascinating place to wander around and, at the end of the day, you can sample Zadar's famous maraschino cherry liqueur.

Orientation

The train and bus stations are adjacent and a 15-minute walk south-east of the harbour and old town.

From the stations, Zrinsko-Frankopanska ulica leads north-west past the main post office to the harbour. Buses marked 'Poluo-tok' run from the bus station to the harbour. Narodni trg is the heart of Zadar.

Information

The official tourist office is Turistička Zajednica, (☎ 212 412), Smiljanića 4. The

American Express representative is the Atlas travel agency (☎ 314 206), Branimirova Obala 12, across the footbridge over the harbour, just north-east of Narodni trg. Croatia Express (☎ 211 660) is on Široka ulica.

Telephone calls can be made from the main post office at Zrinsko-Frankopanska ulica 8 (open from 7 am to 8 pm daily).

There is one left-luggage office for both the train and bus stations, open 24 hours a day.

Things to See

The main things to see are near the circular **St Donatus Church**, a 9th-century Byzantine structure built over the Roman forum. Slabs for the ancient forum are visible in the church and, on the north-western side is a pillar from the Roman era. In summer, ask about musical evenings here (Renaissance and early baroque music). The outstanding **Museum of Church Art** (open daily, except Sunday evening, from 10 am to 12.30 pm and 6 to 7.30 pm) in the Benedictine monastery opposite offers a substantial display of reliquaries and religious paintings. The obscure lighting deliberately re-creates the environment in which the objects were originally kept.

The 13th-century Romanesque **Cathedral of St Anastasia** nearby never really recovered from WWII destruction; the **Franciscan Monastery** a few blocks away is more cheerful. The large Romanesque cross in the treasury behind the sacristy is worth seeing.

Other museums include the **Archaeological Museum** (closed Sunday), across from St Donatus, and the **Ethnological Museum** in the Town Watchtower (1562) on Narodni trg. The latter should reopen as soon as renovations are completed. More interesting is the **National Museum** on Poljana Pape Aleksandra III just inside the Sea Gate. This excellent museum features scale models of Zadar from different periods and old paintings and engravings of many coastal cities. The same admission ticket will get you into the local **art gallery** on Smiljanića. Unfortunately, the captions in all Zadar's museums are in Croatian. Notable churches include the 12th-century St Krševan church, St Simun with a 14th-century gold chest and St Petar Stari with Roman-Byzantine frescoes.

Organised Tours

Any of the many travel agencies around town can supply information on the tourist cruises to the beautiful Kornati Islands (250KN, including lunch and a swim in the sea or a salt lake). As this is about the only way to see these 101 barren, uninhabited islands, islets and cliffs it's worthwhile if you can spare the cash. Check with Kvarner Express (☎/fax 212 215), Kraljice Elizabete Kotromanić 3, Kompas (☎/fax 433 380) on Široka ulica and Croatia Express across the street. Also ask about excursions to Krka National Park which is inaccessible to individual travel. Although there are too few tourists in the region to run the excursion regularly, if there's a group going you can tag along.

Special Events

Major annual events include the town fair (July and August), the Dalmatian Song Festival (July and August), the musical evenings in St Donatus Church (August) and the Choral Festival (October).

Places to Stay

Staying in town is nearly impossible. Most visitors head out to the 'tourist settlement' at Borik, 3km north-west of Zadar, on the Puntamika bus (every 20 minutes from the bus station, 6KN) where there are hotels, a hostel, a camp site and numerous 'sobe' signs; you can arrange a private room through an agency in town. If you arrive in the off season, try to arrange accommodation in advance since hotels, hostels and camp sites will be closed.

Camping *Zaton* (☎ 264 303) is 16km north-west of Zadar on a sandy beach and should be open from May to September but call first. There are 12 buses marked 'Zaton' leaving daily from the bus station. Nearer to Zadar is *Autocamp Borik* (☎ 332 074), only steps away from Borik beach.

Hostels Also near the beach at Borik is the *Borik Youth Hostel* (☎ 331 145; fax 331 190), Obala Kneza Trpimira 76, which is open from May to September. Bed and breakfast costs 70KN and full board is 100KN.

Private Rooms Agencies finding private accommodation include Kompas, Kvarner

ZADAR

Liburnska obàla

Harbour

Istarska obàla

Luke Jelča

Božidara

...berca

Petranović

Bedemi zadarskin pobuna

Pravdonoše

Fra D'Fabunića

Nikšić Matafara

Aleksandra III

Brne Krnarutića

Nadila

Nalka

Zeleni
trg

Benje

S Kožičića

Široka

Juria Dalmatinca

ulica

Obala Kralja Petra Krešimira IV

Excursion
Boat Wharf

Borelli

Dalmatina...

Narodni
trg

Barakovića

Grisogona

E Kotromanić

Smiljanića

Footbridge

Bedemi zadarskin pobuna

Zadar Channel

Varoška

Spire Brusine

Stomarica

Kult Caffe

Pavlinovića

Boškovića

Rudera

Fola

Zvonimira

Obala kralja Petra Krešimira IV

**To Bus &
Train Stations**

0   50   100 m

PLACES TO EAT	
14	Samoposluzivanje Self-Service
28	Dalmacija
31	Kantun

OTHER	
1	Ancona Ferry
2	Jadrolinija
3	Rowing Boat Ride
4	Arsenal
5	Croatia Airlines
6	Jadroagent
7	Franciscan Monastery
8	Serbian Church
9	Cathedral of St Anastasia
10	Main Post Office
11	National Museum
12	St Krševan
13	Croatia Express
15	St Donatus Church
16	Forum
17	Archaeological Museum
18	Kompas
19	Museum of Church Art
20	St Petar Stari
21	Vegetable Market
22	National Theatre
23	Central Kavana
24	Town Watchtower & Ethnological Museum
25	Grocery Store
26	Liburnija Tourist Office
27	Kvarner Express
29	St Simun
30	Turistička Zajednica
32	Kult Caffe
33	Art Gallery
34	Medieval Tower
35	Town Gate
36	Ruins

Express or Marlin Tours (☎/fax 313 194), around the corner from Atlas at Jeretova 3. Liburnija tourist office (☎ 211 039) next to Kvarner Express also might have rooms. Prices vary so check around. Expect to pay around 120KN per person with a 30% surcharge for stays less than three nights. Breakfast is an extra 6KN.

Hotels There are no budget hotels in town and only one regularly operating hotel, the *Hotel Kolovare* (☎ 203 200), Bože Peričića 14, which is being transformed into a luxury establishment. The best bet is to head out to nearby Borik on the Puntamika bus. The B-category *Novi Park* (☎ 206 100) *Zadar* (☎ 332 184), and *Donat* (☎ 332 184), all at Majstora Radovana 7, offer rooms but you must take half-board for 224/369KN a single/double.

Places to Eat
Dalmacija at the end of Kraljice Elizabete Kotromanić is a good place for pizza, spaghetti, fish and local specialities. *Kuntun*, Stomarica 6, serves plates of fried fresh fish for 25KN. The newly renovated *Samoposluzivanje* is a self-service restaurant in the passage off Nikole Matafara 9 which has hot dishes starting at 25KN.

Central Kavana on Široka ulica is a spacious café and hang-out with live music on weekends. *Kult Caffe* on Stomarica draws a young crowd to listen to rap music indoors or relax on the large shady terrace outside. In summer the many cafés along Varoška and Klaića place their tables on the street; it's great for people-watching. There's a *grocery store* on the corner of Grisogona and Barakovića that sells bread and cold cuts for sandwiches and you'll find a number of *burek stands* around the vegetable market.

Entertainment
The National Theatre box office on Široka ulica has tickets to the cultural programs advertised on posters outside. Zadar's most popular disco is *Saturnus*, in Zaton near Zadra. It's the largest disco in Croatia.

Getting There & Away
Bus & Train There are buses to Rijeka (228km), Split (158km), Mostar (four daily,

301km), Dubrovnik (393km, seven daily, 114KN) and Sarajevo (twice daily, 93KN). There are two daily trains to Zagreb (11 hours, 80KN) that change at Knin. The bus to Zagreb (320km, 70KN) is quicker.

The Croatia Express travel agency sells bus tickets to many German cities, including Munich (366KN), Frankfurt (576KN), Cologne (666KN) and Berlin (720KN).

Boat From late June to September the fast boat *Marina* runs from Venice to Zadar twice a week and from Pula to Zadar four times a week, stopping at Mali Lošinj. There are weekly local ferries all year (four times a week in summer) between Mali Lošinj and Zadar (six hours, 30KN) and between Pula and Zadar (eight hours, 58KN). The Jadrolinija coastal ferry from Rijeka to Dubrovnik calls at Zadar four times a week (116KN).

For information on connections to Italy see the Getting There & Away section at the beginning of this chapter and contact Jadroagent (☎ 211 447) on ulica Natka Nodila just inside the city walls. Jadrolinija (☎ 212 003), Liburnska obala 7 on the harbour, has tickets for all local ferries.

On Tuesday and Thursday there's a ferry to Zaglav on Dugi otok island (11KN), which is a good day trip (on other days there's no connection to return to Zadar).

TROGIR
☎ 021
Trogir (formerly Trau), a lovely medieval town on the coast and just 20km west of Split, is well worth a stop if you're coming south from Zadar. A day trip to Trogir from Split can easily be combined with a visit to the Roman ruins of Salona (see the Salona section later in this chapter).

The old town of Trogir occupies a tiny island in the narrow channel between Čiovo Island and the mainland, and is just off the coastal highway. There's many sights on the 15-minute walk around this island. The nearest beach is 4km west at the Medena Hotel.

Orientation
The heart of the old town is a few minutes walk from the bus station. After crossing the small bridge near the station, go through the

North Gate. Trogir's finest sights are around Narodni trg, slightly left and ahead.

Information

The tourist office (☎ 881 554) opposite the cathedral sells a map of the area. There's no left-luggage office in Trogir bus station, so you'll end up toting your bags around town if you only visit on a stopover.

Things to See

The glory of the three-naved Venetian **Cathedral of St Lovro** on Narodni trg is the Romanesque portal of Adam and Eve (1240) by Master Radovan, which you can admire for free at any time. Enter the building through an obscure back door to see the perfect Renaissance Chapel of St Ivan and the choir, pulpit, ciborium and treasury. You can even climb the cathedral tower, if it's open, for a delightful view. Also on Narodni trg is the **town hall**, with an excellent Gothic staircase and Renaissance loggia.

Places to Stay

Vranića Camping (☎ 894 141) is just off the highway to Zadar and about 5km west of Trogir by bus 24. *Seget* (☎ 880 394), 2km west of Trogir, is reliably open from June to September.

The Turist Biro (☎/fax 881 554) opposite the cathedral has private rooms for 150/288KN a single/double plus a 30% surcharge for stays less than three nights. Prices are lower in the off season.

Three kilometres west of Trogir there is the C-category *Hotel Jadran* (☎ 880 008; fax 880 401), which offers rooms for 180/364KN and, a little farther, the B category *Hotel Medena* (☎ 880 588; fax 880 019), with rooms for 252/366KN. Both hotels are on the route of numerous local buses.

Getting There & Away

Southbound buses from Zadar (130km) will drop you off in Trogir. Getting buses north can be more difficult, as they often arrive full from Split.

City bus No 37 runs between Trogir and Split (28km) every 20 minutes throughout the day with a stop at Split airport en route. In Split bus No 37 leaves from the local bus station. If you're making a day trip to Trogir also buy your ticket back to Split, as the ticket window at Trogir bus station is often closed. Drivers also sell tickets if you're stuck.

There's also a ferry once a week between Trogir and Split.

SPLIT
☎ 021

Split (Italian: Spalato), the largest Croatian city on the Adriatic coast, is the heart of Dalmatia. The old town is built around the harbour, on the southern side of a high peninsula sheltered from the open sea by many islands. Ferries to these islands are constantly coming and going. The entire western end of the peninsula is a vast, wooded mountain park, while industry, shipyards, limestone quarries and the ugly commercial-military port are mercifully far enough away on the northern side of the peninsula. High coastal mountains set against the blue Adriatic provide a striking frame to the scene.

Split achieved fame when the Roman emperor Diocletian (245-313 AD), noted for his persecution of early Christians, had his retirement palace built here from 295 to 305. After his death the great stone palace continued to be used as a retreat by Roman rulers. When the nearby colony of Salona was abandoned in the 7th century, many of the Romanised inhabitants fled to Split and barricaded themselves behind the high palace walls, where their descendants live to this day.

First Byzantium and then Croatia controlled the area, but from the 12th to the 14th centuries medieval Split enjoyed a large measure of autonomy, which favoured its development. The western part of the old town around Narodni trg, which dates from this time, became the focus of municipal life, while the area within the palace walls proper continued as the ecclesiastical centre.

In 1420 the Venetians conquered Split, which led to a slow decline. During the 17th century, strong walls were built around the city as a defence against the Turks. In 1797 the Austrians arrived and remained until

1918, with only a brief interruption during the Napoleonic wars.

Since 1945, Split has grown into a major industrial city with large apartment-block housing areas. However, much of old Split remains, which combined with its exuberant nature makes it one of the most fascinating cities in Europe. It's also the perfect base for excursions to many nearby attractions, so settle in for a few days.

Orientation

The bus, train and ferry terminals are adjacent on the eastern side of the harbour, a short walk from the old town. Obala hrvatskog narodnog preporoda, the waterfront promenade, is your best central reference point in Split.

Information

Tourist Office The turistički biro (☎/fax 342 142) is at Obala hrvatskog narodnog preporoda 12.

Money The American Express representative, Atlas travel agency (☎ 343 055), is at Trg Braće Radića.

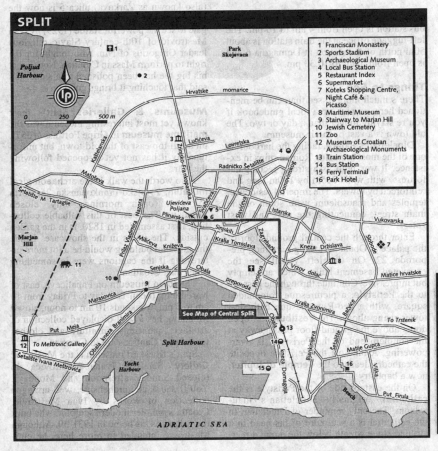

SPLIT

1 Franciscan Monastery
2 Sports Stadium
3 Archaeological Museum
4 Local Bus Station
5 Restaurant Index
6 Supermarket
7 Koteks Shopping Centre, Night Café & Picasso
8 Maritime Museum
9 Stairway to Marjan Hill
10 Jewish Cemetery
11 Zoo
12 Museum of Croatian Archaeological Monuments
13 Train Station
14 Bus Station
15 Ferry Terminal
16 Park Hotel

CROATIA

Post & Communications Poste-restante mail can be collected at window No 7 at the main post office, Kralja Tomislava 9. The post office is open weekdays from 7 am to 8 pm and Saturday from 7 am to noon. The telephone centre here is open daily from 7 am to 9 pm. On Sunday and in the early evening there's always a line of people waiting to place calls, so it's better to go in the morning.

Bookshops Steps away from the Peristyle at Polyana Grgura Ninskog 7, the bookstore Tamaris has a wide selection of English language paperbacks. Look for the sign 'Antikvariyat Grgur'.

Left Luggage The garderoba kiosk at the bus station is open from 4 am to 10 pm. The left-luggage office at the train station is about 50m north of the station at Domagoja 6 and is open from 5 am to 10.30 pm.

Things to See

There's much more to see than can be mentioned here, so pick up a local guidebook if you're staying longer than a day or two. The old town is a vast open-air museum.

Diocletian's Palace, facing the harbour, is one of the most imposing Roman ruins in existence. It was built as a strong rectangular fortress, with walls 215m by 180m long and reinforced by towers. The imperial residence, temples and mausoleum were south of the main street, connecting the east and west gates.

Enter through the central ground floor of the palace at Obala hrvatskog narodnog preporoda 22. On the left you'll see the excavated basement halls, which are empty but impressive. Continue through the passage to the **Peristyle**, a picturesque colonnaded square, with a neo-Romanesque cathedral tower rising above. The **vestibule**, an open dome above the ground-floor passageway at the southern end of the Peristyle, is overpowering. A lane off the Peristyle opposite the cathedral leads to the **Temple of Jupiter**, now a baptistry.

On the eastern side of the Peristyle is the **cathedral**, originally Diocletian's mausoleum. The only reminder of Diocletian in the cathedral is a sculpture of his head in a circular stone wreath below the dome directly above the baroque white-marble altar. The Romanesque wooden doors (1214) and stone pulpit are worth noting. You may climb the tower for a small fee.

The west palace gate opens onto medieval Narodni trg, dominated by the 15th-century Venetian Gothic **old town hall**. Trg Braće Radića, between Narodni trg and the harbour, contains the surviving north tower of the 15th-century Venetian garrison castle, which once extended to the water's edge. The east palace gate leads into the market area.

In the Middle Ages the nobility and rich merchants built residences within the old palace walls; the Papalić Palace at Papalićeva (also known as Žarkova) ulica 5 is now the town museum. Go through the north palace gate to see the powerful **statue** (1929) by Ivan Meštrović of 10th-century Slavic religious leader Gregorius of Nin, who fought for the right to perform Mass in Croatian. Notice that his big toe has been polished to a shine; it's said that touching it brings good luck.

Museums & Galleries Split's least known yet most interesting museum was the **maritime museum** in Gripe Fortress (1657), on a hill top east of the old town, but unfortunately it has not yet re-opened following the war.

Also worth the walk is the **archaeological museum**, Zrinjsko-Frankopanska 25, north of town (open mornings only, closed Monday). The best of this valuable collection, first assembled in 1820, is in the garden outside. The items in the showcases inside the museum building would be a lot more interesting if the captions were in something other than Croatian.

The **town museum** on Papalićeva, east of Narodni trg (open Tuesday to Friday from 10 am to 5 pm, weekends 10 am to noon, closed Monday), has a well-displayed collection of artefacts, paintings, furniture and clothes from Split. Captions are in Croatian.

Split's finest art museum is the **Meštrović Gallery**, Šetalište Ivana Meštrovića 46 (closed Sunday afternoon and Monday). You'll see a comprehensive, well-arranged collection of works by Ivan Meštrović, Croatia's premier modern sculptor, who built the gallery as his home in 1931-39. Although Meštrović intended to retire here, he emigrated to the USA soon after WWII. Bus No 12 passes the gate infrequently. There are beaches on the southern side of the peninsula below the gallery.

From the Meštrović Gallery it's possible to hike straight up **Marjan Hill**. Go up ulica Tonća Petrasova Marovića on the western side of the gallery and continue straight up the stairway to Put Meja ulica. Turn left and walk west to Put Meja 76. The trail begins on the western side of this building. Marjan Hill offers trails through the forest, lookouts, old chapels and the local zoo.

Organised Tours

Atlas runs excursions to Krka waterfalls once a week (215KN). It also offers a canoe picnic on the Cetina River (275KN, including lunch) and a fast boat to Bol beach on Brač every Sunday (120KN return).

Special Events

The Split Summer Festival (mid-July to mid-August) features opera, drama, ballet and concerts on open-air stages. There's also the Feast of St Dujo (7 May), a flower show (May) and the four-day Festival of Popular

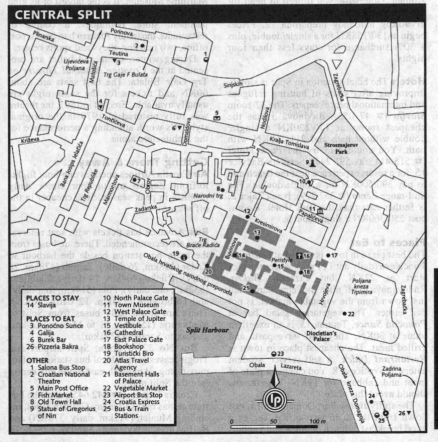

CENTRAL SPLIT

PLACES TO STAY
14 Slavija

PLACES TO EAT
3 Ponoćno Sunce
4 Galija
6 Burek Bar
26 Pizzeria Bakra

OTHER
1 Salona Bus Stop
2 Croatian National Theatre
5 Main Post Office
7 Fish Market
8 Old Town Hall
9 Statue of Gregorius of Nin

10 North Palace Gate
11 Town Museum
12 West Palace Gate
13 Temple of Jupiter
15 Vestibule
16 Cathedral
17 East Palace Gate
18 Bookshop
19 Turistički Biro
20 Atlas Travel Agency
21 Basement Halls of Palace
22 Vegetable Market
23 Airport Bus Stop
24 Croatia Express
25 Bus & Train Stations

Split Harbour

Diocletian's Palace

0   50   100 m

CROATIA

Music (end of June). The traditional February Carnival has recently been revived and from June to September a variety of evening entertainment is presented in the old town.

Places to Stay

Camping The nearest camp site used to be *Autocamp Trstenik* (☎ 521 971), 5km east of the city centre near the beach, but it has been closed for several years. Call to find out if it has reopened. See Trogir for more reliable camping alternatives.

Private Rooms In the summer, you may be met at the bus station by women offering zimmer. Otherwise, you'll need to head for the Turistički biro (☎/fax 342 142), Obala hrvatskog narodnog preporoda 12. Prices begin at 130/158KN for a single/double, plus a 30% surcharge for stays less than four nights.

Hotels The hotel situation in Split is slowly improving after years of housing refugees and international peacekeepers. The 32-room *Slavija* (☎ 47 053), Buvinova 3, has the cheapest rooms at 170/220KN a single/double without bath and 211/260KN with bath. You could also try the *Park Hotel* (☎ 515 411; fax 591 247), Šetalište Bačvice 15, for a resort experience near the beach and to pay 390/500KN for a single/double. The mid-range *Zenta* (☎ 357 229), Ivana Zajca 2, is farther east than the Park Hotel. Rooms cost 250/360KN a single/double.

Places to Eat

The best pizza in town is served at *Galija* on Tončićeva (daily until 11 pm), where the pies start at 22KN, but *Pizzeria Bakra*, Radovanova 2, off ulica Sv Petra Starog and just down from the vegetable market, is not bad either. The vegetarian salad bar at *Ponoćno Sunce*, Teutina 15, is an excellent value at 30KN. They also serve pasta and grilled meat. The cheapest place in town is *Restaurant Index*, a self-service student eatery at Svačićeva 8. You can get a plate of meat and cabbage for 19KN. Vegetarians should avoid this place.

The spiffy *Burek Bar*, Domaldova 13, just down from the main post office, serves a good breakfast or lunch of burek and yoghurt

for about 12KN. The vast *supermarket/delicatessen* at Svačićeva 1 has a wide selection of meat and cheese for sandwiches and nearly everything else you might want for a picnic. You can sit around the fountain and eat your goodies.

Entertainment

In summer everyone starts the evening at one of the cafés along Obala hrvatskog narodnog preporoda, Ujevićeva Poljana or around the cathedral before heading to a disco. *Night Café* is popular. You'll find it in the Koteks shopping centre, a huge white complex a 10-minute walk east of the old town beyond the Maritime Museum. It is the largest of its kind in Dalmatia and includes a supermarket, department store, boutiques, a couple of restaurants, the trendy *Picasso* bar, banks, post office, two bowling alleys and sports centre.

During winter, opera and ballet are presented at the *Croatian National Theatre* on Trg Gaje Bulata. The best seats are about 60KN and tickets for the same night are usually available. Erected in 1891, the theatre was fully restored in 1979 in the original style; it's worth attending a performance for the architecture alone.

Getting There & Away

Air Croatia Airlines operates one-hour flights to/from Zagreb up to four times daily (568KN in peak season, 50% cheaper in the off season).

Bus Advance bus tickets with seat reservations are recommended. There are buses from the main bus station beside the harbour to Zadar (158km, 26 daily), Zagreb (478km, 26 daily), Rijeka (404km, 14 daily), Ljubljana (532km, one daily), Pula (514km, four daily) and Dubrovnik (235km, 12 daily, 70KN). There are seven daily buses from Split to Međugorje (156km), 11 to Mostar (179km) and six to Sarajevo (271km).

Bus No 37 to Solin, Split airport and Trogir leaves from a local bus station on Domovinskog, 1km north-east of the city centre (see the Split map).

Croatia Express (☎ 342 645), near the bus station, has buses to many German cities, including Munich (912km, daily, 378KN) and Berlin (Saturday and Sunday, 738KN).

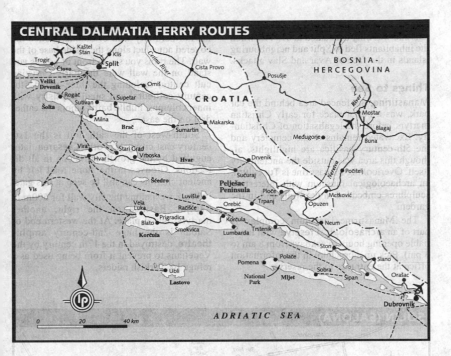

CENTRAL DALMATIA FERRY ROUTES

Agencija Touring (☎ 361 797) at the bus station also has many buses to Germany and a weekly bus to Amsterdam (810KN).

Train There are three or four trains daily between Split and Zagreb (nine hours, 91KN), and two trains daily between Split and Šibenik (74km, 25KN).

Boat Jadrolinija (☎ 355 399), in the large ferry terminal opposite the bus station, handles services to Hvar Island, which operate three or four times a week year-round but the local ferry is cheaper (23KN) and calls at Vela Luka on Korčula Island (25KN) daily.

For information on connections to Italy see the Getting There & Away section at the beginning of this chapter and get the schedule and tickets from Jadroagent in the ferry terminal (open daily from 8 am to 1.30 pm and 5 to 8 pm in the off season; it doesn't close in summer).

Getting Around

The bus to Split airport (20KN) leaves from Obala Lazareta 3, a five-minute walk from the train station. This bus leaves 90 minutes before flight times. You can also get there on bus No 37, as described in Getting There & Away (two-zone ticket).

You can buy a 7KN ticket from a kiosk which is good for two trips but if you buy a ticket from the driver you pay 5KN for only one trip. Validate the ticket once aboard, one end at a time for a two-trip ticket.

SOLIN

The ruins of the ancient city of Solin (Roman: Salona), among the vineyards at the foot of mountains 5km north-east of Split, are about the most interesting archaeological site in Croatia. Today surrounded by noisy highways and industry, Salona was the capital of the Roman province of Dalmatia from the time Julius Caesar elevated it to the status of colony. Salona held out against the barbarians and was only evacuated in 614 AD when the inhabitants fled to Split and neighbouring islands in the face of Avar and Slav attacks.

Things to See

Manastirine, the fenced area behind the car park, was a burial place for early Christian martyrs before the legalisation of Christianity. Excavated remains of the cemetery and the 5th-century basilica are highlights, although this area was outside the ancient city itself. Overlooking Manastirine is **Tusculum**, an archaeological museum with interesting sculptures embedded in the walls and in the garden.

The Manastirine-Tusculum complex is part of an **archaeological reserve** with unreliable opening hours (weekdays from 8 am to 3 pm). Pick up a brochure in the information office at the entrance to the reserve.

A path bordered by cypresses runs south to the northern **city wall** of Salona. Notice the covered aqueduct along the inside base of the wall. The ruins you see in front of you as you stand on the wall were the Early-Christian cult centre, including the three-aisled 5th-century **cathedral** and small **baptistry** with inner columns. **Public baths** adjoin the cathedral on the east.

South-west of the cathedral is the 1st-century east city gate, **Porta Caesarea**, later engulfed by the growth of Salona in all directions. Grooves in the stone road left by ancient chariots can still be seen at this gate.

Walk west along the city wall for 500m to **Kapljuc Basilica** on the right, another martyrs' burial place. At the western end of Salona is the huge 2nd-century **amphitheatre**, destroyed in the 17th century by the Venetians to prevent it from being used as a refuge by Turkish raiders.

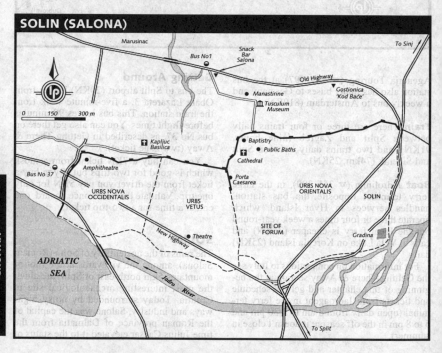

SOLIN (SALONA)

Getting There & Away

The ruins are easily accessible on Split city bus No 1 direct to Salona every half-hour from opposite Trg Gaje Bulata.

From the amphitheatre at Solin it's easy to continue to Trogir by catching a westbound bus No 37 from the nearby stop on the adjacent new highway. If, on the other hand, you want to return to Split, you can use the underpass to cross the highway and catch an eastbound bus No 37 (buy a four-zone ticket in Split if you plan to do this).

HVAR ISLAND
☎ 021

Called the 'Croatian Madeira', Hvar is said to receive more sunshine than anywhere else in the country, 2724 hours each year. Yet the island is luxuriantly green, with brilliant patches of lavender, rosemary and heather. The fine weather is so reliable that hotels give a discount on cloudy days and a free stay if you ever see snow.

Hvar Town

Medieval Hvar lies between protective pine-covered slopes and the azure Adriatic, its Gothic palaces hidden among narrow backstreets below the 13th-century city walls. A long seaside promenade winds along the indented coast dotted with small, rocky beaches. The traffic-free marble avenues of Hvar have an air of Venice; under Venetian rule that Hvar grew rich exporting wine, figs and fish.

Orientation & Information
The big Jadrolinija ferries drop you off in the centre of old Hvar. The barge from Split calls at Stari Grad, 20km east.

The tourist office (☎ 741 059) is in the arsenal building on the corner of trg Sv Stjepana.

The Atlas travel agency (☎ 741 670) facing the harbour, represents American Express. Public telephones are in the post office (open Monday to Friday from 7 am to 8 pm and Saturday from 7 am to 5 pm) on the waterfront. A curious feature of Hvar is its lack of street names. You may stumble across a faded name on a plaque every so often but, in a small town where everyone knows everyone, street names seem superfluous to the residents.

The attendant at the public toilets beside the market adjoining the bus station holds luggage for 6KN apiece, but the toilets are only open during market hours, so check the closing time carefully.

Things to See
The full flavour of medieval Hvar is best savoured on the backstreets of the old town. At each end of Hvar is a monastery with a prominent tower. The **Dominican monastery** at the head of the bay was destroyed by Turks in the 16th century and the local **archaeological museum** is now housed among the ruins. If the museum is closed (as it usually is), you'll still get a good view of the ruins from the road just above, which leads up to a stone cross on a hill top offering a picture-postcard view of Hvar.

At the south-eastern end of Hvar is the 15th-century Renaissance **Franciscan monastery**, with a fine collection of Venetian paintings in the church and adjacent museum, including *The Last Supper* by Matteo Ingoli.

Smack in the middle of Hvar is the imposing Gothic **arsenal**, its great arch visible from afar. The local commune's war galley was once kept here. Upstairs off the arsenal terrace is Hvar's prize, the first **municipal theatre** in Europe (1612), which was rebuilt in the 19th century. Try to get inside to appreciate its delightful human proportions.

On the hill top high above Hvar town is a **Venetian fortress** (1551), well worth the climb for the sweeping panoramic views. Inside is a tiny collection of ancient amphoras recovered from the sea bed. The fort was built to defend Hvar from the Turks, who sacked the town in 1539 and 1571.

The best beach in Hvar is in front of the Hotel Amphora, around the western corner of the cove, but most people take a launch to the naturist islands of Jerolim and Stipanska, just offshore.

Places to Stay
A recent fire on the northern part of the island destroyed the only camp site convenient to Hvar town but there are frequent buses to Jelsa, where you can pitch a tent at *Grebišće* (☎ 761 191) or *Mina* (☎ 761 227).

For private accommodation, try *Mengola Travel* (☎/fax 21 450; mengola-hvar@ st.tel.hr), a right-hand turn from Sv Stjepana along the harbour, or *Pelegrini* (☎/fax 742 250), next to where the Jadrolinija ferries tie up. Expect to pay 100/158KN a single/ double, with a 30% surcharge for stays less than three nights. Outside of the peak season (last week in July through August), you can negotiate a much better price.

The cheapest hotels are the *Dalmacija* (☎/fax 741 120) and the *Delfin* (☎/fax 741 168) on either side of the harbour and charging 270/460KN a single/double with a 20% surcharge for a stay less than four nights. Both hotels open in mid-June. The *Slavija* (☎ 741 820; fax 741 147) is open all year and charges only about 10KN more per person.

Places to Eat The pizzerias along the harbour offer the most predictable but inexpensive eating. For good quality fish, pasta and grilled meat, try *Bounty*, next to the Mengola agency, *Hannibal* on the southern side of trg Sv Stjepana and *Paradies Garden* up some stairs on the northern side of the cathedral. Expect to pay about 45 to 65KN for a meal.

The *grocery store* on Trg Sv Stjepana is your best alternative to a restaurant, and there's a nice park in front of the harbour just made for picnics.

Entertainment Hvar has a lively nightlife when the tourist season is in full swing. On summer evenings there's live music on the terrace of the *Hotel Slavija*, just as you would expect to see in Venice. The disco *Veneranda*, above the Hotel Delfin, provides a reliably good time if you like techno. Otherwise, *Max*, a club outside of town is a good bet; there may be shuttle buses operating between the town and the club.

Getting There & Away The Jadrolinija ferries between Rijeka and Dubrovnik call at Hvar three or four times a week all year, stopping in Hvar Town in winter and Stari Grad in summer before continuing to Korčula. The Jadrolinija agency (☎ 741 132) beside the landing sells tickets.

The local ferry from Split calls at Stari Grad (23KN) three times daily and connects

Hvar town with Vela Luka on Korčula Island in the afternoon.

It's possible to visit Hvar on a (hectic) day trip from Split by catching the morning Jadrolinija ferry to Stari Grad, a bus to Hvar town, then the last ferry from Stari Grad directly back to Split.

Stari Grad

Stari Grad (Old Town), 20km east of Hvar and on the island's north coast, is quite picturesque, though somewhat of a disappointment after Hvar. Stari Grad was the capital of the island until 1331 when the Venetians shifted the administration to Hvar. This explains the extensive medieval quarter still at Stari Grad. The palace of the Croat poet Petar Hektorović (1487-1572) is worth a visit to see the fish pond and garden.

Places to Stay Just off the harbour and in the centre of Stari Grad is *Kamp Jurjevac* (☎ 765 555), open from June to early September. There's no sign, so ask for directions.

Private-room proprietors are less likely to meet the buses and ferries here than in Hvar town and at last report there was no agency renting rooms, so you'll just have to ask around.

Getting There & Away Besides the local ferries that run from Split to Stari Grad, there's a weekly Jadrolinija car-ferry from Stari Grad to Ancona, Italy (244KN), stopping at Split. Buses meet all ferries that dock at Stari Grad.

There are five buses daily from Stari Grad to Hvar town in the summer season (13KN) but services are reduced on Sunday and in the off season.

KORČULA ISLAND
☎ 020

Korčula is the largest island in an archipelago of 48 islets. Rich in vineyards and olive trees, the island was named Korkyra Melaina (Black Korčula) by the original Greek settlers because of its dense woods and plant life. The southern coast is dotted with quiet coves and small beaches linked to the interior by winding, scenic roads.

Korčula Town

The town of Korčula (Italian: Curzola), at the north-eastern tip of the island, hugs a small, hilly peninsula jutting into the Adriatic Sea. With its round defensive towers and compact cluster of red-roofed houses, Korčula is a typical medieval Dalmatian town. In contrast to Turkish cities like Mostar and Sarajevo, Korčula was controlled by Venice from the 14th to the 18th century. Venetian rule left its mark, especially on Cathedral Square. It's a peaceful little place (population 3000), with grey-stone houses nestling between the deep-green hills and gunmetal-blue sea. There are rustling palms all around.

There's lots to see and do, so it's worth planning a relaxed four-night stay to avoid the 30% surcharge on private rooms. Day trips are possible to Lumbarda, Vela Luka, Orebić on the Pelješac Peninsula and the islands of Badija and Mljet.

Orientation The big Jadrolinija car-ferry drops you off below the walls of the old town of Korčula. The passenger launch from Orebić is also convenient, terminating at the old harbour, but the barge from Orebić goes to Bon Repos in Dominče, several kilometres south-east of the centre.

Information The Turist Biro (☎ 711 067) is near the old town. Atlas travel agency (☎ 711 231) is the local American Express representative and there's a Jadrolinija office (☎ 711 101) about 25m up from the harbour.

The post office (with public telephones) is rather hidden next to the stairs up to the old town.

There's no left-luggage office at the bus station.

Things to See Other than following the circuit of the former city walls or walking along the shore, sightseeing in Korčula centres on Cathedral Square. The Gothic **Cathedral of St Mark** features two paintings by Tintoretto (*Three Saints* on the altar and *Annunciation* to one side).

The **treasury** in the 14th-century Abbey Palace next to the cathedral is worth a look; even better is the **town museum** in the 15th-century Gabriellis Palace opposite. The exhibits of Greek pottery, Roman ceramics and home furnishings have explanations in English. It's said that Marco Polo was born in Korčula in 1254; for a small fee, you can climb the tower of what is believed to have been his house. There's also an **icon museum** in the old town. It isn't much of a museum, but visitors are let into the beautiful old **Church of All Saints**.

In the high summer season, water taxis at the Jadrolinija port collect passengers to visit various points on the island as well as **Badija Island**, which features a 15th-century Franciscan monastery (now a D-category hotel) and a naturist beach.

Organised Tours Marko Polo Tours (☎ 715 400; fax 715 800; marko-polo-tours@ du.tel.hr) and Atlas travel agency offer tours to Mljet Island (122KN) and guided tours of Korčula Island (105KN), as well as a half-day boat trip around the surrounding islands (74KN).

Places to Stay Korčula offers quite a range of accommodation, though prices are high in July and August.

Camping The *Autocamp Kalac* (☎ 711 182) is behind Hotel Bon Repos, near a beach, and charges 21KN a person and 14KN a tent.

Private Rooms The Turist Biro (☎ 711 067) and Marko Polo Tours (facing the East Harbour) arrange private rooms, charging 72/108KN for a single/double, except in peak season, when prices increase from 20 to 50%, depending on the period. There are few category II rooms and there is usually a 30% surcharge for stays less than four nights. You may get a better deal from the private operators who meet the boats, but check with the agencies first, since they're only steps from the harbour.

Hotels The B-category *Hotel Bon Repos* (☎ 711 102), overlooking a small beach outside town, and *Hotel Park* (☎ 726 004) in town have the same rates: 280/421KN a single/double with bath and breakfast, except in July and August when prices increase about 22%. You could try the D-category *Badija* (☎ 711 115; 711 746) on Badija Island which has a pool, beach, handball courts and other sports facilities. Singles/doubles are 162/281KN with full board.

Places to Eat Just around the corner from Marco Polo's house, *Adio Mare* has a charming maritime décor and a variety of fresh fish. Restaurant-grill *Planjak*, between the supermarket and the Jadrolinija office in town, is popular with a local crowd which appreciates the fresh, Dalmatian dishes as much as the low prices. A 20-minute walk outside town on the road to Lumbarda takes you to another local favourite, *Gastrionica Hajuk*, for delicious, inexpensive food. The shady terrace at *Hotel Korčula* is a nice place for a coffee.

Entertainment In July and August, there's moreška sword dancing by the old town gate every Thursday at 8.30 pm. Tickets (50KN) can be purchased from the Turist Biro or Marko Polo Tours.

Getting There & Away Connections to Korčula are good. There's a daily bus service from Dubrovnik to Korčula (113km, 42KN) as well as a daily bus to Zagreb (150KN) and two buses a week to Sarajevo (145KN).

Six daily buses link Korčula town to Vela Luka at the west end of the island (1½ hours, 15KN). Buses to Lumbarda run about hourly in the morning (7km, 5KN). No bus runs to Lumbarda on Sunday and service to Vela Luka are sharply reduced on weekends.

Boat Getting to Korčula is easy, as all the Jadrolinija ferries between Split and Dubrovnik tie up at the landing next to the old town. If it's too windy in the east harbour, this ferry moors at the west harbour in front of Hotel Korčula. Once a week from June to September Jadrolinija runs a car-ferry between Korčula and Ancona, Italy (16 hours, 249KN) stopping at Split and Vis. Buy car-ferry tickets at the Jadrolinija office (☎ 715 410).

From Orebić, look for the passenger launch (15 minutes, four times daily year-round except weekends, 8KN one way) which will drop you off at the Hotel Korčula right below the old town's towers. This is best if you're looking for a private room, but if you want to camp or stay at the hotel take the car-ferry to Bon Repos in Dominče

(6.80KN, 15 minutes). The car-ferry is the only alternative on weekends. On Saturday, it connects with the bus from Lumbarda but on Sunday there is only one bus in the morning from Korčula to Orebić and one late afternoon bus returning.

Lumbarda
Just 15 minutes from Korčula town by bus, Lumbarda is a picturesque small settlement, known for its wine, near the south-eastern end of Korčula Island. A good ocean beach (Plaza Pržina) is on the other side of the vineyards beyond the supermarket.

The *Bebić* pension (☎ 712 183) and restaurant has a breathtaking view over the coast and serves good food. A double room or apartment is 200KN with bath and breakfast or 234KN per person with half-board.

The Turist Biro (☎/fax 712 023) arranges private accommodation and there are several small, inexpensive camp sites up the hill from the bus stop.

Vela Luka
Vela Luka, at the western end of Korčula, is the centre of the island's fishing industry because of its large sheltered harbour. There isn't a lot to see and there's no real beaches, so if you're arriving by ferry from Split or Hvar you might jump straight on the waiting bus to Korčula town and look for a room there.

Places to Stay Six kilometres north-west of Vela Luka (no bus service) is *Camping Mindel* (☎ 812 494). The Turist Biro (☎ 812 042), open in summer only, arranges private rooms. It is beside the Jadran Hotel (☎ 812 036) on the waterfront 100m from the ferry landing.

If the Turist Biro is closed your next best bet is the *Pansion u Domaćinstva Barčot* (☎ 812 014), directly behind the Jadran Hotel. This attractive 24-room guesthouse is open all year and its prices are just a little above what you'd pay for private rooms. Some rooms on the 3rd floor have balconies.

Getting There & Away Ferries from Split land at the western end of the harbour and buses to Korčula town meet all arrivals. There's at least one boat daily from Vela Luka to Split (25KN), calling at Hvar five times a week throughout the year. It leaves Vela Luka very early in the morning, so you might want to spend the night if you'll be catching it, although a bus from Korčula does connect with it.

OREBIĆ

Orebić, on the south coast of the Pelješac Peninsula between Korčula and Ploče, offers better beaches than those found at Korčula, 2.5km across the water. The easy access by ferry from Korčula makes it the perfect place to go for the day and a good alternative place to stay.

Things to See & Do

Orebić is great for hiking so pick up a map of the hiking trails from the tourist office. A trail leads up from Hotel Bellevue to an old **Franciscan monastery** on a ridge high above the sea. A more daring climb is to the top of **Mt Ilija** (961m), the bare grey massif that hangs above Orebić. Your reward is a sweeping view of the entire coast.

Places to Stay

The helpful Turist Biro (☎ 713 014; open April to September), next to the post office near the ferry landings, rents out private rooms (50/137KN a single/double) and can provide a town map. If the office is closed, try Orebić Tours (☎ 713 367), Jelačića 84a, or just walk around looking for 'sobe' signs – you'll soon find something.

The best beach in Orebić is Trstenica cove, a 15-minute walk east along the shore from the port. The *Hauptstrand* (☎ 713 399) and *Trstenica* (☎ 713 348) camping grounds overlook the long, sandy beach. The latter rents out rooms with a shared bathroom for 72KN per person, not including breakfast.

Getting There & Away

In Orebić the ferry terminal and the bus station are adjacent. If you're coming from the coast, there are four daily ferries (six in summer) from Ploče to Trpanj which connects with a bus to Orebić. Korčula buses to Dubrovnik, Zagreb and Sarajevo stop at Orebić. See Korčula for additional bus and ferry information.

MLJET ISLAND

Created in 1960, **Mljet National Park** occupies the western third of the green island of Mljet (Italian: Meleda), between Korčula and Dubrovnik. The park centres around two saltwater lakes surrounded by pine-clad slopes. Most people visit on day trips from Korčula but it's possible to come by regular ferry from Dubrovnik, stay a few days and go hiking, biking and boating.

Orientation

Tour boats from Korčula arrive at Pomena wharf at Mljet's western end, where a good map of the island is posted. Jadrolinija ferries arrive at Sobra on the eastern end and are met by a local bus for the 1½-hour ride to Pomena.

Things to See & Do

From Pomena it's a 15-minute walk to a jetty on **Veliko jezero**, the larger of the two lakes. Here the groups board a boat to a small lake islet and are served lunch at a 12th-century **Benedictine monastery**, now a restaurant.

Those who don't want to spend the rest of the afternoon swimming and sunbathing on the monastery island can catch an early boat back to the main island and spend a couple of hours walking along the lakeshore before catching the late-afternoon excursion boat back to Korčula. There's a small landing opposite the monastery where the boat operator drops off passengers upon request. It's not possible to walk right around the larger lake as there's no bridge over the channel connecting the lakes to the sea.

Mljet is good for cycling; the hotels rent out bicycles (60KN a half-day).

Organised Tours

The Atlas travel agency (☎ 711 060) in Korčula offers day trips to Mljet Island twice a week from May to mid-October. The tour lasts from 8.30 am to 6 pm (122KN per person, including the 48KN park entry fee). The boat trip from Korčula to Pomena takes at least two hours, less by hydrofoil. Lunch isn't included in the tour price and meals at the hotels on Mljet are very expensive, so it's best to bring a picnic lunch.

Places to Stay

There's no camping in the national park but there's a small camping ground (☎ 745 071) in Ropa, about a kilometre from the park, open from June to September. The tourist office in Polace (☎ 744 086) arranges private accommodation at 148KN a double room in peak season but it is essential to make arrangements before arrival. Don't count on 'sobe' signs. The only hotel is the luxury *Odisej* in Pomena with rooms at 361KN per person in July and August with half-board, 50% less in the off season.

Getting There & Away

A regular ferry (daily except Sunday; 21KN) leaves from Dubrovnik at 2 pm and goes to Sobra. The return ferry leaves from Sobra at 5:30 am, which means a very early morning departure by local bus from the national park. There are additional ferries in both directions in July and August. The big Jadrolinija coastal ferries also stop at Mljet twice a week in summer and once a week during the rest of the year.

Dubrovnik

☎ 020

Founded 1300 years ago by refugees from Epidaurus in Greece, medieval Dubrovnik (Ragusa until 1918) was the most important independent city-state on the Adriatic after Venice. Until the Napoleonic invasion of 1806, it remained an independent republic of merchants and sailors.

Like Venice, Dubrovnik's fortunes now depend upon its tourist industry. Stari Grad, the perfectly preserved old town, is unique because of its marble-paved squares, steep cobbled streets, tall houses, convents, churches, palaces, fountains and museums, all cut from the same light-coloured stone. The intact city walls keep motorists at bay and the southerly position between Split and Albania makes for an agreeable climate and lush vegetation.

For those who watched the shelling of Dubrovnik on TV in late 1991, here's a bit of good news: the city is still there, as beautiful as ever, with few visible reminders of its recent trauma. Some buildings on the back

streets are still damaged but you won't see it as the shutters will be down and the windows closed. The eight-month siege by the federal army from October 1991 to May 1992 tore through the town's distinctive honey-coloured clay roofs, however. Replacing them with matching tiles was extremely problematic and you'll notice a patchwork of colours as you walk around the city walls. The most severe blow to Dubrovnik was in the catastrophic decline of tourism which left its residents feeling abandoned and apprehensive. The city has recently begun to climb back and in July and August the streets are again crowded with visitors. Whatever the time of year the magical interlay of light and stone is as enchanting as ever. Don't miss it.

Orientation

The Jadrolinija ferry terminal and the bus station are a few hundred metres apart at Gruž, several kilometres north-west of the old town. The camping ground and most of the luxury tourist hotels are on the leafy Lapad Peninsula, west of the bus station.

Information

Tourist Offices The tourist office (☎ 426 354) is on Placa, opposite the Franciscan monastery in the old town. The American Express representative is the Atlas travel agency (☎ 442 222; 411 100) on Brsalje 17, outside Pile gate next to the old town; but mail is held at another office (☎ 432 093) across from Fort Revelin at Frana Supila 2. There's also an office in the harbour at Gruz (☎ 418 001) and another in Lapad at Lisinskog 5 (☎ 442 555).

Post & Communications The main post office is at Ante Starčevića 2, a block from Pile Gate (open Monday to Saturday from 7 am to 8 pm and Sunday from 8 am to 2 pm). Place international telephone calls here. There's another post office-telephone centre at Lapad near Hotel Kompas.

Left Luggage Left-luggage at the bus station is open from 4.30 am to 10 pm. The bus service into town is fairly frequent.

Things to See

You'll probably begin your visit at the city bus stop outside **Pile Gate**. As you enter the city, Placa, Dubrovnik's wonderful pedestrian promenade, extends before you all the way to the clock tower at the other end of town. Just inside Pile Gate is the huge **Onofrio Fountain** (1438) and the **Franciscan monastery**, with the third-oldest functioning pharmacy (since 1391) in Europe by the cloister.

In front of the clock tower at the eastern end of Placa, you'll find the **Orlando Column** (1419) – a favourite meeting place. On opposite sides of Orlando are the 16th-century **Sponza Palace** (now the State Archives) and **St Blaise's Church**, a lovely Italian baroque building.

At the end of the broad street beside St Blaise, Pred Dvorom, is the baroque **cathedral** and, between the two churches, the Gothic **Rector's Palace** (1441), now a museum with furnished rooms, baroque

paintings and historical exhibits. The elected rector was not permitted to leave the building during his one-month term without the permission of the senate. The narrow street opposite this palace opens onto Gundulićeva Poljana, a bustling morning market. Up the stairway at the southern end of the square is the imposing **Jesuit monastery** (1725).

Return to the cathedral and take the narrow street in front to the **aquarium** in Fort St John. Through an obscure entrance off the city walls, above the aquarium, is the **Maritime Museum**. If you're 'museumed out' you can safely give these two a miss.

By this time you'll be ready for a leisurely walk around the **city walls**. Built between the 13th and 16th centuries and still intact, these powerful walls are the finest in the world and Dubrovnik's main claim to fame. They enclose the entire city in a curtain of stone over 2km long and up to 25m high, with two round towers, 14 square towers, two

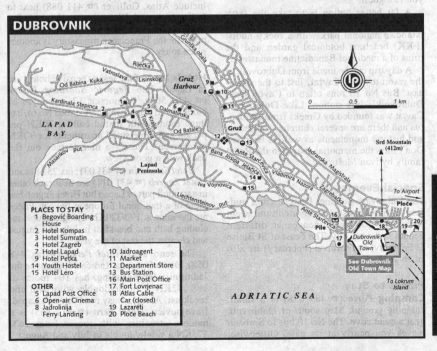

DUBROVNIK

PLACES TO STAY
1 Begović Boarding House
2 Hotel Kompas
3 Hotel Sumratin
4 Hotel Zagreb
7 Hotel Lapad
9 Hotel Petka
14 Youth Hostel
15 Hotel Lero

OTHER
5 Lapad Post Office
6 Open-air Cinema
8 Jadrolinija Ferry Landing

10 Jadroagent
11 Market
12 Department Store
13 Bus Station
16 Main Post Office
17 Fort Lovrjenac
18 Atlas Cable Car (closed)
19 Lazareti
20 Ploče Beach

Gruž Harbour

Grunička obala

Rječka

Vatroslava

Lisinskog

Od Babina Kuka

Kardinala Stepinca

Dalmatinska

Kralja Tomislava

LAPAD BAY

Od Batale

Gruž

Mazarikov put

Lapad Peninsula

Bana Josipa Jelačića

Ante Starčevića

Vladimira Nazora

Iva Vojnovića

Jadranska Magistrala

Zagrebačka

Liechtensteinov put

Ante Starčevića

Srd Mountain (412m)

To Airport

Ploče

Pile

0   0.5   1 km

Dubrovnik Old Town

See Dubrovnik Old Town Map

To Lokrum Island

ADRIATIC SEA

CROATIA

corner fortifications and a large fortress. The views over the town and sea are great – this walk could be the high point of your visit.

Whichever way you go, you'll notice the large **Dominican monastery** in the north-eastern corner of the city. Of all Dubrovnik's religious museums, the one in the Dominican monastery is the largest and most worth paying to enter.

Dubrovnik has many other sights, such as the unmarked **synagogue** at ulica Žudioska 5 near the clock tower (open from 10 am to noon on Friday and from 5 to 7 pm on Tuesday). The uppermost streets of the old town below the north and south walls are pleasant to wander along.

Beaches   The closest beach, Ploče, to the old city is just beyond the 17th-century **Lazareti** (former quarantine station) outside Ploče Gate. There are also 'managed' hotel beaches on the **Lapad Peninsula**, but you could be charged admission unless they think you're a guest.

A far better option is to take the ferry which shuttles hourly in summer to **Lokrum Island**, a national park with a rocky nudist (FKK) beach, a botanical garden and the ruins of a medieval Benedictine monastery.

A day trip can be made from Dubrovnik to the resort town of **Cavtat**, just to the southeast. Bus No 10 runs often to Cavtat from Dubrovnik's bus station. Like Dubrovnik, Cavtat was founded by Greeks from Epidaurus and there are several churches, museums and historic monuments as well as beaches. Don't miss the memorial chapel to the Račič family by Ivan Meštrović.

Special Events

The Dubrovnik Summer Festival from mid-July to mid-August is a major cultural event with over 100 performances at different venues in the old city. The Feast of St Blaise (3 February) and carnival (February) are also celebrated.

Places to Stay

Camping   *Porto* (☎ 487 078) is a small, camping ground, 8km south of Dubrovnik near a quiet cove. The No 10 bus to Srebeno leaves you nearly at its gate. Otherwise,

there's the much larger *Zaton* (☎ 280 280), about 15km west of the city.

Hostels   The *YHA hostel*, (☎ 423 241; fax 412 592) up Vinka Sagrestana from Bana Josipa Jelačića 17, is newly opened and completely refurbished. A bed in a room for four with breakfast is 75KN. Lunch and dinner can be arranged but the hostel is on one of the liveliest streets in Lapad, full of bars, cafés and pizzerias.

Private Rooms   The easiest way to find a place to stay is to accept the offer of a sobe from one of the women who may approach you at the ferry terminal. Their prices are lower than those charged by the room-finding agencies and, unless you arrive in July or August, they are open to bargaining.

Officially, there are no single rooms but in the off season you may be able to knock 20% off the price of a double room, which begins at 108KN in May, June and September. Agencies that handle private accommodation include Atlas, Gulliver (☎ 411 088) next to Jadroagent, and Globtour (☎ 428 144; fax 426 322) on Placa. The tourist office on Placa opposite the Franciscan monastery is another place to try.

Hotels   Most of the less expensive hotels are in Lapad. The *Begović Boarding House* (☎ 428 563), Primorska 17, a couple of blocks from Lapad post office (bus No 6), has three rooms with shared bath at 70KN per person and three small apartments for 90KN per person. There's a nice terrace out the back with a good view.

Hotel Sumratin (☎ 431 031; fax 23 581) and *Hotel Zagreb* (☎ 431 011) are near each other in a tranquil part of Lapad but Hotel Zagreb has more of a traditional European flavour. Prices are the same at 190/320KN a single/double including bath and breakfast in July and August and cheaper the rest of the year.

The renovated *Hotel Petka* (☎/fax 418 058), Obala Stjepana Radića 38, opposite the Jadrolinija ferry landing, has 104 rooms at 198/342KN a single/double with bath and breakfast. Along a busy road through Lapad, Iravojnovica, *Hotel Lero* (☎ 411 455) is a modern structure with rooms from 263/373KN a single/double in July and August.

DUBROVNIK - OLD TOWN

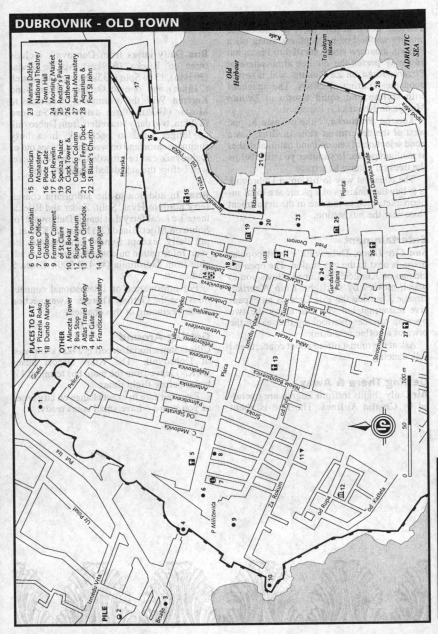

23 Marina Držića
   National Theatre/
   Town Hall
24 Morning Market
25 Rector's Palace
26 Cathedral
27 Jesuit Monastery
28 Aquarium &
   Fort St John

15 Dominican
   Monastery
16 Ploče Gate
17 Fort Revelin
19 Sponza Palace
20 Clock Tower &
   Orlando Column
21 Lokrum Ferry Dock
22 St Blaise's Church

6 Onofrio Fountain
7 Tourist Office
8 Globtour
9 Former Convent
   of St Claire
10 Fort Bokar
12 Rupe Museum
13 Serbian Orthodox
   Church
14 Synagogue

PLACES TO EAT
11 Pizzeria Roko
18 Dundo Maroje

OTHER
1 Minčeta Tower
2 Bus Stop
3 Atlas Travel Agency
4 Pile Gate
5 Franciscan Monastery

ADRIATIC
SEA

To Lokrum
Island

Old
Harbour

PILE

CROATIA

Places to Eat

You can get a decent meal at one of the touristy seafood or pasta places along ulica Prijeko, a narrow street parallel to Placa, but you may prefer the quieter atmosphere at *Pizzeria Roko* on Za Rokum, which serves good pies starting at 28KN. The spaghetti with shrimp and squid risotto at *Dundo Maroje* on Kovačka is excellent.

Konoba Primorka, Nikole Tesle 8, just west of the department store in Gruž, has a good selection of seafood and national dishes at medium prices. In summer you dine below the trees on a lamp-lit terrace.

The cheapest way to fill up in Dubrovnik is to buy the makings of a picnic at a local supermarket, such as the one in the department store near the bus station.

Entertainment

Sun City Disco, Dubrovnik's most popular disco, is next to the bus station. The open-air cinema on Kumičića in Lapad allows you to watch movies by starlight. *Club Nautika*, Brsalje 3 outside the Pile Gate, is an expensive restaurant but you can enjoy the two open-air terraces overlooking the sea for the price of a coffee or a drink.

Ask at the tourist office about concerts and folk dancing.

Getting There & Away

Air Daily flights to/from Zagreb are operated by Croatia Airlines. The fare is about 620KN one way in the summer but much less in the off season.

Bus Daily buses from Dubrovnik include three to Rijeka (639km), six to Zadar (393km), 13 to Split (235km), eight to Zagreb (713km) and one to Orebić (113km) and Korčula. With the resumption of services to Mostar (143km, three daily) and Sarajevo (278km, two daily) travellers from Dubrovnik no longer need to backtrack. In a busy summer season and on weekends, buses out of Dubrovnik can be crowded, so book a ticket well before the scheduled departure time.

Boat In addition to the Jadrolinija coastal ferry north to Hvar, Split, Zadar and Rijeka, there's a local ferry that leaves Dubrovnik for Sobra on Mljet Island (2½ hours, 21KN) at 2 pm daily, except Sunday, throughout the year. Information on domestic ferries is available from Jadrolinija (☎ 418 000), Obala S Radića 40.

For information on international connections see the Getting There & Away section at the beginning of this chapter.

Getting Around

Čilipi international airport is 24km south-east of Dubrovnik. The Atlas airport buses (20KN) leave from the main bus terminal 1½ hours before flight times.

Pay your fare in exact change on city buses as you board – have small coins ready.

Czech Republic

In the middle of Europe lie Bohemia and Moravia that together make up the Czech Republic, a nation on the edge of the Germanic and Slavic worlds. It's one of Europe's most historic countries, full of fairy-tale castles, chateaux, manors and museums. The medieval cores of several dozen towns have been carefully preserved and there's so much to see that you could make repeated visits.

The Czech Republic is doubly inviting for its cultured, friendly people and excellent facilities. The transportation network is equalled only in Western Europe. Ninety per cent of English-speaking visitors limit themselves to Prague but the clever few who escape the hordes and high prices in the capital soon experience just how helpful the Czech people can be. (Almost everything outside Prague is still off the beaten tourist track.)

Facts about the Czech Republic

HISTORY

In antiquity the Bohemian basin was inhabited by the Celtic Boii tribe that gave the region its present name, and was never part of the classical Roman Empire. Germanic tribes conquered the Celts in the 4th century AD, and between the 5th and 10th centuries the West Slavs settled here. From 830 to 907, the Slavic tribes united in the Great Moravian Empire. They adopted Christianity after the arrival of the Thessalonian missionaries Cyril and Methodius in 863, who invented the first Slavic alphabet.

Towards the end of the 9th century, the Czechs seceded from the Great Moravian Empire and formed an independent state. In 995, the Czech lands were united under the native Přemysl dynasty as the principality of Bohemia. The Czech state became a kingdom in the 12th century and reached its peak under Přemysl Otakar II from 1253 to 1278. Many towns were founded at this time.

The Přemysls died out in 1306, and in 1310, John of Luxembourg gained the Bo-

AT A GLANCE

Capital	Prague
Population	10.29 million
Area	78,864 sq km
Official Language	Czech
Currency	1 koruna (Kč) = 100 haleru
GDP	US$115 billion (1996)
Time	GMT/UTC+0100

hemian throne through marriage and annexed the kingdom to the German Empire. His son, Charles IV (depicted on the new 100 Kč banknote), became King of the Germans in 1346 and Holy Roman Emperor in 1355. Inclusion in this medieval empire led to a blossoming of trade and culture. The capital, Prague, was made an archbishopric in 1344 and in 1348 Charles University was founded. These kings were able to keep the feudal nobility in check, but under Wenceslas IV (1378-1419) the strength of the monarchy declined. The church became the largest landowner.

In 1415, the religious reformer Jan Hus,

CZECH REPUBLIC

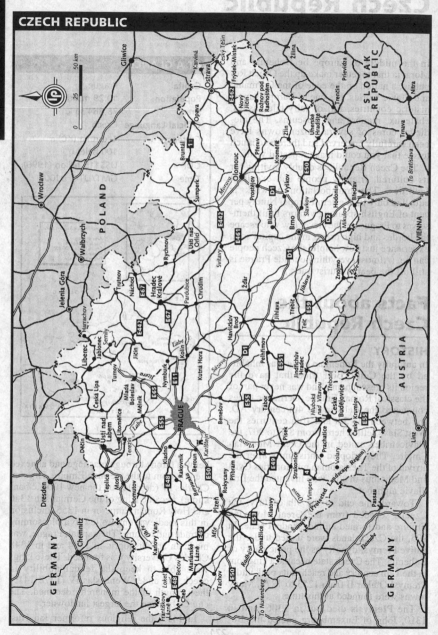

rector of Charles University, was burnt at the stake in Constance. His ideas inspired the nationalistic Hussite movement which swept Bohemia from 1419 to 1434. After the defeat of the Hussites, the Jagiello dynasty occupied the Bohemian throne. Vladislav Jagiello merged the Bohemian and Hungarian states in 1490.

With the death of Ludovic Jagiello at the Battle of Mohács in 1526, the Austrian Habsburg dynasty ascended to the thrones of Bohemia and Hungary. Thus Bohemia, which was strongly affected by the Protestant Reformation, became subject to the Catholic Counter-Reformation backed by the Habsburgs. The Thirty Years' War, which devastated Central Europe from 1618 to 1648, began in Prague, and the defeat of the uprising of the Czech Estates at the Battle of White Mountain in 1620 marked the beginning of a long period of forced re-Catholicisation, Germanisation and oppression.

The Czechs began rediscovering their linguistic and cultural roots in the early 19th century during the so-called National Revival. Despite the defeat of the democratic revolution of 1848, the Industrial Revolution took firm hold here as a middle class emerged.

As a result of WWI, during which Czech and Slovak nationalists strived for a common state, the formation of the Czechoslovak Republic was accomplished on 28 October 1918. The first president was Tomáš Garrigue Masaryk (who appears on the new 5000 Kč banknote), followed in 1935 by Eduard Beneš, who later headed a government-in-exile in London. Three-quarters of the Austro-Hungarian monarchy's industrial potential fell within Czechoslovakia, as did three million Germans.

After annexing Austria in the Anschluss of March 1938, Hitler turned his attention to Czechoslovakia. By the infamous Munich Pact of September 1938, Britain and France surrendered the border regions of Bohemia and Moravia – the Sudetenland – to Nazi Germany, and in March 1939 the Germans occupied the rest of the country (calling it the Protectorate of Bohemia and Moravia). Slovakia became a clero-fascist puppet state.

On 29 May 1942 the acting Nazi Reichs-Protector, Reinhard 'Hangman' Heydrich, was assassinated by Czechoslovaks who had been parachuted in from London for the purpose. As one of the reprisals, the Nazis razed the village of Lidice, 25km north-west of Prague, shot all the males and deported all the females and children to concentration camps. Czechs fought with the Allied forces on all fronts. At the end of WWII West Bohemia was liberated by US troops, while the rest of the country was liberated by the Soviet army. Unlike Germany and Poland which were devastated during WWII, Czechoslovakia was largely undamaged.

Post-WWII

After the liberation of the regional capital of Košice (Slovakia), a National Front was formed, which was covertly controlled by the Czechoslovak Communist Party and fully backed by the Soviets. In April 1945, even before the rest of the country had been freed, a program for national reconstruction was laid out, which was a Communist Party blue print for the takeover of the country. After the Munich sellout, resentment against the west was rife and the strength of the Communist Party grew. In the Constituent National Assembly elections of May 1946, the Communists won 36% of the votes and the Social Democrats 15.6%, together forming a National Front majority. Communist Party chairman Klement Gottwald became prime minister.

A power struggle then developed between the communist and democratic forces. In early 1948, the Social Democrats withdrew from the coalition in protest against the anti-democratic activities of the Communists. The result was that the Communists staged the 'February coup d'état' with the backing of the Soviet Union. The new Communist-led government then revised the constitution and the voting system, and set up the dictatorship of the proletariat. In July, Klement Gottwald replaced Beneš as president.

The whole industrial sector was nationalised and the economic policies nearly bankrupted the country. The 1950s were years of harsh repression when thousands of non-Communists fled the country. Many people were imprisoned, and hundreds were executed or died in labour camps, often for little more than a belief in democracy or religion. A series of Stalinist purges was organised by the Communist Party, during which many people, including top members of the party itself, were executed.

In April 1968, the new first secretary of the Communist Party, Alexander Dubček, introduced liberalising reforms to create 'socialism with a human face'. Censorship ended, political prisoners were released and rapid decentralisation of the economy began. Dubček refused to bow to pressure from Moscow to withdraw the reforms and this led to a political crisis.

On the night of 20 August 1968 the 'Prague Spring' came to an end as Czechoslovakia was occupied by 200,000 Soviet and Warsaw Pact soldiers. The Czechs and Slovaks met the invaders with passive resistance. The 'revisionists' were removed from office and conservative orthodoxy was re-established. One enduring reform of 1968 was the federative system, which established equal Czech and Slovak republics.

In 1969, Dr Gustav Husák replaced Dubček as first secretary, and Dubček was exiled to the Slovak forestry department. In 1975, Husák became president and led Czechoslovakia through two decades of renewed dictatorship. Around 14,000 Communist Party functionaries and 500,000 members who refused to renounce their belief in 'socialism with a human face' were expelled from the party and lost their jobs. Many educated professionals were made street cleaners and manual labourers. Totalitarian rule was re-established and dissidents were routinely imprisoned.

In 1977 the trial of the rock music group The Plastic People of the Universe inspired the formation of the human-rights group Charter 77. (The puritanical communist establishment saw in the nonconformism of the young musicians a threat to the status quo, while those disenchanted with the regime viewed the trial as part of a pervasive assault on human rights.) Made up of a small assortment of Prague intellectuals, including Václav Havel, Charter 77 functioned as an underground opposition throughout the 1980s.

By 1989, Gorbachev's *perestroika* was sending shock waves through the region and the fall of the Berlin Wall on 9 November raised expectations that changes in Czechoslovakia were imminent. On Friday 17 November 1989, an officially sanctioned student march in memory of students executed by the Nazis in 1939 was ruthlessly broken up by police in Prague's Národní třída. Daily demonstrations ensued, and the following Monday 250,000 people gathered in Václavské náměstí (Wenceslas Square) to protest against the Communist government. The protests widened, with a general strike on 27 November 1989, culminating in the resignation of the Communist Party's Politburo. The 'Velvet Revolution' was over.

Civic Forum (Občanské Forum), an umbrella organisation of opponents of the regime formed in the wake of the 17 November violence, was led by playwright-philosopher Václav Havel, Prague's best known 'dissident' and ex-political prisoner. Havel took over as the country's interim president, by popular demand, in the free elections of June 1990, Civic Forum and its counterpart in Slovakia, Society Against Violence, were successful. The Communist Party, however, still won 47 seats in the 300-seat Federal Parliament.

Velvet Divorce

With the strong central authority provided by the Communists gone, old antagonisms between Slovakia and Prague re-emerged. The Federal Parliament tried to stabilise matters by approving a constitutional amendment in December 1990, which gave each of the Czech and Slovak republics full federal status within the Czech and Slovak Federative Republic (ČSFR), as Czechoslovakia was now known. Yet these moves failed to satisfy Slovak nationalists. Meanwhile Civic Forum had split into two factions, the centrist Civic Movement, and the Civic Democratic Party (ODS). In Slovakia several separatist parties emerged.

The ODS instigated a purge of former Communist officials and alleged secret-police informers in 1991, a process known as *lustrace*. But the Communists who committed many crimes against humanity (torture and murder of innocent people) have not been brought to trial.

The June 1992 elections sealed the fate of Czechoslovakia. Václav Klaus' ODS took 48 seats in the 150-seat Federal Parliament, while 24 seats went to the Movement for a Democratic Slovakia (HZDS), a left-leaning Slovak nationalist party led by Vladimír Mečiar.

The incompatibility of Klaus and Mečiar soon became apparent with the former pushing for shock-therapy economic reform while the latter wanted state intervention to save key industries in Slovakia. Mečiar's strident demands for Slovak sovereignty convinced Klaus and his associates that Slovakia had become an obstacle on the road to fast economic reform. Calls from president Havel for a referendum on national unity were rejected by opportunistic politicians on both sides who only wanted to be masters of their own fiefs. In August 1992, Klaus and Mečiar agreed that the Czechoslovak federation would cease to exist at midnight on 31 December 1992. The peaceful 'velvet divorce' was over.

In January 1993, the Czech Parliament elected Václav Havel president of the Czech Republic for a five-year term, and re-elected him by a margin of one vote in 1998. Prime Minister Klaus staked his political future on the success of rapid economic reforms but these were not as far reaching as required and by 1996 the economy was slowing down. Among other major problems were corruption, an ineffective judiciary, and a lack of openness in business, all contributing to restrain foreign investment. In the 1996 elections, ODS won most of the votes but could only form a minority government (two seats short of a majority). ODS found it difficult to run an efficient government but it also lacked the will to make necessary changes. In late 1997, Klaus was forced to resign after a financial scandal involving ODS and a new government, headed by former central bank boss Josef Tošovský, was formed to govern until the June 1998 elections.

At the end of July 1998 president Havel named the new minority government of the Social Democrats (ČSSD) headed by their leader and new prime minister, Miloš Zeman. In order for the Social Democrats to govern, a deal was struck in which the major opposition ODS party provided parliamentary support in exchange for ministerial positions, the axing of some policies and the appoint-

ment of opposition leader and former prime minister Václav Klaus as parliamentary speaker.

GEOGRAPHY & ECOLOGY

The Czech Republic is a landlocked country of 78,864 sq km squeezed between Germany, Austria, Slovakia and Poland. The Bohemian Massif, which is much older than the Carpathian Mountains, forms the broad, rounded ranges of the Czech Republic. Bohemia nestles between the Šumava Mountains along the Bavarian border, the Ore Mountains (Krušné hory) along the eastern German border and the Giant Mountains (Krkonoše) along the Polish border east of Liberec. The Czech Republic's highest peak, Mt Sněžka (1602m), is in the Giant Mountains. In between these ranges are rolling plains mixed with forests and farm land.

The Czech Republic has been called 'the roof of Europe' because no rivers or streams flow into the country. The Morava River flows out of Moravia and enters the Danube just west of Bratislava. Bohemia's most famous river is the Vltava (Moldau in German), which originates near the German border and flows north through Český Krumlov, České Budějovice and Prague. At Mělník it joins the Labe, which becomes the Elbe in Germany.

The 120-sq-km Moravian Karst north of Brno features limestone caves, subterranean lakes and the Macocha Abyss, which is 138m deep. Despite centuries of clear-felling for cultivation, forests – mainly spruce – still cover about one-third of the country. Dwarf pine is common near the tree line and above it (1400m) there is little but grasses, shrubs and lichens.

The forests of northern Bohemia and Moravia have been devastated by acid rain resulting from the burning of poor-quality brown coal at factories and thermal power stations that spew millions of tonnes of sulphur dioxide, nitrogen oxide and carbon monoxide into the atmosphere, creating one of Europe's most serious environmental disaster areas. The most affected region is the eastern Ore Mountains where the majority of trees are dead. In the past few years sulphur dioxide levels in Prague have declined, while carbon monoxide pollution from cars and trucks has increased. The only functioning nuclear generating station is the ageing Soviet reactor at Dukovany (between Znojmo and Brno).

The most common types of wildlife in the mountains are wildcats, marmots, otters, marten and mink. In the woods and the fields there are plenty of pheasants, partridges, deer, ducks and wild geese. Rarer are eagles, vultures, osprey, storks, bustards, grouse and lynxes.

GOVERNMENT & POLITICS

The present constitution was passed by the parliament in 1992. The country is a parliamentary democracy headed by president Havel who faces election by parliament every five years. Real power lies with the prime minister and the cabinet. The parliament can also override the president's veto on most issues by a simple majority. There are two chambers in the parliament – the House of Representatives and the Senate – whose members are elected by Czech citizens every four and six years respectively.

The largest party is the left of centre Social Democrats (ČSSD) led by Miloš Zeman, the current prime minister. The opposition Civic Democratic Party (ODS) is led by Václav Klaus, the pivotal character in economic reform and referred to as a Thatcherite. However Klaus was never that far right and, while in power, his policies were a mix of much-needed reform and socialist-style pragmatism.

The Czech Communist Party is one of the few left in the world that still adheres to the Marxist-Stalinist doctrine and has a solid core of elderly followers. In the 1998 elections it received 11% of the popular vote, an increase of 0.7% from the 1996 elections.

The traditional lands of Bohemia and Moravia are divided into nine administrative regions, consisting of Prague, Brno, five regions in Bohemia, and two regions in Moravia.

ECONOMY

Bohemia and Moravia have specialised in light industry since the Industrial Revolution, and during the 1930s their combined industrial output was second only to that of Germany. Under Communist rule, industry and agriculture were nationalised and heavy industry was introduced along Stalinist lines.

Steel and machinery production are the main forms of heavy industry. Other important products include armaments, vehicles, cement, ceramics, plastics, cotton and beer. In the later years of Communist rule the country's industrial equipment was becoming obsolete and there was much economic inefficiency. Increased production was sought with scant regard for the environment, and in recent times the price has been paid in terms of public health.

The largest industrial area is around Ostrava in North Moravia, with coal mining, chemicals, a steel mill and car production, while the second largest is in the Chomutov/Most/Teplice region of North Bohemia.

Privatisation was carried out in three stages after the fall of communism. The first was the restitution to the original owners of some 100,000 small businesses and commercial properties that were confiscated by the Communists. Then about 30,000 small retail outlets or service facilities throughout the former Czechoslovakia were auctioned off to owner-operators. The third and most difficult stage of privatising 1500 medium and large-sized companies is not yet finished. Some companies were auctioned off and the majority were privatised by a voucher scheme the government devised in which hundreds of millions of shares in 1200 state corporations were distributed to Czechs. Every adult citizen was entitled to purchase 1000 voucher points for 1000 crowns (US$36), that could be used to bid for shares in companies being privatised. Many people assigned their points to investment funds which would act on their behalf, but many funds ripped-off their customers. Privatisation has been dogged by corruption. In April 1993, the Prague stock market opened, and trading began in June of that year.

A handful of large-sized companies, including most of the major banks, are still in government hands. This is partly due to the downturn in the economy as many of the privatised companies were bought by the government owned banks. Productivity is low and companies still employ too many people.

Agriculture is a small part of the Czech economy, employing about 5% of a workforce that is 30% less productive than its EU counterparts. Most of the land has been returned to the previous owners or privatised, but many people decided to form their own co-operatives based on the former government co-operatives. Major crops are sugarbeet, wheat, potatoes, corn, barley, rye and hops, while cattle, pigs and chickens are the preferred livestock.

In 1998 the Czech economy, considered for years as one of the best in the former eastern bloc, went through a slump. Inflation in 1997 increased to 10.8%, and the gross domestic product (GDP) growth rate decreased to 1%, which has serious implications for the increasing unemployment rate of 4.8%. The country recorded its first budget deficit (1% of GDP) since 1993. Other problems are a drop in foreign investment, increasing public and government debt (170 billion Kč), slow privatisation of banks, lack of strong laws in the business sphere and keeping the *koruna* overvalued (in 1997 it was devalued by 12%). The average wage in 1998 was about US$340 (10,894 Kč) a month.

POPULATION & PEOPLE

The Czech Republic is fairly homogeneous; of its population of 10.29 million people, 94% are Czech, while 4% are Slovak. A small Polish minority lives in the borderlands near Ostrava. After WWII three million Sudeten Germans were evicted from the country, and today only about 150,000 Germans remain.

The major cities and their populations are: Prague (1,214,000), Brno (388,000), Ostrava (327,000), Plzeň (173,000) and Olomouc (106,000).

ARTS

Czech culture has a long and distinguished history. Prague University, the oldest in Central Europe, was founded in 1348, about the time that the Gothic architect Petr Parléř was directing the construction of St Vitus Cathedral, Karlův most (Charles Bridge) and other illustrious works.

In the early 17th century, the region was torn by the Thirty Years' War and the educational reformer Jan Ámos Comenius (1592-1670) was forced to flee Moravia. In exile Comenius (Komenský in Czech) produced a series of textbooks that were to be used throughout Europe for two centuries. His *The Visible World in Pictures*, featuring woodcuts made at Nuremberg, was the forerunner of today's illustrated school book. (Comenius' portrait appears on the new 200 Kč banknote.)

Literature

The National Revival period of the early 19th century saw the re-emergence of the Czech language as a vehicle of culture. Late 19th-century romanticism is exemplified in the historical novels of Alois Jirásek (1851-1930), whose works chronicled the entire history of the Czechs. His finest, published in 1915, was *Temno* (Darkness), which dealt with the period of national decline. Karel Čapek (1890-1938) brought the Czech word *robot* (imitation human being) into international usage through a 1920 play featuring a human-like machine that almost manages to enslave humanity.

Another literary genius, Franz Kafka, wrote in German but was, nevertheless, a son of Prague. He was born and lived there most of his life, haunted by the city he both hated and needed. His novel *The Trial* (1925) gives an insight into his world.

After the 1968 Soviet invasion, Czech novelist Milan Kundera saw his works banned. *The Book of Laughter and Forgetting* combines eroticism with political satire, for which the Communist government revoked Kundera's Czech citizenship.

One of the Czech Republic's foremost resident writers is Ivan Klíma, whose works were also banned from 1970 to 1989. Klíma's novels such as *Love and Garbage* (1986) tackle the human dimension behind the contradictions of contemporary Czech life.

Perhaps one of the best contemporary Czech novelists is Bohumil Hrabal (see the later Books section under Facts for the Visitor in this chapter), while by far the most brilliant plays are by the current president Václav Havel – among the most popular are *Audience* and *Largo desolato*.

Music

During the 17th century, when Bohemia and Moravia came under Austrian domination and German was the official language, Czech culture survived in folk music. Moravian folk orchestras are built around the *cymbalum*, a copper-stringed dulcimer of Middle Eastern origin which stands on four legs and is played by striking the strings with two mallets.

Bohemia's pre-eminent baroque composer was Jan Dismas Zelenka (1679-1745) who spent some of his life in Dresden, where he was a composer to the Saxon court. He was greatly esteemed by his contemporary, Bach, for the symbolism and subtle expression of Zelenka's last masses are unique expressions of his introverted, restrained character.

The works of the Czech Republic's foremost composers, Bedřich Smetana (1824-84) and Antonín Dvořák (1841-1904), express nostalgia, melancholy and joy – all aspects of the Czech personality. In his operas, Smetana used popular songs displaying the innate peasant wisdom of the people to capture the nationalist sentiments of his time. Smetana's symphonic cycle *Má Vlast* (My Country) is a musical history of the country. Dvořák attracted world attention to Czech music through his use of native folk materials in works such as *Slavonic Dances* (1878).

The composer Leoš Janáček (1854-1928) shared Dvořák's intense interest in folk music and created an original national style by combining the scales and melodies of folk songs with the inflections of the Czech language. One of his best known works is *Jenůfa* (1904).

Dance

Bohemia's greatest contribution to dance floors is the polka, a lively folk dance in which couples rapidly circle the floor in three-four time with three quick steps and a hop. Since its appearance in Paris in 1843, the form has been popular worldwide. Smetana used the polka in his opera *The Bartered Bride* (1866). In some of Moravia's villages whirling couples dance the *vrtěná*, while the *hošije* and *verbuňk* are vigorous male solo dances.

SOCIETY & CONDUCT

The best way to see traditional Bohemian and Moravian folk customs, dress, song, dance, music and food is to attend one of the many weekend folk festivals that are held in remote villages around the Czech Republic from spring to autumn. Some of the best are in the south-eastern part of Moravia's Slovácko region. Strážnice and Vlčnov festivals are among the best known, while north of the Slovácko region several festivals are held each year in Rožňov pod Radhoštěm's open-air museum. Folk songs and dances can also be seen at the Chod Festival in Domažlice (see the Public Holidays & Special Events section of Facts for the Visitor in this chapter for information about the Strážnice and Chod festivals).

When it comes to attending classical music concerts, opera and traditional theatre, Czechs are quite conservative and all dress formally. Foreign visitors are expected to do the same. Contemporary dress is fine for all other venues. It is customary to say 'good day' *(dobrý den)* when entering a shop, café or quiet bar, and 'goodbye' *(na shledanou)* when leaving. If you are invited to a Czech home bring fresh flowers and when entering someone's home remember to remove your shoes, unless you're told not to bother. On public transport, young people readily give up their seats to the elderly, the sick, pregnant women or women carrying children.

RELIGION

A majority of the people are Catholic (40%) and there's a saying that it took 40 years of Communism to make good Catholics of the Czechs! Despite this, church attendance is extremely low. Various Protestant sects account for a small percentage of the population, while the Jewish community, which was 1% of the population in 1918, today numbers only a few thousand. Religious tolerance is well established and the Church makes little attempt to involve itself in politics.

LANGUAGE

German is predominantly understood by the older generations. Under the Communists everybody learned Russian at school but this has now been replaced by English.

Czech seems an outlandish language to native speakers of English, who must abandon some linguistic habits to learn it. Its peculiarity is a great aversion to the use of vowels. Many words contain nothing that we could identify as a vowel. One famous tongue twister goes *strč prst skrz krk* which means 'stick your finger through your neck' and is pronounced just as it's spelt!

Czech and Slovak are closely related and mutually comprehensible West Slavic languages. In the 19th century, Jan Hus' Czech spelling was adopted to render other Slav languages such as Slovene and Croatian in Latin letters.

An English-Czech phrasebook will prove invaluable, so consider Lonely Planet's *Central* or *Eastern Europe phrasebook*. Some useful Czech words that are frequently used in this chapter are: *most* (bridge), *nábřeží* (embankment), *náměstí* (square), *nádraží* (station), *ostrov* (island), *třída* (avenue) and *ulice* (street). Toilets might be marked *záchody* or *WC*, while men's may be marked *páni* or *muži* and women's *dámy* or *ženy*. To open and close doors you will find the signs *sem* (pull) and *tam* (push). See the Language Guide at the back of the book for pronunciation guidelines and useful words and phrases.

Facts for the Visitor

HIGHLIGHTS
Historic Towns
The Czech Republic boasts many historic towns. The five most authentic and picturesque are Prague, Litoměřice, Český Krumlov, Kutná Hora, Tábor and Telč (see the relevant sections later in this chapter).

Museums & Galleries
The Prague Jewish Museum in the former Prague ghetto is easily the largest and most authentic of its kind in Central Europe. Prague's finest art galleries are in the castle area; of particular interest are the collections of the National Gallery in the Šternberský Palace and the Basilica of St George. The Brewery Museum in Plzeň highlights one of this country's noblest contributions to humanity.

Castles
Holy Roman Emperor Charles IV's Karlštejn Castle looks like something out of Disneyland. Its genuine 14th-century structure underwent heavy reconstruction during the 19th century. Konopiště and Český Krumlov castles have the same effect. Prague Castle is packed with art treasures. Brno's 17th-century Špilberk Castle is a symbol of Habsburg repression.

SUGGESTED ITINERARIES
Depending on the length of your stay, you might want to see and do the following things in the Czech Republic:

Two days
  Visit Prague
One week
  Visit Český Krumlov, Litoměřice, Prague and
  Kutná Hora
Two weeks
  Visit Prague, Litoměřice, Kutná Hora, Český
  Krumlov, Telč and Brno
One month
  Visit all places mentioned in this chapter

PLANNING
Climate & When to Go
The Czech climate is temperate, with cool and humid winters, warm summers and clearly defined spring and autumn seasons. Prague has average daily temperatures above 14°C from May to September, above 8°C in April and October, and below freezing point in December and January. In winter dense fog (or smog) can set in anywhere.

Books & Maps
In *The Good Soldier Švejk*, Jaroslav Hašek (1883-1923) satirises the pettiness of the government and military service. In this Czech classic, a Prague dog-catcher is drafted into the Austrian army before WWI, and by carrying out stupid orders to the letter he succeeds in completely disrupting military life.

Probably the best Czech novelist of this century is Bohumil Hrabal, and one of his finest works is *The Little Town That Stood Still*, a novel set in a small town and showing in a humorous way how the close-knit community interacts.

Before the fall of communism in 1989, the clandestine works of dissident authors were circulated in typewritten *samizdat* editions of a few dozen carbon copies, and the best were smuggled out and published abroad. For an anthology of these underground writings get a copy of *Goodbye samizdat!* edited by M Goetz-Stankiewicz (published in 1993).

Ludvík Vaculík gives an insight into the mood of dissident Prague writers during the 1980s in his collection of chronicles, *A Cup of Coffee with My Interrogator* (1987), which has an introduction by Václav Havel.

The collection of papers entitled *Václav Havel or Living in Truth* (1986), edited by Jan Vladislav, includes Havel's famous 1978 essay 'The power of the powerless'. Havel describes the conformity of those who simply accepted the 'post-totalitarian system' as 'living within the lie'. In contrast, dissidents who dared to say 'the emperor is naked!' endured many difficulties but earned respect by 'living within the truth'. Michael Simmons' *The Reluctant President: A Political Life of Václav Havel* portrays this captivating figure well.

Lonely Planet's *Czech & Slovak Republics* by John King, Scott McNeely and Richard Nebeský gives extensive information on the nuts and bolts of travelling in the Czech Republic.

The maps in this guide are useful as initial references, but you should still obtain standard maps once you are in the country. There are good maps of the Czech Republic available outside the country by some German publishers and by Austrian publishers such as Freytag & Berndt.

Some of the best Czech country maps are by Kartografie Praha; its *Česká republika – automapa* (1:500,000) is good, as are its town plans. Excellent hiking and cycling maps that cover all of the Czech Republic's countryside are by Klub českých turistů – Vojenský kartografický ústav (VKÚ; 1:50,000).

What to Bring

Of course bring as little as you can. Toilet paper, toothpaste and all similar items are available. You need to keep all your valuables in a cotton money belt that fits under your clothing. Hostellers do not need to bring their own bedding. However, it might be an idea to pack the following items, even though they are available in the country: pocket knife, water bottle, universal sink plug, torch, compass, sewing kit, medical kit and length of cord that can be used as a washing line.

TOURIST OFFICES
Local Tourist Offices

In Prague the municipal information office is the Prague Information Service (PIS) and the staff are very knowledgeable about sightseeing, food and entertainment. Receptionists in the expensive hotels are often helpful with information when they're not busy. Throughout the rest of the country there is a network of municipal information centres (*městské informační centrum/středisko*) in all major tourist areas.

The former government tourism monopoly Čedok has offices around the country which you can consult if you wish to change money, or want accommodation, travel or sightseeing arrangements made. It is, however, oriented towards the top end of the market. Čedok staff are sometimes willing to answer general questions, although this is now a commercial travel agency and they're not paid to provide free information. Staff at the American Express office in Prague are in a similar position.

In the Czech Republic there are several youth travel bureaus including CKM (Cestovní kancelář mládeže) in Prague, while the other former CKM offices in Plzeň, České Budějovice and Brno are now all independently owned companies that still offer information. GTS international is another bureau in Prague. Its offices are a better source of information on money-saving arrangements than Čedok's and it also sells ISIC, ITIC, GO25 and Euro <26 cards.

Czech Tourist Authority Offices Abroad

The following Czech Tourist Authority (ČCCR) offices abroad provide information about the whole of the Czech Republic, but they do not book hotels or transportation:

Canada
  (☎ 416-367 3432) Exchange Tower, 2 First Canadian Place, 14th Floor, Toronto, Ontario
UK
  (☎ 0171-291 9925) 95 Great Portland St, London W1N 5RA
USA
  (☎ 212-288 0830) 1109-1111 Madison Ave, New York, NY 10028

VISAS & EMBASSIES

Everyone requires a passport which won't expire within the following eight months. US and Singaporean citizens require no visa for a stay of 30 days. Most citizens of EU countries, Switzerland and New Zealand can stay for three months without a visa, while for UK, Irish and Canadian citizens the limit is six months. Australians need a visa; it costs $56 in advance from the Sydney consulate. Citizens of Japan, South Africa and most other non-European countries also need to pay for a visa, which should be obtained in advance at a consulate.

Visas are only available at three highway border crossings – one from Germany (Waidhaus/Rozvadov) and two from Austria (Wullowitz/Dolní Dvořiště and Klein Haugsdorf/Hatě) – and at Prague's Ruzyně airport for 1500 Kč. Elsewhere you'll be refused entry if you need a visa and arrive without one. Visas are never issued on trains.

Czech tourist and transit visas are readily available at consulates throughout Central Europe at a cost of 600 Kč (about US$19) per entry. You will need two photos per entry (maximum two entries per visa). Don't get a transit visa; it costs the same and cannot be changed to a tourist visa upon arrival. You'll be asked how many days you wish to stay in the Czech Republic, up to a maximum of 30 days, and this number will be written on your visa. You can use your visa at any time within six months of the date of issue.

There's a space for hotel stamps on the back of the visa form and although the old requirement of police registration is seldom enforced these days a difficult official can bring it up if he or she feels in the mood. So ask hotels and camping grounds or travel agencies to stamp your visa form.

You can extend your stay in the country at police stations inside the Czech Republic for about 200 Kč. The offices handling these matters open for short hours and have long queues, so don't leave it till the last day.

Czech Embassies Abroad

The following addresses and telephone numbers are for Czech embassies/consulates:

Australia
Consulate (☎ 2-9371 8878), 169 Military Rd, Dover Heights, NSW 2030

Canada
(☎ 613-562 3875) 541 Sussex Dr, Ottawa, Ontario

Netherlands
(☎ 3170-346 9712) Paleisstr. 4, 2514 JA The Hague

New Zealand
(☎ 4-564 6001) 48 Hair St, PO Box 43035, Wainuiomata, Wellington

UK
(☎ 171-243 7943) 28 Kensington Palace Gardens, London, W8 4QY

USA
(☎ 202-274 9100) 3900 Spring of Freedom St NW, Washington, DC 20008

Foreign Embassies in the Czech Republic

Most embassies/consulates are open weekdays from 9 am to noon.

Albania
(☎ 02-37 93 29) Pod kaštany 22, Bubeneč, Praha 6 (metro: Hradčanská)

Australia
(☎ 02-24 31 07 43), Na Ořechovce 38, Střešovice, Praha 6 – this is only an honorary consul and emergency assistance will be provided (eg a stolen passport); otherwise contact the Australian embassy in Vienna

Bulgaria
(☎ 02-22 21 12 60) Krakovská 6, Nové Město, Praha 1 (metro: Muzeum)

Canada
(☎ 02-24 31 11 08) Mickiewiczova 6, Hradčany, Praha 6 (metro: Hradčanská)

Croatia
(☎ 02-312 04 79) V průhledu 9, Střešovice, Praha 6

Hungary
(☎ 02-36 50 41/44) Badeniho 1, Praha 6 (metro: Hradčanská)

New Zealand
(☎ 02-25 41 98) – this is only an honorary consul and assistance will be given (eg stolen passport but by appointment only); otherwise the nearest NZ embassy is in Bonn, Germany

Poland
Consulate (☎ 02-57 32 06 78), Václavské náměstí 49 (metro: Muzeum)

Romania
(☎ 02-57 32 04 94) Nerudova 5, Malá Strana, Praha 1 (metro: Malostranská)

Russia
Consulate (☎ 02-37 37 23), Korunovační 34, Bubeneč, Praha 6 (metro: Hradčanská)

Slovakia
(☎ 02-32 05 21) Pod hradbami 1, Střešovice, Praha 6 (metro: Dejvická)
Slovenia
(☎ 02-24 31 51 06) Pod hradbami 15, Střešovice, Praha 6 (metro: Dejvická)
UK
(☎ 02-57 32 03 55) Thunovská 14, Malá Strana, Praha 1 (metro: Malostranská)
USA
(☎ 02-24 21 98 44/6) Tržiště 15, Malá Strana, Praha 1 (metro: Malostranská)
Yugoslavia
(☎ 02-57 32 00 31) Mostecká 15, Malá Strana, Praha 1 (metro: Malostranská)

CUSTOMS

You can import, taxed and duty-free, reasonable amounts of personal effects and up to about 6000 Kč worth of gifts and other 'non-commercial' goods. If you're over 18, you can bring in 2L of wine, 1L of spirits, and 250 cigarettes. Theoretically, any consumer goods valued at over 30,000 Kč are taxable at 22%. Customs officers can be strict about antiques and will confiscate goods if they are slightly suspicious. You cannot export genuine antiques. If you have any doubt about what you are taking out, talk to curatorial staff at the National Museum or the Museum of Decorative Arts, both in Prague.

There is no limit to the amount of Czech or foreign currency that can be taken in or out of the country. Arriving visitors are occasionally asked to prove that they have the equivalent of at least US$270.

MONEY

The Czech *koruna* was made fully convertible in 1996. There is no longer a black market; anyone who approaches you offering such a deal is a thief. Most hotels, restaurants and shops accept major credit cards.

The best way to carry money is a credit card. You can take out money as a cash advance in a bank or use automatic teller machines (ATMs). Your own bank will charge a commission of about US$1 to US$3 and at least 1% exchange fee for using the ATMs (cash advances normally attract lower charges), but it is still more favourable than commissions and exchange rates charged on travellers cheques.

Currency

The Czech Republic has had new currency since 1993; don't accept anything with 'Korun Československých' on it. Banknotes come in denominations of 20, 50, 100, 200, 500, 1000, 2000 and 5000 Czech crowns or *Korun českých* (Kč); coins are of 10, 20 and 50 *haléřů* (hellers) and one, two, five, 10, 20 and 50 Kč. Always have a few small 1 Kč and 2 Kč coins for use in public toilets, telephones and transport machines.

Exchange Rates

Since early 1991 the exchange rate has been fairly steady, with about 10% annual inflation.

Australia	A$1	=	18.64 Kč
Austria	AS1	=	2.46 Kč
Canada	C$1	=	20.33 Kč
euro	€1	=	34.11 Kč
France	1FF	=	5.16 Kč
Germany	DM1	=	17.32 Kč
Japan	¥100	=	21.23 Kč
New Zealand	NZ$1	=	15.70 Kč
Poland	zl1	=	8.95 Kč
Slovakia	Sk 1	=	0.88 Kč
United Kingdom	UK£1	=	50.24 Kč
United States	US$1	=	30.76 Kč

Costs

Food, transportation and admission fees are fairly cheap; it's mostly accommodation that makes this one of the most expensive countries in Central Europe. If you really want to travel on a low budget you'll have to spend a little more time looking for a cheap place to stay (hostels or camping), eat in pubs or stand-up cafeterias and/or be prepared to rough it. You might be able to get away with US$15 a day in summer. In a private home or a better hostel, with meals at cheap restaurants and using public transport, you can count on US$25 to US$30. Get out of the capital and your costs will drop dramatically.

A disappointing side of the Czech concept of a 'free market economy' is the official two-price system in which foreigners pay up to double the local price for most hotel rooms, international airline and bus tickets, and museum and concert tickets. Some exchange bureaus charge Czechs a lower commission, or none at all, and give better exchange rates to locals than to foreigners. A 'tourist price' for theatre tickets exists in Prague, as most tickets are snapped up by scalpers and travel agencies, who resell them to foreigners at several times their original price. Sometimes simply questioning the price difference results in an 'error correction'; if not, you either pay the higher price or go elsewhere. When you do get something for the local price (eg beer or domestic train tickets), you'll find it very inexpensive. Students usually get 50% off the entry price at museums, galleries, theatres, fairs etc.

Changing Money

Changing money in the Czech Republic can be a hassle as many private exchange offices, especially in Prague, deduct exorbitant commissions (*výlohy*) of up to 10%. Some of these advertise higher rates on large boards but don't mention their sky-high commission – if in doubt, ask first.

Hotels charge about 5% commission at lower rates while Čedok travel agencies and Post Offices charge 2% at similar rates as the banks. Banks take only 1 to 3% on better rates, but their opening hours are short and they are closed on weekends and holidays.

The Komerční, IPB or Živnostenská are usually efficient about changing travellers cheques for a standard 2% commission. Československá obchodní banka has a 1% commission and we list some of its branches throughout this chapter, but you should always ask about the commission as it seems to vary from branch to branch. Most banks are open weekdays from 8 or 9 am to 5 or 6 pm and in smaller towns may close for lunch between noon and 1 pm.

The American Express and Thomas Cook offices in Prague change their own and some other companies travellers cheques without commission, but their rates are slightly lower than those offered by the banks.

Now that the koruna is a fully convertible currency it is easy to re-exchange a few thousand crowns when you leave the country. However, if you have more than 5000 Kč to change you will be required to show exchange receipts. It is possible to exchange Czech *koruny* in Germany, Austria and the Netherlands, and theoretically it should be the case in most other EU countries, too.

There is a large network of ATMs, or *bankomat*, throughout the country. Most accept Visa/Plus and MasterCard/Cirrus/Euro cards.

Tipping & Bargaining

Tipping in restaurants is optional but if the service is good you should certainly round up the bill to the next 10 Kč (or to the next 10 to 20 Kč if the bill is over 100 Kč) when you pay. Never leave coins worth less than 1 Kč as your only tip or you risk having them thrown back at you.

The same applies to tipping taxi drivers. If your driver is honest and turns on the meter then you should round up the fare at the end of your journey.

Consumer Tax

The value-added tax (VAT) is only 5% on food but up to 22% on hotel rooms, restaurant meals and luxury items. This tax is included in the sticker price and not added at the cash register, so you shouldn't notice it directly.

POST & COMMUNICATIONS
Post

Postage costs are low in the Czech Republic. Czech mail moves much faster than Polish mail (two weeks to the USA). Always use air mail. Most post offices are open on weekdays from 8 am to 7 pm.

Postcards cost 6 Kč to other European countries and 7 Kč air mail overseas. Letters cost 8 Kč and 11 Kč, respectively. A 2kg parcel costs 250 Kč to other European countries by land or sea, while air mail overseas is 560 Kč.

To send parcels weighing more than 2kg abroad, you will need to go to a post office with a customs section. Although the main post offices often don't have a customs section, staff there will be able to tell you which post office you should go to. These post offices are usually open from 8 am to 3 pm. Air mail is about double the cost of surface mail for parcels. When sending books you'll have to be persistent to get the book rate (ask for M-pytel) and these can be sent from any post office. For fast and secure delivery, the expensive Express Mail Service (EMS) is available.

Don't bother sending a parcel containing antiques or anything valuable, for it is quite likely that it will not reach its destination.

General delivery mail should be addressed to Poste Restante, Pošta 1, in most major cities. In the case of Prague, the following information should also be included in the address: Jindřišská 14, 11000 Praha 1, Czech Republic.

American Express card-holders can receive mail addressed c/o American Express, Václavské náměstí 56, 11000 Praha 1, Czech Republic. American Express holds letters for 30 days, but parcels and registered mail are not accepted and will be returned to sender. This is a reliable place to receive mail.

Telephone

Czech Telecom is still replacing the antiquated telephone system with a digital system, so changing telephone numbers will continue to be a problem for a few years to come.

You can make international telephone calls at main post offices or directly from telephone booths. Three minute operator-assisted international telephone calls cost 193 Kč to Australia, New Zealand, and Japan; 169 Kč to Canada; 158 Kč to the USA; 113 Kč to the UK and slightly less to most other European countries. All calls have a three-minute minimum. Check the rates with the clerk before placing your call and ask for a receipt. Czech Telecom prices are higher than in Western European countries, so it is better to call direct numbers for direct connections to operators in a particular country, either for collect, account or credit-card calls. Get the direct access numbers from your home or Czech telephone offices.

Local telephone calls cost 3 Kč from public blue/grey telephone booths. More common around the country are blue or grey card phones and phonecards (100-unit cards cost 300 Kč) are easily obtainable at newsstands and post offices. The international access code is ☎ 00.

To call the Czech Republic from abroad, dial your international access code, ☎ 420 (the country code for the Czech Republic), the area code and the number. When dialling from within the Czech Republic you must add ☎ 0 before the area code.

Fax & Telegraph

Telegrams can be sent from most post offices, while faxes can only be sent from certain major post offices.

INTERNET RESOURCES

Email is available at Internet cafés in Prague, Brno, Plzeň and Kutná Hora; see relevant sections for more details. The usual charge is about 50 Kč for a half-hour. If you are carrying a laptop computer and a modem, you can make a connection through a telephone line but it is not always easy due to poor quality lines and erratic central exchanges (the telephone tone is 'A', which is a repeating short tone and a long pause when engaged tone is a repeating short fast tone, which is shorter than in the USA or UK). Crossed lines and connections to the wrong number are commonplace. Most new telephone plugs are US RJ-11 type. If the telephone plug is an old type, it is possible to buy new plugs with adapters in local electronic shops. It is not easy to connect to the Internet through most hotels, except the upmarket ones which charge their usual high call rates for modem connections too. Many hotels do not know what to do or what to charge when asked about connecting to the Internet and some just reject it outright. If you do manage to connect, the hotel might charge from 5 to 12 Kč or even more per minute.

The Czech Ministry of Foreign Affairs (www.czech.cz) has an excellent site packed with country and travel information, and lots of links while the Czech Press Agency (ČTK) is at www.ctknews.com/. Many Czech towns now have their own Web sites like Kutná Hora (www.webhouse.cz/kutna–hora). Upmarket hotels in the Czech Republic can be booked at www.travel.cz.

NEWSPAPERS & MAGAZINES

The *Prague Post* is a good weekly newspaper founded by a group of young US expats in October 1991. The *Post*'s thick 'Culture' section contains basic practical visitor information but isn't as extensive as it was. There are also several business papers, like the *Central European Business Weekly* and the glossy *Prague Tribune*.

Major European and US newspapers and magazines are on sale at some kiosks in bigger cities.

RADIO & TV

In Prague (101.1 FM) and Brno (101.3 FM), the BBC broadcasts news and other programs in English on the hour from 1 to 5 am, 9 to 11 am, 5 and 10 pm and midnight. Several other radio stations have English programs, but these change, so see the *Prague Post* for details.

On TV, Euronews in English is on channel ČT 2 every early morning.

PHOTOGRAPHY & VIDEO

Kodak, Fuji and Agfa colour print films are available in most places for a reasonable price. Kodak's Ektachrome Elite is the most widely available slide film, sold here at lower prices than in Western Europe. Surprisingly, professional Fuji and Agfa slide films are also reasonably priced – when you can find them. There are plenty of one hour developing places in major cities and these are fine for developing print film. It is safer and faster to have slide film developed at home, except at the ČTK lab, Opletalova 6-7 in Prague. The situation is improving and there might be other reliable labs.

Most video films are widely available at reasonable prices.

TIME

The time in the Czech Republic is GMT/UTC plus one hour. At the end of March the Czech Republic switches to summer time and clocks are set forward an hour. At the end of October they're turned back an hour.

ELECTRICITY

The electric current is 220V, 50Hz.

WEIGHTS & MEASURES

The metric system is used in the Czech Republic.

LAUNDRY

There are only a few self-service laundrettes in Prague. Everywhere else you have to rely on laundrettes or dry cleaners (*prádelna* or *čistírna*) that can take up to a week to wash clothes. Some top-end hotels have an expensive overnight laundry service.

TOILETS

Public toilets in the Czech Republic usually charge 2 to 4 Kč but as there are only a few in the country, you may have to resort to using the facilities of restaurants or pubs; in tourist areas some toilets also charge about 2 Kč.

In central Prague most of the handful of public toilets are in metro stations. McDonald's and KFC are handy in emergencies.

HEALTH

All health care is not free to citizens of the Czech Republic. The National Health Scheme is an insurance-type policy fund into which employers and employees pay set fees. However, first aid is provided free to visitors in case of an accident. For emergencies call ☎ 155 anywhere in the country, but don't expect the person who answers to be able to speak English. In other instances, foreigners must pay a fee. EU nationals receive free medical attention.

Water

Many Czechs do not drink tap water because of its unpleasant taste – the result of heavy doses of chlorine. In remote parts of the country and even in some Prague suburbs the tap water can be polluted. Given that about 50% of fresh water is contaminated, most visitors prefer bottled water.

Thermal Baths

There are hundreds of curative mineral springs and dozens of health spas in the Czech Republic which use mineral waters, mud or peat. Most famous are the spas of West Bohemia (Františkovy Lázně, Karlovy Vary and Mariánské Lázně).

Unfortunately, the spas are reserved for the medical treatment of patients. Yet all the spas have colonnades where you may join in the 'drinking cure', a social ritual that involves imbibing liberal quantities of warm spring water and then parading up and down to stimulate circulation. Admission is free but you need to bring your own cup or buy the special *lázeňský pohárek*.

Though the resorts are pleasant to visit, to receive medical treatment at a spa you must book at least two months in advance through Balnea (☎ 02-21 10 53 06/05; fax 24 21 42 11), Národní 28, 11001 Praha 1. The recommended stay is 21 days though you can book for as few as three days. Daily prices begin at US$47/80 for a single/double in the cheapest category in the winter season, and US$60/100 during the main summer season. Accompanying people not taking a spa treatment get about a third off these prices. From October to April prices are reduced. The price includes medical examination and care, spa curative treatment, room and board, and the spa tax. The clientele tends to be elderly. Čedok offices abroad will have full information about spa treatments.

WOMEN TRAVELLERS

Sexual violence has been on the rise in the Czech Republic but is still much lower than in the west. Nevertheless, solo female travellers should avoid deserted and unlit areas, especially at night. Some women experience routine cat calls and whistling.

GAY & LESBIAN TRAVELLERS

The gay and lesbian monthly magazine SOHO provides information but only in Czech. The SOHO Union of Homosexual Organisations (☎ 02-24 22 38 11; soho @bbs.infima.cz; www.gay.cz/soho), can provide information on activities and places to go. The crisis line for gays and lesbians is ☎ 0602-33 80 92.

Czechs are not accustomed to seeing homosexuals showing affection for each other in public but their reaction will most likely be just a surprised look.

DISABLED TRAVELLERS

No attention used to be paid to facilities for disabled people but this is changing slowly. Ramps for wheelchair users in Prague are becoming more common, especially at the more expensive hotels and major street crossings. Transport is a major problem as buses and trams have no wheelchair access. In Prague,

only Hlavní nádraží and Holešovice railway stations, and a handful of metro stations, have self-operating lifts. The Czech Railways (ČD) claim that any larger station has ramps and lifts for wheelchairs onto the train but the harsh reality is that the service is very poor. McDonald's and KFC entrances and toilets are wheelchair friendly.

Disabled people planning to travel with ČSA need to inform the airline of their needs when booking the ticket. The Stavovské Theatre in Prague has wheelchair access (as several other theatres have) and is equipped for the hearing-impaired. Most pedestrian crossings that are equipped with lights in central Prague give off a ticking noise when the light is green, signalling that it is OK to cross the street.

For more information contact the Prague Wheelchair Users Organization (Pražská organizace vozíčkářů), ☎ 02-232 58 03 or ☎ 02-24 81 62 31; pov@server1gts.cz) at Benediktská 6, Josefov. It can organise a guide and transportation at about half the price of a taxi. The Czech Blind United (Sjednocená unie nevidomých a slaboz-rakých v ČR, ☎ 02-24 81 83 98/73 93; sons–zahr@braillnet.cz), Karlínské náměstí 12, Karlín, Prague 8, can provide some information about Prague for the blind but it does not have any services.

DANGERS & ANNOYANCES

Emergency telephone numbers in the Czech Republic are ☎ 158 (police), ☎ 155 (ambulance) and ☎ 150 (fire). Lost Visa cards can be reported on ☎ 02-24 12 53 53 and MasterCards/Euro cards on ☎ 02-24 42 31 35.

Confusingly, buildings on some streets have two sets of numbers. The blue number is the actual street number while the red number is the old registration number. To make matters worse, the streets themselves are sometimes poorly labelled.

Crime is low compared with levels in the west and only a real problem in Prague's tourist zone (see that section for more details). Prague's international Ruzyně airport is also a haven for thieves. Another problem is the increasing number of robberies that take place on international trains passing through the country. The victims are usually sleeping passengers, some of whom have been gassed to sleep in their compartments and then relieved of their valuables. Groups of skinheads occasionally gang up on darker skinned people and beat them up.

BUSINESS HOURS

On weekdays, shops open at around 8.30 am and close at 5 or 6 pm, although some major department stores stay open until 8 pm and until 6 pm on Saturday. Some bakeries and grocery stores open as early as 7 am. Many small shops, particularly those in country areas, close for up to an hour for lunch between noon and 2 pm. Almost everything closes between 11 am and 1 pm on Saturday and all day Sunday. Many department stores and tourist-oriented shops (especially those in the centre of Prague) are also open on weekends but are usually closed by 4 or 5 pm. Some grocery stores open on weekends. Most restaurants are open every day but smaller ones in Prague's suburbs and in the rest of the country start running out of food after 7 pm and close their kitchens at 9 pm.

Most museums are closed on Monday and the day following a public holiday, but in Prague there are some that are open seven days a week, especially in summer. Many gardens, castles and historic sites in the Czech Republic are closed from November to March and open on weekends only in April and October. In spring and autumn you may have to wait around for a group to form before being allowed in; it's better to go on weekends. In winter, before making a long trip out to some attraction in the countryside, be sure to check that it's open. Staff at some isolated sights take an hour off for lunch. At any sight where a guided tour is required the ticket offices close an hour or so before the official closing time, depending on the length of the tour.

The main town museums stay open all year. Many churches remain closed except for services.

PUBLIC HOLIDAYS & SPECIAL EVENTS

Public holidays include New Year's Day (1 January), Easter Monday (March/April), Labour Day (1 May), Liberation Day (8 May), Cyril and Methodius Day (5 July), Jan Hus Day (6 July), Republic Day (28 October) and Christmas (24 to 26 December). On New Year's Eve many restaurants and bars will either be rented out for private parties or closed.

While there are too many festivals to all be mentioned here, the following are some of the major ones.

Since 1946 the Prague Spring International Music Festival has taken place during the second half of May (most performances are sold out well in advance). In June there's a festival of brass-band music at Kolín. In August the Frédéric Chopin Music Festival occurs in Mariánské Lázně. Karlovy Vary holds the International Film Festival in July and Dvořák Autumn Music Festival in September. Brno has a New Music festival in October and the International Jazz Festival in December.

Moravian folk-art traditions culminate in late June at the Strážnice Folk Festival between Brno and Bratislava. In mid-August the Chod Festival at Domažlice, 57km south of Plzeň, affords you a chance to witness the folk songs and dances of South and West Bohemia. Medieval festivals are held in Český Krumlov and Tábor (see those sections for more details).

The Brno International Trade Fair of consumer goods takes place every spring. In August or September an agricultural exhibition is held in České Budějovice.

ACTIVITIES

Hiking

Excellent day hikes are possible in the forests around the West Bohemian spas, Karlovy Vary and Mariánské Lázně. The Moravian Karst area, north of Brno, is another easily accessible hiking area. The Šumava range in the southern part of Bohemia offers some of the best hiking in the country.

Skiing

The Czech Republic's main ski resorts are Špindlerův Mlýn and Pec pod Sněžkou in Krkonoše National Park, north-west of Svoboda nad Upou along the Polish border. The main season here is from January to March. The resorts are small and downhill runs are generally gentle, while cross-country skiing is good. Prime cross-country ski areas are the Jeseník and Šumava ranges.

Cycling

For information on bicycle rentals and suggested trips, see Activities in the Prague and Český Krumlov sections of this chapter.

Canoeing & Yachting

For canoeing and yachting possibilities turn to the Český Krumlov section of this chapter. A number of rivers are good for canoeing, including the Otava, on which you can take a five-day trip from Sušice to Putim near Písek in South Bohemia. In summer, it is possible to transport canoes on trains.

Golf

There are now over a dozen golf courses around the country, including Prague, but only the Karlštejn and Mariánské Lázně courses have 18 holes.

COURSES

The Information-Advisory Centre of Charles University (☎ 02-96 22 80 36; IPC@ruk.cuni.cz), Školská 13a, Nové Město, Prague 1, provides information about the university, its courses etc, and sells ISIC, ITIC, GO25 and Euro <26 cards.

The Institute of Linguistics and Professional Training at Charles University (☎ 02-24 23 00 27; fax 420-2-24 22 94 97), Jindřišská 29, 11000 Praha 1, runs a three-week Czech course for foreigners from mid-July to early August. Participants have the choice of studying in Prague (US$780 including accommodation) or at Poděbrady, 50km east (US$910 including accommodation and all meals). Single rooms are US$75 extra per month, breakfast US$1.50 per day and group excursions are additional. Students at Poděbrady are able to use the facilities of the local spa. The application deadline is 22 June. No prior knowledge of the Czech language is required and everyone is welcome.

Charles University also offers regular 10-month winter Czech courses (from September

to June) for those interested in further study at Czech universities or specialisation in Slavic studies at a foreign university. (Students wishing to have credits transferred to their home university should obtain written approval from the head of their department before enrolling.) The cost of tuition and materials is US$2370 with 25 hours a week instruction, US$3090 with 35 hours weekly. You can also opt for one or two four-month semesters at US$1210 each (25 hours a week). Special six-week language courses (US$410 tuition) are available from time to time and individual tutors can be hired at US$16 an hour. Participants are eligible for inexpensive accommodation in student dormitories, and in addition to Prague, can study at Dobruška, Mariánské Lázně, Poděbrady or Teplice.

WORK

Unless you can speak Czech or have a job with a foreign English-speaking company the most readily available work is English teaching. It's easier to find a job in provincial towns and your living costs will be much lower. In Prague, look in the Czech advertising paper *Annonce*, the *Prague Post*, several of the expat cafés and US and UK cultural centres.

To obtain work legally you need working and residency permits. More information can be found at the Foreigners' Labour Office (Úřad práce), Zborovská 11, Prague (metro: Anděl), but your employer will obtain the working permit while you will have to get the residency permit from the Foreigners' Police. Companies employing foreigners without working permits face fines of over US$8000.

The Klub mladých cestovatelů (KMC; ☎/fax 02-24 23 06 33), Karolíny Světlé 30, Prague (metro: Národní Třída), organises international work camps from June to August renovating historical buildings, maintaining national parks, teaching children English etc. Contracts are for a minimum of three weeks with no pay, but room and board are provided. The registration fee is US$50 to US$100 for some work camps and free for others. You're supposed to book months ahead through volunteer or HI organisations in your home country.

ACCOMMODATION

Unless otherwise stated, all prices quoted for rooms are for a single/double/triple/quad.

Camping

There are several hundred camping grounds in the Czech Republic, which are usually open from May to September. Most camping grounds are primarily used by motorists so you're often surrounded by noisy caravans and car campers. The grounds are often accessible on public transport, but there's usually no hot water. Most of these places have a small snack bar where beer is sold and many have small cabins for rent which are cheaper than a hotel room. Pitching your own tent in these camping grounds is definitely the least expensive form of accommodation. Camping on public land is prohibited. Camping gas and Coleman fuel is available and called *technický benzín*, while methylated spirits for cooking stoves is *líh*.

Hostels

The Hostelling International (HI) handbook lists an impressive network of hostels in the Czech Republic, but you often find that they're full. Some of the places listed in the handbook are rather luxurious 'Juniorhotels' with single and double rooms, especially those in Prague and Mariánské Lázně.

In July and August many student dormitories become temporary hostels and in recent years a number of such dormitories in Prague have been converted into year-round western-style hostels. In central Prague, some normal schools also turn into temporary hostels. Český Krumlov is the only other place with a solid network of backpacker hostels.

Hostelling is controlled by the Klub mladých cestovatelů (KMC), or Club of Young Travellers (☎/fax 02-24 23 06 33), Karolíny Světlé 30, Prague (metro: Národní Třída). GTS international (☎ 02-96 22 43 00), Ve Smečkách 27, Prague 1, can also assist with hostels and has offices in České Budějovice, Brno and Plzeň. To get into a hostel, it's sometimes best to book ahead. You can book hostels in Prague and Brno from anywhere in the world through the computerised international booking network (IBN) that is linked to the HI booking

service. An HI membership card is not usually required to stay at hostels, though it will usually get you a reduced rate. An ISIC, ITIC, GO25 or Euro <26 cards may also get you a discount.

There's another category of hostel not connected with HI. The tourist hostels (*Turistické ubytovny*) provide very basic and cheap dormitory accommodation without the standards and controls associated with HI hostels (ie they often have mixed dormitories, allow smoking in the rooms, don't impose curfews etc). Ask about tourist hostels at information and Čedok offices and watch for the letters 'TU' on accommodation lists published in languages other than English.

Similarly, the letters 'UH' refer to an *Ubytovací hostinec*, which is a pub or inn offering basic rooms without private facilities.

Private Rooms & Pensions

Private rooms (look for signs reading '*privát*' or '*Zimmer frei*') are usually available in tourist centres, and some tourist information offices and travel agencies like Čedok can book them. Some have a three-night minimum-stay requirement.

In Prague, many private travel agencies now offer private rooms, and though their charges are higher than those of Čedok, the service is available daily and during evenings. This is the easiest way to find accommodation in Prague if you don't mind paying at least 550 Kč per person a night.

Many small pensions (often just glorified private rooms) exist, especially on Prague's outskirts and in South Bohemia, and these offer more personalised service than the hotels at lower rates.

Hotels

The Czech Republic has a good network of hotels covering the entire country. In Prague and Brno the hotels are expensive, whereas hotels in smaller towns are usually cheaper and more likely to have rooms. Czechs pay less than half as much as foreigners at many hotels.

There are five categories of hotels, which used to be rated by an ABC system but nowadays most rate themselves with stars, the five and four being luxury establishments. The three-star hotels are about 1100/1400 Kč and the two-star hotels usually offer reasonable comfort for about 400/600 Kč a single/double with shared bath or 550/900 Kč with private bath (about 50% higher in Prague). In small towns and villages, there are sometimes also one-star hotels. In places well off the beaten track, the police may be able to help you find a place where you can stay if all else fails.

Many hotels will not rent rooms till 2 pm during the peak travel seasons, so leave your luggage at the station. If you have a room with shared bath, you may have to pay about 60 Kč extra to use the communal shower and get the key from the reception. Hotel receptionists usually sell soft drinks and beer for just slightly more than shop prices but these drinks are often kept under the counter, so ask.

FOOD

The cheapest places to eat are self-service restaurants (jídelna) or (samoobsluha). Sometimes these places have really tasty dishes like barbecued chicken or hot German sausage – just right for a quick cooked lunch between sights. Train stations in some large cities often have good cheap restaurants or buffets but the best value meals are to be had in busy beer halls. If the place is crowded with locals, is noisy and looks chaotic, chances are it will have great lunch specials at low prices. As a general rule a restaurant calling itself *restaurace* is usually cheaper than a 'restaurant'.

You'll rarely have trouble finding a place to eat, but when you do, try the dining room of any large hotel. The restaurants in one to three-star hotels are reasonable in dollar terms, though the atmosphere is often stuffy and formal. These places will usually have menus in English or German with fish dishes available, and even vegetarians should be able to find something suitable. Hotel restaurants stay open later and they don't close on weekends.

Lunches are generally bigger and cheaper than dinners in the less expensive places. Dinner is eaten early and latecomers may have little to choose from. Don't expect to be served at any restaurant if you arrive within half an hour of closing time. Some waiters will tell tourists that all the cheaper dishes are finished to get them to order something more expensive.

Always check the posted menu before entering a restaurant to get an idea of the price range. If no menu is displayed inside or out, insist on seeing one before ordering. If the person serving refuses to show you a written menu, you should walk out as you will get overcharged. Some Prague restaurants are notorious for overcharging foreigners (see Places to Eat in the Prague section). The Czech for menu is *Jídelní lístek*. It is mostly in Czech, except in touristy areas where menus are also in German and English. Touristy areas close to the German and Austrian borders have menus predominantly in German thus you will find Lonely Planet's *Central* or *Eastern Europe phrasebook* useful. The main menu categories are *předkrmy* (hors d'oeuvres), *polévky* (soups), *studené jídlo* (cold dishes), *teplé jídlo* (warm dishes), *masitá jídla* (meat dishes), *ryby* (fish), *zelenina* (vegetables), *saláty* (salads), *ovoce* (fruit), *zákusky* (desserts) and *nápoje* (drinks). Anything that comes with *knedlíky* (dumplings) will be a hearty local meal.

Most beer halls have a system of marking everything you eat or drink on a small piece of paper which is left on your table. Waiters in all Czech restaurants, including the expensive ones, whisk away empty plates from under your nose before you manage to swallow your last dumpling.

There are great little pastry shops called *kavárna* or *cukrárna* throughout the country. These offer cakes, puddings and coffee as good as anything you'll find in neighbouring Austria at a fraction of the price.

Local Specialities

Czech cuisine is strong on sauces and gravies and weak on fresh vegetables. *Pražská šunka* (smoked Prague ham) is often taken as an hors d'oeuvre with Znojmo gherkins, followed by a thick soup, such as *bramborová polévka* (potato soup) and *zeleninová polévka* (vegetable soup). *Dršťková polévka* (tripe soup) is a treat not to be missed. The Czechs love meat dishes with knedlíky, flat circular dumplings that can be potato (bramborové) or bread (houskové) and/or sauerkraut. Carp (kapr) from the Bohemian fish ponds can be crumbed and fried or baked. Vegetarian dishes are mostly *bez masá* (meat less) and include *smažený sýr* (fried cheese) or *knedlíky s vejci* (scrambled eggs with dumplings). Czech fruit dumplings *(ovocné knedlíky)*, with whole fruit inside, come with cottage cheese or crushed poppy seed and melted butter.

DRINKS

The Czech Republic is a beer drinker's paradise – where else could you get two or three 500ml glasses of top quality Pilsner for under a dollar? The Czechs serve their draught beer with a high head of foam.

One of the first words of Czech you'll learn is *pivo* (beer); alcohol-free beer is called *nealkoholické pivo*. Bohemian beer is about the best in the world and the most famous brands are Budvar (the ONLY original Budweiser) and Plzeňský Prazdroj (the original Pilsner). The South Moravia and Mělník regions produce good white wine *(bílé víno)*, but red wines *(červené víno)* are so-so. You can be sure of a good feed at a *vinárna* (wine restaurant).

Special things to try include Becherovka (an exquisite bittersweet Czech liqueur), *zubrovka* (vodka with herb extracts) and *slivovice* (plum brandy). *Grog* is rum with hot water and sugar – a great pick-me-up. *Limonáda* is a good nonalcoholic drink and the word is often used to refer to any soft drink, not just lemonade.

ENTERTAINMENT

Theatres and concert-hall admission prices are still well below those in Western Europe and most of the programs are first-rate.

In Prague, unfortunately, most of the best theatre tickets are snapped up by scalpers and travel agencies who demand higher prices (these are still inexpensive), but in smaller centres like Karlovy Vary, Plzeň, České Budějovice and Brno you can see top performances at minimal expense. Check the theatres listed early in the day. The Czech Republic is a conservative country when it comes to social customs and you are expected to dress up when going to the theatre. Most theatres are closed in summer.

Outside Prague, the nightlife is rather limited, though after 9 pm there's usually a band playing in the bar of the best hotel in town and on weekends a disco will be

pumping up somewhere so just ask. You often have to contend with overbearing door attendants and contemptuous waiters.

Movies are always cheap and usually shown in the original language with local subtitles.

SPECTATOR SPORT

European handball is the national sport but the most popular is soccer *(fotbal)*. Ice hockey is followed with more passion than the two above-mentioned sports as the Czech national team is world class. Tennis is also popular.

Among the best Czech ice hockey teams are HC Petra Vsetín (a South Moravian team) and HC Sparta Praha (a Prague city club). Outstanding soccer teams include SK Slavia Praha and AC Sparta Praha (Prague city clubs).

Cross-country ski racing is popular in winter.

THINGS TO BUY

Good buys include china, Bohemian crystal, costume jewellery, folk ceramics, garnets, fancy leather goods, special textiles, lace, embroidery, wooden toys, shoes, colour-photography books, classical CDs and souvenirs. The hardback, blank-page notebooks available at stationery shops in small towns (not Prague) make excellent journals.

Garnet, ruby and amber jewellery has been a speciality in Bohemia for over a century. The ancient Egyptians used the semiprecious garnet gemstone as a kind of travel insurance that was guaranteed to protect the wearer from accidents.

In most shops and supermarkets the number of people inside is controlled by the number of shopping carts or baskets available. Often it can be difficult to enter without one, so pick one up at the door or stand in line and wait for someone to leave. Shopping baskets are even required in shoe shops! Outside Prague the largest department store chain is Tesco.

Before making any major purchases, be aware that goods worth over 30,000 Kč purchased in the Czech Republic may be subject to export duties as high as 22%. Typical souvenirs are supposed to be exempt but even then Czech customs officers have been known to levy excessive duties. Antiques and valuable artworks are closely scrutinised.

Getting There & Away

AIR

The national carrier, Czech Airlines (ČSA), flies to Prague from Abu Dhabi, Al-Ain, Amman, Bahrain, Bangkok, Beirut, Bratislava, Košice, Cairo, Dubai, Istanbul, Kuwait, Larnaca, Montreal, New York, Tel Aviv, Toronto, and many European cities. Fare structures are complicated and variable.

From Western Europe some return excursion and weekend flights are cheaper than a one-way ticket but they're nonrefundable once purchased and flight dates cannot be changed. All fares are seasonal, so check with your travel agent.

The Slovak carrier Tatra Air has daily flights from Bratislava to Košice and five flights a week to Prague. Air Ostrava (☎ 02-24 88 93 83) is a growing Czech airline that flies from Ostrava to Prague, Košice, Berlin, Hannover, Strasbourg, Vienna and Ljubljana.

LAND

Bus

There's a bus several times a day from Vienna (Mitte Busbahnhof) to Brno (three hours, 225 Kč). Try to buy your ticket the day before.

From London, the Kingscourt Express (☎ 0181-673 7500), 15 Balham High Road, London SW12 9AJ, and Capital Express (☎ 0171-243 0488), 57 Princedale Rd, Holland Park, London W11 4NP, have buses to Prague several times a week year-round (1277km, 23 hours). Youth and senior citizen discounts are available. Returning to Britain, check the Prague departure point carefully.

A bus operates between Paris and Prague (16½ hours, 1980 Kč one way) five times a week year-round. From April to September this bus runs daily. In Paris tickets are available at Eurolines Paris, Gare Routière Internationale Galliéni (☎ 01 49 72 51 51), 28 Ave du Général de Gaulle (metro: Galliéni).

There's a Eurolines bus service twice a

week throughout the year from Amsterdam to Prague (19 hours, 1950 Kč one way, with a 10% discount for those aged under 26 or over 59). From June to September this bus runs four times a week. This trip is rather tiring because it follows a roundabout route via Rotterdam, Antwerp and Brussels. For tickets contact Budget Bus/Eurolines (☎ 020-627 5151), Juliana plein (Amstel station), Amsterdam, or Eurolines (☎ 2-203 0709), rue du Progrès 80, Brussels.

Bus services to and from Western Europe are still much cheaper than train services. See Information in the Prague section of this chapter for the names of local offices selling tickets for these buses.

Both Eurolines and the new Eurobus offer bus passes for travel around Europe and it is possible to get off and on anywhere on the route. While Eurolines covers most major cities on the Continent, Eurobus so far has only three routes, the northern one of which covers Munich, Salzburg, Vienna, Budapest, Prague, Berlin and Hamburg. A two-month Eurolines pass is £249, while a Eurobus pass is £139.

Youth discounts are available and bookings are a must during the summer peak season.

Train

The easiest and most comfortable way to get from Western Europe to the Czech Republic is by train. Keep in mind that train fares within the Czech Republic are less expensive than the amount you might otherwise pay for that section of a ticket to or from Western Europe. When travelling between Western and Eastern Europe, buy as little of the Czech portion as you can and use border towns such as Děčín, Cheb, Plzeň, České Budějovice and Břeclav as entry or exit points. In other words, buy tickets that terminate or begin in these towns.

Sample 2nd-class international train fares from Prague are 977 Kč to Budapest (616km, nine hours), 438 Kč to Kraków, 628 Kč to Vienna (354km, six hours), 693 Kč to Warsaw (740km, 12 hours), 994 Kč to Nuremberg (371km, six hours) and 1288 Kč to Berlin (377km, 5½ hours).

In the Czech Republic you should purchase international train tickets in advance from Czech Railways (ČD) ticket offices (which use the computerised booking service ARES that's linked to the European train reservation system) or ČD travel agencies and other travel agents. All international tickets are valid for two months with unlimited stopovers. Students get a 25% discount on train tickets to other Eastern European countries. Eurail passes are not accepted in the Czech Republic, and while Inter-Rail passes (sold to European residents only) are accepted, they will work out to be more expensive than locally paid train fares.

Most of the major 'name trains' travel daily throughout the year and require compulsory seat reservations. First-class sleepers and 2nd-class couchettes are available on almost all of these trains.

Western Europe Prague is on the main line used by all direct trains from Berlin to Vienna and Budapest, so access from those cities is easy. Some express trains link Vienna to Prague via Tábor. It's also possible to travel twice a day north-west from Vienna on local 2nd-class trains by changing at Gmünd and České Velenice, the border points. There are five trains from Vienna (Nordbahnhof or Süd) to Břeclav (146km, 1½ hours). Four times a day there's a service between Linz, Austria, and České Budějovice (125km, four hours).

From western Germany and/or Paris (18 hours) you'll probably go through Nuremberg and Cheb on your way to Prague. Local railcars shuttle between Cheb and Schirnding, Germany, three times a day (13km, 15 minutes). Trains from Zürich and Munich go via Furth im Wald and Plzeň. Three times a day there's an unreserved local train from Furth im Wald, Germany, to Domažlice (25 minutes). Unreserved local trains from Bad Schandau, Germany, to Děčín (22km, 30 minutes), and Zittau, Germany, to Liberec (27km, one hour) operate every couple of hours.

Central & Eastern Europe All express trains running between Budapest and Berlin-Lichtenberg pass through Bratislava, Brno and Prague. Reservations are recommended. Some nationals require a separate Slovak visa to transit Slovakia on their way to Hungary.

Connections between Warsaw, Poland,

and Prague will go through either Wroclaw (12 hours) or Katowice (11 hours). All of these trains avoid Slovakia.

Car & Motorcycle

Travelling by car or motorbike, you will enter the country through one of many border crossings which are marked on most road maps. Drivers from Europe, USA, Canada, Australia and New Zealand don't need an International Driving Permit; only a full domestic licence, along with the vehicle registration. If the car is owned by someone else you need a notarised letter from the owner allowing you to drive it. You'll also need a certificate of insurance – a 'green card' – showing you have full liability insurance. If you don't you will be required to take out insurance (3000 Kč for a car and 600 Kč for a motorcycle) at the border, but not all border crossings issue these.

A vehicle needs to be equipped with a first-aid kit, a red-and-white warning triangle and display a nationality sticker on the rear.

The ride-along service similar to the German *Mitfahrzentrale* – where you can go as a paying passenger in a private car or, if you have a car, take on passengers – is now available from (and within) the Czech Republic to anywhere in Europe, even Moscow, for about half the price of a bus ticket. There are two agencies in Prague that are associated with *Mitfahrzentrale*: Town to Town (☎ 02-22 07 54 07; fax 22 07 54 08), Národní 9, Prague 1, and Bezstarostná jízda (☎ 02-602 22 67 22; ☎/fax 90 02 98 06; jizda@ login.cz), Sázavská 12, Prague 2.

Walking

If you want to avoid the hassle or expense of getting an international train ticket, consider walking across the border! To or from Poland, the easiest place to do this is at Český Těšín, which is on the opposite side of the Olše (Olza) River from Cieszyn, Poland. Both towns have good onward train or bus services, making this a viable option for the slightly adventurous traveller. Two bridges, each with traffic in only one direction, link the towns; the Czech train station is about 500m from the bridges, the Polish station about 1km away. Train services from Český Těšín are good. There are seven trains a day to Prague (397km, five hours), eight to Žilina (69km, two hours) and four to Košice (311km, 4½ hours). For Brno (209km) change at Bohumín or Česká Třebová.

If you want to walk into Austria, a good place to do it is from Mikulov, an unspoiled Moravian town with a large chateau on one hill and a church on another. Mikulov is on the railway line from Břeclav to Znojmo and the station is very close to the Austrian/Czech border point. From Brno, it's much faster to come by bus (50km). You could easily cross on foot and then hitchhike the 77km south to Vienna.

For information on crossing into Germany on foot turn to Getting There & Away in the Cheb section.

LEAVING THE CZECH REPUBLIC
The airport departure tax on international flights leaving the Czech Republic is included in the price of the ticket.

Getting Around

AIR
ČSA only flies between Brno and Prague during trade fairs in Brno otherwise it runs buses four times a day on weekdays and twice a day on weekends (305 Kč). Air Ostrava has several daily Prague-Ostrava flights.

BUS
Within the Czech Republic, the express buses of Czech Automobile Transportation, or Česká automobilová doprava (ČSAD), are often faster and more convenient than the train. Buses and trains are about the same price but some train routes are cheaper than bus routes and vice versa – by European standards both are cheap. Count on spending about 80 Kč for every 100km of bus travel. You sometimes have to pay a small additional charge for checked luggage. There are also several internal long-distance bus companies, including Čebus and Bohemian Express.

Because of numerous footnotes, posted bus timetables are almost impossible to read, so patronise information counters. Two crossed hammers as a footnote means the bus

only operates on working days Monday to Friday. As more buses leave in the morning, it's better to get an early start. Many bus services don't operate on weekends – trains are more reliable at that time. Buses, especially if full, are known to leave a few minutes early, so it is best to get to the station about 10 minutes prior to the stated departure time.

Since bus ticketing is computerised at main stations like Prague and Karlovy Vary, you can often book a seat ahead and be sure of a comfortable trip. At large stations, make sure you're in the right ticket line. Way stations are rarely computerised and you must line up and pay the driver. Reservations can only be made in the originating station of the bus, and at peak periods you may have to stand part of the way if you don't have a reservation.

All over the Czech Republic, if you want to find a bus station or bus stop, write the letters ČSAD on a piece of paper and show it to someone. If you want to find a train station, write ČD (which stands for Czech Railways) on the paper.

Most bus and train stations have a left-luggage room (úschovna). If you lose the receipt, you'll have to pay a fine to recover your bag.

TRAIN
The Czech Railways, or České dráhy (ČD), provides clean (except for the toilets that can be filthy), efficient train service to almost every part of the country. However, over the last seven years there have been over 700 train services cancelled due to lack of passengers, thus making some remote parts of the country harder or impossible to get to by train.

Using the Czech railway system successfully involves a little ingenuity. Some trains operate only on certain days, but the footnotes on the posted timetables are incomprehensible. The clerks at the information counters seldom speak English (not even in major stations), so to get a departure time, try writing down your destination and the date you wish to travel, then point to your watch and pray. All railway information and ticket offices in the Czech Republic are

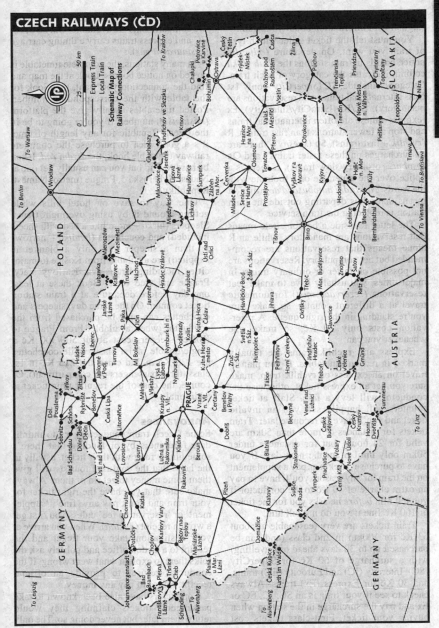

CZECH RAILWAYS (ČD)

Schematic Map of
Railway Connections

Express Train
Local Train

0   25   50 km

computerised and will give you a print out in English with information about your train.

You must tell the ticket seller which type of train you want. On departure (*odjezdy*) notice boards in train stations the *druh vlaku* column indicates the category of each train. Categories include: **SC** (*SuperCity* – only 1st class international trains, and reservations are mandatory), **EC/IC** (EuroCity/InterCity), **Ex** (express – these are often international trains and stop at fewer stations than fast trains), **R** (*rychlík* – fast trains), **Sp** (*spěšný* – there are no surcharges on these faster trains) and **Os** (*osobní* – ordinary slow trains). If there is a notice over the timetable or a footnote with the words '*Náhradní autobusová doprava*', it means that a bus departing outside the train station is replacing the train service.

The letter R inside a box or circle means that reservations are mandatory, while an R alone means that reservations are recommended but not compulsory. Reservations are not possible on faster or ordinary trains. In major cities, you usually have to make seat reservations (*rezervace míst*) for domestic travel at a different counter, so make sure you're standing in the right queue. A reservation costs only 30 Kč, so make one whenever you can.

Express and rychlík trains are usually marked in red on timetables. If you plan to travel on an express or rychlík train, make sure you get an express ticket, otherwise the conductor will levy a fine. Staff at ticket counters will happily sell you an invalid ticket and you'll have no recourse later. Train tickets for distances of more than 50km are valid for 24 hours, but for distances under 50km only until 6 am the next day. If you have to purchase a ticket or pay a supplement on the train for any reason, you'll have to pay an extra charge of 10 Kč to the conductor if you tell him *before* he asks you for the ticket or 100 Kč fine if you do not tell him.

Train tickets are very reasonable at about 53 Kč for 100km in 2nd class (and can be purchased up to 30 days ahead of travelling) with a surcharge of 60 Kč for SuperCity (SC), Intercity (IC) and Eurocity (EC) trains, and 30 Kč for Express (Ex) trains. Always check to see if your train is an SC, IC, EC or Ex and pay the surcharge in the station when buying your ticket. First-class tickets cost

50% more than 2nd-class ones and nonsmoking compartments are available. Only SC, IC, EC and express trains carry a dining carriage (*restaurační vůz*).

In many stations, the complete timetable is posted on notice boards. Look at the map and find the connection you want, then look for the table with the corresponding number. Posted timetables usually give the platform (*nástupiště*) number. If you're going to be in the Czech Republic for any length of time, it's a good idea to purchase the complete railway timetable book, the *Jízdní řád*. It can be hard to find but you can usually get one at Nadas, Hybernská 5, Prague (metro: Náměstí Republiky).

One way to save on hotel bills while getting around is by using overnight trains. Sleepers (*lůžko* – more like a bed with sheets included) and couchettes (*lehátko* – narrower than a sleeper and only a blanket is supplied) are available from Košice to major cities including Bratislava, Karlovy Vary, Prague and vice versa. Book these at least one day before departure at a train station ticket counter. On the same day, sleepers and couchettes can only be purchased from the conductor, when available. From Prague to Košice sleepers cost about 500/300 Kč a single/double in 1st class, while couchettes are 128 Kč in 2nd class and 215 Kč in 1st class (three passengers per compartment). Of course, the cost of the regular train ticket is additional.

Annoyances

Some Czech train conductors try to intimidate foreigners by pretending that there's something wrong with their ticket, usually in the hope that the confused tourists will give them some money to get rid of them. Always make sure that you have the right ticket for your train and don't pay any 'fine', 'supplement' or 'reservation fee' unless you first get a written receipt (*doklad*). When you arrive at your destination, take your ticket and the receipt to a Čedok office and politely ask the folks there to explain what went wrong. If the conductor refuses to provide an official receipt, refuse to pay any money.

Conductors have also been known to take passengers' tickets claiming they would return them later but never doing so. The only circumstance in which a conductor has the right to hold your ticket is when you board a train on which you've reserved a couchette or sleeper, in which case the attendant will keep your ticket overnight so you don't have to be woken up for ticket controls. Don't forget to ask for your ticket back.

Several travellers have reported having problems with some types of lockers at train and bus stations. The trick is to remember that they have two combination dials, one inside and the other outside the door. You set the inside dial with your combination, and when you return, you have to duplicate the same code on the outside dial to open the locker.

CAR & MOTORCYCLE

The types of petrol available at almost all petrol stations around the whole country are special (91 octane), super (96 octane), unleaded is natural (95 octane) or natural plus (98 octane), diesel and LPG. Unleaded petrol costs about 22 Kč or 27 Kč per 1L respectively. LPG gas (about 12 Kč per 1L) is available in every region but there are very few stations that sell it (only five in Prague).

Road Rules

You can drive in the Czech Republic using your normal driving licence (ie an international driving licence is not required).

Speed limits are 40km/h or 50km/h in built-up areas, 90km/h on open roads and 130km/h on motorways; motorbikes are limited to 80km/h. At level crossings over railway lines the speed limit is 30km/h. Beware of speed traps on the autoroutes as the police are empowered to levy on-the-spot fines of up to 2000 Kč and foreigners are the preferred targets. Most of the major freeways now have an 800 Kč annual toll charge (see the country map) and this is payable at most border crossings. If you are caught on a freeway without the toll sticker displayed on the windscreen of your vehicle, the fine will be up to 5000 Kč.

Driving and parking around Prague are a nightmare so it's best to leave your vehicle somewhere safe and use public transport. Unmetered parking in the historic centre of Prague is only allowed if you have a permit.

Car theft by organised gangs is routine, with expensive western cars disappearing across the country's borders within hours.

Rental

The main car rental chains operating in the Czech Republic are A Rent Car, Avis, Budget, Europcar and Hertz. A Rent Car is the cheapest, charging 797 Kč a day plus 6 Kč a kilometre, or 1990/1316 Kč daily/weekly with unlimited mileage, for a Škoda Felicie. Its 'weekend rate' from 1 pm Friday to 9 am Monday is 3577 Kč, including 600km of mileage. Collision insurance (CDW) for up to six days is 214 Kč and passenger insurance is 63 Kč extra, and there's a 285 Kč surcharge if you pick up your vehicle from one of the company's hotel or airport locations. Europcar is 50% more expensive, while other major rental companies are up to 100% more expensive than either of these. None of the prices quoted above includes the 5% VAT.

Most companies allow one-way rentals to their other locations in the Czech Republic at no additional charge. When comparing rates, note whether the 5% VAT is included. The police single out foreign cars for traffic fines, so try to get a Škoda when you rent a car.

BICYCLE

The Czech Republic is small enough to be traversed on a bicycle. It is fairly safe for cyclists as most drivers will do their utmost to avoid them. Cyclists should still be careful as the roads are very narrow and potholed, and in towns the cobblestones and tram tracks can be a dangerous combination, especially when it has been raining. Theft is a problem, especially in Prague and other large cities, so a good long chain and lock are a must.

Many locals use bicycles, so it's fairly easy to transport them on trains. First purchase your train ticket and then take it with your bicycle to the railway luggage office. There you fill out a card which will be attached to your bike; on the card you write your name, address, destination and departing station. You will be given a receipt that should include all the accessories that your bicycle has, such as lights and dynamo. You are not allowed to leave any luggage on the bicycle, and it is advisable to take off the pump and water bottles, as they could disappear along the way. The cost of transporting a bicycle is usually one-tenth of the train ticket. It is best to collect the bicycle from the goods carriage as soon as you arrive at your destination. You can also transport bicycles on most buses if they are not crowded and if the bus driver is willing.

HITCHING

Hitching is never entirely safe in any country in the world, and we don't recommend it. Travellers who decide to hitch should understand that they are taking a small but potentially serious risk.

The Czech Republic is no safer than other European countries when it comes to hitching; many hitchhikers are assaulted and/or raped, and each year a few are killed. Yet despite the usual dangers, many Czechs, including young females, choose to hitch.

LOCAL TRANSPORT

Buses and trams within cities operate from around 4.30 am to 11.30 pm daily. In Prague, buses and trains on some main routes operate every 40 minutes all night long. Tickets sold at newsstands must be validated once you're aboard, as there are no conductors. Tickets are hard to find at night, on weekends and out in residential areas, so carry a good supply. Yellow automatic ticket machines at Prague metro stations sell tickets that can be used on all forms of public transport in Prague.

Taxi

Taxis have meters – just make sure the meter is switched on. Some Prague taxi drivers are highly experienced at overcharging tourists. See the Prague chapter for more details.

Prague

☎ 02

Prague (Praha in Czech) has almost a magical feel about it and is like a history lesson come to life. As you walk among the long stone palaces or across the Karlův most (Charles Bridge), with Smetana's Vltava flowing below and pointed towers all around, you'll feel as if history had stopped back in the 18th century. Goethe called Prague the prettiest gem in the stone crown of the world. A millennium earlier in 965 the Arab-Jewish merchant Ibrahim Ibn Jacob described Prague as a town of 'stone and lime'. For these reasons the city is on the UNESCO World Heritage list.

This story-book city in the centre of Bohemia experienced two architectural golden ages: a Gothic period under Holy Roman Emperor Charles IV and then a baroque period during the Habsburg Counter-Reformation. In the 18th century, Czech culture was suppressed, so it's not at all surprising that Prague's two greatest baroque architects, Christopher and Kilian Dientzenhofer, were Germans.

Today Prague is a city of over a million inhabitants, the seat of government and leading centre of much of the country's intellectual and cultural life. Unlike Warsaw, Budapest and Berlin, which were major battlefields during WWII, Prague escaped almost unscathed and after the war, lack of modernisation prevented haphazard modern development. Since 1989, however, central Prague has been swamped by capitalism as street vendors, cafés and restaurants take over pavements, streets and parks.

How you feel about Prague's current tourist glut may depend on where you're coming from. If you're arriving from London, Paris or Rome it may all seem quite normal, but if you've been elsewhere in Eastern Europe for a while, you'll be in for a bit of a shock. As you're being jostled by the hawkers and hordes of tourists, you may begin to feel that Prague has become a tacky tourist trap, but try to overcome that feeling and enjoy this great European art centre for all it's worth.

And remember, if you're in Prague on a Monday, many museums and galleries will be closed. However, the Jewish Quarter, the Mozart Museum, the National Museum, the Bethlem Chaple, the Strahov Library, St Vitus Cathedral and many attractions in Prague Castle, the old town hall and most sights in Vyšehrad citadel will still be open.

Orientation

Almost exactly midway between Berlin and

to take bus No 112 to the zoo (see the Nearby Palaces section earlier in this chapter) and catch the 11 am or the 5 pm boat from the zoo back to Prague. Allow 15 minutes to walk from the zoo to the landing.

Other cruises that operate throughout the day include a two-hour sightseeing cruise (200/450 Kč without/with lunch) or a three-hour cruise (600 Kč with dinner).

From the Kampa landing next to Karlův most there are 50-minute cruises (200 Kč) hourly between June and September from 11 am to 8 pm, in May from 11 am, and March, April and October to December from noon to 5 pm. This is an excellent alternative to signing up for an expensive bus tour to sights you can easily visit on your own.

The excursion boats of the Evropská vodní doprava (EVD), which leave from a landing behind the Inter-Continental Hotel, have a one-hour tour (200 Kč) daily every hour from 10 am to 6 pm, a two-hour tour including lunch and music (550 Kč) and an evening three-hour tour with dinner and music (650 Kč).

You can row yourself up and down the Vltava in a boat rented from several places along the river (including Slovanský Island).

Places to Stay

Unless otherwise stated, all prices quoted for rooms are for a single/double/triple/quad.

Camping The *University Sport Club Caravan Camp* (☎ 52 47 14) is Prague's most convenient camping ground since it's right on Plzeňská, west of the city, next to tram line Nos 4 and 9 (stop: Hotel Golf). Camping costs 120 Kč per person and 90 Kč per tent.

If this camping ground is full, walk three minutes back along Plzeňská towards Prague and you'll see a large sign pointing up the hill to the *Sport Camp* (☎ 57 21 30 80). Otherwise take tram No 4 or 9 from Anděl metro station to the Poštovka stop, then walk 1km up the hill. Night tram No 58 passes every 40 minutes throughout the night. This site is a stiff 10-minute climb from the tram stop. Camping is 140 Kč per person, plus 110 Kč per tent, and the site has 60 small bungalows for 400 Kč a double, 500 Kč a triple or 600 Kč for four people. The reception is open from 7 am to 9 pm daily. Both camping grounds are

under the same management, so you can ask about one at the other, and they're open from April until the end of October.

Hostels One of the most central places is *Hostel Sokol* (☎ 57 00 73 97) at Hellichova 1, which you enter from Všehrdova 42 (take the metro to Malostranská and then tram No 12 or 22 two stops south). Dorms here are 220 Kč per bed, but check them out before you accept a bed.

Another very central hostel is *Express* (☎ 24 21 18 01), Skořepka 5, in the heart of the Staré Město. The very popular place fills up fast and a bed costs 350 Kč (200 Kč for students in the off-season) in rooms with two/three/four beds. Rooms with bathroom are 800/1200 Kč.

On the opposite side of Staré Město is one of the many Traveller's Hostels establishments, *Pension Dlouhá* (☎ 231 13 18; hostel@terminal.cz), Dlouhá 33. The basic but clean and newly renovated rooms are from 350 Kč in dorms or 490 Kč/bed in a double room. There are seven other Traveller's Hostels available from mid-June to August and ideally located around central Prague in *domov mládeže* (youth homes) locations.

The HI handbook lists in southern Nové Město near Karlovo náměstí, the *Hostel in Club Habitat* (☎ 29 03 15), Na Zbořenci 10 (metro: Karlovo Náměstí). Accommodation in a room with two or more beds is 450 Kč.

The *Juniorhotel* (☎ 29 13 20), at Žitná 12 (metro: Karlovo Náměstí), is often full. Dorm beds are 500 Kč (or 400 Kč with ISIC card). Hotel rooms are 1500/2200/2820 Kč with bath and breakfast. There are no discounts here for HI members.

In the heart of Žižkov is the popular *Clown & Bard Hostel* (☎ 27 24 36), Bořivojova 102, Prague 3 (metro: Jiřího z Poděbrad). A bed in a dorm is 200 Kč, in rooms with two or more beds from 250 Kč, and in doubles including a kitchen for 350 Kč. Around the corner there's the *Purple House* (☎ 27 14 90), Krasová 25, where a space in four-bed rooms is 330 Kč.

Penzion Jana (☎ 25 06 88), Dykova 20 (metro: Jiřího z Poděbrad), has accommodation in rooms with two to five beds for 400 Kč and 350 Kč respectively, including breakfast. There is a large garden where volleyball is played and a parking lot.

Another HI handbook place is the *Hotel Standart* (☎ 87 52 58), Přístavní 1, a large six-storey hotel on a quiet street north of the centre. Rooms with shared bath are 620/800/1100/1400 Kč or 350 Kč per bed in shared rooms if you have an HI card. This is good value and you actually do have a chance of getting in. It's a 10-minute walk from Nádraží Holešovice metro station/Praha-Holešovice train station. Walk east on Vrbenského to Ortenovo náměstí, then right and south five short blocks on Osadní to the hotel. If the Standart is full you could check *Pension Vltava* (☎ 80 97 95), Dělnická 35, just around the corner, with rooms at 500/800 Kč.

In Dejvice, a three-minute walk from Dejvice metro station is *Hostel Orlík* (☎ 23 31 12 40), Terronská 6, where a bed in single/double/triple rooms is 390/350/330 Kč. Walk north-east from the roundabout up Verdunská, and Terronská is second on the left. Another hostel is a 15-minute walk further up Terronská at No 28. Here the *Berhanu CK Hostel* (☎ 24 31 11 05) has beds in doubles for 250 Kč or 350 Kč with bathroom.

Another popular place is *Hostel Boathaus* (Slavoj-Wesico; ☎ 402 10 76), V náklích 1A, where dorm beds are 250 Kč. To get there from Praha-hlavní nádraží train station take tram No 3 at Jindřišská in the direction of Modřany to tram stop Černý kůň and follow the bus signs to the river.

If it's getting late and you still don't have a bed, consider spending the night at the *Turistická ubytovna TJ Sokol Karlín* (☎ 231 51 32) on Malého, a five-minute walk from Florenc bus station (metro: Florenc). To get there, walk east along Křižíkova past the Karlín Theatre and turn right on Pluku just after the railway bridge. The hostel is just before the next railway bridge. The doors don't open until 6 pm and a dorm bed is from 260 Kč.

Student Dormitories *Hostel Jednota*

(☎ 24 21 17 73), Opletalova 38, near Praha-hlavní nádraží train station, has beds priced from 345 Kč (or 100 Kč for a free bed anywhere) including breakfast. Its *Pension* at the same address has beds for 455 Kč/person. If you pre-book a bed with Universitas Tour

(☎ 26 04 26, fax 21 22 90) there is a 50 or 60 Kč discount. It also has two other pensions in Prague.

One of the easiest places to arrange hostel accommodation on the spot is at the *Strahov student dormitory complex* opposite Spartakiádní stadión west of the centre. Bus Nos 143, 149 and 217 run directly there from Dejvická metro station. As you get off the bus you'll see 11 huge blocks of flats. Though the capacity is great, the whole complex does occasionally get booked out by groups. The 11 blocks of flats operate as separate hostels in July and August, while in the off season only three will be open at minimum capacity. The travel agencies in the train stations will book beds at Strahov for a few dollars. Noisy discos operate from 7 pm to 2 am downstairs in *blok* Nos 10 and 11, and until 4 am at No 1.

The *Hostel SPUS* (☎ 57 21 07 64; spus@praha.czcom.cz) in *blok* 4 has rooms with two or three beds for 300 and 250 Kč per person respectively. It also has two seasonal hostels in Nové Město and two that are open all year south of the centre – *Hostel U melouna*, Ke Karlovu 7, Prague 2, (metro: IP Pavlova) and *Hostel Podolí* (☎ 61 21 17 76), Na lysině 12, *blok* B, Prague 4 (from metro station Pražského povstání take bus No 148 to Děkanka stop).

The *Hostel ESTEC* (☎ 57 21 04 10; estec@jrc.cz) in *blok* 5 has crowded dorms for 190 Kč per person or 400 and 290 Kč beds in three or four-bed rooms. It is also a travel agent and can book other accommodation and transportation. At the rear of the complex at *blok* 11 is *Müller Hostel* where a bed is 240 Kč per person.

A similar place is *Kolej Kajetánka* (☎ 20 51 31 18), Radimova 12, Building 1. Take bus No 108 or 174 west from Hradčanská metro to 'Kajetánka' and look for two tall white towers. If the porter doesn't speak English go to the 'Ubytovací kancelář' office inside the building. Kolej Kajetánka has 150 single (395 Kč) and double rooms at 345 Kč per bed.

Room-Finding Services AVE Limited

(☎ 24 22 32 26, reservations ☎ 57 31 29 85) at Praha-hlavní nádraží and Praha-Holešovice train stations and Ruzyně airport rents a variety of *private rooms* at around 400 Kč per person, while *private apartments* begin around 1000 Kč per person. AVE gives discounts for longer stays. It also knows about hostel accommodation (200 Kč per person). The AVE branch at Praha-hlavní nádraží is open daily from about 6 am to 10 pm.

Vesta/Baleno Tour at Praha-hlavní nádraží train station has *private rooms* on the metro line for around 1000 Kč per person.

ESTEC Travel Agency (☎ 57 21 04 10, fax 57 21 52 63; estec@jrc.cz) in *blok* 5 at Vaníčkova 1, Prague 6, can arrange accommodation and transportation.

Top Tour (☎ 232 10 77), Rybná 3, is more expensive. First-category rooms (with private bath) are 830/1280 Kč and 2nd-category rooms (with shared bath) are 630/1050 Kč. Apartments are also available (2000 Kč a double). Rooms are available in the city centre for an additional 10%, and the office is open all year daily until 7 pm.

Stop City Accommodation (☎ 24 22 24 97), Vinohradská 24, about six blocks from Praha-hlavní nádraží train station, arranges *private rooms* in the centre or on a metro line from 550 Kč and apartments from 800 Kč per person. It's open year-round daily from 11 am to 8 pm and staff speak English.

You can also rent a *private room* unofficially from householders you meet at train and bus stations or in the street. They'll ask from about 350 to 800 Kč per person, depending on the location – a bargain if you think the price is too high and check the location on a good map before going.

Pensions An interesting place to stay in the old town is *Unitas Pension* (☎ 232 77 00), Barto-lomějská 9 (metro: Národní Třída). The former prison has 40 dull rooms that were once prison cells (president Havel did some time in one of them) with shared bath at 1020/1200 Kč and a generous breakfast is included. It's a pleasant place to stay but is often fully booked by noisy youth groups.

South of the centre, the five-room *AV Pension Praha* (☎ 795 17 26), Malebná 1172, is a four-minute walk from Chodov metro station. Bed and breakfast is 890/1280 Kč. The quality of the accommodation is high.

North-west of the centre, the friendly and family-run *Pension Bob* (☎ 311 44 92/78

35), Kovárenská 2, Lysolaje (Praha 6), has bright and clean rooms with a bathroom and TV at 965/1530 Kč, including breakfast. It has a bar and secure parking. Take bus No 160 or 355 from Dejvická metro station to the Žákovská bus stop.

Hotels There are no longer any cheap hotels in central Prague due to the many big spending Western European and American tourists. The city is an extremely popular destination; if you're thinking of visiting during Christmas, Easter or summer then bookings are strongly recommended.

Also, many cheaper hotels charge foreigners 50 to 100% more than they charge Czechs for the same rooms.

City Centre An unbelievably well-priced central place is *Libra Q Hostel* (☎ 24 23 17 54), Senovážné náměstí 21 (metro: Náměstí Republiky), which has rooms with shared bathroom at 750/890/1320/1560 Kč and rooms with bathroom at 980/1380/1630 Kč.

Good for the money is the *Hotel Balkán* (☎ 54 07 77), třída Svornosti 28, two blocks from Anděl metro station. Rooms in this attractive old four-storey building are 1100/1400/1700/1950 Kč with bath or shower. The hotel also has a good restaurant and is just a block from the Vltava River.

The five-storey, 65-room *Merkur Hotel* (☎ 232 39 06), Těšnov 9, a five-minute walk from Florenc bus station, is 2800/3200 Kč with bath or shower, breakfast included.

The fading *Grand Hotel Evropa* (☎ 24 22 81 17), Václavské náměstí 25 (metro: Můstek), is an Art Nouveau extravaganza, brimming with old-world atmosphere. The run-down rooms are 1280/2160/2790/3640 Kč without bath and 2450/3400/4350/5200 Kč, breakfast included. Considering the alternatives, this is good value.

Also in the big splurge category is the *Admirál Botel* (☎ 57 32 13 02), Hořejší nábřeží, about four blocks from Anděl metro station. This gigantic luxury barge permanently moored on the Vltava River has 84 double cabins at 2640/2760 Kč including breakfast. The four four-bed cabins go for 4270 Kč a triple, 4630 Kč a quad. Ask for a room facing the river.

The splendid Art Nouveau *Hotel Paříž* (☎ 24 22 21 51), U obecního domu 1, is a real splurge in a historical monument. Doubles with all the extras are about 8250 Kč, including breakfast.

Libeň District A number of good places to stay exist in the Libeň district north of the centre. One of the strangest (and best) is *Pension V sudech* (☎ 688 04 28), Zenklova 217. You sleep in a small bungalow shaped like a Budvar beer keg (no joke!) for 200 Kč per person in a double. The kegs are 'uncorked' from April to October only. Or there is the pension accommodation from 400 Kč per person. Get there on tram No 5, 17 or 25 from Nádraží Holešovice metro station to 'Ke Stírce' and walk straight through the folk restaurant here to the hotel reception in the back yard. (If the restaurant is closed go around the block to the back gate.)

A block from the Na Vlachovce is *Hotel Apollo Garni* (☎ 688 06 28), Kubišova 23, a modern four-storey hotel with rooms with bath at 1090/1730 Kč, breakfast included.

Outskirts The *Hotel Petynka* (☎ 20 51 32 83), Na Petynce, Střešovice, Prague 6, has rooms with shower/WC for 1580/1850 Kč, including breakfast. From Hradčanská metro station take bus No 108 or 174 three stops to Kajetánka.

If a 20-minute metro ride doesn't deter you, consider the 23-storey *Hotel Business* (☎ 67 99 51 11), Kupeckého 842, very close to Háje metro station. When you come out of the station look for the tallest building around. It's 1000/1700 Kč, with each two rooms sharing a toilet and shower. This is another favourite haunt of the cheap bus tour set and it should be treated only as a last resort.

Places to Eat

Tourism has had a heavy impact on the Prague restaurant scene and cheaper restaurants have almost disappeared from the historical centre, while most of the restaurants in the old town, the castle district and along Václavské náměstí are now more expensive.

If you're on a low budget it might be worth walking a few streets away from the tourist centres or taking the metro to an outlying station and eating there. The suburbs of Žižkov and Smíchov have plenty of inexpensive places.

Be aware that the serving staff in some Prague restaurants in the tourist centre shamelessly overcharge foreigners. Annually, the Czech inspectorate finds that it is being overcharged on about 37% of its bills, so imagine what happens to foreigners. Some restaurants in touristy areas have two menus, one in Czech and the other in German, English and French with higher prices. Insist on a menu with prices; if the waiter refuses to show you one listing specific prices, just get up and walk out. Don't be intimidated by the language barrier.

A good idea is to have a glance at the price of the beer on the menu, as this varies a lot and can cancel your savings on lower meal prices. If the drink prices aren't listed expect them to be sky high (unless, of course, it's only a beer hall). At lunchtime the waiter may bring you the more expensive dinner menu.

Even if you do check the menu price, the waiter may claim you were served a larger portion or he may bring you a different, cheaper dish but still charge the higher price of whatever it was you asked for. Extras like a side salad, bread and butter sometimes incur an added charge, so if you're served something you didn't order and don't want, send it back. Many restaurants add a 10 or 20 Kč cover charge *(couvert)* to the bill and this is hard to find on the menu.

It is best if you note all the dishes and prices before you order and check them against the bill. If you are paying by credit card, be sure the date and the price have been clearly and correctly entered. Don't let your card out of sight as unscrupulous proprietors may make several imprints of the card and copy your signature.

We've tried to weed out the bad apples but we can't guarantee that you won't be cheated. You make your choice and take your chances. However, if you're sure you were unfairly treated, let us know and we'll consider dropping the offending establishment. Seen from the other side, many Prague locals are pretty pissed off about the way their favourite haunts have been invaded and taken over by high-spending tourists.

Václavské Náměstí & Around In a courtyard through a passage on Václavské náměstí 48 is the decent *Hospůdka Václavka* with good Czech pub food from 50 Kč.

The *Česká hospoda v Krakovské*, Krakovská 20 (metro: Muzeum), just around the corner from American Express, offers good inexpensive food, pleasant décor, fast friendly service and reasonable prices. Its menu in English, German and Italian includes a couple of vegetarian items, and dark Braník beer is on tap.

A bit farther away from the square is *Jihočeská restaurace u Šumavy*, Štěpánská 3, serving better inexpensive South Bohemian food, but it's closed on Saturday.

If you're dying for a steak, try the midrange *Americká Restaurant Chicago* in the basement at Štěpánská 63. This isn't just a crass US transplant but it represents the USA as the Czechs see it, which makes it fun. Next door is the cheaper *Mayur Indický Snack Bar*, Štěpánská 65, with a dozen tasty choices for vegetarians. Don't confuse the snack bar with the more expensive Indian restaurant adjacent.

An interesting menu that includes local food and Czech versions of Indian or Chinese cuisine is found at *Restaurace U Jindřišské věže*, Jindřišská 26.

Staroměstské Náměstí & Around The *Staroměstská restaurace*, Staroměstské náměstí 19, not far from the old town hall has food and beer prices on the terrace outside that are up to 50% higher than those charged inside. The menu is extensive and the food good with pleasant service. Don't expect to find any bargain eateries in a tourist area like this.

At Templová 2, off Celetná, *Pivnice Radegast* has good cheap food. Try the excellent guláš but ignore the service.

The *Restaurant U černého slunce*, Kamzíková 9, in a tiny alley off Celetná between U supa and the square, is a cosy, romantic (and inexpensive) place to eat.

Off the square at Dlouhá 2, the self-service *Bona Vita*, has plenty of chicken, vegetarian and soya dishes. Try the Sojový guláš for 39 Kč. At No 8, the *Mikulka's Pizzeria* has pricier but good pizzas with unusual toppings, including a sweet pizza with chocolate topping.

South of the square in a passage on Melantrichova 15, the *Country Life* is the healthiest place to eat in Prague. There are inexpensive salad sandwiches, pizzas, goulash and vegetarian food.

Probably the cheapest pub in the old town is *Hostinec U rotundy*, Karolíny Světlé 17, which doesn't serve meals.

Národní Třída & Around Breakfast is good in the Art Nouveau *Louvre Gany's Café*, Národní 22, where you can get eggs done in any way. It is also open for lunch and dinner but prices are higher.

A Prague institution and now a tourist trap is *U Fleků*, Křemencova 11, a German-style beer hall and garden where you can sit at long communal tables. It is increasingly clogged with tour groups high on oompah music. Waiters circulate periodically with mugs of the excellent but overpriced dark 13° ale that is brewed in-house. The food prices are even more shamelessly touristic.

If you don't like the atmosphere at U Fleků, check *Snack Bar Rytmus*, Křemencova 10, just across the street. Its inexpensive menu in English includes a few Chinese dishes and the waiters are friendly, though of course, there's not the setting of U Fleků.

The *U kotvy restaurace*, Spálená 11, is similar to U Fleků but cheaper.

Still in Nové Město but in the northern part is the vegetarian *U Góvindy*, Soukenická 27, run by Hare Krishnas but nobody's preaching. A donation of at least 60 Kč gets you a full lunch from Monday to Saturday.

Malá Strana Many slightly upmarket tourist restaurants are at or around Malostranské náměstí, including the popular ex-pat hang-out *Jo's Bar* at No 7 with Mexican food. Not far away, on the corner of Nerudova and Zámecká, is *Hostinec U kocoura*, one of president Havel's favourites, which still serves inexpensive Bohemian beer snacks and pub grub.

A good place for a splurge is the *Pálffy Palác club restaurace*, Valdštejnská 14 (metro: Malostranská), in one of the rooms of the Pálffy Palace. It has mainly fish and meat dishes with mouthwatering sauces. Main courses cost from 220 to 480 Kč.

In the southern part of Malá Strana, the **Bohemia Bagel**, Újezd 18, has different sorts of bagels with various toppings and is a great place to eat all day and one of the few early morning breakfast places. It is open from 7 until 2 am daily.

Hradčany You'll see many touristy restaurants and cafés here with prices as high as Hradčany itself. If you're on a tight budget have something filling to eat just before heading up this way. If you need a drink try **Bonal** in a corner of Golden Lane.

Big mugs of draught beer and basic meals can be had at **U Černého vola**, Loretánské náměstí 1, just up from the Loreta Convent.

Further west on Pohořelec 3, is the excellent **Sate indonéské kuchyně** with the usual Indonesian dishes for around 100 Kč.

Around Town *Restaurace Dejvická Sokolovna*, Dejvická 2, just outside Hradčanská metro station and near Laundry Kings, serves cheap pub lunches in the rear dining room. Be prepared to choose at random from the Czech menu.

A good local hang-out that includes a sauna (70 Kč per hour) is **U radnice**, Havlíčkovo náměstí 7, in Žižkov, Prague 3 (take tram No 26 from náměstí Republiky four stops to tram stop Lipanská). The food is good and it can be washed down with a mug of Budvar.

On the other side of the river in Smíchov is **Hospoda Starý lev**, Lidická 13 (metro: Anděl), similar for food and prices but no sauna.

Cafés The classy Art Deco **Kavárna Slávie**, Národní 1, has finally been opened after many years but is of course on the pricey side with lukewarm service. The coffee and cakes are not good at the touristy Art Nouveau café of the **Grand Hotel Evropa**, Václavské náměstí 25, which is Prague's most elegant (but come before 3 pm when they start collecting a music cover charge).

The relaxed atmosphere at **Hogo Fogo**, Salvártorská 4 (metro: Staroměstská) is a change from the busy Prague streets outside. It is popular with the young crowd. See the Bookshops section earlier in this chapter for two other similar cafés that double up as bookshops.

Self-Service A cheap stand-up buffet is at the rear of a butcher's shop. **Maso uzeniny**, Václavské náměstí 36, has good stodge but it's best before 1 pm. Only slightly higher in price and definitely worthwhile is **Rybárna** in the Jalta passage, Václavské náměstí 43. It specialises in fish and has three tables to sit at.

In the Krone department store the **Imbiss Krone**, Václavské náměstí 21, offers tasty grilled chicken and other pre-cooked food.

Great ice cream and fruit specialities are found at **Laguna**, Štěpánská 6.

The **Delicatesse Buffet** at the Palace Hotel, opposite the main post office, near the corner of Jindřišská and Panská, has a self-service salad bar. There are tables to sit at.

Fans of Middle Eastern snacks can find felafels, kebabs or gyros at **Adonis buffet**, Jungmanova 30.

Bílá Labuť, Tesco, Kotva and Krone department stores all have **supermarkets** in their basements. In the suburbs the **Delvita** chain of supermarkets offers low prices and a wide selection of groceries.

Entertainment

Prague has an amazing array of entertainment. While it has long been one of the European centres of classical music and jazz, it is now known for its rock and post-rock scenes as well.

In such a vibrant city, it is inevitable that some of the places listed here will have changed by the time you arrive. For the most up-to-date information, refer to the *Prague Post*, *Culture in Prague*, PIS's free *Cultural Events* and *Do města Downtown*. However, even these publications will not list everything, so keep an eye on posters and bulletin boards whenever you are out and about.

For classical music, opera, ballet, theatre and some rock concerts – even the most 'sold-out' (*vyprodáno*) events – you can often find a ticket or two on sale at the box office 30 minutes or so before concert time. In addition, there are plenty of ticket agencies around Prague that will sell the same tickets at a high commission. Touts also sell tickets at the door, but avoid these people unless you have no other option. Although some more-expensive tickets are set aside for foreigners, at the box office non-Czechs normally pay the same price as Czechs. Tickets can cost as little as 10 Kč for standing room only to over 900 Kč for the best seats in the house, but the average price is about 400 Kč.

Cinema is good in Prague and tickets are under 100 Kč. Most films are shown in the original language with Czech subtitles. The *Prague Post* carries complete listings of what's on, with times and cinema addresses.

Ticket Agencies A number of travel agencies specialise in selling theatre tickets for about the same price as the scalpers. The advantage of dealing with the agencies is that they are computerised, quick, some accept credit cards and make advance reservations. One of the largest tourist ticket agencies of this kind is Ticketpro (☎ 24 81 40 20), Salvatorská 10, which also has many branches around Prague.

Some music stores and other outlets also act as its agents – look for the Ticketpro sticker. Another is Best Tour in Hotel Meran (☎ 90 03 27 76), Václavské náměstí 27, which has English-speaking staff. Most agencies charge the same prices for the following shows: the Laterna Magika (650 Kč), opera (150 Kč to 830 Kč), National Theatre and National Marionette Theatre (490 Kč), and 'Bohemian Fantasy' (540 Kč for the show only or 900 Kč with dinner). Tickets to the tacky folklore shows by the Czech Song and Dance Ensemble are 340 Kč.

Bohemia Ticket International (☎ 24 22 78 32; fax 21 61 21 26), Malé náměstí 13, Praha 1, has another branch at Na příkopě 16 and accepts reservations. Laterna Magika tickets should be ordered at least two months in advance.

Other main tourist ticket agencies include Čedok, Pařížská 6; American Express, Václavské náměstí 56; the Prague Information Service, Na příkopě 20; and Čedok, Na příkopě 18.

The best place to buy tickets for rock concerts is Ticketpro's Melantrich in the Rokoko arcade at Václavské náměstí 38; its offerings are advertised on posters.

Concert tickets are available from the FOK Symfonický Orchestr office Rudolfinum, náměstí Jana Palacha. It is open weekdays from 10 am to 12.30 pm and 1.30 to 6 pm, weekends from 1.30 to 7.30 pm and one hour before the concert.

Classical Music Prague's main concert venue is the neo-Renaissance *Rudolfinum*, náměstí Jana Palacha (metro: Staroměstská), where the Prague Spring Music Festival is held in late May.

Prague's wonderful Art Nouveau municipal concert hall, *Smetana Hall*, in Obecní dům, at náměstí Republiky 5 right next to the Powder Gate, is not used very often (it always hosts Prague Spring concerts), but when it is, tickets are available from FOK.

Lots of organ concerts in old churches and recitals in historic buildings are put on for tourists, and you'll see stacks of fliers advertising these in every tourist office and travel agency around Prague. Seat prices begin at around 300 Kč, but the programs change from week to week so it's hard to give any specific recommendations.

Jazz There are many jazz clubs. The *Reduta Jazz Club*, Národní 20 (metro: Národní Třída) was founded in 1958 and is one of the oldest in Europe. It is open from 9 pm to midnight, and there is a 120 Kč cover charge. Tickets are sold after 3 pm on weekdays or after 5 pm on Saturday and 7 pm on Sunday.

You can see and hear live jazz every night from 9 pm to midnight at the unpretentious *AghaRTA jazz centrum*, Krakovská 5 (metro: Muzeum).

The cosy *U malého Glena*, Karmelitská 23 (metro: Malostranská), has jazz bands in the basement every evening from 9 pm.

Rock, Clubs & Discos Adjacent to the Reduta Jazz Club is the *Rock Cafe*, Národní 20, with a music shop selling rock and punk T-shirts, skull and crossbones necklaces and rings etc. From 8 pm to 3 am there's hard rock music here (at least 60 Kč cover charge, standard drink prices). Wear black clothing if you can. *Batalion*, downstairs at 28. října 3, offers local rock or jazz-rock bands weekdays, while DJs spin discs on the weekends.

At the student accommodation in Strahov, *Klub 007 Strahov*, blok 7 in Chaloupeckého 7, Prague 6, has rock bands or DJs playing Monday to Saturday from 8 pm. *Klub Újezd*, Újezd 18 (open from 8 pm daily) has a varied clientele.

The *Lucerna Music Bar*, Vodičkova 36, inside the passage, has bands every evening performing a great variety of music, anything from folk or jazz, to pop or rock.

The prime dance venue is *Club Radost FX*, Bělehradská 120, Prague 2 (metro: IP Pavlova), with famous European and local DJs spinning disks. *Astra*, on the 1st floor of Václavské náměstí 22 (metro: Můstek), is a tacky and touristy disco which is open from 9 pm to 4 am.

Alternative Venues A place with a difference is *Palác Akropolis*, Kubelíkova 27, where local bands perform, but on some nights there are plays, films or other cultural shows.

A variety of performances can be heard at *Malostranská beseda*, Malostranské náměstí 21 (metro: Malostranská), including jazz, folk, country, rock and rock opera. The café is open nightly, and most programs begin at 8.30 pm.

Theatres Opera, ballet and classical drama (in Czech) are performed at the neo-Renaissance *National Theatre* (1883), Národní 2 (metro: Národní Třída). Next door is the modern *Laterna Magika* (1983), Národní 4, which offers a widely imitated combination of theatre, dance and film. Regular tickets, however, are usually sold out two months in advance. The ticket offices for the Laterna Magika and National Theatre (Národní divadlo) are both just inside the Laterna Magika.

Opera and ballet are also presented at the neo-Renaissance *State Opera* on Wilsonova (metro: Muzeum), which has its own ticket office at the theatre. The neoclassical *Stavovské Theatre* (1783), Ovocný trh 1 (metro: Můstek), often presents opera. Headphones providing simultaneous translation into English are available for some of its Czech plays. Its ticket office is opposite the theatre at Ovocný trh 4.

For operettas and musicals in Czech go to the *Karlín Theatre of Music*, Křižíkova 10, near Florenc bus station (metro: Florenc). Because it's a little out of the way and not as famous as some other venues, tickets are often available; it is highly recommended. The ticket office is open Monday to Saturday from 10 am to 1 pm and 2 to 6 pm.

Musicals like *Hair* or *Dracula* were shown at the *Divadlo Spirála* in Výstaviště (Fair-

grounds; metro: Nádraží Holešovice) and the Congress Centre (Palace of Culture), 5.května 65 (metro: Vyšehrad). These have finished but other musicals are planned.

Several theatres around town stage 'black theatre' or 'magic theatre' performances combining mime, film, dance, music or whatever. *Black Theatre of Jiří Srnec*, Štěpánská 61, Nové Město, and *Ta Fantastika*, Karlova 8, Staré Město, are such touristy places. Admission to some is as low as 370 Kč.

Plays in the Czech language by Václav Havel are often put on at the *Na zábradlí Theatre*, Anenské náměstí 5 (metro: Staroměstská).

Puppet Theatres The *Divadlo Minor*, Senovážné náměstí 28 (metro: Náměstí Republiky), offers a mix of puppets and pantomime which is great fun. Performances are at 3 or 7.30 pm on weekdays and you can usually get a ticket at the door just before the show.

The so-called *National Marionette Theatre*, or Říše loutek, at Žatecká 1 (metro: Staroměstská), is a puppet theatre strictly for tourists. Notices in the entrance hall tell what's on and tickets are available at the door.

Free Entertainment In the evening you can stroll along Na příkopě, where buskers play for the throng, or Václavské náměstí, where fast-food stands, cinemas and night bars stay open till late. Můstek and Perlová are thick with prostitutes after dark and black-market moneychangers during the day are found along Můstek, Václavské náměstí and Na příkopě. The floodlit Staroměstské náměstí and the Karlův most are other magical nocturnal attractions.

Things to Buy
You'll find many interesting shops along Karlova and Celetná, between Staroměstské náměstí and náměstí Republiky. The Kotva department store on náměstí Republiky is the largest in the country. There's also the Tesco (Máj) department store, on the corner of Národní and Spálená (metro: Národní Třída) and the expensive Krone, Václavské náměstí.

For Bohemian crystal check the two Sklo Glass shops in the Alfa Cinema Arcade, Václavské náměstí 28. Ceramics with unusual folk designs are worth checking out at Keramika, inside the passage of Václavské náměstí 41.

Getting There & Away

Air Czech Airlines, or ČSA (☎ 20 10 46 20), V celnici 5 (metro: Náměstí Republiky), books daily flights from Prague to Bratislava (5888 Kč).

Bus Buses to Karlovy Vary (122km), Brno (210km, 2½ hours) and most other towns in the Czech Republic depart from the Florenc bus station, Křižíkova 4 (metro: Florenc). Seven express buses a day cover the 321km (from 195 Kč) from Florenc to Bratislava in 4½ hours (as compared to 5½ hours on the train). Reservations are recommended on all these services.

Most international buses (Eurolines depart from Želivského bus station and Bohemian Express from Praha-Holešovice train station) to Western Europe also arrive/depart from the Florenc bus station (for tickets, see Travel Agencies near the beginning of this section).

The left-luggage room at the Florenc bus station is upstairs above the information office (open daily from 5 am to 11 pm).

Tickets Reservations at Prague's Florenc bus station are computerised. To obtain a ticket, first determine the departure time (*odjezdy*) of your bus by looking at the posted timetable beside platform No 1 or asking at the information counter. Then get in line at any of the ticket counters. Make sure that your bus isn't on the sold-out (*vyprodáno*) list on the TV screens here. If it is, pick another bus. Make reservations as far in advance as possible – they can be made up to 10 days before the departure date. Your bus ticket indicates the platform number (*stání*) and seat number (*sed*). You may be charged extra for baggage. The coaches are quite comfortable (no standing) and fares are reasonable.

Tickets for two of the private bus companies with buses to Brno are not sold in the main station but Čebus is at a kiosk on the pavement under the highway overpass behind the Municipal Museum, and Český národní expres has moved to the parking lot above the Praha-hlavní nádraží train station. Eurolines'

bus station is near Želivského metro station, in front of Hotel Don Giovanni between Vinohradská and Jana Želivského.

Train Trains run from Berlin to Prague (386km, five hours) via Dresden six times a day. There's a service twice a day from Nuremberg (372km, 6½ hours) via Cheb and twice daily from Linz, Austria (295km, 5¼ hours), via České Budějovice. Many trains arrive from Budapest (630km, 10 hours) via Brno and Bratislava. From Poland you have the choice of arriving via Wroclaw or Katowice. See Getting There & Away in the chapter introduction for more information.

From Praha-Holešovice and Praha-hlavní nádraží, sleepers and couchettes are available on the nightly *Excelsoir* express train to Bratislava, Žilina, Poprad and Košice. This is an excellent way to save one night's accommodation expenses while getting somewhere. A 1st-class sleeper from Prague to Bratislava will be 444 Kč including the ticket.

Train Stations Prague has four main train stations. International trains between Berlin and Budapest often stop at Praha-Holešovice station (metro: Nádraží Holešovice) on the northern side of the city. Other important trains terminate at Praha-hlavní nádraží (metro: Hlavní Nádraží) or Masarykovo nádraží (metro: Náměstí Republiky), both of which are close to the city centre. Some local trains to the south-west depart from Praha-Smíchov station (metro: Smíchovské Nádraží).

Praha-hlavní nádraží handles trains to Benešov (49km, one hour), České Budějovice (169km, 2½ hours), Cheb via Plzeň (220km, four hours), Karlovy Vary via Chomutov (199km, four hours), Košice (708km, 10 hours), Mariánské Lázně (190km, three hours), Plzeň (114km, two hours) and Tábor (103km, 1½ hours). Trains to Brno (257km, 3½ hours) and Bratislava (398km, 5½ hours) may leave from either Praha-hlavní nádraží, Praha-Holešovice or Masarykovo nádraží.

This is confusing, so carefully study the timetables posted in one of the stations to determine which one you'll be using, then confirm the time and station at the information counter. To go to Kutná Hora (73km, 1½ hours) you may use Praha-Holešovice or, more frequently, Masarykovo nádraží. Karlštejn trains always depart from Praha-Smíchov.

Praha-hlavní nádraží is Prague's largest train station with several exchange offices and accommodation services on levels 2 and 3, and a tourist information booth on level 2. The various snack stands on levels 2 and 3 are not exciting, but on level 4 in the Art Nouveau hall is the pleasant *Fantova kavárna*. Be extremely careful in the train station, as there are many thieves preying on unsuspecting foreigners. It is not the safest place during the day and even worse at night.

The 24-hour left-luggage office (note their three half-hour breaks) is on level 1, so drop your bags off upon arrival and stroll into town to look for a room or a meal (you pay the left-luggage fee when you pick the bags up).

International tickets, domestic and international couchettes and seat reservations are sold on level 2 at the even-numbered windows from 10 to 24 to the right of the stairs up to level 3. Domestic tickets are sold at the odd-numbered windows from 1 to 23 to the left of the stairs.

At Praha-Holešovice station, windows ARES 1 and 2 are for booking international tickets and couchettes. There are currency exchange facilities in all these stations but high commissions are charged.

Getting Around

To/From the Airport
Ruzyně airport is 17km west of the city centre.

Public transport operates to the airport daily from 4.30 am to 11.30 pm on city bus Nos 119 and 254 from Dejvická metro station (about a 20-minute trip). Every hour from 5 to 7.30 am and 7 to 10 pm daily, a Cedaz airport microbus (90 Kč) departs from náměstí Republiky, across from Kotva department store (metro: Náměstí Republiky) and picks up passengers about 30 minutes later at Dejvická metro station on Evropská. Buy your ticket from the driver. Welcome Touristic Company runs buses between the airport and the ČSA office, V celnici 5, every half-hour between 7.30 am and 6.30 pm for 95 Kč.

The information desk at the airport will direct you to Airport Fix-Cars whose prices are regulated by the airport administration and which cost about 560 Kč (20% discount for return trip) into the centre of Prague (a regular taxi fare from central Prague is about 315 Kč). If you take regular taxis, there's a very good chance you will be ripped off.

There's a 24-hour left-luggage office.

Public Transport
All public transport in Prague has two fare rates with different conditions.

The 12 Kč tickets valid on trams, city buses, metro and 2nd-class trains are sold by yellow automatic ticket machines at the entrance to all metro stations, Department of Transportation (DP) ticket windows in major metro stations, some tram and bus stops, or at newsstands. Buy a good supply whenever you have the chance, then validate your ticket as you enter the vehicle or metro. For a large piece of luggage or a bicycle, you must cancel one additional half-price ticket.

Once validated, tickets are good for 60 minutes on weekdays from 5 am to 8 pm, 90 minutes from 8 pm, and 24 hours on weekends and holidays. A cancelled ticket also allows changes between any of the following modes of transport available – metro, tram, bus and train. The 8 Kč-ticket can only be used for 15 minutes on buses and trams, or for four stops on the metro, and no changes are allowed (not valid on night trams and buses).

Being caught 'black' without a ticket entails a 200 Kč fine. Inspectors will often demand a higher fine from foreigners and pocket the difference, so insist on a receipt (*potvrzení*) before paying.

Season tickets (*jízdenka síťová*) valid on all forms of public transport are sold for periods of one (70 Kč), three (180 Kč), seven (250 Kč) or 15 (280 Kč) days. These tickets are always available at the DP information counters in Muzeum and Můstek metro stations (Můstek entry: Jungmannovo náměstí) daily from 7 am to 9 pm, and Karlovo náměstí (entry: Palackého náměstí) and Nádraží Holešovice weekdays from 7 am to 6 pm and many other ticket offices in metro stations. Compare the price of a monthly pass (*měsíční jízdenka*) if you're staying for over two weeks.

PRAGUE RAILWAYS

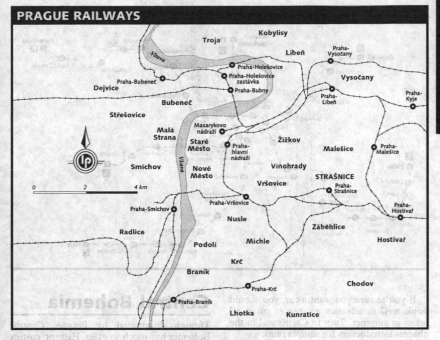

Kobylisy
Troja
Libeň
Praha-Vysočany
Praha-Holešovice
Praha-Holešovice zastávka
Praha-Bubeneč
Vysočany
Dejvice
Praha-Bubny
Praha-Libeň
Praha-Kyje
Bubeneč
Střešovice
Masarykovo nádraží
Malá Strana
Žižkov
Staré Město
Praha-hlavní nádraží
Malešice
Praha-Malešice
Smíchov
Nové Město
Vinohrady
STRAŠNICE
Vršovice
Praha-Strašnice
Praha-Smíchov
Praha-Vršovice
Praha-Hostivař
Nusle
Radlice
Zábehlice
Hostivař
Podolí
Michle
Krč
Braník
Chodov
Praha-Krč
Praha-Braník
Lhotka
Kunratice

0   2   4 km

Metro The first line of the Prague Metro, built with Soviet assistance, opened on 9 May 1974. The metro operates from 5 am to midnight with three lines connecting all bus and train stations, as well as many tourist attractions. Don't get into the rear carriage, as station names are poorly displayed. In general, though, using the metro is easy and the recorded announcements are strangely reassuring.

Line A runs from the north-west side of the city at Dejvická to the east at Skalka; line B runs from the south-west at Zličín to the north-east at Počernická; line C runs from the north at Nádraží Holešovice to the south-east at Háje. Line A intersects line C at Muzeum; line B intersects line C at Florenc; line A intersects line B at Můstek.

A monitor at the end of the platforms tells how long it has been since the last train went through. The way out is marked *výstup*.

After the metro closes down at midnight, trams (Nos 51 to 58) and buses (Nos 501 to 512) still rumble across the city about every 40 minutes all night. If you're planning a late evening, find out if one of these services passes anywhere near where you're staying as taxis can be a rip-off late at night.

Car A Rent Car (☎ 24 28 10 53), Washingtonova 9, is almost opposite the State Opera. Europcar (☎ 24 81 12 90), Pařížská 28, is near the Inter-Continental Hotel (metro: Staroměstská) and Budget has a desk inside the Inter-Continental itself. Avis (☎ 21 85 12 25) is at Klimentská 46, (metro: Náměstí Republiky). Most Čedok offices also rent cars at competitive rates. Avis, Budget, Hertz and Europcar all have offices at Ruzyně airport; however, you'll be charged about 300 Kč surcharge if you use them. There are also several small local car rental places that are much cheaper. One such is Discar Marcel Vlasák (☎ 687 05 23), Hovorčovice 192, Prague 9, north of Třeboradice.

PRAGUE METRO

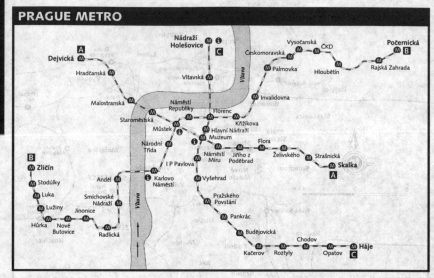

If you're sure you want a car, you should book well in advance as they're often all taken in summer. Turn to Car Rental in the chapter introduction for sample rates.

Bicycle Rental A Landa (☎ 24 25 61 21), Šumavská 33, Vinohrady, Prague 2 (metro: Náměstí Míru), rents bicycles from 120 Kč a day.

Taxi Taxis are reasonable, but only if the meter is turned on. If the driver won't turn on the meter, find another taxi or clearly establish the price before you set out, otherwise you'll end up paying far more than normal. Taxi prices are regulated and to enter a taxi is 25 Kč plus 17 Kč per kilometre. Only four passengers are allowed in a taxi.

Avoid taking taxis from tourist areas, Václavské náměstí or luxury hotels as these are much more expensive. If you feel you're being overcharged ask for a bill (*účet*) which the driver is obliged to provide. A reliable taxi company is AAA (☎ 10 80, 24 32 24 32).

Public transport is so good in Prague that taking a taxi is really a luxury.

Central Bohemia

Though dominated by Prague, Central Bohemia has much to offer. Historic castles and chateaux rise out of the forests at Český Šternberk, Dobříš, Karlštejn, Kokořín, Konopiště, Křivoklát, Mělník, Žleby and elsewhere, while Kutná Hora is a picturesque medieval town. Tourism is sharply focused on these sights. Transport around the region is good and all destinations can be visited as day trips from the capital.

KARLŠTEJN

An easy day trip from Prague is **Karlštejn Castle**, 33km south-west. Erected by Emperor Charles IV in the mid-14th century, this towering, fairy-tale castle crowns a ridge above the village, a 20-minute walk from the train station.

A highlight of Karlštejn Castle is the Church of Our Lady (1357), with its medieval frescoes, including the king's private oratory, the walls of which are covered with precious stones. Even more magnificent is the Chapel of the Holy Rood in the Big Tower, where the coronation jewels were kept until 1420. Some

128 painted panels by Master Theodoric covering the walls make this chapel a veritable gallery of 14th-century art.

The castle is open Tuesday to Sunday in July and August, from 9 am to noon and from 1 to 7 pm, but closes in May/June and September at 6 pm, in April and October at 5 pm and the rest of the year at 4 pm. On 24 December, 1 January and the day after a holiday the castle is closed. The 45-minute guided tours in English cost 150 Kč and in Czech 50 Kč.

Getting There & Away

Trains leave for Karlštejn about once an hour from Praha-Smíchov train station (35 minutes).

KONOPIŠTĚ

Midway between Prague and Tábor, 2km west of Benešov train station, is **Konopiště Castle**. The castle dates back to the 14th century, but the Renaissance palace it shelters is from the 17th century.

Archduke Franz Ferdinand d'Este, heir to the Austro-Hungarian throne, had Konopiště renovated in 1894 and added a large English park and rose garden. Ferdinand's huge collection of hunting trophies and weapons on display at the castle will shock animal rights activists.

Konopiště Castle is open from April to October, Tuesday to Sunday from 9 am to noon and 1 to 3 pm but on weekends to 4 pm, and it closes from May to August at 5 pm. There are three tours of the castle, each covering a different part of the complex. Tours I and II last 45 minutes each and in English cost 110 Kč and in Czech 60 Kč. Tour III (one hour) is 240 Kč and 120 Kč respectively. Huge tour groups frequent the castle so get there early.

Getting There & Away

Ten fast trains leave Prague's Praha-hlavní nádraží for Benešov (49km, one hour). Most trains to and from Tábor (54km, one hour) and České Budějovice (120km, two hours) also stop here. There are occasional buses from Benešov train station to the castle.

KUTNÁ HORA
☎ 0327

In the 14th century, Kutná Hora, 66km east of Prague, was the second-largest town in Bohemia after Prague. This was due to the rich veins of silver below the town itself, and the silver *groschen* minted here was the hard currency of Central Europe at the time. During the 16th century, Kutná Hora's boom ended, and mining ceased in 1726, so the medieval townscape is basically unaltered. In 1996 it was added to UNESCO's World Heritage List.

Orientation

The main train station, Kutná Hora hlavní nádraží, is 3km east of the centre. The bus station is more conveniently located just on the north-eastern edge of the old town.

The easiest way to visit Kutná Hora on a day trip is to arrive on the morning express train from Prague's hlavní nádraží train station, then take a 10-minute walk from Kutná Hora hlavní nádraží train station to Sedlec to visit the ossuary (see the following Things to See section). From there it's another 15-minute walk or a five-minute bus ride to old Kutná Hora.

Information

The helpful municipal Information Centre (☎ 51 55 56; kv.info.kh@pha.pvtnet.cz), Palackého náměstí, sells local maps. Staff can book accommodation and tours. They also have one Internet computer for public use (50 Kč for a half-hour). Komerční banka is at Tylova 9/390. A good map is *Kutná Hora* (1:10,000) by Žaket.

Things to See

At Sedlec, only 1km from the train station on the way into town (turn right when you see a huge church), is a cemetery with a Gothic **ossuary** *(kostnice)* decorated with the bones of some 40,000 people. In 1870, František Rint, a local woodcarver, arranged the bones in the form of bells, a chandelier, monstrances and even the Schwarzenberg coat-of-arms, a truly macabre sight (30 Kč).

Continue 2km south-west along Masarykova. As you enter the old town on Na náměti you'll see the Gothic **Church of Our Lady** on the left. Keep straight and turn right on Tylova which will take you up into

324 Czech Republic – Central Bohemia

KUTNÁ HORA & SEDLEC

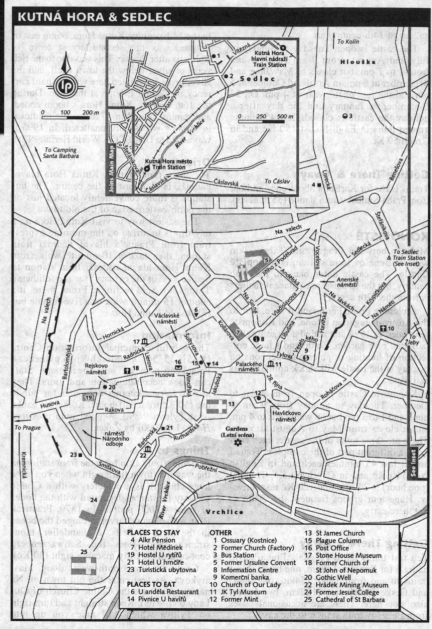

PLACES TO STAY
4 Alkr Pension
7 Hotel Medínek
19 Hostel U rytířů
21 Hotel U hrnčíře
23 Turistická ubytovna

PLACES TO EAT
6 U anděla Restaurant
14 Pivnice U havířů

OTHER
1 Ossuary (Kostnice)
2 Former Church (Factory)
3 Bus Station
5 Former Ursuline Convent
8 Information Centre
9 Komerční banka
10 Church of Our Lady
11 JK Tyl Museum
12 Former Mint

13 St James Church
15 Plague Column
16 Post Office
17 Stone House Museum
18 Former Church of St John of Nepomuk
20 Gothic Well
22 Hrádek Mining Museum
24 Former Jesuit College
25 Cathedral of St Barbara

Palackého náměstí, a quaint square enlarged when the Gothic town hall was demolished after a fire in 1770.

From the upper end of Palackého náměstí, Jakubská – a lane to the left – leads directly to the tall tilting tower of the **St James Church** (1330), just past which is the Gothic former **Royal Mint** (Vlašský dvůr), or Italian Court, now a mint museum (daily, 50 Kč) and it's worth viewing the historical rooms. Master craftsmen from Florence began stamping silver coins here in 1300.

From the front entrance to St James a series of cobbled, signposted streets slope down and up to the **Hrádek Mining Museum** (35 Kč). This 15th-century palace contains an exhibit on the mining that made Kutná Hora wealthy. Note the huge wooden device used in the Middle Ages to lift up to 1000kg of rock from shafts that were 200m deep. The museum's main attraction, however, is the 45-minute guided tour through 500m of **medieval mine shafts** on one of the 20 levels below Kutná Hora. You don a white coat and helmet, and pick up a torch, but the tour only begins when a group of at least three people gathers. The museum is closed on Monday and from October to April.

Just beyond Hrádek is the 17th-century **former Jesuit college**, which has baroque sculpture in front of it and a good view of the Vrchlice River Valley from the promenade. Nearby is Kutná Hora's greatest monument, the **Cathedral of St Barbara** (closed Monday, 20 Kč), begun in 1388 by Petr Parléř, the architect of St Vitus Cathedral in Prague, and finished in 1547. The exquisite net vault above the central nave is supported by double flying buttresses in the French high-Gothic style.

From St Barbara retrace your steps past the Jesuit College and the Hrádek and continue straight along Barborská till it ends at Komenského náměstí. Turn left, then right, and right again down Husova two blocks till you see a baroque **plague column** on the left in Šultysova. Walk up the street behind the column to Václavské náměstí, turn left onto Radnická and walk until you see an old building with a high triangular gable bearing figures of knights jousting, across the car park on the left. This is the **Stone House** (1485), Václavské náměstí 24, that hosts temporary historical exhibits.

Walk north-east back down Václavské náměstí, which becomes Jiřího z Poděbrad, to the former **Ursuline convent** (1743) at No 13 on the left, which houses an exhibition of antiques. The bus station is straight ahead and down Lorecká to the left.

Places to Stay
Camping *Camping Santa Barbara* (51 29 51) is north-west of town off Česká, near the cemetery (u hřbitova).

Private Rooms The Information Centre has priváty priced from around 300 to 500 Kč per person.

Hostels A friendly, welcoming place to stay is the hostel *U rytířů* (☎ 51 22 56), Rejskovo náměstí 123, just off Husova across the street from the large Gothic well in the middle of the road. The 20 rooms vary in price and start at 320 Kč per person. Most rooms are doubles with private bath.

At a pinch you could also try the *Turistická ubytovna* (☎ 51 34 63), náměstí Národního odboje 56, where a basic dormitory is 160 Kč per person or 20 Kč less with youth cards. The reception opens only from 8 to 9 am and 4.30 to 5.30 pm.

Hotels The *Hotel Mědínek* (☎ 51 27 41), a prefabricated four-storey hotel on Palackého náměstí, costs 740/1140 Kč with bath and breakfast included.

A better choice for a room in Kutná Hora is the *Hotel U hrnčíře* (☎ 51 21 13), Barborská 24, just down the street from the Hrádek. The five rooms in this quaint privately owned inn go for 500 Kč per person including breakfast, and they're often fully booked. Even if you don't stay here, the U hrnčíře is an excellent place for a genteel lunch, which is served in the garden in summer.

Alkr Pension (☎ 51 24 69), Lorecká 7, right near the bus station, has comfortable rooms with private bath and a small kitchenette for 350 Kč per person.

Places to Eat
U anděla, Václavské náměstí 8, is a decent place to eat. In front of the plague column nearby is *Pivnice U havířů* (closed Monday),

a local beer hall where inexpensive meals are served, with a more sedate *vinárna* at the back.

Getting There & Away

Kutná Hora is on the main railway line between Prague and Brno via Havlíčkův Brod, but many express trains don't stop here (you may have to change at Kolín). Four fast trains from Prague hlavní nádraží (73km, 55 minutes) and one fast train from Masarykovo nádraží stop at Kutná Hora hlavní nádraží, about 3km east of the centre at Sedlec, and eight local trains arrive from Prague's Masarykovo nádraží (73km, 1½ hours) via Kolín. From the Sedlec station there are 15 daily local trains to Kutná Hora město station just on the outskirts of the town centre.

On weekdays there are five ordinary and two express buses to Prague (70km) but far fewer buses operate on weekends. If your timing doesn't coincide with a bus direct to Prague, take one to Kolín (12km), where there are better connections to Prague. At Kutná Hora bus station, buses to Prague leave from stand No 6, those to Kolín from stand Nos 2 and 10.

North Bohemia

Tourists tend to be shy of North Bohemia, perceived as little more than an arc of polluted factory towns but there are many unspoiled attractions away from the Chomutov/Most/Ústí and Labem industrial region such as Litoměřice, Ploskovice Chateau and great hiking among the Sandstone Rocks of Labe.

LITOMĚŘICE
☎ 0416

The old picturesque historical centre has many baroque buildings and churches, some of which were designed by the 18th century architect Ottavio Broggio, who was born in the town. Litoměřice had a Slavic fortress on its hilltop from the 9th century and was founded by German colonists in the 13th century. Five hundred years later, under Ferdinand III, the town's new status as a royal seat and bishopric brought it more prosperity.

Orientation & Information

From the train station or adjacent bus station, the old centre begins just across the road to the west, past the best preserved part of the 14th century town walls. Walk down Dlouhá to the central square, Mírové náměstí.

The information centre (☎ 73 24 40) is in the House at the Chalice, the present town hall, on Mírové náměstí. The Komerční banka, Mírové náměstí 37, has a Visa/MasterCard ATM. The post and telephone office is on Osvobození, two blocks north of Mírové náměstí.

Things to See

Dominating the beautiful square is the Gothic-turned-baroque **All Saints Church**. Opposite is the **old town hall** with a small town museum. Across the square is the lavishly decorated **House of Ottavio Broggio**. Compare it to the simple and oldest (on the square) Gothic house on your left at No 16. It is now a **Museum and gallery of Litoměřice** with an art collection from St Stephen Cathedral in ornate Gothic rooms (closed Monday).

West of the square at Michalská 7 is another house where Broggio left his fine touch, the excellent **North Bohemia Fine Arts Gallery** with its priceless panels from the Litoměřice Altarpiece (closed Monday).

Cathedral Hill is south-west of Mírové náměstí, and despite its abandoned appearance Domské náměstí – the site of an ancient Slavic fortress – is the town's historical centre. A true baroque gem, the St Wenceslas Church, is off the square at Domská. On top of Cathedral Hill is the town's oldest church, St Stephen Cathedral, built in the 11th century and rebuilt in the 17th. Behind it is the former Bishop's Palace.

Places to Stay

Autocamp Slavoj (☎ 73 44 81) is on Střelecký ostrov just south of the train and bus stations. It's open May through September.

The best bargain in town is *Penzion U pavouka* (☎ 73 16 37), Pekařská 7, where small doubles are 550 Kč, including breakfast. Another well priced place is the basic prefabricated *Lovochemie Hotel* (☎ 73 54 36), Vrchlického 10, a 15-minute walk northeast of the main square. Rooms with bathroom and TV start from 560/920 Kč, including breakfast.

In the House at the Black Eagle is the best place in town, *Hotel Salva Guarda* (☎ 73 25 06), Mírové náměstí 12, where cosy rooms with bathroom and TV are 800/1200 Kč.

Places to Eat

There is a *Potraviny* (supermarket) on Dlouhá. A good bakery is *Pekárna Kodys & Hamele* at Novobranská 18.

Restaurace U sv Jiří, Lidická 9/56, on the first floor is a good inexpensive place to eat. Look for the Krušovice sign on the street. On Mírové náměstí 21, the *Radniční sklípek*, is a pricier but more pleasant place.

Getting There & Away

The train trip is tedious but Prague is only 1¼ hours away on the hourly buses.

AROUND LITOMĚŘICE
Terezín

The infamous former 18th century fortress was a jail and concentration camp during WWII. It's only 3km south of Litoměřice on one of the hourly buses that connect the towns and makes a good day trip. In 1940, the Gestapo established a prison in the Lesser Fortress and at the end of 1941 evicted the residents from the Main Fortress and turned it into a transit camp and ghetto.

The bus will drop you off at the main square, náměstí Československé armády, in the Main Fortress, where the interesting **Museum of the Ghetto** documents life in the ghetto. The Lesser Fortress is a 10-minute walk east across the Ohře River. You can take a self-guided tour through the prison barracks, isolation cells, workshops, morgues, execution grounds and former mass graves. Both the Main Fortress and Lesser Fortress museums are open daily and there is a combined ticket for 110 Kč.

West Bohemia

Cheb and Plzeň are the western gateways to the Czech Republic. All trains from western Germany pass this way and the stately old imperial spas, Karlovy Vary and Mariánské Lázně, are nearby. South-west of Plzeň is Domažlice, centre of the Chod people, where folk festivals are held in August.

KARLOVY VARY
☎ 017

Karlovy Vary is the largest and oldest of the Czech Republic's many spas. According to a local tradition, Emperor Charles IV discovered the hot springs by chance while hunting a stag. In 1358, he built a hunting lodge here and gave the town his name. From the 19th century onwards, famous people such as Beethoven, Bismarck, Brahms, Chopin, Franz Josef I, Goethe, Liszt, Metternich, Paganini, Peter the Great, Schiller, Tolstoy, Karl Marx and Yuri Gagarin came here to take the waters, and the busts of a few of them grace the promenades. Ludvík Moser began making glassware at Karlovy Vary in 1857 and today Bohemian crystal is prized around the world.

There are 12 hot springs at Karlovy Vary containing 40 chemical elements that are used in the medical treatment of diseases of the digestive tract and metabolic disorders. If you have diarrhoea or constipation, this is the place to come. Mineral deposits from the springs form stone encrustations which are sold as souvenirs. Karlovy Vary's herbal Becherovka liqueur is known as the 13th spring.

Karlovy Vary still has a definite Victorian air. The elegant colonnades and boulevards complement the many peaceful walks in the surrounding parks. The picturesque river valley winds between wooded hills, yet the spa offers all the facilities of a medium-sized town without the bother.

Orientation

Karlovy Vary has two train stations. Express trains from Prague and Cheb use Karlovy Vary horní nádraží, across the Ohře River, just north of the city. Trains to and from Mariánské Lázně stop at Karlovy Vary dolní nádraží, which is opposite the main ČSAD bus station. The Tržnice city bus station is in front of the market (*tržnice*), three blocks east of Karlovy Vary dolní nádraží. TG Masaryka, the pedestrian mall in Karlovy Vary's city centre, runs east to the Teplá River. Upstream is the heart of the spa area.

If you decide to walk from town to Karlovy Vary horní nádraží, you'll see a huge building labelled 'okresní úřad' directly in front of you as you cross the bridge. Go around behind this building and straight

KARLOVY VARY

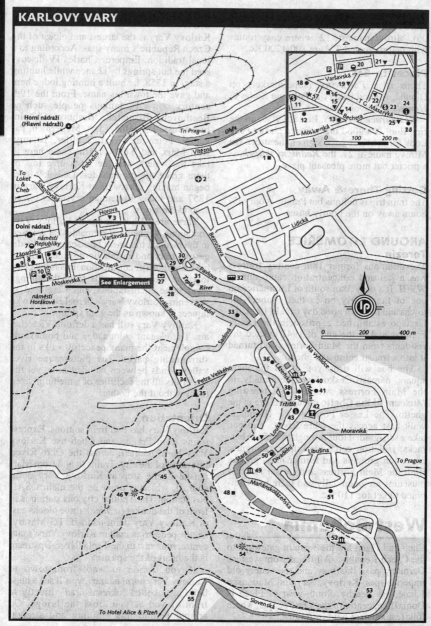

KARLOVY VARY

PLACES TO STAY		OTHER			
1	Penzión Hestia	2	Hospital & Polyclinic	31	Thermal Sanatorium
6	Hotel Adria	4	W-privat Accommodation	32	Open-Air Pool
16	Hotel Kavalerie		Agency	33	Sadová Colonnade
28	Hotel/Pension Kosmos	5	Bus Tour ČSAD Agency	34	Church of SS Peter and Paul
48	Grandhotel Pupp	7	Long-distance Bus Stand &	35	Karl Marx Monument
55	Gejzírpark Hotel		Buses to Nuremberg &	36	Mlýnská Colonnade
			Frankfurt		& Bandstand
PLACES TO EAT		8	Aesculap Pharmacy	37	Golden Key Museum
3	Městská tržnice	9	24-hour Clinic	38	Zámecká Tower
	(supermarket)	10	Autoturist Travel Agency	39	Moser Glasswork Shop
14	Langoš & French	11	IPB banka	40	Incentive (Amex)
	Pancakes	12	Propaganda Music Club		Travel Service
15	Restaurant Fortuna	13	Čedok Travel Bureau	41	Čokoládovny Kolonáda
19	Trumf Bakery &	17	Foreigners' Police	42	Church of Mary Magdalene
	Public Transport	18	Becher Factory Outlet	43	Vřídelní Colonnade
	Office (MHD)	20	Local & Regional Bus		& Kurf-info
21	Bistro Pupík		Station & Market	45	Diana Funicular Railway
22	K Grill	23	Česká spořitelna	47	Diana Lookout Tower
25	McDonald's	24	City Info	49	Karlovy Vary Museum
30	Linie Grill &	26	Čas Cinema	50	Vítězslava Nezvala Theatre
	Cake Shop	27	Post & Telephone	51	Imperial Sanatorium
44	Café Elefant		Office	52	Art Gallery
46	Café	29	Poštovní Bridge	53	Open-Air Cinema
				54	Karla IV Lookout Tower

ahead until you see a signposted way on the left which leads through a tunnel and straight up to the station.

There's no left-luggage office at the bus station. Both train stations have left-luggage rooms but the one at Karlovy Vary horní nádraží is larger and open 24 hours a day.

Maps One of the best new city maps is *Karlovy Vary City Guide Map* (1:20,000), by Paret 2.

Information

The main information office, Kur-Info (☎ 322 40 97), Vřídelní Colonnade has maps and brochures, including the monthly *Promenáda* booklet full of all the latest information for Karlovy Vary. It also arranges spa treatment for foreigners at 2100 Kč per person a day including room and board. An information kiosk, City Info (☎ 233 51), TG Masaryka, can also advise on accommodation.

Money Česká spořitelna, TG Masaryka 14, has an exchange office while IPB bank on the corner of Bechera and Bělehradská has a Visa/MasterCard ATM.

Incentive Travel Service (☎ 322 53 17) is an American Express representative and has an exchange office on Vřídelní 51.

Post & Communications The telephone centre at the main post office, TG Masaryka 1, is open daily from 7.30 am to 7 pm, but closes on Saturday at 1 pm and on Sunday at noon.

Medical & Emergency Services The Foreigners' Police (Cizinecká policie) office is inside a passage off Bechera 24. A 24-hour clinic (☎ 322 46 79) is on Krymská 2a. The pharmacy Aesculap is on náměstí Dr M Horákové 8.

Things to See

As you follow the riverside promenade south from the stations, you'll pass the modern **Thermal Sanatorium** (1976) and the neoclassical **Mlýnská Colonnade** (1881), designed by Josef Zítek. The **Golden Key Museum**, Lázeňská 3, with paintings of the spa from the Karlovarské Theatre was closed for renovations. On a nearby hill is the old castle tower (1608) on the site of Charles IV's 1358 hunting lodge. Today it's a restaurant. Down the hill from the castle is the **House of the Three Moors**, or Dagmar House, Tržiště 25, where Goethe stayed during his many visits to Karlovy Vary.

Opposite this building is a bridge which leads to the pulsing heart of Karlovy Vary, the Vřídlo or Sprundel Spring (1975, formally Yuri Gagarin) in the **Vřídelní Colonnade**. Here 2000I, a minute, of 72.2°C water shoot up 12m from a depth of 2500m. Throngs of Czech tourists, funny little special spa cups (*lázeňský pohárek*) in hand, pace up and down the colonnade, taking the drinking cure (you can as well).

Just above the Vřídelní Colonnade is the baroque **Church of Mary Magdalene** (1736) designed by Kilian Dientzenhofer. Follow the Teplá River south-west past the **Vítězslava Nezvala Theatre** (1886) till you reach the **Karlovy Vary Museum** (closed Monday and Tuesday), Nová Louka 23, which has history and natural history displays on the local area.

Return to the Vřídelní Colonnade, cross the bridge again and follow the promenade west along the river towards the **Grandhotel Pupp**, a former meeting place of the European aristocracy.

Just before the hotel you'll see Mariánská, an alley on the right leading to the bottom station of the **Diana Funicular Railway**, which ascends 166m every 15 minutes from 9 am to 5 pm (until 7 pm in summer, 20 Kč). Take a ride up to the **Diana Tower** for great views and pleasant walks through the forest. If the railway is closed, follow the network of footpaths that begins near this station. A café adjoins the Diana Tower.

Activities

Top off your sightseeing with a swim in the large **open-air thermal pool** (*bazén*) on the hill above the Thermal Sanatorium. Karlovy Vary's numerous sanatoriums are reserved for patients undergoing treatment prescribed by physicians – in fact this is the only place which will let you in.

The bazén is open daily from 8 am to 8.30 pm (on weekends from 9 am to 9.30 pm), admission is 30 Kč per hour. The bazén is closed every third Monday. There's also a

sauna (daily from 3 to 7 pm), a solarium and a fitness club, all open daily. A board at the entrance explains it all in English.

Places to Stay

Camping The nearest camping ground is *Rolava* camp site (☎ 452 24) on a little lake of the same name, about 3km north-west of town.

Private Rooms On weekends Karlovy Vary fills up with Germans on mini holidays and accommodation is tight. City Info can send you to *private homes*, which cost from about 380 Kč. Čedok (☎ 322 22 92), Bechera 21, can suggest *private rooms* from 370 Kč per person.

W-privat Accommodation Agency (☎/fax 322 77 68), náměstí Republiky 5, has *private rooms* priced from 360 Kč per person; it usually has something available.

Hotels There is a 12 to 15 Kč spa tax per person added on top of hotel rates. *Penzión Hestia* (☎ 322 59 85), Stará Kysibelská 45, is about a half-hour walk east of the centre, or you can take bus No 5 from Tržnice bus station. It has clean rooms for 310 Kč per person, with shared facilities.

The *AB Servis Penzión* (☎ 480 25), Sokolovská 72, is in an untouristed neighbourhood about 1km west of Karlovy Vary horní nádraží train station. It charges 720/980/1140 Kč a double/triple/quad with shared bath and breakfast or 770 Kč a double with shower in this renovated 1902 building almost opposite the city brewery. There are several cheap bars and restaurants in the vicinity but it's on the opposite side of town from the spa. If you're only staying for one night, a good bet is the *Adria Hotel* (☎/fax 322 37 65), Západní 1, opposite the ČSAD bus station (832/1408/2032 Kč with bathroom).

In the centre is the newish *Hotel Kavalerie* (☎/fax 322 96 13), TG Masaryka 43, which has cosy rooms for 900/1500 Kč with shower. Cheaper are several pensions along Zahradní, such as *Hotel/Pension Kosmos* (☎ 322 31 68) at No 39. Rooms without bathrooms are 440/360/330 Kč per person in single/double/triple rooms and with are 750/670/560 Kč.

Karlovy Vary's premier address is the *Grand-hotel Pupp* (☎ 310 91 11), Mírové náměstí 2, an imposing 358-room hotel founded in 1701 and operated from 1773 to 1945 and 1990 to the present by the Pupp family. A room here with bath and breakfast will set you back 4300/5255 Kč or more, or you can play the big shot for a lower price by dining at one of the hotel's pretentious restaurants.

There is a hotel along Slovenská just south of the spa centre, which you can reach from the market on bus No 7 bearing the sign 'Březová'. The friendly *Gejzírpark Hotel* (☎ 322 26 62) beside the public tennis courts, has singles/doubles at 820/1440 Kč with bath; rooms without bath are much cheaper. You can use the 14 adjacent tennis courts for 180 Kč an hour – ask the hotel receptionist. The hotel restaurant has good food.

Places to Eat
There is a good *buffet* inside the entrance to the market, which itself is a large supermarket. *Restaurant Fortuna*, Bechera 16, tries to be a US-style steak house.

Good grilled chicken is at *K-Grill*, Jugoslávská 4. Langoše and French pancakes are great snacks on Zeyerova 4.

A popular grill and cake shop called *Linie* is just across the Poštovní Bridge. There is a little *Pizza P+P* a few doors down.

Bars & Cafés A good cake shop and bakery is *Trumf*, Zeyerova 17. The upmarket *Café Elefant*, Stará Louka 30, is perhaps Karlovy Vary's most popular and elegant nonhotel café.

The *Bistro Pupík'*, Horova 2, next to the Tržnice city bus station, has cheap beer on tap.

Entertainment
Karlovy Vary's main theatre is the *Divadlo Vítězslava Nezvala*, Divadlo náměstí, not far from the Vřídelní Colonnade. From mid-May to mid-September concerts are held in the colonnade daily, except Monday.

The *Propaganda Music Club*, Jaltská 7, has occasional live bands or just taped modern rock/pop music nightly.

Among the many cultural events are the Jazz Festival in March/April, the Dvořák Singing Contest in June, the International Film Festival in July, the Dvořák Autumn Festival and the International Festival of Touristic Films in September.

Seeing a movie at *Čas* cinema, TG Masaryka 3, is another option.

Things to Buy
You can buy a box of the famous Lázeňské oplatky wafers at Čokoládovny Kolonáda, Vřídelní 57, next to Pošta No 3 (post office).

Lovers of fine liqueurs will wish to stand outside the Becherova distillery, TG Masaryka 57, and view the displays in the shop window.

Getting There & Away
Bus There are direct trains to Prague, but it's faster and easier to take one of the hourly buses (122km). To Cheb, however, the bus (53km, 1½ hours) takes considerably longer than a local train. The only way to go directly to Plzeň (84km, 1½ hours) and České Budějovice (220km, four hours) is by bus. Seats on express buses can and should be reserved in advance by computer at the ČSAD bus station, which is open weekdays from 6 am to 6 pm and Saturday 7.30 am to 12.30 pm.

Train From Karlovy Vary to Nuremberg, Germany, or beyond, you'll have to change at Cheb. Mariánské Lázně (53km, 1½ hours) and Cheb (52km, one hour) are connected to Karlovy Vary by daily local trains. Couchettes and sleepers are available to and from Košice (897km) on the *Vsacan* and *Excelsior* express trains.

Getting Around
Before boarding a city bus, buy some tickets (6 Kč) from an automatic ticket machine. A good service to know about is bus No 11, which runs hourly from Karlovy Vary horní nádraží train station to the Tržnice city bus station at the market, then over the hills to Divadlo náměstí and the Vřídelní Colonnade. The more frequent city bus No 13 also runs to the market from Karlovy Vary horní nádraží.

Bus No 2 runs between the market and the Grandhotel Pupp (Lázně I) every half-hour or less daily from 6 am to 11 pm.

AROUND KARLOVY VARY
Loket
☎ 0168

If you have an afternoon to spare, take a ČSAD bus (eight daily, 16km, half-hour), which passes about every two hours, 8km south-west to Loket, where you'll find an impressive 13th-century castle (closed Monday, 60 Kč) on the hilltop in the centre of town. A museum in the castle is dedicated to the china made in Loket since 1815. On the façade of the Hotel Bílý Kůň, in Loket's picturesque town square, is a plaque commemorating Goethe's seven visits. You might even consider staying at the *Hotel Goethe* (☎ 68 41 84) at TG Masaryka 21 (740/1070 Kč a single/double), which also has a restaurant where you can get lunch.

You can walk back to Karlovy Vary from Loket in about three hours. Follow the blue-and-white trail down the left bank of the Ohře River, which flows between Cheb and Karlovy Vary, to the Svatošské Rocks. Here you cross the river on a footbridge and take the road to Doubí (serviced by Karlovy Vary city bus No 6). This riverside path down the forested valley is scenic.

CHEB
☎ 0166

This medieval town on the Ohře River, near the western tip of the Czech Republic, is an easy day trip by train from Karlovy Vary or Mariánské Lázně. You can also visit Cheb as a stopover between Karlovy Vary and Mariánské Lázně, as train services to both are good. Only a few kilometres north of the Bavarian border, Cheb retains a strong German flavour.

Orientation & Information

The train station at the south-eastern end of třída Svobody is open all night, so you can wait there if you arrive or depart at an ungodly hour. The left-luggage office at the train station is open 24 hours a day.

The office of the Cultural Information Service (☎ 42 27 05), náměstí krále Jiřího z Poděbrad 33, sells maps, guidebooks, theatre and concert tickets, and can organise guides.

Money The Agrobanka on třída Svobody, near Čedok, has an exchange counter and a Visa/MasterCard ATM.

Post & Communications The main post office is on náměstí krále Jiřího z Poděbrad 38.

Medical Services The 24-hour pharmacy (lékárna), náměstí krále Jiřího z Poděbrad 6, has a red bell you can press if an emergency occurs outside normal business hours.

Things to See

Only a few minutes from the ugly train station area, up třída Svobody, is the picturesque town square, náměstí krále Jiřího z Poděbrad. Burgher houses with sloping red-tile roofs surround the square and in the middle is Špalíček, a cluster of 16th-century Gothic houses which were once Jewish shops. Behind these is the Cheb Museum (closed Monday, 30 Kč) which has an excellent historical exhibition. The Thirty Years' War military commander Duke Albrecht Wallenstein was murdered in the building in 1634 and the museum devotes a room to him. Also on the square is the baroque, former new town hall (1728), now the city art gallery (20 Kč).

At the back of the Cheb Museum is St Nicholas Church, a massive Gothic structure with a sculpture-filled interior. Notice the portal (1270) and the Romanesque features, such as the twin towers. A few blocks away is Cheb Castle (open from April to October, closed Monday), erected in the 12th century by Friedrich I Barbarossa, leader of the Eastern crusades. The Black Tower dates from 1222 but the exterior fortifications were built in the 17th century. In the castle is a 12th-century Romanesque chapel, a rare sight in the Czech Republic.

Places to Stay

The nearest camping grounds are at Dřenice (☎ 315 91) on Jesenice Lake 5km east of Cheb, and Lake Amerika (☎ 54 25 18), 2km south-east of Františkovy Lázně. Both are open from mid-May to mid-September.

The *Slávie Hotel* (☎ 43 32 16), třída Svobody 75, charges 459/750 Kč with bath.

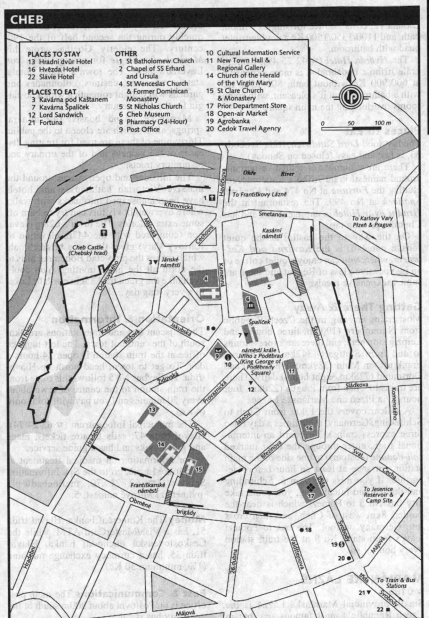

CHEB

PLACES TO STAY
13 Hradní dvůr Hotel
16 Hvězda Hotel
22 Slávie Hotel

PLACES TO EAT
3 Kavárna pod Kaštanem
7 Kavárna Špalíček
12 Lord Sandwich
21 Fortuna

OTHER
1 St Batholomew Church
2 Chapel of SS Erhard and Ursula
4 St Wenceslas Church & Former Dominican Monastery
5 St Nicholas Church
6 Cheb Museum
8 Pharmacy (24-Hour)
9 Post Office
10 Cultural Information Service
11 New Town Hall & Regional Gallery
14 Church of the Herald of the Virgin Mary
15 St Clare Church & Monastery
17 Prior Department Store
18 Open-air Market
19 Agrobanka
20 Čedok Travel Agency

The friendly *Hradní dvůr Hotel* (☎ 42 20 06), Dlouhá 12, costs 900 Kč for singles without bath, and 1100/1350/1500 Kč a double/triple/quad with bathroom.

The *Hvězda Hotel* (☎ 42 25 49), náměstí krále Jiřího z Poděbrad 4, is more expensive at 600/900 Kč without bath, 800/1500 Kč with a bathroom, but it's pleasant, with some rooms overlooking the main square.

Places to Eat

The fast food *Lord Sandwich*, třída Svobody 33, is fast and easy (closed on Sunday).

There are a number of tourist restaurants around náměstí krále Jiřího z Poděbrad, including the *Fortuna* at No 474 and *Kavárna Špalíček* at No 499. The restaurant at the *Hradní dvůr Hotel* is unpretentious and has Chebské pivo on tap.

On the way to the castle, at the quiet Jánské náměstí, is the *Kavárna pod Kaštanem*, where you can enjoy a quiet coffee or an inexpensive glass of Regent and there are some inexpensive meals.

Getting There & Away

Most trains arriving in the Czech Republic from Nuremberg (190km, three hours) and Leipzig stop here, and there are express trains to and from Stuttgart (342km, six hours), Frankfurt am Main (389km, five hours) and Dortmund (728km, eight hours) daily. There are trains to Cheb from Prague (220km, four hours) via Plzeň and Mariánské Lázně.

A railcar covers the 13km from Cheb to Schirnding, Germany, three times a day (also three express trains). To board an international train, enter through the door marked *zoll-douane* (customs) to one side of the main station entrance at least an hour before departure. If you miss the train to Schirnding and don't mind hitchhiking, you could take city bus No 5 to Pomezí which is near the border, 8km west of Cheb, and then cross into Germany on foot. The bus to Pomezí leaves from stand No 9 at the train station every hour or so.

MARIÁNSKÉ LÁZNĚ
☎ 0165

Small, provincial Mariánské Lázně is the Czech Republic's most famous spa, but in many ways it ranks second to the larger, more urbane Karlovy Vary. The resort developed quickly during the second half of the 19th century. The elderly Goethe wrote his *Marienbader Elegie* for young Ulrika von Levetzow here. The town's grand hotels, stately mansions, casinos, colonnades and gardens will delight romantics with a nostalgia for the 19th century.

Mariánské Lázně boasts 140 mineral springs, all of which are closed to the public. Thirty-nine of these are used for treating diseases of the kidneys and of the urinary and respiratory tracts.

The hillsides and open spaces around the massive Victorian bathhouses and hotels have been landscaped into parks with walks where overweight visitors can try to burn off some extra calories. The town's 628m elevation (compared with the 447m elevation of Karlovy Vary) gives the spa a brisk climate which makes the pine-clad Bohemian hills to the north all the more inviting. You could even hike the green trail 35km north to Loket in a very long day.

Orientation & Information

The adjacent bus and train stations are 3km south of the centre of town. The left-luggage office at the train station is open 24 hours a day. To get to town, head north up Hlavní třída. Trolleybus No 5 follows this route from the train station to the centre of town about every 20 minutes and you pay with coins only (4 Kč).

The municipal Infocentrum (☎ 62 24 74), Hlavní třída 47, sells theatre tickets, maps and guidebooks and has a guide service.

For information on medical treatment at Mariánské Lázně, go to the Spa Information Service, (☎ 62 21 70; marienbad@plz .pvt.net.cz) Mírové náměstí 5.

Money The Komerční banka, Hlavní třída 51, has a Visa/MasterCard ATM, while the Československá obchodní banka, Hlavní třída 35, has a currency exchange machine (1%, minimum 30 Kč).

Post & Communications The main post office is on Poštovní about 200m south of the main city bus stand.

MARIÁNSKÉ LÁZNĚ

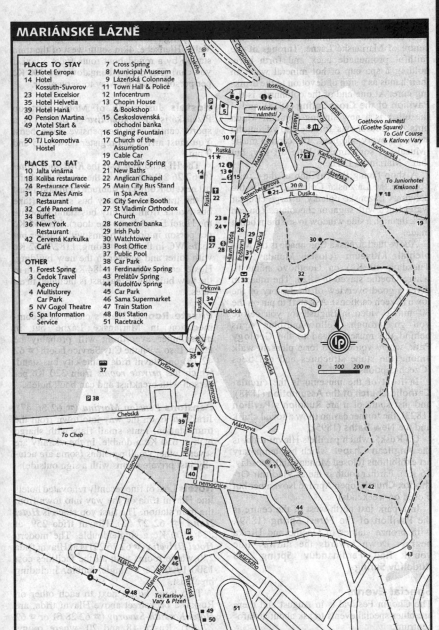

PLACES TO STAY
2 Hotel Evropa
14 Hotel
  Kossuth-Suvorov
23 Hotel Excelsior
35 Hotel Helvetia
39 Hotel Haná
40 Pension Martina
49 Motel Start &
  Camp Site
50 TJ Lokomotiva
  Hostel

PLACES TO EAT
10 Jalta vinárna
18 Koliba restaurace
24 Restaurace Classic
31 Pizza Mes Amis
  Restaurant
32 Café Panoráma
34 Buffet
36 New York
  Restaurant
42 Červená Karkulka
  Café

OTHER
1 Forest Spring
3 Čedok Travel
  Agency
4 Multistorey
  Car Park
5 NV Gogol Theatre
6 Spa Information
  Service

7 Cross Spring
8 Municipal Museum
9 Lázeňská Colonnade
11 Town Hall & Police
12 Infocentrum
13 Chopin House
  & Bookshop
15 Československá
  obchodní banka
16 Singing Fountain
17 Church of the
  Assumption
19 Cable Car
20 Ambrožův Spring
21 New Baths
22 Anglican Chapel
25 Main City Bus Stand
  in Spa Area
26 City Service Booth
27 St Vladimír Orthodox
  Church
28 Komerční banka
29 Irish Pub
30 Watchtower
33 Post Office
37 Public Pool
38 Car Park
41 Ferdinandův Spring
43 Prelátův Spring
44 Rudolfův Spring
45 Car Park
46 Sama Supermarket
47 Train Station
48 Bus Station
51 Racetrack

Things to See

The **Lázeňská Colonnade** (1889) is the centre of Mariánské Lázně. Throngs of the faithful promenade back and forth here, holding a spa cup of hot mineral water in their hands as a sign of devotion to the drinking cure. At one end of the colonnade is the **Pavilion of the Cross Spring** (1818), and at the other is a new singing fountain which puts on free shows for the crowd on the stroke of every odd hour. The canned music (Muzak) is sometimes a little off key, but that's Mariánské Lázně.

A shop facing the Pavilion of the Cross, opposite the Lázeňská Colonnade, sells the delicious Lázeňské oplatky, a large circular wafer filled with sugar or chocolate. You can look through a side window to see them being made.

Above the Lázeňská Colonnade is the **Municipal Museum** (closed Monday and Tuesday, 40 Kč) on Goethovo náměstí, where Goethe stayed in 1823. The museum gives a good overview of the history of the town (Czech captions). Ask staff to put on the 30-minute video in English for you before you go through. Yellow-and-blue signs behind the museum lead to the **Geology Park**, where you can go for a pleasant walk among the stone structures and old trees (Czech captions).

In front of the museum is the circular **Catholic Church of the Assumption** (1848), and just south of it are **Rudolph's Pavilion** (1823), the former casino (now a social club), and the **New Baths** (1895).

On Ruská, which parallels Hlavní třída, is the **Anglican Chapel**, which has temporary art exhibitions (closed Monday and Tuesday, 15 Kč). Farther south is the **St Vladimír Orthodox Church** (open April to November but closed on weekends).

In a park just north-west of the centre is the **Pavilion of the Forest Spring** (1869), with bronze statues of Goethe and Ulrika nearby. Down towards the railway line you'll find **Ferdinandův Spring** and **Rudolfův Spring**.

Special Events

The Chopin Festival is in August and there are other special events to ask about at Infocentrum.

Places to Stay

Camping *Autocamp Luxor* (☎ 35 04) is at Velká Hleďsebe, 4km south-west of the train station by a roundabout route (take a taxi if you can). The double bungalows are 300 Kč per person. It's open May to September.

Hostels Just south of Motel Start on Plzeňská is *TJ Lokomotiva* (☎ 62 39 17), a sports centre with inexpensive dorm beds. You must arrive and register between 5 and 9 pm.

The HI handbook lists the *Krakonoš Hotel* (☎ 62 26 24) which is at the top of the chairlift next to Koliba Restaurant, 6km north-east of the train and intercity bus stations (take bus No 12 from the city bus stand opposite the Hotel Excelsior to the door). It's 365 Kč per person in double rooms with shower but share WC in the old building, 1182/1862 Kč with toilet and shower in the new building. Hostel card-holders pay 484 Kč per person in the new building. Breakfast is included in all rates.

Private Rooms There's plenty of accommodation in Mariánské Lázně but in midsummer everything will probably be taken. If so, visit the City Service booth (☎ 62 42 18) on Hlavní třída at the city bus stand, which has *private rooms* from 320 Kč per person with breakfast and can book hotels.

Pensions *Pension Martina* (☎ 62 36 47), Jiráskova 6, on the way into town from the train station, rents small flats with shared bath at 650 Kč a double. In the vicinity are several other small pensions (some are actually just private rooms with a sign outside).

Hotels Lots of fine recently renovated hotels line Hlavní třída on the way into town from the train station. The first you reach is *Hotel Haná* (☎ 62 27 53), Hlavní třída 259, at 824/1100 Kč a single/double. The modern *Hotel Helvetia* (☎ 62 26 29) is at Hlavní třída 230 where rooms with all the facilities cost 1500/1900 Kč a single/double, including breakfast.

Two large hotels next to each other on Ruská, a backstreet above Hlavní třída, are *Hotel Kossuth-Suvorov* (☎ 62 28 61 or ☎ 62 27 59), Ruská 18 and 20, where rooms without facilities are 450/600 Kč, and with shower/WC 510/790 Kč.

One of the cheapest regular hotels is the basic *Evropa* (☎ 62 20 63), Třebížského 2, with rooms at 400/600/800 Kč without bath, 600/950/1200 Kč with bath. In fact, everything about the Evropa is cheaper.

Motels On Plzeňská beside the stadium, only a five-minute walk from the stations, is *Motel Start* (☎ 62 20 62). Rooms in this prefabricated building without any of the character of the town's hotels are 360 Kč per person – poor value. The walls between the rooms are made of a cardboard-like material.

Places to Eat

The *Jalta vinárna*, upstairs on Hlavní třída 43, serves good food. A stand-up *Bistro*, Hlavná 145, has good salads.

The *Restaurace Classic*, Hlavní třída 50, next to the Excelsior Hotel is a bit more pricey. Its lunch and dinner menus have a special vegetarian section, plus assorted salads and reasonable meat dishes. On the other side of Hlavná, at Poštovní 330, the *Pizza Mes Amis Restaurant* has a varied menu and pizzas under 100 Kč.

Koliba, on Dušíkova 592 at the northeastern edge of town, is an upmarket, folk-style restaurant.

Entertainment

Check the *NV Gogol Theatre* (1868) for musical programs. Many events are held at *Chopin Haus*, Hlavní třída 47. There are regular daily Colonnade Concerts at the Spa Colonnade from May to September. For details ask at the Infocentrum.

On Thursday nights, jazz bands play at the *New York Restaurant*, Hlavní třída 233, from 8 to 11 pm. In a courtyard behind Hlavní 96, follow the sign to the *Irish Pub*, that has a cosy wooden decor and Guinness. It's open until 3 am.

Getting There & Away

There are direct buses between Mariánské Lázně and Cheb, Plzeň and Prague. If you'd like to stop off somewhere between the spas, choose Bečov nad Teplou, where you'll find a castle in a wooded valley.

Train services to Cheb (30km, 30 minutes), Plzeň (76km, 1¼ hours) and Karlovy Vary (53km, 1½ hours) are good. Most international express trains between Nuremberg and Prague stop at Mariánské Lázně.

PLZEŇ
☎ 019

The city of Plzeň (Pilsen), midway between Prague and Nuremberg, is the capital of West Bohemia. Located at the confluence of four rivers, this town was once an active medieval trading centre. An ironworks was founded at Plzeň in 1859, which Emil Škoda purchased 10 years later. The Škoda Engineering Works became a producer of high-quality armaments and attracted heavy bombing at the end of WWII. The rebuilt Škoda Works now produces machinery and locomotives.

Beer has been brewed at Plzeň for 700 years and the town is famous as the original home of Pilsner. The only original Pilsner trademark is Plzeňský Prazdroj, or Pilsner Urquell in its export variety. Plzeň has sights enough to keep you busy for a day. Devoted beer drinkers will not regret the pilgrimage.

Orientation

The main train station, Plzeň hlavní nádraží, is on the eastern side of town. The central bus station (*autobusové nádraží*) is west of the centre on Husova, opposite the Škoda Works. Between these is the old town, which is centred around náměstí Republiky.

Tram No 2 goes from the train station to the centre of town and on to the bus station. The left-luggage office at the bus station is open weekdays from 8 am to 8 pm. The left-luggage office at the train station is open 24 hours.

Information

The municipal Information Centre, náměstí Republiky 41, was closed for renovations as we went to press.

Motorists in need of assistance can turn to the Autoklub Plzeň (☎ 722 07 36), Havlíčkova 6, or Autoturist (☎ 722 00 06), Sady Pětatřicátníků 3.

Money The Komerční banka, Zbrojnická 4, changes travellers cheques for a 2% commission and has a Visa/MasterCard ATM. There is a Visa/MasterCard ATM at Československá obchodní banka, Americká, opposite Tesco.

Post & Communications There's a telephone centre in the main post office on Solní 20.

Cybercafés The Net Café (internetová kavárna) is on the 1st floor, Americká 34. The first half-hour is 50 Kč and each successive hour 40 Kč. It's open weekdays from 12.30 to 8.30 pm.

Bookshop The Universitní knihkupectví on the corner of Sedláčkova and Solní has books and maps.

Cultural Centres The British Council (☎ 723 73 76), náměstí Republiky 12, has a library and is closed Sunday and Monday. The American Centre in Plzeň (☎ 723 77 22; amcenter@mbox.vol.cz), Dominikánská 9, is mainly a business resource centre.

Churches & Museums
The Gothic **St Bartholomew Church** in the middle of náměstí Republiky, the old town square, has the highest tower in Bohemia (102m); you can climb it daily for 18 Kč. Inside the soaring 13th-century structure are a Gothic Madonna (1390) on the high altar and fine stained-glass windows. On the back of the outer side of the church is an iron grille. Touch the angel and make a wish. Outstanding among the many gabled buildings around the square is the Renaissance **town hall** (1558).

Just south on Františkánská is the 14th-century **Assumption Church**. Behind this church, around the block in the Franciscan Monastery, is the **West Bohemian Museum**, with natural history exhibits and paintings (closed for renovations).

There is a private gallery in Vodárenská věž (Water Tower) on the corner of Pražská and Sady 5. května. Another art gallery in the former Butchers' Stalls has been temporarily moved to Pražská 13.

Brewery Museum
Plzeň's most interesting sight by far is the Brewery Museum (40 Kč), Veleslavínova 6,

north-east of náměstí Republiky. Located in an authentic medieval malt house, the museum displays a fascinating collection of artefacts related to brewing. Ask for the explanatory text in English or German. If all that reading makes you thirsty, visit the Pivnice Na Parkánu, which is right beside (or behind) the Brewery Museum.

Underground Corridors
Just around the corner at Perlova 4 is an entrance to one section of the 9km of medieval underground corridors (*Plzeňské historické podzemí*) below Plzeň. These were originally built as refuges during sieges, hence the numerous wells. Some were later used to store kegs of beer.

To enter you must wait for a group of at least five people to gather, then follow them on a tour (if there is no English speaking guide ask for the text in English). The underground corridors are closed on Monday and Tuesday.

Pilsner Urquell Brewery
The famous Pilsner Urquell Brewery is only a 10-minute walk from the underground corridors, a little north of Plzeň hlavní nádraží train station. The twin-arched gate dated 1842-92, which appears on every genuine Pilsner label, is here.

A one-hour tour of the brewing room and fermentation cellar is offered to individuals Monday to Friday at 12.30 pm (40 Kč including a film on the process). Groups are shown through the brewery throughout the day. Near the gate is the Restaurace Na spilce (see Places to Eat), with not so cheap meals and brews.

Places to Stay
Camping There are two camping grounds with bungalows: *Bílá hora* (☎ 53 49 05), 28. října 55, and *Oestende* (☎ 52 01 94), Malý Bolevec 41. Both are at Bílá Hora, 5km north of the city (bus No 20), and both are open from May to mid-September.

Hostels The *Sou H* (☎ 28 20 12) is a year-round hostel (*ubytovna*) at Vejprnická 56, about 3km west of town but easily accessible on tram No 2 (direction Skvrňany) from the

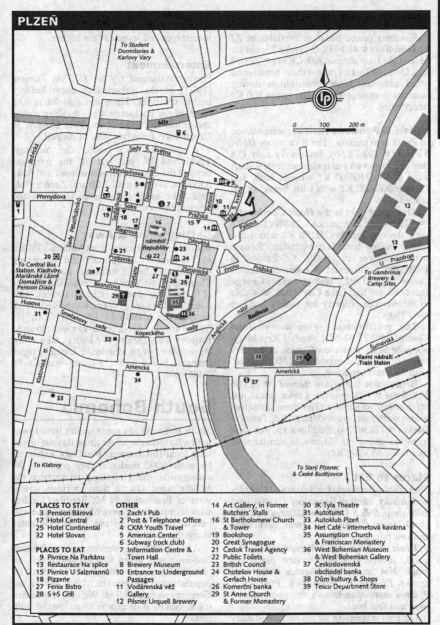

PLZEŇ

To Student
Dormitories &
Karlovy Vary

0   100   200 m

PLACES TO STAY
3 Pension Bárová
17 Hotel Central
25 Hotel Continental
32 Hotel Slovan

PLACES TO EAT
9 Pivnice Na Parkánu
13 Restaurace Na spilce
15 Pivnice U Salzmannů
18 Pizzerie
27 Fenix Bistro
28 S+S Grill

OTHER
1 Zach's Pub
2 Post & Telephone Office
4 CKM Youth Travel
5 American Center
6 Subway (rock club)
7 Information Centre &
   Town Hall
8 Brewery Museum
10 Entrance to Underground
    Passages
11 Vodárenská věž
    Gallery
12 Pilsner Urquell Brewery

14 Art Gallery, in Former
    Butchers' Stalls
16 St Bartholomew Church
    & Tower
19 Bookshop
20 Great Synagogue
21 Čedok Travel Agency
22 Public Toilets
23 British Council
24 Chotěšov House &
    Gerlach House
26 Komerční banka
29 St Anne Church
    & Former Monastery

30 JK Tyla Theatre
31 Autoturist
33 Autoklub Plzeň
34 Net Café - internetová kavárna
35 Assumption Church
    & Franciscan Monastery
36 West Bohemian Museum
    & West Bohemian Gallery
37 Československá
    obchodní banka
38 Dům kultury & Shops
39 Tesco Department Store

train or bus station. Beds are 190 Kč per person and everyone is welcome.

Similarly priced beds are available at *TJ Lokomotiva* (☎ 480 41), Úslavská 75, not far behind the train station. Ask CKM (☎ 723 75 85), Dominikánská 1, about these hostels and other accommodation possibilities during summer in student dormitories (from 200 Kč per person).

Hotels & Pensions Hotel accommodation in Plzeň is expensive. The B-category *Hotel Slovan* (☎ 722 72 56), Smetanovy sady 1, a fine old hotel with a magnificent central stairway, is 500/740/900 Kč without bath, and 1300/1600/1600 Kč with bath, breakfast included.

Also impressive is the *Hotel Continental* (☎ 723 64 79), Zbrojnická 8, at 960/1460 Kč with shower, and 1492/2150 Kč with bathroom, buffet breakfast included. Rooms without shower are 548/802 Kč. Erected in 1929, the Continental is home to Plzeň's casino. (In 1992, photographer George Janeček from Salt Lake City, Utah, was able to recover the property his family had run until 1945.)

The prefabricated seven-storey *Hotel Central* (☎ 722 67 57), náměstí Republiky, opposite St Bartholomew Church in the very centre of town, is overpriced at 1500/2548 Kč with bath and breakfast.

Better value is *Pension Bárová* (☎ 723 66 52), Solní 8, in a renovated town house just off náměstí Republiky. The three attractive rooms with bath are 695/1020 Kč. *Pension Diaja* (☎ 722 40 34), Budilova 15, just west from the centre off Husova, is similar with rooms for 550/900 Kč.

Places to Eat
There is a *supermarket* in Tesco and *Cukrárna lahůdky*, náměstí Republiky 7, is a decent cake shop. *S & S Grill*, Sedláčkova 7, half a block from Čedok, has great barbecued chicken priced by weight.

Fénix Bistro, náměstí Republiky 18, is a good, inexpensive self-service place for lunch. Not far from the square is the well known *Pivnice U Salzmannů*, Pražská 8, Plzeň's institution known for good-quality food and fine beer.

Decent inexpensive pizzas are served daily at *Pizzerie*, Solní 9. The *Restaurace Na spilce*, at the Urquell Brewery, is a bit of a tourist trap and its prices are higher.

Entertainment
For entertainment, try the *JK Tyla Theatre* (1902) or the ultramodern *Dům kultury* beside the river. There are also interesting tours of the backstage area, dressing rooms and below the stage of the Tyla Theatre, in Czech only, from late June to August.

A popular rock club, the *Subway*, Truhlářská 19, just left off the overpass beyond the corner of Rooseveltova and Sady 5.května, is open until 2.30 am. *Zach's Pub*, Palackého náměstí 2, serves Guinness and English beers until 1 am.

Getting There & Away
All international trains from Munich (330km via Furth im Wald, 5½ hours) and Nuremberg (257km via Cheb, four hours) stop at Plzeň. There are fast trains to České Budějovice (136km, two hours), Cheb (106km, two hours) and Prague (114km, two hours). Train services to Mariánské Lázně (76km, 1½ hours) are also good, but if you want to go to Karlovy Vary (83km, two hours), take a bus. Buses also run to Mariánské Lázně, Prague (express buses take 1½ hours) and České Budějovice.

South Bohemia

South Bohemia has many quaint little towns with a Bavarian or an Austrian flavour mixed with local folk baroque buildings, enhanced by some 5000 medieval carp ponds in the countryside, many of them dating from the Middle Ages. On the Šumava ridge, southwest of Prachatice, is Mt Boubín (1362m) with its primeval forest of spruce, pine and beech trees. The Vltava River originates along this ridge.

After WWI, the southern part of South Bohemia was given to Czechoslovakia on historical grounds, although over half of its population was German. After WWII the Germans were expelled. Well off the beaten track, South Bohemia is overflowing with history.

ČESKÉ BUDĚJOVICE
☎ 038

České Budějovice (Budweis), the regional capital of South Bohemia, is a charming medieval city halfway between Plzeň and Vienna. Here the Vltava River meets the Malše and flows northwards to Prague. Founded in 1265, České Budějovice controlled the importation of salt and wine from Austria and was a Catholic stronghold in the 15th century. Nearby silver mines made the town rich in the 16th century. After a fire in 1641 much was rebuilt in the baroque style. In 1832, the first horse-drawn railway on the Continent arrived at České Budějovice from Linz.

High-quality Koh-i-Noor pencils are made here but the city is more famous as the original home of Budvar (Budweiser) beer.

České Budějovice is a perfect base for day trips to many local attractions, and picturesque little Bohemian towns within easy commuting distance include Český Krumlov, Jindřichův Hradec, Písek, Prachatice, Tábor and Třeboň.

Orientation & Information

It's a 10-minute walk west down Lannova třída from the adjacent bus and train stations to náměstí Přemysla Otakara II, the centre of town. The left-luggage office at the bus station is open weekdays from 6.30 am to 6.30 pm, Saturday until 2 pm and Sunday 2 to 6 pm, and at the train station daily from 2.30 am to 11 pm.

The Tourist Information and Map Centre (☎/fax 635 25 89; map-cent@mbox.vol.cz) is in a courtyard and you enter through a passage on náměstí Přemysla Otakara II 26. It sells maps, theatre tickets and Lonely Planet guidebooks. Its staff are good at answering questions, and can arrange tour guides and book accommodation (at no commission). The municipal information centre (☎ 731 28 40), Přemysla Otakara II 2, sells maps and can also arrange accommodation.

Motorists can turn for help to the Jihočeský autoklub (☎ 565 66), Žižkova třída 13.

Money The Komerční banka, Krajinská 19, next to Masné krámy beer hall, changes travellers cheques and has a Visa/MasterCard ATM.

Post & Communications The 24-hour main post office is on Pražská 69, with a branch on Senovážné náměstí.

Medical & Emergency Services A 24-hour pharmacy (☎ 731 44 44) is at 'poliklinika JIM' on Matice školské. The hospital (☎ 82 19 11) is on B Němcové 54 and the police station (☎ 260 17) is on Pražská 5.

Things to See

Náměstí Přemysla Otakara II, a great square surrounded by 18th-century arches, is one of the largest of its kind in Europe. At its centre is **Samson's Fountain** (1727), and to one side stands the baroque **town hall** (1731). On the hour a tune is played from its tower. The allegorical figures on the town hall balustrade – Justice, Wisdom, Courage and Prudence – are matched by four bronze dragon gargoyles. Looming 72m above the opposite side of the square is the **Black Tower** (1553), with great views from the gallery (open from March to November, closed Monday, 6 Kč). Beside this tower is the **Cathedral of St Nicholas**.

The backstreets of České Budějovice, especially Česká, are lined with old burgher houses. West near the river is the former **Dominican monastery** (1265) with another tall tower and a splendid pulpit. You enter the church from the Gothic cloister. Beside the church is a medieval warehouse where salt was kept until it could be sent down the Vltava to Prague. Stroll south along the riverside behind the warehouse, past the remaining sections of the 16th-century walls. The **Museum of South Bohemia** (closed Monday, 20 Kč) is just south of the old town.

You are supposed to book a visit to the **Budvar Brewery** (☎ 770 52 01), on Pražská on the corner of K Světlé, and only groups of five or more will be accepted (a one-hour tour costs 70 Kč and a beer is 16 Kč) weekdays from 8.30 am to 2.30 pm. It is easier to make a booking with the tourist office.

This brewery is in an industrial area several kilometres north of the centre (take bus No 2) and lacks the picturesque appearance of the Urquell Brewery in Plzeň. The Restaurace Budvarka at the brewery is good and serves vegetarian dishes.

ČESKÉ BUDĚJOVICE

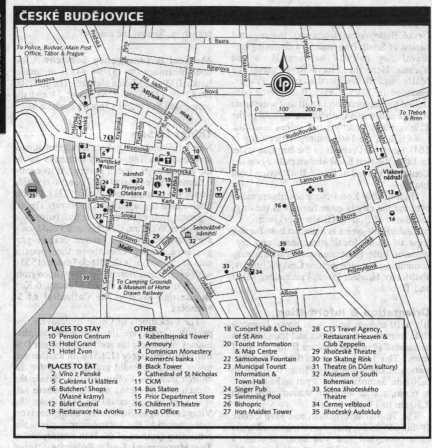

PLACES TO STAY
10 Pension Centrum
13 Hotel Grand
21 Hotel Zvon

PLACES TO EAT
2 Víno z Panské
5 Cukrárna U kláštera
6 Butchers' Shops (Masné krámy)
12 Bufet Central
19 Restaurace Na dvorku

OTHER
1 Rabenštejnská Tower
3 Armoury
4 Dominican Monastery
7 Komerční banka
8 Black Tower
9 Cathedral of St Nicholas
11 CKM
14 Bus Station
15 Prior Department Store
16 Children's Theatre
17 Post Office

18 Concert Hall & Church of St Ann
20 Tourist Information & Map Centre
22 Samsonova Fountain
23 Municipal Tourist Information & Town Hall
24 Singer Pub
25 Swimming Pool
26 Bishopric
27 Iron Maiden Tower

28 CTS Travel Agency, Restaurant Heaven & Club Zeppelin
29 Jihočeské Theatre
30 Ice Skating Rink
31 Theatre (in Dům kultury)
32 Museum of South Bohemian
33 Scéna Jihočeského Theatre
34 Černej velbloud
35 Jihočeský Autoklub

Places to Stay

Accommodation can be all booked out during one of the regular fairs held here throughout the year. Check with Tourist Information before coming to Budějovice.

Camping The *Motel Dlouhá Louka – Autocamp* (☎ 721 06 01), Stromovka 8, is a 20-minute walk south-west of town (take bus No 6 from in front of Dům kultury). Tent space is available here from May to September, and motel rooms (780/980/1200 Kč with breakfast) are available all year. The showers

are clean and the water hot, but beware of bar prices. The restaurant is said to be good.

Stromovka Autocamp (☎ 721 05 97), just beyond Dlouhá louka autocamp, has two, three and four-person bungalows for about 379/480/575 Kč. It is open from April to October.

Hostels CKM youth travel agency (☎ 257 50), Lannova třída 63 (open weekdays from 9 am to 5 pm), the Tourist Information and Map Office, and Tourist Information arrange accommodation in dormitories from around

150 Kč per person. From July to September, the *Kolej jihočeské university* (☎ 777 42 01), Studentská 800/15, has beds from 240 Kč a double.

Private Rooms Both of the tourist information offices have private rooms from around 300 Kč per person. Another good place with similarly priced rooms is CTS Travel Agency (☎ 375 57), náměstí Přemysla Otakara II 38.

Pensions Small private pensions around town are a better deal than the hotels, but the quality varies, so you ought to ask to see the room before accepting it.

We have had good reports about *Pension Centrum* (☎ 635 20 30), Mlýnská stoka 6, just off Kanovnická as you enter the old town. Double rooms with bath are 850 Kč, including breakfast. Another similarly priced place is *AT Pension* (☎ 731 25 29), Dukelská 15.

Hotels The *Hotel Grand* (☎ 565 03), Nádražní 27 opposite the train station, is 700/900 Kč without bath and 1200 Kč for doubles with bath.

The fine *Hotel Zvon* (☎ 731 13 84), náměstí Přemysla Otakara II 28, is good value for a splurge at 1600/2000 Kč with bath and also has cheaper rooms without bath.

Places to Eat

Try the local carp, which is on many restaurant menus. The Prior Department Store has a large *supermarket*.

Bufet Central, Lannova třída 32, is a good place for a self-service breakfast on the way to the train station as it opens at 6 am on weekdays and 7 am on Saturday (closed Sunday).

The *Masné krámy* beer hall in the old meat market (1560), on the corner of Hroznová and 5.května, has been a town institution for centuries. Now it is touristy and expensive with unfriendly waiters, but still worth a look for the ambience.

A more locally oriented beer hall is *Na dvorku*, Kněžská 11. A good wine bar that also has vegetarian and chicken dishes is *Víno z Panské*, Panská 14 (open Monday to

Friday). Its wine is served straight from barrels.

In the evenings the *Restaurant Heaven* turns into *Club Zeppelin*, on the 3rd floor at náměstí Přemysla Otakara II 38, a popular rock bar. *Singer Pub*, Česká 55, is an Irish-type pub.

Cafés The *Cukrárna U kláštera*, Piaristická 18 just off the main square, is great for coffee and cakes (closed Sunday). *Café filharmonie* in the concert hall, Kněžská on the corner of Karla IV, is perhaps the town's most elegant café.

Entertainment

Regular classical music concerts are at the *Chamber Orchestra of South Bohemia* in Church of St Anne, Kněžská 6 and also at the *Conservatory*, Kanovnická 22.

The *Jihočeské Theatre*, by the river on dr Stejskala, usually presents plays in Czech, but operas, operettas and concerts are also performed.

Rock bands play occasionally at *Černej velbloud* (U velblouda), U tří lvů 4. Another popular club is *Hudební klub 2*, Sokolovský ostrov 2, near the soccer stadium.

Getting There & Away

There are fast trains to Plzeň (136km, two hours), Tábor (66km, one hour), Prague (169km, 2½ hours) and Jihlava (132km, two hours). For shorter distances you're better off travelling by bus. The bus to Brno (182km, four hours) travels via Telč (100km, two hours).

Twice a day there are trains to and from Linz, Austria (125km, three hours). On three other occasions you can go to Linz with a change of trains at the border stations (Horní Dvořiště and Summerau). Connections with trains between Prague and Vienna are made at České Velenice, 50km south-east of České Budějovice.

A bus to Vienna's Mitte Bahnhof departs from České Budějovice bus station on Friday, and to Linz via Český Krumlov on Wednesday and Saturday. In July and August this bus operates daily, except Sunday, and two buses go on to Salzburg. Pay the driver.

AROUND ČESKÉ BUDĚJOVICE
Hluboká nad Vltavou
☎ 038

One side trip not to miss takes in the neo-Gothic Tudor palace at Hluboká nad Vltavou, 10km north, which is easily accessible by bus. The 13th-century castle was rebuilt between 1841 and 1871 in the style of Windsor Castle and the extensive park laid out by the landowning Schwarzenberg family. The palace's 144 rooms were inhabited right up to WWII.

The information centre (☎ 96 53 29) at Masarykova 35, opposite the church, can assist with accommodation (open only from June to September). The romantic palace interiors with their original furnishings are closed from November to March and every Monday (admission 120 Kč for an English guide or 60 Kč for a Czech one), but the park is open any time. Also open throughout the year, in the former palace riding school, is the **Alšova jihočeská galerie** (15 Kč), an exceptional collection of Gothic painting and sculpture and Dutch painting.

ČESKÝ KRUMLOV
☎ 0337

Český Krumlov, a small medieval town 25km south of České Budějovice, is one of the most picturesque towns in Europe, its appearance almost unchanged since the 18th century. It has become a haven for Austrian tourists and backpackers. It is built on an S-shaped bend of the Vltava River, its 13th-century castle occupying a ridge along the left bank. The old town centre sits on the high tongue of land on the right bank. Southwest are the Šumava Mountains, which separate Bohemia from Austria and Bavaria.

Český Krumlov's Gothic border castle, rebuilt into a huge Renaissance chateau by 16th-century Italian architects, is second only to Prague Castle as a fortified Bohemian palace and citadel. The Renaissance lords of Rožmberk seated here possessed the largest landed estate in Bohemia, which was given to the Eggenbergs in 1622 and then to the Schwarzenbergs in 1719. In 1992 the town was added to UNESCO's World Heritage List.

Information

The municipal Infocentrum (☎ 71 11 83; ckinfo@ck.bohem-net.cz), náměstí Svornosti 1, provides excellent information about the town and region. It books accommodation and concert and festival tickets, sells maps and guides, and organises tour guides.

Money The IPB, náměstí Svornosti, changes travellers cheques and has an ATM (Visa/MasterCard).

Post & Communications The telephone centre is in the post office, Latrán 81 (open weekdays from 7 am to 6 pm and Saturday until 11 pm).

Medical & Emergency Services The police (☎ 71 14 06) are at the Zámek (castle). A hospital (*nemocnice*; ☎ 76 19 11) is on Kaplická 158.

Things to See

Get off the bus from České Budějovice at Český Krumlov Špičák, the first stop in town. Just above this stop is **Budějovická Gate** (1598), which leads directly into the old town. On the right, two blocks south, is the **castle** entrance. The oldest part of the castle is the lower section with its distinctive **round tower** and great views from the top (25 Kč), but it's the massive upper castle which contains the palace halls that are open to visitors. It is said that the castle is haunted by a white lady who appears from time to time to forecast doom.

You enter the castle across a bridge and below in a pit are several bears. The ticket office between the 2nd and 3rd courtyards sells tickets for three tours of the castle – the Renaissance Rooms, Schwarzenberg Gallery (both 110 Kč, one hour) and the unique Rococo **chateau theatre** (1767; half-hour tour for 150 Kč). Behind this, a ramp to the right leads up to the former **riding school**, now a restaurant. Cherubs above the door offer the head and boots of a vanquished Turk. Above this are the Italian-style castle **gardens**. The **'Bellarie' summer pavilion** and a modern revolving open-air theatre are features of these gardens. The castle interiors are open from April to October only, but you

ČESKÝ KRUMLOV

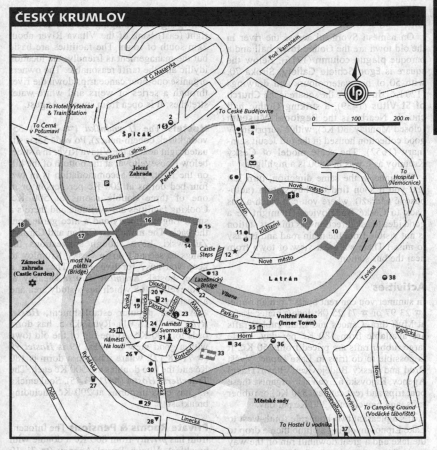

To Hotel Vyšehrad & Train Station
To Černá v Pošumaví
To České Budějovice
To Hospital (Nemocnice)
To Camping Ground (Vodácké tábořiště)
To Hostel U vodníka

Špičák
Chvalšinská silnice
Jelení Zahrada
Poleśnice
Zámecká zahrada (Castle Garden)
most Na plášti (Bridge)
Castle Steps
Nové město
Latrán
Klášterní
Latrán
Nové město
Lazebnický Bridge
Vltava
Dlouhá
Panská
Radniční
Masná
Parkán
Široká
Soukenická
náměstí Svornosti
náměstí Na louži
Horní
Kostelní
Kájovská
Dlouhá
Rybářská
Linecká
Městské sady
Vltava
Vnitřní Město (Inner Town)
Pod kamenem
T G Masaryka
Latrán
Tavírna
Rooseveltova
Tavírna
Nová
Kaplická

ČESKÝ KRUMLOV

PLACES TO STAY
4 Hostel 99
19 Travellers' Hostel
24 Hotel Krumlov
29 Hostel Ryba
34 Hotel Růže
37 Krumlov House

PLACES TO EAT
20 Cikánská jizba
22 Restaurace Vegetarián
26 Hospoda Na louži

28 Pizzeria U dvou opic

OTHER
1 ČSOB Visa/ MasterCard ATM
2 Špičák Bus Stop
3 Budějovická Gate
5 Post Office
6 Čedok
7 Convent of the Poor Clares
8 Church of Božího Těla

9 Minorite Monastery
10 Brewery
11 Red Gate
12 Police
13 Former Church St Jošt
14 Round Tower
15 Bear Pit
16 Castle
17 Chateau Theatre
18 Former Riding School
21 Černý klobouk Nightclub

23 Infocentrum, Town Hall & Police
25 Egon Schiele Gallery
27 U Matesa
30 Vltava Travel Agency & Pension
31 Plague Column
32 IPB (bank)
33 Church of St Vítus
35 Museum
36 Boat Rental
38 Bus Station

can walk through the courtyards and gardens almost any time.

On náměstí Svornosti across the river in the old town are the Gothic **town hall** and a baroque **plague column** (1716). Below the square is **Egon Schiele Gallery**, Široká 70, with 50 of his watercolours and drawings (120 Kč). Just above the square is the **Church of St Vitus** (1439), a striking Gothic hall church. Nearby is the **Regional Museum** (closed Monday, 30 Kč), with a surprisingly good collection housed in the old Jesuit seminary (1652). The scale model of Český Krumlov as it was in 1800 is a highlight.

Continue in the same direction, turn left and you'll soon find the bus station (autobusové nádraží), where you can catch a bus back to České Budějovice. (It might be a good idea to ask directions, as this bus station is not visible from the main road and is easy to miss.) There's a great view of town from near the bus station.

Activities

In summer you can rent boats from an outlet (☎ 23 97 or ☎ 71 25 08; lode@malecek.cz) at Myší díra. Canoes and small rubber rafts are available from 180 Kč per day, while large rubber rafts are priced from 250 Kč. It is possible to do trips to Lake Lipno, Vyšší Brod and Český Budějovice. Vltava Travel Agency, Kájovská 62, can also organise these boat trips and rent canoes (320 Kč) or rubber rafts, and bicycles for 300 Kč per day.

It's a pleasant two-hour ride south-west to Lake Lipno, involving a climb then a drop to the lake and a great downhill run on the way back. There are plenty of places to eat in Horní Planá. If the weather turns bad you can take your bike back to Český Krumlov from Horní Planá by train (there is a service six times a day).

Special Events

Infocentrum sells tickets to major festivals, including the Classical Music Festival in late June and early July and the Folk Music Festival in mid-September. The Pětilisté růže (Five-Petalled Rose) Festival in mid-June features three days of street performances, parades and medieval games.

Places to Stay

Camping The *camping ground* is on the right (east) bank of the Vltava River about 2km south of town. The facilities are basic but the management is friendly, the location idyllic and the tariff reasonable. The owners organise one-hour canoe trips down the river through a series of weirs and white-water stretches. It is open from June to August.

Hostels The *U vodnika* (☎ 71 19 35; vodnik@ck.bohem-net.cz), Po vodě 55, is situated right next to the Vltava River in a street below Rooseveltova, at the bottom of the hill on the right. The accommodation is in two four-bed dorms at 200 Kč per person or in one of three double rooms at 500 Kč. Cooking facilities are available and there's a small English library and a nice garden out the back. The managers, Callon and Carolyn Zukowski, have enough suggestions for things to see and do in Český Krumlov to keep you busy for five days. They have a larger hostel, *Krumlov House*, nearby at Rooseveltova 68 which has a study area and a washing machine.

Another popular establishment, *Hostel Ryba* (☎ 71 18 01), Rybářská 5, has dorm beds for 200 Kč. At the top of the old town with a good view in Věžní 99 is *Hostel 99* (☎ 71 28 12), where a bed in a dorm is 180 Kč and the two doubles are 500 Kč each. The *Travellers' Hostel* (☎ 71 13 45), Soukenická 43, has beds in dorms at 200 Kč, including breakfast.

Private Rooms & Pensions The Infocentrum has *priváty* from 800 Kč a double with breakfast. Vltava Travel Agency (☎ 71 19 88), Kájovská 62, also has *private rooms*. You may also be offered a private room by someone on the street. This is fine, but check the location before you set out.

There are quite a few small pensions around town, and new ones are appearing all the time, so these are a good option when the private-room offices are closed. Rooseveltova near the bus station has one pension after another.

Hotels The *Hotel Krumlov* (☎ 71 15 65) is on náměstí Svornosti and rooms are 1100/1650 Kč. The very expensive *Hotel*

Růže (☎ 71 11 41), Horní 154, is in a Jesuit college building dating from 1588, opposite the Regional Museum.

Places to Eat

A very popular place to eat is *Cikánská jizba*, Dlouhá 31. Vegetarians can choose from a large menu at the *Restaurace Vegetarián*, Parkán 105. If it is pizza you're after, try *Pizzeria U dvou opic*, on the corner of Rybářská and Kájovská.

Good tasting Czech food can be found at *Hospoda Na louži*, náměstí Na louži, and occasionally guests show off their talents playing the restaurant's piano. Eggenberg beer is brewed in Český Krumlov.

Entertainment

A good nightclub is *Černý klobouk* on Panská. If you're just after a drink, try the popular *U Matesa*, Rybářská 24, about 100m on the left past Hostel Ryba.

Getting There & Away

The best way to come to Český Krumlov is by bus, and the service from České Budějovice is quite fast. Trains are more frequent but slower and the station is several kilometres north of town (though it's an easy downhill walk into town).

AROUND ČESKÝ KRUMLOV
Zlatá Koruna

Above the Vltava in the village of Zlatá Koruna is one of the best preserved Gothic Cistercian monasteries, founded in 1263 by Přemysl Otakar II. The monastery cathedral is clearly Gothic despite its baroque facelift. The walled complex also houses the **Museum of South Bohemian Literature** (closed Monday and from November to March). Trains from Český Krumlov are much more frequent than buses.

ŠUMAVA

The Šumava is a heavily wooded mountain region stretching for about 125km in South Bohemia along the border with Austria and Germany. It is a UNESCO protected region and 685 sq km of Šumava is a national park.

The Vltava river originates in Šumava and the highest peak is Plechý (1378m) west of Horní Planá. The range is popular for hiking, cycling and cross-country skiing. There is an almost endless number of hiking opportunities but some of the more well known trails are the Bear Trail, Povydří, Boubínský prales or walk the length of the national park, from Nová Pec, at the northern tip of Lake Lipno, up to Nýrsko, south-west of Klatovy.

Maps

The best hiking map is Klub českých turistů's *Šumava* (1:50,000) and for cyclists there is ShoCart's *Šumava Trojmezí velká cykloturistická* (1:75,000) map.

National Park Walks

The **Povydří** trail along the Vydra river is one of the most scenic walks in the park. The 7km trail is between Čeňkova Pila and Antýgl, which is a canyon-like forested river valley. The Vydra river itself runs between huge rounded boulders. The walk takes about 2½ hours. There are about five buses a day that run between Sušice and Modrava, stopping at Čeňkova Pila and Antýgl. Most of these places have plenty of accommodation.

The 46 hectare **Boubín prales** (virgin forest) around the peak of Boubín (1362m) is the only part of the Šumava forest which is regarded as completely untouched. The head trail is 2km north-east from the zastávka Zátoň (train stop not the Zátoň town train station) at Kaplice, where there is a carpark and a basic camp site. From Kaplice it's an easy 2.5km to U pralesa Lake on blue and green trail. To reach Boubín peak stay on the blue trail and it's 7.5km to the top. To return follow the trail south-west to complete the loop. The whole loop should take about five hours.

Getting There & Away

Šumava can be approached along three roads: road 169 via Sušice, road 4 via Strakonice and Vimperk, or road 141 via Prachatice and Volary. Regular buses and trains cover these routes. Up to seven trains a day run between the scenic route of Volary and Strakonice, stopping at Lenora, zastávka Zátoň and Horní Vltavice, both of the former stops are several kilometres from their respective towns (Kubova Huť and Vimperk).

TÁBOR
☎ 0361

God's warriors, the Hussites, founded Tábor in 1420 as a military bastion in defiance of Catholic Europe. The town was organised according to the biblical precept that 'nothing is mine and nothing is yours, because the community is owned equally by everyone'. New arrivals threw all their worldly possessions into large casks at the marketplace and joined in communal work. This extreme nonconformism helped to give the word Bohemian the connotations we associate with it today.

Planned as a bulwark against Catholics in České Budějovice and farther south, Tábor is a warren of narrow broken streets with protruding houses which were intended to weaken and shatter an enemy attack.

Below ground, catacombs totalling 14km provided a refuge for the defenders. This friendly old town, 100km south of Prague, is well worth a brief stop.

Orientation & Information
From the train station walk west through the park past the bus station. Continue west down 9.května, the major shopping street, until you reach a major intersection. Žižkovo náměstí, the old town square, is straight ahead on Palackého třída, a 15-minute walk from the stations. The left-luggage office at the bus station closes at 11 pm, the facility at the train station is open from 2 am to 11.30 pm.

The municipal Infocentrum (☎ 25 23 85), Žižkovo náměstí 2, is very helpful and informative. It sells maps, books accommodation and guided tours, and stocks bus and train timetables.

Unless otherwise stated, all museums are open between April and October daily from 8.30 am to 5 pm and during the rest of the year Monday to Friday.

Money The Komerční banka, on třída 9.května, halfway into town from the stations, changes travellers cheques. Agrobanka, náměstí FR Křižíka, has a Visa/MasterCard ATM.

Post & Communications The post office, incorporating the telephone centre, is in the pink building on the opposite side of Žižkovo náměstí from the museum.

Things to See
A statue of the Hussite commander Jan Žižka graces Žižkovo náměstí, Tábor's main square. Žižka's military successes were due to the novel use of peasant wagons (see one in the Hussite Museum) against crusading Catholic knights.

Around the square are the homes of rich burghers, spanning the period from the late Gothic to the baroque. On the northern side is the Gothic Church of the Transfiguration of Our Lord on Mt Tábor (built between 1440 and 1512), with Renaissance gables and a baroque tower (1677). It is open in summer when the weather is fine.

The other imposing building on Žižkovo náměstí is the early Renaissance town hall (1521), now the Museum of the Hussite Movement (40 Kč), with the entrance to a visitable 650m stretch of the underground passages. You can visit the underground passages only when a group of five people forms. The passages, constructed in the 15th century as refuges during fires or times of war, were also used to store food and to mature lager.

The arch, Žižkovo náměstí 22, beside the old town hall, leads into Mariánská and then Klokotská, which runs south-west to the Bechyně Gate (open May to October), now a small historical museum which focuses on the lives of peasants.

Kotnov Castle, founded here in the 12th century, was destroyed by fire in 1532; in the 17th century the ruins were made into a brewery which is still operating. The castle's remaining 15th-century round tower (open from May to October) may be climbed from the Bechyně Gate museum for a sweeping view of Tábor, the Lužnice River and the surrounding area.

Special Events
During the second weekend in September, Tábor holds the colourful annual Hussite Festival of Tábor when the locals dress in Hussite costumes.

Places to Stay
Camping *Autokemping Malý Jordán* (☎ 321 03) is 1km north of the town near Lake Jordán. Only a few buses a day come to

this cheap camp site, open from mid-June through September.

Hostels On Martina Koláře 2118, the *Domov mládeže* (☎ 25 28 37), has dorm beds from 110 Kč per person.

Another hostel is at *Zimní stadion* (☎ 23 10 88), Václava Soumara 2300, with dorm beds for 100 Kč per person and a bed in a three-bed room is 200 Kč per person.

Private Rooms & Pensions The Infocentrum has private rooms from 300 Kč per person and the staff know of plenty of pensions.

If you arrive at night or on a weekend when these offices are closed, walk into town looking for pension and 'Zimmer frei' signs.

Closest to the stations is *Pension Dáša* (☎ 25 62 53), Bílkova 735, in a deluxe spot with carpark and garden, priced at 700/900 Kč. The friendly *Pension Alfa* (25 61 65), Klokotská 107, is right in the centre of town, with doubles for 800 Kč.

Hotels There are only two expensive hotels left in Tábor. The classiest *Hotel Kapitál* (☎ 25 60 96/8), třída 9.května 617, has rooms at 985/1558/1865 Kč including shower and breakfast.

Places to Eat
A good place for a quick meal is the *Pizza Restaurant*, Kostnická 159, to the left off Palackého třída just before you reach Žižkovo náměstí.

Standard Bohemian cuisine is available at *Beseda Restaurant* next to the church on Žižkovo náměstí.

West of Žižkovo náměstí in the little streets behind Infocentrum there are plenty of little pubs that are popular drinking places where the young Taborites meet. One such place is *U dvou koček*, Svatošová 9.

Entertainment
Tábor's two theatres, the *Městské divadlo* and *Divadlo Oskara Nedbala*, are next to one another on Palackého třída.

Getting There & Away
Tábor is on the main railway line between Prague and Vienna. The line from České Budějovice to Prague also passes through here.

To go from Tábor to Telč by train you must change at Horní Cerekev and Kostelec u Jihlavy, and although the connections are fairly good, the whole 107km trip by local train takes three or four hours through unspoiled countryside. Otherwise take a bus to Jihlava (74km) and another bus on to Telč (29km) from there.

To Plzeň (113km) or Brno (158km) it's easier to take a bus. Eastbound buses to Jihlava and Brno leave every two or three hours and the posted timetable bears numerous footnotes, so reconfirm your departure time at the information window.

Moravia

Moravia, the other historic land of the Czech Republic, is usually overlooked by tourists visiting Bohemia. This is an attraction in itself, but Moravia also has its own history and natural beauties, such as the karst area north of Brno. The theatres and art galleries of Brno, the capital, are excellent, and quaint towns like Kroměříž, Mikulov, Telč, Znojmo and the Rožnov pod Radhoštěm skansen await discovery. The Moravian Gate between Břeclav and Ostrava is a natural corridor between Poland and the Danube basin. Heavy industry is concentrated in North-East Moravia, which is next to Polish Silesia, whereas fertile South Moravia produces excellent wines. Well placed in the geographical centre of Europe, Moravia is a great place to explore.

TELČ
☎ 066
Telč was founded in the 14th century by the feudal lords of Hradec as a fortified settlement with a castle separated from the town by a strong wall. The artificial ponds on each side of Telč provided security and a sure supply of fish. After a fire in 1530, Lord Zachariáš, then Governor of Moravia, ordered the town and castle rebuilt in the Renaissance style by Italian masons. Profits from gold and silver mines allowed Lord and Lady Zachariáš to enjoy a regal lifestyle.

After the death of Zachariáš in 1589, building activity ceased and the complex you see today is largely as it was then. The main square of this most charming of Czech towns is unmarred by modern constructions, and the fire hall at náměstí Zachariáše z Hradce 28 is poignant evidence of local concern to keep it that way. In 1992, Telč was added to UNESCO's World Heritage List.

Orientation & Information

The bus and train stations are a few hundred metres apart on the eastern side of town, a 10-minute walk along Masarykova towards náměstí Zachariáše z Hradce, the old town square.

A left-luggage service is available at the train station 24 hours a day – ask the station-master.

There's an Information Office (☎ 96 22 33) just inside the town hall that provides the usual services and can book accommodation. Public toilets are in the castle.

Money There is a Visa/MasterCard ATM at Komerční banka, náměstí Zachariáše z Hradce 40, where you can also change travellers cheques.

Post & Communications The post office is on Staňkova, a block from the train station. The telephone section is open weekdays from 7.30 am to noon and 1 to 5.30 pm and Saturday from 8 to 11 am.

Things to See

Telč's wonderful old town square is bordered on three sides by 16th-century Renaissance houses built on the ruins of their Gothic predecessors after the 1530 fire, and forming a covered arcade running almost all the way around it.

Though from other eras, the 49m Romanesque **tower** east of the square and the baroque **Marian column** (1717) in the square do not detract from the town's character.

Telč's greatest monument is the splendid Renaissance **Water Chateau** (1568) at the square's western end. Each tour of the chateau (closed Monday and from November to March) with a Czech-speaking guide is 50 Kč; with an English-speaking guide it's 100 Kč.

There are two routes: *Trasa A* takes you through the Renaissance chateau while *Trasa B* goes through apartment rooms. While you're waiting for your guide to arrive, you can visit the local **historical museum**, which you can enter from the chateau courtyard, or the **Art Gallery Jana Zrzavého**, which is in a wing of the chateau that faces the formal garden to the right. A scale model of Telč in the historical museum dated 1895 shows that the town hasn't changed since. The All Saints Chapel in the chateau houses the tombs of Zachariáš of Hradec and his wife, Catherine of Valdštejn.

The baroque church of Jesus' Name (1655) in the former **Jesuit college** is opposite the chateau; **St James Church** (1372) beyond is Gothic.

Through the gate beside St James Church is the large English-style park surrounding the duck ponds, which were once the town's defensive moat. The park is good for restful walks and views of medieval towers.

Places to Stay

Private Rooms & Pensions The Information Office can book *private rooms* (from 300 Kč per person) and pensions. There are several 'Zimmer frei' signs advertising *private rooms* east along Štěpnická and at náměstí Zachariáše z Hradce 11, 29 and 32.

Hotels The friendly *Hotel Pod kaštany* (☎ 721 30 42), Štěpnická 409, just outside the old town, charges 336/660 Kč a single/double with bath. It gives a 10% discount to ISIC card-holders. The walls are thin here. If Pod kaštany is full try *Pension Relax* (☎ 721 31 26) farther east along Štěpnická on Na posvátné 29, where rooms with bathroom and TV are 450/900 Kč, including breakfast. Another similarly priced place is *Pension Vacek* (☎ 721 30 99) on Furchova.

Hotel Celerin (☎ 96 24 77) on the main square at No 43 has modern rooms at 1020/1120 Kč.

Places to Eat

The Krusý restaurant at the *Černý orel* is good and dinner outside on the terrace, as the sun sets over the square, is most enjoyable. The restaurant at the *Hotel Pod kaštany* is also very reasonable and has cheaper beers.

Restaurace U Marušky, Palackého 29, serves basic but tasty Moravian cuisine.

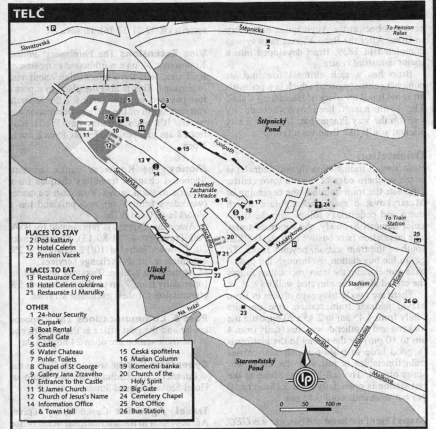

TELČ

PLACES TO STAY
2 Pod kaštany
17 Hotel Celerin
23 Pension Vacek

PLACES TO EAT
13 Restaurace Černý orel
18 Hotel Celerin cukrárna
21 Restaurace U Marušky

OTHER
1 24-hour Security
 Carpark
3 Boat Rental
4 Small Gate
5 Castle
6 Water Chateau
7 Public Toilets
8 Chapel of St George
9 Gallery Jana Zrzavého
10 Entrance to the Castle
11 St James Church
12 Church of Jesus's Name
14 Information Office
 & Town Hall

15 Česká spořitelna
16 Marian Column
19 Komerční banka
20 Church of the
 Holy Spirit
22 Big Gate
24 Cemetery Chapel
25 Post Office
26 Bus Station

A nice little place for coffee and cakes or a shot of plum brandy is the Hotel Celerin *cukrárna* on the square at No I/43 and there's also a good restaurant downstairs with tables in the garden.

Getting There & Away

The railway line through Telč is pretty useless, as it dead ends at Slavonice on the Austrian border. Instead consider using the frequent buses from Telč to Jihlava (29km).

Buses travelling between České Budějovice and Brno stop at Telč about two times a day – it's about a 100km, two-hour trip from Telč to either city. Four buses a day run to Prague (210km, 2½ hours).

There's no information, ticket office or left-luggage area at the bus station. Tickets are sold by the drivers and timetables are posted.

BRNO
☎ 05

Halfway between Budapest and Prague, Brno has been the capital of Moravia since 1641 and its large fortress was an instrument of Habsburg domination. The botanist Gregor

Mendel (1822-84) established the modern science of heredity through his studies of peas and bees at the Augustinian monastery in Brno. After the Brno-Vienna railway was completed in 1839, Brno developed into a major industrial centre.

Brno has a rich cultural life and its compact centre (most of which is a pedestrian zone) holds a variety of fascinating sights. The town hasn't been overwhelmed by tourism the way Prague has. If you're a city slicker, you'll like Brno for a few days.

Orientation

Brno's main train station (hlavní nádraží) is at the southern edge of the old town centre. Opposite the train station is the beginning of Masarykova, a main thoroughfare which trams and pedestrians follow into the triangular náměstí Svobody, the centre of town. The bus station (autobusové nádraží) is 800m south of the train station, beyond Tesco. To get to the bus station, go through the pedestrian tunnel under the train tracks, then follow the crowd along the elevated walkway.

There are two left-luggage offices in Brno hlavní nádraží train station, one upstairs (daily from 4.45 am to 2.45 am) opposite the lockers, and another downstairs (daily from 4 am to 10 pm) by the tunnel to the platforms (a good little map shop which also carries train timetables is just opposite the downstairs office). The left-luggage office at the bus station is open daily from 5.15 am to 10 pm but weekends until 6.15 pm.

Maps One of the latest and best maps is *GEO Club Brno plán města* 1:15,000 (Geodezie).

Information

The information office (☎ 42 21 10 90), or Kulturní a informační centrum (open weekdays from 8 am to 6 pm and weekends from 9 am to 5 pm), in the old town hall, Radnická 8, has computers which can answer almost any question. Its accommodation service can book a room to suit your pocket. It also sells the monthly *Kam v Brně* (also available in bookshops), which is full of detailed information on what's around in Brno. Look out for the free fortnightly *Do města Downtown* leaflet that lists what's on in cinemas, theatres, galeries and *klubs*.

Motorists can turn to the Autoklub České republiky (☎ 42 21 50 30), Bašty 8, or to Autoturist (☎ 42 21 37 16), Husova 8a.

Visa Extensions The Foreigners' Police, Kounicova 24, on a northbound extension of Rašínova, will have information about visa extensions. This is also the place to report a lost passport or visa. Look for the separate entrance north of the main police station entrance. It's open Monday and Wednesday from 8 am to 5 pm, and Friday from 8 am to 1 pm.

Money The Komerční banka, náměstí Svobody, changes travellers cheques for a 2% commission, gives Visa cash advances (weekdays from 8 am to 5 pm) and has a Visa/MasterCard ATM.

American Express is represented by BVV Fair Travel (☎ 42 21 80 13), Starobrněnská 20. Čedok, Nádražní 10/12, charges a 2% commission for its exchange services.

At the train station, Taxatour and Natour (open daily from 7 am to 10 pm) charge a 5% commission for their exchange services.

Post & Communications The telephone centre and the post office at the western end of the train station are open 24 hours a day.

Cybercafés Surf the worldwide Web at the @Internet café, Lidická 17, just south of Hotel Slovan (closed Sunday).

Travel Agencies České dráhy Travel Agency, next to the international ticket office in the train station, sells bus tickets to Western Europe (1950 Kč to Amsterdam, 3600 Kč to London).

The youth travel GTS international (☎ 42 21 31 47), Skrytá 2, in the former CKM office, sells international bus and train tickets, as does Čedok (☎ 42 32 12 67), Nádražní 10/12.

Bookshops Knihkupectví, náměstí Svobody 18, has a good selection of English-language books. For maps and travel guides, Geokart, Vachova 8, is the place.

Medical & Emergency Services The police station is on náměstí Svobody near the corner of Běhounská. The hospital is on Bratislavská 2. First aid (☎ 511 31 13), náměstí 28.října 23, is available Monday to Friday from 7 pm to 6 am, and 24 hours a day on weekends, and there is also a dental section. A 24-hour pharmacy (☎ 42 21 09 30) is on Kobližná 7.

Dangers & Annoyances There are about four cases of pickpocketing reported daily. Car break-ins and theft of cars are becoming more common. According to the local police an area just east of the centre, surrounded by the streets Cejl, Francouzská, Příkop and Ponávka is too dangerous to enter, especially at night.

Things to See

As you enter the city on Masarykova, turn left into Kapucínské náměstí to reach the **Capucine monastery** (1651). In the ventilated crypt below the church are the intact mummies of monks and local aristocrats deposited here before 1784. At the western end of Kapucínské náměstí is the Dietrichstein Palace (1760), with the **Regional Moravian Museum** including a mock medieval village. Nearby, at Zelný trh 8, is **Biskupský Yard Museum** (closed Monday and Sunday) with flora, fauna and numismatic exhibits.

The street in front of the monastery soon leads into Zelný trh and its colourful **open-air market**. Carp used to be sold from the waters of the baroque Parnassus Fountain (1695) at Christmas. The nearby **Reduta Theatre** is where Mozart performed in 1767 and the operettas usually presented here are on hold until restorations are completed.

On Radnická, just off the northern side of Zelný trh, is Brno's 13th-century **old town hall**, which has a splendid Gothic portal (1511) below the tower, which is well worth climbing for 10 Kč. For 20 Kč you can also see the town hall's interior, including Crystal Hall, Fresco Hall and Treasury. The Panorama, another Brno curiosity, which is a rare apparatus made in 1890 that offers continuous showings of the wonders of the Czech Republic in 3-D, is part of the Technological Museum exhibit that was moved here temporarily. Inside the passage behind the portal are a stuffed crocodile, or 'dragon', and a wheel, the traditional symbols of the city.

One legend tells how the dragon once terrorised wayfarers approaching the nearby Svratka River; the wheel was supposedly made by a cartwright who rolled it by hand to Brno from Lednice.

Continue north and take a sharp left to the **Church of St Michael** (1679) and the former Dominican convent. Facing the square on the far side of the church is the 16th-century **new town hall** with its impressive courtyard, stairways and frescoes. Around the corner at Husova 14 is the **Moravian Gallery of Applied Art** (closed Monday and free on Friday).

In the large park on the hill above this gallery is the sinister silhouette of **Špilberk Castle**. Founded in the 13th century and converted into a citadel and prison during the 17th century, it held opponents of the Habsburgs until 1855. In the castle itself, the **Municipal Brno Museum** has three exhibits in various locations: art from the Renaissance era until today; historical moments of Brno; and architecture in Brno (40 Kč). The casemates, which contain an exhibit of prison life, are also open to the public (20 Kč). All are closed Monday and a combined ticket is 50 Kč. There's a good view from the ramparts.

From the park surrounding the castle go south on Husova one block to Šilingrovo náměstí on the left. An unmarked street in the south-eastern corner of the square leads directly towards an old five-storey green building in Biskupská, which will take you up Petrov Hill to the neo-Gothic **Cathedral of SS Peter and Paul**, hidden behind high buildings. The cathedral, rebuilt in the late 19th century on the site of an older basilica, occupies the site where the city's original castle stood. The Renaissance **Bishop's Palace** adjoins the cathedral. In 1645, the Swedish general Torstensson who was besieging Brno declared that he would leave if his troops hadn't captured the city by noon. At 11 am the Swedes were about to scale the walls when the cathedral bell keeper suddenly rang noon. True to his word, the general broke off the attack; since that day the cathedral bells have always rung noon at 11 am.

From Petrov Hill descend Petrská into Zelný trh and continue on Orlí to Minoritská to the **Church of St John** (rebuilt in 1733) with fine altarpieces, an organ and painted ceilings.

BRNO

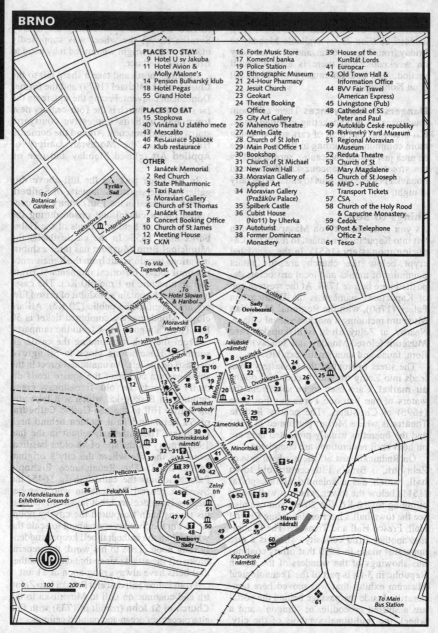

PLACES TO STAY
9 Hotel U sv Jakuba
11 Hotel Avion &
   Molly Malone's
14 Pension Bulharský klub
18 Hotel Pegas
55 Grand Hotel

PLACES TO EAT
15 Stopkova
40 Vinárna U zlatého meče
43 Mescalito
46 Restaurace Špalíček
47 Klub restaurace

OTHER
1 Janáček Memorial
2 Red Church
3 State Philharmonic
4 Taxi Rank
5 Moravian Gallery
6 Church of St Thomas
7 Janáček Theatre
8 Concert Booking Office
10 Church of St James
12 Meeting House
13 CKM

16 Forte Music Store
17 Komerční banka
19 Police Station
20 Ethnographic Museum
21 24-Hour Pharmacy
22 Jesuit Church
23 Geokart
24 Theatre Booking
   Office
25 City Art Gallery
26 Mahenovo Theatre
27 Měnín Gate
28 Church of St John
29 Main Post Office 1
30 Bookshop
31 Church of St Michael
32 New Town Hall
33 Moravian Gallery of
   Applied Art
34 Moravian Gallery
   (Pražákův Palace)
35 Špilberk Castle
36 Cubist House
   (No11) by Uherka
37 Autoturist
38 Former Dominican
   Monastery

39 House of the
   Kunštát Lords
41 Europcar
42 Old Town Hall &
   Information Office
44 BVV Fair Travel
   (American Express)
45 Livingstone (Pub)
48 Cathedral of SS
   Peter and Paul
49 Autoklub České republiky
50 Biskupský Yard Museum
51 Regional Moravian
   Museum
52 Reduta Theatre
53 Church of St
   Mary Magdalene
54 Church of St Joseph
56 MHD - Public
   Transport Tickets
57 ČSA
58 Church of the Holy Rood
   & Capucine Monastery
59 Čedok
60 Post & Telephone
   Office 2
61 Tesco

On nearby náměstí Svobody is a striking plague column (1680). At Kobližná 1, in a corner of the square, is the **Ethnographic Museum** (30 Kč) which has Moravian folk costumes and implements. Just north is the parish church, **St James** (1473), with a soaring nave in the purest Gothic style. This is Brno's most powerful church. The **Church of St Thomas** and the former **Augustinian monastery**, Moravské náměstí 1A, now the Moravian Gallery, are just north of St James.

Also worth seeing is the **City Art Gallery** (Dům umění), Malinovského náměstí 2, beside the Mahenovo Theatre. Excellent art exhibitions are sometimes staged in this gallery (free Wednesday).

Other museums worth seeing are the Moravian Gallery at **Pražákův Palace**, Husova 18, with a 20th-century Czech art exhibit, and the **Janáček Memorial Museum**, Smetanova 14, which is a house-museum dedicated to the composer (open weekdays).

Mendel also has a museum dedicated to him – the **Mendelianum**, Mendlovo náměstí 1. **Pavilion Anthropos**, Pisárecká, has an interesting exhibition on evolution and prehistory, while the functionalist **Vila Tugendhat**, Černopolní 45, is a shrine for fans of modern architecture (closed Monday and Tuesday, 80 Kč).

All museums are closed Monday, unless otherwise stated.

Language Courses

If you'd like to learn Czech, contact either Lingua centrum (☎ 42 21 96 71), Anenská 10, or U tří kohoutů (☎ 42 32 13 09), Masarykova 32. Rates for one student are from about 145 Kč per hour.

Special Events

The annual Brno Motorcycle Grand Prix is held at the end of August.

Places to Stay

During February, March, April, August, September and October, Brno hosts international trade fairs. Before arriving, check carefully that your visit does not coincide with one of these fairs, as hotels fill, their rates increase by about 25% and all public facilities are very overcrowded.

Camping The *Motel Boubrava* (☎ 42 21 60 57) is just beyond Modřice, 12km south of the city. Take tram No 2 or 6 to the end of the line, then walk the remaining 3km. Otherwise take a local train to Popovice train station, 500m from the camping ground (get the times of returning trains before leaving Brno as no information is available at Popovice). Camping costs are 36 Kč per person and 90 Kč per tent. Two-bed cabins are 233 Kč and four-bed cabins are 360 Kč, while rooms with shower, hot water and toilet in the motel are from 270 to 980 Kč per double. The restaurant is good and is open year-round.

The *Obora Camping* (☎ 79 11 05) at the Brněnská přehrada (Brno dam) is only open from May to September. To get there from the main train station, take tram No 1 to the zoo and there change to bus No 103. The camping ground is at the seventh stop.

Hostels CKM youth travel, Skrytá 2, knows of accommodation in student dormitories during July and August.

South of the centre, the HI-listed *Hotel Interservis* (☎ 45 23 43 35/31 65), Lomená, rents beds in double rooms for 305 Kč per person. Take tram No 9 or 12 south to the end of the line, go through the underpass and follow Lužná east for three blocks, then turn right on Lomená. The hostel is the tall modern building about two blocks down on your left.

Another place on the HI list is *Hotel Přehrada* (☎ 46 21 01 67), Kníničky 225, Brno Přehrada, that has rooms with shared facilities from 440/580 Kč and doubles with bathroom at 780 Kč, including breakfast. Student and youth card holders pay 150 Kč per person for a bed. It is open from March to November. Take tram No 1 from the main train station to the zoo and there cross the road west to náměstí 28.dubna and take bus No 54 to the end.

Year-round you can get a room at *Palacký roh – vysokoškolské koleje* (☎ 41 32 12 63), Kolejní 2, block K-1, on the northern side of the city, for 840/1060 Kč. This large student complex is easy to get to by taking tram No 13 north to the end of the line, then taking trolleybus No 53 right to the hostel.

The cheapest and most central accommodation is in *Pension Bulharský klub* (☎ 42 21 10 63), Skrytá 1, where a bed in basic two or three-bed rooms costs 350 Kč. Bathroom is shared.

Hotel Slovan (☎ 41 32 12 07), Lidická 23, gives 10% discount to holders of student and youth cards.

Private Rooms Čedok arranges rooms in *private homes* from 500 Kč per person a night. Most are far from the centre but can easily be reached on public transport. The Infocentrum also has *private rooms* from 500 Kč.

Taxatour (☎ 42 21 33 48) in the train station arranges *private rooms* from 500 Kč per person.

Hotels The modern *Hotel Avion* (☎ 42 21 50 16), Česká 20, is reasonable at 645/845 Kč without shower, 845/1360 Kč with shower.

The friendly but ageing *Hotel U sv Jakuba* (☎ 42 21 07 95), Jakubské náměstí 6, costs 990/1490 Kč with shower. The hotel restaurant is good. The U sv Jakuba is clean, well-managed and relatively free of tram noise.

The *Hotel Pegas* (☎ 42 21 01 04), Jakubská 4, in an old building that was renovated a few years ago, is on a quiet street right in the centre of town. Bright and clean rooms with bath and breakfast are 1074/1611 Kč.

One of the top hotels is the *Holiday Inn* (☎ 43 12 21 11) near the Exhibition Grounds at Křižkovského 20 at 2800/3900 Kč.

Places to Eat

Restaurants The *Haribol*, Lužanecká 4, is a vegetarian restaurant open from 11 am to 5 pm weekdays. The touristy *Pivnice Pegas*, Jakubská 4, is an attractive restaurant with an extensive menu in English. The food is so-so, but it brews its own dark and light beer on the premises in two huge copper vats. *Stopkova plzeňská pivnice*, Česká 5, is a little more staid than Pegas.

Unusual dishes (meat or vegetarian) are found at *Mescalito*, Starobrněnská 3. Try an Aztec mushroom hamburger. This is also a popular bar for the young in the evenings. Good Moravian food is served at *Restaurace Špalíček*, Zelný trh 12.

A pleasant place to order a bottle of local wine with your meal is *Vinárna U zlatého meče*, Mečová 3.

Klub restaurace (☎ 42 21 13 76), Pod Petrovem, is fine dining and an ideal place for a splurge.

Self-Service The stand-up *Bufet Sputnik*, on the 1st floor at Česká 1, has good grilled chicken, draught beer, coffee and strawberry milkshakes!

About the best ice-cream cones in town are dispensed by *Diana*, Česká 25.

There's a good *supermarket* in the basement of Tesco behind the train station on the way to the bus station – perfect if you need to stock up on groceries for a long trip.

Entertainment

Except in midsummer when the artists are on holiday, Brno's theatres offer excellent performances. In Brno, the tickets aren't all cornered by scalpers and profiteers as they are in Prague, but you are expected to dress up a bit.

Opera, operettas and ballet are performed at the modern *Janáček Theatre* (Janáčkovo divadlo), Sady osvobození. This large theatre which opened in 1966 is named after composer Leoš Janáček, who spent much of his life in Brno.

The nearby neo-baroque *Mahenovo Theatre* (Mahenovo divadlo; 1882), a beautifully decorated old-style theatre designed by the famous Viennese theatrical architects Fellner and Hellmer, presents classical drama in Czech and operettas.

Operettas used to be held at the historic *Reduta Theatre* (1734), Zelný trh 3, but at the time of writing it was closed for renovations.

The *State Philharmonic Brno*, in Besední dům, Komenského náměstí 8 (the entrance is from Husova), has regular concerts. Tickets can be bought from SFB in Besední.

For tickets to the Janáček, Mahenovo and Malá scéna theatres, go to Předprodej (☎ 42 32 12 85), Dvořákova 11, a small booking office behind the Mahenovo Theatre. It is open weekdays from 9 am to 5.30 pm, but on Saturday it closes at noon.

If you're around on Sunday, don't miss the *Radost Puppet Theatre*, Bratislavská 32,

which puts on shows
kids' stuff but great
enjoyed puppets for a

The Kulturní a info
booking office (Cent
Běhounská 16. It sells t
concerts at a variety of

Bars & Clubs

A basic pub pop
young locals is *Livingstone*, Starobrněnst
it's open till 3 am. Another is the cosy Irish
pub *Molly Malone's*, adjacent to Hotel Avion.

Alterna, Kounicova 48, *blok* B, is an alternative *klub* where you can enjoy rock, punk, jazz and other alternative entertainment. It's open from 7 pm to 12.30 am. From Česká take trolleybus No 134 or 136 three stops north.

The largest disco in the Czech Republic is in the *Boby centrum*, Sportovní 2. This place can overload your senses with two bars, a night club and four restaurants. From the intersection of Koliště and Cejl take bus 67 north.

Things to Buy

Forte Plus music store, náměstí Svobody 22, has a good selection of local compact discs and staff don't mind playing things for you.

Getting There & Away

Bus The bus to Vienna (Mitte Bahnhof) departs from platform No 20 at the bus station twice a day (127km, 225 Kč one way).

For shorter trips buses are faster and more efficient than trains. A bus is better if you're going to Telč (96km), Trenčín (134km) or anywhere in South Bohemia.

Train All trains between Budapest and Berlin stop at Brno. If you're going to or from Vienna, change trains at Břeclav. To go to or from Košice, change trains at Přerov. Direct trains from Bratislava (141km, two hours) and Prague (257km, three hours) are frequent.

An overnight train with couchettes and sleepers runs between Brno and Košice. Reserve international tickets, couchettes or sleepers at windows to the right of the main entrance in the train station.

Around Benešova 22 (open weekdays 6 pm and weekends from 7 am tickets for public transport. tickets are 8 Kč and 90- a 24-hour ticket is 40 Kč is 180 Kč. Tickets are shops displaying the shops.

On the Three rolling count Slavkov u Brna (Austerlitz 'Battle of Bonaparte defeated the in the open, Emperor Franz I (Austria) and Brno and der I (Russia), defenders of the Napoleon feudal past. The battle was decided at Pracký kopec, a hill 12km west of Slavkov u Brna where a monument was erected in 1912. After the battle Napoleon spent four days concluding an armistice at the baroque **chateau** (1705) in Slavkov u Brna.

Slavkov u Brna is 21km east of Brno and is easily accessible by bus or train from Brno (ask about times and platform numbers at the information counter). The chateau's historical exhibit on Napoleon's life, the decorated palace rooms and the gallery wing are open Tuesday to Sunday from April to November. Unfortunately, Pracký kopec is difficult to reach by public transport. You can try getting a bus from Brno's bus station to Prace, from where it is a 3km walk south to the top of the hill, or by the more frequent Brno-Slavkov train, getting off at Ponětovice and walking 4km south through Prace.

Moravian Karst

☎ 0506

The caves, chasms and canyons of the Moravský kras (Moravian Karst), 20km north of Brno, have been created by the underground Punkva River and are the most treasured in the country. You can walk 1km through the deepest caves, admiring the stalactites and stalagmites, ending up at the foot of the Macocha Abyss. There you board a small boat for a 400m ride down the Punkva River out of the cave.

CZECH REPUBLIC

Information
služba of Moravi... ...s
Mlýn provides i... 75
dation and tick... pen all
...een April

The Caves
(50 Kč but in... me year they
minutes and...
year from 8... he same opening
and Septe... ept in winter when
are open
Caves (3... d they are closed from
hours as...ary. On weekends and in
they op...uckets will usually have been
Nove...
mids...rs or more before the tours are
sold
due ... mmence, so arrive early. A so-called
'eco...y train' *(Eko-expres)* on wheels
carr... motorists from the parking lot at
Skalní Mlýn to the caves every 30 minutes
for 30 Kč.

From Punkevní it's a 15-minute hike, or an easy gondola ride (40 Kč one way or 60 Kč for a combined ticket with the ecology train), up to the top of the 139m deep Macocha Abyss. Other caves to be visited in this area include Balčárka and Sloupsko-Sošuvské (both have similar hours as Kateřinská – contact the information

...races of prehistoric humans have ...und in the caves.

Places to Stay & Eat Near the Macocha Abyss is *Útulna na Macoše* (☎ 31 55), where dorm beds are 160 Kč per person. There is also a restaurant here. In Skalní Mlýn, the pricier *Hotel Skalní Mlýn* (☎ 41 81 13) has modern rooms at 1190/1490 Kč.

Getting There & Away To get there, take a train (16 a day) to Blansko, then walk over to the adjacent bus station. This is where your problems will start as there is only one regular bus between Blansko and Skalní Mlýn at 7.40 am, which means that you have to catch the 6.35 am train from Brno – leaving you about four minutes to catch the bus. There is a return bus at 3.25 pm. The fit can take the 8km trail from Blansko to Skalní Mlýn and hitching is also easy.

Another option is to catch the Obůrka bus from stand No 12 to Nové Dvory, from which it's a pleasant 40-minute walk through the forest to Punkevní. It's also possible to take a bus from stand No 40 at Brno bus station to Jedovnice (29km). Buses depart every couple of hours. From Jedovnice follow the yellow hiking trail 7km to the Macocha Abyss via Kateřinská Caves.

which puts on shows during the day. It's kids' stuff but great fun if you haven't enjoyed puppets for a while.

The Kulturní a informační centrum has a booking office (Centrální předprodej) at Běhounská 16. It sells tickets to rock and folk concerts at a variety of venues.

Bars & Clubs A basic pub popular with young locals is *Livingstone*, Starobrněnská 1; it's open till 3 am. Another is the cosy Irish pub *Molly Malone's*, adjacent to Hotel Avion.

Alterna, Kounicova 48, *blok* B, is an alternative *klub* where you can enjoy rock, punk, jazz and other alternative entertainment. It's open from 7 pm to 12.30 am. From Česká take trolleybus No 134 or 136 three stops north.

The largest disco in the Czech Republic is in the *Boby centrum*, Sportovní 2. This place can overload your senses with two bars, a night club and four restaurants. From the intersection of Koliště and Cejl take bus 67 north.

Things to Buy

Forte Plus music store, náměstí Svobody 22, has a good selection of local compact discs and staff don't mind playing things for you.

Getting There & Away

Bus The bus to Vienna (Mitte Bahnhof) departs from platform No 20 at the bus station twice a day (127km, 225 Kč one way).

For shorter trips buses are faster and more efficient than trains. A bus is better if you're going to Telč (96km), Trenčín (134km) or anywhere in South Bohemia.

Train All trains between Budapest and Berlin stop at Brno. If you're going to or from Vienna, change trains at Břeclav. To go to or from Košice, change trains at Přerov. Direct trains from Bratislava (141km, two hours) and Prague (257km, three hours) are frequent.

An overnight train with couchettes and sleepers runs between Brno and Košice. Reserve international tickets, couchettes or sleepers at windows to the right of the main entrance in the train station.

Getting Around

The MHD at Benešova 22 (open weekdays from 6 am to 6 pm and weekends from 7 am to 4 pm) sells tickets for public transport. Single 60-minute tickets are 8 Kč and 90-minute are 12 Kč, a 24-hour ticket is 40 Kč and a 15-day ticket is 180 Kč. Tickets are also available from shops displaying the MHD sticker and Tabák shops.

AROUND BRNO
Slavkov u Brna

On 2 December 1805, the famous 'Battle of the Three Emperors' took place in the open, rolling countryside between Brno and Slavkov u Brna (Austerlitz). Here Napoleon Bonaparte defeated the combined armies of Emperor Franz I (Austria) and Tsar Alexander I (Russia), defenders of the aristocratic, feudal past. The battle was decided at Pracký kopec, a hill 12km west of Slavkov u Brna where a monument was erected in 1912. After the battle Napoleon spent four days concluding an armistice at the baroque **chateau** (1705) in Slavkov u Brna.

Slavkov u Brna is 21km east of Brno and is easily accessible by bus or train from Brno (ask about times and platform numbers at the information counter). The chateau's historical exhibit on Napoleon's life, the decorated palace rooms and the gallery wing are open Tuesday to Sunday from April to November. Unfortunately, Pracký kopec is difficult to reach by public transport. You can try getting a bus from Brno's bus station to Prace, from where it is a 3km walk south to the top of the hill, or by the more frequent Brno-Slavkov train, getting off at Ponětovice and walking 4km south through Prace.

Moravian Karst
☎ 0506

The caves, chasms and canyons of the Moravský kras (Moravian Karst), 20km north of Brno, have been created by the underground Punkva River and are the most treasured in the country. You can walk 1km through the deepest caves, admiring the stalactites and stalagmites, ending up at the foot of the Macocha Abyss. There you board a small boat for a 400m ride down the Punkva River out of the cave.

CZECH REPUBLIC

Information The Ústřední informační služba of Moravský kras (☎ 35 75) at Skalní Mlýn provides information, books accommodation and tickets for the caves.

The Caves The visit to the Punkevní Caves (50 Kč but in July/August it's 70 Kč) takes 75 minutes and they are the only ones open all year from 8.20 am to 3.50 pm between April and September, but the rest of the year they are open from 9 am to 2 pm. Kateřinská Caves (30 Kč) also have the same opening hours as Punkevní, except in winter when they open at 10 am and they are closed from November to January. On weekends and in midsummer, all tickets will usually have been sold two hours or more before the tours are due to commence, so arrive early. A so-called 'ecology train' *(Eko-expres)* on wheels carries motorists from the parking lot at Skalní Mlýn to the caves every 30 minutes for 30 Kč.

From Punkevní it's a 15-minute hike, or an easy gondola ride (40 Kč one way or 60 Kč for a combined ticket with the ecology train), up to the top of the 139m deep Macocha Abyss. Other caves to be visited in this area include Balčárka and Sloupsko-Sošuvské (both have similar hours as Kateřinská – contact the information

service). Traces of prehistoric humans have been found in the caves.

Places to Stay & Eat Near the Macocha Abyss is *Útulna na Macoše* (☎ 31 55), where dorm beds are 160 Kč per person. There is also a restaurant here. In Skalní Mlýn, the pricier *Hotel Skalní Mlýn* (☎ 41 81 13) has modern rooms at 1190/1490 Kč.

Getting There & Away To get there, take a train (16 a day) to Blansko, then walk over to the adjacent bus station. This is where your problems will start as there is only one regular bus between Blansko and Skalní Mlýn at 7.40 am, which means that you have to catch the 6.35 am train from Brno – leaving you about four minutes to catch the bus. There is a return bus at 3.25 pm. The fit can take the 8km trail from Blansko to Skalní Mlýn and hitching is also easy.

Another option is to catch the Obůrka bus from stand No 12 to Nové Dvory, from which it's a pleasant 40-minute walk through the forest to Punkevní. It's also possible to take a bus from stand No 40 at Brno bus station to Jedovnice (29km). Buses depart every couple of hours. From Jedovnice follow the yellow hiking trail 7km to the Macocha Abyss via Kateřinská Caves.

Hungary

Hungary is just the place to kick off an Eastern European trip. A short hop from Vienna, this land of Franz Liszt and Béla Bartók, Romani (Gypsy) music and the romantic Danube River continues to enchant visitors. The allure of Budapest, once an imperial city, is obvious at first sight, but other cities like Pécs, the warm heart of the south, and Eger, the wine capital of the north, have much to offer travellers, as does the sprawling countryside.

Here you'll find much of the glamour and excitement of Western Europe at less than half the cost.

Facts about Hungary

HISTORY

The Celts occupied Hungary in the 3rd century BC but were conquered by the Romans around the beginning of the Christian era. Until the early 5th century AD, all of Hungary west of the Danube (Transdanubia) was included in the Roman province of Pannonia. The Roman legion stationed at Aquincum (Budapest) guarded the northeastern frontier of the empire. The Romans planted the first vineyards in Hungary and built baths near the region's thermal waters.

The Romans were forced to abandon Pannonia in 451 by the Huns, whose short-lived empire was established by Attila. The Huns were followed by the Goths, Lombards and finally the Avars, a powerful Turkic people. They were subdued by Charlemagne in 796.

Seven Magyar tribes under the leadership of Árpád – the *gyula* (chief military commander) – swept in from beyond the Volga River in 896 and occupied the Danube Basin. The Magyars terrorised Europe with raids as far as Spain, northern Germany and southern Italy until they were stopped at the battle of Augsburg in 955 and subsequently converted to Christianity. Hungary's first king and patron saint, Stephen I (István), was crowned on Christmas Day in 1000 AD, marking the

AT A GLANCE

Capital	Budapest
Population	10.4 million
Area	93,030 sq km
Official Language	Hungarian
Currency	1 forint (Ft) = 100 filler
GDP	US$74.7 billion (1996)
Time	GMT/UTC+0100

foundation of the Hungarian state. After the Mongols sacked Hungary in 1241, killing an estimated one-third of its two million people, many cities were fortified.

Medieval Hungary was a powerful state which included Transylvania (now in Romania), Slovakia and Croatia. The so-called Golden Bull, a kind of Magna Carta limiting some of the king's powers in favour of the nobility, was signed at Székesfehérvár in 1222, and universities were founded in Pécs (1367) and Buda (1389).

In 1456 at Nándorfehérvár (now Belgrade) Hungarians under János Hunyadi stopped the

HUNGARY

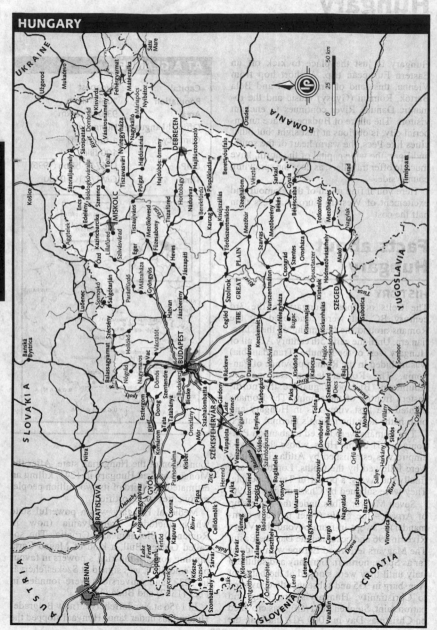

Ottoman Turkish advance into Hungary and under Hunyadi's son, Matthias Corvinus (ruled 1458-90), Hungary experienced a brief flowering of Renaissance culture. Then in 1514 a peasant army turned on the landowners. The serfs were eventually suppressed and their leader, György Dózsa, was burned alive on a red-hot iron throne, but Hungary was seriously weakened. In 1526 the Turks defeated the Hungarian army at Mohács.

Buda Castle capitulated in 1541 and Hungary was divided into three. The central part was in Turkish hands while Transdanubia and what is now Slovakia were governed by the Austrian House of Habsburg assisted by the Hungarian nobility based in Pozsony (Bratislava). The principality of Transylvania, east of the Tisza River, prospered as a vassal state of the Ottoman Empire.

When the Turks were expelled in 1686 by the Austrian, Hungarian and Polish armies, Hungary was subjected to Habsburg domination. From 1703 to 1711 Ferenc Rákóczi II, Prince of Transylvania, led an unsuccessful war of independence against the Austrians.

Hungary never fully recovered from these disasters and from the 18th century it had to be rebuilt almost from scratch. But under the 'enlightened absolutism' of the Habsburg monarchs Maria Theresa (1740-80) and her son Joseph II (1780-90), the country made great steps forward economically and culturally.

The revolution of 1848 led by Lajos Kossuth and the poet Sándor Petőfi demanded freedom for the serfs and independence. Although it was put down a year later, the uprising shook the oligarchy. In 1866 Austria was defeated by Prussia and the next year a compromise was struck between Austrian capitalists and Hungarian landowners, and an Austro-Hungarian monarchy was formed. This proved unfortunate because Hungary came to be viewed by its neighbours as a tool of Habsburg oppression.

After WWI and the collapse of the Habsburg Empire, Hungary became independent, but the 1920 Trianon Treaty stripped the country of 68% of its territory and 58% of its population. Many of the problems Trianon created remain, and it still colours Hungary's relations with some neighbours.

In August 1919, a short-lived communist government led by Béla Kun was overthrown and thousands were killed, imprisoned or forced to flee the country. In March 1920, Admiral Miklós Horthy established a repressive rightist regime.

In 1941 Hungary's desire to recover its lost territories drew it into war alongside the Nazis. When Horthy tried to make a separate peace with the Allies in 1944, the occupying Germans ousted him and put the fascist Arrow Cross Party in power, which immediately began deporting hundreds of thousands of Jews to Auschwitz and other labour camps, where they were brutally murdered, starved or succumbed to disease.

In December 1944 a provisional government was established at Debrecen, and by early April 1945 all of Hungary had been liberated by the Soviet army.

The Communist Era

After the war the communists divided the large estates among the peasantry and nationalised industry.

On 23 October 1956 student demonstrators demanding the withdrawal of Soviet troops were fired upon. The next day Imre Nagy, a reform-minded communist, was made prime minister. On 28 October Nagy's government offered an amnesty to all those involved in the violence and promised to abolish the AVO, the hated secret police, but the fighting intensified with some Hungarian military units joining the rebels. Soviet troops, who had become directly involved in the conflict, began a slow withdrawal.

On 31 October hundreds of political prisoners were released and there were widespread reprisals against AVO agents. On 1 November, Nagy announced that Hungary would leave the Warsaw Pact and become neutral. At this, the Soviet forces began to redeploy and on 4 November Soviet tanks moved into Budapest, crushing the uprising. The fighting continued until 11 November, resulting in 3000 Hungarians being killed and another 200,000 fleeing to neighbouring Austria. Nagy was arrested and deported to Romania where he was executed two years later. In 1989 Nagy was officially 'rehabilitated' and reburied in Budapest. A striking monument was unveiled near the Parliament building in Budapest in 1996.

HUNGARY

The role of Radio Free Europe (a Cold War propaganda station beamed into communist countries from the west) in the events of 1956 is still debated. Broadcasts encouraged the uprising and seemed to promise western assistance. This never materialised and Hungarians felt totally friendless.

After the revolt, the Hungarian Socialist Workers' Party was reorganised, and János Kádár took over as president. In 1961 Kádár turned an old Stalinist slogan around to become, 'He who is not against us is with us', to symbolise the new social unity. After 1968 Hungary abandoned strict central economic control for a limited market system.

In June 1987 Károly Grósz took over as premier and in May 1988, after Kádár's forced retirement, became party secretary general. Under Grósz, Hungary began moving towards full democracy.

Post Communism

At a party congress in October 1989 the communists agreed to give up their monopoly on power, paving the way for free elections in March 1990. A new program advocating social democracy and a free-market economy was adopted.

This was not enough to shake off the stigma of four decades of autocratic rule, however, and the 1990 vote was won by the centrist Hungarian Democratic Forum (MDF), which advocated a gradual transition towards capitalism. As Gorbachev looked on, Hungary changed political systems with scarcely a murmur and the last Soviet troops left in 1991.

In coalition with two smaller parties, the MDF oversaw the painful transition to a full market economy, which has resulted in declining living standards for most people. In 1991 most state subsidies were removed, leading to a severe recession. Beggars appeared on the streets and free education and health care programs were cut. Disillusionment with this ugly side of the market economy resulted in the 1994 elections being won by the Socialist Party.

This in no way implied a return to the past, and party leader Gyula Horn was quick to point out that it was his party that had initiated the whole reform process in the first place.

GEOGRAPHY & ECOLOGY

Hungary (slightly larger than Portugal) occupies the Carpathian Basin in the very centre of Eastern Europe. The 417km Hungarian section of the Danube River cuts through a southern extension of the Carpathian Mountains at the majestic Danube Bend north of Budapest. The Danube divides Hungary's 93,030 sq km into the Great Plain (Nagyalföld) in the east and Transdanubia (Dunántúl) in the west. The 598km-long Tisza River crosses the Great Plain about 100km east of the Danube. Hungary's 'mountains' are actually hills that seldom exceed an elevation of 1000m. The highest peak is Kékes (1014m) in the Mátra range north-east of Budapest.

Two-thirds of Hungary is less than 200m above sea level. The almost treeless *puszta* (another name for the Great Plain) between the Danube and Romanian border is a forerunner of the Ukrainian Steppes. Lake Balaton, covering 598 sq km between the Danube and Austria averages only 2 to 3m in depth, and the waters warm up quickly in summer.

Hungary is home to more than 2000 flowering plant species, many of which are not normally found at this latitude. There are a lot of common European animals (deer, wild hare, boar, otter) as well as some rare species (wild cat, lake bat, Pannonian lizard), but three-quarters of the country's 450 vertebrates are birds, especially waterfowl.

There are five national parks. The two on the Great Plain – Hortobágy and Kiskunság – protect the wildlife and the fragile wetlands and saline grasslands of the open puszta. Two are in the north: the almost completely wooded Bükk Hills and the Aggtelek region with its extensive system of karst caves. The smallest park is at Lake Fertő on the Austrian border.

Pollution is a large and costly problem. Low-grade coal that fuels some industry and heats homes creates sulphur dioxide and acid rain. The over-use of nitrate fertilisers in agriculture has caused the groundwater beneath the plains to become contaminated with phosphates and threatens Lake Balaton.

CLIMATE

Hungary has a temperate Continental climate with Mediterranean and Atlantic influences. Winters are cold, cloudy and damp or windy, the summers warm and sometimes very hot. May, June and November are the rainiest months, although more rain usually falls in the west and south-west than in the east. The number of hours of sunshine a year varies between 1900 and 2500 – among the highest in Europe. From April to the end of September, you can expect the sun to shine for about 10 hours a day. July is the hottest month (average temperature 23.2°C) and January the coldest (-1.3°C). The average annual temperature is 11°C.

GOVERNMENT & POLITICS

Hungary's head of state is the president, currently Árpád Göncz. Real power resides with the prime minister, leader of the majority party (or coalition) in parliament. The current prime minister is Viktor Orbán.

The largest political parties are: MSZP (Hungarian Socialist Party), SZDSZ (Alliance of Free Democrats), Fidesz (Hungarian Civic Party), MDF (Hungarian Democratic Forum) and FKGB (Independent Smallholders Party). Horse-trading between these and smaller parties are a feature of political life, and a party's platform can change radically. For example, the SZDSZ began life as an anticommunist party but joined the ex-communist MSZP in a governing coalition. Fidesz was once a radical liberal party but is now slightly right-wing, while MDF has moved from slightly left to slightly right. The populist FKGB espouses right-wing and nationalist views.

In the elections of 1998, Fidesz won office in coalition with MDF and FKGB.

ECONOMY

Hungary's painful economic restructuring appears to be paying off for those lucky enough to be in the re-emerging middle class. Many Hungarians are optimistic that they will approach the economic level of their western neighbours in the coming years. For many others, though, a return to the bad old days of abject poverty looms. Inflation is a big problem and the unemployment rate

(which was negligible under communism) seems likely to remain high.

Taking advantage of the country's low wages and skilled-labour base, European, Asian and North American companies have established automobile-assembly plants, high-tech electronics factories and light manufacturing works. However, most of the jobs are in relatively prosperous Budapest and Transdanubia. The north-east part of Hungary, traditionally an economic 'black hole', has largely been passed over, and unemployment still reaches double digits in many towns and villages there.

The sale of utilities and state enterprises, mostly to western investors, is beginning to show tangible benefits. For instance, Hungary leads Eastern Europe in the modernisation of its antiquated telephone system.

Reducing the social security bill has been one of the toughest challenges facing the government. Because of the large role the so-called shadow (or black market) economy plays, Hungary simply cannot raise enough funds through taxes to meet its budget commitments.

Hungary is determined to become a member of the EU. Nearly two-thirds of all exports go to EU countries, and it's likely Hungary will be invited to join the EU early next century. In order to qualify Hungary must get its economic house in order. This explains why politicians, whatever their party persuasion, are united in continuing the tough economic reforms.

POPULATION & PEOPLE

Neither a Slavic nor a Germanic people, the Ugric Hungarians were the last major ethnic group to arrive in Europe during the period of the Great Migrations. Some 10.4 million Hungarians live within the national borders, with another five million abroad. The estimated two million ethnic Hungarians in Transylvania constitute the second-largest national minority in Europe (after the Albanians of Yugoslavia), and large numbers of Hungarians live in Slovakia, Yugoslavia, Croatia, Ukraine, Austria, the USA and Canada. Minorities within Hungary include Germans (1.6%), Slovaks (1.1%), South Slavs (0.9%) and Romanians (0.2%). The estimated quarter of a million Hungarian Roma (Gypsies) live mostly in the north-eastern corner of the country.

Almost two-thirds of all Hungarians live in cities, just over two million of them in Budapest. The country's next largest cities are Debrecen (220,000), Miskolc (211,000), Szeged (185,000), Pécs (179,000) and Győr (130,000). Hungary has Europe's highest rate of suicide (39 per 100,000 people), well ahead of Russia, which ranks second with 26 per 100,000. The literacy rate is about 98%. Education is compulsory for children until age 16.

Hungarians are generally friendly and polite, with a love of dogs, children and each other – public displays of affection between people of all ages are surprisingly common.

ARTS

Although the Renaissance flourished briefly here during the late 15th century, Hungary was isolated from the mainstream of European culture during Turkish rule (1526-1686). Then came domination by the Habsburgs until 1918 and, more recently, Nazi Germany and the USSR. It's not surprising that the work of Hungarian writers and artists reflect the struggle against oppression.

Music

Franz (or Ferenc) Liszt (1811-86) liked to describe himself as part Gypsy, and some of his works, notably *Hungarian Rhapsodies*, echo that people's music. Ferenc Erkel (1810-93) is the father of Hungarian opera and two of his works – the stirringly nationalist *Bánk Bán* and *László Hunyadi* – are standards at the State Opera House in Budapest. Erkel also composed the music for the Hungarian national anthem.

Béla Bartók (1881-1945) and Zoltán Kodály (1882-1967) made the first systematic study of Hungarian folk music, travelling and recording throughout the linguistic region in 1906. Both integrated some of their findings into their own compositions – Bartók in *Bluebeard's Castle*, for example, and Kodály in his *Peacock Variations*. Bartók composed and made a further study of Balkan folk music; Kodály went on to estab-

lish his own method of musical education with initial emphasis on voice instruction.

Romani and Hungarian folk music are often confused and it's important to know the difference. Romani music as it is known and played in Hungarian restaurants from Budapest to Boston is urban schmaltz and based on recruiting tunes *(verbunkos)* played during the Rákóczi independence war. At least two fiddles, a bass and a cymbalom (a curious stringed instrument played with sticks) are *de rigueur*; if you want to hear this saccharine *csárdás* music, the restaurants in Budapest's Castle District can oblige, or you can buy a tape by Sándor Lakatos or his son Déki.

To confuse matters further, real Romani music does not use instruments but is sung a cappella (though it is sometimes backed with guitar and percussion); a very good tape of Hungarian Romani folk songs is *Magyarországi Cigány Népdalok* (Hungarian Gypsy Folk Songs), produced by Hungaroton. The best modern Romani group is Kalyi Jag (Black Fire), led by Gusztav Várga.

A *táncház* is an excellent place to hear Hungarian folk music and, incidentally, to learn how to dance. It's all good fun and they're easy to find in Budapest, where the dance-house revival began about 20 years ago. Hungarian folk musicians play zithers, hurdy-gurdies, bagpipes and lutes on a five-note scale.

Traditional Yiddish music was once closely associated with Central European folk music. Until WWI, Jewish klezmer dance bands were led by the violin and cymbalom, but the influence of Yiddish theatre and the first wax recordings inspired a switch to the clarinet which predominates today. In 1990 the Budapest Klezmer Band was formed to revive this happy mix of jazz and the big-band sound.

Literature

Sándor Petőfi (1823-49) is Hungary's most celebrated and accessible poet, and a line from his work *National Song* became the rallying cry for the 1848-49 War of Independence, in which he fought and died. Petőfi's comrade-in-arms, János Arany (1817-82), whose name is synonymous with impeccable Hungarian, wrote epic poetry *(Toldi Trilogy)* and ballads. Another friend, the prolific novelist and playwright Mór Jókai (1825-1904), gave expression to heroism and honesty in such wonderful works as *The Man with the Golden Touch* and *Black Diamonds*. This author, known as the 'Hungarian Dickens', still enjoys widespread popularity.

Hungary's finest 20th-century lyric poet, Endre Ady (1877-1919), attacked narrow materialism, provoking a storm of indignation from right-wing nationalists. The work of the poet Attila József (1905-37), a perennial favourite among Hungarian youth, expresses the alienation felt by individuals in the technological age. The novels of Zsigmond Móricz (1879-1942) examined the harsh reality of peasant life in turn-of-the-century Hungary.

György Konrád (1933-) and Péter Esterházy (1950-) are two important contemporary writers. *A Hungarian Quartet* (paperback, 1700 Ft) contains four short stories by contemporary writers, including Esterházy.

Visual Arts

Hungary has one of the richest folk traditions in Europe but you are unlikely to see good examples of weaving, pottery, woodcarving and the like outside museums.

In fine art, favourite painters from the 19th century include the realist Mihály Munkácsy (1844-1900) – the 'painter of the puszta' – and Tivadar Csontváry (1853-1919), who has been compared with Van Gogh. Victor Vasarely (1908-), who as Vásárhelyi Győző emigrated to Paris in 1930, is considered the 'Father of Op Art'.

SOCIETY & CONDUCT

In general Hungarians are not uninhibited like the Romanians or the sentimental Slavs, who will laugh or cry at the drop of a hat (or a drink). They are a somewhat reserved, formal people. Forget about the impassioned, devil-may-care Roma stereotype – it doesn't exist. There's a tendency to *honfibú*, literally 'patriotic sorrow' but really a penchant for the blues, although if you're here in the spring you'll see extraordinary numbers of lighthearted amorous couples.

There are few rules governing interpersonal relationships or conduct. If you're invited to someone's home, bring a bunch of flowers (available in profusion all year) or a bottle of good local wine. You can talk about almost anything, but money is a touchy subject. Traditionally, the discussion or manifestation of wealth was considered gauche. Your salary – piddling as you may think it is – will astonish most Hungarians.

Hungarians were prepared to die to liberate their land from the USSR, but this doesn't mean that they have uncritically embraced capitalism. Socialism's emphasis on communal responsibility struck a chord with a clannish people who have always seen themselves as different from the rest of the world. Socialism brought benefits that the majority had never enjoyed under any previous system of government, and which are being eroded by the market economy. Many people are uneasy that national assets are being sold to foreigners, and that some people go hungry while others drive fancy cars.

RELIGION

Of those Hungarians declaring religious affiliation, about 68% say they are Roman Catholic, 21% Reformed (Calvinist) Protestant and nearly 6% Evangelical (Lutheran) Protestant. There are also small Greek Catholic and Orthodox congregations. Hungary's Jews number about 80,000, down from a prewar population of almost 10 times that size.

LANGUAGE

Hungarians speak Magyar, a member of the Finno-Ugric language group that is related very, very distantly to Finnish, Estonian and about a dozen other very minor languages in Russia and western Siberia. Hungarian is not an Indo-European language, meaning that English is closer to French, Russian and Hindi than it is to Hungarian. As a result you'll spot few words that you are likely to recognise – with the exception of words like *disco*.

Many older Hungarians understand German but it's unusual to meet someone on the street who understands English. If you have trouble making yourself understood, try writing down what you want to say. Travel agencies usually have at least one staff member who can speak some English.

HUNGARY

Some useful words to learn are: *utca* or *utcája* (street), *körút* (boulevard), *út* or *útja* (road), *tér* or *tere* (square), *sétány* (promenade), and *híd* (bridge). Public toilets (WC) are marked *női* for women and *férfi* for men. A plural is indicated by a final 'k'. *Nem* indicates a negative.

Hungarians put surnames before given names: John Smith is always Smith John in Hungarian. To avoid confusion, all Hungarian names in this chapter are written in the usual western manner – first name first – including the names of museums and theatres if they are translated into English; the Arany János színház in Budapest is the János Arany Theatre in English. Addresses are always written in Hungarian: Kossuth Lajos utca, Arany János tér etc.

See the Language Guide at the back of the book for pronunciation guidelines and useful words and phrases. Lonely Planet's *Eastern Europe phrasebook* contains a complete chapter on Hungarian.

Facts for the Visitor

HIGHLIGHTS
Historic Towns
Many historic towns, including Eger, Győr and Veszprém, were rebuilt in the baroque style during the 18th century. Sopron and Kőszeg are among the few towns with a strong medieval flavour. The greatest monuments of the Turkish period are in Pécs.

Castles & Palaces
Hungary's most famous castles are those that resisted the Turkish onslaught in Eger, Kőszeg, Siklós and Szigetvár. Though in ruins, Visegrád Citadel evokes the power of medieval Hungary. Among Hungary's finest palaces are the Esterházy Palace at Fertőd, the Festetics Palace at Keszthely and the Széchenyi Mansion at Nagycenk.

Museums & Galleries
The following museums stand out not just for what they contain but for how they display it: the Christian Museum in Esztergom (Gothic paintings), the Storno Collection in Sopron (Romanesque and Gothic furnishings), the Zsolnay Museum (Art Nouveau porcelain)

and the Csontváry Museum in Pécs (symbolist painting), the Ferenc Móra Museum in Szeged (Avar finds and a mock yurt), the Imre Patkó Collection (Asian and African art) in Sopron, and the Commerce and Catering Museum (antique cookware) in Budapest.

SUGGESTED ITINERARIES
Depending on the length of your stay, you might want to see and do the following things:

Two days
  Visit Budapest
One week
  Visit Budapest, the Danube Bend and one or two of the following cities and towns: Sopron, Kőszeg, Pécs, Győr, Szeged or Eger
Two weeks
  Visit Budapest, the Danube Bend, Győr, Kőszeg, Hévíz, the north shore of Lake Balaton and either Sopron, Pécs, Szeged or Eger
One month
  Visit all the places included in this chapter

PLANNING
Climate & When to Go
Every season has its attractions. Though it can get pretty wet in May and early June, spring is excellent. Summer is warm and sunny and unusually long, but the resorts are crowded. If you avoid Lake Balaton, you'll do OK. The summer fashions and beach wear are daringly brief in summer, even by western standards. Like Paris, Budapest comes to a grinding halt in August.

Autumn is beautiful, particularly in the hills around Budapest and in the north. In Transdanubia and on the Great Plain it's harvest and vintage time.

Maps & Brochures
In this small country you can get by with the map *Road Map Hungary*, free from the Hungarian Tourist Board (HTB). Otherwise, pick up Cartographia's excellent road atlas.

The HTB produces many free brochures and pamphlets in English. Some of them are just colourful pap while others are extremely useful. They are often available at HTB, Ibusz and Malév Hungarian Airlines offices abroad; inside Hungary you'll find them at HTB's tourist information offices called Tourinform, as well as at independent travel bureaus and agencies, Malév offices and expensive hotels.

Two publications to get hold of are the monthly *Programme in Ungarn/in Hungary* and the annual *Preliminary Calendar of Events*, which list just about every event. Also useful are the *Accommodation* and *Camping* booklets.

What to Bring

There are no particular items of clothing to remember – an umbrella in late spring and autumn, a warm hat (everyone wears them) in winter – unless you plan to do some serious hiking or other sport. A swimsuit for use in the mixed-sex thermal spas and pools is a good idea as are sandals or thongs (flip-flops).

If you plan to stay in hostels, pack a towel and a plastic soap container. Bedclothes are usually provided, though you might want to bring your own sheet bag. An immersion coil to heat water in a cup is handy if you don't fancy weak Hungarian tea or ersatz coffee in the morning. You'll sleep easier with a padlock on one of the storage lockers provided at hostels.

TOURIST OFFICES
Local Tourist Offices

The HTB has a chain of tourist information offices called Tourinform in most towns and cities with tourist attractions, and these are the best places to ask general questions and pick up brochures.

If your query is about private accommodation, international train transport or changing money, visit a commercial travel agency; every Hungarian town has several. Ibusz remains the largest (though it is scaling back) and has representative offices abroad (see the following section). At least one member of the staff should speak some English.

The travel agency Express used to serve the youth and student market exclusively, but it now also sells outbound package tours to local people. Express sells Hostelling International (HI) cards (700 Ft) but you'll need Hungarian student ID to buy an ISIC card (700 Ft). It will sell discounted BIJ train tickets to anyone under 26. Some Express offices also know about beds in student accommodation in July and the first three weeks of August.

Tourist Offices Abroad

The HTB has offices in various countries including:

Austria
(☎ 0222-513 9122; fax 0222-513 1201) Parkring 12, III/6, 1010 Vienna
Germany
(☎ 069-929 1190; fax 069-9291 1918) Berliner Strasse 72, 60311 Frankfurt-am-Main
Netherlands
(☎ 070-320 9092; fax 070-327 2833) 2509 EE The Hague
UK
(☎ 0891 171 200; fax 0891 669 970) PO Box 4336, London SW18 4XE
USA
(☎ 212-355 0240; fax 212-207 4103) 150 East 58th St, New York NY 10155

For countries without an office, contact Malév, which has offices in three dozen countries.

VISAS & DOCUMENTS

Everyone needs a valid passport. Citizens of the USA, Canada, most European countries and South Africa do not require visas to visit Hungary for stays of up to 90 days. Nationals of Australia, Hong Kong, Japan and New Zealand (among others) still require visas. Check current visa requirements at a consulate or any HTB or Malév office.

Single-entry visas valid for 30 days are issued at Hungarian consulates upon receipt of US$32/£26 and three photos. A double-entry tourist visa costs US$60/£48 and you must have five photos. (If you know you'll be visiting Hungary twice, get a double-entry visa to avoid having to apply again somewhere else.) Some consulates charge US$15/£10 extra for express service (10 minutes as opposed to overnight).

Be sure to get a tourist rather than a transit visa; the latter – available for both single (US$30/£25) and double (US$50/£42) entries – is only good for a stay of 48 hours and cannot be extended. On a transit visa you must enter and leave through different border crossings and have a visa (if required) for the next country you visit. A tourist visa can be extended at the central police station (*rendőrkapitányság*) of any city or town, provided you do so 48 hours before it expires.

HUNGARY

Visas are no longer issued at border crossings (both road and rail) nor at the airport in Budapest.

Hungarian Embassies Abroad

Hungarian embassies around the world include the following:

Australia
(☎ 02-6282 3226) 17 Beale Crescent, Deakin, ACT 2600; or (☎ 02-9328 7859) Suite 405, Edgecliff Centre, 203-233 New South Head Road, Edgecliff, NSW 2027

Austria
(☎ 0222-533 2631) 1 Bankgasse 4-6, 1010 Vienna

Canada
(☎ 613-230 2717) 7 Delaware Ave, Ottawa, Ont K2P 0Z2; or (☎ 416-923 3596) Suite 1005, 102 Bloor St, West, Toronto, Ont M5S 1M8

Croatia
(☎ 041-610 430) Ul Cvijetno Naselje 17b, 41000 Zagreb

France
(☎ 01 43 54 66 96) 92 Rue de Bonaparte, 75006 Paris

Germany
(☎ 0228-371 112) Turmstrasse 30, 53175 Bonn (Plittersdorf); or (☎ 089-911 032) Vollmannstrasse 2, 81927 Munich

Japan
(☎ 3-798 8801) 14-17 Mita 2-chome, Minato-ku, Tokyo 108

Netherlands
(☎ 070-350 0404) Hogeweg 14, 2585 JD The Hague

Romania
(☎ 090-614 6621) Strada Calderon 63-65, Bucharest

Slovakia
(☎ 07-330 541) Sedlárska ul 3, 81425 Bratislava

Slovenia
(☎ 061-131 5168) Dunajska cesta 22, IV, 61000 Ljubljana

South Africa
(☎ 012 433 0330UK) 959 Arcadia Street, Pretoria

UK
(☎ 0171-235 2664) 35b Eaton Place, London SW1X 8BY

USA
(☎ 202-362 6730) 3910 Shoemaker St NW, Washington, DC 20008; or (☎ 212-752 0661) 223 East 52nd St, New York, NY 10022

Yugoslavia
(☎ 011-444 0472) Ul Ivana Milutinovica 74, Belgrade 11000

Foreign Embassies in Hungary

Selected countries with representation in Budapest (where the telephone code is ☎ 1) follow. The Roman numerals preceding the street name indicate the *kerület*, or district, in the capital.

Australia
(☎ 201 8899) XII Királyhágó tér 8-9

Austria
(☎ 351 6700) VI Benczúr utca 16

Canada
(☎ 275 1200) XII Budakeszi út 32

Croatia
(☎ 155 1522) XII Nógrádi utca 28b

France
(☎ 132 4980) VI Lendvay utca 27

Germany
(☎ 251 8999) XIV Stefánia út 101-103

Japan
(☎ 275 1275) XII Zalai utca 7

Netherlands
(☎ 326 5301) II Füge utca 5-7

Romania
(☎ 268 0271) XIV Thököly út 72

Slovakia
(☎ 251 1700) XIV Stefánia út 22-24

Slovenia
(☎ 325 9207) II Cseppkő utca 68

South Africa
(☎ 267 4566) VIII Rákóczi utca 1-3

UK
(☎ 266 2888) V Harmincad utca 6

Ukraine
(☎ 155 9609) XII Nógrádi utca 8

USA
(☎ 267 4400) V Szabadság tér 12

Yugoslavia
(☎ 342 0566) VI Dózsa György út 92b

CUSTOMS

You can bring the usual personal effects, 500 cigarettes, three bottles of wine and 1L of spirits into Hungary. Importing illegal drugs, pirated CDs and cassettes, offensive weapons and paprika (!) is taboo. You are not supposed to take valuable antiques out of Hungary without a 'museum certificate' (available from the shop). Restrictions on the import/export of forint won't affect most travellers; the limit is 300,000 Ft.

Customs inspections at most borders and the airport are pretty cursory. The exception is Romania. Hungarian police believe this country has become a conduit for drug traffickers from Asia into Western Europe since the collapse of Yugoslavia. In summer there may be very long delays for motorists.

MONEY
Currency

The Hungarian forint (Ft) is divided into 100 fillér, worthless little aluminium coins that are no longer minted but remain in circulation for now. There are coins of 10, 20 and 50 fillér and one, two, five, 10, 20, 50, 100 and 200 Ft.

Notes come in denominations of 200, 500, 1000, 5000 and 10,000 Ft. You might still see 50 and 100 Ft notes but they are being withdrawn.

Exchange Rates

Australia	A$1	=	131 Ft
Canada	C$1	=	145 Ft
euro	€1	=	243 Ft
France	1FF	=	37 Ft
Germany	DM1	=	124 Ft
Japan	¥100	=	151 Ft
New Zealand	NZ$1	=	110 Ft
United Kingdom	UK£1	=	359 Ft
United States	US$1	=	220 Ft

Changing Money

You'll find automatic teller machines (ATMs) accepting any number of credit cards and some cash cards throughout the country. It's always useful to carry a little foreign cash, preferably US dollars or Deutschmarks, or perhaps travellers cheques. American Express, Visa and Thomas Cook are the most recognisable brands.

You can exchange cash, travellers cheques and Eurocheques at banks (the national savings bank – Országos Takarékpenztár or OTP – has branches almost everywhere and charges no commission on travellers cheques) and travel offices, which take a commission of 1 to 2%. K&H banks everywhere give you a cash advance on your Visa card.

Post offices change Eurocheques, Postcheques and cash, and allow withdrawals from German and Austrian postal savings accounts. They will soon give credit card cash advances.

American Express is at V Deák Ferenc utca 10 in the capital, and there's an ATM there dispensing cash forints and travellers cheques in US dollars at a fee and a poor rate. Using private money-change bureaus is convenient but expensive.

It's senseless to use the black market to change money. The advantage is virtually nil, and you are almost sure to be ripped off.

Credit cards are widely accepted, especially Visa and MasterCard. You can use them at upmarket restaurants, shops, hotels, car-rental firms, travel agencies and petrol stations.

Having money wired to Hungary through American Express' Moneygram system is fairly straightforward; you don't need to be a card holder and it takes less than a day. You should know the sender's full name, the exact amount and the reference number when you're picking up the cash. With a passport or other ID you'll be given the amount in US dollars or forints. The sender pays the hefty service fee.

Don't get stuck with too many forints. You are allowed to change leftover forints back into hard currency, but you need to have the official exchange receipts with the date and your passport number clearly legible. The limit is about half the total on each of your transactions up to US$300, and you'll be charged commission.

Costs

High inflation and the devaluation of the forint have made life very difficult for people earning local salaries, but for foreign travellers the country remains a bargain destination. If you stay in private rooms, eat at medium-price restaurants and travel 2nd-class on trains, you should get by on US$25 a day without scrimping.

Because of the rapidly changing value of the forint, many hotels quote their rates in Deutschmarks. In such cases, we have done the same.

Tipping

Hungarians routinely tip waiters, hairdressers, taxi drivers and even doctors, dentists and some petrol-station attendants about 10%. In restaurants, do this immediately on payment of the bill (the waiter gives you change at the table) – don't wait to leave money on the table. If you were less than impressed with the service at the restaurant, the joyride in the taxi or the way someone cut your hair, leave next to nothing or nothing at all. They will get the message.

Taxes & Refunds

ÁFA, a value-added tax (VAT) of 16%, covers the purchase of almost all new goods. It's usually included in the quoted price but sometimes it's on top, so beware. Visitors are not exempt, but they can claim refunds for total purchases (of goods only – you can't claim the VAT on hotel accommodation, for example) of more than 50,000 Ft. You must take the goods out of the country within 90 days. The ÁFA receipts (available from the shops where you made the purchases) should be stamped by customs at the border and the claim has to be made within six months of the purchase.

Two outfits in Budapest that can help with refunds are Europe Tax Free Shopping Hungary (☎ 1-212 4734) at II Bég utca 3-5 and Interimport (☎ 1-204 4355) at XI Budafoki út 111. They charge a fee of at least 10%.

Some car-rental firms can exempt you from paying the ÁFA by having you sign a statement saying you do not intend to stay more than 180 days.

POST & COMMUNICATIONS
Post

Surface mail to Europe costs 27 Ft to neighbouring countries and 90 Ft to the rest of Europe. Foreign air mail costs 102 Ft for a 20g letter to the UK (postcards 72 Ft) and 212 Ft (84 Ft) to most countries outside Europe.

When collecting poste restante mail, look for the sign 'postán maradó küldemények'. Don't forget identification, although it's best to also write your name on a piece of paper. Otherwise, the clerk reading the name in your passport might assume that your first name is your family name and look in the wrong pigeon-hole.

You can have your mail delivered to American Express (1052 Budapest, Deák Ferenc utca) if you have an American Express credit card or travellers cheques.

Telephone

You can make domestic and international calls from most public telephones, which usually work. There are both coin and card phones; buy a telephone card from any post office. These come in message units of 50 (800 Ft) and 120 (1800 Ft). Telephone boxes with a black and white arrow and red target on the door and the word 'visszahívható' display a telephone number, so you can be phoned back.

All localities have a two-digit area code, except for Budapest, which simply has '1'. Local codes appear under the destination headings in this book.

To make a local call, pick up the receiver and listen for the continuous dial tone. Then dial the local number. For a long distance call within Hungary dial ☎ 06 and wait for the second, more musical, tone. Then dial – and don't forget the area code.

The procedure for making an international call is the same except that you dial ☎ 00 (not 06), followed by the country code and the area code and then the number. International phone charges are: 100 Ft per minute to neighbouring countries; 138 Ft for most of Western Europe; and 150 Ft to North America, Australia, New Zealand, Japan and South Africa.

You can get straight through to an operator in your home country by dialling the 'Country Direct' number from a public phone, but you need a coin or phonecard for the initial connection. Some of the services listed below are very expensive, although they will still be cheaper than a normal call from a phone in a hotel room. Country Direct services generally require you to make a reverse charge (collect) call.

Australia Direct	☎ 00-800 06111
Britain Direct (BT)	☎ 00-800 44011
France	☎ 00-800 03311
Canada Direct	☎ 00-800 01211
New Zealand Direct	☎ 00-800 06411
South Africa	☎ 00-800 0270
	+city code
Sweden	☎ 00-800 04611
USA – Direct (AT&T)	☎ 00-800 01111
– MCI	☎ 00-800 01411
– Sprint Express	☎ 00-800 01877

HUNGARY

Useful phone numbers include the international operator (☎ 199) and international directory inquiries in English (☎ (1) 267 5555).

Fax & Telegraph
You can send telegrams and faxes from most main post offices.

INTERNET RESOURCES
The HTB has a Web site at www.hungary-tourism.hu – it's informative. Internet cafés come and go rapidly in Budapest and some of that city's year-round hostels offer email. Public Internet connections in the provinces are much harder to find.

BOOKS
Guidebooks
You won't find a better independent guidebook to Hungary than Lonely Planet's *Hungary*.

History & Politics
Books on history and politics are good value and many titles are available in English. Most English translations of Hungarian works are published by the Corvina company.

The Corvina History of Hungary, edited by Péter Hanák, is fairly comprehensive but rather dull. *Hungary: A Brief History* is a light, almost silly history by geologist-cum-journalist István Lázár. *A History of Modern Hungary* by Jörg K Hoensch covers the period from 1867 to 1994 in a balanced though somewhat dry fashion. Another serious work is *The Hungarian Revolution of 1956* edited by György Litván. For an interpretation of what led to the collapse of communism in 1989, read Misha Glenny's updated *The Rebirth of History*.

NEWSPAPERS & MAGAZINES
Two weekly English-language publications are the glossy *Budapest Week* (96 Ft), which concentrates on nightlife and entertainment listings, and the excellent *Budapest Sun* (128 Ft), which will keep you abreast of Hungarian news as well as providing entertainment listings. Both are hard to find outside Budapest.

Some western newspapers, such as the *International Herald Tribune*, are available on the day of publication at kiosks and big hotels in Budapest. Many more, mainly British, French and German, are sold a day late. International news magazines are also available.

RADIO & TV
State-owned Magyar Televízió has three stations (TV 1, 2 and 3), and there are four local cable stations, including Top TV, the Hungarian response to MTV. If you stay in a hotel or pension and have a TV in your room, it will almost certainly receive satellite stations, such as CNN and Sky TV, as well.

Hungarian Radio has three stations, named after Lajos Kossuth, Sándor Petőfi and Béla Bartók. There are also an increasing number of commercial stations, such as Budapest's Slager, Juvuntus and the good StarRadio (FM 92.9).

PHOTOGRAPHY & VIDEO
Major brands of film are readily available and one-hour processing places are common in Budapest.

Film prices vary but basically 24 exposures of 100 ASA Kodacolor II, Agfa or Fujifilm cost about 700 Ft, and 36 exposures 875 Ft. Ektachrome 100 is 1800 Ft. Developing print film costs about 450 Ft a roll; for the prints themselves, you choose the size (9x13cm prints cost 45 Ft each if you wait a day, 52 Ft in an hour). Slide film costs 550 Ft to process. Video tape like TDK EHG 30/45 minutes costs 760/1030 Ft.

TIME
Time is GMT plus one hour. The clock is put an hour forward at the end of March and an hour back at the end of September. In Hungarian, 'half eight' means 7.30 and not 8.30.

ELECTRICITY
The electric current is 220V, 50Hz AC. Plugs are the European type (so-called europlugs) with two round pins.

WEIGHTS & MEASURES
Hungary uses the metric system. There's a conversion table at the back of this book.

LAUNDRY
Most hostels and camping grounds have some sort of laundry facilities, or access to them. Staff at other places to stay might be willing to do your laundry but if not, you'll need to plan ahead. Commercial laundries often take days to do your wash, and they aren't cheap. Self service laundries are rare.

TOILETS
Public toilets are invariably staffed by an old *néne* (auntie), who mops the floor continuously, hands out sheets of Grade A sandpaper and has seen it all. The usual charge is from 30 to 60 Ft a go.

HEALTH
No special inoculations are needed before visiting Hungary, and there are no troublesome snakes or creepy-crawlies to worry about. Mosquitoes are a scourge around lakes and rivers, so be armed with insect repellent (*rovarírtó*).

One insect that can bring on more than just an itch is the forest tick (*kullancs*), which burrows under the skin causing inflammation and even encephalitis. You might consider getting an FSME (meningo-encephalitis) vaccination if you plan to do a lot of hiking and camping, especially between May and September.

The number of AIDS cases is relatively low, but remember that the border has only really been open for a few years, so the number could multiply in a short time. An AIDS hotline in English can be reached on ☎ 1-166 9283.

First-aid and ambulance services are free for citizens of the UK, Scandinavian and most Eastern European countries, though follow-up treatment must be paid for.

Treatment at a public outpatient clinic (*rendelő intézet*) costs little, but doctors working privately sometimes charge much more. Very roughly, a consultation in a doctor's surgery (*orvosi rendelő*) starts at 2500 Ft, while a home visit costs from 5000 Ft.

Dental work is usually of a high standard and cheap by western standards. Some dentists advertise in the English-language press.

Most large towns and Budapest's 22 districts have an all-night pharmacy open every day; a sign on the door of any pharmacy will help you locate the closest 24-hour one.

WOMEN TRAVELLERS
Hungarian men can be very sexist in their thinking, but women do not suffer any particular form of harassment (although rape and domestic violence get little media coverage). Most men – even drunks – are effusively polite with women. Nevertheless the usual care should be taken.

Two useful organisations are:

Women United Against Violence (NANE)
   PO Box 660, Budapest 1462 (☎ 1-216 5900, helpline ☎ 1-216 1670)
Feminist Network
   PO Box 701, Budapest 1399

GAY & LESBIAN TRAVELLERS
There's not much gay or lesbian life beyond Budapest, but a couple of national organisations might be able to help with information. See the Budapest section for listings in the capital.

Rainbow Association for Homosexual Rights
   PO Box 690, Budapest 1293
Mások
   PO Box 388, Budapest 1461 (☎ 1-137 0327)

DISABLED TRAVELLERS
A law requiring equal access for people with disabilities was passed recently, and Budapest buses will eventually become wheelchair-friendly. For the foreseeable future, though, wheelchair ramps, toilets fitted for the disabled and the like will remain rare. You could try contacting:

Hungarian Disabled Association (MEOSZ)
   San Marco utca 76, Budapest 1035 (☎ 1-388 2387; fax 1-388 2339)

DANGERS & ANNOYANCES
Hungary is hardly a violent or dangerous society, but crime increased dramatically in

the 1990s (from a communist-era base of virtually nil). Violence is seldom directed against travellers though racially motivated attacks against Roma, Africans and Arabs are not unknown.

As a traveller you are most vulnerable to pickpockets and taxi louts (see Getting Around in the Budapest section) and maybe car thieves.

In an emergency anywhere in Hungary, the following are the most important national numbers:

Police	☎ 107
Fire	☎ 105
Ambulance	☎ 104
Car assistance nationwide	☎ 06-1-155 0379
Hungarian Auto Club	☎ 1-252 8000

BUSINESS HOURS

Grocery stores and supermarkets open weekdays from about 7 am to 7 pm, department stores from 10 am to 6 pm. Most shops stay open until 8 pm on Thursday but on Saturday close at 1 or 2 pm. Post offices open weekdays from 8 am to 6 pm, and Saturday from 8 am to 1 pm. Banking hours vary but banks usually close no later than 4 pm Monday to Thursday and as early as 1 pm on Friday. With few exceptions, museums are open 10 am to 6 pm Tuesday to Sunday from April to October and to 4 pm on the same days the rest of the year.

PUBLIC HOLIDAYS & SPECIAL EVENTS

Hungary's nine public holidays are: New Year's Day (1 January), 1848 Revolution Day (15 March), Easter Monday, International Labour Day (1 May), Whit Monday (May/June), St Stephen's Day (20 August), 1956 Remembrance Day (23 October), Christmas Day and Boxing Day (25 and 26 December).

The most outstanding annual events include the Budapest Spring Festival (mid-March to mid-April), Hortobágy Equestrian Days (late June), Sopron Early Music Days (late June), Búcsú (Farewell) Festival in Budapest (late June), Győr Summer Cultural Festival (late June to late July), Pannon Festival in Pécs (July and August), Szentendre

Summer Festival (July), Kőszeg Street Theatre Festival (late July), Savaria International Dance Competition in Szombathely (July), Debrecen Jazz Days (July), Szeged Open-Air Festival (mid-July to August), Eurowoodstock on Diáksziget (Student Island) north of Budapest (August), Eger Wine Harvest Festival (September), and Budapest Autumn Arts Festival (mid-September to mid-October).

St Stephen's Day (20 August) is celebrated with sporting events, parades and fireworks nationwide. On the same day there's a Floral Festival in Debrecen and a Bridge Fair in nearby Hortobágy. Formula 1 car races are held in early August at the Hungaroring near Mogyoród, 24km north-east of Budapest.

ACTIVITIES
Water Sports

Wherever there's water, a bit of wind and a camp site, you'll find sailboards for rent, but the main place for the sport is Lake Balaton, especially at Kiliántelep and Balatonszemes. Qualified sailors can rent yachts on the lake. Motorboats are banned so the only place you'll get to do any water-skiing on Balaton is at Füred Camping in Balaton-füred, where a cable tow does the job.

Many canoe and kayak trips are available. Following the Danube from Rajka to Mohács (386km) or the Tisza River from Tiszabecs to Szeged (570km) are obvious choices, but there are less congested waterways and shorter trips like the 210km stretch of the Körös and Tisza rivers from Békés to Szeged or the Rába River from Szentgotthárd to Győr (205km).

The HTB publishes a brochure titled *Water Tours in Hungary*, which is a gold mine of information for planning itineraries and rentals and learning the rules and regulations.

Cycling

The possibilities for cyclists are many. The slopes of northern Hungary can be challenging, whereas Transdanubia is much gentler and the Great Plain flat though windy (and in summer, hot). The problem is bicycle rentals; they're hard to come by. Your best bets are camping grounds, resort hotels or Budapest's

Margaret Island in season. Bicycles can be taken on trains but not on buses or trams.

Remember when planning your itinerary that bicycles are banned from the motorways (and national highways Nos 0 to 9), and they must be equipped with lights and reflectors. Riding mountain bikes is becoming increasingly popular, especially in the Buda Hills and in the Börzsöny Hills north of the Danube Bend.

The HTB publishes a pamphlet called *Hungary by Bike* with recommended routes and basic sketch maps. *Hungary by Bicycle*, in Hungarian, German and English, can be found in some Budapest bookshops. Frigoria publishes a useful trilingual map called *Budapest on Bike*.

The Bicycle Touring Association of Hungary (MKTSZ) in Budapest at VI Bajcsy-Zsilinszky út 31 (☎ 1-332 7177) can supply more information.

Hiking

You can enjoy good hiking in the forests around Visegrád, Esztergom, Badacsony, Kőszeg and Budapest. North of Eger are the Bükk Hills and south of Kecskemét the Bugac Puszta, both national parks with marked trails. Pick up detailed hiking maps in Budapest as these are not always available locally. Cartographia produces 1:60,000 and 1:40,000 hiking maps.

Horse Riding

The Magyars say they were 'created by God to sit on horseback' and, judging from the number of stables, riding schools and courses around the country, that still holds true today. Prices vary, but are usually around DM10 per hour.

It's risky – particularly in the high season – to show up at a riding centre without a booking. Do this through the local tourist office, or in Budapest contact Pegazus Tours (☎ 1-117 1644) at V Ferenciek tere 5 which organises a wide range of rides and riding tours throughout the country.

Thermal Baths

More than 100 thermal baths are open to the public. The Romans first developed the baths of Budapest, and the Turks and Habsburgs followed suit. The thermal lake at Hévíz is probably Hungary's most impressive spa.

Public thermal pools at Budapest, Eger, Győr, Harkány and Szeged are also covered in this book.

LANGUAGE COURSES

Language schools teaching Hungarian to foreigners have proliferated (at least in Budapest) but they vary tremendously in quality, approach and success rates. Reliable schools include:

Hungarian Language School
   (☎ 1-112 5899) VI Eötvös utca 25a
Arany János Language School
   (☎ 1-111 8870) VI Csengery utca 68

Debrecen Summer University organises intensive two and four-week courses in July and August and 80-hour advanced courses in winter. The emphasis is not just language but the whole Magyar culture. Contact the Debreceni Nyári Egyetem (☎/fax 52-329 117), PO Box 35, Debrecen 4010.

WORK

Travellers on tourist visas are not supposed to work but some end up teaching or even working for foreign firms without permits.

Check the telephone book or advertisements for English-language schools in *Budapest Week* or *Budapest Sun*; there are also job listings but pay is generally pretty low. You can do much better teaching privately once you've built up the contacts.

Obtaining a work permit (and thus a one-year renewable residency) involves a Byzantine paper chase. You'll need a letter of support from your prospective employer, copies of your birth certificate, and your academic record officially translated into Hungarian (about 1500 Ft). A medical exam and AIDS test (about 4000 Ft) is mandatory. The office in Budapest dealing with foreigners' registrations is KEOKH (☎ 1-118 0800) at VI Városligeti fasor 46-48.

ACCOMMODATION
Camping

Hungary has more than 200 camping grounds. Small, private camping grounds are usually preferable to the large, noisy, 'official' camping grounds. Prices vary widely from about 500 to 2000 Ft for two adults plus tent. The sites around Lake Balaton are more expensive. Some sites on the Great Plain have poor drainage.

Most camping grounds open from May or June to September (though some open in April and close in October) and also rent small bungalows (from 3000 Ft). In midsummer the bungalows may all be booked, so it pays to check with the local tourist office before making the trip. Members of the International Camping & Caravanning Club (FICC) and holders of student cards sometimes get a 10% discount. Camping 'wild' is prohibited.

Hostels
Despite all the 'hostels' listed in the HI/Hungarian Youth Hostel Federation handbook, an HI card doesn't get you very far. Generally the only year-round hostels are in Budapest.

Hostel beds cost about 2000 Ft in Budapest, less in low season and less outside Budapest. An HI card is not required although you occasionally get 10% off with one. There's no age limit at the hostels, they remain open all day and they are often good places to meet other travellers.

From 1 July to 20 August, the cheapest rooms are in vacant student accommodation where dorm beds begin around 800 Ft per person and there are sometimes private rooms. Express offices can generally tell you where to try, and they'll sometimes call ahead to reserve your bed.

Tourist Hostels
A tourist hostel (turista-szálló) offers beds in separate dormitories for men and women and usually private rooms as well. Tourist hostels used to be found in many cities (they catered to locals holidaying on a budget) but because of privatisation many have closed or have been converted to more upmarket hotels.

Private Rooms
Private rooms are assigned by travel agencies which take your money and give you a voucher bearing the address or sometimes even the key to the flat. If the first room you're offered seems too expensive, ask if they have a cheaper one. There are usually several agencies offering private rooms. In

Budapest, individuals at train stations approach anyone looking vaguely like a traveller and offer private rooms. Until you suss out the pitfalls you're probably better off getting a room from a travel agency.

There's often a 30% supplement if you stay less than four nights, and single rooms are hard to come by.

You'll usually share a house or flat with a Hungarian family. The toilet is usually communal but otherwise you can close your door and enjoy as much privacy as you please. Some places offer kitchen facilities. In Budapest you may have to take a room far from the centre of town, but public transport is good and cheap. In Budapest and elsewhere, the distinction between the more expensive private rooms and pensions is becoming blurred.

In resort areas look for houses with signs reading 'szoba Kiadó' or the German 'Zimmer frei', advertising private rooms.

Pensions
Pensions (panzió) are really just little hotels charging from 2500 Ft in the provinces (from 4000 Ft in tourist centres) and from 5000 Ft in Budapest for a double. Many charge a lot more than this. They are usually clean and often have an attached restaurant, bar or coffee shop. You'll find pensions in the main tourist areas and sometimes along highways.

Hotels
Hotels, called szálló or szálloda, run the gamut from luxurious five-star palaces to the derelict Béke (Peace) Hotel that you might still find in some towns. Unfortunately, there's a real gap in the market between rock-bottom places on the verge of closing and revamped hotels catering to supposedly wealthy tourists.

Even if you do find a good cheap hotel it will be more expensive than private rooms, charging at least 5000 Ft a double. A hotel may be the answer if you're only staying one night or if you arrive too late to get a private room through an agency. Two-star hotels usually have rooms with a private bathroom, whereas at one-star hotels the bathroom is usually down the hall. Breakfast is almost always included in the room price.

Farmhouses

'Village tourism', which means staying at a farmhouse, is in no way as developed as it is in, say, Slovenia. Most of the places are truly remote, but they can be cheap. Contact Falusi Turizmus Centrum (☎ 1-321 4396) in Budapest at VII Dohány utca 86 for detailed brochures.

FOOD

Hungary has a tasty national cuisine all its own. Many dishes are seasoned with paprika (a spice made from certain varieties of red pepper), which appears on restaurant tables as a condiment beside the salt and pepper. Although hot paprika originated in Central America, the peasants of Szeged have been growing it since the early 18th century and it's now as important to Hungarian cuisine as the tomato is to Italian cooking.

Hungarian goulash *(gulyás)* is a thick beef soup cooked with onions and potatoes and usually eaten as a main course. What we think of as goulash is actually *pörkölt*, meat stewed with onions and paprika. Turkey, chicken and pork are the most common meats, and if you don't eat pigs you'll have to be careful, as pork finds its way into many dishes.

Cabbage is an important vegetable, either stuffed *(töltött káposzta)* or made into a thick cabbage soup *(káposzta leves)*. Other delicacies include goose liver *(libamaj)* prepared in a variety of ways and roast goose leg *(sült libacomb)*. Chicken paprika *(csirke paprikás)* served with tiny dumplings *(galuska)* is always a crowd-pleaser.

Fisherman's soup *(halászlé)* is a rich mixture of several kinds of poached fish, tomatoes, green peppers and paprika. It's a meal in itself. Noodle dishes with cheese like *sztrapacska* go well with fish dishes.

Strudel *(rétes)* is a layered pastry filled with apple, cherry, poppy-seed, curd or cheese. Look out for *lángos*, fried dough eaten with garlic, salt, cheese and sour cream. It's a very popular snack.

Some dishes for vegetarians to request are *rántott sajt* (fried cheese), *gombafejek rántva* (fried mushroom caps), *gomba leves* (mushroom soup), *gyümölcs leves* (fruit soup), *sajtos kenyer* (sliced bread with soft cheese)

and *túrós csusza* (Hungarian pasta with cheese). *Bableves* (bean soup) sometimes contains meat. Pancakes/crêpes *(palacsinta)* may be made with cheese *(sajt)*, mushrooms *(gomba)*, nuts *(dió)* or poppy seeds *(mák)*.

Supermarket chains like Csemege, Julius Meinl and Kaiser's sometimes sell takeaway salads in plastic containers. Healthy brown bread is widely available.

Restaurants

Restaurants *(etterem* or *vendéglő)* are relatively inexpensive. Meal prices begin at around 300 Ft in a self-service restaurant, 750 Ft in a local restaurant and 1500 Ft in a tourist restaurant. For many Hungarians, lunch is the main meal of the day. Many restaurants, even the upmarket places, offer a set lunch *(menü)* on weekdays and this is usually very good value. It consists of soup, a side salad, a main course and occasionally a dessert. You'll pay around 300 Ft in a restaurant where ordering the items individually would cost about 1000 Ft.

Restaurant menus are often translated into German and sometimes into English. The main categories on a menu are *előételek* (appetisers), *levesek* (soups), *saláták* (salads), *készételek* (ready-to-serve meals which are just heated up), *frissensült* (freshly prepared meals), *halételek* or *halak* (fish dishes), *szárnyasok* (poultry dishes), *tészták* (desserts) and *sajtok* (cheeses).

If garnishes *(köretek)* such as rice, pommes frites, potatoes *(burgonya)* or vegetables *(zöldseg)* are individually listed in a separate section of the menu, it probably means they're not included with the main plate and will cost extra, though main courses always include some sort of garnish.

It's not very common, but a waiter may try to charge you extra for a dish you didn't order or serve you imported bottled beer when all you wanted was ordinary Hungarian draught. If you ask for a *pohár* (glass) or a *korsó* (half-litre mug) by name and don't just say 'beer' *(sör)*, they're less likely to try this trick.

Always insist on seeing a menu with prices listed to get an idea of how much your meal will cost. Some places add a 10% service charge to the bill, which makes tipping unnecessary. Tourist restaurants sometimes feature Romani music after 6 pm and these roving minstrels are accustomed to receiving tips. Give them 100 Ft and they'll move to the next table.

A *csárda* is an old-style inn or tavern offering traditional fare and wine. *Borozó* denotes a wine bar, *pince* is a beer or wine cellar and a *söröző* is a pub offering draught beer (*csapolt sör*) and sometimes meals. A *bisztró* is an inexpensive restaurant that is often self-service (*önkiszolgáló*). A *büfé* is the cheapest place, although you may have to eat standing at a counter. Pastries, cakes and coffee are served at a *cukrászda*, while an *eszpresszó* is a café.

DRINKS

Wine has been produced here for thousands of years and you'll find it available by the glass or bottle everywhere. For dry whites, look for Badacsonyi Kéknyelű or Szürkebarát, Mőcsényi or Boglári Chardonnay or Debrői Hárslevelű. Olasz Rizling and Egri Leányka tend to be on the sweet side, though nowhere near the Tokaji Aszú dessert wines. Dependable reds are Villányi Merlot, Pinot Noir and Cabernet Sauvignon, Szekszárdi Kékfrankos and Nagyrédei Cabernet Franc. The celebrated Egri Bikavér (Eger Bull's Blood) is a full-bodied red high in acid and tannin.

An alcoholic drink that is as Hungarian as wine is *pálinka*, a strong brandy distilled from a variety of fruits but most commonly apricots or plums. Hungarian liqueurs are usually unbearably sweet and taste artificial, though the Zwack brand is reliable. Zwack also produces Unicum, a bitter apéritif that has been around since 1790. Austrian Emperor Joseph II christened the liqueur when he exclaimed *'Das ist ein Unikum!'* ('This is a unique drink!'). It's an acquired taste.

Some beers are sold nationally (eg Dreher and Kőbanyai) though some are found only near where they are brewed (Kanizsai in Nagykanizsa and Szalon in Pécs). Bottled Austrian and German beer are readily available, as are excellent Czech imports Pilsner Urquell and Staropramen.

ENTERTAINMENT

Hungary is a paradise for culture vultures. In Budapest there are several musical events to choose from each evening and excellent opera tickets cost between 1000 Ft and 4500 Ft. Besides the traditional opera, operetta and concerts, there are rock and jazz concerts, folk dancing, pantomime, puppet shows, movies in English, discos, floor shows and circuses to keep you entertained.

Excellent cultural performances can also be seen in provincial towns such as Eger, Győr, Kecskemét, Pécs, Szeged, Veszprém and Szombathely, all of which have fine theatres. Information about events is readily available at tourist offices. Some useful words to remember are *színház* (theatre), *pénztár* (box office), *jegy* (ticket) and *elkelt* (sold out).

In mid-June many theatres close for the summer holidays, reopening in late September or October. Summer opera, operetta and concert programs especially designed for tourists are more expensive than the normal programs in winter. On the other hand, there are many summer festivals from late June to mid-August, though the period from 20 August (St Stephen's Day) to late September is culturally dead.

Going to the cinema (*mozi*) can be hit or miss as the programs advertised outside may be coming attractions or even what's showing in some other cinema across town. Write in Hungarian the name of the film you think you're going to see with a large question mark after it and show it to the ticket seller before you pay. Also be aware that many foreign films are dubbed into Hungarian, so try asking the ticket seller if the film is dubbed (*szinkronizált* or *magyarul beszélő*), or only has Hungarian subtitles (*feliratos*) and retains the original soundtrack.

Admission prices are low (about 400 Ft). The English-language papers in Budapest list what films are being shown in their original language in the capital, but elsewhere around the country you're on your own. Unfortunately good films by such noted Hungarian directors as István Gaál, Miklós Jancsó, András Jeles, Róbert Koltai, Károly Makk, Pál Sándor and István Szabó are likely to be in Hungarian with no subtitles; see them at an art cinema at home.

HUNGARY

THINGS TO BUY

Shops are well stocked and the quality of products generally high. Food, alcohol, books and folk-music recordings are affordable and there is an excellent selection. Traditional products include folk-art embroidery and ceramics, wall hangings, painted wooden toys and boxes, dolls, all forms of basketry and porcelain (especially Herend, Zsolnay or the cheaper Kalocsa). Feather or goose-down goods like pillows or duvets (comforters) are of excellent quality. Foodstuffs that are expensive or difficult to buy elsewhere – goose liver (both fresh and potted), caviar and some prepared meats like Pick salami – make nice gifts (if you are allowed to take them home) as do the many varieties of paprika. Some of Hungary's new 'boutique' wines – especially the ones with imaginative labels – make good, inexpensive gifts. A bottle of five or six-*puttonyos* dessert Tokay always goes down well.

Getting There & Away

AIR

Malév Hungarian Airlines flies direct to Budapest Ferihegy airport (☎ 1-296 9696) to/from the USA and more than 30 European cities. Other destinations include Bangkok, Cairo, Damascus, Larnaca and Tel Aviv.

Malév doesn't offer student discounts on flights originating in Hungary, but youth fares are available to people aged under 26. These might not always be cheaper than a discounted ticket, though. Discounted return flights (you must stay away at least one Saturday night) to other cities in the former Soviet bloc include: Moscow, 53,740 Ft; Warsaw, 39,320 Ft; and Prague 39,750 Ft.

LAND

Budapest has excellent land (and river) transport connections.

Bus

Most international buses are run by Eurolines or its Hungarian associate Volánbusz. Eurolines has 30/60-day passes allowing unlimited travel in many European countries. You are not allowed to travel on the same line more than twice. Adults pay US$299/379 (or the equivalent) and the youth/senior passes cost US$239/299.

There are two international bus stations in Budapest, Erzsébet tér and Nepstadion. See the Budapest Getting There & Away section for more information on these, and note than Erzsébet tér will be relocated in the fairly near future.

You don't necessarily have to leave Hungary from Budapest. From Harkány, 22km south of Pécs, you can catch a bus to several towns in Croatia, from Pécs to Osijek in Croatia, from Barcs and Nagykanizsa to Zagreb, from Lenti to Ljubljana in Slovenia and from Szeged to Arad and Timişoara in Romania. Several services between Budapest and Western Europe stop in Győr.

Eurolines services between Budapest and Western Europe include:

Berlin
13,400 Ft one way; departs Berlin Friday and Saturday, plus Tuesday and Wednesday in season; 15 hours; some services connect with Hamburg (15,000 Ft) or Copenhagen (19,600 Ft)
London
20,900 Ft one way; departs London Monday, Friday and Saturday, plus Wednesday and Thursday in season; 25 hours via Brussels (16,900 Ft)
Paris
16,900 Ft one way; departs Paris Wednesday and Sunday, plus Friday in season; 22 hours via Reims (16,900 Ft)
Rome
13,900 Ft one way; departs Rome Thursday and Sunday, plus Monday and Friday in season; 20 hours via Florence (11,300 Ft)
Rotterdam
19,400 Ft one way; departs Rotterdam Monday, Friday and Saturday, daily in season; 23 hours via Frankfurt (16,100 Ft), Düsseldorf (17,100 Ft) and Amsterdam (19,400 Ft)
Vienna
3690 Ft one way; at least three buses daily and more in summer; 3¾ hours or less, depending on stops

The cheapest and easiest way to go from Hungary to Romania is by bus. There are buses from Budapest to Oradea/Nagyvárad (2200 Ft, at least once daily, six hours), Arad (2260 Ft, daily except Sunday, eight hours),

Timişoara/Temesvár (2760 Ft, Saturday, eight hours) and Cluj-Napoca/Kolozsvár (about 4000 Ft, daily, 9½ hours). The Hungarian names of the Romanian cities are given as these are the ones you'll see written on the timetables. There can be long delays at highway border crossings into Romania (especially in summer), though it's worse westbound than eastbound.

Other useful international buses include those to Bratislava/Pozsony (1660 Ft, daily, four hours); Prague (4190 Ft, at least once daily, 8¾ hours); Subotica/Szabatka in Yugoslavia (1790 Ft, daily, 4½ hours), Tatranská Lomnica/Tatralomnic in Slovakia (about 2400 Ft, twice weekly, seven hours) and Zakopane in Poland (twice weekly, 2580 Ft). The last two places are on opposite sides of the Tatra Mountains, a route poorly served by train. There are three buses a week to Llubljana in Slovenia.

Train

Trains arrive in Budapest from every neighbouring capital. The main entry points for international trains include: Sopron and Hegyeshalom (from Vienna and most of Western Europe); Szombathely (from Graz); Komárom and Szob (from Prague and Berlin); Miskolc (from Košice, Kraków and Warsaw); Nyíregyháza (from Lvov, Moscow and St Petersburg); Békéscsaba (from Bucharest via Arad and Timişoara); Szeged (from Subotica); Pécs (from Osijek); and Nagykanizsa (from Zagreb and Ljubljana).

In Budapest, most international trains arrive and depart from Keleti (eastern) station (☎ 1-113 6835); trains to Oradea in Romania leave from Nyugati (western) station (☎ 1-149 0115) while Déli (southern) station (☎ 1-175 6293) handles trains to/from Zagreb and Rijeka. But these are not hard-and-fast rules, so always make sure you check which station the train leaves from when you buy a ticket.

If you just want to get across the border, local trains are cheaper than international expresses, especially if you're on a one-way trip.

Tickets & Discounts To reduce confusion, specify your train by the name listed under the following sections or on the posted schedule when requesting information or buying a ticket. You can do both at the three train stations in Budapest that serve international

trains, but it's easier to communicate with the information staff at MÁV's central ticket office in Budapest.

There are big discounts on return fares to former communist countries: 30% to Belarus, Czech Republic, Bulgaria, Latvia, Lithuania, Poland and Slovenia; 50% to Croatia, Russia and Ukraine; 40% to Yugoslavia (Belgrade); and a massive 70% to Romania and Slovenia. There are sometimes even better deals to selected cities in the region.

For tickets to Western Europe you'll pay the same as everywhere else unless you're aged under 26 and qualify for the 30% BIJ discount (ask at MÁV or Express).

The following are sample one-way 2nd class fares from Budapest (return trip is double): Amsterdam 42,000 Ft; Berlin 21,700 Ft; London 51,000 Ft; Munich 18,500 Ft; and Rome 21,600 Ft. There's a discounted return fare to Vienna of 9400 Ft if you return to Budapest within four days. Three daily Euro-City (EC) trains to Vienna and points beyond charge a supplement of about 1500 Ft. The 1st-class seats are always 50% more expensive than in 2nd class.

An international seat reservation costs 600 Ft. Fines are levied on passengers without tickets or seat reservations where they are mandatory. Costs for sleepers depend on the destination, but a two-berth sleeper in a 1st-class cabin is 7600 Ft per person to Munich and about 5000 Ft in 2nd class. A couchette in a compartment for six people is 3100 Ft. Tickets are valid for 60 days from purchase, and stopovers are permitted.

Budapest is no longer the bargain basement for tickets on the trans-Siberian railway that it once was. In fact, MÁV will only write you a ticket to Moscow; you have to buy the onward ticket from there. Of course, if you are coming back to Budapest from Moscow you get the 40% discount.

MÁV sells Inter-Rail passes in one to seven zones to European citizens (only) under 26 years of age. Hungary is in Zone D along with the Czech Republic, Slovakia, Poland, Croatia, Bulgaria and Romania. It's almost impossible for a Eurail pass to pay for itself in Hungary, so plan your Eurail travel days carefully.

You cannot buy tickets with travellers cheques or credit cards.

Western Europe Some eight trains a day link Vienna with Budapest (3¼ hours) via Hegyeshalom. Most leave from Vienna's Westbahnhof, including the *Orient Express* from Paris (18 hours) via Munich, the *Arrabona* from Vienna to Debrecen via Budapest, the Eurocity *Bartók Béla* from Frankfurt (12 hours) via Salzburg, the Eurocity *Liszt Ferenc* from Dortmund (15 hours) via Frankfurt, the *Dacia Express* to Bucharest (15 hours), and the *Avala* bound for Belgrade (11 hours). The early-morning Eurocity *Lehár*, however, departs from Vienna's Südbahnhof and the *Beograd Express* arrives and departs from Budapest's 'fourth' station – Kelenföld in Buda. None requires a seat reservation, though they're highly recommended in summer.

Up to 10 trains leave Vienna's Südbahnhof every day for Sopron (75 minutes) via Ebenfurth; as many as a dozen a day also serve Sopron from Wiener Neustadt (easily accessible from Vienna). Some seven trains daily make the three-hour trip from Graz to Szombathely.

Czech Republic & Germany Four trains a day run from Berlin's Lichtenberg station to Budapest (about 14 hours) via Prague and Bratislava: the *Metropol*, the Eurocity *Commenius* (from Hamburg), the *Hungária* and the *Csárdás* (from Malmö). The *Pannónia* runs from Prague to Budapest (nine hours).

Slovakia & Poland Every day two trains, the *Polonia* and the *Báthory*, leave Warsaw for Budapest (12 hours) via Katowice, Bratislava and Štúrovo. The *Karpaty* from Warsaw passes through Kraków and Košice before reaching Miskolc, where you can change for Budapest. The *Cracovia* runs from Kraków to Budapest (12 hours) and Pécs via Košice.

Another train, the *Rákóczi*, links Košice with Budapest (four hours) and in summer there's an extension to Poprad Tatry, 100km northwest of Košice. The *Bem* connects Szczecin in north-western Poland with Budapest (18 hours) via Poznań, Wrocław and Lučenec.

Five local trains a day (two hours) cover the 90km from Miskolc and Košice. The 2km hop from Sátoraljaújhely to Slovenské Nové Mesto is only a four-minute ride by train.

Romania From Bucharest to Budapest (14 hours) you can choose between the *Alutus*, the *Dacia Express*, the *Ister* and the *Pannónia*, all via Arad. Three of these require seat reservations. The *Karpaty* goes to Bucharest from Miskolc.

There are two daily connections from Cluj-Napoca to Budapest (seven hours, via Oradea): the *Corona* (from Braşov) and the *Claudiopolis*. These trains require a seat reservation. The *Partium* links Budapest and Oradea only.

There's only one local train a day linking Baia Mare in northern Romania with Budapest (eight hours) via Satu Mare and Debrecen. Otherwise you'll have to take one of two local trains from Debrecen across the border to Valea lui Mihai and catch a Romanian train.

Bulgaria & Yugoslavia The *Balkán*, departing from Istanbul (28 hours), links Budapest with Sofia (15 hours) via Belgrade. Other trains between Budapest and Belgrade via Subotica (six hours) include the *Beograd Express*, the *Hunyadi*, the *Avala* and the *Hellas* (which runs from Thessaloniki in Greece via Skopje and takes 23 hours). Be warned that the *Beograd Express* arrives and departs from Kelenföld station in Buda. You must reserve your seats on some of these trains.

The *Pushkin* from Belgrade and Subotica to Moscow goes through Szeged, Kecskemét, Szolnok and Debrecen. Otherwise there are five local trains (no reservations needed) making the 1¾-hour journey between Subotica and Szeged every day.

Croatia & Slovenia You can get to Budapest from Zagreb (six hours) on four trains, all of them via Siófok on Lake Balaton: the *Adriatica* from Rijeka (11 hours), *Maestral* from Split (16 hours), the *Avas* and the *Venezia Express* via Ljubljana (eight hours). The *Dráva*, which originates in Venice, also travels via Ljubljana.

Ukraine & Russia From Moscow to Budapest (28 hours) there's only the *Tisza Express*, which travels via Kiev and Lvov in Ukraine. The *Pushkin Express* between Belgrade and Moscow can be caught in Szeged,

Kecskemét, Szolnok or Debrecen. The *Tisza Express* has an extension to/from St Petersburg, which joins the line at Lvov. Most nationalities require a transit visa to travel through Ukraine.

Car & Motorcycle

Of the 70 border crossings Hungary maintains with its seven neighbours, 15 (mostly in the north and north-east) are restricted to local citizens. That no longer includes the Esztergom-Štúrovo ferry crossing, which is now one of the easiest and most central ways to enter Hungary from Slovakia. (See Visas & Embassies in the Facts for the Visitor section of this chapter for details of Hungary's main overland border crossings.)

Walking & Cycling

Many border guards frown on walking across borders, particularly in Romania, Yugoslavia and Croatia; try hitching a ride instead. Cyclists may have a problem crossing at Hungarian stations connected to main roads since bicycles are banned on motorways and national highways with single-digit route numbers.

There are three crossings to/from Slovakia where you won't have any problems: the Esztergom-Štúrovo ferry (which carries bikes); the bridge connecting Komárom with Komárno; and at Sátoraljaújhely, north-east of Miskolc, another highway border crossing over the Ronyva River which links the centre of Sátoraljaújhely with Slovenské Nové Mesto.

To/from Romania, the easiest place to cross on foot is Nagylak/Nădlac between Szeged and Arad. There are eight local trains a day from Szeged to Nagylak (47km, 1¼ hours) near the border. After crossing into Romania you must walk or take a taxi 6km to Nădlac, where you'll find trains to Arad (52km, 1½ hours).

Slovenia-bound, take a train from Budapest to Zalaegerszeg (252km via Tapolca, four hours by express train), then one of 10 daily trains from Zalaegerszeg to Rédics (49km, 1½ hours), which is only a couple of kilometres from the main highway border crossing into Slovenia. From the border it's an interesting 5km downhill walk through

Lendava to the bus station, where you'll have a choice of six daily buses to Ljubljana (212km, four hours) and many more to Maribor (92km).

BOAT

A hydrofoil service on the Danube between Budapest and Vienna (282km, 6½ hours) via Bratislava operates daily from April to early November, twice daily from mid-July to late August. Fares are high – Austrian Schilling (AS) 750/1100 one-way/return – but ISIC student-card holders pay only AS 590/900 and Eurail Pass holders get a 50% discount, with some restrictions. Taking along a bicycle costs ATS 200 each way.

Ferries arrive and depart from the International Ferry Pier *(Nemzetközi hajóállomás)* on Belgrád rakpart in Budapest, just north of Szabadság Bridge on the Pest side. In Vienna, the boat docks at the Reichsbrücke pier near Mexikoplatz.

In Budapest contact Mahart Tours (☎ 1-118 1704) at the pier, open from 8 am to 4 pm on weekdays, 8 am to noon on weekends. In Vienna, contact Mahart Tours (☎ 0222-729 2161/62) at Karlsplatz 2-8.

Getting Around

AIR

There are no scheduled flights within Hungary. The cost of domestic air taxis within the country is prohibitive – eg 45,000 Ft from Budapest to Szeged and back (you must pay the return) – and the trips can take almost as long as an express train when you add the time required to get to/from the airports.

BUS

Volán buses are a good alternative to trains, and fares are only slightly more expensive than comparable 2nd-class train fares.

In southern Transdanubia or parts of the Great Plain, buses are essential unless you are prepared to make several time-consuming changes on the train. For short trips on the Danube Bend or Lake Balaton areas, buses are recommended. Tickets are usually available from the driver, but ask at the station to be sure. There are sometimes queues for inter-city buses so it's wise to arrive early.

Timetables are posted at stations and stops. Some footnotes you could come across include *naponta* (daily), *hétköznap* (week-days), *munkanapokon* (on workdays), *mun-kaszüneti napok kivételével naponta* (daily except holidays), *szabadnap kivételével naponta* (daily except Saturday), *szabad és munkaszüneti napokon* (on Saturday and holi-days), *munkaszüneti napokon* (on holidays), *iskolai napokon* (on school days) and *sza-badnap* (on Saturday).

A few large bus stations have luggage rooms, but they generally close by 6 pm.

TRAIN

Magyar Államvasutak (MÁV, pronounced 'maav') operates comprehensive, reliable and not overcrowded train services. Second-class train fares are 234 Ft for 50km, 570 Ft for 100km, 1140 Ft for 200km and 2080 Ft for 500km. First class is 50% more. If you buy your ticket on the train rather than in the station, there's a 400 Ft surcharge (1400 Ft on Intercity trains). Seat reservations may be compulsory (indicated on the timetable by an 'R' in a box), mandatory on trains departing from Budapest (an 'R' in a circle) or simply available (just plain 'R').

There are several types of train. Express (Ex on the timetable) trains often require a seat reservation (90 Ft). The two dozen or so InterCity (IC) trains levy a 290 Ft supplement and you must book a seat. IC trains stop at main centres only and are the fastest and most comfortable trains.

The other types of train are *gyorsvonat* (fast trains) and *személyvonat* (passenger trains), which don't move very fast even when they aren't stopped at yet another village – Trabants sprint past.

An unlimited travel pass for all trains costs 7780/11,670 Ft 2nd/1st class for seven days, and 11,200/16,800 Ft for 10 days, but you'd have to travel like the wind to make it pay for itself. Reservation charges and the IC sup-plement are additional.

If you'll be using trains extensively, you can buy the complete timetable *(menetrend)* for 400 Ft. This is probably excessive if you're only visiting a few places, but it's a good idea to pick up the small IC timetable.

In all stations a yellow board indicates de-partures *(indul)* and a white board arrivals *(érkezik)*. Express trains are indicated in red, local trains in black. In some stations, large black-and-white schedules are plastered all over the walls. To locate the table you need, first find the posted railway map of the country, which indexes the route numbers at the top of the schedules.

All train stations have left-luggage offices, many of which stay open 24 hours a day. You often have to pay the fee (about 80 Ft per item) at another office (usually marked *pénztár*).

The following are distances and approxi-mate times to provincial cities from Budapest (usually via express trains).

Transdanubia		
Győr	131km	two hours
Sopron	216km	three hours
Szombathely	236km	3½ hours
Pécs	228km	three hours
Danube Bend		
Esztergom	53km	1½ hours
(slow trains only)		
Szentendre	20km	40 minutes
(on the HÉV commuter railway)		
Lake Balaton		
Siófok	115km	1½ hours
Balatonfüred	132km	two hours
Veszprém	112km	1¾ hours
Székesfehérvár	67km	50 minutes
Great Plain		
Szolnok	100km	1¼ hours
Kecskemét	106km	1½ hours
Debrecen	221km	three hours
Békéscsaba	196km	2½ hours
Szeged	191km	2½ hours
Northern Hungary		
Nyíregyháza	270km	four hours
Eger	143km	two hours
Miskolc	183km	2¼ hours
Sátoraljaújhely	267km	3½ hours

CAR & MOTORCYCLE

Roads are generally good and there are three basic types. Motorways, preceded by an 'M', link Budapest with Lake Balaton and Vienna via Győr and run part of the way to Miskolc and Kecskemét. National highways are num-bered by a single digit and fan out mostly

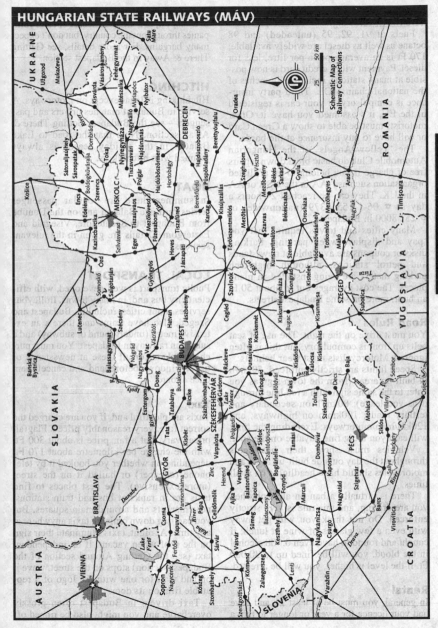

from Budapest. Secondary and tertiary roads have two or three digits.

Fuels of 91, 92, 95 (unleaded) and 98 octane as well as diesel are widely available; 170 Ft is an average price per litre, less for diesel. Payment with a credit card is now possible at many stations, including branches of the national chain MOL. Third-party insurance is compulsory. If your car is registered in the EU, it's assumed you have it. Other motorists must be able to show a Green Card or will have to buy insurance at the border.

The 'Yellow Angels' of the Hungarian Automobile Club do basic breakdown repairs free of charge if you belong to an affiliated organisation such as AAA in the USA or AA in the UK. They can be reached 24 hours a day at ☎ 06-1-155 0379 (nationwide) or ☎ 252 8000 in Budapest.

Many cities and towns require that you 'pay and display' when parking. Parking disks or coupons are available at newsstands and petrol stations, although high-tech parking meters are being installed in many places. The cost averages out to about 50 Ft an hour, more on some Budapest streets.

Road Rules

You must drive on the right. The use of seat belts up front is compulsory, but this is often ignored. Motorcyclists must wear helmets.

Speed limits are strictly enforced: 50km/h in built-up areas (from the town sign as you enter to the same sign with a red line through it as you leave); 80km/h on secondary and tertiary roads; 100km/h on highways; and 120km/h on motorways. Exceeding the limit will earn you a big fine payable on the spot.

Vehicles must show their headlights throughout the day outside built-up areas and motorcycles should have headlights on at all times.

There is virtually a ban on alcohol when you are driving, and this rule is *very* strictly enforced. Do not think you will get away with even a few glasses of wine at lunch; if caught and found to have even 0.008 alcohol in the blood, you will be fined up to 30,000 Ft. If the level is higher, you will be arrested.

Rental

In general, you must be at least 21 and have had your licence for a year or longer to rent a car. All the big international firms have offices in Budapest, and there are scores of local companies throughout the country, but don't expect many bargains. For more details, see Getting There & Away in the Budapest section.

HITCHING

Hitchhiking is legal except on motorways. A service in Budapest matches drivers and passengers – see the Budapest Getting There & Away section. Note that the road to Lake Balaton in the holiday season is always jammed with hitchhikers.

BOAT

In summer there are regular passenger ferries on Lake Balaton and on the Danube from Budapest to Szentendre, Visegrád and Esztergom. Details are given in the relevant sections.

LOCAL TRANSPORT

Public transport is well developed, with efficient city bus and, in many towns, trolleybus services. Four cities, including Budapest and Szeged, also have trams and there's an extensive metro (underground or subway) and a suburban railway in Budapest. You must purchase tickets for all these at newsstands or ticket windows beforehand and cancel them once aboard.

Taxi

Taxis are plentiful and, if you are charged the correct fare, very reasonably priced. Flagfall prices vary, but a fair price is about 300 Ft, with the charge per kilometre about 170 Ft, depending on whether you booked it by telephone (cheaper) or hailed it on the street (more expensive). The best places to find taxis are in ranks at bus and train stations, near markets and around main squares. But you can flag down cruising taxis anywhere at any time. At night, taxis illuminate their sign on the roof when vacant. If an independent taxi (see the Getting Around section of the Budapest section) stops on the street, wave it on and wait for one with the logo of a reputable firm on its door.

Taxi drivers in Budapest often grossly overcharge and you might also be ripped off in a town that sees a lot of tourists, such as Győr. An old Lada taxi is less likely to overcharge than a new Audi. Always make sure that the meter is switched on, but this doesn't guarantee a fair rate as some meters run lightning-fast for foreigners. If all goes well, passengers usually tip drivers about 10% (or round up to the nearest 100 Ft, even if it means tipping a little less or a little more).

Budapest

☏ 1

The capital of Hungary straddles a curve of the Danube River where Transdanubia meets the Great Plain. More romantic than Warsaw, more cosmopolitan than Prague, Budapest is the 'first city' of Eastern Europe. One Hungarian in five lives in Budapest.

Strictly speaking, the story of 'Budapest' only begins in 1873 when hilly, residential Buda merged with flat, industrial Pest to form what was at first called Pest-Buda. But a lot of water had flowed under the Danube bridges by that time; the Romans built the town of Aquincum here, and you can still see their aqueduct in the north of the city. Layer upon layer of history blankets Buda's Castle District, and Pest's ring roads are a testament to the Hungarian and Austrian engineers and architects of the 19th century. Add to this parks brimming with attractions, a chair lift and cog-wheel railway in the nearby Buda Hills, riverboats plying upriver to the scenic Danube Bend, and hot thermal baths in Turkish-era bathhouses and you have Budapest.

The city has many more fascinating aspects. Many Eastern Europeans and Russians come here to make money or get a taste of the west, while westerners revel in the affordable nightlife, theatres, museums, restaurants and cafés. Few cities are more striking than this 'Queen of the Danube'.

Orientation

Budapest is 249km south-east of Vienna, exactly halfway between Sofia and Berlin. The Danube (*Duna*) is Budapest's main artery, dividing historic Buda from commercial Pest. All the eight bridges now spanning the Danube at Budapest were destroyed during WWII and have been rebuilt.

Budapest is divided into 22 kerület (or districts), each with a Roman numeral.

Maps The best folding map to the city is Cartographia's *Budapest City Map* available everywhere for 400 Ft. If you plan to see the city thoroughly or stay beyond a few days, the *Budapest Atlas* (900 Ft), also from Cartographia, is indispensable. It's quite small and easy to carry around.

If you arrive at Keleti train station you'll find a guy selling these and other maps in the sunken forecourt near the metro entrance. He charges more than the shops but not much.

Cartographia has its own outlet at VI Bajcsy-Zsilinszky út 37 (metro: Arany János utca), but it's not self-service. A better bet would be Calypso – see the Bookshops section later in this section.

Train Stations Most visitors arrive at one of the three main train stations: Keleti (east) or Nyugati (west) in Pest, or Déli (south) in Buda. All are on the metro lines which converge at Deák tér on the northern edge of the city's 'inner town'.

At Keleti, the accommodation offices mentioned in this book, the left luggage lockers (50 Ft coins required) and the K&H Bank are all off the large entrance hall on the north side of the station (on the right as the train arrives), accessible from the platforms. There's another hall on the south side which is currently being renovated, so some places could move. Note that the sign saying 'Information' above the flight of steps leading down from the end of the platforms refers to train information, not tourist information. To get to the metro station, go down these steps and keep going straight ahead through a scrappy arcade then across the sunken forecourt.

At Nyugati the tourist information counter is on platform 10. On platform 13 there's a small 24-hour ABC (supermarket). The metro station is accessible through a large system of underground arcades. It might be simpler to leave the station and take one of the street entrances to the metro.

It's easy enough to work out Déli station; just go down the stairs at the end of the platform and you'll find shops, money changers and the metro entrance.

HUNGARY

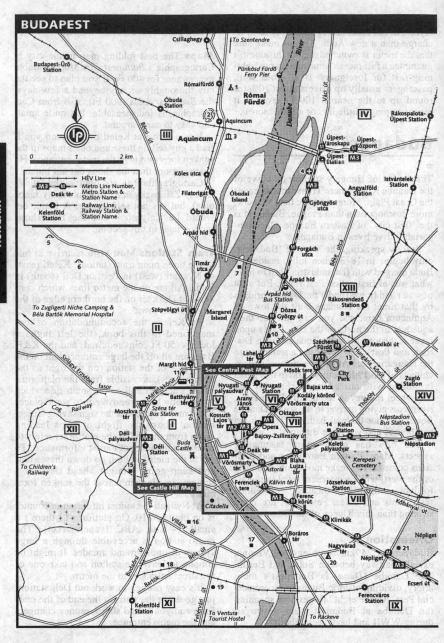

BUDAPEST

Csillaghegy

To Szentendre

Budapest-Úrö
Station

Rómaifürdő

Óbuda
Station

Pünkösd Fürdő
Ferry Pier

Római
Fürdő

Danube River

IV Rákospalota-
Újpest Station

Aquincum

III Aquincum

Újpest-
Városkapu

Újpest-
központ

Újpest
Station M3

Istvántelek
Station

Köles utca

Filatorigát

Óbudai
Island

M3

Angyalföld
Station

Gyöngyösi
utca

HÉV Line

M3 **M** Metro Line Number,
Metro Station &
Station Name

Deák tér

Kelenföld
Station Railway Line,
Railway Station &
Station Name

0   1   2 km

Óbuda

Árpád híd

Forgách
utca

5

6

Timár
utca

Árpád híd

XIII Rákosrendező
Station

To Zugligeti Niche Camping &
Béla Bartók Memorial Hospital

Szépvölgyi út

II

Margit
Island

Árpád híd
Bus Station

Dózsa
György út

8

Lehel utca

M3

Szécheny
Fürdő

Mexikói út

M1

9

13

City
Park

Hungária körút

Zugló
Station

XIV

To Zugligeti Niche Camping &

Margit híd

11

12

Batthyány
tér

Moszkva
tér

Széna tér
Bus Station

I

Szilágyi Erzsébet fasor

Cog Railway

XII

Déli
pályaudvar M2

To Children's
Railway

15

See Castle Hill Map

See Central Pest Map

Hősök tere

Nyugati
pályaudvar Nyugati
Station

V Arany
János
utca VI

Bajza utca

Kodály körönd

Vörösmarty utca

Oktagon

VII

Margit körút

Buda
Castle

Kossuth
Lajos
tér M2 M3

Opera

M1

Bajcsy-Zsilinszky út

Deák tér

14 Keleti
Station

Keleti
pályaudvar

Népstadion
Bus Station

M2 Népstadion

Alkotás utca

Astoria

Blaha
Lujza tér

Kerepesi
Cemetery

Vörösmarty
tér M2

Ferenciek
tere

Kálvin tér

Józsefváros
Station

Citadella

M3

Ferenc
körút

VIII

Kőbányai út

Klinikák

Népliget

16

17

Borâros
tér

Nagyvárad
tér

20

21

Népliget

M3

Villány út

18

19

Bartók út

Béla út

Budaörsi út

Fehérvári út

Kelenföld
Station XI

To Ventura
Tourist Hostel

To Ráckeve

Ecseri út

Ferencváros
Station

IX

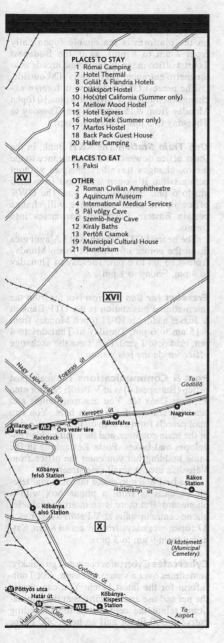

PLACES TO STAY
1 Római Camping
7 Hotel Thermál
8 Goliát & Flandria Hotels
9 Diáksport Hostel
10 Ho(s)tel California (Summer only)
14 Mellow Mood Hostel
15 Hotel Express
16 Hostel Kek (Summer only)
17 Martos Hostel
18 Back Pack Guest House
20 Haller Camping

PLACES TO EAT
11 Paksi

OTHER
2 Roman Civilian Amphitheatre
3 Aquincum Museum
4 International Medical Services
5 Pál völgy Cave
6 Szemlò-hegy Cave
12 Király Baths
13 Pertöfi Csarnok
19 Municipal Cultural House
21 Planetarium

Pest Pest is very much the heart of Budapest. It's quite easy to orient yourself here as most roads follow a regular pattern, with two semi-circular 'ring' roads and major roads radiating from the centre. The exception is the central 'inner town', south and west of Deák tér, where interlocking squares and winding old streets mean that *everyone* is confused at least some of the time.

From Deák tér, leafy Andrássy út runs north-east to City Park (Városliget), while the 'little ring road', composed of Károly körút, Múzeum körút and Vamház körút, swings around to Szabadság Bridge and Gellért Hill. The 'big ring road' is made up of Szent István körút, Teréz körút, Erzsébet körút, József körút and Ferenc körút.

Óbuda is at the western end of Árpád Bridge north of Buda, and Aquincum beyond that.

Information

Tourist Offices Your best source of information about Budapest and all of Hungary is Tourinform (☎ 117 9800; fax 117 9578), Sütő utca 2 (metro: Deák tér), which is open daily from 8 am to 8 pm. Pick up a free copy of *Budapest Panorama*, which lists upcoming events and details attractions.

In Nyugati train station next to platform No 10, there's a tourist information office (☎ 302 8580, open daily from 7 am to 8 pm) and in the large underground arcade connecting Nyugati train station with the Nyugati metro station there's a Budapest Tourism office.

Assistance and advice for motorists is available at the Magyar Autóklub (☎ 088 for assistance in English or German), II Rómer Flóris utca 4a off Margit körút near Margaret Bridge. There's another Magyar Autóklub office just opposite the Budapest Operetta Theatre at VI Nagymező utca 20.

Money As elsewhere in Hungary, the OTP Bank changes travellers cheques without commission, but get there at least an hour before closing to be sure the foreign-exchange counter will still be open. The big OTP branch opposite American Express on V Deák Ferenc utca doesn't do exchange, but it has two ATMs and a foreign-currency exchange machine outside. The closest OTP branch to Deák tér is at VII Károly körút 1, open Monday from 8.15 am to 6 pm, Tuesday to Thursday to 3 pm, Friday to 1 pm (metro: Astoria).

The Welcome Hotel Service (☎ 118 4848, 118 5776), V Apáczai Csere János utca 1 near the Duna Marriott Hotel, changes travellers cheques round the clock.

The K&H Bank at Váci utca 40 is open Monday to Thursday from 8 am to 1 pm, Friday to noon, and changes US dollar travellers cheques into dollars cash for a 3% commission.

The American Express office (☎ 267 2022) at V Deák Ferenc utca 10, a block up from Vörösmarty tér towards Deák tér, changes its own travellers cheques at a rate about 3% lower than the banks. To convert US dollars travellers cheques into dollars cash costs about 7% commission.

Credit Lyonnais and Citibank are both near the south-west corner of Erzsébet tér (see the Central Pest map).

Some flashy private exchange offices around town deduct exorbitant 10% commissions. Others have huge signs reading 'no commission' but give 10% below the normal bank rate. Few people offer to change money on the street and most of them are thieves; see Money in the introductory Facts for the Visitor section for more information about the black market.

Keleti Train Station The K&H Bank, off the entrance hall (on your right as the train comes in) changes travellers cheques at a good rate. It's open on weekdays from 8 am to 6.30 pm, Saturday to 1 pm. The GWK counter on the platform gives a fair rate for cash and a slightly less fair rate for travellers cheques. The advantage is that it's open daily from 6 am to 9 pm. There's at least one ATM at Keleti.

Avoid using the other change counters at Keleti without comparing the rates with those at K&H and GWK, and beware of small print saying that you have to change 50,000 Ft or receive an even lower rate.

The nearest OTP branch is at VIII Rákóczi út 84, corner of Huszar, (open Monday 8.15 am to 6 pm, Tuesday to Thursday to 4 pm, Friday to 1 pm).

Nyugati Train Station The GWK exchange bureau next to the tourist information office on the platform is reasonable (open daily from 7 am to 8 pm), as is the Budapest Tourist office in the underground arcade near the metro entrance. There's an ATM outside.

The nearest OTP branch with foreign exchange facilities is at XIII Tátra utca 10 (open Monday from 8.15 am to 6 pm, Tuesday to Thursday to 3 pm, Friday to 1 pm).

Déli Train Station The K&H Bank, in the Ibusz office downstairs at the entrance to the metro, changes travellers cheques without commission. It's open weekdays from 8.15 am to 6 pm, Saturday to 1 pm. The GWK office in the same concourse will change certain Eastern European currencies into forints.

The nearest OTP branch is at I Alagút utca 3, on the corner of Attila út (open Monday from 8.15 am to 6 pm, Tuesday to Thursday to 4 pm, Friday to 1 pm).

Erzsébet tér Bus Station Not far from the international bus station is the OTP Bank at V József nádor tér 10-11 (open Monday from 8.15 am to 6 pm, Tuesday to Thursday to 4 pm, Friday to 1 pm). Don't use the exchange office inside the bus station.

Post & Communications The main post office (Budapest 4) is at V Petőfi Sándor utca 13, near Deák tér. You can mail letters and send telexes and faxes from here. You can mail parcels from a room on the opposite side of the main counters, and they sell padded envelopes and boxes. Poste Restante is in the same building but you enter the office from Városház utca, a small side street.

The best place to make international telephone calls is from a phone box with a phonecard. But there is an international telephone centre upstairs at V Petőfi Sándor utca 17 (open weekdays from 8 am to 8 pm, Saturday from 9 am to 3 pm).

Cybercafés Cybercafés come and go quickly, sometimes over a summer season. Ask Tourinform for the latest batch. You can access the net and use email facilities at the international telephone centre (see the preceding entry) at 300 Ft for half an hour, 500 Ft for an hour. The Goethe Institute at VI Andrássy út 24 has free Internet access from 2 to 7 pm, although you'll probably have a long wait.

Travel Agencies The MÁV ticket office (☎ 322 8405) at VI Andrássy út 35 (metro: Opera) sells international train tickets and can make advance seat reservations for domestic express trains at the same price you'd pay at the station. It accepts cash only and is open weekdays from 9 am to 5 pm (6 pm in summer). Get there early to avoid the queues.

If the queues are long at MÁV, head for Ibusz at VII Dob utca 1 (metro: Astoria or Deák tér), which sells the same tickets and can also make seat reservations. It's open weekdays from 8 am to 6 pm and on Saturday from 9 am to 1 pm.

Express (☎ 111 6418), V Zoltán utca 10 (metro: Kossuth Lajos tér), open Monday to Thursday from 8 am to 4 pm, Friday to 3 pm, sells BIJ train tickets with a 30% discount on fares to Western Europe to those under the age of 26. The main Express office (☎ 117 8600) is at V Semmelweis utca 4 (metro: Astoria).

You must have an ISIC card to get the student fare on international tickets. There are no student fares on domestic train travel.

Bookshops The best English-language bookshop is Bestsellers, V Október 6 utca 11 (metro: Arany János), which has novels, travel guides, magazines and newspapers. There's another new branch at the Central European University on the corner of Nádor utca and Zrínyi utca.

The Calypso bookshop in Párizsi Udvar (a neo-Gothic arcade well worth a look, despite its dilapidation) sells travel guides, including a lot of Lonely Planet titles. It also has a fair selection of books in English and other languages, both translated Hungarian works and originals. Atlantisz Book Island, V Váci utca 32, is also worth trying.

Laundry One central laundrette (and one of the few self-service places in the country) is at VII Rákóczi út 8b (metro: Astoria). It's small, so there might be queues.

Medical Services International Medical Services (☎ 329 8423), XIII Váci út 202

(metro: Újpest-Városkapu) is a private medical clinic open 24 hours a day. Consultations usually cost from 3000 Ft. Home visits cost around 4500 FT.

A dental clinic specialising in treating foreigners is Dental Co-op (☎ 394 3411), XII Zugligeti út 60 (bus No 158), open weekdays from 9 am to 6 pm (from 1 pm on Thursday).

Emergency If you need to report a lost or stolen passport or credit card or a crime, go to the central police station (☎ 112 3456) at V Deák tér 16-18. If possible, bring along a Hungarian speaker. Tourinform might be able to help. The office dealing with foreigners' registrations is KEOKH (☎ 118 0800) at VI Városligeti fasor 46-48 (metro: Hösök tere).

Things to See
The Budapest Card is sold at many outlets in the centre of Pest. It gives free admission to most museums and galleries and is also a public transport pass. At 2000 Ft it nearly pays for itself with a 1400 Ft discount on the Ibusz city tour. However it's only valid for two days, so many travellers prefer buying a transport pass (see Getting Around later in the Budapest section) and paying the admission charges, which average under 200 Ft.

Buda Most of what remains of medieval Budapest is on **Castle Hill** (Várhegy), perched above the Danube. The easiest way to get there is to take the metro to Moszkva tér, cross the bridge above the square and continue straight up Várfok utca to the **Vienna Gate**. A minibus marked 'Budavári Sikló' follows this same route from the bridge, shuttling every few minutes from Moszkva tér to the funicular near Buda Castle. Or you could take the sikló itself, the funicular that whisks passengers up from Clark Ádám tér to Szent György tér in two minutes. It runs between 7.30 am and 10 pm daily (180 Ft). It's closed on the second and fourth Monday of the month.

Once through Vienna Gate, take a sharp right on Petermann bíró utca past the **National Archives**, with its majolica-tiled roof, to Kapisztrán tér. The **Magdalen Tower** is all that's left of a Gothic church destroyed here in WWII. The white neoclassical building facing the square is the **Museum of Military**

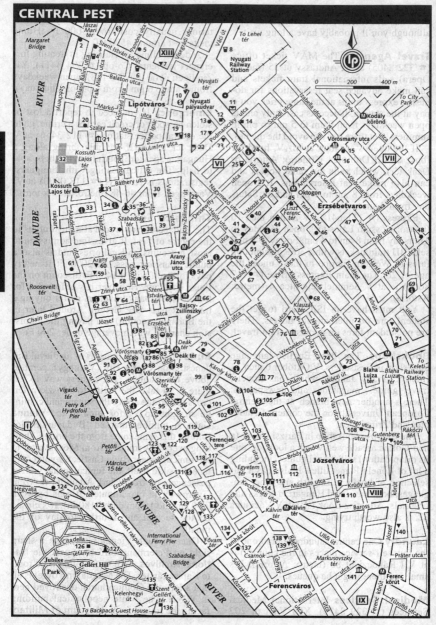

CENTRAL PEST

CENTRAL PEST

PLACES TO STAY
12 Yellow Submarine
14 Best Youth Hostel
22 Hostel Bánki
28 Medosz Hotel
45 Caterina Hostel
74 Marco Polo
86 Corvinus Kempinski Hotel
93 Duna Marriott Hotel
110 Museum Hostel
116 Hostel (Summer Only)
126 Citadella Hostel/Hotel
136 Gellért Hotel & Baths

PLACES TO EAT
7 Okay Italia
9 Okay Italia
17 Sir Lancelot
19 Semiramis
23 Crazy Café
27 Mirtusz
30 Market & Tükör Restaurant
47 Jorgosz Restaurant
50 Felafel Faloda
51 Művesz Café
57 Kisharang Étkezde
59 Gandhi
60 Self-Service Restaurant
63 Duna Palota
64 Coquan's Kavé
70 New York Café
75 Hannah
89 Gerbeaud Café
103 Café Talk Talk
109 Görög Csemege
115 Brooklyn Café
117 Vegetárium
118 Cabar
123 Bölcs Bagoly
128 Taverna Dionysos
129 Govinda
133 Fatál
134 Stop
138 Coquan's Kavé
139 Iran Persian Sandwich Club
140 Il Treno

BARS & CLUBS
4 Jazz Café
6 Franklin Trocadero
8 Bahnhof
18 Becketts Irish Bar
25 Bamboo
39 Mystery Bar
72 Old Man's Music Pub
99 Merlin Jazz Club

111 Nothing But the Blues Club
113 Irish Cat Pub
114 Action Bar
130 Kalamajka Táncház (Club)

TOURIST OFFICES & BOOKING AGENCIES
20 Cooptourist
24 Volántourist
33 Express (Train Tickets)
34 Express (Hostel Bookings)
43 MÁV Ticket Office
53 Színházak Központi Jegyiroda (Ticket Office)
54 Dunatours
62 Budapest Tourist
69 Village Tourism
78 Ibusz (Train Tickets)
90 Nemzeti Filharmónia Jegyiroda (Ticket Office)
91 Malév Office
94 Welcome Hotel Service (24-hour Accommodation Booking)
98 Tourinform
102 Express (Main Office)
119 Ibusz Main Office (Private Rooms)

MUSEUMS
16 Ferenc Liszt Museum
21 Ethnography Museum
66 Post Office Museum
76 Electrotechnology Museum
77 Jewish Museum
112 National Museum
141 Museum of Applied Arts

OTHER
1 OTP Bank
2 White House
3 Antikvárium Bookshop & Báv Shop
5 Vígszínház (Gaiety Theatre)
10 OTP Bank
11 Post Office
13 Kaiser's Supermarket
15 Puppet Theatre
26 Muvesz Cinema
29 Cartographia Map Store
31 Imre Nagy Monument
32 Parliament
35 Soviet Army Memorial
36 US Embassy
37 Hungarian Television Building

38 Hungarian National Bank Building
40 Budapest Operetta Theatre
41 Thalia Theatre
42 Goethe Institute
44 Ferenc Liszt Music Shop
46 Liszt Academy of Music
48 National Theatre
49 Madách Theatre
52 State Opera House
55 St Stephen's Basilica
56 Bestsellers Bookshop
58 Central European University
61 Academy of Science
65 Inka Car Rental
67 János Arany Theatre
68 Ghetto Market
71 Julius Meinl Supermarket
73 Rothschild Kosher Supermarket
77 Great Synagogue
79 1-hr Photos & Pro Film Supplies
80 Erzsébet tér Bus Station
81 OTP Bank
82 Credit Lyonnaise
83 UK Embassy
84 Central Police Station
85 Airport Bus Stop
87 Citibank
88 American Express
92 Pesti Vigadó (Concert Hall)
95 Folkart Centrum
96 Main Post Office
97 International Telephone Centre
100 Holló Atelier (Folk Craft)
101 City Hall
104 K&H Bank
105 OTP Bank
106 Laundrette
107 Uránia Cinema
108 Kenguru Ride Service
120 Parizsi Udvar
121 Atlantisz Book Island
122 Inner Town Parish Church
124 Rác Baths
125 Rudas Baths
127 Independence Monument
131 K&H Bank
132 Serbian Orthodox Church
135 Cliff Chapel
137 Central Market Hall (Nagycsamarok)

HUNGARY

HUNGARY

top floor - Hung "Famous Eight"

History, which you enter from the ramparts side on Tóth Árpád sétány. Walk south-east along Tóth Árpád sétány, the ramparts promenade, enjoying the views of the Buda Hills. The long white building below you is Déli train station. Halfway along the ramparts you'll catch a glimpse of the neo-Gothic tower of **Matthias Church** on Szentháromság utca. The church (rebuilt in 1896) has a colourful tiled roof, murals inside and the **Museum of Ecclesiastical Art**, which you enter through the crypt. The church is open daily but is closed from mid January to mid February.

Franz Liszt wrote the *Hungarian Coronation Mass* for the coronation of Franz Joseph and Elizabeth here in 1867. Behind the church is an equestrian statue of St Stephen (977-1038), Hungary's first king. Behind that is the **Fisherman's Bastion**, a late 19th-century structure offering great views of Pest, the Parliament building and the Danube.

If you take a little detour north-west up Fortuna utca to No 4, you'll come to the charming **Commerce and Catering Museum**, where an entire 19th-century cake shop has been relocated, complete with pastry kitchen and all the old equipment.

From the **Holy Trinity Statue** in the centre of Szentháromság tér, Tárnok utca runs south-east to the gate of the **Royal Palace**. The palace enjoyed its greatest splendour under King Matthias in the second half of the 15th century but has been destroyed and rebuilt many times since then.

Today the palace contains two important museums. The **National Gallery** has a huge collection of Hungarian works of art from Gothic to contemporary. It's open daily, except Monday, from 10 am to 6 pm and admission is 200 Ft. The **Budapest History Museum** in Wing E to the south traces the city's 2000 years of history. It's open daily in summer and daily, except Tuesday, the rest of the year; admission costs 250 Ft.

From the castle terrace take the **funicular railway** or walk down the steps to Clark Ádám tér at the Buda end of **Chain Bridge**, which was opened in 1849 and was the first bridge to span the Danube in Hungary. In the park in front of the lower funicular station is the **Zero Kilometre Stone**, from which all highway distances in Hungary are measured.

Go through the small pedestrian tunnel under the end of the Chain Bridge and take tram No 19 south along the right bank of the Danube. Get off at Móricz Zsigmond körtér, the second stop after the Gellért Hotel (1918). Walk back a little, round the corner to the left and board bus No 27 on Villányi út. This bus will take you right up to the Citadella on Gellért Hill, but it's just as easy to walk from the Gellért Hotel up Kelenhegyi út.

The commanding fortress on top, the **Citadella**, was built by the Habsburgs after the 1848-49 Revolution to 'defend' the city from further insurrection. By the time it was ready the political climate had changed and the Citadella had become obsolete. To walk up here (it's pretty steep) from Pest, cross Erzsébet Bridge and take one of the stairs leading up by the 'waterfall'. At the top choose a path – there are several – and keep climbing.

The **Independence Monument**, the lovely lady with the palm proclaiming freedom throughout the city at the southern end of the Citadella, was erected in tribute to the Soviet soldiers who died liberating Hungary in 1945. But many Hungarians choose not to remember that any more and both the victims' names in Cyrillic letters on the plinth and the statues of the soldiers have been removed. You'll see your most memorable views of Budapest and the Danube from this hill. At night, with the city lit up below you, the views are spectacular.

Pest Industrialisation allowed Budapest to develop rapidly during the late 19th century, and one of the nicest places to get a feel for this period is in **City Park**, north-east of the centre. Take metro No 1 (the yellow line) to Széchenyi Fürdő.

This line, the oldest underground railway on the continent, opened in 1896 and was renovated for its centenary. You'll come out of the station right in the middle of the park beside the **Széchenyi Baths** (1913), behind which is the **Vidám Park**, with amusement rides, the **Grand Circus** and the **Budapest Zoo**.

Cross the busy boulevard to the south-east and you'll come to **Vajdahunyad Castle** (1896), partly modelled after a fortress in Transylvania but with Gothic, Romanesque and baroque wings and additions to reflect architectural styles from all over Hungary. The **Agricultural Museum** is housed in the castle.

City Park's dominant feature is the entrance at **Hősök tere** with a great monument erected in 1896 for the millennium of the Magyar conquest of the Carpathian Basin. The Tomb of the Unknown Soldier is also here. On the south-east side of the square is the **Múcsarnok**, an exhibition hall built for the Millenary Exhibition in 1896, now fully restored and used for art exhibits. On the other side of the square is the **Museum of Fine Arts** (1906), housing Hungary's richest collection of foreign art. The collection of Spanish paintings is one of the best outside Madrid. It's open daily, except Monday, from 10 am to 6 pm (4 pm from January to mid-March) and admission is 200 Ft.

From Hősök tere, stately Andrássy út runs straight into the heart of Pest. To save yourself a long walk, take the metro to Opera. The **State Opera House** was built in 1884 in the neo-Renaissance style and the daily tours at 3 and 4 pm are worth taking, especially if you can't catch a performance. Many of the other great buildings along this section of Andrássy út date from this time, including **Drechsler House** opposite, which now houses the State Ballet Institute. Proceed south-west on this fashionable avenue and round the corner onto Bajcsy-Zsilinszky út. You'll see the 96m-high neo-Renaissance dome of **St Stephen's Basilica** (1906) looming before you. The right hand – the so-called Holy Right or Holy Dexter – of St Stephen is kept in the chapel at the rear of the church. Take the passage on the left near the altar. There's a 100 Ft charge to turn on the light to see the hand. The ticket office just inside the basilica charges 100 Ft admission to the treasury, not to the basilica itself.

Cross the square in front of the basilica and continue straight ahead for a block on Zrínyi utca, then right on Október 6 utca. Proceed straight ahead onto Szabadság tér with the Art Nouveau **National Bank** (1900) to the right and the **Hungarian Television Building** (1906), formerly the Budapest Stock Exchange, to the left. At the end of the square in front of the US Embassy at No 12 is the **Soviet Army Memorial** (1945), one of the few such monuments left in the city.

As you look up Vécsey utca from the memorial you see the great neo-Gothic silhouette of the **Parliament building** (1904) on Kossuth Lajos tér. Tours in English are available but leave at different times depending on whether Parliament is sitting. Ask Tourinform for details. The **Ethnography Museum** (1896; 500 Ft) also faces Kossuth Lajos tér at No 12. It's open daily, except Monday, and admission costs 200 Ft.

There's a metro station on the south side of Kossuth Lajos tér and for a more dramatic view of the Parliament building, take the metro for one stop over to Batthyány tér on the Buda side, where you'll also find a large public market hall and some old churches.

Óbuda & Aquincum Óbuda – Old Buda – is most easily reached by taking the HÉV suburban railway from Batthyány tér to the stop at Árpád Bridge. The **Vasarely Museum**, with its op art collection at III Szentlélek tér 6, greets you right outside the station.

Walk through Szentlélek tér to Fő tér, the beautifully restored heart of Óbuda. The **Town Hall** is at III Fő tér 3, but the most interesting building is the baroque **Zichy Mansion** (1752) at Fő tér 1. At the back of the courtyard is an art gallery and upstairs the unique **Kassák Museum**, a three-room exhibition with some gems of early 20th-century avant-garde art.

Return to the HÉV and take a train three stops farther north to Aquincum. Aquincum was the key military garrison of the Roman province of Pannonia. A **Roman aqueduct** used to pass this way from a spring in the nearby park and remains have been preserved in the median strip of the highway alongside the HÉV railway line. The 2nd-century civilian **amphitheatre** is right beside the station. A few hundred metres away is a large excavated area and the outdoor **Aquincum Museum**. It's open daily, except Monday, and closes between November and March. Admission is 150 Ft. From Aquincum you have a choice of returning to Budapest or taking the HÉV on to Szentendre (see the Danube Bend section).

Other Museums Two museums in central Pest are worthy of special attention. The twin-towered **Great Synagogue** (1859) at VII Dohány utca 2-8, the largest functioning synagogue in Europe, contains the **Jewish Museum** (closed Saturday and from November to April; admission 400 Ft). The former Jewish ghetto extends behind this synagogue between Dohány utca, Kertész utca and Király utca, an area worth exploring.

The **National Museum**, VIII Múzeum körút 14-16, has the nation's main collection of historical relics in a large neoclassical building (1847), including the most cherished object in all of Hungary – the **Crown of St Stephen**. It's open from 10 am to 6 pm (5 pm in winter) Wednesday to Sunday. Admission is 250 Ft, free on Wednesday.

Margaret Island When your head begins to spin from all the sights, take a walk from one end of Margaret Island (Margit sziget) to the other. Bus No 26 from beside Nyugati train station covers the island or you can get there on tram No 4 or 6, both of which stop halfway across Margaret Bridge. As you stroll among the trees and statues, you'll come across the ruins of two medieval monasteries, a small zoo, a rose garden, an open-air theatre, cafés, swimming pools, a pseudo-Japanese garden and hot springs at the Hotel Thermál. The island is such a relaxing, restful place you'll feel as if you're several miles from the busy city.

Unfortunately the island is no longer considered safe at night, and you should not walk there alone after dark.

Graves & Statues Budapest's Highgate or Pére Lachaise is **Kerepesi Cemetery**, on VIII Fiumei út near Keleti train station. Built over a century ago, it's the final resting place of Hungary's wealthiest and most prominent people. The most notable built themselves huge mausoleums, which now stand alongside memorials to communists of yesteryear. Half the streets in Hungary are named after people buried here.

Monumental communist-era statues have been gathered together in **Statue Park**, at XXII Balatoni út (corner of Szabadkai utca) in the south-west of Buda. It's advertised as 'Tons of Socialism' and is worth a look. Entry is 200 Ft. To get there from central Pest take bus No 7 to the terminal at Kosztolányi tér and from there take a yellow bus from stand No 6.

Activities

Thermal Baths Budapest is a major spa centre with numerous **thermal baths** open to the public. The Danube follows the geological fault separating the Buda Hills from the Great Plain and over 40 million litres of warm mineral water gush forth daily from more than 100 thermal springs.

Some bathhouses require you to wear a bathing suit while others do not. Have one with you and go with the flow. Most of the public baths hire out bathing suits and towels if you don't have your own. Some of the baths become gay venues on male-only days – especially the Király and Rác. Not much actually goes on except for some intensive cruising.

Begin your bathhouse tour with the **Gellért Baths** (enter through the side entrance of this eclectic-style hotel on XI Kelehegyi út). The pools here maintain a constant temperature of 44°C and a large outdoor pool is open in summer. A price list 2m long in English and German is beside the ticket booth. Entry to the pool costs 1200 Ft, or 600 Ft after 5 pm on weekdays and after 2 pm on weekends. A thermal bath costs 450 Ft. You must wear a bathing cap (supplied) in the swimming pool. Men and women are separated in the communal baths and if you're a couple paying for a two-person tub bath make sure you'll be allowed in together!

Therapeutical services such as traction cure, ultrasonic, inhalation and short-wave treatments are available. Everything but the swimming pool is closed after 2 pm on weekends.

There are two bathing establishments near the Buda end of Erzsébet Bridge where you'll meet far more locals than tourists. The **Rudas Baths** beside the river at I Döbrentei tér 9 were built by the Turks in 1566 and retain a strong Turkish atmosphere. They are open daily for men only (closed Saturday afternoon and Sunday). Women should make for the **Rác Baths** at the foot of the hill, on the opposite side of the bridge, at I Hadnagy utca 8-10. The Rác Baths are reserved for women on Monday, Wednesday and Friday and for men on Tuesday, Thursday and Saturday. Admission is 350 Ft at both.

The *ivócsarnok*, or well room (closed weekends), is below the bridge and within

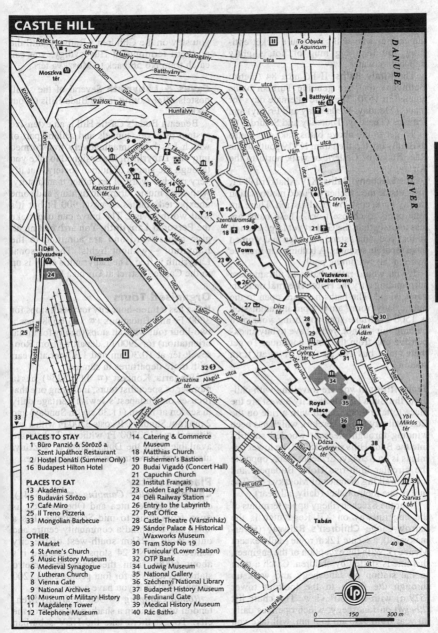

CASTLE HILL

HUNGARY

PLACES TO STAY
1 Büro Panzió & Söröző a Szent Jupáthoz Restaurant
2 Hostel Donáti (Summer Only)
16 Budapest Hilton Hotel

PLACES TO EAT
13 Akadémia
15 Budavári Söröző
17 Café Miro
25 Il Treno Pizzeria
33 Mongolian Barbecue

OTHER
3 Market
4 St Anne's Church
5 Music History Museum
6 Medieval Synagogue
7 Lutheran Church
8 Vienna Gate
9 National Archives
10 Museum of Military History
11 Magdalene Tower
12 Telephone Museum
14 Catering & Commerce Museum
18 Matthias Church
19 Fishermen's Bastion
20 Budai Vigadó (Concert Hall)
21 Capuchin Church
22 Institut Français
23 Golden Eagle Pharmacy
24 Déli Railway Station
26 Entry to the Labyrinth
27 Post Office
28 Castle Theatre (Várszínház)
29 Sándor Palace & Historical Waxworks Museum
30 Tram Stop No 19
31 Funicular (Lower Station)
32 OTP Bank
34 Ludwig Museum
35 National Gallery
36 Széchenyi National Library
37 Budapest History Museum
38 Ferdinand Gate
39 Medical History Museum
40 Rác Baths

0   150   300 m

sight of the Rudas Baths. You can buy drinking water from nearby springs from here. Pay the cashier who will give you a ticket entitling you to a big mug of hot, slightly radioactive water.

The **Király Baths**, II Fő utca 84 (metro: Batthyány tér), are genuine Turkish baths erected in 1570. There are alternate days for males (Monday, Wednesday and Friday) and females (Tuesday, Thursday and Saturday).

To get to the above baths, take the metro to Batthyány tér, then tram No 19 south to the Rác, Rudas or Gellért, or walk north to the Király.

The **Széchenyi Baths**, XIV Állatkerti út 11, just outside the Széchenyi Fürdő metro station in City Park, cost 350 Ft admission. There are nine pools to choose from. These baths are less touristy than the Gellért yet large enough so that you won't stand out. Men and women have separate sections. A bathing cap must be worn in the swimming pool.

If you would rather bathe in ultramodern surroundings, try the **Hotel Thermál** on Margaret Island. The baths here are open to the public daily from 7 am to 8 pm and admission is 1500 Ft. Make sure you bring your own bathing suit – if not, you'll have to buy an expensive one from the hotel boutique. To get there, take bus No 26 from Nyugati train station.

Train Rides If you are travelling with children, the Buda Hills to the city's west are the place to take them. Begin with a ride on the **Cog Railway** (Fogaskerekű), which has been winding through pleasant wooded suburbs into the Buda Hills since 1874. The lower terminus is on Szilágyi Erzsébet fasor, opposite the circular high-rise Hotel Budapest and within walking distance of Moszkva tér. The fare is one metro ticket (daily, all year).

Near the Széchenyihegy upper terminus of the cog railway on XII Rege utca is the narrow-gauge **Children's Railway** (Gyermekvasút), a scenic 12km route (daily except Monday). With the exception of the engineer, this line is staffed by children. Catch a train to the station on Jánoshegy and walk up through the forest to the lookout tower (529m) with its 360° view. The **chair lift** (libegő) on Jánoshegy, which operates daily all year from 9.30 am to 5 pm, will take you

down to XII Zugligeti út, where you can catch the No 158 bus back to Moszkva tér. If you stay on the Children's Railway until the northern terminus at Hűvösvölgy, you can catch tram No 56 back to Moszkva tér.

Caves & Labyrinth Several of the small hostels offer **caving** in the Buda Hills (about 2000 Ft).

Beneath Buda's Castle Hill is an extensive system of caves, tunnels and cellars, part of which has been imaginatively transformed into **The Labyrinth**. It's designed to take you through the stages of human society, but it's very much a work of art rather than history, with eerie music, dramatic lighting and some unexpected statues. It costs 900 Ft but it's well worth a visit. The brave can undertake the **Personal Labyrinth**. You arrive at night, give a password and are admitted to the Labyrinth – without lights! The Personal Labyrinth is free. The Labyrinth's entry is up in the Castle District at Úri utca 9.

Organised Tours

Ibusz has a three-hour city tour with stops for 3600 Ft and Budatours (☎ 153 0558) has a two-hour tour without stops (handy for initial orientation) for 2900 Ft, departing from Roosevelt tér at 10.30 am and 1.30 pm all year, with more departures in summer.

Hungaria Koncert (☎ 117 2754) has a number of specialist tours, including one that focuses on Budapest's Jewish heritage daily in season at 11 am (11.30 am on Sunday) and 2 pm (not Sunday). It costs 3300 Ft with a traditional meal, 2700 Ft without. Tickets are available from the Duna Palota at V Zrínyi utca and at the entrance to the synagogue.

Places to Stay

Camping *Haller Camping* (☎ 215 5741), corner of Haller utca and Óbester utca, is open from June to mid-September. It's a small place behind a community centre and only about 2.25km south-west of the city centre. Tram No 24 stops outside and it's about 600m from the Nagyvárad metro station. A tent site for four people costs 1200 Ft, plus 400 Ft if you have a car.

Római Camping (☎ 368 6260), III Szentendrei út 189, is in a shady park north of the city. To get there take the HÉV suburban railway from the Batthyány tér metro station to the Római Fürdő station, which is within sight of the camping ground. A tent site for two people costs 2300 Ft. Though it's open all year, cabins are only available from mid-April to mid-October for 2100 Ft a double in 3rd category, 4800 Ft for three in 2nd category. There are about 45 cabins but they're often full. Use of the adjacent swimming pool is included.

Zugligeti Niche Camping (☎ 200 8346), XII Zugligeti út 101, is at the bottom station of the Buda Hills chair lift (take bus No 158 from Moszkva tér to the terminus). Camping on one of the small hillside terraces costs 450 Ft per tent plus 150 Ft per person. It's another 650 Ft if you have a car. There's one on-site caravan at 3500 Ft a double, one bungalow at 3500 Ft for two people, and a couple of rooms. Zugligeti Niche is open all year and the friendly staff speak English.

Hostels In July and August backpackers are often approached at train stations by hostel touts offering free minibus rides to their hostels. This is fine, but if you want a double room get a firm commitment that one will be available that night. Otherwise you could be stuck in a dormitory for days on end waiting for someone to leave. Hostels rarely have single rooms.

There are two types of hostel in Budapest: student accommodation which is leased over summer by private operators and run as hostels (a few student places run year-round), and the burgeoning number of small hostels, most in apartments close to the Pest city centre.

Small Hostels These hostels run all year, are very personal (but cramped) and are probably the best places to stay. Most have cooking facilities and some have laundries. Even in winter it pays to book ahead at these places. The prices quoted here can be expected to rise in summer and perhaps fall in winter. Few hostels offer singles or doubles in summer but many can arrange them in winter.

Yellow Submarine (☎ 327 283), Teréz Körút 56, 3rd floor, close to Nyugati train and metro stations, is one of the best places – it's well run and has lots of information for travellers. Dorms cost from 1350 Ft. Diagonally opposite on the corner of Teréz Krt and Pod-

maniczky utca, *Best Youth Hostel* (☎ 332 4934) is cheaper but not as good.

Mellow Mood (☎ 351 8862), Baross tér 15, 5th floor (there's a lift), is a reasonable place diagonally opposite Keleti train station. From the main entrance on the north side of the station, look left until you see the McDonald's sign, then look farther down the street until you see the less obvious Pizza Hut sign. The entrance to the hostel's apartment building is immediately left of Pizza Hut. Dorms cost from 1200 Ft.

Not far from the centre of town, the *Museum Hostel* (☎ 318 9508, lotus@ freemail.c3.hu), on the 1st floor at Mikszáth Kálmán tér 4, is a friendly, small place, charging from 1000 Ft. The nearest metro station is Kálvin tér.

On classy Andrássy Ave, No 47, *Caterina Hostel* (☎ 291 9538) is also in an apartment, but this building was once a posh place. The hostel is just as cramped as the others but there are high ceilings and a bit of opulence. Caterina herself is very friendly (although her English is limited) and runs a tight ship. Dorm beds cost US$6 and singles/doubles are US$10 per person. The nearest metro station is Oktogon. If the hostel is full, Caterina can arrange apartments from US$10 per person.

The *Back Pack Guest House* (☎ 185 8946), XI Takács Menyhért utca 33, in the south of Buda, is one of the original small hostels. Because it isn't in the city centre it's a house, with a pleasant lawn area. Dorms cost from 1000 Ft and doubles from 1500 Ft per person. It's a well-run and friendly place. Access is relatively easy on bus No 7 or 7A (green numbers) from Keleti train station, tram No 49 or 47 across Erzsébet Bridge or tram No 17 or 18 from Buda.

Other Hostels The Travellers company (it used to be called More Than Ways) is associated with Hostelling International (HI) and runs many of the summer hostels in student accommodation.

The Travellers/HI office at Keleti train station (☎ 0660 322 719; open daily from 7 am to 11 pm, 9 pm in winter) makes bookings at Travellers hostels and maybe at the others as well. All the Travellers hostels are open 24 hours a day and you can check in any time, but you must depart by 9 am or pay for

HUNGARY

another night. There's no curfew, and an HI card is not required.

Travellers also has two year-round places: the big *Diáksport Hostel* (☎ 340 8585), a two-minute walk south from Dózsa György út metro station at XIII Dózsa György út 152 and the well-located *Marco Polo* (☎ 342 9587), VII Nyár utca 6. The Marco Polo is smaller and looks good from the outside but it was 'closed due to technical difficulties' when we called by, so we can't vouch for the interior. Dorms cost 1200 Ft, singles/doubles (all year) are 7600/8800 Ft.

Diáksport used to be crowded, noisy and chaotic but it was popular with party animals, with a 24-hour bar. It was undergoing a complete renovation at the time of writing, so that might change. Dorms cost between 1600 and 1950 Ft, depending on the number of beds, and rooms cost from 2200 to 2650 Ft per person, depending on the size (of the room, not the person).

Another year-round hostel in student accommodation is *Martos Hostel* (☎ 463 3777), XI Sztoczek utca 5-7. It's well-located near the Danube in Buda, between Petőfi and Szabadság bridges. Singles cost as little as 1800 Ft and doubles, triples and quads cost from 1400 Ft per person. There are also small apartments. In summer there's free email and net access.

Travellers' summer hostels include: *Ho(s)tel California* (☎ 140 8585), XIII Váci utca 21, mid-June to late August; *Hostel Bánki* (☎ 312 5268), VI Podmaniczky utca 8, early July to late August; *Hostel Donáti* (☎ 201 1971), II Donáti utca 46, mid-June to September; and *Hostel Kek* (☎ 371 0066), XI Szüret utca 2-18, July to late August.

Private Rooms Assigned by local travel agencies, private rooms are reasonable value. They generally cost from 2000 Ft per person, with a 20% supplement if you stay less than four nights. To get a single or a room in the centre of town, you may have to try several offices. There are lots of rooms and even in July and August you'll be able to find something. You'll probably need an indexed city map to find your room.

Although there are lots of 'traditional' private rooms, where you share a flat with a family, others are run by entrepreneurs who

rent empty flats and sublet them as private rooms. You'll have more privacy in a place like this but you'll also have other guests – maybe travellers or maybe heavy-drinking Russian workers.

The following is a list of various agencies, beginning with those closest to the transportation terminals. Most are open only during normal business hours, so if you arrive late or on a weekend, try the 24-hour Welcome Hotel Service at V Apáczai Csere János utca 1 near the Duna Marriott Hotel (metro: Ferenciek tere). This office was thinking of relocating at the time of writing – if it does, it will be nearby in the same street, with the same phone number. If you arrive at Keleti train station between 11.10 pm and 4.30 am when the metro isn't running, catch night bus No 78 from outside the nearby Grand Hotel Hungária at VII Rákóczi út 90 to Erzsébet Bridge.

You may be offered a private room by entrepreneurs at the railway stations and elsewhere. These vary considerably and cases of travellers being promised an idyllic room in the centre of town, only to be taken to a dreary, cramped flat in some distant suburb, are not unknown. You really have to use your own judgment.

Keleti Train Station The Ibusz office in the Keleti train station (☎ 342 9572; open weekdays to 6 pm and Saturday to 4 pm) has private rooms from 1800 Ft per person, but there are few singles. Express, next to Ibusz, has private rooms from about Ft 2300 per person.

Nyugati Train Station The tourist information office on platform 10 arranges expensive private rooms from 5000/6500 Ft and pensions from DM40/46. Also try Budapest Tourist (open weekdays from 9 am to 4.30 pm) in the underground concourse at the entrance to the metro below Nyugati train station. More rooms are for rent at Volántourist, VI Teréz körút 38, also near Nyugati. A Cooptourist office is in the opposite direction at V Kossuth Lajos tér 13 across from the Parliament (metro: Kossuth Lajos tér).

Erzsébet Tér Bus Station Dunatours at VI Bajcsy-Zsilinszky út 17 behind St Stephen's

Basilica has reasonable rooms. Also nearby is Ibusz at V Október 6 utca 8. One of the largest offices in the city offering private rooms is Budapest Tourist (☎ 118 6600), V Roosevelt tér 5 (open weekdays from 9 am to 5 pm). Singles/doubles start around 3000/4000 Ft.

Near the International Ferry Pier Some of Budapest's least expensive private rooms are available from Ibusz, V Ferenciek tere 10 (metro: Ferenciek tere), open weekdays to 7 pm and Saturday to 2 pm. The 24-hour Welcome Hotel Service (☎ 118 4848, 118 5776), V Apáczai Csere János utca 1 near the Duna Marriott Hotel, is also within walking distance of both the pier and the international bus station. It has singles/doubles from 2500/3000 Ft.

Near Déli Train Station At Déli train station private rooms are arranged by Ibusz, at the entrance to the metro and open weekdays to 6 pm and Saturday to 1 pm, or by Budapest Tourist, in the mall in front of the station. Also try Cooptourist, I Attila út 107, directly across the park in front of Déli train station.

Hotels – Budget A hotel room costs more than a private room, though the management doesn't mind if you stay only one night. There are no cheap hotels right in the city centre, but *Domnik Panzió* (☎ 343 7655), XIV Cházár András utca 3, beside a large church on Thököly út, is just two stops northeast of Keleti train station on bus No 7 (black number). The 33 rooms with shared bath are 3900/4600 Ft a single/double. The price includes breakfast. This friendly pension is a convenient place to stay for a few nights.

Hotel/Hostel Flandria (☎ 350 3181), XIII Szegedi út 27, is easily accessible on tram Nos 12 and 14 from Lehel tér metro station. Rooms with shared bath in this big tourist hotel cost DM32/44/54/64 a single/double/triple/quad, less in winter. There are also hostel-style rooms from DM10. *Hotel/Hostel Góliát* (☎ 270 1456), XIII Kerekes utca 12-20, is two blocks away from the Flandria and charges about the same. This huge 11-storey block accommodates workers as well as tourists.

If you've always dreamed of staying in a castle on the Danube consider the *Citadella Hotel* (☎ 166 5794) in the Citadella above the Hotel Gellért. But check it out carefully first as it's deteriorating and (apart from the location) not great value unless you are in a group. Big, clean (if musty) rooms go for 6780 Ft for one or two people, with shared bath; 7400 Ft with a leaky shower. However, the toilets are communal and they're some of the most unpleasant this side of Bombay. Dorm beds cost 1280 Ft but they are often usually booked by groups.

Hotel Express (☎ 175 3082), XII Beethoven utca 7-9, several blocks southwest of Déli train station (take tram No 59 for two stops), charges from 2330 Ft per person in twin rooms with shared bathroom and also has dorms from 1410 Ft.

Hotels – Mid-Range There's a shortage of mid-range hotels. The best is the *Medosz Hotel* (☎ 374 3000), VI Jókai tér 9 (metro: Oktogon). It's close to everything and the rooms are reasonable. The drawback is that it's often full (especially the single rooms), so book well in advance. All rooms have private bath and satellite TV but no phone, and cost DM40/60 in low season, DM56/80 in high. The hotel takes cash only – no credit cards, no travellers cheques.

Büro Panzió (☎ 212 2929), II Dékán utca 3, off the north side of Moszkva tér, looks basic from the outside but the rooms (which cost DM60/80/100 a single/double/triple, less in low season) are comfortable and all have a bathroom and TV.

If both the Medosz and the Büro are full you'll have to compromise on quality, location or both. The old *Park Hotel* (☎ 313 1420), VIII Baross tér 10, directly across from Keleti train station, costs 4950/5950 Ft for a small single/double without bath, from 8900 Ft with shower. It's bearable but it does provide a time-trip back into the dingy communist past.

Hotel Touring (☎ 250 3184), III Pünkösd Fürdő utca 38, at the north-west end of Budapest, has singles/doubles with shower for DM55/65 (less in winter) and DM43/55 with shared bath. Triples/quads with shared bath cost DM74/87. It's a 10-minute walk from Békásmegyer HÉV Station (ask directions from the station).

Hotels – Top End Choose any of the following for their location, special amenities or 'face-giving' qualities: the old world *Gellért Hotel* (☎ 185 2200) at XI Szent Gellért tér 1 with singles/doubles from DM207/348; the *Budapest Hilton* (☎ 214 3000) on Castle Hill at I Hess András tér 1 (from DM270/360); and *Hotel Thermál* (☎ 311 1000) on Margaret Island (DM193/240). These hotels have lower winter rates and also offer weekend packages and other deals.

Places to Eat
Pest Restaurants *Café Talk Talk*, Magyar utca near the corner of Reáltanoda utca, is a hip and handy city-centre place for a drink, a snack or a meal. Breakfast costs 390 Ft, felafels are 180 Ft and more substantial main courses start around 500 Ft. It doesn't get many tourists.

Stop, V Váci utca 86 at Fővám tér (metro: Kálvin tér), offers a good variety of fish and meat dishes plus several vegetarian selections. Prices are reasonable (most dishes 300 to 400 Ft), the menu is in many languages, and it's open almost 24 hours a day. Even better is the ever popular (and nearby) *Fatál*, V Váci utca 67, which serves massive Hungarian meals on wooden platters. Main courses are around 1000 Ft. Typical Hungarian meals are also served at *Alföldi*, V Kecskeméti utca 4 (metro: Kálvin tér). Most main courses cost between 200 and 600 Ft.

The friendly *Karcsi*, VI Jókai utca 20, a block back from Teréz körút and four blocks from Nyugati train station, serves very reasonable Hungarian meals weekdays from 11 am to 9 pm. Most main courses cost under 450 Ft.

The popular Italian-run *Okay Italia* has branches at XIII Szent István körút 20 and V Nyugati tér 6. You'll spend around 1200 Ft for a couple of courses, coffee and a beer. Also in the Nyugati area at Jókai utca 30 (corner of Podmaniczky utca), *Crazy Café* is a laid-back bar (with 100 bottled beers and 25 on tap) and a good restaurant, serving Hungarian standards and Italian dishes at reasonable prices. Across the road at Podmaniczky utca 14, *Sir Lancelot* is a medieval theme restaurant serving enormous portions. The *Mongolian Barbecue*, XII Malvány utca 19a, offers all the food you can eat and all the

beer you can drink for 1500 Ft before 5 pm, 1900 Ft after. It's popular with backpackers.

For excellent Greek food go to *Jorgosz* at VII Csengery utca 24. It isn't cheap (starters from 250 Ft, main courses between 750 and 1200 Ft) but it's worth it.

There are some good vegetarian restaurants. *Gandhi*, in a cellar at V ker Vigyázó Ferenc utca 4, is excellent and is open from noon until late daily. The menu is limited but changes daily and a very large serve costs about 750 Ft and a small serve 550 Ft. Salad is sold by weight, at 180 Ft per 100g. Other places well worth trying include *Vegetárium*, V Cukor utca 3 just off Ferenciek tere (noon to 10 pm daily), and the more stodgy *Mirtusz*, VI Zichy Jenö utca 67, where the daily set lunch costs under 400 Ft. The Hari Krishna-run *Govinda*, an Indian vegetarian restaurant, is at V Belgrád rakpart 18.

For a kosher lunch, head for *Hannah*, in a courtyard behind the Orthodox Synagogue at VII Dob utca 35 (open weekdays from 11.30 am to 4 pm only). Nearby at 31 Kazinsky, *Carmel Restaurant* isn't kosher but does specialise in Central European Jewish dishes.

Dine in style (and empty your wallet) at the restaurant upstairs at *Duna Palota*, V Zrínyi utca 5 (open daily from noon to 11 pm). Most dishes cost well over 1000 Ft. This elegant palace, erected in 1894, was formerly a military officers' club. If you're not discouraged by the prospect of spending something like 5000 Ft per person for dinner, *Gundel*, next to the zoo directly behind the Museum of Fine Arts at XIV Állatkerti út 2 (metro: Széchenyi Fürdő), is probably Budapest's fanciest restaurant, with a tradition dating back to 1894. Budapest cognoscenti, though, have abandoned Gundel to the expense-account brigade and flock to *Bagolyvár*, Gundel's little sister next door. It's open daily from noon to 11 pm. See the New York Café in the later Cafés section for less expensive dining in magnificent surroundings.

Buda Restaurants Expensive restaurants popular with tourists and *nouveau riche* Hungarians abound in the Castle District. *Budavári Sörözo*, across from the Hilton, is a cosy pub that's a little less expensive than most. *Café Miro*, Úri utca 30, is a bright, modern place, good for a coffee or a meal such as sandwiches (190 Ft), ham and eggs (350 Ft) or steak (800 Ft).

Away from the Castle District, hearty Hungarian meals are served at *Söröző a Szent Jupáthoz*, II Retek utca 16 a block north of Moszkva tér. The menu is posted outside in English and it's open 24 hours a day. Recommended by locals for its Hungarian cuisine, *Paksi* isn't a cheapie but it's reasonable, with most dishes well under 1000 Ft and steaks from 1100 Ft. It's on Margit körút three or four blocks south-west of Margit Bridge.

Il Treno, XII Alkotás utca 15, is an upbeat location across the street from Déli train station. Pastas starts around 450 Ft and pizzas cost between 650 and 910 Ft. The salad bar makes this place a good choice for vegetarians. *Gerber Banya-Tanya*, half a block up from Il Treno on XII Nagyented utca, is a good local place.

The simple but excellent Italian fare at *Marcello*, XI Bartók Béla út 40, attracts students from the nearby university.

Fast Food & Cheap Eats Fast-food places like McDonald's, Pizza Hut, Kentucky Fried Chicken and Wendy's outlets abound, but old-style self-service restaurants, the mainstay of both white and blue-collar workers in the old regime, where full meals can cost under 400 Ft, are disappearing fast. One of the few left in Pest is *Bölcs Bagoly*, V Váci utca 33 (metro: Ferenciek tere), open weekdays from 11.30 am to 3 pm. There's a similar *self-service* place at V Arany János utca 5 open weekdays from 11.30 am to 4 pm only and another, *Tranzit*, near Keleti on the corner of Hernád and Dembinszky utcas.

Oddly enough, there are two self-service restaurants in the Castle District: *Akadémia* above the police station at I Országház utca 30 (take the lift to the 3rd floor) is open from 11.30 am to 2 pm, and there's another above the *Fortuna Spaten restaurant*, directly across the street from the Hilton Hotel on I Fortuna utca. Go into the arched passage and the entrance is on the left. It's open weekdays from 11 am to 2.30 pm.

Bear in mind that, while cheap, self-service restaurants usually serve mediocre food. Much better value at lunch are the butcher shops that serve cooked sausage and occasionally roast chicken, like *Gasztró Hús-Hentesáru* at II Margít körút 2, opposite the first stop of tram Nos 4 and 6 on the west side of Margaret Bridge.

Even better are the wonderful little restaurants called *étkezde* – not unlike British caffs – that serve simple dishes that change every day. One of the best is *Kisharang*, V Október 6 utca 17 (open weekdays to 8 pm, weekends to 3.30 pm) with main courses for under 200 Ft.

Middle Eastern food is served at *Semiramis*, V Alkotmány utca 20 (additional seating upstairs). One of the healthiest and least expensive places to eat in is *Felafel Faloda*, VI Paulay Ede utca 53 (metro: Opera or Oktogon). It's strictly vegetarian, and you pay a fixed price to stuff a piece of pitta bread or fill a plastic container yourself from the great assortment of salad bar options. There's also a large selection of teas. The bright, modern décor attracts a young crowd (open weekdays from 10 am to 8 pm only).

Cabar, V Iranyi utca 25, around the corner from the Vegetárium restaurant, has Israeli-style shwarma and felafel, which you eat standing up. There's a self-service salad bar – you'll be charged by the weight of the food you select. It's open Monday to Saturday from 10 am to 11 pm. Another place for Middle Eastern food (mainly gyros and cakes) is the tiny *Iran Persia Sandwich Club*, on IX Ráday utca near Coquan's Kavé.

Cafés Like Vienna, Budapest is famous for its cafés and cake shops and the most famous of the famous is *Gerbeaud*, on the west side of V Vörösmarty tér, a fashionable meeting place for the city's elite since 1870. But sorry to say that in recent years this place has become pretentious and overpriced.

Művész, VI Andrássy út 29, almost opposite the State Opera House, is a more interesting place to people-watch than Gerbeaud and has a better selection of cakes at lower prices. It's open 24 hours a day, although there isn't much more than coffee on offer in the early hours. Cheaper yet is nearby *Perity*, VI Andrássy út 37, with unbelievably rich desserts, great ice cream and drinks with prices clearly displayed.

The sumptuous *New York Café*, VII Erzsébet körút 9-11 (metro: Blaha Lujza tér), has been a Budapest institution since 1895. The turn-of-the-century décor glitters around the literati who still meet here. There's also a restaurant and prices aren't too bad (main courses between 1500 and 2500 Ft), considering the surroundings and the service. To help pay for the upkeep there's a door charge of 250 Ft, which is deducted from your bill if you give your receipt to the waiter. It's open from noon to midnight.

For the best coffee in town head for one of the two *Coquan's Kavé* cafés at V Nádor utca 5 and IX Ráday utca 15. They have a long list of coffees and a few cakes, plus toasted bagels for breakfast. A bonus is that they are non-smoking. Another non-smoking place is *Brooklyn Café*, Kecskeméti utca, not far from the corner of Múzeum körút. There's nothing special about it, but it's not far from the National Museum so it's a handy refuelling stop.

The perfect place for coffee and cakes up in the Castle District is the very crowded *Ruszwurm*, I Szentháromság utca 7 near Matthias Church. Two more good cafés on the Buda side are *Angelika*, I Batthyány tér 7 and the untouristy *Caffé Déryné* at I Krisztina tér 3.

Markets The *Nagycsarnok* (central market hall) on Fővám tér (metro: Kálvin tér) is Budapest's finest. There are some quite good food stalls on the upper level serving everything from Chinese spring rolls to enormous German sausages.

There are large supermarkets everywhere including the *Julius Meinl* supermarket on Blaha Lujza tér and *Kaiser's* opposite Nyugati train station in Pest. *Rothschild* is another large chain; its branch at VII Nyár utca 1 sells kosher products only.

Entertainment

Opera & Operetta You should pay at least one visit to the *State Opera House*, VI Andrássy út 22 (metro: Opera), to hear a concert and to see the frescoes and incredibly rich decoration inside. The box office is on the left-hand side of the building behind the tour office (closed on Monday).

Budapest has a second opera house, the modern (and ugly) *Erkel Theatre* at VIII Köztársaság tér 30 near Keleti train station. Tickets are sold just inside the main door

(Tuesday to Saturday from 11 am to 7 pm, Sunday from 10 am to 1 pm and 4 to 7 pm).

Operettas are presented at the *Budapest Operetta Theatre* at VI Nagymező utca 17. Tickets are sold at the box office at No 19 of the same street, and it's worth checking here in summer as there are often special programs.

Musicals are performed at the *Madách Theatre*, VII Erzsébet körút 31-33 (metro: Blaha Lujza tér). The Madách presents an interesting mix of rock operas, musicals and straight drama in Hungarian – it's worth investigating.

Classical Music The *Koncert Kalendárium* lists all concerts each month, and most nights you'll have several to choose from. The motto of the Budapest Spring Festival in late March is '10 days, 100 venues, 1000 events' and you'll have a good selection of musical events each night. Budapest's main concert hall is the *Pesti Vigadó*, V Vigadó tér 2 (metro: Vörösmarty tér). Other concerts are held at the stunning *Liszt Academy of Music* at VI Liszt Ferenc tér 8 (metro: Oktogon).

Tánchaz & Dance Authentic folk-music workshops (*tánchaz* or 'dance house') are held at least once a week but unfortunately usually not between July and September. Venues include the *Municipal Cultural House* (Fővárosi Művelődési Ház) at XI Fehérvári út 47 in Buda; the *Kalamajka Tánchaz* at V Molnár utca 9; and the *Marczibányi Művelődési Ház*, II Marczibányi tér 5a.

Most people come to tánchaz evenings to learn the folk dances that go with the music. These workshops have nothing to do with tourism and are a great opportunity to hear musicians practising and get involved in a local scene at next to no expense. You become part of the program instead of merely watching others perform.

The Hungarian State Folk Ensemble performs at the *Budai Vigadó*, I Corvin tér 8 (metro: Batthyány tér); the Danube Folk Ensemble at the stately *Duna Palota*, V Zrínyi utca 5, just off Roosevelt tér; and the Rajkó Folk Ensemble at the *Bábszinház*, Andrássy Ave 69. Tickets to each of these cost 3300 Ft and you can make reservations on ☎ 117 2754.

Every Monday, Friday and Saturday from May to mid-October at 8.30 pm, the more touristy Folklór Centrum presents Hungarian dancing accompanied by a Romani orchestra at the *Municipal Cultural House*. This performance is one of the best of its kind.

Pubs & Clubs *Nothin' But the Blues*, VIII Krúdy utca 6, is cheap and popular with backpackers, and has music every night. Check the crowded *Old Man's Music Pub*, VII Akácfa utca 13, with a lively bar area, a cramped music venue (nightly from 9 pm) and a pizzeria (3 pm to 3 am). Less grungy is the *Irish Cat Pub*, V Múzeum körút 41. There's sometimes music. *Beckett's Irish Bar*, V Bajcsy-Zsilinzky u'72 is another lively pub.

One of Budapest's top discos is *Bahnhof*, VI Váci út 1. It attracts a 20-something crowd and is open Wednesday to Saturday from 9 pm. It doesn't play techno. *Franklin Trocadero*, VI Szent István körút 15, is older and plays great canned Latin, with live acts usually from Wednesday to Sunday. *Bamboo*, not far from Nyugati station at VI Dessewffy utca 44, is open from 7 pm and closes 'when you drop dead'. It's into funk.

Tilos az Á, VIII Mikszáth Kálmán tér 2, off Baross utca (metro: Kálvan tér), presents live blues or rock-and-roll groups from Thursday to Saturday nights and sometimes also on Wednesday. Some of the best music in Budapest is heard here.

Jazz The *Merlin Jazz Club*, V Gerlóczy utca 4, around the corner from Károly körút 28 (metro: Deák tér), has live music nightly from 10 pm.

The *Jazz Café* in a cellar at V Balassi Bálint 25 is flooded in blue light that makes the smoky air appear more dense, and the music starts at 8 pm on Monday, Wednesday, Friday and Saturday.

Gay & Lesbian Venues There are no women-only clubs, but lesbians frequent *Angel*, VII Szövetség utca 33, a gay venue that is becoming increasingly mixed. *Mystery Bar*, V Nagysándor József utca 3, is a quiet gay bar (open from May), a good place to take a date, while the name of the *Action Bar*, V Magyar utca 42, says it all. Take the usual precautions.

Circus The *Grand Circus* in the City Park at XIV Állatkerti körút 7 (metro: Széchenyi Fürdő), has performances on weekends at 10 am; Wednesday, Thursday, Friday and Saturday at 3 pm; and Wednesday, Friday, Saturday and Sunday at 7 pm (closed in summer). The matinées are occasionally booked out by school groups, but there's almost always space in the evening. Seats at weekday performances cost from 300 to 600 Ft, 50 Ft more on weekends.

Planetarium & Puppets The *Planetarium* (☎ 263 0871; metro: Népliget) features exciting laser light shows to the accompaniment of music ranging from Pink Floyd to Mozart, with different music on different days. Shows are held from Monday to Saturday at 7 and 9 pm. Tickets (1190 Ft) are sold at the door from 6 pm and at most ticket agencies.

The *Puppet Theatre*, VI Andrássy út 69 (metro: Vörösmarty utca), presents shows designed for children during the day and occasional evening programs for adults. The kids' shows are generally held at 3 pm Monday to Thursday and at 10.30 am and 4 pm Friday to Sunday. Tickets cost 180 Ft during the week and from 200 to 350 Ft on weekends. The theatre is closed all summer.

Ticket Agencies The busiest theatrical ticket agency is the *Színházak Központi Jegyiroda*, VI Andrássy út 18 (metro: Opera), open weekdays from 9 am till 6 pm. It has tickets to numerous theatres and events (including visiting rock acts), although the best are gone a couple of days in advance. The staff are aggressively non-English-speaking. For opera or ballet tickets, go to the office next door at No 20. It's open weekdays from 10 am to 5.30 pm. For concert tickets try *Nemzeti Filharmónia Jegyiroda*, V Vörösmarty tér 1 (metro: Vörösmarty tér). It's open weekdays from 10 am to 6 pm, to 2 pm on Saturday.

Things to Buy

Before you do any shopping for handicrafts at street markets, have a look in the Folkart Centrum, V Váci utca 14 (metro: Ferenciek tere), a large store where prices are clearly marked. It's open till late at night. Most of the stuff for sale at folk-art shops (népművészeti bolt) is created for the tourist trade, but much is still pretty and unique to Hungary. You might still be able to buy 'real' crafts from Transylvanian women at Moszkva tér or at the market on the corner of Fehérvári út and Schönherz utca in Buda's District XI.

Upstairs at the far back corner of the central market hall on Fővám tér (metro: Kálvin tér), a number of stalls sell Hungarian folk costumes, dolls, painted eggs, embroidered tablecloths etc.

The Zeneszalon on the Danube side of Vörösmarty tér has CDs of Hungarian folk music, including a few by the excellent Romani band Kalyi Jag, and the popular Hungarian folk group Muzsikás. For locally produced classical CDs and tapes, try the Liszt Ferenc Zeneműbolt at VI Andrássy út 45.

There's an excellent selection of Hungarian wines at the Boutique des Vins at V József Attila utca 12 – enter on Hild tér. Ask the staff to recommend a label if you feel lost.

Getting There & Away

Air The main ticket office for Malév Hungarian Airlines is at V Dorottya utca 2 near Vörösmarty tér. For information call ☎ 235 3804 or free-call outside Budapest on ☎ 06-8021 2121. Other major carriers and their locations are as follows:

Aeroflot
   (☎ 118 5892) V Váci utca 4
British Airways
   (☎ 118 3299) VIII Rákóczi út 3
Lauda
   (☎ 266 3169) V Aranykéz utca 4-6
Lufthansa
   (☎ 266 4511) V Váci utca 19-21
SAS
   (☎ 266 2633) V Bajcsy-Zsilinszky út 12
Swissair
   (☎ 267 2500) V Kristóf tér 7-8

See also To/From the Airport in the following Getting Around section.

Bus For details of international bus services see the general Getting There & Away section earlier in this chapter.

There are three important bus stations. Most buses to Western Europe as well as to Prague, Bratislava, Slovenia and Croatia leave from the international bus station at Erzsébet tér (☎ 117 2562 for international services, 117 2345 for national services; metro: Deák tér). There's a left-luggage office inside the station open daily from 6 am to 6 pm (8 pm Friday). The international ticket office, upstairs, is open weekdays from 6 am to 7 pm (6 pm in winter) and 6.30 am to 4 pm on weekends. Note that a new theatre is being built next to this bus station; it will eventually move out to Kelenfold train station in Buda.

Some buses for Eastern Europe and destinations east of the Danube as well as Turkey and Sweden leave from the bus station at Népstadion (☎ 252 1896 for international services, 252 4496 for national services; metro: Népstadion), XIV Hungária körút 48-52. The left-luggage office there keeps similar hours to the one at Erzsébet tér. The international ticket window is open weekdays from 5.30 am to 6 pm, Saturday 5.30 am to 4 pm. On Sunday try paying the driver. The clerks at Népstadion speak very little English, so study the posted timetables and then write down what you want. Also, many of the buses here originate in other countries, so the information window (open from 5.30 am to 9 pm) might not have the latest information.

Buses to the Danube Bend leave from the bus station next to Árpád híd metro station.

Train The three main train stations are each on a metro line.

Keleti train station at Baross tér (metro: Keleti pályaudvar) handles domestic trains to and from the north and north-east. Trains for the Great Plain and the Danube Bend arrive and depart from Nyugati train station (metro: Nyugati pályaudvar). For trains bound for Transdanubia and Lake Balaton, go to Déli (pronounced 'daily') train station (metro: Déli).

The handful of secondary stations are of little importance to travellers. Occasionally, though, a through train in summer will stop only at Kőbánya-Kispest train station (the terminus of the blue metro line) or even at Kelenföld train station in Buda. When the new metro line connects Kelenföld with central Pest it's possible that more trains will be routed here.

For details of international trains, see Getting Around, earlier in this chapter.

Car & Motorcycle Prices are very high. One of the cheapest outfits is Inka (☎ 117 2150), V Bajcsy-Zsilinszky út 16. Its least expensive car – a Suzuki Swift – costs US$24/151 a day/week plus US$0.24 per kilometre, or US$420 a week with unlimited kilometres. Insurance is US$12 a day extra. You have to be aged 23 or over. The big international companies charge even more.

The 25% ÁFA (value-added tax) doesn't apply to foreigners who sign an affidavit saying they do not intend to stay in Hungary more than 180 days.

Hitching Super Kenguru (☎ 266 5857), VIII Kőfaragó út 15 (metro: Blaha Lujza tér), matches up drivers and riders for a fee – mostly to points abroad. The cost is around 6.5 Ft per kilometre, and approximate one-way fares include: Amsterdam 9300 Ft, London 10,900 Ft, Munich 4700 Ft, Paris 9900 Ft, Prague 3500 Ft and Vienna 1800 Ft. The office is open weekdays from 8 am till 6 pm, weekends from 10 am to 2 pm.

Boat Mahart ferries (☎ 118 1704) to Vienna depart from the International Ferry Pier (*Nemzetközi hajóállomás*) on Belgrád rakpart, just north of Szabadság Bridge on the Pest side in District V. For fares, see the introductory Getting There & Away section.

Mahart river ferries and, in summer, hydrofoils link Budapest with the towns of the Danube Bend (see that section for fares and schedules). In the capital the boats leave from below Vigadó tér (metro: Vörösmarty tér) on the Pest side. The first stop is at Batthyány tér in Buda.

Getting Around
To/From the Airport
There are two terminals about 5km apart at Ferihegy airport, which is 16km south-east of Budapest. Malév, Delta, Lufthansa, Alitalia and Air France flights arrive and depart from Terminal 2; all other airlines use Terminal 1. This could change, so ask which terminal you're departing from when confirming your flight.

With much cheaper options for getting to/from Ferihegy, it would be senseless to take a taxi and risk a major rip-off.

The Airport Minibus Service (☎ 296 8515/55) picks up passengers wherever they're staying – hotel, hostel or private home. But there are drawbacks: you have to book 24 hours in advance and, as the van seats about half a dozen people, it can be a time-consuming process. When you book they ask what flight you're catching and time the pick-up to get you there in time. This apparently works. The fare is 1200 Ft. Tickets into the city are available in the airport arrival halls.

An easier way to go is on the Centrum Bus, which runs every half-hour between 5.30 am and 9.30 pm and charges 600 Ft. It takes about 30 minutes to Terminal 1 and 40 minutes to Terminal 2. The stop (which has a timetable) is across from Erzsébet tér on the corner of Miatyárk utca, outside the big Corvinus Kempinsky Hotel. The yellow metro line's Deák tér entrance is close by.

6x6 Volán Taxi (☎ 1 666 666) offers a 2200 Ft fare to the airport if you make a phone booking.

The cheapest way to go is to take the blue metro to the end of the line (the Kőbánya-Kispest stop) and board bus No 93. Note that both the red express and black No 93 are good for Ferihegy 1; only the red one carries on to Ferihegy 2. This costs about half what you pay on the Centrum Bus but is much more nerve-wracking if you're hurrying for a flight.

The general flight information phone number at the airport is ☎ 296 9696.

Public Transport Three underground metro lines meet at Deák tér: M1, the little yellow line from Vörösmarty tér to Mexikoi út; M2, the red line from Déli train station to Örs vezér tere; and M3, the blue line from Újpest-Központ to Kőbánya-Kispest. A possible source of confusion on M1 is that one stop is called Vörösmarty tér and another is Vörösmarty utca. The HÉV (pronounced 'heave') suburban railway, which runs north from Batthyány tér, is almost like a fourth metro line.

A new metro line linking Kelenföld train station with the existing metro network is planned.

There's also an extensive network of tram, trolleybus and bus services; you'll seldom wait more than a few minutes for any of them. On certain bus lines the same numbered bus may have a black or a red number. The red-numbered bus is the express, which makes limited stops. An invaluable transit map detailing all services is available at most metro ticket booths.

The metro operates from 4.30 am till just after 11 pm. Certain tram and bus lines operate throughout the night. After 8 pm you must board buses through the front doors and show the driver your ticket or transit pass.

Travelling 'black' (ticketless) is more risky than ever; with increased surveillance (including a big crackdown in the metro), there's a good chance you'll get caught. Tickets are always checked on the HÉV. The on-the-spot fine is 1000 Ft, which rises dramatically if you pay later at the BKV office at VII Akácfa utca 22.

We've heard stories about scams connected with metro fines (pay them only to officials with good ID) and some people seem to resent the fact that they are caught travelling without a ticket. If you do get nabbed, do us all a favour – shut up and pay up. The inspectors (and your fellow passengers) hear the same stories every day.

Fares & Transit Passes To use public transport you must buy tickets at a kiosk, newsstand or metro entrance. To travel on trams, trolleybuses, regular buses and the HÉV (as far as the city limits) the fare is a flat 70 Ft. On the metro the fare is 30 Ft if you are just going three stops within 30 minutes. Five stops in one hour with one change (transfer) at Deák tér to another metro line costs 45 Ft. Unlimited stops travelled with one transfer is 110 Ft. You must always travel in one continuous direction on a metro ticket; return trips are not allowed. Tickets have to be validated in machines at metro entrances and on the other vehicles.

Life is much simpler if you buy a pass. Passes are valid on all trams, buses, trolleybuses, HÉV (to city limits) and metro lines, and you don't have to worry about validating your ticket each time you get on. Passes will also save you money.

A seven day pass costs 1450 Ft. Longer periods are available but you'll need a photo. All but the monthly passes are valid from midnight to midnight, so buy them in advance and specify the date(s) you want. The easiest place to buy a pass is at the ticket window of a metro station. If the clerk's English and your Hungarian aren't good, try saying, eg *hetijegy* (one week).

Taxi Taxis aren't cheap and, considering the excellent public transport network, you won't have to use them much. Overcharging (due to rigged meters or long detours) is common and we've even heard from readers who were threatened by taxi drivers. Taxis with no name on the door and only a removable light box on the roof are the most likely to cheat you. Never get into a taxi that does not have a yellow licence plate (as required by law), the logo of a reputable taxi firm on the side doors and a table of fares posted on the dashboard inside.

As a rule of thumb, avoid taxis which are expensive cars, and don't take one from a rank outside an upmarket hotel. A trip from, say, City Park to Deák tér should cost under 1000 Ft. Fares are lower if you phone a taxi rather than hailing one on the street.

Following are the telephone numbers of reliable taxi firms. You can call them from anywhere (the dispatchers usually speak English), and they'll arrive in a matter of minutes. Make sure you know the number of the phone you're calling from, as that's how they establish your address.

City	☎ 211 1111
Tele 5	☎ 155 5555
Fő	☎ 122 2222
Rádió	☎ 177 7777
Volán	☎ 166 6666
Buda	☎ 233 3333

MÁV, the railway company, runs minibuses between train stations for 600 Ft and 'anywhere in Budapest' for 1900 Ft. These prices aren't great compared with an honest taxi and if there are other passengers the trip could take a while.

Boat Between May and September passenger ferries depart from Boráros tér, beside Petőfi Bridge, and Pünkösd Fürdő north of

Aquincum, with many stops along the way. Tickets (70 to 250 Ft) are usually sold on board. The ferry stop closest to the Castle District is Batthyány tér, and Petőfi tér is not far from Vörösmarty tér, a convenient place to pick up the boat on the Pest side.

Private boats at the foot of Margaret Bridge on the Pest side will take you to Római Fürdő from Thursday to Sunday. You can return to Budapest on the HÉV from there.

Daily from May to late August and on April weekends there are 1½-hour Mahart cruises (700 Ft) on the Danube, departing at noon. Buy your ticket and board the boat at a small ticket office by the river at Vigadó tér (metro: Vörösmarty tér). In season there's a choice of evening cruises, at 7 pm (700 Ft) and a slightly longer cruise at 7.45 pm, with folk music (800 Ft).

The Danube Bend

Between Vienna and Budapest, the Danube breaks through the Pilis and Börzsöny hills in a sharp bend. Here medieval kings once ruled Hungary from majestic palaces overlooking the river at Esztergom and Visegrád. East of Visegrád, the river divides, with Szentendre and Vác facing different branches and long, skinny Szentendre Island in the middle. Today the historic monuments, easy access, good facilities and forest trails combine to put this scenic area at the top of any visitor's list. This is the perfect place for a Danube River cruise.

Getting There & Away
You can reach the Danube Bend from Budapest by rail, road, and river. The HÉV suburban railway runs to Szentendre, while local trains from Budapest's Nyugati train station serve Nagymaros and Esztergom. Szentendre, Visegrád and Esztergom are accessible by bus from the bus station at Árpád Bridge. All of these services are fairly frequent and in summer Mahart riverboats stop at most of the places described in this section.

SZENTENDRE
☎ 26
If you only have a short time in Hungary, a trip to Szentendre (St Andrew in English), 19km north of Budapest on an arm of the Danube, should be on your itinerary. A stroll through the narrow, winding streets between the city's exotic Serbian Orthodox churches or along the Danube embankment is an enchanting experience.

Not so enchanting are the fleets of international tour buses that roll in, and the tourist traps that cater to them. Travellers who have a few days to spare can find similar enchantment with far less commercialism in towns and cities farther afield.

In the late 17th century Serbian merchants fleeing the Turks settled here, giving the place something of a Balkan flavour. Although most of them returned home in the 19th century, the Serbian appearance remained. In the early years of this century, Szentendre became a favourite of painters and sculptors, who founded an artists' colony here. It has been known for its art and artists ever since and galleries abound.

Orientation
From the HÉV and bus station, it's a short walk under the subway and up Kossuth Lajos utca to Fő tér, the centre of the old town. The Duna korzó – the river embankment – is a block east of this square. The Mahart riverboat terminal at the end of Czóbel Béla sétány and the camping ground on Pap Island are one and 2km farther north. There's no left-luggage office at Szentendre's HÉV and bus station.

Information
Tourinform (☎ 317 965), Dumtsa Jenő utca 22, has brochures and information on other parts of Hungary as well as Szentendre. It's open weekdays from 10 am to 4 pm, to 2 pm on Saturday and Sunday. The main post office is at Kossuth Lajos utca 23-25 across from the stations.

Money Beware of the exchange offices on Fő tér, which give a much lower rate than the bank. The OTP Bank is at Dumtsa Jenő utca 6, just off Fő tér. There's a K&H Bank at Bogdányi utca 11 with an ATM.

Things to See
Begin your sightseeing with Fő tér, which on summer evenings becomes a stage for

theatrical performances. Many of the buildings around this colourful square date from the 18th century, as does the plague cross (1763) in the centre and the **Blagoveštenska Church** (1752), the Greek Orthodox church on the north-east corner.

In an alley off the east side of Fő tér is the **Margit Kovács Museum**, in an 18th-century salt house at Vastagh György utca 1 (250 Ft). Kovács (1902-77) was a ceramicist who combined Hungarian folk, religious and modern themes to create Gothic-like figures. The **Ferenczy Museum**, Fő tér 6 beside the Orthodox church, displays the artwork of the Ferenczy clan, pioneers of the Szentendre artists' colony (90 Ft).

Narrow stepped lanes lead up from Fő tér to Castle Hill and the **Parish Church of St John** (rebuilt in 1710), from where you get splendid views of the town. In the warmer months, a weekend folk market is held in the square here. The **Béla Czóbel Museum** (90 Ft) is opposite the church. Just north is the tall red tower of **Belgrade Church** (1764), the finest of the town's Serbian churches. Beside the church is the **Serbian Ecclesiastical Art Collection** (100 Ft).

All of the museums are closed Monday and the ecclesiastical collection shuts on Tuesday as well.

The very large **Hungarian Open-Air Ethnographic Museum**, which includes reassembled houses and buildings from around the country, is quite a way north-west of Szentendre on Sztaravodai út. Buses from stand No 8 at the bus station run there about 10 times a day. It's open daily, except Monday, from 9 am to 5 pm April to October only. There's often a seasonal festival or everyday village activities going on, and tickets are a bargain at 250 Ft, or 4000 Ft for a guided tour in English, German, French or Italian.

Activities

You can rent bicycles in the courtyard behind Kossuth Lajos utca 17-19 from 200 Ft for one hour (less for longer rentals). Take the hourly ferry across to Szentendre Island and you'll have kilometres of uncrowded cycling. The Hajós restaurant, in the boat moored next to the posh Duna Club Hotel at Duna korzó 5 just north of the centre, rents boats and jet skis.

Places to Stay

You can easily see Szentendre on a day trip from Budapest, but the town makes a good base for the Danube Bend.

Camping Two km north of Szentendre near the Danube riverboat landing is *Pap Sziget Camping* (☎ 310 697), open May to October. Camping is 1500 Ft for two persons with a tent, and bungalows with bath cost DM50 for two people. The motel rooms with shared bath are DM8 per person. Reception is open from 8 am to 4 pm only. To get there, take bus No 1, 2 or 3.

Private Rooms Both Ibusz and Dunatours on Bogdányi utca organise private rooms from around 3500 Ft, but you might not find either office open outside peak times.

Pensions & Hotel There are quite a few pensions, most relatively expensive. Dunatours might be able to find you a double room for 4000 Ft. The most central pension is *Bükkös* (☎ 312 021), halfway between the stations and Fő tér at Bükkös 16. Good singles/doubles with bath are DM55/65. Other places that are cheaper but less convenient include *Villa Apollo* (☎ 310 909), just off the ring road at Méhész utca 3; the nearby *Coca-Cola* (☎ 310 410), Dunakanyar körút 50; and *Villa Castra* (☎ 311 240), farther north at Ady Endre út 54.

Out of season, the upmarket *Danubius Hotel* (☎ 312 489), by the river at Ady Endre utca 28, has specials such as doubles for DM50.

Places to Eat

Régimódi, on the corner of Fő tér and Futó utca just down from the Margit Kovács Museum, occupies an old Szentendre house. Another old stand-by is *Rab-Ráby* at Péter-Pál utca 1.

There are a couple of Italian places on Duna korzó: *Ristorante da Carlo* at No 6-8 is a relatively expensive restaurant with tables outside in summer, while *Pizza Andreas* at No 5a is a more simple affair.

Dixie Chicken, Dumtsa Jenő utca 16, is your standard local fast-food joint, but it does have a salad bar and you can sit in the back courtyard. Check the *lángos stall*, halfway

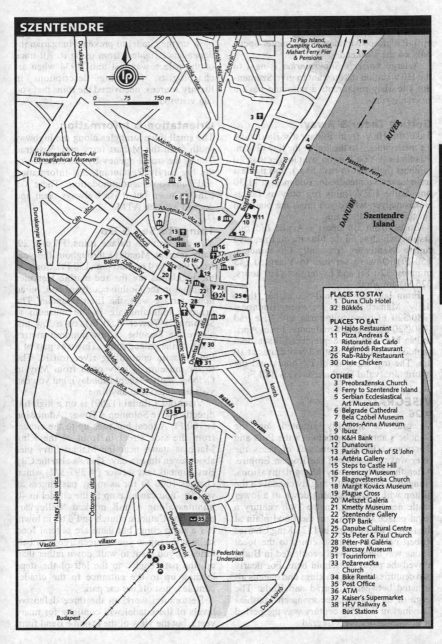

SZENTENDRE

To Pap Island,
Camping Ground,
Mahart Ferry Pier
& Pensions

1 ■
2 ▼

0   75   150 m

RIVER

Passenger Ferry

DANUBE

Szentendre
Island

HUNGARY

To Hungarian Open-Air
Ethnographical Museum

Dunakanyar körút

Dunakanyar

Istáló-Béla utca

Bartók-Béla utca

Bogdányi utca

Duna körző

Martinovics utca

Pátriárka utca

Cseh utca

Alkotmány utca

Rákóczi

F   Fő tér

Bajcsy-Zsilinszky utca

Kossuth Lajos utca

Kucsera Ferenc utca

Duna körző

Bükkös Part

Papírmalmi utca

Bükkös
Stream

Kanonok utca

Dumtsa Jenő utca

Kossuth Lajos utca

Ortorony utca

Nagy Lajos utca

Vasúti   villasor

Dunakanyar körút

Pedestrian
Underpass

To
Budapest

Duna körző

3 ✝
5 🏛
6 ✝
7 🏛
8 🏛
9
10 ●
11
12 ●
13 🏛 Castle
14   Hill
15
16
17
18 🏛
19 ⚓
20
21
22
23
24 $
25 ●
26 ▼
27
28
29 🏛
30 ▼
31
32 ■
33 🏛
34 ●
35 ✉
36 $
37
38

PLACES TO STAY
1 Duna Club Hotel
32 Bükkös

PLACES TO EAT
2 Hajós Restaurant
11 Pizza Andreas &
   Ristorante da Carlo
23 Régimódi Restaurant
26 Rab-Ráby Restaurant
30 Dixie Chicken

OTHER
3 Preobraženska Church
4 Ferry to Szentendre Island
5 Serbian Ecclesiastical
   Art Museum
6 Belgrade Cathedral
7 Bela Czóbel Museum
8 Ámos-Anna Museum
9 Ibusz
10 K&H Bank
12 Dunatours
13 Parish Church of St John
14 Artéria Gallery
15 Steps to Castle Hill
16 Ferenczy Museum
17 Blagoveštenska Church
18 Margit Kovács Museum
19 Plague Cross
20 Metszet Galéria
21 Kmetty Museum
22 Szentendre Gallery
24 OTP Bank
25 Danube Cultural Centre
27 Sts Peter & Paul Church
28 Péter-Pál Galéria
29 Barcsay Museum
31 Tourinform
33 Požarevačka
   Church
34 Bike Rental
35 Post Office
36 ATM
37 Kaiser's Supermarket
38 HÉV Railway &
   Bus Stations

up Váralja lépcsö, the narrow set of steps between Fő tér 8 and 9 going up to Castle Hill. It's closed Monday and in winter opens only on the weekend.

A large *Kaiser's Supermarket* is next to the HÉV station if you want to give Szentendre's touristy restaurants a miss and have a riverside picnic.

Getting There & Away

Take the HÉV from Budapest's Batthyány tér metro station to the end of the line (21km, 40 minutes). You'll never wait longer than 20 minutes (half that in rush hour), and the last train leaves Szentendre for Budapest at 11.30 pm. Some HÉV trains run only as far as Békásmegyer, where you cross the platform for the Szentendre train.

Buses from Budapest's Árpád híd bus station, which is on the blue metro line, also run to Szentendre frequently (30 minutes, 150 Ft). Onward services to Visegrád (45 minutes, 220 Ft) and Esztergom (1½ hours, 325 Ft) are good.

From late May to mid-September, three daily Mahart ferries between Budapest (780/520 Ft one-way/return) and Visegrád (780/520 Ft) stop at Szentendre. From April to late May and late September till seasonal shutdown, only one boat a day operates at 10 am. The trip takes about 1½ hours and the return fare (valid for three days) is 560 Ft.

VISEGRÁD

☎ 26

Visegrád is superbly situated, on the Danube's abrupt loop between the Pilis and Börzsöny hills. For hundreds of years the river was the border of the Roman Empire. After the 13th century Mongol invasions, Hungarian kings built a mighty citadel on the hilltop with a wall running down to a lower castle near the river. In the 14th century a royal palace was built on the flood plain at the foot of the hills and in 1323 King Charles Robert of Anjou, whose claim to the local throne was being fiercely contested in Buda, moved the royal household here. For nearly two centuries Hungarian kings and queens alternated between Visegrád and Buda. The reign of the Renaissance monarch Matthias Corvinus in the 15th century was the period of greatest glory for Visegrád.

The destruction of Visegrád came with the Turks and later in 1702 when the Habsburgs blew up the citadel to prevent Hungarian independence fighters from using it. All trace of the palace was lost until 1934 when archaeologists, following descriptions in literary sources, uncovered the ruins that you can visit today.

Orientation & Information

The small town straggles along the highway south from the Mahart ferry pier. Visegrad Tours, the travel agency by the entrance of the big Sirály Restaurant, has information and can book accommodation. There's a bank in town but it isn't always open and doesn't have an ATM.

Things to See & Do

You can visit the **palace ruins**, Fő utca 29, daily (except Monday) throughout the year from 9 am to 4 or 4.30 pm (150 Ft). Some of the highlights are the red-marble Hercules Fountain in the Gothic courtyard and, on an upper terrace wall, the Lion Fountain. The original fountains are in the museum at **Solomon's Tower** (150 Ft), on a low hill above the Danube, a few hundred metres north of the palace ruins. This was part of a lower castle controlling river traffic. The tower museum is only open from May to October, daily (except Monday), but you can visit the exterior at any time.

Visegrád Citadel (1259) is on a high hill directly above Solomon's Tower. Admission is 180 Ft. A local bus runs up to the citadel from the side street in front of the King Matthias statue near the Mahart ferry pier about seven times a day. There's also the City Bus minibus taxi service (☎ 397 372) which charges 1000 Ft for as many passengers as will fit. You can hike up to the citadel in 40 minutes along a trail marked 'Fellegvár' behind the Catholic church on Fő tér in town. It's a steep climb but there are several food stalls at the top so you can recharge your batteries. If you want to walk down rather than up, the path begins to the left of the steps leading up to the entrance to the citadel complex, just off the car park.

Restoration work on the three defensive levels of the citadel will continue for many years, but the view of the Danube Bend from

VISEGRÁD

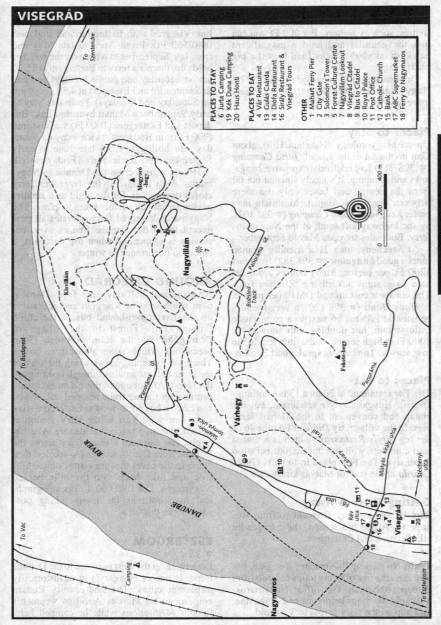

PLACES TO STAY
6 Jurta Camping
19 Kék Duna Camping
20 Haus Honti

PLACES TO EAT
4 Vár Restaurant
13 Gulás Csárda
14 Diófa Restaurant
16 Sirály Restaurant & Visegrád Tours

OTHER
1 Mahart Ferry Pier
2 City Gate
3 Solomon's Tower
5 Forest Cultural Centre
7 Nagyvillám Lookout
8 Visegrád Citadel
9 Bus to Citadel
10 Royal Palace
11 Post Office
12 Catholic Church
15 Bank
17 ABC Supermarket
18 Ferry to Nagymaros

the walls is well worth the climb. There's a small museum and some quasi-medieval activities, such as archery. For 200 Ft you can don the gauntlet and hold a magnificent hawk, or, if you're lucky (and brave) a big puszta eagle.

On another hill nearby is the 377m **Nagyvillám Lookout Tower**, which offers more fabulous views.

Places to Stay

Up on Mogyoróhegy (Hazelnut Hill), about 2km north-east of the citadel, *Jurta Camping* (☎ 398 217) has relatively expensive bungalows and camping. It's nicely situated but far from the centre, and buses only run there between June and August. Motorists may prefer *Kék Duna Autos Camping* (☎ 398 102), by the highway just south of the Nagymaros ferry. Both sites are open May to September.

At Széchenyi utca 21 a friendly woman rents a good *bungalow* (☎ 398 382) from just 1200 Ft per person. Many houses along Fő utca have signs advertising 'Zimmer frei'. The cheapest cost around DM10 per person.

Haus Honti (☎ 398 120), a very friendly pension at Fő utca 66 next to a picturesque little stream, has doubles with shower for 2000 Ft in high season, and a little less in the low season. The owners speak good English.

Places to Eat

The *Vár* restaurant at Fő utca 13 is a nothing-special, Hungarian-style restaurant, but it's cheap and convenient to the Mahart ferry pier. In the village, try *Diófa* at Fő utca 46 or the big *Sirály Restaurant* which is a tourist trap complete with live music, but isn't too expensive. The best place in town is *Gulás Csárda* at the start of Mátyás király utca.

Getting There & Away

Bus Buses are very frequent to/from Budapest's Árpád híd station, the Szentendre HÉV station and Esztergom.

Train No railway line reaches Visegrád, but you can take one of many trains to Szob from Budapest-Nyugati. Get off at Nagymaros-Visegrád, six stops before the end of the line, and hop on the ferry across to Visegrád.

Ferry & Hydrofoil Between late May and mid-September, three daily Mahart ferries link Visegrád with Esztergom and Budapest (840/560 Ft). From April to late May and from late September to whenever the weather holds up, there's a ferry to Esztergom at 11.20 am on Saturday and public holidays and one to Szentendre and Budapest at 4.30 pm (4 pm on Saturday and holidays). From late May to early September a Mahart hydrofoil links Budapest and Esztergom (1000 Ft) via Visegrád (900 Ft from Budapest) twice a day on Saturday and holidays; from late June to early September these ferries run on Friday as well.

Hourly ferries cross the Danube to Nagymaros. Don't panic if the large car ferry closes down early for the night as a smaller passenger launch usually takes its place. The Nagymaros-Visegrád ferry operates all year except when the Danube freezes over, but service is suspended when fog descends, a common occurrence in winter.

AROUND VISEGRÁD

An excellent half-day hike from **Dömös**, 6km south-west of Visegrád and accessible on the Esztergom-bound bus, is the climb through Pilis Forest to the village of **Dobogókő** via the Rám szakadék (Rám precipice), which takes about three hours. There are sweeping views along the way of the river and mountains through openings in the forest. At Dobogókő there's an excursion centre with further trails mapped out, or you can catch a bus north-west to Esztergom (five a day) or south-east to the HÉV station at Pomáz, one stop before Szentendre. Alternatively, you can take a small ferry across the Danube from Dömös to Dömösi átkéles, then climb to the caves that are visible on the hillside and hike back into the hills behind Nagymaros. The 1:40,000 *A Pilis* topographical map outlines the many hiking possibilities in this area.

ESZTERGOM
☎ 33

Esztergom, at the west entrance to the Danube Bend, is one of Hungary's most historically important cities. The 2nd-century Roman emperor-to-be Marcus Aurelius wrote his famous *Meditations* while he camped here.

Stephen I, founder of the Hungarian state, was born and crowned at Esztergom, and it was the royal seat from the late 10th to the mid-13th centuries. After the Mongol invasion of 1241, the king moved the court to Buda, but Esztergom continued as the ecclesiastical centre of Hungary and remains so today. Originally the clerics lived by the riverbank while royalty lived in the hill-top palace. When the king departed, the archbishop moved up and occupied the palace, maintaining Esztergom's prominence. In 1543 the Turks ravaged the town and much was rebuilt in the 18th and 19th centuries.

Esztergom can be reached by ferry to/from Štúrovo, making the city an important gateway to Slovakia.

Orientation

The train station is at the southern edge of town, a 10-minute walk south of the bus station. From the train station, walk north on Baross Gábor út, then along Ady Endre utca to Simor János utca. The ticket clerk at the train station holds luggage (open 24 hours), but no left-luggage service is available at the bus station.

While the Cathedral area and the banks of the Danube and Little Danube are peaceful and pretty, the small town centre is a bad mixture of drab architecture and relatively heavy traffic (this is surprising, given the importance of the town to Hungarians).

Information

Three travel agencies which might be able to help with information are Komturist (☎ 312 082), Lörincz utca 6; Gran Tours (☎ 417 052), Széchenyi tér 25; and Express (☎ 313 113), Széchenyi tér 7.

For an honest taxi phone ☎ 340 403.

Money The OTP Bank on Rákóczi tér in the centre of town is open Monday from 8 am to 3.30 pm, Tuesday to Thursday from 8 am to 2.30 pm and Friday from 8 am to 12.30 pm. There's a K&H branch with an ATM diagonally across the square.

Post The post office is at Arany János utca 2, just off Széchenyi tér.

Things to See & Do

The bus station is a couple of blocks southeast of Széchenyi tér and the **Town Hall** (1773). A block south is the **Inner City Parish Church** (1757), near a branch of the Danube lined with small houseboats. Cross the footbridge to Primas Island and follow Gőzhajó utca directly across to the Mahart riverboat landing on the main Danube channel.

Around 200m north stand the ruins of the **Mária Valéria Bridge**, the only bridge that spanned the Danube between Budapest and Komárom. The bridge was destroyed by the retreating Germans at the end of WWII and was never rebuilt.

Continue north along the river and cross the bridge to the **Watertown Parish Church** (1738). Esztergom's **Christian Museum** (closed Monday; 100 Ft) is in the adjacent Primate's Palace (1882) at Berényi Zsigmond utca 2. This is the best collection of medieval religious art in the country. A plaque on the side of the Primate's Palace bears the name 'József Mindszenty' and is dated 26 December 1948. Cardinal Mindszenty was arrested that day for refusing to allow the Catholic schools of Hungary to be secularised; in 1949 he was sentenced to life imprisonment for treason. Freed during the 1956 uprising, Mindszenty was soon forced to seek refuge in the US Embassy in Budapest where he stayed until 1971. In 1974 Mindszenty was sacked as Primate of Hungary for his criticism of the Pope's dealings with the communist regime and he died in Vienna in 1975. Nearby at Pázmány Péter utca 13 is the **Bálint Balassi Museum** (closed Monday; 50 Ft) with objects of local interest. The poet Balassi died defending Esztergom from the Turks in 1594.

You can't miss **Esztergom Cathedral**, built on a hill high above the Danube and the largest church in Hungary. The building was rebuilt in the neoclassical style in the 19th century, but the white and red marble **Bakócz Chapel** (1510) on the south side was moved here from an earlier church. Underneath the cathedral is a large **crypt** (entry 150 Ft); among those at rest down here is the late Cardinal Mindszenty, whose remains were brought here in 1991. Most interesting is the **treasury** (150 Ft) to the right behind the altar. Many priceless and artistically beautiful medieval objects are kept here, including the historically important 13th-century Hungarian coronation cross. Sometimes the staircases to the top of the cathedral are open to visitors.

Beside the cathedral, at the southern end of the hill, is the **Castle Museum** (closed Monday; 150 Ft) with partially reconstructed remnants of the medieval royal palace (1215). The views from this hill are great. If you want to continue on to Visegrád after visiting the cathedral, there's no need to

return to the bus station – you can pick up the bus on nearby Iskola utca.

The **Danube Museum** (closed Tuesday), Kölcsey Ferenc utca 2, provides much information on the river through photos and models, though most of the captions are in Hungarian. Along the way, at Imaház utca 4, you'll pass the **Technical House** (1888), which once served as a synagogue for Esztergom's Jewish community, the oldest in Hungary.

The outdoor **thermal baths** (100/70 Ft) are open May to September from 9 am to 6 pm.

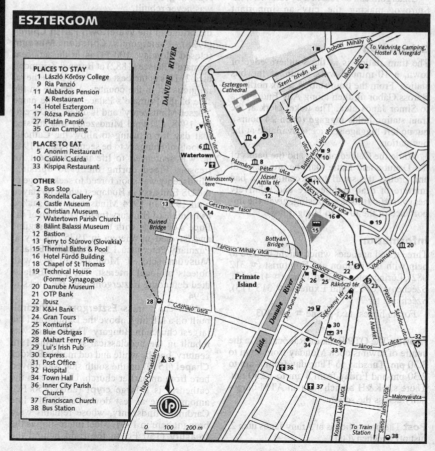

ESZTERGOM

PLACES TO STAY
1 László Kőrösy College
9 Ria Panzió
11 Alabárdos Pension & Restaurant
14 Hotel Esztergom
17 Rózsa Panzió
27 Platán Pansió
35 Gran Camping

PLACES TO EAT
5 Anonim Restaurant
10 Csülök Csárda
33 Kispipa Restaurant

OTHER
2 Bus Stop
3 Rondella Gallery
4 Castle Museum
6 Christian Museum
7 Watertown Parish Church
8 Bálint Balassi Museum
12 Bastion
13 Ferry to Štúrovo (Slovakia)
15 Thermal Baths & Pool
16 Hotel Fürdő Building
18 Chapel of St Thomas
19 Technical House (Former Synagogue)
20 Danube Museum
21 OTP Bank
22 Ibusz
23 K&H Bank
24 Gran Tours
25 Komturist
26 Blue Ostrigas
28 Mahart Ferry Pier
29 Lui's Irish Pub
30 Express
31 Post Office
32 Hospital
34 Town Hall
36 Inner City Parish Church
37 Franciscan Church
38 Bus Station

0   100   200 m

You can use the indoor pool the rest of the year from 6 am to 6 pm (Saturday to 1 pm, Sunday to noon).

Places to Stay

Camping *Gran Camping* (☎ 402 513 or ☎ 489 563) is by the Danube, down a quiet lane. It's open from May to the end of September, although it might be open at other times if there's a group. A tent site for two people costs about DM19, a dorm bed is DM10, a four-person self-contained bungalow is DM70 and a double room is DM50.

Private Rooms & Hostel See Gran Tours for private rooms (from 1400 Ft) or apartments (about 4000 Ft). Express can help with summertime dormitory rooms for about 800 Ft at the *trade school* near the train station at Budai Nagy Antal utca 38 and *László Kőrösy College*, Szent István tér 16.

Pensions & Hotel The large *Platán Panzió* (☎ 411 355), Kis-Duna sétány 11, charges just 1200 Ft for a single with shared bath, or 3000 Ft for a double with a bathroom shared with the room next door. This place is good for travellers on a tight budget, although the rooms are small (but clean) and there's a bit of an institutional atmosphere.

Another cheap place is *Rózsa Panzió* (☎ 313 581) above Bajcsy-Zsilinszky utca at Török Ignác utca 11, with doubles from 3000 Ft. Nearby are two nicer, but more expensive, places: *Alabárdos* (☎ 312 640) down the hill and around the corner at Bajcsy-Zsilinszky utca 49 with singles/doubles for 4500/5500 Ft, and the *Ria Pension* (☎ 313 115), Battyany Lajos utca 11, with singles/doubles in both a new and an older building for 4500/6000 Ft.

Hotel Esztergom (☎ 350 0377) looks like it might be a 1970s hotel now in decline, but it's actually quite good. It's also well located, overlooking the Danube and close to everything but without traffic noise. Room rates are 4900/9500 Ft and there's a reasonable restaurant.

Places to Eat & Drink

Csülök Csárda, Batthyány utca 9, is popular with both visitors and locals and serves good home cooking and huge main courses from 700 Ft. *Anonim*, in a historical townhouse at Berényi Zsigmond utca 4, is convenient to the museums in Watertown but closes at 9 pm. A popular old-style place is *Kispipa* at Kossuth Lajos utca 19, east of Széchenyi tér.

For a drink and snack, try *Luis' Irish Pub*, Széchenyi tér, or *Blue Ostrigas*, a small, local bar on Lörincz utca.

Getting There & Away

Bus Buses from Budapest's Árpád híd bus station are frequent. Buses from Budapest to Esztergom may travel via Dorog (75 minutes) or via Visegrád and Szentendre (two hours).

Buses to Budapest run about every half-hour from 5 am to 8 pm, to Vise-grád and Szentendre hourly from 6 am to 8.40 pm and to Sopron and Győr twice daily.

Train Trains to Esztergom depart from Budapest's Nyugati train station (53km, 1½ hours) up to a dozen times a day. To get to western Transdanubia from Esztergom, take one of the three daily trains to Komárom. This trip takes nearly two hours to cover about 50km because for a long way the train runs (well, walks) slowly along the wooded bank of the Danube. It's a slow but pretty trip.

Ferry & Hydrofoil A ferry crosses the Danube to Štúrovo in Slovakia 10 times a day between 7.20 am and 4.20 pm and it costs another 250/150 Ft to take a car/bicycle along.

Mahart riverboats travel to/from Budapest (900/600 Ft one-way/return, 3¾ hours) three times a day from late May to late September, but you must change at Visegrád. From April to late May and late September to seasonal shutdown, there's only one a day on Saturday and holidays.

From late May to early September a hydrofoil links Budapest and Esztergom (1000 Ft) via Visegrád twice a day on Saturday and holidays; from late June to early September this runs on Friday as well.

Western Transdanubia

Beyond the Bakony Hills, north-west of Lake Balaton, lies western Transdanubia, a region bounded by the Danube and the Alps. Conquered by the Romans but never fully occupied by the Turks, this enchanting corner of Hungary contains picturesque small towns and cities with a decidedly European air. The old quarters of Sopron and Győr are brimming with what were once the residences of prosperous burghers and clerics, Kőszeg offers an intact medieval castle, Fertőd a magnificent baroque palace and Pannonhalma a functioning Benedictine monastery. This region is also a convenient gateway to/from Austria and Slovakia and points farther north and west.

Getting There & Away

Many trains link Sopron to Austria and you can cross into Slovakia from Komárom. From Budapest's Déli train station there are trains to Komárom, Győr, Sopron and Szombathely. Rail links to/from the Danube Bend (Komárom-Esztergom) and Lake Balaton (Komárom-Székesfehérvár as well as Győr-Veszprém) are also good, though travelling south-east from Sopron and Szombathely is often easier by bus.

KOMÁROM
☎ 34

Komárom is the gateway to Hungary for visitors arriving from Komárno in Slovakia. Until 1920 these two towns were one. Komárom's position is the only thing that makes it of interest to travellers. There's a good camping ground next to the public thermal baths within walking distance of the train station and border crossing, and a couple of inexpensive hotels should you arrive late in the afternoon and want to spend the night. But you'll be gone in the morning, no doubt about it.

Orientation & Information

The train station is very close to the highway bridge to/from Slovakia; the bus station is 100m to the south. The train station in Komárno is 2km to the north of the bridge.

Komturist (☎ 341 767), a travel agency, is at Mártírok útja 19a in the centre of town (open weekdays from 8 am to 3.30 pm). Walk straight south from the bridge down Igmándi út to Jókai Mór tér and you'll find it a block to the east on the right-hand side. A map of this area is in the Komárno section of the Slovakia chapter.

The OTP Bank, just east of Komturist at Mártírok útja 21, is open Monday from 8 am to 5 pm, Tuesday to Thursday to 3 pm and Friday to 2 pm. The post office is near the Béke Hotel on the corner of Kállai Tivadar utca and József Atilla utca.

Things to See & Do

Among the sights of Komárom are two large 19th-century fortifications that were built by the Habsburgs. Csillagvár (Star Castle) is near the river just north-east of the Hotel Thermál. The Igmándi Fortress is on the south side of town. Right next to Hotel Thermál are the thermal baths. To get there from the bridge, go south for two blocks and then turn east on Táncsics Mihály utca.

Places to Stay

Komturist should have private rooms for about 1400 Ft per person, but they're usually fully booked. The closest hotel to the Danube bridge is the Béke Hotel (☎ 340 333), Bajcsy-Zsilinszky út 8. It's a bit dingy but cheap, at 3800/4000 Ft a single/double with shared bath.

Thermal Hotel & Camping (☎ 342 447), Táncsics Mihály utca 38, charges 4000/5300 Ft a single/double (less in winter) and motel-style units are 1500 Ft for up to three people without bath or breakfast, but they're only available from mid-April to mid-October. There's also a hostel section charging 800 Ft. It costs from 520 to 650 Ft to pitch a tent.

Hotel Karát (☎ 342 222), Czuczor Gergely utca 54, two blocks west of the baths, charges 6000/8000 Ft for a single/double, not bad for a three-star hotel.

Getting There & Away

Though there are hourly runs to Tata, bus services from Komárom are generally limited. Count on only two a day to Budapest, four to Esztergom, three to Győr, one to Sopron and, on weekdays only, five to Komárno, where you can catch a local train to Bratislava (100km).

On the other hand, train services from Komárom to Budapest (94km, 1½ hours), Győr (37km, 35 minutes) and Sopron (122km, two hours) are fairly frequent. (Most trains on this line depart from Budapest-Keleti but some use Budapest-Déli.) For the Danube Bend, catch a train to Esztergom (three daily, 53km, 1¾ hours), and for Lake Balaton go via Székesfehérvár (nine daily, 82km, 1½ hours).

GYŐR
☎ 96

Győr (Raab in German) is a historic city midway between Budapest and Vienna at the point where the Mosoni-Danube, Rábca and Rába rivers meet. In the 11th century, Stephen I established a bishopric here on what was the site of a Roman town named Arrabona. In the mid-16th century a fortress was erected at Győr to hold back the Turks.

Győr (pronounced 'jyeur') is Hungary's third-largest industrial centre, but you'd never know it standing in the charming old centre. Most travellers give it a miss, but it's less touristy than Esztergom, Sopron or Eger and well worth a visit.

In March, Győr hosts many events in conjunction with Budapest's Spring Festival.

Orientation
The large neo-baroque City Hall (1898) rises up across from the train station. The left-luggage office at the station (open daily from 5 am to midnight) is next to the exit from one of the two tunnels under the tracks (the one farther away from the city). This same tunnel leads directly through to the main bus station, which is just south of the train station. Baross Gábor utca, which leads to the old town and the rivers, lies diagonally across from City Hall.

Information
There's a Tourinform office (☎ 311 771) in the pedestrian mall on the corner of Árpad út and Baross Gábor utca. Ciklámen Tourist (☎ 96-311 557) is at Aradi vértanúk útja 22, a block north of the train station.

There's a 24-hour shop on the corner of Teleki László and Schweidel utcas (and a tiny 24-hour bar next door).

If you catch a taxi in Győr, keep your eyes on the meter, as some operators aren't all they could be.

Money There's an OTP Bank at Árpád út 36 next to the Rába Hotel and another one at Baross Gábor utca 16. Both are open weekdays only. If both are closed, the reception desk at the Rába Hotel will change travellers cheques. There are quite a few ATMs around the town centre.

Post There's a post office next to the train station. The main one is at Bajcsy-Zsilinszky út 46.

Things to See
Follow Aradi vértanúk útja north to Bécsí kapu tér, where you'll find the enchanting **Carmelite church** (built in 1725 and recently renovated) and many fine baroque palaces. On the north-west side of the square are the fortifications built in the 16th century to stop the Turks. A short distance east at Király utca 4 is **Napoleon House**, where Monsieur Bonaparte spent his only night in Hungary in 1809. It's now a picture gallery.

Continue north on the narrow street up to Chapter Hill (Káptalandomb), the oldest part of Győr. The large baroque **Cathedral** on the hill was originally Romanesque, but most of what you see inside dates from the 17th and 18th centuries. The baroque ceiling frescoes are fine, but don't miss the Gothic **Héderváry Chapel** on the south side of the church, which contains a glittering 15th-century bust of King (and St) Ladislas. Opposite the cathedral is the fortified **Bishop's Castle** in a mixture of styles.

The streets behind the cathedral are full of old palaces, and at the bottom of the hill on Jedlik Ányos utca is the outstanding **Ark of the Covenant**, a large baroque statue dating from 1731. A colourful open-air market unfolds on nearby Dunakapu tér to the north-east. There's a good view of the rivers from the bridge.

One of the nicest things about Győr is its atmospheric old streets. Take a stroll down Bástya utca, Apáca utca, Rákóczi Ferenc

GYŐR

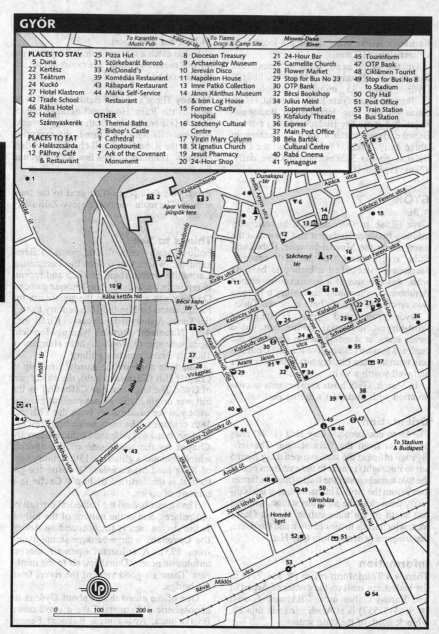

To Karantén Music Pub
Kálóczy-tér
To Tiamo Disco & Camp Site
Mosoni-Duna River

PLACES TO STAY
5 Duna
22 Kertész
23 Teátrum
24 Kuckó
27 Hotel Klastrom
42 Trade School
46 Rába Hotel
52 Hotel Szárnyaskerék

PLACES TO EAT
6 Halászcsárda
12 Pálfrey Café & Restaurant

25 Pizza Hut
31 Szürkebarát Borozó
33 McDonald's
39 Komédiás Restaurant
43 Rábaparti Restaurant
44 Márka Self-Service Restaurant

OTHER
1 Thermal Baths
2 Bishop's Castle
3 Cathedral
4 Cooptourist
7 Ark of the Covenant Monument

8 Diocesan Treasury
9 Archaeology Museum
10 Jereván Disco
11 Napoleon House
13 Imre Patkó Collection
14 János Xánthus Museum & Iron Log House
15 Former Charity Hospital
16 Széchenyi Cultural Centre
17 Virgin Mary Column
18 St Ignatius Church
19 Jesuit Pharmacy
20 24-Hour Shop

21 24-Hour Bar
26 Carmelite Church
28 Flower Market
29 Stop for Bus No 23
30 OTP Bank
32 Bécsi Bookshop
34 Julius Meinl Supermarket
35 Kisfaludy Theatre
36 Express
37 Main Post Office
38 Béla Bartók Cultural Centre
40 Rabá Cinema
41 Synagogue

45 Tourinform
47 OTP Bank
48 Ciklámen Tourist
49 Stop for Bus No 8 to Stadium
50 City Hall
51 Post Office
53 Train Station
54 Bus Station

To Stadium & Budapest

0   100   200 m

utca, Liszt Ferenc utca and Király utca, where you'll see many fine buildings. The late Renaissance **palace** at Rákóczi Ferenc utca 6 was once a charity hospital. Go inside to see the courtyards.

Széchenyi tér is the heart of Győr and features a **Column of the Virgin** (1686) in the middle. **St Ignatius Church** (1641) is the finest church in the city with superb pulpit, pews and ceiling frescoes. At Széchenyi tér 9 is the **Jesuit Pharmacy** (closed weekends), a fully operational baroque institution! Cross the square to visit the **János Xantus Museum**, Széchenyi tér 5, which is in a palace built in 1743. Beside it at Széchenyi tér 4 is the **Iron Log House**, which still sports the beam into which itinerant artisans would drive a nail to mark their visit. The building now houses the **Imre Patkó Collection** of paintings and Asian and African art, one of Hungary's finest small museums.

Pannonhalma Abbey If you have a half-day to spare, it's worth visiting Pannonhalma Abbey, on top of a 282m hill some 21km south of Győr. English-language tours (600 Ft) include the Gothic cloister (1486), into the Romanesque basilica (1225) and down to the 11th-century crypt. A half-dozen organ and choral concerts are held in the basilica between April and December.

Pannonhalma is best reached from Győr by bus (up to a dozen a day) as the train station is a couple of kilometres south-west of the abbey (though up to six local trains between Győr and Veszprém stop at Pannonhalma every day).

Activities

Győr's well-maintained **thermal baths** (open daily May to September) are west of the Rába River. To get there, cross Rába kettős híd (Rába Double Bridge) over the little island and walk north to Ország út 4. The covered pool is open all year from 6 am to 8 pm on weekdays, 7 am to 6 pm at weekends. The pools and grassy strand are open between May and September.

Places to Stay

Camping *Kiskút-liget Camping* (☎ 411 042), near the stadium some 3km north-east of town, has a motel open all year (2500/3200

Ft a single/double, 3500/4700 Ft triples/quads) and unpleasant bungalows for up to four people (3000 Ft) open between mid-April and mid-October. Tent sites cost about 300 Ft. Bus No 8 from beside the City Hall runs here.

Private Rooms & Hostels Private rooms are available from Ciklámen Tourist and Ibusz, Kazinczy utca 3. Singles are scarce and these offices close at about 4.30 pm.

Ask Express, Bajcsy-Zsilinszky út 41 (open weekdays from 8 am to 3.45 pm) about dormitory accommodation in summer at the huge *college*, at Ságvári Endre utca 3 north of the river, or at the trade school west of the old town on the corner of Erkel Ferenc utca and Kossuth Lajos utca opposite the old synagogue.

Pensions Győr is full of small private pensions and, while not the cheapest places to stay, they are usually very central and in some of the city's most colourful old buildings.

Kuckó (☎ 316 260), in an old townhouse at Arany János utca 33, has eight doubles with bath from 3600/4200 Ft for singles/doubles. The smaller *Kertész* (☎ 317 461) at Iskola utca charges 4500/5600 Ft. The pick of the crop, though, and under the same management, are *Teátrum* (☎ 310 640) at No 7 of the pedestrianised Schweidel utca and the *Duna* (☎ 329 084), with antique furniture at Vörösmarty utca 5. Singles/doubles at both are 4500/5500 Ft; triples/quads are 6000/7500 Ft. Prices rise in summer.

Hotels *Hotel Szárnyaskerék* (☎ 314 629), at Révai Miklós utca 5 directly opposite the train station, charges 3150 Ft for a double with washbasin and 4700 Ft for one with a bath. The hotel's name means 'flying wheel', which is the symbol of MÁV.

Cheaper but not as central, *Hotel Stop* (☎ 416 999), Mészáros Lőrinc utca 20, is about a 25-minute walk north-east of the centre. To get there, follow Baross híd across the railway overpass and turn left onto Hunyadi/Csaba utca, which then becomes Mészáros Lőrinc utca. It's a classic run-down 'modern' hotel, but the rooms are large (most are two-room apartments) and the manager friendly. The tariff for two/three people is

3300 Ft/4300 Ft. Bus No 23 from the city centre stops outside.

The four-star *Hotel Klastrom* (☎ 315 611), just off Bécsi kapu tér at Zehmeister utca 1 charges from DM106 a night for rooms in a 250-year-old Carmelite convent. This is a great place if you can afford it.

Places to Eat
Rábaparti, Zehmeister utca 15, serves tasty, reasonably-priced Hungarian fare in an unpretentious (though rather gloomy) restaurant. The *Pálfrey* café on the north-west corner of Széchenyi tér is an obvious place for a snack or drink, inside or at the outdoor tables. Downstairs there's a good restaurant where a decent meal costs around 1700 Ft.

A typical inn with fish dishes near the market is *Halászcsárda*, Apáca utca 4. The lunch menu can cost as little as 250 Ft. *Komédias Restaurant*, Czuczor Gergely utca is also worth trying, with most main courses around 600 Ft and a set-menu meal from 280 Ft.

For a cheap self-service meal, try *Márka*, Bajcsy-Zsilinszky út 30 (set-menu meal from 150 Ft), open weekdays from 7.30 am to 4.30 pm, weekends from 7 am to 2.30 pm.

A decent wine cellar is the *Szürkebarát Borozó*, Arany János utca 20 (closed Sunday). A stairway in the courtyard leads down into this vaulted restaurant. Only cold dishes are available at lunch.

There's a *Pizza Hut*, *McDonald's* and a *Julius Meinl Supermarket* on Baross Gábor utca.

Entertainment
The celebrated Győr Ballet and the city's opera company and philharmonic orchestra all perform at the modern *Kisfaludy Theatre*, Czuczor Gergely utca 7, a technically advanced though rather unattractive structure covered in op art tiles by Victor Vasarely. The *Béla Bartók Cultural Centre*, which stages less highbrow performances like folk dances and rock operas, is at Czuczor Gergely utca 17. Győr Summer is a month-long festival of music, theatre and dance from late June to late July.

Jereván in the middle of the island in the Rába River and *Tiamo* on Héderváry utca north of the centre are Győr's most popular clubs.

Getting There & Away
Bus Buses of possible interest include those to Balatonfüred (eight daily, 99km), Budapest (at least hourly, 123km), Esztergom (two daily, 87km), Hévíz (two daily, 214km), Kecskemét (one daily, 208km), Keszthely (five daily), Pannonhalma (hourly, 21km), Pécs (two daily, 241km), Székesfehérvár (eight daily, 87km) and Vienna (four daily, 122km). To get to Fertőd, you must take the Sopron bus to Kapuvár (up to 12 a day) and change there.

Train Győr is well connected by express train to Budapest's Déli and Keleti train stations (125km, 1½ hours) and to Sopron (85km, one hour). Other trains go to Szombathely (117km, 1¾ hours) via Celldömölk. To go to Lake Balaton there's a secondary line with five or six local trains a day going south to Veszprém (79km, 2½ hours) via Pannonhalma.

To go to/from Vienna's Westbahnhof (126km) you may have to change trains at Hegyeshalom since some express trains don't pick up passengers at Győr. Another route to Austria is through Sopron, an infrequent service run by a private concern called GySEV and not part of the MÁV system.

SOPRON
☎ 99
Sopron (Ödenburg in German) sits right on the Austrian border, 217km west of Budapest and only 69km south of Vienna. In 1921 the town's residents voted to remain part of Hungary, while the rest of Bürgenland (the region to which Sopron used to belong) went to Austria, thus explaining the town's location in a little knot of Hungarian land jutting into Austria.

Sopron has been an important centre since the time of the Romans, who called it Scarbantia. The Mongols and Turks never got this far, so numerous medieval structures remain intact to this day. In the small, horseshoe-shaped old town, still partially enclosed by medieval walls built on Roman foundations, almost every building is historically important. This is Sopron's principal charm and wanderers among the Gothic and baroque houses are rewarded at every turn. Some of the buildings are now museums, and you can peek into the courtyards of many others.

Sopron is popular with Hungarians mainly because of the wooded hills that rise up behind the city. It's popular with Austrians because of the many dentists and optometrists, who presumably charge less than those in Austria.

Orientation

From the main train station, walk north on Mátyás király utca, which becomes Várkerület after a few blocks. Várkerület and Ógabona tér form a loop right around the old town, following the line of the former city walls. There are two entrances to the old town: the Előkapu (Front Gate) and the Hátsókapu (Back Gate). Sopron's Fire Tower is between Előkapu and Fő tér, the old town's central square.

The bus station is on Lackner Kristóf utca running north-west off Ógabona tér. The left-luggage office in the main train station is open from 3 am to 11 pm. There's no left-luggage area at the bus station.

Scruffy Deák tér is the city's 19th-century boulevard.

Information

Tourinform (☎ 338 892) is at Liszt Ferenc utca 1, beside the casino.

Ciklámen Tourist (☎ 312 040), a travel agency, is at Ógabona tér 8 on the corner of Lackner Kristóf utca. Express (☎ 312 024) is at Mátyás király utca 7 between the train station and the old town.

Money The OTP Bank at Várkerület 96 is open weekdays from 7.45 am to 3.30 or 4 pm. In the old town there's a Postabank with an ATM at Új utca 8. Ciklámen Tourist will change travellers cheques, but gives a mediocre rate.

Things to See

The 60m-high **Fire Tower** above the old town's northern gate is a true architectural hybrid. The 2m-thick square base, built on a Roman gate, dates from the 12th century, the cylindrical middle and arcaded balcony were built in the 16th century, and the baroque spire was added in 1680. You can climb up to the top for a marvellous view of the city

daily, except Monday. **Fidelity Gate** at the bottom of the tower pictures Hungaria receiving the *civitas fidelissima* (most loyal citizenry) of Sopron. It was erected in 1922 after that crucial plebiscite.

In the centre of Fő tér is the magnificent **Holy Trinity Column** (1701) and beyond this the 13th-century **Goat Church**, whose name comes from the heraldic animal of its chief benefactor. Below the church is **Chapter Hall**, part of a 14th-century Franciscan monastery with frescoes and stone carvings.

There are several excellent museums on Fő tér. **Fabricius House** at No 6 is a comprehensive historical museum with rooms on the upper floors devoted to domestic life in the 17th and 18th centuries and impressive Roman sculpture in the Gothic cellar. **Storno House** at No 8 is a famous Renaissance palace (1560) that is now a museum and gallery of Romanesque and Gothic art.

A unique museum of Jewish life is housed in the 14th-century **Old Synagogue** (closed Tuesday and October to February) at Új utca 22. Jews were an important part of the community until their expulsion in 1526. In the Ikva district north of the old town are several more interesting museums, including the excellent **Zettl-Langer Collection** of ceramics, paintings and furniture, Balfi út 11 (open only from 10 am to noon from Tuesday to Sunday) and the wonderful **Bakery Museum**, Bécsi tér 5 (open Wednesday, Friday and Sunday from 10 am to 2 pm, and Tuesday, Thursday and Saturday from 2 to 6 pm).

To see some of Sopron's surrounds, take bus No 1 or 2 to the Lővér Hotel and hike up through the forest to the **Károly Lookout** for the view. You can't miss **Taródi Castle** at Csalogány köz 8, a 'self-built private castle' owned by the obsessed Taródi family. It's a bizarre place with a half-baked, neo-Gothic feel to it. To get to the castle, take bus No 1 from the station and get off at the Lővér Baths. Follow Fenyves sor and Tölgyfa sor north for three blocks and turn left on Csalogány köz. The castle is on your right up the hill.

Places to Stay

Camping *Lővér Camping* (☎ 311 715), at Pócsidomb on Kőszegi út about 5km south of the city centre, has more than 100 small bungalows available between mid-April and

SOPRON & LŐVÉR HILLS

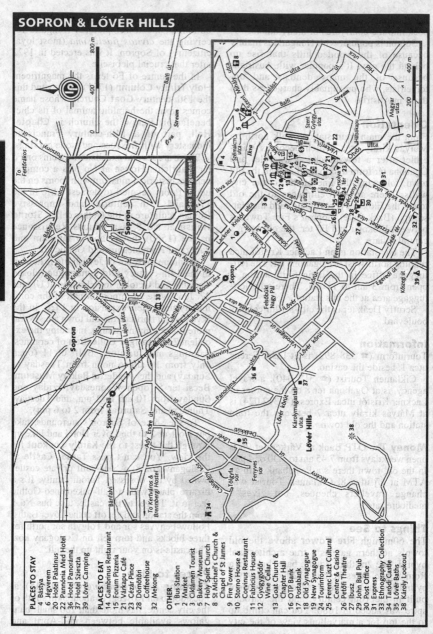

PLACES TO STAY
4 Bástya
6 Jégverem
20 Hotel Palatinus
22 Pannónia Med Hotel
36 Hotel Panoráma
37 Hotel Sziesta
39 Lővér Camping

PLACES TO EAT
14 Gambrinus Restaurant
15 Forum Pizzeria
21 Várkapu Café
23 Cézár Pince
28 Dömötöri
32 Mekong
 Coffeehouse

OTHER
1 Bus Station
2 Market
3 Cikámen Tourist
5 Bakery Museum
7 Holy Spirit Church
8 St Michael's Church &
 Chapel of St James
9 Fire Tower
10 Storno House &
 Corvinus Restaurant
11 Fabricius House
12 Gyógygödör
 Wine Cellar
13 Goat Church &
 Chapter Hall
16 OTP Bank
17 Postabank
18 Old Synagogue
19 New Synagogue
24 Tourinform
25 Ferenc Liszt Cultural
 Centre & Casino
26 Petőfi Theatre
27 Ibusz
29 John Bull Pub
30 Post Office
31 Express
33 Ethnography Collection
34 Tarodi Castle
35 Lővér Baths
38 Károly Lookout

mid-October. Doubles with shared bath are about 2500 Ft and camping costs about 800 Ft. Bus No 12 from both the bus and train stations stops directly in front of the camp site. If you take bus No 1 or 2, get off at Citadella Park and walk down Sarudi utca to Kőszegi utca. The camp site is just to the south.

Hostel The *Tájékoztató* hostel (☎ 313 116) on Brennbergi út is pretty far to the west of the city centre (take bus No 3 or 10 from the bus station). Beds cost 1300 Ft in the pension section and 965 Ft in the hostel section. It's open from mid-April to mid-October.

Private Rooms Ciklámen Tourist has private rooms for about 2300/3300 Ft a single/double. All rooms are sometimes full in summer and singles may have to pay for a double.

You can also find quite a few private rooms by taking bus No 1 from the train station to the Hotel Szieszta, Lövér körút 37, then walking back down the hill looking for houses with 'Zimmer frei' signs.

Pensions & Hotels Most pensions are pretty expensive. *Bástya* (☎ 325 325) at Patak utca 40, a 10-minute walk north of the old town up Szélmalom utca, charges 6000/7900 Ft for singles/doubles. The more central *Jégverem* (☎ 312 004), with five rooms in an 18th-century ice cellar, at Jégverem utca 1 in the Ikva district charges 6000 Ft a room.

Hotel Panoráma (☎ 312 745), Panoráma utca 38, is on a hillside about 1km (as the crow flies) to the south-west of the city centre. It's a pension-style place with good prices; singles/doubles are 2800/3900 Ft. Bus Nos 1 and 2 running along Lövér körút will get you near the hotel.

Hotel Palatinus (☎ 311 395) couldn't be more central at Új utca 23. Reasonable singles/doubles are DM80/120. Sopron's grand old hotel is the 100-year-old *Pannónia Med Hotel* (☎ 312 180) at Várkerület 75. It's a very nice place but the rooms aren't really worth the price; from DM100/130 and way up.

Places to Eat

The best place for an inexpensive lunch or light meal is *Cézár Pince*, in a medieval

cellar at Hátsókapu 2 off Orsolya tér (open till 9.30 pm).

Corvinus, with its café tables on Fő tér, is a great place for a pizza in the warmer months. For something more substantial, try *Gambrinus*, open till 10 pm across the square at No 3. The *Forum* at Szent György utca 3 also does pizza.

Deák, Erzsébet utca 20 on the corner of Deák tér, specialises in game dishes, though fish is also on the menu. In the evening there's live music and the place is popular with Austrian border-jumpers.

Mekong, a short distance to the south-east at Deák tér 46, has passable Chinese (main courses from 500 Ft) and opens nightly till midnight.

Have at least a cup of coffee and a slice of cake at *Várkapu Café* on the corner of Hátsókapu and Várkerület. More impressive (but usually crowded and smoky) is *Dömötöri*, on Széchenyi tér next to the John Bull pub (which is another reliable eatery). As well as coffee and cake there are light meals, such as ham and eggs for just 250 Ft.

Sample Sopron's wines in the *Gyógygődőr*, a deep, deep cellar at Fő tér 4.

Entertainment

The *Ferenc Liszt Cultural Centre* off Széchenyi tér at Liszt Ferenc tér 1 is the place to go for music and other events. The beautiful *Petőfi Theatre* is around the corner on Petőfi tér. Those who want to take a chance should head for the nearby *Sopron Casino*.

Getting There & Away

Buses of interest from Sopron include two a day to Balatonfüred (160km), five to Budapest (210km), two to Esztergom (174km), hourly or better to Fertőd and Fertőrákos, hourly to Győr (87km), three daily to Hévíz and Keszthely (141km), seven to Kőszeg (53km), about every half-hour to Nagycenk (13km), one daily to Pécs (287km), two to Székesfehérvár (174km) and nine to Szombathely (73km). There's also a bus to Vienna on weekdays at 8 am and another on Monday, Thursday and Friday at 9.20 am, plus another on Friday at 8.55 am.

Express trains en route to Vienna's Südbahnhof pass through Sopron three times a day, though local services to Ebenfurth and

Wiener Neustadt (where you can transfer for Vienna) are much more frequent. There are four express trains a day to Budapest-Keleti via Győr and Komárom, and eight to 10 local trains to Szombathely.

AROUND SOPRON

An hourly bus from the main bus station in Sopron runs 9km north-east to **Fertőrákos** where the mammoth halls and corridors of the old limestone quarry are an impressive sight (open daily all year). The quarries were worked by the Romans, and the pliable limestone was later used to decorate many of the buildings around the Ring in Vienna, including the Votivkirche. From late June to late August concerts and operas are performed in the acoustically perfect Cave Theatre.

Nagycenk, 13km south-east of Sopron, was once the seat of the Széchenyi clan, whose most celebrated member was Count István Széchenyi (1791-1860), a notable reformer who founded the National Academy of Sciences, improved communications and wrote a series of books intended to convince the nobility to lend a hand in modernising Hungary. The Chain Bridge in Budapest was one of his many projects.

The baroque **Széchenyi Mansion** (1758) contains a memorial museum to Count István and an expensive three-star hotel. The café just outside the hotel restaurant serves great cakes and ice cream. Other attractions include the park with its 2.5km 'avenue' of linden trees, the Széchenyi family mausoleum in the village cemetery, a 3.5km narrow-gauge steam train to Fertőboz and a stud farm where you can ride horses. From Sopron, Nagycenk is accessible by bus every half-hour and by up to eight trains daily bound for Szombathely.

FERTŐD
☎ 99

Don't miss the 126-room **Esterházy Palace** (1766) at Fertőd, 27km east of Sopron and readily accessible by bus. This magnificent Versailles-style baroque palace, easily the finest in Hungary, is open daily all year, except Monday, from 9 am to 4 or 5 pm. You must visit the palace with a guide. From April to August there are piano and string quartets

performing in the concert hall on most Saturday evenings at 6 pm and on some Sunday mornings at 11 am.

Joseph Haydn was court musician to the princely Esterházy family from 1761 to 1790, and many of his works were first performed in the concert hall.

Places to Stay & Eat
You can spend the night in the palace. Clean, simple rooms in the Kastély Hotel (☎ 370 971) on the 3rd floor cost 2500 Ft a double and are available all year. To find the hostel, look for the arrow near the ticket office that points up to the 'szálloda' to the left. If you arrive to find the Kastély full, don't let yourself be talked into staying at the Esterházi Panzió nearby at Fő utca 20. Instead, see if the *hostel* in the Udvaros Ház, an outbuilding of the palace at Fő utca 1, has a bed.

The café in *Grenadier House* opposite the palace's rococo wrought-iron gate is pleasant enough, and there are several decent restaurants in the village, including the *Haydn* in the Udvaros Ház.

KŐSZEG
☎ 94

Kőszeg (Güns in German) is a small town at the foot of the Kőszeg Hills just 3km from the Austrian border. Mt Írottkő (882m), southwest of town and straddling the border, is the highest point in Transdanubia. At its centre is the old town, a well-preserved medieval precinct.

In 1532 Kőszeg's castle garrison held off a Turkish army of 100,000, and this delay gave the Habsburgs time to mount a successful defence of Vienna, ensuring Kőszeg's place in national history. The houses along the street in front of the castle were erected in a saw-toothed design in order to give defenders a better shot at the enemy.

Jurisics tér, Kőszeg's delightful main square, hasn't changed much since the 18th century.

Orientation & Information
The train station is a 15-minute walk to the south-east of the old town on Alsó körút; buses stop just a block from Várkör on Liszt Ferenc utca. The train station doesn't have a

left-luggage office, but the staff will probably agree to hold your bags for the usual fee.

For information try Savaria Tourist (☎ 360 238) at Várkör 69, or Express (☎ 360 247) around the corner at Városház utca 5. The OTP Bank at Kossuth Lajos utca 8 has an ATM and a foreign currency exchange machine.

Things to See

The **Heroes' Gate**, which leads into Jurisics tér, was erected in 1932 to mark the 400th anniversary of the Turkish onslaught. The tower

above is open to visitors and offers wonderful views (and photographs) of the square. In the General's House next to the gate at Jurisics tér 4-6 is a branch of the **Miklós Jurisics Museum** (closed on Monday), which contains exhibits on folk art, trades and crafts, and the natural history of the area.

The painted Renaissance façade of the **Town Hall** is at No 8 of the square. A statue of the Virgin Mary (1739) and the town fountain (1766) in the middle of the square adjoin two fine churches. The **Church of St Henry** (1615) is closer to the gate. Behind it is the

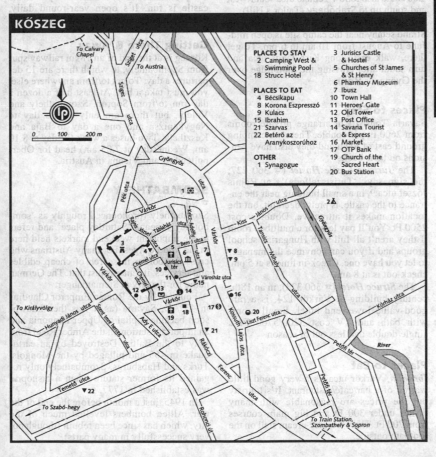

KŐSZEG

PLACES TO STAY
2 Camping West & Swimming Pool
18 Strucc Hotel

PLACES TO EAT
4 Bécsikapu
8 Korona Eszpresszó
9 Kulacs
15 Ibrahim
21 Szarvas
22 Betérő az Aranykoszorúhoz

OTHER
1 Synagogue
3 Jurisics Castle & Hostel
5 Churches of St James & St Henry
6 Pharmacy Museum
7 Ibusz
10 Town Hall
11 Heroes' Gate
12 Old Tower
13 Post Office
14 Savaria Tourist & Express
16 Market
17 OTP Bank
19 Church of the Sacred Heart
20 Bus Station

Church of St James (1403), a splendid Gothic structure with three 15th-century frescoes. At Jurisics tér 11 is a baroque **pharmacy**, which is now a museum.

The other highlight of Kőszeg is **Jurisics Castle** (1263), now a historical museum (closed Monday). The courtyard and towers of this Gothic bastion have an almost fairytale air about them.

A pleasant way to spend a few hours is by walking up to the baroque chapel on 393m **Kálváriahegy** (Calvary Hill) north-west of the town centre, or into the vineyards of Királyvölgy (King's Valley) west of the castle. You could also follow Temető utca south-west and south up to **Szabóhegy** (Tailor's Hill).

The **swimming pool** and 'beach' on Strand sétány near the camp site is open mid-June to August from 10 am to 6 pm. To get there, walk east along Kiss János utca and turn south after crossing the footbridge over the Gyöngyös River.

Places to Stay

Savaria Tourist can arrange private rooms from 2600 Ft per double. There's a camping ground east of town and they also have pensions on their books.

The *Jurisics Castle Hostel* (☎ 360 227; the sign says 'Turistszalloda)') at Rajnis József utca 9, in a small building near the entrance to the castle, is pretty decrepit, but the location makes it attractive. Doubles cost 2500 Ft. You'll pay less for a multibed room if they aren't all full with Hungarian school groups and if you can convince the manager to let you have one. Check-in time is at 5 pm, check-out is at 8 am.

The *Strucc Hotel* (☎ 360 323), in an 18th-century building at Várkör 124, is a rare good-value lower-end hotel. Small rooms with bath and TV cost 3200/5700 Ft a single/double and less out of season.

Places to Eat

Ibrahim, Várkör utca, is a very good little warren of a bar/café/restaurant. It's touristy but the prices are reasonable with many dishes under 300 Ft and big main courses from 700 Ft. There's an ice-cream stall on the footpath outside.

Bécsikapu at Rajnis József utca 5, almost opposite St James Church, is a pleasant little place close to the castle; *Kulacs* at Várkör 12 is more convenient to the bus stops. Other options include *Szarvas*, in an attractive 19th-century house at Rákóczi utca 12, with many main courses around 600 Ft, and *Betérő az Aranykoszorúhoz* at Temető utca 59 (the name is quite a mouthful, but it just means 'Visitor at the Sign of the Golden Wreath'). It has excellent food but closes at 9 pm and all day Monday.

For coffee and cakes you can't beat *Korona Eszpresszó*, Várkör 18, open daily from 8 am to 6 pm. After dinner, a drink at the *pub* in the castle is fun. It's open year-round daily, except Monday, and shuts at midnight.

Getting There & Away

Kőszeg is at the end of an 18km railway spur from Szombathely, to which there are 15 departures a day. To get to/from anywhere else, you must take a bus. At least half a dozen a day run to/from Sopron, Szombathely and Velem, but there are only two a day to Nagykanizsa and one a day to Baja and Keszthely. Two buses a week (Friday at 8.10 am, Wednesday at 7.05 am) head for Oberpullendorf and Vienna in Austria.

SZOMBATHELY
☎ 94

Szombathely (pronounced roughly as 'sombot-hay') means 'Saturday place' and refers to the important weekend markets held here in the Middle Ages. For many Austrians who cross the border in search of cheap edibles and services, it remains just that. The German name for the city is Steinamanger.

Founded by the Roman Emperor Claudius in 43 AD, Savaria (as it was then known) soon became capital of Upper Pannonia and an important station on the Amber Road from Italy to the Baltic. Destroyed by an earthquake in 455 and pillaged by the Mongols, Turks and Habsburgs, Szombathely only regained its former stature when a bishopric was established in 1777.

In 1945, just a month before the end of the war, Allied bombers levelled much of the city, which has since been rebuilt (though not very successfully in many parts).

Although there's no compelling reason to visit, you might find yourself passing through as it's a transport crossroad.

Orientation

Szombathely is made up of narrow streets and squares with the centre at leafy Fő tér, one of the largest squares in Hungary. To the west are Berzsenyi Dániel tér and Templom tér, the administrative and ecclesiastical centre of town. The train station is five blocks east of Mártírok tere at the end of Széll Kálmán út. The bus station is on Petőfi Sándor utca, north of the cathedral.

Information

Savaria Tourist (☎ 312 348) is at Mártírok tere 1.

Money There's an ATM at the train station. The OTP Bank, diagonally opposite Savaria Tourist at Király utca 10, is open on Monday from 8 am to 5 pm, Tuesday to Thursday 8 am to 3 pm, and Friday 8 am to 1 pm.

Things to See

There are a few sights to keep you occupied while waiting for a train or bus. The rebuilt **Szombathely Cathedral** (1797) is on Templom tér. Behind the cathedral is the **Garden of Ruins** (Romkert), with Roman Savaria relics. On the other side of the cathedral is the baroque **Bishop's Palace** (1783), and beyond this at Hollán Ernő utca 2 is the **Smidt Museum** (closed Monday), containing a fascinating assortment of things collected by the squirrel-like physician Smidt before his death in 1975.

Szombathely Gallery, Rákóczi Ferenc utca 12, is one of the best modern art galleries in Hungary (closed Monday and Tuesday). The lovely twin-towered Moorish building across the street at No 3 is the former **synagogue** (1881). A monument marks the spot from which '4228 of our Jewish brothers and sisters were deported to Auschwitz on 4 July 1944'.

The **Vas County Museum Village**, on the western bank of the fishing lake on Árpád utca, is an outdoor ethnographic museum with a dozen 18th and 19th-century farm-

houses moved from various villages in the Őrség region south-west of Szombathely. Bus No 7 from the train station goes here.

In **Ják**, a small village 12km south of Szombathely, is one of the finest examples of Romanesque architecture in Hungary, the **Abbey Church** (1214). It's open from 8 am to 6 pm April to October and 10 am to 2 pm the rest of the year. Buses from Szombathely are frequent and will drop you at the bottom of the hill a few minutes walk from the church.

Places to Stay

Private rooms (2600 to 3500 Ft a double) are assigned by Savaria Tourist. In summer, ask Express, Király utca 12, about dormitory rooms at the *student hostels* on Ady Endre tér and Nagykar utca 1-3 (about 1000 Ft).

The *Liget Hotel* (☎ 314 168), west of the centre at Szent István park 15, is the most affordable hotel (get there on bus No 7 from the train station); pricey *Hotel Savaria* (☎ 311 440), Mártírok tere 4 in the very centre of town, is the nicest.

Getting There & Away

Bus The bus service is not so good to/from Szombathely, though up to 20 buses leave every day for Ják and about 10 go to Kőszeg, Sárvár and Velem. Other destinations include: Baja (one departure daily), Budapest (two), Győr (six), Kaposvár (two), Keszthely via Hévíz (three), Nagykanizsa (seven), Pécs (two), Sopron (six), Szentgotthárd (one) and Zalaegerszeg (six). One bus a week departs for the Austrian cities of Graz (Friday at 7 am) and Vienna (Wednesday at 6.40 am).

Train Express trains to Budapest-Déli (236km, 3½ hours) go via Veszprém and Székesfehérvár. Other express trains run to Győr (117km, 1¾ hours) via Celldömölk. Frequent local trains run to Kőszeg (18km, 30 minutes) and Sopron (64km, 1½ hours). There's also an early morning express train to/from Pécs (244km, 4½ hours).

Szombathely is only 13km from the Austrian border, and there are direct trains to/from Graz (146km, three hours). Some of the Graz services involve a change of trains at Szentgotthárd on the border.

428 Hungary – Lake Balaton

Lake Balaton

Lake Balaton, 77km long, is the largest fresh-water lake in Europe outside Scandinavia. The south-eastern shore is shallow and in summer the warm, sandy beaches are a favourite family holiday spot. Better scenery, more historic sites and deeper water are found on the north-western side.

The Bakony Hills and the extinct volcanoes of the Tapolca Basin lie to the north of the lake. Several ruined castles, such as those at Sümeg and Nagyvázsony, remind visitors that during the Turkish period the border between the Ottoman and Habsburg empires ran down the middle of the lake; the Turks actually maintained a fleet based at Siófok. Veszprém and Székesfehérvár, north and north-east of Balaton, are ancient towns full of monuments, and one of Hungary's finest 18th-century palaces is at Keszthely. The Benedictine crypt in Tihany's Abbey Church is the oldest religious structure extant in Hungary.

The many towns and villages on Balaton, particularly along its northern shore, are serious wine-making centres. Scenic train lines encircle the lake, and there are upwards of 40 camping grounds on its shores. 'Zimmer frei' (or 'szoba Kiadó') signs are everywhere. Balaton's very popularity is its main drawback, with the south-eastern shore particularly crowded and honky-tonk in July and August.

Private motorboats are prohibited, making Balaton a favourite yachting centre. Continuous breezes from the north speed sailors and sailboarders along. Other common activities are tennis, horse riding and cycling, and the thermal baths of Hévíz are nearby. If you want to hike, buy the *A Balaton* 1:40,000 map, available at bookshops.

Places to Stay

As well as the places listed under the towns in this section, you'll find HI-affiliated hostel accommodation in other lakeside towns, including *Sport Motel* (☎ 88-352 011), Nike körút, Balatonfüzfö (1100 Ft); *Vendégház* (☎ 88-352 011), Bugyogóforrás utca 19, Balatonfüzfö (1700 Ft); *College Panzió* (☎ 88-338 888), Rákóczi utca 39, Balatonalmádi (1600 Ft, late June to September only); and *Hotel Ezüstpart* (☎ 84-350 622), Liszt Ferenc sétány 2-4, Siófok.

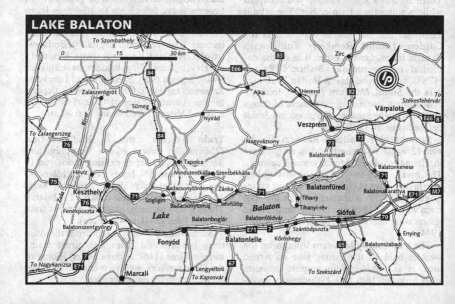

LAKE BALATON

Getting There & Away

Trains to Lake Balaton leave from Budapest's Déli train station and buses leave from the bus station at Erzsébet tér. If you're travelling north or south from the lake to towns in western or southern Transdanubia, buses are usually preferable to trains.

Getting Around

Train services on both the northern and southern sides of the lake are fairly frequent. A better way to see Lake Balaton up close, though, is on a Mahart passenger ferry.

Ferries operate on the route between Siófok, Balatonfüred, Tihany and Tihanyirév and Balatonföldvár from late March to late October, with more frequent sailings in July and August.

During the main summer season, which is from June to early September, ferries ply the entire length of the lake from Balatonkenese to Keszthely (five hours) with frequent stops on both shores. There are also car ferries across the lake between Tihanyirév and Szántódirév (from early March to late November), and Badacsony and Fonyód (from late March to late October). There are no passenger services on the lake in winter.

Adults pay 240 Ft for distances of one to 10km, 440 Ft for 11 to 20km, 500 Ft for 21 to 40km and 580 Ft for 41 to 70km. Children pay half-price, and return fares are slightly less than double the one-way fare.

BALATONFÜRED
☎ 87

Balatonfüred, a spa town with the easy-going grace that highly commercialised Siófok on the opposite shore totally lacks, has attracted heart patients for centuries because of its curative thermal waters. It has been the most fashionable bathing resort on the lake since the late 18th century, when a medicinal bathing centre was established here. In the early 19th century it became an important meeting place for Hungarian intellectuals, and some parts of town still bear an aristocratic air – in other parts there are topless bars.

Although Balatonfüred is a major spa centre, the mineral baths are reserved for patients. But because it's a health resort, much is open throughout the year; with Keszthely,

Balatonfüred is probably the best place on the lake to visit in the off season.

Orientation & Information

The adjacent bus and train stations are on Dobó István utca, 1km north-west of the spa centre and lake. The left-luggage office at the train station is open from 7.15 am to 9 pm. Buses to/from Tihany also stop near the ferry landing below the Round Church on Jókai Mór utca. Blaha Lujza utca runs from in front of the church directly into Gyógy tér, under which the thermal waters bubble.

Tourinform (☎ 342 237) is at Petőfi Sándor utca 8 and Balatontourist (☎ 343 471) is near the ferry pier, in the same building as Vitorlás restaurant.

The OTP Bank is at Jókai Mór utca 15, next to a large supermarket.

Things to See

The heart of the old spa town is **Gyógy tér**. In the centre of this leafy square, **Kossuth Spring** (1853) dispenses slightly sulphuric water that you can drink.

The park along the nearby lakeshore is worth a promenade. Near the wharf you'll encounter the bust of the Bengali poet Rabindranath Tagore before a lime tree that he planted in 1926 to mark his recovery from illness after treatment in Balatonfüred. The poem 'Tagore', which he wrote for the occasion, is reproduced on a plaque in slightly dodgy English.

A little inland, diagonally opposite the **Round Church** (1846), is the **Mór Jókai Museum** in the acclaimed novelist's former summerhouse (closed from November to April and on Monday).

The picturesque buildings and surrounds of **Veszprém**, 16km north of Balatonfüred, make it a worthwhile day trip. Balatontourist, on pedestrianised Kossuth Lajos utca between the bus station and the old town, can provide a map. The best way to get there from Balatonfüred is by bus, as the bus station is central while the train station is 3km from town.

Activities

Balatonfüred has three public beaches (admission about 150 Ft); the best is Aranyhíd to the east of Tagore sétány. There are other

HUNGARY

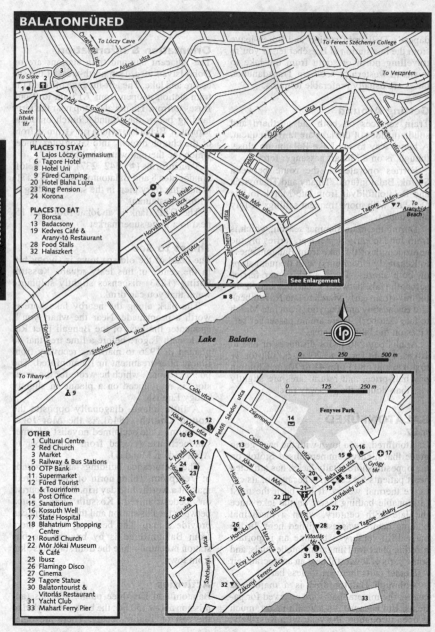

BALATONFÜRED

PLACES TO STAY
4 Lajos Lóczy Gymnasium
6 Tagore Hotel
8 Hotel Uni
9 Füred Camping
20 Hotel Blaha Lujza
23 Ring Pension
24 Korona

PLACES TO EAT
7 Borcsa
13 Badacsony
19 Kedves Café &
    Arany-tó Restaurant
28 Food Stalls
32 Halaszkert

OTHER
1 Cultural Centre
2 Red Church
3 Market
5 Railway & Bus Stations
10 OTP Bank
11 Supermarket
12 Füred Tourist
    & Tourinform
14 Post Office
15 Sanatorium
16 Kossuth Well
17 State Hospital
18 Blahatrium Shopping
    Centre
21 Round Church
22 Mór Jókai Museum
    & Café
25 Ibusz
26 Flamingo Disco
27 Cinema
29 Tagore Statue
30 Balatontourist &
    Vitorlás Restaurant
31 Yacht Club
33 Mahart Ferry Pier

To Lóczy Cave
To Ferenc Széchenyi College
To Veszprém
To Siske
Szent István tér
To Tihany
To Aranyhíd Beach

Lake Balaton

See Enlargement

Fenyves Park

0   250   500 m

0   125   250 m

beaches attached to various places to stay. The beach at the camp site has water-skiing by electric cable tow (1800 Ft/hour).

Bicycle rental places come and go. Ask Tourinform about the latest.

In July the Anna Ball is held at Hotel Arkad, and it's a prime event on the Hungarian social calendar. Tickets cost about 20,000 Ft. Concerts and other events accompany the ball; keep your eyes peeled if you're here in July.

Places to Stay

Camping There's only one camping ground but it can accommodate 3500 people. *Füred Camping* (☎ 343 823), Széchenyi utca 24, is beside Hotel Marina on the lake, 3km from the train station. Camping (April to mid-October) for three people with a tent or caravan costs from DM18 to DM27.50, depending on the season. There are also bungalows but to get one you have to arrive during office hours (8 am to 1 pm and 3 to 7 pm daily). The cheapest cost DM40 to a massive DM80 in mid-summer.

Hostels *Lajos Lóczy Gymnasium* on Ady Endre utca near the stations, and the far-flung *Ferenc Széchenyi College* on Iskola utca, 3km to the north-east of the resort, charge about 800 Ft for dorm beds in summer.

Private Rooms & Pensions As elsewhere around Lake Balaton, private room prices are inflated, much more so in summer. Balatontourist and Füred Tourism (☎ 481 605/06, next to Tourinform) are among the places to try. Other agencies open in summer. In season you'll pay from 6000/8000 Ft a single/double at Füred Tourism, perhaps a little less at Balatontourist.

The *Ring Pension* (☎ 342 884) at Petőfi Sándor utca 6a is so-named because the owner was a champion boxer, not a jeweller. Neat, clean singles/doubles with shared bath cost from DM40/65 (much more in season). The nearby *Korona* (☎ 343 278), with 18 rooms at Vörösmarty Mihály utca 4, charges about the same.

Hotels The most central place is the cosy *Hotel Blaha Lujza* (☎ 343 094) on Blaha Lujza utca – the nicest street in town. This was once the holiday home of the much-loved 19th-century actress-singer Lujza Blaha. Singles/doubles/triples with shower and TV cost 2400/4000/5300 Ft in the low season; doubles (only) are 5000 Ft in summer.

There are several other hotels in town and some are good value in the low season. The high-rise *Hotel Uni* (☎ 341 822), right on the foreshore, feels like a motel and charges from just 2900/3750 Ft in winter, rising by increments to 8230/9800 Ft from 10 July to 23 August.

Places to Eat

The eastern end of Tagore sétány is a strip of pleasant bars and terraced restaurants including *Bella Italia*, with good pizza and pastas, and the *Borcsa* restaurant, very popular with local residents, although they aren't cheap.

Jókai Mór utca is another good hunting ground for restaurants. The *Badacsony* has a mutilingual menu and is popular with young tourists.

Halászkert, west of Vitorlás tér on Zákonyi Ferenc utca, still serves the best 'drunkard's fish soup' (korhely halászlé) in Hungary. It costs 890 Ft, but it's worth it. The restaurant at *Hotel Blaha Lujza* is upmarket though still affordable.

The *food stalls* on the north-east side of Vitorlás tér are great for something fast and cheap, especially the large pieces of fried carp and catfish sold by weight.

Getting There & Away

Balatonfüred is two hours by express train from Budapest-Déli (132km) and a weary three hours by local train. The line continues to Tapolca via Badacsony. If you come from Budapest by local train, note that there are several stations before Balatonfüred with 'Balaton' in their name, and at least one with 'füred'. The two stations before Balatonfüred are Csopak and Balatonarács.

There are Mahart ferries to Siófok from late March to late October (440 Ft).

Buses for Tihany (11km) and Veszprém (16km) leave continually throughout the day, and there are buses to Győr (seven a day), Esztergom (one a day), Sopron (two a day) and Kecskemét (one a day).

HUNGARY

SIÓFOK

The milky-green Sió River drains Lake Balaton into the Danube at Siófok, the largest and busiest settlement on Balaton's south-eastern shore. It's a useful transit point, but there's no reason to stay. A strip of pricey high-rise hotels, a half-dozen large camping grounds, holiday cottages, tacky discos and a sleazy nightlife attract big crowds. In mid-summer bedlam reigns and the confused travel agency staff in charge of issuing private rooms won't even consider stays of one or two nights, and singles are unavailable. In winter Siófok is dead.

Siófok can be convenient, however, if you're just passing through as the train and bus stations are adjacent in the centre of town on Váradi Adolf tér just off Fő utca (the main drag), and the Mahart ferry pier is an easy 10-minute walk to the north-west.

TIHANY

☎ 87

The Tihany Peninsula almost bisects the eastern end of Lake Balaton. Consensus has it that this is the most beautiful place on the lake, and in summer Tihany gets more than its fair share of tourists. After visiting the famous Abbey Church, you can easily shake the hordes by hiking to the hilly peninsula's Inner Lake (Belsőtó), with its abundant birdlife. Outer Lake (Külsőtó) has almost completely dried up and is now a tangle of reeds.

If you don't have your own transport, however, check the town before deciding to stay here, as it's high on a bluff and quite a walk to the lake.

Orientation & Information

Tihany's Abbey Church sits on a ridge above a ferry landing on the eastern side of the peninsula's high plateau. The village of Tihany is perched above Inner Lake, just below the abbey. Lake boats also stop at Tihanyirév, the car-ferry landing at the southern end of the peninsula.

Balatontourist (☎ 448 804) is at Kossuth Lajos utca 20 (open April to mid-October only) and Tihany Tourist (☎ 448 481) is No 11.

Things to See & Do

Tihany's twin-towered **Abbey Church** (1754) is outstanding for its carved baroque altars, pulpit and organ; pride of place, however, goes to the 11th-century **crypt** below the front of the church containing the tomb of the abbey's founder, King Andrew I. The abbey's Deed of Foundation, now in the archives of the Benedictine Abbey at Pannonhalma near Győr, is the earliest document in existence containing Hungarian words. In summer, organ concerts are held in the church.

The monastery beside the church contains the **Abbey Museum** (open May to October, closed Monday) with exhibits relating to Lake Balaton and a library of manuscripts. Archaeological finds are in the cellar. The view of Lake Balaton from behind the abbey is excellent.

Pisky sétány, a promenade running along the ridge north from the church to Echo Hill, passes a cluster of folk houses which have now been turned into a small **open-air museum** (same hours as the Abbey Museum). From Echo Hill you can descend Garay utca to the inner harbour or continue up onto the green and red-marked **hiking trails**. The red trail crosses the peninsula between the two lakes to **Csúcs Hill**, which offers fine views (two hours). Following the green trail north-east of the church for an hour will bring you to a **Russian Well** (Oroszkút) and the ruins of the **Old Castle** (Óvár), where Russian Orthodox monks, brought to Tihany by Andrew I, hollowed out cells in the soft basalt walls. The trails are poorly marked but are a delightful respite from the tourist trappings in the village.

Places to Stay & Eat

Tihany Tourist has *private rooms* from DM40 per double in the low season and DM50 in the high season. Many houses along Kossuth Lajos utca and on the little streets north of the Abbey Church have 'Zimmer frei' signs, so in the off season you could try there. Tihany's *pensions* and *hotels* are very expensive.

Rege Café in the former monastery stables next to the Abbey Church serves light meals and offers a panoramic view from its terrace, but you would do better to eat at the *Kecskeköröm Csárda*, Kossuth Lajos utca

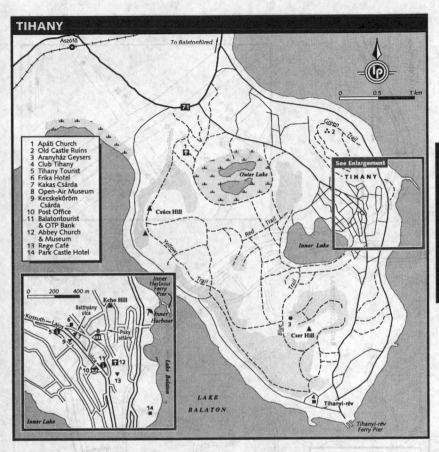

TIHANY

1 Apáti Church
2 Old Castle Ruins
3 Aranyház Geysers
4 Club Tihany
5 Tihany Tourist
6 Frika Hotel
7 Kakas Csárda
8 Open-Air Museum
9 Kecskekörom
   Csárda
10 Post Office
11 Balatontourist
   & OTP Bank
12 Abbey Church
   & Museum
13 Rege Café
14 Park Castle Hotel

To Balatonfüred

Aszófő

Green Trail

Outer Lake

Csúcs Hill

Red Trail

Inner Lake

Yellow Trail

See Enlargement

TIHANY

HUNGARY

Blue Trail

Cser Hill

Trail

Inner Harbour Ferry Pier

Echo Hill

Batthyány utca

Kossuth Lajos

Pisky sétány

Inner Harbour

utca

Lake Balaton

Inner Lake

LAKE BALATON

Tihanyi-rév

Tihanyi-rév Ferry Pier

13, a few hundred metres north-west on the main road, or at the **Kakas Csárda** almost opposite at Batthyány utca 1. **Don Pietro** in Tihanyirév is reliable for pizzas and pastas.

Getting There & Away

Buses cover the 11km from Balatonfüred's train station to and from Tihany about 20 times a day (110 Ft). The bus stops at both ferry landings before climbing to the village of Tihany where it turns around and returns the same way.

Passenger ferries stop at Tihany from late March to late October. Catch them at the pier below the abbey or at Tihanyirév, about 3km to the south-west at the tip of the peninsula. From early March to late November the car ferry crosses the narrow stretch of water between Tihanyirév and Szántódirév.

BADACSONY

Badacsony lies between Balatonfüred and Keszthely in a picturesque region of basalt peaks that can claim some of the best hikes in Hungary. Vineyards hug the sides of Badacsony's extinct volcanic cone; the gentle

HUNGARY

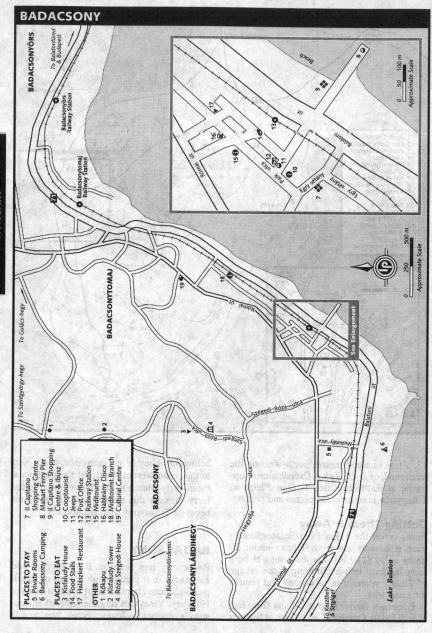

BADACSONY

BADACSONYÖRS

To Balatonfüred & Budapest

Badacsonyörs Railway Station

Badacsonytomaj Railway Station

To Gulács-hegy

To Szentgyörgy-hegy

BADACSONYTOMAJ

Római út

Szegedi–Róza–utca

Szegedi–Róza–utca

Hegyalja

BADACSONY

BADACSONYLÁBDIHEGY

To Badacsonytördemic

Balatoni út

Muskotály-utca

To Keszthely & Szigliget

Lake Balaton

See Enlargement

Beach

Park utca

Római út

Egry sétány

Balatoni út

PLACES TO STAY
5 Private Rooms
6 Badacsony Camping

PLACES TO EAT
3 Kisfaludy House
14 Food Stalls
17 Halászkert Restaurant

OTHER
1 Kökapu
2 Kisfaludy Tower
4 Róza Szegedi House
7 Il Capitano Shopping Centre
8 Mahart Ferry Pier
9 Il Capitano Shopping Centre & Ibusz
10 Cooptourist
11 Jeeps
12 Post Office
13 Railway Station
15 Miditourist
16 Hableány Disco
18 Miditourist Branch
19 Cultural Centre

0   50   100 m
Approximate Scale

0   250   500 m
Approximate Scale

climate and rich soil make this an ideal wine-making area.

From October to April or as late as mid-May almost all of the travel agencies, pensions and restaurants mentioned here are closed. You should still be able to find a room by looking for 'Zimmer frei' or 'szoba Kiadó' signs or by asking around, but bring some food with you just in case. The left-luggage office at the train station is open from 8 am to 8 pm.

Things to See & Do

The **József Egry Museum** at Egry sétány 52 in town is devoted to the Balaton region's leading painter (1883-1951) and is open from May to October.

The slopes and the vineyards above the town are sprinkled with little press houses and 'folk-baroque' mansions. One of these is the **Róza Szegedi House** (1790), which belonged to the actress wife of the poet Sándor Kisfaludy of Sümeg. It contains a literary museum.

The flat-topped forested massif overlooking the lake is just the place to escape the tipsy herd. If you'd like a running start on your hiking, catch one of the topless jeeps marked 'Badacsonyhegyi járat', which depart from opposite the post office May to September from 10 am to dusk whenever at least six paying passengers climb aboard (380 Ft per person). The jeep will drop you at the Kisfaludy House restaurant, where a map of the trails is posted by the parking lot. **Kisfaludy Tower** offers splendid views.

The tiny **beach** is reedy; you would do better to head a few kilometres east to Badacsonytomaj or Badacsonyörs for a swim.

Places to Stay

The closest camping ground is *Badacsony Camping* (☎ 87-431 091) at the water's edge about 1.5km west of the ferry pier and open from May to early September. It's a casual place but be sure to bring mosquito repellent. It costs from DM4 to DM5.20 for a tent and the same per person.

Private rooms are available from a number of agencies, including Balatontourist and Ibusz in the Il Capitano shopping centre near

the ferry pier. There are several small pensions among the vineyards on the road above the railway line, a 10-minute walk from the station, but they close from October to April or mid-May.

Places to Eat

The best place for a meal or drink is the terrace of the *Kisfaludy House* restaurant, on the hill overlooking the vineyards and the lake. The *Halászkert restaurant* at Park utca 5 is crowded and touristy, but the fish dishes are excellent. *Pizzeria Il Capitano* is in the shopping centre by the ferry pier. There are *food stalls* with picnic tables dispensing sausage and fish soup between the train station and Park utca.

Getting There & Away

There are three buses a day to Balatonfüred and Veszprém. Other destinations include: Hévíz (two trips daily), Keszthely (one), Nagykanizsa (one), Révfülöp (three), Tapolca (two or three) and Zalaegerszeg (four).

Badacsony is on the rail line linking all the towns on Lake Balaton's northern shore with Budapest-Déli and Tapolca. To get to Keszthely you must change at Tapolca, but there's often an immediate connection.

Ferries between Badacsony and Fonyód are fairly frequent between late March and late October; in Fonyód you can get a connection to southern Transdanubia by taking a train direct to Kaposvár (53km, 1½ hours), then a bus on to Pécs from there.

A boat ride to Badacsony from Siófok or Balatonfüred is the best way to get the feel of Lake Balaton. Boats operate from June to early September. Ferries also travel on to Keszthely at this time.

KESZTHELY
☎ 83

Keszthely (pronounced 'kest-hay') is a fairly large old town with some attractions, good facilities and boat services on the lake from June to early September. It's the only town on Lake Balaton that has a life of its own; since it isn't entirely dependent on tourism, it's 'open' all year.

Orientation

The bus and train stations, side by side at the end of Mártírok útja, are fairly close to the lake ferry terminal. The left-luggage office inside the train station is open 24 hours. From the stations follow Mártírok útja up the hill, then turn right onto Kossuth Lajos utca into town.

Information

Tourinform (☎ 314 144), Kossuth Lajos utca 28, is an excellent source of information on the whole Balaton area.

The OTP Bank, Kossuth Lajos utca 3, is open Monday to Thursday from 8 am to 2.30 pm, Friday to noon. The main post office is at Georgikon utca 3.

Things to See

Keszthely's most important sight is the **Festetics Palace**, the one-time residence of the wealthy Festetics family, built in 1745 and extended a century and a half later. The palace is open all year from 10 am to 6 pm daily, except Monday, and costs 700 Ft plus 300 Ft if you want to take photos. A highlight of the 100-room palace (you only get to see a dozen or so rooms) is the Helikon Library.

The palace is on Kastély utca at the northern end of Kossuth Lajos utca.

In 1797 Count György Festetics, an uncle of the reformer István Széchenyi, founded Europe's first agricultural institute, the Georgikon, here and even today Keszthely is noted for its large agricultural university. Part of the original school at Bercsényi Miklós utca 67 is now the **Georgikon Farm Museum** (open from May to October, closed Monday). The **Balaton Museum**, not far from the train station on the corner of Mártírok útja and Kossuth Lajos utca, has exhibits on the history of navigation on the lake and fascinating photographs of summer frolickers there at the turn of the century. It's open from early April to early September; it's closed Mondays.

Places to Stay

Camping There are several camping grounds near the lake, all of which have bungalows and are open from May to September. As you leave the train station, head south across the tracks and you'll soon reach *Sport Camping* (☎ 313 777) at Csárda utca. But

wedged between the railway tracks and a road, it's noisy and not very clean. Carry on south for 20 minutes to *Zalatour Camping* (☎ 312 998), a much bigger place with large bungalows for four people from DM60 to DM90, and smaller holiday houses from DM25. There are tennis courts, and the site has access to Helikon Beach. *Castrum Camping* (☎ 312 120), north of the stations at Mora Ferenc utca 48, has its own beach but is really for foreign caravans.

Hostels In July and August you can stay in the student accommodation at *Ferenc Pethe College* (☎ 311 290), Festetics György út 5, for about 1500 Ft per person. Ask Express, Kossuth Lajos utca 22, about summer dormitory rooms at the more central *Pannon Agricultural University* on the corner of Széchenyi utca and Deák Ferenc utca.

Private Rooms Private rooms are available from three agencies on Kossuth Lajos utca from about 1500 Ft per person: Ibusz at No 27; Zalatour at No 1; and Keszthely Tourist at No 25. Ask around, as prices differ.

If you're only staying one night, some of the agencies levy exorbitant surcharges, making it worthwhile to forgo their services and go directly to houses with 'szoba' signs, where you may be able to bargain with the owners.

Hotels The *Hotel Georgikon* (☎ 315 730), in one of the original Georgikon buildings on the corner of Bercsény Miklós utca and Georgikon utca, has singles/doubles for 4400/6500 Ft (less in the low season). Avoid the rooms facing Georgikon utca as they are very noisy.

In the off season it's worth checking for specials at the upmarket hotels along the lakefront. The three star *Beta Hotel Phoenix* (☎ 312 631), Balatonpart 5, goes as low as DM38/48 and it's dearest rates are DM65/79.

Places to Eat

The *Hungária Gösser* pub-restaurant, in a lovely historical building with stained-glass windows at Kossuth Lajos utca 35 (the corner of Fő tér), has pizza, Hungarian dishes and a salad bar. The renovated *Béke*, Kossuth

HUNGARY

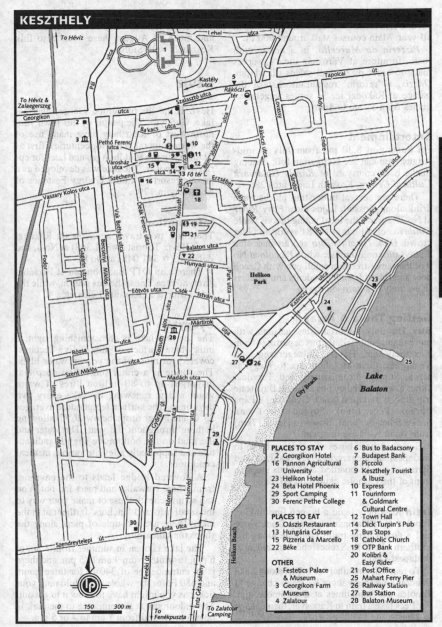

KESZTHELY

To Hévíz
To Hévíz & Zalaegerszeg
Georgikon utca
Lehel utca
Kastély utca
Szalasztó utca
Rákóczi tér
Tapolcai út
Pethő Ferenc utca
Bakacs utca
Városház utca
Széchenyi
Vaszary Kolos utca
Deák Ferenc utca
Vak Bottyán utca
Berzsenyi Miklós utca
Fő tér
Erzsébet királyné utca
Kossuth Lajos utca
Balaton utca
Hunyadi utca
Eötvös utca
Csók utca
István utca
Mártírok utca
Rózsa utca
Szent Miklós utca
Madách utca
Gagárin utca
Fodor utca
Imre utca
Festetics György út
Kossuth Lajos utca
Szendreytelepi út
Római utca
Honvéd utca
Csárda utca
Fenéki út
Erhz Géza sétány

Rákóczi utca
Lovassy utca
Ady utca
Endre utca
Móra Ferenc utca
Sándor utca
Apát utca
Bem József utca
Park utca
Kapency utca

Helikon
Park

Lake
Balaton

City Beach

Helikon Beach

To Fenékpuszta
To Zalatour
Camping

0   150   300 m

PLACES TO STAY	OTHER
2 Georgikon Hotel	1 Festetics Palace
16 Pannon Agricultural	& Museum
University	3 Georgikon Farm
23 Helikon Hotel	Museum
24 Beta Hotel Phoenix	4 Zalatour
29 Sport Camping	6 Bus to Badacsony
30 Ferenc Pethe College	7 Budapest Bank
	8 Piccolo
PLACES TO EAT	9 Keszthely Tourist
5 Oászis Restaurant	& Ibusz
13 Hungária Gösser	10 Express
15 Pizzeria da Marcello	11 Tourinform
22 Béke	& Goldmark
	Cultural Centre
	12 Town Hall
	14 Dick Turpin's Pub
	17 Bus Stops
	18 Catholic Church
	19 OTP Bank
	20 Kolibri &
	Easy Rider
	21 Post Office
	25 Mahart Ferry Pier
	26 Railway Station
	27 Bus Station
	28 Balaton Museum

Lajos utca 50, has a reasonable menu with several fish dishes, a decent café and is open all year. Main courses start around 600 Ft.

Pizzeria da Marcello, in a cellar with rustic furniture at Városház utca 4, serves made-to-order pizzas and salads till 11 pm. *Oászis*, a 'reform' restaurant east of the palace at Rákóczi tér 3, serves vegetarian dishes from 11 am to 4 pm.

Entertainment
On Sunday at 8.30 pm from July to mid-August you can see Hungarian folk dancing in the back courtyard of *Károly Goldmark Cultural Centre*, Kossuth Lajos utca 28.

There are several interesting places for a drink along Kossuth Lajos utca. *Easy Rider* at No 79 attracts the local young bloods while *Kolibri* cocktail bar at No 81 is for an older crowd. *Dick Turpin's Pub* at Városház utca 2 plays the coolest music while *Piccolo* at No 9 of the same street is a small pub with Czech beer and full of friendly students and soldiers (Keszthely is a garrison town).

Getting There & Away
Bus The only important destinations with more than about 10 daily bus departures from Keszthely are Hévíz, Zalaegerszeg and Veszprém; there are about six to Nagykanizsa, Sümeg, Szombathely and Tapolca. Other towns served by bus include: Baja (one trip daily), Budapest (one), Győr (one), Pápa (three), Pécs (one), Sopron (two) and Székesfehérvár (one). Buses to Hévíz (7km) from stand No 4 are frequent.

Some of these buses – including those to Budapest, Zalaegerszeg, Nagykanizsa and Sümeg – can be boarded at the bus stops in front of the Catholic church on Fő tér.

Train Keszthely is on a branch line linking Tapolca and Balatonszentgyörgy, from where half a dozen daily trains continue along the southern shore to Székesfehérvár and also Budapest-Déli.

To reach Szombathely or towns along Lake Balaton's northern shore by train, change at Tapolca and sometimes at Celldömölk, too. For Pécs take a train to Kaposvár, then change to a bus.

Ferry Mahart ferries travel to/from Badacsony from June to early September. In July and much of August these boats also link Keszthely with Siófok.

HÉVÍZ
☎ 83
Hévíz is the site of Europe's largest thermal lake, Gyógytó. The people of this town 7km north-west of Keszthely have made use of the warm mineral water for centuries, first as a tannery in the Middle Ages and later for curative purposes. The lake was developed as a private resort by Count György Festetics of Keszthely in 1795.

Information
There are two travel agencies on Rákóczi utca: Hévíz Tourist (☎ 341 348) at No 4, and Zalatour (☎ 341 048) at No 8.

There's an OTP Bank branch at Erzsébet királynő utca 7 near the bus station, while the post office is at Kossuth Lajos utca 4.

Gyógytó
The thermal lake is an astonishing sight: a milky-blue surface of almost five hectares, covered for most of the year in water lilies. The spring is a crater some 40m deep that disgorges up to 80 million litres of warm water a day, renewing the lake every two days or so. The surface temperature averages 33°C and never drops below 26°C, allowing bathing throughout the year. The water and the mud on the bottom are slightly radioactive and supposedly alleviate various medical conditions.

A covered bridge leads to the pavilion, from where catwalks and piers fan out. You can swim beneath these or make your way to the small rafts and 'anchors' farther out in the lake. There are a couple of piers along the shore for sunbathing.

The lake is open in summer from 8 am to 6 pm, in winter from 9 am to 5 pm, and there is an entrance fee of 340 Ft for three hours and 680 Ft for the whole day. Hold onto your ticket as you might have to show it to get out. The indoor spa at the entrance to the park is open year-round from 7 am to 4 or 5 pm.

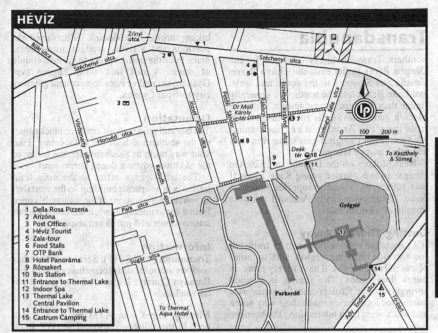

HÉVÍZ

1 Della Rosa Pizzeria
2 Arizóna
3 Post Office
4 Hévíz Tourist
5 Zala-tour
6 Food Stalls
7 OTP Bank
8 Hotel Panoráma
9 Rózsakert
10 Bus Station
11 Entrance to Thermal Lake
12 Indoor Spa
13 Thermal Lake
   Central Pavilion
14 Entrance to Thermal Lake
15 Castrum Camping

Places to Stay

Castrum Camping (☎ 343 198), on the southern end of the lake at the start of Tópart, is the only camp site in town. It's a new free-enterprise operation and is expensive, with packages aimed at Austrian and German tourists visiting the baths.

Zalatour and Hévíz Tourist (see the Information section) can find you a private room from 4000 Ft per double, though things could be tight in summer. You'll see 'Zimmer frei' and 'szoba Kiadó' signs on Kossuth Lajos utca and Zrínyi utca, where you can make your own deal for less.

Most hotels are expensive. A former union guest house, *Arizóna* (☎ 340 482) at Széchenyi utca 23, has singles/doubles with shared bath from 1500 Ft per person and with bath from 2750/4400 Ft a single/double. Add a tax of 200 Ft per person to these prices. The high-rise *Hotel Panorama* (☎ 341 074), charges DM52/75 and about 20% less in winter.

Places to Eat

The best place for a quick bite is Deák tér near the bus station, which has cafés (including the *Grill Garten*). A block north, at the end of Somogy Béla utca, you'll find *food stalls* selling lángos, sausages and fish. For a proper meal, try *Rózsakert* with a huge beer garden at Rákóczi utca 3, the *Hársfa* restaurant and wine bar just up from Kossuth Lajos utca at Honvéd utca 13, or *Della Rosa Pizzeria* on Széchenyi utca open daily till 9 pm.

Getting There & Away

Hévíz doesn't have a train station, but a bus goes to Keszthely almost every half-hour from stand No 3 (7km, 30 minutes). There are also plenty of departures to Sümeg and Zalaegerszeg and some to Badacsony, Balatonfüred and Veszprém. Other destinations with at least a couple of buses a day include Budapest, Győr, Pécs, Sopron and Szombathely.

Southern Transdanubia

Southern Transdanubia is bordered by the Danube River to the east, the Dráva River, Croatia and Slovenia to the south and west, and Lake Balaton to the north. It's generally flatter than western Transdanubia, with the Mecsek and Villány hills rising in isolation from the plain. At times it can feel almost Mediterranean though it gets more rain than any other part of Hungary.

Near Mohács on the Danube in 1526, the Hungarian army under young King Lajos II was routed by a vastly superior Ottoman force. The gracious city of Pécs still bears the imprint of Turkish rule.

Getting There & Away

It's easy to get to/from Budapest by train, but for travel within the region and to other places in Hungary you'll have to rely more on buses than trains. The region is a good springboard for Croatia and Slovenia as a number of local buses make their way south and south-west from towns along the borders.

PÉCS
☎ 72

Pécs (pronounced 'pairch') is a large, historical city between the Danube and Drava rivers. Its fine location on the southern slopes of the Mecsek Hills gives the city a relatively mild climate. Zsolnay porcelain and Pannónia sparkling wine are made here.

For 400 years the settlement of Sophianae was the capital of the Román province of Lower Pannonia. Christianity flourished here in the 4th century and by the 9th century the town was known as Quinque Ecclesiae for its five churches (it's still called Fünfkirchen in German). In 1009 Stephen I made Pécs a bishopric. The first Hungarian university was founded here in the mid-14th century, and the 15th-century bishop Janus Pannonius, who wrote some of Europe's most celebrated Renaissance poetry, was based here.

City walls were erected after the Mongol invasion of 1241, but 1543 marked the start of almost a century and a half of Turkish domination. The Turks left their greatest monuments at Pécs and these, together with imposing churches and a lovely synagogue, over a dozen museums, possibilities for hiking through the Mecsek Hills, varied excursions and a lively student atmosphere, make Pécs the perfect place to spend a couple of days. A rail link with Zagreb (via Gyékényes) makes Pécs an excellent gateway city to/from Croatia.

Orientation

The bus and train stations are three blocks apart on the southern side of the town centre. Find your way north to Széchenyi tér, the centre of the old town where a dozen streets meet.

The left-luggage office at the main train station is in a separate building, to the west (left as you leave the station) of the station. It's open from 4 am to midnight, while the one at the bus station closes at 4 pm (6 pm some days).

Information

Tourinform (☎ 213 315), Széchenyi tér 9, has copious amounts of information on Pécs and Baranya County. It's open daily (until 2 pm on weekends).

Money There's an ATM on the footpath outside the railway station. The OTP Bank branch opposite the National Theatre at Király utca 11 is open Monday to Wednesday from 7.45 am to 3 pm, Thursday from 9.15 am to 5.30 pm, and Friday from 7.45 am to 2 pm. M&M Exchange at Király utca 16 offers a decent rate and opens daily from 8 am to 2.30 pm and 3.30 to 10 pm.

Post The main post office is in a beautiful Art Nouveau building (1904) at Jókai Mór utca 10.

Bookshops The Corvina Art Bookshop at Széchenyi tér 7-8 has one of the best selections of books in English in Hungary.

Things to See

Széchenyi tér is the bustling heart of Pécs, dominated on the north by the former Gazi Kassim Pasha Mosque, the largest Turkish building in Hungary. Today it's the Inner Town Parish Church, more commonly known as the **Mosque Church**. Islamic elements inside, such as the mihrab (prayer niche) on the south-eastern side, are easy to spot.

Behind the Mosque Church at Széchenyi tér 12 is the **Archaeological Museum**.

From here go west along Janus Pannonius utca for a block to the **Csontváry Museum** at No 11, displaying the work of surrealist painter Tivadar Csontváry (1853-1919).

Káptalan utca, which climbs north-east from here, is lined with museums. Behind the **Endre Nemes Museum** at No 5 is the Erzsébet Schaár *Utca* or 'Street', a complete artistic environment in which the sculptor has set her whole life in stone. The **Vasarely Museum** at No 3 houses op art. Victor Vasarely, a long-time resident of southern France, was born in this house in 1908 as Vásárhelyi Győző. Across the street at No 2 is the **Zsolnay Porcelain Museum**, which has examples of famous porcelain from the factory's early days in the mid-19th century to the present.

Walk westward to Dóm tér and the enormous four-towered **Basilica of St Peter**. The oldest part of the building is the 11th-century crypt, but the entire complex was rebuilt in a neo-Romanesque style in 1881. In summer there are organ concerts on Friday evenings. West of the **Bishop's Palace** (1770), which stands in front of the cathedral, is a 15th-century **barbican**, the only stone bastion to survive from the old city walls.

To the south of Dóm tér is leafy Szent István tér. Here you'll see a stairway down to an excavated 4th-century **Christian chapel** with striking frescoes of Adam and Eve, and Daniel in the lion's den. There's a later **Roman mausoleum** a little farther south at Apáca utca 14.

Follow your map south-west a few blocks from Szent István tér to the 16th-century **Hassan Jakovali Mosque**, wedged between a school and a hospital at Rákóczi út 2. It's the best-preserved Turkish monument in Hungary.

Follow Pécs' attractive pedestrian malls, Ferencesek utcája and Király utca, east across the city. You'll pass three beautiful old churches and the neo-rococo **National Theatre**. Just beyond the **Church of St Stephen** (1741), turn right from Király utca into Felsőmalom utca 9, where you'll find an excellent **City History Museum**.

The **synagogue** (1869) on Kossuth tér, an oblong square south of Széchenyi tér, is open to visitors from May to October, closed Saturday.

All of Pécs' museums, except the synagogue, are closed Monday.

After exploring Pécs, take a trip up into the **Mecsek Hills**. Bus No 35 from in front of the train station climbs hourly to the 194m **TV Tower** on Misina Peak (534m). You could also take bus No 35 from Hunyadi János út just outside the old town wall. There's a restaurant below the viewing balcony high up in the tower (open daily).

Well-marked hiking trails fan out from the TV Tower – the 1:40,000 *A Mecsek* topographical map shows them all. Armed with this map, you could also take a bus from the bus station to **Orfű** (with an attractive lake) or **Abaliget** (with a 450m-long cave) and hike back over the hills. Much of this area has been logged over, but doesn't attract many visitors, making it peaceful and uncrowded.

Places to Stay
Camping *Mandulás Camping* (☎ 315 981), up in the Mecsek Hills at Angyán János utca 2, has sites and bungalows with shared shower from DM35 and a hotel which has doubles with bath from DM45. Some bungalows are let as hostel accommodation for about 2000 Ft. It's a long and steep way from the city centre but bus No 34 from the train station runs past.

Hostel In July and August, *Janus Pannonius University* (☎ 251 203), west of the centre at Szánto Kovács János utca 1c, accommodates travellers in three-bed dorm rooms for about 1000 Ft per person. Ask Tourinform about other college dorms.

Private Rooms Mecsek Tours (☎ 213 855), Széchenyi tér 1, and Ibusz, Apáca utca 1, arrange private rooms from 1200/2000 Ft for singles/doubles and apartments from 3500 Ft. Unless you stay more than three nights there's a 30% surcharge on the first night. One place that has been recommended is at Jokai Mór utca 5, close to Szechenyi tér. The phone number is ☎ 336 427 and a bed costs about 2000 Ft.

Hotels A very central place to stay is the *Főnix Hotel* (☎ 311 680), Hunyadi János út 2.

Singles/doubles cost 3600/4700 Ft with shared bath, more with attached bath.

Hotel Laterum (☎ 252 113), Hajnóczy utca 37-39 is a long way from the centre, on the far west side of town. Take bus No 4 from the train station or the market on Bajcsy-Zsilinszky utca near the bus station to the end of the line at Uránváros. There's a six-bed dorm room that costs 900 Ft per person, minimum 2700 Ft and a four-bed room with shared bathroom that costs 3600 Ft. Singles/doubles/triples with bath cost 3000/5000/6000 Ft. This is where NATO troops

heading for Bosnia stay, so there aren't always vacancies.

Wander into the old *Hotel Palatinus* (☎ 233 022), Király utca 5, for a look at the opulent foyer. If you can't afford DM104/112 a single/double (less in winter) don't regret it too much – the rooms aren't anywhere near as impressive as the public areas.

Several slightly upmarket places to stay are up in the Mecsek Hills near the TV Tower. Their prices are high because of the views and the surrounding woods, but if you don't have transport you might feel cut off

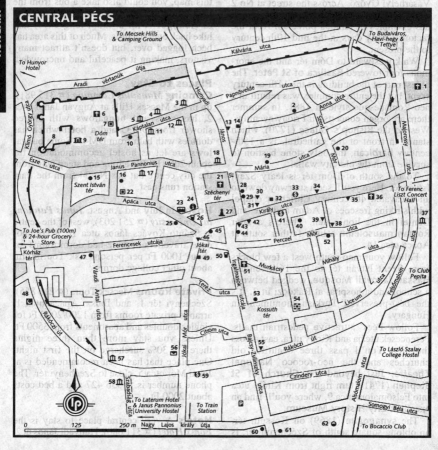

CENTRAL PÉCS

from the city. *Hotel Kikelet* (☎ 310 777), Károlyi Mihály utca 1, has rooms with shared bath at 4200/5800 Ft a single/double. Bus Nos 34 and 35 run to the hotel from the train station. The two-star *Hotel Fenyves* (☎ 315 996), Szőlő utca 64, has a great view of the city and charges 5640/8120 Ft a single/ double. Take bus No 34 or 35 to Hotel Kikelet, then walk down to the Fenyves.

Places to Eat

Walk east along Kiraly utca, from *McDonald's* on the corner and the surprisingly good *John Bull's Pub* next door (an 'energy salad' costs 750 Ft, comes with grilled turkey and is an excellent snack), to a range of places farther on. *Dóm Snack* (up an alley) has pizza and pasta for under 500 Ft. Next door, a meal at the good *Dóm Vendéglö* restaurant costs around 1700 Ft. For breakfast (egg dishes 225 Ft) or any other meal, or just a drink, *Vasváry* is a pleasant bar/café. It plays good music and stays open late. Diagonally opposite, *Caflisch Café* is the place for coffee and cake, or try *Mecsek Cukrászda* at Széchenyi tér 16 near the old Nádor Hotel.

Az Elefánthoz, just off the south-west corner of Széchenyi tér, is a bustling Italian restaurant, also serving Hungarian standards. You'll spend about 2500 Ft on a big meal. Behind the Főnix Hotel at Hunyadi utca 2, the underground *Cellarium* has a prison theme.

There's a cheap *buffet* up a lane near the Apollo Cinema and a *nonstop grocery store* at Hungária utca 18 west of Petőfi tér.

Entertainment

Pécs has well-established opera and ballet companies. If you're told that tickets to the *National Theatre* on Király utca are sold out, try for a cancellation at the box office an hour before the performance. This theatre is closed all summer so ask Tourinform about concerts and other events elsewhere.

House of Artists (or Művészetek Háza) at Széchenyi tér 7-8 advertises its many programs outside. This is the place to ask about classical music concerts.

Some of Pécs' most popular discos are *Club Pepita* on 48-as tér near the university east of the centre; *A Gyár* (The Factory), an 'alternative culture and rock music club'

CENTRAL PÉCS

PLACES TO STAY		
14	Főnix Hotel	
32	Hotel Palatinus	
49	Private Room	

PLACES TO EAT		
13	Cellarium	
30	Dóm Vendéglö	
31	Dóm Snack	
34	Vasváry	
35	Caflisch Café	
38	Apolló Takeaway Restaurant	
39	Buffet	
42	John Bull's Pub	
43	McDonald's	
46	Az Elefánthoz	
55	Pizza Hut	

OTHER		
1	St Augustine Church	
2	Croatian Theatre	
3	Zsolnay Porcelain Museum	
4	Modern Hungarian Art Gallery I	

5	Ferenc Martyn Museum
6	Basilica of St Peter
7	Jug Mausoleum
8	Barbican
9	Bishop's Palace
10	Kioszk Café
11	Endre Nemes Museum
12	Vasarely Museum
15	Tomb Chapel
16	Pannonvin Champagne Factory
17	Csontváry Museum
18	Archaeology Museum
19	Café Jazz
20	Puppet Theatre
21	Mosque Church
22	Roman Mausoleum
23	Lajos Nagy Swimming Pool
24	Tourinform
25	Ibusz
26	Nothing But the Blues
27	Trinity Column
28	Nádor Hotel Building

29	Mecsek Cake Shop
33	OTP Bank
36	Church of St Stephen
37	City History Museum
40	National Theatre
41	M&M Exchange
44	Mecsek Tours
45	House of Artists & Corvina Art Bookshop
47	Memi Pasha Baths
48	Hassan Jakovali Mosque
50	Áfium Bar & Restaurant
51	Church of the Good Samaritan
52	Apollo Cinema
53	Town Hall
54	Synagogue
56	Main Post Office
57	Ethnology Museum
58	Modern Hungarian Art Gallery II
59	Main OTP Bank
60	Express
61	Market
62	Bus Station

open Tuesday to Saturday from 8 pm to 4 am at Czindery utca 3-5; and the *Ajima Club* on Irgalmasok utcája. Students drink at *Nothin' but the Blues* on Apáca utca and *Joe's Pub* on Hungária utca. For jazz, try *Café Jazz* on Mária utca.

Getting There & Away

Bus Daily buses departing from Pécs include two to Hévíz (164km), seven to Kaposvár (67km), two to Kecskemét (176km), hourly to Siklós (32km), three to Siófok (122km), one to Sopron (287km) and six to Szeged (189km, four hours). The bus is more direct than the train on all these routes. In summer there are two dozen daily departures to Abaliget and Orfű, and eight or so a day in winter.

Train Some 10 trains a day connect Pécs with Budapest-Déli (229km, three hours; less by IC). You can reach Nagykanizsa and other points north-west via a rather circuitous but scenic line along the Dráva River. From Nagykanizsa, three or four trains a day continue on to Szombathely. One early morning express (at 5.40 am) follows this route from Pécs all the way to Szombathely.

Croatia A daily train runs between Pécs and Zagreb (267km, five hours), leaving Pécs in the very early morning and Zagreb in the late afternoon. Buses run about five times a day from Barcs to Zagreb (202km), and there are also two afternoon buses a day from Pécs to Osijek.

AROUND PÉCS

An easy day trip from Pécs by train or bus is to **Szigetvár**, 33km west, where some 2500 Hungarians and Croats held off Turkish forces numbering up to 100,000 for over a month in 1566. As the moated 'island castle' (which is the meaning of its name) was about to fall, the remaining defenders sallied out under Miklós Zrínyi to meet their end in bloody hand-to-hand combat. The Turks suffered tremendous losses, including that of Sultan Suleiman I, and their march on Vienna was halted.

Szigetvár's **Zrínyi Castle** (1420) with its four corner bastions contains a museum focusing on the 1566 battle. Inside the complex is a mosque built soon after the fall of Szigetvár in honour of the sultan. Only the

base remains of the minaret. A second mosque, the **Ali Pasha Mosque** (1569), now a Catholic church, stands in the centre of town.

Harkány
☎ 72

The hot springs at Harkány, 26km south of Pécs, feature medicinal waters with the richest sulphuric content in Hungary. There are large open-air thermal pools open in summer and indoor baths open year round.

Harkány is a transit point for people travelling between Croatia and Yugoslavia. The Drávaszabolcs/Donji Miholjac border crossing to/from Croatia is 9km south of town. However, unless you're interested in the thermal pools there isn't much reason to stay here. Push on to Pécs.

Information The left-luggage office at the bus station is open Monday to Thursday from 8 am to 4 pm, Friday to 2 pm.

K&H Bank has an exchange office at the entrance to the spa. The OTP Bank has a kiosk between the bus station and the baths open May to September only.

Places to Stay & Eat *Thermál Camping* (☎ 480 117), Bajcsy-Zsilinszky utca 6, has a motel (DM21 to DM24 a double), a hotel (from DM31/33/45 for one/two/three people) and bungalows with two double rooms and kitchen from DM50 to DM68. Tent sites cost DM3.50 to DM5. The complex is open between mid-April and mid-October.

Mecsek Tours (☎ 480 322), at the main entrance to the baths at Bajcsy-Zsilinszky utca 4, books *private rooms* from about 2000 Ft a person, but for a one-night stay you may be better investigating the possibilities yourself by strolling east on Bartók Béla utca, where 'Zimmer frei' signs proliferate.

There's a bunch of faintly depressing hotels on Bajcsy-Zsilinszky utca opposite the baths entrance. The *Baranya Hotel* (☎ 480 160) is typical and has singles/doubles for 2740/5500 Ft.

You're not going to starve in this town of sausage stands and wine counters, but if you want to sit down, try the *Robinson* with pizza and other dishes at Kossuth Lajos utca 7. For Serbian grills like čevapčiči and pleskavica try the terrace of *Hotel Bosna*, across from the baths entrance.

Getting There & Away All buses between Pécs and Siklós stop here. Four buses a day link Harkány to Croatia: two to Osijek (at 12.30 and 5.30 pm, 87km) and one each to Našice (weekdays at 10 am, 71km) and Slavonski Brod (5.15 pm, 125km).

Siklós

Siklós, surrounded by the wine-producing Villány Hills is 6km east of Harkány. On a hilltop stands a well-preserved 15th-century castle, now the **Castle Museum**. The Gothic chapel and the dungeon with its implements of torture are also worth a look.

Siklós is connected to Pécs (32km) by hourly bus via Harkány. The bus and train stations are on opposite sides of Siklós, each about a 10-minute walk from the castle.

The Great Plain

The Great Plain (Nagyalföld) of south-eastern Hungary is a wide expanse of level puszta (or prairie) drained by the Tisza River. It has for centuries figured in poems, songs, paintings and stories. Parts of the plain have been turned into farmland but other regions are little more than grassy, saline 'deserts'. In the blazing heat of the summer more than a few people have witnessed distinct mirages floating over the scorched and windy plain.

Visitors to the region are introduced to the lore of the Hungarian horse, cow and shepherds and their unique animals: Nonius horses, long-horned grey cattle and *racka* sheep. Two national parks, Kiskunság in the Bugac Puszta and Hortobágy in the Hortobágy Puszta, protect this special environment.

KECSKEMÉT
☎ 76

Lying exactly halfway between Budapest and Szeged and near the geographical centre of Hungary, Kecskemét is a clean, leafy city famous for its apricots, potent *barack pálinka* (apricot brandy), fine architecture and level puszta. It's known as the garden city of Hungary for the fruit trees in the surrounding area; wine is also produced here. Among

Kecskemét's most renowned native sons are the beloved playwright József Katona (1791-1830) and the composer Zoltán Kodály (1882-1967).

Central Kecskemét has more than it's share of impressive public and religious architecture, but it also has been invaded by ugly modern buildings. These dominate just south of the centre but on the north side Rákcóczi utca is a leafy boulevard, like Budapest's Andrássy Ave on a small scale. You find little old streets (some paved with brick) west of here.

Orientation

Kecskemét is a city of squares which run into one another, and can be a little confusing at first. The bus and main train stations are opposite one another in József Katona Park. A 10-minute walk south-west along Nagykőrösi utca will bring you to the first of the squares, Szabadság tér. The left-luggage office at the train station is open from 7 am to 7 pm.

Information

Tourinform (☎ 481 065) is on the west side of the Town Hall at Kossuth Lajos tér 1. It's open from 8 am to 5 pm on weekdays (6 pm in summer) and from 9 am to 1 pm on Saturday.

Money OTP Bank has a branch at Szabadság tér 5 next to the former synagogue and is open Monday to Wednesday from 7.45 am to 3.30 pm, Thursday to 4.30 pm and Friday to 1 pm. Among the ATMs in town you'll find one at the main post office.

Post The main post office is at Kálvin tér 10.

Things to See

Kossuth tér is surrounded by historic buildings. Dominating the square is the massive Art Nouveau **Town Hall** (1897) with a carillon that plays on the hour. Flanking the Town Hall are the neoclassical **Great Church** (1806) and the earlier **Church of St Nicholas**, dating (in parts) from the 13th century. The **Kodály Institute of Music Education** occupies the baroque monastery directly behind it at Két templom köz 1. Nearby on Katona József tér is the magnificent **József Katona**

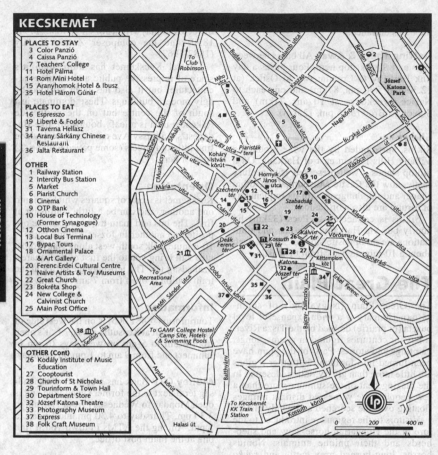

KECSKEMÉT

PLACES TO STAY
3 Color Panzió
4 Caissa Panzió
7 Teachers' College
11 Hotel Pálma
14 Rom Mini Hotel
15 Aranyhomok Hotel & Ibusz
35 Hotel Három Gúnár

PLACES TO EAT
16 Espresszo
19 Liberté & Fodor
31 Taverna Hellasz
34 Arany Sárkány Chinese Restaurant
36 Jalta Restaurant

OTHER
1 Railway Station
2 Intercity Bus Station
5 Market
6 Piarist Church
8 Cinema
9 OTP Bank
10 House of Technology (Former Synagogue)
12 Otthon Cinema
13 Local Bus Terminal
17 Bypac Tours
18 Ornamental Palace & Art Gallery
20 Ferenc Erdei Cultural Centre
21 Naive Artists & Toy Museums
22 Great Church
23 Bokréta Shop
24 New College & Calvinist Church
25 Main Post Office

OTHER (Cont)
26 Kodály Institute of Music Education
27 Cooptourist
28 Church of St Nicholas
29 Tourinform & Town Hall
30 Department Store
32 József Katona Theatre
33 Photography Museum
37 Express
38 Folk Craft Museum

Theatre (1896) with a baroque statue of the Trinity (1742) standing in front of it.

Of the many museums and art galleries, the most interesting is the **Museum of Naive Artists** in the Stork House (1730), on Gáspár András utca just off Petőfi Sándor utca. In the art gallery below the museum you can buy original paintings almost as good as those on display upstairs, at reasonable prices. Another museum that's worth a look is the **Photography Museum**, in an Orthodox synagogue at Katona József tér 12. It's open Wednesday to Sunday from 10 am to 6 pm.

Places to Stay

Camping *Autós Camping* (☎ 329 398) is on Sport utca, on the south-western side of Kecskemét, nearly 5km from the train station and crammed with German and Dutch tourists in caravans. It's open from mid-April to mid-October. Bus Nos 1 and 11 run to the camp site from the train station.

Hostels The best in-expensive accommodation is at Hotel Pálma – see the Hotels section below.

About three blocks from the camping ground is *GAMF College* (☎ 321 916), Izsáki út 10 with summer accommodation for 800 Ft. Officially it's only open mid-June to August, but you can sometimes get a bed during other months. Catch bus No 1 or 11 at the train station. Various other colleges also have accommodation – see Tourinform.

Private Rooms & Pensions *Color Panzió* (☎ 483 246), Jókai utca 26, is a small pension charging 3800 Ft a double. *Caissa Panzió* (☎ 481 685), Gyenes tér 18, charges 4900 Ft a double. Tourinform has a brochure listing more places and Ibusz at the Aranyhomok Hotel, at Kossuth Lajos tér 2, makes bookings.

Hotels *Hotel Pálma* (☎ 321 045), in the centre of town at Arany János utca 3, is a very friendly church-owned hotel offering good value. Shared rooms in the tourist section cost 2400/4200 Ft for singles/doubles, 4800/5800 Ft for triples/quads with shared bathroom. In the hotel section you'll pay 3800/5000/6000 Ft a single/double/triple with bath, phone and TV. These rates include breakfast. It has another 80 dorm beds in a nearby building, so you should get one.

Rom Mini Hotel (☎ 483 174), Széchenyi tér 14, is above a shop in a small shopping plaza, across from the local bus station. The rooms are small but have attached bathroom and TV – not bad value at 4200 Ft for singles or doubles. *Hotel Három Gúnár* (☎ 483 611), close to the centre at Batthyány utca 1-7, charges DM64/70 a single/double with bath, and is very comfortable. A popular bowling alley and bar are in the hotel basement.

Places to Eat

For a coffee or a snack, ignore McDonalds, across from Szabadság tér, and go to *Espresszo*, a café next door. *Jalta*, Batthyány utca 2, opposite the Hotel Három Gúnár, is a rather homy wine cellar with a menu in both English and German. Its speciality is grilled South Slav dishes.

Modern *Taverna Hellasz*, behind the shopping centre on the corner of Lechner and Kisfaludy utcas, has excellent Greek meals and snacks. Order a gyros (650 Ft) and you'll get a platter of lamb and salad that bears no resemblance to the dodgy stuff that goes by that name in the United Kingdom.

The pizza at *Italia* on Koháry István körút has improved in recent years but you can opt instead for black olives and feta cheese by crossing the street to *Görög Udvar*. *Arany Sárkány* is a Chinese restaurant at Erkel Ferenc utca 1a, south-east of Katona József tér.

If you want to splurge, you couldn't do better than at *Liberté* in a historical building next to Pusztatourist on Szabadság tér, one of the best restaurants in provincial Hungary. You can have coffee and cake for under 400 Ft. The best ice cream and cakes are at *Fodor*, in the same building as the Liberté restaurant on Szabadság tér.

Entertainment

Kecskemét is a city of music and theatre; you'd be crazy not to attend at least one performance here. The *Ferenc Erdei Cultural Centre* at Deák Ferenc tér 1 sponsors some events and is a good source of information for other venues. The 19th-century *József Katona Theatre* on Katonpa József tér stages dramatic works as well as operettas and concerts by the Kecskemét Symphony Orchestra. *Club Robinson*, Akadémia körút 2 (closed Monday and Tuesday) is a large, popular disco. *Roger's Club*, under the cinema at the top end of Rákcóczi utca, has music nightly.

Getting There & Away

There are almost hourly buses to Budapest (85km), buses every couple of hours to Szeged (86km) and at least one a day to Pécs (176km; 7.30 am, 1400 Ft). Buses also run to Arad (191km) in Romania about four times a week and to Subotica (130km) in Yugoslavia a couple of times daily, but check this information before making plans.

Kecskemét is on the rail line linking Budapest-Nyugati with Szeged. To get to Debrecen and other cities and towns east, you must change at Cegléd (33km, 30 minutes).

KISKUNSÁG NATIONAL PARK

Totalling 35,000 sq hectares, Kiskunság consists of half a dozen 'islands' of land. Much of the park's alkaline ponds, dunes and grassy 'deserts' are off limits to casual visitors, but you can get a close look at this environmentally fragile area – and see the famous horseherds go through their paces – at **Bugac**, 30km south-west of Kecskemét.

The easiest but priciest way is to join a tour in Kecskemét with Bugac Tours (☎ 481 643, bugac@mail.datanet.hu), at the north-east end of Szabadság tér. For about 6500 Ft, they'll bus you to the park, take you by carriage to the horse show, and serve you lunch at a touristy csárda.

Alternatively, take the 8.25 am narrow-gauge train from Kecskemét KK station – not the main train station. Kecskemét KK is on Halasi út, which is the southern continuation of Batthyány utca; you can walk from the centre of Kecskemét or take bus No 2 or 13 from the local bus station. Get off at the Bugac felső station (31km; 1¼ hours) and not the Bugacpuszta or Bugac train stations, which come before it.

From the station, walk north for 15 minutes to the Bugaci Karikás Csárda and the park entrance (800 Ft admission). There you can board a horse carriage for DM10 or walk another 3km to the **Herder Museum**, filled with stuffed flora and pressed fauna of the Kiskunság. It's open daily (except Monday) from April to September.

The **horse show** starts at 1 pm from April to the end of September (this can vary slightly; ask at the park entrance). The horseherds crack their whips, race one another bareback and ride 'five-in-hand', a breathtaking performance in which one *csikós* (cowboy) gallops five horses at full speed while standing on the backs of the rear two.

The **Bugaci Karikás Csárda**, with its folk-music ensemble and its gulyás, is a lot more fun than it first appears to be. There are horses for riding (1400 Ft per hour) and a *camp site* for 60 people. Bugac Tours, with offices in Kecskemét and at the park entrance, has rustic *cottages* for rent nearby from DM60 for two people. It also offers various riding packages and training in two-in-hand and four-in-hand carriage driving.

Unless you entertain yourself with bird-watching or drinking apricot pálinka at the csárda, you have a lot of time to kill between the end of the horse show and the next train at 6.35 pm. You can catch a bus back to Kecskemét from the main highway (route No 54) near the csárda (four a day).

SZEGED
☎ 62

Szeged (Segedin in German), the most important city on the southern Great Plain, straddles the Tisza River just before it enters Yugoslavia. The Maros River from Romania enters the Tisza just east of the centre.

Disaster struck in 1879 when the Tisza swelled its banks and almost washed the city off the map. Szeged was redesigned with concentric boulevards and radial avenues. Sections of the outer boulevard are named for the cities that provided aid after the flood, including Vienna, London, Paris, Berlin, Brussels and Rome.

Szeged is more architecturally homogeneous than many other cities, with few modern buildings intruding on the stately city centre. It's large and lively with lots of students, and in midsummer it comes to life during the Szeged Festival. Szeged is also celebrated for its edibles: Szeged paprika, which mates so wonderfully with fish from the Tisza in *szegedi halászlé* (spicy fish soup), and Pick, Hungary's finest salami.

Orientation

The main train station is south of the city centre on Indóház tér; tram No 1 connects the train station to town. The bus station, to the west of the centre on Mars tér, is within easy walking distance via pedestrian Mikszáth Kálmán utca. The left-luggage office at the train station is open from 4 am to 11 pm.

A taxi from the station to the centre of town shouldn't cost more than 350 Ft but there's at least one driver who charges three times that amount.

Information

Tourinform (☎ 311 711) is at Victor Hugo utca 1. Szeged Tourist (☎ 321 800) is on Klauzál tér, just off Victor Hugo utca.

Money The OTP Bank at Klauzál tér 2 is open Monday from 7.45 am to 4.30 pm, Tuesday to Thursday to 3 pm, and Friday to 11.30 am. It also has a foreign-currency exchange machine.

Post The main post office is at Széchenyi tér 1.

Things to See

The symbol of Szeged is the twin-towered **Votive Church**, an ugly brick structure that was pledged after the flood of 1879 but not completed until 1930. The cavernous interior is covered with frescoes, and the organ has 11,500 pipes.

The Romanesque **St Demetrius Tower** beside the church is all that remains of a church dating from the 13th century, which was demolished to make room for the present one. Have a look inside the **Serbian Orthodox Church** (1778) behind the Votive Church at the fantastic iconostasis – a central gold 'tree' with 60 icons hanging off its 'branches'.

By the Inner Town Bridge (Belvárosi híd) over the Tisza is the **Ferenc Móra Museum** in a huge neoclassical building (1896). Downstairs is a good collection of Hungarian painting (including several representations of the 1879 flood) and an exhibit on the Avar people who occupied the Carpathian Basin from the 5th to 8th centuries. The upper floor is dedicated to the folk art. The park just north (Várkert) contains ruins of what was Szeged's 18th-century fortress and the very informative **Castle Museum**.

There are many fine buildings around Széchenyi tér in the centre of town, including the **Old Town Hall**. Don't miss the **Reök Palace** (1907), a mind-blowing Art Nouveau structure on Kölcsey utca.

The **Great Synagogue** (1903), Gutenberg utca 13, is the most beautiful Jewish house of worship in Hungary, and is still in use. There are a few other buildings of interest in the neighbourhood including the **Old Synagogue** (1843), Hajnóczy utca 12.

Places to Stay

Camping *Partfürdő Camping* (☎ 430 843) is off Közép kikötő sor in Újszeged (New Szeged) along the river opposite the city centre. Camping is about 450 Ft per person and per tent and there are hotel rooms from 2500 Ft per double. Guests have free use of the swimming and thermal pools. Partfürdő is open from May to October.

A second (and much less attractive) site is *Napfény Camping* (☎ 421 800), Dorozsmai út 2, across a large bridge near the western terminus of tram No 1.

Student Accommodation Plenty of student accommodation is open to travellers in July and August, including at the central *István Apáthy College* (☎ 323 155), Eötvös utca 4 next to the Votive Church. Private rooms with bath cost 3500 Ft per person and dorms cost around 850 Ft. *Loránd Eötvös College* (☎ 310 641), Tisza Lajos körút 103, charges a little less for dorms. Go directly to the hostels or ask for information at Express, Kígyó utca 3.

Private Rooms Your best bet for a private room is Szeged Tourist, which charges from 1600/2800 Ft a single/double (30% more for one-night stays) and from 3500 Ft for an apartment (minimum four nights).

Hotel & Pensions The fine old two-star *Hotel Tisza* (☎ 478 278), Wesselényi utca 1 just off Széchenyi tér, is no longer cheap but it's still reasonable value at 4000/5500 Ft a single/double with shared bathroom, 6700/7700 Ft with bath (less out of season).

If you arrive by bus you'll be within walking distance of *Sára Panzió* (☎ 498 206), Zákány utca 13, where singles/doubles cost about 3000/4000 Ft. If it's full there's the slightly more upmarket *Pölös Panzió* on the opposite corner at Pacsirta utca 17a, charging from 3500/4800 Ft.

Places to Eat

Hági, an old Szeged stand-by at Kelemen utca 3 in the centre, serves reliable and reasonably priced Hungarian and South Slav dishes. *Lesö Harcsa Halászcsárda* – that's the Eager Catfish Fishermen's Inn – at Roosevelt tér 14 is a Szeged institution and serves up szegedi halászlé by the cauldron. *Numero Uno Pizza*, on Vörösmarty utca facing Széchenyi tér, is a casual place with good food. A mini pizza costs just 200 Ft. It's open till midnight (11 pm on Sunday).

Boszorkánykonyha, Híd utca 8, just off Széchenyi tér, is an unappetising, but very cheap, self-service place. Better yet, try the *Festival* self-service in the modern building on Oskola utca directly across the street from the entrance to the Votive Church. There's also *Jumbo Grill*, Mikszáth Kálmán utca 4, with almost-real salads and excellent grilled chicken.

SZEGED

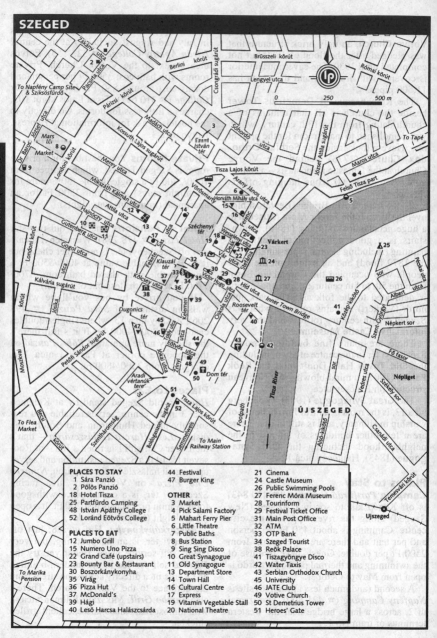

0   250   500 m

PLACES TO STAY
1 Sára Panzió
2 Pölös Panzió
18 Hotel Tisza
25 Partfürdo Camping
48 István Apáthy College
52 Loránd Eötvös College

PLACES TO EAT
12 Jumbo Grill
15 Numero Uno Pizza
22 Grand Café (upstairs)
23 Bounty Bar & Restaurant
30 Boszorkánykonyha
35 Virág
36 Pizza Hut
37 McDonald's
39 Hági
40 Lesõ Harcsa Halászcsárda

44 Festival
47 Burger King

OTHER
3 Market
4 Pick Salami Factory
5 Mahart Ferry Pier
6 Little Theatre
7 Public Baths
8 Bus Station
9 Sing Sing Disco
10 Great Synagogue
11 Old Synagogue
13 Department Store
14 Town Hall
16 Cultural Centre
17 Express
19 Vitamin Vegetable Stall
20 National Theatre

21 Cinema
24 Castle Museum
26 Public Swimming Pools
27 Ferenc Móra Museum
28 Tourinform
29 Festival Ticket Office
31 Main Post Office
32 ATM
33 OTP Bank
34 Szeged Tourist
38 Reök Palace
41 Tiszagyöngye Disco
42 Water Taxis
43 Serbian Orthodox Church
45 University
46 JATE Club
49 Votive Church
50 St Demetrius Tower
51 Heroes' Gate

Upstairs on Deák Ferenc utca, behind the Belvárosi cinema, *Grand Café* is a good place for a snack and a quiet coffee. There are usually some English-language magazines. For something both nearby and completely different, go to the posh *Bounty Bar*, Wesseléyi utca opposite the National Theatre, for a drink (there's a long list of whiskies) or a meal. Check *Virág* on Klauzál tér, one of the nicest cake and coffee shops in Hungary. The outlet at No 8 is for stand-up service and takeaway, No 1 has tables inside and on the square.

Szeged is loaded with fast-food places (all those students, no doubt) including: *Pizza Hut* at Kárász utca 10; *McDonald's* at Kárász utca 11; and *Burger King* at Árpád tér 1.

For fresh-squeezed orange juice (a rarity in Hungary), go to the stall in the department store on the corner of Tisza Lajos Körút and Attila utca.

Entertainment

Your best sources of information in this culturally active city are Tourinform or the *Béla Bartók Cultural Centre* at Vörösmarty utca 3. The *National Theatre* (1883) across the street has always been the centre of cultural life in Szeged and usually stages opera and ballet.

The Szeged Open-Air Festival (mid-July to August) unfolds on Dóm tér with the two towers of the Votive Church as a backdrop. The outdoor theatre here seats some 6000 people. Main events include an opera, an operetta, a play, folk dancing, classical music, ballet and a rock opera. Tickets and information are available from the festival ticket office at Deák Ferenc utca 30 (open weekdays from 10 am to 5 pm, and to 3 pm in summer).

Szeged isn't all highbrow: there's a vast array of bars, clubs and other night spots in this student town, especially around Dugonics tér.

The *JATE Club* at Toldy utca 1 is the best place to meet students on their own turf. The huge *Tiszagyöngye Disco* on Közép kikötő sor in Újszeged is open on summer weekends until 4 am.

Sing Sing Disco occupies a huge pavilion at Mars tér and Dr Baross János utca near the bus station. It's open Wednesday, Friday and Saturday from 10 pm to 4 am.

Getting There & Away

Bus Bus services are good, with seven daily departures to Budapest, two to Debrecen, two to Eger, eight to Kecskemét, six to Pécs, four to Székesfehérvár and two to Veszprém.

To Romania, buses run to Arad from Tuesday to Saturday at 5.10 pm and to Timişoara on Tuesday and Friday at 6.30 am. Buses run to Senta (Hungarian: Zenta) in Yugoslavia twice daily and to Subotica Tuesday to Saturday at 6 am and 12.30 pm.

Train Szeged is on a main train line to Budapest-Nyugati. Another line connects the city with Hódmezővásárhely and Békéscsaba, where you can change trains for Gyula or Romania. Southbound local trains leave Szeged for Subotica in Yugoslavia five times a day.

Boat From June to late August, on Saturday and holidays only, a Mahart ferry plies the Tisza River between Szeged and Csongrád (70km), leaving Szeged at 7 am and Csongrád at 4 pm. Though it's a pleasant way to travel, the five-hour trip is more than twice as long as the bus, making a half-dozen stops along the way.

Northern Hungary

Northern Hungary is the most mountainous part of the country. The southern ranges of the Carpathian Mountains stretch east along the Slovakian border in a 1000m-high chain of woody hills from the Danube Bend almost to the Ukrainian border. Historic Eger offers an ideal base for sightseers and wine tasters. Just to the north is Szilvásvárad, home of the snow-white Lipizzaner horses, and farther afield the karst caves near Aggtelek. To the east is the famous Tokaj wine-growing area.

Getting There & Away

The peripherals of northern Hungary are well served by train, but if you want to venture into the hills, you'll have to go by bus.

HUNGARY

EGER
☎ 36

Eger (Erlau in German) is a lovely baroque city full of historic buildings. It was at Eger Castle in 1552 that 2000 Hungarian defenders temporarily stopped the Turkish advance into Europe and helped to preserve Hungary's identity. The Turks returned in 1596 and captured the castle but were thrown out by the Austrians in 1687. Eger played a central role in Ferenc Rákóczi II's attempt to overthrow the Habsburgs early in the 18th century, and it was then that a large part of the castle was razed by the Austrians.

It was the bishops and later the archbishops of Eger who built the town you see today. Eger possesses some of Hungary's finest examples of Copf (Zopf in Hungarian) architecture, a transitional style between late baroque and neoclassicalism found only in Central Europe.

Today Eger is famous for its potent Bull's Blood (Egri Bikavér) red wine. Dozens of wine cellars are to be seen in Szépasszonyvölgy (Valley of the Beautiful Women), just a 20-minute walk south-west of the centre.

Orientation

The train station is a 15-minute walk south of town on Vasút utca, just west of Deák Ferenc utca, while the bus station is above Széchenyi István utca, Eger's main drag. Egervár train station, which serves Szilvásvárad and other points north, is a five-minute walk north of the castle. The left-luggage office at the train station is open from 6.30 am to 6.30 pm only; the one at the bus station stays open as long as the ticket windows do.

Information

Staff at Tourinform (☎ 321 807), Dobó István tér 2, are very friendly and several speak fluent English. One can speak French – a rare talent in Hungary!

The OTP Bank, Széchenyi utca 2, is open weekdays from 7.45 am to 3 pm (1 pm on Friday).

Things to See & Do

The first thing you see as you come into town from the bus or train station is the neoclassical Eger Cathedral (1836) on Eszterházy tér. Directly opposite is the Copf-style Lyceum (1765) with a frescoed library on the 1st floor and the 18th-century observatory on the 6th floor. Climb three more floors up to the observation deck for a great view of the city and surrounding vineyards. There is also a 200-year-old periscope here that allows you to spy on Eger unobserved. You can visit the Lyceum (250 Ft) daily in summer from 9.30 am to 3.30 pm, between Christmas and mid-March on weekend mornings only and the rest of the year every morning except Monday.

Kossuth Lajos utca has some fine buildings, including the baroque County Hall at No 9 (1761); the Provost's House at No 4; Franciscan church at No 14, completed in 1755 on the site of a mosque; and the former Orthodox synagogue (1893) at No 17. The ruins of an earlier neoclassical synagogue (1845) can be seen on Hibay Károly utca, which runs north off Kossuth utca.

At the eastern end of Kossuth utca, across Dózsa György tér, a cobblestone lane leads up to Eger Castle, erected in the 13th century after the Mongol invasion. Inside are the foundations of St John's Cathedral, which was destroyed by the Turks. Models and drawings in the castle's István Dobó Museum show how the cathedral once looked. This museum, in the former Bishop's Palace (1470), is named after the national hero who led the resistance to the Turks in 1552. Below the castle are underground casemates hewn from solid rock, which you may tour with a guide (250 Ft for the museum and casemates).

The Minorite church (1773) on Dobó István tér is one of the most beautiful baroque buildings in Hungary. In front of the church is a statue of Dobó as well as sculptures depicting the battle against the Turks. In the shadow of the castle in the old town along Knézich Károly utca is the 40m minaret topped with a cross. Nonclaustrophobes can brave the 100 narrow spiral steps to the top.

After so much history, unwind in the Archbishop's Garden (Érsek kert), once the private reserve of papal princes. It has open-air and covered swimming pools (open from 8.30 am to 7 pm) as well as thermal baths dating from Turkish times.

EGER

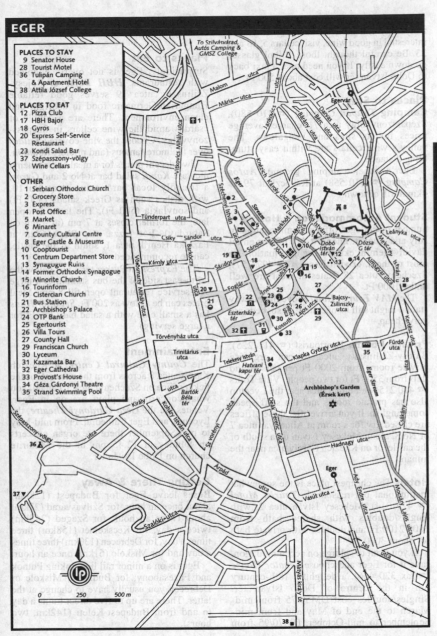

PLACES TO STAY
9 Senator House
28 Tourist Motel
36 Tulipán Camping
   & Apartment Hotel
38 Attila József College

PLACES TO EAT
12 Pizza Club
17 HBH Bajor
18 Gyros
20 Express Self-Service
   Restaurant
23 Kondi Salad Bar
37 Szépasszony-völgy
   Wine Cellars

OTHER
1 Serbian Orthodox Church
2 Grocery Store
3 Express
4 Post Office
5 Market
6 Minaret
7 County Cultural Centre
8 Eger Castle & Museums
10 Cooptourist
11 Centrum Department Store
13 Synagogue Ruins
14 Former Orthodox Synagogue
15 Minorite Church
16 Tourinform
19 Cistercian Church
21 Bus Station
22 Archbishop's Palace
24 OTP Bank
25 Egertourist
26 Villa Tours
27 County Hall
29 Franciscan Church
30 Lyceum
31 Kazamata Bar
32 Eger Cathedral
33 Provost's House
34 Géza Gárdonyi Theatre
35 Strand Swimming Pool

To Szilvásvárad,
Autós Camping &
GMSZ College

Egervár

Malom ━ utca

Mária ━ utca

Vitkovics Mihály utca

Jankovics utca

Bérc ━ utca

Darvas ━ utca

Kmetty utca

Kossuth Lajos utca

Bartók utca

Kretich Károly utca

Eger ━ Stream

Széchenyi István ━ utca

Tündérpart ━ utca

Csíky ━ Sándor ━ utca

Vörösmarty Mihály utca

Kármly ━ utca

Sándor

Foglár

Eszterházy tér

Törvényház utca

Trinitárius utca

Telekesy István ━ utca

Hatvani kapu tér

Bartók Béla tér

Király

Kohárý István utca

Sz vezérei

Árpád

Szépasszony-völgy ━ utca

Szalóki utca

Eger Castle & Museums

Dobó István tér

Dózsa G tér

Leányka ━ utca

Melcey Isrey utca

Almagyar utca

Bajcsy-Zsilinszky utca

Kertész utca

Fürdő utca

Eger Stream

Csákyr utca

Archbishop's Garden
(Érsek kert)

Klapka György utca

Hadnagy ━ utca

Eger

Vasút utca

Mátyás király út

Sas utca

Mocsáry Lajos utca

Aby István utca

Deák Ferenc utca

0   250   500 m

The choice of **wine cellars** at Szépasszonyvölgy can be a bit daunting. If you're interested in good wine, visit cellars 5, 13 and 23. Be careful though; those 100ml glasses go down easily. If you need one, a taxi back to Dobó István tér will cost about 500 Ft.

Places to Stay

Camping *Tulipán Camping* (☎ 410 580), Szépasszonyvölgy utca 71, charges average prices for its sites and bungalows. The valley's wine cellars are within easy stumbling distance.

Eger's other camping ground, *Autós Camping* (☎ 310 558) at Rákóczi út 79, is 4km north of town.

Student Accommodation & Hostels A
number of colleges offer accommodation in July and August. Phone ☎ 411 686 or email davidi@gemini.ektf.hu for information on most of them, or visit Express (☎ 427 757), Széchenyi utca 28. Rates at most are well under 1000 Ft.

The *MÁV Tourist Hotel* above the railway station might still be operating. If so, beds are very cheap.

Private Rooms Egertourist (☎ 411 225), Bajcsy-Zsilinszky utca 9, can organise private rooms from 2000 Ft per person and flats from 3500 Ft for two people. Villa Tours (☎ 410 215) on Fellner utca near the Lyceum also has private rooms and the staff speak some English. If you arrive after these offices are closed, try for a room at Almagyar utca 7 or No 8, along Mekcsey István utca south of the castle, or on Knézich Károly utca near the minaret.

Hotels The cheapest place is the somewhat institutional but reasonable *Tourist Motel* (☎ 429 014), Mekcsey István utca 2, with singles/doubles with shared bath from 1600/2100 Ft and doubles with private bath for about 3000 Ft.

If you want to splurge on accommodation, save it for Eger and choose *Senator House* (☎/fax 320 466), a delightful 18th-century inn in the centre of Dobó István tér. Singles/doubles cost DM50/75 from mid-March to the end of May and from mid-September to mid-October, DM70/95 from

June to mid-September and DM40/60 the rest of the year.

Places to Eat
Surprisingly, Eger is not overly endowed with restaurants. *HBH Bajor* at Bajcsy-Zsilinszky utca 19 serves good reliable Hungarian/Germanic food in a bright and clean environment. There are a couple of csárdas amid the wine cellars in Szépasszonyvölgy. Choose the vine-covered *Kulacs* over the more famous (and pricier) *Ködmön*.

Two decent places for a meal on Széchenyi utca are *Kondi* salad bar at No 2 and *Gyros*, a friendly local bar/restaurant at No 10, with dishes such as Greek salads (300 Ft) and souvlakia (600 Ft). The latter is open late; the former closes at 7 pm (at 4 pm on Saturday). For pizza, the *Pizza Club* at Fazolka Henrik utca 1, south of the castle, can be recommended.

The *Express*, at Pyrker tér 4 just below the north-east side of the bus station, is a large self-service restaurant open till 8 pm. Meal prices can be as low as 200 Ft. *Setantor Haus* has a small café with a salad bar (300 Ft for a large serving).

Entertainment
The *County Cultural Centre* at Knézich Károly utca 8 across from the minaret, or the ticket office on Széchenyi utca 3, can tell you what concerts and plays are on in Eger. Venues are the *Géza Gárdonyi Theatre*, the Lyceum, and Eger Cathedral. From mid-May to mid-September there are organ concerts on Sunday at 12.45 pm in the Minorite church on Dobó István tér.

Getting There & Away
Buses leave Eger for Budapest (128km) about once an hour, for Szilvásvárad (27km) about twice an hour, for Szeged (245km) twice a day, for Kecskemét (158km) three times a day, for Debrecen (130km) three times a day and for Miskolc (61km) once an hour.

Eger is on a minor rail line linking Putnok and Füzesabony; for Budapest, Miskolc or Debrecen you usually have to change at the latter. There are up to five direct trains a day to and from Budapest-Keleti (142km, two hours).

SZILVÁSVÁRAD
☎ 36

To the north of Eger is the Bükk range of hills, most of which falls within the 388-sq-km **Bükk National Park**. A good place to begin a visit is the village of Szilvásvárad, 27km north of Eger. It's an ideal base for hiking and is also the centre of horse breeding in Hungary, with some 250 prize Lipizzaners. It's also the place to ride on a delightful narrow-gauge train.

Orientation & Information

Get off the train at Szilvásvárad-Szalajkavölgy, and follow Egri út east for about 10 minutes to the centre of town. The main station is about 2km to the north. The bus from Eger will drop you off in the centre of town.

There's no tourist office but Tourinform in Eger can provide you with whatever information you need and sell you Cartographia's *A Bükk*, the best map of the Bükk region (300 Ft).

An OTP Bank branch is at Egri út 30a. The post office is at No 12.

Things to See & Do

Some people come to Szilvásvárad just to ride the **narrow-gauge railway** into the Szalajka Valley. The open-air train leaves seven times a day from May to September (more often on weekends), with three daily departures in April and October. The station is next to the open racecourse.

The little train chugs along for about 5km to **Szalajka-Fátyolvízesés**. Stay on the train for the return trip or walk back along well-trodden, shady paths, taking in the sights along the way. The open-air **Forest Museum** has some interesting exhibits, including a 16th-century water-powered saw.

From Szalajka-Fátyolvízesés, you can walk for 15 minutes to the **Istállóskő Cave**, where Palaeolithic pottery shards were discovered, or climb 958m **Mt Istállóskő**, the highest peak in the Bükk.

In Szilvásvárad, both the covered and the open **racecourses** put on Lipizzaner parades and coach races on weekends throughout the summer, but times are not fixed.

For horse riding (from 1800 Ft per hour) or coach driving, head for the **Lipizzaner Stud Farm** at the top of Fenyves utca. You'll learn more about these intelligent horses at the **Horse Museum** in an 18th-century stable at Park utca 8. At Miskolci út 58, a 17th-century farmhouse called **Orbán House** displays flora, fauna and geology of Bükk National Park.

You can rent **mountain bikes** at the entrance to the park at Szalajka-Fatelep, an easy walk from the centre of Szilvásvárad. Prices range from 300 Ft for one hour to 1200 Ft for a day.

Places to Stay

Hegyi Camping (☎ 355 207) at Egri út 36a, a stone's throw from the Szilvásvárad-Szalajkavölgy train station, has small holiday houses for two for 3000 Ft. Camping costs around 500 Ft for a tent and 500 Ft per person. *Szalajka* (☎ 355 257), a pension at Egri út 2, charges 2400 to 2700 Ft for a double room with shared bath.

Getting There & Away

Buses to/from Eger are very frequent and they're faster than the train.

TOKAJ
☎ 47

Although it's just a small town in Hungary's poor north-east region, Tokaj (pronounced 'tok-eye') has been synonymous with fine wine since the 17th century. Actually, this is just one of many winemaking villages in the area but for some reason Tokaj was the name that stuck.

King Louis XIV called Tokaj 'the wine of kings, the king of wines' but to modern tastes it's often too sweet. The dessert wines are especially sugary and are rated according to the number of *puttony* (butts) of sweet Aszú added. But Tokaj also produces less sweet wines: Szamorodni (not unlike dry sherry), Furmint and Hárslevelű, the driest of them all.

As well as vineyards and cellars, Tokaj is home to nesting storks, whose huge nests can be seen around the town.

Information

Tourinform (☎ 352 259) is at Serház utca 1. The OTP bank has an ATM.

Things to See

Tokaj Museum, Bethal Gábor utca 7, open daily (except Monday) from May to November, leaves nothing unsaid about the history of Tokaj, the region and the production of its wines. Just up the road, in an 18th-century Greek Orthodox church, the *Tokaj Gallery* exhibits works by local artists daily (except Monday) from April to September.

Wine Tasting

Private cellars *(pincék)* offering wine tastings are scattered throughout the town, including those at Rákóczi út 2, Óvári utca 36 and 40, and Bem József utca 2. If the cellars seem closed just ring the bell and someone will appear. For the ultimate in tasting locales go to the 600-year-old cellar at 13 Kossuth tér (near the Rákóczi Pince wine bar), where bottles of wine mature in corridors several kilometres long.

Start with the 100ml glasses; you may consume more than you think. If you're serious, the correct order of sampling Tokaj wines is: Furmint, dry Szamorodni, sweet Szamorodni and then the Aszú wines – from three to six puttony.

Places to Stay

Tisza Camping (☎ 352 012), along the river just south of the bridge, has sites and relatively inexpensive bungalows.

Makk Marci Panzió (☎ 352 336), Liget köz 1, is worth a look and charges 2464/3584 Ft for singles/doubles and there are also three and four-bed rooms for 4816 Ft and 6084 Ft. Prices rise in summer. The big *Tokaj Hotel* (☎ 352 344), Rákóczi utca 5, looks completely out of place but the rooms are quite good. In the low season you'll pay from 3000/3200 Ft a single/double and 3600/3900 Ft in summer. There are also some rooms with a shower rather than a bath that cost about 500 Ft less.

Places to Eat

Bacchus Étterem serves standard dishes at reasonable prices if you choose carefully, although it isn't especially pleasant. *Makk Marci Panzió* has a pizza restaurant or you could try the dining room at the *Tokaj Hotel*.

Getting There & Away

Tokaj is not well served by buses. There are a couple of direct trains to/from Budapest's Keleti station, including the Bartók Eurocity express (2½ hours, reservations required). Otherwise you'll usually have to change trains to cover any distance.

A Mahart ferry departs from the pier at Hösök tér and makes the 2½-hour run to the architecturally interesting little city of Sáospatak on weekends between April and November. The current timetable allows you to get there and back in a day if you catch the 7.30 am ferry from Tokaj, but check this.

Macedonia (Македонија)

The Former Yugoslav Republic of Macedonia (FYROM) is at the south end of what was once the Yugoslav Federation. Its position in the centre of the Balkan Peninsula between Albania, Bulgaria, Serbia and Greece has often made it a political powder keg. The mix of Islamic and Orthodox influences tell of a long struggle which ended in 1913 when the Treaty of Bucharest divided Macedonia among its three neighbours. Serbia got the northern part while the southern half went to Greece. Bulgaria received a much smaller slice. Only in 1992 did ex-Yugoslav Macedonia become fully independent.

In this book, Lonely Planet uses the name Macedonia rather than the Former Yugoslav Republic of Macedonia. This is to reflect what its inhabitants prefer to call their country and is not intended to prejudice any political claims.

For travellers Macedonia is a land of contrasts, ranging from space-age Skopje with its modern shopping centre and timeworn Turkish bazar, to the many medieval monasteries of Ohrid. Macedonia's fascinating blend of Orthodox mystery and the exotic Orient combine with the world-class beauty of Lake Ohrid to make the country much more than just a transit route on the way to somewhere else.

Facts about Macedonia

HISTORY

Historical Macedonia (whence Alexander the Great set out to conquer the ancient world in the 4th century BC) is today contained mostly in present-day Greece, a point Greeks are always quick to make when discussing contemporary Macedonia's use of that name. The Romans subjugated the Greeks of ancient Macedonia and the territory to the north in the mid-2nd century BC, and when the empire was divided in the 4th century AD this region became part of the Eastern Roman Empire ruled from Constantinople. Slav

AT A GLANCE

Capital	Skopje
Population	2 million
Area	25,333 sq km
Official Language	Macedonian
Currency	1 Macedonian denar (MKD) = 100 deni
GDP	US$2 billion (1996)
Time	GMT/UTC+0100

tribes settled here in the 7th century, changing the ethnic character of the area.

In the 9th century the region was conquered by the Bulgarian tsar Simeon (893-927) and later, under Tsar Samuel (980-1014), Macedonia was the centre of a powerful Bulgarian state. Samuel's defeat by Byzantium in 1014 ushered in a long period when Macedonia passed back and forth between Byzantium, Bulgaria and Serbia. After the crushing defeat of Serbia by the Turks in 1389, the Balkans became part of the Ottoman Empire and the cultural character of the region again changed.

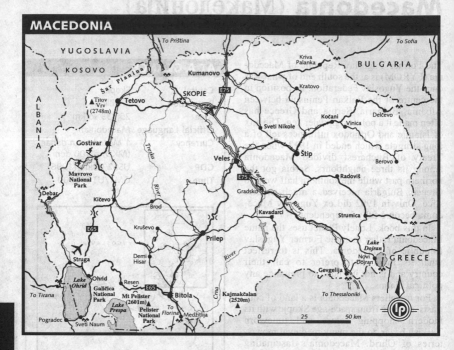

MACEDONIA

In 1878 Russia defeated Turkey, and Macedonia was ceded to Bulgaria by the Treaty of San Stefano. The Western powers, fearing the creation of a powerful Russian satellite in the heart of the Balkans, forced Bulgaria to give Macedonia back to Turkey.

In 1893 Macedonian nationalists formed the Internal Macedonian Revolutionary Organisation (IMRO) to fight for independence from Turkey, culminating in the Ilinden uprising of May 1903 which was brutally suppressed three months later. Although nationalist leader Goce Delčev died before the revolt he has become the symbol of Macedonian nationalism.

The First Balkan War in 1912 brought Greece, Serbia and Bulgaria together against Turkey. In the Second Balkan War in 1913 Greece and Serbia ousted the Bulgarians and split Macedonia between themselves. Frustrated by this result IMRO continued the struggle against royalist Serbia; the interwar government in Belgrade responded by ban-

ning the Macedonian language and even the name Macedonia. Though some IMRO elements supported the Bulgarian occupation of Macedonia during WWII, many more joined Tito's partisans, and in 1943 it was agreed that postwar Macedonia would have full republic status in future Yugoslavia. The first Macedonian grammar was published in 1952 and an independent Macedonian Orthodox Church was allowed to form. By recognising Macedonians as an ethnic group distinct from both Serbs and Bulgarians, the Belgrade authorities hoped to weaken Bulgarian claims to Macedonia.

On 8 September 1991 a referendum on independence was held in Macedonia and 74% voted in favour, so in January 1992 the country declared its full independence from former Yugoslavia. For once Belgrade cooperated by ordering all federal troops present to withdraw and, because the split was peaceful, road and rail links were never broken. In mid-1993, however, about 1000 United Nations troops were sent to Macedonia to monitor the border with Yugoslavia, especially near the potentially volatile province of Kosovo.

Greece delayed diplomatic recognition of Macedonia by demanding that the country find another name, alleging that the term Macedonia implied territorial claims on northern Greece. The concern of Greece is that if the Macedonians use the term Macedonia they may aspire to greater de facto legitimacy to the ambit of ancient Macedonia, which included (and still includes) a large part of Greece. At the insistence of Greek officials, Macedonia was forced to use the absurd 'temporary' title FYROM (Former Yugoslav Republic of Macedonia) for the purpose of being admitted to the UN in April 1993. After vacillating for two years, six of the European Union (EU) countries established diplomatic relations with FYROM in December 1993 despite strong objections from Greece, and in February 1994 the USA also recognised FYROM. At this, Greece declared an economic embargo against Macedonia and closed the port of Thessaloniki to the country's trade. The embargo was lifted in November 1995 after Macedonia changed its flag and agreed to enter into discussions with Greece about the name of the country. Shortly after these decisions were made, president Kiro Gligorov was almost assassinated in a car-bombing. To date, there has been no final resolution of this thorny issue.

Relations with Greece on the trade front nonetheless are looking healthy, though recently introduced visa restrictions for both sides has meant time-wasting visits to embassies in Athens and Skopje for casual travellers, and Macedonians wishing to take a vacation in Greece are often subjected to numbing delays at the border. Macedonians wishing to visit other Western European countries also face many visa requirements.

Macedonia is in the process of seeking possible admission to the EU.

GEOGRAPHY

Much of 25,713-sq-km Macedonia is a plateau between 600 and 900m high. The Vardar River cuts across the middle of the country, passing the capital, Skopje, on its way to the Aegean Sea near Thessaloniki. Ohrid and Prespa lakes in the south-west drain into the Adriatic via Albania. These lakes are among the largest on the Balkan Peninsula, and Lake Ohrid is also the deepest (294m compared to Prespa Lake's 35m). In the north-west the Šar Planina marks Macedonia's border with Kosovo; Titov Vrv (2748m) in this range is Macedonia's highest peak. The country's three national parks are Pelister (west of Bitola), Galičica (between lakes Ohrid and Prespa) and Mavrovo (between Ohrid and Tetovo).

GOVERNMENT & POLITICS

The current government under president Kiro Gligorov is nominally a democratically elected parliament following the American presidential system. However, cronyism and corruption are widely thought to exist and power is still in the hands of the old guard pseudo-communists of the former Yugoslavia and little grass-roots democracy is yet practised.

ECONOMY

Macedonia is a rich agricultural area which feeds itself and exports tomatoes and cucumbers to Western Europe. Cereals, rice, cotton and tobacco are also grown and Macedonian mines yield chromium, manganese, tungsten, lead and zinc. The main north-south trade route from Western Europe to Greece via the valleys of the Danube, Morava and Vardar rivers passes through the country. Tourism is concentrated around Lake Ohrid. At present Macedonia is gradually recovering its economic equilibrium after the lifting of UN sanctions against Yugoslavia which, together with Greece, had provided the ports and land routes for Macedonia's trade. Economic relations with Greece, though not what they once were, are slowly improving.

With the changes in Eastern Europe and especially with the separation of Macedonia from Yugoslavia, a new east-west trading route is developing from Turkey to Italy via Bulgaria, Macedonia and Albania. Over the next decade US$2.5 billion is to be invested in a new railway and motorway corridor linking Sofia, Skopje and Tirana. At present this route is covered only by

MACEDONIA

narrow secondary roads, a legacy of the political policies of former regimes.

Since the late 1960s, tens of thousands of Macedonians have emigrated, and remittances from the 100,000 Macedonians now resident in Germany and Switzerland are a major source of income.

POPULATION & PEOPLE

Of the republic's present population of over two million, 66% are Macedonian Slavs who bear no relation whatsoever to the Greek-speaking Macedonians of antiquity. The Macedonian language is much closer to Bulgarian than to Serbian and many ethnographers consider the Macedonians ethnic Bulgarians. The official position of the Bulgarian government is that Macedonians are Bulgarians, though only a minority of Macedonians support this view.

The largest minority groups are ethnic Albanians (22%), Turks (4%), Serbs (2%), Roma (2%) and others (4%). The birth rate of the mostly rural Albanians is three times the national average. Albanians are in a majority in the region between Tetovo and Debar in the north-west of the republic and there have been demonstrations in defence of the right to education in Albanian.

The 50,000 Macedonians living in northern Greece are subject to assimilatory pressures by the Greek government, which calls them 'Slavophone Greeks'. Education in Macedonian is denied and human rights groups such as Helsinki Watch have documented many cases of police harassment of Greek Macedonians who publicly protested against these policies.

ARTS
Music

The oldest form of Macedonian folk music involves the *gajda* (bagpipes). This is played solo or is accompanied by *tapan* (two-sided drum), each side of which is played with a different stick to obtain a different tone. These are often augmented by *kaval* (flute) and/or *tambura* (small lute with two pairs of strings). Macedonia has also inherited (from the long period of Turkish influence) the *zurla* (double-reed horn), also accompanied by the *tapan*, and the '*Čalgija*' music form

involving clarinet, violin, *darabuk* (hourglass shaped drum) and *džumbuš* (banjo-like instrument).

Bands playing these instruments may be heard at festivals such as the folklore festival in Ohrid in mid-July or the Ilinden festival in Bitola around August 2, and you may catch a stage performance in Skopje or Ohrid at other times. If you're really lucky you may get to see a wedding procession. However, in most restaurants and night spots, synthesiser, drum kit and guitar are the order of the day. Nearly all Macedonian traditional music is accompanied by dancing.

Folk Dancing

The most famous Macedonian folk dance is probably *Teškoto* (The Difficult One). It is a male dance for which music is provided by the *tapan* and *zurla*. It starts very slowly and becomes progressively faster. The finale is dynamic and beautiful to watch. During the dance, a number of symbolic actions take place. At one point, the dance leader climbs on to the tapan, for example. This dance is often included in festivals or concerts, and is always performed by dancers in traditional Macedonian costume.

Other dances often included in performances are *Komitsko*, symbolising the struggle of Macedonian freedom fighters against the Turks and *Tresenica*, a women's dance from the Mariovo region.

SOCIETY & CONDUCT

Macedonians are a proud and hospitable people and welcome visitors. If invited out for a meal, it is assumed that your host will pay for you. Insist on contributing if you must, but don't overdo it. Show respect to your hosts by learning a few words of Macedonian. Be aware that churches and mosques are not built for tourists, but are working places of worship. Dress and behave accordingly. Tread carefully when talking politics, especially about Greeks and Albanians.

RELIGION

Most of the Albanians and Turks are Muslim, while the Slavs are Orthodox.

LANGUAGE

Macedonian is a South Slavic language divided into two large groups, the western and eastern Macedonian dialects. The Macedonian literary language is based on the central dialects of Veles, Prilep and Bitola. Macedonian shares all the characteristics which separate Bulgarian from the other Slavic languages, evidence that it's closely related to Bulgarian.

The Cyrillic alphabet is based on the alphabet developed by two Thessaloniki brothers, St Cyril and St Methodius, in the 9th century. It was taught by their disciples at a monastery in Ohrid, Macedonia, whence it spread across the eastern Slavic world.

The Cyrillic alphabet is used predominantly in Macedonia. Street names are printed in Cyrillic script only, so it is imperative that you learn the Cyrillic alphabet if you don't want to get lost. Road signs use both Cyrillic and Latin scripts.

Lonely Planet's *Mediterranean Europe phrasebook* contains a complete chapter on Macedonian with Cyrillic spellings provided. For a quick introduction to Macedonian, see the Language chapter at the end of this book.

Facts for the Visitor

HIGHLIGHTS

The Byzantine monasteries of Ohrid, particularly Sveti Sofija and Sveti Kliment, are worth a visit. Lake Ohrid itself is simply beautiful. The Čaršija (old Turkish bazar) in Skopje is very colourful.

SUGGESTED ITINERARIES

Depending on the length of your stay, you might want to see and do the following things in Macedonia:

Two days
  Visit Skopje
One week
  Visit Skopje and Ohrid
Two weeks
  As above, plus some hiking in Pelister and Galičica national parks between Ohrid and Bitola

PLANNING
Climate & When to Go

Macedonia's summers are hot and dry. In winter, warm Aegean winds blowing up the Vardar Valley moderate the continental conditions prevailing further north. However, Macedonia receives a lot of snowfall, even if temperatures are warmer than those further north.

Books & Maps

A couple of good background books are *Who Are the Macedonians?* by Hugh Poulton, a political and cultural history of the region, and *Black Lambs and Grey Falcons* by Rebecca West, a between-the-wars Balkan travelogue.

Baedeker's Greece map also covers Macedonia. In Macedonia you should be able to get hold of the excellent *Republic of Macedonia* map, published by GiziMap of Hungary.

What to Bring

You can find most things in Macedonia, but do bring along a universal sink plug since hotels rarely have them.

TOURIST OFFICES

Makedonijaturist (☎ 115 051), based in the Hotel Turist in Skopje, is the state tourist organisation. Private agencies are also appearing on the scene.

VISAS & EMBASSIES
Visas

British and Yugoslav passport-holders do not require visas. Canadians, Americans and Australians need a visa but it's issued free of charge at the border. New Zealanders and South Africans need pre-arranged visas. However, if it is at all feasible, a visa should be obtained beforehand so as to avoid any possible delays or hassles.

Macedonia Embassies Abroad

Macedonian embassies are found in the following countries. There are no embassies as yet in Australia or New Zealand.

France
  (☎ 01-45 77 10 50; fax 01-45 77 14 84) 21 rue Sébastien Mercie 15e, Paris

MACEDONIA

Netherlands
  (☎ 070-427 4464) Laan van Meerdervoort 50/C, 2517 AM, The Hague
UK
  (☎ 0171-499 5152) 19a Cavendish Square, London, W1M 8DT 5JJ
USA
  (☎ 202-337 3063) 3050 K Street NW, Washington DC, 20007

Foreign Embassies in Macedonia

The following embassies are in Skopje:

Albania
  (☎ 614 636; fax 614 200) ul H T Karpoš 94
Bulgaria
  (☎ 229 444; fax 116 139) ul Zlatko Šnajder 3 (weekdays from 9 am to noon)
Romania
  (☎ 370 114; fax 361 130) ul Londonska 11a
UK
  (☎ 116 772; fax 117 555) ul Dimitrija Čupkovski 26 (weekdays from 10 am to 4 pm)
USA
  (☎ 116 180; fax 117 103) Bulevar Ilindenska (weekdays from 10 am to 4 pm)
Yugoslavia
  (☎ 362 697; fax 361 288) Knez Hacon 2-7-9

Visa requirements and costs for travellers to all nearby countries change frequently, so check with the embassies in question, or see the relevant country chapter.

CUSTOMS

Customs checks are generally cursory. However, if you are carrying photographic or electrical items customs officers may record them in your passport to ensure that you will carry them out when you depart.

MONEY

Colourful Macedonian denar (MKD) banknotes come in denominations of 10, 50, 100, 500, 1000 and 5000 and there are coins of one, two and five denari. The denar is now a stable currency, but outside Macedonia it is worthless.

Travellers cheques can be changed into Macedonian denari at most banks with no commission deducted. Small private exchange offices can be found throughout central Skopje and Ohrid and the rate they offer is generally good.

Exchange Rates

Conversion rates for major currencies in mid-1998 are listed below:

Australia	A$1	=	37 MKD
Canada	C$1	=	40 MKD
France	1FF	=	9.2 MKD
Germany	DM1	=	31 MKD
UK	UK£1	=	89.9 MKD
USA	US$1	=	54.9 MKD

Tipping

It is common practice to round up restaurant bills to the nearest convenient figure and waiters may indeed assume that this is what you intend and keep the expected change anyway. Consequently, don't give the waiter more than you are prepared to part with as a tip.

Taxi drivers will expect a round-up to the nearest convenient figure unless you have agreed on a fee beforehand.

POST & COMMUNICATIONS
Post

Mail addressed c/o Poste Restante, 91000 Skopje 2, Macedonia, can be claimed at the post office next to Skopje train station, weekdays from 8 am to 1 pm. Mail addressed to 91101 can be picked up at the main post office by the river.

Mail addressed c/o Poste Restante, 96000 Ohrid, Macedonia, can be picked up at Ohrid's main post office near the bus station.

Telephone

Long-distance phone calls cost less at main post offices than in hotels. To call Macedonia from abroad dial the international access code, ☎ 389 (the country code for Macedonia), the area code (without the initial zero) and the number. Area codes include ☎ 091 (Skopje), ☎ 096 (Ohrid) and ☎ 097 (Bitola). For outgoing calls the international access code in Macedonia is ☎ 99. Card phones are now available in major centres. You can purchase phonecards, in 100 (75 MKD) or 200-unit (150 MKD) denominations, from post offices.

The approximate cost of a three-minute call to the USA or Australia is about 337 MKD.

While Macedonia has a digital mobile phone network (MOBIMAK), it is unlikely that your own provider has a roaming agreement with Macedonia's domestic network. Check with your own provider to be sure.

INTERNET RESOURCES
A couple of useful World Wide Web sites are www.b-info.com/places/macedonia/republic (*Macedonia Information Almanac*), and www.vmacedonia.com/index2.html (*Virtual Macedonia*). Both sites have useful background and practical information. A number of private Internet service providers operate in Skopje, but the most practical way to access the Net is through Internet cafés.

NEWSPAPERS & MAGAZINES
There are three local Macedonian-language papers, along with an Albanian and a Turkish daily. English-language papers and magazines can be bought at most central kiosks, but *Svet World Press* on the corner of Dame Gruev and Partizanski in Skopje has a wide selection of foreign publications. There is also an English-language monthly called *Skopsko Metro* that you may be able to find at tourist locations.

RADIO & TV
You have a choice of two state TV stations and any number of private and satellite channels, including CBC, Eurosport and Euronews. There are many local FM radio stations. The BBC World Service is found on 104.4, the Voice of America on 107.5 FM.

PHOTOGRAPHY & VIDEO
Film sales and same-day developing services are widespread, at least in Ohrid and Skopje and are reasonably cheap. You are advised to develop your slide film at home. Video paraphernalia is not easy to find, so come supplied with everything you might need.

TIME
Macedonia goes on daylight-saving time at the end of March when clocks are turned forward one hour. On the last Sunday of September they're turned back an hour. Bulgaria and Greece are always one hour ahead of Macedonia while Yugoslavia and Albania keep the same time as Skopje.

ELECTRICITY
Macedonia uses 220V AC, 50 Hz. A circular plug with two round pins is used.

WEIGHTS & MEASURES
Macedonia uses the metric system.

LAUNDRY
There are currently no self-wash laundry services anywhere in Macedonia. Handwash as you go, or your hotel just might be able to wash your clothes for a fee. Dry cleaning (*chemisko chistenye*) is available, but you'll have to ask around to find an outlet.

TOILETS
Public toilets are invariably of the grotty 'squattie' type and are universally in bad shape. Take toilet paper with you if you must use them, but make use of hotel and restaurant toilets whenever you can.

HEALTH
Basic health services may be available free to travellers from state health centres. Health insurance to cover private health services is recommended.

WOMEN TRAVELLERS
Women travellers should feel no particular concern about travel in Macedonia. Other than possible cursory interest from men, travel is hassle-free and easy.

GAY & LESBIAN TRAVELLERS
Homosexuality in Macedonia is technically legal. However, the profile of gays in the country is so low as to be invisible. Given its tenuous social acceptability, a low profile should always be maintained.

DISABLED TRAVELLERS
Few public buildings or streets have facilities for wheelchairs. Access could be problematic. Newer buildings do provide wheelchair ramps.

DANGERS & ANNOYANCES

Macedonia is a safe country in general. Travellers should be on the lookout for pickpockets in bus and train stations and exercise common sense in looking after belongings.

BUSINESS HOURS

Office and business hours are 8 am to 8 pm weekdays, 8 am to 2 pm on Saturday.

PUBLIC HOLIDAYS & SPECIAL EVENTS

Public holidays in Macedonia are New Year (1 and 2 January), Orthodox Christmas (7 January), Old New Year (13 January), Easter Monday and Tuesday (March/April), Labour Day (1 May), Ilinden or Day of the 1903 Rebellion (2 August), Republic Day (8 September) and 1941 Partisan Day (11 October).

ACTIVITIES

Macedonia's top ski resort is Popova šapka (1845m) on the southern slopes of Šar Planina west of Tetovo. Hiking in any of the three national parks is a good way to get to know the countryside, but there do not seem to be organised outings for visitors.

COURSES

The American Language Company offers 'Survival Courses in Macedonian for Foreigners'. For full details call ☎ 237 614 between 4 and 9 pm. Check also Via Media (☎ 114 669) at Dame Gruev 1/14.

ACCOMMODATION

Macedonia's hotels are very expensive but there are camping grounds and private-room agencies in Ohrid and Skopje. Skopje's convenient HI hostel is open throughout the year, and the Ohrid hostel opens in summer. Beds are available at student dormitories in Skopje in summer. Prices in more expensive hotels are usually quoted in deutschmarks (DM) or US dollars (US$).

FOOD

Turkish-style grilled mincemeat is available almost everywhere and there are self-service cafeterias in most towns for the less adventurous. Balkan *burek* (cheese or meat pie) and yoghurt makes for a cheap breakfast. Look out for a sign sporting *burekdžilnica* if you want burek for breakfast. Watch for Macedonian *tavče gravče* (beans in a skillet) and Ohrid trout, which is priced according to weight.

Other dishes to try are *teleška čorba* (veal soup), *riblja čorba* (fish soup), *čevapčinja* (small skinless sausages), *mešena salata* (mixed salad) and *šopska salata* (mixed salad with grated white cheese).

DRINKS

Skopsko Pivo is the local beer. It's good and reasonably cheap. Other brand name European beers are also available. There is a good number of commercially produced wines of average to better quality and the national firewater is *rakija,* a strong distilled spirit made from grapes. *Mastika,* an ouzo-like spirit, is also popular.

ENTERTAINMENT

Entertainment for Macedonia's hip generation consists of hanging out in smart cafés and bars until the early hours. Movies are popular and all the latest Hollywood blockbusters can be watched at a fraction of the price back home. Live traditional Macedonian music can often be heard in restaurants and Skopje has a couple of bars with live jazz bands.

THINGS TO BUY

Look out for rugs and small textiles, paintings, traditional costumes, antique coins, handmade dolls and, from Ohrid, wood carvings for mementos to take home.

Getting There & Away

AIR

Jugoslavian Airlines (JAT), Macedonian Airlines (MAT), Adria (SLO), Croatia Airlines (HR) and Avioimpex (MK) offer flights from Skopje to a number of European destinations, many via Belgrade. Sample one-way discount prices are: Amsterdam (9765 MKD); Belgrade (3875 MKD); Düsseldorf (8680 MKD); Rome (7000 MKD); and Vienna

(7750 MKD). Return prices are usually a better deal and all prices are usually linked to and quoted in DM.

Any travel agent in Skopje or Ohrid can book these flights. In Skopje, Mata Travel (☎ 239 175), next to the international bus station, or Marco Polo Travel (☎ 222 340), on the corner of ul Maksim Gorki, are two agencies that you may like to approach.

LAND
Bus
The international bus station in Skopje is next to the City Museum. Mata Travel Agency (☎ 239 175; fax 230 269), at the international bus station, has buses to Sofia (twice to three times daily, 6½ hours, 500 MKD), İstanbul (four daily, 16 hours, 1630 MKD), Belgrade (daily, 5½ hours, 1050 MKD) and Munich (once a week, 27 hours, 4300 MKD). Some international buses also leave from a station behind the Stopanska Banka on the Čaršija side of the River and from a parking lot near the Grand Hotel.

To/from Croatia you must head for Belgrade and change for a bus to the Croatian border where you will change to a Croatian bus. Ask about overnight buses from Skopje to Belgrade and Podgorica. Buses between Skopje and Prizren in Kosovo, Yugoslavia (117km), are fairly frequent. To/from Albania you can travel between Skopje and Tirana by bus, or walk across the border at Sveti Naum (see the Ohrid section).

Train
Express trains run three times a day between Skopje and Belgrade (nine hours, 1178 MKD), via Niš. Sleepers are available on the overnight Skopje-Belgrade train. Trains run twice a day between Skopje and Thessaloniki.

Sample 2nd-class international train fares from Skopje are 676 MKD to Thessaloniki (five hours), 1780 MKD to Athens (14 hours), 2762 MKD to Budapest (15 hours) and 4076 MKD to Vienna (20 hours).

Greece-bound, it's cheaper to buy a ticket only to Thessaloniki and get another on to Athens from there. There's no direct rail link between Macedonia and Bulgaria and the train is not recommended for travel between

Sofia and Skopje as you must change trains in Yugoslavia and a visa will be required.

All the timetables and arrivals/departures boards at Skopje train station are in Cyrillic script only. For information in English go upstairs to Feroturist Travel Agency (open daily 7 am to 8.30 pm), which also sells international train tickets and books sleepers to Belgrade.

Note that Thessaloniki in Macedonian is 'Solun'.

Car & Motorcycle
There are several main highway border crossings into Macedonia from neighbouring countries.

Yugoslavia You can cross at Blace (between Skopje and Uroševac) and Tabanovce (10km north of Kumanovo).

Bulgaria The main crossings are just east of Kriva Palanka (between Sofia and Skopje), and east of Delčevo (26km west of Blagoevgrad) and Novo Selo (between Kulata and Strumica).

Greece There are crossings at Gevgelija (between Skopje and Thessaloniki), Dojran (just east of Gevgelija) and Medžitlija (16km south of Bitola).

Albania The crossings are Sveti Naum (29km south of Ohrid), Ćafa San (12km south-west of Struga) and Blato (5km northwest of Debar).

LEAVING MACEDONIA
The airport departure tax at Skopje and Ohrid is 510 MKD (20 DM).

Getting Around

BUS
Bus travel is well developed in Macedonia with fairly frequent services from Skopje to Ohrid and Bitola. Always book buses to/from Ohrid well in advance.

TRAIN
You won't find Macedonia's trains of much use, except perhaps for the overnight train

from Skopje to Belgrade and trains to Greece. The local train from Skopje to Bitola takes four hours to cover 229km. There are also local services from Skopje to Kičevo and Gevgelija on the Greek border.

CAR & MOTORCYCLE

Petrol costs are somewhat cheaper than most western European countries, and leaded and unleaded petrol and diesel are widely available. The cost is 36.5 MKD per litre for unleaded and 38.5 MKD for leaded petrol. Diesel is about 27.5 MKD per litre.

Motorway tolls along the main highway between Yugoslavia and Greece work out to approximately 200 MKD per 100km.

Speed limits for cars and motorcycles are 120km/h on motorways, 80km/h on open roads and from 50 to 60km/h in towns. Speeding fines are very high (4000 to 12,000 MKD) and inflexibly enforced by radar-equipped highway police who just love to catch offenders, so never speed! Parking tickets average 2000 MKD and wearing a seatbelt is compulsory.

The Macedonia-wide number for emergency highway assistance is ☎ 987.

HITCHING

Hitching can be undertaken in Macedonia, but you will probably have to wait a long time for a ride. LP does not recommend hitching as a form of transport.

LOCAL TRANSPORT

A quick way of getting around the country if the buses are not convenient is by taxi, especially if there are two or more of you to share the cost. An 88km trip, say from Ohrid to the Greek border at Medžitlija, will work out at around 1500 MKD.

ORGANISED TOURS

Very little in Macedonia is geared to the international visitor market, so you will have to ask around the travel agents for any useful leads. Monthly shopping trips to Thessaloniki and other jaunts are organised by the local expat community. Call ☎ 131 412 for current details.

Around the Country

SKOPJE (СКОПЈЕ)
☎ 091

Macedonia's capital, Skopje (population 600,000), is strategically set on the Vardar River at a crossroads of Balkan routes almost exactly midway between Tirana and Sofia, capitals of neighbouring Albania and Bulgaria. Thessaloniki, Greece, is 260km south-east, near the point where the Vardar flows into the Aegean. The Romans recognised the location's importance long ago when they made Scupi the centre of Dardania Province. Later conquerors included the Slavs, Byzantines, Bulgarians, Normans and Serbs, until the Turks arrived in 1392 and managed to hold onto Uskup (Skopje) until 1912.

After a devastating earthquake in July 1963 killed 1066 people, aid poured in from the rest of Yugoslavia to create the modern urban landscape we see today. It's evident that the planners got carried away by the money being thrown their way, erecting oversized, irrelevant structures which are now crumbling due to lack of maintenance. The post office building and telecommunications complex next to it are particularly hideous examples of this architectural overkill. Fortunately, much of the old town survived, so you can still get a glimpse of the old Skopje.

Orientation

Most of central Skopje is a pedestrian zone, with the 15th-century Turkish stone bridge (Kamen Most) over the Vardar River linking the old and new towns. South of the bridge is Ploštad Makedonija (the former Ploštad Maršal Tito), which gives into ul Makedonija leading south. The new train station is a 15-minute walk south-east of the stone bridge. The old train station, with its clock frozen at 5.17 am on July 27 the moment the earthquake struck, is now the home of the City Museum and is at the south end of ul Makedonija. The domestic bus station is just over the stone bridge. Further north is Čaršija, the old Turkish bazar.

The left-luggage office at the bus station is open from 5 am to 10 pm. Each item left costs 40 MKD. Left luggage at the train station is open 24 hours.

Information
Tourist Offices The tourist information office is opposite the Daud Pasha Baths on the viaduct between the Turkish bridge and Čaršija. There is also a tourist office inside the Trgovski Centar, the main shopping mall.

The office of the Automoto Sojuz or Automobile Club of Macedonia (☎ 116 011) is at Ivo Ribar Lola 51 just west of the city centre.

Money The Stopanska Banka facing the Turkish bridge opposite the bus station changes travellers cheques on weekdays from 7 am to 7 pm, on Saturday from 7 am to 1 pm. There are many private exchange offices scattered throughout the old and new towns where you can change your cash at a good rate.

There are ATMs on Partizanski Odredi in the Bunjakoveć Shopping Centre; in Trgovski Centar off Ploštad Makedonija; at the SBS Agrobank near Ploštad Makedonija; and at Skopje airport.

Post & Communications Poste-restante mail is held both at the train station post office and the main post office. The telephone centre in the main post office near the city centre is open 24 hours and the post office is open from 7.00 am to 7.30 pm and to 2.30 pm on Sunday.

Cybercafé The Café Astoria (☎ 128 404; astoria@mkinter.net) in the Bunjakoveć Shopping Centre at Partizanska 27a, Skopje, charges 100 MKD per hour for online time. Visit its site at www.astoria.com.mk.

Travel Agencies Mata Travel Agency (☎ 239 175; fax 230 269) is at the international bus station next to the City Museum. Feroturist Travel Agency (daily 7 am to 8.30 pm) is upstairs in the Skopje train station.

Medical & Emergency Services The city hospital (☎ 221 133) is on the corner of ul 11 Oktomvri and Moše Pijade. The Neuromedica private clinic (☎ 215 780) is at ul Partizanski 3-1-4, near the British Embassy.

Things to See
As you walk north from the Turkish bridge you'll see the **Daud Pasha Baths** (1466) on the right, once the largest Turkish baths in the Balkans. The **City Art Gallery** (closed on Monday, 100 MKD) now occupies its six domed rooms. Almost opposite this building is a functioning Orthodox church **Sveta Dimitrija**.

North again is Čaršija, the old market area, which is well worth exploring. Steps up on the left lead to the tiny **Church of Sveti Spas** with a finely carved iconostasis done in 1824. It's half buried because when it was constructed in the 17th century no church was allowed to be higher than a mosque. In the courtyard at Sveti Spas is the tomb of Goce Delčev, a mustachioed IMRO freedom fighter killed by the Turks in 1903.

Beyond the church is the **Mustafa Pasha Mosque** (1492), with an earthquake-cracked dome. The 100-MKD ticket allows you to ascend the 124 steps of the minaret. In the park across the street from this mosque are the ruins of **Fort Kale**, with an 11th-century Cyclopean wall and good views of Skopje. Higher up on the same hill is the lacklustre **Museum of Contemporary Art** (closed Monday; 50 MKD), where temporary exhibitions are presented.

The lane on the north side of Mustafa Pasha Mosque leads back down into Čaršija and the **Museum of Macedonia**. This has a large collection which covers the history of the region fairly well, but much is lost on visitors unable to read the Cyrillic captions and explanations, even though the periods are identified in English at the top of some of the showcases. The museum is housed in the modern white building behind the **Kuršumli Han** (1550), a caravanserai or inn used by traders during the Turkish period. With the destruction of Sarajevo, Skopje's old Oriental bazar district has become the largest and most colourful of its kind left in Europe.

Places to Stay
Camping From April to mid-October you can pitch a tent at *Feroturist Autocamp Park* (☎ 228 246) for 160 MKD per person and tent. Basic camping caravans are for hire year-round at 400 MKD per person. Late-night music from the restaurant can be a problem. This camping ground is between the river and the stadium, just a 15-minute walk

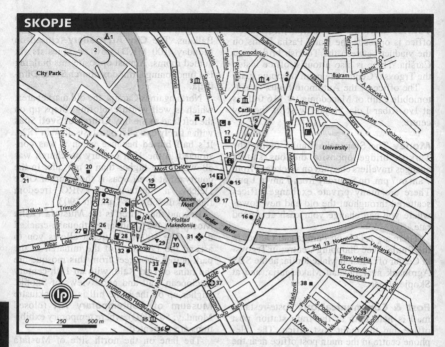

SKOPJE

upstream from the Turkish stone bridge along the right (south) bank. It's always a good bet.

Hostels The HI *Dom Blagoj Šošolčev Hostel* (☎ 114 849; fax 235 029; mkeuro26@mkinter.net), Prolet 25, is near the train station and is by far the best bet for travellers. The two, three and four-bed dorms are 540 MKD for members, 610 MKD for nonmembers. The newly renovated and air-conditioned double rooms with private bathroom are 830 MKD per person for members, 1350 MKD for nonmembers (including breakfast). Open all year, 24 hours a day, this hostel is often full with groups. Book beforehand if possible.

Private Rooms The tourist information office (☎ 116 854), on the viaduct two blocks north of the Turkish stone bridge, has singles/doubles in private homes beginning at 1050 MKD per person, but they're in short supply and there's no reduction for stays longer than one night. At this price insist on something in the centre.

Hotels The *Hotel Ambasador* (☎/fax 202 603) at ul Pirinska 38 is an unusual private hotel with pleasant rooms at an approachable price. Single/double rooms go for 2170/3100 MKD. You'll understand why it's unusual after you have spotted the statue on the roof. The central 91-room *Hotel Turist* (☎ 115 051; fax 114 753) just up ul Makedonija charges a hefty 3920/6050 MKD for singles/doubles. There are at least a dozen other hotels in town, but their prices are similar to those above.

Places to Eat
The *Bit Pazar* next to the Čaršija is a colourful and lively market where you can stock up on salad items, and the well-stocked *Kamfood Supermarket* in the basement of the Trgovski Centar is a good place to get your dairy and delicatessen items. There is a

PLACES TO STAY		
1	Feroturist Autocamp Park	
20	Hotel Ambasador	
33	Hotel Turist	
38	HI Youth Hostel	

PLACES TO EAT
9 Fontana Restaurant
11 Pivnitsa An
29 Ischrana Self-Service
30 Dal Met Fu Restaurant

OTHER
2 Stadium
3 Museum of Contemporary Art
4 Museum of Macedonia

5 Bit Pazar
6 Kuršumli Han
7 Fort Kale
8 Mustafa Pasha Mosque
10 Sultan Murat Mosque
12 Church of Sveti Spas
13 Tourist Information
14 Sveta Dimitrija Orthodox Church
15 Daud Pasha Baths
16 Macedonian National Theatre
17 Stopanska Banka
18 Domestic Bus Station
19 Main Post Office
21 Astoria Internet Café; Bunjakoveć Shopping Centre

22 JAT & MAT Airline Offices
23 Svet World Press (Newspaper & Magazine Shop)
24 Marco Polo Travel
25 Neuromedica Clinic
26 British Embassy
27 Lady Blue 2
28 Colosseum Disco
31 Trgovski Centar; Kamfood Supermarket
32 Svet World Press
34 Concert Hall; Lady Blue 1
35 City Museum
36 International Bus Station
37 City Hospital
39 Train Station

cheap restaurant in the basement of the Youth Hostel (see Places to Stay) which is open to the public.

There are two easy-to-find restaurants in the modern city centre close to Ploštad Makedonija on the south side of Kamen Most. The *Dal Met Fu Restaurant* is fairly obvious across the square at the beginning of ul Makedonija, on the left as you come from the bridge. This place is good for pizza and pasta. The *Ischrana Self-Service* is a no-frills self-service joint half a block away down the next street over to the right. Look for the vertical sign reading 'Restaurant' in large blue letters.

Colourful small restaurants in Čaršija serving *kebabi* and *čevapčinja* reflect a Turkish culinary heritage still dear to the stomachs of many Macedonians. Try the *Fontana* restaurant. It is on a little square with a fountain in the Čaršija. The grills are good and the atmosphere is great. The *Pivnitsa An* nearby is an atmospheric place in an old Turkish inn (*hani*) for a relaxing evening meal.

Entertainment
Check the *Concert Hall*, ul Makedonija 12, for performances. *Club MNT*, downstairs below the Macedonian National Theatre, cranks up around 10 pm and is open in summer. The *Silex Disco* at the stadium is a hot spot as is the unmarked *Coloseum Disco*

a block east of the British Embassy on Dimitri Čupkovski. Live jazz, blues and rock music can be heard at the *Lady Blue 1* and *Lady Blue 2* clubs, the latter on the corner of Ivo Ribar Lola and Sveti Kliment Ohridski and the former in the Concert Hall complex.

Getting There & Away
Bus There are buses to Ohrid, Bitola, Priština, Prizren, Peć, Podgorica and Belgrade. Book a seat on the bus of your choice the day before, especially if you're headed for Lake Ohrid.

There are two bus routes from Skopje to Lake Ohrid: the one through Tetovo (167km) is much faster and more direct than the bus that goes via Veles and Bitola (261km). If you just want to get to the Adriatic from Skopje, catch the overnight bus to Podgorica in Montenegro (382km).

If for some reason you can't take the direct bus to Sofia (see the Getting There & Away section earlier this chapter) there are 12 buses daily to Kriva Palanka (96km), 13km short of the Bulgarian border. Onward hitching should be possible.

Train All trains between central Europe and Greece pass through Skopje. There are two daily trains to/from Thessaloniki (five hours, 676 MKD) and Athens (14 hours, 1780 MKD).

Three trains run daily to Belgrade (nine hours, 1178 MKD), and six local trains run to Bitola (four hours, 194 MKD) and, for what it's worth, five trains to Kičevo (two hours, 150 MKD). Couchettes are available to Belgrade. Feroturist Travel Agency upstairs in the Skopje train station sells international tickets and books couchettes and sleepers (800 MKD).

Warning Beware of illegal taxi touts who meet trains. Do *not* get into a taxi that does not have an official taxi sign. You will be ripped off and at worse have your luggage and personal belongings stolen. Official taxis are OK.

Getting Around
To/From the Airport There are 11 special airport buses daily which all pick up at the international bus station as well as major hotels. A ticket costs 100 MKD. A taxi should cost between 800 and 1000 MKD.

Bus Inner-suburban city buses in Skopje cost 10 MKD per trip and outer-suburban buses 30 MKD per trip. Pay as you enter the bus. You can purchase 10-trip tickets for outer suburban buses at major stops for 130 MKD.

OHRID (ОХРИД)
☎ 096
Lake Ohrid, a natural tectonic lake in the south-west corner of Macedonia, is the deepest lake in Europe (294m) and one of the world's oldest. One third of its 450-sq-km surface area belongs to Albania. Nestled amid mountains at an altitude of 695m, the Macedonian section of the lake is the more beautiful, with striking vistas of the water from the beach and hills.

The town of Ohrid is *the* Macedonian tourist mecca and is popular with visitors from Macedonia and neighbouring countries. Some 30 'cultural monuments' in the area keep visitors busy. Predictably, the oldest ruins readily seen today are Roman. Lihnidos (Ohrid) was on the Via Egnatia, which connected the Adriatic to the Aegean, and part of a Roman amphitheatre has been uncovered in the old town.

Under Byzantium, Ohrid became the epis-copal centre of Macedonia. The first Slavic university was founded here in 893 by Bishop Kliment of Ohrid, a disciple of St Cyril and St Methodius, and from the 10th century until 1767 the patriarchate of Ohrid held sway. The revival of the archbishopric of Ohrid in 1958 and its independence from the Serbian Orthodox Church in 1967 were important steps on the road to modern nationhood.

Many of the small Orthodox churches with intact medieval frescos have now been adapted to the needs of ticketed tourists. Neat little signs in Latin script direct you to the sights, but even these tourist touches don't spoil the flavour of enchanting Ohrid.

Orientation
Ohrid bus station is next to the post office in the centre of town. To the west is the old town and to the south is the lake.

Information
Tourist Offices Biljana tourist office (☎ 22 494; fax 24 114) is at Partizanska 3 in front of the bus station.

Automoto Sojuz (☎ 22 338) is on Galičica at Lazo Trpkoski, behind the large 'Mini Market' on the corner of Jane Sandanski and Bulevar Turistička, a major intersection on the east side of town.

Money The Ohridska Banka agency, on Sveti Kliment Ohridski mall (Monday to Saturday from 8 am to 8 pm, Sunday 7 am to 1 pm), changes travellers cheques and cash without commission. Travel agencies often exchange cash as well.

Post & Communications The telephone centre in the modern post office near the bus station is open Monday to Saturday from 7 am to 9 pm, and Sunday from 9 am to noon and 6 to 8 pm. Phonecard phones are located outside the post office.

Note that Ohrid is gradually shifting to six-digit phone numbers, so that some of the numbers listed here may have changed by the time you read this.

Travel Agencies Putnik, Partizanska 4 opposite the bus station, sells train and plane tickets.

Left Luggage The left-luggage office at the bus station is open from 5 am to 8.20 pm daily. Cost is 50 MKD per piece per day.

Things to See

The picturesque old town of Ohrid rises from Sveti Kliment Ohridski, the main pedestrian mall, up towards the Church of Sveti Kliment and the citadel. A medieval town wall still isolates this hill from the surrounding valley. Penetrate the old town on Car Samoil as far as the **Archaeological Museum** in the four-storey dwelling of the Robevu family (1827) at No 62. Admission is 100 MKD. Further along Car Samuil is 11th-century **Sveti Sofija**, also worth the 100/30 MKD (foreigner/student) admission price. Aside from the frescos there's an unusual Turkish *mimbar* (pulpit) remaining from the days when this was a mosque, and an upstairs portico with a photo display of the extensive restoration work. An English-speaking guide is on hand.

From near here ul Ilindenska climbs to the North Gate, then to the right is the 13th-century **Church of Sveti Kliment**, (100 MKD admission), almost covered inside with vividly restored frescos of biblical scenes. An icon gallery is opposite this church with a fine view from the terrace. The walls of the 10th-century **citadel** to the west offer more splendid views.

In the park below the citadel are the ruins of an Early Christian **basilica** with 5th-century mosaics covered by protective sand, and nearby is the shell of **Sveti Pantelejmon**, now a small museum. The tiny 13th-century **Church of Sveti Jovan Bogoslov Kaneo**, on a point overlooking the lake, occupies a very pleasant site. There's a rocky beach at the foot of the cliffs and in summer young men perform death-defying leaps into the water from the clifftop above the lake. All churches and museums at Ohrid are open daily,

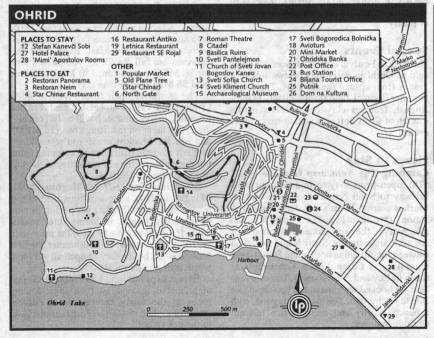

OHRID

PLACES TO STAY
12 Stefan Kanevči Sobi
27 Hotel Palace
28 'Mimi' Apostolov Rooms

PLACES TO EAT
2 Restoran Panorama
3 Restoran Neim
4 Star Chinar Restaurant

16 Restaurant Antiko
19 Letnica Restaurant
29 Restaurant SE Rojal

OTHER
1 Popular Market
5 Old Plane Tree (Star Chinar)
6 North Gate

7 Roman Theatre
8 Citadel
9 Basilica Ruins
10 Sveti Pantelejmon
11 Church of Sveti Jovan Bogoslov Kaneo
13 Sveti Sofija Church
14 Sveti Kliment Church
15 Archaeological Museum

17 Sveti Bogorodica Bolnička
18 Avioturs
20 Mini Market
21 Ohridska Banka
22 Post Office
23 Bus Station
24 Biljana Tourist Office
25 Putnik
26 Dom na Kultura

MACEDONIA

except Monday, from 9 am to 3 pm with a morning break from 10.30 to 11 am.

The better part of a second day at Ohrid could be spent on a pilgrimage to the Albanian border to see the 17th-century **Church of Sveti Naum** on a hill above the lake, 29km south of Ohrid by bus. From here you get a view of the Albanian town of Pogradec across the lake and inside the church is a finely carved iconostasis.

In summer you can also come by boat but it only leaves when a group is present; ask about times at the Putnik office opposite the bus station at the wharf the day before. The fare is around 100 MKD each way. The mountains east of Lake Ohrid, between it and Prespa Lake, are included in Galičica National Park.

There's frequent bus service from Ohrid to **Struga**. This small Macedonian town at the northern end of the lake is divided by the Crni Drim River, which drains Lake Ohrid into the Adriatic near Shkodra, Albania. On Saturday there's a large market at Struga. Each year at the end of August, poets converge on Struga for an international festival of poetry.

Special Events

The Balkan Festival of Folk Dances & Songs, held at Ohrid in early July, draws folkloric groups from around the Balkans. The Ohrid Summer Festival, held from mid-July to mid-August, features classical concerts in the Church of Sveti Sofija as well as many other events.

Places to Stay

Camping The *Autocamp Gradište* (☎ 22 578), open from May to mid-September, is halfway to Sveti Naum. A secluded nudist beach is nearby. There's also *Autocamp Sveti Naum* (☎ 58 811) 2km north of the monastery of the same name. Both camp sites are accessible on the Sveti Naum bus. Just between the Albanian border and Sveti Naum monastery is *Camp Vasko Karandžgleski* (open in July and August only). The caravans here are booked well ahead but you should be able to pitch a tent. The location is good, with a beach nearby and boat service to/from Ohrid in summer.

Private Rooms Private rooms are your best bet at Ohrid as the camping grounds and hostel are far from town and the hotels are pricey. Private rooms from the Biljana tourist office (☎ 22 494; fax 24 114), Partizanska 3, beside the bus station, cost from 250 to 310 MKD per person in a double room, plus 20 MKD per person per day tax. Women who unofficially rent private rooms often wait just outside the Biljana office. Popular with the diplomatic community, *'Mimi' Apostolov Rooms* (☎/fax 31 549) at ul Strašo Pinđura 2 has several comfortable, heated rooms with phone and satellite TV for 800 MKD including breakfast. For real rustic flavour right on the lake the *sobi* (rooms) of Stefan Kanevči (☎ 34 813) in Kaneo are hard to beat. A room goes for 310 MKD plus an extra 150 MKD for a hearty breakfast, if you want it.

Other private rooms are available from Putnik (☎ 32 025; fax 31 606) opposite the bus station or Avioturs (☎/fax 32 110) on Kosta Abraš.

Hostels & Hotels The HI *Mladost Hostel* (☎ 21 626; fax 35 025) is located on the lakeside a little over 2km west of Ohrid, towards Struga. A bed in a dorm or a small four-berth caravan will cost around 200 MKD per person including breakfast. Even if all the caravans are full they'll let you pitch a tent for 80 MKD per person, 150 MKD per tent (and 56 MKD per person tax).

The hostel is open from April to mid-October and YHA membership cards are not essential. In midsummer it will be full of children. Get there on the Struga bus (15 MKD) and ask for Mladost or, if you're walking, turn left after the fifth minaret, counting from the one opposite the old plane tree at the top of Sveti Kliment Ohridski.

Mladinski Centar-Hotel Magnus (☎ 21 671; fax 34 214), a modern hotel next to the hostel, charges 620 MKD per person in two or three-bed rooms, including three meals daily. If you have a hostel card, the price will be 10 to 20% lower. In midsummer they're booked solid, but as they're open all year it's worth trying other months.

Expect to pay around 1560/2400 MKD per night, including breakfast, for a single/double room at the fairly central *Hotel Palace* (☎ 260 440; fax 35 460) on Partizanska, close to the bus station.

Places to Eat

Picnic-minded travellers can stock up on fresh vegetables at the busy *Popular Market* just north of the Old Plane Tree. There is a *mini-market* for meat and dairy produce on Sveti Kliment Ohridski.

There are a number of fast-food and pizza joints in the old town area, but the easiest place to eat at is the *Letnica Self-Service Restaurant* on Bulevar Makedonski Prosvetiteli not far from the little harbour. The food is basic and cheap.

About 100m west of the Old Plane Tree are two low to mid-priced restaurants that warrant a visit. The *Restoran Neim* on the south side of Goce Delčev does some good *musaka* or *polneti piperki* (stuffed peppers) and the *Restoran Panorama* opposite offers similar fare.

A very pleasant mid-range restaurant is the *SE Rojal* at Jane Sandanski 2, about 200m south-east along the lakefront. Despite its smart décor, a meal is very affordable and the owner Sotir speaks English. The *Star Chinar* (Old Plane Tree) is a neat, modern restaurant near the Old Plane Tree and does some tasty local specialities. Try *chulban* – lamb, beef and rice patties in sauce. The smartest and most atmospheric eating place is the *Restaurant Antiko*, Car Samoil 30, in an old house in the old town. It is expensive and ordering Lake Ohrid trout will probably blow your budget.

Entertainment

Ohrid's movie theatre is *Dom Na Kultura* at Grigor Prličev, facing the lakeside park. Various cultural events are also held here. However, entertainment is mainly of the people-watching kind in the many street cafés or night-time bars, though many locals have taken a shine to playing bingo in recent times.

Getting There & Away

Air There is not much choice when it comes to flying to/from Ohrid. MAT and Avioimpex fly from Ohrid to Zürich (320 Sfr); MAT flies to Belgrade (5,890 MKD) and there are occasional summer flights from Ohrid to Amsterdam and one or two cities in Germany, but schedules and prices change too rapidly to rely on. Check with Putnik for current details.

Bus No less than 10 buses a day run between Ohrid and Skopje (167km, three hours, 265 MKD), via Kičevo. Another three go via Bitola and another two via Mavrovo. The first route is much shorter, faster, more scenic and cheaper, so try to take it. It pays to book a seat the day before.

There are six buses a day to Bitola (1¼ hours, 115 MKD). Buses to Struga (7km) leave about every 15 minutes (5 am to 9 pm) from stand No 1 at the bus station. Enter through the back doors and pay the conductor (35 MKD).

Yugoslavia An overnight bus from Ohrid to Belgrade (694km, 1510 MKD), via Kičevo, leaves Ohrid at 5.45 pm, reaching Belgrade 14 hours later. Another two buses go to Belgrade via Bitola, leaving at 5 am and 3.30 pm (1650 MKD).

Albania To go to Albania catch a bus or boat to Sveti Naum monastery, which is very near the border crossing. In summer there are six buses a day from Ohrid to Sveti Naum (29km, 65 MKD), in winter three daily. The bus continues on to the border post. From Albanian customs it's 6km to Pogradec but you may find a taxi to take you if you don't feel like walking.

Greece To get to Greece you can take a bus from Ohrid to Bitola (72km), then hitch or take a taxi 16km to the Medžitlija border crossing. Alternatively, you can try heading for Veles or even Skopje and pick up a train to Thessaloniki from there. Coming from Greece, try to get a cross-border taxi (10,000 drachmas) from Florina to Bitola directly, otherwise you may be stuck on the Macedonian side. Call (☎ 0385-23 851) for one of the cross-border taxi drivers in Florina.

BITOLA (БИТОЛА)
☎ 097

Bitola, the southernmost city of the former Yugoslavia and second largest in Macedonia, sits on a 660m-high plateau between mountains 16km north of the Greek border. The old bazar area (Stara Čaršija) is colourful but the facilities at Bitola are poor.

Private rooms are unavailable and the hotels overpriced. No left-luggage office is provided at either the bus or train stations and the city is useless as a transit point to/from Greece as there's no bus or train to the border (Medžitlija). You must hitch the 16km, or take a taxi. Bus services to Ohrid (72km) and Skopje (181km), on the other hand, are good.

The bus and train station are adjacent to each other, about 1km south of the town centre. It's probably not worth dragging your luggage into town just to see Bitola's Turkish mosques and bazar but the **Heraclea ruins** beyond the old cemetery, 1km south of the

bus/train stations, are recommended (admission 50 MKD, photos 500 MKD and video an exorbitant 1000 MKD extra). Founded in the 4th century BC by Philip II of Macedonia, Heraclea was conquered by the Romans two centuries later and became an important stage on the Via Egnatia. From the 4th to 6th centuries AD it was an episcopal seat. Excavations continue but the Roman baths, portico and theatre can now be seen. More interesting are the two Early Christian basilicas and the episcopal palace, complete with splendid mosaics. There's also a small museum and refreshment stand.

Poland

In both area and population, Poland is by far the largest country in Eastern Europe. The next largest, Romania, is only two-thirds the size of Poland and none of the other countries of the former Eastern Bloc is more than a third as big. Poland is just a bit smaller than reunified Germany and about the same size as the US state of New Mexico.

Always open to invaders from east and west, Poland has had a tumultuous past. The weight of history is on Kraków, the illustrious royal city; Gdańsk (Danzig), the former Hanseatic trading town where WWII began; Auschwitz, a reminder of the depths to which humanity can descend; and rebuilt Warsaw, symbol of the resilient Polish spirit.

As well as the historical and cultural aspects of this subtle land of Chopin and Copernicus, there's the gentle beauty of Baltic beaches, quiet north-eastern lakes and forests, and majestic mountains in the south – all requiring time to be appreciated. Poland has a number of regions each with its own character: Mazovia (around Warsaw), Małopolska ('Little Poland', in the south-east), Silesia (in the south-west), Wielkopolska ('Great Poland', in the west), Pomerania (in the north-west) and Masuria (in the north-east). Palpable differences remain between the areas once controlled by Austria, Germany and Russia. Yet, bound together by Catholicism, language, nationality and a common experience, Poland has a unity few other nations in the region can match.

In 1944 Stalin commented that fitting communism onto Poland was like putting a saddle on a cow. The truth of this became evident in 1989, when Poland changed the course of history by becoming the first Eastern European state to break free of communism. Since then, the economic, social and psychological changes have been tremendous.

For visitors, Poland is now an easy and attractive destination. Once you have a visa (where required) there are few additional hassles. The shortages of food and consumer goods are long gone, and there are no travel restrictions. Foreigners are now accepted everywhere on the same footing as Poles. Of

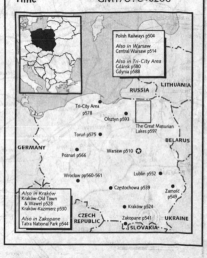

AT A GLANCE

Capital	Warsaw
Population	38.5 million
Area	312,677 sq km
Official Language	Polish
Currency	1 zloty (Zl) = 100 groszy
GDP	US$246 billion (1996)
Time	GMT/UTC+0200

course prices have gone up, but compared to Western Europe, Poland is still good value.

Facts about Poland

HISTORY
Early History
In the 6th and 7th centuries AD the West Slavs pushed north and west and settled large areas of what is now Poland. By the 10th century the Polanian tribe in Wielkopolska attained dominance over other Slavic groups of the region. Its tribal chief, Duke Mieszko I adopted Christianity in 966, considered to

POLAND

BALTIC SEA

Map labels: Ustka, Łeba, Hel, Gulf of Gdańsk, Kaliningrad, RUSSIA, To Vilnius & St Petersburg, Kaunas, Słupsk, Gdynia, Sopot, LITHUANIA, Kołobrzeg, Koszalin, Gdańsk, Frombork, Lidzbark Warmiński, Gizycko, Suwałki, Świnoujście, Elbląg, Mikołajki, Augustów, Hrodna, Szczecin, Szczecinek, Malbork, Ostróda, Olsztyn, Grudziądz, Łomża, Białystok, Piła, Bydgoszcz, Chełmno, Toruń, BIAŁOWIEŻA NP, Gorzów Wielkopolski, Warta, Ostrołęka, Ciechanów, Białowieża, Frankfurt/Oder, Włocławek, Płock, BELARUS, Poznań, Gniezno, Konin, Kutno, WARSAW, Odra, To Berlin, Zielona Góra, Leszno, Kalisz, Łowicz, Siedlce, Brest, Cottbus, Sieradz, Łódź, Vistula, GERMANY, To Dresden, Zgorzelec, Wrocław, Wieluń, Piotrków Trybunalski, Radom, Puławy, Kazimierz Dolny, Lublin, Jelenia Góra, Brzeg, Kielce, Chełm, Wałbrzych, Opole, Częstochowa, Sandomierz, Zamość, Kłodzko, Nysa, Gliwice, Tarnobrzeg, Hradec Králové, Katowice, Kraków, Rzeszów, Łańcut, Lviv, PRAGUE, Ostrava, Oświęcim, Tarnów, Przemyśl, Bielsko-Biała, To Kiev & Odessa, Cieszyn, Rabka, Nowy Sącz, Sanok, Olomouc, Zakopane, Rysy 2499m, Prešov, UKRAINE, Poprad, CZECH REPUBLIC, SLOVAKIA, Košice, To Budapest, To Vienna & Bratislava

0 50 100 km

be the date of the formation of the Polish state, and in 1000 the Gniezno Archbishopric was founded. Mieszko's son, Boleslav the Brave, took the title of king in 1025 and his descendant, Boleslav the Bold, consolidated the power of the Piast dynasty over a territory quite similar to the Poland of today.

There was constant pressure from the west as the Germans pushed into Pomerania and Silesia, so to be less vulnerable the royal seat was moved in 1038 from Poznań to Kraków. In the mid-12th century the country was divided into four principalities and a weakened

Poland soon fell prey to invaders. In 1226 the Teutonic Knights, a Germanic military and religious order founded in Palestine during the Third Crusade (1198), were invited to Poland by the prince of Mazovia to subdue the restive Prussians of the north-east. Once the knights had subjugated the Baltic tribes they turned their attention to the Poles. The order set up a state in the lower Vistula, which they ruled from their castle at Malbork. Tatar invasions devastated southern Poland in 1241 and 1259. Though Poland was reunified in 1320, the knights held onto Pomerania and Prussia.

POLAND

A Great Power

From the 14th to 17th centuries Poland was a great power. It's said that the 14th-century king, Casimir III the Great, last of the Piast dynasty, 'found a Poland made of wood and left one made of masonry'. When Casimir died without an heir, the throne passed to the daughter of the king of Hungary, Princess Jadwiga, who in 1386 married the duke of Lithuania, uniting the two countries under the Jagiellonian dynasty.

In 1410 combined Polish-Lithuanian forces under Ladislaus Jagiełło defeated the Teutonic Knights at Grunwald, south of Olsztyn. After the Thirteen Years' War (1454-66) the Teutonic order was broken up and in 1525 the secular Duchy of Prussia became a fiefdom of the Polish crown.

The early 16th-century monarch, Sigismund I the Old, brought the Renaissance to Poland and in 1543 Nicolaus Copernicus published his treatise *De Revolutionibus Orbium Coelestium*. At a time when much of Europe was being torn apart by religious wars and persecutions, there was relative peace and tolerance in Poland. Lithuania and Poland were formally united as one country in 1569, to oppose Russian expansion, and the Polish-Lithuanian Commonwealth became the largest country in Europe, stretching from the Baltic Sea to the Black Sea.

After the death of Sigismund Augustus in 1572, the Jagiellonian dynasty became extinct and it was decided future kings would be elected by the Sejm (parliament). In the absence of a serious Polish contender, a foreign candidate would be considered. Sigismund III, an elected king from the Swedish Vasa line, moved the capital from Kraków to Warsaw in 1596. He also embroiled Poland in Swedish dynastic wars and, though the country successfully held off Sweden and Moscow for a time, from 1655-60 a Swedish invasion devastated Poland's towns. King Jan III Sobieski led a crusade against the Turks which resulted in their removal from Hungary after 1683.

Decline

Weak leadership, constant wars and the domination of the gentry over the middle class led to the decline of Poland in the 18th century. In the first partition of Poland in 1773, Russia, Prussia and Austria took 29% of the national territory. Poland's last king, Stanislaus Poniatowski, tried to reverse the situation with reforms, but the powerful magnates resisted strongly, which resulted in civil war and a pretext for foreign intervention. In 1791 the king granted Poland a democratic constitution (the second in the world) but the magnates again revolted, leading to a second partition in 1793. A year later Tadeusz Kościuszko, a veteran of the American Revolution, led a war of independence against the invaders but was defeated in 1795. A third partition that year wiped Poland off the map of Europe until 1918.

The oppressed Poles supported Napoleon, who set up a duchy of Warsaw in 1807 from where he led his Grand Army to Moscow in 1812 (the beginning of a special Franco-Polish relationship which has continued until today). After 1815 the duchy came under tsarist Russia. There were unsuccessful uprisings against tsarist rule in 1831, 1848 and 1864 with Poland's position worsening after each one. A Russification and Germanisation policy was enforced in the areas controlled by those powers; only in the Austrian-occupied part were Poles permitted to maintain some of their identity.

WWI & WWII

Poland was completely overrun by the Germans during WWI, but in 1919 the Polish state was re-established by the Treaty of Versailles. Then the Polish military struck east and took big chunks of Lithuania, Belarus and Ukraine from a weakened Soviet Union.

In 1926 Marshal Józef Piłsudski, an ex-commander of the Polish Legions which had fought alongside Austria in WWI, staged a military coup and set himself up as dictator. Under his rule to his death in 1935, Poland gained a measure of prosperity.

WWII began on 1 September 1939 in Gdańsk (at that time the Free City of Danzig) where 182 Poles at Westerplatte held out for a week against the battleship *Schleswig Holstein*, Stuka dive bombers and thousands of German troops. To the west the Polish Pomeranian Brigade of mounted cavalry met General Guderian's tanks – medieval lances against modern armour – in a final suicidal

POLAND

charge. Polish resistance continued for almost a month and German losses during the campaign were as great as subsequent combined losses during the Western European, Balkan and North African invasions of 1940-41. On 17 September 1939 the Soviet Union invaded from the east and took back the territories lost in the 1919-21 Polish-Soviet War. Poland had been partitioned for the fourth time.

During WWII Poland was the only country in Europe not to produce any quislings to serve in a German-dominated puppet government. The Nazi governor general, Hans Frank, ruled those areas not directly incorporated into the Reich, and Poles resident in the areas which had been annexed by Germany were deported east. Yet two resistance groups, the London-directed Armia Krajowa (Home Army) and the communist Gwardia Ludowa (People's Guard), later the People's Army, fought on inside Poland.

The five-year Nazi occupation triggered many acts of armed resistance, including two heroic uprisings in Warsaw. During the Ghetto Uprising of April 1943, some 70,000 poorly armed, starving Jews led by Mordechai Anielewicz held out against the full weight of the Nazi army for 27 days. The victorious Nazis reduced the Jewish quarter to rubble.

The second act, the Warsaw uprising, was begun on 1 August 1944 by the Home Army as Soviet forces approached the right bank of the Vistula. The intention was to evict the retreating Germans from Warsaw and have a non-communist force in place to greet the Red Army, but the uprising was premature. By 2 October, when the remaining partisans surrendered with honour, some 250,000 Poles had died, many of them civilians slaughtered en masse by SS troops. The remaining inhabitants were then expelled from the city and German demolition teams levelled Warsaw street by street.

During these appalling events, the Red Army, which was sitting just across the Vistula, didn't lift a finger. It wasn't until 17 January 1945 that the Soviet troops finally marched in to 'liberate' Warsaw, which by that time was little more than a heap of empty ruins. Ironically the Germans set the stage for a postwar communist Poland by physically eliminating the bulk of the non-communist resistance within the country.

Six million Poles – a fifth of the prewar population – died during the war, half of them Jews. The country and its cities lay in ruins. About 85% of Warsaw's buildings were damaged. Of the large cities, only Kraków miraculously escaped destruction.

At the Yalta Conference in February 1945, Churchill, Roosevelt and Stalin decided to leave Poland under Soviet control. They agreed that Poland's eastern frontier would roughly follow the Nazi-Soviet demarcation line of 1939. In effect, the Soviet Union annexed some 180,000 sq km of prewar Polish territory. In August 1945 at Potsdam, Allied leaders established Poland's western boundary along the Odra (Oder) and Nysa (Neisse) rivers, thereby reinstating about 100,000 sq km of the country's western provinces after centuries of German control. Millions of people were dislocated by these changes, which eventually resulted in 98% of Poland's population being ethnically Polish.

Communist Poland

After the war a Soviet-style communist system was installed in Poland and the country was run according to five and six-year plans. The emphasis on heavy industry led to chronic shortages of consumer goods while the *nomenklatura* of party bureaucrats enjoyed many privileges. Intellectual freedom was curtailed by the security apparatus and individual initiative stifled. In 1956, when Nikita Khrushchev denounced Stalin at the Soviet 20th Party Congress, Bolesław Bierut, the Stalinist party chief in Poland, died of a heart attack!

In June 1956 workers in Poznań rioted over low wages, and in October, Władysław Gomułka, an ex-political prisoner of the Stalin era, took over as party first secretary. Gomułka introduced a series of superficial reforms reducing Soviet domination of Poland and freeing political prisoners, but the basic system continued unchanged. After the Arab-Israeli War of 1967, party hardliners used an 'anti-Zionist' purge to enforce discipline, but by December 1970 living conditions had declined to the point where workers in northern Poland went on strike over food price increases. When 44 of them were shot down during demonstrations, Edward Gierek replaced Gomułka as party leader and persuaded the strikers to return to work by promising sweeping changes.

Gierek launched Poland on a reckless program of industrial expansion to produce exports which could be sold on world markets. This was financed by 17 capitalist governments and 501 banks. However, many of the ill-founded heavy industry schemes ended in failure, and by 1981 the country had run up a hard-currency debt of US$27 billion.

This decade of mismanagement left Poland bankrupt. Living standards fell sharply as Poland was forced to divert goods to export from domestic consumption, to earn hard currency with which to service the debt. The election of a Pole to the papacy in October 1978, and the visit to Poland by John Paul II in June 1979, also changed the atmosphere in a country where the party was supposed to play the 'leading role'.

In 1980 a wave of strikes over sharp food price increases forced Gierek out and marked the emergence of Lech Wałęsa's Solidarity trade union. It soon had 10 million members, a million of whom had come from the Communist Party's ranks! At first the government was conciliatory, but under growing pressure from both the Soviets and local hardliners, it became increasingly reluctant to introduce any significant reforms and rejected Solidarity's proposals. In the absence of other legal options, strikes became the union's main political weapon. The political tensions rose while the economy continued to deteriorate.

On 13 December 1981 martial law was declared by General Wojciech Jaruzelski, and thousands of Solidarity leaders and activists were interned as the government broke up the union. In October 1982 Solidarity was dissolved by the courts and life returned to the usual Soviet-style norm. By July 1983 martial law was lifted.

Jaruzelski tried to introduce some economic reforms, but his initiatives lacked public support and the economy remained in desperate shape. In a referendum held in November 1987, Poles cast a vote of no confidence in the communist government. Meanwhile the underground Solidarity movement had been biding its time, and in 1988 fresh strikes followed government attempts to remove food subsidies. The big pay increases won by the striking workers clearly revealed government weakness, and officials agreed to meet with the opposition to discuss reform, realising that without a compromise Poland would explode.

In April 1989, in the so-called round-table agreements between the government, the opposition and the Church, Solidarity was re-established and the opposition was allowed to stand for parliament. The sweeping Solidarity victory in the June 1989 elections soon caused the communist coalition to fall apart, and Tadeusz Mazowiecki was picked to head a Solidarity-led coalition, thus becoming the first non-communist prime minister in Eastern Europe since WWII. Though Jaruzelski was elected to serve as a transitional president by parliament, the communist era in Poland had in effect come to an end. The two-million-member Polish United Workers Party dissolved itself at its congress in January 1990.

Postcommunist Poland

The Mazowiecki government adopted a 'shock therapy' economic program to switch Poland from a planned to a free-market economy. On 1 January 1990 price and currency exchange controls were removed, allowing both to find their real levels. During the first month, prices jumped 79% but the markets suddenly filled with products. Inflation was eventually brought under control as the złoty stabilised against western currencies, though at the cost of wages losing 30% of their purchasing power in 1990 and industrial production falling by 25%. The Mazowiecki team also prepared for privatisation by cutting subsidies to overstaffed state industries, thereby sending unemployment up from zero to 7.5% in 1990.

In September 1990 General Jaruzelski stepped down and Lech Wałęsa was elected president three months later. Parliamentary elections with no allotted seats were held in October 1991, but Poland's system of proportional representation resulted in 29 political parties winning seats although only two got over 10% of the vote. In January 1992 Jan Olszewski formed a centre-right coalition government which was defeated after only five months in office and in July

1992 Hanna Suchocka of the centrist Democratic Union (UD) cobbled together a coalition of seven parties to become Poland's first woman prime minister.

Abortion had been legal in Poland since 1956 but parliament came under intensive lobbying from the Catholic Church and in January 1993 an anti-abortion law was pushed through by the Christian National Union, one of Suchocka's coalition partners. Abortion became illegal except in cases of incest, rape, deformed foetus or serious danger to the mother. Public opinion surveys showed a large majority of Poles against this move and the conservative politicians strongly resisted having the matter put to a referendum. Moderates did manage to have amendments attached to the law requiring that contraceptives be made available and that Polish schools begin providing sex education for the first time.

Political instability combined with lowered living standards and soaring unemployment had made the successive centrist governments unpopular among those hardest hit by economic austerity, especially pensioners, industrial workers and low-ranking civil servants. When Suchocka's government was defeated in a vote of no confidence over a labour dispute in May 1993, President Wałęsa ordered fresh elections to be held under a new rule restricting parliamentary representation to parties winning over 5% of the vote.

The parliamentary elections of September 1993 saw a strong swing to the left, with two ex-communist parties, the Democratic Left Alliance (SLD) and the Polish Peasant Party (PSL), capturing 66% of seats in the Sejm. The PSL leader, Waldemar Pawlak, became prime minister. The new government slowed down the pace of economic reform, particularly in the areas of privatisation and foreign investment. Pawlak was later replaced with Józef Oleksy, a former senior Communist Party official.

The November 1995 presidential election put SLD leader Aleksander Kwaśniewski in the top office. This smooth-talking one-time communist technocrat won by a narrow margin over Wałęsa, the only other significant contender. Soon afterwards Włodzimierz Cimoszewicz, another former party official,

took the post of prime minister, following Oleksy's stepping down after being accused of collaborating with the KGB. In effect, the postcommunists gained a stranglehold on power, controlling the presidency, government and parliament – a 'red triangle', as Wałęsa warned. Many of the old-time communists were discreetly put back into key political and administrative posts, and they also enjoyed priorities in the economic sector. Yet the social benefits promised in the presidential campaign haven't materialised.

The electorate seems to have realised that the pendulum swung too much to the left; the popular mood was reflected in the results of the parliamentary elections of September 1997, won by the alliance of some 40 small Solidarity offshoot parties, the Solidarity Election Action (AWS). The alliance formed a coalition with the centrist liberal Freedom Union (UW), pushing ex-communists into opposition. Jerzy Buzek became prime minister. A fully new constitution was finally passed in April 1997, to replace the Soviet-style document which had been in force since 1952 (though it had been much amended to correspond with the postcommunist status quo). The new government has pushed ahead with the privatisation program, and Poland's economic indicators are now about the highest among the Eastern European countries.

GEOGRAPHY & ECOLOGY

Poland covers an area of 312,677 sq km. It's a low, square-shaped country, roughly 600 x 600km, bordered in the south by the mountain ranges of the Sudetes and Carpathians. Poland's highest mountains are the rocky Tatras, a section of the Carpathian range that it shares with Slovakia. The highest peak of the Polish Tatras is Mt Rysy (2499m).

Lowland predominates in central Poland, a region of great north-flowing rivers such as the Vistula, Odra, Warta and Bug. The entire drainage area of the 1047km Vistula, the mother river of Poland, lies within Poland's boundaries and most of the rest of the country is drained by the Odra.

Poland has more postglacial lakes than any country in Europe except Finland. The plain along the broad, sandy, 524km Baltic coastline is spotted with sand dunes and seaside lakes.

Poland's fauna numbers some 90 species of mammals, of which the most common ones include the hare, red deer and wild boar. Some elks live in the woods of the north-east, while occasional brown bears and wildcats can be found in the mountain forests. Several hundred European bison, which once inhabited the continent in large numbers but were brought to the brink of extinction early this century, live in Białowieża National Park and some other limited areas.

Birds are represented by some 420 species, including the white eagle, Poland's national bird which appears in the Polish emblem. Forests cover about 27% of Poland's territory.

Poland has 22 national parks (*parki narodowe*) which together account for about 3000 sq km, a mere 0.95% of the country's area. A few new parks are planned for the near future. The parks are administered by a special department of the Ministry of Environment.

No permit is necessary to visit the parks, but most have introduced small entry fees which you pay at the park's office or at an entry point. Camping in the parks is not allowed, except for specified sites.

Apart from the national parks, there's a network of not-so-strictly preserved areas called *parki krajobrazowe* or landscape parks. There are about 100 of them scattered in all regions and together they cover about 20,000 sq km, or 6.5% of the country.

GOVERNMENT & POLITICS

Poland is a parliamentary republic. The president is elected in a direct vote for a five-year term as head of state and is empowered to nominate the prime minister.

The parliament consists of two houses, the 460-seat lower house, the Sejm or Diet, and the 100-seat upper house, the Senat or senate. The senate was only created in 1989; before that there was just the one-house parliament based on the Sejm.

Before 1989 the Polish United Workers Party was constitutionally the leading political force and was guaranteed a majority of seats in the Sejm. Today the party no longer exists and a myriad of new political parties have appeared on the scene.

ECONOMY

Bituminous coal has traditionally been Poland's chief mineral resource, with the largest deposits concentrated in Upper Silesia. The quality, low-sulphur coal is mostly exported, while brown lignite is burned locally for electricity and to fuel industry. The country's oil resources are insignificant. On the other hand, Poland possesses considerable reserves of sulphur, zinc and lead, and smaller ones of copper and nickel.

Hydroelectric power is responsible for only a small fraction of electricity production, and the potential is not great. A nuclear reactor based on Soviet technology was started in the early 1980s near Gdańsk but construction was abandoned in 1990.

Approximately half of Poland's territory is arable. Among the main agricultural crops are rye, potatoes, wheat, sugar beets, barley and oats. Unlike the rest of the ex-communist bloc, over 80% of farmland in Poland remained in the hands of individual farmers after WWII.

Many of Poland's huge state-owned factories dating from the period of the postwar rush towards industrialisation are still in operation. Their major products include steel, chemicals (fertilisers, sulphuric acid), industrial machinery and transport equipment (ships, railway cars and motor vehicles).

Yet, in the few short years since the fall of communism, the situation has changed dramatically. While the old state-owned industries have been falling apart, a plethora of new, private enterprises have soared. Trade has shifted towards the west, yet Poland wisely maintains and expands economic links with the countries of the ex-Soviet bloc, to preserve its position as a bridge between west and east.

More than half of Poland's GDP is now produced by the private sector, which employs about 60% of the workforce. The 1997 GDP growth was about 6% and is likely to remain similarly high in the near future. The level of unemployment peaked at 17% in mid-1994, but since diminished and stood at about 10% by mid-1998. It is believed, however, that a third of those on the dole work and are paid under the table. Average monthly wages in mid-1998 were about

US$350. The 1997 inflation rate was 13.5%
but was expected to drop below 10% within
a couple of years.

POPULATION & PEOPLE

Poland's population in 1998 stood at about
38.5 million. The rate of demographic increase, which was pretty high in the postwar
period, has dropped gradually over recent
decades to stabilise at about 0.7%, a figure
comparable to those of Western Europe.

There were massive migratory movements
in Poland in the aftermath of WWII, and the
ethnic composition of the nation is now
almost entirely homogeneous. Poles make up
98% of the population, Ukrainians and Be-
larusians about 1%, and the remaining 1% is
composed of all other minorities – Germans,
Jews, Lithuanians, Tatars, Gypsies, Lemks,
Boyks and a dozen other groups.

Today's ethnic picture differs significantly from before WWII. Poland was for
centuries one of Europe's most cosmopolitan
countries, and had the continent's largest
community of Jews. Right before the outbreak of WWII they numbered around 3.3
million, but only about 5000 to 6000 Jews
live in Poland today.

Population density varies considerably:
Upper Silesia is the most densely inhabited
area while the north-eastern border regions
remain the least populated.

Over 60% of the country's inhabitants live
in towns and cities. Warsaw (1.7 million) is
by far the largest city and is followed by Łódź
(825,000), Kraków (720,000), Wrocław
(650,000), Poznań (590,000) and Gdańsk
(470,000).

According to rough estimates, between
five and 10 million Poles live abroad. The
largest Polish émigré community lives in the
USA with the biggest group being in
Chicago. Poles sometimes joke that Chicago
is the second-largest Polish city, as nearly a
million of them live there. Poles refer to the
overseas Polish community as 'Polonia'.

ARTS
Visual Arts & Literature

Poland is a land of remarkable individuals, so
many in fact that visitors often lose their way
among the unfamiliar names.

As well as Copernicus and Chopin one
soon becomes acquainted with Jan Matejko
(1838-93), whose monumental historical
paintings hang in galleries throughout
Poland. By creating dramatic visual images
of decisive moments in Polish history,
Matejko inspired his compatriots at a time
when Poland was under foreign domination.

A kindred spirit was the Romantic poet,
Adam Mickiewicz (1798-1855), who sought
the lost motherland in his writings. Mickiewicz explored the ethical and moral
problems of a Poland subject to Russia and
held out the hope of eventual redemption, in
the same way that Christ was resurrected.

Henryk Sienkiewicz (1846-1916) wrote
historical novels which gave Poles a new
sense of national identity and won the author
a Nobel Prize in 1905 for Quo Vadis?. His
book The Teutonic Knights published in 1900
makes fascinating reading in light of the Nazi
attack on Poland four decades later.

Stanisław Wyspiański (1869-1907) was
the most outstanding figure of Young Poland,
an artistic movement which developed in
Kraków at the turn of the 19th century. A
painter, dramatist and poet, he's as much
known for his literary achievements – particularly The Wedding, one of the greatest
Polish dramas – as for his pastels and drawings. He also designed a number of amazing
stained-glass windows.

Another exceptionally gifted artist
working in many fields was Stanisław Ignacy
Witkiewicz (1885-1939), commonly known
as Witkacy. A philosopher, painter, dramatist
and photographer, he left behind an extensive
collection of expressionist paintings, but he's
possibly more acclaimed for his novels (such
as Insatiability) and plays (Mother, Cobblers,
New Deliverance). Witkacy was the creator
of the theatre of the absurd long before
Ionesco made it famous.

The postwar period imposed a choice on
many writers: sell out to communism or take
a more independent path. Czesław Miłosz
(born 1911), who broke with the regime,
gives a fascinating analysis of this moral
dilemma in The Captive Mind. Miłosz occupies the prime position in Polish postwar
literature, and the Nobel Prize awarded him
in 1980 was a recognition of his achievements. He started his career in the 1930s and

expresses himself equally brilliantly in poetry and prose.

Polish literature was once again honoured with a Nobel Prize in 1996, this time for Wisława Szymborska (born 1923), a brilliant Kraków poet who by the time of the award was little known beyond the boundaries of her motherland.

Stanisław Lem is Poland's best internationally known science-fiction writer, while Ryszard Kapuściński is well known for his journalistic accounts. Works of both have been translated into a dozen languages.

Music

Polish folk music goes back far beyond the first written records of the mid-16th century. Different musical rhythms, all with their corresponding dance forms, evolved in different regions. Some of the more popular are the *krakowiak*, an old folk dance from the Kraków region, and the *mazurek* (mazurka), a spirited Mazovian genre similar to a polka, which originated in central Poland. Danced by a circle of couples in three-four time with much improvisation, mazurkas were originally accompanied by goatskin bagpipes.

The *polonez* (polonaise) is a dignified ceremonial dance that originated as a formal march in the 16th century. During the 17th and 18th centuries the polonaise was used to open functions at the royal court. Arrayed according to their social station, couples would promenade around the ballroom in three-four time, knees bending slightly on every third gliding step.

The romantic composer, Frédéric Chopin (in Polish, Fryderyk Szopen; 1810-49) raised these folk and court dances (mazurkas, polonaises and waltzes) to the level of concert pieces. Written at a time when central Poland was under Russian domination, Chopin's music displays the melancholy and nostalgia which became hallmarks of the Polish national style.

Stanisław Moniuszko (1819-72) 'nationalised' 19th-century Italian opera music by introducing folk songs and dances onto the stage. His *Halka* (1858), about a peasant girl abandoned by a young noble, was the first Polish national opera, and is a staple of the national opera houses.

Another composer inspired by folklore,

Karol Szymanowski (1882-1937) strove to merge the traditions of Polish music with those of Europe. His ballet *Harnasie*, based on folk rhythms from the Tatra Mountains, employed modern technical devices also used by the Russian Igor Stravinsky.

Poland has produced several outstanding composers of contemporary music, including Witold Lutosławski (1913-94), Krzysztof Penderecki (born 1933) and Henryk Górecki (born 1933).

SOCIETY & CONDUCT

By and large, Poles are more conservative and traditional than westerners and there's a palpable difference between the city and the village. While the way of life in large urban centres increasingly mimics Western European and, in particular, North American patterns, the traditional spiritual culture is still very much in evidence in the more remote countryside. Religion plays an important role in this conservatism, the other factor being the still limited and antiquated infrastructure of services and communications. All in all, travelling in some rural areas can be like going back a century in time.

Poles don't keep as strictly to the clock as people do in the west. You may have to wait a bit until your friend arrives for an appointed meeting in the street or in a café. Poles often collide with each other on the street and rarely apologise. They're not being rude, it's just the way they do things.

In greetings, Poles, particularly men, are passionate hand-shakers. Women, too, often shake hands with men, but the man should always wait until the woman extends her hand first. You may occasionally see the traditional polite way of greeting when a man kisses the hand of a woman. Here, again, it's the woman who suggests such a form by a perceptible rise of her hand.

RELIGION

Poland is a strongly religious country and about 90% of the population are practising Roman Catholics. The 1978 election of the 'Polish pope', John Paul II, has strengthened the position of the Church in Poland.

In 966 Poland became the easternmost Roman Catholic country in Europe, while

Russia and most of the Balkan countries converted to Eastern Orthodox Christianity. Since then, Poland has always been on the borderline between Rome and Byzantium, and both faiths have been present for most of its history. After WWII Poland's borders shifted towards the west and consequently the Orthodox Church is now present only along a narrow strip on the eastern frontier. Its adherents number about 1% of the country's population, yet it is the second-largest creed practised in Poland.

The narrow line between the Church and the state has always been difficult to define in Poland. The Church openly supported Solidarity throughout the years when it was banned, and the overthrow of communism was as much a victory for the Church as it was for democracy. It's no coincidence that Catholic religious instruction was introduced in public schools just as the teaching of Marxist ideology was dropped. Legislation passed in 1993 requires both public and private radio and TV to espouse 'Christian values' in their broadcasts. In the same year, a strong anti-abortion law was introduced. The Church has demanded the return of property confiscated not only by the communists but also by the Russian tsars.

Omnipresent and growing in power, the Catholic Church has recently begun to lose both popular support and its adherents. Ironically, it has become the victim of its own victories. It is alienating an increasing number of Poles, who rebel against such open clerical militancy.

LANGUAGE

Most ordinary Poles don't speak any language other than Polish. This includes attendants at public services such as shops, post offices, banks, bus and train stations, restaurants and hotels (except for some top-end ones), and you may even encounter language problems at tourist offices. This is also true for phone emergency lines, including the police, ambulance and fire brigade.

Ideally, everyone who wants to travel in Poland should know some basic Polish. A phrasebook and a small dictionary are essential.

English and German are the best known foreign languages in Poland, though they're by no means commonly spoken or understood. English is more commonly heard in larger urban centres among the better educated. German is in large part a heritage of prewar territorial divisions, and is therefore mainly spoken in the regions which were once German, such as Masuria, Pomerania and Silesia. See the Language Guide at the back of the book for pronunciation and basic vocabulary.

Facts for the Visitor

HIGHLIGHTS
Nature
Poland excels in mountains, lakes and sea coast. Those wishing to commune with the Baltic will find the beaches of Łeba unending and the sand dunes inspiring. Mikołajki is a fine place to begin exploring the 3000 Masurian lakes, while Zakopane is the launching pad for hikes into the Tatras, Poland's most magnificent mountain range. The primeval Białowieża Forest on Poland's eastern border is home to the largest remaining herd of European bison and other wildlife. Each of these environments is distinct and equally worth experiencing.

Historic Towns
Of all Poland's cities, only Kraków has a fully authentic old centre, almost untouched by WWII. The damaged historic cores of Poznań, Toruń and Wrocław have been masterfully restored. The old towns in Gdańsk and Warsaw were destroyed almost totally and rebuilt from scratch, with amazingly good results. All are well worth visiting. Among smaller urban centres, Zamość in south-east Poland is a 16th-century Renaissance town.

Museums
Warsaw's National Museum holds Poland's largest art collection, though national museums in Kraków, Wrocław, Poznań and Gdańsk are also extensive and worth visiting. The Auschwitz Museum at Oświęcim is perhaps the most touching and meaningful.

Anyone interested in traditional rural architecture and crafts should visit some of Poland's 29 *skansens* (open-air museums), the best of which include those at Sanok and Nowy Sącz.

Castles

The imposing Malbork Castle, one-time seat of the Teutonic Knights, is reputedly the largest surviving medieval castle in Europe. Other remarkable castles built by the knights include those in Lidzbark Warmiński and Kwidzyn. For hundreds of years the mighty Wawel Castle in Kraków sheltered Polish royalty, most of whom are buried in the adjacent cathedral. True castle lovers will also seek out Pieskowa Skała Castle near Kraków. All these castles are now museums.

Palaces

Warsaw contains Poland's two most magnificent royal palaces: the 17th-century Wilanów Palace and the 18th-century Łazienki Palace. In the countryside feudal magnates built splendid Renaissance, baroque and rococo palaces, the best of which include those in Łańcut, Nieborów, Kozłówka, Rogalin and Pszczyna, all open as museums.

SUGGESTED ITINERARIES

Your itinerary will largely depend on your particular interests, the length of your stay in Poland, the season, the direction you are coming from and where you're heading. Regardless of how short your visit is, however, try not to miss Kraków. With a month or so in Poland, you'll be able to visit a good part of the places included in the Highlights section.

PLANNING
Climate & When to Go

Poland has a moderate continental climate with considerable maritime influence along the Baltic coast, which makes conditions variable from year to year and day to day. Spring is a time of warm days and chilly nights, while summer can be hot. Autumn brings some rain and there can be snow from December to March. In the mountains the snow lingers until April or even May. From late October to February it gets dark around 5 pm (about 4 pm in December). July is the hottest month, February the coolest.

The tourist season runs roughly from May to September, that is, from mid-spring to early autumn. Its peak is in July and August. These are the months of school and university holidays, and most Polish workers and employees take their annual leave in that period. Most theatres and concert halls are closed in July and August.

If you want to escape the crowds, probably the best time to visit is either late spring (mid-May to June) or the turn of summer and autumn (September to mid-October). These are pleasantly warm periods, ideal for general sightseeing and outdoor activities such as walking, biking, horse riding and canoeing. Many cultural events take place in both these periods.

The rest of the year, from mid-autumn to mid-spring, is colder, darker and perhaps less attractive for the average visitor. However, this doesn't mean that it's a bad time to visit city sights and enjoy the cities' cultural life, which is not much less active than during the tourist season. Understandably, hiking and other outdoor activities are less prominent in this period, except for skiing in winter (December to March). Most camp sites and youth hostels are closed at this time.

Books & Maps

Lonely Planet's *Poland* is a comprehensive travel guide to the country, and is well worth picking up if you'll be spending much time in Poland. For walkers, Bradt's *Hiking Guide to Poland and Ukraine* is worth considering. Hippocrene Books' *Poland's Jewish Heritage* is good for anybody interested in the subject, even though its practical information is scanty.

God's Playground: a History of Poland by Norman Davies is possibly the best key to understanding the history of the Polish nation. This two-volume work is beautifully readable and has at the same time a rare analytical depth.

The Polish Way: a Thousand-Year History of the Poles and their Culture by Adam Zamoyski is a superb cultural history of Poland full of maps and illustrations which bring the past 1000 years to life. This book reads as smoothly as a novel though it's 100% factual.

Bookshops and tourist offices in Poland sell excellent city and regional maps for under US$2. Tram and bus routes are shown on the maps, which is handy. There's also a choice of detailed road maps, including comprehensive book-format road atlases.

POLAND

What to Bring
The first and most important rule is to bring
as little as possible. The time when shelves in
Poland were empty is long over and you can
now buy almost anything you might need.
Clothes, toiletries, stationery, sports and
camping equipment and the like, both locally
produced and imported, are easily available
in shops and markets.

TOURIST OFFICES
Local Tourist Offices
Most larger cities have municipal tourist
offices, which are usually good sources of information and most sell maps and tourist
publications. If you can't find any, try Orbis,
the largest travel agency in Poland with
offices and its own hotels in cities and towns
throughout the country. Orbis doesn't focus
on providing free information to travellers,
yet staff may occasionally help if they're not
too busy, and in most offices there's someone
who speaks English.

Another possible information source is the
Polish Tourists Association (PTTK) which
has offices and its own hostels in towns and
resort areas. It sells maps and arranges
guides, and may provide some information,
but English is seldom spoken.

Almatur is the Student Travel & Tourism
Bureau and has offices in major provincial
capitals. It operates summer student hostels,
sells international transport tickets, organises
inexpensive two-week sailing, canoeing and
horse-riding holidays (which foreigners may
join), and issues ISIC cards (US$7). The ISIC
card gives reductions on museum admissions
(normally by 50%), Polferry ferries (20%),
LOT domestic flights (10%) and urban transport in Warsaw (50%).

Tourist Offices Abroad
Polish tourist offices abroad include:

Belgium
  Bureau du Tourisme Polonais (☎ 2-511 81 69;
  fax 511 80 05) 18/24 Rue des Colonies, 1000
  Brussels
Germany
  Polnisches Fremdenverkehrsamt (☎ 30-210
  0920) Marburger Strasse 1, 10789 Berlin

Netherlands
  Pools Informatiebureau voor Toerisme (☎ 20-
  625 35 70; fax 623 09 29) Leidsestraat 64, 1017
  PD Amsterdam
Sweden
  Polska Statens Turistbyra (☎ 8-21 60 75 or 21
  81 45; fax 21 04 65) Kungsgatan 66, Box 449,
  S-10128 Stockholm
UK
  Polish National Tourist Office (☎ 0171-580
  8811; fax 580 8866) 1st floor, Remo House,
  310-312 Regent St, London W1R 5AJ
USA
  Polish National Tourist Office (☎ 312-236 9013
  or 236 9123; fax 236 1125) 33 North Michigan
  Ave, Suite 224, Chicago, IL 60601
  (☎ 212-338 9412; fax 338 9283) 275 Madison
  Ave, Suite 1711, New York, NY 10016

You can also try offices of the Polish travel
agencies, the widest network of which has
Orbis. As in Poland, they focus on selling
their services and have package holidays
which may include skiing, sailing or horse
riding. They can book Orbis hotels for you
and arrange a rental car. As well, they may
provide tourist information and have free
tourist publications on Poland. Orbis offices
abroad appear under the name of either Orbis
or Polorbis and include:

Austria
  Austro Orbis Touristik (☎ 1-214 76 88 or 212
  13 56; fax 214 76 89) Lilienbrunngasse 5, 1020
  Vienna
Belgium
  Polorbis Benelux Sprl (☎ 2-513 13 22; fax 502
  12 61) 18/24 Rue des Colonies, 1000 Brussels
France
  SPTOV Polorbis (☎ 01 47420742; fax 49
  249436) 49 Ave de l'Opéra, 75002 Paris
Germany
  Polorbis Reiseunternehmen GmbH
  (☎ 221-95 15 34; fax 52 82 77) Hohenzollern-
  ring 99-101, 50672 Cologne
  (☎ 40-33 76 86 or 24 81 03; fax 32 42 10) Ernst
  Merck Strasse 12-14, 20099 Hamburg
  (☎ 30-294 13 94 or 294 13 95; fax 294 96 48)
  Warschauer Strasse 5, 10243 Berlin
  (☎ 711-61 24 20 or 61 37 11; fax 61 21 06)
  Rotebühl Strasse 51, 70178 Stuttgart
Hungary
  (☎ 1-117 05 32; fax 117 14 74) Orbis Budapest
  Kft, Vörösmarty tér 6, 1051 Budapest

POLAND

Israel
(☎ 3-566 07 50; fax 566 46 25) Polish Travel Office Orbis, 95 Allenby Rd, Tel Aviv 65 134

Italy
Orbis Italia (☎ 6-488 34 17 or 488 34 37; fax 482 11 09) Via Barberini 11, 00 187 Rome

Sweden
Orbis Resor AB (☎ 8-23 53 45 or 10 05 90; fax 10 89 65) Birger Jarlsgatan 71, 104 32 Stockholm
Orbis Resor AB (☎ 40-10 05 65; fax 12 85 19) Kalendegatan 9, 211 35 Malmö

UK
Polorbis Travel Ltd (☎ 0171-637 4971, or 580 8028 or 580 1704; fax 436 6558) 82 Mortimer St, London W1N 8HN

USA
Orbis Polish Travel Bureau (☎ 212-867 5011; fax 682 4715) 342 Madison Ave, New York, NY 10173

VISAS & EMBASSIES

Citizens of Austria, Belgium, Denmark, Finland, France, Germany, Ireland, Italy, Luxembourg, the Netherlands, Norway, Portugal, Spain, Sweden, Switzerland, the UK and the USA do not require visas for a stay of up to 90 days (Britons up to six months). Other nationals should check with one of the Polish consulates and apply for a visa if they need one.

Visas are issued for a period of up to 180 days, and the price is the same regardless of the visa's duration, about US$40 to US$60, varying from country to country. Some consulates may give shorter visas if you apply by mail. You can stay in Poland in the period specified in the visa, so work out the dates of your planned entry and exit which you have to indicate in the application form. You can extend your visa in Poland for a period of up to 90 days (see the Warsaw section for information on visa extensions).

There are also 48-hour transit visas (onward visa required) if you just need to pass through Poland. Visas are generally issued in a few days, with an express same-day service available in some consulates if you pay 50% more.

Polish Embassies Abroad

Polish embassies and consulates are found in Belgrade, Bratislava, Bucharest, Budapest, Prague, Sofia and Zagreb. Others include:

Australia
(☎ 02-6273 1208) 7 Turrana St, Yarralumla, ACT 2600 (Canberra)
(☎ 02-9363 9816) 10 Trelawney St, Woollahra, NSW 2025 (Sydney)

Canada
(☎ 613-789 0468) 443 Daly Ave, Ottawa 2, Ontario K1N 6H3
(☎ 514-937 9481) 1500 Ave des Pins Ouest, Montreal, Quebec H3G 1B4
(☎ 416-252 5471) 2603 Lakeshore Blvd West, Toronto, Ontario M8V 1G5
(☎ 604-688 3530) 1177 West Hastings St, Suite 1600, Vancouver, BC V6E 2K3

UK
(☎ 0171-580 4324) 47 Portland Place, London W1N 4JH
(☎ 0171-580 0475) 73 New Cavendish St, London W1N 7RB
(☎ 0131-552 0301) 2 Kinnear Rd, Edinburgh EH3 5PE

USA
(☎ 202-234 3800) 2640 16th St NW, Washington, DC 20009
(☎ 212-889 8360) 233 Madison Ave, New York, NY 10016
(☎ 312-337 8166) 1530 North Lake Shore Drive, Chicago, IL 60610
(☎ 310-442 8500) 12400 Wilshire Blvd, Suite 555, Los Angeles, CA 90025

Foreign Embassies in Poland

The following embassies are all in Warsaw and have attached consular offices. There are also foreign consulates in other Polish cities, including Kraków (see that section later in this chapter for consulates located there).

Australia
(☎ 617 60 81) ul Estońska 3/5

Belarus
(☎ 617 39 54) ul Ateńska 67

Bulgaria
(☎ 629 40 71) Al Ujazdowskie 33/35

Canada
(☎ 629 80 51) ul Matejki 1/5

Czech Republic
(☎ 628 72 21) ul Koszykowa 18

Estonia
(☎ 646 44 80) ul Karwińska 1

France
(☎ 628 84 01) ul Piękna 1

Germany
(☎ 617 30 11) ul Dąbrowiecka 30

Hungary
(☎ 628 44 51) ul Chopina 2

Israel
(☎ 825 00 28) ul Krzywickiego 24
Japan
(☎ 653 94 30) Al Jana Pawła II 23
Latvia
(☎ 48 19 47) ul Rejtana 15
Lithuania
(☎ 625 34 10) Al Szucha 5
Romania
(☎ 628 31 56) ul Chopina 10
Russia
(☎ 621 34 53) ul Belwederska 49
Slovakia
(☎ 628 40 51) ul Litewska 6
Sweden
(☎ 640 89 00) ul Bagatela 3
UK
(☎ 628 10 01) Al Róż 1
Ukraine
(☎ 629 64 49) Al Szucha 7
USA
(☎ 628 30 41) Al Ujazdowskie 29/31

Some of the Eastern European embassies only open Monday, Wednesday and Friday for a few hours in the morning and may need a while to issue a visa; plan ahead.

CUSTOMS
Customs procedures are usually a formality now, on both entering and leaving Poland, and your luggage is likely to pass through with only a cursory glance.

When entering Poland, you're allowed to bring duty-free articles for personal use required for your travel and stay in Poland. They include clothes, books etc; two still cameras, one cine and one video camera plus accessories; portable self-powered electronic goods such as a personal computer, video recorder, radio set, cassette player and the like plus accessories; a portable musical instrument; sports and tourist equipment such as a sailboard, kayak (up to 5.5m in length), bicycle, tent, skis etc; and medicines and medical instruments for your own use. You'll rarely be asked to declare these things.

Unlimited amounts of foreign currency and travellers cheques can be brought into the country, and the equivalent of up to 2000 ECU can be taken out by every foreigner without a declaration. If you enter with more than 2000 ECU and want to take it all out of Poland, fill in a currency-declaration form

upon arrival and have it stamped by customs officials. In practice, probably nobody will ask you how much money you're taking in and out. You're allowed to import or export Polish currency, but there's no point in doing so. Narcotics, naturally, are forbidden and you'd be asking for trouble smuggling them in or out.

When leaving the country, you may take out duty-free gifts and souvenirs to a total value not exceeding US$100. The export of items manufactured before 9 May 1945 is prohibited.

MONEY
An essential question for many travellers is what to bring: cash, travellers cheques or a credit card. Any of the three forms of carrying money is OK in Poland, though it's probably best to bring a combination of the three to allow yourself maximum flexibility. Travelling in Poland is generally safe, so there are no major problems in bringing some hard currency in cash, which is easiest to change. Travellers cheques are safer but harder to change and you get about 2% to 3% less than for cash. Finally, with the recent rash of ATMs (*bankomaty*), credit cards are becoming the most convenient option of getting local currency in the cities, though still not so in the countryside.

Currency
The official Polish currency is the złoty (literally 'gold'), abbreviated to zł. It is divided into 100 units called the grosz, abbreviated to gr. New notes and coins were introduced on 1 January 1995, and include five paper bills (10, 20, 50, 100 and 200 złotys) and nine coins (1, 2, 5, 10, 20 and 50 groszy, and 1, 2 and 5 złotys). The bills feature Polish kings, have different sizes and are easily recognisable. The new currency has replaced the old złoty bills and coins, which were gradually withdrawn from circulation and since 1 January 1997 are no longer legal tender.

Exchange Rates
Polish currency is now convertible and easy to change either way. There's no longer a black market in Poland and the official exchange rate roughly represents the currency's

actual value. The złoty's rate of depreciation against hard currencies has slowed down significantly over the past few years, but it's still high – about 10% per year.

At the time we went to press the approximate rates were:

Australia	A$1	=	2.12 zł
Canada	C$1	=	2.39 zł
euro	€1	=	4.10 zł
France	1FF	=	0.63 zł
Germany	DM1	=	2.10 zł
Japan	¥100	=	2.64 zł
United Kingdom	UK£1	=	6.25 zł
United States	US$1	=	3.73 zł

Changing Money

Changing Cash The place to exchange cash in Poland is the *kantor*, the private currency-exchange office. Kantors are ubiquitous; in the centre of the major cities they dot every second block. They're so numerous we don't usually bother listing them in this chapter: when you need one you'll probably find one. Just ask anybody for a kantor. The kantors are either self-contained offices or just desks in the better hotels, travel agencies, train stations, post offices, department stores etc. The farther out from the cities you go, the less numerous they are, but you can be pretty sure that every medium-size town has at least a few of them. Kantors are usually open on weekdays between roughly 9 am and 6 pm and till around 2 pm on Saturday, but some work longer and a few stay open 24 hours.

Kantors change cash only (no travellers cheques) and accept most of the major world currencies. The most common and thus the most easily changed are the US dollar, the Deutschmark and the pound sterling (in that order). Australian dollars and Japanese yen are somewhat exotic to Poles and not all kantors will change them. There's no commission on transaction – you get what is written on the board (every kantor has a board displaying the exchange rates of currencies it changes). The whole operation takes a few seconds and there's no paperwork involved. You don't need to present your passport or fill in any forms.

Kantors buy and sell foreign currencies, and the difference between the buying and

selling rates is usually not larger than 1%. Don't forget to change your extra złotys back to hard currency before you leave Poland, but don't leave it to the last minute as exchange offices on the border and at airports tend to give poor rates, and some may be unwilling to change back altogether.

Exchange rates differ slightly from city to city and from kantor to kantor (about 1%). Smaller towns may offer up to 3% less, so it's advisable to change money in large urban centres.

One important thing to remember before you set off from home is that banknotes must be in good condition, without any marks or seals. Kantors can refuse to accept banknotes which have numbers written on them in pen or pencil (a common practice of western bank cashiers totalling bundles of notes) even if they are in otherwise perfect condition.

Street moneychangers are slowly becoming an extinct species, but some still hang around touristy places. Give them a miss – most are con men. Particularly, beware of moneychangers in Gdańsk.

Changing Travellers Cheques This is not as straightforward as changing cash, but is still pretty easy. The usual place to change travellers cheques is a bank, but not all banks handle these transactions. The best known bank which offers this facility is the Bank Pekao SA. It has a dozen offices in Warsaw and branches in all major cities.

Several other banks, including Bank Gdański, Bank Zachodni, Bank Śląski, Powszechny Bank Kredytowy and Powszechny Bank Gospodarczy, also provide this service, and they too have many regional branches.

Banks in the larger cities are usually open weekdays from 8 am to 5 or 6 pm (some also open on Saturday till 2 pm), but in smaller towns they tend to close earlier. They change most major brands of cheque, of which American Express is the most widely known.

The exchange rate is marginally lower than in kantors, and banks charge a commission (*prowizja*) on transactions, which varies from bank to bank (somewhere between 0.5% to 2%). Most banks also have a set minimum charge of US$1.50 to US$3. For example, the Bank Pekao's commission on changing cheques into złotys is 1.5% with a minimum charge of US$2.

Some banks also exchange travellers cheques for US cash dollars and the commission is usually lower (eg the Bank Pekao charges 0.5% with a minimum of US$1.25). Once you have US cash dollars you can go to any kantor and change them into złotys at the usual kantor's rate.

Banks can be crowded and inefficient; you'll probably have to queue a while and then wait until they complete the paperwork. It may take anything from 10 minutes to an hour. You'll need your passport in any transaction. Some provincial banks may insist on seeing the original receipt from when you bought your travellers cheques, and if you don't present it, they can simply refuse to change your cheques. If you have a receipt, bring it with you.

You can also change travellers cheques to złotys (but not to US cash dollars) in American Express offices, but there are only two offices in Warsaw and one in Kraków. They are efficient, speak English and change most major brands of cheque. Their rates are a bit lower than those of the banks, but they charge no commission, so you may get more złotys for your cheques here than in the bank.

American Express card-holders can also have mail sent c/o American Express Travel, Dom Bez Kantów, Krakowskie Przedmieście 11, 00-068 Warszawa, Poland. Mail is kept for three months.

Cash enough travellers cheques to last until you set foot in another big city before setting off for a trip into more remote regions.

Credit Cards

Credit cards are becoming increasingly popular for buying goods and services, though their use is still limited to upmarket establishments, mainly in the major cities. Among the more popular cards accepted in Poland are American Express, Diners Club, Eurocard, Access, MasterCard and Visa.

Credit cards are also useful for getting cash advances in the banks, and the procedure is faster than changing travellers cheques. The best card to bring is Visa, because it's honoured by the largest number of banks, including the Bank Pekao and all the other banks listed in the earlier Travellers Cheques

section. The Bank Pekao will also give cash advances on MasterCard.

The first ATMs appeared in July 1996 and spread like wildfire. Today almost every office of a major bank has its own bankomat, and there are also a lot of others, strategically placed in the key points of the city central areas. They accept most major cards, including Visa and MasterCard. The main ATM shark in Poland is Euronet which had about 350 ATMs as we went to press. Euronet ATMs accept 17 different credit cards.

Costs

Visitors now pay for everything in Poland (except visas) in local currency, as do the Poles. Everyone pays the same price for food, accommodation, transport and admissions – unlike some other Eastern European countries where foreigners are sometimes charged higher prices than locals.

You should be able to see Poland in relative comfort for under US$30 per person per day following the recommendations in this book. This amount would cover accommodation in budget hotels, food in medium-price restaurants and moving at a reasonable pace by train or bus, and would still leave you a margin for some cultural events, a few beers and occasional taxis. Couples, families and small groups sharing hotel rooms will spend less, and if you camp or sleep in youth hostels, and eat only at self-services you could easily end up spending under US$20 per person per day. Museum admission fees are usually around US$1 to US$2 (half that price for students), and most museums have one free-entry day during the week (different from place to place). Before congratulating yourself on how cheap it is, remember that Polish workers only make the equivalent of about US$350 a month.

POST & COMMUNICATIONS

Post services are operated by the Poczta Polska, while communications facilities are provided by the Telekomunikacja Polska. Both companies usually share one office, called the post office (*poczta*), although recently the Telekomunikacja has been opening its own communications-only offices. Yet in most cases you can use the poczta for everything: buying stamps, sending letters, receiving poste restante, placing long-distance calls and sending faxes. In the cities there will be a dozen or more post offices, of which the Poczta Główna (main post office) will usually have the widest range of facilities, including poste restante and fax. Larger post offices in the cities are normally open weekdays from 8 am to 8 pm, and one will stay open round the clock. In smaller localities business hours may only be on weekdays till 4 pm and international calls are not always possible.

Sending Mail

Air-mail letters sent from Poland take about a week to reach a European destination and up to two weeks if mailed to other continents. The rates for postcards and letters are reasonably low, but air-mail parcels are expensive, with prices comparable to those in Western Europe.

Receiving Mail

Poste restante doesn't seem to be very reliable. If you want mail sent to you, stick to the large cities, such as Warsaw, Kraków and Gdańsk (see those sections for details). Mail is held for 14 working days, then returned to the sender.

Telephone

The Polish telephone system is antiquated and unreliable. Public telephones are few and far between by western standards, and not infrequently out of order. Go to a post office: each should have at least one functioning public phone. Old phones operate on tokens (żetony) which can be bought at the post office. However, these phones have almost disappeared, and will probably be extinct within a few years.

Newly installed telephones only operate on magnetic phonecards. It's well worth buying a phonecard (at the post office) if you think you'll be using public phones from time to time. Cards come in three kinds: a 25-unit card (US$1.75), a 50-unit card (US$3.50) and a 100-unit card (US$7). One unit represents one three-minute local call. Cards can be used for domestic and international calls.

Apart from the regular phone network, there are several cellular phone providers, including the analog Centertel and the digital

Era and Plus. Mobile phones are quickly becoming popular, both as a status symbol and as a more reliable alternative to the jammed stationary lines and scarce and often inoperable public phones.

Intercity direct dialling is possible to almost anywhere in the country. In this chapter telephone area-code numbers are listed just below the heading of the town or city. They all begin with '0', after which you get another, usually fainter dial tone; you then dial the rest of the area code and the local phone number.

Telekomunikacja Polska is upgrading the telephone system to a uniform seven-digit system. When this book was researched, the company was somewhere halfway through the process, with a massive change of phone numbers. This unfortunately means that some numbers included in this chapter may be already invalid by the time you read this.

You can now dial directly to just about anywhere in the world. When dialling direct, a minute will cost around US$0.75 to Europe and US$1.50 anywhere outside Europe. If you place the call through the operator at the post office, the minimum charge is for a three-minute call which will cost about US$2.50 to Europe and US$5 elsewhere. Every extra minute costs a third more. For a person-to-person call, add an extra minute's charge.

Collect calls are possible to most major countries around the world. Inquire at any Telekomunikacja Polska office for the toll-free number to the operator in the country you want to call, then call from any public or private telephone. These numbers include:

Australia	☎ 00 800 61 111 61
France	☎ 00 800 33 111 33
Germany	☎ 00 800 49 111 49
UK	☎ 00 800 44 111 44
USA (AT&T)	☎ 00 800 1 1111 11

To call a telephone number in Poland from abroad, dial the international access code of the country you're calling from, the country code for Poland (☎ 48), the area code (drop the initial '0') and the local phone number. To call abroad from Poland, dial ☎ 00 (the Polish international access code) before the country code of the country you are calling.

POLAND

INTERNET RESOURCES

Though it's still way behind Western Europe, the Internet is becoming popular in Poland and there are a number of service providers. Cybercafés offering Internet service to the public are beginning to open in the big cities. An hour of surfing the Web or emailing costs about US$2, though it can be twice as much in some places in Warsaw. Some of the cafés use quite dated (and accordingly painfully slow) equipment.

NEWSPAPERS & MAGAZINES

Each large city has at least one local newspaper. The *Gazeta Wyborcza* was the first independent daily in postwar Eastern Europe and is now the major national paper with countrywide distribution. The *Rzeczpospolita* is the main business daily. The *Wprost* is the biggest weekly magazine, whereas the *Poradnik Domowy* (Home Adviser) is the best-selling Polish monthly.

The major Polish publication in English is *The Warsaw Voice* – a well edited and interesting weekly. It gives a good insight into Polish politics, business and culture, and includes a tourist section which lists local events. It's distributed in top-class hotels, airline offices and embassies, and can be bought from major newsagencies (US$1.50). It's hard to find outside big cities.

Major foreign newspapers and weeklies are easy to find in large urban centres. The best places to look for them are the EMPiK bookstores, existing in most sizable cities. Alternatively try foreign-language bookshops or the newsstands in the lobbies of the upmarket hotels. Traditionally, *Time* and *Newsweek* are the most widely distributed.

RADIO & TV

The state-run Polish Radio (Polskie Radio) is the main broadcaster. The Warsaw-based Radio Zet and the Kraków-based RFM are two nationwide private broadcasters. Plenty of other private competitors operate locally on FM. Apart from the headline news in English broadcast by some of the private stations, all programs are in Polish.

There are two state-owned countrywide TV channels: the general program I and the more education and culture-focused program II. The third countrywide venture is the private PolSat. Some of the larger cities also have local programming.

Satellite TV has become very popular, and most major hotels have it. Rough estimates indicate that, except for France and the UK, Poland owns more satellite dishes than any other country in Europe.

PHOTOGRAPHY & VIDEO

Kodak and Fuji films are the most popular and Agfa is not far behind. You can buy both slide and negative film in several commonly used speeds. High-quality B&W Ilford films are also available from specialist photo shops, as are Fujichrome professional series including Velvia and Provia. The prices are comparable to those in Western Europe. Stock up in major cities.

As for processing, you can easily have your prints done, often within an hour, in any of the numerous photo minilabs. Slides are more of a problem, because not all labs seem to do a good job.

As for photo equipment, the choice is limited and the prices high. Bring along your own reliable gear. Getting your camera repaired in Poland can be a problem if you have an uncommon make and any original spare parts are necessary. General mechanical faults can usually be fixed quite easily.

VHS is the standard format for recording from TV and viewing rented films at home. SECAM used to be the standard image registration system in Poland, but most of the new video equipment entering the market is additionally set up for PAL and/or NTSC. Video 8mm is a favourite system used by amateurs shooting their own videos. Equipment for both systems is available, but the variety is limited, and it's expensive.

TIME

All of Poland lies within the same time zone, GMT/UTC+1. Poland puts the clocks forward an hour in late March and back again in late September.

ELECTRICITY

Electricity is 220V, 50Hz. Plugs with two round pins are used, the same as in the rest of Continental Europe.

WEIGHTS & MEASURES

Poland uses the metric system.

LAUNDRY

Dry cleaners (*pralnia*) exist in the larger cities but it will take them up to a week to get your clothes cleaned. A more expensive express service is available and can cut this time by half. Top-class hotels offer laundry facilities for their clients and are faster. Self-service laundrettes are unheard of so far, but there are some which offer service washes.

TOILETS

Self-contained public toilets in the cities are few and far between. If you're really desperate, look for a restaurant. Hotels, museums and train stations are other emergency options. It may be helpful to know that the toilet is labelled 'Toaleta' or simply 'WC'. The gents will be labelled 'Dla Panów' or 'Męski' and/or marked with a triangle (an inverted pyramid), and the ladies will be labelled 'Dla Pań' or 'Damski' and/or will be marked with a circle.

The use of a public toilet (including those in restaurants and train stations) costs from US$0.10 to US$0.50. Charges are pasted on the door and collected by attendants sitting at the door, who will give you a piece of toilet paper. It's a good idea to carry a roll of paper at all times.

HEALTH

The medical services and the availability of medications are not as good as in the west. Sanitary conditions still leave much to be desired and heavy pollution contaminates water and air. Public-hospital conditions are bad and medical equipment is outdated and scarce. Private clinics are on the increase and are better but more expensive.

Most minor health problems can be solved by a visit to the *apteka* or pharmacy. There are plenty of them and they have qualified staff, some of whom speak English. In the case of a more serious illness or injury you should seek a specialised doctor. Your embassy or consulate should be able to advise on a place to go. If you can't find help, ask for the *przychodnia* or an outpatient clinic. These clinics

have physicians of various specialities and are the places where ordinary Poles go when they get ill. Charges are relatively small. Citizens of the UK receive free treatment if they can prove coverage back home.

The countrywide emergency phone number for the ambulance service is ☎ 999 but don't expect the operator to speak English. Ask any Pole around to call for you.

Avoid unboiled tap water; it is heavily chlorinated, tastes awful and, more importantly, is polluted. Stick to bottled water for drinking; it's readily available in shops and supermarkets.

Bring a travel-insurance policy to cover theft, loss and medical problems. No vaccinations are necessary for Poland, but you are advised to get vaccinated against hepatitis A or at least get a gamma globulin jab. Due to poor sanitation, hepatitis A is still a problem in Poland. Mosquitoes are bastards in humid areas in summer, so if you plan on sailing, canoeing or trekking, an efficient insect repellent is a good idea.

The incidence of AIDS is high in Poland by European standards, and perhaps as many as 100,000 people are HIV-positive. Polish condoms are of bad quality, so it would be wise to bring your own. Not all chemists have contraceptives on display, and some simply don't stock them – this is, after all, a strong Catholic country. Tampons and syringes are available.

WOMEN TRAVELLERS

Travel for women in Poland is pretty much hassle-free except for occasional encounters with local drunks. Harassment of this kind is almost never dangerous, but can be annoying. Steer clear of drunks and avoid places considered male territory, particularly cheap drink bars.

On the other hand, a woman travelling alone, especially in remote rural areas, may expect to receive more help, hospitality and generosity from the locals than would a man on his own.

GAY & LESBIAN TRAVELLERS

The Polish gay and lesbian movement is still very much underground and pretty faint. Warsaw has the most open scene and is the

POLAND

easiest place to make contacts and get to know what's going on – get as much information here as you can, because elsewhere in Poland it can be difficult to contact the community. Warsaw's best source of information is the Rainbow/Lambda centre (☎ 628 52 22; Tuesday, Wednesday and Friday from 6 to 9 pm, English spoken), ul Czerniakowska 178 m 16.

DANGERS & ANNOYANCES

Poland is a relatively safe country to travel in, even though there has been a steady increase in crime since the fall of communism; you should keep your eyes open and use common sense. The problems mostly occur in big cities, with Warsaw being perhaps the least safe place in Poland. Take care when walking alone at night, particularly in the centre and the Praga suburb, and be alert at Warsaw central train station, the favourite playground for thieves and pickpockets. Other large cities appear to be quieter, but keep your wits about you. By and large, the smaller the town, the safer it is.

Don't venture into run-down areas, dubious-looking suburbs and desolate parks, especially after dark. Use taxis if you feel uncertain about an area. Keep a sharp eye on your pockets and your bag in crowded places such as markets or city buses and trams. Watch out for groups of suspicious male characters hanging around markets, shady bars and bus and train stations, and stay a safe distance from them.

Theft from cars is becoming a plague these days – keep your vehicle in a guarded car park (*parking strzeżony*) and don't leave any bags visible which may attract the attention of thieves. Pirate or 'mafia' taxis are a problem in Warsaw and some other large cities (see Taxi under Getting Around later in this chapter). Theft on international trains has also reached a plague proportion (see Train under Getting There & Away).

Hotels are generally safe, though you shouldn't leave valuables in your room; in most places you can deposit them at the reception desk. Lock your luggage if you can. By removing the temptation you'll usually eliminate the danger.

Heavy drinking is unfortunately a way of life in Poland and drunks may at times be disturbing. Poles smoke a lot and so far there has been no serious anti-tobacco campaign. Polish cigarettes are of low quality and the smoke they produce is hardly tolerable for anyone unused to them, let alone a nonsmoker.

Slow and impolite service in shops, offices and restaurants is slowly being eradicated by the competitive market economy, though you can still occasionally experience it. Cheating is not common but there are some areas, especially those connected with foreign tourism, where you should be alert. Worst are probably taxi drivers, particularly those who wait at airports or in front of plush hotels and hunt for foreign tourists. Simply avoid them.

Since WWII Poland has been ethnically an almost homogeneous nation and Poles, particularly those living in rural areas, have had little contact with foreigners. That's why travellers looking racially different, eg of African or Asian background, may attract some stares from the locals. In most cases, this is just curiosity, without any hostility in mind. On the other hand, there have been some acts of racism in the cities, though it's still not a social problem by any definition.

If your passport, valuables and/or other belongings are lost or stolen, report it to the police. They will give you a copy of the statement which serves as a temporary identity document; if you have insurance, you'll need to present it to your insurer in order to make a claim. English-speaking police are rare, so it's best to take along an interpreter if you can. Don't expect your things to be found, for the police are unlikely to do anything. They earn next to nothing and can be rather cynical about a 'rich' foreigner complaining about losing a few dollars.

BUSINESS HOURS

Most grocery shops are open on weekdays from 7 or 8 am to 6 or 7 pm and half a day on Saturday. Delicatessens and supermarkets usually stay open longer, until 8 or 9 pm, and there's at least one food shop which is open 24 hours in every major town and every district of the city. All such night shops have a section selling beer, wine and spirits. General stores (selling clothing, books, stationery, household appliances etc) normally open at 10 or 11 am and close at 6 or 7 pm (at 2 or 3 pm on Saturday).

The opening hours of museums and other tourist sights vary greatly. As a rough guide, they tend to open between 9 and 11 am and close anywhere from 3 to 6 pm. The overwhelming majority of museums are open on Sunday but closed on Monday; most of them also stay closed on the day following public holidays. Most museums close one or two hours earlier in the off season.

PUBLIC HOLIDAYS & SPECIAL EVENTS

Official public holidays include New Year (1 January), Easter Monday (March or April), Labour Day (1 May), Constitution Day (3 May), Corpus Christi (a Thursday in May or June), Assumption Day (15 August), All Saints' Day (1 November), Independence Day (11 November) and Christmas (25 and 26 December).

Poland's many annual festivals provide the opportunity to experience the best in music, theatre and folklore amid an exciting cultural milieu. Many cultural events take place in May/June and September/October.

Among the classical music highlights, you should be in Łańcut in May for the Old Music Festival, in Warsaw in June/July for the Mozart Festival, and in Wrocław in September for Wratislavia Cantans with its oratorios and cantatas. The best of contemporary music is presented at the Warsaw Autumn International Festival in September. If you are a jazz fan there's possibly nothing better than the Warsaw Summer Jazz Days in June and the Jazz Jamboree, also in Warsaw, in late October.

Major theatre festivals take place in Warsaw (January), Kalisz (May) and Toruń (May). Film comes to the fore in Kraków (May/June), Warsaw (October) and Toruń (November/December). For traditional music, the last week of June in Kazimierz Dolny is a must if you want to listen to genuine folk bands and singers from all over the country, but if you are interested in international folk songs and dances of highlanders, you should be in Zakopane in late August.

Apart from the cultural events, a variety of religious celebrations take place all over the country. Given the strong Catholic character of the nation, these events are much celebrated, especially among the more traditional rural population. Among the most important dates are Easter (the best known celebrations are in Kalwaria Zebrzydowska), Corpus Christi (the procession in Łowicz is the most famous), the Assumption (a pilgrimage to Częstochowa is a must for many Poles), All Souls' Day and Christmas.

ACTIVITIES

Zakopane, Poland's premier mountain resort, features hiking in summer and skiing in winter. With a little effort you could also get in some rafting on the nearby Dunajec River. Hikers less interested in meeting their fellows along the trails may consider other mountain areas such as the Bieszczady, the Beskid Sądecki or the Karkonosze.

Mikołajki and Giżycko in the Great Masurian Lakes district are major yachting centres with boats available for rent. Canoeists and kayakers will be quite at home here, and this part of Poland is flat enough also to appeal to cyclists, as is most of northern Poland.

See Organised Tours under the introductory Getting Around section later in this chapter for information on package tours built around these activities.

COURSES

Polish-language courses are available in most major cities. Warsaw's language schools include:

Polonicum, Warsaw University (☎/fax 022-826 54 16) ul Krakowskie Przedmieście 26/28
Linguae Mundi (☎ 022-654 22 18; fax 654 22 19) ul Złota 61
Schola Polonica 19 (☎ 022-625 26 52; fax 625 08 17) ul Jaracza 3 m
Berlitz (☎ 022-624 96 50; fax 624 96 87) ul Elektoralna 26

In Kraków, the major facility is the Polonia Institute of the Jagiellonian University (☎ 012-421 98 55; fax 421 98 77), ul Jodłowa 13. On the coast, there's the Sopot School of Polish (☎ 058-550 32 84; fax 550 06 96) in

Sopot, Al Niepodległości 763. In Poznań, try Berlitz (☎ 061-852 34 23; fax 852 34 18), ul Ratajczaka 10/12. Berlitz also operates in Wrocław (☎ 071-72 35 45; fax 44 70 18), ul Krupnicza 2/4.

ACCOMMODATION
Camping

There are hundreds of camping grounds in Poland, many offering small timber cabins which are often good value. International Federation of Camping & Caravanning (IFCC) card-holders get a 10% discount on camping fees. Theoretically, most camping grounds are open May to September, but they tend to close early if things are slow. The opening and closing dates listed in official brochures (and in this book) are only approximate. The *Polska Mapa Campingów* map lists most camping grounds and is available at tourist offices, large bookshops and PTTK offices.

Youth Hostels

Polish youth hostels (*schroniska młodzieżowe*) are operated by Polskie Towarzystwo Schronisk Młodzieżowych (PTSM), a member of Hostelling International. There are currently about 130 all-year hostels and 440 seasonal ones, open in July and August only. They are distributed more or less uniformly throughout the country, and there's at least one in every major city.

The all-year hostels are more reliable and have more facilities, including showers, a place to cook and a dining room. The seasonal hostels are usually installed in schools (while the pupils are off for their holidays) and their amenities may be scarce.

Many previously strict hostel rules have been relaxed or abandoned. Youth hostels are now open to all, members and nonmembers alike, and there is no age limit. Curfew is 10 pm, but some hostel staff may be flexible about this. Some hostels may admit both sexes in one dorm – not bad for a Catholic country. Most hostels are closed between 10 am and 5 pm. Checking-in time is usually till 9 pm, but this varies from place to place.

Hostels cost some US$4 to US$7 (depending on the hostel's category) per bed in a dorm for Poles, and about US$1 more for foreigners. Singles and doubles, if there are any, cost about 20% to 50% more. The youth hostel card gives a 25% discount off these prices for nationals and, in some places, for foreigners. If you don't have your own bed sheet or a sleeping bag, the staff will provide a sheet for about US$1.25.

Given the low prices, hostels are popular with travellers and are often full. A particularly busy time is early May to mid-June when hostels are crowded with Polish school groups.

PTTK Hostels & Mountain Refuges

PTTK runs an array of its own hostels, called Dom Turysty or Dom Wycieczkowy. They are aimed at budget travellers, providing them with simple shelter for the night. They rarely have singles, but always have a choice of three and four-bed rooms with shared facilities, where you can usually take just a bed, not the whole room, and which cost between US$4 and US$7. Some of the PTTK hostels, especially those in the large cities, are now under private management and are more expensive.

PTTK also runs a chain of mountain refuges (*schroniska górskie*) which are an essential help for trekkers. Conditions are usually simple, but you don't pay much and the atmosphere can be great. They also serve cheap hot meals. The more isolated refuges are obliged to take in all comers, regardless of how crowded they get, which means that in the high season (summer and/or winter) it can be hard to find even a space on the floor. Refuges are open all year though you'd better check at the nearest regional PTTK office before setting off.

Student Hostels

These are the hostels set up in student dormitories during the summer holiday period (July to mid-September) when students are away. In each major university city there are at least a few student dorms, some of which are open as student hostels in summer, and the picture may change from year to year.

Each year the Almatur student agency runs one dorm in Warsaw, Gdańsk, Kraków and Poznań. Accommodation costs US$17/26 a single/double for students and a dollar more for nonstudents. To use these hostels you need an Almatur voucher, which can be bought from Almatur offices.

Many other student dorms open in summer as hostels and run independently. They don't need vouchers, take in all comers and are usually cheaper than the Almatur hostels, though their standards can be lower.

Private Rooms

In some major cities, you'll find an agency, usually called the Biuro Zakwaterowania or the Biuro Kwater Prywatnych, which arranges accommodation in private homes. The rooms on offer are mostly singles and doubles and cost around US$16/24. The staff in the office show you what's available; you then decide, pay and go to the address they give you. The most important thing is to choose the right location, taking into consideration both distance and transport. Some places are a long way from the centre and you'd do far better to pay more for a central hotel and save hours travelling on public transport.

During the high season, there will probably be some people hanging around outside the office offering accommodation, often at lower prices (and open to bargaining) than those in the office. If you decide to deal with them, check exactly where the place is before committing yourself.

In popular holiday resorts, you'll find plenty of signs at the entrances to private homes saying *pokoje* (rooms) or *noclegi* (lodging), which indicate where to knock and ask for a room. They are usually cheaper than in the cities – US$7 a head will be sufficient in most cases.

Hotels

There's a variety of old and new hotels ranging from ultra-basic to extra-plush. The rudimentary outlets are mostly confined to the smaller provincial towns, whereas the upmarket establishments dot the central areas of big cities. Various state-run lodging networks, previously accessible to few, have now opened to all. The latter category includes the sports hotels (built within sports centres in order to create facilities for local and visiting teams) and workers' hotels (built to provide lodging facilities for

workers), both of which fall into the bottom price bracket.

Most hotels have single and double rooms, and some also offer triples. As a rule, single rooms work out proportionally more expensive than the doubles; a double usually costs only 20% to 40% more than a single. Taking a triple between three people gives a further saving as it is likely to cost only slightly more than a double. Rooms with private bath can be considerably more expensive than those with shared facilities, sometimes as much as twice the price. In Poland everyone, both locals and foreigners, pays the same price for hotel rooms.

Hotel prices vary according to the season and these are different in the various regions of Poland. At Zakopane the high ski season is from mid-December to March, while in Poznań hotel rates increase dramatically at trade-fair time. Rates are usually posted on a board at hotel reception desks.

If possible, check the room before accepting. Don't be fooled by the hotel reception areas, which may look great in contrast to the rest of the establishment. If you ask to see a room, you can be pretty sure that they won't give you the worst one, which might happen otherwise.

FOOD

Poles start off their day with breakfast (*śniadanie*) which is roughly similar to its western counterpart and may include bread and butter (*chleb z masłem*), cheese (*ser*), ham (*szynka*), eggs (*jajka*), and tea (*herbata*) or coffee (*kawa*).

The most important and substantial meal of the day, the *obiad*, is normally eaten somewhere between 2 and 5 pm. Obiad has no direct equivalent in English: judging by its contents, it is closer to western dinner than to lunch. The third meal is supper (*kolacja*), which is often similar to breakfast.

Etiquette and table manners are more or less the same as in the west. When beginning a meal, whether it's in a restaurant or at home, it's good manners to wish your fellow diners *smacznego*, or 'bon appetit'. When drinking a toast, the Polish equivalent of 'cheers' is *na zdrowie* (literally 'to the health').

Polish Specialities

Poland was for centuries a cosmopolitan country and its food has been influenced by various cuisines. The Jewish, Lithuanian, Belarusian, Ukrainian, Russian, Hungarian and German traditions have all made their mark. Polish food is hearty and filling, with thick soups and sauces, abundant in potatoes and dumplings, rich in meat but not in vegetables.

Poland's most internationally known dishes are the *bigos* (sauerkraut with a variety of meats), *pierogi* (ravioli-like dumplings stuffed with cottage cheese or minced meat or cabbage and wild mushrooms) and *barszcz* (red beetroot soup, originating from Russian borsch). Favourite Polish ingredients and herbs include dill, marjoram, caraway seeds and wild mushrooms.

Typical starters include *tatar* (raw minced beef accompanied by chopped onion and raw egg yolk), *śledź w oleju* (herring in oil), *śledź w śmietanie* (herring in sour cream) and *nóżki w galarecie* (jellied pig's knuckles).

Poland is a land of hearty soups such as *żurek* (rye-flour soup thickened with sour cream), *botwinka* (beet greens soup), *kapuśniak* (sauerkraut soup), *krupnik* (barley soup), *flaki* (seasoned tripe cooked in bouillon with vegetables) and *chłodnik* (cold beetroot soup with sour cream and fresh vegetables).

Among the main courses, the most common dishes include *kotlet schabowy* (crumbed pork cutlet), *golonka* (boiled pig's knuckle served with horseradish), *zraz* (stewed beef in cream sauce), *gołąbki* (cabbage leaves stuffed with minced beef and rice) and *schab pieczony* (roast loin of pork seasoned with prunes and herbs).

Wild mushrooms (*grzyby*) have always been great favourites in Poland, either boiled, pan-fried, stewed, sautéed, pickled or marinated. Cucumbers are served freshly sliced in sour cream (*mizeria*) or dill (*ogórek kiszony*). *Ćwikła* is a boiled and grated beetroot with horseradish. Potatoes are made into dumplings, patties or pancakes (*placki ziemniaczane*). *Kopytka* are chunks of dough served with a semi-sweet sauce, while *knedle* are dumplings stuffed with plums or apples. A traditional Polish dessert is *mazurek* (shortcake). In early summer you can get fresh strawberries, raspberries or blueberries with cream.

Places to Eat

With the move towards capitalism, there has been dramatic development in the gastronomic scene. A constellation of western-style eating outlets – almost nonexistent in communist Poland – such as bistros, snack bars, pizza houses, salad bars and fast-food joints sprang up to serve things which were previously uncommon or unobtainable. Most of the famous international fast-food chains, including McDonald's, Burger King, KFC and Pizza Hut, have already conquered Polish cities, and a myriad of Polish imitations have settled in.

A good proportion of the old drab restaurants have either closed down or been revamped, and the pavements filled with food stalls and open-air café-bars. Many cafés, which were once essentially meeting places rather than eating places, have introduced meal menus, which may be more attractive and cheaper then those of some restaurants.

The prices have obviously gone up in the process, but you now have a more decent choice, can eat and drink till late, and it's all still cheaper than in the west.

Milk Bars The cheapest place to eat is a milk bar (*bar mleczny*), a sort of no-frills self-service cafeteria which serves mostly vegetarian dishes. The 'milk' part of the name is to suggest that a good part of the menu is based on dairy products. You can fill yourself up for about US$2.

Milk bars open around 7 to 8 am and close at 6 to 8 pm (earlier on Saturday); only a handful are open on Sunday. The menu is posted on the wall. You choose, then pay the cashier who gives you a receipt which you hand to the person dispensing the food. Once you've finished your meal, carry your dirty dishes to a designated place, as you'll see others doing. Milk bars are popular and there are usually lines to the counter, but they move quickly. Smoking is not permitted and no alcoholic beverages are served.

Milk bars were created to provide cheap food for the less affluent, and were subsidised by the state. The free-market economy forced many to close, but a number have survived and some do a good job.

Restaurants Restaurants (*restauracja*) are more expensive than milk bars, but are more numerous, open longer and may provide a proper meal with table service in enjoyable surroundings. They range from unpretentious cheap eateries where you can have a filling meal for less than US$5, all the way up to luxurious establishments that may leave a sizable hole in your wallet. Most restaurants serve Polish food, but there has been a considerable expansion of ethnic outlets in the large cities, principally in Warsaw.

Restaurants generally open either around 9 to 10 am (and then they usually have a breakfast menu) or about noon. Closing time varies greatly from place to place and from city to province. In smaller towns it may be pretty hard to find somewhere to eat after 8 pm, whereas in big cities there are always some places which stay open until 11 pm or midnight. Among these are the restaurants at top-end hotels.

Most of the top-class restaurants have their menus in Polish and English and/or German, but don't expect foreign-language listings in cheaper eateries, nor waiters speaking anything but Polish. The menu is split into several sections, including soups (*zupy*), main courses (*dania drugie*) and accompaniments (*dodatki*). The price of the dish doesn't usually include the accompaniments such as potatoes, chips, salads etc which you choose from the dodatki section; you then tally up the price of the components to get the complete cost of the dish. Also note that the weight of a portion of some dishes (particularly fish and poultry) is hard to determine beforehand, so the price in the menu is given for 100g. However, if you are not precise when ordering, they will probably serve you the whole fish, which will weigh much more than 100g, and you'll be charged accordingly. To avoid surprises in the bill (*rachunek*), study the menu carefully and make things clear to the waiter.

The service charge is included in the price so you just pay what's on the bill. Tipping is up to you and there don't seem to be any hard and fast rules about it. In low-price restaurants guests rarely leave a tip; they might, at most, round the total up to the nearest whole figure. In upmarket establishments it's customary to tip 10% of the bill.

DRINKS

Vodka (*wódka*) is the national drink, which the Poles claim was invented here. In Poland vodka is drunk neat, not diluted or mixed, and it comes in a number of colours and flavours, including *myśliwska* (vodka flavoured with juniper berries), *wiśniówka* (flavoured with cherries), *żubrówka* (flavoured with grass from the Białowieża Forest) and *jarzębiak* (flavoured with rowanberry). Other notable spirits include *krupnik* (honey liqueur), *śliwowica* (plum brandy) and *winiak* (grape brandy).

Under the communists the only alcoholic beverage you could usually get was vodka. Now a fair choice of beer (*piwo*) is available in restaurants, cafés, bars and pubs, though not all cheap establishments serve it cold. Ask for *zimne piwo* (cold beer) when ordering. Polish beer is much cheaper than imported ones, and is quite good. The top brands include Żywiec, Okocim and EB.

Wine is imported from the ex-Eastern Bloc and the west. Hungarian and Bulgarian wines are quite acceptable and cheap, but western wines can be expensive. Pay attention to the price on the menu, which may be for a glass, not a bottle.

ENTERTAINMENT

Cinemas run the usual western fare with several months delay. The majority come from the USA, while the number of Polish films is minimal. All films are screened with original soundtrack and Polish subtitles. The entrance fee is around US$3 to US$4.

Polish theatre, long recognised at home and abroad, continues to fly high. Language is obviously an obstacle for foreigners, but theatre buffs may want to try some of the best theatres if only to see the acting. The productions range from Greek drama to recent avant-garde with room for great classics from Shakespeare to Beckett. Local authors are well represented, with a particular focus on all those who were officially forbidden during the communist era. Most theatres are closed on Monday and in July and August. Tickets are roughly US$4 to US$8.

Some of the largest cities have proper opera houses. You'll probably find the best productions in Warsaw and Łódź and they are definitely worth the money – about US$10 at most.

POLAND

For classical music, the Filharmonia Narodowa is the place to head. Almost all larger cities have their philharmonic halls and concerts are usually held on Friday and Saturday, for next to nothing. You might occasionally come upon some of the greatest national and international virtuosi. The repertoire ranges from medieval music to the latest works from the pillars of Polish contemporary music, though most of the fare is somewhere between Bach and Stravinsky.

Polish jazz is as good as any in Europe, and big international jazz names visit the country quite frequently. Warsaw and Kraków have the liveliest jazz life.

Discos are popular in Poland, usually opening at 9 pm from Thursday to Saturday.

THINGS TO BUY

For local handicrafts, go to Cepelia shops. There's a network of them in all large cities and they sell artefacts made by local artists. The most common Polish crafts include papercuts, woodcarvings, tapestries, embroidery, paintings on glass, pottery and hand-painted wooden boxes and chests.

Amber is typically Polish. It's a fossil resin of vegetable origin, which appears in a variety of colours from pale yellow to reddish brown. You can buy amber necklaces in Cepelia shops, but if you want it in a more artistic form, look for jewellery shops or commercial art galleries. Prices vary enormously, with the quality of the amber and even more with the level of craftwork. Possibly the best choice of amber jewellery is in Gdańsk and Warsaw.

Polish contemporary paintings, original prints and sculptures are renowned internationally and sold by private commercial art galleries. The best places to look for them are Warsaw and Kraków. Polish posters are among the world's best – a tempting souvenir. The best selection of them is, again, in Warsaw and Kraków.

Poland publishes quite an assortment of well edited and lavishly illustrated coffee-table books about the country, many of which are also available in English and German. Check the large bookshops of the main cities.

Polish music (pop, folk, jazz, classical and contemporary) is now commonly produced on CD and is increasingly easy to buy. Polish CDs cost about US$10 to US$15; imported CDs are US$15 to US$20.

Getting There & Away

AIR

The national carrier, LOT Polish Airlines, links Warsaw with Bangkok, Beijing, Cairo, Chicago, Damascus, Istanbul, Montreal, New York, Tel Aviv, Toronto and numerous European cities. LOT has retired its fleet of gas-guzzling, Russian-made Tupolevs and Ilyushins and now flies exclusively western aircraft.

Regular one-way fares to Warsaw are not cheap: US$570 from Frankfurt/Main, US$600 from Amsterdam, US$650 from Paris and US$525 from London. Ask travel agents about special excursion and advance-purchase excursion fares on LOT and note the restrictions. LOT sometimes has promotional fares from New York to Warsaw beginning from about US$800 return. In the USA call LOT for information at ☎ 800-223 0593 toll-free (in Canada ☎ 800-668 5928). A US travel agency specialising in Poland is Fregata (☎ 212-541 5707; fax 212-262 3220), 250 West 57th St, New York, NY 10107.

Bucket shops in Europe and Asia sell LOT tickets at large discounts, usually on fares from Asia to Western Europe or vice versa with a free stopover in Warsaw. Ask around the budget travel agencies in Singapore, Penang, Bangkok, London or Amsterdam for deals.

Although Poland isn't a mecca for people in search of cheap long-distance flights, an increasing number of local travel agencies try to offer competitive fares. Warsaw has the largest number of agencies and is possibly the best place to shop around. The *Gazeta Wyborcza*'s weekend travel section has advertisments for most major operators. Of course, you could probably do better in Berlin, Amsterdam or London, but you'll have to add the cost of getting there and your expenses while shopping around and waiting for a reservation.

LAND

Train

Quite a number of international trains link Poland with other European countries to the west, south and east. On the whole, train travel is not cheap and, on longer routes, the price of an ordinary train ticket can be almost as much as that of a discounted air fare.

Fortunately, there's a choice of special train tickets and rail passes, including the Inter-Rail pass, which gives European residents under 26 years of age unlimited 2nd-class travel for a month on most of the state railways of Western and Central Europe (including Poland), and Eurotrain which gives under-26s a substantial discount off the ordinary fare.

Domestic train fares in Poland are cheaper than international ones. Accordingly, you'll save money by buying a ticket to the first city you arrive at inside Poland, then taking a local train.

International trains to Poland, as well as those to other Eastern European countries, have recently become notorious for theft. Keep a grip on your bags, particularly on the Berlin-Warsaw and Prague-Warsaw overnight trains.

Western Europe From London, you can travel to Warsaw via either the Channel Tunnel or Ostend. The ordinary return fares in the high season are around £290 and £220 respectively (£230 and £170 in the low season). People under 26 can get a Eurotrain return fare to Warsaw for around £160 and a one-month Inter-Rail pass for £250. Both ordinary and Eurotrain tickets are valid for two months and you can break the journey as many times as you wish. Tickets can be bought from British Rail ticket offices or travel centres. The agencies that specialise in travel to Poland, including Fregata (☎ 0171-734 5101 or ☎ 451 7000), 100 Dean St, London W1 6AQ and (☎ 0161-226 7227), 117 Withington Rd, Manchester MI6 7EU and the Polish Travel Centre (☎ 0181-741 5541), 246 King St, London W6 0RF, may offer cheaper fares.

Plenty of Western European cities are linked by train (direct or indirect) with the major Polish cities. Direct destinations to/from Warsaw include Berlin, Brussels, Cologne, Dresden, Frankfurt/Main, Leipzig and Vienna.

The Warsaw-Berlin route (via Frankfurt/Oder and Poznań) is serviced by several trains a day, including two EuroCity express trains which cover the 569km distance in 6½ hours. There are also direct trains between Berlin and Gdańsk (via Szczecin), and Berlin and Kraków (via Wrocław).

Czech Republic & Austria Trains between Prague and Warsaw (three a day) travel via either Wrocław (740km, 12 hours) or Katowice (10 hours). Between Wrocław and Prague (339km), there are four trains a day and the journey takes about seven hours. There's also a train between Prague and Kraków (via Katowice).

Two trains per day travel between Vienna and Warsaw (753km, 11 hours) via Břeclav and Katowice.

Slovakia, Hungary & Romania There are two trains daily between Budapest and Warsaw (837km, 12 hours) via Bratislava and Katowice. These trains are routed through a short stretch of the Czech Republic, so get a Czech visa if you require one.

A different route through Košice in eastern Slovakia is followed by the train between Budapest and Kraków (598km, 12 hours). The train between Bucharest and Warsaw (31 hours) also travels via Košice, Nowy Sącz and Kraków (missing Budapest).

Ukraine, Belarus, Lithuania & Russia Warsaw has direct train links with Kiev in Ukraine, Minsk and Hrodna in Belarus, Vilnius in Lithuania, and both Moscow and St Petersburg in Russia. These trains only have sleeping cars and you'll be automatically sold a sleeper when buying your ticket. Remember that you need transit visas for the countries you will be passing through en route. For example, the Warsaw-Vilnius-St Petersburg rail line goes via Hrodna in Belarus, and the Belarusian border guards come aboard and slap unsuspecting tourists with a US$30 Belarusian transit visa fee (which is reportedly valid for a return trip). You may avoid this by taking a bus from Poland direct to Lithuania.

Bus

International bus travel to almost anywhere in Europe is serviced by dozens of Polish companies and the prices are attractive. Tickets are sold by many travel agencies, which you'll find in most major cities.

Western Europe The cheapest way to travel to Poland from the UK, France, the Netherlands and many other Western European countries is by bus, which costs much less than by train or plane. In Britain, call Eurolines National Express (☎ 0171-730 8235), 52 Grosvenor Gardens, Victoria, London SW1W 0AC. Fregata and the Polish Travel Centre (see Train earlier in this section) may be a little cheaper. The Fregata buses leave Victoria coach station for Warsaw and Kraków daily in summer and twice weekly the rest of the year. Fares from London to either destination are £70 one way, £110 return with reductions for those aged under 26 and over 59 years.

Budget Bus/Eurolines (☎ 020-627 5151), Rokin 10, Amsterdam, runs buses from Amsterdam to Kraków, Warsaw and Gdańsk. The fare on all these services is about US$90/140 one way/return (10% reduction for students and persons aged under 26 or over 59 years). For information on similar buses from Brussels to Warsaw contact Eurolines (☎ 02-217 0025), Place de Brouckere 50, Brussels.

Hungary There are buses a few times a week between Budapest and Kraków (US$25, 10 hours).

Ukraine, Belarus & Lithuania The Polish PKS bus company runs daily buses from Warsaw to Lviv (US$17), Minsk (US$21) and Vilnius (US$19). These routes shouldn't normally take more than 12 hours, though the actual time depends on traffic lines at the border and customs. There are also half-hourly buses between Przemyśl and Lviv (US$7, four hours), and four buses a day between Suwałki and Vilnius (US$9, five hours).

Car & Motorcycle

Travelling by car or motorbike, you'll pass the frontier via one of the designated border road crossings. Following is the list of border road crossings open 24 hours. The localities listed are the settlements on the Polish side of the border and you can find them on road maps. (Some of these crossings don't allow buses through.)

German border (north to south) – Lubieszyn, Kołbaskowo, Krajnik Dolny, Osinów Dolny, Kostrzyn, Słubice, Świecko, Gubin, Olszyna, Łęknica, Zgorzelec, Sieniawka, Porajów

Czech border (west to east) – Zawidów, Jakuszyce, Lubawka, Kudowa-Słone, Boboszów, Głuchołazy, Pietrowice, Chałupki, Cieszyn

Slovak border (west to east) – Chyżne, Łysa Polana, Piwniczna, Konieczna, Barwinek

Ukrainian border (south to north) – Medyka, Hrebenne, Dorohusk, Zosin

Belorusian border (south to north) – Terespol, Kuźnica Białostocka

Lithuanian border – Budzisko, Ogrodniki

Russian border (east to west) – Bezledy, Gronowo

The lines of cars on some eastern border crossings can be several kilometres long and the waiting time may occasionally reach a few days. Fortunately, on the German, Czech and Slovak borders, customs checking is much smoother and you shouldn't experience long delays.

SEA

Scandinavia

Poland has a regular ferry service to/from Denmark and Sweden operated by the Unity Line, Stena Line and Polferries. The Unity Line covers the Świnoujście-Ystad route (daily, nine hours). The Stena Line runs between Gdynia and Karlskrona (six days a week, 11 hours). Polferries services the Świnoujście-Copenhagen route (five times a week, 10 hours), the Świnoujście-Malmö route (daily, nine hours), and the Gdańsk-Oxelösund and Gdańsk-Nynäshamn routes (several days a week, 18 hours each). All routes operate year-round.

The deck tickets normally don't need to be booked. Cabins of different classes are available and reservation is recommended in the high season. You can bring along your car, but book in advance. Bicycles go free. A return ticket costs about 20% less than two singles and is valid for six months. Students and senior citizens get a 20% discount. There's a variety of other discounts for families, larger parties, groups plus car etc, which vary from route to route. Depending on the type of fares and discounts the one-way fare is between US$50 and US$70. Any travel agent in Scandinavia will have tickets; in Poland inquire at an Orbis office.

LEAVING POLAND

The airport tax is US$10 for international departures from Warsaw, and around US$8 for departures from other Polish airports servicing international flights. You don't pay the tax at the airport itself, as it is automatically added to the price of your air ticket when you buy it.

As currency exchange rates at the airports are poor, change your remaining złotys back to foreign currency beforehand at any kantor, leaving only a small reserve for the airport.

Getting Around

AIR

LOT Polish Airlines operates domestic flights daily from Warsaw to Gdańsk, Kraków, Poznań, Szczecin and Wrocław. There are no direct flights between these cities – all must go via Warsaw and connections aren't always convenient. On domestic routes, LOT uses the French-Italian, new-generation ATR 72 turbo aircraft exclusively.

The regular one-way fare on any of the direct flights to/from Warsaw is around US$140, except for Szczecin (US$170). Any combined flight via Warsaw (eg Szczecin-Kraków or Gdańsk-Wrocław) will cost around US$175. Tickets can be booked and bought at any LOT and Orbis offices and from some travel agencies.

Senior citizens over 60 years of age pay 80% of the full fare on all domestic flights. Foreign students holding an ISIC card get a 10% discount. There are attractive stand-by fares (about 25% of the regular fare) for young people below 20 and students below 26; tickets have to be bought immediately before scheduled departure. There are also promotional fares for everybody on some flights in some periods (eg early or late flights, weekend flights etc); they can be just a third of the ordinary fares.

You must check in at least 30 minutes before departure. Have your passport at hand: you'll be asked to show it. There's no airport tax on domestic flights.

TRAIN

Polish Railways (PKP) operates over 27,000km of railway line, allowing you to reach almost every town by rail.

Express trains (pociągi ekspresowe) with seat reservations are the fastest way to travel. Fast trains (pociągi pospieszne) are a bit slower and don't usually require reservations, but may be more crowded. Ordinary trains (pociągi osobowe) are OK for short trips and never require reservations. Polish trains usually run on time.

Intercity trains have been introduced on some major routes out of Warsaw, including Gdańsk, Katowice, Kraków, Poznań and Szczecin. They don't stop en route and are still faster than the express trains; their average speed is about 100km/h. They require seat reservations and a light meal is included in the price.

Almost all trains carry two classes: 2nd class (druga klasa), and 1st class (pierwsza klasa), which is 50% more expensive. The carriages of long-distance trains are usually divided into compartments: the 1st-class compartments have six seats, the 2nd-class ones contain eight seats. Smoking is allowed in some compartments and the part of the corridor facing them, but many Poles are chain smokers, so it's better to book a seat in a nonsmoking compartment and go into the smoking corridor if you wish to smoke.

The couchette compartments have either four or six beds, with two or three to a side. Sleepers come in both 2nd and 1st class: the former sleep three to a compartment, the latter only two, and both have a washbasin, sheets and blankets.

Train Stations

Most larger train stations are purpose-built and of reasonable standard. They have a range of facilities including waiting rooms, snack bars, newsstands, left-luggage rooms and toilets. The biggest stations in the major

POLISH RAILWAYS

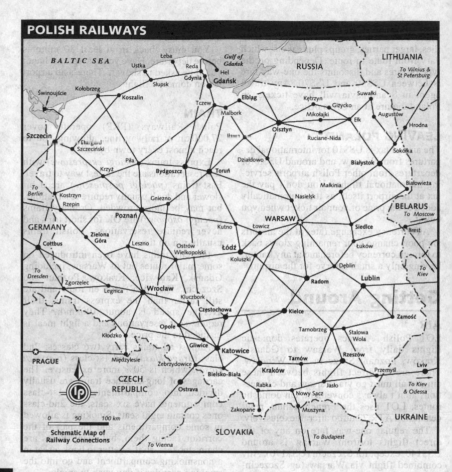

BALTIC SEA

Gulf of Gdańsk

RUSSIA

LITHUANIA

To Vilnius & St Petersburg

Łeba
Ustka
Reda
Słupsk
Gdynia
Hel
Gdańsk
Elbląg
Suwałki
Kętrzyn
Giżycko
Augustów
Hrodna
Świnoujście
Kołobrzeg
Koszalin
Tczew
Malbork
Mikołajki
Ełk
Olsztyn
Ruciane-Nida
Sokółka

Szczecin
Stargard
Szczeciński
Piła
Krzyż
Bydgoszcz
Toruń
Iława
Działdowo
Białystok
Białowieża

To Berlin
Kostrzyn
Rzepin
Gniezno
Nasielsk
Małkinia

Poznań
WARSAW
Siedlce
BELARUS
To Moscow
Brest

GERMANY
Cottbus
Zielona Góra
Leszno
Ostrów Wielkopolski
Kutno
Łowicz
Łuków

Łódź
Koluszki
Dęblin
To Kiev

Zgorzelec
Legnica
Wrocław
Radom
Lublin

To Dresden
Kluczbork
Kielce
Zamość

Częstochowa

Opole
Tarnobrzeg
Stalowa Wola

Kłodzko
Gliwice
Katowice
Tarnów
Rzeszów

PRAGUE
Międzylesie
Zebrzydowice
Kraków
Przemyśl
Lviv

CZECH REPUBLIC
Bielsko-Biała
Rabka
Jasło
To Kiev & Odessa

Ostrava
Nowy Sącz

Zakopane
Muszyna
UKRAINE

0   50   100 km

SLOVAKIA
To Budapest

Schematic Map of
Railway Connections

To Vienna

cities may also have a restaurant, a kantor and even a post office. If there are several train stations in a city, the main one is identified by the name 'Główny' and is the one which handles most of the traffic including all express trains.

Large train stations have left-luggage rooms (*przechowalnia bagażu*), which are usually open round the clock and are secure. There's a low basic daily storage charge per item (about US$0.40), plus 1% of the declared value of the luggage which includes insurance. Consequently, the value you

declare will largely affect the cost of the storage. One thing to remember is that the cloakrooms usually close once or twice a day for an hour or so. The times of these breaks are on display. Reserve some time for possible queuing and paperwork while collecting your bags. You pay the charge when you pick your luggage up, not when you deposit it.

Timetables

Train departures (*odjazdy*) are usually listed on a yellow board while arrivals (*przyjazdy*) are on a white board. The ordinary trains are marked in black print, fast trains in red, and if you spot an additional 'Ex', this means an express train. InterCity trains are identified by the letters 'IC'. The letter 'R' in a square indicates the train with compulsory seat reservation. There may also be some letters and/or numbers following the departure time; always check them in the key below. They usually say that the train *kursuje* (runs) or *nie kursuje* (doesn't run) in particular periods or days. The timetables also indicate which platform (*peron*) the train departs from.

Tickets

Since most of the large stations have been computerised, buying tickets (*bilety*) is now less of a hassle than it used to be, but queuing is still a way of life. Be at the station at least half an hour before the departure time of your train and make sure you are queuing at the right ticket window. As cashiers rarely speak English, the easiest way to buy a ticket is to have all relevant details written down on a piece of paper. These should include the destination, the departure time, and the class (*klasa pierwsza* or *klasa druga*). If seat reservation is compulsory on your train, you'll automatically be sold a reserved seat ticket (*miejscówka*); if it's optional, you must state whether you want a miejscówka or not.

If you are forced to get on a train without a ticket, you can buy one directly from the conductor for a small supplement, but you should find him/her right away. If the conductor finds you first, you'll be fined for travelling without a ticket.

Couchettes (*kuszetki*) and sleepers (*miejsca sypialne*) can be booked at larger stations at special counters; it's advisable to reserve them in advance. Advance tickets for journeys of over 100km, couchettes and sleepers can also be bought at Orbis offices, which may be quicker.

Fares

Fast-train tickets are 50% dearer than those for ordinary trains, and an express train costs 33% more than a fast train (twice as much as an ordinary train). First class is 50% more expensive than 2nd class. Sample 2nd-class fares for a 100/300km trip are US$3.20/5.80 by ordinary train, US$4.80/8.70 by fast train, and US$6.40/11.60 by express train.

A reserved seat ticket costs US$2 (US$3 on IC trains) regardless of the distance. A couchette costs US$14/11 in a four/six bed compartment. The 1st/2nd-class sleeper costs US$32/21.

The approximate fares on InterCity trains (including the compulsory seat reservation) from Warsaw to Gdańsk, Katowice, Kraków or Poznań are US$17/23 in 2nd/1st class, and US$19/26 to Szczecin.

As yet, there are no discounts for foreign students on domestic trains, but there may be a discount (possibly 25%) for ISIC holders, if and when the lengthy negotiations between Almatur and PKP come to a successful end. Check for news when you arrive.

Polrail Pass

A Polrail Pass providing unlimited travel on trains throughout Poland is available from North American travel agencies through Rail Europe (it can also be bought in Poland). The passes come in durations of eight days (US$65/95 for 2nd/1st class), 15 days (US$75/110), 21 days (US$85/130) and 30 days (US$110/160). Persons aged under 26 years on the first day of travel can buy a 'Junior' pass for about 25% less. Seat reservation fees are included.

BUS

Long distances are often better covered in Poland by train than by bus, but buses can be more convenient on short routes and in the mountains, where trains are slow and few.

Most bus transport is operated by the state bus company PKS. It has bus terminals in all the cities and towns, and provides two kinds of bus service: the ordinary buses (marked in black on timetable boards), which cover mostly regional routes and stop at all stops on the way, and the fast buses (marked in red or in bold), which cover mainly long-distance routes and ignore minor stops. As a rough guide, the ordinary/fast bus fares over a distance of 100km are US$3/4.

Timetables are posted on boards either inside or outside PKS bus terminals. Always check any additional symbols which accompany the departure time of your bus, which can mean that the bus runs only on certain days or in certain seasons. The key at the end

POLAND

of the timetable lists these irregularities. Terminals in the larger cities have a separate information desk.

Of the private bus operators, the biggest is Polski Express, a joint venture with Eurolines National Express based in Britain, which runs several major long-distance routes out of Warsaw, including Białystok, Bydgoszcz (via Toruń), Gdańsk (via Elbląg), Kraków (via Łódź and Katowice), Olsztyn, and Rzeszów (via Lublin). It is faster, more comfortable and cheaper than PKS, and may be an interesting alternative to train travel.

PKS tickets have to be bought at the terminal itself; Orbis doesn't handle this service. Tickets on long routes serviced by fast buses can be bought up to 30 days in advance but those for short local routes are only available the same day. Tickets for Polski Express buses can be bought at the terminals where they arrive/depart (PKS or the company's own), and from major Orbis offices.

CAR & MOTORCYCLE

Poland's 260,000km of roads are mostly narrow, but by and large they are in an acceptable condition for leisurely driving. Over the next 15 years Poland plans to build a 2600km network of toll motorways stretching from the Baltic to the Czech border and Germany to Ukraine.

To drive a car into Poland you'll need your driver's licence, the car registration card and liability insurance ('green card'). If your insurance isn't valid for Poland you must buy an additional policy at the border. The car registration number will be entered in your passport.

In recent years petrol has become readily available at gas stations, which have mushroomed throughout Poland. They sell several kinds and grades of petrol, including the 94-octane leaded (US$0.60 per litre), 95-octane unleaded (US$0.60), 98-octane unleaded (US$0.65) and diesel (US$0.50). Most petrol stations are open from 6 am to 10 pm (Sunday 7 am to 3 pm), though some work around the clock. You can import or export up to a maximum 10L of fuel in a spare tank.

Car theft is a problem in Poland, so always try to park your vehicle at a guarded car park (*parking strzeżony*). If you can't, take your luggage to your hotel or at least hide your bags to make the car look empty. The radio/cassette player in the car is usually the first thing that attracts thieves' attention.

The Polski Związek Motorowy or PZM (Polish Motoring Association), which has offices in most large cities and at border crossings, can provide breakdown service (*pomoc drogowa*) and other assistance to motorists. If you're a member of an automobile club at home, bring along your membership card with an international letter of introduction, as this could entitle you to free breakdown service and legal advice from the PZM. The PZM's nationwide emergency breakdown number is ☎ 981.

Road Rules

The speed limit is 110km/h on highways and motorways, 90km/h on other open roads and 60km/h in built-up areas. Motorcycles cannot exceed 90km/h anywhere. At the entrance to small towns, if the background of the sign bearing the town name is white you must reduce speed to 60km/h. If the background is green there's no need to reduce speed, unless the road signs state otherwise.

Radar-equipped police are very active, especially in villages where you must slow down to 60km/h, and speeding fines up to US$40 are levied frequently. Approaching cars often flash their lights in warning. Seat belts are compulsory in the front seat.

Unless signs state otherwise, cars may be parked on pavements, as long as a minimum 1.5m-wide walkway is left for pedestrians. Parking in the opposite direction to the flow of traffic is allowed. The permitted blood alcohol level is 0.02%, so it's best not to drink at all before driving. Cyclists are not allowed to ride two abreast on highways.

Rental

Avis, Budget, Hertz and some other international agencies are now well represented in Poland, and there are also plenty of local operators. Car rental is not cheap – the prices are comparable to, or even higher than, full-price rental in Western Europe – and there are seldom any promotional discounts.

Some companies offer one-way rentals within Poland, but almost all will insist on keeping the car within Poland. Avis is possibly the only company which allows you to rent the car in Warsaw and return it in Prague.

Rental agencies will require you to produce your passport, a driver's licence held for at least one year, and a credit card. You need to be at least 21 or 23 years of age to rent a car, although renting some cars, particularly luxury models and 4WDs, may require a higher age.

As a rough guide only, economy models offered by reputable companies begin at around US$60 a day plus US$0.35 a kilometre, or US$100 daily with unlimited kilometres. Add US$10 to US$30 (depending on the model) a day for compulsory insurance. All companies have discount rates if you are going to use the car for a longer time, a week being the usual minimum period.

It's usually cheaper to prebook your car from abroad rather than to front up at an agency inside Poland. Furthermore, this will ensure that you have the car you need upon arrival in Poland; otherwise you may have to wait for a few days or, sometimes, a few weeks.

It would be cheaper to rent a car in the west, say in Berlin, and drive it into Poland, but few rental companies will allow you to take their car eastward.

Car-rental information is not included in the main text of this chapter, but top-class hotels, tourist offices and travel agencies will be happy to inform you about where to go.

HITCHING

Hitchhiking (*autostop*) does take place in Poland, though it's not very popular. Car drivers rarely stop to pick up hitchhikers, and large commercial vehicles (which are easier to wave down) expect to be paid the equivalent of a bus fare.

BOAT

There are no regular passenger-boat services on the main rivers or along the coast. Several cities, including Szczecin, Gdańsk, Toruń, Wrocław and Kraków, have local river cruises in summer, and a few coastal ports (Kołobrzeg, Gdańsk) offer sea excursions.

On the Masurian Lakes, excursion boats run in summer between Giżycko, Mikołajki, Węgorzewo and Ruciane-Nida. Tourist boats also operate in the Augustów area where they ply a part of the Augustów Canal. The most unusual canal trip is the full-day cruise along the Elbląg Canal from Elbląg to Ostróda where the boats are carried up and down ramps on rail-mounted platforms. There is also a spectacular raft trip through the Dunajec Gorge in the Pieniny Mountains.

LOCAL TRANSPORT
Bus, Tram & Trolleybus

Most cities have both buses (*autobus*) and trams (*tramwaj*), and some also have trolley buses (*trolejbus*). Public transport operates from around 5 am to 11 pm and may be crowded during rush hours. The largest cities also have night-time services, on either bus or tram. Timetables are usually posted on the stops, but don't rely too much on their accuracy.

In most cities, there's a flat-rate fare for local transport, but if you change vehicle you need another ticket. The ordinary fare is around US$0.40; night services are more expensive. An ISIC card gives a 50% discount in Warsaw only. Bulky luggage is an additional ordinary fare.

There are no conductors on board; you buy tickets beforehand from Ruch kiosks and punch or stamp them upon boarding. Buy a bunch of them if you are going to use public transport frequently. Buy enough tickets on Saturday morning to last you until Monday, as few kiosks are open on Sunday. Tickets purchased in one city cannot be used in another.

The plain-clothed ticket inspectors control tickets more often today than they did before, and foreign backpackers are their favourite prey; make sure you punch the ticket for yourself (and your luggage if applicable). If you are caught without a ticket, it's best to pay the fine straight away. Never give an inspector your passport, even if they threaten you with police intervention if you don't.

Taxi

Taxis in Poland are easily available and not too expensive by western standards. As a rough guide, a 5km taxi trip will cost around US$3, and a 10km ride shouldn't cost more than US$5. Taxi fares are 50% higher at night (10 pm to 6 am) and outside the city limits. The number of passengers (usually up to four) and the amount of luggage don't affect the fare.

There are plenty of taxi companies, including the once monopolist state-run Radio Taxi (☎ 919), which is the largest and operates in most cities. Taxis are recognisable by large boards on the roof with the company's name and its phone number. There are also some pirate taxis (called the 'mafia' by Poles), which usually have just a small 'taxi' label on the roof without any name or phone number. Mafia taxis are a plague in Warsaw (see Warsaw later in this chapter for further information) and are recently spreading to some other large cities, principally Kraków and Łódź. They are mostly to be found at major tourist haunts such as airports, top-class hotels and important tourist sights. They tend to overcharge up to several times the normal fare and should be avoided at all cost.

Taxis can be waved down on the street, but it's much easier to go to a taxi stand (*postój taksówek*) where you'll almost always find a line of them. There are plenty of such stands and everybody will tell you where the nearest one is. Taxis can also be ordered by phone, and there's usually no extra charge for this service. Taxis should normally arrive within 10 minutes unless you request one at a specified time.

Taxis have meters, but due to constant inflation some meters may not be adjusted to the current tariff. In this case the fare shown on the meter has to be multiplied by a factor which should be displayed in the taxi. The factor may vary from city to city and from taxi to taxi depending on when the last adjustment was made.

When you get into a taxi, make sure the driver turns on the meter. Also check whether the meter has been switched to the proper rate: a typical drivers' scam for foreigners is to drop the flag at the higher 'night' rate during the daytime. The meter shows the rate, which is identified by the number: '1' is the daytime rate, whereas '2' is the night rate.

Remember to carry smaller bills, so you'll be able to pay the right fare. If you don't, it's virtually impossible to get change back from the driver who's intent on charging you more. It's always a good idea to find out beforehand how much the right fare should be by asking the hotel staff or an attendant at the airport.

ORGANISED TOURS

A number of tours to Poland can be arranged from abroad. Orbis has traditionally been the major operator and offers a choice of packages, usually one to two weeks long, from sightseeing in historic cities to skiing and horse-riding holidays. Orbis addresses of overseas offices are listed in the Tourist Offices section earlier in this chapter. Polish-run travel agents who deal with transportation tickets, including Fregata and the Polish Travel Centre (see the Getting There & Away section earlier) also have a selection of packages around Poland. Other UK-based agencies operated by Polish émigrés include Tazab Travel (☎ 0171-373 1186), 273 Old Brompton Rd, London SW5 9JB; Bogdan Travel (☎ 0181-992 8866), 5 The Broadway, Gunnersbury Lane, London W3 8HR; and the New Millennium (☎ 0121-711 2232), 20 High St, Solihull, Birmingham B91 3TB.

Exodus Expeditions (☎ 0181-675 5550), 9 Weir Rd, London SW12 0LT, has a 14-day Historic Poland tour which includes Warsaw, Gdańsk, Poznań, the Masurian Lakes and Białowieża National Park. It also offers a 14-day hiking trip in the Tatras and Beskids, with accommodation in mountain refuges.

Martin Randall Travel (☎ 0181-742 3355), 10 Barley Mow Passage, Chiswick, London W4 4PH, has several tours to Poland, including a 10-day 'Monasteries, Mansions and Country Towns' tour of Warsaw, Kraków and the south and east of the country; and the 'Amber Route' which goes to Gdańsk and the Baltic Coast.

In the USA, apart from Orbis, the main operator to Poland is the Polish American Tours (☎ 1-800-388 0988 or ☎ 413-747 7702), 1053 Riverdale Rd, West Springfield, MA 01089, which offers a 12-day 'Best of Poland' tour, plus a choice of other packages.

Affordable Poland (☎ 1-800-801 1055), 2833 Junction Ave, Suite 207, San Jose, CA 95134, has standard and deluxe tours covering Poland's highlights, and a range of independent packages, so you can build your own tour and explore destinations of your choice at your own pace.

Some of the new breed of Polish travel agencies based in Poland have begun to focus on incoming tourism and sell their tours abroad. One good example is Kampio (see Organised Tours under Warsaw).

Almatur (with its offices in Poland's larger cities, listed in those sections later in this chapter) offers two-week sailing, kayaking and horse-riding holidays in July and August. These trips are intended mainly for students and are priced very reasonably.

OZGT in Olsztyn (see that section later in this chapter) runs regular 10-day kayak tours along the Krutynia River from June to August and occasionally in spring and autumn.

Orbis offices and private travel agencies around Poland offer organised city sightseeing tours in Warsaw, Kraków and other cities. Information is given in the relevant sections.

Warsaw

☎ 022

The capital of Poland, Warsaw (Warszawa) is a city of about 1.7 million inhabitants and the major focus of the political, scientific and educational life of the nation. It's Poland's most cosmopolitan, dynamic and progressive urban centre, a thrilling, busy melting pot catching up with the west.

Warsaw began its life in the 14th century as a stronghold of the Mazovian dukes. When Poland and Lithuania were unified in 1569, Warsaw's strategic central location came to the fore, and the capital was transferred here from Kraków in 1596-1609.

Like the rest of Poland, Warsaw fell prey to the Swedish invasion of 1655-60, but it soon recovered and continued to develop. Paradoxically, the 18th century – a period of catastrophic decline for the Polish state – witnessed Warsaw's greatest prosperity. It was then that a wealth of splendid palaces, parks and churches emerged, and cultural and artistic life flourished. In 1791, the first constitution in Europe was signed in Warsaw.

The 19th century was a period of decay with Warsaw as a mere provincial town of the Russian Empire. Yet this was nothing compared with WWII, during which 700,000 residents (over half of the city's prewar population) perished and 85% of Warsaw's buildings were destroyed. Very few of the 350,000 Jews living in Warsaw in 1939 escaped the death camps. No other Eastern European city suffered such immense loss of life or such devastation.

Immediately after the war the gigantic task of restoration began and Warsaw re-emerged like a phoenix from the ashes. Parts of the historic city, most notably the Old Town (Stare Miasto), have been meticulously rebuilt to their previous shape, but most of the urban landscape is modern and includes everything from dull Stalinist edifices to spanking steel-and-glass towers of the most recent generation. The war also changed Warsaw's socio-cultural structure with the place of many of the city's prewar inhabitants taken by newcomers.

In a way, Warsaw epitomises the Polish nation. It's a blend of the old and the new, in both appearance and spirit, respecting tradition but racing towards the future. Warsaw is an interesting layered cake you'll need several days to digest.

Orientation

The main part of the city sits on the western, left bank of the Vistula. Here is the Old Town, the historic nucleus of Warsaw and possibly the most important focal point for tourists. To the south stretches the new city centre with the monstrous Palace of Culture & Science overlooking the area; this is not a place to go for historic monuments but for the bustling commercial atmosphere of contemporary Warsaw. A few kilometres to the south-east is the beautiful Łazienki Park, linked to the Old Town by the 4km Royal Way (Szlak Królewski). Many tourist sights are along this route.

Finding your way around upon arrival is relatively easy. If you arrive by air at Okęcie airport, urban bus No 175 or the AirportCity bus will take you to the centre, passing the youth hostel and a number of hotels on the way. Coming by train, you arrive at the central train station right in the city centre. Whichever way you come, consider buying a city map (plan miasta) which has urban transport routes marked on it.

Information
Tourist Offices & Publications The city tourist office (☎ 94 31), Plac Powstańców Warszawy 2, is open weekdays from 8 am to 8 pm, Saturday from 9 am to 5 pm, Sunday

WARSAW

To Gdańsk
To Kampinos NP
To Białystok
Wisłostrada
Modlińska
Generalska
Marymoncka

0 1 2 km

Żeromskiego
ŻOLIBORZ
Powązkowska
Popieluszki
Warszawa Gdańska
Warszawa Wileńska
Warszawa Wschodnia
PRAGA
Grochowska
Warszawa Stadion
Powstańców Śląskich
Jana Pawła II
Okopowa
Marszałkowska
Waszyngtona
Górczewska
Wolska
WOLA
Kasprzaka
Warszawa Ochota
To Lublin
To Poznań
Połczyńska
Warszawa Zachodnia
Al Jerozolimskie
Grójecka
Zwirki i Wigury
Al Niepodległości
Puławska
Trasa Łazienkowska
OCHOTA
Hynka
Wołoska
Sobieskiego
Wiłanowska
MOKOTÓW
Al Krakowska
To Kraków
& Katowice
Willanowska

PLACES TO STAY
1 Hotel Cytadela
2 Youth Hostel
   (ul Międzyparkowa)
5 Youth Hostel
   (Wał Miedzeszyński)
8 Youth Hostel
   (ul Karolkowa)
9 Camping Rapsodia
   & Hotel Rapsodia
10 Camping Nr 123
   Majawa &
   Hotel Majawa
11 Camping Nr 34
   Gromada
14 Hotel Hera
15 Hotel Karat
16 Hotel Agra
17 Camping Nr 260 &
   Hotel Stegny

OTHER
3 Zoo
4 10th Anniversary
   Stadium (Market)
6 Powązki Cemetery
7 Jewish Cemetery
12 Botanical Gardens
13 Łazienki Park
   & Palace
18 Okęcie Airport
19 Wilanów Park
   & Palace

See Central Warsaw Map

---

from 9 am to 3 pm. It has outlets at the airport, in the Rotunda on the corner of ul Marszałkowska and Al Jerozolimskie, and in the Historical Museum of Warsaw at the Old Town Square. The staff in these offices are very helpful.

Another city tourist office (☎ 524 51 84) is at the Warsaw central train station, and is open daily from 9 am to 7 pm (May to August till 8 pm on weekdays). The private tourist office (☎ 635 18 81), Plac Zamkowy 1/13 opposite the Royal Castle, is open weekdays from 9 am to 6 pm, Saturday from 10 am to 6 pm, Sunday from 11 am to 6 pm (may stay open until 8 pm in July and August).

All three tourist offices are knowledgeable and helpful, and all can find and book a hotel or hostel for you (the private office will charge for this service).

Pick up a copy of the free monthly magazines *Warszawa, What, Where, When* and *Welcome to Warsaw* at the tourist offices or at a luxury hotel. Both include a map of central Warsaw and current information about tourist facilities. The best however, is the comprehensive *Warsaw Insider* monthly (US$1.25).

Also consider buying *The Warsaw Voice* weekly (US$1.50) to know what's happening in local politics.

A booklet listing youth hostels in Poland is available (for US$1.50) from Polskie Towarzystwo Schronisk Młodzieżowych (PTSM; ☎ 49 83 54), room 426, 4th floor, ul Chocimska 28, (open weekdays from 8 am to 3 pm).

Visa Extensions Your visa can be extended for up to 90 days at the Urząd Wojewódzki, Wydział Spraw Obywatelskich, Oddział d/s Cudzoziemców (☎ 625 59 04 or ☎ 622 02 31), ul Krucza 5/11 (open weekdays except Wednesday from 10 am to 3 pm). The paperwork takes four working days and the cost of the visa is US$15 regardless of whether you need one day or 90.

Money Kantors are everywhere; in the city centre, you will find a kantor on every second block. There has also been a rash of ATMs, so they are now easy to find around the centre.

Travellers cheques are probably best changed at the American Express office (☎ 635 20 02), ul Krakowskie Przedmieście 11 (weekdays from 9 am to 6 pm), which exchanges its own cheques as well as those of other major banks and charges no commission. The staff speak English and there are no crowds, unlike in the banks. It's here that you report the loss or theft of American Express cheques and apply for a refund. The office has a poste restante service for AmEx cardholders. There's also the American Express outlet (☎ 630 69 52) in the Hotel Marriott. It's open weekdays from 8 am to 8 pm, weekends from 10 am to 6 pm, and also changes travellers cheques.

The Bank Pekao has a dozen offices in the city, including those at Plac Bankowy 2, ul Mazowiecka 14, ul Czackiego 21/23, ul Grójecka 1/3 and Al Jerozolimskie 65/79. The bank changes travellers cheques into cash dollars or złotys, whichever you prefer. You can also get cash advances on Visa and MasterCard, either from the cashier or the bank's ATM.

Post & Communications The main post office, ul Świętokrzyska 31/33, is open from 8 am to 8 pm for mail and round the clock for telephones. You can also send faxes from here.

Poste restante is at window No 12. If you want letters sent to you, they should be addressed care of Poste Restante, Poczta Główna, ul Świętokrzyska 31/33, 00-001 Warszawa 1. The mail is kept for 14 working days.

Warsaw has both six and seven-digit phone numbers (the former are currently being changed to make way for the uniform seven-digit system).

Cybercafés As we went to press, Warsaw had just two Internet cafés: the overpriced Cyberia (☎ 828 14 47), ul Krakowskie Przedmieście 4/6, and PDI (☎ 622 66 11), ul Nowogrodzka 12 m 29.

Travel Agencies Student travel is handled by Almatur (☎ 826 35 12 or 826 26 39), ul Kopernika 23. It operates the summertime International Student Hostels and organises inexpensive two-week sailing, kayaking and horse-riding holidays in July and August. It also sells international air, bus and ferry tickets, and may have attractive discounts for students and people under 26 years. The Almatur outlet (☎ 828 53 07), ul Kopernika 8/18, issues ISIC cards (US$7).

Trakt (☎ 827 80 68), ul Kredytowa 6, offers guides in several major languages, English included (US$90 per group for any period up to five hours and US$15 for each extra hour). The private tourist office can also arrange a foreign-language guide, for marginally less.

Our Roots (☎ 620 05 56), ul Twarda 6 next to the Nożyk Synagogue, is the Jewish tourist bureau. The agency stocks some guidebooks and general publications referring to Jewish issues, and offers tours around Jewish monuments in Warsaw and beyond.

Bookshops The widest selection of maps and guidebooks (including Lonely Planet guidebooks) is to be found in the Sklep Podróżnika (☎ 822 54 87), ul Kaliska 8/10.

The American Bookstore (☎ 826 01 61), ul Krakowskie Przedmieście 45, is the best place to try for English-language publications, including literature, coffee-table books, specialist fare and magazines. It also has most Lonely Planet titles.

The best bookshop with French-language literature is the Marianne (☎ 826 62 71), in the French Institute, ul Senatorska 38, which also has a decent selection of French press.

Foreign newspapers and magazines are available from some larger newsagencies, or you can try the foyers of the top-class hotels. The widest selection, however, is to be found in EMPiK Megastore, ul Nowy Świat 15/17.

Laundry Alba self-service laundry (☎ 831 73 17), ul Karmelicka 17, on the corner of ul Anielewicza (weekdays from 9 am to 5 pm, Saturday from 9 am to 1 pm) charges US$6 to wash and dry up to 6kg. Call a couple of days ahead to make a reservation. Bring your own detergent or buy some in the laundry.

Medical & Emergency Services There's a wide network of pharmacies in Warsaw, and some of them stay open all night. The Swiss Pharmacy (☎ 628 94 71), Al Róż 2, near the British Embassy, is well stocked with imported medicines and some of the staff speak English.

If you happen to get sick, call ☎ 827 89 62 (business hours, English sometimes spoken) for information on private outpatient clinics. The Medical Centre (☎ 621 06 46 or ☎ 630 51 15), in the Hotel Marriott building (3rd floor), has specialist doctors, carries out laboratory tests and attends house calls. It's open weekdays from 7 am to 9 pm, Saturday from 8 am to 8 pm, Sunday from 9 am to 1 pm. Capricorn (☎ 831 76 07 or ☎ 831 86 69), ul Podwale 11, handles general and dental surgery and has an ambulance service. It's open 24 hours. Ring your embassy for other recommendations. The city ambulance service can be called on ☎ 999 or ☎ 628 24 24, but don't count on them speaking English.

Don't drink Warsaw's tap water – it's of poor quality. Bottled water is easily available from shops and supermarkets.

Things to See

Old Town The main gateway to the Old Town is the Castle Square (Plac Zamkowy). On a tall pillar in the centre of the square is a statue of King Sigismund III Vasa (who moved the capital from Kraków to Warsaw).

The massive **Royal Castle** on the east side of the square developed over the centuries as successive Polish kings added wings and redecorated the interior. In 1945 all that

remained was a heap of rubble, but from 1971 to 1984 the castle was rebuilt and is now a museum (open daily). The entrance is on the north side of the building, but castle tickets must be purchased at the Zamek Królewski-Kasy Biletowe, around the corner at ul Świętojańska 2. The most important parts of the interiors are the king's apartments on the 1st floor, which are visited in groups guided in Polish (US$4, US$2 for students). A guide in English, German or French will cost an extra US$14 per group. Sunday is a free-entry day and there's no guide service; you can visit all the castle's exhibitions. In summer, demand outstrips supply, so arrive early and be prepared to wait.

Enter the Old Town along ul Świętojańska. You'll soon come to the 14th-century Gothic **St John's Cathedral**, and then to the **Old Town Square** (Rynek Starego Miasta). Try to catch the 15-minute film screened at noon at the **Historical Museum of Warsaw** (closed Monday), Rynek Starego Miasta 42, which unforgettably depicts the wartime destruction of the city. It's hard to believe that all the 17th and 18th-century buildings around this square have been completely rebuilt from their foundations.

Continue north a block on ul Nowomiejska to the **Barbican**, part of the medieval walled circuit around Warsaw. North of here is the **New Town** (Nowe Miasto), centred around New Town Square (Rynek Nowego Miasta). The delightful streets and buildings in both the old and new towns are best explored casually on your own.

The Royal Way (Szlak Królewski) This is a 4km route from the Royal Castle to Łazienki Palace, the royal summer residence. The route follows ul Krakowskie Przedmieście, ul Nowy Świat and Al Ujazdowskie, and includes a good number of sights.

Just south of the Royal Castle is **St Anne's Church**, one of the most beautiful churches in the city. A few hundred metres farther south along ul Krakowskie Przedmieście is the **Carmelite Church**, and beside it, the powerful **Radziwiłł Palace**, the Polish White House. Next to the palace is the elegant **Hotel Bristol** (1901) with the neoclassical **Hotel Europejski** (1877) across the street. Behind the Europejski are the Saxon Gardens with

POLAND

the **Tomb of the Unknown Soldier** occupying a fragment of an 18th-century royal palace destroyed in WWII. The ceremonial changing of the guard takes place here on Sunday at noon.

North of the tomb is the massive **Grand Theatre** (1833, rebuilt in 1965), while to the south is the **Zachęta Modern Art Gallery** (closed Monday) which often stages great art shows. To the south, beyond the circular Evangelical Church, is the **Ethnographic Museum** (closed Monday), ul Kredytowa 1. This large museum has collections of tribal art from Africa, Oceania and Latin America, as well as Polish folklore.

From the museum follow ul Traugutta east a block back to the Royal Way. Just around the corner on the right is the 17th-century **Church of the Holy Cross**. The heart of Chopin is preserved in the second pillar on the left-hand side of the main nave. It was brought from Paris (where Chopin died of tuberculosis aged only 39) in accordance with his will. In front of the nearby 19th-century Staszic Palace (now the seat of the Academy of Sciences) stands a statue of Copernicus by the Danish sculptor Bertel Thorvaldsen. Below the academy towards the river is the **Chopin Museum**, ul Tamka 41, with such memorabilia as Chopin's last piano and a collection of Chopin manuscripts.

Returning to the Royal Way, head south along ul Nowy Świat (New World St), crossing Al Jerozolimskie (Jerusalem Ave) to the former Party Headquarters. This is where the Central Committee of the Polish United Workers Party (PZPR) used to meet. In 1991 the top floor of this building became the Warsaw Stock Exchange.

A few paces towards the river is the large **National Museum** (closed Monday) which has a magnificent collection of Polish sculpture and painting, from the medieval period to the present. Probably the most famous work here is the gigantic *The Battle of Grunwald* by Matejko.

Next to the National Museum is the **Polish Army Museum** (closed Monday and Tuesday) with a large assortment of old guns, tanks and planes on the terrace outside.

Farther south along the Royal Way, close to the busy motorway of Trasa Łazienkowska, is the interesting **Centre of Contemporary Art** (closed Monday), accommodated in the reconstructed Ujazdów Castle from the 1620s. Nearby to the south are the small **Botanical Gardens**, and just behind them stretches the vast Łazienki Park.

Łazienki This park and palace complex is best known for its 18th-century **Palace upon the Water** (closed Monday), summer residence of Stanisław August Poniatowski, the last king of Poland, who was deposed by a Russian army and a confederation of reactionary Polish magnates in 1792.

The nearby **Old Orangery** houses the 18th-century court theatre and gallery of sculpture (closed Monday). The **Chopin Monument** (1926) is just off Al Ujazdowskie. On summer Sundays piano recitals are held here. Wander about the park to see some other structures scattered around, including the Myślewice Palace, the amphitheatre and the New Orangery.

Wilanów This is another park and palace complex, about 6km south-east of Łazienki (take bus No 116 from Al Ujazdowskie). The centrepiece is the mighty **Wilanów Palace**, a former summer residence of King Jan III Sobieski who defeated the Turks at Vienna in 1683, ending their threat to Central Europe forever. Today it's a museum (closed Tuesday). All visitors are guided in groups; one-hour tours in Polish cost US$3 (US$2 for students). Foreign-language tours are available for US$40 per group of up to 10 people. Weekdays are essentially for prebooked groups, so it's better to come on weekends or a holiday when the palace is reserved for individuals; in summer arrive early and be prepared to stand in line. Summaries in English and French are posted in most rooms.

In the well kept park behind the palace is the **Orangery** which houses an art gallery. The **Poster Museum** (Muzeum Plakatu) in the former royal stables beside the palace has changing exhibitions of posters (closed Monday). Don't miss it – Polish posters are among the world's best.

Other Attractions The giant **Palace of Culture & Science**, near the central train station, is an apocalyptic piece of Stalin-era architecture. A 'gift of friendship' from the Soviet Union to the Polish nation, the palace

POLAND

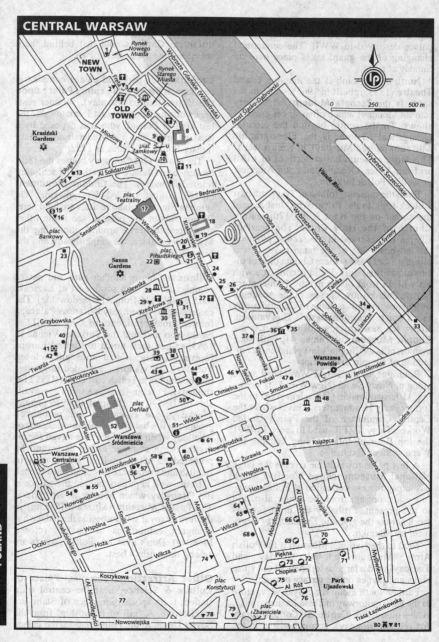

CENTRAL WARSAW

NEW TOWN

Rynek Nowego Miasta

Rynek Starego Miasta

OLD TOWN

Krasiński Gardens

Miodowa

Długa

Al Solidarności

plac Zamkowy

plac Teatralny

Bednarska

Wierzbowa

Senatorska

plac Bankowy

Saxon Gardens

Krakowskie

Przedmieście

plac Piłsudskiego

Królewska

Dobra

Browarna

Topiel

Tamka

Solec

Dobra

Jaracza

Krucza

Wisłostrada

Most Śląsko-Dąbrowski

Wybrzeże Gdańskie (Wisłostrada)

Vistula River

Wybrzeże Kościuszkowskie

Most Syreny

Wybrzeże Szczecińskie

Kredytowa

Jasna

Mazowiecka

Grzybowska

Zielna

Twarda

Świętokrzyska

Emilii Plater

plac Defilad

Warszawa Śródmieście

Warszawa Centralna

Al Jerozolimskie

Nowogrodzka

Chmielna

Nowy Świat

Kopernika

Foksal

Smolna

Warszawa Powiśle

Al Jerozolimskie

Kruczkowskiego

Książęca

Ludna

Rozbrat

Widok

Żurawia

Wspólna

Hoża

Nowogrodzka

Emilii Plater

Poznańska

Marszałkowska

Wilcza

Chałubińskiego

Oczki

Hoża

Wilcza

Koszykowa

plac Konstytucji

Piękna

Chopina

Al Róż

plac Zbawiciela

Nowowiejska

Al Niepodległości

Mokotowska

Al Ujazdowskie

Wiejska

Krucza

Piękna

Park Ujazdowski

Myśliwiecka

Trasa Łazienkowska

0   250   500 m

POLAND

CENTRAL WARSAW

PLACES TO STAY	35 Salad Bar Tukan	37 Almatur
10 Dom Literatury	46 Bar Mleczny Familijny	39 Main Post Office
13 Pokoje Gościnne Federacja	50 Bar Krokiecik	40 Jewish Theatre
Metalowcy	57 Bar Mleczny Średnicowy	41 Nożyk Synagogue
19 Hotel Bristol	62 Pizzeria da Elio	42 Our Roots Jewish
20 Hotel Europejski	63 Bar Mleczny Szwajcarski	Tourist Bureau
23 Hotel Saski	64 Bar Mleczny Bambino	43 Filharmonia Narodowa
26 Hotel Harenda	74 Bar Mleczny Złota Kurka	(National Philharmonic)
32 Hotel Mazowiecki	78 Leniwa Gospodyni	45 City Tourist Office
33 Hotel Na Wodzie	79 Bistro Carino	48 Polish Army Museum
34 Hotel Belfer	81 Qchnia Artystyczna	49 National Museum
38 Hotel Warszawa		51 City Tourist Office
44 Dom Chłopa	**OTHER**	52 Palace of Culture & Science
47 Youth Hostel	5 Historical Museum	53 Polski Express Bus Stop
55 Hotel Marriott	of Warsaw	54 LOT Office
58 Hotel Polonia	7 St John's Cathedral	56 Fotoplastikon
59 Hotel Metropol	8 Royal Castle	61 Kasy Teatralne ZASP
60 Hotel Forum	9 Private Tourist Office	65 Biuro Kwater Prywatnych
	11 St Anne's Church	Syrena Univel (Private Rooms)
PLACES TO EAT	12 American Bookstore	66 Bulgarian Embassy
1 Restauracja Ekologiczna	15 Bank Pekao	67 Parliament House
Nowe Miasto	17 Grand Theatre	68 Visa Extensions
2 Restauracja pod Samsonem	18 Radziwiłł Palace	69 US Embassy
3 Sklep z Kawą Pożegnanie	21 American Express Office	70 Canadian Embassy
z Afryką	22 Tomb of the Unknown	71 French Embassy
4 Bar Mleczny pod	Soldier	72 Hungarian Embassy
Barbakanem	24 Warsaw University	73 Romanian Embassy
6 Restauracja Fukier	27 Church of the Holy Cross	75 Czech Embassy
14 Restauracja Tay-Ho	28 Zachęta Modern Art Gallery	76 British Embassy
16 Salad Bar Tukan	30 Ethnographic Museum	77 Warsaw Technical University
25 Bar Mleczny Uniwersytecki	31 Bank Pekao	80 Ujazdów Castle & Centre
29 Salad Bar Tukan	36 Chopin Museum	of Contemporary Art

was built in the early 1950s and is still Poland's largest and tallest (234m) building. It has a huge congress hall, three theatres, a cinema and a Technical Museum. An elevator will carry you up to the observation terrace on the 30th floor for a panoramic view. Poles often joke that this is the best view in the city because it's the only one which doesn't include the Palace of Culture itself!

The **Fotoplastikon**, Al Jerozolimskie 51, just south of the palace, is reputedly the last working example in Europe of a once-popular apparatus, which allows you to see images in 3D. Each 20-minute session (US$1) consists of 48 stereoscopic slides, some in colour, dating from the turn of the century. It's a family-run business, which has been operating here since 1901.

The large street market selling everything from imported beer to car tyres at the eastern foot of the palace, and the large department stores, Junior, Wars and Sawa, farther to the east, are good places to get a feel for the current state of Polish consumerism. Another impressive demonstration of the country's free-market era is the huge bazaar at the **10th Anniversary Stadium** (Stadion Dziesięciolecia) in the suburb of Praga, considered the largest bazaar in Eastern Europe. Its average daily turnover is thought to be around US$2 million. It's open daily until around noon, and is busiest on Saturday and Sunday.

A five-minute walk north-west of the Palace of Culture, right behind the Jewish Theatre, is the neo-Romanesque **Nożyk Synagogue** (1902). It's Warsaw's only synagogue that managed to survive WWII, albeit in a sorry state. It was restored and today is open for religious services (Thursday only for tourists). The vast area of the Mirów

POLAND

and Muranów districts stretching to the north-west beyond the synagogue was once inhabited predominantly by Jews. During WWII the Nazis established a ghetto there and after the crushing of the Ghetto Uprising razed the quarter to the ground. Few remnants of the Jewish legacy are left. Possibly the most moving of these is the vast **Jewish Cemetery** (closed Friday and Saturday), ul Okopowa 49/51. It was founded in 1806 and today boasts over 100,000 tombstones – the largest collection of its kind in Europe.

Organised Tours

Mazurkas Travel (☎ 629 18 78) in the lobby of the Hotel Forum, ul Nowogrodzka 24/26, is Warsaw's major tour operator. It offers tours in the city (US$25 per person) and beyond, including trips to Kraków and Gdańsk. Weco-Travel (☎ 658 17 59) in the Hotel Jan III Sobieski, Plac Zawiszy 1, also offers regular city tours, covering and costing much the same.

Kampio (☎ 823 70 70; fax 823 71 44), ul Maszynowa 9 m 2, focuses on ecotourism, organising kayaking, biking and birdwatching trips to out-of-the-way areas.

Special Events

Warsaw's major annual events include the International Book Fair in May, the Warsaw Summer Jazz Days in late June, the Mozart Festival from mid-June to mid-July, the 'Warsaw Autumn' Festival of Contemporary Music in September and the 'Jazz Jamboree' International Jazz Festival in late October.

Places to Stay

Warsaw is the most expensive Polish city to stay in. It has an increasing collection of up-market hotels, whereas the cheaper places are not that numerous. Furthermore, the latter are scattered throughout the city, sometimes a long way from the centre, and there isn't any obvious budget hotel area to head for upon arrival. If you don't book in advance try to arrive in the city reasonably early in the day so as to have enough time to track down a room. The tourist offices will help you to find and book a room somewhere (the private office will charge a US$1.50 service fee per person).

Camping Warsaw has several camping grounds. The largest, most central and most popular among westerners is the *Camping Nr 34 Gromada* (☎ 825 43 91), ul Żwirki i Wigury 32, in the Ochota suburb. It's open May to September and has budget cabins and a large pavilion with hotel-style rooms. The place is friendly, helpful and clean, but it may close down in 1999 – check for news when you come. The camping ground is accessible from the airport on bus Nos 175 and 188, and from the central train station on bus Nos 136 and 175.

In the same suburb, close to the central bus terminal, is the smaller *Camping Nr 123 Majawa* (☎ 823 37 48), ul Bitwy Warszawskiej 1920r 15/17. It has all-year heated cabins (US$20/30 a double without/with bath) and also the all-year *Hotel Majawa* (US$30/38/44 a double/triple/quad without bath).

Camping Nr 260 (☎ 42 27 68), ul Inspektowa 1, in the Stegny suburb on the way to Wilanów, is open from mid-May to around mid-September. It has no shade and no cabins, but there is the the all-year *Hotel Stegny* in the grounds where triple rooms without bath cost US$30.

Camping Rapsodia (☎ 634 41 65), ul Fort Wola 22, in the Wola suburb is open June to September, and it also has a an all-year facility, the *Hotel Rapsodia* (US$15/20 a double/triple without bath, US$30/34 with bath).

Youth Hostels There are two all-year youth hostels, far too few for a capital city and insufficient for the needs of tourists. Neither is particularly good or large and both are often full.

The 110-bed *youth hostel* (☎ 827 89 52), ul Smolna 30, close to the National Museum, is accessible by bus No 175 from the airport and by any eastbound tram from the train station. It has large dormitories and charges about US$7 per person. Curfew is at 11 pm. The other *youth hostel* (☎ 632 88 29), ul Karolkowa 53a, is 2km west of the train station in the Wola suburb and is accessible by tram No 24 (there's no direct transport from the airport). The hostel has some smaller rooms that afford more privacy.

There are also two seasonal youth hostels, but they are smaller and poorer. The *youth hostel* (☎ 831 17 66), ul Międzyparkowa 4/6, on the northern outskirts of the New Town, is open 1 April to 31 October. Bus No 174 from the train station, or No 175 from the airport will take you there. The other *youth hostel* (☎ 617 88 51) is at Wał Miedzeszyński 397 on the eastern side of the Vistula close to the Trasa Łazienkowska (the main west-east city motorway). It's open 15 April to 15 October. Take bus No 501 from the train station, or No 188 from the airport.

Student Hostels The tourist offices may know which student dorms are open as hostels (normally from early July to mid-September). Of those that have been open each summer over the past few years, you could try the *Dom Studenta Nr 1* (☎ 668 63 07) and *Dom Studenta Nr 2* (☎ 822 24 07), in two large blocks next to one another at ul Żwirki i Wigury 97/99 and 95/97; *Dom Studenta* (☎ 822 18 69), ul Spiska 16; *Hermes* (☎ 49 67 22), ul Madalińskiego 6/8; *Grosik* (☎ 49 23 02), ul Madalińskiego 31/33; and *Sabinki* (☎ 646 32 00), Al Niepodległości 147. Any of these will cost US$8 to US$10 per bed in doubles or triples with shared facilities.

Private Rooms Accommodation in private homes is arranged by the Biuro Kwater Prywatnych Syrena Univel (☎ 628 75 40), ul Krucza 17 (Monday to Saturday from 9 am to 7 pm, Sunday from 9 am to 5 pm). Try to get there reasonably early, as later there may be not much to choose from. The rooms are in the central districts and cost US$17/25 a single/double.

Hotels – Budget & Middle This section includes hotels which cost up to about US$50 a double. There are not that many central hotels in this price bracket and they tend to fill up fast. The hotels farther out from the city centre are more likely to have vacancies. Also consider the hotel and cabin facilities of the camp sites (listed earlier in this chapter), which fall into the budget price bracket, even though most are far from the centre.

The ideally located *Dom Literatury* (☎ 635 39 20), ul Krakowskie Przedmieście 87, is just off the Old Town. It's not a regular hotel, but it rents out rooms (six doubles and one triple in all) on its top floor for about

US$23 per person. Most rooms provide a superb view over the Castle Square.

Another place close to the Old Town is the *Pokoje Gościnne Federacja Metalowcy* (☎ 831 40 21), ul Długa 29. It costs US$14/22/34 a single/double/quad without bath – it's hard to find a cheaper hotel in central Warsaw.

A few blocks south is the more stylish *Hotel Saski* (☎ 620 46 11), Plac Bankowy 1. Rooms without bath are US$33/44 a single/double (breakfast included); ask for one facing the interior courtyard, away from tram noise. The hotel has real character and a fine location.

The *Hotel Mazowiecki* (☎ 682 20 69), ul Mazowiecka 10, is a former army dorm once reserved for military officers but now open to everyone. Rooms with shared facilities cost US$32/44/50 a single/double/triple.

Hotel Belfer (☎ 625 26 00) is at Wybrzeże Kościuszkowskie 31/33, on the Vistula bank. This large former teachers' hotel has singles/doubles without bath at US$27/36 and singles/doubles/triples with bath and breakfast at US$38/52/62. Rooms on the upper floors provide good views.

The nearby *Hotel Na Wodzie* (☎ 628 58 83) is in two boats, *Anita* and *Aldona*, anchored to the river shore between the railway and Poniatowski bridges. It operates from around April to November and offers single/double cabins without bath for US$20/25.

South of the city centre, in the Mokotów district, you can try *Hotel Hera* (☎ 41 13 08), ul Belwederska 26/30, south of the Łazienki Park. It has singles/doubles without bath at US$25/34, with own bath at US$50/62, breakfast included.

Hotel Agra (☎ 49 38 81) is also in Mokotów, at ul Falęcka 9/11, and has singles/doubles/triples for US$34/38/50. The bath is shared between two adjacent rooms.

Hotels – Top End This section is for those who can afford to pay more than around US$50 for a double. Central Warsaw has quite a number of such hotels. Most hotels listed serve breakfast, which is included in the room price.

One of the cheapest is the old-fashioned *Hotel Polonia* (☎ 628 72 41), Al Jerozolimskie 45, a short walk from the central train

station. It costs US$40/60 a single/double
without bath, US$60/90 with bath. Just round
the corner, at ul Marszałkowska 99a, is the
newer if unstylish *Hotel Metropol* (☎ 629 40
01), where rooms are US$75/100 with bath.

The refurbished *Hotel Harenda* (☎ 826 26
25), conveniently located at ul Krakowskie
Przedmieście 4/6, has singles/doubles with
bath for US$50/75.

Dom Chłopa (☎ 827 92 51), Plac
Powstańców Warszawy 2, is unexciting but
well located. Rooms go for US$75/90 with
bath. The nearby *Hotel Warszawa* (☎ 827 14
72), Plac Powstańców Warszawy 9, costs
marginally more.

Hotel Cytadela (☎ 687 72 36), ul Krajew-
skiego 3/5, a 10-minute walk north-west of
the New Town, is good value. This army-run
hotel opened in 1993 and costs US$60/80 a
double/triple with bath. Another reasonable
choice is the small *Hotel Karat* (☎ 601 44
11), ul Słoneczna 37, in Mokotów, which
offers singles/doubles for US$75/100.

For a splurge, you have half a dozen luxury
hotels, including the classy old-style *Hotel
Bristol* (☎ 625 25 25), ul Krakowskie Przedmieście 42/44. It reopened in 1993 after a
US$36 million renovation. Rooms begin at
US$200/250 a single/double. The US$36
Sunday brunch here (from 12.30 to 4 pm) is
superb with unlimited champagne and a
buffet that includes smoked salmon, caviar,
salads, cheeses, meats, several main dishes,
sweets and coffee. Reservations are required;
make them a couple of days in advance.

Places to Eat
Warsaw has a wider range of eating places
than any other Polish city, in every price
bracket. It's the only city which offers a fair
variety of ethnic cuisines. There has been a
virtual explosion of small modern bistros,
pizzerias, snack bars and big international fast-
food chains, which are replacing the old, drab,
run-down places. Yet a number of genuine
milk bars still exist, providing some of the
cheapest food in town. There's also a spectacular proliferation of pubs, which have spread
like wildfire since the fall of communism.

Old Town & Around The *Bar Mleczny
pod Barbakanem*, ul Mostowa 27/29 next to
the Barbican, is a popular milk bar which has

successfully survived the fall of the iron
curtain and continues to serve cheap, unpretentious food.

Restauracja pod Samsonem, ul Freta 3/5,
is one of the best inexpensive restaurants in
the area. The interior is rather dull but the
food – a mix of Polish and Jewish cuisine –
is decent and tasty.

Restauracja Ekologiczna Nove Miasto,
Rynek Nowego Miasta 13/15, serves vegetarian dishes plus a variety of salads,
reputedly prepared from organically grown
vegetables, in bright cheerful surroundings.
The food is not that cheap but it's fine and
tasty. The *Salad Bar Tukan*, ul Nowomiejska 5, has plenty of wonderful salads, though
if you really want to fill up with them, it
won't be a budget meal.

The Old Town boasts some of Warsaw's
best restaurants specialising in traditional
Polish cuisine, including the *Restauracja
Bazyliszek* and *Restauracja Fukier*, both on
the Old Market Square. Also on the square is
the *Dom Restauracyjny Gessler* – don't miss
going downstairs to its amazing karczma, a
traditional country inn serving typical food.

The Old Town also shelters some fine
Asian eateries, including *Restauracja Tay-
Ho*, ul Długa 29 (Vietnamese fare), *Restauracja Bliss*, ul Boczna 3 (Chinese food)
and *Restauracja Maharaja*, ul Szeroki Dunaj
13 (Thai cuisine).

Arguably the best coffee in town is served
in the *Sklep z Kawą Pożegnanie z Afryką*, ul
Freta 4/6. This tiny coffee shop, one of about
10 outlets of the chain scattered around
Poland's major cities, offers nothing but
coffee (30-odd varieties) – but what coffee!

At least a dozen open-air cafés spring up
every summer on the Old Town Square, a
pleasant place to sit and chat over a drink and
watch the world go by. Some of the best ice
cream in the Old Town is to be found in the
small takeaway *Lody* ice-cream shop, ul
Nowomiejska 9, a few paces north of the
square.

New Centre & Around This section
covers the large area to the south of the Old
Town, including the Royal Way.

Three milk bars have survived along the
Royal Way at comfortably short walking intervals: *Bar Mleczny Uniwersytecki*, ul

Krakowskie Przedmieście 20, *Bar Mleczny Familijny*, ul Nowy Świat 39 and *Bar Mleczny Szwajcarski*, ul Nowy Świat 5. All are good and very cheap. To the west of the Royal Way, you have the busy *Bar Mleczny Średnicowy*, Al Jerozolimskie 49, near the central train station, *Bar Mleczny Bambino*, ul Krucza 21, and *Bar Mleczny Złota Kurka*, ul Marszałkowska 55/73.

The self-service *Bar Krokiecik*, ul Zgoda 1, is deservedly popular thanks to its good inexpensive food. The *Grill Bar Zgoda* across the street at ul Zgoda 4 is a bit more expensive but worth it. You'll find a number of other inexpensive snack bars and bistros in the area.

A chain called the *Salad Bar Tukan* has opened at several locations, including Plac Bankowy 2 (in the blue skyscraper), ul Kredytowa 2, ul Tamka 37, and ul Nowomiejska 5, and offers just about the widest choice of salads in town.

The *Leniwa Gospodyni*, ul Nowowiejska 12/18, and *Bistro Carino*, ul Nowowiejska 6, have cheap lunches. The *Pizzeria da Elio*, ul Żurawia 20, offers inexpensive Italian food, including pizzas, pastas and meats, plus a salad bar.

The *Qchnia Artystyczna* in the Ujazdów Castle, Al Ujazdowskie 6 (which houses the large Centre of Contemporary Art), serves good food (including delicious salads) at affordable prices in artistic 'postmodern' surroundings.

There's a cluster of white-and-red plastic cabins on the east side of Plac Konstytucji, some of which are run by Vietnamese who cook budget Oriental food. Similar Vietnamese cabin eateries have sprung up at other busy locations throughout the central area.

For Asian specialities in better appointed surroundings (and considerably more expensive), you can try the *Restauracja Mekong*, ul Wspólna 35 (Chinese food), *Restauracja Ha Long*, ul Emilii Plater 36 (Vietnamese cuisine) and *Restauracja Maharaja*, ul Marszałkowska 34/50 (Indian food).

There are plenty of cafés along the Royal Way, of which the *Café Blikle*, ul Nowy Świat 33, is one of the most popular with locals. It has delicious doughnuts and other pastries, several set breakfasts, light lunches, salads, milk shakes etc.

Wedel on the corner of ul Szpitalna and ul Górskiego, adjacent to the Wedel chocolate shop, is the place for a cup of hot chocolate and chocolate waffles.

The *Restauracja Adler*, ul Mokotowska 69, serves hearty Bavarian and Polish food at reasonable prices. Farther south, in the Mokotów district, the *Restauracja Flik* (☎ 49 44 34), ul Puławska 43, combines fine cooking and an enjoyable setting. The focus is on Polish food, and its lunch buffet is excellent value – so good that it needs an advance booking.

Entertainment

Check the *Gazeta Wyborcza* local paper for what's on. Its Friday edition has the *Co Jest Grane* entertainment section, which details theatres, cinemas, museums, night spots etc. Another good source of information is the *iks* monthly. The *Warsaw Insider* (see Information earlier) is a good help for dining and drinking out. The Kasy Teatralne ZASP, Al Jerozolimskie 25, sells tickets for most of the city theatres, opera, musical events and visiting shows.

Cinema Most of the city's cinemas screen the usual, mostly US-made commercial fare. Cinemas where you are likely to see more thought-provoking films include *Kino Agrafka*, Plac Żelaznej Bramy 2, *Kino Foksal*, ul Foksal 3/5, *Kino Iluzjon*, ul Narbutta 50a, *Cinema Paradiso*, Al Solidarności 62, and *Kino Rejs*, ul Krakowskie Przedmieście 21/23.

Theatre Warsaw has about 20 theatres, the best of which include the *Centrum Sztuki Studio* in the Palace of Culture, the *Teatr Ateneum*, ul Jaracza 2, and the *Teatr Powszechny*, ul Zamoyskiego 20. Most of the theatres close in July and August for their annual holidays.

Opera & Ballet The main venue for opera and ballet performances is the *Teatr Wielki* (Grand Theatre). Advance booking is recommended. The *Opera Kameralna* (Chamber Opera), Al Solidarności 76b, performs operas in a more intimate but splendid setting.

POLAND

Classical Music The *Filharmonia Narodowa* (National Philharmonic), ul Jasna 5, has a concert hall (enter from ul Sienkiewicza 10) and a chamber hall (enter from ul Moniuszki 5). Regular concerts are held in both halls, usually on Friday and Saturday, by the brilliant Warsaw Orchestra and visiting ensembles.

Piano recitals are held in Łazienki Park next to the Chopin Monument, every Sunday from May to September. Chamber concerts are staged in summer in the Old Orangery in the park.

Jazz The *Jazz Club Akwarium*, ul Emilii Plater 49 behind the Palace of Culture, is Warsaw's only regular jazz club. Live jazz is performed nightly at 8.30 pm. *Klub Remont* has live jazz every Thursday except from July to September. *Pub Harenda* may have jazz in its cellar. In July and August, open-air jazz concerts are staged at the Old Town Square, on Saturday at 7 pm.

Student Clubs & Discos Warsaw's main student clubs include *Remont*, ul Waryńskiego 12, *Stodoła*, ul Batorego 10, *Hybrydy*, ul Złota 7/9, *Park*, ul Niepodległości 196 and *Proxima*, ul Żwirki i Wigury 99a. They all have weekend discos (and during the week in July and August). They are inexpensive and, furthermore, students get discounts on entry fees.

The dearer, non-student discos include *Ground Zero*, ul Wspólna 62, (one of the most popular among westerners), and the techno *Blue Velvet*, ul Krakowskie Przedmieście 5.

Bars & Pubs Warsaw is flooded with bars and pubs these days. *The Irish Pub*, ul Miodowa 3, is one of the popular drinking haunts in the Old Town area, and stages live music most nights (Irish, folk, country etc).

If you prefer something more local, go to *Pub pod Baryłką*, ul Garbarska 5/7, on the Mariensztat Square. It's a Polish pub offering 20-plus kinds of Polish beers – a good testing ground for visiting beer connoisseurs.

Pub Harenda, ul Krakowskie Przedmieście 4/6, next to Hotel Harenda is a trendy and lively spot and is open longer than most other places of this kind.

Other pubs you might want to try include the Irish *Morgan's*, ul Okólnik 1 (enter from

ul Tamka), the *Zanzi Bar*, ul Wierzbowa 9/11, and the *Grand Kredens,* Al Jerozolimskie 111.

Getting There & Away

Air Okęcie airport, 10km south-west of the city centre, handles all domestic and international flights. The small but functional terminal has international arrivals downstairs and departures upstairs. The domestic section occupies a small separate part of the same building.

The international section houses the tourist office (on the arrivals level), which has good information, sells city maps and can help to find a place to stay. A few ATMs on the same level accept some major credit cards, including Visa and MasterCard. Avoid the Orbis office which charges astronomical fees for its services and has a kantor which gives outrageously low rates; go upstairs to the Powszechny Bank Kredytowy which exchanges cash and travellers cheques at possibly the best rates in the terminal, though not the best rate in town. Change just enough to get to the city where any of the numerous kantors will pay you more for your dollars. By the same token, before you leave Poland change your extra złotys back to a hard currency in the city. Note that the duty-free shops are beyond passport control, and there are no exchange facilities there.

The arrivals level houses several car-rental companies, a left-luggage room and a newsagency – the place to buy public transport tickets. Buses and taxis depart from this level.

LOT and foreign carriers link Warsaw with Europe and beyond. Pick up the LOT timetable which lists all international flights to/from Poland, along with domestic flights. Tickets can be booked and bought from the main LOT office in the building of the Marriott Hotel, Al Jerozolimskie 65/79, or from any of the Orbis offices and other travel agencies.

Train Warsaw has several train stations of which Warszawa Centralna, (Warsaw central station), opposite the Marriott Hotel in the city centre, handles the overwhelming majority of traffic including all international trains. When you arrive, get off the train quickly as the central station is not the terminus.

The station includes a spacious main hall on street level (which houses ticket counters, post office, newsagency, the helpful tourist office, an ATM, snack bars and some other facilities) and a subterranean level with tracks and platforms, right underneath the hall. On an intermediate level between the hall and the platforms is an extensive array of passageways. Here you'll find more fast-food outlets, half a dozen kantors (one of which is open 24 hours), a left-luggage office (open 7 am to 9 pm), lockers (almost always occupied), several Ruch kiosks (for city transport tickets and city maps), a bookshop (well stocked with regional and city maps from all over the country) and plenty of shops selling food, clothing etc.

Watch your belongings closely on all levels, and particularly in the passageways which are usually crowded. Be alert on platforms and while boarding the train – pickpocketing and theft are on the increase here.

Warsaw central handles trains to just about every corner of the country. InterCity trains run to Gdańsk (333km), Katowice (303km), Kraków (292km), Lublin (175km), Poznań (311km) and Szczecin (525km). International destinations include Berlin, Bratislava, Brussels, Bucharest, Budapest, Cologne, Dresden, Frankfurt/Main, Hrodna, Kiev, Leipzig, Minsk, Moscow, Prague, St Petersburg, Vienna and Vilnius.

Domestic and international train tickets are available either directly from the counters at the station (allow at least an hour for possible queuing) or from any Orbis office. International train tickets can also be bought from Almatur and other travel agencies.

Other major train stations include Warszawa Zachodnia (West Warsaw) next to the central bus terminal, and Warszawa Wschodnia (East Warsaw) in the Praga suburb. Warszawa Śródmieście station, a couple of hundred metres east of Warsaw central, handles local trains.

Bus Warsaw has two PKS bus terminals. Dworzec Centralny PKS (the central bus terminal) operates all domestic buses which head towards the south and west. The terminal is west of the city centre, adjoining Warszawa Zachodnia train station. To get there from the centre, take the commuter train from Warszawa Śródmieście station (two stops).

Dworzec PKS Stadion (Stadium bus terminal), behind the main city stadium, adjoining the Warszawa Stadion train station (and also easily accessible by the commuter train from Warszawa Śródmieście), handles all domestic bus traffic to the north, east and south-east. Bus tickets are sold at the respective terminals.

The Polski Express bus company runs its coaches from Okęcie airport. They all call (and can be boarded) at the carrier's bus stop on Al Jana Pawła II next to the central train station. Polski Express' destinations include Białystok, Lublin, Olsztyn, Puławy, Rzeszów and Toruń. These cities are serviced by train, but bus travel is cheaper and in many cases almost as fast as the train. Tickets for Polski Express are available from either of its offices and from selected Orbis outlets, but they cannot be bought at PKS terminals. Information is available on ☎ 620 03 30.

International buses are operated by a few dozen bus companies and depart from either the central PKS bus terminal or Warsaw central train station. Tickets are available from the companies' offices, selected Orbis offices, Almatur and a number of other travel agencies. A wide range of options for travel to Western Europe are offered by Anna Travel (☎ 825 53 89) at Warsaw central train station and the Bus Travel Center (☎ 628 62 53), Al Jerozolimskie 63. PKS has daily departures to Vilnius (US$19), Minsk (US$21) and Lviv (US$17).

Getting Around

To/From the Airport

The cheapest way of getting from the airport to the city (and vice versa) is by bus No 175, which will take you right into the centre and up to the Old Town, passing en route Warsaw central train station and the youth hostel at ul Smolna. Watch your bags and pockets closely all the way – this line has become a favourite playground for thieves. Don't forget to buy tickets for yourself and your luggage at the airport's newsagency, and to punch them upon boarding the bus.

The next cheapest option is the Airport-City special bus which goes to the Bristol and Europejski hotels, calling at Warsaw central train station. The bus runs from 6 am to 11 pm, every 20 minutes on weekdays and every half an hour on weekends. The fare of US$2 (US$1 for students) covers the luggage and is paid directly to the driver.

Don't even think about taking a taxi from the taxi stand in front of the arrivals hall – they are operated by 'mafia' drivers who will try to charge an astronomical fare.

Bus & Tram There are about 30 tram routes and over 100 bus routes, which are clearly marked on the city transport map (tram routes in red, bus routes in blue) and at the stops.

Public transport operates from about 5 am to about 11 pm. At night (from 11 pm to 5 am), several bus lines link major suburbs to the city centre. The night 'terminal' is at ul Emilii Plater behind the Palace of Culture, from where buses depart every half-hour.

Warsaw's public transport is pretty frequent and cheap. The fare is a flat US$0.40 (US$1.20 on night buses) for either bus or tram, regardless of distance. Students below 26 years of age with an ISIC card pay half the fare in Warsaw (there are as yet no ISIC student concessions in other cities). Bulky luggage (according to the regulations, any that exceeds 60 x 40 x 20cm) costs an extra, ordinary fare. Daily, weekly and monthly passes are available from the Dział Sprzedaży Biletów office, ul Senatorska 37.

There are no conductors on board; you buy a ticket beforehand from Ruch kiosks, then board the tram or bus and punch the ticket (on the side that doesn't have a metal strip) in one of the small machines inside. Inspections are not unusual and fines are high: US$25 for travel without a validated ticket and US$10 for luggage. There's a new breed of tough and rude plain-clothes inspectors, who literally hunt for foreign tourists.

Watch out for pickpockets on crowded city buses and trams (especially bus No 175 and trams running along Al Jerozolimskie). Some are highly skilled and can easily zip open a bag you thought was in front of you. Don't become separated from your companion by people reaching between you to grab hold of the handrail. The pleasant looking young man who says hello may only be trying to distract you.

Metro The 12.5km stretch of the metro, from the Ursynów suburb (Kabaty station) at the southern city limits to the city centre (Centrum station) is in operation. It's planned to be extended up to the northern Młociny suburb by around 2004.

You use the same kind of tickets as on trams and buses (US$0.40); the differences are that you punch them on the opposite side (where there's a silver metal strip), and that you do it at the entrance to the platform, not on the train itself.

Car The condition of Warsaw's street surfaces is disastrous. They are full of potholes – some more dangerous than the others – so driving needs constant attention. The local government plans to introduce paid parking on the central streets. At the time of writing, you could park free almost anywhere, on the road or on the pavement. See how the locals park their cars and follow their lead. For your security, try to park your car in a guarded car park (*parking strzeżony*). There are some in central Warsaw, including one on ul Parkingowa behind Hotel Forum.

Taxi There are about 20 taxi companies, including Radio Taxi (☎ 919), Super Taxi (☎ 96 22), Lux Taxi (☎ 96 66) and Sawa Taxi (☎ 644 44 44), all of which are pretty reliable. The daytime charge (from 6 am to 10 pm) is US$1.20 for the first kilometre plus US$0.50 per each additional kilometre; night-time fares are US$1.20 and US$0.70, respectively.

Most taxis in Warsaw now have their meters adjusted to the current tariff, so you just pay what the meter says. When you board a taxi, make sure the meter is turned on in your presence, which ensures that you don't have the previous passenger's fare added to yours.

Taxis can be waved down on the street, but it's much easier to walk to the nearest taxi stand, which are plentiful. You can also order a taxi by phone and there's no extra charge for this service.

Beware of 'mafia' taxis parked in front of the luxury hotels, at the airport, the Warsaw central train station, the Rotunda (on the corner of ul Marszałkowska and Al Jerozolimskie) and in the vicinity of tourist sights.

Małopolska

Małopolska (literally 'Little Poland') encompasses the whole of south-eastern Poland, from Mazovia in the north down to the Carpathian Mountains along the country's southern border. Together with Wielkopolska (Great Poland), Małopolska was the cradle of the Polish state, and it became of prime importance after the capital was moved to Kraków in 1038. As the royal province, the region enjoyed the special attention of the kings, who built a fine array of castles to protect it. It was always one of the most 'Polish' regions of the country, and it retains much of that flavour to this day.

It is a region of softly rolling hills and green valleys, sprinkled with villages and towns, and much of it still bears a gentle bucolic air of bygone times. You'll see people working the fields as they have for centuries, and long wooden horse carts along the roads.

Nearly every foreign visitor makes it to Kraków, Poland's former capital and one of the great art centres of Europe. Some also join the hordes of Polish excursionists on their way to the mountains around Zakopane. There's much more to south-eastern Poland, however, such as the holy sanctuary of Jasna Góra at Częstochowa, the Renaissance town of Zamość, the superb baroque palace at Łańcut, and the horrors of Auschwitz, Birkenau and Majdanek. It's easy to lose the crowds in the unspoiled mountains along the southern border. Here is Poland to be savoured.

KRAKÓW
☎ 012

Kraków (population 720,000) is the third largest city in Poland, and one of the oldest: the first traces of its existence date from the 7th century. In 1000 the bishopric of Kraków was established, and in 1038 Kraków became the capital of the Piast kingdom. The kings ruled from Wawel Castle until 1596, but even afterwards, when the capital moved to Warsaw, Polish royalty continued to be crowned and buried in Wawel Cathedral.

At this crossing of trade routes from Western Europe to Byzantium and from southern Europe to the Baltic, a large medieval city developed. Particularly good times came with the reign of King Casimir the Great, a generous patron of art and scholarship. In 1364 he founded the Kraków Academy (later renamed the Jagiellonian University), the second-oldest university in Central Europe after the one in Prague. Copernicus, who would later develop his heliocentric theory, studied here in the 1490s.

In January 1945 a sudden encircling manoeuvre by the Soviet army forced the Germans to quickly evacuate the city, and Kraków was saved from destruction. As such, Kraków is Poland's only large city that has preserved its old architecture almost intact.

In order to balance the clerical/aristocratic traditions of the old capital, in the early 1950s the communists built the vast industrial suburb of Nowa Huta centred around gigantic steelworks, just 8km east of Kraków's historic centre. Far from acting as a bulwark of the regime, a May 1988 strike by 20,000 steelworkers here contributed greatly to its eventual fall. Yet the tens of thousands of tonnes of carbon monoxide, sulphur dioxide and particles emitted annually by the steel mill have seriously damaged Kraków's monuments. Now a restructuring program is underway to cut both the workforce and pollution, while the city's historical monuments are being gradually restored.

No other city in Poland has so many historic buildings and monuments, and nowhere else will you encounter such a vast collection of works of art (2.3 million). In 1978 UNESCO included the historic centre of Kraków on its first World Cultural Heritage list. The Old Town harbours world-class museums and towering Gothic churches, while Kazimierz, the now silent Jewish quarter, tells of a sadder recent history, revealed to the world by Steven Spielberg's film, Schindler's List. Kraków is a city with character and soul, and has traditionally been the major centre of Polish culture. This is the one Polish city you simply cannot miss.

Orientation

The great thing about Kraków is that almost all you need is at hand. There's no other city in Poland where you have so many things – both historic buildings and also good tourist

KRAKÓW

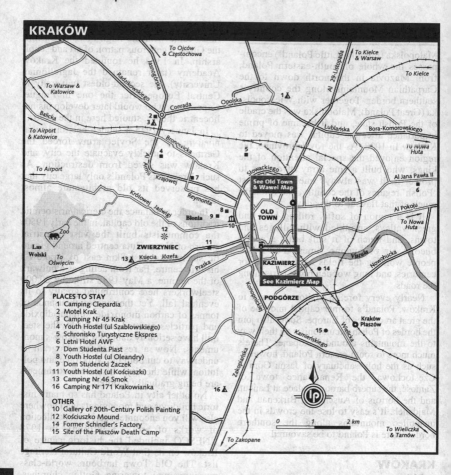

PLACES TO STAY
1 Camping Clepardia
2 Motel Krak
3 Camping Nr 45 Krak
4 Youth Hostel (ul Szablowskiego)
5 Schronisko Turystyczne Ekspres
6 Letni Hotel AWF
7 Dom Studenta Piast
8 Youth Hostel (ul Oleandry)
9 Dom Studencki Żaczek
11 Youth Hostel (ul Kościuszki)
13 Camping Nr 46 Smok
16 Camping Nr 171 Krakowianka

OTHER
10 Gallery of 20th-Century Polish Painting
12 Kościuszko Mound
14 Former Schindler's Factory
15 Site of the Płaszów Death Camp

facilities – so conveniently squeezed into the small compact area of the Old Town. Some 800m wide and 1200m long, the historic quarter has the Rynek Główny, the Main Market Square, in the middle, and is surrounded by the green ring of the Planty, that was once a moat. On the southern tip of the Old Town sits the Wawel castle, and farther south stretches the district of Kazimierz.

The bus and train stations – where you're most likely to arrive – are next to each other on the north-eastern rim of the Old Town. The tourist office is right opposite the train station and nearly 10 hotels covering all price brackets within a 500m radius. Rynek Główny is a 10-minute walk from the station.

Information

Tourist Offices The KART city tourist office (☎ 422 04 71 or ☎ 422 60 91), ul Pawia 8 opposite the train station, is a good source of information. It's open weekdays from 8 am to 6 pm, Saturday from 9 am to 1 pm (October to May from 8 am to 4 pm weekdays only).

Two private travel agencies have opened their own tourist information desks: the Jordan tourist office (☎ 939), ul Floriańska 37 (weekdays from 8 am to 6 pm, weekends from 9 am to 3 pm), and the Dexter tourist office (☎ 421 77 06), in the Cloth Hall in the middle of the Rynek Główny (weekdays from 9 am to 6 pm, Saturday from 9 am to 1 pm). Kraków also has a knowledgeable Cultural Information Centre (☎ 421 77 87), ul Św Jana 2.

Watch out for two free monthly magazines: *Welcome to Cracow* and *Kraków: What, Where, When*. They are distributed through tourist offices, travel agencies, some upmarket hotels etc. And buy a copy of the useful *Krakow Insider* magazine, which covers museums, hotels, restaurants, cafés, pubs etc.

Foreign Consulates All the consulates are in or near the city centre and include:

Austria
  (☎ 421 97 66) ul Cybulskiego 9
Denmark
  (☎ 421 71 20) ul Floriańska 37
France
  (☎ 422 18 64) ul Stolarska 15
Germany
  (☎ 421 84 73) ul Stolarska 7
Hungary
  (☎ 422 56 79) ul Mikołajska 26
Russia
  (☎ 422 83 88) ul Westerplatte 11
Ukraine
  (☎ 656 23 36) ul Krakowska 41
USA
  (☎ 422 97 64) ul Stolarska 9

Money Cash can easily be exchanged in any of the numerous kantors scattered throughout the Old Town. Some trade on Sunday, but the rates are usually poorer then; change enough money on Saturday to last you until Monday.

Change your travellers cheques at the American Express counter in the Orbis office, Rynek Główny 41 (weekdays from 8 am to 7 pm, Saturday from 8.30 am to 1 pm), which charges no commission. You can also change cheques in Bank Pekao, Rynek Główny 31, but it charges commission.

Cash advances on Visa and MasterCard are obtainable at Bank Pekao, either from the cashier inside or the ATM outside, and there are many more ATMs throughout the central area.

Post & Communications The main post office, ul Westerplatte 20, has poste restante. Mail should be addressed care of Poste Restante, Poczta Główna, ul Westerplatte 20, 31-045 Kraków 1, Poland, and can be collected at window No 1.

There's a telephone centre in the main post office (open 24 hours), or you can use the more central phone office at Rynek Główny 19 (open till 10 pm). There's also a post/phone office that has a 24-hour telephone service at ul Lubicz 4, opposite the central train station.

Cybercafés The oldest and best known place in town is the Cyber Café u Luisa, set in a spectacular vaulted cellar at Rynek Główny 13. Yet it has painfully slow connections, so if speed is more important than the ambience check one of the following:

Cyber Net Café
  (☎ 421 89 64) Plac Matejki 5
KKI Caffe Internet
  (☎ 421 22 79) 2nd floor, ul Starowiślna 20
Looz Internet Café
  ul Mikołajska 11

Travel Agencies A number of travel agencies operate tours in and around Kraków (see Organised Tours later in the Kraków section for details). As well as offering activity-based tours, Almatur (☎ 422 46 68), ul Grodzka 2, issues ISIC student cards.

Bookshops For English-language literature check the English Book Centre, Plac Matejki 5, and the Inter Book, ul Karmelicka 27. The Księgarnia Edukator in the French Institute, ul Św Jana 15, has probably the best selection of books in French.

The Księgarnia Odeon, Rynek Główny 5, and the Księgarnia Znak, Sławkowska 1, also have a selection of both French and English books.

The widest choice of publications related to Jewish issues is to be found at the Jarden Jewish Bookshop, ul Szeroka 2, in Kazimierz.

Some of the best selection of regional and city maps is in Sklep Podróżnika, ul Jagiellońska 6 and ul Szujskiego 2; the latter is perhaps the only place in Kraków which sells Lonely Planet guidebooks.

POLAND

Medical Services Profimed (☎ 421 79 97), Rynek Główny 6, has private doctors of different specialities. Dent America (☎ 421 89 48), Plac Szczepański 3, is a Polish-American dental clinic. The US consulate department of citizen services (☎ 422 12 94) has a list of recommended doctors speaking English.

The ambulance emergency phone number is ☎ 999.

Things to See

Main Market Square You'll probably want to begin your visit on Rynek Główny, Kraków's wonderful market square, the largest medieval town square in Europe. The 16th-century Renaissance **Cloth Hall** (Sukiennice) dominates the centre of the square and there's a large craft market on the ground floor. Upstairs is the **Gallery of 19th-Century Polish Painting** (one of the six branches of the National Museum), which includes several well known historical works by Matejko. Take note of the opening hours of the other branches (posted on the door) and consider buying a special ticket (US$5, US$3.50 for students) which allows admission to all branches and is cheaper than a total of individual entry fees.

The 14th-century **St Mary's Church** fills the north-east corner of the square. The huge main altarpiece (1489) by Wit Stwosz (Veit Stoss) of Nuremberg is the finest (and largest) sculptural work of Gothic art in Poland. The altar's wings are opened daily at noon. A trumpet call (*hejnał*) occurs hourly from the higher of the church's towers; it recalls a 13th-century trumpeter, who in the middle of sounding a warning of invasion, was cut down by a Tatar arrow.

On the opposite side of the Cloth Hall is the 15th-century **Town Hall Tower**. You can go to the top in summer. The town hall itself was dismantled in the 1820s. Also visit the **Historical Museum of Kraków**, Rynek Główny 35 (closed Monday and Tuesday).

Around the Old Town Take ul Floriańska (the town's liveliest street) northwards to the **Florian Gate** (1307), the only one existing of the original seven gates. Behind it is the **Barbican**, a defensive bastion built in 1498.

Visit the Czartoryski Museum, ul Św Jana 19, which features a valuable art collection from Europe and beyond. The most famous works here are Leonardo da Vinci's *Lady with an Ermine* and Rembrandt's *Landscape with the Good Samaritan*. Don't miss the **Szołajski Museum**, Plac Szczepański 9, which has one of the best selections of late Gothic and early Renaissance altarpieces and Madonnas in Poland. Both these places are branches of the National Museum.

Farther south, at ul Jagiellonska 15, is the 15th-century **Collegium Maius**, the oldest surviving part of the Kraków Academy. Inspect its magnificent arcaded Gothic courtyard and visit the museum (open weekdays from 11 am to 2.30 pm, Saturday till 1.30 pm). Just round the corner is the opulent, baroque **St Anne's Church**.

At Plac Wszystkich Świętych, where the tram tracks cut across ul Grodzka, are two powerful 13th-century monastic churches, the **Dominican Church** on the east and the **Franciscan Church** on the west, the latter noted for the Art Nouveau stained-glass windows designed by Stanisław Wyspiański.

South on ul Grodzka is the early 17th-century Jesuit **Church of SS Peter & Paul**, the first baroque church built in Poland. The Romanesque **St Andrew's Church** (1086) alongside was the only building in Kraków which resisted the Tatar attack of 1241. The parallel ul Kanonicza (arguably Kraków's most picturesque street) boasts the **Wyspiański Museum**, dedicated to this renowned poet, painter, playwright and stained-glass designer, and the **Archdiocesan Museum** featuring religious art.

Wawel Just south of the Old Town is Wawel, a hill topped with a castle and a cathedral, both of which are the very symbols of Poland and the guardians of national history.

Wawel Cathedral (1364) was for four centuries the coronation and burial place of Polish royalty, and 100 kings and queens are interred in the crypt. There's a maze of sarcophagi, tombstones and altarpieces inside the church. The Sigismund Chapel (1539), on the south side with the golden dome, is considered to be the finest Renaissance construction in Poland. Climb the bell tower housing Poland's largest bell (11 tonnes) and visit the crypts. The cathedral is open daily except Sunday morning; the ticket office is diagonally opposite its entrance.

The 16th-century **Wawel Castle** (closed Monday) is behind the cathedral. The tickets you buy at the gate admit you to the different museum departments around the great Italian Renaissance courtyard. Wawel is famous for its 16th-century Flemish tapestry collection, but there is much else of interest including the 17th-century Turkish tents and the 13th-century Piast coronation sword, the 'Szczerbiec'.

Reserve at least three hours for the castle and the cathedral. In summer, it's best to arrive early, as later there may be long queues for tickets. Avoid weekends when Wawel is besieged by visitors. Guide services in English, French and German are available upon request (about US$30 per group for a three-hour tour). The guides' office (☎ 422 09 04) is in the alley going up the Wawel hill.

Kazimierz Today one of Kraków's inner suburbs within walking distance south-east of Wawel, Kazimierz was until the 1820s an independent town with its own municipal charter and laws. The town was founded in 1335 by King Casimir the Great (Kazimierz Wielki in Polish) and swiftly developed thanks to numerous privileges granted by the king, and by the Jews who came here in the late 15th century, after they had been expelled from Kraków. They settled in a relatively small prescribed area north-east of the Christian quarter, and the two sectors were separated by a wall.

The Jewish quarter became home to Jews fleeing persecutions from all corners of Europe, and it grew particularly quickly, gradually determining the character of the whole of Kazimierz. At the outbreak of WWII it was populated by about 70,000 Jews. During the war the Germans relocated Jews to a walled ghetto in Podgórze, just south of the Vistula River, and then exterminated them in the nearby Płaszów death camp. Spielberg's *Schindler's List* tells the story. The current Jewish population in the city is estimated at around 100.

Today's Kazimierz reveals its two historically determined sectors. Its western,

Catholic part is dotted with churches, of which the Gothic **St Catherine's Church** (1363) boasts a singularly imposing 17th-century gilded high altar, while the **Corpus Christi Church** (1340) is crammed with baroque fittings. The **Ethnographic Museum** in the old Kazimierz town hall (closed Tuesday) has a good collection of regional crafts and costumes.

The eastern part, the Jewish quarter, is punctuated with synagogues, which miraculously survived the war. Of these, the most important is the justifiably named late 15th-century Old Synagogue (the oldest Jewish religious building in Poland), today housing the **Jewish Museum** (closed Monday and Tuesday). A short walk north is the small 16th-century **Remu'h Synagogue** (the only one open for religious services), which can be visited on weekdays. Behind the synagogue is the **Remu'h Cemetery** boasting some extraordinary Renaissance gravestones. You can also visit the recently restored **Izaak's Synagogue** (closed Saturday).

Of the places portrayed in *Schindler's List*, Płaszów death camp no longer exists (only a memorial stands on the site), but the Schindler factory is still there, at ul Lipowa 4 in Podgórze, relatively unchanged since WWII. It's now the Krakowskie Zakłady Elektroniczne 'Telpod' (Telpod Electrical Works). You can look around the place, but ask permission first.

Wieliczka Wieliczka, 15km south-east of Kraków's centre, is famous for its **salt mine**, part of which can be visited. The mine is on the UNESCO World Cultural Heritage list.

You visit three upper levels of the mine, from 64 to 135m below the ground, walking through an eerie world of pits and chambers, all hewn out by hand from solid salt. The highlight is the richly ornamented Chapel of the Blessed Kinga, which is actually a fair-sized church measuring 54 by 17m and 12m high. Every single element here, from chandeliers to altarpieces, is of salt. It took over 30 years (1895-1927) to complete this underground temple, and about 20,000 tonnes of rock salt had to be removed. Occasional masses and concerts are held here.

The last stop is the museum installed in 16 worked-out chambers on the 3rd level, which

POLAND

KRAKÓW - OLD TOWN & WAWEL

0   50   100 m

POLAND

KRAKÓW - OLD TOWN & WAWEL

PLACES TO STAY
6 Hotel Warszawski
7 Hotel Polonia
9 Hotel Europejski
12 Hotel Francuski
18 Dom Gościnny UJ
21 Hotel Pokoje
     Gościnne SARPu
24 Hotel Elektor
26 Hotel Saski
35 Dom Turysty PTTK
57 Hotel Rezydent
67 Hotel Wawel Tourist

PLACES TO EAT
13 Restauracja Cyrano
     de Bergerac
14 Kuchnia Staropolska u
     Babci Maliny
17 Jadłodajnia Sąsiedzi
19 Jama Michalika
29 Sklep z Kawą Pożegnanie
     z Afryką
30 Restauracja u Szkota
31 Jadłodajnia u Pani Stasi
     & Pizzeria Cyklop
32 El Paso Tex Mex Saloon
44 Bistro Piccolo Chicken Grill
46 Kawiarnia u Zalipianek
49 Restauracja Sinus
50 Bar Bistro Różowy Słoń
51 Bar Mleczny Barcelona
52 Pizzeria Grace
53 Jadłodajnia Kuchcik

54 Salad Bar Chimera
55 Restauracja Léonard's
     & Café Malma
56 Ristorante da Pietro
58 Akropolis Grill
65 Bar Wegetariański Vega
66 Restauracja Korsykańska
     Paese
68 Taco Mexicano
69 Restauracja pod Aniołami
72 Restauracja pod Temidą
73 Bar Grodzki
75 Restauracja u Literatów
77 Restauracja Smak Ukraiński
78 Pizza Hut

OTHER
1 English Book Centre
2 Bus No 208 to Airport
    & Minibuses to Wieliczka
3 Central Bus Terminal
4 KART City Tourist Office
5 Biuro Turystyki i
    Zakwaterowania Waweltur
    (Private Rooms)
8 Post Office
10 Barbican
11 Florian Gate
15 French Institute
16 Czartoryski Museum
20 Matejko House
22 Jordan Tourist Office
23 Teatr im Słowackiego
     (Słowacki Theatre)

25 Szołajski Museum
27 Cultural Information Centre
28 Orbis & American Express
33 Hungarian Consulate
34 Russian Consulate
36 St Mary's Church
37 Statue of Adam Mickiewicz
38 Gallery of 19th-Century
     Polish Painting
39 Dexter Tourist Office
40 Cloth Hall
41 Town Hall Tower
42 Bank Pekao
43 Historical Museum of Kraków
45 Teatr Stary (Old Theatre)
47 St Anne's Church
48 Collegium Maius
59 German Consulate
60 US Consulate
61 French Consulate
62 Dominican Church
63 Main Post Office
64 Main Telephone Centre
70 Franciscan Church
71 Filharmonia
     (Philharmonic Hall)
74 Church of SS Peter & Paul
76 Wyspiański Museum
79 Archdiocesan Museum
80 Visa Extensions
81 Wawel Castle
82 Wawel Cathedral
83 Wawel Cathedral Museum
84 Dragon's Cave

holds an extensive collection of objects related to the mine. From here a lift takes you back up to the outer world.

The mine is open 16 April to 15 October daily from 8 am to 6 pm, and the rest of the year from 8 am to 4 pm. All visits are in guided groups and the tour takes about three hours. It's about a 3km walk (wear comfortable shoes) through the mine and, roughly midway, there's a café and toilets where you have a 10-minute break. The temperature in the mine is 14°C.

Most tours are in Polish (US$7), but in summer there are some scheduled tours in English (US$8) – check the current schedule beforehand with the tourist offices. You can also rent an English-language guide (US$45 per group plus the US$5 entry ticket per person). English-language brochures are available at the souvenir kiosk by the entrance to the mine.

Minibus is the easiest way of getting to Wieliczka from Kraków's centre – they depart every 10 minutes all day long from just north of the bus terminal, and let you off close to the mine (US$0.70). There are also trains from Kraków Główny station, but they run irregularly and will leave you farther away from the mine.

Organised Tours

Orbis (☎ 422 40 35), Rynek Główny 41, Jan-Pol (☎ 421 42 06) in the Dom Turysty PTTK, ul Westerplatte 15/16, and Intercrac (☎ 422 58 40) in the Dom Polonii, Rynek Główny 14, jointly operate a set program of tours in and outside Kraków. They include city centre sightseeing by coach (US$20), the traces of

POLAND

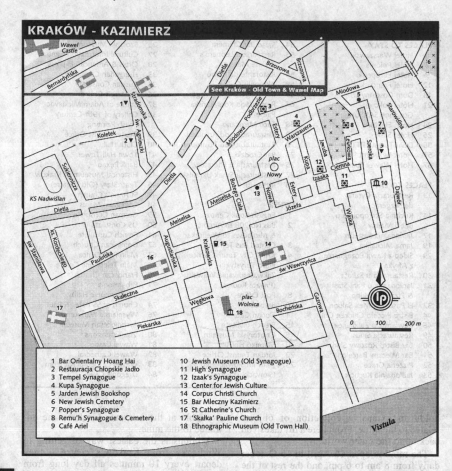

KRAKÓW - KAZIMIERZ

See Kraków - Old Town & Wawel Map

0   100   200 m

1 Bar Orientalny Hoang Hai
2 Restauracja Chłopskie Jadło
3 Tempel Synagogue
4 Kupa Synagogue
5 Jarden Jewish Bookshop
6 New Jewish Cemetery
7 Popper's Synagogue
8 Remu'h Synagogue & Cemetery
9 Café Ariel
10 Jewish Museum (Old Synagogue)
11 High Synagogue
12 Izaak's Synagogue
13 Center for Jewish Culture
14 Corpus Christi Church
15 Bar Mleczny Kazimierz
16 St Catherine's Church
17 'Skałka' Pauline Church
18 Ethnographic Museum (Old Town Hall)

Jewish culture (US$20), the Wieliczka salt mine (US$27) and the Auschwitz-Birkenau death camps (US$25). Students get 25% discount on the Wieliczka and Auschwitz tours. Contact any of the three operators for their free 'Cracow Tours' brochure with a full list and description of the tours.

The Jarden Jewish Bookshop (☎ 421 71 66), ul Szeroka 2, in Kazimierz's Jewish quarter, is the best known agency offering a choice of tours discovering Jewish heritage, including its showpiece – the Retracing Schindler's List tour. This two-hour tour is conducted daily in summer (at other times on request) in a minibus and costs US$14 per person. Alternatively, buy the *Retracing Schindler's List* brochure (US$2) in the bookshop, and set off on your own. Jordan also organises Auschwitz-Birkenau tours (US$27 per person). All the tours mentioned earlier in this section are conducted in English; some tours may go with French and German-speaking guides.

Some hotels, including Hotel Grand (☎ 421 72 55) and Hotel Polonia (☎ 422 12 33) arrange taxi trips on demand to

Auschwitz (US$75 per taxi for up to four people) and to other destinations.

Wędrowiec (☎ 421 89 08), in the kiosk at the car park on ul Powiśle at the foot of the Wawel, has guides in major western languages, who can show you around the city (US$40 per group for any time up to five hours) and the region (US$50).

Almatur (☎ 422 09 02), Rynek Główny 8, offers hiking, kayaking, horse riding, sailing etc holidays in summer.

Special Events

Kraków has one of the richest cycles of annual events in Poland. The major events include the Organ Music Days in April, the Student Song Festival in May, the Polish and International Festivals of Short Films in May/June, the Jewish Culture Festival in June, the International Festival of Street Theatre in July, Music in Old Kraków in August, the All Saints' Day Jazz Festival in October/November and the exhibition of nativity scenes in December. Contact the Cultural Information Centre for full program details.

On Maundy Thursday and Good Friday during Easter week there's the famous Passion Play at nearby Kalwaria Zebrzydowska; on Assumption Day (15 August) a solemn procession in folk costumes is held in the same village. Seven days after Corpus Christi (a Thursday in May or June), a colourful pageant headed by the Lajkonik, a legendary figure disguised as a Tatar riding a hobbyhorse, parades Kraków streets.

In 2000 Kraków will be European City of Culture (along with Avignon, Bergen, Bologne, Brussels, Helsinki, Prague, Reykjavik and Santiago de Compostela) – expect plenty of events. 'Spirituality' is the main theme chosen by Kraków for its Festival 2000.

Places to Stay

Kraków is Poland's premier tourist destination, so finding a bed in summer can be tricky and may involve some legwork. Book in advance or at least try to arrive reasonably early to allow time for possible hotel hunting. All three tourist offices are likely to help you find somewhere to stay.

Camping There are four camping grounds in the city. The *Camping Nr 46 Smok* (☎ 421

02 55), ul Kamedulska 18, 4km west of the centre, is Kraków's only camping ground operating year-round. It's small, quiet and pleasantly located. From Kraków Główny train station, take tram No 2 to the end of the line in Zwierzyniec and change for any westbound bus except No 100.

The *Camping Clepardia* (☎ 415 16 74), ul Mackiewicza, is 4km north of the centre. It's open from mid-June to early September and has no cabins. Take bus No 115 from the train station.

The *Camping Nr 171 Krakowianka* (☎ 266 41 91), ul Żywiecka Boczna 4, on the road to Zakopane 6km south of the centre, is open May to September. It's good and clean and the only one which has cabins. You can get there from Kraków Główny train station by tram No 19 or bus No 119.

The *Camping Nr 45 Krak* (☎ 637 21 22) is next to the Motel Krak, ul Radzikowskiego 99, on the Katowice road about 5km northwest of the centre. It's the city's largest, best equipped and most expensive camping ground and is open May to September. The traffic noise can be considerable. Bus No 238 from Kraków Główny train station goes there.

Youth Hostels Kraków has two all-year youth hostels. The closest to the city is the *youth hostel* (☎ 633 88 22; ☎/fax 633 89 20), ul Oleandry 4, 2km west of the train station (take tram No 15 and get off just past Hotel Cracovia). With its 350 beds (mostly in large dorms), this is the largest youth hostel in the country but is nonetheless often full.

The *youth hostel* (☎ 422 19 51), ul Kościuszki 88, is 1km farther south-west. Installed in a part of a former convent overlooking the Vistula, it's a nicer place to stay, but it has only 110 beds and also fills up quickly. From the train station, take tram No 2 to the end of the line.

There's also a large July-August *youth hostel* (☎ 637 24 41), ul Szablowskiego 1, 4km north-west of the Old Town. Tram No 4 from the station will let you off nearby. It's the least convenient hostel, but possibly least invaded by travellers.

Student Hostels There are several student hostels operating each summer (July to mid-September, approximately), and the picture

POLAND

changes from year to year. Tourist offices
tend to keep track of them, so ask which are
currently open. They are most likely to
include some of the following: the closest to
the centre, *Dom Studencki Żaczek* (☎ 633 54
77), Al 3 Maja 5; the *Letni Hotel AWF*
(☎ 648 02 07), Al Jana Pawła II 82, 4km east
of the train station, midway to Nowa Huta;
and the *Dom Studenta Piast* (☎ 637 49 33),
ul Piastowska 47, 3km west of the station.
Each will cost around US$15/20 a single/
double and each has its own cafeteria. The
Dom Studencki Żaczek may operate some
rooms year-round. Jagiellonian University
may open the dorm-type, cheaper *Schronisko
Turystyczne Nawojka* (☎ 633 52 05), ul Rey-
monta 11.

Other Hostels The big, crowded *Dom
Turysty PTTK* (☎ 422 95 66), ul Westerplatte 15/16, is possibly the cheapest place to stay
in the city centre. Just 500m south of the train
station, it may be a wise first option, especially if you're arriving late or tired. Singles/
doubles/triples are overpriced at US$36/50/65
without bath, US$48/60/85 with bath (all in-
cluding breakfast), but the hostel has a
number of eight-bed dorms which go for
US$9 per person (without breakfast). There's
a cheap cafeteria on the premises (open from
7 am to 10 pm) which is actually the only
place around for an early budget breakfast.
The hotel also has a left-luggage room – a
useful facility if you don't get a bed here and
have to look for one elsewhere.

The all-year *Schronisko Turystyczne
Ekspres* (☎ 633 88 62), ul Wrocławska 91,
2km north-west of the centre, is a cross
between a private guesthouse and a youth
hostel. Unlike youth hostels, it doesn't close
during the day and has no curfew. It has 80
beds distributed in doubles (US$7 per person)
and six-bed dorms (US$6). Advance reserva-
tion is essential. Bus No 130 from the train
station goes there; get off at the fifth stop.

There are a dozen other budget hostels,
mostly former workers' dorms, located in the
outer suburbs, including Nowa Huta. By and
large they are not particularly inspiring, but
can be a shelter if nothing more central or attractive is available. Try, for example, *Hotel
Czyżyny* (☎ 644 98 24), ul Centralna 32
(US$20/35 a double/quad), or the slightly

cheaper *Schronisko Turystyczne Wagabunda*
(☎ 643 02 22), Osiedle Złotej Jesieni 15c. The
tourist offices know more places like these.

Private Rooms Biuro Turystyki i Zakwaterowania Waweltur (☎ 422 19 21 or 422 16
40), ul Pawia 8, next door to the municipal
tourist office, arranges accommodation in
private rooms at around US$18/28 a single/
double. Rooms are scattered around the city
so check the location carefully before deciding.

You may also be offered a private room by
someone on the street outside. The tourist
offices don't recommend these services, but if
you decide to use them, ask to see the location
on the map before agreeing to go, and pay only
after you have seen the room and accepted it.

Hotels There are three affordable hotels by
the train station. *Hotel Warszawski* (☎ 422
06 22), ul Pawia 6, costs about US$36/50/65
a single/double/triple without bath, US$50/
60/75 with bath. The more appealing *Hotel
Polonia* (☎ 422 12 33), ul Basztowa 25, just
around the corner from the Warszawski, is
marginally more expensive. *Hotel Europejski* (☎ 423 25 10), ul Lubicz 5, has been
revamped and is now the nicest of the three.
It costs much the same as Hotel Polonia. All
three are often full and fairly noisy; choose a
room at the back.

Hotel Saski (☎ 421 42 22) is ideally
located in a historic townhouse at ul Sławkowska 3 just off Rynek Główny. It costs
US$35/45/55 for singles/doubles/triples
without bath, US$55/75/85 with bath – good
value so close to the main square. Note the
century-old lift, still in working order.

Hotel Pokoje Gościnne SARPu (☎ 429 17
78), ul Floriańska 39, is also a good place to
stay, if you are lucky enough to get a room
there. This former architects' dormitory
offers six double rooms only, for US$50
each. Two adjacent rooms share one bath,
stove and fridge. The place is on the top, 4th
floor of an old building.

A few doors north is another attractive
(and often full) option, the *Dom Gościnny
UJ* (Jagiellonian University Guest House;
☎421 12 25), ul Floriańska 49. This small
hotel has just five singles (US$55) and seven
doubles (US$85). Rooms are spacious, quiet
and clean, and have large beds, desk, tele-

phone and private bath. Breakfast is included in the price.

It's easier to find a room in the *Hotel Wawel Tourist* (☎ 422 67 65), ul Poselska 22, which has doubles without/with bath for US$44/60.

If money is not a problem, you have quite a choice of upmarket hotels in the Old Town, including *Hotel Rezydent* (☎ 429 54 95), ul Grodzka 9, *Hotel Elektor* (☎ 421 80 25), ul Szpitalna 28 and *Hotel Francuski* (☎ 422 51 22), ul Pijarska 13.

Places to Eat

By Polish standards, Kraków is a food paradise – the Old Town is tightly packed with gastronomic venues, all the way from rock bottom to topnotch. Privatisation has eliminated most of the old dirt-cheap proletarian milk bars, but many excellent little places have popped up in their place offering superior fare at very affordable prices. Pushcart vendors sell obwarzanki, ring-shaped pretzels powdered with poppy seeds, a local speciality.

One of the best budget places for a hearty meal is the self-service *Kuchnia Staropolska u Babci Maliny* in the basement of the Polska Akademia Umiejętności, ul Sławkowska 17, which offers huge plates of well prepared Polish food.

Other inexpensive eateries worth a particular mention include: the legendary *Jadłodajnia u Pani Stasi*, ul Mikołajska 16, just off Mały Rynek; the *Jadłodajnia Kuchcik*, ul Jagiellońska 12; the *Bar Grodzki*, ul Grodzka 47; the *Restauracja pod Temidą* on ul Grodzka; and the *Jadłodajnia Sąsiedzi*, ul Szpitalna 40. Most of these places are open weekdays from 10 or 11 am to 6 or 7 pm, but close earlier on weekends (some don't open at all on Sunday).

Salad Bar Chimera, ul Św Anny 3, is a cosy place in an attractive cellar consisting of several vaults, each with its own atmosphere. In summer, a garden is open at the back of the building. There's an amazing array of fresh, good cheap salads.

Bar Bistro Różowy Słoń (Pink Elephant), ul Straszewskiego 24, is another recommended place. It doesn't offer such a variety of salads, but has spaghetti, crêpes, pierogi, barszcz etc. Next door is one of the last surviving milk bars, the *Bar Mleczny Barcelona*, which is possibly the cheapest place to eat in the centre.

A few steps north of the Pink Elephant, ul Straszewskiego 28, is the *Restauracja Sinus* – a restaurant which has gone through the communist-to-capitalist change untouched. It serves tasty Polish food at low prices in its drab surroundings. In the same area, the *Kawiarnia u Zalipianek*, ul Szewska 24, has a modest choice of popular dishes, including pierogi, in its folksy interior. In summer you can eat on its open terrace facing the Planty.

Bar Wegetariański Vega, ul Św Gertrudy 7, is a clean cheap veggie place which serves tasty pierogi, crêpes, salads etc. The *Bistro Piccolo Chicken Grill*, ul Szczepańska 4, is a popular self-service place offering reasonably cheap food, including roasted chicken.

Restauracja u Literatów, ul Kanonicza 7, serves inexpensive meals and has a pleasant garden with tables at the back of the building, where you can feel as if you've escaped from the city rush. A few doors south, at ul Kanonicza 15, is the Ukrainian centre which has the inexpensive basement *Restauracja Smak Ukraiński*.

Pizza Hut, Plac Św Marii Magdaleny, has attractive vaulted cellars. Among other pizza houses, arguably the best are the *Pizzeria Cyklop*, ul Mikołajska 16, and *Pizzeria Grace* at two central locations, ul Św Anny 7 and ul Św Jana 1.

Taco Mexicano, ul Poselska 20, brings a Mexican breeze to town. *El Paso Tex Mex Saloon* on ul Św Krzyża does much the same at marginally higher prices in a more elegant interior.

Akropolis Grill, ul Grodzka 9, is a Greek eatery serving gyros, souvlaki, moussaka, beef stew, Greek bread and the like at affordable prices. The *Restauracja Korsykańska Paese*, ul Poselska 24, offers Corsican and some mainland French cuisine. The food is good, prices acceptable and the interior bright and cheerful.

Restauracja Chłopskie Jadło, ul Agnieszki 1, a short walk south of Wawel, is arranged as an old country inn and serves typical traditional Polish food at good prices; it's highly recommended. A few steps from there, at ul Stradomska 13, is the tiny *Bar Orientalny*

Hoang Hai which does hearty Chinese-Vietnamese food at low prices.

For Jewish food, go to the *Café Ariel*, ul Szeroka 17 or 18, in Kazimierz (two independent businesses bearing the same name). Both serve traditional Jewish dishes, cakes and desserts, and a hearty kosher beer. In the evening, both cafés have live performances of Jewish, Gypsy and Russian folk songs (for a US$5 admission fee to either).

Among upmarket restaurants, the *Restauracja pod Aniołami*, ul Grodzka 35, offers fine Polish food in some of the most amazing surroundings. Another marvellous setting is the *Restauracja Cyrano de Bergerac*, ul Sławkowska 26 (French cuisine). Other well appointed eateries include *Restauracja u Szkota*, ul Mikołajska 4 (Polish and Scottish food); *Ristorante da Pietro*, Rynek Główny 17 (Italian food); and *Restauracja Léonard's*, Rynek Główny 25 (Polish and French cuisine). These all enjoy a fabulous setting in vaulted cellars.

Cafés The most famous Kraków café is the legendary *Jama Michalika*, ul Floriańska 45, established in 1895. Decorated with works of art of the time, the place gives the impression of a small fin-de-siecle museum. It's nonsmoking – one of the few such cafés in the city.

For the best coffee in town, go to *Sklep z Kawą Pożegnanie z Afryką* (Coffee Shop Farewell to Africa), ul Św Tomasza 21. It is a shop-cum-café which sells about 70 kinds of coffee, half of which can be drunk inside at the tables. Coffee is prepared in sophisticated coffee makers and spring water is used, not tap water which is pretty bad in Kraków. This is also a nonsmoking venue.

Smokers can try *Café Larousse* just a block away at ul Św Tomasza 22. Papered in leaves from a Larousse dictionary (hence its name), this tiny place of only four tables (predictably often full) serves a choice of exotic coffees.

For a cup of good tea, choose between *Herbaciarnia Słodka Dziurka*, ul Mikołajska 5, and *Herbaciarnia Gołębnik*, ul Gołębia 5.

Entertainment

The Cultural Information Centre provides detailed information about what's on. It publishes a comprehensive monthly brochure, *Karnet*, listing cultural events and sells tickets for some of them.

Theatre Best known internationally was the avant-garde Cricot 2, but the theatre was dissolved after its creator and director, Tadeusz Kantor, died in 1990. Theatre buffs may be interested in visiting *Cricoteka*, ul Kanonicza 5, the centre that has documented his work.

Today the best known venue is *Teatr Stary* (Old Theatre), ul Jagiellońska 1, which has attracted the cream of the city's actors. The *Teatr im Słowackiego* (Słowacki Theatre), Plac Św Ducha 1, (built in 1893) focuses on Polish classics and large-scale productions. Opera and ballet performances are also staged here. It was totally renovated in 1991 and its interior is spectacular.

Classical Music *Filharmonia*, ul Zwierzyniecka 1, is home to one of the best orchestras in the country. Concerts are normally held on Friday and Saturday and irregularly on other days.

Jazz The main jazz outlets include *Jazz Club u Muniaka*, ul Floriańska 3 (Thursday to Saturday), *Jazz Klub pod Jaszczurami*, Rynek Główny 8 (mainly Tuesday), *Harris Piano Jazz Bar*, Rynek Główny 28 (Thursday to Saturday) and *Klub u Luisa*, Rynek Główny 13 (weekends). Other places to check include *Piwnica pod Baranami*, Rynek Główny 27, the *Rotunda Student Club*, ul Oleandry 1 and *Jazz Club Kornet*, Al Krasińskiego 19.

Discos Popular haunts include *Equinox*, ul Sławkowska 13/15, *Maxime*, ul Floriańska 32, *Klub pod Papugami*, ul Szpitalna 1 and *Klub Pasja*, ul Szewska 5. All operate nightly, usually except Monday. Most student clubs run discos on Friday and Saturday nights. Try *Klub Rotunda*, ul Oleandry 1, or *Klub pod Przewiązką*, ul Bydgoska 19b.

Bars & Pubs There are more than 50 of these in the Old Town alone. Some offer snacks but most serve just drinks, mainly beer. Many are in vaulted cellars, often very attractive. All are smoking venues, so in some places those sensitive to cigarette smoke might find an oxygen mask essential.

Some pubs are open till midnight, but many don't close until the wee hours of the morning.

To name a few, just to help you start your exploration: *Black Gallery*, ul Mikołajska 24, *Klub Kulturalny*, ul Szewska 25, *Pub pod Papugami*, ul Św Jana 18, *Free Pub*, ul Sławkowska 4, *Pub u Kacpra*, ul Sławkowska 2, *Italica* in the Italian Institute, ul Grodzka 49, *Pub Prohibicja*, ul Grodzka 51 and *Pub pod Jemiołą*, ul Floriańska 20.

Hotel Elektor boasts exquisite medieval cellars, which now house a classy wine bar. Its selection of French and Rhine wines is among the best in town, though it's probably not a proposition for backpackers.

Getting There & Away

Air The airport in Babice, 18km west of the city, is accessible by bus No 208 from just north of the bus terminal and by the more frequent and faster fast bus B from the bus stop across the street from Hotel Europejski. The LOT office, ul Basztowa 15, on the northern edge of the Old Town, deals with tickets and reservations.

Within Poland, the only flights are to Warsaw, but you can get there much more cheaply, centre-to-centre, by train in 2½ hours. LOT has direct flights between Kraków and Frankfurt/Main, London, Paris, Rome, Vienna and Zurich.

Train The central train station, Kraków Główny, on the north-eastern outskirts of the Old Town, handles all international and most domestic rail traffic.

There are two morning, two afternoon and one evening InterCity trains to Warsaw (297km) and the trip takes just two hours and 35 minutes. There are also several express and fast trains to Warsaw which take a bit longer to get there.

To Częstochowa (132km) there are two morning fast trains as well as several evening trains, but the latter are inconvenient as you'll arrive pretty late. Trains to Katowice (78km) run frequently, and there's also good transport farther on to Wrocław (268km), with perhaps a dozen departures a day. Several trains run daily to Zakopane (147km) but it's much faster to go there by bus. A dozen trains travel east to Rzeszów (158km).

To Oświęcim (65km), there are a couple of trains early in the morning and then nothing till the afternoon. There are more trains to Oświęcim from Kraków Płaszów station, though they don't depart regularly either.

Internationally, there are one or two direct trains daily to Berlin, Bratislava, Bucharest, Budapest, Dresden, Frankfurt/Main, Kiev, Leipzig, Odessa, Prague and Vienna.

Tickets and couchettes can be booked directly from Kraków Główny station or from the Orbis office, Rynek Główny 41.

Bus The central bus terminal is next to Kraków Główny train station. Travel by bus is particularly advisable to Zakopane (104km) as it's considerably shorter and faster than by train. Fast PKS buses go there every hour (US$4, 2½ hours). A private company runs nine buses a day to Zakopane, which are faster and cheaper (US$3); tickets are available from Waweltour, ul Pawia 8.

There are two convenient morning departures to Częstochowa (119km), nine buses a day to Oświęcim (64km), one to Lublin (269km), two to Zamość (318km) and eight to Cieszyn (Czech border, 121km).

There are a number of international bus routes originating in Kraków, going to Amsterdam, Budapest, London, Paris, Vienna and a variety of destinations in Germany. Information and tickets are available from a number of travel agencies throughout the town, some of which are close to the bus terminal.

OŚWIĘCIM
☎ 033

Oświęcim is a medium-sized industrial town about 60km west of Kraków. The Polish name may be unfamiliar to outsiders, but the German one – Auschwitz – is not: the largest Nazi concentration camp was here. This is the scene of the largest experiment in genocide in the history of humankind and the world's largest cemetery. It is possibly the most moving sight in Poland.

The Auschwitz camp was established in April 1940 in the prewar Polish army barracks on the outskirts of Oświęcim. It was originally destined to hold Polish political prisoners but it eventually came to be a gigantic centre for the extermination of European Jews. For this purpose, the much

POLAND

larger Birkenau (Brzezinka) camp, also referred to as Auschwitz II, was built in 1941-42, 2km west of Auschwitz, and followed by another one in Monowitz (Monowice), several kilometres to the west of the town. About 40 smaller camps, branches of Auschwitz, were subsequently established all over the region. This death factory eliminated some 1.5 to two million people of 27 nationalities, about 85% to 90% of whom were Jews. The name Auschwitz is commonly used for the whole Auschwitz-Birkenau complex, both of which are open to the public.

Auschwitz

Auschwitz was only partially destroyed by the fleeing Nazis, and many of the original buildings stand to this day as a bleak document of the camp's history. A dozen of the 30 surviving prison blocks today house the museum; some blocks stage general exhibitions, while others are dedicated to victims from particular countries which lost citizens at Auschwitz.

During the communist era, the museum was conceived as an anti-fascist exhibition and the fact that most of the victims were Jewish was played down. Undue prominence was given to the 75,000 Polish Catholics killed here, at the expense of the Jewish dead. This approach has changed: block No 27, dedicated to the 'suffering and struggle of the Jews', now presents Auschwitz more correctly as the place of martyrdom of European Jewry.

From the visitors centre in the entrance building, you enter the barbed-wire encampment through the gate with the cynical inscription 'Arbeit Macht Frei' (Work Makes Free), then visit exhibitions in the prison blocks and finally see the gas chamber and crematorium. You don't need much imagination to take in what happened here.

A 15-minute documentary about the liberation of the camp by Soviet troops on 27 January 1945 is screened in the cinema in the visitors' centre every half-hour, and a few times a day it is also shown with a foreign-language soundtrack (English, French, German, Italian or Russian). Before you set off for the camp check with the information desk at the visitors' centre what time your language version is screened – although the film's message is clear in any language.

The museum opens daily at 8 am and closes at 7 pm in June, July and August; at 6 pm in May and September; at 5 pm in March and November; at 4 pm in April and October; and at 3 pm in December, January and February. Admission is free; there's a US$0.50 fee to enter the cinema. Photos, film and video are permitted free of charge throughout the camp. Anyone under 13 is advised by the museum management not to visit the camp, but the final decision is left up to the accompanying adults. There's a cheap self-service Bar Smak by the entrance, facing the car park. There's also a kantor, a left-luggage room and several bookshops stocked with publications about the place.

Get a copy of a small brochure (available in a number of languages, including Polish, English, French and German) which is quite enough to get you round the grounds. Tours in English and German are organised daily at 11.30 am (US$4 per person). Otherwise you can hire a foreign-language guide for your party at the information desk; they cost US$40 for Auschwitz-Birkenau (three hours).

From 15 April to late October, there is a special bus from Auschwitz to Birkenau (US$0.40). It departs hourly from 10.30 am to 4.30 pm from just outside the entrance to the visitors' centre, opposite Bar Smak. Alternatively, you can walk (2km) or take a taxi.

Birkenau

It was actually at Birkenau, not Auschwitz, that the extermination of large numbers of Jews took place. Vast (175 hectares), purpose-built and 'efficient', the camp had over 300 prison barracks and four huge gas chambers complete with crematoria. Each gas chamber accommodated 2000 people and there were electric lifts to raise the bodies to the ovens. The camp could hold 200,000 inmates at a time.

Though much was destroyed by the retreating Nazis, the size of the place, fenced off with long lines of barbed wire and watchtowers stretching almost as far as the eye can see, will give you some idea of the scale of the crime. Don't miss going to the top of the entrance gate for the view. Some of the surviving barracks are open to visitors. At the back of the complex is the monument to the dead, flanked on each side by the sinister remains of gas chambers.

In some ways, Birkenau is an even more shocking sight than Auschwitz. It can be visited in the same opening hours as Auschwitz and entry is free. Make sure to leave enough time (at least an hour) to walk around the camp – it is really vast.

There are no buses from Birkenau to the train station (2km); walk or go by taxi. Alternatively, take the same special bus back to Auschwitz (departing 11 am to 5 pm at full hours) and change there for one of the frequent buses to the station.

Places to Stay & Eat

For most visitors, Auschwitz-Birkenau camp is a day trip, in most cases from Kraków, and *Bar Smak*, mentioned in the Auschwitz section earlier, is all you need to keep you going. However, if you want to linger longer, Oświęcim has a choice of places to stay and eat.

The Catholic Church-built *Centrum Dialogu i Modlitwy* (☎ 43 10 00), ul Św Maksymiliana Kolbe 1, 700m south-west of the Auschwitz camp, provides comfortable and quiet accommodation in rooms of two, three, four, five, six and 10 beds (most with private bath) and a restaurant. Bed and breakfast costs US$20 (US$15 for students). You can also camp here (US$6 per person).

Another good place is *Międzynarodowy Dom Spotkań Młodzieży* (International Meeting House for the Youth; ☎43 21 07), ul Legionów 11, 1km east of the train station. Built in 1986 by the Germans, the place essentially provides lodging for groups coming for longer stays, but anyone can be accommodated if there are vacancies. Singles/doubles/quads with bath cost US$18/25/34; students pay US$12/20/27, respectively. Inexpensive meals are served in the dining room on the premises. Camping is also possible here.

Hotel Glob (☎ 43 06 32), ul Powstańców Śląskich 16, outside the train station, has decent (if noisy) singles/doubles with bath for US$25/36 and its own restaurant.

Getting There & Away

For most tourists, the jumping-off point for Oświęcim is Kraków, from where many tours

to the camp are organised. Some of them may be good value, costing not much more than what you'd pay for transport coming on your own by train or bus.

There are a few early morning trains from Kraków Główny station via Trzebinia (65km) but then nothing till around 3 pm. More trains depart from Kraków Płaszów station via Skawina (also 65km), though they are not very regular either. Check the schedule the day before to plan properly. Frequent urban buses (Nos 24 to 29) run from Oświęcim train station to Auschwitz camp (1.7km), but none to Birkenau camp (2km).

There are about 10 buses per day from Kraków to Oświęcim (64km); they pass by Oświęcim train station and Auschwitz museum before reaching the terminal on the far eastern outskirts of the town. Don't miss the stop, otherwise you'll have to backtrack 4km to the museum by the infrequent local bus No 2 or 3.

To get back to Kraków, check the schedule of trains at the Oświęcim train station and that of buses at the bus stop across the street from the station, and take whichever passes through first. Better still, take notes of these schedules upon arrival in town and plan your visit accordingly.

If Katowice is your starting point for Oświęcim, there are frequent trains between the two (33km).

CZĘSTOCHOWA
☎ 034

Częstochowa, north of Katowice, is the spiritual heart of Poland and the country's national shrine. It owes its fame to the miraculous icon of the Black Madonna, kept in Jasna Góra (Bright Mountain) Monastery, which has been pulling in pilgrims from all corners of the country and beyond for centuries. Today, Częstochowa attracts some of the largest pilgrimages in the world.

The monastery was founded in 1382 by the Paulites of Hungary, and the Black Madonna was brought soon after. The holy icon was damaged in 1430 by the Hussites, who slashed the face of the Madonna and broke the wooden panel. The picture was restored and repainted, but the scars on the face of the Virgin Mary were left as a reminder of the sacrilege.

POLAND

Early in the 17th century the monastery was fortified, and it was one of the few places in the country which withstood the Swedish sieges of the 1650s, is miracle naturally being attributed to the Black Madonna and contributing to still larger floods of pilgrims. In 1717 the Black Madonna was crowned Queen of Poland.

After WWII, in an attempt to overshadow its religious status, the communists built Częstochowa into a major industrial centre. Today it's a city of 260,000 people which has a large steelworks and a number of other factories complete with a forest of smoky chimneys. Amid them, however, the tower of the Paulite monastery still proudly overlooks the city, showing pilgrims the way to the end of their journey.

Orientation

The main thoroughfare in the city centre is Al Najświętszej Marii Panny (referred to in addresses as Al NMP), a wide, tree-lined avenue with Jasna Góra Monastery at its western end and St Sigismund's Church at the eastern end. Both the train and bus stations are just south of the eastern part of Al NMP. It's about a 20-minute walk from either of the stations to the monastery.

Information

Tourist Office The Centrum Informacji Turystycznej (☎ 24 13 60; ☎/fax 24 34 12), Al NMP 65, is open weekdays from 9 am to 6 pm, Saturday from 10 am to 6 pm, Sunday (15 April to 15 October) from 10 am to 6 pm. It's well stocked with maps from all over the country.

Money You'll find several kantors and ATMs on Al NMP. Bank Pekao, ul Kopernika 19, changes travellers cheques and gives cash advances on Visa and MasterCard.

Cybercafés The Centrum Internetowe (☎ 66 48 13) is on the top floor of the Dom Handlowy Seka, Al NMP 12d (open daily till 10 pm).

Things to See

A vibrant symbol of Catholicism in a secular sea, **Jasna Góra Monastery** retains the ap-

pearance of a fortress. Inside the compound are a number of buildings including a church, a chapel and the monastery. The large baroque church you enter first is beautifully decorated, but the image of the Black Madonna is on the high altar of the adjacent chapel. Upstairs in the monastery is the Knights' Hall (Sala Rycerska) where you can examine a copy of the icon up close.

There are also three museums to visit within the defensive walls (all open daily): the Arsenal with a variety of old weapons; the 600th Anniversary Museum (Muzeum Sześćsetlecia) containing Lech Wałęsa's 1983 Nobel Peace Prize; and the Treasury (Skarbiec) featuring votive offerings presented by the faithful. You can also climb the monastery tower (the tallest church tower in Poland at 106m), open daily April to November.

On weekends and holidays there are long lines to enter all three museums, and the crowds in the chapel may be so thick you're almost unable to enter, much less get near the icon.

The **City Museum** (closed Monday) in the old town hall (1828) on Plac Biegańskiego has an ethnographic collection and modern Polish paintings, plus some temporary exhibitions.

Special Events

The major Marian feasts at Jasna Góra are 3 May, 16 July, 15 August, 26 August, 8 September, 12 September and 8 December, and on these days the monastery is packed with pilgrims. Particularly celebrated is the Assumption (15 August) on which day pilgrims come on foot to Częstochowa from all over Poland. Up to half a million of the faithful can flock to Jasna Góra for this feast.

Places to Stay

The all-year *Camping Nr 76 Oleńka* (☎ 24 74 95), ul Oleńki 10/30 near the monastery, is good and has chalets. Rooms are US$5/10 a single/double without bath, US$23/30/37 for three/four/five people with bath, or you can pitch your tent for US$2 per person. There's an inexpensive snack bar on the grounds.

The *youth hostel* (☎ 24 31 21), ul Jasnogórska 84/90, is also close to the monastery,

CZĘSTOCHOWA

PLACES TO STAY
1 Hotel Sekwana
2 Dom Pielgrzyma
3 Camping Nr 76
Oleńka
4 Hale Noclegowe
19 Hotel Ha-Ga
20 Hotel Polonia
26 Diecezjalny Dom
Rekolekcyjny

PLACES TO EAT
5 Pizzeria Paradiso
8 Vecchia Milano
9 Café Bar Laguna
13 Alamo Restaurant
14 Pizzeria La Bussola
24 Bar Viking
25 Restauracja Viking

OTHER
7 Tourist Office
10 Theatre

11 City Museum
12 Orbis
15 Filharmonia
(Philharmonic Hall)
16 Dom Handlowy Seka
(Centrum Internetowe)
17 St Sigismund's Church
18 Cathedral
21 Main Post Office
22 Bus Terminal
23 Bank Pekao
27 St Barbara's Church

but it's open only in July and August and has modest facilities.

Some of the cheapest accommodation is provided by the Church-run *Hale Noclegowe* (☎ 65 66 88, ext 224), ul Klasztorna 1, just next to the monastery. You pay US$3.50 per head in a four to nine-bed dorm with shared facilities and cold water only, and must be inside before the 10 pm curfew.

The Church's better lodging facility is *Dom Pielgrzyma*, or Pilgrim's Home (☎ 24 70 11), right behind the monastery. This large hostel has singles/doubles/triples with bath

for US$15/18/25, or you can pay US$5 for a bed in a quad without bath. The door closes at 10 pm. There's a cheap cafeteria on the premises. The *Diecezjalny Dom Rekolekcyjny* (☎ 24 11 77), ul Św Barbary 43, a 10-minute walk south of the monastery, offers similar conditions and also has a curfew.

The best place to stay in the monastery's area is the small *Hotel Sekwana* (☎ 24 89 54), ul Wieluńska 24, which costs US$40/60 a single/double with bath. It has a pleasant and reasonably priced French restaurant – good value.

POLAND

There are a few hotels close to the train station, including the basic *Hotel Ha-Ga* (☎ 24 61 73), ul Katedralna 9. It has singles/doubles/triples/quads with shared facilities for US$13/15/18/20 and rooms with bath attached for US$18/22/25/28. The best of the lot is *Hotel Polonia* (also called Centralny; ☎ 24 23 88), ul Piłsudskiego 9, opposite the station. It has been renovated and now costs US$33/40/50/60 with bath and breakfast.

Places to Eat

In the monastery area, apart from the cafeteria of the *Dom Pielgrzyma* and the *Bar Oleńka* at the camping ground (both mentioned in Places to Stay), there's a line of fast-food outlets on ul 7 Kamienic, including the pleasant *Pizzeria Paradiso*.

There are also quite a number of inexpensive eateries along Al NMP, including the *Café Bar Laguna*, Al NMP 57, *Alamo Restaurant*, Al NMP 16, and the *Pizzeria La Bussola* next door. Some of the best ice cream and cappuccinos in town can be found at the *Vecchia Milano*, Al NMP 59.

The upmarket *Restauracja Viking*, ul Nowowiejskiego 10, is one of the best places to eat in the centre. It runs the cheap *Bar Viking* just round the corner, which is good and has a few tables on the terrace.

Getting There & Away

The new, purpose-built train station on ul Piłsudskiego handles half a dozen fast trains to Warsaw (235km) and about the same number to Kraków (132km). Trains run every hour or so to Katowice (86km), from where there are connections to Kraków and Wrocław.

The bus terminal is close to the central train station. Buses departing from here include three daily to Kraków (114km), three to Wrocław (176km) and one to Zakopane (222km).

ZAKOPANE & THE TATRAS
☎ 018

The Tatras, 100km south of Kraków, are the highest range of the Carpathian Mountains and the only alpine type, with towering peaks and steep rocky sides dropping hundreds of metres to glacial lakes. There are no glaciers in the Tatras, but patches of snow remain all year. Winters are long, summers short and the weather erratic.

The whole range, roughly 60km long and about 15km wide, stretches across the Polish-Slovakian border. A quarter of it is Polish territory and was declared the Tatra National Park, encompassing about 212 sq km. The Polish Tatras boast over a score of peaks exceeding 2000m, the highest of which is Mt Rysy (2499m).

Set at the northern foot of the Tatras, Zakopane (population 30,000) is the most famous mountain resort in Poland and the winter sports capital. The town attracts a couple of million tourists a year, with peaks in summer and winter. Though Zakopane is essentially a base for either skiing or hiking in the Tatras, the town itself is enjoyable enough to hang around for a while, and it has lots of tourist facilities.

Since the late 19th century, Zakopane has become popular with artists, many of whom came to settle and work here. The best known of these are the composer Karol Szymanowski and the writer and painter Witkacy. The father of the latter, Stanisław Witkiewicz (1851-1915), was inspired by the traditional local architecture and created the so-called Zakopane style; some of the buildings he designed stand to this day.

Orientation

Zakopane, nestling below Mt Giewont at an altitude of 800 to 1000m, will be your base. The bus and train stations are adjacent in the north-east part of town. It's a 10-minute walk down ul Kościuszki to the town's heart, the pedestrian mall of Krupówki, lined with restaurants, cafés, boutiques and souvenir shops. It's always jammed with Polish tourists parading around in trendy ski or hiking gear.

The funicular to Mt Gubałówka is just off the northern end of Krupówki. The cable car to Mt Kasprowy Wierch is at Kuźnice, 3km to the south.

Information

Tourist Office The helpful Centrum Informacji Turystycznej (☎ 201 22 11), ul Kościuszki 17, is open daily from 7 am to 9 pm.

ZAKOPANE

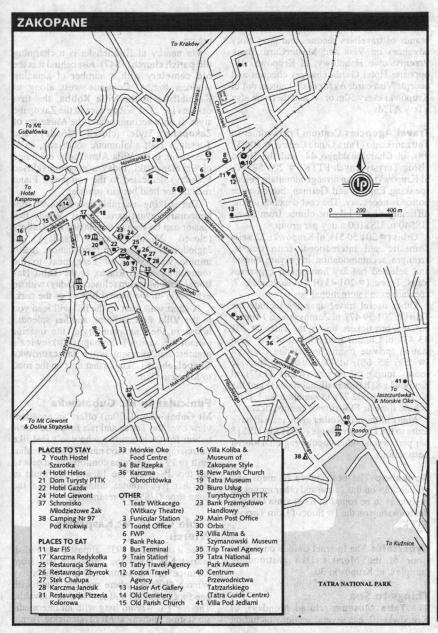

To Kraków

To Mt Gubałówka

To Mt Kasprowy

To Mt Giewont & Dolina Strążyska

0   200   400 m

To Jaszczurówka & Morskie Oko

To Kuźnice

Rondo

TATRA NATIONAL PARK

PLACES TO STAY
2 Youth Hostel Szarotka
4 Hotel Helios
21 Dom Turysty PTTK
22 Hotel Gazda
24 Hotel Giewont
37 Schronisko Młodzieżowe Żak
38 Camping Nr 97 Pod Krokwią

PLACES TO EAT
11 Bar FIS
17 Karczma Redykołka
25 Restauracja Swarna
26 Restauracja Zbyrcok
27 Stek Chałupa
28 Karczma Janosik
31 Restauracja Pizzeria Kolorowa

33 Morskie Oko Food Centre
34 Bar Rzepka
36 Karczma Obrochtówka

OTHER
1 Teatr Witkacego (Witkacy Theatre)
3 Funicular Station
5 Tourist Office
6 FWP
7 Bank Pekao
8 Bus Terminal
9 Train Station
10 Tatry Travel Agency
12 Kozica Travel Agency
13 Hasior Art Gallery
14 Old Cemetery
15 Old Parish Church

16 Villa Koliba & Museum of Zakopane Style
18 New Parish Church
19 Tatra Museum
20 Biuro Usług Turystycznych PTTK
23 Bank Przemysłowo Handlowy
29 Main Post Office
30 Orbis
32 Villa Atma & Szymanowski Museum
35 Trip Travel Agency
39 Tatra National Park Museum
40 Centrum Przewodnictwa Tatrzańskiego (Tatra Guide Centre)
41 Villa Pod Jedlami

POLAND

Money Bank Pekao, ul Gimnazjalna 1, behind the bus terminal changes most major brands of travellers cheques and pays złoty advances on Visa and MasterCard. Bank Przemysłowo Handlowy, ul Krupówki 19, opposite Hotel Gazda changes cheques and accepts Visa card. As for cash, kantors dot ul Krupówki every 50m or so, and there are also a few ATMs.

Travel Agencies Centrum Przewodnictwa Tatrzańskiego ('Tatra Guide Centre; ☎ 206 37 99), ul Chałubińskiego 44, and the Biuro Usług Turystycznych PTTK (☎ 201 58 48), ul Krupówki 12, can arrange mountain guides speaking English and German, but advance notice is necessary. The cost depends on the difficulty of the hike or climb: from about US$40 to US$100 a day per group.

Orbis (☎ 201 50 51), ul Krupówki 22, sells domestic and international train tickets, arranges accommodation in private houses and selected holiday homes and organises tours. Teresa (☎ 201 43 01), ul Kościuszki 7, specialises in international bus tickets.

Other useful travel agencies include the Trip (☎ 201 59 47), ul Zamoyskiego 1 (international bus tickets, tours); the Tatry (☎ 201 43 43), ul Chramcówki 35, just off the train station (private rooms, tours); the Giewont (☎ 206 35 66), ul Kościuszki 4 (private rooms, tours); the Fregata (☎ 201 33 07), ul Krupówki 81b (international tickets) and the Kozica (☎ 201 32 77), ul Jagiellońska 1, right behind the Bar FIS (private rooms, tickets).

Many of these and other agencies will have tours to the Dunajec Gorge (US$15 to US$18 per person) and other popular regional tourist destinations.

Bookshop The best choice of maps and guidebooks on the Tatras and other mountain regions is to be found in Księgarnia Górska, the bookshop on the 1st floor of Dom Turysty PTTK.

Cybercafés The Internet Café is on the 1st floor of the Morskie Oko gastronomic complex, ul Krupówki 30.

Things to See

The **Tatra Museum** (closed Monday), ul Krupówki 10, has several sections including

history, ethnography, geology and flora and fauna and is thus a good introduction to the region.

On nearby ul Kościeliska is a charming **old parish church** (1847). Just behind it is the **old cemetery** with a number of amazing wooden tombs. Continue west along ul Kościeliska to the **Villa Koliba**, the first design (1892) of Witkiewicz in the Zakopane style. It now accommodates the **Museum of Zakopane Style** (closed Monday and Tuesday). Half a kilometre south-east, on ul Kasprusie, is the **Villa Atma**, once the home of Szymanowski, today a museum (closed Monday) dedicated to the composer. Piano recitals are held here in summer.

The striking assemblages of Polish contemporary avant-garde artist Władysław Hasior can be seen at the **Hasior Art Gallery** (closed Monday and Tuesday), ul Jagiellońska 7, near the train station. A 20-minute walk south of here, next to the roundabout called Rondo, is the **Tatra National Park Museum** (closed Sunday) with an exhibition on the natural history of the park.

A short walk east up the hill will lead you to the **Villa Pod Jedlami**, another splendid house in the Zakopane style (the interior cannot be visited). Perhaps Witkiewicz's greatest achievement is the **Jaszczurówka Chapel**, about 1.5km farther east on the road to Morskie Oko.

Funicular to Mt Gubałówka

Mt Gubałówka (1120m) offers an excellent view over the Tatras and is a favourite destination for those tourists who don't feel like exercising their legs too much. The funicular, built in 1938, provides comfortable access to the top. It covers the 1388m-long route in less than five minutes, climbing 300m at the same time (US$2.50 return trip).

Cable Car to Mt Kasprowy Wierch

Since it opened in 1935, almost every Polish tourist has made the cable-car trip from Kuźnice to the summit of Mt Kasprowy Wierch (1985m) where you can stand with one foot in Poland and the other in Slovakia. The route is 4290m long with an intermediate station midway at Mt Myślenickie Turnie

(1352m). The one-way journey takes 20 minutes, and you climb 936m in that time.

There's a great view from the top, clouds permitting, and also a restaurant. Many people return to Zakopane on foot down the Gąsienicowa Valley, and the most intrepid walk the ridges all the way across to Morskie Oko Lake via Pięć Stawów, a strenuous hike taking a full day in good weather.

The cable car normally operates from about mid-December to mid-May and from early June to late October (take these dates as a rough guide only). In midsummer, it runs from 7.30 am to 8 pm; in winter, from 7.30 am to 4 pm.

The one-way/return ticket costs US$5/7. If you buy a return, your trip back is automatically reserved two hours after departure time. Tickets can be bought at the Kuźnice cableway station (for the same day only). You can also buy them in advance from Orbis and some other travel agencies, but normally only if you purchase some of their services. At peak tourist times (both summer and winter), tickets run out fast and there can be long lines in Kuźnice; get there early. PKS buses go to Kuźnice frequently from the bus terminal, and there are also private minibuses that park in front of the Bar FIS.

Hiking in the Tatras

If you plan on hiking in the Tatras, get a copy of the *Tatrzański Park Narodowy* map, which shows all the walking trails in the area. In July and August, the Tatras can be overrun by tourists. Late spring and early autumn seem to be the best times for visits. Theoretically at least, you can expect better weather in autumn (September to October) when the rainfall is lower than in spring.

Like all alpine mountains, the Tatras can be dangerous, particularly during the snowy period, which is roughly November to May. Use common sense and go easy. Remember that the weather can be tricky, with snow or rain, thunderstorms, fog, strong wind etc occurring frequently and unpredictably. Bring good footwear, warm clothing and waterproof rain gear.

There are several picturesque small valleys south of Zakopane, the Dolina Strążyska being arguably the nicest. You can return the same way or transfer by the black trail to either of the neighbouring valleys. You can also continue from the Strążyska by the red trail up to Mt Giewont (1909m, 3½ hours from Zakopane), and then walk down on the blue trail to Kuźnice in two hours.

There are two long and beautiful forested valleys, the Dolina Chochołowska and the Dolina Kościeliska, in the western part of the park, known as Tatry Zachodnie (West Tatras). Each valley has a mountain refuge if you want to eat or stay for the night. Visit the Jaskinia Mroźna (Frosty Cave). Both valleys are serviced by PKS buses and private minibuses from Zakopane.

The Tatry Wysokie (High Tatras) to the east offer quite different scenery: it's a land of bare granite peaks with glacial lakes at their feet. One way of getting there is to take the cable car to Mt Kasprowy Wierch and head eastward along the red trail to Mt Świnica (2301m), and on to the Zawrat pass (2½ hours from Mt Kasprowy). From Zawrat you can descend either north to the Dolina Gąsienicowa along the blue trail and back to Zakopane, or south (also by the blue trail) to the wonderful Dolina Pięciu Stawów (Five Lakes Valley) where you'll find a mountain refuge (1¼ hours from Zawrat). The blue trail heading west from the refuge will bring you to the emerald-green Lake Morskie Oko (Eye of the Sea), acclaimed as being among the loveliest in the Tatras (1½ hours from the refuge).

A far easier way of getting to Morskie Oko is by road from Zakopane, and this is one of the most popular tourist trips in the Tatras. Hence, the lake is swamped with visitors in the peak season, particularly July and August. PKS buses and private minibuses depart from Zakopane for the lake regularly and go as far as the car park at the Polana Palenica (US$1.25, 30 minutes). From there a road continues uphill to the lake (9km), but no cars, bikes or buses are allowed farther up. You can walk the distance in two hours (it isn't steep), or you can take a horse-drawn carriage that brings you to Włosienica, 2km from the lake.

Horse-drawn carriages leave when they collect 15 people. The trip takes about 1¼ hours uphill and costs US$7; to come down takes 45 minutes and costs US$5. In summer, carriages go up until about 4 or 5 pm and return up to around 8 pm. In winter, transport is by horse-drawn four-seater sledges, which are more expensive than carriages.

The Morskie Oko mountain refuge at the lakeside serves hearty bigos and drinks. A stone path circling the lake provides a lovely stroll (40 minutes). You can climb to the upper lake, Czarny Staw, in another 20 minutes or so. The trail continues steeply up to the top of Mt Rysy (2499m). In late summer, when the snow has finally gone, you can climb it in about four hours from the refuge.

Special Events

The International Festival of Mountain Folklore in late August is the town's leading cultural event. In July, a series of concerts presenting music by Szymanowski is held in the Villa Atma.

Places to Stay – Zakopane

Zakopane has heaps of places to stay and, except for occasional peaks, finding a bed is no problem. Even if hotels and hostels are full, there will still be some private rooms around. Incidentally, private rooms provide some of the cheapest and best accommodation in town.

As with all seasonal resorts, accommodation prices in Zakopane fluctuate (sometimes considerably) between the high and the off seasons, peaking in February, July, August and late December/early January. The prices given in the text are for the high season.

Camping The all-year *Camping Nr 97 Pod Krokwią* (☎ 201 22 56) on ul Żeromskiego has large heated bungalows, each containing several double and triple rooms. They cost US$10 per person in July and August (less in other months), but they are often full in that period. To get to the camping grounds from the bus/train stations, take any bus to Kuźnice or Jaszczurówka and get off at Rondo.

Zakopane has several more camping grounds, including the all-year *Camping Nr*

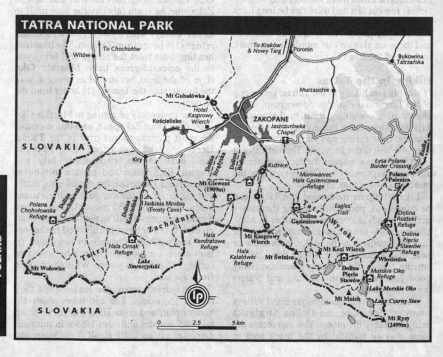

TATRA NATIONAL PARK

160 Harenda (☎ 206 84 06) on the Kraków road; the summer *Camping za Strugiem* (☎ 201 45 66), ul Za Strugiem 39; the *Camping u Daniela* (☎ 206 12 96) in Oberconiówka; and the *Auto Camping Nr 252 Comfort* (☎ 201 49 42), ul Kaszelewskiego 7, on the Kościelisko road.

Youth Hostels Zakopane has the year-round *Youth Hostel Szarotka* (☎ 206 62 03), ul Nowotarska 45, a 10-minute walk from the centre and the same distance from the bus and train stations. With some 250 beds (mostly in eight to 12-bed dorms), this is one of the largest hostels in the country, but it can still get packed, far exceeding its capacity in the high season. The hostel is frequently used by school-excursion groups.

The all-year *Schronisko Młodzieżowe Żak* (☎ 201 57 06), ul Marusarzówny 15, is in a quiet, verdant south-western suburb of the town. Run by Almatur, it's not a regular PTSM youth hostel, but it works on similar principles and costs much the same. It has seven small dorms (US$5 a bed) and two doubles (US$6 a bed); bedclothes are US$1.50 extra if you need any. The place is well run and friendly, and is little known, so it may be easier to find a bed here than in the Szarotka.

Other Hostels The very central 460-bed *Dom Turysty PTTK* (☎ 206 32 07 or ☎ 206 32 81), ul Zaruskiego 5, has heaps of rooms of different sizes, mostly dormitories. Doubles/triples with bath cost US$32/40, rooms with shower only go for US$26/36, and those without bath can be got for US$24/30. You can stay in a dorm with four beds (US$8 per head), eight beds (US$6) or 28 beds (US$5). Like the Szarotka, the place can often be swamped with excited crowds of pre-teens. There's an 11 pm curfew.

Private Rooms The business of private rooms for hire is flourishing. It is run by most travel agencies, including the tourist office, Orbis, PTTK, Tatry and Kozica (see Information earlier in this section). In the peak season, they probably won't want to fix up accommodation for a period shorter than three nights, but in the off season, this shouldn't apply. Expect a bed in a double room to cost US$6 to US$10 in the peak season. Check the location before deciding.

In the peak season, there are usually quite a few locals hanging around the bus and train stations, who approach arriving passengers to offer them rooms in their homes. The prices given up-front may sometimes be absurdly inflated (particularly for foreigners), but they can be swiftly negotiated down to the normal level. As a rule, you shouldn't pay more than when renting a room through an agency. Again, check the location first before setting off for the trip.

Many locals don't rent out rooms through an agency but directly: they simply put boards reading *pokoje*, *noclegi* or *zimmer frei* outside their homes. You'll find many such signs throughout the town. You'll also see a number of places called 'pensjonat' (pension), which may offer better facilities, but are usually more expensive and may insist on selling a bed-and-board package.

Holiday Homes There are plenty of holiday homes in Zakopane. These days, most of them are open to the general public, renting rooms either directly or through travel agencies. The major agent is FWP (☎ 201 27 63) which has its office in the DW Podhale, ul Kościuszki 19. It's open weekdays from 8 am to 5 pm, and in the peak season also on Saturday.

The office rents rooms in 11 FWP holiday homes scattered around the town. Rooms range from doubles to quads; some have private bath, while others don't. You can take just a room or room with board (three meals). As a rough guide, in July and August a bed in rooms without/with bath will cost US$10/18; in the off season it will be US$6/10. Add US$8 for full board. One-night stays are OK.

Hotels Given the abundance of private rooms and holiday homes, plus other cheap options, few travellers bother to look for a hotel, which are more expensive and aren't always good value. However, if you need one, there are a number of them including three central establishments: the *Hotel Gazda* (☎ 150 11), ul Zaruskiego 2; the Orbis-run *Hotel Giewont* (☎ 120 11), ul Kościuszki 1; and the *Hotel Helios* (☎ 138 08), ul Słoneczna 2a. Any of these will cost around US$40/60 (US$30/50 in the off season).

POLAND

Places to Stay – Tatra National Park

Mountain Refuges Camping is not really allowed in the park but there are eight PTTK mountain refuges, which provide simple accommodation (costing around US$5 to US$8 per person in a dorm or US$20 to US$25 per double room). Most refuges are pretty small and fill up fast. In both midsummer and midwinter they are invariably packed far beyond capacity. No one is ever turned away, though you may have to crash on the bare floor if all the beds are taken. Don't arrive too late, and bring along your own bed mat and sleeping bag. All refuges serve simple hot meals, but their kitchens and dining rooms close early, in some places at 7 pm.

The refuges are open year-round but some may be temporarily closed for repairs, usually in November. Before you set off, check the current situation at the PTTK office in Zakopane, which runs the refuges and provides information.

The easiest refuge to get to from Zakopane is the large and decent *Hala Kalatówki Refuge* (84 beds, US$14 per person, breakfast included), a 30-minute walk from the Kuźnice cable-car station. Half an hour beyond Kalatówki on the trail to Giewont is the *Hala Kondratowa Refuge* (20 beds). For location and atmosphere it's great, but note the small size.

Hikers wishing to traverse the park might begin at the *Dolina Roztoki Refuge* (96 beds), accessible via the Morskie Oko bus. An early start from Zakopane, however, would allow you to visit Morskie Oko in the morning and stay at the *Morskie Oko Refuge*, or continue through to the *Dolina Pięciu Stawów Refuge* (70 beds). This is the highest (1700m) and most scenically located refuge in the Polish Tatras and is well worth a visit.

A leisurely day's walk north-west of Pięć Stawów is the *Murowaniec Hala Gąsienicowa Refuge* (100 beds), from which you can return to Zakopane. The Pięć Stawów and Hala Gąsienicowa are the most crowded refuges.

In the western part of the park are the *Hala Ornak Refuge* (75 beds) and *Polana Chochołowska Refuge* (161 beds), connected by trail.

Places to Eat

The central mall, ul Krupówki, boasts heaps of eateries, everything from hamburger stands to well-appointed establishments. Eating cheaply is not a problem in Zakopane – the proliferation of small fast-food outlets is astonishing, and there are also plenty of informal places in private homes in the back streets, displaying boards saying 'obiady domowe' (home-cooked lunches).

Among the cheapest places are the basic *Bar Mleczny*, ul Krupówki 1, the *Bar Rzepka*, ul Krupówki 43, the *Bistro Grota*, ul Kościuszki 5, and the *Bufet* in the building of the Urząd Miasta (local government headquarters), ul Kościuszki 13. Slightly more expensive is the *Restauracja Swarna*, ul Kościuszki 4. If you arrive hungry by bus or train, the large drab *Bar FIS* can be an emergency option.

The folksy *Stek Chałupa*, ul Krupówki 33, has popular Polish dishes at low prices. Opposite, *Restauracja Pizzeria Kolorowa* has been totally revamped and is now a pleasant place to eat, and not only for pizza. *Morskie Oko*, a few steps up the mall, is a large food centre, plus a vast restaurant in the basement.

There's a fair choice of reasonable restaurants serving typical food, most of which are decorated accordingly and even the waiters are decked out in regional costumes. Going from north to south, you have *Karczma Redykołka*, ul Krupówki 2, *Restauracja Zbyrcok*, ul Krupówki 29, *Karczma Janosik*, ul Krupówki 35 and, probably the best of its kind, *Karczma Obrochtówka*, ul Kraszewskiego 10a.

Don't miss trying the smoked sheep's-milk cheese sold at street stands all along ul Krupówki.

Entertainment

The *Teatr Witkacego* (Witkacy Theatre), ul Chramcówki 15, is one of the best theatres in Poland.

Getting There & Away

Most regional routes are covered by bus; the train is useful only for long-distance travel – to Warsaw for example.

Train There are several trains to Kraków (147km) but buses are faster and run more frequently. One train daily (in the high season two) runs to Warsaw (439km). Tickets are available from the station or from Orbis, ul Krupówki 22.

Bus The PKS fast buses run to Kraków (104km) every hour; the trip costs US$4 and takes 2½ hours. There are also nine buses a day to Kraków operated by a private company (departing from ul Kościuszki 19). They are cheaper (US$3) and a bit faster. Tickets are available from the office next to Kozica travel agency. There are several PKS buses daily to Nowy Sącz and single buses to Tarnów, Przemyśl, Rzeszów and Krynica. PKS has introduced a useful direct bus to Kąty (for the Dunajec raft trip).

In the region around Zakopane, bus transport is relatively frequent. PKS buses can take you to the foot of the Kościeliska and Chochołowska valleys as well as to Polana Palenica near Morskie Oko Lake. There are also private minibuses leaving from in front of Bar FIS, which ply the most popular tourist routes.

There are a couple of buses per week to Budapest (US$16, nine hours), and a daily morning bus to Poprad in Slovakia (US$3), where you can catch the express train to Prague, departing around 11 am and arriving about 6.30 pm. You can also take any of the Polana Palenica PKS buses or private minibuses; get off at Łysa Polana (22km), cross the border on foot and continue by bus (regular transport) to Tatranská Lomnica (30km). Southbound this route is easy but northbound you could find the Polana Palenica bus to Zakopane crowded with day-trippers from Morskie Oko (in which case hitch, as the taxi drivers want 20 times the bus fare).

DUNAJEC GORGE

Every year tens of thousands of people go rafting on the Dunajec River, along a stretch where the river cuts through the Pieniny Mountains just before turning north to flow up towards the Vistula. The river runs right along the Polish-Slovakian border here, winding through a spectacular deep gorge with high cliffs on both sides. The mix of deciduous trees and conifers makes for lovely patterns of colour. This is not a white-water experience: the rapids are gentle and you won't get wet.

The trip begins in Kąty, and after a 15km journey you disembark in the spa of Szczawnica. The 2½-hour raft trips operate from May to October with rafts leaving as soon as 10 people sign up (US$8 per person). Each 10-seat raft consists of five wooden coffinlike sections lashed together, guided by two boatmen dressed in embroidered folk costumes. In Szczawnica, the sections are taken apart, loaded onto a truck and carried back to Kąty.

Dunajec raft trips are also offered from Červený Kláštor in Slovakia, but the Slovakian trips are shorter and not as easily arranged.

Getting There & Away

The Dunajec Gorge is an easy day trip from Zakopane. Take the direct PKS bus from Zakopane to Kąty (US$1.75). Alternatively, go to Nowy Targ (frequent service, 24km, 30 minutes, US$1), then take one of the six daily Sromowce Niżne buses from Nowy Targ to Kąty (31km, one hour, US$1). The landing at Kąty is fairly obvious with a large parking lot and a pavilion housing the ticket office and a snack bar.

At Szczawnica, where the trip ends, you can take the direct PKS bus back to Zakopane, or catch one of the 25 daily buses to Nowy Targ (38km, US$1) and change for one to Zakopane, or stay for the night in any of the numerous private rooms in Szczawnica. If you go to Nowy Targ, it's well worth stopping midway at the village of Dębno Podhalańskie, which boasts one of the best timber Gothic churches in Poland.

There are five fast buses from Szczawnica direct to Kraków (118km), and a regular bus service to Nowy Sącz (48km).

There are plenty of tours organised from Zakopane; they include rafting trips and visits to the church in Dębno Podhalańskie and the ruined castle in Czorsztyn. They cost US$16, which is a fair deal.

SOUTH-EAST POLAND

Poland's far south-east doesn't see many foreign visitors, even though it's an attractive region, both culturally and geographically. It is a largely unspoilt, wooded, rugged land sprinkled with historic towns and villages revealing its complex ethnic and religious past, a blend of the west and the east. Some of the region's highlights are briefly outlined below.

POLAND

Nowy Sącz

An easy bus ride from Szczawnica, Nowy Sącz (population 85,000) has a good museum, particularly renowned for its extensive collection of old icons, and one of the best skansens in the country. The town has a fair accommodation infrastructure, including an all-year *youth hostel* at Al Batorego 72. The tourist office, ul Piotra Skargi 2, can give you farther information about the town and the region.

A visit to the nearby sleepy little town of Stary Sącz, featuring a genuine cobbled market square and two splendid churches, is a worthwhile trip. You'll pass through it while coming from Szczawnica.

Biecz

If you decide to wander farther east along the road to Sanok, the small town of Biecz may make an interesting stop. Visit its monumental Gothic church and charming local museum. If you can't find a direct bus, go to Gorlice and change. Biecz has a good year-round *youth hostel* at ul Parkowa 1.

Sanok

Sanok (population 44,000) is another important point on the tourist map, noted principally for having Poland's largest collection of Ruthenian icons, displayed in the castle museum, and an excellent skansen. The town has the usual assortment of hotels, but its *youth hostel*, ul Konarskiego 10, only operates in July and August. Go to the PTTK office, ul 3 Maja 18, for information. Coming from Biecz, you may need to change buses in Krosno.

The Bieszczady

Occupying the far south-eastern corner of Poland, south of Sanok, the Bieszczady is a wild, scantily populated mountain region of thick forests and open meadows. The highest and most spectacular part of the mountains is now a national park, popular with hikers. The major bases for hikes are the villages of Ustrzyki Górne and Wetlina, both offering a choice of budget accommodation and both accessible by bus from Sanok.

Przemyśl

Perched on a hillside and dominated by four mighty historic churches, Przemyśl (population 70,000) is a picturesque sort of place. It also has a museum with yet another good selection of Ruthenian icons. Just 14km from the Ukrainian border, the town is the usual starting or transit point for Lviv (95km) with regular bus services operating on this route. The town has quite a choice of inexpensive accommodation, including the all-year *camping ground* (with cabins) at Wybrzeże Piłsudskiego 8a and the good all-year *youth hostel* at ul Lelewela 6. Call at the tourist office at ul Ratuszowa 8 for more details.

The Renaissance castle in Krasiczyn, 10km west of Przemyśl, is a pleasant short trip.

Łańcut

The town of Łańcut, 67km north-west of Przemyśl (regular transport by both bus and train), boasts a magnificent palace (originally built in 1629 but remodelled later), possibly the best known old aristocratic residence anywhere in Poland. It's now a museum housing an extensive and diverse collection of art. The palace's coach house features 50-odd old carriages, while the stable holds a collection of icons.

There's a reasonable *hotel* and a *restaurant* in the palace, and more places to stay and eat in town. Trains go to Kraków regularly, but if you're heading to Zamość, take a bus.

ZAMOŚĆ
☎ 084

Zamość (population 66,000) was founded in 1580 by Jan Zamoyski, chancellor and commander in chief of Renaissance Poland, who intended to create an ideal urban settlement and impregnable barrier against Cossack and Tatar raids from the east.

The town was designed by the Italian architect Bernardo Morando and was built in one go within a few decades. Its position on the crossroads of the busy Lublin-Lviv and Kraków-Kiev trade routes led merchants of many nationalities to settle here. Zamość was one of Poland's few cities to withstand the Swedish siege of 1656.

During WWII, the Nazis renamed Zamość 'Himmlerstadt' and expelled the Polish inhabitants from the town and its environs. Their place was taken by German colonists to create what Adolf Hitler planned would become an eastern bulwark for the Third Reich.

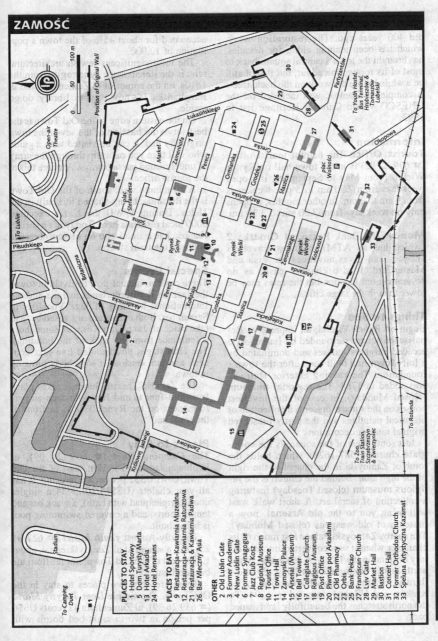

ZAMOŚĆ

0   50   100 m

Position of Original Wall

Open-air Theatre

To Lublin

Piłsudskiego

To Youth Hostel,
Bus Terminal,
Hrubieszów &
Tomaszów
Lubelski

Partyzantów

Okopowa

Łukasińskiego

plac
Wolności

Market

Zamenhofa

Pereca

Ormiańska

Grodzka

Staszica

Bazyliańska

Grecka

plac
Stefanidesa

Solna

Rynek
Solny

Rynek
Wielki

Zamkowięc

Rynek
Wodny

Moranda

Kościuszki

Botaniczna

Akademicka

Pereca

Kołłątaja

Grodzka

Staszica

Kolegiacka

Kołłątaja

Zamkowa

Kolowej Jadwigi

Stadium

To Camping
Duet

To Zoo,
Train Station,
Szczebrzeszyn
& Zwierzyniec

To Rotunda

PLACES TO STAY
1 Hotel Sportowy
5 Dom Turysty Marta
13 Hotel Arkadia
24 Hotel Renesans

PLACES TO EAT
9 Restauracja-Kawiarnia Muzealna
12 Restauracja-Kawiarnia Ratuszowa
21 Restauracja & Kawiarnia Padwa
26 Bar Mleczny Asia

OTHER
2 Old Lublin Gate
3 Former Academy
4 New Lublin Gate
6 Former Synagogue
7 Jazz Club Kosz
8 Regional Museum
10 Tourist Office
11 Town Hall
14 Zamoyski Palace
15 Arsenal (Museum)
16 Bell Tower
17 Collegiate Church
18 Religious Museum
19 Post Office
20 Piwnica pod Arkadami
22 Old Pharmacy
23 Bank Pekao
25 Orbis
27 Franciscan Church
28 Lviv Gate
29 Market Hall
30 Bastion
31 Concert Hall
32 Former Orthodox Church
33 Speluna Artystyczna Kazamat

Zamość's Old Town happily escaped war destruction, and it looks much the same as it did 400 years ago. The restoration work, which has been inching along for decades, has brought the town's central square back to most of its former splendour, but it will still be a while before the work on the backstreets is completed. Zamość was included on the UNESCO World Cultural Heritage list in 1992.

Information

Tourist Office The helpful tourist office (☎ 639 22 92) is in the town hall on Rynek Wielki. From May to September, it's open weekdays from 7.30 am to 5 pm, weekends from 9 am to 2 pm. In other months, it opens only on weekdays from 7.30 am to 3.30 pm.

Money The Bank Pekao, ul Grodzka 2 (which has an ATM), changes travellers cheques and gives advances on Visa and MasterCard. It also changes cash, as do several central kantors, but the rates may be lower than in the large cities.

Things to See

Begin on **Rynek Wielki**, an impressive Renaissance square surrounded by Italian-style arcaded burghers' houses and dominated by a lofty **town hall** built soon after the town's foundation. The curving exterior stairway was added in 1768. The **regional museum** (closed Monday), in one of the loveliest houses on the square, presents a collection of historical paintings and the partly preserved original interior decoration.

Just south-west of the square is the **collegiate church** (1587-1628), which holds the tomb of Zamoyski in the chapel to the right of the high altar. Behind the church is the **religious museum** (closed Tuesday) featuring a collection of sacral art. A short walk west will bring you to the old **Arsenal**, now a museum of old weapons (closed Monday). The nearby **Zamoyski Palace** lost much of its character when it was converted into a military hospital in the 1830s. A few paces to the north-east is the former **Academy**, Poland's third institution of higher education (after Kraków and Vilnius), founded in 1594. To the north stretches the beautifully landscaped park.

The area to the east of the Academy was once inhabited by Jews, who before WWII accounted for about 45% of the town's population of 12,000.

The most significant Jewish architectural relic is the Renaissance **synagogue** from the 1610s, on the corner of ul Zamenhofa and ul Bazyliańska. It's now a public library; do go inside.

On the eastern edge of the Old Town is the best surviving **bastion** of the seven the town originally had. It can be visited with a guide who will take you on a trip through the array of underground passageways. Arrange this at the tourist office.

A 10-minute walk south of the Old Town is the **Rotunda**, a ring-shaped fort built in the 1820s. During WWII the Nazis executed 8000 local residents here. Today it's a shrine. Zamość has a small **zoo** on ul Szczebrzeska opposite the train station.

Special Events

There are two annual jazz festivals in town: the Jazz on the Borderlands in June and the International Meeting of Jazz Vocalists in September. Both events are organised by, and take place at, Jazz Club Kosz, ul Zamenhofa 3 (entrance from the back of the building). The club stages unscheduled live jazz concerts and jam sessions if somebody turns up in town.

The Zamość Theatre Summer takes place from mid-June to mid-July with open-air performances on the Rynek Wielki in front of the town hall.

Places to Stay

The *Camping Duet* (☎ 639 24 99), ul Królowej Jadwigi 14, 1km west of the Old Town, costs US$2 per person to camp. It has all-year chalets (US$14/20/28/34 a single/double/triple/quad with bath), a snack bar and tennis courts, and a covered swimming pool is being built.

The July-August *youth hostel* (☎ 627 91 25) is in a school at ul Zamoyskiego 4, about 1.5km east of the Old Town, not far from the bus terminal.

There are only two places to stay in the Old Town. The simple *Dom Turysty Marta* (☎ 639 26 39), ul Zamenhofa 11, costs US$6 per person in two to eight-bed dorms with shared facilities. More comfortable is the modern *Hotel Renesans* (☎ 639 20 01), ul Grecka 6, which offers singles/doubles with private bath for US$44/62.

Hotel Sportowy (☎ 638 60 11), in the sports centre, ul Królowej Jadwigi 8, is a 10-minute walk from the Rynek. Singles/doubles/triples/quads with bath cost US$20/26/28/32. You can stay in a five or six-bed dorm without bath for US$8.

The brand-new *Hotel Arkadia* (☎ 638 65 07), Rynek Wielki 9, is the best place in town. It has just four rooms: two doubles (US$50 each), one triple (US$60) and one suite (US$85).

There are also several less convenient hotels farther away from the centre; the tourist office will give you information.

Places to Eat

For a simple cheap meal, go to the *Bar Mleczny Asia*, ul Staszica 10. Several cafés, most of which are on the Rynek, serve the usual set of popular dishes such as flaki, barszcz, sausage etc. Also, the *Restauracja-Kawiarnia Ratuszowa* in the town hall has reasonable food at low prices.

Of the more decent places for lunch or dinner, try the *Restauracja-Kawiarnia Muzealna* in a cellar next to the regional museum, the basement *Restauracja Padwa*, ul Staszica 23 (at the Rynek), or the 1st-floor *Restauracja Arkadia* in the hotel of the same name.

Entertainment

For a drink or two, try either of the 'artistic' bars, both located in the old fortifications: the *Speluna Artystyczna Kazamat*, ul Bazyliańska 36 or the *Kawiarnia Artystyczna Brama* in the Old Lublin Gate. You can also try the *Piwnica pod Arkadami*, ul Staszica 25 (at the Rynek), a cellar bar-café with pool tables.

Getting There & Away

The tourist office will inform you about the train and bus schedules, and Orbis, ul Grodzka 18, books and sells train tickets.

Train The train station is about 1km southwest of the Old Town; walk or take the city bus. There are several slow trains to Lublin (118km) but give them a miss – they take a long roundabout route. It's much faster to go by bus, and you will arrive in the centre of Lublin.

Three ordinary trains go directly to Warsaw (293km), but they take over six hours to get there. It's faster to go by bus or take a special PKP bus (departing from the train station) to Lublin at 5 am which goes to Lublin train station and meets the express train to Warsaw at 7 am. The whole trip takes four hours. There's a convenient morning fast train to Kraków, which takes six hours to get there, or you can take the morning Kraków PKS bus.

Bus The bus terminal is 2km east of the centre; frequent city buses link it with the Old Town. Buses to Lublin (89km), either fast or ordinary ones, run roughly every half-hour till about 6 pm, and there are also plenty of private minibuses, which are cheaper. There are two morning buses to Rzeszów (148km), passing Łańcut on the way, and one to Przemyśl (148km). One morning fast bus goes directly to Kraków (318km), one to Sandomierz (157km) and four to Warsaw (247km).

LUBLIN
☎ 081

Long a crossroads of trade, Lublin (population 360,000) was an important point on the Polish map. In 1569 a political union of Poland and Lithuania was signed here, creating the largest European state of the time. Beginning in the 17th century, Lublin saw repeated foreign invasions by Swedes, Austrians, Russians and Germans, culminating in the Nazi death camp at Majdanek. In July 1944, before Poland was liberated, the provisional communist government was installed here by the Soviets.

Luckily, Lublin didn't experience significant wartime damage, so its Old Town has retained much of its historic architectural fabric. However, the early postwar restoration was superficial, and the quarter looks dilapidated and untidy. A more thorough program is currently underway, but it's progressing painfully slowly. The Old Town gets deserted after 9 pm or so and may be positively dangerous; avoid strolling about the streets at night.

POLAND

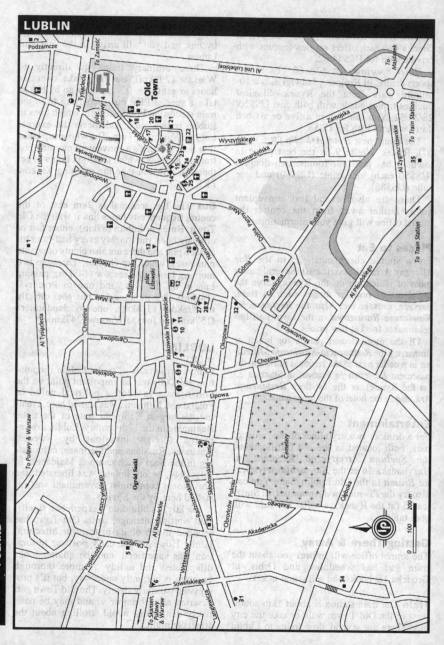

LUBLIN

Podzamcze

To Zamość

Al Tysiąclecia

plac
Zamkowy

Old
Town

Warsaw

To Lubartów

Al Tysiąclecia

Al Unii Lubelskiej

To Majdanek

Zamojska

To Train Station

Al Zygmuntowskie

Wyszyńskiego

Bernardyńska

Lubartowska

Lubartowska

Rynek

Królewska

Ruska

Dolna Panny Marii

Górna

Al Piłsudskiego

To Train Station

Niecała

Radziwiłłowska

plac
Litewski

Narutowicza

Graniczna

Narutowicza

3 Maja

Chmielna

Ogrodowa

Krakowskie Przedmieście

Okopowa

Chopina

Chopina

Spokojna

Lipowa

To Puławy & Warsaw

Al Tysiąclecia

Ogród Saski

Leszczyńskiego

Radziszewskiego

Skłodowskiej - Curie

Obrońców Pokoju

Rajbrego

Głęboka

Cemetery

Akademicka

Dłuższa

Popiełuszki

Weteranów

Al Racławickie

Sowińskiego

Langiewicza

To Skansen, Puławy
& Warsaw

0   100   200 m

N

LUBLIN

PLACES TO STAY					
1	Motel PZM	15	Bar Staromiejski	14	Kraków Gate & Historical
2	Hotel Pracowniczy LPBP	17	Oberża Artystyczna		Museum of Lublin
5	Youth Hostel		Złoty Osioł	16	Old Town Hall &
19	Archidiecezjalny	18	Kawiarnia Szeroka 28		Museum of the
	Dom Rekolekcyjny	24	Bar pod Basztą		Crown Tribunal
21	Wojewódzki Ośrodek	27	Kawiarnia Artystyczna	20	Dominican Church
	Metodyczny	28	Klub Hades	22	Cathedral
30	Dom Nauczyciela			23	Trinitarian Tower &
34	Hotel Studenta	**OTHER**			Archdiocesan Museum
	Zaocznego UMCS	3	Central Bus Terminal	25	Bank Pekao
35	Hotel Bystrzyca	4	Castle, Lublin Museum	26	Teatr im Osterwy
			& Chapel of the		(Osterwa Theatre)
PLACES TO EAT			Holy Trinity	29	Filharmonia Lubelska
6	Karczma Słupska	7	Tourist Office		(Philharmonic Hall) &
9	Restauracja Resursa	8	Bank Przemysłowo		Teatr Muzyczny
11	Bar Uniwersalny		Handlowy		(Musical Theatre)
	Ludowy	10	Bank Depozytowo	31	Chatka Żaka
13	Bar Turystyczny		Kredytowy	32	Orbis
		12	Main Post Office	33	Internet Café

Orientation

Lublin is a fairly big city but as usual you should aim for the centre. Coming by bus you arrive in the city centre, while the train deposits you, less conveniently, 2km south of the town's heart.

The centre consists of the Old Town, where you'll do most of your sightseeing, and the New Town stretching to the west along its main thoroughfare, ul Krakowskie Przedmieście, where the tourist office is. The main hotel area is farther to the west.

Information

Tourist Office The tourist office (☎ 532 44 12), ul Krakowskie Przedmieście 78 (open weekdays from 9 am to 5 pm, Saturday from 10 am to 2 pm) sells maps and is generally helpful.

Money The Bank Pekao, ul Królewska 1, facing the Kraków Gate, changes travellers cheques and gives cash advances on Visa and MasterCard. Bank Depozytowo Kredytowy and Bank Przemysłowo Handlowy, both on ul Krakowskie Przedmieście, handle travellers cheques and Visa card transactions. Plenty of kantors line ul Krakowskie Przedmieście and the adjacent streets, and you'll also find several ATMs there.

Cybercafés The InterCafé (☎ 743 64 06) is in the basement at ul Graniczna 10.

Things to See

Old Town The compact historic quarter is centred around the **Rynek**, the main square, with an oversized neoclassical **old town hall** (1781) plunked in its middle. Its cellars house the **Museum of the Crown Tribunal** (closed Monday and Tuesday). The **Kraków Gate**, the only significant remnant of medieval fortifications, shelters the **Historical Museum of Lublin** (closed Monday and Tuesday). You'll get a view of the town from the top floor. For a better view, go to the top of the nearby **Trinitarian Tower**, which houses the **Archdiocesan Museum** (closed Monday). Next to the tower is the **cathedral** (1596) with impressive baroque frescoes all over its interior. Also interesting is the **Dominican Church**, rebuilt after the fire of 1575. To the right of the entrance is a large historical painting depicting the 1719 fire of the city.

Castle Built atop a hill just north-east of the Old Town, the original 14th-century castle was largely destroyed, and what you see today is actually a neo-Gothic prison put up in the 1820s and functioning until 1944. During the Nazi occupation, over 100,000 people passed through this building, to be

POLAND

deported later to the death camps. Most of the edifice is now occupied by the extensive **Lublin Museum** (closed Monday and Tuesday), which contains several sections including archaeology, ethnography, decorative art, arms, coins and paintings.

Adjoining the eastern end of the building is the 14th-century **Chapel of the Holy Trinity**. Its interior is entirely covered with amazing Russo-Byzantine frescoes painted in the 1410s, possibly the finest medieval wall paintings in Poland. The chapel is open for visitors within the museum opening hours.

Majdanek Death Camp Majdanek, 4km south-east of Lublin's centre, was one of the largest death camps in Europe. About 360,000 people, representing 51 nationalities from 26 countries (including some 100,000 Jews), were exterminated here.

Barracks, guard towers and long lines of formerly electrified double barbed wire remain as they were more than 50 years ago, and you don't need much imagination to feel the horror of those days. There is a sobering exhibition, and a small cinema shows documentaries. Near the road, in front of the camp, is a massive stone monument to the victims of Majdanek, while at the rear of the camp is a domed mausoleum holding the ashes of the victims. Both memorials are impressive.

The museum is open daily except Monday from 8 am to 5 pm (October to April till 3 pm). Entrance is free. Trolleybus No 156 from ul Królewska near the Bank Pekao will take you to Majdanek.

Skansen Lublin has an interesting skansen (closed Monday), about 5km west of the city centre, on the Warsaw road. To get there, take bus No 18 from ul Krakowskie Przedmieście anywhere west of Plac Litewski. Covering an undulating terrain of 25 hectares, it has half a dozen old farmsteads with fully equipped interiors, open to visitors. It all looks like a natural traditional village.

Places to Stay

Lublin has quite a choice of places to stay and they are generally inexpensive. The other side of the coin is that most are poor and some distance from the centre, involving the use of public transport or at least a long walk.

Camping There are three camping grounds in the city; all have chalets and are open May to September, and all are a fair distance from the city centre. The closest one is *Camping Nr 91 Na Sławinku* (☎ 741 22 31), ul Sławinkowska 46, about 5km west of the centre, close to the skansen (bus No 18 from the bus terminal, bus No 20 from the train station).

The other two camping grounds are both on an artificial lake, the Zalew Zemborzycki, about 8km south of the centre. *Camping Nr 65 Marina* (☎ 744 10 70), ul Krężnicka 6, is accessible by bus No 8 from ul Narutowicza opposite the Osterwa Theatre in the centre. From the main train station, take bus No 17, 20, 21 or 27 to the Stadion Sygnał and change for bus No 25. *Camping Nr 35 Dąbrowa* (☎ 744 08 31) is at ul Nad Zalewem 12, right across the lake from the Marina, but a long way around. There's no direct public transport from either the centre or the train station.

Hostels The all-year, 80-bed *youth hostel* (☎ 533 06 28) is at ul Długosza 6, 2km west of the Old Town (take trolleybus No 150 from the train station, bus Nos 5, 10, 18, 31 and 57 from the bus terminal). Just a five-minute walk south of the youth hostel, at ul Akademicka 4, is *Dom Nauczyciela* (☎ 533 82 85), a clean and cheap teachers' hostel, costing US$12/18 a single/double without bath. It's often full.

There are two budget places to stay in the Old Town, but it's hard to find a vacancy there. The 28-bed *Wojewódzki Ośrodek Metodyczny* (☎ 743 61 33), ul Dominikańska 5, charges US$9 per person in a four or five-bed dorm with bath. You have more chance of getting a shelter in the Church-run *Archidiecezjalny Dom Rekolekcyjny* (☎ 532 41 38), ul Podwale 15. Two to seven-bed dorms (some with bath, others without) cost US$7 per person, and you can get budget meals on the premises.

Some student dorms near the Almatur office (☎ 533 32 37), ul Langiewicza 10, open as hostels in summer. The office may have some information about that; otherwise inquire at the tourist office. A more reliable student accommodation, however, is the all-year *Hotel Studenta Zaocznego UMCS* (☎ 525 10 81), ul Sowińskiego 17. It offers singles/doubles/triples for US$20/

23/26. One bathroom is shared between two adjacent rooms.

There are several unsavoury workers' hotels, all located in drab blocks, scattered throughout the city. Their main clientele are visitors from across the eastern border. The most central of these is *Hotel Pracowniczy LPBP* (☎ 747 44 07), ul Podzamcze 7, 500m north-east of the bus terminal. A double/triple/quad with shared facilities costs US$12/14/16. Bus Nos 17 and 33 from the train station area will drop you off at the hotel's door.

If you're arriving late or tired by train, you can try the basic *Hotel Piast* (☎ 532 16 46), ul Pocztowa 2, next to the train station. Singles/doubles/triples with shared facilities cost US$13/17/23, or you can pay US$7 a bed in a four or five-bed dorm.

Hotels The simple *Motel PZM* (☎ 533 42 32), ul Prusa 8, is nothing special but it's within walking distance of the Old Town. Singles/doubles without bath cost US$12/20, while rooms with bath go for US$26/28.

The *Hotel Bystrzyca* (☎ 532 30 03), Al Zygmuntowskie 4, 1km north of the train station, costs US$20/27/32 a single/double/triple; one bathroom is shared by two rooms. The quiet *Hotel Garnizonowy* (☎ 533 05 36), ul Spadochroniarzy 7, 3km west of the Old Town, has neat singles/doubles/triples with bath for US$34/40/44.

Places to Eat
There are still a few milk bars, including *Bar Staromiejski*, ul Jezuicka 1, at the foot of the Kraków Gate, and *Bar Turystyczny*, ul Krakowskie Przedmieście 29. Both are basic. Better places for a budget lunch include *Bar Uniwersalny Ludowy*, ul Krakowskie Przedmieście 60 and *Bar Pod Basztą*, ul Królewska 6.

There are finally some noteworthy eating establishments in the Old Town, which until recently was nearly a ghost town. The *Oberża Artystyczna Złoty Osioł*, ul Grodzka 5a, has a pleasant interior and a cosy inner garden and serves hearty food and drinks. The newer *Kawiarnia Szeroka 28*, ul Grodzka 21, also offers artistic charm and economical dining. Slightly cheaper is another charming place, the *Piwnica u Biesów* in the cellar at Rynek

18 (enter through the best doorway on the square). It is essentially a drink bar but it has a reasonable food menu.

If you are staying in the youth hostel, you can eat in the nearby *Karczma Słupska*, Al Racławickie 22, a place with a slightly folksy décor and acceptably cheap food.

For a more upmarket lunch or dinner, you may consider *Restauracja Resursa*, Krakowskie Przedmieście 68, or *Klub Hades* in the basement of a large building of the Cultural Centre (Dom Kultury), ul Peowiaków 12. The club has a restaurant, open from noon till 3 am, and an adjacent bar with pool tables. Access to both is restricted to club members, but the manager will probably let you in. The club's café, *Kawiarnia Artystyczna* (enter from the opposite, northern side of the building) is open to all and stages live music, including jazz (see the following Entertainment section).

Entertainment
For classical music, check the program of *Filharmonia Lubelska* at its brand-new huge hall at ul Skłodowskiej-Curie 5. Here is also the *Teatr Muzyczny* which stages operettas and a variety of musical events. The main city venue for drama is *Teatr im Osterwy*, ul Narutowicza 17, featuring mostly classical plays with some emphasis on national drama.

Real theatre buffs may be interested in the experimental *Gardzienice Theatre*, one of the most outstanding and accomplished companies currently performing in Poland. The theatre is based and performs in the small village of Gardzienice, 28km south-east of Lublin, but it has an office (☎ 532 98 40 or ☎ 532 96 37) in Lublin at ul Grodzka 5a. It's essential to book well in advance.

As for lighter fare, Kawiarnia Artystyczna of *Klub Hades* has live music (rock, jazz etc) and discos on Friday. The club organises the three-day Hades Jazz Festival in late October.

Chatka Żaka, ul Radziszewskiego 16, is the student club of the Marie Curie University, which has cultural events on some days. Behind the Chatka is a popular student disco, *Art-Bis-Club*.

Getting There & Away
Train The main train station, Lublin Główny, is linked to the Old Town by trolleybus No 160 and several buses including Nos 13 and

17. There are at least half a dozen fast trains daily to Warsaw (175km), Radom (128km) and Kielce (213km), and two fast trains to Kraków (345km). Tickets can be bought directly from the station or from the Orbis office, ul Narutowicza 33a.

Bus The central bus terminal, Dworzec Główny PKS, is at the foot of the castle near the Old Town and handles most of the traffic. Buses to Kazimierz Dolny (44km) run every hour or so (look for the Puławy bus via Nałęczów and Kazimierz). To Zamość (89km), PKS buses run every half-hour, and there are also private minibuses every 20 minutes. There are three buses daily to Sandomierz (110km) – look for the Tarnobrzeg bus in the timetable. Every morning a fast bus goes directly to Kraków (269km). Polski Express buses go to Warsaw every other hour.

There are two morning buses to Kozłówka (38km), and then nothing until about 3 pm. They are hard to detect in the timetable – ask at the information counter.

Four buses a day to Przemyśl (185km) depart from the south terminal next to the train station.

KOZŁÓWKA

The hamlet of Kozłówka, 38km north of Lublin, is famous for its sumptuous late-baroque palace, which until WWII was the residence of the wealthy Zamoyski family. Today it's a museum displaying much of the original decoration, including period furnishings, ceramic stoves, crystal mirrors etc. The most striking feature, however, is an unusually extensive collection of paintings, each one complete with its own distinct ornate frame.

Kozłówka is also noted for its unique collection of socialist-realist art, the official artistic doctrine in postwar Poland until 1954, which is displayed in one of the side wings of the palace. You surely have never seen so many portraits and busts of revolutionary communist leaders – including Stalin, Lenin, Marx and Mao Zedong – in one place.

The palace is open March to November, on Tuesday, Thursday and Friday from 10 am to 4 pm, and on Wednesday, Saturday and Sunday from 10 am to 5 pm. Weekdays are normally intended for prebooked excursions,

but individual tourists can usually tag along with one of the groups. On weekends, individual visitors have priority.

The usual departure point for Kozłówka is Lublin – see that section earlier for transport details. Returning to Lublin, there are buses in the afternoon roughly every hour, or you can hang around the car park for a lift.

KAZIMIERZ DOLNY
☎ 081

Set on the bank of the Vistula at the foot of wooded hills, Kazimierz Dolny is a small, picturesque town with much charm and atmosphere. It has some fine historic architecture, good museums and attractive countryside. The town has become a fashionable weekend and holiday spot for tourists.

Founded in the 14th century by King Casimir the Great, the town was called Dolny (lower) to distinguish it from up-river Kazimierz, today part of Kraków. It soon grew rich as a trading port, sending grain and salt downriver to Gdańsk and farther on for export. A number of splendid burghers' mansions and mighty granaries were built, and some of this heritage can still be seen today.

Information
The PTTK office (☎ 81 00 46), Rynek 27, has information about the town and sells brochures and maps. There are no banks in town and only one kantor (at the post office).

Things to See
The **Rynek** is lined with merchants' houses, of which the finest are the two arcaded **Houses of the Przybyła Brothers** (1615) with extraordinary Renaissance façade decoration in bas-relief. Another fine historic building, the **House of the Celej Family** (1630), accommodates the **Town Museum** (closed Monday), featuring paintings and a large collection of gold and silverwork, including old Judaic cult silverware and jewellery.

The mannerist **parish church** (1613) overlooking the Rynek shelters the ornate carved organ from 1620 which sounds as good as it looks, and organ recitals are held here. There's a fine view from the nearby ruins of the 14th-century **castle**. A wider panorama can be got from the 13th-century **watch-tower**, 200m up the hill.

The **Natural History Museum** (closed Monday), in a large granary from 1591, has geology, mineralogy and flora and fauna sections. It's a 10-minute walk from the Rynek along the Puławy road.

For centuries and right up to WWII, the Jews accounted for roughly half the town's population, but few escaped the death camps. Have a glimpse at the 18th-century **synagogue**, now a cinema, just off the Rynek, and visit the impressive **Jewish monument**, 1km south of the town.

It's worth doing some walking in the picturesque environs of Kazimierz (several marked trails originate at the Rynek), and taking the trip by ferry to the other side of the Vistula, to visit the castle and museum in **Janowiec**.

Special Events
The highly acclaimed Festival of Folk Bands and Singers takes place in Kazimierz during the last week of June, from Friday to Sunday.

Places to Stay & Eat
Kazimierz has plenty of places to stay, yet you might face some problems on summer weekends. At the budget end, the *Camping Nr 36* (☎ 81 00 36), behind Dom Turysty Spichlerz, is open May to September. The PTTK office on the Rynek arranges accommodation in private rooms (US$6 to US$8 per person).

There are two all-year youth hostels: *Pod Wianuszkami* (☎ 81 03 27), ul Puławska 64, on the Puławy road about 1.5km from the Rynek, and the very central *Strażnica* (☎ 81 04 27) in the building of the fire brigade station at ul Senatorska 23a.

Hotel-type accommodation includes the *Zajazd Piastowski* (☎ 81 03 51), ul Słoneczna 3, the *Hotel Łaźnia* (☎ 81 02 98), ul Senatorska 21 and the *Dom Turysty Spichlerz* (☎ 81 00 36), ul Krakowska 61. Alternatively try the small *Pensjonat Pod Wietrzną Górą* (☎ 81 05 43), ul Krakowska 1 (US$16 per person). All four have reasonable restaurants, and there are more places to eat around the town.

Several cafés on and around the Rynek serve fast food. The *Piekarnia Sarzyński*, a

bakery at ul Nadrzeczna 6, has delicious rolls and bread, including some unusual bread in the shape of roosters, crayfish and other animals. Next door is the budget *Grill u Piekarzy*. The *Galeria Herbaciarnia u Dziwisza*, ul Krakowska 8, is a charming, cosy place recommended for a good tea (80-odd tastes to choose from). Diagonally opposite is perhaps the best eatery in town, the *Restauracja Vincent*.

Getting There & Away
Kazimierz can be conveniently visited as a stop on your Lublin-Warsaw route, or as a day trip from Lublin. Buses to Lublin (44km) go roughly every hour, taking a bit over an hour. There are about five fast buses daily straight to Warsaw (140km), taking 3½ hours, or you can go by any of the frequent buses to Puławy (13km) and change to a train to Warsaw.

Silesia

Silesia (Śląsk) in south-western Poland is made up of three geographically distinct regions. Its small south-eastern part, the Silesian Upland or Upper Silesia (Górny Śląsk), is the industrial heart of the country. Occupying only about 2% of Poland's territory, it's home to over 10% of the country's population and provides a fifth of its wealth, including half its steel and 90% of its coal (8% of the world supply). The central part of Upper Silesia around Katowice is Poland's most densely populated, industrialised and polluted area.

To the north-west lies the Silesian Lowland or Lower Silesia (Dolny Śląsk), which stretches along the Odra River for over 300km. The main city of this fertile, predominantly farming region is Wrocław. The devastating flood caused by the overflowing of the Odra in July 1997 (probably the largest flood in Poland's 1000-year history) resulted in an estimated US$2 billion damage, but the region is slowly recovering.

The lowland is bordered on the south-west by the Sudeten Mountains (Sudety), a varied and largely forested range running for over 250km along the Czech border; its highest peak is Mt Śnieżka (1602m).

POLAND

Silesia was settled gradually during the second half of the first millennium AD by Slavic tribes known collectively as the Ślężanie or Silesians, and incorporated into Poland by Duke Mieszko I shortly before 1000. When Poland was split into principalities in the 12th century, Silesia was divided into independent duchies ruled by Silesian Piasts, a branch of the first Polish dynasty. In the 1330s the region was annexed by Bohemia and in 1526 it fell under Austria's Habsburgs. Frederick the Great took Silesia for Prussia in 1741, and the large Polish minority was subjected to Germanisation.

After WWI Polish nationalist uprisings resulted in most of Upper Silesia going to Poland, but the rest, including Lower Silesia, joined Poland only in the aftermath of WWII. The Germans were repatriated into the new Germany and their place was taken by Poles resettled from Poland's eastern provinces lost to the Soviet Union. This chequered history can be traced in the local architecture, the people and the atmosphere.

While tourists may not be attracted to the industrial wonders of Katowice and its vicinity, Wrocław is an old, historic, cultured city deserving a visit. Parts of the Sudeten Mountains, particularly the Góry Stołowe (Table Mountains) west of Kłodzko and the Karkonosze south of Jelenia Góra, will lure hikers and nature lovers.

WROCŁAW
☎ 071

Wrocław was originally founded on the island of Ostrów Tumski on the Odra River. It must have already been a fair-sized stronghold by 1000, judging by the fact it was chosen as one of Piast Poland's three bishoprics, along with Kraków and Kołobrzeg. The medieval town developed to become a prosperous trading and cultural centre of Lower Silesia.

After six centuries in foreign hands – Bohemian, Austrian and Prussian – Wrocław returned to Poland in 1945 in a sorry state. During the final phase of WWII, the Nazis fortified the area and 40,000 German soldiers held out from 15 February to 6 May, only surrendering after Berlin fell on 2 May 1945. In the course of this 81-day siege 70% of the city was destroyed. German residents who hadn't already fled were deported and the ruins resettled with Poles from Poland's prewar eastern regions, mostly Lviv.

Today, this restored enjoyable city of 650,000 inhabitants offers good museums, historic buildings and parks, plus a lovely old market square and a memorable cluster of churches by the river. Wrocław is a lively cultural centre, with theatres, several important annual festivals and a large student community based in 13 institutions of higher education.

Orientation
The train and bus stations are near each other 1km south of the Old Town. Hotels are conveniently close to the city centre and the train station, and almost all major tourist attractions are within walking distance in the central area.

The addresses of the buildings around the edge of the central square are given as 'Rynek', while the block in the middle of the square is referred to in addresses as 'Rynek-Ratusz'.

Information
Tourist Office The municipal tourist office (☎ 44 31 11; fax 44 29 62), Rynek 14, is open weekdays from 9 am to 5 pm, Saturday from 10 am to 2 pm. It's worth picking up the practical Welcome to Wrocław magazine (free). If the tourist office doesn't have it, try one of the travel agencies or upmarket hotels.

Money Bank Pekao, ul Oławska 2, changes travellers cheques and gives advances on Visa and MasterCard. Bank Zachodni is useful for travellers cheques and gives advances on Visa; it can be found at several locations, including ul Ofiar Oświęcimskich 41/43 and Rynek 9/11. For changing cash, there are plenty of kantors throughout the central area, plus two or three in the train station, which trade 24 hours a day. There are also several ATMs in the centre.

Travel Agencies The Orbis office (☎ 343 26 65) is at Rynek 29. PTTK (☎ 343 03 44), Rynek-Ratusz 11/12, can arrange foreign-language guides, but it usually needs to be notified well in advance. Almatur (☎ 44 47 28), ul Kościuszki 34, sells ISIC cards and international transportation tickets for students and nonstudents.

Bookshops English-language books are available from PolAnglo, ul Szczytnicka 28; the bookshop of the English Department of Wrocław University, ul Kuźnicza 22; Columbus, ul Kuźnicza 57/58; and the bookstore, ul Więzienna 16. The best place for maps of Polish cities and regions is Księgarnia Firmowa PPWK, ul Oławska 2, just off the Rynek. EMPiK, Plac Kościuszki 21/23, has the widest choice of foreign-language newspapers and magazines.

Cybercafés Internet Café is at ul Świdnicka 19 (2nd floor).

Things to See
Old Market Square At 173 by 208m, this is Poland's second-largest old market square after the one in Kraków. The middle is occupied by a large block of buildings that incorporate three parallel streets. The **town hall** (1327-1504) on the southern side of the central block is certainly one of the most beautiful in Poland. Inside is the **Historical Museum** (closed Monday and Tuesday), accommodated in splendid period interiors.

In the north-western corner of the Rynek are two small houses called **Jaś i Małgosia**, or Hansel and Gretel, linked by a baroque gate. Just behind them looms the monumental 14th-century **St Elizabeth's Church** with its 83m-high tower, which you can climb for a sweeping view. The south-western corner of the Rynek spills into **Plac Solny**, or Salt Square, which was once the site of the town's salt trade.

Around the Old Town One block east of the Rynek is the Gothic **St Mary Magdalene's Church** with a Romanesque portal from around 1280 incorporated into its southern external wall. The tympanum is on display in the National Museum. Farther east along ul Wita Stwosza, past St Adalbert's Church, is the 15th-century former Bernardine church and monastery which is now home to the **Museum of Architecture** (closed Monday and Tuesday).

In the park behind the museum is the **Panorama Racławicka** (closed Monday), a huge 360° painting of the Battle of Racławice (1794) near Kraków, in which the Polish peasant army led by Tadeusz Kościuszko defeated Russian forces intent on partitioning Poland. Created by Jan Styka and Wojciech Kossak for the centenary of the battle in 1894, the painting is 114m long and 15m high. You're given headphones with an English, French or German commentary, but they screech and the story is difficult to follow. Buy your tickets early (US$5, US$3 for students), as the place may be overrun by tourists.

Just to the east is the **National Museum** (closed Monday) with an extensive collection of masterpieces of medieval Silesian art, plus a good selection of Polish paintings from the 17th century to the present day. The Panorama admission ticket entitles you to a free visit to the museum on the same day.

Cross the Most Pokoju, the bridge over the Odra River beside the museum, taking a glance upstream (east) at the **Most Grunwaldzki** (1910), one of the most graceful of Wrocław's 90 bridges. On the north side of the river, turn left where the tram tracks bend right and walk west into Ostrów Tumski, the cradle of the city inhabited since about the 8th century. Today it's a markedly ecclesiastical district dotted with churches. It's no longer on an island, since an arm of the Odra was filled in during the 19th century.

The focal point is the mighty two-towered Gothic **cathedral**, boasting a triptych (1522) attributed to the school of Veit Stoss in its high altar. Behind the altar are three chapels deserving attention, though they are usually kept securely locked. Next to the cathedral is the **Archdiocesan Museum** (closed Monday), and farther north stretches the lovely, restful **Botanical Gardens** established in 1811.

West from the cathedral is the two-storey Gothic **Church of the Holy Cross** (1288-1350). Cross over the small bridge to the 14th-century **Church of St Mary on the Sand** with its lofty Gothic vaults.

Southbound now, follow the tram tracks across another small bridge to the large, red-brick **market hall** (1908). Next, follow the riverbank downstream to the university quarter. Its centre point is an ornate university building (1728-42) with the spectacular

WROCŁAW

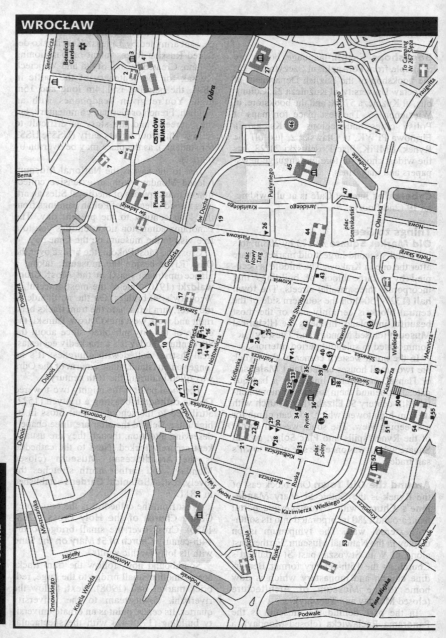

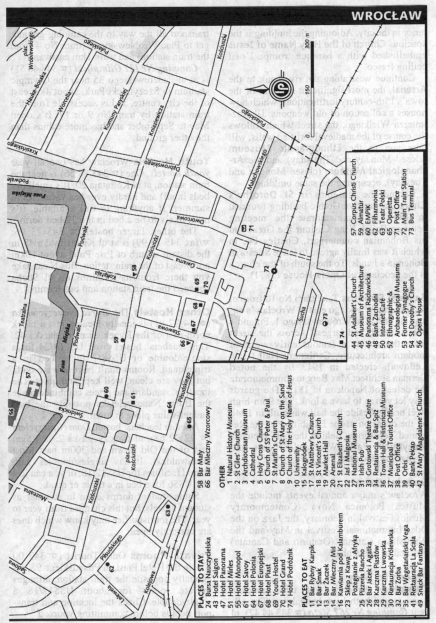

WROCŁAW

PLACES TO STAY
24 Bursa Nauczycielska
43 Hotel Saigon
47 Hotel Panorama
51 Hotel Mities
55 Hotel Monopol
61 Hotel Savoy
64 Hotel Polonia
67 Hotel Europejski
68 Hotel Piast
69 Youth Hostel
70 Hotel Grand
74 Hotel Podróżnik

PLACES TO EAT
11 Bar Rybny Karpik
12 Bar Smak
14 Bar Żaczek
15 Bar Mleczny Miś
16 Kawiarnia pod Kalamburem
23 Sklep z Kawą
25 Pożegnanie z Afryką
26 Pizzeria Rancho
28 Bar Jacek i Agatka
30 Karczma Piastów
32 Karczma Lwowska
30 Restauracja Królewska
29 Bar Zorba
35 Bar Wegetariański Vega
41 Restauracja La Scala
49 Snack Bar Fantasy
58 Bar Mały
66 Bar Mleczny Wzorcowy

OTHER
1 Natural History Museum
2 St Giles' Church
3 Archdiocesan Museum
4 Cathedral
5 Holy Cross Church
6 Church of SS Peter & Paul
7 St Martin's Church
8 Church of St Mary on the Sand
9 Church of the Holy Name of Jesus
10 University
15 Kalogródek
17 St Matthew's Church
18 St Vincent's Church
19 Market Hall
20 Arsenal
21 St Elizabeth's Church
22 Jaś i Małgosia
27 National Museum
31 Irish Pub
33 Grotowski Theatre Centre
36 Restauracja & Bar Spiż
37 Town Hall & Historical Museum
38 Municipal Tourist Office
39 Post Office
40 Bank Pekao
42 St Mary Magdalene's Church
44 St Adalbert's Church
45 Museum of Architecture
46 Panorama Racławicka
48 Bank Zachodni
50 Internet Café
52 Ethnographic &
   Archaeological Museums
53 Former Synagogue
54 St Dorothy's Church
56 Opera House
57 Corpus Christi Church
59 Almatur
60 EMPiK
62 Filharmonia
63 Teatr Polski
65 Operetta
71 Post Office
72 Main Train Station
73 Bus Terminal

POLAND

Aula Leopoldina on the 1st floor (closed Wednesday), regarded as the best baroque interior in the city. Adjoining the building is the spacious **Church of the Holy Name of Jesus** embellished with a baroque trompe l'oeil ceiling fresco.

Continue west along the riverbank to the **Arsenal**, the most significant remnant of the town's 15th-century fortifications, which now houses a collection of old weapons. Ul Kazimierza Wielkiego, the street which follows the course of the medieval fortified walls, will take you to the **Ethnographic Museum** (closed Monday and Thursday) and the **Archaeological Museum** (closed Monday and Tuesday), occupying the same building.

Behind the museums is **St Dorothy's Church**, a massive Gothic building founded in 1351 to commemorate the meeting between Polish King Casimir the Great and his Bohemian counterpart, Charles IV, in which it was finally agreed to leave Silesia in Bohemia's hands. To the south of the church is the neoclassical **Opera House** (1871).

Eastern Suburbs Take tram No 10 from ul Kazimierza Wielkiego east to Wrocław's enjoyable **zoo** at ul Wróblewskiego 1, Poland's oldest (1865) and largest. Across the street from the zoo is a famous early work of modern architecture, **Centenary Hall** (Hala Ludowa), erected in 1913 by the noted German architect Max Berg to commemorate the defeat of Napoleon in 1813. The guards may let you in to have a look. The 96m-high steel needle beside the hall was built in 1948 on the occasion of the Exhibition of the Regained Territories. Behind the hall stretches **Szczytnicki Park**, Wrocław's oldest and largest wooded area.

Special Events
Wrocław's major annual events include the Musica Polonica Nova (Contemporary Music) Festival in February, the Jazz on the Oder International Festival in May and the Wratislavia Cantans (Oratorio and Cantata) Festival in September.

Places to Stay
Camping Wrocław has two camping grounds and both have bungalows. The all-year *Camping Nr 267 Ślęza* (☎ 343 44 42), ul

Na Grobli 16/18, is on the bank of the Odra 2km east of the Old Town. There's no urban transport all the way to the camping ground; get to Plac Wróblewskiego (tram No 4 from the train station) and walk 1km eastward.

Camping Nr 117 Olimpijski (☎ 348 46 51) is at ul Paderewskiego 35 near the Olympic stadium in Szczytnicki Park, about 4km east of the city centre, and is accessible from the train station by tram No 9 or 17. It's open May to September and has more cabins than the other ground.

Youth Hostels Wrocław has two all-year *youth hostels*. One (☎ 343 88 56) is near the train station, at ul Kołłątaja 20. It's small (47 beds in all) and hardly ever has vacancies in summer. If anything is still available, it's most likely to be a bed in the 22-bed dorm.

The other, larger hostel (☎ 345 73 96; ☎/fax 345 73 99) is at ul Kiełczowska 43 in the distant suburb of Psie Pole, about 10km north-east of the train station. Bus N can take you there from its terminus on ul Sucha between the train station and bus terminal.

Other Hostels The *Bursa Nauczycielska* (☎ 44 37 81) is ideally located just a block north-east of the Rynek, at ul Kotlarska 42. This teachers' hostel costs US$14/24 for a single/double or US$8/7 for a bed in a triple/quad. Rooms don't have private bath, but they are clean, well kept and quiet. The location, standard and prices combined make the Bursa Nauczycielska possibly the best budget-value place in town.

Another teachers' hostel, *Dom Nauczyciela* (☎ 22 92 68), ul Nauczycielska 2, is 1.5km east of the Old Town and 300m past Most Grunwaldzki. It has singles/doubles with shared facilities for US$12/18, or you can just pay US$6 for a bed in a triple or quad.

Some student dorms open in summer as student hostels, but this changes from year to year. The tourist office may know which ones are currently open.

Private Rooms Odra Tourist (☎ 343 00 37), in the Hotel Piast, ul Piłsudskiego 98, diagonally opposite the train station, arranges private rooms for about US$12/18 a single/double. Check the location and transport details before committing yourself.

Hotels The noisy *Hotel Piast* (☎ 343 00 33), ul Piłsudskiego 98, is the cheapest hotel in the vicinity of the station but it's hardly inspiring. It costs US$15/27 for singles/doubles without bath and US$33/40 for triples/quads.

The equally noisy *Hotel Grand* (☎ 343 60 71) is just across the street at ul Piłsudskiego 100/102. Grand it is not, but nonetheless it's a bit better than the Piast. It has singles/doubles without bath for US$24/34 and rooms with own bath for US$38/55, breakfast included.

Appreciably quieter is *Hotel Savoy* (☎ 40 32 19 or 344 30 71), Plac Kościuszki 19, within easy walking distance of the station. Singles/doubles with bath cost US$30/40, triples US$50. It's good value and is often full.

You can also try *Hotel Podróżnik* (☎ 73 28 45) on the 1st floor of the bus terminal at ul Sucha 1, where simple doubles/triples/quads with bath cost US$30/38/48.

There are few budget hotels in the Old Town area; *Hotel Mirles* (☎ 341 08 73), ul Kazimierza Wielkiego 45, is one of the cheapest. It has just three doubles (US$30) and two triples (US$42), but it's little known so you have some chance. Baths are shared.

For a bit more comfort try *Hotel Saigon* (☎ 44 28 81), ul Wita Stwosza 22/23, three blocks east of the Rynek. Its rooms have private baths and cost about US$52/58 a single/double.

Of the five Orbis outlets in the city, the stylish *Hotel Monopol* (☎ 343 70 41), ul Modrzejewskiej 2 beside the Opera House, is the cheapest and most colourful. Rooms go for US$38/65 a single/double without bath, US$65/100 with bath, breakfast included. Operating since 1892, the Monopol is the city's oldest hotel. Hitler stayed here whenever he visited Breslau (Wrocław's German name) and addressed the crowds from the balcony.

Places to Eat

Budget eating is no problem in Wrocław. The array of milk bars includes *Bar Mleczny Wzorcowy*, ul Piłsudskiego 86, near the train station; the basic *Bar Mleczny Miś*, ul Kuźnicza 43/45, in the university area; and the best and most central, *Bar Wegetariański Vega*, in the central block of the Rynek next to the town hall.

There are a number of other cheap places, mostly of the newer generation, scattered throughout the Old Town. *Snack Bar Fantasy*, ul Świdnicka 8, is a large self-service cafeteria serving meals (not only snacks) from 11 am to 10 pm. *Bar Smak*, ul Odrzańska 17 (the entrance is from ul Nożownicza), is open from 9 am to 8 pm. Other budget eateries include *Bar Jacek i Agatka*, Plac Nowy Targ 27, *Bar Żaczek*, ul Kuźnicza 43/45, and *Bar Mały* on the corner of ul Kołłątaja and ul Kościuszki.

Bar Rybny Karpik on the corner of ul Grodzka and ul Odrzańska serves cheap fish. *Bar Zorba*, right in the middle of the block in the centre of the Rynek, grills souvlaki and other simple Greek dishes. The cosy *Pizzeria Rancho*, ul Szewska 59, does reasonable pizza.

Most of the city's more decent eating establishments are conveniently around the Rynek. The luxurious *Restauracja Królewska* (King Restaurant), in the gastronomic complex of the Dwór Polski (Polish Court), Rynek 5, is Wrocław's top spot for traditional Polish cuisine in a historic interior. The more informal *Karczma Piastów* (Piast Inn), at the back of the same complex, also has Polish food and is cheaper. *Restauracja La Scala*, Rynek 38, is possibly the best Italian eatery around. The enjoyable *Karczma Lwowska*, Rynek 4 (upstairs), brings some fine Lviv cuisine to town.

The best choice of aromatic coffees is served in the *Sklep z Kawą Pożegnanie z Afryką*, ul Igielna 16, one block north of the Rynek. Typically for the chain, it's a non-smoking venue.

With its Art Nouveau decorations and arty atmosphere, the *Kawiarnia pod Kalamburem*, ul Kuźnicza 29a, is one of the most charming cafés in town. A short menu of light dishes is available at lunchtime.

Entertainment

Wrocław is an important cultural centre, and there's much activity year-round. Local papers have listings of what's on, or pick up the detailed free cultural monthly, *Co Jest Grane*.

Theatre Wrocław is internationally known for the avant-garde Teatr Laboratorium (Laboratory Theatre) of Jerzy Grotowski, created in the early 1960s and dissolved 20 years later after its founder moved to Italy and established a theatre research centre there.

In 1990 the *Grotowski Theatre Centre* was founded in the theatre's former home at Rynek-Ratusz 27, which has documentaries on the Laboratory Theatre and can present them on request. It also invites various experimental groups, occasionally from abroad, to give performances in its small theatre.

Today, the main ambassador for Wrocław theatre is the Wrocławski Teatr Pantomimy created by Henryk Tomaszewski. The theatre is usually on tour somewhere in the country or abroad. Check with the tourist office for news and don't miss it if it is in the city.

Teatr Polski, ul Zapolskiej 3, is the major mainstream city venue, staging classic Polish and foreign drama, while *Teatr Współczesny*, ul Rzeźnicza 12, tends more towards contemporary productions.

Opera & Classical Music The *Opera House* is at ul Świdnicka 35, while the *Operetta* is at ul Piłsudskiego 72. Concerts of classical music are held regularly, usually on Friday and Saturday, in the *Filharmonia* (Philharmonic Hall), ul Piłsudskiego 19.

Jazz The basement *Klub Muzyczny Jazzgot*, ul Rzeźnicza 11, is one of the very few places which stages live jazz. Also check *Czarny Salon*, Rynek-Ratusz 27.

Bars & Pubs The *Irish Pub* at Plac Solny 5, is rather expensive, but has live music on some nights. A cheap watering hole is the open-air *Kalogródek* on the corner of ul Uniwersytecka and ul Kuźnicza, an informal place with an amphitheatre-like patio.

Wrocław's most unusual drinking spot is probably *Restauracja & Bar Spiż*, a subterranean German-style restaurant-cum-bar beside the town hall, which serves beer from its own brewery. The restaurant is upmarket but a mug of its rich brew in the adjacent wood-panelled bar should fit almost anyone's budget and belly, and you can see brass vats used in the production process behind the buffet. There's a beer garden in summer on the square outside.

Getting There & Away

Air The airport in Strachowice, 10km west of the city centre, is accessible by bus No 106 from the Wrocław Świebodzki train station, a 10-minute walk west of the Rynek. There are direct connections with Warsaw (four times a day), Frankfurt/Main (daily), Copenhagen (daily) and Vienna (four days a week). The LOT office (☎ 343 17 44), ul Piłsudskiego 36, and Orbis, Rynek 29, reserve seats and sell tickets.

Train The main train station, Wrocław Główny, was built in 1856 and is a historical monument in itself. Trains are plentiful and can take you to most places in the region and beyond. Fast trains to Katowice (190km) depart every hour or two; many of them continue to Kraków (268km). There are at least half a dozen fast trains plus three express trains to Warsaw (385km) and some stop at Łódź (242km) en route. Wrocław also has regular train links with Poznań (165km), Wałbrzych (70km), Jelenia Góra (126km), Legnica (66km), Zielona Góra (156km) and Kłodzko (96km).

International destinations include Berlin, Budapest, Dresden, Frankfurt/ Main, Kiev and Prague.

Bus The bus terminal south of the main train station handles all bus traffic in the region and beyond, though most tourist destinations can also be reached by train. There are a number of international bus routes to places including Prague and plenty of cities in Western Europe. Tickets are available from Virgo (at the terminal itself), Orbis, Almatur and other travel agencies.

Wielkopolska

Wielkopolska (Great Poland) was the cradle of the Polish nation. Here, along the Warta River, lived the Polanians, a Slavic tribe which gave its name to the whole country. In 966 Mieszko I, duke of the Polanians, was baptised and his son, Boleslaus the Brave, was crowned king in 1025, establishing the Piast dynasty which ruled Poland until 1370.

Despite the royal seat moving to Kraków in 1038, Wielkopolska remained Poland's most important province and an integral part of the country until the second partition in 1793, when it was annexed to Prussia. After Bismarck set up the German empire in 1871, Germanisation and German colonisation of the region became intense. Returned to Poland in 1919, the area was seized by the Nazis in 1939 and devastated during the liberation battles of 1945.

Today, rebuilt Poznań is the region's major industrial, commercial and cultural centre, and an interesting historical city. From here many visitors wander along the so-called Piast Trail through the places where Poland was formed. Gniezno is one of the key spots on the route, and can easily be visited on the way to Toruń. Though German influence is visible, Wielkopolska is as Polish as you can get.

POZNAŃ
☎ 061

Poznań (population 590,000), midway between Berlin and Warsaw, was a focal point of Polish history a millennium ago. A wooden fort was built on the island of Ostrów Tumski in the 9th century, and from 968 to 1038 Poznań was the de facto capital of Poland. By the 12th century the settlement had expanded beyond the island, and in 1253 a new town centre was laid out on the left bank of the Warta River, where it is now.

By the 15th century Poznań was already famous for its fairs, and despite Swedish assaults in the 17th century, the city continued as an important trading centre. In 1793 Poznań fell under Prussian rule to remain so until 1918, when it returned to Poland. The city was under Nazi occupation during WWII and the 1945 battle to liberate it lasted over a month and did a huge amount of damage.

The 1956 massive strike of Poznań's industrial workers, demanding 'bread, truth and freedom', was the first serious popular upheaval in communist Poland. The strike was cruelly crushed by tanks, leaving 76 dead and over 600 wounded.

Since 1925 Poznań has been the site of Poland's largest international trade fairs, which are now held for a few days in most months and attract hordes of visitors and businesspeople. If you are interested in Poznań's historic monuments and varied

museums, it's better to avoid these periods. July and August are the fair-free, relatively quiet months.

Orientation

The Old Town, which contains most of the major tourist attractions, is about 2km northeast of the main train station. Between these two points spreads the new city centre, composed mainly of postwar architecture plus some monumental public buildings from the Prussian era. This area is dotted with offices, stores and restaurants, but has few tourist sights.

Information

Tourist Offices The municipal tourist office (☎ 852 61 56), Stary Rynek 59, is open weekdays from 9 am to 5 pm, Saturday from 10 am to 2 pm. The city tourist office (☎ 851 96 87), ul Ratajczaka 44, is open weekdays from 10 am to 7 pm, Saturday to 5 pm. Glob-Tour (☎ 866 06 67) in the main hall of the main train station is open round the clock. All three offices provide good information and have a selection of maps and tourist publications.

Poznań has a comprehensive what's-on monthly, *iks* (US$1), containing listings and comments (in Polish) on everything from museums to outdoor activities, plus a useful city map. It's available from Ruch kiosks and the tourist offices.

Money Useful banks include Bank Pekao, ul Św Marcin 52/56 and ul Masztalarska 8, Powszechny Bank Kredytowy, Stary Rynek 97/98, and Bank Gdański, ul Paderewskiego 10. Kantors are plentiful throughout the central area, and there are also several ATMs. There's a round-the-clock kantor at the main train station, next to Glob-Tour.

Bookshops Omnibus Bookshop, ul Św Marcin 39, is the best for English-language books, and also has some French and German ones. The newsagency at Café Głos, ul Ratajczaka 39, and EMPiK Megastore, ul Ratajczaka 44, have the largest choice of foreign press in town. For maps, check Księgarnia Turystyczna Globtrotter on ul Żydowska just off the Stary Rynek, which is also the only place in town that sells Lonely Planet guidebooks.

POZNAŃ

POZNAŃ

PLACES TO STAY		32	Pizzeria Tivoli	21	City Tourist Office
1	Hotel Ikar	35	Bistro Avanti	22	EMPiK Megastore
4	Hotel MCM	37	Trattoria Valpolicella	25	Orbis
10	Hotel Lech	38	Bar Wegetariański	26	National Museum
12	Hotel Royal	41	Restauracja Stara	27	Franciscan Church
13	Hotel Wielkopolska		Ratuszowa	28	Museum of Decorative Arts
24	Hotel Rzymski	45	Energia	34	Town Hall & Historical
33	Dom Turysty	46	Restauracja pod Psem		Museum of Poznań
43	Dom Polonii	47	Ristorante Estella	35	Wielkopolska Historical
54	Hotel Poznań				Museum
		OTHER		39	Parish Church
PLACES TO EAT		2	Teatr Wielki	40	Municipal Tourist Office
3	Bar Mleczny Przysmak	5	Bus NB to Kórnik	42	Archaeological Museum
11	Bar Mleczny pod	6	Filharmonia	44	Museum of Musical
	Kuchcikiem	7	Monument to the Victims		Instruments
16	Spaghetti Bar Piccolo		of June 1956	48	Ethnographic Museum
19	Spaghetteria Al Dente	8	Palace of Culture (Kaiserhaus)	49	Palm House
20	Uni-Pozmeat Bar	9	Main Post Office	50	Biuro Zakwaterowania
23	Bar Mleczny Apetyt	14	Internet Club		Przemysław
29	Restauracja Africana	15	Bank Pekao	51	Main Train Station
30	Spaghetti Bar Piccolo	17	Café Głos	52	PKS Bus Terminal
31	Jadłodajnia w Ramce	18	Teatr Polski	53	Teatr Muzyczny

Cybercafés Try Internet Club (☎ 853 78 18), ul Garncarska 10 m 1 (closed Sunday).

Things to See
Old Town Square The Stary Rynek has been restored to its historic shape and looks beautiful, except for two large concrete buildings which were plonked in the middle of the square after the war and are not exactly in harmony with the rest of the architecture. The focal point is the Renaissance **town hall** (1550-60) with its decorative façade facing east. High above the clock two metal goats butt their horns together daily at noon, striking each other 12 times. Inside the building the **Historical Museum of Poznań** (closed Saturday) with its splendid period interiors takes you into Poznań's past.

The **Museum of Musical Instruments** (closed Monday), diagonally opposite the town hall, displays everything from whistles to concert pianos from Europe and elsewhere, dating from the 15th century onward.

The 16th-century Renaissance palace at the south-eastern corner of the square shelters the **Archaeological Museum** (closed Monday), which presents the region's history from the Stone Age to early medieval times.

Note the copy of the famous bronze doors from the Gniezno cathedral.

One of the incongruous modern buildings in the centre of the Stary Rynek houses a peculiar **Military Museum** (closed Monday and Thursday) full of little lead soldiers. The other accommodates an art gallery. Right behind it is the 19th-century neoclassical guardhouse, today the **Historical Museum** featuring temporary exhibitions focused on historical/political issues of the region.

Around the Old Town The 17th-century **Franciscan Church**, one block west of the square, has a beautiful baroque interior complete with wall paintings and rich stucco work. On the hill opposite the church is the **Museum of Decorative Arts** (closed Monday and Thursday) featuring old furniture, silverware, glass, clocks, sundials etc.

The nearby **National Museum** (closed Monday) holds an extensive and varied collection of art, including medieval church woodcarving, Polish paintings of the last two centuries and a reasonable selection of Italian, Flemish, Dutch and Spanish paintings.

Two blocks south of the Stary Rynek is a large baroque **parish church** with a spacious three-naved interior fitted out with

POLAND

monumental altars. A five-minute walk east of here is the **Ethnographic Museum** (closed Monday and Thursday), which boasts an interesting collection of folk woodcarving and traditional costumes of the region.

Ostrów Tumski The cradle of Poznań, the island of Ostrów Tumski, is 1km east of the Old Town (any eastbound tram from Plac Wielkopolski will take you there, or just walk). Its dominant mark is the monumental, double-towered, 14th-century **cathedral**, built on the site of the original pre-Romanesque church from 968 (the relics of which can be seen in the crypt). The Byzantine-style Golden Chapel (1841), mausoleum of Mieszko I and Boleslaus the Brave, is behind the high altar.

Opposite the cathedral is the 15th-century **St Mary's Church**, possibly the purest Gothic building in the city. A couple of hundred metres to the north is the rich **Archdiocesan Museum** (closed Sunday).

Other Sights About 1km north of the Old Town is the 19th-century Prussian **citadel**, where 20,000 German troops held out for a month in February 1945. The fortress was destroyed by artillery fire and a large park has been laid out on the site, which incorporates two war museums and the Commonwealth war cemetery.

Poznań's largest historic building is the massive neo-Romanesque **Kaiserhaus**, ul Św Marcin, built for the German emperor Wilhelm II. Today it's the Palace of Culture, housing various cultural institutions.

A pair of huge crosses bound together in the park beside the palace make up a moving **Monument to the Victims of June 1956**. The dates recall subsequent popular upheavals: 1968 (Warsaw), 1970 (Gdańsk), 1976 (Radom) and 1980 (Gdańsk). Next to the monument is a statue of the Romantic poet Adam Mickiewicz.

In Park Wilsona just west of the fairgrounds is the **Palm House** (Palmiarnia), built in 1910 (closed Monday). Occupying over 4000 sq m, this is one of the biggest greenhouses in Europe. Inside are 19,000 species of tropical and subtropical plants, including reputedly Europe's largest cactus collection and tallest bamboo trees. The adjacent aquarium has a collection of exotic fish.

Special Events

Poznań's pride is the trade fairs, the main ones taking place in January, June, September and October, but there are a dozen minor fairs throughout the year.

Culturally, major events include the Poznań Musical Spring (contemporary music) in April, the 'Malta' International Theatre Festival in late June, and the Wieniawski International Violin Festival which takes place in November every five years (the next one will be in 2001).

Places to Stay

Poznań's hotels and private rooms tend to double their prices when the trade fairs are on. During the major fairs all hotel rooms are likely to be fully booked, and private rooms may be scarce and at distant locations. The prices given in this section are for the off-fair periods. All three tourist offices are knowledgeable about the city's lodging options and may help you to find a bed.

Camping Poznań has three camping grounds, and all have cabins. Closest to the centre is the all-year *Camping Nr 155 Malta* (☎ 876 62 03) on the north-eastern shore of Lake Malta at ul Krańcowa 98, 3km east of the Old Town. Bungalows to sleep two/three/five people, all with private bath and kitchenette, cost US$40/70/100.

The two other camping grounds are on the north-western outskirts of the city, each about 10km from the centre. *Camping Nr 111 Strzeszynek* (☎ 848 31 29) is at ul Koszalińska 15 in the Strzeszynek suburb; *Camping Nr 30 Baranowo* (☎ 848 28 12) is on Lake Kierskie. Both are open from May to September and have much cheaper chalets than the Malta.

Youth Hostels There are four all-year youth hostels in the city. The *youth hostel* (☎ 866 40 40) at ul Berwińskiego 2/3 is a 10-minute walk south-west of the train station along ul Głogowska. It's the smallest and the poorest of the lot and fills up fast.

The *youth hostel* (☎ 848 58 36) at ul Drzymały 3 is 3km north of the train station (take tram No 11) and 3km from the Old Town (tram No 9). It's the newest and best in town.

The two remaining hostels are a long way from the centre. The *youth hostel* (☎ 822 10 63) at ul Biskupińska 27 is about 7km north-west in the suburb of Strzeszyn – bus No 60 from ul Solna on the northern edge of the centre will take you there. The *youth hostel* (☎ 878 84 61) at ul Głuszyna 127 is on the southern city limits over 10km from the centre (there's no direct transport).

Other Hostels The tourist offices should know which student dorms open in summer as student hostels. They will also know about several inexpensive workers' hostels, but most are in the outer suburbs.

Private Rooms Private rooms are run by Biuro Zakwaterowania Przemysław (☎ 866 35 60), ul Głogowska 16, opposite the train station; it's open weekdays from 8 am to 6 pm, Saturday from 10 am to 2 pm (longer at fair times). Rooms normally go for US$10/15 a single/double and are almost always available, but at fair times they cost US$24/32 and there may be fewer rooms to choose from.

Glob-Tour arranges private rooms for marginally more.

Hotels *Dom Turysty* (☎ 852 88 93), set in the 1798 former palace at Stary Rynek 91 (enter from ul Wroniecka), has singles/doubles/triples without bath for US$26/40/45, and singles/doubles with bath for US$36/58. It also has four and five-bed dorms with shared facilities for US$12 a bed. Breakfast is included in the price.

Dom Polonii (☎ 853 19 61), Stary Rynek 51, is the only other place in the heart of the city. It has just two double rooms, both with private bath, costing US$30/50 for single/double occupancy.

The small *Hotel Royal* (☎ 853 78 84), ul Św Marcin 71, midway between the train station and the Old Town, costs US$18/28/40 a single/double/triple without bath, US$20 a single with bath. Next door, at ul Św Marcin 67, *Hotel Wielkopolska* (☎ 852 76 31) costs US$27/44 a single/double without bath, US$35/50 with bath.

An interesting proposition may be *Hotel MCM* (☎ 853 66 69), ul Skośna 1, near the June 1956 Monument, which has beds with magnetic mattresses, reputedly helpful for your health and wellbeing. Doubles with bath cost US$33.

There are several more expensive yet affordable hotels in the central area, including *Hotel Rzymski* (☎ 852 81 21), Al Marcinkowskiego 22, *Hotel Lech* (☎ 853 01 51), ul Św Marcin 74, and *Hotel Ikar* (☎ 857 67 05), ul Kościuszki 118.

Places to Eat

Some of the cheapest food in town is in the modernised *Bar Mleczny Apetyt*, Plac Wolności 1. It has delicious naleśniki, pierogi and pyzy. Other central milk bars include *Bar Mleczny Przysmak*, ul Roosevelta 22, and the basic *Bar Mleczny pod Kuchcikiem*, ul Św Marcin 75.

Uni-Pozmeat Bar, Plac Wolności 14, and *Energia*, ul Woźna 21, are slightly more expensive than milk bars but open a bit longer. Vegetarians can try the simple *Bar Wegetariański*, ul Wrocławska 21.

The very cheap and popular *Bistro Avanti*, Stary Rynek 76, serves tasty plates of spaghetti (US$1); it has a 24-hour outlet at the main train station. *Spaghetti Bar Piccolo*, ul Rynkowa 1, a few steps north of the Stary Rynek, also does spaghetti and is slightly cheaper than the Avanti. It also has an outlet at ul Ratajczaka 37. Yet another budget place of a similar sort is *Spaghetteria Al Dente*, ul 3 Maja. They all have a modest choice of salads.

Restauracja Turystyczna, downstairs from the Dom Turysty hotel, Stary Rynek 91 (enter from ul Wroniecka), has inexpensive Polish food. *Restauracja pod Psem*, ul Garbary 54, is more pleasant and the food is better, though it's more expensive. Another agreeable place with an innovative menu and reasonable prices is *Jadłodajnia w Ramce*, ul Wroniecka 10.

Restauracja Stara Ratuszowa, Stary Rynek 55, has a café on the ground level and a restaurant and bar in the attractive 16th-century cellar, the whole beautifully decorated with old photos and antiques. The food – mostly Polish fare – is good, though not particularly cheap.

For an upmarket Italian meal, choose between *Trattoria Valpolicella*, ul Wrocławska 7, and *Ristorante Estella*, ul Garbary 41. *Restauracja Chińska Bambus*, Stary Rynek 64/65, is said to be the best Chinese eatery in town. African food in appropriate surroundings can be tried at *Restauracja Africana*, ul Zamkowa 3.

POLAND

Entertainment

Poznań has a reasonable cultural menu. Get a copy of *iks* magazine to know what's going on. It's in Polish, but you should be able to work a few things out.

Operas are performed at the *Teatr Wielki* (Grand Theatre), ul Fredry 9. The Polski Teatr Tańca (Polish Dance Theatre), one of the best groups of its kind in Poland, performs here as well. The *Teatr Muzyczny* (Musical Theatre) next to Hotel Poznań features Broadway-style shows.

The main repertory theatres are the *Teatr Polski*, ul 27 Grudnia 8, and the *Teatr Nowy*, ul Dąbrowskiego 5. The former usually has classics in its repertoire, while the latter tends more towards contemporary productions. It's also worth checking the *Teatr Ósmego Dnia* (Theatre of the Eighth Day), which started in the 1970s as an avant-garde, politically involved student theatre. Its office is at ul Ratajczaka 44. The Teatr Biuro Podróży (Travel Agency Theatre) is Poznań's excellent street theatre which has already gained international acclamation.

The *Filharmonia*, ul Św Marcin 81, runs concerts at least every Friday, performed by the local symphony orchestra and often by visiting artists. Poznań has Poland's best boys' choir, the Poznańskie Słowiki (Poznań Nightingales), which sometimes can be heard here.

Rock and jazz concerts are staged in summer in the courtyard of the *Palace of Culture* (Kaiserhaus); enter from Al Niepodległości.

For a beer or two check any of the pubs/bars flooding the old centre. *Harry's Pub*, Stary Rynek 91, was the first establishment of this sort and is still popular, but these days it faces increasing competition from more atmospheric places, including *Pub Stara Piwnica* just across the street, *Pub pod Aniołem*, ul Wrocławska 4, and *Tawerna* around the corner, ul Kozia 4. And don't miss the charming *Klub za Kulisami*, ul Wodna 24.

Getting There & Away

Air Poznań's airport is in the western suburb of Ławica, 7km from the centre and accessible by several bus lines. Direct connections include three flights a day to Warsaw, two to Copenhagen and one to Düsseldorf. The LOT office (☎ 852 28 47) is at ul Piekary 6.

Train Poznań is a busy railway hub. There are about 10 trains daily to Warsaw (311km), including the EuroCity and InterCity trains which run that distance in just over three hours. Equally frequent is transport to Wrocław (165km) and Szczecin (214km), and there are five fast trains direct to Kraków (398km).

Gdańsk (313km) is serviced by four express and two fast trains, and Toruń (142km) by three fast and four ordinary trains, all pass via Gniezno (51km).

Six trains run daily to Berlin (261km), including two EuroCity trains which take just three hours. There are also direct trains to Budapest, Cologne and Moscow.

Bus The PKS bus terminal is a 10-minute walk east of the train station. Buses run half-hourly to Kórnik (20km) and every couple of hours to Rogalin (24 or 31km, depending on the route). You can also get to Kórnik by hourly suburban bus NB from ul Św Marcin near the train track. Buses to Gniezno (49km) depart every hour or so and go via either Kostrzyn or Pobiedziska; the latter pass Lake Lednica en route.

Getting Around

Unlike most other cities, public transport fares depend on how much time the journey takes. Tickets cost US$0.20 for a 10-minute ride, US$0.40 for a half-hour trip, and US$0.80 for a journey of up to one hour. Approximate times of rides are posted at the bus and tram stops.

AROUND POZNAŃ
Kórnik

This small town 20km south-east of Poznań is noted for its **castle** (closed Monday), originally built in the 15th century but extensively remodelled in a mock-Gothic style in the mid-19th century by German architect Karl Friedrich Schinkel. The spectacular Moorish Hall, influenced by the Alhambra in Granada, is the setting for a display of armour and military accessories, and you'll also visit the castle's other interiors, furnished and decorated as they were a century ago.

Behind the castle is a large, English-style **arboretum** (open daily), featuring numerous exotic species of trees and shrubs. The nearby coach house (*powozownia*) houses three 19th-century London coaches.

Kórnik is easily accessible from Poznań by frequent PKS and suburban NB buses. If you plan continuing on to Rogalin, there are about five buses daily (check the timetable before visiting the castle).

Rogalin

This tiny village 13km west of Kórnik boasts a large 18th-century baroque **palace** (closed Monday), once belonging to the aristocratic Raczyński family. The main part of the palace is still closed to visitors because of restoration, but there are some exhibitions in the outbuildings, including the **Gallery of Painting** featuring Polish and European canvases from the 19th and early 20th centuries.

Behind the palace is a French garden, and farther west stretches what once was an English landscaped park, dotted with ancient oak trees. The three most imposing specimens have been fenced off and baptised with the names Lech, Czech and Rus, after the legendary founders of the Polish, Czech and Russian nations.

Buses from Rogalin back to Poznań pass through every couple of hours till late afternoon, but check the timetable before visiting the palace and plan accordingly.

LAKE LEDNICA

Lake Lednica, 30km east of Poznań on the Gniezno road, may be a stop if you are heading this way. The lakeside **skansen** (closed Monday) in Dziekanowice, 500m north of the main road, features a good selection of 19th-century rural architecture from Wielkopolska.

Two kilometres north of the skansen (the signs will direct you) is the **Museum of the First Piasts** (closed Monday), which displays finds excavated on the island of **Ostrów Lednicki**, just opposite the museum and accessible by boat from mid-April to October. The island was one of the major settlements of the first Piasts, rivalling Poznań and Gniezno. In the 10th century a stronghold was built here along with a stone palace and a church, the remains of which can be seen. According to the most recent research, it was here, not in Gniezno as commonly thought, that Mieszko I adopted Christianity in 966.

Getting There & Away

There are several buses a day between Poznań and Gniezno passing the lake. From whichever end you start, take the bus via Pobiedziska, not Kostrzyn, and ask the driver to drop you at the turn-off to Dziekanowice. Trains don't pass this way.

GNIEZNO
☎ 061

Gniezno (population 75,000), 50km east of Poznań, is commonly considered the birthplace of the Polish nation, for it was probably the major stronghold of the Polanie, from where the dispersed tribes of the region were unified by Mieszko I in the 10th century. In 1000 an archbishopric was established in Gniezno, and in 1025 Boleslaus the Brave was crowned in the local cathedral to become the first Polish king. The town has retained its status as Poland's ecclesiastical capital, even though archbishops are only occasional guests these days.

Things to See

Gniezno's pride is its **cathedral**, a large, twin-towered Gothic structure built in the second half of the 14th century after the destruction of the Romanesque cathedral. Inside, the focal point is the elaborate silver sarcophagus (1662) of St Adalbert in the chancel.

St Adalbert was a Bohemian bishop who in 997 passed through Gniezno on a missionary trip to convert the Prussians, a heathen Baltic tribe which inhabited what is now Masuria in north-eastern Poland. Instead the Prussians beheaded the bishop. Boleslaus the Brave recovered the body, paying its weight in gold, then buried it in Gniezno's cathedral in 999. In the same year, Pope Sylvester canonised the martyr, elevating Gniezno to an archbishopric a year later. The life story of the saint appears on the cathedral's famous Romanesque bronze doors (1175), inside below the tower. There are more treasures inside the church.

Behind the cathedral is the rich **Archdiocesan Museum** (closed Sunday). It's also worth visiting the **Museum of the Origins of the Polish State** (closed Monday) on the side of Lake Jelonek, a 10-minute walk from the cathedral.

Places to Stay & Eat

Gniezno has an all-year *youth hostel* (☎ 426 27 80), ul Pocztowa 11, close to the train and bus stations, plus half a dozen hotels including *Hotel Orzeł* (☎ 426 49 25), ul Wrzesińska 25 (US$10/20 a single/double without bath); *Hotel City* (☎ 425 35 35), Rynek 15 (US$24/30 with bath); *Hotel Mieszko* (☎ 426 46 25), ul Strumykowa 2 (US$24/40 with bath); and *Hotel Pietrak* (☎ 426 14 97), ul Chrobrego 3 (US$40/60 with bath and breakfast).

All these hotels have eating facilities, and there are a number of other eating establishments in the centre. Among the cheap options are the snack bar of Hotel Pietrak, whereas *Restauracja Królewska* in the same hotel is more upmarket.

Getting There & Away

The train and bus stations are side by side 1km south-east of the cathedral. Trains run regularly throughout the day to Poznań (51km), and there are several departures daily to Bydgoszcz (102km), Toruń (91km) and Wrocław (216km).

Buses to Poznań via Pobiedziska (eight daily but fewer on weekdays) will let you off at Lake Lednica (18km). For Biskupin (33km), take a bus to Gąsawa and change there for the narrow-gauge train, or just walk the last 2km.

BISKUPIN & AROUND

Biskupin, 33km north of Gniezno, is a fortified **Iron Age township** built on a small island around 550 BC by a tribe of the Lusatian culture, which at that time lived in Central Europe alongside many other groups. The town was accidentally discovered in 1933 and unearthed from a thick layer of turf. It has been partially reconstructed to make it more interesting for the casual visitor.

The nearby **museum** displays the finds excavated in the town, together with some background information about the place and people. Both the town and museum are open daily.

Wenecja, a small village across the lake from Biskupin, is noted for its **Museum of Narrow-Gauge Railways** (open daily).

Getting There & Away

A pleasant way of getting to Biskupin is by the narrow-gauge tourist train, which operates daily from May to September between Żnin and Gąsawa. There are five trains a day in either direction running at intervals of roughly 1¼ hours between around 10 am and 4 pm. The train passes through Wenecja.

Pomerania

Pomerania (Pomorze) stretches along Poland's Baltic coast, from the German frontier in the west to the lower Vistula valley in the east. The region rests on two large urban pillars: Szczecin at its western end and Gdańsk to the east. Between them hangs the sandy coastline dotted with seaside lakes and beach resorts. Farther inland is a wide belt of rugged, forested lakeland.

Szczecin on the Odra River was once the main port of Berlin, but it was largely destroyed in WWII and is now not much more than just another vast industrial city. On the other hand, beautifully restored Gdańsk is one of Poland's loveliest historic cities. The lower Vistula valley is notable for its castles – the best being the one in Malbork – and Toruń, an enchanting, old, riverside town resplendent with Gothic churches.

For those who prefer beaches, there's a long string of seaside resorts all the way from Świnoujście to Hel, with Łeba and its environs being among the most attractive.

Pomerania has long been a battleground between Poles and Germans. Poland never really controlled the Slavic dukedoms of western Pomerania, and from the 12th century the area was gradually absorbed by the Brandenburg margraves. In eastern Pomerania the Germanic Teutonic Knights, invited here in 1226 to help subdue the restive Prussian tribes, played a similar role. From their castles at Malbork and Toruń, the knights defied the king of Poland until their defeat in the 15th century by combined Polish and Lithuanian forces.

In 1621 the Swedes conquered most of the Pomeranian coast, from where they had conducted their devastating war against Poland in the 1550s. In 1720 the Kingdom of Prussia forced the Swedes out and regained control over western Pomerania, and the first partition of Poland (1773) brought everything south as far as Toruń under Prussian control (Toruń itself wasn't annexed by Prussia until 1793).

In 1919 the Treaty of Versailles granted Poland a narrow corridor to the sea from Toruń to Gdańsk, separating East Prussia from Pomerania. Since Gdańsk was not included in the corridor but was made the Free City of Danzig, largely controlled by its dominant German population, the Polish government built a port from scratch at nearby Gdynia.

In 1945 the whole of Pomerania returned to Poland, albeit in a devastated state after a very fierce Soviet offensive. The remaining German inhabitants were expelled and the largely ruined land was repopulated with Poles, mostly from Poland's prewar eastern provinces.

TORUŃ
☎ 056

Toruń (population 210,000) was a wealthy Hanseatic port and the birthplace of Copernicus. Today it's a lovely historic city that retains much of its old architecture, charm and character in its narrow streets, burghers' mansions, vaulted cellars and museums, plus three imposing Gothic churches and a town hall. Toruń offers the chance to step briefly back in history without a lot of other tourists on your heels.

Toruń's Slavic origins go back to the 11th century, but the town really came to life in 1233 when the Teutonic Knights established one of their early outposts here. Its position at a crossing of trade routes on the Vistula River made it an important and swiftly growing port and trading centre; its affiliation with the Hanseatic League in the 1280s gave its development further impetus.

Following the Thirteen Years' War (1454-66) between the Teutonic Order and Poland, a peace treaty was signed in Toruń in 1466, which returned to Poland the town and a large area of land stretching up to Gdańsk, and also presaged the military downfall of the order.

The period of prosperity which followed came to an end with the Swedish wars, and then came the time of Poland's partitions,

during which Toruń remained under Prussian domination (1793-1918). WWII fortunately did relatively little damage to the city, and the medieval quarter was almost unaffected. Partly restored during recent decades, it's perhaps the best preserved Gothic town in the country. In 1997, Toruń's historic quarter was included on the UNESCO World Heritage List.

Orientation
The historic sector of Toruń sits on the northern bank of the Vistula. It is made up of the Old Town (Stare Miasto) to the west, and the New Town (Nowe Miasto) to the east. Both towns, originally separated by walls and a moat, developed around their own market squares, but gradually merged after the walls were taken down in the 15th century. All the major tourist attractions are in this area, as is much accommodation.

The bus station is a five-minute walk north of the historic quarter, while the main train station is south across the river, a short bus ride.

Information
Tourist Office The friendly and knowledgeable municipal tourist office (☎ 621 09 31), ul Piekary 37/39, is open Monday and Saturday from 9 am to 4 pm, Tuesday to Friday from 9 am to 6 pm, and Sunday (May to August only) from 9 am to 1 pm.

Money Bank Pekao, ul Bydgoska 86/88, west of the Old Town, and Bank Gdański, Wały Sikorskiego 15, both exchange travellers cheques and give advances on Visa (Bank Pekao also accepts MasterCard). There are a couple of ATMs on ul Szeroka. Cash can be easily exchanged in any of the numerous kantors in the city centre.

Things to See
The **Old Town Square** (Rynek Staromiejski) is the usual starting point for the visitor. The massive 14th-century brick **old town hall** in the middle now shelters the **Regional Museum**, featuring an extensive and varied collection related to the town's history. It's open from 10 am to 4 pm Tuesday to Saturday (as are the other museums in this section

unless specified otherwise). From May to September you can go to the top of the tower for a fine view.

The **Statue of Copernicus** (1853), near the museum's entrance, is dedicated to the astronomer. The richly decorated house nearby at No 35 accommodates the **Museum of Far Eastern Art** in the original interior, featuring a spiral wooden staircase of 1697.

Just off the north-west corner of the square is the late 13th century **St Mary's Church**, a typical Gothic hall church with all naves of equal height – but what a height! Note the early 15th-century Gothic stalls in the chancel and the organ from 1609, placed unusually on a side wall. Behind the church is the **Planetarium**, installed in an old gas tank, presenting diverse shows several times a day except Monday.

The brick Gothic house at ul Kopernika 15 is where Copernicus was born in 1473. It's now the **Museum of Copernicus**, dedicated to the man who 'stopped the sun and moved the earth'. The museum has a short audiovisual presentation about Copernicus' times in Toruń, with a scale model of the town from that period (an English soundtrack is available on request).

One block east of the museum stands the largest of the city's churches, the **Cathedral of SS John the Baptist & John the Evangelist**, begun around 1260 and completed at the end of the 15th century. Its massive tower houses Poland's second-largest bell (after Wawel Cathedral in Kraków), the Tuba Dei, cast in 1500, which is rung before mass. On the southern side of the tower, facing the Vistula River, is the original 15th-century clock, still in working order. The lofty whitewashed interior, topped with classic Gothic vaulting and crammed with a maze of baroque altars and chapels, is singularly impressive.

Behind the church is the house of the Esken family, today home to a **museum** presenting old weapons and Polish modern paintings, plus temporary exhibitions. Farther east are the ruins of the **Castle of the Teutonic Knights**, destroyed in 1454.

North of the castle ruins lies the New Town centred around the **New Town Square** (Rynek Nowomiejski). The building in the middle is the former Protestant church erected in the 19th century after the town hall was pulled down.

St James' Church, just off the eastern corner of the square, dates from the early 14th century. Unlike its Old Town brothers, this is a basilica-type church and is more elaborate from the outside, including a series of pinnacles adorning the rim of the roof. Its interior is filled with mostly baroque furnishings.

In the park just north of the Old Town is the **Ethnographic Museum** which focuses on traditional fishing, with all sorts of implements, boats and nets. In the grounds behind the museum is a good **skansen**, containing examples of the traditional rural architecture of the region and beyond. Both are open daily.

Special Events
Major annual events include the Probaltica Music & Art Festival of Baltic States in May, the Contact International Theatre Festival in May/June, the International Meeting of Folk Bands in June, and the Camerimage International Film Photography Festival in late November/early December.

Places to Stay
Toruń has a reasonable array of places to stay, and finding a room shouldn't normally present major problems. There's no longer an agency arranging private rooms, but the tourist office should be able to track down a bed for you in one of the city's 20-odd hotels or hostels.

Camping The *Camping Nr 33 Tramp* (☎ 654 71 87) is at ul Kujawska 14, near the south end of the bridge, a five-minute walk from the main train station. It operates from 15 May to 15 September and has simple but cheap cabins (US$12/14/16 a double/triple/quad) and a building with hotel-style rooms (US$12/18 a double/triple). There are only shared facilities.

Hostels The all-year *youth hostel* (☎ 654 45 80) is at ul Św Józefa 22/24, 2km north-west of the centre. Bus No 11 links the hostel with the train station and the Old Town. The hostel has five six-bed dorms, just 30 beds in all.

Bursa Szkolna (☎ 267 37), ul Słowackiego 47/49, 1km west of the Old Town, charges US$5 per bed in dorms of four to eight beds.

TORUŃ

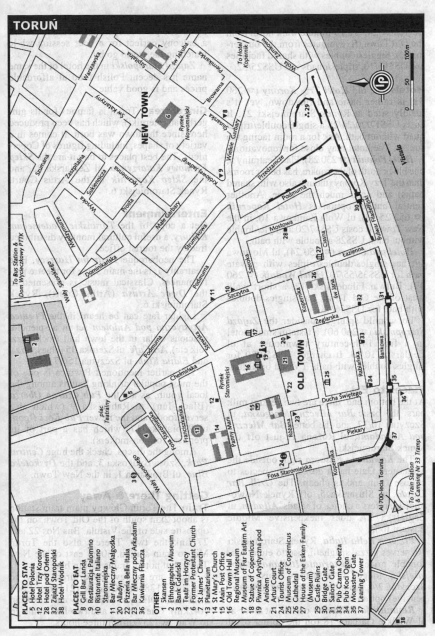

PLACES TO STAY
- 5 Hotel Polonia
- 12 Hotel Trzy Korony
- 28 Hotel pod Orłem
- 32 Zajazd Staropolski
- 38 Hotel Wodnik

PLACES TO EAT
- 8 Grill Bar Landa
- 10 Restauracja Palomino
- Ristorante Italiano
- Staromiejska
- 11 Bar Mleczny Małgośka
- 20 Alladyn
- 22 Pizzeria Bella Italia
- 23 Bar Mleczny pod Arkadami
- 36 Kawiarnia Fliscaza

OTHER
- 1 Skansen
- 2 Ethnographic Museum
- 3 Bank Gdański
- 4 Teatr im Horzycy
- 6 Former Protestant Church
- 7 St James' Church
- 9 Planetarium
- 13 St Mary's Church
- 14 Old Town Hall &
     Regional Museum
- 16 Main Post Office
- 17 Museum of Far Eastern Art
- 18 Statue of Copernicus
- 19 Piwnica Artystyczna pod
     Aniołem
- 21 Artus Court
- 24 Tourist Office
- 25 Museum of Copernicus
- 26 Cathedral
- 27 House of the Esken Family
     (Museum)
- 29 Castle Ruins
- 30 Bridge Gate
- 31 Sailors' Gate
- 33 Pub Czarna Oberza
- 34 Pub Kod Ogon
- 35 Monastery Gate
- 37 Leaning Tower

Dom Wycieczkowy PTTK (☎ 238 55), ul Legionów 24, is a 10-minute walk north from the Old Town (five minutes from the bus terminal). Singles/doubles with shared facilities are US$16/20, triples/quads are US$25/32.

Hotels The old *Hotel Trzy Korony* (☎ 260 31) is rather basic and run-down, yet it's ideally sited at Rynek Staromiejski 21. It costs US$17/20/24/28 a single/double/triple/quad without bath. Ask for a room facing the square. The hotel may close for renovations.

Hotel Polonia (☎ 230 28), Plac Teatralny 5, one block north of the square, has better rooms than the Trzy Korony (though also with shared baths) and costs much the same. Another central budget option is *Hotel Kopernik* (☎ 652 25 73), ul Wola Zamkowa 16, in the New Town. It costs US$17/20 a single/double without bath, US$28 a double with bath.

Hotel pod Orłem (☎ 250 24), ul Mostowa 17, has singles/doubles/triples with private bath for US$35/55/70. *Hotel Wodnik* (☎ 260 49), Bulwar Filadelfijski 12, a short walk west of the Old Town, has singles/doubles with bath for US$36/48.

For a mild splurge consider the *Zajazd Staropolski* (☎ 260 60), a tasteful small hotel in a fine 14th-century townhouse at ul Żeglarska 10/14. It charges US$50/80 for singles/doubles with bath, TV and breakfast.

Places to Eat

At the bottom end, there are two central milk bars: the basic *Bar Mleczny Małgośka*, ul Szczytna 10/12, and the better *Bar Mleczny pod Arkadami*, ul Różana 1, just off the Rynek Staromiejski.

The *Kawiarnia Flisacza* right outside the Monastery Gate has a dozen fish species to choose from and is cheap. The *Grill Bar Landa*, ul Ślusarska 5, off Rynek Nowomiejski, offers a choice of salads. *Alladyn*, ul Żeglarska 27, does inexpensive Middle Eastern food.

Pizzeria Bella Italia, Rynek Staromiejski 10, serves pizza, spaghetti, risotto etc at reasonable prices. *Ristorante Italiano Staromiejska*, lodged in a historic house at ul Szczytna 2/4, is a more decent (and more expensive) option for Italian cuisine.

Restauracja Palomino on the 1st floor at ul Wielkie Garbary 18 (on the corner of ul

Królowej Jadwigi), specialises in grilled meat. The place is open till midnight and has a balcony perfect for a beer session while watching the world go by.

Zajazd Staropolski in the hotel of the same name has decent Polish food at affordable prices and is good value.

Gingerbread Toruń is famous for its gingerbread (pierniki), which has been produced here since the town was born. It comes in a variety of shapes, including figures of Copernicus. The best places to buy it are the *Sklep Firmowy Katarzynka*, ul Żeglarska 25, and the *Sklep Kopernik* in the Artus Court, Rynek Staromiejski 6.

Entertainment

Get a copy of the *Toruńskie Vademecum Kultury*, a useful cultural monthly distributed free by the tourist office.

The neobaroque *Teatr im Horzycy*, Plac Teatralny 1, is the main stage for theatre performances. Classical music is presented in the *Dwór Artusa* (Artus Court), Rynek Staromiejski 6.

Lighter fare can be heard in the *Piwnica Artystyczna pod Aniołem* set in a splendid, spacious cellar in the town hall (rock, jazz, folk etc), *Art Café*, ul Szeroka 35 (blues, jazz), and *Elana Klub*, ul Szczytna 15/17 (jazz).

The earlier-mentioned Piwnica is one of the most popular drinking haunts among the local youth, as are the *Pub Czarna Oberża* (Black Inn), ul Rabiańska 9 (which also serves food), and the newer *Pub Koci Ogon*, ul Rabiańska 17 (which has a part of its premises for nonsmokers).

Among the discos, check the huge *Central Park*, Szosa Bydgoska 3, and the *Dyskoteka Blue*, ul Browarna 1, in the New Town.

Getting There & Away

Train The Toruń Główny main train station is about 2km south of the Old Town, on the opposite side of the Vistula. Bus Nos 22 and 27 link the two. There's also the Toruń Miasto train station, 500m east of the New Town, but not all trains call in here.

There are a few departures daily to Malbork (138km), Gdańsk (211km), Łódź (178km), Olsztyn (163km) and Poznań (142km). One express and two fast trains go to Warsaw (237km) in three hours.

Bus The bus station, close to the northern edge of the Old Town, handles a regular service to Chełmno (41km), Golub-Dobrzyń (43km), Płock (103km) and Bydgoszcz (47km). Polski Express has a dozen departures a day to Warsaw (209km, US$7, 3½ hours).

AROUND TORUŃ

There are some important Teutonic relics around Toruń, including at Chełmno and Golub-Dobrzyń, both easily accessible by bus from Toruń.

Chełmno, a small laid-back town near the Vistula River 41km north-west of Toruń, is completely surrounded by a 14th-century fortified wall protecting a medieval chessboard of streets punctuated with half a dozen Gothic churches, plus a graceful Renaissance town hall on the market square. The town has a few budget lodging and eating options, should you want to linger.

Golub-Dobrzyń, 43km north-east of Toruń, has a red-brick castle built by the Teutonic Knights. There's a café and a budget hotel, and the building's original Gothic interiors house a small museum.

MALBORK

☎ 055

Malbork (population 40,000), about 140km north of Toruń and 50km south-east of Gdańsk, boasts one of the largest medieval fortified castles in Europe and possibly Poland's best.

The castle was built by the Teutonic Knights. Construction began in 1276 and in 1309 the order's capital was shifted here from Venice. Constant territorial disputes with Poland and Lithuania finally culminated in the Battle of Grunwald in 1410. The order was defeated but continued to hold the castle until 1457. From 1773 to 1945 Malbork was incorporated into Prussia and extensive restorations were carried out in the years prior to WWI when the castle was viewed as a romantic symbol of the glory of medieval Germany. It was badly damaged during WWII, after which the Polish authorities continued work to preserve this great monument of Gothic culture. It was placed on the UNESCO World Heritage List in 1997.

Orientation

The train and bus stations are at the eastern end of town, 1km from the castle. As you leave the train station turn right and cut across the busy highway, then head straight down ul Kościuszki to the castle. Lots of taxis park in front of the train station; otherwise it's a 15-minute walk through the modern town.

Castle

The castle, set on the Nogat River (an eastern arm of the Vistula), consists of the 15th-century Lower Castle, the 14th-century Middle Castle where the Grand Master lived, and the 13th-century High Castle complete with a church and chapel. The Lower Castle hasn't survived in its entirety and is now used for service facilities (hotel, restaurant etc), but most of the rooms and chambers in the beautifully restored High and Middle castles are open for visitors, and some feature exhibitions. The amber collection is no doubt one of the highlights, but there's a lot more to see.

The castle is open Tuesday to Sunday from 9 am to 5 pm May to September, 9 am to 2.30 pm October to April. The compulsory two-hour guided tour with a Polish-speaking guide (US$3.50 per person, US$2 for students) departs half-hourly from the ticket office. For a tour in English, French or German an additional US$28 per group must be paid. Arrive at least three hours before closing time.

The best view of the castle is from the opposite side of the river, easily accessible by a pedestrian bridge. You'll also catch a fine glimpse of the castle from the train. Coming from Gdańsk, look on your right when crossing the river.

Places to Stay & Eat

The cheapest place to stay is the all-year *youth hostel* (☎ 72 24 08) in the local school at ul Żeromskiego 45. It has a few doubles (US$5 a bed), but most are dorms sleeping eight or more people.

Hotel Zbyszko (☎ 72 26 40), ul Kościuszki 43, between the station and the castle, costs US$15/22/28 a single/double/triple without bath or US$18/28/36 with bath, breakfast included. It has its own restaurant (open till 9 pm), which is OK and reasonably priced.

TRI-CITY AREA

To Reda, Wejherowo,
Hel, Łeba & Szczecin

Terminal Promowy
(Ferries to Karlskrona)

Gdynia
Leszczynki

Gdynia
Chylonia

Gdynia
Grabówek

Gdynia
Stocznia

Gdynia
Główna

GDYNIA

Gdynia Wzgórze
Św Maksymiliana

Gdynia
Redłowo

Gdynia
Orłowo

GDYNIA
SOPOT

Sopot Kamienny
Potok

SOPOT

Sopot

Sopot Wyścigi

SOPOT
GDAŃSK

Gdańsk
Żabianka

Gdańsk
Oliwa

OLIWA

Gdańsk
Przymorze

ZASPA

Gdańsk
Zaspa

Gdańsk
Wrzeszcz

WRZESZCZ

GDAŃSK

SUCHANINO

JELITKOWO

GULF
OF
GDAŃSK

BRZEŹNO

Gdańsk
Brzeźno

WESTERPLATTE

Gdańsk
Nowy Port

NOWY
PORT

Gdańsk
Politechnika

OLD
TOWN

MAIN
TOWN

Gdańsk
Główny

STOGI

To Kartuzy
& Kościerzyna

To Tczew

To Toruń &
Bydgoszcz

To Elbląg, Frombork,
Olsztyn & Warsaw

0   2   4 km

PLACES TO STAY
1 Youth Hostel
3 Hotel Miramar
4 Camping Nr 19
5 Camping Nr 73
6 Pensjonat Maryla
8 Grand Hotel
10 Camping Nr 67
11 Camping Nr 18
15 Youth Hostel
16 Camping Nr 10
19 Camping Gdańsk-Tourist
20 Dom Nauczyciela
22 Youth Hostel

OTHER
2 Southern Pier
7 Opera Leśna
9 Sopot Pier
12 Oliwa Cathedral
13 Zoo
14 Airport
17 Ferry Terminal
   (Ferries to Oxelösund &
   Nynäshamn)
18 Westerplatte Monument &
   Museum
21 Mac-Tur

POLAND

Hotel Parkowy (☎ 72 24 13), ul Portowa 1, 1.2km north of the castle, has doubles/triples/quads without bath for US$22/28/32 and doubles with bath for US$32. From mid-May to September, the hotel operates *Camping Nr 197* in the grounds, including cabins (US$30 per quad).

At about US$100 a double with bath and breakfast, *Hotel Zamek* (☎/fax 72 33 67), set in a restored medieval building of the Lower Castle, is a splurge. The hotel restaurant is the best place to eat in town − good food, fine surroundings and prices to match.

Getting There & Away

Malbork sits on the busy Gdańsk-Warsaw railway line, so there are a number of trains to both Gdańsk (51km) and Warsaw (278km). There are also regular train links with Elbląg (29km), Grudziądz (76km) and Toruń (138km), and a couple of trains east to Olsztyn (128km).

Given the number of train connections, it's quite easy to visit Malbork as a stopover between Warsaw and Gdańsk, Gdańsk and Olsztyn or Gdańsk and Toruń, or as a day trip from Gdańsk.

GDAŃSK
☎ 058

Gdańsk (population 470,000) is the largest city in northern Poland and an important port and shipbuilding centre on the Baltic Sea. It's the biggest, oldest and by far the most interesting component of the Tri-City, a conurbation comprising Gdańsk, Sopot and Gdynia, which stretches 30km along the Gulf of Gdańsk.

Though in existence as early as the 9th century, Gdańsk really came to the fore after the Teutonic Knights seized it in 1308; within half a century they turned it into a fully fledged medieval town, by then known as Danzig. Joining the Hanseatic League in 1361, the town grew fat on trade and expanded swiftly.

In 1454, in an armed protest against the economic restrictions imposed by the order, the inhabitants destroyed the Teutonic castle and pledged their loyalty to the Polish monarch. In turn, Gdańsk was rewarded with numerous privileges, including a monopoly on the grain trade and a greater degree of political independence than any other Polish city.

By the mid-16th century, Gdańsk had come to control three-quarters of Poland's foreign trade and its population reached 40,000. It was the largest Polish city, bigger than royal Kraków itself, and the Baltic's greatest port, providing access to the sea for much of Central Europe.

Demographically predominantly German and architecturally reminiscent of Flanders rather than Poland, Gdańsk was effectively an independent city-state for most of its history. Wealthy, cultured and cosmopolitan, it has produced many famous citizens, including the astronomer Johannes Hevelius, physicist Daniel Fahrenheit, philosopher Arthur Schopenhauer and writer Günter Grass.

Napoleon was once heard to say that Gdańsk was the key to everything, and Hitler seemed to share this opinion when he started WWII here. Not many European cities were devastated on the scale of Gdańsk, but you'd hardly know it today. Admirably − if somewhat surprisingly − the communist regime rebuilt, brick by brick, house by house, and street by street, the historic core to its former shape.

Though Gdańsk is known best to outsiders as the birthplace of Solidarity, there are many other reasons to come here. This is a real city with bones and a soul − a place to be savoured. Gdańsk celebrated its millennium in 1997; many buildings were restored for the occasion and the centre looks attractive.

Orientation

You're most likely to arrive at the Gdańsk Główny main train station, which is just a 10-minute walk from the heart of the historic quarter. The bus terminal is next to the train station. Sightseeing in Gdańsk is straightforward, as almost all the main attractions are in the city centre just a short walk apart.

The city centre consists of three historic districts: the Main Town in the middle, the Old Town to the north and the Old Suburb to the south. Outside the centre, your itinerary might include a half-day trip to the Oliwa suburb, and a boat trip to the port and Westerplatte.

Gdynia is probably best done as a half-day trip from Gdańsk, but Sopot can be a destination in itself, particularly if you plan on beach life amid crowds of Polish holiday-makers (see the relevant sections later in this chapter).

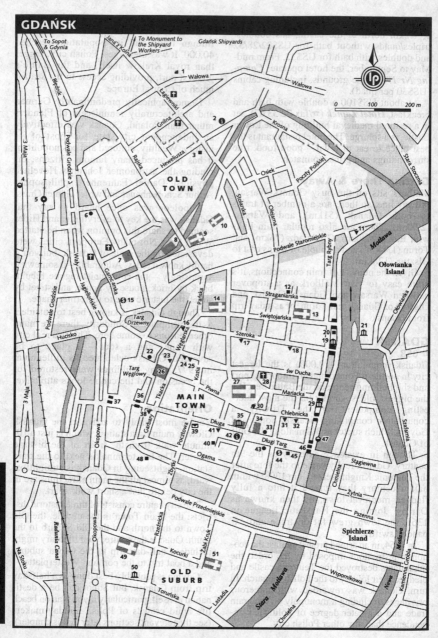

GDAŃSK

To Sopot & Gdynia

To Monument to the Shipyard Workers

Gdańsk Shipyards

0   100   200 m

OLD TOWN

MAIN TOWN

OLD SUBURB

Ołowianka Island

Spichlerze Island

Radunia Canal

POLAND

PLACES TO STAY		38	Bar Złoty Kur	26	Arsenal
1	Youth Hostel	41	Bar Mleczny Neptun	27	St Mary's Church
3	Hotel Hevelius			28	Royal Chapel
12	Dom Aktora	**OTHER**		29	Archaeological Museum
20	Hotel Hanza	2	Municipal Tourist Office	33	Golden House
40	Hotel Zaułek	4	Bus Terminal	34	Artus Court
45	Hotel Jantar	5	Main Train Station	35	Main Town Hall & Historical
48	Dom Harcerza	6	Gdańsk-Tourist		Museum of Gdańsk
			(Private Rooms)	36	Golden Gate
PLACES TO EAT		7	Old Town Hall	37	Upland Gate; PTTK
11	Restauracja Kubicki	8	Great Mill	39	Main Post Office
16	Bar Mleczny Turystyczny	9	St Catherine's Church	42	Agencja Informacji
17	La Pasta	10	St Bridget's Church		Turystycznej
18	Restauracja pod Łososiem	13	St John's Church		(Private Tourist Office)
23	Sklep z Kawą Pożegnanie	14	St Nicholas' Church	43	Almatur
	z Afryką	15	Bank Pekao	44	Bank Gdański
24	Bar Starówka	19	Gdańsk Crane &	46	Green Gate
25	Restauracja Gdańska		Maritime Museum	47	Excursion Boats
30	Restauracja Milano	21	Maritime Museum &	49	Church of the Holy Trinity
31	Pub u Szkota		Museum Ship Sołdek	50	National Museum
32	Jadłodajnia u Plastyków	22	Teatr Wybrzeże	51	Church of SS Peter & Paul

Information

Tourist Offices The private Agencja Informacji Turystycznej (☎ 301 93 27), ul Długa 45, opposite the main town hall is open daily from 9 am to 6 pm and is a good source of information. It's well stocked with maps and brochures.

You can also use the helpful municipal tourist office (☎ 301 43 55; ☎/fax 301 66 37), ul Heweliusza 27, on the northern edge of the Old Town; it's open weekdays from 8.30 am to 4 pm.

Money Bank Pekao is at ul Garncarska 23; Bank Gdański has offices at several central locations, including Wały Jagiellońskie 14/16, Długi Targ 14/16 and the main train station; Powszechny Bank Kredytowy is at ul Ogarna 116. All these and some other banks will exchange most major brands of travellers cheques and give advances on Visa; Bank Pekao will also accept MasterCard. ATMs are easy to find in the centre.

Kantors are plentiful throughout the central area. Ignore the moneychangers who hang around Długi Targ and Długie Pobrzeże and offer foreigners attractive rates. You won't get what you expect!

Post & Communications The main post office is at ul Długa 22. Poste restante is in the same building but you enter through the back door from ul Pocztowa. Mail sent here should be addressed: your name, Poste Restante, ul Długa 22/28, 80-801 Gdańsk 50, Poland.

Travel Agencies Almatur (☎ 301 24 24), Długi Targ 11, provides its usual services, including ISIC student cards and international train and bus tickets.

PTTK (☎ 301 60 96) in the Upland Gate arranges guides speaking English, German and French (US$55 per group for up to five hours plus US$10 for each extra hour).

Orbis (☎ 301 56 31), ul Heweliusza 22, sells ferry tickets, international and domestic train tickets, and international bus tickets. It also organises tours in the city and beyond (Hel, Malbork, Frombork).

Bookshops English Books Unlimited (☎ 301 33 73), ul Podmłyńska 10, has probably the best choice of English-language literature, phrasebooks and dictionaries. Other places to check include the First Book Bank (☎ 346 20 33), ul Heweliusza 11, and Libri Mundi (☎ 305 15 74), ul Rajska 1.

POLAND

Some of these bookshops sell a few English-language newspapers and magazines, but the widest selection (as well as the press in German and French) is to be found in EMPiK Megastore across the street from the main train station. There's another, smaller EMPiK at Długi Targ 25/27.

Cybercafés Try Comptrade (☎ 341 47 14) in Gdańsk Wrzeszcz, room 34, 2nd floor, Al Grunwaldzka 102 (Monday to Friday from 10.30 am to 4 pm), or Cybermind in Gdańsk Żabianka, Al Grunwaldzka 613, behind Bank Gdański (almost on Gdańsk's administrative border with Sopot).

Things to See

Main Town This is the largest, architecturally the richest and best restored part of the three historic quarters. Its main thoroughfare is formed by ul Długa (Long Street) and Długi Targ (Long Market), known as the **Royal Way**, along which Polish kings traditionally paraded during their periodical visits. They entered the Main Town through the **Upland Gate** (1574), then passed through the **Golden Gate** (1614), and proceeded east to the Renaissance **Green Gate** (1568) which was intended to be the kings' residence (though none ever stayed here, opting instead for cosier houses nearby).

The towering Gothic **main town hall** on the west end of Długi Targ contains the good **Historical Museum of Gdańsk** (closed Monday) in its period interiors, the showpiece of which is the 16th-century Red Room. Make sure you go up to the tower for a great view.

Behind **Neptune's Fountain** (1613) stands the **Artus Court** where local merchants once met. Go inside to see Europe's highest (10.65m) Renaissance tiled stove (1546). The nearby **Golden House** (1618) has perhaps the richest façade in town.

Two blocks north of the Green Gate along the waterfront is St Mary's Gate with the **Archaeological Museum** (closed Monday); through this gate is **ul Mariacka** (St Mary's St), the most picturesque street in Gdańsk, lined with 17th-century burgher houses. Follow it west to the gigantic **St Mary's Church** (1343-1502), the largest brick Gothic church in the world. Discover the many trea-

sures inside, including an ornate baroque organ and a 14m-high astronomical clock. You can climb 405 steps to the viewing platform atop the 78m tower.

Continue west on ul Piwna (Beer St) to the Dutch Renaissance **Arsenal** (1609), today housing a supermarket, then take the street running north to the Gothic **St Nicholas' Church**, one of the oldest in town and richly decorated inside. Two blocks east is the large **St John's Church**, currently under restoration.

Nearby on the waterfront is the 15th-century **Gdańsk Crane**, the biggest crane in medieval Europe, capable of hoisting loads up to two tonnes and reputedly the only fully restored relic of its kind in the world. It's now home to the **Maritime Museum** (closed Monday), whose other sections are in the modern building next to the crane, and in three reconstructed granaries across the Motława River (the museum's boat will take you there).

Old Town Destroyed almost totally in 1945, the Old Town wasn't rebuilt to its previous shape, apart from a handful of buildings (mainly churches). The largest and most remarkable of these is **St Catherine's Church**, Gdańsk's oldest church, begun in the 1220s. Opposite is the **Great Mill**, built by the Teutonic Knights around 1350 and operating until 1945. Just before WWII it was producing 200 tonnes of flour per day.

Right behind St Catherine's is **St Bridget's Church** (1514), wrecked in 1945 and reconstructed from scratch. It was Lech Wałęsa's place of worship and, predictably, the church features some contemporary craft works related to Solidarity and to modern Polish history in general.

On the northern outskirts of the suburbs, at the entrance to the shipyards (where Solidarity was born in August 1980), stands the **Monument to the Shipyard Workers**, erected in late 1980 in memory of 44 workers killed in the riots of December 1970. This striking set of three 40m-tall steel crosses was the first monument in a communist regime to commemorate its victims.

Old Suburb This part of the historic town was also reduced to rubble in 1945, and little of the former urban fabric has been reconstructed except for the Franciscan monastery, which today shelters the **National Museum** (closed Monday). The extensive collection includes paintings, woodcarving, silverware, porcelain and furniture dating from Gdańsk's early days onward. Not surprisingly, the museum features a section of Dutch and Flemish paintings, the highlight being Hans Memling's *Last Judgement*.

Adjoining the museum from the north is the former Franciscan **Church of the Holy Trinity**, built at the end of the 15th century. It's the town's second-largest church after St Mary's.

Oliwa The north-westernmost suburb of Gdańsk, about 9km from the centre, Oliwa is known for its soaring **cathedral**, an unusual building with a Gothic-baroque façade and a very long but surprisingly narrow central nave. Its showpiece, the rococo organ (1793), is one of the best in Europe, and short music presentations are held several times a day in summer (check the schedule with the tourist offices before setting off for Oliwa).

The nearby abbots' palace is now a **Modern Art Gallery**, whereas the granary opposite the palace houses the **Ethnographic Museum** (both closed on Monday). A large park surrounding the historic complex supplies a fine natural setting. About 1.5km west is a small **zoo**. Oliwa can be easily reached from central Gdańsk by commuter train; get off at Gdańsk Oliwa station.

Westerplatte Westerplatte, at the entrance to the harbour from the sea 7km north of the city centre, is where WWII broke out at 4.45 am on 1 September 1939, when the German battleship *Schleswig-Holstein* began shelling the Polish naval post. The 182-man garrison held out against ferocious attacks for seven days before surrendering. The site is now a memorial, with some of the ruins left as they were after the bombardment, a small museum and a massive monument in memory of the defenders.

Bus No 106 goes to Westerplatte from the main train station every 40 minutes or so, but a more attractive way to get there is by the excursion boat which departs several times a day from April to October from the landing next to the Green Gate (US$8 return, US$5 for students). The trip provides a fine cross-sectional view of Gdańsk's harbour.

Special Events

The Dominican Fair (Jarmark Dominikański) is the oldest city event, going back to 1260. It takes place over the first two weeks of August at various locations in the historic centre.

The International Organ Music Festival is held in the Oliwa cathedral, with twice-weekly recitals from mid-June till the end of August. Meanwhile, St Mary's Church is the stage for the International Organ, Choir and Chamber Music Festival (on Friday from June to September). St Nicholas' and St Bridget's churches are also used for organ recitals.

July sees the Folklore Festival of the People from the North, featuring groups from such exotic locations as, say, Greenland or Kamchatka. Also in July is the International Street and Open-Air Theatre Festival.

Places to Stay

Both tourist offices provide good information about accommodation options. The private tourist office can also find and book a hotel or hostel for a US$1.75 service charge per reservation.

Camping Gdańsk has four camping grounds. The nearest to the city centre (about 5.5km to the north-east) is *Camping Gdańsk-Tourist* (☎ 307 39 15) in the seaside holiday centre at ul Wydmy 1 in the suburb of Stogi; it's open June to September. Here is possibly Gdańsk's best beach. Tram No 13 from the main train station goes there.

The three remaining camping grounds are open from May to September and all have cabins. *Camping Nr 10* (☎ 343 55 31), ul Hallera 234, in the suburb of Brzeźno is accessible by tram No 13 from the main train station. If you arrive by ferry from Sweden, this is the closest camping ground to the ferry terminal, a short ride by tram No 15.

Camping Nr 18 (☎ 553 27 31) is at ul Jelitkowska 23 in the suburb of Jelitkowo. Take tram No 2 or 6 from the main train station. *Camping Nr 69* (☎ 308 07 39), ul Lazurowa 5, in Sobieszewo, is about 15km east of the city centre. Take bus No 112 from the train station.

Youth Hostels Gdańsk has three all-year youth hostels. The most convenient is the *youth hostel* (☎ 301 23 13) at ul Wałowa 21, a five-minute walk north-east of the main train station. Predictably, it's often full, particularly in summer.

The next closest is the *youth hostel* (☎ 302 60 44) at ul Kartuska 245b, 3.5km west of the main train station. To get there, take bus Nos 161, 167 or 174 from ul 3 Maja at the back of the station, or go by tram No 10 or 12 to the end of the line, then walk west along ul Kartuska for about 10 minutes.

The *youth hostel* (☎ 341 16 60) at Al Grunwaldzka 240/244 is around 6km north-west of the main train station. It's in a sports complex next to the soccer field. Take the commuter train to the Gdańsk Zaspa station and walk north-west for five minutes along Al Grunwaldzka.

Student Hostels From July to September, the Politechnika Gdańska opens 10 hostels in its own student dorms, all of which are in Gdańsk Wrzeszcz. A bed in a double or triple will cost US$5 to US$15, depending on the facilities and standards. The hostels' central office (☎ 347 25 47 or ☎ 347 25 89) is at ul Wyspiańskiego 7a.

Other Hostels There are two budget places conveniently sited in the Main Town. *Dom Harcerza* (☎ 301 36 21), ul Za Murami 2/10, has good doubles/triples without bath for US$32/36, plus dorms of four/five/six/12 beds costing US$9/7/5/4 per bed (but in summer you have to pay for the whole room).

Hotel Zaułek (☎ 301 41 69), ul Ogarna 107/108, is just 100m from the town hall. It's in the five-storey, free-standing building between ul Długa and ul Ogarna. This former workers' dorm offers basic accommodation for US$17/22 singles/doubles, US$25/28 for triples/quads or US$6 for a bed in a five, six or seven-bed dorm. Again, they may refuse renting the room by the bed in the high season. In both these places it's pretty hard to find a vacancy at this time anyway.

Private Rooms Gdańsk-Tourist (☎ 301 26 34), ul Heweliusza 8, near the train station (open daily in summer from 8 am to 7 pm) is the main agency handling private rooms. Singles/doubles in the central area are US$15/24, while rooms farther from the centre (including distant suburbs) cost

US$12/20. When making your choice, don't worry too much about the distance from the centre – work out how close the place is to the commuter train line.

Mac-Tur (☎ 302 41 70), ul Beethovena 8, in the suburb of Suchanino, about 2km west of the main train station (bus No 184 from the front of the station goes there), is a private agency (English spoken) offering accommodation in private houses, including the owners' house where the agency is located. A bed with a filling breakfast costs US$15.

The private tourist office may have some central private rooms for about US$15 per person.

Hotels The old *Hotel Jantar* (☎ 301 27 16), Długi Targ 19, has singles/doubles without bath for US$38/55, and doubles/triples with bath at US$70/80. It's probably not great value for your money in this rather run-down place (which may close for a long-deserved revamping), but you couldn't ask for a more central location. You may be lucky enough to get a front room, but note that the 1st-floor rooms can be noisy due to the band playing on weekends in the restaurant downstairs.

A better central option is *Dom Aktora* (☎/fax 301 59 01), ul Straganiarska 55/56. It has six small apartments sleeping two/three/four guests for US$65/85/100 and its own bistro. Advance booking is essential.

There are some inexpensive hotels outside the historic quarter. The closest is probably *Dom Nauczyciela* (☎ 341 55 87), ul Uphagena 28, in Gdańsk Wrzeszcz. It's a teachers' hotel, offering some simple singles/doubles/triples/quads without bath for US$15/20/24/28, and singles/doubles with bath for US$33/48. The hotel is close to the Gdańsk Politechnika station.

If money is not a problem, the classiest place to stay is the new *Hotel Hanza* (☎ 305 34 27; fax 305 33 86), attractively sited on the waterfront next to Gdańsk Crane. Doubles go for US$150, suites for up to double that price.

Places to Eat
Ultra-budget dining is provided by two central milk bars: *Bar Mleczny Neptun*, ul Długa 33/34, and the more basic *Bar Mleczny Turystyczny*, ul Węglarska 1/4.

There are plenty of other cheap self-service joints, including **Bar Złoty Kur**, ul Długa 4, and **Bar Starówka**, ul Św Ducha.

One of the best places for a tasty, cheap lunch (from noon to 6 pm) is the **Jadłodajnia u Plastyków**, ul Chlebnicka 13/16. The **Bar Bistro** in the Dom Aktora hotel is slightly more expensive but the food is good and worth its price. **La Pasta**, ul Szeroka 32, does some of the better pizzas in town.

Restauracja Kubicki, ul Wartka 5, on the waterfront serves solid tasty Polish food at reasonable prices, as it has since its founding in 1918. **Restauracja Milano**, ul Chlebnicka 4, in the shade of St Mary's Church offers good Italian cuisine at good prices (try their carpaccio).

Pub u Szkota, ul Chlebnicka 10, also called the Scotland Restaurant, is a cosy double-level place combining the functions of a restaurant and a bar. Food is good and affordably priced (drinks perhaps not so), and the place is beautifully decorated and open till midnight.

Central Gdańsk has several upmarket establishments, of which **Restauracja pod Łososiem**, ul Szeroka 54, is probably the classiest and most famous. Founded in 1598, its strong point is fish, particularly the salmon after which the place is named, but it also has some typical meat dishes. Other recommended places for a fine dinner are **Restauracja Gdańska**, ul Św Ducha 16, and **Restauracja Hanza** in the hotel of the same name.

Cafés **Kawiarnia Palowa** in the basement of the town hall is one of Gdańsk's best known cafés, and it now has a reasonable food menu, which makes it a pleasant, though not cheap, place for lunch.

For good milk shakes, pastries and espresso, head for **Cocktail Bar Capri**, ul Długa 59, diagonally opposite the post office. The nearby **Cukiernia Kaliszczak**, ul Długa 74, has good ice cream and excellent pączki (doughnuts). The best selection of exotic coffees is to be found at the **Sklep z Kawą Pożegnanie z Afryką**, ul Kołodziejska 4.

The photogenic ul Mariacka has several romantic little café-bars, with tables on their charming front terraces. You'll find more open-air coffee houses and bars on the waterfront, Długie Pobrzeże.

Entertainment

The **Opera House & Concert Hall** are at Al Zwycięstwa 15 in Gdańsk Wrzeszcz, just off the Gdańsk Politechnika station. The main city theatre is the **Teatr Wybrzeże**, Targ Węglowy 1, next to the Arsenal in the Main Town. There are usually some Polish and foreign classics in the repertoire.

Klub Żak, Wały Jagiellońskie 1, on the western outskirts of the Main Town, is the leading student club, with its own café, theatre and a bar in the basement. Sadly, by the time we went to press, the club was packing its goods and chattels and looking for a new, still unknown location. Inquire in the tourist offices for news.

The main jazz venue is the **Jazz Club**, Długi Targ 39/40, which has live music on weekends; jazz is also staged at the **Cotton Club**, ul Złotników 25/29.

If all you want is a beer or five, some of the most amazing surroundings in which to sit over a bottle are at the **Latający Holender** in the basement of the LOT building, Wały Jagiellońskie 2/4; the **Celtic Pub**, ul Lektykarska 3; and the **Irish Pub** in the fabulous vaulted cellar of the old town hall (the last two may have live music at times).

Things to Buy

Gdańsk is known for amber. It's sold either unset or, more often, in silver jewellery, some of which is of high quality. Most shops selling amber are on ul Mariacka, Długi Targ and Długie Pobrzeże. Although a selection of amber can also be found in Warsaw, Kraków and other major cities, Gdańsk has the best choice. However, beware of some overpriced jewellery and souvenir shops catering to western visitors.

Getting There & Away

Air The airport is in Rębiechowo, 14km west of Gdańsk. Bus No 110 goes there from the Gdańsk Wrzeszcz train station, or you can take the infrequent bus B from the Gdańsk Główny (main) station. The LOT office (☎ 301 11 61) is at ul Wały Jagiellońskie 2/4, next to the Upland Gate.

The only direct domestic flights are to Warsaw (four times a day but fewer in the off season), while international flights go to Copenhagen (daily), Hamburg (daily) and London (twice a week).

POLAND

Train The main train station, Gdańsk Główny, on the western outskirts of the Old Town, handles all incoming and outgoing traffic. Almost all long-distance trains coming from the south go to Gdynia (and usually appear under Gdynia in the timetables). Trains heading south originate not from Gdańsk but from Gdynia. On the other hand, most trains along the coast to western destinations such as Szczecin originate (and terminate) in Gdańsk and stop at Gdynia en route.

A dozen trains a day go to Warsaw (329km), including eight express trains and two InterCity trains (which cover the distance in less than 3½ hours). All these trains go via Malbork (51km) but only the express trains stop there. There are six fast trains daily to Olsztyn (179km), and these too call at Malbork en route.

Two express and three fast trains go to Wrocław (478km); all go through Bydgoszcz (160km) and Poznań (313km). There are also six fast trains to Toruń (211km). Four fast trains depart for Szczecin (374km); one of these continues to Berlin.

Bus The bus terminal is behind the central train station and you can get there by an underground passageway.

There's one morning bus directly to Frombork (112km). Alternatively, take any of the half-hourly buses to Elbląg (61km) from where you have regular transport to Frombork by both bus and train. Four fast buses daily go to Olsztyn (170km) and four to Lidzbark Warmiński (157km). For Łeba, go to Gdynia, from where four direct buses a day run to Łeba in summer, or take a bus or train to Lębork and change there.

There are plenty of connections to Western European cities; travel agencies (including Almatur and Orbis) have information and sell tickets. Two PKS buses depart daily to Kaliningrad (US$8, six hours).

Ferry Car ferries to Oxelösund and Nynäshamn in Sweden depart from Gdańsk, while those to Karlskrona in Sweden start from Gdynia. See Getting There & Away at the beginning of this chapter for details. Information, booking and tickets can be obtained from the Orbis office, ul Heweliusza 22.

Getting Around

Commuter Train A commuter train, known as SKM (Fast City Train), runs constantly between Gdańsk Główny and Gdynia Główna (21km) from 5 am till midnight, stopping at a dozen intermediate stations, including Sopot. The trains run every five to 10 minutes (not so frequently late in the evening) and the Gdańsk-Gdynia trip takes 35 minutes. You buy tickets at ticket offices in the stations or some Ruch kiosks and validate them in the machines at the platform entrance (not on the train itself).

Tram & Bus These are slower than SKM and are advisable only for destinations not connected by the train. They run between around 5 am and 11 pm.

Fares depend on the duration of the journey: US$0.20 for up to a 10-minute trip, US$0.40 for up to a half-hour ride and US$0.60 for an hour's journey. Your ticket is stamped with the date and time you get on.

Boat From mid-May to late September excursion boats go from Gdańsk's wharf near the Green Gate to Sopot (US$8 one way, US$11 return), Gdynia (US$10 one way, US$15 return) and across the Gulf of Gdańsk to the fishing village of Hel on the Hel Peninsula (US$11 one way, US$16 return). Students pay about two-thirds of the normal fare. The trip to Hel is a nice way to get in a sailing mood and do some sightseeing and beach bathing (see the Hel section later in this chapter).

SOPOT
☎ 058

Sopot (population 45,000), just north of Gdańsk, has been one of Poland's most fashionable seaside resorts since Napoleon's doctor, Jean Haffner, built baths here in 1823. During the interwar period, Sopot belonged to the Free City of Danzig, only fully joining Poland in 1945. Sopot has an easy-going resort atmosphere, which makes it a pleasant place to stay for beach-goers. Unfortunately, the Vistula River flushes thousands of tonnes of pollutants into the Gulf of Gdańsk every year, so some consider swimming here unhealthy.

Orientation & Information

The tourist office (☎ 551 26 17) is at ul Dworcowa 4 diagonally opposite the train station. A few minutes walk north from here will bring you to ul Bohaterów Monte Cassino, Sopot's attractive pedestrian mall which leads straight down to the 'molo', Poland's longest pier, jutting 512m into the Gulf of Gdańsk. North of the pier and the old-fashioned Grand Hotel is a seaside promenade, while behind the town, west of the railway line, is a large forest. Here is the Opera Leśna, an amphitheatre capable of seating 5000 people, where the International Song Festival is held in the second half of August.

Places to Stay

Sopot has three camping grounds. The largest and best is *Camping Nr 19* (☎ 550 04 45), ul Zamkowa Góra 25, in the northern end of town (a five-minute walk from the Kamienny Potok train station). It's open May to September and has bungalows. Just south of here at ul Sępia 41/45 is *Camping Nr 73* (☎ 551 07 25), open June to August, which has fewer facilities and no cabins. The third one, *Camping Nr 67* (☎ 551 65 23), ul Bitwy pod Płowcami 69, is in the southern end of Sopot, near the beach. It's a long way from the commuter train line.

Private rooms are handled by the tourist office. Be prepared to pay about US$10/18/24 a single/double/triple in July and August. During this time, there may be some locals hanging around the office who will offer rooms.

Of the regular all-year hotels, one of the cheaper is *Hotel Miramar* (☎ 550 00 11), ul Zamkowa Góra 25. It costs US$28/34/38 a double/triple/quad without bath, or US$36/50 a single/double with bath.

A five-minute walk south of Hotel Miramar is *Pensjonat Maryla* (☎ 551 00 34), ul Sępia 22. It's a good, pension-style place which offers singles/doubles with bath for US$35/50. In summer, it hires out cabins in its grounds (US$25/30 a double/quad).

Across the street is the much larger, modern *Sopot Lucky Hotel* (☎ 551 22 25), ul Haffnera 81/85, which has doubles/triples/quads with bath for US$45/60/75.

If you want to stay where the fashionable once flocked, go to the Orbis-run *Grand Hotel* (☎ 551 00 41; fax 551 61 24), ul Powstańców Warszawy 12/14, by Sopot pier next to the beach. The hotel lived up to its name more before the war than it does today, but it's still a plush place to stay. Singles/doubles go for US$90/120.

Even more elite and plush is *Villa Hestia* (☎ 550 32 51), ul Władysława IV 3/5, which costs US$180 a double.

There are more hotels, pensions and holiday homes, many of which open only in summer. Hotel prices at Sopot are greatly increased in July and August (these are quoted here), so expect to pay less if you come at other times.

Places to Eat

Apart from a number of all-year eating outlets, plenty of bars, bistros, cafés, open-air restaurants and street stands open in summer throughout the town, particularly in the beach area. Sopot's top-end eateries include *Restauracja Balzac*, ul 3 Maja 7 (topnotch French cuisine), *Restauracja Rozmaryn*, ul Ogrodowa 8 (the best Italian food for miles around), and the restaurant of *Villa Hestia*.

Getting There & Away

Train For details of long-distance trains, see the Gdańsk section. Commuter trains to Gdańsk (12km) and Gdynia (9km) run every five to 10 minutes.

Boat Excursion boats (mid-May to the end of September) go daily to Gdańsk (US$8), Gdynia (US$5) and Hel (US$9 one way, US$13 return). The landing site is at the pier.

GDYNIA
☎ 058

North of Sopot is Gdynia, the third component of the Tri-City area. It has nothing of the historic splendour of Gdańsk, nor of the relaxed beach ambience of Sopot. It's just a busy young city of about 250,000 inhabitants, without much style or charm except for the omnipresent atmosphere of a port.

In the aftermath of WWI, when Gdańsk became the Free City of Danzig, the Polish government decided to build a new port on the site of the small fishing village of Gdynia to give Poland an outlet to the sea. With the help of French capital, the construction of the port

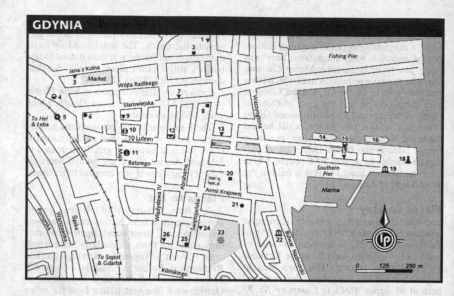

GDYNIA

PLACES TO STAY
- 2 Hotel Neptun
- 8 Hotel Lark
- 20 Hotel Gdynia

PLACES TO EAT
- 1 Restauracja
   La Gondola
- 3 Restauracja Jackfish
- 7 Bar Uniwersalny
- 9 Bistro Prima

- 13 Bistro Kwadrans
- 17 Restauracja Róża
   Wiatrów
- 24 Bar Chata
- 26 Bar Mleczny
   Słoneczny

OTHER
- 4 Bus Terminal
- 5 Gdynia Główna/
   Main Train Station

- 6 Biuro Zakwaterowań
   Turus
- 10 Bank Gdański
- 11 Tourist Office
- 12 Main Post
   Office
- 14 Museum Ship
   Błyskawica
- 15 Excursion Boats
- 16 Museum Ship
   Dar Pomorza

- 18 Monument to
   Joseph Conrad
- 19 Oceanographic
   Museum & Aquarium
- 21 Teatr Muzyczny
- 22 Naval Museum
- 23 Lookout
- 25 EMPiK

began in 1923, and 10 years later Gdynia already had the largest harbour on the Baltic. It was badly damaged during WWII, but was rebuilt and modernised and is now the base for much of Poland's merchant and fishing fleet.

Gdynia hosts the Gdynia Summer Jazz Days in July and the Festival of Polish Feature Films in October.

Orientation & Information

You are most likely to arrive in town at Gdynia Główna main train station. Follow ul 10 Lutego to the waterfront where the major

tourist attractions are. You'll pass near the tourist office (☎ 621 77 51), ul 3 Maja 27, the useful Bank Gdański and the main post office on the way.

Things to See

The southern pier (molo południowe) has most of the sights. Near its tip is the **Oceanographic Museum & Aquarium** (closed Monday). Moored on the northern side of the pier are two **museum ships** (both closed Monday): the WWII destroyer Błyskawica and the three-masted frigate Dar Pomorza built in Hamburg in 1909.

South of the pier, on Bulwar Nadmorski, is the **Naval Museum**, which has an open-air display of guns, war planes, helicopters and rockets arranged in a garden.

Places to Stay

The all-year *youth hostel* (☎ 627 00 05) is at ul Morska 108c, 2km north-west of the centre (get off at the Gdynia Grabówek station).

Private rooms are arranged for US$13/22 a single/double by the Biuro Zakwaterowań Turus (☎ 621 82 65), ul Starowiejska 47 (entrance from ul Dworcowa), opposite the main train station. A minimum stay of three nights is required.

There are a few affordable hotels right in the city centre, including *Hotel Lark* (☎ 621 80 46), ul Starowiejska 1 (US$22/33 a single/ double and US$38/42 a triple/quad with bath) and *Hotel Neptun* (☎ 626 64 77), ul Jana z Kolna 6 (US$24/34 a single/double without bath).

Places to Eat

Gdynia has plenty of eating outlets throughout the city centre. *Bar Mleczny Słoneczny*, on the corner of ul Władysława IV and ul Żwirki i Wigury, is a genuine milk bar with exclusively vegetarian dishes that cost next to nothing. Efficient, clean and good, it's deservedly popular among the locals. Other good budget eating options include *Bar Uniwersalny*, ul Starowiejska 14, and *Snack Bar Liliput*, ul Świętojańska 75.

You won't pay much more at *Bistro Kwadrans*, Skwer Kościuszki 20, or *Bistro Prima*, ul 3 Maja 21. However, possibly the highest prize goes to *Bar Chata*, ul Świętojańska 49, which serves large plates of home-cooked Polish food for US$3 a dish.

Gdynia also has something to offer at the top end of the scale, including *Restauracja La Gondola*, ul Portowa 8 (Italian cuisine), and *Restauracja Jackfish*, ul Jana z Kolna 55 (fish). *Restauracja Róża Wiatrów* on the southern pier has acceptable food and good views.

Getting There & Away

Train See the Gdańsk section for information on long-distance trains. There are several trains daily to Hel (77km) and Lębork (where you change for the bus to Łeba).

Bus The bus terminal is next to the train station. Regional routes include Hel (78km) and Łeba (89km). Two fast buses run daily to Świnoujście (324km).

Boat Ferries to/from Karlskrona, Sweden, depart from and arrive at Terminal Promowy, ul Kwiatkowskiego 60, 5km north-west of central Gdynia. Ask about the free shuttle bus between the terminal and Gdańsk when you book your ticket.

Excursion boats to Gdańsk (US$10), Sopot (US$5) and Hel (US$8 one way, US$12 return) depart from the southern pier from mid-May to the end of September. There are also one-hour excursions to Gdynia harbour; boats go there several times a day from April to October (US$5).

HEL
☎ 058

Hel is an old fishing village, today swiftly developing as a beach resort, at the tip of the narrow, 34km crescent-shaped peninsula separating the Gulf of Gdańsk from the sea. It's a popular day-trip destination for Tri-City area visitors.

The old Gothic church near the harbour is now home to the **fishing museum** featuring exhibits related to fishing and boat-building techniques, plus a collection of old fishing boats outside. A large tank for grey seals is being built nearby, which is going to be another tourist attraction. There are still some fine 19th-century **timber houses** along ul Wiejska, the village's main street. There's a beautiful, wide **beach** on the sea coast and another, less attractive one facing the gulf.

Places to Stay & Eat

Hotel Riviera (☎ 675 05 28), ul Wiejska 130, is Hel's top place (US$30 a double with bath), but you can stay for less next door, at ul Wiejska 132 (☎ 675 05 40), where inexpensive lunches are also served. Private rooms can be arranged at the PTTK (☎ 675 06 21), ul Wiejska 78, or directly with owners by asking around. The usual price is about US$15 per double room, but few locals will want to rent a room for just one night.

POLAND

The town has a reasonable array of summer bars and small restaurants. The most charming places to eat and drink include *Maszoperia*, ul Wiejska 110, and *Pub Captain Morgan*, ul Wiejska 21.

Getting There & Away

Hel can be reached by road and railway (fairly regular services by both train and bus from Gdynia), and by excursion boat from mid-May to the end of September from Gdańsk, Sopot and Gdynia (see those sections for fares). Note that the return ticket is considerably cheaper than two singles. The boat's schedule allows for up to six hours at Hel. There's a small bar aboard where you can get coffee or a beer and the open deck at the back makes for a pleasant trip (if the weather is fine).

The road along the peninsula is open for private cars all the way to Hel.

ŁEBA
☎ 059

Łeba is a small old fishing port of about 4000 people, which these days is also a popular seaside resort. The wide sandy beach here stretches in both directions as far as the eye can see, and the water is reputedly the cleanest on the Polish coast. The nearby Słowiński National Park (see that section later) shelters unusual shifting dunes and relatively undisturbed nature. If you're looking for a Baltic beach resort, Łeba is one of the best places to consider.

Orientation

The train and bus stations are next to each other in the south-western part of Łeba, two blocks west of ul Kościuszki, the town's main drag. This shopping street runs north to the port, set on a brief stretch of the Łeba River which joins Lake Łebsko to the sea. The river divides Łeba's beach in two. The town is nestled behind the eastern beach, and where the main resort area is. The beach on the west side of the river is less crowded, and the broad white sands here stretch back 75m to the dunes, making up some of the best beaches on the entire Baltic. A town plan is posted outside the train station.

Information

The tourist office (☎ 66 25 65) is at ul 11 Listopada 5a, just round the corner from the train station. Cash can be easily exchanged in any of several kantors, including one in the post office, but travellers cheques can be hard to cash.

Places to Stay & Eat

As in most seaside resorts, the lodging and culinary picture varies widely between the high season (July and August) and the rest of the year. Many holiday homes and pensions open their doors in summer; most also have eating facilities and countless fish stalls and snack bars that mushroom around the town. Locals rent out rooms in their homes in summer.

A useful first port of call in town is the Centrum Turystyczne Łeba (☎ 66 22 77), ul Kościuszki 64, which arranges rooms in private homes, pensions and holiday homes. A bed in the high season will cost anywhere between US$7 and US$20. In the off season, prices drop significantly, to between US$4 and US$12 per head. The Biuro Wczasów Przymorze (☎ 66 13 60), Plac Dworcowy 1, diagonally opposite the train station also arranges private rooms.

There are half a dozen camping grounds in Łeba, including *Camping Nr 41 Ambré* (☎ 66 24 72) and *Camping Nr 48 Przymorze* (☎ 66 23 04), next to each other at ul Nadmorska 9 in the resort area; and *Intercamp 84* (☎ 66 22 40), *Camping Nr 21 Leśny* (☎ 66 13 80) and *Camping Nr 145 Rafael* (☎ 66 19 72), all on ul Turystyczna west beyond the Łeba River. Most camping grounds are open June to September and some have their own eating facilities. Be sure to bring a mosquito repellent, or you might be eaten alive.

Among more permanent accommodation (some operating year-round) are the cheap *Dom Wycieczkowy PTTK* (☎ 66 13 24), ul 1 Maja 6, near the station, *Dom Wczasowy Kowelin* (☎ 66 14 40), ul Nad Ujściem 6, *Zespół Wypoczynkowy Mazowsze* (☎ 66 18 88), ul Nadmorska 15, and *Hotel Wodnik* (☎ 66 15 42), ul Nadmorska 10. The closest to the seashore is the expensive *Hotel Neptun* (☎ 66 14 32), ul Sosnowa 1, which has a terrace overlooking the beach and great views of the sunset.

POLAND

Getting There & Away

The usual transit point to/from Łeba is Lębork, a town 29km to the south, where you may need to change bus or train. Trains to Lębork run every three or four hours, and four continue to Gdynia. Buses ply the Łeba-Lębork route every hour or so. There are two buses direct between Łeba and Gdynia (94km) plus two extra ones in summer.

SŁOWIŃSKI NATIONAL PARK

This park begins just west of Łeba and stretches along the coast for 33km. It contains a diversity of habitats, including forests, lakes, bogs, beaches and dunes. The lake wildlife is remarkably rich, particularly in birds. The park is a UNESCO World Biosphere Reserve.

The most unusual feature of the park is the extensive **shifting dunes** that create a desert landscape. They are on the sandbar separating the sea from Lake Łebsko, about 8km west of Łeba. During WWII, Rommel's Afrika Korps trained in this desert and V-1 rockets were fired at England from here.

The dunes are easily reached from Łeba. Take the road west to the hamlet of Rąbka (2.5km) where there's a car park and the gate to the park. Private minibuses ply this road in summer, or you can just walk. The paved road continues into the park for another 3.5km to the site of the rocket launcher (not survived), from where a wide path goes on through the forest for another 2km to the southern foot of the dunes, where trees can be seen half-buried in the sand.

No cars or buses are allowed beyond the car park. You can walk to the dunes (70 minutes), take one of the small electric trolleys (US$5 per three people), take a horse-drawn cart (US$14 per five people) or rent a bicycle (US$0.80 per hour). There are also large electric trolleys, but they only go as far as the launcher (US$0.50), so you'll still have 2km to walk to the dunes. You then can climb the vast 40m-high dunes for a sweeping view of desert, lake, beach, sea and forest. You can walk back to Łeba along the beach with perhaps a stop for a swim – something you can't do in the Sahara!

On the south-western shore of Lake Łebsko is the tiny hamlet of Kluki, once populated by the Słowińcy, the original inhabitants of the region, after whom the park is named. The village's **skansen** brings to life some of this now extinct culture. Kluki is accessible by bus from Słupsk (41km), but not from Łeba. In summer, a boat from Łeba departs for the skansen in the morning and returns in the afternoon (US$8 return).

Warmia & Masuria

Warmia and Masuria lie in north-eastern Poland, to the east of the lower Vistula valley. Here the Scandinavian glacier left behind a typical postglacial landscape including some 3000 lakes, many linked by rivers and canals to create a system of waterways well favoured by yachtspeople and canoeists. The winding shorelines with many peninsulas, inlets and small islands are surrounded by hills and forests, making this picturesque lake district one of the most attractive and varied touring areas in the country. Add to this interesting historical remains and the opportunity to venture into places which seldom see English-speakers, and you'll have all the reasons you need to visit.

Originally inhabited by heathen Prussian and Jatzvingian tribes, the region was conquered in the 13th century by the Teutonic Knights who had been invited in by the Polish Prince Conrad of Mazovia in 1226. The intention was that the knights would convert the Baltic tribes and depart, but instead they created a powerful religious state and turned their attention to the Poles.

The Battle of Grunwald, fought in 1410 just south-west of Olsztyn, turned out to be a pivotal showdown between the knights and the Polish Crown. The knights' defeat at the battle was followed by the Thirteen Years' War, concluded with the Treaty of Toruń (1466) which gave Warmia (the area north of Olsztyn) to Poland for over three centuries. Masuria (the area east of Olsztyn), however, remained in the German sphere of influence and came under the Hohenzollerns of Brandenburg in the 17th century. In 1773 Warmia was annexed to the Kingdom of Prussia, and both regions were returned to Poland only in 1945.

POLAND

OLSZTYN
☎ 089

Olsztyn (population 175,000) is the only significant city in the region and a major transport hub. For travellers, Olsztyn is probably more important as a jumping-off point for attractions in the region rather than a destination in itself. Though the city has reasonable food and accommodation facilities, you can see its historic sites in a few hours.

Founded in the 14th century as the southernmost outpost of Warmia, Olsztyn's history has been a successive overlapping of Prussian and Polish influences. From 1466 to 1773 the town belonged to the Kingdom of Poland, and none other than Nicolaus Copernicus, administrator of Warmia, commanded Olsztyn Castle from 1516 to 1520. Here he made some astronomical observations for his epochal work *On the Revolutions of Celestial Spheres*.

With the first partition of Poland, Olsztyn became Prussian Allenstein and remained so until 1945. The city was heavily damaged during WWII and little of its historical fabric was rebuilt.

Orientation
Olsztyn's main train station and the bus terminal are adjacent on the north-east side of town, a 15-minute walk from the Old Town, which is the focus of tourist interest. Midway is the youth hostel. You'll enter the historic quarter through the High Gate, which houses another good budget place to stay.

Information
Tourist Office The tourist office (☎/fax 527 57 76), in a bookshop at Plac Jana Pawła II 2/3, is open weekdays from 9 am to 6 pm, Saturday from 10 am to 4 pm. It sells maps, although a better selection can be found at the Sklep Podróżnika (Traveller's Shop) behind the High Gate.

Money Useful banks include Bank Pekao, ul 1 Maja 10, and Powszechny Bank Gospodarczy, ul Mickiewicza 2; both have their own ATMs. Kantors are easy to find in the centre.

Things to See
The **High Gate** is all that remains of the 14th-century city walls. Just to the west is the **Museum of Warmia and Masuria** (closed Monday) staging exhibitions related to the city's past.

A little farther west, the 14th-century **castle** contains the good **Regional Museum** (closed Monday) featuring Warmian paintings and silverware, plus an exhibition dedicated to Copernicus (with many explanations posted in English).

The **Rynek**, or old market square, was destroyed during WWII and rebuilt in a style only superficially reverting to the past. To the east, the red-brick Gothic **cathedral** dates from the 14th century, but its 60m tower was added in 1596.

Organised Tours
The Mazury travel agency (☎ 527 40 59; fax 527 34 42) in the PTTK office next to the High Gate runs 10-day canoeing tours from Sorkwity, 50km east of Olsztyn, down the Krutynia River to Ruciane-Nida. The 10-kayak (20-people) tours go daily from late June to mid-August. The US$200 price includes kayak, food, lodging in cabins and a Polish-speaking guide. You can just show up at the Olsztyn office and hope they can fit you into one of the scheduled tours, or fax or write before you leave for Poland and fit their tour into your schedule. Either way, it's worth the effort. The postal address of the office is: Biuro Podróży Mazury przy OZGT PTTK, ul Staromiejska 1, 10-950 Olsztyn.

Places to Stay
Camping Nr 95 Wanda (☎ 527 12 53), ul Sielska 12, 3km west of the Old Town on the shore of Lake Ukiel (also known as Lake Krzywe), is open from May to September. Take bus No 7 from the train station.

The all-year *youth hostel* (☎ 527 66 50), ul Kopernika 45, halfway between the Old Town and the train station, is well run and tidy, though all of its 80 beds are often occupied in summer.

Hotel Wysoka Brama (☎ 527 36 75) is excellently located on the edge of the Old Town. Its old section in the High Gate has dorms (US$4 per bed), whereas the adjacent new building houses singles without bath

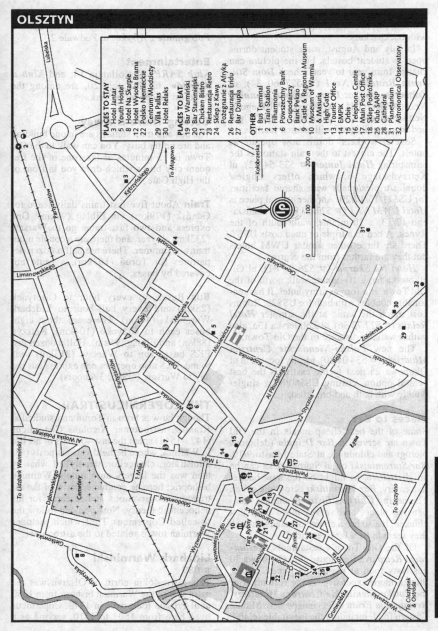

OLSZTYN

PLACES TO STAY
3 Hotel Jantar
7 Youth Hostel
8 Hotel Na Skarpie
12 Hotel Wysoka Brama
22 Polsko Niemieckie
   Centrum Młodzieży
29 Villa Pallas
30 Hotel Relaks

PLACES TO EAT
19 Bar Warmiński
20 Bar Staromiejski
21 Chicken Bistro
23 Restauracja Retro
24 Sklep z Kawą
26 Pożegnanie z Afryką
27 Restauracja Eridu
   Bar Dziupla

OTHER
1 Bus Terminal
2 Train Station
4 Filharmonia
6 Powszechny Bank
   Gospodarczy
   Bank Pekao
9 Castle & Regional Museum
10 Museum of Warmia
   & Masuria
11 High Gate
13 Tourist Office
14 EMPiK
15 Orbis
16 Telephone Centre
17 Main Post Office
18 Sklep Podróżnika
25 Klub SARP
28 Cathedral
31 Planetarium
32 Astronomical Observatory

(map labels: Lubelska, Partyzantów, Kętrzyńskiego, To Mrągowo, To Ostróda, Kościuszki, Limanowskiego, Kłiki, Mickiewicza, Masurska, Głowackiego, Żołnierska, Kościuszki, To Szczytno, Dąbrowszczaków, Partyzantów, Warmińska, Al Wojska Polskiego, To Lidzbark Warmiński, To Cdfwrowskiej, Cemetery, 11 Listopada, Giełkowska, Andzykowa, Warszawska, Zamkowa, Staromiejska, Targ Rybny, Nowowiejskiego, Wyzwolenia, Okopowa, Rynek, Prosta, Pieniężnego, Al Piłsudskiego, 1 Maja, 22-Stycznia, Reja, 22-Stycznia, Kolobrzeska, To Cłsztynek & Ostróda, Grunwaldzka)

200 m
100

POLAND

(US$10) and doubles without/with bath (US$14/18). In summer the hotel is crammed with backpackers.

In July and August, some student dorms open as student hostels, but the picture can change from year to year. Check *Dom Studenta Bratniak Nr 1* (☎ 527 60 34), ul Żołnierska 14b, or *Dom Studenta Bratniak Nr 3* (☎ 526 65 41), Al Wojska Polskiego 1. Neither should cost more than US$7/5 per bed in a double/quad with shared facilities.

Several workers' dorms now operate as hotels. The closest to the train station is the uninspiring *Hotel Jantar* (☎ 533 54 52), ul Kętrzyńskiego 5, which offers singles/doubles/triples/quads with shared facilities for US$11/15/17/20. Another central place is *Hotel UWM Nr 1* (☎ 527 27 80), ul Osińskiego 12/13, a 10-minute walk south of the Rynek. A bed in a triple or quad costs US$7. There are three other similar UWM hotels but they are farther from the centre.

Hotel Na Skarpie (☎ 526 93 81), ul Gietkowska 6a, a 10-minute walk north of the Old Town, is a former army hotel. It has reasonable doubles with bath for US$28. Rooms cost much the same at the simpler *Hotel Relaks* (☎ 527 73 36), ul Żołnierska 13a, also within walking distance of the Old Town.

The new *Polsko-Niemieckie Centrum Młodzieży* (☎ 534 07 80), ideally located at ul Okopowa 25 next to the castle, is the best central option, costing US$60/80 a single/double with bath and breakfast.

Places to Eat

Some of the best cheap meals in the Old Town are served in *Bar Dziupla* (delicious pierogi and chłodnik), ul Stare Miasto 9/10. *Bar Staromiejski* on ul Staromiejska can be an alternative, as might be the new budget fish eatery, *Bar Warmiński* across the street. The nearby *Chicken Bistro* is another inexpensive place, and serves more than just chicken. It also has a choice of salads, though they seem to be a bit overpriced.

Of the Old Town's restaurants, *Restauracja Retro* in a fine house at ul Okopowa 20 has tasty food at reasonable prices. Better, though more expensive, is the restaurant of the *Polsko-Niemieckie Centrum Młodzieży*. *Restauracja Eridu* offers inexpensive Middle Eastern food, including the inevitable felafel.

For a cup of well-prepared coffee (30-odd flavours to choose from) go to *Sklep z Kawą Pożegnanie z Afryką*, ul Podwale 2.

Entertainment

Klub SARP, ul Kołłątaja 14, and *Klub u Artystów*, ul Kołłątaja 20, are among the trendiest places for a drink.

Getting There & Away

The bus and train stations are in one building and are pretty busy. You can walk to the Old Town in 15 minutes or take one of the frequent city buses which drop you in front of the High Gate.

Train About five fast trains daily leave for Gdańsk (179km) via Elbląg (99km). One express and two fast trains go to Warsaw (233km) all year, and there are a couple more trains in summer. There are half a dozen departures for Toruń (163km), a route not covered by buses.

Bus Buses go every hour to Olsztynek (28km) and every half-hour to Lidzbark Warmiński (46km). There are about eight buses each to Giżycko (104km), Kętrzyn (88km) and Elbląg (95km). Half a dozen fast PKS buses run to Warsaw (213km) year round. PKS also operates one express bus per day to Warsaw (US$6, 3¼ hours).

THE COPERNICUS TRAIL

Though he was born in Toruń and studied at Kraków, astronomer Nicolaus Copernicus (1473-1543) spent the last 40 years of his life in Warmia, where he held various posts (administrator, chancellor, deputy) of what by then was the largely autonomous Warmian bishopric; here he conducted most of the astronomic observations and research for his heliocentric theory. Now you can follow the so-called Copernicus Trail which includes Warmian towns related to the astronomer.

Lidzbark Warmiński
☎ 089

This town 46km north of Olsztyn was the main seat of the Warmian bishops from 1350 until Prussia took over in 1773. Copernicus lived here from 1503 to 1510, serving as a doctor and adviser to his uncle, Bishop Łukasz Watzenrode.

Soon after the bishops moved into town, a strong **castle** was built for their residence, which miraculously came through numerous wars unharmed and today houses the **Warmian Museum** (closed Monday). Beginning from a splendid arcaded interior courtyard, virtually unchanged since its construction in the 1380s, you proceed through the castle period rooms featuring various exhibitions, including Warmian medieval sculpture, modern Polish paintings and a collection of old icons.

Lidzbark Warmiński is an easy day trip by bus from Olsztyn, but should you care to linger, the town has a choice of lodging and eating places, including the simple but atmospheric *Dom Wycieczkowy PTTK* (☎ 767 25 21) in the 15th-century High Gate (US$9/12/14 a single/double/triple), the small *Pensjonat Pizza Hotel* (☎ 767 52 59; US$24 a double), and the more upmarket *Hotel Przy Bramie* (☎ 767 32 58; US$48 a double).

Frombork
☎ 055

This small, sleepy town on the shore of the Vistula Lagoon (Zalew Wiślany) was founded in the 13th century and was made the early seat of the Warmian bishopric. A fortified ecclesiastical township was erected on a hill overlooking the lagoon (the so-called Cathedral Hill), and it's still there, much the same as it was six centuries ago.

From 1510 to 1516, and again from 1521 until his death in 1543, Copernicus lived and worked in Frombork and here he wrote his revolutionary *On the Revolutions of the Celestial Spheres*. His unmarked grave is in the powerful red-brick Gothic **cathedral** (closed Sunday) which dominates the Cathedral Hill. Built in 1329-88, it remains the largest Warmian church and perhaps the most magnificent.

The former bishops' palace next to the cathedral is now the **Copernicus Museum** (closed Monday) devoted to the life and work of the astronomer. Other attractions on the hill include the Radziejowski Tower providing sweeping views and a planetarium (both open daily). Just below Cathedral Hill is a tall statue of Copernicus which makes him look rather like Chairman Mao.

Frombork has a few budget accommodation options, including the summer *Camping Nr 12* (☎ 243 73 68), ul Braniewska 14 (which has cabins for US$10/15 a double/triple), the good year-round *youth hostel* (☎ 243 74 53) at ul Elbląska 11 (where you can also camp), and *Dom Wycieczkowy PTTK* (☎ 243 72 52) in the park just west of Cathedral Hill (which costs US$7 a person and also serves cheap meals). Another place for a budget meal is *Restauracja Akcent*, ul Rybacka 4, just off the Rynek.

Frombork can be reached by direct bus from Gdańsk and Lidzbark Warmiński, but there are no major problems in getting there from Malbork and Olsztyn (by bus or train with a change at Elbląg).

THE ELBLĄG CANAL

Linking Elbląg with Ostróda, the 80km Elbląg Canal is Poland's longest navigable canal still in use. It's also the most unusual: the canal deals with the 99.5m difference in water levels by means of a system of five slipways; boats are carried across dry land on rail-mounted trolleys. Each slipway consists of two trolleys tied to a single looped rope, operating on the same principle as a funicular. They are powered by water.

The canal, built in 1848-76, was used for transporting timber from the rich inland forests down to the Baltic. It remains the only one of its kind in Europe operating, now as a tourist attraction.

Theoretically, the excursion boats depart from both ends, Elbląg and Ostróda, daily at 8 am from mid-May to mid-September (11 hours, US$20), but captains can cancel the trip if not enough passengers are around. You should be OK in July and August, particularly on weekends. Call the carrier for information about the availability of tickets and the likelihood of the trip taking place; in Elbląg on ☎ 055 32 43 07, in Ostróda on ☎ 088 46 38 71. Bring your own food as what's sold on board is expensive.

If you plan on taking the trip you'll probably spend the night before departure in either Elbląg or Ostróda (depending on which end you start), and the following night at the other end. Neither town has any spectacular tourist attractions, but both have an array of places to stay and eat, and good transport.

Elbląg, easily accessible from Gdańsk, Malbork, Frombork and Olsztyn, is far larger (130,000 inhabitants) and has more facilities than Ostróda. Budget options include the riverside, cabin-equipped *Camping Nr 61* (☎ 32 43 07), ul Panieńska 14 (from where the canal boats depart), about 1km west of the train and bus stations, and *Hotel Galeona* (☎ 32 48 08), ul Krotka 5, right in the city centre.

Ostróda (population 35,000), serviced regularly by trains from Toruń and Olsztyn, has the inexpensive *Dom Wycieczkowy Drwęcki* (☎ 46 30 35), ul Mickiewicza 7, 500m east of the bus and train stations and just 100m from the boat wharf. There are several other budget options north along the same street.

THE GREAT MASURIAN LAKES

The Great Masurian Lake District east of Olsztyn is a verdant land of rolling hills interspersed with plenty of glacial lakes, healthy little farms, tracts of forest and small towns. The district is centred around Lake Śniardwy (114 sq km), Poland's largest lake, and Lake Mamry and its adjacent waters (104 sq km in all). A fifth of the surface of the area is covered by water and another 30% by forest.

The lakes are well connected by canals, rivers and streams, to form extensive systems of waterways. The whole area has become a prime destination for yachtspeople and canoeists, and is also popular with anglers, hikers, bikers and nature lovers. Tourists arrive in great numbers in July and August, though after 15 August the crowds begin to thin out.

The main lakeside centres are Mikołajki and Giżycko, with two additional ones, Węgorzewo and Ruciane-Nida, at the far northern and southern ends of the lakeland, respectively. They all rent out kayaks and sailing boats, though it may be difficult to get one in July and August.

The detailed Wielkie Jeziora Mazurskie map (scale 1:100,000) is a great help for anyone exploring the region by boat, kayak, bike, car or foot. It shows walking trails, canoeing routes, accommodation options, petrol stations and much more. It's normally available in the region but you're better off buying one at a bookstore in a city before you come.

Getting Around the Lakes Yachtspeople can sail most of the larger lakes, all the way from Węgorzewo to Ruciane-Nida, which are interconnected and are the district's main waterway system. Kayakers will perhaps prefer more intimate surroundings alongside rivers and smaller lakes. The best-established and most popular kayak route in the area originates at Sorkwity and follows the Krutynia River and Lake Bełdany to Ruciane-Nida. Kayaks can be rented in Sorkwity, if any are left after the guided tours have taken their share (see Organised Tours in the Olsztyn section). There's also a beautiful kayak route along the Czarna Hańcza River in the Augustów area farther east (for which tours are arranged by PTTK in Augustów).

If you're not up to sailing or canoeing, you can enjoy the lakes in comfort from the deck of the excursion boats operated by the Masurian Shipping Company. These are large boats with an open deck above and a coffee shop below; you can carry backpacks and bicycles aboard without problems.

Theoretically, boats run between Giżycko, Mikołajki and Ruciane-Nida daily from May to September, and to Węgorzewo from June to August. In practice, the service is most reliable from late June to late August. At other times trips can be cancelled because too few passengers turn up (a minimum of 10 people is normally necessary for the boat to set off).

Sample fares are US$9 from Węgorzewo to Giżycko, US$10 from Giżycko to Mikołajki, and US$9 from Mikołajki to Ruciane-Nida. There are no discounts for foreign students. Schedules are clearly posted at the lake ports. The same company also operates tourist boats out of Augustów.

Getting There & Away Transport is generally good, with three different west-east railway lines running between Olsztyn and Ełk across the lake district, via Giżycko, Mikołajki and Ruciane-Nida. Buses link the settlements on north-south routes, so getting around is easy. There are direct buses to/from Warsaw which are faster than the train.

THE GREAT MASURIAN LAKES

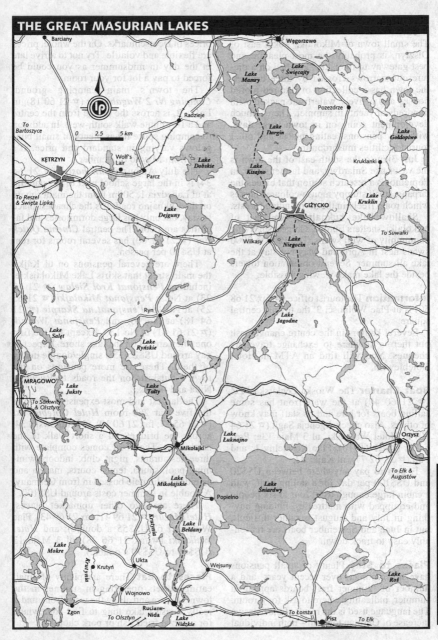

Mikołajki
☎ 087

The small town of Mikołajki, 86km east of Olsztyn, is probably the most pleasant and best gateway to the lakes. Perched on a picturesque narrows crossed by three bridges, the town has a collection of fine red-roofed houses and a lively waterfront packed with hundreds of yachts in summer. There's much development going on in town these days, with new pensions, eating places and other tourist facilities mushrooming.

Just 3km to the south-east of the town is the vast Lake Śniardwy, and farther south, in Popielno, is a research station that breeds the tarpans, small stumpy mouse-coloured horses which roam freely in the surrounding forests.

Shallow Lake Łuknajno, 4km east of Mikołajki, shelters Europe's largest surviving community of wild swans. The 1200 to 2000 swans nest in April and May but stay at the lake all summer. Several observation towers beside the lake make viewing possible.

Information The tourist office (☎/fax 21 68 50) is at Plac Wolności 3, the town's central square.

Several kantors in the centre change cash but there's nowhere to exchange travellers cheques. You will find an ATM in Hotel Gołębiewski.

Boat Charter The Wioska Żeglarska PZŻ (☎ 21 60 40) at the waterfront has some sailing boats for hire and its staff may know of others. Also check Agencja Sagit (☎ 21 64 70) in Hotel Wałkuski, ul 3 Maja 13a; Propeller (☎ 21 69 10), Plac Kościelny 1; and Fun (☎ 21 62 77), ul Kajki 82.

Expect to pay anywhere between US$20 and US$100 per day for a sailing boat, with a cabin large enough to fit four to six people and equipped with mattresses. Finding anything in July and August is rather difficult, but in June and September boats are reasonably easy to track down.

Places to Stay Plenty of small pensions have mushroomed over recent years, and a number of 'zimmer frei' boards appear in summer, indicating where to ask for a room. The language used is the result of the massive increase of German tourism – both individual

and bus tour – in Mikołajki and throughout the region. Many pensions simply list their prices in Deutschmarks. On the whole, prices are flexible and volatile. Try not to arrive late in the day in midsummer as you could be forced to pay a lot for your room.

The town's main camping ground, *Camping Nr 2 Wagabunda* (☎ 21 60 18), ul Leśna 2, is across the bridge from the centre and a 10-minute walk south-west. In addition to camping space it has plenty of small bungalows varying in standard and price. It's open from May to September.

The July-August *youth hostel* (☎ 21 64 34) is in the large school next to the stadium at ul Łabędzia 1, 500m from the main square on the Łuknajno road. It's the cheapest place to stay, but only has large dormitories and facilities are poor. The central *Cinema Quick Bar* (☎ 21 61 60) has several rooms for rent at US$10 per person.

There are several pensions on ul Kajki, the main street that skirts Lake Mikołajskie, including *Pensjonat Król Sielaw* (☎ 21 63 23) at No 5; *Pensjonat Mikołajki* (☎ 21 63 25) at No 18; *Pensjonat na Skarpie* (☎ 21 64 18) at No 96; and *Pensjonat Wodnik* (☎ 21 61 41) at No 130. Except for the first one, they are all on the lake shore. Expect to pay around US$25/35 a single/double in any of them. There are more pensions on the town's outskirts on the roads to Ruciane-Nida and to Ełk.

The largest and most expensive option is the five-star 280-room *Hotel Gołębiewski* (☎ 21 65 17; fax 21 60 10), ul Mrągowska 34, across the bridge and a short walk to the north-west. The hotel comes complete with three restaurants, night club, indoor swimming pool, sauna, tennis courts, marina and an elderly clientele bussed in from Germany. A double in summer costs around US$100.

There are two other upmarket places: *Hotel Mazur* (☎ 21 69 41; fax 21 69 43), Plac Wolności 6 (US$55 a double); and *Hotel Wałkuski* (☎/fax 21 66 28), ul 3 Maja 13 (US$60 to US$90 a double).

Places to Eat There are plenty of small eating outlets operating in summer in the town's centre and along the waterfront, and it really doesn't take long to find somewhere for a pizza, fried fish or pork chop.

POLAND

Cinema Quick Bar, Plac Wolności 9, is inexpensive, as is *Bar Dino* next door. *Pensjonat Król Sielaw* has reasonable food. All the upmarket hotels listed earlier in this section have their own restaurants, with the food prices roughly corresponding to the accommodation rates.

Getting There & Away The sleepy train station is 1km from the centre on the Giżycko road. It handles three trains a day to Ełk and three to Olsztyn.

The bus terminal is in the centre, near the large Protestant church. Buses to Mrągowo (25km) run roughly every hour; change there for Olsztyn or Kętrzyn. Several buses daily go to Giżycko (31km), and there are two to Suwałki (122km). Two or three fast buses depart in the high season to Warsaw (224km) and are much faster than the trains.

Giżycko
☎ 087
Set on the northern shore of Lake Niegocin, Giżycko (population 30,000) is the largest lakeside centre in the area, yet it's a rather ordinary place without charm or historical character. There's nothing much to see here except perhaps the large Boyen Fortress on the western outskirts of the town, built by the Prussians in 1844-55 to protect the border with Russia. The fortifications have survived in pretty good shape and might be of interest to buffs of military engineering. For most travellers, however, Giżycko will just be a base from which to pick up an excursion boat to Mikołajki or Węgorzewo, or to rent a boat.

Information The tourist office (☎ 28 57 60) is at ul Warszawska 7 (enter from ul Kętrzyńskiego).

Powszechny Bank Kredytowy, ul Dąbrowskiego 12, near the train station exchanges travellers cheques and gives advances on Visa. There are some kantors in the centre including one in the Orbis office, ul Dąbrowskiego 3.

Yacht Charter Sailing boats are hired out by a number of operators, including Almatur (☎ 28 59 71), ul Moniuszki 24; Centrum Mazur (☎ 28 54 38) in Camping Nr 1 Zamek,

ul Moniuszki 1; Ośrodek Żeglarski LOK (☎ 28 14 08), ul Lotnicza 4; PUH Żeglarz (☎ 28 20 84), ul Kościuszki 1; COS (☎ 28 23 35), ul Moniuszki 22; and Orbis (☎ 28 51 46), ul Dąbrowskiego 3.

Places to Stay *Camping Nr 1 Zamek* (☎ 28 34 10), ul Moniuszki 1, opens from June to September. The large, basic *youth hostel* (☎ 28 29 59) in the Boyen Fortress operates from May to September.

The well-located but dilapidated *Dom Wycieczkowy PTTK* (☎ 28 29 05), ul Nadbrzeżna 11, costs US$6 per head. It's small and often full in summer. Similarly simple and cheap (US$7 a bed) is the nearby *Hotel Zębiec* (☎ 28 25 30) in the LOK centre, ul Lotnicza 4.

Better is *Hotel Garnizonowy* (☎ 28 14 14), ul Olsztyńska 10a, back off the street behind some apartment blocks. Singles/doubles/triples without bath cost US$13/20/28. *Pokoje Gościnne PKO BP* (☎ 28 54 63), Plac Grunwaldzki 11, offers reasonable singles/doubles/triples at US$16/26/32. The small *Motel Zamek* (☎ 28 24 19), ul Moniuszki 1, has doubles with bath for US$32. A lock-up garage (optional) costs US$5 extra.

From May to September (or longer) you can stay in *COS* (☎ 28 23 35), ul Moniuszki 22, on Lake Kisajno. It's a large sports centre with chalets and rooms in buildings. The latter cost US$32/45/58 a single/double/triple. Next to COS, *Almatur* (☎ 28 59 71), ul Moniuszki 24, also has a collection of chalets and buildings, some of which are heated and open year-round.

The central *Hotel Wodnik* (☎ 28 38 71), ul 3 Maja 2, and *Hotel Jantar* (☎ 28 54 15), ul Warszawska 10, are more upmarket options.

Places to Eat Some of the cheapest meals in town are served in the basic *Bar Omega*, ul Olsztyńska 4. Marginally more expensive is *Bar Zamek*, ul Moniuszki 1. There are many other budget places throughout the central area.

Karczma pod Złotą Rybką, ul Olsztyńska 15, has about the widest choice of fish in town and good prices. Crayfish is available at times. The *Motel Zamek*, *Hotel Jantar* and *Hotel Wodnik* have their own restaurants.

Getting There & Away The train station is on the southern edge of town near the lake. Around eight trains run daily to Ełk (47km), Kętrzyn (30km) and Olsztyn (120km), and two fast trains run to Gdańsk (299km). Trains to Warsaw (353km) take a roundabout route – it's faster to go by bus.

Just next to the train station, the bus terminal offers a regular service to Węgorzewo (26km) and Mrągowo (41km). Half a dozen buses daily run to Mikołajki (31km), Kętrzyn (31km), Olsztyn (104km) and Suwałki (91km). There's a bus or two to Lidzbark Warmiński (93km), and several fast buses to Warsaw (251km) in summer.

Wolf's Lair
☎ 089

History buffs will probably want to visit **Hitler's wartime headquarters**, the Wolfschanze or Wolf's Lair (Wilczy Szaniec in Polish), at Gierłóż, 30km west of Giżycko. Hitler arrived in the Wolf's Lair on 26 June 1941 (four days after the invasion of the Soviet Union) and stayed until 20 November 1944, with only short trips to the outside world. The base had its own train station and airfield surrounded by minefields, anti-aircraft guns and camouflaging. As the Red Army approached, the Germans blew up the Wolfschanze on 24 January 1945 and only cracked concrete bunkers remain.

Over 70 ruined bunkers are scattered through the forest. A large map of the site is posted at the entrance and all the bunkers are clearly numbered: Bormann No 11, Hitler No 13, Goering No 16 etc. The roofs of the eight most important ones are 8m thick!

An assassination attempt was made on Hitler at the Wolf's Lair in July 1944, by a group of pragmatic high-ranking German officers who considered continuation of the war

suicidal. They planned to negotiate with the Allies after eliminating Hitler.

The leader of the plot, Claus von Stauffenberg, arrived from Berlin on 20 July on the pretext of informing Hitler of the newly formed reserve army. A frequent guest in Giełoż, he enjoyed the confidence of the staff and had no problems getting in with a bomb in his briefcase. He placed his briefcase beneath the table a few feet from Hitler and left the meeting to take a pre-arranged phone call from an aide. The explosion killed two members of Hitler's staff and wounded half a dozen others, but Hitler himself suffered only minor injuries and was even able to meet Mussolini, who arrived later the same day. Stauffenberg and some 5000 people involved directly or indirectly in the plot were executed.

Admission to Wolfschanze is US$2 per person, plus another US$2 if you have to park a car. English and German-speaking guides wait at the entrance and charge US$15 per group for a one-hour tour of the site. You can buy booklets about the place (available in English and German).

Places to Stay & Eat The renovated *Dom Wycieczkowy* (☎ 752 44 29) at the site costs US$20/28/38 a single/double/triple with bath and breakfast. At the opposite end of the same building is a restaurant and a bar. Diagonally opposite is a basic *camping ground*, open June to September; enquire at the ticket office.

Getting There & Away The town of Kętrzyn, 8km west of the bunkers, is the usual starting point for most visitors. Buses between Kętrzyn and Węgorzewo run several times a day and stop at the entrance to the bunker site. In summer, there's also the hourly suburban bus from Kętrzyn's train station to the bunkers.

Romania

Romania is a surprise package filled with unexpected delights. No other Eastern European country offers the variety of sights you'll find here, from medieval castles and monasteries to Black Sea beaches and alpine ski resorts; from colourful old Transylvanian cities to the Danube Delta's nature and wildlife reserves; from quaint peasant villages to modern cities where the two lifestyles often overlap. Much of Romania's charm derives from it being a developing country, struggling to catch up with the west since the end of communism, yet retaining many of its ancient customs. Of course, this also results in certain inconveniences, inefficiencies and problems, like some food and product limitations, slow and often rude service and occasional hot water shortages. But if you see this as a unique transitional period in modern history, your experience is vastly more rewarding than visiting a fully developed, westernised country. Most of our readers' letters declare Romania to be the most exciting, best-value destination for the adventurous budget traveller in Eastern Europe.

Romania straddles the rugged Carpathian Mountains, with rich green valleys and farms spread throughout the countryside. It borders Ukraine and Moldova to the north, Hungary to its west, Bulgaria and Yugoslavia to the south and ends at the Black Sea to the east, offering a variety of cultures. The towns of Transylvania are straight out of medieval Hungary or Germany, while the exotic Orthodox monasteries of Moldavia suggest Byzantium. Western Romania bears the imprint of the Austro-Hungarian empire, in contrast to the Roman and Turkish influences in Constanţa. Bucharest, once known as 'the Paris of the East', has a Franco-Romanian character all its own and is working hard to recapture its old mystique.

The secret here is balance: Romania's historical cities can be fascinating, but make an effort to explore the rural countryside as well. Romania's museums and monuments are rewarding and you could spend weeks touring nothing but churches and ancient monasteries. But for many travellers the most

AT A GLANCE

Capital	Bucharest
Population	22.5 million
Area	237,500 sq km
Official Language	Romanian
Currency	1 leu (L) = 100 bani
GDP	US$113 billion (1996)
Time	GMT/UTC+0200

cherished memories are of mountain hikes, beer gardens, quiet villages and chats with the warm and welcoming local people.

Facts about Romania

HISTORY

Ancient Romania was inhabited by Thracian tribes. The Greeks called them the Getae, the Romans called them Dacians, but they were actually a single Geto-Dacian people. From the 7th century BC the Greeks established trading colonies along the Black Sea at

ROMANIA

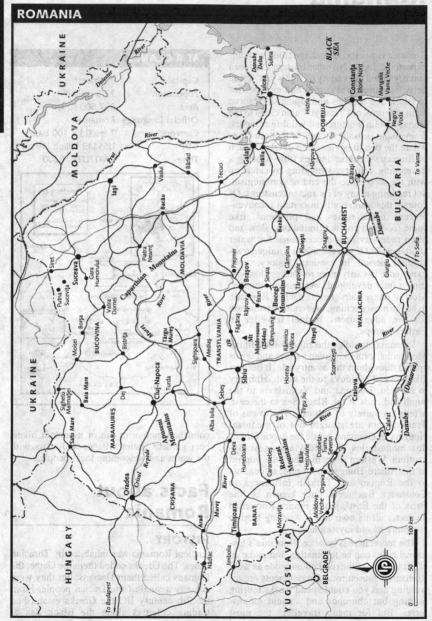

ROMANIA

UKRAINE

MOLDOVA

BLACK
SEA

Danube
Delta

Dniester River

Prut River

Siret

Putna
Sucevița

Suceava

Gura
Humorului

Vatra
Dornei

Borșa

Moisei

Bistrița

BUCOVINA

Vaslui

Bârlad

Bacău

Iași

Tecuci

Galați

Brăila

Tulcea

Sulina

Histria

DOBRUJA

Hârșova

Constanța
Eforie Nord

Mangalia
Vama Veche

Negru
Vodă

To Varna

Călărași

BULGARIA

Danube

To Sofia

Giurgiu

BUCHAREST

Snagov

Ploiești

Buzău

Câmpina

Târgoviște

Târgu Mureș

Sighișoara

Mediaș

Prejmer

Brașov

Sinaia

Bran

Râșnov

Fǎgǎraș

Bucegi
Mountains

▲ Mt
Moldoveanu
(2544m)

Câmpulung

Râmnicu
Vâlcea

Curtea de
Argeș

Pitești

Scornicești

Horezu

WALLACHIA

Olt River

Craiova

Târgu Jiu

Jiu River

Drobeta-
Turnu
Severin

Băile
Herculane

Orșova

Moldova
Veche

Calafat

Danube (Dunărea)

BELGRADE

YUGOSLAVIA

Moravița

Jimbolia

Nădlac

Timișoara

BANAT

Arad

Deva

Hunedoara

Caransebeș

Retezat
Mountains

Alba Iulia

Sebeș

Turda

Cluj-Napoca

Dej

Baia Mare

Sighetu
Marmației

Satu Mare

MARAMUREȘ

Oradea

CRIȘANA

Crișul Repede

Mureș River

Crișul

HUNGARY

To Budapest

UKRAINE

Apuseni
Mountains

TRANSYLVANIA

Olt

Siret River

Mureș

Carparthian Mountains

Piatra
Neamț

MOLDAVIA

Caparthian
Mountains

0   50   100 km

N

Callatis (Mangalia), Tomis (Constanţa) and Histria. In the 1st century BC, a Dacian state was established to counter the Roman threat. The last king, Decebalus, consolidated this state but was unable to prevent the Roman conquest in 105-6 AD.

The Romans recorded their expansion north of the Danube (most of present Romania, including the Transylvanian plateau, came under their rule) on two famous monuments: Trajan's Column in Rome and the 'Tropaeum Trajani' at Adamclisi, on the site of their victory in Dobruja. The slave-owning Romans brought a superior civilisation and mixed with the conquered tribes to form a Daco-Roman people who spoke Latin. A noted visitor during the Roman period was the Latin poet Ovid, who was exiled to Constanţa on the Black Sea by the Roman emperor Augustus (for unknown reasons).

Faced with Goth attacks in 271 AD, Emperor Aurelian decided to withdraw the Roman legions south of the Danube, but the Romanised Vlach peasants remained in Dacia. Waves of migrating peoples, including the Goths, Huns, Avars, Slavs, Bulgars and Magyars (Hungarians), swept across this territory from the 4th to the 10th centuries. The Romanians survived in village communities and gradually assimilated with the Slavs and other peoples who settled there. By the 10th century a fragmented feudal system ruled by a military class had appeared.

From the 10th century the Magyars expanded into Transylvania, north and west of the Carpathian Mountains, and by the 13th century all of Transylvania was an autonomous principality under the Hungarian crown (although Romanians still comprised the majority of the population). German Saxons first came to Transylvania after the devastating Tatar raids of 1241 and 1242, when King Bela IV of Hungary offered the Saxons free land and tax incentives to settle and defend the crown's south-eastern flank.

In the 14th and 15th centuries the Romanian speaking principalities of Wallachia and Moldavia offered strong resistance to the Ottomans' northern expansion. Mircea the Old, Vlad Ţcpcş and Ştefan the Great became legendary figures in this struggle.

Vlad Ţepeş (The Impaler), ruling prince of Wallachia in 1456-62 and 1476-77, is perhaps more famous as the inspiration for Bram Stoker's Count Dracula. Vlad was called Dracula (meaning 'son of the dragon') after his father, Vlad Dracul, a knight of the Order of the Dragon, although today *drac* means 'devil' in Romanian. (The vampires originated in the imagination of the 19th-century Irish novelist.)

When the Turks conquered Hungary in the 16th century, Transylvania became a vassal of the Ottoman Empire, retaining its autonomy by paying tribute to the sultan. After the Ottoman victory in Transylvania, Wallachia and Moldavia also paid tribute to the Turks but maintained their autonomy (this indirect control explains why the only Ottoman buildings in Romania today are in Dobruja, the area between the Danube and the Black Sea). In 1600 the three Romanian states were briefly united under Michael the Brave (Mihai Viteazul) at Alba Iulia.

This semi-independence meant that Hungarians and Saxons in Transylvania could convert from Catholicism to Protestantism in the 16th century, leading to a schism with the Catholic Habsburg rulers. Yet hope for an independent Transylvania was dashed after the Turks were defeated at the gates of Vienna in 1683. In 1687 Transylvania came under the rule of the Habsburgs and between 1703 and 1711 the Austrian Habsburgs suppressed an independence struggle led by the Transylvanian prince Ferenc Rákóczi II.

Turkish suzerainty persisted in Wallachia and the rest of Moldavia well into the 19th century despite unsuccessful revolutions in 1821 and 1848. After the Russian defeat in the Crimean War (1853-56), Romanian nationalism grew and in 1859, with French support, Alexandru Ioan Cuza was elected to the thrones of Moldavia and Wallachia, creating a national state, which took the name Romania in 1862. The reform-minded Cuza was forced to abdicate in 1866 and his place was taken by the Prussian prince Karl of Hohenzollern, who took the name Carol I. With Russian assistance, Romania declared independence from the Ottoman Empire in 1877 and, after the 1877-78 War of Independence, Dobruja became part of Romania.

WWI & WWII

In 1916 Romania entered WWI on the side of the Triple Entente (Britain, France and Russia) with the objective of taking Transylvania – where 60% of the population was Romanian – from Austria-Hungary. The Central Powers (Germany and Austria-Hungary) occupied Wallachia, but Moldavia was defended by Romanian and Russian troops. With the defeat of Austria-Hungary in 1918, the unification of Banat, Transylvania and Bucovina with Romania was finally achieved.

In the years leading to WWII, Romania, under foreign minister Nicolae Titulescu, sought security in an alliance with France and Britain and joined Yugoslavia and Czechoslovakia in the Little Entente. Romania also signed the Balkan Pact with Yugoslavia, Turkey and Greece, and established diplomatic relations with the USSR. These efforts were weakened by the western powers' appeasement of Hitler and by Romania's King Carol II, who declared a dictatorship in February 1938. Romania was isolated after the fall of France in May 1940 and in June 1940 the USSR occupied Bessarabia (taken from Russia after WWI). On 30 August 1940 Romania was forced to cede northern Transylvania (43,500 sq km) and its 2.6 million inhabitants to Hungary by order of Nazi Germany and Fascist Italy. In September 1940 southern Dobruja was given to Bulgaria.

These setbacks sparked off widespread demonstrations. To defend the interests of the ruling classes, General Ion Antonescu forced King Carol II to abdicate in favour of the king's son Michael, then imposed a fascist dictatorship with himself as *conducător* (supreme leader). German troops were allowed to enter Romania in October 1940; in June 1941 Antonescu joined Hitler's anti-Soviet war. The results were gruesome: 400,000 Romanian Jews and 36,000 Roma (Gypsies) were murdered at Auschwitz and other camps. (After the war, Antonescu was executed as a war criminal.)

Throughout WWII, anti-Nazi resentment smouldered among the Romanian soldiers and people. On 23 August 1944 Romania suddenly changed sides, captured 53,159 German soldiers and declared war on Nazi Germany. By this act, Romania salvaged its independence and dramatically shortened the war. By 25 October, Romanian and Soviet armies had driven the Hungarian and German forces from Transylvania. Romania continued fighting in Hungary and Czechoslovakia. Some 670,000 Romanian soldiers died during the war.

The Communist Era

Before 1945 Romania's communists had little influence; their post-war ascendancy was a consequence of backing from Moscow. The Soviet-engineered return of Transylvania enhanced the prestige of the left-wing parties, which won the parliamentary elections of November 1946. A year later the monarchy was abolished and the Romanian People's Republic proclaimed. At about the same time the name 'Rumania' was replaced by 'Romania', to emphasise the country's Roman heritage.

Soviet troops withdrew in 1958 and after 1960 Romania adopted an independent foreign policy under two leaders, Gheorghe Gheorghiu-Dej (ruled 1952-65) and his protégé Nicolae Ceauşescu (1965-89), who were both imprisoned during WWII.

Unlike other Warsaw Pact countries, Romania deviated from the official Soviet line and did not participate in joint military manoeuvres after 1962. Romania never broke with the USSR, as did Tito's Yugoslavia and Mao's China, but Ceauşescu refused to assist the Soviets in their 1968 'intervention' in Czechoslovakia and condemned the invasion publicly, earning him praise and economic aid from the west. Romania condemned the Soviet war in Afghanistan and participated in the 1984 Los Angeles Olympic Games despite a Soviet-bloc boycott.

In contrast to its skilful foreign policy, Romania suffered from inept government at home during Ceauşescu's 25-year reign. In 1974 the post of president was created for Ceauşescu, who placed his wife, Elena, son Nicu and three brothers in important political positions during the 1980s.

Ceauşescu's domestic policy was chaotic and megalomaniacal. Only two of his grandiose projects can be considered successes: the Trans-Făgăraş Highway and the Bucharest Metro (opened in 1985). Others were expensive failures: the Danube Canal from Agigea to Cernavo, which opened in 1984; the agricultural development and toxic waste processing in the Danube Delta; the costly House of the People and disruptive redevelopment of southern Bucharest into a new political centre between 1983 and 1989; and his plan to 'systematise' Romanian agriculture by transferring 7000 rural villagers into hastily constructed concrete apartment blocs.

By the late 1980s, with the Soviet bloc quickly disintegrating, the United States withdrew Romania's most favoured nation trading status. Undaunted, Ceauşescu continued spending millions of dollars to build the House of the People and transform Bucharest into a showcase socialist capital. His great blunder was the decision to export Romania's food to help finance his projects.

In November 1987 workers rioted in Braşov to demand better conditions; during the winter of 1988-89 the country suffered its worst food shortages in decades. Tensions simmered as the population endured prolonged scarcities of almost everything.

The 1989 Revolution

The spark that ignited Romania came on 15 December 1989, when Father Lászlo Tökés spoke out publicly against the dictator from his small Hungarian church in Timişoara. The following evening people protested against the decision of the Reformed Church of Romania to remove him from his post and by 9 pm this had turned into a noisy demonstration. When the police began to make arrests, the unrest spread and armoured cars began patrolling the streets.

On 17 December a huge crowd on Timişoara's Blvd 30 Decembrie (now Piaţa Victoriei) was confronted by the Securitate and regular army troops. The army used tanks and armoured cars to clear the vast square. Despite this, further clashes took place in nearby Piaţa Libertăţii.

In Bucharest, the Executive Political Committee condemned the 'mild' action taken by the army and ordered that real bullets be used; this was the start of civilian casualties. On 19 December, the army in Timişoara switched to the demonstrators' side.

The next day newly arrived Securitate units began firing on the demonstrators. Ceauşescu, just back from a state visit to Iran,

proclaimed martial law in Timiş County. Trainloads of troops were dispatched with orders to crush the rebellion.

On 21 December Ceauşescu decided to address a mass rally in front of the Central Committee building in Bucharest, to show the world that the workers of Romania 'approved' of the military action against the 'hooligan' demonstrators in Timişoara.

As Ceauşescu began speaking from the balcony of the building, youths held back by three cordons of police started booing. Tension mounted in the crowd and suddenly Ceauşescu was cut off in mid-sentence by shouts of disapproval. For a second the dictator faltered, his amazement at being directly challenged written across his face. Pandemonium erupted as the youths attempted to break through the police lines while the assembled workers tried to escape. Ceauşescu attempted to continue his speech even as police cleared the square, finally ending as the tape with pre-recorded applause and cheers was switched off.

Meanwhile the anti-Ceauşescu demonstrators retreated to the boulevard between Piaţa Universităţii and Piaţa Romană. About 2.30 pm riot police with clubs and shields were deployed and plain-clothes police began making arrests. As more police and armoured cars arrived, the growing number of demonstrators became concentrated in the two squares. About 5 pm, with crowds still refusing to disperse, the police at Piaţa Romană first fired warning shots and then used gunfire and armoured cars to crush the demonstrators.

Armoured cars also drove into the crowd on Piaţa Universităţii. Drenched by ice-cold water from fire hoses, the demonstrators there refused to submit and began erecting barricades, watched by western journalists in the adjacent hotel. At 11 pm the police began their assault on Piaţa Universităţii, using a tank to smash the barricades. By dawn the square had been cleared and the corpses removed.

At 7 am on 22 December demonstrators began reassembling in Piaţa Romană and Piaţa Universităţii. By 11 am huge crowds faced a phalanx of army troops, tanks and Securitate units. Rumours began circulating about General Milea, the minister of defence, who allegedly had been forced to commit suicide for refusing to order his troops to fire on the people. Gradually the crowd began to chant 'The army is with us!' and to mix with the troops arrayed against them, offering the soldiers flowers and cigarettes.

At 11.30 am Bucharest Radio announced the 'suicide' of the 'traitor' Milea and the proclamation of a state of emergency. As thousands of people moved towards the Central Committee building, the Securitate drew back. At noon Ceauşescu again appeared on the balcony to speak, but people began booing and throwing objects at him, forcing him to duck back inside the building. The crowd then surged in past unresisting police. Ceauşescu and his wife escaped by helicopter from the roof.

The helicopter took the Ceauşescus to their villa at Snagov, north of Bucharest. The plan was to proceed to an air base near Piteşti, where a waiting jet would take them into exile. Halfway to Piteşti, however, the helicopter pilot feigned engine trouble and set the chopper down beside a highway, where two Securitate officers commandeered a passing car. The party then drove to Tîrgovişte, where the Ceauşescus were arrested and taken to a military base.

On 25 December Nicolae and Elena Ceauşescu were tried together by an anonymous court, condemned and summarily executed by a firing squad. The next day their bodies were exhibited on TV.

Reports of casualties in the revolution were wildly exaggerated. At the Ceauşescus' trial it was claimed that 64,000 people died in the revolution; after a week the number of victims had been reduced to 7000 and the final count was 1033. In Timişoara, 115 people died, not the 4000 reported.

Democracy

The National Salvation Front (FSN) led by Ion Iliescu took over. It is believed that reformers in the Communist Party had been preparing a coup d'état against Ceauşescu and his family for at least six months when the December 1989 demonstrations forced them to move their schedule forward. Once in power, the FSN easily won the 20 May 1990 election and control of the National Assembly and Senate. Romania's new democratic government was being run by former communists.

Students protested against the FSN's ex-communist party leadership but, on 13 June 1990, 20,000 coal miners from the Jiu River area travelled to Bucharest for a counter-riot. Many injuries were sustained, and it was later revealed that secret police had infiltrated the miners and provoked the violence.

In September 1991 the miners returned to Bucharest to force the resignation of Prime Minister Petre Roman, whose free-market economic reforms had led to worsening living conditions. Roman's departure was a serious setback for the whole reform process.

In 1992 a new constitution was ratified and after elections in September 1992 the left-wing Democratic National Salvation Front (DFSN, successor to the FSN) formed a coalition government with several smaller communist or ultra-nationalist parties and promised to slow down economic reforms. In October 1992 Ion Iliescu was re-elected president. The political scene eventually stabilised, with President Iliescu leading under the banner of the Party of Social Democracy (PDSR).

In April 1996 Romania applied for full NATO membership, although it was rejected. It also signed associate-member agreements with the European Union (EU).

In September 1996 Emil Constantinescu of the Democratic Convention in Romania (CDR) was elected president. Internal party bickering further delayed the promised economic reforms, however, and caused the people to demonstrate their new democracy by demanding a change of government. On March 30 1998 prime minister Victor Ciorba and his ministers were forced to step down after just 15 months in office. President Constantinescu then appointed Radul Vasile prime minister; Vasile's new cabinet was approved in April 1998.

Romania Today

Romanians now enjoy open contact with foreigners, can hold foreign currency and can speak freely. Bustling food markets and trendy shops have replaced the empty shelves of the old government stores. Since 1993 when subsidies on food, transportation and energy were scrapped, prices have skyrocketed. Rampant inflation has caused declining living standards for some Romanians, whose average monthly wage is about 830,000 lei (US$100). The economy seems to have stabilised, however, and many Romanians are capitalising on the new financial opportunities, opening businesses of their own or joining the many international companies that have set up offices and factories in Romania. Corruption and inefficiency still exist, as it takes time to unlearn the old ways; but progress, while slower than in some other former eastern bloc countries, is finally on a steady track forward. Romanians value and appreciate their new personal freedoms and, despite the economic problems, few would wish to be back in the suffocating grip of the old communist system. Yet it's fascinating to ask people what they think of Ceauşescu and to hear them compare the present to the recent past. Be prepared for some unexpected comments.

GEOGRAPHY & ECOLOGY

Covering 237,500 sq km, oval-shaped Romania is larger than Hungary and Bulgaria combined. The Danube River drains the whole of Romania (except the Black Sea coast) and completes its 2850km course through nine countries in Romania's Danube Delta. Most of Romania's rivers are tributaries of the Danube.

Most of central and northern Romania is taken up by the U-shaped Carpathian Mountains. The highest point is Mt Moldoveanu (2544m), part of the Făgăraş range south-east of Sibiu. The Transylvanian Plain, a plateau with hills and valleys, occupies the centre of the U, while the Moldavian plateau lies to the east. Earthquakes are common in the south and south-west.

The Carpathian Mountains account for about one-third of the country's area, with alpine pastures above and thick fir, spruce and oak forests below. Another third of Romania is covered by hills and tablelands full of orchards and vineyards. The final third is a fertile plain where cereals, vegetables, herbs and other crops are grown.

Rural Romania has thriving animal populations, including chamois, lynx, fox, deer, wolf, bear and badger. The birdlife is most varied in the Danube Delta, though you'll see eagles, hawks and vultures almost everywhere.

GOVERNMENT & POLITICS

Romania now has a constitutional republic government with a multi-party parliamentary system consisting of the Chamber of Deputies and the Senate. The president is elected by the people; his nominations for prime minister and the cabinet must be approved by parliament. There are many political parties, but the most powerful include the National Peasant-Christian Democratic Party (NP-CDP), the Social Democratic Union (USD) and the Hungarian Democratic Union of Romania (UDMR). The government's current priorities are economic reform, the privatisation of state-owned properties, the fight against corruption, and entry into NATO and the EU.

ECONOMY

Fifty per cent of Romania's economy is based on industry (metallurgy, petrochemicals, machinery, textiles and manufactured goods), 33% on its growing service sector and 17% on agriculture. The change from a centrally planned economy to a market economy has been slow and difficult. The restructuring of Romania's business and industrial environment has caused soaring inflation and 9% unemployment.

Romania's communist government promoted huge heavy industry and infrastructure projects in hydropower, natural gas, petrochemicals, iron and steel and nuclear power. Excessive development led to extreme oversizing, heavy costs and gross inefficiencies. The old emphasis on heavy industry was very much in line with the communists' goal of self-reliance but it led to shortages of food and consumer goods and left Romania with uneconomic industries that are technologically unable to compete on world markets. These industries are being restructured with the help of foreign investment.

The government wants to shut down inefficient industries and privatise those with economic potential. It is encouraging foreign investment with new regulations benefiting those buying shares from the State Ownership Fund (SOF).

The largest foreign companies in Romania include Daewoo, Mobil Rom, Shell, Coca Cola, Unilever and Colgate-Palmolive. Plus

McDonald's has 24 restaurants in Romania and four more under construction.

Bucharest's stock exchange (BVB) is growing too. Two years after its opening in November 1995, it had 94 quoted companies, expecting to soon reach 100. Trading now takes place daily, with an average transaction volume for 1997 of over US$1 million.

POPULATION & PEOPLE

Romania has a population of 22.5 million, 53% of whom live in towns and cities. Bucharest (2.1 million) is by far the largest city, followed by Constanţa (350,000), Iaşi (338,000), Timişoara (325,000), Galaţi (324,000), Braşov (324,000), Cluj-Napoca (322,000) and Craiova (303,000). The main educational centres are in Bucharest, Iaşi, Cluj-Napoca and Timişoara.

The number of Germans in Romania has fallen drastically in the last 60 years. During WWII, 175,000 Romanian Germans were killed or left the country and since then many Transylvanian Saxons and Banat's Swabians have emigrated to Germany. Some 227,000 left between 1976 and 1991; the number of Germans in Romania has dropped from 745,000 in 1930 to 119,000 in 1992.

The government estimates that only 400,000 Roma live in Romania, but a more accurate figure would be one million, making it the largest Roma community in the world. Unfortunately there is much anti-Roma sentiment. Roma villages have been burned by Romanian nationalists with official complicity. One bright spot was the formation in 1996 of the Romani Alliance, a coalition of Roma groups which will enable Roma leaders to compete in national elections for the first time.

For decades the situation of the 1.6 million Hungarians in Romania has soured relations with Hungary. Under Ceauşescu, Hungarian-language newspapers and magazines in Romania were closed down, and official plans to relocate 7000 Romanian villages, many of them in Transylvania, threatened Romania's Hungarians with cultural assimilation. Now the constitution guarantees minority rights and the UDMR is represented in both the Romanian Senate and Chamber of Deputies.

Most accounts of ethnic conflicts in Romania published in the west show justified concern for the Hungarian minority, yet ignore the fact that the Romanian majority in Transylvania was subjected to forced 'Magyarisation' under Hungarian rule before WWI. While Hungarians and Bulgarians tend to look down on Romanians, the Romanians consider themselves the direct heirs of ancient Rome and thus on a higher plain than the descendants of barbaric Slav and Hungarian tribes. Interestingly, Romania has always had friendly relations with Yugoslavia.

ARTS

Painter Nicolae Grigourescu (1838-1907) absorbed French impressionism and created canvases alive with the colour of the Romanian peasantry. You can see his work in art galleries in Bucharest, Iaşi and Constanţa.

Although primarily a resident of France after 1904, abstract sculptor Constantin Brâncuşi (1876-1957) endowed his native Tîrgu Jiu with some of his finest works in 1937. Brâncuşi revolutionised sculpture by emphasising essential forms and the beauty of the material itself.

The Romantic poet Mihai Eminescu (1850-89) captured the spirituality of the Romanian people in his work. In his plays, satirist Ion Luca Caragiale (1852-1912) decried the impact of precipitous modernisation on city life and showed the comic irony of social and political change. The Romanian writer best known internationally is perhaps playwright Eugene Ionesco (1912-1994), a leading exponent of the 'theatre of the absurd', who lived in France after 1938. Former dissident Paul Goma, born in 1935, is Romania's most renowned contemporary novelist. His *My Childhood at the Gate of Unrest* recently appeared in Britain in an English translation, though all his books are worth reading.

Romanian cinema has blossomed since the revolution. In 1994 Lucian Pintilie's *O Vara de Neuiţat* (Unforgettable Summer) made a small splash at Cannes. Other films to look out for are Mircea Daneliuc's *Senatorul Melcilor* (Senator of the Snails) and Radu Gabrea's *Rosenemil, o Tragica Lubire* (The Tragic Love Story of Rosenemil). In 1996

Fox Studios paid US$1.5 million for film rights to *Almost Adam*, a novel by Romanian-born Petru Popescu.

Music

Traditional Romanian folk instruments include the *bucium* (alphorn), the *cimpoi* (bagpipes), the *cobză* (a pear-shaped lute) and the *nai* (a panpipe of about 20 cane tubes). Many kinds of flute are used, including the *ocarina* (a ceramic flute) and the *tilinca* (a flute without finger holes). The violin, which is of more recent origin, is today the most common folk instrument. Romania's most famous composer, George Enescu (1881-1955), was a virtuoso violinist who used Romanian folk themes in his work.

The *doină* is an individual, improvised love song, a sort of Romanian blues with a social or romantic theme. The *baladă*, on the other hand, is a collective narrative song steeped with feeling.

Couples may dance in a circle, a semicircle or a line. In the *sîrbă* males and females dance quickly in a closed circle with their hands on each other's shoulders. The *horă* is another fast circle dance and in the *brîu* (belt dance) the dancers form a chain by grasping their neighbour's belt.

Modern Romani or 'Tzigane' music has absorbed many influences and professional Roma musicians play whatever their village clients desire. The *lăutari* (musicians) circulate through the village inviting neighbours to join in weddings, births, baptisms, funerals and harvest festivals. Improvised songs *(cîntec)* are often directed at a specific individual and are designed to elicit an emotional response (and a tip). To appeal to older people, the *lăutari* sing traditional ballads (*baladă*) or epic songs *(cîntece epice)* in verse, often recounting the exploits of Robin Hood-style *haiducs* (outlaws) who apply justice through their actions.

Professional Roma ensembles or *tarafs*, such as the famous Taraf de Haiducs from Clejani village south-west of Bucharest, use the violin, accordion, guitar, double bass, *ţambal* (hammered dulcimer), *fluier* (flute) and other instruments.

Under communism, an urbanised folk music was promoted by the state to bolster Romanian national identity. In this genre virtuoso *nai* and *ţambal mare* (concert cymbalum or dulcimer) players are backed by large orchestras seldom seen in Romanian villages. You may either love or despise the music of Gheorghe Zamfir, Romania's self-proclaimed 'Master of the Panpipe'.

SOCIETY & CONDUCT

The Romanians' egocentric Latin temperament is apparent when they do things like turn on loud music without consulting those nearby, push in front of others in the queue, monopolise the pavement and generally insist on being served first. Some bad-mannered Romanians rudely interrupt conversations at ticket and information windows. It's also common for Romanians to squeeze close together in queues and on buses; the notion of 'personal space' has yet to catch on here.

On the other hand, many Romanians go out of their way to assist foreign visitors. They will often feed, and even house, a foreigner, refusing any payment.

RELIGION

Eighty-six per cent of the population is Romanian Orthodox, 5% is Roman Catholic, 3.5% is Protestant, 1% is Greek Orthodox, 0.3% is Muslim and 0.2% is Jewish.

LANGUAGE

Romanian is closer to classical Latin than other Romance languages. Some Slavic words were incorporated in the 7th to 10th centuries as the Romanian language took definite shape. English and French are the first foreign languages taught in Romanian schools and German is useful in Transylvania. Speakers of Italian, Spanish and French should be able to understand some Romanian. This is one Eastern European country where Russian won't get you very far.

A few terms of use in getting around are *bloc* (building), *bulevardul* (boulevard), *calea* (avenue), *intrarea* (entrance), *piaţa* (square), *scara* (stairway), *şoseaua* (highway) and *strada* (street). In Romania, you can use the French *merci* to say 'thank you' – many locals do.

See the Language chapter at the back of the book for pronunciation guidelines and useful words and phrases.

Facts for the Visitor

HIGHLIGHTS
Museums & Galleries

Constanţa's archaeological museum has one of the better collections of Greek and Roman artefacts in Eastern Europe. The ethnographical museum in Cluj-Napoca, the Museum of Popular Techniques at Sibiu and Bucharest's Village Museum contain excellent displays of Romanian folk culture. Romania's oldest and finest art gallery is the Brukenthal Museum in Sibiu. Finally, the Danube Museum in Drobeta-Turnu Severin is outstanding for history and natural history, with an aquarium of fish from the Danube.

Castles

Bran Castle near Braşov is on everyone's 'must see' list (even if Count Dracula never slept there), but don't ignore nearby Râşnov Castle. Peleş Castle at Sinaia is actually a royal palace, but it's an amazing palace and easily the finest in Romania.

Historic Towns

Romania's best preserved medieval towns – Sighişoara, Sibiu, Braşov and Cluj-Napoca – are in Transylvania. Oradea is an elegant 19th-century Habsburg town in Crişana.

SUGGESTED ITINERARIES

Depending on the length of your stay, you might want to see and do the following things in Romania:

Two days
  Visit Braşov and Sinaia
One week
  Visit Braşov, Sinaia, Bran/Râşnov, Sighişoara and perhaps Cluj-Napoca. If you're heading south to Bulgaria, add a day or two in Bucharest
Two weeks
  Visit Bucharest, Braşov, Sinaia, Bran/Râşnov, Sighişoara, Sibiu, Cluj-Napoca and Oradea with at least one mountain hike. Or skip Cluj-Napoca and Oradea and visit the monasteries of Bucovina
One month
  Concentrate on Bucharest, Transylvania, Bucovina, the Danube Delta and the Black Sea

PLANNING
Climate & When to Go

The average annual temperature is 11°C in the south and on the coast, but only 2°C in the mountains. Romanian winters can be extremely cold and foggy with lots of snow from mid-December to mid-April. In summer there's usually hot, sunny weather on the Black Sea coast. Annual rainfall is 600 to 700mm, much of it in spring. The mountains get the most rain and the Danube Delta the least.

May and June are by far the best months to visit, followed by September and early October. Spring in Romania is a pastiche of wildflowers, melodious bird song and rivers flowing with melted snow. At higher elevations snow lingers as late as early May and the hiking season doesn't begin in earnest until mid-June. Along the Black Sea coast, the resorts start filling up in June and stay packed until August. Romania is famous for its harsh winters, when tourism focuses on ski resorts like Poiana Braşov and Sinaia.

Books & Maps

A History of Romania produced by the Centre for Romanian Studies in Iaşi is the absolute best history book around, combining a clear account of events with biographies, photos and maps. It's also available on CD-ROM. *Athene Palace* by RG Waldeck is a memoir of Bucharest's grand hotel and the political intrigues carried on there before WWII. Another colourful portrait of Romania at the outbreak of WWII is Olivia Manning's novel *The Balkan Trilogy*.

Kiss the Hand You Cannot Bite: the Rise and Fall of the Ceauşescus by Edward Behr provides fascinating background on the 1989 revolution. Hannah Paluka's *Marie, Queen of Romania* focuses on the half-English, half-Russian granddaughter of Queen Victoria whose persuasive charm at the 1919 Trianon Peace Conference helped Romania obtain Transylvania.

Serious hikers should get the *Hiking Guide to Romania* by Tim Burford. For maps, brochures and other information, it's best to contact your country's resident Romanian National Tourist Office or cultural centre as these are difficult to find in Romania.

What to Bring

A first-aid kit, insect repellent, toilet paper and a small torch (flashlight) will come in handy. Bring your own gear if you plan to hike or camp.

Motorists intending to camp should bring a detailed road map and stock up on canned foods, powdered soups, and tea bags in Hungary, as these can be hard to find in rural Romania. You're not allowed to bring in fresh meat and dairy products. You can usually find tomatoes, peppers, onions, potatoes, carrots, apples and bread in Romania. Supermarkets in larger cities carry imported foods at western prices.

Most importantly, bring western currency in cash, which can be changed to local currency anywhere. Several city shops now take credit cards and you can get Visa and MasterCard cash advances in city banks; some even have ATMs, called Bancomats. Travellers cheques are only accepted at banks, tourist offices and large hotels. American Express has an office in Bucharest. (Small hotels and most stores will require payment in local currency.)

TOURIST OFFICES
Local Tourist Offices

ONT Carpaţi is the state-run tourism agency in Romania. Visit ONT offices for free travel brochures or to plan trips to the countryside.

The service and information at the Agenţia de Turism Intern (ATI) offices are hit-or-miss. They cater to Romanian tourists but often book private rooms and day trips for foreigners. For town maps, ATI is often the only hope.

Touring ACR, the travel agency of the Romanian Automobile Club (Automobil Clubul Român), has desks in several hotels around Romania which are helpful for reservations at upmarket hotels and providing general information for visiting motorists (and others). You can usually get a free copy of a Romanian highway map. All offices are listed in this chapter.

Private travel agencies have opened across Romania, but their main business is organising package holidays for Romanians. Some do, however, arrange private rooms and sightseeing tours.

Tourist Offices Abroad

Romanian National Tourist Offices are the best places to get information and maps before you travel. Their addresses include:

France
(☎ 01 40 20 99 33; fax 01 40 20 99 43) 12 rue des Pyramides, F-75001 Paris
Germany
(☎ 069-295 278; fax 069-292 947) Zeil 13, D-60313 Frankfurt-am-Main (☎/fax 030-589 2684)
Frankfurter Tor 5, D-10243 Berlin
Netherlands
(☎/fax 020-623 9044) Weteringschans 165, C-1017 XD, Amsterdam
UK
(☎/fax 0171-224 3692) 83a Marylebone High St, London, W1M 3DE
USA
(☎ 212-545-8484; fax 212-251-0429) 14 E 38th St, 12th Floor, New York, NY 10016

VISAS & EMBASSIES

American citizens with valid passports may travel visa-free for 30 days in Romania. All other western visitors require a tourist or transit visa to enter. Romania issues three types of visas: transit, single entry and multiple entry. Costs vary depending on your country.

A single transit visa (US$21) is good for three days and one entry. Double entry visas (US$50) are valid for three days too, but you can enter twice. They must be used within one month of issue date. Single entry visas (US$35 to $62) are good for 30-day visits. Multiple-entry visas (US$70 to $94) are valid for three or six months.

Single entry transit visas and 30-day visas can be bought at the border and at Otopeni airport in Bucharest.

If you lose the 'exit card' (ie the scrappy piece of paper) that officials put in your passport upon arrival, you'll be fined the cost of a new 30-day visa and could even be detained for a few hours. The same penalties apply to travellers who overstay their original visa.

Visa Extensions

Once inside Romania, it's possible to extend your stay by reporting to a passport office – any local tourist office will have the address. The Bucharest office is at Str Nicolae Iorga 7 near Piaţa Romană. You must apply before your current visa expires.

Romanian Embassies Abroad

Romanian embassies and consulates around the world (in addition to Romanian embassies in Belgrade, Budapest, Bratislava, Prague, Sofia, Warsaw and Zagreb listed elsewhere in this book) include the following:

Australia
(☎ 02-6286 2343, fax 02-6286 2433) 4 Dalmar Crescent, O'Malley, ACT 2606

Canada
(☎ 613-789 5345; fax 613-789 4365) 655 Rideau St, Ottawa, Ont K1N 6A3
(☎ 416-585 5802; fax 416-585 4798) 111 Peter St, Suite 530, Toronto, Ont M5V 2H1
(☎ 514-876 1792; fax 514-876 1797) 1111 St Urbain, Suite M 01, Montreal, Que H2Z 1Y6

France
(☎ 01 40 62 22 35) 3-5 rue de l'exposition, F-75007 Paris

Netherlands
(☎ 070-354 3796; fax 070-354 1587) Catsheuvel 55, 2517 KA, The Hague

UK
(☎ 0171-937 9666; fax 0171-937 8069) 4 Palace Green, London W8 4QD

USA
(☎ 202-332-4848; fax 202-232-4748) 1607 23rd St NW, Washington, DC 20008
(☎ 212-682-9120; fax 212-972-8463) 200 E 38th St, New York, NY 10016
(☎ 310-444-0043; fax 310-445-0043) 11766 Wilshire Blvd, Suite 560, Los Angeles, CA 90025

Foreign Embassies & Consulates in Romania

These embassies and consulates are in Bucharest:

Albania
(☎ 212 0190) Aleea Modrogan 4 (embassy)

Australia
(☎ 312 9097) Blvd General Magheru 29, room 45 (consulate)

Bulgaria
(☎ 211 1106) Str Vasile Lascăr 32 (consulate)

Canada
(☎ 222 9845) Str Nicolae Iorga 36 (embassy)

Croatia
(☎ 312 1600) Blvd Hristo Botev 3 (consulate)

Czech Republic
(☎ 615 9142) Str Ion Ghica 11 (consulate)

France
(☎ 312 0217) Str Biserica Amzei 13-15
(☎ 312 0217) Intrarea Christian Tell 6 (consulate)

Germany
(☎ 230 0332) Str Rabat 19 (consulate)
(☎ 230 2580) Str Rabat 21 (embassy)

Hungary
(☎ 614 6622) Str Jean Louis Calderon 65 (embassy)

Japan
(☎ 210 0790) Str Polona 4 (embassy)

Moldova
(☎ 666 5720) Str Câmpina 47 (consulate)

Poland
(☎ 230 2715) Aleea Alexandru 23 (embassy)

Slovakia
(☎ 312 6833) Str Oţetari 3 (consulate)

UK
(☎ 312 0303) Str Jules Michelet 24 (embassy)

Ukraine
(☎ 223 2702) Str Tuberozelor 5 (consulate)

USA
(☎ 211 6630) Str Nicolae Filipescu 26 (consulate)

Yugoslavia
(☎ 210 0359) Calea Dorobanţilor 34 (consulate)

CUSTOMS

Romanian customs regulations are complicated but not often enforced. Gifts worth up to a total of US$100 may be imported duty free. For foreigners, duty-free allowances are 4L of wine, 1L of spirits and 200 cigarettes.

Officially, you're allowed to import hard currency up to a maximum of US$50,000. Valuable goods and foreign currency over US$1000 should be declared upon arrival. Border officials may stamp your passport if you have a video camera or laptop computer. You must pay a hefty fine if you leave Romania without them, even if they were lost or stolen. This does not apply to personal stereos and standard cameras.

MONEY
Currency

There are coins of 50 and 100 lei and notes of 500, 1000, 5000, 10,000, 50,000 and 100,000 lei.

Exchange Rates

At the time of going to press, the Romanian leu (plural: lei) was officially worth:

Australia	A$1	=	L5212
Canada	C$1	=	L5703
euro	€1	=	L9566
France	1FF	=	L1447
Germany	DM1	=	L4853
Japan	¥100	=	L6056
New Zealand	NZ$1	=	L4405
UK	UK£1	=	L14,147
USA	US$1	=	L8740

All prices in US dollars quoted in this chapter were obtained by converting from lei at the official rate.

Costs

Romania is a relatively inexpensive country for foreigners. Restaurant meals, drinks, public transport, museum admissions, theatre tickets and private rooms (outside Bucharest) are less expensive in Romania than in any other European country. Foreigners may pay a higher rate than Romanians to sleep in the same hotel or for domestic air flights, and car rentals are expensive, but almost everything else is priced to be affordable for the locals. On average you'll pay US$20 to $35 per night for budget accommodation and less than US$10 per day for meals and drinks.

However, bear in mind that average Romanians earn the equivalent of only US$80 a month. When discussing prices with Romanians it's far better to express sympathy with their situation instead of raving about how cheap everything is, which will breed resentment and encourage the overcharging of foreigners.

Changing Money

You can now change travellers cheques and get Visa and MasterCard cash advances from most branches of BANCOREX, Bancă Comercială Română and Banc Post on weekdays from 9 am to 2 pm. ATM machines giving 24-hour advances (Cirrus, Plus, Visa, MasterCard, Eurocard) are becoming more common too, with at least one in every major city.

Banks charge a 3 to 5% commission to change travellers cheques for either lei or US dollars. Some private exchange houses will also cash travellers cheques at a rate competitive with the official bank rate.

Whether you change money at a bank or tourist office, you'll need your passport. You are also given a receipt which you should keep for reference, although almost everything can be paid for in lei without this proof that you have obtained your lei legally. Receipts are required to change excess lei back into hard currency, which you can do at main branches of the banks listed and at the exchange desk at Bucharest's Otopeni airport (US$50 maximum). Bulgarian leva cannot be changed in Romania and Hungarian forints are only accepted by black marketeers in Transylvania.

Black Market

By law Romanians are allowed to purchase only US$125 in foreign currency a year, which is why there's a black market offering 10 to 25% above the official bank rate for cash US dollars, British pounds and Deutschmarks.

Changing money on the street is illegal and risky. People who offer to change money on the street are often professional thieves who only want to trick you out of your cash. The amount of money you will be given the first time will always be 'short' and in the process of correcting the 'error' the real money disappears. The moneychangers flash a thick wad of notes, count out the agreed price for your dollars or Deutschmarks, roll the money up into a tight roll, then switch rolls at the last instant. Later, when you take the money out to count it again, you discover a roll of newsprint or worthless Yugoslav banknotes with a lei note on top. These operators will insist that you change at least US$50 or DM100, which is one way to recognise them.

Another favourite trick is to take your dollars and give you the correct amount, then just as you're walking off they rush back shouting 'not good, not good'. The operators will then insist on giving 'your' money back in exchange for theirs. As soon as they have the lei in hand again, they'll quickly disappear and you'll find that your US$20 and

ROMANIA

US$50 bills have been swapped for US$1 bills or counterfeit notes.

Beware of anyone who's too pushy or works with a partner. Given any chance at all, they'll rob you.

If you're set on cutting your costs by 25%, deal with people you meet in camping grounds or hotels rather than on the street. Take the money from them first, examine it carefully, put it away and only then show your money. Don't be in a hurry.

This book has included warnings on this subject since the first edition and we still get letters from readers who thought they knew what they were doing and ended up being cheated. Once again, be careful.

Tipping

Tipping is not yet common in Romania, though you should always round the bill up to the nearest 100 lei (some waiters and taxi drivers do this automatically). Tips should not be offered to officials, including train conductors.

POST & COMMUNICATIONS
Sending Mail

Mailboxes in Bucharest are red and labelled *Poşta Română* (elsewhere they may be yellow). One slot is for Bucharest addresses, the other for all other destinations.

Main post offices are open from Monday to Saturday until 8 pm and Sunday until noon. When mailing purchases home from Romania, you may be asked to pay an export duty of 20% of their value. The Romanian postal service is improving, but to limit language problems, buy your stamps *(timbre)* at a main post office in a city.

Receiving Mail

Post restante mail (c/o Poste Restante, Posta Romană Oficiul Bucureşti 1, Strada Mateo Millo 10, RO-70700 Bucureşti, ROMANIA) can be collected at the main post office in Bucharest on Str Matei Millo, in the room with the post-office boxes. Collection times are on weekdays from 7.30 am to 8 pm and Saturday from 8 am to 1 pm. Incoming mail will be held for one month.

Telephone

The phone service is being upgraded. Making a call is the same as anywhere else. To use the bright orange pay phones for either local, regional or international calls you must purchase a magnetic phonecard *(cartela telefonică)* at either the telephone building in Bucharest or at post offices. The minimum amount per card is 60,000 lei (about US$7) which is good for about four minutes to the USA. (Times allowed per card to all international destinations are posted in the telephone building.) As with other phonecards, the cost of each completed call is deducted.

You can dial your international destination direct or try ringing an English-speaking operator: ☎ 01-800 4444 (British Telecom), ☎ 01-800 4288 (AT&T USA Direct), ☎ 01-800 1800 (MCI Worldwide) and ☎ 01-800 0877 (Sprint). Romania's international operator is reached by dialling ☎ 971. You'll need more than one card for anything but the briefest of calls to Western Europe and the USA.

To call Romania from abroad dial the international access code, Romania's country code (40), the area code (minus the first 0) and the number.

Fax & Telegram

Sending an international fax from a main post office is easy and costs US$2 to $5 per page at any central post office, or in Bucharest from any Telex-Fax office. The average charge for international telegrams is US$0.20 per word.

INTERNET RESOURCES

Romania is fast embracing the Internet. Many businesses in Romania now have Web sites and email accounts. Cybercafés are popping up in the major cities, allowing email and Internet access for about US$3.50 per hour.

There are many online resources for information about Romania, including the Romanian Press Review, published electronically each month (www.business-romania.ro). Bucharest Online (bucharest .com/bol) highlights local news and also lists hundreds of Romania-related Web sites. Virtual Romania (www.info.polymtl.ca/romania) has current news and dozens of

Romania links. A good Romanian newsgroup is soc.culture.romanian.

NEWSPAPERS & MAGAZINES

The most popular Romanian daily papers are *Adevârul*, which favours the PDSR, *România Libera*, an opposition voice, and *Evenimentul Zilei*, a popular mainstream paper.

Nine O'Clock is Bucharest's free daily English-language newspaper, found in several local pubs and hotels, as is the weekly *The Business Review* and the monthly *Romanian Business Journal*. *Romania Libera* also publishes a weekly English edition. Newsstands in larger cities sell *Newsweek*, *Time* and the *Economist*. Hotels often sell the *International Herald Tribune*, *Wall Street Journal* and other international papers.

TIME

Romanian time is GMT/UTC plus two hours, which means there's a one-hour difference between Romania and Hungary and Yugoslavia. Romania starts daylight-savings time at the end of March, when clocks are turned forward an hour. At the end of September, they're turned back an hour.

ELECTRICITY

The electric current is 220V, 50Hz AC.

HEALTH

Other than diarrhoea (watch what you eat and drink, and bring a remedy just in case), there's little to fear in Romania. Your embassy can easily provide a list of English-speaking doctors in Romania. In the countryside, go to the nearest 1st-class hotel if you're suffering serious health problems.

One-third of all European sources of mineral or thermal waters are concentrated in Romania, which has more than 160 spas. The mud baths on Lake Techirghiol at Eforie Nord go well with the salty lake water and the nearby Black Sea. Other important spas are Băile Felix (near Oradea) and Băile Herculane (known since Roman times). Ask for the brochure *Health Sources & Original Treatments in Romania* at Romanian National Tourist Offices abroad.

WOMEN TRAVELLERS

It's generally safe for women to travel in Romania, but do not wander alone late at night, especially in Bucharest. Avoid sitting in empty compartments on long-distance and overnight trains. A few strong words often discourage offensive behaviour, as does shouting for the *poliția!* Women travellers may also be unnerved by the way some Romanian men eye them constantly and deliberately bump into them on trains or on the street.

GAY & LESBIAN TRAVELLERS

Homosexuality in Romania is illegal and punishable by five years imprisonment but pressure from the international community will probably force a change in the law soon. Gay and lesbian Romanians rarely show affection in public. The Orthodox Church considers homosexuality a sin, and a surprising number of young Romanians feel that gay and lesbian relationships are 'unnatural'. Hotel managers might turn away openly gay couples, so be discreet if you're travelling with a same-sex partner.

DISABLED TRAVELLERS

Disabled travellers will find it difficult, if not downright impossible, to conquer Romania. Street surfaces are woefully uneven, while ramps and specially equipped toilets and hotel rooms are virtually unheard of. There is not a single wheelchair-accessible train or bus in the country. Consider joining a package tour that will cater to your specific needs (see Getting There & Away at the beginning of this book).

DANGERS & ANNOYANCES

Be prepared for heavy pollen (spring is murder for allergy sufferers), year-round pollution in the larger cities and swarms of mosquitoes in summer. Water and power cuts occasionally still occur, but are rare.

Romania has a stray dog problem, but authorities are working to control it. Keep your distance from roaming packs of dogs. Barking dogs are a major nuisance at night; these include pets as well as strays. Ear plugs are your best defence against the noise.

Beware of theft in Romania. This is a poor country, so it's unwise to display your wealth. Be on guard if walking late at night, as muggings are not unknown. Keep to well-lit streets and look purposeful. If you are attacked, don't expect much help from bystanders or the police. Apart from the danger of having things stolen while camping or being ripped off while changing money on the street, also take care in hotels by locking valuables in your pack or suitcase when you go out.

If you have a car, bring valuables into your hotel room rather than leaving them in the boot overnight. (The Black Sea coast and Braşov are said to be the worst areas for car break-ins.) Always check that your car doors and windows are properly closed.

Occasionally beggars can be a nuisance. Be especially wary of professional beggars, typically women carrying babies. Groups of beggar children have been known to mob travellers, smiling and waving as they search their pockets.

Beware of scams, particularly the 'tourist-police' one:

I heard of an unusual trick being used at Constanţa and Neptun. A man will walk up to you and ask if you want to change money. If you say 'no' and walk on, another man will appear and 'arrest' the first man. He'll flash some fake ID-card at you telling you that he is from the 'tourist police' and that he wants to see your passport and check your money. If you give them to him he'll say he needs them as 'evidence' and they'll both be off.

Michael Van Verk, The Netherlands

The man may also say he is investigating counterfeit currency. Either way, never show your passport or cash to anyone. Simply walk away. If they flash a badge, politely explain that you will happily accompany them to the nearest police station. Follow them only if you believe they are absolutely authentic – taking a taxi with a thief is not a good idea. Ideally, try to attract the notice of a uniformed police officer.

BUSINESS HOURS
Banking hours are weekdays from 9 am to 2 or 3 pm. Most shops and markets close on

Sunday. All museums close on Monday. Theatrical performances and concerts usually begin at 7 pm, except on Monday; in summer most theatres are closed.

PUBLIC HOLIDAYS & SPECIAL EVENTS
Public holidays are New Year (1 and 2 January), Easter Monday (March/April), National Unity Day (1 December) and Christmas (25 and 26 December).

Many festivals take place in summer, including the three-day Bucharest carnival in June and the Golden Stag international pop music festival in Braşov in July. Folklore festivals include Hora la Prislop in Maramureş in July and the International Festival of Danubian Folklore in Tulcea in August. In September there's Sibiu's Cibinium music festival and, the next month, Cluj-Napoca's Musical Autumn. In December the Days of Bihor Culture takes place in Oradea and Sighet Marmaţiei celebrates its Christmas festival.

Ask the local tourist agencies for information and festival schedules.

ACTIVITIES
Skiing
Romania's most famous ski resorts are Sinaia, Buşteni, Predeal and Poiana Braşov, all in the Carpathian Mountains between Bucharest and Braşov. They are fully developed, with cable cars, chair lifts and modern resort hotels. The ski slopes at Sinaia vary in altitude from 400 to 2800m, with level differences up to 585m. On top of the Bucegi Plateau above the Sinaia resort is an 8km cross-country route; there is also a 13-bend bobsled track. Poiana Braşov boasts 20km of ski slopes and sledding runs at varying degrees of difficulty. As this resort is off the main railway line, it's less crowded and preferred by serious skiers.

The ski season runs from December to mid-March and you can hire gear at the main hotels for US$8 to $12 per day. Courses at the ski school at Poiana Braşov last from four to six days and run for four hours a day, with about 12 students in each class.

Hiking

Romania's Carpathian Mountains offer endless opportunities for hikers; the most popular areas are the Bucegi and Făgăraş ranges, south and west of Braşov. Other Carpathian hiking zones include the Retezat National Park, north-west of Tîrgu Jiu; the Şureanu Mountains, between Alba Iulia and Târgu Jiu; the Apuseni Mountains, south-west of Cluj-Napoca; and the Ceahlău Massif, between Braşov and Suceava. Detailed hiking maps are hard to come by – check at tourist offices and shops such as SurMont Sports (in Sibiu and Sinaia).

ACCOMMODATION

You may pay all accommodation charges in lei, although some hotels may accept credit cards. There's no requirement to register with the police or to account for every night spent in the country.

Camping

As there are few youth hostels in Romania, camping is one of the few ways to travel on a low budget. Of course you'll need to come in summer and have a tent. Dozens of official camping grounds have been set up along the Black Sea coast, the perfect place to relax for a few days and meet young Romanians. Camping grounds with bungalows are called *popas turisticas*. Many Romanian camping grounds are in bad condition. Some are without toilets and showers and most only open from mid-May or June to around mid-September. When choosing a site at a camping ground keep in mind that your Romanian neighbours will probably have their radios on fairly loudly until the wee hours.

Freelance camping is prohibited in cities and in the Danube Delta, but not necessarily elsewhere. Such camping on the Black Sea coast is fairly common. If you see Romanian tourists camping in an open field or on a beach, there's nothing to prevent you from joining them. If you're camping alone, try to keep out of sight of the road. If you wish to sleep in your car or van, it's safer to park at a camping ground or near a hotel, as vehicles parked along roads can attract unwelcome attention. If anyone hints that there could be a problem about camping somewhere, believe them and go elsewhere. Wherever you camp, take care of your gear.

Mountain Huts

Although you can pitch a tent anywhere you like in the mountains, you may find it too cold. In most mountain areas there's a network of cabins or chalets *(cabana)* with restaurants and dormitories. They are cheaper than hotels and no reservations are required, but arrive early if the cabana is in a popular location, for example next to a cable-car terminus. Expect to find good companionship rather than cleanliness or comfort at these places. Many are open year-round and in winter cater for skiers, but it's always wise to confirm at a tourist office in advance.

Private Rooms

Only since 1990 have Romanians been allowed to rent rooms in their homes to foreigners, but this type of accommodation is becoming very popular. Only a few tourist offices arrange private rooms *(cameră particulară)*. It's more common to rent from locals you meet at train stations or on the street. They usually charge US$7 to $15 per person.

Agrotourism (B&B in the countryside) is a booming new business. The two main organisations in this field are the National Association of Rural, Ecological and Cultural Tourism (ANTREC) and the Belgian-based Opération Villages Roumains (OVR). Both have a network of offices throughout Romania which finds accommodation in rural homes for US$10 to $15. ANTREC also has an office in Bucharest on Calea Stirbei Vodă 2-4 (☎ 315 3206; fax 312 0148; antrec@rolink.iiruc.ro).

Hostels

There are four hostels in Romania, two of them in Bucharest. The Villa Helga hostel is open year-round and costs US$12, including breakfast and laundry. The YMCA also runs a hostel charging US$15 a night. The other two hostels, in Cluj-Napoca and Sighişoara, are in student dormitories and only open in July and August, when students are on holiday.

Hotels

Rooms in a good, modern hotel often cost only about US$10 more than you'd pay for a fleapit, so this is one country where the cheapest isn't always the best value. It may be better value in the long run to take a room with a private bathroom.

All accommodation prices in this chapter were calculated at the official rate. Low-budget hotels generally require payment in lei, but better hotels may take credit cards.

Romanian hotels are rated by the government on a star system, one-star being the lowest (and cheapest) and five-star the highest. One-star hotels, while generally clean, often have a shared bath and toilet, but ask to be sure; they charge from US$10 to $24. Two-star hotels are good value with clean rooms with TV and private bath for between US$20 and $40. The three-stars will charge US$45 to $100 for a double with in-room phone and cable TV. At some hotels breakfast *(mic dejun)* is often included in the price (but ask).

FOOD

Romanian restaurants are affordable; it would be difficult to spend more than US$10 per day on food. On the other hand, restaurants can be hard to find and/or very basic, offering the same things with unnerving consistency: grilled pork, grilled chicken, fried cheese and french fries.

Private restaurants are scarce in rural areas. If you have trouble finding a decent place to eat, try the dining room of a major hotel. In many towns they are still the only places serving proper meals from regular menus.

Even at upmarket restaurants you'll rarely pay over US$20 for dinner for two, a bottle of wine included, and one person alone drinking only mineral water can have a good meal for US$3. All restaurant meals can be paid for in lei. You should show your appreciation for good, honest service by rounding the bill up to the next even figure.

Always have a look at the menu, even a menu in Romanian. If it's a first-class place and you're told there's no menu with prices clearly listed (usually untrue), consider walking out rather than being forced to ask the price of every dish. Many cheaper places don't have menus but are still quite OK.

Some of the things on the menu won't be available. Vegetarians will have problems in Romania, as almost every restaurant dish is meat-based with few alternatives. Vegetarians should look for dishes based on cheese *(brînză/cascaval)*, tomatoes *(roşii)*, peppers *(ardei)*, mushrooms *(ciuperci)* and eggs *(ou)*. When you order a salad at a restaurant it's usually a plate of sliced tomatoes and cucumbers *(castraveţi)*. Pastries and cakes are available everywhere. Always check your bill for 'mistakes', but remember that vegetables, bread and even ketchup are often extra.

Romanian Specialities

Romanian favourites include *ciorbă de perişoare* (a spicy soup made with meatballs and vegetables), *ciorbă de burtă* (tripe soup), *ghiveciu* (vegetable stew), *tocană* (onion and meat stew) and *ciorbă de legumă* (vegetable soup often cooked with meat stock). Restaurants and beer gardens typically offer *mititei* or *mici* (pronounced 'meech'; grilled meatballs). Other common dishes are *muşchi de vaca/porc/miel* (cutlet of beef/pork/lamb), *ficat* (liver), *piept de pui* (chicken breast), *cabanos prajit* (fried sausages) and *cascaval pane* (breaded fried cheese). Cooking styles include grilled *(la grătar)*, fried *(prajit)*, boiled *(fiert)* and roasted on a spit *(la îrigare)*. Almost every dish comes with *cartofi* (potatoes) or *orez* (rice).

Folk dishes are hard to find but worth the search, especially *ardei umpluti* (stuffed peppers) and *sarmale* (cabbage or vine leaves stuffed with spiced meat and rice). *Mămăligă* is a cornmeal polenta that goes well with everything. Typical desserts include *plăcintă* (turnovers), *paturi cu brinză* (cheese pastries), *clătite* (crêpes) and *cozonac* (a brioche).

DRINKS

Romania is noted for its excellent wine, while the local beer is notable mostly for its low price (about US$0.75 for a half-litre). Imported Hungarian and German beers are available but more expensive. Among the best Romanian wines are Cotnari, Murfatlar, Odobesti, Tîrnave and Valea Calugareasca. Red wines are called *negru* and *roşu*, while white wine is *vin alb*. Also look for the words *sec* (dry), *dulce* (sweet) or *spumos* (sparkling) on the labels. *Vin de masă* is table wine. Even at the restaurant of a two-star hotel, a bottle of decent Romanian wine shouldn't be more than US$4.

Must is a fresh unfermented wine available during the wine harvest. *Ţuică* (plum brandy) and *palinca* (apricot brandy) are strong liqueurs drunk at the beginning of a meal. *Crama* refers to a wine cellar and a *berarie* is a pub or beer hall. A couple of toasts are *poftă bună* (bon appétit) and *noroc!* (cheers!).

Beware of *Ness*, an awful instant coffee made from vegetable extracts. It's always served supersweet and tepid. Proper cafés serve *cafea filtru* (filtered coffee) and espresso (but don't get your hopes up). Unless you specifically ask, coffee and *ceai* (tea) are almost never served *cu lapte* (with milk). *Apă minerală* (mineral water) is cheap and widely available.

ENTERTAINMENT

Ask at tourist offices about local festivals or cultural events. Also ask about local events at the main theatre and concert hall and visit any theatre ticket offices you can find. Opera companies exist in Bucharest, Cluj-Napoca, Iaşi and Timişoara. In large towns buy the local paper and try to decipher the entertainment listings. Hotel bars are often dull and pretentious, and discos often feature sleazy erotic shows and prostitutes. There are few decent bars in Romania, except in Bucharest, where there are lots of cool places.

THINGS TO BUY

Traditional purchases in Romania include plum brandy, embroidered blouses and handicrafts. The latter is easiest to find at major tourist sights, for example Bran Castle and Bucovina's painted monasteries. Romarta stores sell glassware, textiles, women's clothing and ceramics, and Muzică stores sell Romanian records. You're not supposed to export books printed before 1973. If in doubt about a price at stores, offer the vendors a pen and paper and ask them to write it down. Always count your change.

Getting There & Away

AIR

Romania's state-owned carrier TAROM has flights to Bucharest from Amsterdam, Berlin, Brussels, Budapest, Chicago, Düsseldorf, Istanbul, London, Madrid, New York, Paris, Prague, Rome, Sofia, Tel Aviv, Vienna, Warsaw, Zagreb, Zürich and many other cities worldwide. For prices contact TAROM in Britain (☎ 0171-224 3693, 0181-745 5542) or the USA (☎ 212-687-6013, 773-871-3012).

Other airlines that fly to/from Romania include Aeroflot, Air France, Air Moldova, Alitalia, Austrian Airlines, Balkan Air, British Airways, Czech Airlines, DAC Air, Delta Airlines, El Al Israeli Airlines, KLM-Royal Dutch Airlines, LOT Polish Airlines, Lufthansa Airlines, MALEV-Hungarian Airlines, Olympic Airways, Swissair and Turkish Airlines.

Most international flights arrive at Bucharest's Otopeni airport; a few also fly to Timişoara and Constanţa. There's no airport departure tax in Romania.

LAND
Train

Travelling by train is one of the most interesting ways to visit Romania because you can relax and enjoy the gorgeous scenery. In Romania, international train tickets are sold only at CFR offices in town – look for the 'Agenţie de Voiaj CFR' signs.

If you're travelling on an Inter-Rail pass, seat reservations (US$2 to $4) are mandatory on express trains within Romania. Even if you're not travelling with a rail pass, most of the international trains require seat reservations. If you already have a ticket, you may be able to make reservations at the station an hour before departure, preferably at least one day in advance. (Seat reservations are included in tickets purchased in Romania.)

Hungary & Beyond The *Alutus* runs from Berlin, through Bratislava, Prague and Budapest, to Arad, Braşov and Bucharest. The *Pannonia* arrives from Munich, via Vienna, Prague, Bratislava and Budapest. The *Dacia*

Expres comes from Vienna via Budapest to Bucharest. The *Ister* and *Ovidius* trains travel only between Budapest and Bucharest. The ride from Bucharest to Budapest takes about 12 hours (873km).

The easiest way of travelling between Romania and Hungary is on one of the two daily local Hungarian trains that shuttle between Oradea and Budapest-Nyugati (five hours). No reservations are required, but in Romania try to buy an open Oradea-Budapest ticket at a CFR office well ahead of time. If this is impossible, board the train at Episcopia Bihor, following the instructions given in the Oradea section of this chapter.

Local trains also depart from Békéscsaba, Hungary, for Oradea (90km) and Arad (68km) three times daily.

The *Carpaţi* from Warsaw via Kraków and Braşov to Bucharest takes about 27 hours (1645km).

The *Romania Expres* travels from Bucharest to Moscow, stopping in Chişinău, Moldova (13 hours) and in Kiev (28 hours); total time to Moscow is 42 hours.

Yugoslavia The *Bucureşti Expres* and *Banat* trains shuttle daily between Belgrade-Dunav and Bucharest (693km, 13 hours) via Timişoara and Drobeta-Turne Severin. If you can't get a ticket or reservation for this train, you can get an unreserved early morning train from Timişoara Nord to Jimbolia (39km), where you change to another local train to reach Kikinda, Yugoslavia.

Bulgaria & Turkey Train service between Romania and Bulgaria is slow and crowded but cheap. Between Sofia and Bucharest (12 hours) there are two trains, the *Bulgaria Expres* from Moscow and two without names, all of which stop in Ruse. A Bucharest-Ruse single ticket (2nd class) is US$4. Bucharest-Sofia costs about US$33/23 for a single 1st-class/2nd-class ticket. This train continues on to Thessaloniki.

The overnight *Bucureşti-Istanbul Expres* (803km, 17 hours) travels through eastern Bulgaria; also stopping at Ruse. A single 2nd-class fare is US$38.

Bus

There's little reason to ride a bus to Romania with such good train service available. Romania's public bus system is terrible and the private bus companies can be expensive. The exception is the trip to Istanbul, where the bus (12 to 14 hours) is both cheaper and faster than the train.

Many private bus companies operate daily buses between Western Europe and Romania. Tickets can be bought from ticketing agencies in Romania's larger cities; these are listed in the relevant sections.

To/from Hungary the cheapest option is the Hungarian Volanbus; a Budapest-Oradea trip costs US$8. Private buses charge about US$18 for a single Bucharest-Budapest fare.

Private buses travel to Sofia, Bulgaria from Bucharest for about US$11. There's also a weekly bus from Constanţa to Bulgaria.

Numerous buses a day shuttle between Bucharest and Istanbul (see Getting There & Away in the Bucharest section). Istanbul buses can also be used to reach Bulgaria.

Car & Motorcycle

Drivers need vehicle registration papers, liability insurance and a driving licence. Make sure your car is in good condition and carry a petrol can, oil and basic spares. Car rental is very expensive.

Border Crossings When crossing the border by car, expect long queues at Romanian checkpoints, especially on weekends. Carry some food and water for the wait. Avoid the temptation to bribe Romanian officials and beware of unauthorised people charging dubious 'ecology', 'disinfectant', 'road' or 'bridge' taxes at the border. (Ask for a receipt.)

The Romanian highway border crossings listed below are open 24 hours, except those to/from Ukraine and Moldova, which are open from 8 am to 8 pm.

Hungary There are border crossings at Petea (11km north-west of Satu Mare), Borş (14km north-west of Oradea), Vărşand (66km north of Arad) and Nădlac (between Szeged and Arad).

Yugoslavia You may cross at Jimbolia (45km west of Timişoara), Moraviţa (between

Timişoara and Belgrade), Naidăş (120km east of Belgrade) and Porţile de Fier (Iron Gate; 10km west of Drobeta-Turnu Severin).

Bulgaria You can cross at Calafat (opposite Vidin, Bulgaria), Giurgiu (opposite Ruse), Călăraşi (opposite Silistra), Negru Vodă (37km north-east of Tolbuhin) and Vama Veche (10km south of Mangalia). The Giurgiu bridge toll across the Danube is US$10/3 for cars/motorcycles. Its car ferry costs US$6 plus a Bulgarian ecological tax of US$3.50. The Calafat ferry costs US$3.50/2 and Călăraşi's ferry is US$1.20.

Moldova If you're going to/from Moldova, cross the border at Albiţa (65km south-east of Iaşi) or at Sculeni (24km north of Ungheni). Officials will check your car thoroughly.

Ukraine Use Siret, 45km north of Suceava on the road to Cernăuţi, to travel to the Ukraine.

Walking

You can walk in or out of Romania at most of its border crossings, except those with Moldova and Ukraine. Hitch a ride instead. Pedestrians are not allowed to use the so-called 'Friendship Bridge' to/from Ruse, Bulgaria, but you can go by taxi (US$29) or ferry.

BOAT

Between May and September a ferry runs twice weekly between Constanţa and Istanbul. The trip takes 20 hours and costs US$40/55 single/return. This is an amazing bargain if you don't mind skipping Bulgaria.

There are passenger and car ferries year-round into Bulgaria from Calafat and Giurgiu in Romania (see the Border Crossings section).

LEAVING ROMANIA

There is no departure tax in Romania. You will need to show your 'exit card' (that wee piece of paper placed in your passport upon entering Romania) or risk having to buy a new 30-day visa as a punishment. Also be sure to get an exit stamp in your passport.

Getting Around

AIR

The state-owned carrier TAROM has an extensive network of domestic flights from Bucharest. Many flights to Constanţa operate only in July and August, but you can fly out of Bucharest's Băneasa domestic airport to every other part of the country year-round. Very few TAROM flights operate on Sunday.

Foreigners pay much higher fares than Romanians on TAROM's domestic flights, which makes it very expensive. A single fare is usually US$50 to $60. Prices are listed in US dollars, but you must pay in Romanian lei. Only 10kg of luggage is carried free but overweight charges are minimal.

TRAIN

Căilor Ferate Române (CFR; Romanian State Railways) runs trains over 11,106km of track. There are four types of trains: local *(persoane)* and three expresses *(accelerat, rapid* and inter-city or *IC).*

On express trains you pay a supplement of US$0.50 to $3 for the required seat reservation. First-class express is about twice the price of 2nd class, but it's still cheap: a train ticket for a journey of 100km costs US$1.50 on a local train and US$4 for 1st-class on an express. A 500km ticket is US$4/10 on local trains/1st-class express.

If you're caught riding in the wrong class you must pay a US$6 penalty. If you board a train without a ticket you'll be hit with a penalty of US$8 to $11.

Considering the low cost, it's wise to travel 1st class *(clasă întîi).* At major stations there are separate ticket lines for 1st and 2nd class; you'll be relieved to see how much shorter the 1st-class line is. First-class has six seats per cabin; second-class compartments seat eight. Some, however, are open cars.

If possible, buy tickets for express trains a day in advance at a CFR office, but remember that most are closed on weekends. Also note that CFR offices do not sell tickets for express trains leaving the same day; you must buy a ticket at the station *no more than one hour* before departure. However, CFR offices do sell same-day tickets for local trains. Got all that?

ROMANIA

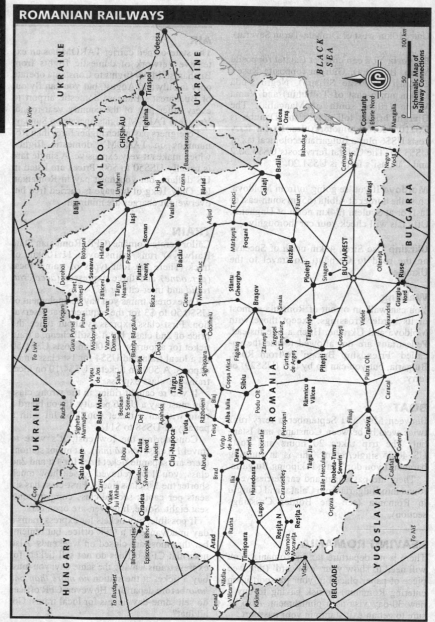

ROMANIAN RAILWAYS

Schematic Map of Railway Connections

0   50   100 km

In those cases when you must buy a ticket at the station (on weekends or for same-day express trains), you're not guaranteed a seat or even a ticket if the queue is too long. Arrive early and be sure to get in the correct queue, as tickets for different destinations are sold at different ticket windows (a list should be posted near each window).

If you have to change trains somewhere and board another express you'll need a new reservation, which you can make at the ticket window in the station an hour before departure. Your reservation ticket will give the code number of your train along with your assigned carriage (vagon) and seat (locul).

Often several trains leave within 30 minutes of each other for the same destination, so make sure you get on the right one by noting the train number, then check the carriage number (posted on metal signs on every train carriage). If you miss your train, have your ticket stamped at the Information window, so you can use it for the next train.

If you have an international ticket right through Romania, you're allowed to make stops along the route but must purchase a reservation ticket each time you reboard an accelerat or rapid train. If the international ticket was issued in Romania, you must also pay the express train supplement each time.

Express trains often have dining cars; a meal with a main meat dish, side salad and large beer will cost about US$4. Local trains have no dining cars, so take food and water with you.

Sleepers (vagons de dormit) are available between Bucharest and Arad, Cluj-Napoca, Oradea, Suceava, Timişoara, Tulcea and other points, and are a good way to cut accommodation expenses. First-class sleeping compartments have two berths and a sink, second-class sleepers have three berths and second-class couchettes have six berths. Book these well in advance at a CFR office in town. A 1st-class sleeper costs US$19 for a 500km trip (seven hours). Overnight trips on unreserved local trains are also good if you buy a 1st-class ticket and board the train early at the originating station. You can travel from Braşov to Iaşi this way.

If you'll be travelling much in Romania, look out for the railway timetable booklet, the Mersul Trenurilor, which is sold at CFR offices and at some stations. It costs US$1.50 and is invaluable. On posted timetables, sosire means arrivals and plecare means departures.

Rail Passes

Inter-Rail passes (sold to European residents only) are accepted in Romania, but Eurail passes are not. Even with a pass you must buy a reservation in the station every time you reboard an express. No supplements or fees are required for local trains.

BUS

Romania's buses are less reliable and more crowded than its trains, and on rural routes only one or two buses may run daily. The schedules posted in bus stations are often incomplete or out of date, so always ask at the ticket window. You usually have to purchase your ticket before boarding and if you haven't done so at a bus station (autogară), you could have problems with the driver. If the bus is the only way to get somewhere, try to reserve a seat by buying a ticket the day before and arriving early at the station.

With the advent of private buses (such as those from Braşov to Bran Castle), things are slowly improving.

CAR & MOTORCYCLE

Do not attempt to drive in Romania unless your car is in good shape and has been serviced recently. Repair shops are common but, unless you're driving a Renault (the same as Romania's Dacia) or a Citroën (the basis of Romania's Oltcit model), parts are hard to come by.

Some major roads are being resurfaced, but even major highways are in poor condition, with unexpected potholes and irregular signposting. Secondary roads can become dirt tracks, while mountain roads are often impassable after heavy rains. Concrete roads were often constructed without gaps for expansion and are now quickly deteriorating. Level crossings over railway lines should be approached with caution, as the roads can become very rough at these points. Open manhole covers are a hazard in cities such as Bucharest and Constanţa. Check the pressure of your tyres before entering Romania because it's often impossible to do so at Romanian petrol stations. Punctures can be repaired at shops labelled vulcanizare.

ROMANIA

Drive carefully as roadwork warnings are not posted and vehicles tend to stop suddenly in the middle of the road. You'll come across slow-moving horse-carts loaded with peasants. (It's against the law to honk at horse-carts lest you scare the horses.) Trucks and bicycles sometimes don't have lights and many drivers lack discipline.

Breakdowns

Members of major foreign automobile clubs (AA, AAA) are automatically covered by Romania's Automobil Clubul Român (ACR). Of course you still must pay: emergency road service costs US$5 to $10, and towing is US$0.50 per kilometre. In the event of a breakdown, call ACR's 24-hour emergency service number (☎ 927).

Fuel

Petrol is no longer rationed in Romania, and PECO and Royal Dutch Shell have built new stations all over the country. There is at least one 24-hour PECO station in every major Romanian city.

The types of petrol (benzină) available in Romania are normal or regular (88-90 octane), unleaded (95 octane), premium or super (96-98 octane) and diesel. You can pay for all petrol in lei. Some PECO stations and many Shell stations accept Visa and MasterCard.

Road Rules

The speed limit for cars is 60km/h in built-up areas or 80km/h on the open road. Motorbikes are limited to 60km/h in built-up areas and 70km/h on the open road. Drink driving is severely punished in Romania; the blood alcohol limit is 0.01 per cent.

If you are fined for a traffic violation, insist on a receipt before producing any money. Don't accept only a written statement that doesn't specify the exact amount, otherwise the money may go straight into the police officer's pocket.

It's wise to check with ACR offices for driving information and road maps.

Rental

It's no longer difficult to hire a car in Romania. Avis, Budget, Hertz and Europcar have offices in most cities. The new problem

is price, about US$80 per day for unlimited kilometres or US$25 per day plus $0.25 per kilometre. Average weekly rates are US$140 (not including kilometres). The extra daily insurance charge averages US$17. Credit-card insurance is not accepted – everyone must pay the additional fee. Most companies accept payment by credit card.

HITCHING

Hitchhiking in Romania is variable as the small cars are usually full and there isn't much traffic on secondary roads, where you may really need a ride. Your chances improve if it's obvious that you're a westerner. Hitching from near bus stops is the best option as you can always jump on any bus that comes along. It's common practice to pay the equivalent of the bus fare to the driver. Occasionally drivers even solicit business at bus and train stations as a way of covering their fuel costs.

You may be able to guess where a car is going by the letters on its licence plate: AB (Alba Iulia), AR (Arad), BV (Braşov), B (Bucharest), CJ (Cluj-Napoca), CT (Constanţa or Mangalia), DJ (Craiova), GL (Galaţi), GR (Giurgiu), IS (Iaşi), BH (Oradea), PH (Ploieşti), SB (Sibiu), SV (Suceava), TM (Timişoara) and TL (Tulcea).

BOAT

NAVROM offers regular passenger boat service from Galaţi and Tulcea to Sulina on the Black Sea throughout the year. In summer a hydrofoil speeds from Galaţi to Tulcea (see the Danube Delta section for details).

LOCAL TRANSPORT
Public Transport

Public transport within towns and cities is fairly good, though often overcrowded. Tram, bus and trolleybus services usually run from 5 am to 11 pm daily. Most routes have numbers and, if you ask the best-dressed person at the stop for advice on which number to take, you'll find that getting around is no problem. You must purchase tickets at kiosks marked bilet or casă de bilet and then validate them once aboard. Some tickets are good for one trip (calatori) while others are for two trips, each end of the ticket being valid for one ride. Tickets cost less than US$0.30.

Taxi

Government taxis are distinguishable by a chequered design on the side and meters (you pay what the meter displays). Unmetered private taxis with the letters 'P' or 'PO' on the roof are more expensive but often easier to find. If there's no meter, bargain for a price beforehand. The official rate is US$0.20 per kilometre. It's always cheaper to phone for a taxi.

ORGANISED TOURS

Most local travel agencies offer guided tours around Romania, enabling you to see the prime sights in a minimum of time, but you may have to become part of a group.

Many agencies, local and abroad, arrange stays at Romanian health resorts, as well as package tours to ski resorts such as Sinaia, Buşteni, Predeal and Poiana Braşov. All package tours are based on dual-occupancy hotel rooms. (If you can't or don't wish to share a room, you must pay a single supplement.)

The Transylvanian Society of Dracula (☎ 01-222 5195; fax 01-312 3056) organises tours of Vlad Ţepeş' old haunting grounds – Tîrgovişte, Sighişoara, Braşov and Bran Castle. The tours start in Bucharest and the cost includes meals, accommodation and transport.

Ronedo (☎/fax 40 33-231 306; ronedo@ decebal.ro) in Piatra Neamţ offers steam train tours of Moldavia, as well as monastery tours and Dracula tours.

Bucharest

☎ 01

Tree-lined boulevards, park-girdled lakes and pompous public monuments give Bucharest (Bucureşti) a smooth Parisian flavour. The city is at its best in spring and summer, when relaxed crowds fill the beer gardens and parks. As well as having the usual complement of museums, Bucharest has a gentle Latin air that goes well with the mysticism of its Orthodox churches.

Founded by a legendary shepherd named Bucur on the plains between the Carpathian foothills and the Danube River, Bucharest became the capital of Wallachia in 1459, during the reign of Vlad Ţepeş (Dracula).

Today a city of 2.1 million people, Bucharest is the largest and wealthiest metropolis in Romania and has been the national capital since 1862.

During the 1980s the city was transformed by Nicolae Ceauşescu's attempt to recast Bucharest as a grandiloquent socialist capital, with the behemoth House of the People as its centrepiece. The revolution of December 1989 put an end to its Stalinist makeover, yet reminders of the Ceauşescu era remain – from ugly bloc-style apartments to neglected buildings and streets.

Bucharest is now on a fast-track to recovery, though. Many of its grand old edifices have been restored and fashionable new shops, restaurants and night spots are opening everywhere. There is plenty to see and do in Bucharest, so try to allow several days to fit it all in.

Orientation

Bucharest's main train station, Gara de Nord, is a few kilometres north-west of central Bucharest.

The metro connects Gara de Nord with the centre, either at Piaţa Victoriei on the northern side or to Piaţa Unirii to the south; bus Nos 79, 86 and 133 will take you mid-centre to Piaţa Romană. The main boulevard (and the north-south metro line) runs between Piaţa Victoria, Piaţa Romană, Piaţa Universităţii and Piaţa Unirii and changes its name three times. These squares are your main focal points.

Maps Book vendors around Piaţa Universităţii sometimes have maps of Bucharest. Librărie Noi on Blvd Nicolae Bălcescu often has maps, too.

Information

Tourist Offices ONT Carpaţi (☎ 614 0759), Blvd General Magheru 7, supplies travel brochures, books sightseeing tours, answers questions and changes currency. It is open on weekdays from 8 am to 8 pm and Saturday from 8 am to 3 pm.

Touring ACR (☎ 650 7076), part of the Automobil Clubul Român (ACR) network, Str Cihoschi 2 near Piaţa Romană, is open on weekdays from 8 am to 8 pm. The helpful, English-speaking staff assist visiting motorists, and rent out Eurodollar cars. The main

ACR office (☎ 650 2595; fax 312 0434), off Blvd Magheru at Str Take Ionescu 27, books package trips and guided caravan tours throughout Romania.

Money Currency exchanges are all over the city and accept US dollars, British pounds, Deutschmarks, French francs and most other major currencies. Changing money on the street is illegal and it's likely that you'll be swindled. The risk is not worth the few cents you might save. It's better to compare rates at the private exchange offices along Blvd Bălcescu north of Piaţa Universităţii. Most change cash commission-free but charge 7% to change travellers cheques in US dollars. It's harder to change British pounds and Deutschmarks travellers cheques – try one of the banks listed.

The Bancă Comercială Română (BCR), Blvd Republicii 14, changes travellers cheques into US dollars or lei, gives cash advances on Visa/MasterCard (in lei only) and has an outside ATM (Plus, Cirrus, Visa, MasterCard, Eurocard), as does its branch at Calea Victoriei near Piaţa Victoriei. Both are open from 8 am to 2.30 pm.

BANCOREX, BCIT and Bancă Agricola all give cash advances in dollars or lei on credit cards. BANCOREX has branches at Blvd Bălcescu 11, Calea Victoriei 22 and Calea Victoriei 155 by Piaţa Victoriei, open from 8.30 am to 2 pm and with ATMs which accept Visa. BCIT has a branch west of Piaţa Victoriei at Şoseaua N Titulescu 1 and another at Str Doamnei 12; both are open weekdays from 9 am to 2.30 pm. Bancă Agricola has branches at Str Lipscani 27 and Str Smâdan 3.

Marshal Turism (☎ 650 2347; fax 223 1203; office@marshal.eunet.ro), Blvd Magheru 43, is the local American Express agent, open weekdays from 9 am to 6 pm. It can replace lost travellers cheques.

TAROM operates an exchange at Băneasa airport. At Otopeni airport you can get cash advances for Visa/MasterCard at the exchange near the information desk in the arrival hall; there is also an ATM.

Post & Communications The main post office is at Str Matei Millo 10, behind the telephone building near Hotel Continental.

Poste-restante letters can be collected here. It's open weekdays from 7.30 am to 8 pm and Saturday from 7.30 am to 2 pm. Branch offices are dotted throughout town.

To mail a parcel you must take it unsealed to Post Office No 67, Str Virgiliu 45, between Gara de Nord and Eroilor, on weekdays from 8 am to 2.30 pm. All packages are carefully inspected. Express Mail Service (EMS) is available on weekdays from 8.30 am to 5 pm.

The telephone centre (Oficiul Telefonic de Cabina), entrance around the corner from Calea Victoriei on Str Matei Millo, is open 24 hours and sells the magnetic phonecards (cartela telefon) to use in all orange street phones for local or international calls. Cards cost US$7 (good for about four minutes to the USA). A board lists the call length per card to every country.

You can also send and receive faxes at the telephone centre: it costs US$1 per page within Bucharest, US$1.50 per page to elsewhere in Romania and US$2 per page for international. Private 'Telex-Fax' offices are around the city, too.

Cybercafés Bucharest has several places where you can buy time on the Internet and send emails.

The 24-hour Internet Cafe (icafe@icafe .kapp.ro), Blvd Carol I 25 at Piaţa Rosetti, charges US$1.80 for 30 minutes.

The French Institute (☎ 210 224; adm@ instfrbuc.ro), Blvd Dacia 77, operates a cyber-café, Le Bistro, where 30 minutes online costs US$1.50; it's open from 10 am to 11 pm.

There's also the Web Club (☎ 650 6417; web@web.club.ro), Blvd 1 Mai 12, which is open 24 hours and charges US$7 per hour.

Travel Agencies There are many private agencies that book hotel rooms and countryside excursions. Peter Express (☎ 659 5761; peter@kappa.ro), Blvd Magheru 32-36, books private accommodation in guest houses and countryside trips; Paralela 45 Turism (☎ 613 4450), Blvd Kogălniceanu 7-9, arranges city and regional tours; Nouvelles Frontieres/Simpa Turism (☎ 615 9615; fax 312 7465) on Blvd Republicii and Str Jean Louis Calderon books day trips, folk evenings and trips to the Danube Delta.

ANTREC (☎ 315 3206; fax 312 01 48; antrec@rolink.iiruc.ro), Calea Stirbei Vodă 2-4, in the Lars Turism office across from the Hilton organises rural accommodation in private homes around the countryside.

Bookshops Librărie Noi, Blvd Bălcescu 18, stocks English-language art and history books. Galeria Halelor on Splaiul Independentei north of Piaţa Unirii has English literature and travel guides; Librărie Minerva, Calea Victoriei 116, has a small selection of English novels, mostly 19th-century classics. Magazine kiosks throughout the city sell *Time, Newsweek* and the *Economist*. The English-language newspaper *Nine O'Clock* (free) is usually found in pubs.

Left Luggage You can leave your luggage at the special 24-hour foreigners-only cloakroom (*bagaje de mîna*) at Gara de Nord on the right side of the central hall when your back is to the train platforms.

Medical & Emergency Services Foreigners with non-emergency medical problems are referred to the Policlinic Batiştei (☎ 613 3480), Str Tudor Arghezi 28, opposite the US consulate. Many physicians here speak English; consultations cost from US$30. It's open weekdays from 7 am to 9 pm.

Unirea Medica Centre (☎ 336 1696), Blvd Unirii 27, bloc 15, scara 3, near Dunkin' Donuts, has English and German-speaking doctors; it's open weekdays from 8 am to 7 pm.

Rombus Medical (☎/fax: 211 4717), Intrarea Spatarului 1, is an American diagnosis, treatment and ambulatory surgery centre; it's open Monday to Saturday from 8 am to 8 pm.

For emergencies go to the 24-hour Spitalul de Urgenta (☎ 679 6490), Calea Floreasca 8 on the corner of Şoseaua Ştefan cel Mare. Call an ambulance on ☎ 961.

Novident (☎ 336 1223) Str Apolodor 13-15, scara B, apartment 52, is an American dental clinic.

The 24-hour Farmacia No 5, Blvd Magheru 20 next to Teatrul Nottara, stocks imported health aids.

Dangers & Annoyances Bucharest is not especially dangerous, and crime is no worse here than in other capital cities. Women are advised not to walk alone late at night, especially near Gara de Nord.

Bucharest's pickpockets are becoming more daring, so be wary of people on the street making close physical contact with you. A common trick is to admire your 'very nice' pants, casually feel what's in the pockets and then 'accidentally' bump into you.

Things to See & Do

In Bucharest, admission to most churches and monasteries is free. Admission to museums is rarely more than US$0.75.

Central Bucharest From the north-western corner of Piaţa Unirii, across the river and just west of Blvd Brătianu, find the narrow Str Sepcari. Enter the old city on this street and view the ruins of Vlad Ţepeş' **Curtea Veche** (Old Court; 1462) and the oldest church in Bucharest (1546) on Str Iuliu Maniu. Go across the road, into the courtyard of **Hanul Manuc** (1808), an old inn and caravansary with a lovely beer garden.

Walk west on Str Iuliu Maniu a few blocks and, when you see a large white church, turn right onto Str Poştei and continue to **Stavropoleos Church** (1724) and its adjoining courtyard.

Follow Str Stavropoleos west to Calea Victoriei and Bucharest's most important museum, the **National History Museum** (closed Monday) in the former Post Office Palace (1900). The 41 rooms on the 1st and 2nd floors tell the story of the country from prehistoric times to WWI. The highlight is the fabulous treasury in the basement, full of gold objects and precious stones. There's also a complete plaster cast of Trajan's Column which depicts the conquest of Dacia by Rome. Information in English and French is posted in most rooms.

Proceeding north on Calea Victoriei, you'll come to **Str Lipscani**, the old trading bazaar street that runs through to Blvd Brătianu.

A short detour west at Blvd Regina Elisabeta (also named Blvd Kogalniceanu) will bring you to lovely **Cişmigiu Garden**. Amid the lush gardens, there's a rowing-boat lake, a beer garden and often music playing in the gazebo.

Resuming the walk north on Calea Victoriei, after about four blocks, you'll arrive at

ROMANIA

BUCHAREST

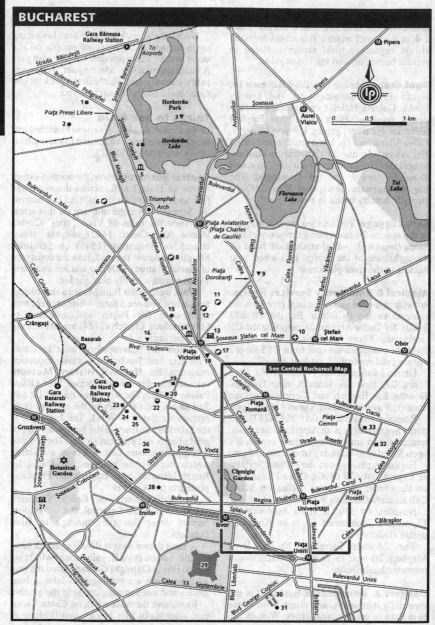

Gara Băneasa
Railway Station

To Airports

Strada Băiculești

Bulevardul Poligrafiei

Șoseaua Băneasa

Piața Presei Libere

1

2

Herăstrău Park

3

Herăstrău Lake

4

Șoseaua Kiseleff

Blvd Mărăști

5

Aviatorilor

Bulevardul

Pipera

Pipera

Aurel Vlaicu

Șoseaua

0   0.5   1 km

Bulevardul 1 Mai

6

Triumphal Arch

Piața Aviatorilor (Piața Charles de Gaulle)

Bulevardul

Mircea

Elade

Floreasca Lake

Tei Lake

Calea Grivitei

Calea Floreasca

Strada Barbu Văcărescu

Bulevardul Lacul tei

7

8

Piața Dorobanți

9

Șoseaua Kiseleff

Averescu

Bulevardul 1 Mai

Bulevardul Aviatorilor

Calea Dorobanților

11

12

15

16

14

13

Șoseaua Ștefan cel Mare

10

Ștefan cel Mare

Obor

Crângași

Basarab

Blvd Titulescu

Piața Victoriei

17

18

Calea Griviței

Gara de Nord Railway Station

19

21

20

23

22

24

25

26

Știrbei Vodă

Strada

Gara Basarab Railway Station

Grozăvești

Dâmbovița River

Plevnei

Botanical Garden

Șoseaua Cotroceni

27

28

Bulevardul

Eroilor

Splaiul Independenței

Izvor

See Central Bucharest Map

Lascăr Catargiu

Piața Romană

Blvd Magheru

Calea Victoriei

Bulevardul Dacia

Piața Gemini

Strada Rosetti

Piața Universității

Cișmigiu Garden

Blvd Bălcescu

Regina Elisabeta

Bulevardul Carol 1

Piața Rosetti

Bulevardul

Calea Moșilor

33

32

Piața Unirii

Calea

Călărașilor

Bulevardul Carol 1

29

Calea 13 Septembrie

Blvd Libertății

Blvd George Coșbuc

Blvd Brătianu

Bratianu

30

31

Bulevardul Unirii

PLACES TO STAY		9	White Horse Pub	12	Albanian Embassy
1	Hotel Parc; Hotel Turist		& Restaurant	13	Victoriei Palace
7	Hotel Triumf	16	Dubliner Irish Pub	14	Natural History Museum
19	Hotel Marna	18	Sydney Bar & Grill	15	Web Club
20	Hotel Grivița			17	Hungarian Consulate
21	Hotel Dunărea	**OTHER**		22	Bus Station
23	Hotel Bucegi	2	RomExpo	26	Post Office No 67
24	Hotel Cerna	4	Boat Rentals	27	Cotroceni Palace
25	Hotel Astoria	5	Muzeul Satului	28	Opera Română
32	YMCA Hostel		(Village Museum)		(Romanian Opera House)
33	Villa Helga Hostel	6	Moldovian Consulate	29	Parliament Palace
		8	Ukrainian Consulate	30	Patriarchal Cathedral
PLACES TO EAT		10	Spitalul de Urgenta	31	Chamber of Deputies
3	Lake Herestrau Cafés	11	Polish Consulate		

Piața Revoluției and see **Crețulescu Church** (1722) on the left, a red-brick structure badly damaged in the 1989 revolution. To its north is the massive **Royal Palace** (1937), formerly the king's palace and the scene of heavy fighting during the revolution; the extensive collection of Romanian and European art in its four-storey **National Art Museum** was badly damaged. The palace has been under renovation, so check to see if the main museum is open. It's closed on Monday and Tuesday.

Ceaușescu made his last speech from the balcony of the former **Central Committee of the Communist Party** building, the long, white-stone edifice across the square from Crețulescu Church. The **University Library** (1895), between the former party building and the Ateneul Român, was gutted but has since been rebuilt. The skeletal building directly behind the library has been left charred and bullet-riddled, in honour of those who died in the 1989 revolution.

Just north of the library is the neoclassical **Ateneul Român** (1888), the city's main concert hall, built by French architect Albert Galleron. Try to see its magnificent interior. Check the ticket office for performance schedules; seats cost about US$3. Next door is the historic **Athenee Palace** hotel, recently renovated and reopened as a Hilton hotel.

North again at Calea Victoriei 107 is the **Ceramics Museum**. The nearby **Muzeul Colecțiilor de Artă** (closed Monday and Tuesday), Calea Victoriei 111, was formed from several private art collections. Note the many fine works by the 19th-century painter Nicolae Grigourescu.

Turn right onto Str Piața Amzei to find the city's bustling open **food market** tucked between Bucharest's two main boulevards. This is the place to buy your fresh fruit and vegetables.

The centre's other main artery is the multi-named Blvd Lascar Catargiu/Blvd Magheru/Blvd Nicolae Bălcescu/Blvd Brătianu, running parallel to Calea Victoriei. This is the centre's busiest commercial street, lined with shops, bookstores, travel offices, hotels, banks, groceries, cafés, churches and the University of Bucharest. The metro runs along this street stopping at Piața Victoria, Piața Romană, Piața Universității and Piața Unirii. It is also a major city bus route, including the airport bus No 783.

The **fountain** at Piața Universității and facing Blvd Bălcescu is where Romanian students held antigovernment protests in June 1990, until they were ruthlessly squashed by coal miners loyal to the post-revolutionary regime. On the south-western corner of the piața at Blvd Brătianu 2, is the **Muzeul al Municipiului București** in Sutu Palace (1835), a municipal museum with displays on turn-of-the-century Bucharest (closed Monday).

Southern Bucharest In the last years of the Ceaușescus' reign, the southern section of Bucharest around **Piața Unirii** was redesigned to create the new civic centre. From Piața Unirii metro station walk over to the large ornamental **fountain** in the middle of

ROMANIA

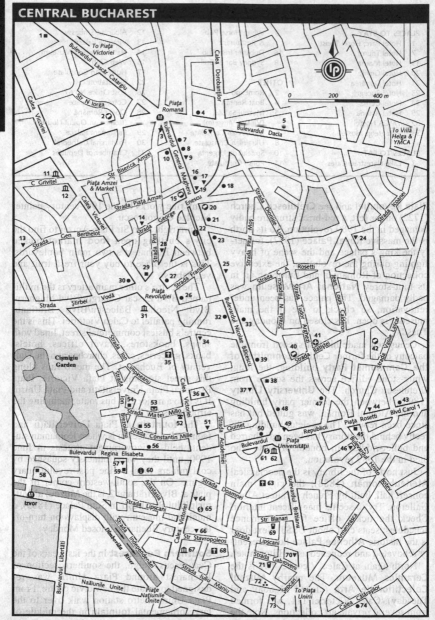

CENTRAL BUCHAREST

PLACES TO STAY		
1	Hotel Minerva & Nan Jing	
30	Athenee Palace (Hilton)	
38	Intercontinental Hotel	
45	Hotel Banat	
54	Hotel Carpaţi	
55	Hotel Palas	
58	Hotel Dîmboviţa	
59	Hotel Central	

PLACES TO EAT		
3	Bererie Turist	
6	Pizza Hut	
9	KFC	
13	Hanul Maramureş	
14	Casa Veche	
17	Gas Station	
19	McDonald's	
25	Restaurant Moldova	
26	Cofetăria Ambasador	
29	Bistro Ateneu	
34	Cofetăria Le Bistro	
37	Restaurantul Pescarul	
44	McMoni's	
46	Paradise	
49	Pizza Apollo	
51	Brăutria Deutschland	
57	McDonald's	
64	Cofetăria Victoria	

66	Caru cu Bere	
70	Sheriff's Fast Food	
73	Hanul Manuc	

OTHER		
2	Canadian Embassy	
4	Touring ACR	
5	French Institute &	
	Le Bistro	
7	Peter Express Agency	
8	Bus Stop for Airport Bus	
10	Marshal Turism	
11	Muzeul Colecţiilor de Artă	
12	Ceramics Museum	
15	Honorary Consulate	
	of Australia	
16	Automobil Clubul Român	
	(ACR) Main Office	
18	Vox Maris Supermarket	
20	British Embassy	
21	Nottara Theatre	
22	Farmacia No5	
23	ONT Carpaţi	
24	Patria Cinema	
27	Central University Library	
28	Ateneul Român	
31	ANTREC & Lar Tours	
32	Royal Palace &	
	National Art Museum	

33	Unic Supermarket	
35	Former Communist	
	Party Building	
36	Creţulescu Church	
39	Librărie Noi	
40	US Consulate	
41	Policlinic Batiştei	
42	Bulgarian Consulate	
43	Internet Cafe	
47	American Cultural Centre	
48	National & Operetta	
	Theatres & Lapteria Enache	
50	University of Bucharest	
52	Telephone Centre	
53	Main Post Office	
56	Cinema Festival;	
	Cinema Corso	
60	CFR & TAROM offices	
61	Bancă Comercială Română	
62	Muzeul al Municipiului	
	Bucureşti	
63	Russian Church	
65	BANCOREX	
67	Natural History Museum	
68	Stavropoleos Church	
69	Club A	
71	Hard 'n' Heavy	
72	Old Princely Court	
74	Market	

the square to get your bearings. On the north-eastern side of the square is the **Unirea Department Store** and a McDonald's restaurant; shops and small vendor kiosks line the eastern and western sides of the square.

Walk south-west from the fountain, across Blvd Unirii and up Blvd George Coşbuc for 200m to the **Patriarchal Cathedral** (1658) and **Patriarch's Palace** (1875). Surrounding the church are the **Chamber of Deputies** (1907), a belfry (1698) and three 16th to 17th-century stone crosses.

West from the fountain, Blvd Unirii runs directly towards the enormous **Parliament Palace**, Ceauşescu's House of the People, an incredible Stalinist structure that was almost finished when Ceauşescu was overthrown in 1989. Some 20,000 workers and 400 architects toiled for six years on this massive palace at a cost of 16 billion lei. Virtually all of the materials used were Romanian. The building is 360,000 sq m in area and contains

over 1000 rooms, with halls ranging from 100 to 2600m. It is the second-largest building in the world after the US Pentagon, and many historic structures were demolished to make way for it. Today the palace houses Romania's parliament and is also an international conference centre. Tours are conducted between 10 am and 6 pm, but only on Friday, Saturday and Sunday when parliament is in session. Entrance is on the southern side.

Across the street are several government ministry headquarters. The converging streets are lined with towering apartment buildings once intended to house Ceauşescu's bureaucrats. To the north, a small park extends toward the river. Cross the Izvor bridge, walk in one block and turn right to return to the centre of town.

Northern Bucharest Exiting the Piaţa Victoriei metro station you'll see **Victoria Palace** (1938), the Romanian government building

ROMANIA

on the north-eastern side of the square. On the north-western side is the worthwhile **Natural History Museum**, with a large collection of stuffed animals. It's closed on Monday and Tuesday.

Walk up tree-lined Şoseaua Kisselef, or continue on the metro one stop north to Piaţa Charles de Gaulle (formerly Piaţa Aviatorilor), then walk 500m west, to the **Triumphal Arch** (Arcul de Triumf; 1936), commemorating the reunification of Romania in 1918. Its resemblance to the Arc de Triomphe in Paris was intentional and gives evidence of the strength of French-Romanian cultural ties before WWI.

A short walk north is one of Bucharest's best sights, the **Muzeul Satului** (Village Museum), with full-scale displays of nearly 300 churches, wooden houses and farm buildings, first assembled here in 1936 in a rich mixture of styles (closed Monday). It is surrounded by beautiful **Herăstrău Park**, with lush gardens and a lake filled with all manner of boats in summer. At the northern rim of the lake are several outdoor cafés and a go-cart track.

Ten km farther north is **Băneasa Forest** with a zoo (☎ 233 0502) and picnic grounds, open from 8 am to 8 pm. Admission is US$0.30, but it costs extra to bring a camera. There are fast food kiosks and beer gardens serving traditional mititei sausages. To get there, take bus No 301 from Piaţa Romană.

Western Bucharest To begin this walk you can either take the M3 metro from Piaţa Unirii west to Eroilor stop, or walk west on Splaiul Independenţii along the Dîmboviţa river. You could also walk west along Blvd Kogalniceanu, past Cişmigiu Garden, until you reach the **Opera Română** (Romanian Opera House), then cross the road. From Piaţa Eroilor walk west along Blvd Eroii Sanitari to Blvd Marinescu and the wall of **Cotroceni Palace**, built in 1893 for Queen Marie. It's now the president's residence and houses the **National Cotroceni Museum** (☎ 638 7975) exhibiting 17th and 18th century art. Visits must be prearranged; the entrance is at Blvd Geniului 1. (Closed on Monday.)

Nearby is Bucharest's **Botanical Garden**. Walk north on Blvd Marinescu to Şoseaua Cotroceni 32. The garden, with 10,000 plant species, is open daily, but the Botanical Museum and greenhouse are open on Tuesday, Thursday and Sunday from 9 am to 1 pm (US$0.15).

Places to Stay

Camping The nearest camping grounds are at Snagov Lake, 34km north of Bucharest.

Private Rooms Peter Express (☎ 659 5761), Blvd Magheru 32 near Piaţa Română, arranges rooms near its office at US$15/22 for a single/double.

Occasionally people at the station or on the street outside offer private rooms. Evaluate these people carefully and ask them to point out the location of their rooms on a map.

Hostels The clean and friendly *Villa Helga* hostel (☎/fax 610 2214), Str Salcamilor 2, provides a bed in a shared room, breakfast, kitchen facilities and free laundry for US$12 a night, plus great information about what to see in Romania. It's conveniently located in the centre, east of Piaţa Romană, just past Piaţa Gemini (formerly Piaţa Galaţi). Take bus No 79, 86 or 133 from Gara de Nord for six stops to Piaţa Gemini or bus No 783 from Otopeni airport to Piaţa Română, then walk or take a local bus east two stops to Piaţa Gemini. It's open 24 hours.

In the same area on Str Silvestru 33, the *YMCA* (☎ 210 0909; fax 665 7046) also has a hostel with shared rooms and kitchen access for US$15 a night. From Gara de Nord take bus No 133 or 123, or trolley bus No 26 to Moşilor station. Reception hours are from 2 pm to 6 pm.

Hotels There are lots of one and two-star hotels in Bucharest. Prices average US$20/35 for a single/double with shared bath, but are higher for a private bath; check whether breakfast is included in the price. Rooms facing a busy road can be noisy. There are two clusters of inexpensive hotels: one around the train station and another in the city centre.

Around Gara de Nord As you exit the station, turn right and walk for 30m to the noisy but surprisingly clean *Hotel Bucegi* (☎ 637 5225), Str Witing 2. It charges US$10/15/20 for a good single/double/triple without bath, US$18/ 24 a single/double with bath. Across the street, the comparable *Hotel Cerna* (☎ 637 4087), Blvd Golescu 29, charges US$10/20 for a single/double without bath, US$23/36 with bath. Rooms at the nice two-star *Hotel Astoria* (☎ 637 7640; fax 638 2690), Blvd Golescu 27, near the Cerna have baths and cost US$50/77 a single/ double, breakfast included. There's a wonderful pastry shop next door, too.

To the north-east of the station, across the road is *Hotel Dunărea* (☎ 222 9820), Calea Griviţei 140, the nicest in the neighbourhood despite the noise from passing trams. It charges US$12/18 without bath, US$17/25 with bath. Farther down the same street is *Hotel Griviţa* (☎ 650 2327), Calea Griviţei 130, which charges US$13/18 for rooms without bath. The bar here is smoky and off-putting and women travelling solo should head elsewhere. Two blocks down and around the corner to the left is *Hotel Marna* (☎ 650 6820), Str Buzeşti 3. It charges US$12/18 without bath and US$30 for a double with bath.

City Centre The entrance to quiet *Hotel Dîmboviţa* (☎ 615 6244), Blvd Schitu Măgureanu 6, is actually off Str Gutenberg. Singles/doubles cost US$25/42 with bath, US$21/34 without.

A short walk away is the renovated *Hotel Carpaţi* (☎ 615 7690), Str Matei Millo 16. It's the nicest in the area, with rooms equipped with TV and phone; singles/ doubles cost US$38/40 with bath, US$17/23 without. Nearby *Hotel Palas* (☎ 615 3710), Str Constantin Mille 18, has been renovated to two-star status; doubles with bath are US$35, while singles without bath are US$15. Next to the McDonald's at Str Brezoianu 13 is two-star *Hotel Central* (☎ 312 1549) with unrenovated/renovated singles for US$32/53 and doubles for US$40/66 with baths, including breakfast (credit cards accepted). *Hotel Muntenia* (☎ 614 6010), Str Academiei 21, is noisy but has a great location near the university. It's US$25/32 for a double/triple with bath, and US$13/23/30 for a single/double/triple without.

For a splurge, the three-star *Hotel Minerva* (☎ 650 6010; fax 312 2734), Str Gheorghe Manu 2-4, is near Piaţa Romană. Singles/ doubles cost US$70/90.

North of the City Centre *Hotel Turist* (☎ 222 8450), Blvd Poligrafiei 5, has rooms for US$14/23. It shares a swimming pool with the more expensive Hotel Parc (the pool is open to non-guests). Near Piaţa Presei Libere is the 14-storey, two-star *Hotel Parc* (☎ 222 8480; fax 222 5938). Get a room on one of the upper floors to escape the disco beat; they cost US$62/96 for a single/double, breakfast included. Two-star *Hotel Triumf* (☎ 222 3172; fax 223 2411) on tree-lined Şoseaua Kiseleff 12, is a lovely brick edifice in a garden setting; it has singles/doubles for US$38/56.

Places to Eat
Restaurants Bucharest has a range of reasonable restaurants.

Near Piaţa Victoriei Friendly *Sydney Bar & Grill* on Piaţa Victoriei serves Australian-style steaks and salads and has a vast drink menu. Its large terrace is filled at night.

Farther north is the English *White Horse Pub & Restaurant* at Str G Calinescu 4A, just off Piaţa Dorobanţi, with a full menu upstairs and bar food downstairs.

A short walk west of Piaţa Victoriei, is *Dubliner Irish Pub* at Blvd Titulescu 18, with sandwiches, meat pies and Irish beer.

All are great places for English-speaking travellers and stay open until 3 am.

Near Piaţa Romană On the southern side of Piaţa Romană, *Berarie Turist* serves a few small dishes and big mugs of draught beer. This is a good place to sit outside in summer.

The *Gas Station* bar and restaurant on Str Tache Ionescu 14, behind McDonald's, has good international food and stays open late.

Charming *Casa Veche* (☎ 615 7897) on Str G Enescu 15-17, west of Blvd Magheru serves 40 varieties of pizza, good wine and has a lovely outdoor terrace (credit cards accepted).

The more upmarket *Nan Jing*, in the Hotel Minerva on Blvd Lascar Catargiu serves expensive but exquisite Chinese food (Visa accepted).

Near Piaţa Revoluţiei One of Bucharest's best spots is *Bistro Ateneu* (☎ 613 4900) on Str Episcopiei opposite the Ateneul Român. The good food and cosy elegance draw crowds, so make a reservation. It's a nice place to stop in the afternoon, too. Food is served until 1 am.

Hanul Maramureş, Str General Berthelot 24, serves traditional dishes and local beers in a rustic wooden house typical of the Maramureş region at reasonable prices.

Around Piaţa Universităţii Though rather touristy, the restaurant at historic *Hanul Manuc*, Str Iuliu Maniu 62, has a great atmosphere. The beer garden is pleasant and the indoor restaurant closes at 8 pm.

The *Carul cu Bere* on Sr Stavropoleos, close to the Natural History Museum, is Bucharest's oldest (1875) and most ornate beer hall, in the best German tradition. The food is reasonably priced and there is live folk music on some nights.

The *Restaurantul Pescarul*, on Blvd Bălcescu 9a, across the street from the Intercontinental Hotel, offers a range of fish dishes in a small, smoky setting. It's closed on Sunday.

Paradise, Blvd Hristo Botev 10, off Piaţa Rosetti is a casual place serving Lebanese vegetarian food; felafel sandwiches are about US$0.60.

Moldova Gradină de Vară, off Str JL Calderon, east of Blvd Bălcescu, serves Moldavian cuisine in a garden setting.

Cafés There are *cofetărias* all over Bucharest specialising in delicious sweets and Turkish coffee. You'll find incredibly rich cakes at *Cofetăria Victoria*, Calea Victoriei 18. *Cofetăria Ambasador*, next to Hotel Ambasador, Blvd Magheru 10, serves some of the best coffee and cakes in Bucharest. *Cofetăria Le Bistro* on Blvd Bălcescu 32 is a small modern pastry café and bar. *Cofetăria Ema*, Blvd Dinicu Golescu 24, south of Gara de Nord by hotels Cerna and Astoria, has wonderful doughnuts and pastries.

Fast Food There are *McDonald's* restaurants on Blvd Magheru, on Blvd Regina Elizabeta near Cişmigiu Garden and at Piaţa Unirii; all are open until 1 am. *Pizza Hut* is on Blvd Dacia just off Piaţa Romană; *KFC* is on Blvd Magheru, near McDonald's. *McMoni's* on Piaţa Rosetti 3 has good sand-

wiches and pizzas. *Sheriff's Fast Food* on Blvd Brătianu serves burgers, pizza and pastries. You can get a beer and a slice at *Pizza Apollo* in Piaţa Universiaţii's underground metro concourse, among other goodies. *Panipat* sells delicious breads, pastries and take-out pizzas; there are branches in Gara de Nord, on Blvd Brătianu and on Str CA Rosetti just east of Blvd Magheru. Romanian cheese and fruit pastries are sold from kiosks everywhere. Hot dog kiosks are popping up around town, too.

Self Catering Two *open-air markets* have fresh fruit and vegies: one at Piaţa Amzei between Calea Victoriei and Blvd Magheru; the other is east of Piaţa Unirii. The *Vox Maris* supermarket on Str George Enescu behind McDonald's stocks imported foods. *Unic* at Blvd Bălcescu 33 is a more basic grocery. German breads and sweets can be found at tiny *Brutărie Deutschland* on Str Edgar Quinet, an alley that runs from Piaţa Universitatii's fountain to Calea Victoriei.

Entertainment

Cinemas Bucharest's cinemas show current films in their original language with Romanian subtitles for about a dollar. The *Patria*, *Scala*, and *Studio* cinemas are clustered along Blvd Magheru; the *Luceafarul* is on Blvd Brătianu. The *Corso*, *Lumina* and *Festival* cinemas are on Blvd Regina Elisabeta, between Calea Victoriei and Cişmigiu Garden.

Bars & Discos *Hard 'n' Heavy*, Str Gabroveni 14 off Blvd Brătianu, mixes live hard rock with recorded rock. Some nights there's a US$1.50 cover charge.

Club A, Str Blanari 4 off Blvd Brătianu, has trendy downstairs digs with its bar separate from the dance floor (cover charge US$1.50).

The *Big Mamou* on Blvd Ferdinand 79 is a cavernous club with live rock music weeknights and jazz and blues Friday and Saturday at 10 pm.

Laptaria Enache, Blvd Bălcescu 2 in the National Theatre on the 4th floor, is a cool club with live jazz on Friday, Saturday and Sunday from 9 pm to 2 am (small cover charge). Its entrance is on the northern side.

Theatres Most productions cost less than US$3 and begin early, between 6 and 7 pm. All theatres are closed in July and August.

The *National Theatre* is at Blvd Bălcescu 2 at Piaţa Universitatii. The ticket office is on the southern side of the building and open Monday to Saturday from 11 am to 6 pm. Next door is the *Ion Dacian Operetta Theatre*; tickets are sold daily from 11 am to 6.30 pm.

The *Nottara Theatre* is at Blvd Magheru 20; its box office is open daily from 10 am to 2.15 pm and 2.45 to 7 pm.

Ateneul Român, Bucharest's elegant concert hall in Piaţa Revoluţiei, has a ticket office on its northern side.

The *Opera Română* is at Blvd Kogăl-niceanu 70-72, west of Cişmigiu Park (take the metro to Eroilor).

Getting There & Away

Air Romania's national airline, TAROM, has two main offices in Bucharest. The domestic branch (☎ 659 4185) is off Piaţa Victoriei at Str Buzeşti 59 and is open weekdays from 7.30 am to 7.30 pm and Saturday from 7.30 am to 1.30 pm. The international office (☎ 615 0499) at Str Brezoianu 10 above the CFR office is open weekdays from 8 am to 7.30 pm and Saturday from 8 am to noon. All domestic flights depart from Băneasa airport. TAROM has flights several times a week from Bucharest to Arad, Baia Mare, Cluj-Napoca, Iaşi, Oradea, Satu Mare, Sibiu, Suceava, Târgu Mureş and Timişoara. In summer there are also flights to Constanţa and Tulcea. Fares are quoted in relevant chapters but don't expect any bargains; foreigners are charged higher fares than Romanians.

International airlines with offices on Blvd Bălcescu/Blvd Magheru include: Air France (☎ 312 0085), Austrian Airlines (☎ 311 1266), British Airways (☎ 303 2222), KLM-Royal Dutch Airlines (☎ 312 0149), LOT Polish Airlines (☎ 659 2575), Lufthansa Airlines (☎ 312 9559), MALEV-Hungarian Airlines (☎ 312 0427), Swissair (☎ 312 0238) and Turkish Airlines (☎ 311 2410). There's another cluster of offices around Str Batiştei near the US embassy: Air Moldova (☎ 312 1258), Alitalia (☎ 210 4111), Balkan Air

(☎ 614 8501), Czech Airlines (☎ 312 0984) and DAC Air (☎ 311 1083).

The Otopeni airport information number is ☎ 212 0122; Băneasa airport's is ☎ 633 0030.

Train Romania has a comprehensive train network linking Bucharest to most towns and villages. Almost all express trains and many local trains use Bucharest's Gara de Nord. Local trains to/from Snagov and a couple of seasonal accelerat trains to/from Mangalia sometimes use Gara Băneasa, on the northern side of town.

At Gara de Nord there are separate ticket halls for 1st and 2nd class. Different windows sell tickets to different destinations, as noted on small posted signs. Express train tickets are only sold at the station two hours before departure. Timetables are posted overhead in the main hall. You can usually buy a timetable book, called *Mersul Trenurilor*, at the information desk – it's invaluable if you plan to roam the country.

You can avoid long queues at the station by buying your ticket in advance at a CFR office. The main office (☎ 613 2644) at Domniţa Anastasia 10-14, a block past the McDonald's at Str Brezoianu, handles both international and domestic train tickets. It's open on weekdays from 7.30 am to 7 pm. There's also a domestic CFR office near Gara de Nord at Calea Griviţi 139 (☎ 650 7247).

International trains depart from Bucharest for Belgrade, Berlin, Bratislava, Budapest, Istanbul, Kiev, Kraków, Moscow, Munich, Prague, Sofia, Thessaloniki, Vienna and Warsaw.

Bus Bucharest's central bus station is on Calea Griviţei. Services are poor and schedules change regularly, so check the timetables stuck on lamp posts at the bus stop. You buy your ticket from the driver.

Various bus agencies on the square between Gara de Nord and Hotel Cerna have daily buses to Athens, Budapest, Chişinău in Moldova, Istanbul, Sofia, Warsaw, cities in Germany and more. Compare prices and check out visa requirements for your destination. Major bus companies to Turkey include Toros Trans (☎ 638 2424), Str Gării de Nord; Ortadoğu Tur (☎ 637 6778), Piaţa Gara de Nord 1; and Ö Murat (☎ 618 4095), Str

ROMANIA

Dinicu Golescu 31. The leading bus companies to Germany and Western Europe include Atlas Reisen (☎ 230 7980), Str Ankara 4; Double T (☎ 613 3642), Calea Victoriei 2; and Touring (☎ 633 1661), Str Sofia 26.

Getting Around

To/From the Airports Going to the city centre from Otopeni, catch bus No 783 immediately outside the main terminal; buy a magnetic ticket at the kiosk to the right. From Băneasa, exit the terminal and cross to the opposite side of the busy Bucharest-Piteşti

road. Every 30 minutes from 6.30 am to 9 pm you can take bus No 783 to Otopeni and Băneasa airports from Piaţa Unirii and Piaţa. It takes 20 minutes to reach Băneasa (it's not obvious where to get off, so ask someone to point out the stop) and 30 minutes to reach Otopeni (the end of the line).

Don't believe taxi drivers if they say the airport buses have stopped running or don't exist. And don't pay more than US$10 to $15 to/from Otopeni or US$8 to $10 to/from Băneasa.

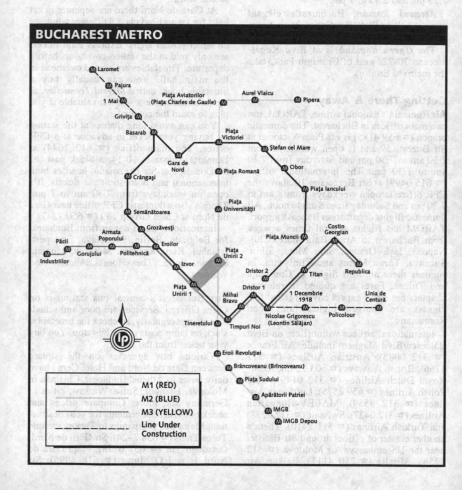

BUCHAREST METRO

- M1 (RED)
- M2 (BLUE)
- M3 (YELLOW)
- Line Under Construction

Public Transport For buses, trams and trolleybuses, buy tickets (US$0.20) at streetside kiosks marked '*casă de bilet*' or simply '*bilet*', and validate one end of the ticket on board. Tickets are checked regularly by inspectors and there's a US$6 fine if you're caught without one. Public transport runs daily from 5 am to 11 pm, with a reduced service on Sunday.

Metro Bucharest's metro system has three lines and is great for getting around the city centre. Trains run every five to seven minutes. To use the metro buy a magnetic ticket for either two rides (US$0.36) or 10 rides (US$1.50) at the subterranean kiosks.

Red line M1 circles the centre from Republica, moving west across the south-centre, swinging north at Eroilor to Gara de Nord, then continuing east across the north-centre to end at Dristor. Blue line M2 travels north-south from Pipera to IMGB, stopping at the main central piaţas (Victoriei, Română, Universităţii and Unirii). Transfer between lines M1 and M2 at Piaţa Victoriei or Piaţa Unirii. The yellow M3 line goes west from Eroilor to Industriilor.

Sit near the front of the train for a better chance of seeing the station names. At platform level, the name of the station where you are is the one with a box around it; the others indicate the direction the train is going. The final destination is also shown on the front of the first car.

Taxi Licensed taxis have a registration number in black and white on the door. If the taxi doesn't have a meter, agree on a price before getting in. At the time of writing the official rate was US$0.20 per kilometre. It's best to call a taxi by phoning ☎ 922, ☎ 942, ☎ 953 or ☎ 988.

Wallachia

Wallachia is a flat, tranquil region of farms and small-scale industrial complexes, stretching across the Danube plain north to the crest of the Carpathian Mountains. Although the Danube River flows right along the southern edge of Wallachia, it is best seen between Moldova Veche and Drobeta-Turnu Severin

in the west, where it breaks through the Carpathians at the legendary Iron Gate, a gorge of the Danube River on the Romanian-Yugoslav border.

Towns such as Calafat and Giurgiu are industrial river ports with little to offer – most travellers quickly pass through on the way to/from Bulgaria by ferry, car, or foot. Other towns, including Curtea de Argeş and Târgu Jiu, are jumping-off points for the southern Carpathians. The national capital is in Wallachia.

History

Before the formation of Romania in the 19th century, the Romanians were known as Vlachs, hence Wallachia. These days the name Wallachia is seldom used in Romania since both it and the term *Vlach* are considered derogatory – they originated in the 3rd century as the Goth word for 'foreigner'.

Founded by Radu Negru in 1290, this principality was subject to Hungarian rule until 1330, when Basarab I defeated the Hungarian king Charles I and quickly declared Wallachia independent. The Wallachian princes *(voivodes)* built their first capital cities – Câmpulung, Curtea de Argeş and Târgovişte – close to the protective mountains, but in the 15th century Bucharest gained ascendancy.

After the fall of Bulgaria to the Turks in 1396, Wallachia faced a new threat and in 1417 Mircea the Old was forced to acknowledge Turkish suzerainty. Other Wallachian princes such as Vlad Ţepeş and Michael the Brave became national heroes by defying the Turks and refusing to pay tribute. In 1859 Wallachia was united with Moldavia, paving the way for the modern Romanian state.

SNAGOV
☎ 018

Snagov, 38km north of Bucharest, is a favourite picnic spot for city dwellers, with a famous 16th-century **church** tucked away on a small island on Snagov Lake. The first monastery was built on the island in the 11th century, and in 1456 Vlad Ţepeş built fortifications and a prison near the church. The present church dates from 1521, with paintings done in 1563. The body of Vlad Ţepeş is reputedly buried below the dome. You can hire a boat to the island from outside the Dolce Vita restaurant for about US$7.

The early 20th-century **Snagov Palace**, just across the lake from the island, was built by Prince Nicolae, brother of King Carol II, in the Italian Renaissance style. During the Ceauşescu era it was used for meetings of high-level government officials and today houses the Snagov Complex restaurant. Ceauşescu had a summer home on Snagov Lake, **Villa No 10**, which is now rented out to rich and famous tourists.

There are two *camping grounds* in the lakeside oak forest plus a few *beer gardens* and *food stands*. The lakeside *Dolce Vita* restaurant and bar serves Romanian dishes.

Getting There & Away
From June to September two unreserved local trains a day run from Bucharest's Gara de Nord to Snagov Plajă at 7.25 and 8.25 am, returning at 7.15 and 9.40 pm (one hour). In winter there's one daily train from Bucharest's Gara Băneasa.

CALAFAT
☎ 051
The small town of Calafat on the Danube opposite Vidin in Bulgaria makes a convenient entry/exit point to/from Bulgaria. Car ferries cross the river hourly and there are frequent local trains to/from Craiova, from where you can catch an express train to Bucharest or Timişoara. Apart from the **Muzeul de Artă** on Str 22 Decembrie and a monument to the 1877-78 war of independence against the Turks, there isn't much to see or do in Calafat.

Orientation & Information
The ferry landing is right in the centre of Calafat, about four blocks from the train station. To use the left-luggage office at the train station, first buy a baggage ticket at the ticket window, then look for the baggage room in a small building just down the track.

It's impossible to change a travellers cheque in Calafat. Exiting the ferry you'll see several exchange kiosks near customs. Bancă Agricola, opposite the post office on the way from the ferry to the train station, changes cash at the official rate.

Places to Stay & Eat
The *Hotel Dunărea Calafat* (☎ 231 303) on a slight hill near the ferry terminal charges US$24/37 for a single/double with bath. The accommodation situation is better in Vidin, so continue to there if it's not too late.

Getting There & Away
There are six local trains a day to/from Craiova (2½ hours). If you're continuing to Bucharest or elsewhere, buy a ticket to your final destination and, as soon as you reach Craiova, go into the station and purchase a compulsory seat reservation for your onward express train.

Bulgaria The car ferry crosses the Danube hourly year-round (30 minutes, US$3.50 in hard currency only). Cars can spend several hours waiting to cross but pedestrians can just walk past the car queues in both directions. There are small 24-hour cafés along the line where you can buy food and drinks. For information about the other side, see the Vidin section in the Bulgaria chapter.

DROBETA-TURNU SEVERIN
☎ 052
Drobeta-Turnu Severin is on the Danube, bordering Yugoslavia, with two local buses crossing the border. Though of ancient origin, the present town was laid out in the 19th century and has a pleasant series of parks in the centre. A three-hour stop is enough to see the best of Drobeta-Turnu Severin.

Orientation & Information
From the train station follow Blvd Republicii east for 1.5km to the Hotel Parc at the intersection of Str Coştescu. From here walk one block north and turn right onto Str Decebal, where you'll find the post, CFR and tourist offices.

Money Change money, cash travellers cheques or get cash on Visa/MasterCard at BANCOREX on the corner of Str Bibiescu and Str Unirii, or at Bancă Comercială Română, two blocks south on the corner of Str Coştenescu and Str Aurelian, on weekdays from 8.30 am to 2 pm.

Post & Communications
The post office, open weekdays from 7 am to 9 pm and Saturday from 8 am to noon, is adjacent to the telephone office at Str Decebal 41. The telephone office is open weekdays from 7.30 am to 8 pm and weekends from 8 am to 2 pm.

Things to See
At the east end of Blvd Republicii is the **Muzeul Porţile de Fier** (Iron Gate Museum; closed Monday), with a fine exhibit on the natural history of the Danube River. Other sections of the museum cover history and ethnography, including a scale model of the Roman bridge constructed across the Danube in 103 AD by Apolodorus of Damascus on the orders of the emperor Trajan. The bridge stood just below the site of the present museum, and alongside the museum are the ruins of **Castrul Drobeta**, a 2nd to 3rd-century Roman fort that protected the bridge.

West of Drobeta-Turnu Severin, the train runs along the northern bank of the Danube through the famous **Iron Gate**, passing a huge concrete hydroelectric power station (1972), on top of which is a road that links Romania to Yugoslavia. You get a good view of everything from the train window.

Places to Stay
There's no camping ground at Drobeta-Turnu Severin. ANTREC (☎/fax 220 833), Str Avram Iancu 38, arranges rooms in private houses for about US$10 a night. The cheapest hotel is friendly *Hotel Severin* (☎ 212 074), Str Eminescu 1, off Blvd Republicii, where singles/doubles cost US$12/20. *Hotel Traian* (☎ 311 799), Blvd Vladimirescu 74, has singles/doubles for US$25/33 and a 24-hour billiard bar.

Getting There & Away
All express trains between Bucharest and Timişoara stop here. Local trains make slower, more frequent trips in both directions.

Transylvania

To most people, the name Transylvania conjures images of haunted castles, werewolves and vampires. Certainly the 14th-century castles at Râsnov and Bran appear ready-made for a Count Dracula movie, perhaps filmed against the medieval skyline of a town like Sighişoara.

Yet the charms of Transylvania are far more diverse – mountain scenery, some of Romania's best hiking and skiing, plus scores of rural villages that haven't changed much since the 18th century.

For lovers of medieval art and history, it's an unparalleled chance to escape the tourist hordes in Budapest and Prague and have an overlooked part of the old Austro-Hungarian empire all to themselves. Many readers have written in saying Transylvania was their favourite part of Romania, particularly Braşov and Sighişoara.

History
For 1000 years, right up to WWI, Transylvania was associated with Hungary. In the 10th century a Magyar tribe, the Szeklers, settled in what they called Erdély (Beyond the Forest). They were followed in the 12th century by Saxon merchant-knights, who were invited in to help defend the eastern frontiers of Hungary. The seven towns the Saxons founded – Bistriţa (Bistritz), Braşov (Kronstadt), Cluj-Napoca (Klausenburg), Mediaş (Mediasch), Sebeş (Muhlbach), Sibiu (Hermannstadt) and Sighişoara (Schässburg) – gave Transylvania its German name, Siebenbürgen (Seven Cities). Before 1989 there were an estimated 370,000 ethnic Germans living in Romania, mostly in Transylvania. After the revolution huge numbers migrated to Germany and by 1992 only 119,000 Germans remained. In 1995 Romania's German population was estimated at less than 62,000. Left behind are many small villages around Sibiu and Sighişoara that seem to have been lifted directly out of 19th-century Germany.

Medieval Transylvania was an autonomous unit ruled by a prince responsible to the Hungarian crown. The indigenous Romanians were mere serfs; their presence is only noted in the chronicles in relation to peasant revolts. After the defeat of Hungary by the Turks in 1526 the region became independent, though it still recognised Turkish suzerainty (and paid tribute). This independence was maintained in the early 17th

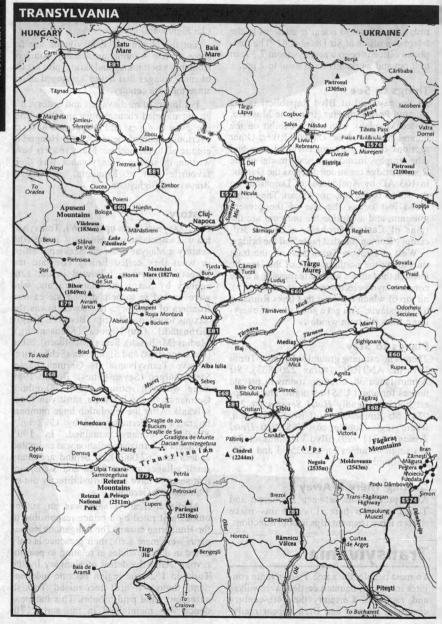

TRANSYLVANIA

HUNGARY

UKRAINE

Carei

Satu Mare

Baia Mare

Borşa

Cârlibaba

Iacobeni

Tăşnad

E81

Târgu Lăpuş

Pietrosul (2305m)

Marghita

Şimleu-Silvaniei

Coşbuc

Tihuţa Pass

Vatra Dornei

Ip

Jibou

Someş

Salva

Năsăud

Liviu Rebreanu

Piatra Fântânele

E576

Mureşeni

Zalău

Dej

Livezile

Bistriţa

Pietrosul (2100m)

Aleşd

Treznea

E81

Gherla

Deda

Ciucea

Zimbor

Nicula

Topliţa

To Oradea

Poieni

Huedin

E576

Sărmaşu

Reghin

Apuseni Mountains

Bologa

E60

Cluj-Napoca

Someşul Mic

Vlădeasa (1836m)

Mănăstireni

Beiuş

Stâna de Vale

Lake Fântânele

Turda

Câmpii Turzii

Târgu Mureş

Sovata

Praid

Pietroasa

Şei

Horea

Muntelui Mare (1827m)

Buru

Ludus

E60

Mureşul Mic

Corund

Bihor (1849m)

Gârda de Sus

Albac

Câmpeni

Roşia Montană

Târnăveni

Mică

Odorheiu Secuiesc

E79

Avram Iancu

Aiud

E81

Târnava

Mare

Abrud

Bucium

Târnava

Sighişoara

To Arad

Brad

Zlatna

Mediaş

Copşa Mică

E60

Rupea

Deva

E68

Mureş

Alba Iulia

Sebeş

Blaj

Agnita

Băile Ocna Sibiului

Slimnic

Hunedoara

Orăştie

E81

Cristian

Sibiu

Olt

Făgăraş

E68

Oţelu Roşu

Densuş

Hateg

Orăştie de Jos Bucium Orăştie de Sus Gradiştea de Munte Dacian Sarmizegetusa

Transylvanian

Pălţiniş

Cisnădie

Victoria

Făgăraş Mountains

Bran

Zărneşti

Măgura

Peştera

Ulpia Traiana-Sarmizegetusa

Petrila

Cindrel (2244m)

A l p s

Negoiu (2535m)

Moldoveanu (2543m)

Moieciu Fundata

Şimon

Retezat Mountains

Petroşani

Podu Dâmbovita

Retezat National Park

Peleaga (2511m)

Lupeni

Parângul (2518m)

Brezoi

Trans-Făgăraşan Highway

E574

Câmpulung Muscel

Dâmboviţa

Târgu Jiu

Bengeşti

Olt

Horezu

E81

Călimăneşti

Râmnicu Vâlcea

Curtea de Argeş

Argeş

Baia de Aramă

Jiu

To Craiova

Olt

Piteşti

To Bucharest

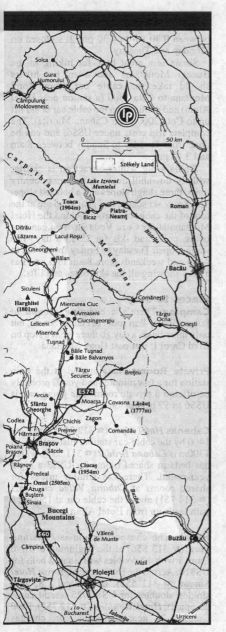

century by playing the Ottoman sultan off against the Habsburg emperor.

In 1683 Turkish power was broken at the gates of Vienna and in 1687 Transylvania came under Habsburg rule. The Catholic Habsburg governors sought to control the territory by favouring first the Protestant Hungarians and Saxons, and then the Orthodox Romanians. In 1848, when the Hungarians revolted against the Habsburgs, the local Romanian population sided with the Austrians. After 1867 Transylvania was fully absorbed into Hungary, to the dismay of the increasingly nationalist Romanians, who massed at Alba Iulia in 1918 to demand Transylvania's union with Romania.

Transylvania's absorption into Romania has never been fully accepted by Hungary and from 1940 to 1944 much of the region was annexed by Hungary's pro-Nazi fascists. After the war the communists squelched nationalist sentiments, but since 1989 Hungarian and Romanian nationalists have revived the issue. The 'Transylvania Question' continues to cast a small but persistent cloud over relations between the two countries.

SINAIA
☎ 044

This popular winter ski resort snuggles at an altitude of 800 to 930m in the narrow Prahova Valley, at the foot of the fir-clad Bucegi Mountains. Sinaia is a convenient day trip from Bucharest or Braşov.

Although its monastery has existed since the 17th century, Sinaia developed into a major resort only after King Carol I decided to build his summer residence, the magnificent Peleş Castle, there in 1870.

A railway line from Bucharest followed in 1879 and the local elite soon arrived en masse, constructing imposing residences and villas along the wooded slopes. Until 1920 the Hungarian-Romanian border ran along Predeal Pass just north of Sinaia. For convenience this area has been included in the Transylvania section, even though, strictly speaking, it is in Wallachia.

Orientation & Information
The train station is directly below the centre of town. From the station go up the stairway

across the street and climb up to busy Blvd Carol I. The Hotel Montana and cable car are toward the left, the monastery and palace are uphill to the right.

Palace Agenție de Turism, Str Octavian Goga 11 opposite Villa Parc, sells hiking maps of the Bucegi Mountains and is open on weekdays from 8 am to 8 pm, Saturday from 9 am to 2 pm and Sunday from 9 am to noon. Maps can also be found at the Hotel Montana reception desk.

SurMont Sports, a few doors down, sells hiking maps, skis, tents and imported outdoor gear.

There are currency exchanges inside hotels International, Sinaia and Montana along Blvd Carol I. Bancă Comercială Română, just past the Hotel Montana, gives cash advances on Visa/MasterCard from 8 am to 11 am on weekdays and has an ATM outside. Bank Post, also on Blvd Carol I, has an outside ATM for Visa.

The left-luggage office at the train station is open 24 hours.

Things to See & Do

From the train station walk up the stairway to town, turn left and make a quick right onto Str Octavian Goga, then curve left at the casino. There's a stairway here, at the top of which is **Sinaia Monastery**, named after Mt Sinai. The large Orthodox church dates from 1846 and an older church (1695) with its original frescoes is in the compound to the left. Beside the newer church is a small history museum, which is open from 10 am to 6 pm daily, except Monday and Tuesday.

Just past the monastery begins the road to **Peleş Castle** (1883), the former royal palace. Admission is US$4.50, paid at a small kiosk on the road. The palace with 160 rooms was built in the German-Renaissance style for the Prussian prince Carol I, first king of Romania (ruled 1866-1914). The queue can be long on weekends, but it's worth waiting as the interior rooms are magnificent. This is one of Romania's finest castles. Tours are given from 9 am to 3 pm in various languages. It's closed Monday and Tuesday.

A few hundred metres uphill from the main palace is the smaller **Pelişor Palace**, in mock-medieval style. Pelişor was built for Carol I's son, Ferdinand, and was decorated

in the Art Nouveau style by Queen Marie. Admission is US$3 for a 20-minute tour between 9.30 am to 4.30 pm. It's closed on Monday and Tuesday.

Sinaia is a great base for **hiking** in the Bucegi Mountains and even non-hikers should take the **cable car** from Hotel Montana to Cota 1400 (a station near Hotel Alpin) and continue on the cable car or ski lift up to Cota 2000 (near Cabana Miorița). The complete trip costs under US$6, and can be done from Tuesday to Sunday between 8 am and 3.45 pm.

Sinaia's big winter attraction is **skiing**, with 10 downhill tracts, three cross-country trails, three sleigh slopes and a bobsled slope. The Snow ski school and gear shop are at the foot of the cable-car station behind the Hotel Montana at Str Cuza Voda 2a. You can rent boots, poles and skis for US$5 a day. The station, open Tuesday to Friday from 8 am to 4 pm and weekends from 8 am to 5 pm, has a map showing all the ski routes and lifts.

Places to Stay

Camping There's a *camping ground* at Izvorul Rece, 4km south of central Sinaia, but only three buses a day go there from a stop on Blvd Carol I, just past Hotel Montana.

Private Rooms Hang around at the train station for a few minutes and you'll probably be offered a private room. The going rate is US$6 to $9 per person.

Cabanas *Hotel Alpin* (☎ 312 351) is at Cota 1400 by the cable-car station. Just below it at 1300m is *Cabana Brădet* (☎ 311 551), which has beds in shared rooms for US$3 a night year-round. There are similar prices for shared rooms at *Cabana Valea cu Brazi* (☎ 314 751) above the cable car at 1500m; a path leads up from Hotel Alpin.

Hotels The cheapest option is *Pensiuna Parc* (☎ 313 856) at the beginning of Blvd Carol I with 12 doubles with shared bath for US$10. Across the road is the high-rise *Hotel Sinaia* (☎ 311 551), Blvd Carol I 8, with singles/ doubles for US$17/25 (credit cards accepted). *Hotel Montana* (☎ 312 751), Blvd Carol I 24 near the cable car, charges

US$22/36 for a single/double. Farther down at Blvd Carol I 65 is the attractive old *Hotel Păltiniş* (☎ 314 651); singles/doubles with private bath cost US$10/25.

Villa Parc (☎ 313 856), Str Octavian Goga 2, has doubles with/without bath for US$14/10. Directly across from Hotel Palace is the renovated *Hotel Tanţi*, where singles/doubles with bath go for US$18/30 (credit cards accepted). Founded in 1911, *Hotel Palace* (☎ 312 051), Str Octavian Goga 4, is an elegant splurge at US$33/45 a single/double (credit cards accepted). Behind the Hotel Palace, overlooking the park, is the *Hotel Caraiman* (☎ 311 151), its entrance on Blvd Carol I, with singles/doubles for US$28/37.

Getting There & Away
Sinaia is on the Bucharest-Braşov rail line – 126km from the former and 45km from the latter. All express trains stop here and local trains to Buşteni (8km), Predeal (19km) and Braşov are quite frequent.

THE BUCEGI MOUNTAINS
The Bucegi Mountains are Romania's best-kept secret, rivalling Slovakia's Tatra Mountains and even the Alps when it comes to trekking. Getting lost is difficult, thanks to a network of marked trails, while most mountain huts (cabanas) are open year-round for hikers and cross-country skiers. The only danger is the weather: winter is severe, waist-deep snow lingers as late as May and summertime thunderstorms are common. Day hikes from Sinaia and Buşteni require no special equipment, but freelance campers should bring food, water and warm clothes to combat the elements. If you sleep in cabanas, it's still a good idea to bring extra food.

Day Hikes
Catch a morning train from Braşov or Sinaia to Buşteni, then take the Buşteni cable car (US$2.40; open Wednesday to Monday from 8 am to 4 pm) up to **Cabana Babele** (2206m). From Babele you hike south to **Cabana Piatra Arsă** (1950m), where you pick up a blue trail that descends to Sinaia via **Poiana Stânii** (a five-hour walk in total). The beginning of the blue trail is poorly marked at Piatra Arsă, so study the large map on the

wall in the cabana carefully. Once you're actually on the trail, it's no problem. This trip across alpine pastures and through the forest is varied and downhill all the way.

A variation on the above involves taking the Sinaia cable car up to Cabana Mioriţa (1957m), near the crest. You then walk north to Cabana Piatra Arsă (1½ hours) and on to Cabana Babele (another hour), where you can catch the Buşteni cable car down the mountain. The problems with this hike are that it's uphill (350m gain) and you must take two cable cars.

Longer Hikes
A more ambitious expedition involves taking one of the two cable cars mentioned above and hiking north-west across the mountains to Bran Castle, where there are buses to Braşov. You can do this in one strenuous day if you get an early start from Babele, but it's preferable to take two days and camp freelance or spend a night at Cabana Omul.

As you look north from Babele, you'll see a red-and-white TV transmitter on a hill. To the left is a yellow-marked trail that leads to **Cabana Omul** (two hours) on the summit (2505m). North of Babele the scenery gets dramatic, with dizzying drops into valleys on either side.

To go from Omul to Bran Castle takes another six hours and involves a tough 2000m. The yellow-triangle trail is easy to follow and chances are that you will have this glorious landscape all to yourself. From Omul, begin by crossing Mt Scara (2422m) before dropping into Ciubotea Gorge (the grassy valley at the bottom of the gorge is ideal for freelance camping). Once you clear the tree-line the trail descends through thick forest. Eventually you come out on a logging road beside a river, which you follow for 2½ hours to Bran Castle.

You could extend this hike by a day or two by including **Cabana Padina** and any of a dozen well-marked trails, but make sure you have a hiking map (buy one at the tourist office in Sinaia).

Places to Stay & Eat
Both *Cabana Babele* (☎ 311 750), *Cabana Caraiman* (☎ 320 617) and *Cabana Piatra Arsă* (☎ 311 751) charge US$3 to $9 per

THE BUCEGI MOUNTAINS

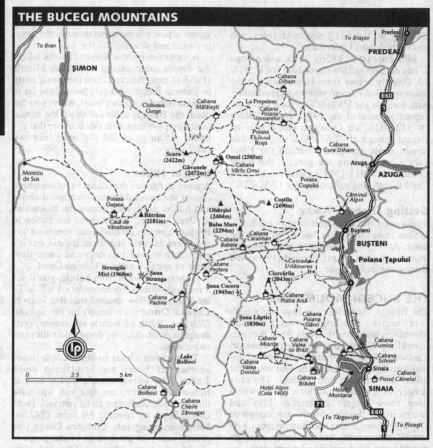

person, depending on whether you want a bed in a double room or a mattress in the dormitory. Cabana Piatra Arsă is a large, modern chalet with 112 beds. All of the above (and *Cabana Miorița* farther south) serve inexpensive meals and drinks. Babele is open year-round, while Caraiman and Piatra Arsă operate in summer only.

Cabana Vârfu Omul (☎ 320 677) is small and basic, with 35 mattresses in a dormitory for US$2 per person. Meals (soup, bread and omelette) are served only occasionally, so bring your own food. Although blankets are

provided, a sleeping bag would be useful. Omul is open from May to September. It's always best to check with the local tourist office about which cabanas are open.

BRAŞOV
☎ 068

Braşov (Brassó in Hungarian) is one of Romania's most visited cities – and for good reason. Piaţa Sfatului, the central square, is the finest in the country, lined with baroque façades and pleasant outdoor cafés. Within easy reach by bus and train are the ski resorts of Sinaia and Poiana Braşov, the castles of Bran and Râşnov and trails that lead into the dramatic Bucegi Mountains.

A pleasant medieval town flanked by verdant hills on both sides, Braşov started as a German mercantile colony named Kronstadt. Its strategic location at the meeting point of three principalities helped it to become a major medieval trading centre. The Saxons built ornate churches and townhouses, all protected by a brawny wall that still remains. The Romanians lived at Scheii, just outside the walls to the south-west.

Contemporary Braşov is Romania's sixth-largest city, with a population of 324,000. Today Braşov's tractor, truck and soap factories have more importance than commerce and endless rows of concrete apartment blocks have risen to house the proletariat. Fortunately, these are far enough away to not spoil Braşov's photogenic old town.

Orientation

The train station is to the north-east and far from the centre of town. Take bus No 4 (buy your ticket at a kiosk) to Parcul Central or Str Mureşenilor. Strada Republicii, Braşov's pedestrian-only promenade, is crowded with shops and cafés from Parcul Central to Piaţa Sfatului.

Braşov has two main bus stations: Autogara 1, next to the train station, and Autogara 2, west of the train station at Str Avram Iancu 114. Take local bus No 12 or 22 into the centre from the Stadion Tineretului stop on Str Stadionului.

Information

Tourist Offices There's a tourist desk in the lobby of the Hotel Aro Palace, Blvd Eroilor 25, but it's not of much use except for the expensive town map it sells.

The Touring ACR desk (☎ 118 920) in Hotel Capitol on Blvd Eroilor provides assistance for motorists. The main ACR office (☎ 135 476) is north of the city centre at Calea Bucureşti 68.

Money The IDM currency exchange on Piaţa Sfatului is open weekdays from 8 am to 7.30 pm, Saturday from 9 am to noon and changes Eurocheques; another office at Str Apollonia

Hirscher is open weekdays from 10 am to 6 pm and Saturday from 10 am to 2 pm.

BANCOREX, Str Republicii 20a, changes travellers cheques and gives cash advances on Visa/MasterCard. It's open weekdays from 8.30 am to 2 pm.

The Bancă Comercială Română, Str Republicii near the CFR office, also gives cash advances weekdays from 8 am to 2 pm, as does BCIT, on the corner of Str Republicii and Str Weiss from 9 am to 2 pm.

There is also an ATM outside the Hotel Aro Palace restaurant on Blvd Eroilor.

Post & Communications The main post office is opposite the Heroes Cemetery and open from 7 am to 8 pm.

Braşov's telephone centres are at Str Republicii 12 (open weekdays 10 am to 6 pm); Blvd Eroilor, between the Capitol and Aro Palace hotels (open daily from 7 am to 10 pm); and one street farther east off Blvd Eroilor (open weekdays 7 am to 7 pm).

Travel Agencies Dimm Travel (☎/fax 151 084), Str Iuliu Maniu 13, can arrange private rooms in Braşov and other towns; it's open weekdays from 9 am to 6.30 pm and Saturday from 10 am to 2 pm.

Nouvelles Frontieres/Simpa Turism (☎ 151 173) on Piaţa Sfatului changes cash at a good rate and has cheap deals on international plane tickets; it's open weekdays from 9 am to 5 pm.

Bookshops There's a small selection of English-language novels at Librărie George Coşbuc, Str Republicii 29. Librărie Aldus, Str Apollonia Hirscher 4, has maps, postcards and guidebooks.

Left Luggage The left-luggage office (open 24 hours) in the train station is in the underpass that leads out from the tracks.

Things to See

In the middle of Piaţa Sfatului is the Council House (1420), now the **Braşov History Museum** (closed Monday). The 58m Trumpeter's Tower above the building dates from 1582.

The Gothic **Black Church** (1384-1477), still used by German Lutherans, looms just south of the square. The church's name comes from its appearance after a fire in 1689. As you walk around the building to the entrance, you'll see statues on the exterior of the apse. The originals are now inside at the back of the church, and Turkish rugs hang from every balcony.

In summer, recitals are given on the 1839 organ on Thursday and Saturday at 6 pm (US$0.25). The church is closed to sightseers on Sunday.

Go south-west a little to the neoclassical **Schei Gate** (1828), then walk 500m up Str Prundului to Piaţa Unirii. As soon as you pass through Schei Gate the urban landscape changes, from the sober rows of Teutonic houses in the walled old town to the smaller, simpler houses of the former Romanian settlement.

On Piaţa Unirii you'll find the black-spired Orthodox **Church of St Nicolae din Scheii** (1595). Beside the church is the **First Romanian School Museum**, which houses a collection of icons, paintings on glass and old manuscripts. The clock tower (1751) was financed by Elizabeth, empress of Russia. At the time of writing the museum and clock tower were inexplicably closed.

Go back the way you came and turn right just before Schei Gate to reach the 16th-century **Weavers' Bastion**, which is a little hidden above the sports field. This corner fort on the old city walls has a museum with a fascinating scale model of Braşov in the 17th century. The model itself was created in 1896.

Above the bastion is a pleasant promenade through the forest overlooking Braşov. Halfway along you'll come to the **Tâmpa cable car** (Telecabina), which operates daily until 8 pm in summer (closed Monday in winter; US$2.50 return). The cable car rises from 640 to 960m and offers a stunning view of the entire area. The hike to the top, following a series of zigzagging trails, takes 45 minutes and is well worth the effort.

The art gallery inside the **Muzeul de Etnografie**, Blvd Eroilor 21, next to the Hotel Capitol, has a good Romanian collection upstairs.

Cetatea Braşov, a whitewashed fort on a hill overlooking the old town, was built in 1580 to defend Kronstadt's Saxon merchants from marauding Turks. Today it houses two good beer patios, a so-so disco and an expensive restaurant.

Places to Stay
Camping The closest camping ground, *Camping Darste* (☎ 259 080), is 3km south-east of the centre at Calea Bucureşti 285, with wooden huts for US$5 a night and tent space. The only other area near Braşov is at Râşnov (see the Râşnov & Bran section).

Private Rooms You may be approached at the train station by several people offering rooms for about US$8 to $10 as well as local tourist advice. Maria and Grig Bolea (☎ 311 962) might seem a bit pushy but their rooms are fine. Radu Jiga (☎ 413 886) also offers rooms and tours to Bran.

Hotels The *Hotel Postăvarul* (☎ 144 330/40; fax 141 505) on Str Politechnicii 2 in the city centre has rooms with shared bath for US$14/20 a night; doubles with private bath are US$22. Next door is the two-star *Hotel Coroana* (☎ 144 330; fax 154 427), Str Republicii 62, where every room has a private bath (US$34/54).

The *Hotel Aro Sport* (☎ 142 840), Str Sf Ioan 3, behind the Aro Palace Hotel, charges US$11/16 for rooms with shared bath.

The three-star high-rise *Hotel Capitol* (☎ 118 920; fax 115 834), Blvd Eroilor 19, offers singles/doubles for US$36/60 with breakfast (Visa and Amex accepted).

The four-star *Aro Palace* (☎ 142 840; fax 150 427) on Blvd Eroilor, facing Parcul Central, has plush rooms, cable TV, phone and fridge if you can afford US$48/110 (Visa, Amex and Master-Card accepted).

Places to Eat
Pizza Iulia, a pizza and pasta spot on Str Nicolae Bălcescu, has good food, low prices and friendly staff. It's open until 10.30 pm.

Sirena Gustari on Piaţa Sfatului, is a good place to try Romanian specialities such as *sarmale* (stuffed grape leaves) and *mămăligă* (corn polenta), and has an English menu.

Adjacent and in the Saxon-built Hirscher House (1545) is Braşov's most famous

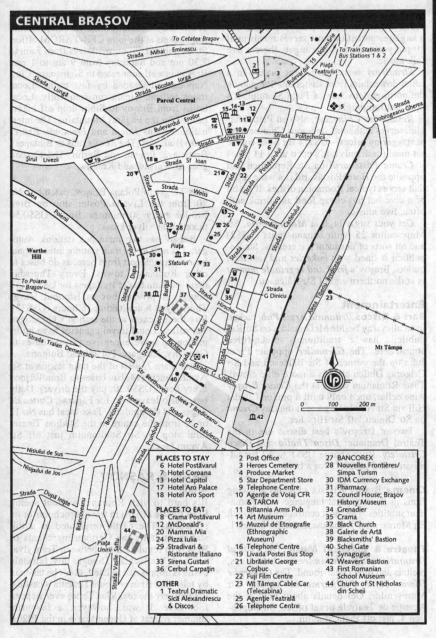

CENTRAL BRAŞOV

Strada Mihai Eminescu
To Cetatea Braşov

Bulevardul 15 Noiembrie
Piaţa Teatrului
To Train Station & Bus Stations 1 & 2

Strada Lungă

Strada Nicolae Iorga

Parcul Central

Strada Dobrogeanu Gherea

Bulevardul Eroilor

Strada Politechnicii

Strada Sadoveanu

Şirul Livezii

Strada Sf Ioan

Strada Republicii

Strada Postăvenului

Strada Weiss

Strada Amata Română

Strada Nicolae Bălcescu

Strada Castelului

Calea Poienii

Strada Mureşenilor

Warthe Hill

Strada Diaconu Coresi

Piaţa Sfatului

Strada Zidurl

Strada Dupa

To Poiana Braşov

Strada Gheorghe Bariţiu

Strada Baritiu

Strada G Dinicu

Strada Hirscher

Strada Porta Scheii

Strada Cerbului

Strada Richter

Mt Tâmpa

Strada Traian Demetrescu

Strada Beethoven

Aleea Tiberiu Brediceanu

Strada G Coşbuc

Aleea Saguna

Aleea T Brediceanu

Strada Dr G Baiulescu

Strada Brâncoveanu

Strada Prundului

Nisiului de Sus

Nisiului de Jos

Strada După Iniţe

Piaţa Unirii

Strada Vasile Saftu

0   100   200 m

PLACES TO STAY
6 Hotel Postăvarul
7 Hotel Coroana
13 Hotel Capitol
17 Hotel Aro Palace
18 Hotel Aro Sport

PLACES TO EAT
8 Crama Postăvarul
12 McDonald's
20 Mamma Mia
29 Stradivari & Ristorante Italiano
33 Sirena Gustari
36 Cerbul Carpaţin

OTHER
1 Teatrul Dramatic Sică Alexandrescu & Discos

2 Post Office
3 Heroes Cemetery
4 Produce Market
5 Star Department Store
9 Telephone Centre
10 Agenţie de Voiaj CFR & TAROM
11 Britannia Arms Pub
14 Art Museum
15 Muzeul de Etnografie (Ethnographic Museum)
16 Telephone Centre
19 Livada Postei Bus Stop
21 Librăirie George Coşbuc
22 Fuji Film Centre
23 Mt Tâmpa Cable Car (Telecabina)
25 Agenţie Teatrală
26 Telephone Centre

27 BANCOREX
28 Nouvelles Frontières/ Simpa Turism
30 IDM Currency Exchange
31 Pharmacy
32 Council House; Braşov History Museum
34 Grenadier
35 Crama
37 Black Church
38 Galerie de Artă
39 Blacksmiths' Bastion
40 Schei Gate
41 Synagogue
42 Weavers' Bastion
43 First Romanian School Museum
44 Church of St Nicholas din Scheii

restaurant, *Cerbul Carpaţin*. The wine cellar opens in summer from 7 pm to midnight, and a large restaurant upstairs serves meals until 10 pm year-round. Some nights there's live folk music.

Stradivari serves excellent pizzas in a cellar downstairs from Ristorante Italiano on the north-eastern side of Piaţa Sfatului; it's open until midnight.

Restaurant Chinezesc, also on Piaţa Sfatului, serves authentic, delicious Chinese food at staggering prices – US$14 for a six-course set meal (cash only); it's open until 11 pm.

Crama Postăvarul on Str Republicii and opposite the Hotel Postăvarul is a wine cellar that serves typical Romanian dishes. It's a bit of a dive but has cheap food and drink and, often, live music.

Get your sugar high at *Mamma Mia*, Str Mureşenilor 25, with banana splits (US$2) and all sorts of decadent ice creams. Str Republicii is lined with *bakeries* and fast food outlets. Braşov's *fruit and vegetable market* is at the northern end of Str Bălcescu.

Entertainment
Bars & Discos *Britannia Arms Pub*, tucked in an alleyway beside McDonald's on Str Republicii, has a traditional smoke-filled atmosphere. The *Grenadier* opposite Pizza Julia on the corner of Str Bălcescu and Str Grigoraş Dinicu attracts a more elite crowd. Taste Romanian wines at the *Cetate Braşov* wine cellar, open only until 8 pm, on Citadel Hill via Str Nicole Iorga or at the tiny *Crama* on Str Dinicu, off Str Hirscher.

Two of Braşov's best discos are in the Teatrul Dramatic: *Disco Thalia* and *Disco Cristolety*. Both charge US$1 to $2 for admission and US$0.75 for a beer.

Cinema Braşov has six cinemas showing films in their original language with Romanian subtitles. The most central are the *Royal*, Str Mureşenilor 7, and the *Astra*, Str Lunga 1.

Theatre & Classical Music The *Teatrul Dramatic Sică Alexandrescu* has plays, recitals and opera year-round. The *Gheorghe Dima State Philharmonic* is on Str Mureşenilor. Get details about both at the Agenţie de Teatrală ticket office, Str Republicii 4, just off Piaţa Sfatului.

Getting There & Around
Train Buy domestic and all international train tickets at the joint CFR-TAROM office, Str Republicii 53, on weekdays from 7 am to 7.30 pm and Saturday from 9 am to 1 pm. Braşov is well connected to Sighişoara, Cluj-Napoca and Oradea by fast trains. Local trains to/from Sinaia run frequently. Local trains from Braşov to Sibiu drop off hikers headed for the Făgăraş Mountains. The international trains *Dacia* and *Pannonia Expres* go to Budapest. The *Alutus* runs to Budapest, Bratislava, Prague and Berlin. The *Carpati* goes to Warsaw and Kraków.

Bus To get to Poiana Braşov, catch bus No 20 from the Livada Postei stop on Blvd Eroilor every 30 minutes. Buy a US$0.50 ticket at the silver kiosk.

Braşov has two main bus stations. Autogara 1 is next to the train station; international buses arrive/depart from here, as do buses to other Romanian towns. Every Thursday there's a 7 am bus to Budapest for US$15 (17 hours). A private bus to Istanbul leaves Thursday at 8 am, taking 16 hours (US$33). Buy these tickets at the station's Ortadoğuu Tur office. Local travel agencies have information on more expensive private buses to Germany, Hungary, Poland and Bulgaria.

Autogara 2, west of the train station at Str Avram Iancu 114, has buses to Bran/Râşnov every hour (US$0.30; pay the driver). Daily buses also leave here for Făgăraş, Curtea de Argeş and Câmpulung. Take local bus No 12 or 22 from the centre to the Stadion Tineretului stop on Str Stadionului just off Str Avram Iancu.

BRAN & RÂŞNOV
☎ 068

It's hard to visit Romania without seeing **Bran Castle** (1378) in travel brochures or on postcards. The castle originated as a toll station built by the German merchants of Braşov to regulate trade between Transylvania and Wallachia. Though this fairytale castle is impressive in itself, don't be taken in by tales that Bran is Count Dracula's castle – it's unlikely the real Vlad Ţepeş ever stepped foot here. It was, however, a favourite summer retreat of Queen Marie in the 1920s.

Still, it's fun to run through the castle's 57 rooms. Beside the entrance to the castle is an ethnographic village museum with a collection of Transylvanian farm buildings. Your ticket (US$2.50, US$1.50 with a student card) admits you to the farmhouses, castle and the Vama Bran Museum below the castle. They all open from 9 am to 5 pm and are closed on Monday.

Râşnov offers the dual attraction of a convenient camping ground and the ruins of 13th-century **Râşnov Castle**, which is closed on Monday (admission is US$0.50). Everyone who makes the trip agrees that Râşnov's hill-top fortress is more dramatic and a lot less touristy than the castle at Bran.

Places to Stay & Eat

You can camp for free in the field across the stream from the Vama Bran Museum, just below Bran Castle. Otherwise, *Cabana Bran Castel* (☎ 236 404), a rustic chalet on the hillside about 600m behind the castle, provides accommodation at US$5 per person in a dorm room. Meals are served and it's open year-round, but in summer it's often full.

Bran Imex (☎ 236 642; fax 152 598), the agent for ANTREC in Bran, at Str Aurel Stoian 395 arranges inexpensive accommodation in 250 private homes in Bran and the surrounding villages. It's open daily from 8 am to 9 pm in summer and 10 am to 6 pm in winter.

The one-star *Hotel Bran* (☎ 236 556), two blocks from the castle, charges US$10 per person for a bed in a double room with private shower; hot water flows from 8 pm to midnight. The front terrace is a good place for a meal. The *Casă de Creatie* (☎ 236 738), opposite the main bus stop on Str Principală, has 25 beds in double/triple rooms with shared bath for $3 a night, plus breakfast. The large chalet-style building at the foot of the castle has no sign, but its restaurant is open from 10 am to 10 pm. The *Bran Benzin* petrol station (☎ 151 675) at the northern end of Bran has six rooms above the station. Doubles with private/shared bath are US$10/9 a night.

Râşnov's camping ground, *Camping Valea Cetaţii* (☎ 186 346), is directly below the castle on the road to Poiana Braşov, less than 1km from Piaţa Unirii or about 2km

from the bus stop to/from Braşov. There are 30 cabins at US$5 per person and camping is US$2.50 per tent. It's reliably open from June to August only.

Getting There & Away

Buses to Bran and Râşnov leave hourly from Braşov's Autogara 2. The ride takes under an hour and costs about US$0.30. It's best to visit Bran first and then stop at Râşnov on the way back. Return buses leave Bran every hour between 5.40 am and 7.40 pm.

From the bus stop in Bran the castle is easy to spot. From the stop in Râs, walk 100m east towards the mountains, turn right at Piaţa Unirii and watch for the hillside stairs in the courtyard of the unmarked Casă de Cultură (on your left). The castle is a 15-minute walk uphill.

POIANA BRAŞOV
☎ 068

Take bus No 20 from Braşov's Biblioteca Judeteana at Livada Postiei to the winter ski resort of Poiana Braşov (1020m), nestled in the mountains 13km away (buy your ticket at the central kiosk for about US$0.50). Poiana has seven ski lifts, one gondola, and two cable cars *(telecabina)*, a few of which operate services year-round to the summit of **Postăvarul Massif** (1799m), from which there's a splendid view of the Carpathian Mountains. A large map by the bus stop indicates where the cable cars and hotels are. The information centre and tourist office (☎ 262 310; fax 150 504) is by the Complex Favorit. Buses back to Braşov run regularly through the evening.

Activities

Telecabina B is near the Hotel Sport and Telecabina A and the adjacent gondola are near the Hotel Teleferic. All three drop you high on the mountain near Cabana Cristianul Mare. All three cost US$3.50 each way and are open daily from 9 am to 4 pm.

From Cabana Cristianul Mare it's possible to hike down to Timişu de Jos (on the rail line from Sinaia to Braşov) in four hours. Otherwise hike back down to Poiana Braşov via Cabana Postăvarul in under two hours. A direct 9km road links Poiana Braşov to Râşnov, a pleasant downhill walk.

The Centrul de Echitaţie, (☎ 262 161), 300m down the road to Braşov, has **horse riding** for US$7 per hour between 10 am and 6 pm. The trails here are stunning. Winter **sleigh rides** are US$5 an hour.

You can use the sauna and swimming pool at Hotel Alpin for US$8.

If you want to go **skiing**, single-day lift tickets are US$11 and a four/five/six-day pass costs US$40/50/60. Private lessons cost US$15 per hour. Rent skis, boots and poles from either the ski school at the tourist centre or its hotel reps for US$12 per day; cross-country skis are US$10 per day.

Places to Stay & Eat

The cheapest hotel is the *Poiana Ursului* (☎ 252 216), next to the tourist village. Double/triple rooms with shared bath are US$14/19. The 66-room *Hotel Caraiman* (☎/fax 262 061) has single/double rooms with private bath for US$14/20. Next door, the *Piatra Mare* (☎ 262 226) charges US$32/55 for a single/double. Close by is *Hotel Şoimul* (☎ 262 111) with 107 doubles costing US$23. Most travel agencies in Braşov take bookings for hotels in Poiana Braşov.

The *Cabana Cristianul Mare* at 1690m offers beds in shared rooms at US$3 per person. This large wooden chalet and the attached restaurant are open throughout the year, except for a few weeks in November. Fifteen minutes downhill from Cristianul Mare is the calmer *Cabana Postăvarul* (☎ 186 356), at 1585m. It also has shared rooms at US$3 per person.

Private rooms in local villas are arranged by the tourist centre for about US$20 a night.

PREJMER & HĂRMAN

Prejmer (Taertlauer) is an unspoiled Saxon town with a picturesque 15th-century **citadel** surrounding the 13th-century **Gothic church** in its centre. The 275 small cells on four levels lining the inner citadel wall were intended to house the local population during sieges. It makes an interesting side trip from Braşov. Make a day of it by catching a train south to Hărman before returning to Braşov.

Hărman (Honigburg) is a small Saxon village with a 16th-century citadel at its centre. Inside the thick walls is a weathered **clock tower** and a **15th-century church**. The colourful houses facing the main square are typical of the Saxon era, with large rounded doors and few windows. Like Prejmer, rural Hărman hasn't changed that much since the 19th century.

Getting There & Away

From Braşov trains leave for Ilieni (the station closest to Prejmer Citadel) at 7.55 am and 12.23, 1.20 and 4.05 pm. The 14km trip takes 20 minutes. As you arrive at Ilieni look for the tall tower of the citadel church, to the right (south) of the railway line. Walk south on Str Nouă for about 500m, then left on Str Alexandru Ioan Cuza, which you follow to the end. Turn left to reach Str Şcolii on the right. The citadel is straight ahead.

From Ilieni trains leave for Hărman and Braşov at 9.13 am and 1.52, 4.30, 5.33 and 9.42 pm. If you decide to visit Hărman, walk 200m north-east from its station, turn left, cross the highway and continue straight for 2km to the centre of town.

SIGHIŞOARA
☎ 065

Sighişoara (Schässburg in German, Segesvár in Hungarian), birthplace of Vlad Ţepeş, is a perfectly preserved medieval town in beautiful hilly countryside. Eleven towers stand along Sighişoara's intact city walls, inside which are sloping cobblestone streets lined with 16th-century burgher houses and untouched churches. All trains between Bucharest and Budapest (via Oradea) pass through here, as do several trains a day from Braşov. Many readers have written to us saying Sighişoara was their favourite town in Romania.

Orientation

Follow Str Gării south from the train station to the Soviet war memorial, where you turn left to the large Orthodox church. Cross the Târnava Mare River on the footbridge here and take Str Morii to the left, then keep going all the way up to Piaţa Hermann Oberth and the old town. Many of the facilities you'll want to use are found along a short stretch of Str 1 Decembrie.

Information

Tourist Offices Steaua Agenţie de Turism, Str 1 Decembrie 10, arranges private rooms and has information on weekly buses to Hungary and Germany. It is open on weekdays from 9 am to 5 pm and Saturday from 9 am to 2 pm.

Money Change travellers cheques and get Visa/MasterCard cash advances at BANCOREX, Str 1 Decembrie 39, open weekdays from 8.30 am to 2 pm, or at Bancă Agricola, Str Justitiei 7, which is open weekdays from 8 am to noon.

The currency exchange inside Steaua Agenţie de Turism is open weekdays from 9 am to 5 pm and Saturday from 9 am to 1 pm. The IDM exchange on Piaţa Hermann Oberth gives cash advances on Visa/MasterCard weekdays from 9 am to 6 pm.

Post & Communications The telephone centre in the main post office on Piaţa Hermann Oberth is open daily from 7 am to 8.30 pm.

Left Luggage The left-luggage office is on the main platform at the train station (open 24 hours).

Things to See

The first tower you reach above Piaţa Hermann Oberth is the massive **clock tower** on Piaţa Muzeului (the 1648 clock still keeps time). The 14th-century tower is now a **museum** (closed Monday) with a good collection of WWI-era photographs, a scale model of the town and a superb view from the walkway on top. Next to the tower is the 15th-century **Biserica Mănăstirii** (Monastery Church), which has a collection of Oriental rugs hanging on each side of the nave. Unfortunately, it is usually closed.

Across Piaţa Muzeului is the house where Vlad Ţepeş (the Impaler) was born in 1431; it's now a restaurant. Also known as Draculea because he was the son of Vlad Dracul (the Dragon), Vlad Ţepeş became a Wallachian prince who led Romanian resistance against Ottoman expansion in the 15th century.

A house between the restaurant and the clock tower contains a **museum** with antique firearms and a small Dracula exhibition, though at the time of writing it was closed for no obvious reason.

Piaţa Cetăţii, surrounded by fine old houses, is the heart of old Sighişoara. Turn left up Str Şcolii from the square to the 172 steps of the **covered stairway** (1642). This leads to the 14th-century **schoolhouse** and the Gothic **Bergkirche** (1345), undergoing a DM5 million restoration paid for by the city of Munich. Behind the hill, along the fortress wall, is the old German **cemetery**.

Places to Stay

Camping You can camp on a hill above the town, but it's a stiff half-hour hike up from the train station. Walk east along the train tracks to a bridge, then cross the tracks and turn left onto a road leading up. At the end of this road is the *Dealul Gării Restaurant* (☎ 771 046), where you can camp for US$3 or rent a bungalow for US$10 a double.

There's a better camping ground at Hula Daneş (☎ 771 052), 4km out of town on the road to Mediaş; 11 buses a day marked 'Cris' travel here from the *autogară* (bus terminal) beside the train station. Bungalows cost US$9 a double.

Private Rooms The *Steau Agenţie de Turism*, Str 1 Decembrie 10, arranges rooms in private homes starting at US$5 per person. Advance notice is preferred.

Hostels Run by a local student, *Bobby's Hostel* (☎ 772 232), Str Take Ionescu 18, is open between 15 June and 1 September only and based in the technical school dormitory. Double rooms cost US$6 and a bed in a dormitory is US$5. Hot water runs between 9 and 10 am and 8 and 9 pm in the shared bathrooms. It's a 25-minute walk from the train station, but Bobby will meet backpackers at the station. The reception is in the building behind the Grupul Şcoala de Industrie Uşoar.

Hotels The best deal is the small, clean *Hotel Chic* (☎ 775 901), Str Libertăţii 44, directly opposite the train station with doubles and shared bath for US$10. Its sign reads 'Non-Stop Hotel Restaurant'.

ROMANIA

SIGHIŞOARA

PLACES TO STAY
3 Hotel Chic
15 Hotel Steaua
31 Bobby's Hostel

PLACES TO EAT
8 Hermes Fast Food
11 Alimentara
12 Pizza 4 Amici
13 Pizza 4 Amici
19 Pizzeria Perla
21 P & I
25 Restaurantul Cetatea
27 Boema

OTHER
1 Train Station
2 Bus Station
4 Market
5 Soviet War Memorial
6 Saint Treime
   Orthodox Church
7 Black Box Disco
9 Cinema Lumina
10 BANCOREX
14 Grădină de Vară Disco
16 Steaua Agenţie de Turism
17 Agenţie de Voiaj CFR
18 Main Post Office &
   Telephone Centre
20 IDM Currency Exchange
22 Clock Tower & Museum
23 Biserica Mănăstirii
24 Collection of
   Medieval Arms
26 Roman Catholic Church
28 Church on the Hill
29 Cemetery
30 Bancă Agricola

The **Hotel Steaua** (☎ 771 594; fax 771 932), Str 1 Decembrie 12, is a comfortable two-star place. It charges US$18/23/30 for a single/double/triple with bath (US$14/19/25 without). breakfast included.

Hotel Rex (☎ 166 615) is a nice, modern hotel 1km east of the old town at Str Dumbravei 18, off Str Mihai Viteazul. All 24 double rooms with bath and cable TV cost US$24, including breakfast (Visa/Master-Card accepted).

A 20-minute walk (or drive) from the centre through a charming rural neighbourhood is

Motel Poeniţa (☎ 772 739), Str Dimitrie Cantemir 24. It's a large new villa with a restaurant and small outdoor pool. Double rooms with bath and TV are US$20, including breakfast.

Places to Eat

Dracula freaks can dine at **Restaurantul Cetatea**, in Vlad Dracula's former house in the citadel. There's a good restaurant upstairs and a *berarie* (pub) downstairs.

Boema, in a courtyard off Str Şcolii, serves pizza and pastries and has the only outdoor dining in the citadel.

Popular *Ristorante Pizzeria 4 Amici* has two outlets: one at Str Morii 7 and another at Str Octavian Goga 12. Both have outside tables and are open from noon to midnight.

Pizzeria Perla on Piaţa Hermann Oberth has a good selection of pizza, pasta, soups and cutlets; it's open daily until 11 pm in summer (9 pm in winter).

P & I is a large, terrace pâtisserie and café above the park at Piaţa Hermann Oberth 7; it's open from 10 to 2 am.

Hermes Fast Food, Str 1 Decembrie 54, serves burgers daily from 8 am to 10 pm.

The daily *market* off Str Tîrnavei has a good selection of fruit, vegetables and cheeses. There is a large *alimentara* (supermarket) on the corner of Str Podului and Str Morii.

Entertainment

Grădină de Vară disco is down the alley and through the iron gates under the archway at Str 1 Decembrie 8, near the Hotel Steaua. It's open until 2 am. The *Black Box* disco at Str Horea Teculescu 35 is more upmarket.

Small *Cinema Lumina*, Str 1 Decembrie at Şoseaua Mihai Viteazul, shows films in their original language (usually English).

Getting There & Away

The Agenţie de Voiaj CFR (☎ 771 820) on Str 1 Decembrie 2 sells domestic and international train tickets weekdays from 7.30 am to 7.30 pm. All trains between Bucharest (via Braşov) and Cluj-Napoca stop at Sighişoara. For Sibiu (95km) you must change trains at Mediaş or Copşa Mică.

Buses from the bus station (☎ 771 260), adjacent to the train station, include two to Sibiu (92km) and one to Făgăraş (86km). The Steaua Agenţie de Turism has information on weekly buses to Hungary and Germany.

SIBIU
☎ 069

Beautiful Sibiu (population 91,000) is just far enough off the beaten track to be spared the tourist tide that occasionally engulfs Braşov. Founded in the 12th century on the site of the former Roman village of Cibinium, Sibiu (Hermannstadt to the German Saxons, Nagyszében to Hungarians) has always been one of the leading cities of Transylvania. De-stroyed by the Tatars in 1241, the town was later surrounded by strong walls that enabled the citizens to resist the Turks. Under the Habsburgs from 1703 to 1791 and again from 1849 to 1867, Sibiu served as the seat of the Austrian governors of Transylvania. Much remains from this colourful history, especially in the old town, which is one of the largest and best preserved in Romania. Sibiu is also a gateway to the Făgăraş Mountains and has shops that sell hiking gear and trail maps.

Orientation
The adjacent bus and train stations are near the centre of town. Exit the station and stroll up Str General Magheru four blocks to Piaţa Mare, the historic centre.

Information
Tourist Offices The tourist desks in the lobbies of the Bulevard and Împăratul Romanilor hotels can answer basic questions but can't arrange private rooms. The Automobil Clubul Român (ACR; ☎ 447 359), Str General Vasile Milea 13, is two blocks east of Hotel Continental.

Money There are IDM exchanges giving cash advance on Visa/MasterCard at Piaţa Mică 9, Str Papiu Ilarian 12, and Parcul Tineretului 20; all are open weekdays from 8 am to 8 pm and Saturday from 9 am to 2 pm. There are also currency exchanges inside the Bulevard and Împăratul Romanilor hotels.

BANCOREX, Str Tribunei 6, near Hotel Bulevard, changes travellers cheques and arranges Visa/MasterCard cash advances. It is open on weekdays from 8.30 am to 2 pm.

Bancă Comercială Română, Str Nicolae Bălcescu 11, changes travellers cheques, gives cash advances and has an outside ATM; it's open weekdays from 8.30 am to noon.

Post & Communications The main post office on Str Mitropoliei is open weekdays from 7 am to 8 pm. Sibiu's telephone centre, Str Bălcescu 13, is open daily from 7 am to 7 pm.

You can send email and access the Internet at PVD Net-Group, Str Bălcescu 5, through the courtyard. Access for 30 minutes/one hour is US$1/1.20; it's open weekdays from 9 am to 6 pm.

ROMANIA

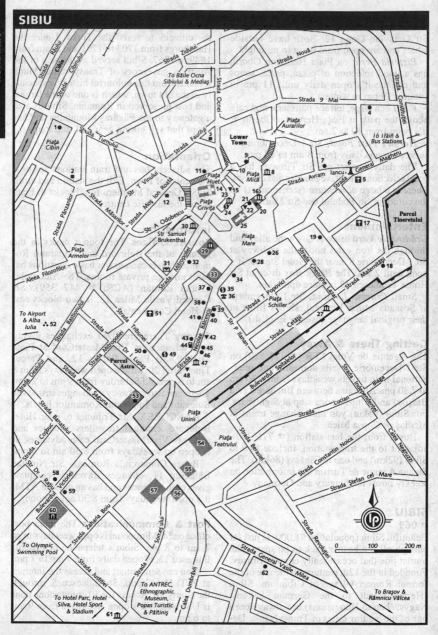

SIBIU

To Băile Ocna
Sibiului & Mediaş

Lower
Town

Piaţa Cibin

Piaţa Turnului

Piaţa Aurarilor

Train &
Bus Stations

Parcul
Tineretului

To Airport
& Alba
Iulia

Piaţa Huet

Piaţa Griviţa

Str Samuel
Brukenthal

Piaţa Armelor

Piaţa Mare

Piaţa Mică

Piaţa Schiller

Piaţa Popovici

Parcul
Astra

Piaţa Unirii

Piaţa Teatrului

To Olympic
Swimming Pool

To Hotel Parc, Hotel
Silva, Hotel Sport
& Stadium

To ANTREC,
Ethnographic
Museum,
Popas Turistic
& Păltiniş

To Braşov &
Râmnicu Vâlcea

0   100   200 m

PLACES TO STAY		13	Staircase Passage		39	Magazin Centrală
2	Hotel Halemadero	14	Evangelical Church		40	Agenţie de Teatrală
3	Hotel La Podul Minciunilor	16	Council Tower &		41	Librărie Humanitas
12	Pensiune Leu		History Museum		43	Trans-Europa Travel Agency
33	Hotel Împăratul Romanilor	17	Franciscan Church		44	Scorpion Bar
53	Hotel Bulevard	18	Haller Bastion		45	Cinema Pacea
56	Hotel Continental	19	Philharmonic & Art Café		46	Librărie Mihai Eminescu
		21	Librărie Thausib		47	Art Gallery
PLACES TO EAT		23	Franz Binder Museum of		49	BANCOREX
15	Domar Cofetărie & Patisserie		World Ethnology		50	Agenţie de Turism Păltiniş
20	La Turn	24	IDM Currency Exchange		51	Orthodox Cathedral
22	Dori's	25	Catholic Cathedral		52	Soldisch Bastion
42	Restaurant Mara	26	Haller's House		54	Radu Stancu State Theatre
48	Restaurant Bumita	27	Natural History Museum		55	Magazinal Dumbrava
		28	Librărie Dacia Traian		57	Disco Bar Mega Vox;
OTHER		29	Brunkenthal Museum			Casă de da Cultură
1	Market	30	Primaria Municipiului &			(Culture House)
4	Mihu Reisen Travel Agency		City History Museum		58	University, German &
5	Ursuline Church	31	Main Post Office			American Libraries
6	Statue of Nicolaus Olahus	32	House where Avram		59	University, British &
7	SurMont Sports;		Iancu stayed			Romanian-American
	Boua Bikes Club	34	PVD Net-Group			Libraries
8	Pharmaceutical Museum	35	Bancă Comercială Română		60	Palace of Justice
9	Artist's House	36	Telephone Centre		61	Museum of Hunting
10	Iron (Liars') Bridge	37	Agenţie de Voiaj CFR			Weapons & Trophies
11	Staircase Tower	38	TAROM		62	Automobil Clubul Român

Travel Agencies The CFR office, Str Nicolae Bălcescu 6, next to the Împăratul Romanilor Hotel, is open weekdays from 10 am to 6 pm.

Bookshops The Librărie Dacia Traian, Piaţa Mare 7, has English-language novels, postcards and some maps. Librărie Thausib, Piaţa Mică 3, also has English books.

Left Luggage The left-luggage office at the train station is at the western end of the main platform near track 1 (open 24 hours).

Things to See & Do

Central Sibiu is a perfectly preserved medieval monument and the best way to begin your visit is by strolling along Str Nicolae Bălcescu and Piaţa Mare, the main square. The old council tower (1588), now the **History Museum**, overlooks the square with colourful houses and guild halls; climb to the top for a superb view (closed Monday).

Walk through the piaţa past the baroque **Catholic cathedral** (1728) to the **Brukenthal**

Museum at No 4-5, the oldest and finest art gallery in Romania. Founded in 1817, the museum is in the palace (1785) of Baron Samuel Brukenthal, former governor of Transylvania. Along with the paintings, it contains excellent archaeological and folk-art collections. It's open daily, except Monday, from 9 am to 5 pm.

Just west along Str Samuel Brukenthal at Str Mitropoliei 2 is the **Primaria Municipiului** (1470), now the City History Museum.

Nearby on Piaţa Huet is the Gothic **Evangelical Church** (1300-1520), its great five-pointed tower visible from afar. Note the four magnificent baroque funerary monuments on the upper nave and the organ with 6002 pipes (1772). The tomb of Mihnea Vodă cel Rău (Prince Mihnea the Bad), son of Vlad Ţepeş (Dracula), is in the closed-off section behind the organ. This prince, who ruled Wallachia from 1507 to 1510, was murdered in the church square after attending a service in March 1510. Don't miss the splendid fresco of the Crucifixion (1445) in the sanctuary. The church is open weekdays from

ROMANIA

9 am to 1 pm; organ concerts are held at 6 pm on Wednesday (check the schedule outside for dates).

To reach the lower town from here, walk down the 13th-century **Staircase Passage**, on the opposite side of the church from where you entered, or cross the photogenic **Iron Bridge** (1859) on nearby Piaţa Mică to the steep stairway. It is nicknamed 'Liars' Bridge', because it's thought that it will collapse if anyone tells a lie while standing on it.

Also on Piaţa Mică are the **Pharmaceutical Museum**, with a collection of antique drug jars and medical tools, and the **Artists' House**, hosting various temporary exhibitions.

Walk south-west from Piaţa Mică, along Str Mitropoliei to the **Orthodox cathedral** (1906), a monumental building styled after the Hagia Sofia in Istanbul. Next, turn left onto Strada Tribunei and follow it across Piaţa Unirii to Str Cetăţii, turning left to begin a pleasant walk north-east along a narrow park and the 16th-century **city walls** and watch towers. At the far end is the **Haller Bastion** (1551) and the **Natural History Museum** dating from 1849. Take a narrow street on your left to return to Piaţa Mare.

If you have an extra afternoon, it's worth taking in the **Museum of Popular Techniques** in Dumbrava Park, south of the city centre (take trolleybus No T1 from the train station). It's open from May to October daily, except Monday, between 10 am and 5 pm. Many authentic rural buildings and houses have been reassembled in the park to create an **open-air ethnographic museum**. At the adjacent **zoo** you can hire a boat and row around the lake.

Places to Stay

Camping There are two near Sibiu. The closest camping ground is *Popas Turistic* (☎ 422 831), beside the Hanul Dumbrava Restaurant 4km south-west of the town centre (take trolleybus No T1 from the train station direct to the site). There are 204 rooms in worn-out cabins at US$11 for a single or double. Pitch your tent on the shady lawn for US$4.50. There's plenty of space and it's open from June to September.

Fourteen km north of Sibiu on the railway line to Copşa Mică is Băile Ocna Sibiului,

with a large *camping ground* in the forest. The site is next to the station and all trains stop here. The many natural pools and geological curiosities around Ocna Sibiului make it a popular bathing resort.

Private Rooms ANTREC (☎ 220 179), Calea Dumbrăvii 120, arranges rooms in private houses for about US$10 a night, including breakfast.

Hotels Most hotels are in two main areas: the city centre and south of the centre.

City Centre On the first side street below the Iron Bridge is *Hotel La Podul Minciunilor* (☎ 217 259), a small three-room pension at Str Azilului 1 (US$16/18 a single/double). Below Piaţa Huet, just off Str Turnului is the *Pensiune Leu* (☎ 218 392), Str Moş Ion Roată 6, with rooms for US$5/9. The proprietors speak German. Similar is the three-room *Hotel Halemadero* (☎ 212 509), Str Măsarilor 10, which overlooks a pleasant garden and patio and charges US$16/22 for a single/double. The adjacent bar is a friendly hangout.

Sibiu's most colourful hotel is the three-star *Hotel Împăratul Romanilor* (☎ 216 500; fax 213 270), Str Bălcescu 4. Founded in 1555, it took its name in 1773 after a visit by Habsburg emperor Josef II. It has two room grades (A and B), each with a private shower/bath and colour TV; singles/doubles range from US$28/32 to US$46/50, breakfast included (Visa and MasterCard accepted).

Another appealing old place is the two-star *Hotel Bulevard* (☎ 216 060), Piaţa Unirii 2-4, a worthwhile splurge at US$20/31, breakfast included.

The nearby 15-storey *Hotel Continental* (☎ 218 100), Calea Dumbrăvii 2-4, caters for business travellers. Every room has a direct-dial phone and colour TV. The cost is US$44/72, breakfast included.

South of the City Centre There's a cluster of hotels next to the municipal stadium, a few blocks south of Hotel Continental (a taxi from the train station costs US$1.50). The largest is the grim, eight-storey *Hotel Parc* (☎ 424 455), Str Scoala de Înot 3, which charges US$11/17.

A better choice is *Hotel Silva* (☎ 442 141; fax 217 945), Str Aleea Eminescu 1, 30m to the right of Hotel Parc. Rooms in this modern three-storey building overlook a tranquil park. You'll pay US$17/23.

Much better value than either of these, though not as comfortable, is the old two-storey *Hotel Sport* (☎ 422 472), Str Octavian Goga 2, on the eastern side of Hotel Parc. Rooms are US$4 per person, but it's often fully booked by sporting groups.

Places to Eat

Sibiu has a shortage of private restaurants, which means you may eat more than one meal in a hotel restaurant. The one in the *Împăratul Romanilor* is rather stuffy, but several readers have commented that they found the food superb. The *Restaurant Bumita* farther down Str Bălcescu is cheaper, more local and has nice wooden tables with red tablecloths on the street. *Restaurant Mara*, Str Bălcescu 21, is a small, quiet bistro with an English-language menu. Everything here, except the spaghetti, is good.

La Turn, next to the old council tower on Piaţa Mare, has a terrace overlooking the square and serves traditional Romanian cuisine, but it can get noisy from traffic moving through the tower.

Dori's at Piaţa Mica 14 is a cheap pâtisserie serving only freshly baked breads and yoghurt; it's open weekdays from 8 am to 8 pm and Saturday from 10 am to 8 pm. Across the square is the trendy *Domar Cofetărie & Patisserie* with a great selection of cakes and pastries, and excellent coffee.

There are several small bakeries and food shops along Str Bălcescu. Stock up on vegetables and fruit at the *market* on Piaţa Cibin, north-east of Str Măsarilor near Hotel Halemadero.

Entertainment

Events at the *Philharmonic* on Str Filharmonicii off Str Magheru, and the *Radu Stanca State Theatre*, Blvd Spitelor 2-4, just off Piaţa Unirii, are worth seeing. Buy tickets at the Agenţie de Teatrală, Str Bălcescu 17, weekdays from 10 am to 1 pm and 5 to 6.15 pm.

Disco-Bar Meridan inside the Cinema Tineratului complex is an alternative cellar club with blues and funky jazz. The bar is open 24 hours, the disco from 10 pm to 5 am. *Disco Bar Mega Vox*, downstairs in the Casă de Cultură in front of Hotel Continental (entry from the rear of the building), is popular on summer weekends.

On Str Bălcescu, opposite the Prima food shop, is the *Scorpion Bar* with blacked-out windows and a dark, smoky atmosphere; it's open from noon to midnight.

Cinema Tineretului, adjoining the hip Bar Meridan on Str Alexandru Odobescu, is an auditorium-cum-bar with sofas and coffee tables from which you can relax over a beer while watching your favourite Hollywood film; it has four screenings daily. The more conventional *Cinema Pacea*, Str Bălcescu 29, has five screenings daily.

Things to Buy

SurMont Sports, Str Avram Iancu 25, has tents, climbing ropes and water bottles, plus a good selection of hiking maps (some for sale, some for reference only). It's open weekdays from 9 am to 5 pm.

Getting There & Away

Air TAROM has morning and evening flights to Bucharest on Monday, Wednesday and Friday. Single/return tickets (US$25/50) are sold at TAROM (☎ 211 157), Str Bălcescu 10, weekdays from 8 am to 7 pm and Saturday from 8 am to noon. TAROM runs a shuttle bus from its office to/from the airport, 5km west of the centre.

Train The Agenţie de Voiaj CFR office (☎ 216 441) at Blvd Nicolae Bălcescu 6 is open weekdays from 7 am to 7.30 pm. The train station is at the eastern end of Str General Magheru on Piaţa 1 Decembrie.

From Sibiu there are seven daily trains to Braşov, one express train to Cluj-Napoca, one express train to Timişoara, seven local trains to Copşa Mică, five express trains to Bucharest and one overnight train to Iaşi. For Sighişoara, you have to change at Copşa Mică or Mediaş.

Bus The bus station is opposite the train station. There's a daily service to Cluj-Napoca and two daily to Sighişoara.

Mihu Reisen (☎ 211 744), Str 9 Mai 52, has buses to Germany. It's open weekdays from 8 am to 8 pm. Touring Eurolines (☎ 218 100), inside the Hotel Continental, books private buses to Germany, too. Trans-Europa (☎ 211 296), Str Bălcescu 41, sells bus tickets to Western Europe.

THE FĂGĂRAŞ MOUNTAINS

In summer a small but steady stream of back-packers descend on the Făgăraş Mountains, a section of the Carpathian Mountains in the centre of Romania. They soon get lost in the alpine glory of Făgăraş, the most spectacular hiking area in the country.

The main drawback is getting there: from train stations along the Sibiu-Braşov line, most trailheads are 8 to 15km south, poorly serviced by bus and difficult to hitch to (few cars can accommodate a group of hikers and their packs).

To hike the Făgăraş you must be in good physical shape and have warm clothing and sturdy boots. The trails are well marked, but keep the altitude in mind and be prepared for cold and rain at any time.

From November to early May these mountains are snow covered; August and September are the best months. Basic food is available at the cabanas but carry a supply of biscuits and your water bottle. You'll meet lots of other hikers eager to tell you of their adventures, and with a good map you'll soon know exactly where to go. SurMont Sports in Sibiu sells hiking maps, or try tourist offices and reception desks at hotels.

Routes & Places to Stay

The easiest access is from Sibiu, and local trains on the Făgăraş line to Braşov pass many starting points.

One of the best places to get off is Gară Sebeş Olt (24km from Sibiu), from where you can hike to *Cabana Suru* (1450m, 60 beds) in about five hours via Sebeşu de Sus (450m). The first leg is rather boring, but the

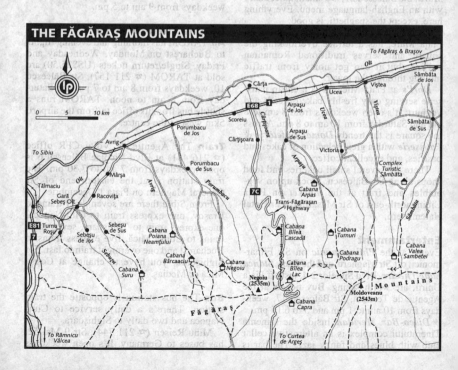

scenery is stunning once you start the ascent. The next morning head for **Cabana Negoiu** (1546m, 170 beds), seven hours east of Cabana Suru across peaks up to 2306m high.

If you've had enough, hike seven hours downhill to the railway line at Porumbacu de Jos (41km from Sibiu). Otherwise, eight gruelling hours east of Cabana Negoiu is *Cabana Bîlea Lac* (2034m, 170 beds), where there's a cable car down to *Cabana Bîlea Cascadă* (1234m, 63 beds) and to a road leading out of the mountains. On this section you will pass Mt Negoiu (2535m), the second-highest peak in Romania. If you decide to end your trip here by hitching or hiking north from Bîlea Cascadă to the railway at Cârţa (51km from Sibiu), check out the ruins of a fortified 13th-century Cistercian monastery about 1km north of Cârţa station.

A seven-hour hike east of Cabana Bîlea Lac is *Cabana Podragu* (2136m, 100 beds), which you can use as a base to climb Mt Moldoveanu (2543m), Romania's highest peak. It's a tough uphill climb, but the views from the summit are unbeatable. From Cabana Podragu you can descend to the railway at Arpaşu de Jos (420m) or Ucea, 59km from Sibiu, in a day.

CLUJ-NAPOCA
☎ 064
Cut in two by the Someşul Mic River, Cluj-Napoca (population 322,000) is as Hungarian as it is Romanian and known as Klausenburg to the Germans and Kolozsvár to the Hungarians. Its position near the middle of Transylvania made it a crossroads, which explains its role as an educational and industrial centre. The old Roman name of Napoca has been added to the city's official title to emphasise its Daco-Roman origin, but it is simply referred to as Cluj.

The history of Cluj-Napoca goes back to Dacian times. In 124 AD, during the reign of Emperor Hadrian, Napoca attained municipal status and Emperor Marcus Aurelius elevated it to a colony. Documented references to the medieval town date back to 1183. German merchants arrived in the 12th century and after the Tatar invasion of 1241 the medieval earthen walls of *castrenses de Clus* were rebuilt in stone. From 1791 to 1848 and again

after the union with Hungary in 1867, Cluj-Napoca served as the capital of Transylvania.

Because Cluj is a major university town it has a relaxed, inviting atmosphere, fine architecture and several good museums. It's well worth a few days visit. Nearby Turda Gorge is also worth a look.

Orientation
The train station is 1.5km north of the city centre, so walk left out of the station, buy a ticket at the red Coca-Cola kiosk across the street and catch tram No 101 or a trolleybus south down Str Horea. On the trolleybus get off immediately after crossing the river; on tram No 101 go two stops, then walk south until you cross the river.

Cluj-Napoca has two bus stations. Autogară No 2 (with buses to Hungary) is over the bridge from the train station, north of town. Autogară No 1 is on Str Aurel Vlaicu on the far eastern side of town (no left luggage). Trolleybus No 4 connects Autogară No 1 to the centre of town and the train station.

Information
Tourist Offices The Transylvanian Ecological Club (☎ 197 399) at Blvd Eroilor 2, open weekdays from 9 am to 6 pm, arranges tours and activities in rural areas of Transylvania and publishes the *EcoForum* magazine.

The Automobil Clubul Român (☎ 116 503) is at Str Memorandumului 27.

Money Change travellers cheques and get Visa/MasterCard cash advances at BANCOREX on Str Gheorghe Doja 8 and at Piaţa Unirii 10, which is open on weekdays from 9 am to 2 pm and Saturday from 10.30 am to 1 pm. The Str Doja bank has an outside ATM, as does Bank Post, just across the street.

Bancă Comercială Română, Piaţa Unirii 7, also gives cash advances and cashes travellers cheques on weekdays from 8.30 am to 12.30 pm.

Black-market moneychangers lurk around Piaţa Unirii, Hotel Continental and the Agenţie de Turism Km0. Most change forints for lei and vice versa, but be extremely careful (scams are common).

Post & Communications The telephone centre is behind the main post office, Str Doja 33; both are open weekdays from 7 am to 8 pm and Saturday from 7 am to 1 pm. A smaller telephone office at Piaţa Unirii 5 is open weekdays from 7 am to 9 pm.

Travel Agencies Consus Travel (☎ 192 928; fax 193 044), at Str Georghe Sincai 15 books hotel rooms and arranges trips to Maramureş and the Apusini Mountains; it's open from 9 am to 5 pm. Both Visa and MasterCard are accepted.

Bookshops Librărie Universiţăţii, on Piaţa Unirii opposite the Continental Hotel, stocks English-language novels. Newsstands on Piaţa Unirii often sell current copies of *Newsweek* and the *Economist*. The English-language newspaper *Nine O'Clock* is harder to find.

Left Luggage The left-luggage office inside the train station is near the restaurant (open 24 hours).

Things to See
St Michael's Church, a 15th-century Gothic hall church with a neo-Gothic tower (1859),

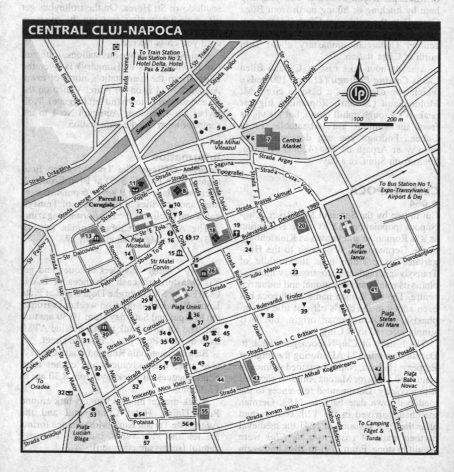

CENTRAL CLUJ-NAPOCA

towers impressively above Piața Unirii. Flanking it on the south is a huge **equestrian statue** (1902) of the famous Hungarian king Matthias Corvinus (ruled 1458-90). On the eastern side of the square is the excellent **National Art Museum** (closed Monday and Tuesday) in the baroque Banffy Palace (1785). A **pharmaceutical museum** is diagonally across the street at Str Doja 1, on the site of Cluj-Napoca's first apothecary (1573). It is open from 10 am to 4 pm.

Strada Matei Corvin leads from the northwestern corner of the square to **Corvinus' birthplace** (in 1440) at number 6 (closed to the public). A block farther is the beautifully decorated **Franciscan Church**.

To the west and left on Piața Muzeului is the interesting **History Museum of Transylvania** (closed Monday), which has been open since 1859. Though none of the captions are in English it's still worth walking through. An **ethnographic museum** with Transylvanian folk costumes and farm implements is at Str Memorandumului 21.

South at Str Republicii 42 is the fragrant **Botanical Gardens**, which includes green-

houses, a museum and a Japanese garden. In summer allow several hours to explore it.

The **Tailors' Bastion** on Piața Baba-Novac was built in the 1550s by the local tailors' guild; it was restored in 1982. The history museum inside is closed indefinitely.

For an overall view of Cluj-Napoca, climb up the steps behind Hotel Astoria to the **citadel** (1715), which sounds more impressive than it is. After climbing all those steps, you can stop for a beer on the terrace at Hotel Transilvania.

Places to Stay

Camping Up in the hills, 7km south of Cluj-Napoca is *Camping Făget* (☎ 196 234). Open from mid-May to mid-October, the site's 143 bungalows go for US$5/7 a double/triple. It's US$2/3/5 a single/double/triple to camp with a tent. The summer-only restaurant closes at 8 pm. To reach the camping site take bus No 35 from Piața Mihai Viteazul south down Calea Turzii to the end of the line. From here it's a marked 2km hike to the site.

CENTRAL CLUJ-NAPOCA

PLACES TO STAY		
10	Hotel Vlădeasa	
20	Hotel Victoria	
25	Hotel Central-Melody	
50	Hotel Continental	

PLACES TO EAT	
6	McDonald's
9	Restaurant Specializat
23	Boema Grădină de Vară
24	Hubertus
38	P&P Ristorante
39	Primăvara Pizza
51	Continental Cafe
52	Napoca 15

OTHER	
1	Synagogue
2	Cinema Favorit
3	Cinema Republicii
4	TAROM
5	Agenție de Voiaj CFR
7	Complex Commercial Mihai Viteazul

8	Central Department Store & Cafe Mihai Viteazul
11	Main Post Office; Telephone Centre
12	Franciscan Church
13	History Museum of Transylvania
14	Birthplace of Matthias Corvinus
15	Pharmaceutical Museum
16	Bank Post
17	BANCOREX
18	24-Hour Grocery
19	Hungarian Reform Church
21	Orthodox Cathedral
22	Cinema Victoria
26	National Art Museum
27	St Michael's Church
28	Harley Davidson Club
29	Diesel Bar
30	Ethnographic Museum
31	Automobil Clubul Român (ACR)
32	Post Office

33	Consus Travel
34	Pharmacy
35	BANCOREX; Agenție de Tourism KMO
36	Statue of Matthias Corvinus
37	Archeological Dig
40	Agenție de Teatrală
41	National Theatre; Opera House
42	Tailors' Bastion
43	Stat Philharmonic
44	Babeș-Bolyai University
45	Transylvanian Ecological Club
46	Telephone Office
47	Bancă Comercială Român
48	University Bookshop
49	Cinema de Artă Română
53	Student Club
54	Laundrette
55	German Cultural Centre; American Library; US Embassy Information Bureau
56	British Council Library
57	ANTREC

Private Rooms ANTREC (☎ 215 585) at
Piaţa Avram Iancu 15 arranges rooms in
private houses around Cluj for US$15 a night
(meals extra).

Opération Villages Roumains (☎/fax 420
516) arranges rural accommodation in villages throughout the Cluj district and
Transylvania through its office at Str Groza-
vescu 13. It charges US$10 to $12 a night
with breakfast.

Hostels Between 1 July and 1 September
Hostel Mi-Do (☎/fax 186 616), Str Braşov 2-
4, offers a bed in a dormitory for US$7 a
night, including breakfast. The hostel has
lockers. From the train station take trolleybus
No 3 three stops to Piaţa Cipariu, then walk
south along Str Andrei Mureşanu, then take
the first left along Str Zrínyi Miklós. At the
end of the street turn left onto Str Braşov and
go 50m to the right.

Hotels The five-storey *Hotel Delta* (☎ 132
507), at bus station No 2, across the bridge
from the train station, is convenient and
cheap at US$3 for bed in a shared room with
communal bath.

Opposite the train station *Hotel Pax*
(☎ 136 101), Piaţa Gării 2, is noisy but clean.
Singles/doubles/triples with shared bath are
US$18/33/39. Some 150m east along Str Câii
Ferate – a three-minute walk from the train
station – is the *Hotel Junior* (☎ 432 028)
with simple, modern doubles/singles with
private bath for US$14 per person.

The cheapest option in the city centre is
Hotel Vlădeasa (☎ 194 429), Str Doja 20; it's
good value at US$20/32 without bath, US$38
with bath. The reception is through an
archway adjacent to the Restaurant Vlădeasa.

The renovated *Hotel Central-Melody*
(☎ 197 465), Piaţa Unirii 29, overlooks the
square and charges US$33/21 for a double
with/without bath.

At the elegant old *Continental Hotel*
(☎ 191 441) on the south-western corner of
Piaţa Unirii you'll pay US$17/23 with shared
bath, US$40/60 with private bath.

Places to Eat

P&P Ristorante, Blvd Eroilor 12b, serves
good pizza and breakfast omelettes and meat
dishes. It's open from 10 am until 11 pm.

Primăvara Pizza at Blvd Eroilor 26 has a
terrace and is open weekdays from 8 am to 9
pm, Saturday from 10 am to 9 pm and
Sunday from noon to 8 pm.

Trendy *Napoca 15* has a streetside terrace
at Str Napoca 15. Try its *cascaval pane* (hot
breaded cheese). It's open daily from 9 am to
midnight.

Restaurant Specializat, near Hotel
Vlădeasu on Str Doja, serves hearty portions
of meat, potatoes and soups, spicy meatballs
and breaded cheese. It's open daily from 9
am to 11 pm.

If you want game or quail, head for *Hu-
bertus*, Blvd 21 Decembrie 1989. It has a
small courtyard decorated with hunting
motifs. Cognac is the traditional start to a
meal here. It's closed on Sunday.

Good old *McDonald's* is on Piaţa Mihai
Viteazul; it's open from 7 am to midnight.
For fresh produce, the *central market* is next
door. Str Gheorghe Doja is lined with pastry
and snack vendors. A small *grocery* on the
corner of Str Memorandumului and Str David
Ferenc is open 24 hours.

Cafés The *Boema Grădină de Vară* at Str
Iuliu Maniu 34 is a pleasant terrace café in a
courtyard off the main street. It has live
music some evenings and is open daily from
10 am to 11 pm. The *Continental Cafe* adjoining the Hotel Continental at Str Napoca 1
has delicious cakes.

Entertainment

Bars & Discos A stylish, young crowd is attracted to *Diesel Bar*, on the western side of
Piaţa Unirii.

Disco Bianco e Negro, in the Clubul Cultural Studenţesc on the corner of stradas
Universităţii and Kogălniceanu, is open after
9 pm from Thursday to Sunday year-round.

The *Student Club*, in the Casă de Cultură
Studenţească on Piaţa Lucian Blaga, hosts
weekly discos during the school year
(October to mid-May); check the notice
board outside for schedules.

Theatre & Classical Music The neo-
baroque *National Theatre* (1906) on Piaţa
Ştefan cel Mare was designed by the famous
Viennese architects Fellner and Hellmer. The

Hungarian State Theatre & Opera is at the northern end of Str Emil Isac, near the river. Also look out for performances at the *puppet theatre* in the courtyard at Blvd Eroilor 8. The Agenţie de Teatrală, Blvd Eroilor 36, sells tickets for most events.

Getting There & Away
Train Buy domestic and international train tickets at the CFR office, Piaţa Mihai Viteazul 20, which is open weekdays only from 7 am to 8 pm. There are express trains from Cluj to Oradea (2½ hours), Sighişoara (three hours), Braşov (five hours), Timişoara (six hours) and Bucharest (eight hours). Through trains run to Iaşi via Gura Humorului and Suceava. For Sibiu you may have to change at Copşa Mică. Sleepers are available to Bucharest.

Bus A Hungarian Volanbus to Budapest leaves from bus station No 2, across the bridge from the train station, three times a week (399km, US$6). Tickets are sold at the bus station.

From bus station No 1 on Str Aurel Vlaicu east of the city centre there are daily buses to Alba Iulia (96km), Sibiu (173km) and other centres.

TURDA
Turda, 30km south-east of Cluj-Napoca, was the seat of the Transylvanian *diet* in the mid-16th century; today this small market town preserves a number of stately baroque and Magyar façades. Yet the reason to visit is strictly practical – to hike or catch a bus to Turda Gorge (Cheile Turzii), 9km west.

Turda Gorge
Turda Gorge is a short but stunning break in the granite mountains south-west of Turda. You can hike the gorge's length in under an hour, so plan on camping for a night or two to explore the surrounding network of marked trails – the map outside the cabana's restaurant details half a dozen different routes.

A good two-hour trek is the red-cross trail through the gorge, then the steep red-dot trail up and over the peak before returning to the cabana.

It's also possible to go all the way from Turda Gorge to Cluj, along the vertical red-stripe trail via Deleni and Camping Făget (on the outskirts of Cluj). This 29km hike will take 10 to 12 hours.

Places to Stay & Eat
Turda's lone hotel is the *Potaissa* (☎ 311 625) on Piaţa Republicii, charging US$14/22 for a single/double. You're better off camping freelance in the grassy valley at the gorge's northern end. You could also camp at noisy *Cabana Cheile Turzii*, at the southern foot of Turda Gorge. It's US$2.50 per tent or US$12 per person for a room in the main building. An on-site *restaurant* serves simple meals.

Getting There & Away
There are three daily buses from Cluj's Piaţa Ştefan cel Mare to Turda (reduced service on weekends). The last bus back from Turda to Cluj leaves about 5.30 pm.

From Turda you can hike to the gorge in 2½ hours. Starting at Piaţa Republicii follow signs for Cîmpeni and, 1km past the village of Mihai Viteazu, turn right at the 'Cheile Turzii' sign. From here it's another 5km. Follow the paved road uphill past the quarry and go left at the fork. If you're driving, do not attempt this steep road after heavy rains.

Shave a few kilometres off the walk by catching a Coroneşti or Cîmpeni-bound bus from Turda's Piaţa Republicii and get off at the turn-off past Mihai Viteazu.

Crişana & Banat

The plains of Crişana and Banat, divided in two by the Mureş River, merge imperceptibly into Yugoslavia's Vojvodina and Hungary's Great Plain. From the late 9th century until the Ottoman conquest in 1552, the territory was under Hungarian rule. In 1699 the Turks relinquished Hungary to Austria, but held onto Banat until their defeat by Habsburg Prince Eugene of Savoy in 1716. In 1718 Banat became part of the Austro-Hungarian empire, after which Swabians from south-western Germany arrived to colonise the region. Until 1918 all these regions were governed jointly as part of the Habsburg Empire.

The Treaty of Trianon in 1920 split the territory among Romania, Hungary and Yugoslavia and set their current borders.

The Hungarian element is still strong throughout Crişana region, especially in architecture. In Banat you'll see the influence of the Swabians, despite the mass exodus of Germans since WWII and the collapse of communism.

Crişana and Banat are the door to Romania, and all trains from Hungary and Yugoslavia pass through one of its gateway cities: Timişoara, Arad and Oradea. They're all good places to stop and get your bearings.

ORADEA
☎ 059

Oradea (population 107,000), only a few kilometres east of the Hungarian border is the seat of Bihor County. It's also the centre of the Crişana region, a fertile plain drained by the Alb, Negru and Repede rivers at the edge of the Carpathian Mountains.

Of all the cities of the old Austro-Hungarian empire, Oradea (Nagyvárad in Hungarian, Grosswardein in German) is probably the one that has best retained its 19th-century elegance. When Oradea was ceded to Romania in 1920, this example of Habsburg majesty became the backwater it remains today, a time capsule for romantics in search of a simpler world. Băile Felix with its hot thermal springs is a suburb. Oradea is a great place to stop and spend your remaining Romanian currency and to prepare yourself for a return to the ruthless west.

Orientation

The train station is a few kilometres north of town; tram Nos 1 and 4 run south from Piaţa Bucureşti (across the road from the station) to Piaţa Unirii on the southern bank of the Crişul Repede River. Tram No 4 also stops at the northern end of Str Republicii – a five-minute walk south to the centre.

The main square north of the river is Piaţa Republicii (also called Piaţa Ferdinand I), a pedestrianised mall just across the bridge from Piaţa Unirii, beginning at the Teatrul de Stat.

Information

Tourist Offices The Agenţie de Turism Crişul (☎ 130 737), next door to Hotel Crişul at Str Libertăţii 8, is open weekdays from 9 am to 4 pm.

The Automobil Clubul Român (ACR; ☎ 130 725), next to BANCOREX at Piaţa Independenţei 31 is open weekdays from 8 am to 3 pm and Saturday from 8 am to 1 pm. Dac Air's office (☎/fax 135 098) at Piaţa Independenţei 47 is open weekdays from 9 am to 7 pm and Saturday from 9 am to noon. It also sells tickets for TAROM, MALEV, JAT, Air France, KLM and British Airways.

Money BANCOREX at Piaţa Independenţei 31 cashes travellers cheques and gives Visa/MasterCard cash advances on weekdays from 8.30 am to 2 pm. Bancă Comercială Română at the southern end of Piaţa Independenţei does the same and has an ATM outside; it is open weekdays from 8.30 am to 6.30 pm and Saturday from 9 am to 1 pm.

Post & Communications The post office at Str Roman Ciorogariu is open weekdays from 8 am to 8 pm. The telephone office is down the alley near the Hotel Parc at Piaţa Republicii 5; it's open daily from 7 am to 9 pm.

Left Luggage The left-luggage office at the train station is beside the restaurant on the main platform and is open 24 hours.

Things to See

Oradea's most imposing sights are on piaţas Unirii and Republicii. On Piaţa Unirii, overlooking the Crişul Repede river is the magnificent yellow **Vulturul Negru** (Black Vulture) hotel and shopping mall dating from 1908. The mall, with its fabulous stained-glass ceiling, links Piaţa Unirii with Str Independenţeii. The **Orthodox church** (1784) on the piaţa is known as the 'Moon church' for a 3m sphere on the tower which shows the phases of the moon. The other churches and civic palaces on this square are an interesting mix of rococo, baroque, Renaissance and Art Nouveau. Listen for the trumpet tune playing from the **Town Hall** every hour.

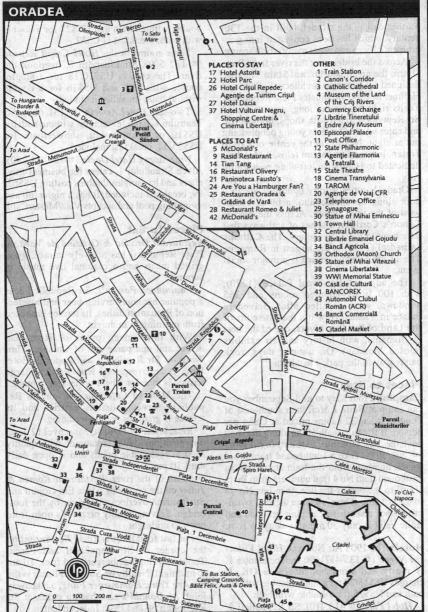

ORADEA

PLACES TO STAY
17 Hotel Astoria
22 Hotel Parc
26 Hotel Crişul Repede;
   Agenţie de Turism Crişul
27 Hotel Dacia
37 Hotel Vultural Negru,
   Shopping Centre &
   Cinema Libertăţii

PLACES TO EAT
5 McDonald's
9 Rasid Restaurant
14 Tian Tang
16 Restaurant Olivery
21 Paninoteca Fausto's
24 Are You a Hamburger Fan?
25 Restaurant Oradea &
   Grădină de Vară
28 Restaurant Romeo & Juliet
42 McDonald's

OTHER
1 Train Station
2 Canon's Corridor
3 Catholic Cathedral
4 Museum of the Land
   of the Cris Rivers
6 Currency Exchange
7 Librărie Tineretului
8 Endre Ady Museum
10 Episcopal Palace
11 Post Office
12 State Philharmonic
13 Agenţie Filarmonia
   & Teatrală
15 State Theatre
18 Cinema Transylvania
19 TAROM
20 Agenţie de Voiaj CFR
23 Telephone Office
29 Synagogue
30 Statue of Mihai Eminescu
31 Town Hall
32 Central Library
33 Librărie Emanuel Gojudu
34 Bancă Agricola
35 Orthodox (Moon) Church
36 Statue of Mihai Viteazul
38 Cinema Libertatea
39 WWI Memorial Statue
40 Casă de Cultură
41 BANCOREX
43 Automobil Clubul
   Român (ACR)
44 Bancă Comercială
   Română
45 Citadel Market

Just east of Piaţa Unirii is **Parcul Central** with the **Casă de Cultură** at its eastern end. Farther east is the **citadel**, built in the 13th century, which has been converted into government offices and is not really worth seeing.

Across the bridge over the river from Piaţa Unirii, the green neoclassical **State Theatre**, designed by Viennese architects Fellner and Hellmer in 1900, dominates Piaţa Republicii. To its right begins the long, pedestrianised Str Republicii, lined with shops, bookstores, and cafés where Oradea's young people hang out at night. Nearby, in the centre of **Parcul Traian**, is a small **museum** (closed Monday) dedicated to Hungarian left-wing poet Endre Ady.

Oradea's other worthy buildings are in a park along Str Stadionului, a block southwest of the train station. Across the road is **Canon's Corridor**, a series of archways that date back to the 18th century. The **Catholic cathedral** (1780) is the largest in Romania. The 11 am Sunday service is a major social event.

The adjacent Episcopal Palace (1770), with 100 fresco-adorned rooms and 365 windows, was modelled after Belvedere Palace in Vienna. Now it's the **Museum of the Land of the Criş Rivers**, one of the best in Romania, with history and art exhibits (closed Monday). On summer days, rock bands play in the park's bandstand.

Places to Stay

Camping From May to mid-September you can camp at **Băile 1 Mai**, 9km south-east of Oradea. It has 32 cabins priced at US$4 per person. If it's full, walk 500m along the road past the bus terminus to **Camping Venus** (☎ 261 507). Take a southbound tram No 4 (black number) from the train station or an eastbound tram No 4 (red number) from Piaţa Unirii to the end of the line, then bus No 15 to the last stop. There's a large thermal swimming pool near these camping grounds and Băile Felix is only 30 minutes away by foot.

Hotels The 1908 Art Nouveau *Hotel Vulturul Negru* (☎ 135 417), Str Independenţei 1, is musty and worn but otherwise OK. It charges US$13/20 for a single/double without bath and US$25 for a double with bath.

Hotel Parc (☎ 418 410), Str Republicii 5, on the pedestrian promenade is friendly, clean and charges US$17/23 for a single/double without bath and US$27 for a double with bath; breakfast is US$2.

Some rooms at the *Hotel Crişul Repede* (☎ 132 509), Str Libertăţii 8, overlook the river. The cost is US$10/18 for a single/double with bath and US$16 for a double without bath, breakfast included.

Two-star *Hotel Astoria* (☎ 131 663), Str Teatrului 1, has a few singles without bath for US$10 or doubles with shower/bath for US$25/34, breakfast included.

Nine-storey *Hotel Dacia* (☎/fax 411 280), Aleea Ştrandului 1, caters for business travellers and has singles/doubles costing US$62/99, breakfast included. It has a nightclub and swimming pool and accepts Visa/MasterCard.

Places to Eat

Restaurant Oradea & Grădină de Vară on Piaţa Republicii has a lovely terrace, good grilled meats and occasional live music in summer.

Paninoteca Fausto's, Str Republicii 3, is a popular hangout serving beer and a selection of Romanian dishes. Its terrace is packed from morning to midnight.

With three menu pages of Romanian dishes and one paragraph of Chinese, *Tian Tang* on Str Republicii and opposite Hotel Parc, is an overpriced letdown. The large terrace is nice for a beer or dessert, though.

The *Minerva Cofetăria*, also on Str Republicii, serves delicious pastries and its terrace is great for people watching.

Restaurant Olivery, Str Moscovei 12, is an unpretentious cellar restaurant with quality food at reasonable prices and is open daily until 10 pm.

South of the river, *Restaurant Romeo & Juliet* on the corner of Aleea Em Gojdiu and Str Română overlooks the river by the footbridge. Serving mainly pizza, it's open from noon to midnight.

For fast food there is *Rasid Restaurant* on the corner of Str Republicii and Parcul Traian, serving hamburgers and fries, 10 am to midnight. Nearby on Str Aurel Lazăr is the hip *Are You a Hamburger Fan?*, a takeaway joint. *McDonald's* also has an outlet at Str Republicii 30 and Piaţa Independenţei.

Entertainment

Cinema *Cinema Libertăţii* in the Vulturul Negru building at Str Independenţei 1 shows films in their original language with Romanian subtitles, as does the *Cinema Transylvania* on Piaţa Republicii.

Theatre & Classical Music The Agenţia Filarmonica & Teatrală, Str Republicii 6, has schedules and sells tickets for performances at the *State Philharmonic* (Filarmonica de Stat) and *State Theatre* (Teatrul de Stat) weekdays from 10 am to 4 pm and Saturday from 10 am to 1 pm. The ticket office inside the theatre is open daily from 10 am to 1 pm and 5 to 7 pm.

Getting There & Away

Air TAROM operates two daily flights on weekdays and one on Saturday to Bucharest for US$55/110 one way/return. Tickets are sold at the TAROM office (☎/fax 131 918), Piaţa Republicii 2, open weekdays from 6.30 am to 8 pm and Saturday from 11 am to 2 pm.

Train The Agenţie de Voiaj CFR, Str Republicii 2, is open weekdays only from 7 am to 8 pm. International tickets must be purchased at the CFR office in advance, not at the station.

Express trains run north to Satu Mare, south to Arad and east to Cluj-Napoca daily.

Four trains run each day from Oradea to Budapest-Nyugati station: the *Claudiopolis* and *Corona* express trains and two local trains, the *Varadinium* and the *Partium*. Fares to Budapest are US$16. Also ask about the three daily local trains from Oradea to Békéscsaba (90km).

If you don't already have an international train ticket, take bus No 11 from Oradea's train station directly to the border at Episcopia Bihor, where you can easily buy a train ticket to Hungary with lei.

Bus From Oradea bus station there are two daily services to Beiuş and Deva and one to Satu Mare.

A daily bus to Budapest departs from outside the train station at 6 pm and takes 10 hours. Tickets (US$6/11 one way/return) are sold at the bus station, inconveniently located at Str Războieni 81 on the south-eastern side of town (bus No 12 from Piaţa Unirii). If the bus is not full you can purchase a ticket from the driver before departure. The daily bus to Debrecen in Hungary departs from Oradea's bus station at 5 am. One way/return tickets cost US$4/7.

Most of the travel agencies can arrange buses to Budapest, Kraków and cities throughout Austria and Germany.

BĂILE FELIX
☎ 059

People come to Băile Felix, a famous year-round health spa only 8km south-east of Oradea, to splash in swimming pools and nap in the sun. In summer the atmosphere is rowdy in the best sense. There's a large, open-air, thermal swimming pool and several smaller thermal pools covered by the rare *Nymphea lotus thermalis*, a white water lily.

The most popular public pools are Strand Apollo and Strand Felix, by the Staţia Băile Felix bus stop. Both are open daily from 7 am to 6 pm from May to October and charge US$1 for day use. Bring your own bathing suit and towel.

Places to Stay

The nearest official *camping grounds* are 3km away at Băile 1 Mai (see under Places to Stay in Oradea).

Hotel Felix (☎ 136 532) is behind *Hotel Lotus* (☎ 261 361) in the centre of the resort. The *Hotel Thermal* (☎ 261 215), near the train station, has an on-site thermal swimming pool. *Hotel Nufărul* (☎ 343 994), 50m beyond Strand Apollo, has a good restaurant and accepts Visa. *Hotel Poeniţa* (☎ 261 172), on the eastern side of town, has a pool and accepts Visa and Amex. All these hotels charge US$20/26 for single/double with bath.

Getting There & Away

Three local trains a day run from Oradea to Băile Felix (11km, 20 minutes), but it's easier to take tram No 4 (red number) east from Piaţa Unirii, or tram No 4 (black number) south from Oradea's train station to the end of the line at Cartierul Nufărul. From here bus No 14 runs directly to the spa (US$0.30, pay the driver), stopping first at Staţia Băile Felix before circling past the major hotels. Returning, it's quickest to

ROMANIA

board at Staţia Strand Apollo, 50m south of Staţia Băile Felix.

PEŞTERA URŞILOR

Although it's not easy to reach, Peştera Urşilor (Bear Cave), named for the bear skeletons found by quarry workers in 1975, is one of Romania's finest caves and well worth a day trip from Oradea, 82km north-west. Compulsory guided tours allow you to spend an hour or so exploring the cold stalactite-filled chambers. The site is dependably open from May to September only, Tuesday to Sunday from 10.30 am to 5 pm. Admission is US$2.50 with an additional US$3.50 for cameras.

Places to Stay & Eat

Camping Fluturi, in the centre of nearby Chişcău, has a dozen wooden cabins with bedding and shared bathrooms for US$3.50 a night, but no running hot water.

Getting There & Away

Oradea's Agenţie de Turism Crişul charges US$20 per person for a return trip to the site.

Otherwise there are three daily trains to Beiuş, from where you can catch the one daily bus to 'Chişcău', within 1km of the cave. Check with Agenţie de Turism Crişul before heading out.

TIMIŞOARA
☎ 056

Timişoara (Temesvár in Hungarian, Temeschburg in German) is Romania's fourth-largest city (population 400,000), with outdoor cafés and regal, Habsburg-era buildings fronting its three main squares. Justly called the 'garden city', Timişoara has thriving opera and drama scenes, thanks in part to its 8000 university students. It was also the centre of protests in December 1989, igniting the countrywide protests that eventually toppled Ceauşescu.

Timiş County, of which Timişoara is the administrative centre, is the richest agricultural area in Romania. The Banat plain around Timişoara is an eastward extension of Yugoslavia's Vojvodina, and the Bega Canal

which curves through the city leads into the Tisa River in Yugoslavia.

Orientation

Timişoara Nord train station is just west of the city centre. Walk east on Blvd Republicii to the Opera House and Piaţa Victoriei. A block north is the verdant Piaţa Libertăţii. Piaţa Unirii, the old town square, is two blocks farther north.

If you'd rather ride, trolleybus Nos 11 and 14 travel from the station east down Blvd Republicii, then turn north onto Str 1 Mai.

Timişoara's bus station is beside the Idsefin Market, three blocks from the train station. Take Str General Dragalina south to the canal, which you cross and follow west to the next bridge.

Information

Tourist Offices The friendly Agenţie de Turism Banatul (☎ 198 862), Str 1 Mai 2, on the eastern side of Hotel Timişoara, sells town maps. Cardinal (☎ 191 911), Blvd Republicii 6, is an agent for Malev, Delta and TAROM. Neither agency arranges private rooms.

The Automobil Clubul Român (☎115 819), Str Hector 1, is opposite Beraria Bastion in the old city wall, a block from the Hotel Continental.

Foreign Consulate Yugoslavia has a consulate at Str Remus 4 where you can apply for travel visas Monday to Thursday from 9 am to noon. Coming from town, cross the bridge leading to Blvd 16 Decembrie 1989, make a sharp left along the canal to Str Caraiman (the first street on the right). Follow it west a block to Piaţa Plevnei, turn left and walk two blocks straight to the consulate.

Money Cash travellers cheques and get Visa/MasterCard cash advances at Bancă Comercială Română, Blvd Revoluţiei 1, opposite Hotel Continental (open weekdays from 8.30 am to noon and Saturday from 9 am to 1 pm) or at BANCOREX, Str 9 Mai just off Piaţa Libertăţii (open weekdays from 9 am to 1.30 pm). The currency exchange inside the Hotel Continental also gives cash advances on major credit cards.

Post & Communications The telephone office is on Blvd Mihai Eminescu, just off Piaţa Victoriei and open daily from 7 am to 9 pm. The main post office is on Blvd Revoluţiei 1989, two blocks east of the Hotel Continental; it's open weekdays from 7 am to 8 pm and Saturday from 8 am to noon.

Left Luggage The left-luggage office at the train station is at the beginning of the underground passageway to the tracks, and is open 24 hours.

Things to See

The centre of town is **Piaţa Victoriei**, a beautifully landscaped pedestrian mall lined with shops, cinemas and cafés, with the **Opera House** at its head. Just east of the piaţa is the 15th-century **Huniades Palace**, which houses the **Banat history museum** (closed Monday). On the piaţa, **Galeria Helios** is an art gallery with a good collection of local work and **Librărie Mihai Eminescu** sells some English-language books. In the centre of the promenade, note the column topped with the figures of **Romulus and Remus**, a gift from the city of Rome.

Towering over the mall's south-western end is the exotic Romanian Orthodox **Metropolitan Cathedral** (1946), in front of which are memorials to the people who died in the fighting here in December 1989. Next to the cathedral is **Parcul Central**, and just south of it the **Bega Canal** runs along tree-lined banks. The revolution began on 15 December 1989 at the **Biserica Reformed Church** (Biserica Reformată Tökés), Str Timotei Cipariu 1, south of the Bega, just off Blvd 16 Decembrie 1989, a Reformed Protestant church that serves the local Hungarian community.

Heading north from the Opera House, pedestrianised Str Alba Iulia leads to the gardens of **Piaţa Libertăţii** and the **old town hall** (1734). Two blocks north, **Piaţa Unirii** is Timişoara's most picturesque square featuring a baroque **Catholic cathedral** (1754), the **Serbian cathedral** (1754), fountains and the **Museum of Fine Arts**. Walk east down Str Palanca to the **ethnographic museum**, Str Popa Şapcâ 8, with Banat folk costumes and crafts. It's closed on Monday.

Places to Stay

Camping The *Pădurea Verde* camping ground is in the Green Forest on the opposite side of town from Timişoara Nord train station. From the station catch tram No 1 (black number) and ask to be let off at the 'camping'. The route from the tram stop is unmarked – follow one of the trails leading through the forest. The site has 50 small cabins for US$3 per person, and tent camping is US$2 for two people. There's a small restaurant on the premises. It's open from June to mid-September.

Hotels Timişoara's cheapest hotel is *Casă Tineretului* (☎ 162 419), a large, modern building on Str Arieş about 2km south of the city centre. Rooms with shared bath are US$6 per person. From the train station take tram No 8 to Calea Martirilor.

Of Timişoara's city-centre hotels, the most reasonably priced is *Hotel Banatul* (☎ 191 903), Blvd Republicii 5. Rooms in the adjoining annexe were partially renovated in 1995, though even the 'old' rooms are OK. It's US$15/26 for a single/double with bath, US$7/12 without.

More expensive is *Hotel Central* (☎ 190 091; fax 190 096), Str Lenau 6, next door to Cinema Studio. It charges US$21/36 for a double/apartment with bath, TV and breakfast.

The modern 11-storey *Hotel Timişoara* (☎ 198 854; fax 199 450), Str 1 Mai 2 behind the Opera House, charges US$35/53 for a two-star single/double, breakfast included.

The three-star *Hotel Continental* (☎ 131 144), Blvd Revoluţiei 3 near Parcul Civic, is more expensive at US$45/60 but takes credit cards.

Places to Eat

Restaurantul Bulevard, on Piaţa Victoriei opposite the Opera House, is very elegant with a beer garden. There's a restaurant at *Hotel Banatul*, nearby on Blvd Republicii.

The *Brasserie Opera* on Str Hector serves mostly pizzas, pastries and beer inside and out.

The *Cina Restaurant*, Str Piatra Craiului 4, shares a kitchen with *Hotel Banatul restaurant* but earns higher marks for atmosphere.

The best spot on Piaţa Unirii is *Restaurant Unirea*, next to the Catholic cathedral, with

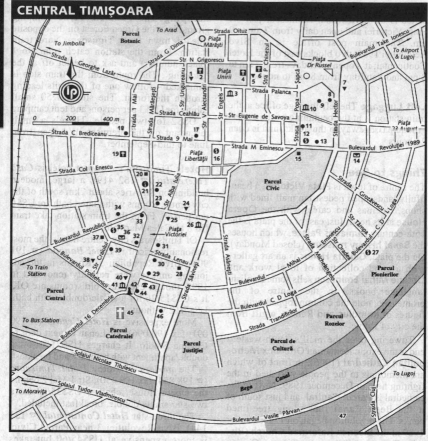

CENTRAL TIMIȘOARA

tables on the square and a small dining room indoors.

The smell alone recommends nearby *BM Croissant*, Str Ungureanu 10, an honest-to-goodness bakery with fresh pastries. Many items sell out by 10 am. It's closed on Sunday.

The *Crama Bastion*, in a section of the city's 18th-century fortifications, is a wine cellar and has a small menu of meat and rice dishes. There's also a large beer garden.

There are several casual cafés and bakeries along Str Alba Iulia and Piaţa Victoriei, in-

cluding *Violeta's*, serving pizzas and pastries. There's also the Contimalimenta *grocery* on the piaţa and a colourful *produce market* on Str Brediceanu near the intersection of Str 1 Mai.

Entertainment

Discos From October to May there's a disco in the Casă de Cultură a Studenţilor, Blvd Tineretii 9, near the corner of Str General Dragalina and three blocks south of the train station. Tram No 1 passes this way.

PLACES TO STAY		8	Automobil Clubul	29	Unic Alimentara
15	Hotel Continental		Român (ACR)	30	Cinema Studio
20	Hotel Timişoara	9	Complex Expo Bastion	31	Contimalimenta Grocery
28	Hotel Central	10	Ethnographic Museum	32	Librărie Mihai Eminescu
37	Hotel Banatul	11	DAC Air; MALEV	33	Agenţie de Voiaj CFR
		12	Bancă Comercială	34	Cardinal Agenţie
PLACES TO EAT			Română	35	Currency Exchange
1	BM Croissant	13	TAROM	36	Post Office
5	Restaurant Unirea	14	Main Post Office	39	Sport Volaj Sporting
7	Crama Bastion	16	BANCOREX		Goods
24	Brasserie Opera	17	Old Town Hall	41	Galeria Helios
25	McDonald's	18	Market	42	Memorial to Victims
38	Cina Restaurant	19	Greco-Catholic Church		of Revolution
40	Violeta's	21	Agenţie de Turism	43	Telephone Office
			Banatul	44	Cinema Timiş
OTHER		22	Agenţie de Teatrală	45	Metropolitan Cathedral
2	Serbian Cathedral	23	National Theatre	46	State Philharmonic
3	Museum of Fine Arts;		& Opera House		Theatre
	Prefecture Palace	26	Huniades Palace;	47	University
4	Catholic Cathedral		Banat Museum		
6	Lutheran Cathedral	27	Bancă Agricola		

Cinemas Films in their original language (generally English) are screened at *Cinema Studio*, Str Leanu next to Hotel Central, and *Cinema Timiş* on Piaţa Victoriei near the telephone centre.

Theatre & Classical Music The theatre ticket office (agenţie teatrală) is at Str Mărăşeşti 2, across from the Hotel Timişoara. There are professional and student-directed performances year-round at the *Opera House* and *State Philharmonic Theatre*.

Getting There & Away

Air TAROM (☎/fax 190 150), Blvd Revoluţiei 3-5 opposite Hotel Continental, has daily flights (except Sunday) to Bucharest, Iaşi and Constanţa. DAC Air (☎ 221 555) on Str Popa Şapcâ flies twice daily weekdays to Bucharest and once daily to Cluj-Napoca. The Cardinal agency books international Malev and Delta flights.

Train Direct express trains link Timişoara to Iaşi via Cluj-Napoca and Suceava. By local train Timişoara is 1½ hours south of Arad (57km). The service to Bucharest is fairly frequent via Băile Herculane, Drobeta-Turnu

Severin and Craiova. Sleepers are available to/from Bucharest (eight hours). The CFR office, Blvd Republicii 1, is open weekdays from 8 am to 8 pm. International tickets can only be bought at CFR.

Yugoslavia Two daily express trains connect Timişoara with Belgrade. The *Bucureşti* leaves Timişoara Nord at 5.02 am and arrives in Belgrade at 9.23 am. The *Banat* leaves at 6.09 pm and arrives at 10.15 pm (advance reservations are required for both).

It's also possible to reach Yugoslavia by taking a local train to the Romanian town of Jimbolia (one hour) and then a connecting train to Kikinda (two daily, 19km). Two unreserved local trains also run daily from Timişoara to Vršac (76km) on the line to Belgrade.

Bus Daily buses connect Timişoara to Békéscsaba (138km), Baja (257km) and Szeged (157km). There's a weekly service to Budapest (eight hours, US$8). The international ticket window is open on weekdays from 9 am to 5 pm, otherwise you can usually pay the driver.

ROMANIA

Maramureş

A visit to the valleys of Maramureş is like stepping back in time. Cut off by a natural fortress of mountains, it has remained largely untouched by the 20th century. Life here operates much as it did 200 years ago.

Maramureş was never conquered by the Romans, earning the region the title 'land of the free Dacians'. Social activities revolve around the tall-steepled, wooden village churches dating from the 15th and 16th centuries. Traditional folk costumes are worn in most villages, although the colourful costumes, each bearing motifs typical to each village, are donned only on special holidays. Horse carts share the roads with automobiles.

Maramureş is practically impossible to explore without private transport.

History

Maramureş, with Sighetu Marmaţiei as its capital, was first attested in 1199. Hungary gradually exerted its rule over the region from the 13th century onwards. Tartar invasions of the Hungarian-dominated region continued well into the 17th and 18th centuries, the last battle being documented on the Prislop Pass in 1717. Numerous churches sprang up in Maramureş around this time to mark the Tartars' final withdrawal from the region.

Maramureş was annexed by Transylvania in the mid-16th century. In 1699 the Turks ceded Transylvania to the Austrian empire and it was not until 1918 that Maramureş, with the rest of Transylvania, was returned to Romania.

Between 1940 and 1944 the Maramureş region – along with the rest of northern Transylvania – fell under pro-Nazi Hungarian rule.

SIGHETU MARMAŢIEI
☎ 062

Sighetu Marmaţiei is the northernmost town in Romania, lying at the confluence of the Tisa, Iza and Ronişoara rivers, 2km from the Ukrainian border.

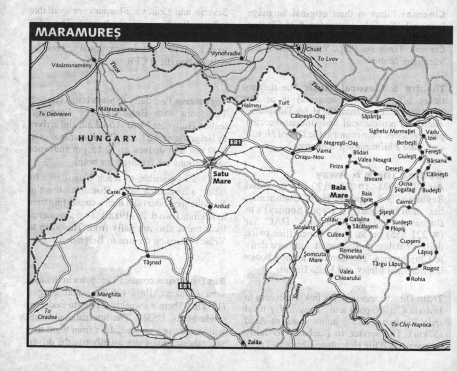

MARAMUREŞ

Sighet (as it's called locally) is a farming town of 40,000, famed for its vibrant winter festival and peasant costumes.

Information

Tourist Offices The official tourist office at Piaţa Libertăţii 21 runs a currency exchange and can rent you a car (price negotiable). It's open weekdays from 8 am to 4 pm and Saturday from 9 am to 1 pm.

Post & Communications The post and telephone office is opposite the Maramureş Museum on Str Ioan Mihaly de Apşa. Send faxes and email and access the Internet from the privately run Sighetu Business Centre (☎/fax 313 887; lazin@sintec.ro) in an apartment block at Str Independenţei, bloc 2, stairway A, apartment 23. It costs US$0.75 to send an email or US$3 for 30 minutes online; the centre is open weekdays from 7 am to 7 pm and weekends from 8 to 10 am.

Money The Bancă Comercială Română on Str Iuliu Maniu is open weekdays from 8.30 am to 12.30 pm and gives cash advances on Visa.

Things to See

Piaţa Libertăţii & Around Sighet, first documented in 1328, was a strong cultural and political centre. On Piaţa Libertăţii is the **Hungarian Reformed Church**, built during the 15th century. Close by is the **Roman Catholic Church**, constructed in the 16th century.

Off Piaţa Libertăţii at Str Bogdan Vodă 1 is the **Maramureş Museum**, an ethnographic museum in which colourful folk costumes, rugs and carnival masks are displayed. It is open daily, except Monday, from 9 am to 5 pm. For handmade crafts visit the **Artis Ruzzel** gallery at Piaţa Libertăţii 21.

Just off the square at Str Bessarabia 10 is Sighet's only remaining **synagogue**. Before WWII there were eight synagogues serving a large Jewish community, which comprised 40% of the town's population.

The Jewish writer and 1986 Nobel peace prize winner, Elie Wiesel, who coined the term 'Holocaust' was born in and later deported from Sighet. His house on the corner of Str Dragoş Vodă and Str Tudor Vladimirescu, is now a **memorial museum**.

On Str Gheorghe Doja, at Str Mureşan, there is a **monument** to the victims of the Holocaust.

Serious art lovers should also visit the private collection displayed in the **Pipaş Museum**, 2km east of Sighet in Tisa village.

Sighet Prison Sighet's former maximum-security prison is now a museum, although little evidence remains of the horror it housed. In May 1947 the communists embarked on a reign of terror, imprisoning, torturing, killing and deporting thousands of Romanians. Between 1948 and 1952, 180 of Romania's academic and government elite were imprisoned here.

Today four white marble plaques covering the barred windows of the prison list the 51 prisoners who died in the Sighet cells. Eight more plaques list those prisoners who survived the torture.

The prison, in the old courthouse on Str Corneliu Coposu, was closed in 1974. In

ROMANIA

1989 it opened as a private **Museum of Arrested Thoughts and International Study Centre of Totalitarianism**. Since 1997 it has been open to the public. Photographs are displayed and you can visit the torture chambers and cells. The museum is open daily, except Monday, from 9.30 am to 1 pm, and from 3 to 5 pm.

Village Museum Traditional peasant houses from the Maramureş region have been reassembled in Sighet's outstanding open-air Village Museum (Muzeul Satului), on the right as you approach the town from the south. The museum is open daily, except Monday, from 10 am to 6 pm.

Places to Stay & Eat

Sighet's one central hotel, the **Hotel Tisa** (☎ 312 645) at Piaţa Libertăţii 8, has 40 doubles, most of them recently renovated. A double with private bathroom, TV and telephone is US$21, including breakfast.

The grotty **Hotel Ardealu** (☎ 312 172), opposite the train station on Str Iuliu Maniu, has basic single and double rooms with no bath, no shower and no hot water, just a communal toilet and sink. Beds cost US$3.

A short walk from the centre, overlooking Eminescu Park is the **Hotel Marmaţia** (☎ 512 241; fax 515 484) at Str Mihai Eminescu 54. Singles/doubles with private bath are US$10/16 a night.

The upmarket, two star **Motel Topliţa** (☎ 513 174; fax 515 484), just out of town on the road to Borşa at Str Tepliţei 56, has four double rooms with private bath, TV and telephone for US$28 a night, including breakfast.

Cheap snacks and light meals are served at the fun **Snack Bar No 7** on Str Traian, a real eye-opener into the local scene.

Getting There & Away

Train The CFR office is near the tourist office at Piaţa Libertăţii 25; it's open weekdays from

SIGHETU MARMAŢIEI

0   100   200 m
Approximate Scale

To Motel Topliţa, Tisa
Vişeu De Sus & Borşa

Strada Horia
Strada Tilibreului
Strada Cării
Str Iuliu Maniu
Strada Pievnei
Strada Dragoş Vodă
Strada
Strada A Irasiuc
Strada Trandatinlor
Strada N Grigorescu
Strada Pintea Viteazul
Strada Mihai Viteazul
Str George Coşbuc
Piaţa Libertăţii
Str Tudor Vladimirescu
Bulevardul Unirii
Strada Traian
Strada Ioan Mihaly de Apşa
Piaţa 1 Decembrie
Str Bogdan Vodă
To Village Museum, Vadu Izei, Ocna Şugatag, Berbeşti & Baia Mare
Strada Avram Iancu
To Săpânţa, Merry Cemetery, Negreşti & Satu Mare
Str Gheorghe Doja
Gheorghe Şincai
Str Cornelui Copoşu
Strada Ştefan cel Mare
Str Gh Lazăr
Strada Independenţei
Strada Zimbrului
Strada Eroilor
Strada Mihai Eminescu
Strada Izei

Parcul Grădină Morii
Iza   To Vadu Izei

PLACES TO STAY	OTHER	
3 Hotel Ardealu	1 Train Station	9 Synagogue
16 Hotel Tisa	2 Bus Station	10 Elie Wiesel House
19 Hotel Marmaţia	4 Bancă Comercială Română	12 Former Sighet Prison
	5 Roman Catholic Church	13 Post & Telephone Office
PLACES TO EAT	6 Artis Ruezzel Art Gallery	14 Maramureş Museum
11 Snack Bar No 7	7 Tourist Office & Currency Exchange	15 Hungarian Reformed Church
	8 Agenţie de Voiaj CFR	17 Hungarian Monument
		18 Sighetu Business Center

8 am to 6 pm. There are five trains daily to Vişeu de Jos (two hours), two to Cluj-Napoca (six hours) and one to Bucharest (12 hours).

Bus The bus station is opposite the train station on Str Gării. Local buses include six daily to Baia Mare (65km); two to Borşa and Ocna; five to Budeşti; three to Vişeu de Sus; and one to Bârsana, Botiza, Călineşti, Coştiui, Glod, Ieud, Mara, Săpânţa and Târgu Lăpuş.

SĂPÂNŢA
☎ 062

Săpânţa, 12km north-west of Sighetu Marmaţiei, is famous for its Merry Cemetery, which is unique for the colourfully painted wooden markers above the tombstones. Săpânţa's crosses attract coachloads of tourists every year. Villagers sit outside their cottages, their fenceposts strung with colourful rugs and handwoven bags for sale. Buses run daily trips to/from Sighet.

Merry Cemetery
Săpânţa's Merry Cemetery was the creation of Ioan Stan Pătraş, a simple wood sculptor who in 1935 began carving crosses to mark graves in the church cemetery. Each cross depicts the deceased at their trade with humorous epitaphs inscribed below. Since Pătraş' death, Dumitru Pop, his apprentice, has carried on the tradition.

Places to Stay
Camping Poieni, 3km south of Săpânţa, has two-bed wooden cabins for US$3 per person a night, including breakfast. Tents can also be pitched. The camp site is only open in summer.

IZEI VALLEY
The Izei Valley follows Izei river eastward to Moisei. The valley is lined with small peasant villages where daily life continues as it has for centuries. They are renowned for their elaborately carved wooden gates and tall wooden churches. Tourism is gradually developing in this region, providing visitors the opportunity to sample traditional cuisine or try their hand at wood carving, wool weaving and glass painting.

In mid-July, Vadu Izei, together with the neighbouring villages of Botiza and Ieud, hosts the Maramuzical Festival, a lively four-day international folk music festival. Guests stay in local homes or in tents.

Vadu Izei
☎ 062
Vadu Izei is at the confluence of the Izei and Mara rivers, 6km south of Sighetu Marmaţiei. Its museum is in the oldest house in the village (1750).

Fundaţia Turistică Agro-Tur (☎/fax 330 171) sells maps and guides of the region and can arrange for a French or English-speaking guide for US$10 a day. It also sells local crafts. Its office is in house No 161 at the northern end of the village. If it's closed, contact Denisia Covrig (☎ 330 076; English and French-speaking) at house No 58 or Petru Negrea (☎ 330 083; French-speaking) at house No 319. Agro-Tur arranges guided tours of Maramureş' wooden churches; wood carving, icon painting and wool weaving workshops; traditional folk evenings; and fishing trips.

Places to Stay & Eat Agro-Tur arranges accommodation in private homes. Some 20 families offer beds for US$10 a night (half/full board is US$13/15). Bookings can be made through the Agro-Tur office or directly at the homes involved. Some homes are signposted and their owners welcome guests knocking at their door.

Bârsana
Continue south-east for 12km to Bârsana. Dating from 1326, the village acquired its first church in 1720 (its interior paintings were done by local artists). The Orthodox **Bârsana Monastery** is a popular pilgrimage spot in Maramureş. It was the last Orthodox monastery to be built in the region before Serafim Petrovai, head of the Orthodox church in Maramureş, converted to Greco-Catholicism in 1711.

Rozavlea
Continue south past Stâmtura to Rozavlea, first documented under the name of Gorzohaza in 1374. Its fine church, dedicated to the

ROMANIA

archangels Michael and Gabriel, was built between 1717 and 1720 in another village, then erected in Rozavlea on the site of an ancient church destroyed by the Tartars.

Botiza

From Rozavlea continue south for 3km to Sieu, then take the turn-off for Botiza. Botiza's old church, built in 1694, is overshadowed by the large new church that was constructed in 1974 to serve the 500 or so devout Orthodox families. The weekly Sunday service (9 am) is the major event of the week.

Places to Stay & Eat Villagers in Botiza have formed their own agrotourism scheme. Half/full board in a local home is US$10/23 a night. The society is led by wealthy weaver and wife of the local priest Viktoria Berbecaru (☎ 062-334 991; ext 7 'casă preotului'). Her home is the large house by the church. She also sells bottles of home-made ţuică for US$1.20.

Ieud

The oldest wooden church in Maramureş dating from 1364, is in Ieud, 6km south of the main road.

Ieud was first documented in 1365. In 1364 its fabulous Orthodox 'Church on the Hill' was built from fir wood and housed the first document known to be written in Romanian (1391-92), in which the catechism and church laws pertaining to Ieud were coded. The church was restored in 1958 and in 1997. It is generally locked but you can get the key from the porter's house, distinguishable by a simple wooden gate opposite the *textile incaltaminte* in the centre of the village.

Ieud's second church, Greco-Catholic, was built in 1717. The church is unique to the region as it has no porch. It houses one of the largest collections of icons on glass found in Maramureş. The church is at the southern end of the village.

Places to Stay Opération Villages Roumains runs a small agrotourism scheme in Ieud. You can make advance bookings through the office in Vadu Izei or go straight to the local representative, Gavrila Chindris,

at house No 665. A bed for the night starts at US$10, including breakfast.

Bogdan Vodă

Bogdan Vodă was renamed in honour of Moldavian prince Bogdan I (1359-65), who marched south-east from former Cuhea to found the state of Moldavia in 1359. A statue of the great prince is being erected outside the village church (1718). Some of the interior paintings in the pine church draw upon the traditional method of painting on linen, while others are painted on wood. A rope carved in wood wraps around the four sides of the church. The church, dedicated to St Nicholas, is on the left as you enter the village from the north.

Moisei

Moisei lies 7km north-east of Săcel, at the junction of route 17C and route 18. A small town at the foot of the Rodna massif, known for its traditional crafts and customs, Moisei gained fame in 1944 when retreating Hungarian (Horthyst) troops gunned down 31 people before setting fire to the village.

In 1944, following the news that the front was approaching Moisei, villagers started to flee, including those forced labour detachments stationed in the village. Occupying Hungarian forces organised a manhunt to track down the deserters. Thirty-one were captured and detained in a small camp in Vişeu de Sus without food or water for three weeks. On 14 October 1944 Hungarian troops brought the 31 prisoners to a house in Moisei, locked them inside, then shot them through the windows. Before abandoning the village, the troops set it on fire, leaving all 125 remaining families homeless.

Only one house in Moisei survived the blaze: the one in which the prisoners were shot. Today, it houses a small **museum** in tribute to those who died in the massacre. Photographs of the 29 who died as well as the two who survived the bloodbath adorn its walls. Opposite the white cottage, on a hillock above the road and railways line, is a circular **monument** to the victims. The 12 upright columns symbolise the sun and light. Each column is decorated with a traditional carnival mask, except for two which bear human faces based on the features of the two survivors.

The museum and monument are at the most eastern end of the village. If the museum is locked, knock at the pink house next door and ask for the key.

Borşa

Ore has been mined at Borşa, 12km east of Moisei, since the mid-14th century. The area was colonised in 1777 by German miners from Slovakia; later, Bavarian-Austrian miners moved to Baia Borşa, 2km north-east of the town, to mine copper, lead and silver.

The Complex Turistic Borşa, a small ski resort and tourist complex 10km east of Borşa town, is a main entrance to the **Rodna mountains**, part of which form the Pietrosul Rodnei Nature Reservation (5900 hectares). Hiking trails leading into the massif are listed inside the two-star *Hotel Ştibina* (☎ 062-343 466), Str Fântâna 23. Double rooms with private bath cost US$24 a night.

In winter, you can ski down the 2030m-long ski-run in the complex. The ski lift (☎ 343 703, 344 442), Str Brâdet 10, is open daily from 7 am to 6 pm; ski hire is not available.

PRISLOP PASS

Prislop Pass is the main route from Mara-mureş into Moldavia. Hikers can trek from Borşa to the east across the Prislop Pass. From Moldavia you can bear north-east to Câmpulung Moldovenesc and on to the monasteries of Bucovina.

At 1416m, a roadside monument honours the site of the last Tartar invasion before their flight from the region in 1717. Nearby is *Hanul Prislop*, site of the Hora de la Prislop festival, held every August. The festival has its origins in a traditional sheep market. Today it's just for merrymaking with friends from the surrounding villages. The hora dancers stamp their feet, swing their upper body, and clap vigorously to the rhythm of a *ţâpurituri*, a chanted rhyme drummed out by three musicians on a traditional *zongora* (viola tuned in the key of A minus the C#), a *cetera* (shrill violin), and a *doba* (bongo made from fir or maple wood, covered with goat or sheep hide).

Moldavia

With its forest-clad hills and tranquil valleys, Moldavia rivals mighty Transylvania when it comes to rich folklore, natural beauty and turbulent history. Prince Bogdan won Moldavian independence from Hungary in 1349, after which the centre of the medieval principality, tucked away in the easily defended Carpathian foothills, became known as Bucovina (meaning 'beech wood').

From Suceava, Ştefan cel Mare (Ştefan the Great), called the 'Athlete of Christ' by Pope Pius VI, led the resistance against the Turks from 1457 to 1504. This prince and his son, Petru Rareş, erected fortified monasteries throughout Bucovina. Many have miraculously survived centuries of war and weather, with their stunning exterior frescoes intact. Only with the defeat of Petru Rareş by the Turks in 1538 did Moldavia's golden age wane. Moldavia regained a measure of its former glory after it was united with the principality of Wallachia by Prince Alexandru Ioan Cuza in 1859 – a date that marks the birth of the modern Romanian state.

Medieval Moldavia, however, was much larger than the portion incorporated into Romania in 1859. Bessarabia, the portion east of the Prut River, was conquered and claimed by Russia in 1812. Despite being recovered by Romania from 1918-40 and again from 1941-44, Bessarabia is now split between Ukraine and the Republic of Moldova. Northern Bucovina was annexed by the Soviets in 1940 and is now also part of Ukraine. Only southern Bucovina belongs to Romania today, but its 15th-century painted monasteries are some of the most fascinating sights in Romania.

Southern Bucovina

The painted churches of southern Bucovina are among the greatest artistic monuments of Europe – in 1993 they were collectively designated a world heritage site by UNESCO. Erected at a time when northern Moldavia was threatened by Turkish invaders, the monasteries were surrounded by strong defensive walls. Great popular armies would gather inside these fortifications, waiting to

ROMANIA

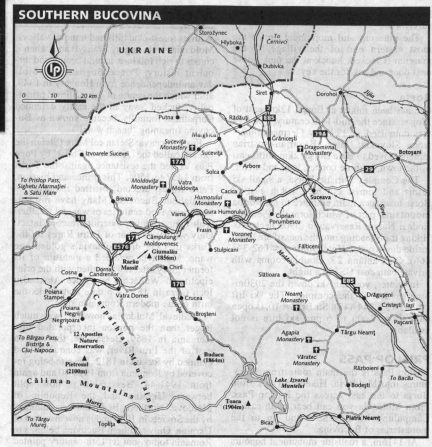

SOUTHERN BUCOVINA

do battle. To educate the illiterate peasants who were unable to understand the liturgy, biblical stories were portrayed on the church walls in colourful pictures. The exteriors of many of the churches are completely covered with these magnificent 16th-century frescoes. Remarkably, most of the intense colours – from the greens of Suceviţa to the blues of Voroneţ and the reds of Humor – have been preserved despite five centuries of rain and wind.

The church domes are a peculiar combination of Byzantine pendentives and Moorish crossed arches with larger-than-life paintings of Christ or the Virgin peering down from inside.

Bucovina's monasteries are generally open daily from 9 am to 5 or 6 pm. Admission is less than US$1. If your time is limited, the Voroneţ, Humor and Moldoviţa monasteries, all accessible by bus and train, provide a representative sample of what Bucovina has to offer.

To do a complete circuit of Suceava, Voroneţ, Humor, Moldoviţa, Suceviţa and Putna on your own will require three days.

You can save time by hiring a tour guide with car to show you around or renting a car in Suceava for a day and driving yourself.

Apart from the religious art and monasteries, Bucovina is well worth visiting for its folklore, picturesque villages, bucolic scenery and colourful locals, all as good as anything you'll find elsewhere in Romania.

SUCEAVA
☎ 030

Suceava was the capital of Moldavia from 1388 to 1565 and a thriving commercial centre on the Lviv-Istanbul trading route. Today it's the seat of Suceava County and gateway to the painted churches of Bucovina. Its few old churches and historic fortress are easily seen in a day.

Orientation

Piața 22 Decembrie is the centre of town. Suceava has two train stations, Gara Suceava and Gara Suceava Nord, both a few kilometres north of the city centre and easily reached by trolleybus.

From Gara Suceava, cross the street, buy a ticket at a kiosk and take trolleybus No 2 or 3 to the centre of town (about six stops from the station at the top of a small hill). From Gara Suceava Nord take trolleybus No 5.

Information

Tourist Offices Head straight for Bucovina Estur (see Travel Agencies) across the main square. Its staff have the best information and are friendly and helpful.

The Automobil Clubul Român (☎ 210 997), Str Nicolae Bălcescu 8, sells road maps. It's open weekdays from 8 am to 4 pm.

Money The Platinum currency exchange inside Bucovina Estur is open weekdays from 9 am to 5 pm and Saturday from 9 am to 1 pm.

BANCOREX at Str Curtea Domnească and Str Firmu changes travellers cheques and gives Visa/MasterCard cash advances; it's open on weekdays from 8.30 am to noon. Bancă Comercială Română, at Str Ștefan cel Mare 31, cashes travellers cheques on weekdays from 8.30 to 1.30 pm and Saturday from 10 am to 1 pm. It also has a Visa/MasterCard ATM outside.

Post & Communications The telephone centre, in the main post office on the corner of Str Nicolae Bălcescu and Str Firmu, is open weekdays from 7 am to 8 pm and Saturday from 8 am to noon.

Travel Agencies Bucovina Estur (☎ 213 095, 223 259; fax 223 259), Str Ștefan cel Mare 24, arranges private rooms, has a variety of monastery tour programs and rents out cars. A car with driver costs US$35 for five hours; a minibus is US$53. You can also rent a bicycle for US$1/8 per hour/day. The office is open weekdays from 9 am to 8 pm and Saturday from 9 to 11 am. The staff speak English.

Left Luggage The left-luggage office at Gara Suceava is at the information window on the main platform (open 24 hours).

Things to See

The **Casă de Cultură** (House of Culture) is at the western end of Piața 22 Decembrie. North of the bus stop along Blvd Ana Ipatescu lie the foundations of the 15th-century **Princely Palace**. The large church to the west is **St Dimitru's church** built by Petru Rareș in 1535. Beyond the church is Suceava's main **vegetable market**.

West of Piața 22 Decembrie, behind the Casă de Cultură on Str Ciprian Porumbescu 5, is **Hanul Domnesc**, a princely 16th-century guesthouse that now houses an ethnographic museum (closed Monday). Its collection of folk costumes is quite good.

Return to Piața 22 Decembrie and follow Str Ștefan cel Mare south past **Parcul Central** (Central Park) to the surprisingly informative **Bucovina History Museum** at No 33. The presentation comes to an abrupt end at 1945 and old paintings now hang in rooms that formerly glorified the communist era. The captions are in Romanian only (closed Monday).

Backtrack a little to the park and take Str Mitropoliei south-east to the **Monastery of Saint John the New** (1522). The paintings on the outside of the church are badly faded, but they give you an idea of the painted churches that Bucovina is famous for.

Continue on Str Mitropoliei, keeping left on the main road out of town, till you see a

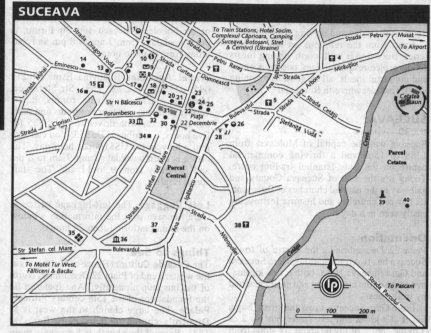

SUCEAVA

large wooden gate marked 'Parcul Cetatii' on the left. Go through it and, when the ways divide, follow the footpath with the park benches around to the left to the huge **equestrian statue** (1966) of the Moldavian leader, Ştefan cel Mare. Twenty metres back on the access road to the monument is another footpath on the left, which descends towards the **Cetatea de Scaun** (1388), a fortress that in 1476 held off Mehmed II, conqueror of Constantinople (Istanbul).

On the hillside opposite the fortress is **Mirăuţi Church** (1390), the original Moldavian coronation church, which was rebuilt in the 17th century. Get here by taking the path down through the park on the western (left) side of the fortress.

Places to Stay

Camping Near the Suceava River, between Gara Suceava Nord and Suceava, is *Camping Suceava* (☎ 214 958) on Str Cernăuţi. It has

been privatised but is in bad shape, with two-bed wooden huts that could use a good cleaning. A bed costs US$3.50 a night.

Private Rooms *Bucovina Estur* (see Information) arranges nice rooms in private homes for US$12 to $22 per person in Suceava and surrounding villages.

Hotels Five-storey *Hotel Socim* (☎ 258 297; fax 522 662), Str Jean Bart 24, is 200m up the street from Gara Suceava. A bed in a double/triple room with shared shower and toilet is US$2.80/3.50 a night. Hot water is only available from 6 to 9 am and 4 to 9 pm.

Better value is the central *Hotel Gloria* (☎ 521 209; fax 520 087) at Str Mihai Vasile Bumbac 4. Singles/doubles are US$11/15, breakfast included.

Hotel Balada (☎ 223 198; fax 520 087), Str Mitropoliei 1, is a privately run two-star hotel with direct-dial phones and cable TV. Double/triple rooms are US$45/64 (Visa/

PLACES TO STAY		5	Domniţelor Church	22	ONT Office
16	Hotel Arcaşul	6	Princely Palace Ruins	23	Supermarket
21	Hotel Suceava &	7	St Dimitru's Church	24	TAROM
	Restaurant Suceava	8	Synagogue	25	Pharmacy Nr 1
34	Hotel Gloria	9	Post Office	26	Buses to/from Train Station
37	Hotel Bucovina	10	BANCOREX	29	Bucovina Estur
		12	Kodak Express	30	Artizant Souvenir Shop
PLACES TO EAT		13	Cinema Modern	31	Casă de Cultură & Club 33
2	Café Olmasil	14	Eurostela 24-hour Shop	32	Taxi Rank
11	Restaurant Aida	15	St Nicholas Church	33	Hanul Domnesc &
27	Poftă Bună Patisserie		& Monument		Ethnographic Museum
28	Poftă Bună Fast Food	17	Automobil Clubul	35	Universal Department Store
			Român (ACR) Office	36	Bucovina History Museum
OTHER		18	Post Office &	38	Monastery of St John
1	Bus Station; Hotel		Telephone Centre		the New
3	Central Market	19	BTT	39	Statue of Ştefan cel Mare
4	Mirăuţi Church	20	Agenţie de Voiaj CFR	40	Cemetery

MasterCard accepted). Book through Bucovina Estur and get a 10% discount.

The *Hotel Suceava* (☎ 222 497; fax 521 080), Str Bălcescu 2, is a modern four-storey hotel in the centre of town. Rooms with bath are US$45/60, breakfast included.

Hotel Arcaşul (☎ 210 944; fax 227 598), Str Mihai Viteazul 4-6, charges the same as Hotel Suceava, but breakfast costs US$3 extra.

At 10-storey *Hotel Bucovina* (☎ 217 048), Str Ana Ipătescu 5, singles/doubles with bath are US$45/90, breakfast included.

Places to Eat

Eating options in Suceava are rather limited. *Restaurant Suceava* at Str Nicolae Bălcescu 2 has a tasty charcoal-grilled beef steak for US$2. It's open daily from 10 am to 10 pm.

A local favourite is *Country Pizza* near the stadium at Blvd 1 Decembrie 1918. It has a small selection of pizza slices, with a variety of generous toppings, which cost US$1.20; it's open daily from 10 am to midnight.

Restaurant Aida on Str Curtea Domnească has the usual plates of pork and potatoes; it's open from 8 am to 9 pm. *Cafe Olmasil* on Str Curea Domnească has billiard tables and is open daily from 8 am to 10 pm. There's a *fast food outlet* at Str Meseriasilor 10 open daily from 8 am to midnight.

Next to the bus stop on Piaţa 22 Decembrie is the *Poftă Bună Patisserie* and adjoining fast food outlet. The cakes and pastries are

heavenly and you can get breakfast. Hot dogs and hamburgers are sold in *Poftă Bună fast food* open 24 hours.

There's a *supermarket* opposite Restaurant Suceava on Str Ştefan cel Mare which is open until 8 pm. *Eurostela* opposite St Nicholas Church on Str Mihai Eminescu is open 24 hours.

Entertainment

Cinema Modern, facing the roundabout at the western end of Str Bălcescu, screens films in their original language. There's also a small cinema inside the Casă de Cultură on Piaţa 22 Decembrie.

Club 33 inside the House of Culture is open daily from noon to midnight.

Getting There & Away

Train Express trains to Bucharest (seven hours), Iaşi (1½ hours) and Cluj-Napoca (6½ hours) are fairly regular. Local trains go to Gura Humorului, Putna, Câmpulung Moldovenesc and Vatra Dornei.

The CFR office (☎ 214 335) is at Str Bălcescu 8; it's open weekdays from 7 am to 8 pm.

Bus The bus station (☎ 216 089) is in the centre of town at Str Armenească. Tickets for international destinations are sold at window No 4. Eight buses a day run between Suceava and Cernăuţi in Ukraine (90km).

Buses to Romanian destinations include eight daily to Gura Humorului (47km), 10 to Rădăuţi and Botoşani (62km) and one to Iaşi (141km).

GURA HUMORULUI
☎ 030

This small logging town, 36km west of Suceava on the main railway line to Cluj-Napoca, is an ideal centre for visiting the monasteries. Most trains stop here and the adjacent train and bus stations are a seven-minute walk from the centre of town.

The post office is on the corner of Str Bucovinei and Str 9 Mai. The CFR office, Str Republicii 10, is opposite the Cinema Lumina.

Things to See

The **Ethnographic Museum**, Blvd Bucovina 21, is on the main street, east of the post office (closed Monday).

Voroneţ and Humor monasteries are the main reasons to visit Guru Humorului (see these sections later in the chapter). There are several buses a day taking visitors to Voroneţ and Humor; on Sunday the bus service is greatly reduced. You can also walk the 4km south to Voroneţ through beautiful farmland. It's a 6km hike north to Humor monastery from the town centre. In summer both monasteries stay open until 8 pm.

Places to Stay

The unappealing *Hotel Carpaţi* (☎ 231 103), Str 9 Mai 3, beside the post office, has single/double rooms with communal showers for US$7/11 per person; it has no hot water.

Otherwise, try *Cabana Ariniş* at the foot of the wooded hills, 1km south of town (US$5 per person). Coming from the stations on foot, don't cross the river and enter town, but follow the right embankment downstream till you reach a bridge at the entrance to Parc Dendrologic. Go through the park to a suspension bridge that leads directly to the cabana. By car the cabana is accessible from the Voroneţ road (turn left just south of the bridge). You could easily walk from here to Voroneţ in under an hour. Meals are served at the cabana and in the large terrace restaurant by the suspension bridge.

Places to Eat

Basic places for pork and soup are the *Moldova*, on the left just after the bridge as you come from the stations, and the *Bucovina*, on the right behind the cinema.

Better is *Restaurant Select* at Str Bucovinei 1, with a Romanian-French-English menu; it's open daily from 10 am to midnight. Next door is a *Mini Market* for supplies if you'll be hiking to the monasteries.

Getting There & Away

Gura Humorului is on the main railway line between Suceava and Cluj-Napoca.

Buses from Gura Humorului's station at Str Ştefan cel Mare 37 include eight daily to Suceava, seven to Humor, four to Voroneţ, seven to Humor, one to Arbore, two to Rădăuţi and to Piatra Neamţ and nine to Câmpulung Moldovenesc. On weekends the service is greatly reduced. If you have limited time, you can bargain with taxi drivers here for tours to the monasteries.

VORONEŢ

The *Last Judgment*, which fills the entire western wall at Voroneţ monastery, is perhaps the most marvellous of Bucovina's frescoes. At the top, angels roll up the signs of the zodiac to indicate the end of time. The middle fresco shows humanity being brought to judgment. On the left St Paul escorts the believers, while on the right Moses brings forward the nonbelievers. Below is the Resurrection. Even the wild animals give back pieces of bodies to complete those rising from the graves.

The northern wall depicts the book of Genesis. The southern wall features the Tree of Jesse with the genealogy of biblical personalities. Inside, facing the iconostasis, is the famous portrait of Ştefan the Great offering Voroneţ Church to Christ. The vibrant blue pigment used throughout the frescoes here is known worldwide as 'Voroneţ blue'.

If you arrive early in the day, you may be able to attend a service and hear the nuns performing a traditional board-tapping ritual dating from the days when church bells were banned.

HUMOR

At Humor, an active monastery run by kindly nuns, the predominant colour is deep red. On the church's southern exterior wall (1530 AD) the 1453 siege of Constantinople is depicted, with the parable of the return of the prodigal son beside it. On the porch is the *Last Judgment* and, in the first chamber inside the church, scenes of martyrdom. Humor has the most impressive interior frescoes of all the monasteries.

MOLDOVITA

Moldovita monastery (1532) is in the middle of a quaint Romanian farming village with a life of its own. Moldovita consists of a strong fortified enclosure with towers and brawny gates, with a magnificent painted church at its centre. The monastery has undergone careful restoration in recent years.

The fortifications here are actually more impressive than the frescoes. On the church's southern exterior wall is a depiction of the defence of Constantinople in 626 AD against Persians dressed as Turks, while on the porch is a representation of the *Last Judgment*, all on a background of blue. Inside the sanctuary, on a wall facing the original carved iconostasis, is a portrait of Prince Petru Rareş (Moldovita's founder) and his family offering the church to Christ. All these works date from 1537. In the monastery's small museum is Petru Rareş' original throne.

Places to Stay & Eat

Popas Turistic, between the train station and the monastery, has small cabins at US$4.50 per person (open mid-June to around mid-September). You can also camp here. There's no running water, but you can draw water from the caretaker's well next door.

A simple restaurant in the *Complex Commercial*, near the camping ground on the road to Vama, serves mititei and draught beer.

Getting There & Away

Moldovita monastery is right above Vatra Moldovitei's train station (be sure to get off at Vatra Moldovitei, not Moldovita). From Suceava there are seven daily trains to Vama (1½ hours). From Vama two trains daily leave for Vatra Moldovitei (50 minutes) at 7.09 am and 2.51 pm, returning to Vama at noon and 5.57 pm.

SUCEVITA

Sucevita monastery is the largest and finest of Bucovina's monasteries. The church inside the fortified quadrangular enclosure (built between 1582 and 1601) is almost completely covered in frescoes. Green and red colours dominate. As you enter you first see the *Virtuous Ladder* fresco covering most of the northern exterior wall, which depicts the 30 steps from hell to paradise. On the southern exterior wall is a tree symbolising the continuity of the Old and New Testaments. The tree grows from the reclining figure of Jesse, who is flanked by a row of ancient philosophers. To the left is the Virgin as a Byzantine princess, with angels holding a red veil over her head. Mysteriously, the western wall remains blank. Legend has it that the artist fell off his scaffolding and died, thus the wall was left unfinished. Apart from the church, there's a small museum at Sucevita monastery.

Places to Stay & Eat

It's worth spending a night here and doing a little hiking in the surrounding hills, which are forest-clad and offer sweeping views. Freelance *camping* is possible in the field across the stream from the monastery. Otherwise *Hanul Sucevita*, a restaurant about 1km north-east towards Rădăuţi, offers rooms with bath in the main two-storey building at US$4.50 per person; the hotel only runs hot water if 14 or more of its rooms are occupied and then only between 7 and 10 am and 8 and 11 pm. The restaurant has basic meals and is open year-round.

Popasul Bucovinean is an excellent Moldavian restaurant which also rents out rooms. Double rooms cost between US$8.50 and $11, depending on room and bed size. A ham and egg breakfast is US$2 extra. Some rooms have private bathrooms. There are also 10 wooden double huts for US$4.20 per hut. Popasul Bucovinean is 5km south of Sucevita on the road to Vatra Moldovitei.

Getting There & Away

Sucevita is the most difficult monastery to reach on public transport. There are four buses from Rădăuţi (17km), one in the morning and three in the afternoon. Two daily buses connect Suceviţa to Moldoviţa (36km), one in the early morning and another around mid-afternoon. The road connecting the two monasteries winds up and over a high mountain pass (1100m), through forests and small alpine villages. The road is stunning and offers unlimited freelance camping opportunities, but you need a car to explore it fully (hiking up would be madness). It's possible to hike the 20km north to Putna in about five hours.

PUTNA

Putna Monastery, built by Ştefan cel Mare in 1466, is still home to an active religious community with groups of monks chanting mass just before sunset. Ştefan and his family are buried in the church, to the right as you enter. The large building behind the monastery contains a small *museum* of medieval manuscripts, rare 15th-century textiles and the holy book of the great prince. The 60 monks living at Putna practise icon painting, shepherding and wood sculpturing. Putna is easy to reach by train and makes a good day trip from Suceava.

Places to Stay & Eat

The *Cabana Putna*, signposted 50m off the main road through the village leading to the monastery, has three and four-bed cabins with shared bathrooms for US$20 per person, including breakfast.

Almost opposite the turn-off for the cabana is the *Complex Turistic Putna*, a shabby hotel and hut complex with a restaurant. Double/triple/four to eight-bed rooms with shared bath are US$11/10/6 per person, including breakfast. A bed in one of its eight huts is US$4.50.

Some people camp freelance in the field opposite the rock-hewn *Daniel the Hermit's cave* at Chilia 2km from the train station. To get there, follow the river upstream to a wooden bridge, cross over and continue straight ahead.

Getting There & Away

Local trains travel to Putna from Suceava eight times a day (two hours). The monastery

is at the end of the road, just under 2km from the station.

You can hike the 20km from Putna to Suceviţa monastery in about five hours. Follow the trail marked with blue crosses in white squares that starts near the hermit's cave. About 4km down the road you turn off to the left.

RĂDĂUŢI

Rădăuţi is a large and boring market town. The only reason to come is to catch a bus for Suceviţa Monastery. If you don't arrive in time for a convenient departure, take a bus to Margin and walk or hitchhike the last 9km to the monastery.

Orientation & Information

The bus station is on Blvd Ştefan cel Mare, a block from Rădăuţi's train station on Str Gării. The centre of town, Piaţa Unirii, is an eight-minute walk along Blvd Ştefan cel Mare.

The left-luggage office at the train station is open 24 hours.

Things to See

The *Muzeul Etnografik* (open daily), opposite the Hotel Nordic, features local folk pottery and embroidered coats. In the central courtyard of the museum is a workshop where traditional pottery is made and items can be purchased. A large market is held in Rădăuţi on Friday.

Nine km west of Rădăuţi towards Suceviţa is the village of Marginea, famous for its black pottery.

Places to Stay & Eat

The only hotel open at the time of writing was the 16-room *Hotel Azur* (☎/fax 464 718), a 10-minute walk from the centre at Calea Cernăuţi 29. Doubles and four/five-bed rooms with private bath are US$6 per person a night.

Getting There & Away

There are direct trains from Suceava to Rădăuţi (1½ hours) daily at 8.19 am and 12.20, 1.50 and 5.22 pm. There are eight trains daily to Putna (one hour) and Dorneşti (11 minutes). From Dorneşti there are direct trains to Suceava (1½ hours) and other stops along the Suceava-Bucharest line.

Buses from Rădăuţi include eight a day to Suceava (62km), seven to Suceviţa (17km) and two to Guru Humorului. Oddly, only one bus, at 3 pm on Friday, goes to Putna. Double-check the times posted in the bus station with a ticket clerk. Bus tickets are sold only one hour before departure.

Dobruja

Dobruja, the land between the Danube River and the Black Sea, was joined to Romania in 1878 when a combined Russo-Romanian army drove the Turks from Bulgaria. In antiquity the region was colonised first by the Greeks and then by the Romans, both of whom left behind a great deal for visitors to admire. Histria, 70km north of Constanţa, is the oldest ancient settlement in Romania, founded by Greek merchants in 657 BC. From 46 AD, Dobruja was the Roman province of Moesia Inferior. At Adamclisi the Romans scored a decisive victory over the Geto-Dacian tribes, which made possible their expansion north of the Danube. Dobruja later fell under Byzantium and in 1418 was conquered by the Turks.

Today the soft, sandy beaches along the 245km southern half of Romania's tideless Black Sea coast are the country's main tourist spots. Each summer the trains are jammed with Romanians in search of fine white sand, warm water and sunshine; in midsummer the Black Sea coast resembles a massive outdoor party, with beachfront barbecues and plenty of beer.

The high season runs from mid-May to late September. From October to late April, the beaches are quiet and the weather is cold. During the off season only a few hotels remain open to house the trickle of tourists and spa clients.

There are nine main resorts lining the seacoast: Mamaia, Eforie Nord, Eforie Sud, Costineşti, Neptun-Olimp, Jupiter, Venus-Aurora, Saturn and Mangalia. Mamaia, the largest resort and the only one north of Constanţa, has numerous sport facilities and a freshwater lake for sailing and water skiing and is popular with families. Eforie Nord has

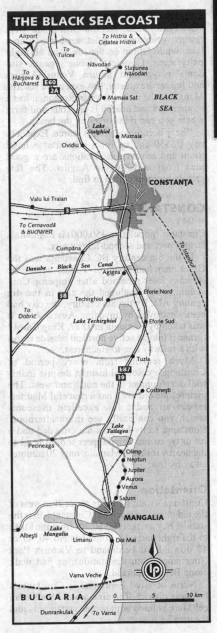

THE BLACK SEA COAST

a famous health spa and the therapeutic Techirghiol lake. Neptun-Olimp are twin resorts – Neptune is quiet, set back along a lake, while Olimp on the sea is an all-night party scene. Costineşti is one gigantic students' playground. Saturn, Venus, Aurora and Jupiter are quieter, less expensive resorts. Mangalia, the oldest town in Romania, has a modern spa and nearby is an Arab stud farm where you can ride horses by the beach.

Cheap accommodation is scarce. Expect to pay US$30 and up for a comfortable hotel room and advance reservations are a good idea from mid-June to August. The few private rooms are hard to find.

CONSTANŢA
☎ 041

Constanţa (population 350,000) is Romania's largest port and second-largest city.

In the 6th century BC Constanţa was the Greek merchant town of Tomis, which the Romans later renamed after emperor Constantin, who developed the city in the 4th century AD. By the 8th century, the city had been destroyed by invading Avars. After it was taken by Romania in 1877, King Carol I turned it into an active port and seaside resort with a railway line to Bucharest.

Much remains from every period of Constanţa's colourful history, despite industrial development to the north and west. The picturesque old town has a peaceful Mediterranean air and a few excellent museums which you can easily see in an afternoon. Constanţa's city beaches are crowded and a bit dirty, so sun-worshippers should head to the nearby resort of Mamaia, only 20 minutes away by bus.

Orientation

Constanţa's train station is about 2km west of the old town. To reach old Constanţa, exit the station, buy a ticket (US$0.20) from the kiosk to the right and take trolleybus No 40, 41 or 43 down Blvd Ferdinand to Victoria Park (four stops from the station); or just walk along Blvd Ferdinand.

North of Blvd Ferdinand is Constanţa's business district. The area around Str Ştefan cel Mare is lined with shops, restaurants and theatres.

Information

Tourist Offices The Agenţie de Turism Intern (☎/fax 611 429), Blvd Tomis 46, is useless except for its maps (open weekdays from 8 am to 5 pm and Saturday from 8 am to noon).

Foreign Embassies If you need a visa to enter Turkey, the Turkish Consulate is a short walk from the train station at Blvd Ferdinand 82 (weekdays 8 am to noon).

CONSTANŢA

1 Hotel Perla
2 Hotel Parc
3 Pescărie Bus Stop
4 Planetarium; Dolphinarium
5 China Restaurant
6 Northern Bus Station (Autogară Nord)
7 Stadionul 1 Mai; Childrens' Park
8 Automobil Clubul Român (ACR)
9 Culture House
10 Southern Bus Station (Autogară Sud)
11 Train Station

Money BANCOREX, Str Traian 2, changes travellers cheques and give cash advances on Visa/MasterCard on weekdays from 8.30 am to 2 pm. Next door, Bancă Comercială Română, Str Traian 1, has an ATM outside accepting Visa/MasterCard. Both are on the way to/from the train station. Bancă Agricola at Piaţa Ovidiu 9 and on the corner of Str Cuza Vodă and Str General Manu also gives advances and changes travellers cheques on weekdays from 8 am to 11 am. BCIT on Str Ştefan cel Mare 32-34 is open weekdays from 9 am to 2.30 pm. The Danubius Exchange at Blvd Ferdinand 44 changes money at good rates. Most hotels and supermarkets have exchange outlets, too.

Post & Communications The telephone centre is in the main post office, Blvd Tomis 79. The telephone section is open daily from 7 am to 10 pm, while the post office's hours are weekdays from 9 am to 5 pm.

Travel Agencies The Danubius travel agency's friendly, English-speaking staff sell tickets for ferries to Istanbul and arrange day trips to the Danube Delta and Murfatlar winery. It has offices at Piaţa Ovidiu 11 (☎ 613 103) and Blvd Ferdinand 36 (☎ 670 129), both open weekdays from 9 am to 7 pm and Saturday from 9 am to 2 pm.

Left Luggage The left-luggage office in the train station is downstairs inside the passageway from the main hall to the tracks (open 24 hours).

Dangers & Annoyances Constanţa is plagued with street hustlers and thieves. Don't change money on the streets and beware of boys who crowd around you acting friendly – they'll pick your pockets and steal your pack.

Things to See

The first place you'll notice in the centre of town is **Parcul Victoriei** on Blvd Ferdinand, which has remains of the 3rd-century **Roman city wall**, pieces of Roman sculpture and a modern **Victory monument**. On the corner of Blvd Tomis is the **Museum of Art** and the adjoining **small gallery** where contemporary

art exhibits are held. As you walk south on Blvd Tomis you come to the worthwhile **Muzeul de Artă Populară** (Folk Art Museum) in an ornate building on the left at No 32 (closed Monday). You will also pass the **Geamia Hunchiar Mosque**, built in 1868 with stones from the old gate of the former Ottoman fortress.

Constanţa's most renowned attraction is the **History & Archaeological Museum** at Piaţa Ovidiu 12, with exhibits on three floors (closed Monday and Tuesday). It includes 24 2nd-century Roman statues discovered under the old train station in 1962. The most unusual objects are kept in the treasury downstairs. Don't miss the 2nd-century AD sculpture of Glykon, a serpent with the muzzle of an antelope and the eyes, ears and hair of a human. Most cases have captions in English and German.

The archaeological fragments of Roman Tomis spill over onto the surrounding square. Facing these is a glass museum, which shelters a gigantic 3rd-century **Roman mosaic** discovered in 1959. The **statue of Ovid**, erected on Piaţa Ovidiu in 1887, commemorates the Latin poet exiled to Constanţa in 8 AD.

A block south and on Str Muzeelor is Mahmudiye **mosque** (1910), with a 140-step minaret you can climb when the gate is unlocked. Two blocks farther down the same street is an **Orthodox cathedral** (1885). One block to the right is the **Saligny monument**, overlooking the modern harbour.

From the monument, a peaceful promenade meanders along the waterfront, offering sweeping views of the Black Sea. On summer evenings this is a popular hangout for kids, entwined couples and old men playing chess. Have a beer or coffee on the terrace of Constanţa's French baroque **casino** (1910). Farther along the promenade is the **Genoese lighthouse** (1860) and pier, with a fine view of old Constanţa.

The **Naval History Museum**, Str Traian 53, has detailed exhibits on early Romanian history. The captions are in Romanian, but the illustrations are informative (closed Monday).

Places to Stay

Camping The nearest camping ground is in Mamaia, but an easy 20-minute trolleybus ride will take you there.

ROMANIA

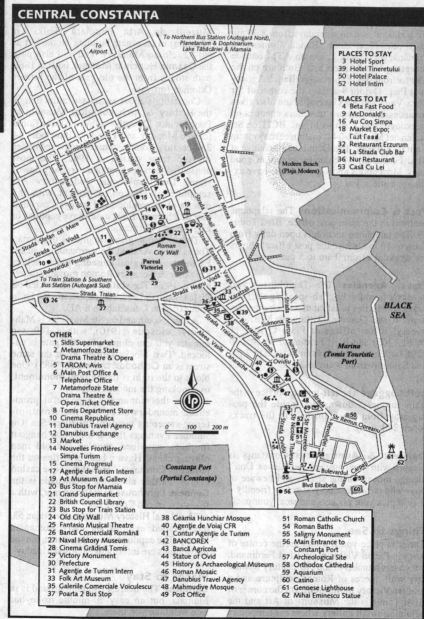

CENTRAL CONSTANȚA

To Northern Bus Station (Autogară Nord),
Planetarium & Dophinarium,
Lake Tăbăcăriei & Mamaia

To Airport

Modern Beach
(Plaja Modern)

Strada Sarmisegetuza
Strada Răscoalei din 1907
Strada Cenzal Manu
Strada Mihai Viteazul
Bulevardul Tomis
M. Eminescu Blvd
Strada Mihail Kogălniceanu
Strada Mircea cel Bătrân
Strada Ecaterina Varga

Roman City Wall

Strada Ștefan cel Mare
Strada Cuza Vodă
Bulevardul Ferdinand

Parcul Victoriei

To Train Station & Southern Bus Station (Autogară Sud)
Strada Traian

Strada Negru Vodă
Strada Karatzali

Strada Marcus Aurelius
Bulevardul Tomis
Suimona

Aleea Vasile Canarache
Strada Traian

Constanța Port
(Portul Constanța)

Piața Ovidiu

Strada Revoluției
Strada Nicolae Titulescu
Strada Ovidiu
Strada Mirzicilor
Str Mirzicilor
Str Nicolae Titulescu

Str Remus Opreanu

Bulevardul Carpați
Blvd Eilsabeta

BLACK SEA

Marina
(Tomis Touristic Port)

0   100   200 m

PLACES TO STAY
3   Hotel Sport
39 Hotel Tineretului
50 Hotel Palace
52 Hotel Intim

PLACES TO EAT
4   Beta Fast Food
9   McDonald's
16 Au Coq Simpa
18 Market Expo;
    Fast Food
32 Restaurant Erzurum
34 La Strada Club Bar
36 Nur Restaurant
53 Casă Cu Lei

OTHER
1   Sidis Supermarket
2   Metamorfoze State
    Drama Theatre & Opera
5   TAROM; Avis
6   Main Post Office &
    Telephone Office
7   Metamorfoze State
    Drama Theatre &
    Opera Ticket Office
8   Tomis Department Store
10 Cinema Republica
11 Danubius Travel Agency
12 Danubius Exchange
13 Market
14 Nouvelles Frontières/
    Simpa Turism
15 Cinema Progresul
17 Agenție de Turism Intern
19 Art Museum & Gallery
20 Bus Stop for Mamaia
21 Grand Supermarket
22 British Council Library
23 Bus Stop for Train Station
24 Old City Wall
25 Fantasio Musical Theatre
26 Bancă Comercială Română
27 Naval History Museum
28 Cinema Grădină Tomis
29 Victory Monument
30 Prefecture
31 Agenție de Turism Intern
33 Folk Art Museum
35 Galeriile Comerciale Voiculescu
37 Poarta 2 Bus Stop

38 Geamia Hunchiar Mosque
40 Agenție de Voiaj CFR
41 Contur Agenție de Turism
42 BANCOREX
43 Bancă Agricola
44 Statue of Ovid
45 History & Archaeological Museum
46 Roman Mosaic
47 Danubius Travel Agency
48 Mahmudiye Mosque
49 Post Office

51 Roman Catholic Church
54 Roman Baths
55 Saligny Monument
56 Main Entrance to
    Constanța Port
57 Archeological Site
58 Orthodox Cathedral
59 Aquarium
60 Casino
61 Genoese Lighthouse
62 Mihai Eminescu Statue

Hotels The two-star *Hotel Tineretului* (☎ 613 590; fax 611 290), Blvd Tomis 24, is a five-storey hotel with neat, clean rooms costing US$21/31 for a single/double with breakfast.

The elegant *Hotel Intim* (☎ 618 285), Str Nicolae Titulescu 9, offers two-star singles/doubles at US$27/36 and three-star rooms for US$37/48, breakfast included.

Hotel Palace (☎ 614 696), Str Remus Opreanu 7 in the old town, is in a beautiful location that overlooks the sea, but it's rather expensive at US$26/40 for a two-star double/triple and US$65/84 for a three-star single/double, breakfast included.

North of Blvd Ferdinand, the *Hotel Sport* (☎ 617 558; fax 611 009) at Str Cuza Vodă 2 is a nice modern hotel by the beach. It charges US$29/40/53 for single/double/triple (the triple has a bunk bed), breakfast included. Some rooms have balconies overlooking the beach. The hotel is usually full with athletic groups.

Places to Eat

Constanţa's eating scene is not great, so stock up on fruit, cheese and vegies at the market off Str Răscoaiei 1907, behind the bus stop. The *Grand Supermarket* at Blvd Tomis 57 is open 24 hours and has good cakes and sweets. The *Sidis Supermarket* at Blvd Tomis 99 has everything; it's open Monday to Saturday from 8 am to 9 pm.

There are fast-food outlets at the modern *Galeriile Comerciale Voiculescu* shopping arcade on Blvd Tomis. *Beta Fast Food* in the park opposite TAROM on Str Ştefan cel Mare has a terrace where you can drink beer and eat traditional mititei; it's open from 10 am until dusk. *McDonald's* is on Str Ştefan cel Mare by the Tomis department store.

The trendy *La Strada Club Bar* at Str Vasile Alecsandri 7 serves great cappuccino and is open 24 hours.

For authentic Turkish food there's *Restaurant Erzurum*, Blvd Tomis near the Folk Art Museum, open daily from 10 am to 6 pm; or *Nur Restaurant* on Str Traian 24.

The French *Au Coq Simpa* at Str Ştefan cel Mare is open from 11 am to midnight.

Constanţa's modest splurge is the *Casă Cu Lei* (meaning 'House of the Lions') at Str Dianei 1, west of Piaţa Ovidiu. It's an elegant 1887 building with three salons and a cosy bar.

Entertainment

Foreign films are presented in their original language (with Romanian subtitles) at *Cinema Progresul*, Str Ştefan cel Mare 33, and *Cinema Republica*, Blvd Ferdinand 58.

The *Metamorfoze State Drama Theatre and Opera* is in the park at Str Mircea cel Brân 97. Tickets are sold at Blvd Tomis 97, next to the post office. The *Fantasio Musical Theatre*, Blvd Ferdinand 11, offers musicals and cabarets.

Getting There & Away

Air In summer there are international flights to/from Constanţa's airport, 25km from the city centre.

Between May and September TAROM (☎ 662 632), Str Ştefan cel Mare 15, runs flights daily, except Sunday, from Constanţa to Bucharest; one way/return is US$50/100. TAROM's office is open weekdays from 9 am to 5 pm and Saturday from 9 am to 1 pm. It runs a free shuttle for ticket holders from its office to the airport 1½ hours before flight departures.

Train Constanţa's train station is by the bus station at the western end of Blvd Ferdinand. The CFR office (☎ 614 960) is at Aleea Vasile Canarache 4, behind the archaeological museum. It's open weekdays from 7.30 am to 7 pm and Saturday from 7.30 am to 1 pm.

Constanţa is well connected to Bucharest's Gara de Nord by express train (three hours). In summer there are also direct trains to Oradea, Timişoara, Arad, Iaşi, Suceava, Braşov and Satu Mare; the *Ovidius* express train runs overnight between Constanţa and Budapest-Keleti (17 hours) via Bucharest and Arad.

Local trains run north to Tulcea (179km via Medgidia), south to Mangalia (43km) and west to Bucureşti-Obor and Braşov. For northern Romania, take a Bucharest-bound train west to Feteşti (79km) and change for Făurei (for Iaşi) or Buzău (for Suceava).

Bus If you're travelling south down the Black Sea coast, buses are infinitely more convenient than the trains. Exit Constanţa's train station and walk 50m to the right, to the queue of buses. Private minivans leave every 30 minutes for Mangalia, stopping at Eforie Nord, Eforie Sud, Neptun-Olimp, Venus and

Saturn for US$1.25. Blue buses Nos 10, 11, 12 and 20 also travel south to resort towns via the main highway; you may have to walk a kilometre or two from the stop to reach the coast. Rates by destination are posted inside the bus; pay the driver.

Trolleybus No 41 to Constanţa's centre continues north to Mamaia. For city buses buy a ticket at a kiosk, then validate it once aboard.

There is a daily bus to Istanbul (17½ hours, US$17/23 one way/return) via Bulgaria, departing from Autogară Sud, next to the train station, at noon.

From Constanţa's northern bus station (Autogară Nord) daily services include one to Histria (52km) and five to Tulcea (125km).

Ferry The Constanţa-Istanbul ferry operates from 1 May to 1 September, takes 20 hours and costs US$40/55 single/return for a deck seat (payable in hard currency or by Visa). It also offers a variety of expensive cabins. At the time of writing, there were two departures a week to Istanbul. Danubius (☎ 615 836; fax 618 010), Blvd Ferdinand 36, sells tickets a day in advance for the ferry and is open on weekdays from 9 am to 6 pm. The agency runs a free shuttle bus for its passengers from its Piaţa Ovidiu office to the port. You can also buy tickets two hours before departure from the ticket office on the ferry, docked at the southern end of Blvd Elisabeta.

MAMAIA
☎ 041

Just north of Constanţa, Mamaia, an 8km strip of beach between Lake Siutghiol and the Black Sea, is Romania's most popular resort with 61 hotels. Mamaia is an above-average example of the Black Sea resorts you'll find farther south, with abundant greenery and a festival-like atmosphere.

The main things to do here are swim and sunbathe, drink beer and stroll along the boardwalk. Best of all, Constanţa is just a bus ride away (No 41).

Information
Tourist Offices The Litoral tourist office (☎ 831 334) on the highway side of Hotel Perla south of the casino arranges car rentals and guided tours (April to October 15, weekdays from 9 am to 3 pm).

Money Every hotel has a currency exchange, but to change travellers cheques or get a cash advance you must go to Constanţa. Most of the large hotels accept credit cards.

Post & Communications The telephone centre and post office share an office on the boardwalk, 200m south of the Cazino complex. It's open weekdays from 8 am to 8 pm.

Things to See & Do
In summer a boat ferries tourists across freshwater Lake Mamaia to **Ovidiu Island** every hour or two in the afternoon. The boat leaves from the wharf near **Mamaia Cazino**, on the lake side of the strip, behind the Cazino Bazar. A return ticket costs US$2.

All kinds of **water sports**, such as sailboarding, water-skiing, yachting, rowing and pedal boating, are available on Lake Mamaia.

The tennis courts at Grăvina Boema, on the highway between the Doina and Victoria hotels, cost US$7 per hour including equipment rental.

Places to Stay
Camping The *Popas Tabăra Turist* is at the far northern end of Mamaia's 8km strip. It's small and always full in summer. It costs US$1 to pitch a tent and US$4 for a bed in a wooden hut. Take bus No 23 from Pescări bus stop to the Statia Tabăra Turist bus stop. There's a disco next to the site.

Popas Mamaia is 2km farther north than Tabăra, but larger. It costs US$2 for a tent and US$3.50 for a bed in a hut. Bus No 23 stops outside the site.

The *Popas Hanul Piraţilor* is 1km farther north of Popas Mamaia, between the main road and the beach (again, take bus No 23). It has double/triple huts for US$6/10 and a two-room villa for US$20.

Beach Chalets The *Cazino Delta Pensiune* (☎ 831 665) inside the Cazino complex and on the southern side of the main building, offers terraced chalets overlooking the beach (they're basically rooms with mattresses). A double chalet with shared bathroom and cold water costs US$6 a night.

The *Mini-Hotel* (☎ 831 878) on the northern side of the Cazino main building rents out chalets, too. Its five triple rooms and 50 doubles cost US$3.50 per person in May, US$5 in June and September and US$6 in July and August.

Hotels The *Hotel Victoria* (☎ 831 153; fax 831 253), 300m north of the Cazino on the boardwalk, is a family-run hotel on the beach. It has 10 double rooms with private bath for US$15 a night.

Friendly *Hotel Albatros* (☎ 831 381; fax 831 346) is 50m south of the Victoria. Singles/doubles with bath are US$20/35. It's 20m left of the Statia Cazino bus stop turn. Next door to the Albatros is the two-star *Hotel Condor* (☎ 831 142; fax 831 906). Doubles with private bath are US$20 a night.

Hotel Perla (☎ 831 670) and *Hotel Parc* (☎ 831 670) are high-rises at the southern end of the boardwalk, near the Pescărie bus stop. Both have standard rooms and mid-range prices: US$22/35/40 for a single/double/triple.

Places to Eat

Almost every hotel has an adjoining restaurant serving the usual pork and grilled meatballs. *Fast-food stands* along the boardwalk suffice for lunch and hot snacks. The casino's *Delta Restaurant* has slow service, but the food and beach views are good. Across the road from the Popas Hanul Piraților is the touristy *Hanul Piraților Restaurant*, where you can enjoy a good mixed grill and plenty of wine.

Ovidiu Island's thatched-roof *Rustic Restaurant* is famous for seafood and worth a visit.

Getting There & Away

Travelling between Constanța and Mamaia by trolleybus is simple and quick. Trolleybus No 40 runs from the train station to the centre of Constanța down Blvd Ferdinand, then on to the Pescărie bus stop near Hotel Parc, at the southern end of Mamaia. Here you can change to trolleybus No 23 or 47, which run north past Mamaia's major hotels. In summer a shuttle runs up and down Mamaia's 5km boardwalk.

EFORIE NORD
☎ 041

Eforie Nord, 17km from Constanța, is the first large resort south of the city. The beach is below 20m cliffs on the eastern side of the town, and walls built out into the sea trap additional sand. Tiny Lake Belona, just behind the southern end of the beach, is a popular bathing spot, as its water is warmer than the Black Sea. Because Eforie Nord is close to Constanța it tends to be overcrowded; the beaches are better and cleaner farther south.

Just south-west of Eforie Nord is Techirghiol Lake, a former river mouth famous for its black sapropel mud, effective against rheumatism. The cold mud baths are the only place in Romania where nudism is allowed (separate areas are designated for women and men). The lake's waters are four times as salty as the sea; the lake is 2m below sea level.

Eforie Nord has 44 hotels accommodating some 19,000 tourists every year. If you don't like crowded beaches and blaring pop music, stay away.

Orientation

The train station is only a few minutes walk from the post office and main street, Blvd Republicii. Exit the station and turn left; turn left again after Hotel Belvedere and then right onto Blvd Republicii. City maps are posted at the station and around town. Buses from Mangalia and Constanța stop in the centre of town on Blvd Republicii.

Most hotels and restaurants are on Str Tudor Vladimirescu, which runs parallel to Blvd Republicii along the beach. The beach is a 10m drop from the road.

Information

The Agenție de Turism Intern (☎ 741 188), Blvd Republicii 4, 50m north of the bus stop, arranges private rooms for US$10 per person (open April to September, Monday to Saturday from 8 am to 4 pm).

There are currency exchanges at nearly every hotel, supermarket and street corner.

Post & Communications The telephone centre at the main post office on Blvd Republicii 119 is open daily from 7 am to 10 pm; the post office is open weekdays from 9 am to 6 pm.

Places to Stay

Camping The budget traveller's first stop should be *Camping Sincai*, a few hundred metres west of Eforie Nord's train station. Walk west to the far end of the railway platform, cross the tracks and follow a path to a breach in the wall. As well as camping space, there are five two-room huts at US$5 per person and a lovely but dilapidated old villa right by the lake (US$5 per person).

There are better facilities at *Camping Meduza*, behind the Minerva and Prahova hotels at the northern end of the beach. Walk north along Str Tudor Vladimirescu and turn immediately left after Club Maxim. It's closer to the beach but farther from the train station. Tent spaces are US$1.50 per person.

Hotels The *Europa Hotel* (☎ 742 990), Blvd Republicii 19 in the centre of town, is Eforie Nord's most upmarket address. It charges US$30/45 for a single/double with bath.

Two-star *Hotel Delfin*, *Hotel Meduza* and *Hotel Steaua* are high-rises, side-by-side at Str Tudor Vladimirescu 39-43 at the northern end of the beach. They're owned by the same company (☎ 742 483; fax 742 980) and specialise in natural cures and mud baths. Single/double rooms in all three start at US$20/35.

Places to Eat

The *Cofetăria Pescărus* opposite the post office has great pastries. The adjacent restaurant is loud and crowded in summer. *Restaurant Berbec*, Str 1 Mai, at the northern end of the beach, is famous for its folk-dancing shows. It charges US$10 for a meal and music. *Nunta Zamfirei* has folk song-and-dance shows. Walk north along Blvd Republicii and turn left onto the small track opposite the thermal baths.

Getting There & Away

The CFR office, next to the post office, sells tickets for express trains. All trains between Bucharest and Mangalia stop at Eforie Nord, but you're better off on a private minibus (see Getting There & Away under Constanţa). Slower and only slightly cheaper are city bus Nos 10 and 11, which leave for Eforie Nord from the street beyond the tram stop, just south of Constanţa's train station.

NEPTUN-OLIMP
☎ 041

Before the 1989 revolution, Neptun-Olimp was the exclusive tourist complex of Romania's Communist Party. Since 1989 the hotels have been privatised and are now open to everyone. The resort offers a range of activities: tennis, windsurfing, sailing, jet-skiing, mini-golf, billiards, bowling and, at night, the discos. Neptun-Olimp is perhaps the nicest and most chic of Romania's Black Sea resorts.

Orientation

Neptun-Olimp is really two resorts in one. Olimp, a huge complex of hotels facing the beach, is the party place. Neptun, 1km south, is separated from the Black Sea by two small lakes amid lush greenery. Together they form a vast expanse of hotels and discos. A paved road and local minibuses connect the towns.

Information

The Dispecerat Cazare (room dispatcher; ☎ 701 300) can give you information on hotels and take bookings. It can also arrange camp sites and sometimes rooms in private houses. The office is inside the Levent Market on the main street; it's open 24 hours between June and September.

Most hotels have tourist desks with English-speaking staff who will help you with organised tours along the coast.

BANCOREX, next to Hotel Decebal at Neptun, changes travellers cheques for a US$3 commission on weekdays from 10 am to 1 pm. So does Bancă Comercială Română, next door, on weekdays from 8.30 am to 11.30 am.

The post office and telephone centre is a block north of Hotel Decebal in Neptun.

Places to Stay

Camping Both of Neptun-Olimp's camping grounds are packed in summer. *Camping Neptun* (☎ 731 220) at the southern end of Lake Neptun II is open year-round. In July and August, a double room in the main building is US$10, a double hut with running water is US$8 per person and camping is US$4 per person.

Camping Olimp (☎ 731 314) at the northern end of Olimp's tourist strip charges similar prices for its 140 basic wooden huts.

Hotels Neptun-Olimp's hotels are not for budget travellers. There are 44 two and three-star hotels charging from US$22/36 for a double room, without breakfast. Without reservations you'll pay more. It's best to have a travel agency in Bucharest or Constanţa book a room for you.

Places to Eat

There are numerous fast-food joints, but a nicer place to eat is the *Restaurant Insula*, a series of wooden rafts moored on Lake Neptun I, which serves traditional Romanian food. It's open from noon until past midnight.

Known for their cuisine and folklore shows are the *Calul Bălan*, on the left as you enter Neptun's main street from the south, and *Popasul Căproarelor* at the north-western end of Neptun in Comorova forest.

Getting There & Away

Train Halta Neptun station is within walking distance of the Neptun-Olimp hotels, midway between the two resorts. All trains travelling from Bucharest or Constanţa to Mangalia stop at Halta Neptun.

The CFR office is inside Neptun's Hotel Apollo, north-west of Lake Neptun II.

Bus Private minivans run between resort towns and from Mangalia to Constanţa (see Getting There & Away under Constanţa).

Buses from Constanţa and Mangalia will drop you on the main highway, 2.5km from Neptun-Olimp's hotels. City bus Nos 15 and 20 travel 9km south to Mangalia, while city bus No 20 runs 38km north to Constanţa.

MANGALIA
☎ 041

Formerly ancient Greek Callatis, Mangalia, founded in the 6th century BC, contains several minor archaeological sites. It is a quiet town, not a place for partying, and attracts many elderly European tour groups.

Orientation

Mangalia's train station is 1km north of the centre. Turn right as you exit and follow Şoseaua Constanţei (the main road) south. At the roundabout, turn left for Hotel Mangalia and the beach or continue straight for the

pedestrianised section of Şoseaua Constanţei, where most facilities are. Private and city buses stop in front of the train station and at Staţia Stadion, south of the roundabout on Şoseaua Constanţei.

Information

Tourist Offices Your best bet is the reception desk of the Hotel President. Staff speak English, French and German and sell maps for Mangalia and other coastal resorts. There are also information boards in the Hotel Mangalia. The hotel's tourist office organises day trips to Murfatlar vineyards (US$23).

Money Most hotels have currency exchanges. Cash travellers cheques and get Visa/MasterCard cash advances at Bancă Comercială Română at Şoseaua Constanţei 25 (weekdays from 8 to 11 am; with outside ATM) or at Bancă Agricola on the beachfront at Str Teilor 7 (weekdays from 8 to 11.30 am and Saturday from 8 am to noon).

Post & Communications The telephone centre and post office are at Ştefan cel Mare 16 (the former is open daily from 7 am to 10 pm, the latter open weekdays from 7 am to 8 pm).

There is an Internet café inside the Hotel President, open weekdays from noon to midnight.

Things to See & Do

At the roundabout, a street runs left straight down to Hotel Mangalia and the beach, with the ruins of a 6th-century **Palaeo-Christian basilica** and a fountain dispensing sulphurous mineral water. The numerous apartment blocks around Hotel Mangalia were built towards the end of the Ceauşescu era.

Return to the roundabout and continue south on Şoseaua Constanţei. You'll soon reach the **Callatis Archaeological Museum** on the left, with a good collection of Roman sculpture (closed Monday). Just past the high-rise building next to the museum are some remnants of a 4th-century necropolis.

Continue south on Şoseaua Constanţei for another 500m to the centre of town. On most summer evenings cultural events take place in the **Casă de Cultură**, with the large mural on the façade (on the right). Farther ahead along the same street is the Turkish **Sultan**

Esmahan Mosque (1460). All these sights can easily be seen in two hours.

The Mangalia Stud Farm (☎ 751 325) is 3km north of Mangalia at the southern tip of Venus. It has a small racecourse and experienced riders can ride for US$6 an hour.

At Saturn, just 1km north of Mangalia, you can rent paddleboats on the beach.

Places to Stay

Camping The nearest camping ground is *Popas Saturn*. A tent space costs US$2, plus there are 56 small cabins for US$4 per person. The site is shady and has snack and beer bars, occasional warm showers and easy access to the beach. It's open from June to mid-September. To get here, follow Şoseaua Constanţei 1km north from Mangalia's train station to the Art-Deco 'Saturn' sculpture, turn right, go 50m and turn left. You could also take bus Nos 14, 15 and 20 from the train station to the Saturn sculpture (two stops).

There are similar camping grounds in Venus and Jupiter, all accessible by bus and operating beyond capacity.

Private Rooms ANTREC (☎ 750 473) has an office at Str Aurora 13, block D, apartment 2. It arranges rooms in private homes in Mangalia and other coastal resorts starting at US$10 a night.

Hotels Three two-star hotels on the promenade, the *Hotel Zenit* (☎ 751 646), *Hotel Astra* (☎ 751 673) and *Hotel Orion* (☎ 751 156) at Str Teilor 7, 9 and 11 are quite pleasant and charge US$20 a night for a double with private bath. A popular choice with tour groups for its spa treatments is *Hotel Mangalia* (☎ 752 052; fax 753 510), Str Rozelor 35, with single/double rooms for US$25/35.

There are countless high-rise hotels along the beach between Mangalia and Saturn, with double rooms averaging US$30 in summer. Most are open from June to September only.

Places to Eat

Hotel restaurants are the main dinner option. Get fresh pastries and good coffee at *Patiseria Peach-Pit* on Şoseaua Constanţei, near the archaeological museum. *Four Seasons*, next door to the museum, has pizza, sandwiches and ice cream but closes at 6 pm.

Stock up on packed-lunch delights at the *food market* on Piaţa Agroalimentară, behind Hotel Zenit at Str Vasile Alecsandri.

Getting There & Away

Train From Constanţa there are 18 trains daily in summer (1¼ hours) but only five daily in winter. Many of these trains are direct to/from Bucharest's Gară de Nord (4½ hours). In summer there are express trains to/from Arad, Iaşi, Oradea, Sibiu, Suceava and Timişoara.

The CFR office adjoins the post office at Str Ştefan cel Mare 16; it's open weekdays from 9 am to 5 pm.

Bus Private buses from Constanţa stop throughout the day at Mangalia's train station and near the roundabout (see Getting There & Away under Constanţa). City bus No 12 also travels the main highway to Constanţa.

Bus No 14 runs from Mangalia's train station to the Bulgarian border at Vama Veche, 10km south of Mangalia, six times a day. After crossing on foot, it's a 6km hike to Durankulak.

The Danube Delta

At the end of its long journey across Europe the mighty Danube river empties into the Black Sea just south of the Ukrainian border. Here the Danube splits into three channels – the Chilia, Sulina and Sfântu Gheorghe, creating a 5800 sq km wetland of marshes, floating reed islets and sandbars, sanctuary for 300 species of birds and 160 species of fish. Reed marshes cover 156,300 hectares, constituting one of the largest single expanses of reed beds in the world.

The Danube Delta (Delta Dunarii) is protected under the Administration of the Danube Delta Biosphere Reserve (ARBDD), set up in response to the ecological disaster that befell the Delta during Ceauşescu's attempt to transform it into an agricultural region. Now 18 protected reserves – 50,000 hectares including the 500-year-old Leţea forest and Europe's largest pelican colony – are off-limits to tourists or anglers. The Delta is also included in UNESCO's world heritage list.

THE DANUBE DELTA

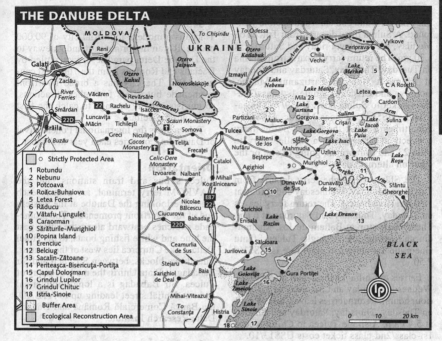

Strictly Protected Area
1 Rotundu
2 Nebunu
3 Potcoava
4 Roăca-Buhaiova
5 Letea Forest
6 Răducu
7 Vătafu-Lungulet
8 Caraorman
9 Sărăturile-Murighiol
10 Popina Island
11 Erencluc
12 Belciug
13 Sacalin-Zătoane
14 Periteașca-Bisericuța-Portița
15 Capul Doloșman
16 Grindul Lupilor
17 Grindul Chituc
18 Istria-Sinoie

Buffer Area

Ecological Reconstruction Area

The part of the Delta most accessible to foreigners is the middle arm, which cuts directly across from Tulcea to Crișan and Sulina (71km). Most river traffic uses the Sulina arm, including the ferries and touring boats from Tulcea. The villages along the Sfântu Gheorghe arm are also becoming popular with travellers.

Getting Around
Most hotels and travel agencies in Tulcea arrange day trips through the delta on small motorboats. You can also approach local boat operators directly and arrange a private trip for an agreed price.

The government-subsidised NAVROM operates passenger ferries and hydrofoils to several towns and villages in the delta. However, you'll need small boats to see the most interesting wildlife, as commercial traffic and passenger ferries have driven the birds deeper into the delta. It's easy to hire rowing boats from village anglers and this is

the only way to penetrate the more exotic backwaters (fishermen charge US$15 to $20 for a few hours).

All visitors need a permit to travel in the delta. As a tourist, you're fined US$100 if you enter a protected area without a permit. Permits cost US$1 and are sold in Tulcea's travel agencies and at hotel receptions in Crișan, Sulina and Murighiol. Permits are automatically included in organised tours. You need a special permit to fish or camp. You'll also need lots of mosquito repellent!

Hydrofoils NAVROM runs hydrofoils from Tulcea to Crișan and Sulina, with a reduced service in winter. Hydrofoils to Sulina leave Tulcea on Tuesday and Thursday at 4.30 pm. The trip takes 1½ hours and costs US$13. Return hydrofoils depart from Sulina on Wednesday, Friday and Sunday at 7.30 am.

From mid-May to September there's a daily hydrofoil from Tulcea to Galați at 12.15 pm (three hours, US$6).

ROMANIA

Ferries The ferries serve all three channels. They have 1st and 2nd class and operate year-round. A Sulina ferry departs from Tulcea on Monday, Wednesday, Friday and Saturday at 1.30 pm. The return ferry departs from Sulina on Tuesday, Thursday, Saturday and Sunday at 7 am. It stops at Partizanul, Maliuc, Gorgova and Crişan. A single 1st-class/2nd-class ticket to Sulina costs US$9/7 (Tulcea-Crişan US$6/4, Tulcea-Maliuc US$5/4). Four times a week the Tulcea-Sulina ferry connects at Crişan with a smaller ferry to Mila 23 and Caraorman, going to one or the other on alternate days.

The Sfântu Gheorghe ferry departs from Tulcea on Monday, Wednesday and Friday at 1.30 pm (five hours). The return ferry leaves on Tuesday, Thursday and Saturday at 6 am. These boats stop at Balteni de Jos, Mahmudia and Murighiol. A single Tulcea-Sfântu Gheorghe 1st-class/2nd-class fare is US$10/7.50.

Ferries to Chilia-Veche depart on Monday, Wednesday, Friday and Saturday at 1.30 pm (four hours). Return ferries leave Chilia-Veche on Tuesday, Thursday, Saturday and Sunday at 5.45 am. A single Tulcea to Chilia-Veche 1st-class/2nd-class ticket costs US$13/10.

Ferry and hydrofoil tickets are sold at Tulcea's NAVROM terminal from 11.30 am to 1.30 pm. In summer the queues are long, so get in the correct line early (each window sells tickets to a different destination). The classic ferries have 1st and 2nd class, though it's unlikely you'll want to stay in the stuffy 1st-class lounge for long. If it's a nice day take 2nd class and sit outside.

Organised Tours Tulcea's hotels and travel agencies offer day trips on the Delta from mid-May to September (see Information under Tulcea).

Ibis Tours in Tulcea (π/fax 040-511 261; Str Grivitei1, bloc C1, apartment 9) arranges wildlife tours in the Delta and Dobruja led by professional ornithologists for about US$25 a day, including accommodation in a private home. A longer day trip is from Tulcea to Murighiol by bus, followed by two to three hours on a small boat touring bird colonies.

TULCEA
π 040

Tulcea is a modern industrial city of 90,000 people. It's an important port and gateway to the Danube Delta paradise. It was settled by Dacians and Romans from the 7th to 1st centuries BC. The city has a broad riverfront promenade but offers few other attractions, so tourists usually arrange to catch the first ferry into the delta.

Tulcea hosts the International Folk Festival of Danubian Countries each year in August.

Orientation

Tulcea's bus and train stations, and the NAVROM ferry terminal, are next to each other overlooking the Danube at the western end of the riverfront promenade. The promenade stretches eastward along the river, past the blue and white fishing boats, to the Hotel Delta. Lake Ciuperca lies west of the stations. Inland two blocks, between Str Păcii and Str Babadag, is Piaţa Unirii, the modern centre of Tulcea. Str Babadag is a long commercial and residential street leading up to ATBAD, the Bancă Comercială Română and Danube Delta Research Institute.

Information

Tourist Offices The ARBDD (π 550 950) has a tourist information centre 3km from the city centre at Str Taberei 32 at the western end of the city, open weekdays from 10 am to 4 pm. It sells maps of the delta and travel permits. ARBDD plans to open a central tourist office behind the Culture House on the riverfront in 1999.

Fishing and hunting permits are sold at the Fishing & Hunting Association (π 511 404) at Str Isaccea 10. The office is open Monday through Saturday, 7 am to 1 pm, and on Wednesday and Friday again from 5 to 8 pm. A map in the window highlights the areas where tourists are allowed to fish and hunt. (Next door is a fishing tackle shop where you can buy camping gear, open weekdays from 10 am to 6 pm and Saturday from 7 am to 1 pm).

The Automobil Clubul Român (ACR; π 515 151) has an office on the riverfront. It organises boat trips for US$20 and books rooms on its floating hotel.

Money All the hotels have currency exchanges. You can cash travellers cheques and get Visa/MasterCard cash advances at Bancă Comercială Română on Str Toamnei, at the top of Str Babadag. It's open weekdays from 8 to 11 am and has an ATM outside. Bancă Agricola is on Str 9 Mai.

Post & Communications The post office and telephone centre are at Str Păcii 6, open weekdays from 7 am to 8 pm and Saturday from 8 am to noon.

Travel Agencies Danubius Travel Agency (☎ 515 836) on Str Păcii, inside the Hotel Europolis, arranges boat day trips to Crişan from mid-May to September for US$19, including lunch. It's open daily from 8.30 am to 6.30 pm.

Nouvelles Frontières/Simpa Turism (☎/fax 515 753) inside the Hotel Delta arranges day trips along the Sulina arm to Crişan and back

along the Old Danube via Mila 23. The cost is US$26/20 per person for 1st class/2nd class. The same trip can be booked through the Hotel Egreta for US$25 per person.

Private motorboats cost US$11 an hour for up to 15 people. The *SC Gomoescu* (☎ 526 616) moored opposite the ACR office is one of the many boats in the harbour to do day trips.

Left Luggage The left-luggage office at the train station is open daily 24 hours.

Things to See

As you stroll along the river note the **Independence Monument** (1904) on Citadel Hill, at the far eastern end of town. You can reach this by following Str Gloriei from behind the Egreta Hotel to its end; the views are superb. The **History and Archaeology Museum** is just below the monument. On your way back, look for the minaret of **Azizie Mosque** (1863) down Str Independenţei.

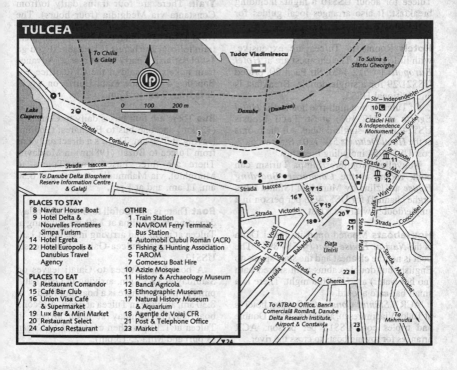

TULCEA

To Chilia & Galaţi

Tudor Vladimirescu

To Sulina & Sfântu Gheorghe

Lake Ciaperca

Danube (Dunărea)

Str–Independenţei

To Citadel Hill & Independence Monument

0   100   200 m

Strada Portului

Strada Isaccea

To Danube Delta Biosphere Reserve Information Centre & Galaţi

Strada Isaccea

Str Chindei

Strada 9 Mai

Strada Water

Strada Victoriei

Strada Unirii

Strada Concordei

Strada Păcii

Strada Mahmudia

Piaţa Unirii

Str M Vodă

Str C Doja

Strada C D Gherea

Babadag

To ATBAD Office, Bancă Comercială Română, Danube Delta Research Institute, Airport & Constanţa

To Mahmudia

PLACES TO STAY
8 Navitur House Boat
9 Hotel Delta & Nouvelles Frontières Simpa Turism
14 Hotel Egreta
22 Hotel Europolis & Danubius Travel Agency

PLACES TO EAT
3 Restaurant Comandor
15 Café Bar Club
16 Union Visa Café & Supermarket
19 Lux Bar & Mini Market
20 Restaurant Select
24 Calypso Restaurant

OTHER
1 Train Station
2 NAVROM Ferry Terminal; Bus Station
4 Automobil Clubul Român (ACR)
5 Fishing & Hunting Association
6 TAROM
7 Gomoescu Boat Hire
10 Azizie Mosque
11 History & Archaeology Museum
12 Bancă Agricola
13 Ethnographic Museum
17 Natural History Museum & Aquarium
18 Agenţie de Voiaj CFR
21 Post & Telephone Office
23 Market

At the southern end of Str Gloriei, turn left onto Str 9 Mai; the **Ethnographic Museum** at No 2 has traditional costumes, fishing gear and carpets among its exhibits.

The **Natural History Museum and Aquarium**, Str Progresului 32, has a good collection of Danube fish and detailed exhibits on delta wildlife. In front of the Greek Orthodox church opposite the museum is a memorial to local victims of the 1989 revolution.

Tulcea's museums are open daily, except Monday, from 8 am to 6 pm (US$0.40).

Places to Stay

Camping A no-camping regulation within Tulcea's city limits is strictly enforced by police. Seek local advice from BTT at Str Babadag 2. BTT operates a camping ground at Lake Roşu, south of Sulina in the Delta.

Private Rooms ANTREC (☎/fax 515 753), Str Isaacea 2 in Hotel Delta, arranges accommodation in private homes in and around Tulcea for about US$10 a night, including breakfast. It also arranges local guides for US$10 a day.

Hotels Rooms in Tulcea are expensive, with little choice. The cheapest are at **Hotel Europolis** (☎ 512 443), Str Păcii 20, priced US$21/29 for a single/double. Breakfast is an additional US$2.

Of Tulcea's two high-rise hotels, the **Hotel Egreta** (☎ 517 103) at Str Păcii 1 costs US$24/31 for a single/double. All the rooms at the **Hotel Delta** (☎ 514 720), Str Isaccea 2, cost US$43/54 including breakfast.

Nouvelles Frontières/Simpa Turism can book rooms at the **Cormoran Boarding House** at Uzlina by Murighiol (Sfântu Gheorghe channel) for US$24/38 per person in a single/double with breakfast.

Houseboats Moored opposite Hotel Delta is the **Navitur House Boat** (☎ 518 894). The boat is not the cleanest and the staff speak no English, but double cabins with shared bath (no hot water) are US$10 a night. There is a small bar-café aboard.

ACR's **Sfântul Constantin** floating hotel is at Tudor Vladimirescu, across the river. Double and triples cost US$18 per person. ACR arranges for rowing boats to cross the river.

Places to Eat

Restaurant Select at Str Păcii 6 has a large menu and good food; it's open from 10 am to midnight. The **Calypso Restaurant** up Str Babadag, just a bit past the synagogue, is an attractive private restaurant with delicious food at reasonable prices (US$2 to $4). The menu is in English.

For fresh fish afloat, try the large **Restaurant Comandor** moored at the riverfront promenade. It's air-conditioned and open daily from 10am to 10 pm.

The **Union Visa** outdoor café on Str Unirii is good for a beer and to snack; its adjoining grocery has all the basics. Across the street are the **Lux Bar** (in the courtyard) and the seedy **Cafe Bar Club**. There are beer gardens along the riverfront promenade, too.

Stock up on cheese, fruit and vegies at the **produce market** at the end of Str Păcii, 100m past Hotel Europolis next to the small park.

Getting There & Away

Train There are four trains daily to/from Constanţa via Medgidia (four hours). The daily express train from Bucharest's Gară de Nord takes five hours (335km). The local train to/from Bucharest is bearable if you go 1st class; arrive early to get a seat. Advance train tickets are sold at the CFR office, Str Babadag 4 opposite Piaţa Unirii, on weekdays from 9 am to 4 pm.

Bus There are four buses daily to Constanţa (123km) and one bus to Bucharest (263km) leaving at 5.30 am. There's a direct daily bus from Tulcea to Buzău (198km) in Moldavia. There are three buses from Tulcea to Murighiol, via Mahmudia, departing at 6.30 am, 11 am, and at 1 pm.

Boat There is a hydrofoil to Galaţi on Friday, departing from Sulina at 7.30 am, stopping at Tulcea at noon, and arriving in Galaţi at 1.30 pm. A single Tulcea-Galaţi ticket costs US$13.

A boat from Tulcea to Galaţi leaves on Saturday at 12.15 pm, arriving in Galaţi at 5 pm. From Galaţi there is a boat on Monday at 8.30 am, arriving in Tulcea at noon. A second boat leaving Monday at noon arrives in Tulcea at 1.30 pm, then continues to Crişan (3 pm) and Mila 23 (5 pm).

MALIUC & CRIŞAN

The Tulcea-Sulina ferry's first stop is at **Partizani**, a small fishing village with the *Ilgani de Sus Cabana*. Next stop is Maliuc, a popular stop for tour groups that lunch at the *Hotel Salcia* (☎ 511 515). Single/double rooms cost US$9/14 with breakfast. Ask at reception about camping behind the hotel. From Maliuc you can hire fishing boats for tours of smaller waterways to the north for US$10 to $15 per hour. North of Maliuc is **Lake Furtuna**, a snare for birdwatchers.

The ferry's next stop is the junction with Old Danube, a riverstream 1km upstream from Crişan. At the junction's tip is the rustic 1st-class *Hotel Lebăda* (☎ 543 778), which charges US$40 for a double. Next door is ARBDD's **Ecological Information Centre** featuring wildlife displays, a library, and a video room. It's open weekdays from 8 am to 4.30 pm. At the main Crişan ferry dock, ask about side trips to **Mila 23** or **Coraorman** (you'll need a permit), and about renting a rowing boat. Be sure to take some food and water on any expedition into the Delta. Warning: do not drink Danube water!

SULINA

☎ 040

Sulina is a romantic spot on the eastern edge of Europe. Its riverfront promenade is lovely at sunset, as the sun drops behind the Danube. About 8000 people live here – half of the delta's population. Sulina is not connected to the European road network so there are only a few vehicles in town (boats are the preferred mode of transport).

As the ferry sails through the centre you'll pass derelict old dredges and freighters – many noble ships have ended their careers at Sulina's scrapyard.

A canal dug between 1880 and 1902 shortened the length of the Tulcea-Sulina channel from 83.3 to 62.6km, ensuring Sulina's future as the Danube Delta's main commercial port. After WWI Sulina was declared a 'free port' and trade boomed. Greek merchants dominated business here until their expulsion in 1951. The Sulina channel has been extended 8km out into the Black Sea by two lateral dikes.

Although not as good a base as Maliuc or Crişan for seeing delta wildlife, Sulina is a pleasant place with a beach, a 19th-century lighthouse and an old cemetery with Romanian, Ukrainian, Turkish, Greek, Jewish and British graves, testimony to the colourful ethnic mix that once passed through the town's docks. If you get a cheap room you may want to stay for a while.

Orientation & Information

Sulina is small and easy to navigate. The ferry dock is in the centre of town, with a few shops and bars to the west, the Hotel Sulina and Black Sea to the east. There are no banks. The ARBDD plans to open a tourist information centre here.

Things to See

The only specific attractions at Sulina are a few old **churches**, the defunct 18.5m **lighthouse** (1870) and an overgrown 19th-century **British cemetery** you pass on the way to the beach. The **beach** itself, 2km from town, has an accumulation of Danube silt that has required the creation of a channel far out into the Black Sea. You'll also see a long line of Romanian radar installations among the dunes, pointed out to sea.

Places to Stay

Camping You can camp in the cow pasture opposite the Hotel Sulina and lots of people also camp free along the beach, though it can be rather windy.

Private Rooms As you're getting off the ferry, watch for people offering private rooms. The going rate is about US$6 per person.

Hotels The three-storey *Hotel Europolis*, next to the Sulina Cinema, is US$8 per person for a spacious but plain room with shared bath. You'll spot it as your ship is arriving.

A few hundred metres west along the riverfront from the Europolis, past the bookshop, is a small sign pointing to the *Hotel Ochiş*, which you enter from the rear. Rooms here are US$6 per person.

The government-owned *Hotel Sulina* (☎ 543 017), Str Deltei 207, charges foreigners US$20 per person.

Getting There & Away

For information on ferries and hydrofoils, see Getting Around at the beginning of the chapter and Getting There & Away under Tulcea.

UPRIVER FROM TULCEA

The ferry trip between Tulcea and Galaţi (pronounced 'ga-lahts') is especially interesting since the Danube here marks the boundary between Romania and Ukraine.

Galaţi (population 326,000) is a large industrial city with a steel mill, shabby shipyards and massive housing complexes. Inexpensive accommodation is hard to find, so walk straight through the town to the train station, which has four daily local trains to Bîrlad (2½ hours), where you change for Iaşi. If your timing doesn't coincide with these trains, take one of the 13 daily trains to Tecuci (two hours), where there are more connections for Iaşi and Suceava. Four express trains a day run from Galaţi to Bucharest (3½ hours), in addition to an overnight local train.

Slovakia

Europe's youngest country, Slovakia emerged in 1993 from 74 years of junior partnership in Czechoslovakia. The rugged High Tatra Mountains along the Polish border, the gentler natural beauty of the Malá Fatra near Žilina, and the Slovenský raj east of Poprad offer some of the best terrain in Europe for outdoor activities. Best of all, these places are off the beaten tourist track as most visitors do not venture beyond Bratislava. The possibilities for hikers are so numerous this book can only scratch the surface. In winter Slovakia is easily one of the best ski countries in Europe in terms of value for money.

Slovakia is also rich in architecture, arts and folk culture. In East Slovakia, a string of unspoiled 13th-century medieval towns founded by Saxon Germans shelter Gothic artworks of the first order, while Bratislava is a cosmopolitan city with a rich cultural life. There are about 180 quaint castles and castle ruins in Slovakia, the largest and most photogenic being Spišský hrad, east of Levoča.

The rural Slovaks still adhere to their peasant traditions and this is evident in the folk costumes you'll see in remote Slovak villages on Sunday and the colourful handicrafts. For 900 years Slovakia was Hungarian and many ethnic Magyars still reside here. You'll find the Slovaks to be extremely warm, friendly people prepared to go out of their way to help you enjoy their country.

AT A GLANCE

Capital	Bratislava
Population	5.4 million
Area	48,845 sq km
Official Language	Slovakian
Currency	1 koruna (Sk) = 100 halierov
GDP	US$42.8 billion (1996)
Time	GMT/UTC+0100

SLOVAKIA

Railways of the Slovak Republic (ŽSR) p716

Also in Bratislava
Central Bratislava p721

POLAND

POLAND

CZECH REPUBLIC

Levoča p743 • Bardejov p745
• Malá Fatra p730
Vysoké Tatry (High Tatras) p733 • Spišská Nová Ves & Slovenský raj p740-741
Trenčín p727 • Košice p749

UKRAINE

Bratislava p719

AUSTRIA   HUNGARY

Facts about Slovakia

HISTORY

Slavic tribes occupied what is now Slovakia in the 5th century AD. In 833, the prince of Moravia captured Nitra and formed the Great Moravian Empire, which included all of present Central and West Slovakia, the Czech Republic and parts of neighbouring Poland, Hungary and Germany. The empire converted to Christianity with the arrival of the Thessaloniki brothers and missionaries, Cyril and Methodius, in 863. To facilitate the translation of the Bible, Cyril created the first Slavic alphabet, the forerunner of contemporary Cyrillic.

In 907, the Great Moravian Empire collapsed as a result of the political intrigues of its rulers and invasion by Hungary. By 1018 the whole of Slovakia was annexed to Hungary and remained so for the next 900 years, although the Spiš region of East Slovakia belonged to Poland from 1412 to 1772.

The Hungarians developed mining (silver, copper and gold) and trade (gold, amber and furs). After a Tatar invasion in the 13th century, the Hungarian king invited Saxon Germans to settle the depopulated northeastern borderlands.

SLOVAKIA

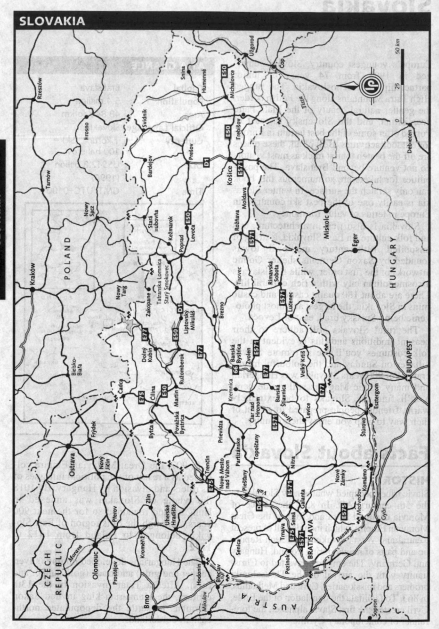

SLOVAKIA

When the Turks overran Hungary in the early 16th century, the Hungarian capital moved from Buda to Bratislava. Only in 1686 was the Ottoman presence finally driven from Hungary south of the Danube.

In the mid-19th century the poet Ľudovít Štúr (1815-56) created a literary Slovak language, and the democratic revolution of 1848 further stimulated Slovak national consciousness.

Yet the formation of the dual Austro-Hungarian monarchy in 1867 gave Hungary autonomy in domestic matters and a policy of enforced Magyarisation was instituted in Slovakia between 1868 and 1918. In 1907 Hungarian became the sole language of elementary education.

As a reaction to this, Slovak intellectuals cultivated closer cultural relations with the Czechs, who were themselves dominated by the Austrians. The concept of a single Czecho-Slovakian unit was born for political purposes and, after Austro-Hungarian defeat in WWI, Slovakia, Ruthenia, Bohemia and Moravia united as Czechoslovakia.

The centralising tendencies of the sophisticated Czechs alienated many Slovaks and, after the 1938 Munich agreement that forced Czechoslovakia to cede territory to Germany, Slovakia declared its autonomy within a federal state. Hungary took advantage of this instability to annex a strip of southern Slovakia including Košice and Komárno. The day before Hitler's troops invaded Czech lands in March 1939, a clero-fascist puppet state headed by Monsignor Jozef Tiso (executed in 1947 as a war criminal) was set up, and Slovakia became a German ally.

In August 1944, Slovak partisans (both communist and noncommunist) started the Slovak National Uprising (SNP) against the Tiso regime, an event that is now a source of national pride. It took the Germans several months to crush the uprising. In the wake of Soviet advances in early 1945, a Czechoslovak government was established at Košice two months before the liberation of Prague.

The second Czechoslovakia established after the war was to have been a federal state, but after the communist takeover in February 1948 the administration once again became centralised in Prague. Many of those who resisted the new communist dictatorship were ruthlessly eliminated by execution, torture and starvation in labour camps.

Although the 1960 constitution granted Czechs and Slovaks equal rights, only the 1968 'Prague Spring' reforms introduced by Alexander Dubček (a rehabilitated Slovak communist) implemented this concept. In August 1968, Soviet troops quashed democratic reform, and although the Czech and Slovak republics theoretically became equal partners in a federal Czechoslovakia in 1969, the real power remained in Prague.

The fall of communism in Czechoslovakia during 1989 led to a resurgence of Slovak nationalism and agitation for Slovak autonomy. In February 1992 the Slovak parliament rejected a treaty that would have perpetuated a federal Czechoslovakia.

The rift deepened with the June 1992 elections, which, in Slovakia, brought to power the left-leaning nationalist Movement for a Democratic Slovakia (HZDS) headed by Vladimír Mečiar. In July the Slovak parliament voted to declare sovereignty.

Mečiar held negotiations with his Czech counterpart Václav Klaus, as neither was able to form a government, but he could not reach a compromise. In August 1992 it was agreed that the federation would peacefully dissolve on 1 January 1993.

Mečiar's semi-authoritarian rule has gained him control of most of the media. The passing of anti-democratic laws has brought criticism from human rights organisations, EU and the US government.

The second election in Slovakian history is due to be held in September 1998. Most polls are showing the five-party opposition Slovak Democratic Coalition (SDK) a few points ahead of Mečiar and the HZDS. Mečiar might be helped by the inability of the Slovak parliament to vote in a new president, which it has tried and failed to do seven times since January 1998. If there is no president then most presidential powers – including nominating someone to form a government – pass on to the premier.

GEOGRAPHY & ECOLOGY

Slovakia sits in the heart of Europe, straddling the north-western end of the Carpathian Mountains. This hilly 49,035-sq-km country forms a clear physical barrier between the plains of Poland and Hungary. Almost 80% of Slovakia is over 750m above sea level.

Slovakia south of Nitra is a fertile lowland stretching down to the Danube (Dunaj in Slovak), which forms the border with Hungary from Bratislava to Štúrovo/Esztergom. The Váh River joins the Danube at Komárno and together they flow south-east to the Black Sea.

The town of Žilina is between the Beskydy of Moravia and the Malá Fatra (Little Fatra) of Central Slovakia, and to the east are the Vysoké Tatry (High Tatra). At 2655m Gerlachovský štít is the highest of the mighty peaks in this spectacular alpine range, which Slovakia shares with Poland. The Nízke Tatry (Low Tatra) are between Poprad and Banská Bystrica.

There are five national parks: Malá Fatra (east of Žilina), Nízke Tatry (between Banská Bystrica and Poprad), Vysoké Tatry (north of Poprad), Pieniny (along the Dunajec River) and Slovenský raj (near Spišská Nová Ves). In this book we cover all these parks except Nízke Tatry.

Forests, mainly beech and spruce, cover 40% of the country despite centuries of deforestation. The rich wildlife includes bears, wolves, lynxes, marmots, chamois, otters and mink that live in the High Tatras. The national parks outside the Tatras include most of these animals in smaller numbers. Deer, pheasants, partridges, ducks, wild geese, storks, grouse, eagles and other vultures can be seen throughout the countryside.

The Slovak countryside is not as badly polluted as other European countries. It's the larger towns that have seen rapid industrialisation since WWII that suffer from industrial pollution, especially Bratislava and Košice, but also Banská Bystrica, Žilina and Trenčín. According to government figures, the pollution of air and land actually decreased in 1996.

GOVERNMENT & POLITICS

Slovakia is a parliamentary republic. The head of the government is the president, who is elected for a five year term by the national council, with a minimum three-fifths majority. The highest government body is the cabinet, headed by the prime minister. The president appoints and dismisses ministers. The national council is the only house of parliament and has 150 members, who are elected every four years by proportional representation.

ECONOMY

For centuries Slovakia was a backward agricultural area from which people sought to escape through emigration (nearly two million people of Slovak origin live in the USA today). In 1918 Slovakia united with the far more advanced Czech lands, stimulating limited industrial development. During WWII, however, most existing Slovak factories were adapted to the needs of the German war effort, and later the communists developed heavy industry and arms production: 65% of the former Czechoslovakia's military production came from Slovakia. Attempts since 1989 to convert these plants to other uses have led to widespread unemployment in Central Slovakia and created severe problems for Slovakia's heavy manufacturing industry. In 1997, inflation was 6.4%, unemployment was 12.4% and the average wage was 10,400 Sk (US$296) a month.

The Slovak economy has been improving since 1995. It grew by 6.5% in 1997 and is one of the leading former eastern bloc economies. Most of the success is due to exports (up by 9.2% in 1997), mainly in convenience foods and raw materials, by several major industrial state-owned giants including Bratislava Slovnaft and East Slovak Ironworks Košice. Not all is well and some of the problems that need to be solved are a restrictive monetary policy, the absence of effective bankruptcy laws, inefficiency and a high gross foreign debt (US$9.896 billion in 1997, a 26.7% increase on the previous year). The limited investment (41.2 billion Sk or 1% of GDP) is a reflection of the Slovak government's 'socially oriented' market economy and the suspension of the privatisation process.

Under communism, agriculture was neglected and the connection of farmers to their land was disturbed by Soviet-style collectivisation. Agriculture remains an important part of the economy with 1.78 million hectares of arable land. Slovakia's cooperative farms are now owned by those who work on them, and only a fraction of land is in private farms.

The first Soviet-designed VVER-440 nuclear power station was built at Jaslovské Bohunice near Trnava in the 1970s and supplies about one third of Slovakia's electricity. A second plant at Mochovce, east of Nitra, had its first reactor activated in June 1998, attracting major protests from Austria.

The Gabčíkovo hydroelectric project on the Danube west of Komárno became highly controversial after Hungary backed out of the joint project in 1989 because of environmental considerations. Both countries are still negotiating about their differences on the project. Gabčíkovo produces enough electricity to cover the needs of every home in Slovakia and its canal allows the largest river vessels to reach Bratislava year-round.

POPULATION & PEOPLE

Slovakia has a population of 5.4 million, of which 85.6% are Slovaks, 10.7% Hungarians, 1.5% Roma and 1% Czechs. The 600,000 ethnic Hungarians live mostly in southern and eastern Slovakia.

The September 1992 Slovak constitution guarantees the rights of minorities, with three-quarters of Hungarian children receiving schooling in their mother tongue. For historical reasons, some antagonism exists between Slovaks and Hungarians, and the Slovak government aggravated the situation in 1996 by passing a law making Slovak the only official language. This means that, officially, the large Hungarian minority cannot use their mother tongue in public places.

The nomadic culture of the Roma has been destroyed in the process of assimilation into mainstream Slovak life under communist rule. Recently, as heavy industrial jobs have disappeared, many Slovakian Roma have migrated to the Czech Republic. As elsewhere in eastern Europe, there is much prejudice against Roma.

The largest cities are Bratislava (population 452,000), Košice (241,900), Nitra (87,100), Prešov (93,000), Banská Bystrica (85,000), Žilina (86,700) and Trnava (70,200).

ARTS

Despite 900 years of Hungarian domination, a national revival began with the creation of the Slovak literary language by the 19th-century nationalist Ľudovít Štúr (based on an earlier version by Anton Berlák). This led to the emergence of Slovak national consciousness. One of the leading artists in the National Revival was poet Pavol O Hviezdoslav, whose works have been translated into several languages. Other artists, such as portraitist Petr Bohúň, expressed their nationalistic feelings on canvas. In music, Ján Levoslav Bela used folk motifs in his classical compositions, one of his best being the opera *Blacksmith Wieland*.

Slovakia has many outstanding architectural wonders, paintings and sculptures by both foreign and local artists. Some of the most notable Gothic masterpieces can be found in the St James' Church in Levoča, and there are magnificent Renaissance buildings in Bardejov.

The very short history of Slovak cinematography first made its mark during the 1960s 'New Wave'. Some of the era's classic films are *Death Calls Itself Engelchen* (1963) by the director Ján Kádar and *The Shop On the Main Street* (1965) by Elmar Klos.

Music

Traditional Slovak folk instruments include the *fujara* (a 2m-long flute), the *gajdy* (bagpipes) and the *konkovka* (a strident shepherd's flute). Folk songs helped preserve the Slovak language during Hungarian rule, and in East Slovakia ancient folk traditions are still a living part of village life. The songs tell of love, lament, anticipation and celebration, and vigorous dancing helps dispel the uncertainty of life.

In classical music, the 19th century Ján L Bela and the symphonies of Alexander Moyzes have gained world recognition since the mid-20th century.

SOCIETY & CONDUCT

Slovaks are very polite people and it is customary to say 'good day' (*dobrý den*) when you enter a shop, hotel or restaurant, and 'goodbye' (*do videnia*) when you leave. Despite the general surliness that Slovaks show to each other in service industries they are friendly and hospitable people. On public transport, younger people readily give up their seats to the elderly, sick, and to women who are pregnant or with small children.

If you are invited to someone's home remember to bring flowers for your hosts. It is important that if the host removes their shoes you do the same. When attending a classical concert or theatre, men wear a tie and a suit while women wear a dinner dress. Casual dress is fine in contemporary venues, such as theatre or rock/jazz concerts.

RELIGION

Religion is taken seriously by the folksy Slovaks. Catholics form a majority but Evangelicals are also numerous, and in East Slovakia there are many Greek Catholics and Orthodox believers.

LANGUAGE

Although many people working in tourism have a good knowledge of English, in rural Slovakia very few people speak anything other than Slovak. German is probably the most useful non-Slavic language here.

An aspect of Slovak nationalism is pride in the language and Slovaks can get a little hot under the collar when Slovak is given short shrift in comparison with other Slavic languages. As a visitor, you won't be taken to task if you mix Czech with Slovak, but any effort to communicate in the local language will be appreciated.

See the Language Guide at the end of this book for details on Slovak pronunciation and some useful words and phrases. Lonely Planet's *Eastern Europe phrasebook* has a complete chapter on Slovak.

Facts for the Visitor

HIGHLIGHTS

Epicureans will enjoy Bratislava's wine museum. The Šarišské Museum at Bardejovské Kúpele has one of the best collections of reassembled traditional dwellings in eastern Europe. The Slovak National Uprising Museum in Banská Bystrica, a political museum built by the communists, survives because of the crucial period it documents in Slovakia's history. Finally, at the museum of the Tatra National Park at Tatranská Lomnica, you have the rare opportunity of stepping out the door and exploring the very things you saw in the exhibits.

Spišský hrad, in the remote Spišské Podhradie, is the largest castle in the country, and Trenčín Castle is well known as having been the most strategic.

Three of Slovakia's most picturesque historic towns are Bardejov, Levoča and Košice. Old Bratislava is also scenic.

SUGGESTED ITINERARIES

Depending on the length of your stay, you could do the following things:

Two days
    Visit Bratislava
One week
    Visit Bratislava, Bardejov, Levoča and the Tatra Mountains
Two weeks
    Visit most of the places in this chapter

PLANNING
Climate & When to Go

Slovakia experiences hot summers and cold winters. The warmest, driest and sunniest area is the Danube lowland east of Bratislava. Because of the altitude spring and autumn are much shorter in the High Tatra Mountains. The High Tatras experience the highest rainfall.

Books & Maps

For a readable history of Slovakia try Stanislav J Kirschbaum's *A History of Slovakia – The Struggle for Survival*. William Shawcross' *Dubček & Czechoslovakia* is a biography of the late leader and an account of the 1968 Prague Spring. One of the few works readily available in English translation is *The Year of the Frog* by Martin Šimečka – a story about a young intellectual who is made a social outcast by the communist government for his political views.

Lonely Planet's *Czech & Slovak Republics* by John King and Richard Nebeský gives extensive information on the nuts and bolts of travelling in Slovakia.

The Austrian publisher Freytag & Berndt has a good map of Slovakia (*Slovenská republika*, 1:500,000). Excellent hiking maps that cover all of Slovakia's mountain regions are published by Vojenský kartografický ústav (VKÚ; 1:50,000). It also has more detailed skiing and hiking maps (1:25,000). The Mountain Rescue Service (Horská služba) has a series of four hiking maps for the High and Low Tatras that show cycling trails (1:100,000).

What to Bring

For details see the Czech Republic chapter.

TOURIST OFFICES

Slovakia has an extensive network of well informed municipal information centres (*Mestské informačné centrum*, ☎ 186) that form an Association of Information Centres of Slovakia (AiCES). They have computers and exchange facilities, can organise sightseeing tours and guides, and assist with accommodation, and the staff speak English. They are normally open Monday to Saturday during summer (June to August) from 8 am to 6 pm (on Saturday until noon) but only on weekdays from 9 am to 5 pm at other times of the year.

Commercial agencies include Satur, Tatratour and Slovakoturist, which all have offices around the country.

The Euro <26, ISIC and GO25 cards are available from some major Satur offices.

VISAS & EMBASSIES

Nationals of most European countries and Canada do not need a visa for stays of up to 90 days (UK and Irish citizens for up to 180 days) and US, and South African citizens for up to 30 days. Australian and New Zealand citizens need a visa; 30-day visas cost about 700 Sk. If you need a visa, two photos are required. The visa consists of a full-page stamp in your passport and two separate sheets (make sure the clerk doesn't forget to give you these), one of which should include your photo. For drivers, 30-day Slovak visas are available only at Petržalka border crossing during business hours and at the officials' discretion. Visa extensions cost 500 Sk.

Slovak Embassies Abroad

Slovak embassies abroad include:

Australia
(☎ 61-2-6290 1516) 47 Culgoa Circuit, O'Malley, Canberra, ACT 2606
Canada
(☎ 1-613-749 4442) 50 Rideau Terrace, Ottawa, KIM 2A1
Netherlands
(☎ 31-70-416 7777) Parkweg 1, 2585 JG The Hague
UK
(☎ 44-171-727 9432) 25 Kensington Palace Gardens, London W8 4QY
USA
(☎ 1-202-445 3804) 2201 Wisconsin Ave NW, Suite 250, Washington, DC 20007

Foreign Embassies in Bratislava

Australia and New Zealand do not have embassies in Slovakia; the nearest are in Vienna. Irish and Commonwealth citizens can use the UK Embassy.

Austria
(☎ 07-533 29 85) Ventúrska 10
Bulgaria
(☎ 07-533 59 71) Kuzmányho 1
Canada (Consulate)
(☎ 07-35 21 75) Kolárska 4
Croatia
(☎ 07-36 14 13) Grösslingová 47
Czech Republic
(☎ 07-536 12 07) 29 Augusta 5
France
(☎ 07-533 57 45) Hlavné nám 7
Hungary
(☎ 07-533 05 41) Sedlárska 3
Poland
(☎ 07-580 34 12) Hummelova 4
Russia
(☎ 07-531 34 68) Godrova 4
Romania
(☎ 07-39 16 65) Fraňa Kráľa 11
South Africa
(☎ 07-580 33 81/72) Jančova 8
UK
(☎ 07-531 96 32) Grösslingová 35
Ukraine
(☎ 07-533 16 72) Radvanská 35
USA
(☎ 07-533 08 61) Hviezdoslavovo nám 4

CUSTOMS

You can import reasonable amounts of personal effects and up to about 3000 Sk worth

SLOVAKIA

of gifts and other 'noncommercial' goods. If you're over 18, you can bring in 2L of wine, 1L of spirits, and 250 cigarettes. Theoretically, any consumer goods valued at over 3000 Sk to 8000 Sk are dutiable from 5 to 50% (depending on the type of goods), and anything over 8000 Sk is dutiable at up to 100%, plus 6 to 25% VAT depending on the type of goods. Customs officers can be strict about antiques and will confiscate goods if they are slightly suspicious. You cannot export genuine antiques. If you have any doubt about what you are taking out, talk to curatorial staff at the National Museum in Bratislava.

It is illegal to import or export any Slovak currency. Arriving foreigners are required to have at least US$15 a day for each day of their stay but this is rarely enforced. If you have saved your encashment receipts you can sell unused Slovak crowns at your port of exit.

MONEY
Currency
Slovakia's currency is the Slovak crown, or Slovenská koruna (Sk). There are coins of 10, 20 and 50 hellers (halierov) and one, two, five and 10 crowns (Sk). Banknotes come in denominations of 20, 50, 100, 200, 500, 1000 and 5000 crowns.

Exchange Rates

Australia	A$1	=	22.75 Sk
Canada	C$1	=	24.31 Sk
Czech Republic	1 Kč	=	1.04 Sk
euro	€1	=	38.99 Sk
Germany	DM1	=	19.33 Sk
Hungary	Ft1	=	0.20 Sk
Poland	zl1	=	11.43 Sk
United Kingdom	UK£1	=	58.93 Sk
United States	US$1	=	34.79 Sk

Changing Money
The easiest place to change travellers cheques is at a branch of the Všeobecná úverová banka (VÚB – General Credit Bank), Slovenská sporiteľňa (Slovak Savings Bank) or the Investičná banka (Investment Bank) where you'll be charged a standard 1% commission. Satur offices (see Tourist Offices) and post office exchange windows deduct 2%. Banks often give a slightly better

rate for travellers cheques than for cash. Most banks are open from 8 or 9 am to 4 or 5 pm weekdays (some close for 30 minutes between noon and 1.30 pm for lunch).

Credit cards (mainly Visa, MasterCard, Eurocard and American Express) can be used in most major hotels, restaurants and shops. Some of the larger branches of major banks may give cash advances from credit cards. ATMs (bankomat) are becoming quite common, and the most common network for Visa, MasterCard, Eurocard, Plus and Cirrus.

Some exchange places might not accept damaged or torn US dollar notes.

Costs
The Slovakian koruna is not fully convertible, and the country is likely to remain a bargain for a while. You'll find food, admissions and transport cheap and accommodation manageable except in Bratislava. If you camp or stay in hostels, eat in local pubs and take local transport expect to spend about US$15 to US$20 a day. The value-added tax (VAT) in Slovakia is 23% (5% on food).

Taxes & Refunds
Satur office in Bratislava refunds 13% of the VAT for all foreign visitors on purchases of more than 1000 Sk but very few stores stock the forms you need to get the refund.

POST & COMMUNICATIONS
Post
Mail is reliable and fast. Express Mail Services are available from most post offices, but if you are mailing a parcel over 2kg from Slovakia, it has to be sent from a customs office (colnica; open weekdays from 8 am to 3 pm). These are separate from normal post offices but post office staff will tell you where they are. Don't post anything valuable. Poste-restante mail can be sent to major post offices in larger cities and will be kept for one month, and should be addressed to Poste Restante, Pošta 1. American Express cardholders can have their mail sent c/o Tratatour (see the Bratislava section).

A postcard/letter to other European countries is 7/12 Sk and elsewhere 10/16 Sk (air mail). A 2kg parcel by airmail to other European countries costs 319 Sk and elsewhere

704 Sk. Most post offices are open from 7 or 8 am to 5 or 8 pm weekdays and 8 am to noon Saturday. In large towns like Bratislava and Košice they open on Sunday, from 8 am till noon.

Telephone

The telephone system isn't the best. It can be difficult to get through and crossed lines are common. Calls are most easily placed from main post offices or telephone centres although you can also make them from blue coin or card phones on the street. Coin phones often do not work. A three-minute operator assisted call from Slovakia will cost about 97 Sk to the UK, 145 Sk to the USA or Australia and 187 Sk to New Zealand or South Africa. If you dial the number yourself it will be 25 Sk cheaper. Card phones can be found throughout the country, but keep some 2 Sk coins for villages. There are 140, 180 and 360 Sk phone cards available from post offices and any store displaying the phone card logo.

To call Slovakia from abroad, dial the international access code, ☎ 421 (the country code for Slovakia), the area code and the number. When dialling from within Slovakia you must add a 0 before the area code. The international access code is ☎ 00.

The system is being modernised and numbers are being changed throughout the country. Wherever possible we have used the new numbers but you may find that some numbers do not work. If so, ring directory assistance on ☎ 120 (for numbers in the local region) and ☎ 121 or 0120 (for numbers elsewhere in Slovakia).

Most major countries now have arrangements with Slovakian Telekomunikácie for direct connections to an operator in the foreign country, so you pay your home country rate rather than the higher Slovakian rate. Get the access numbers from your own telephone company or a telephone office in Slovakia.

Fax & Telegram

Telegrams can be sent from most post offices, while faxes can only be sent from certain major post offices.

INTERNET RESOURCES

If you are carrying a lap top computer and a modem, it is possible to make a connection through a telephone line (but see Telephone information above). The telephone tone is 'A'. Most new telephone plugs use US RJ-11. Cost is a major problem for making a connection in a hotel. Any call is charged by what is called an *impuls* (one impuls is 40 or 80 seconds long and costs 2.10 Sk for a local call). All hotels add their surcharge of up to 6 Sk/impuls but some hotels can also charge up to 300% more for internet use.

Email/Internet access is available at the Internet caffé (see Cybercafes under Information in Bratislava section). Some of the business-oriented top-end hotels offer Internet access at the excessive rate of 200 Sk per hour.

EU Net web site provides regional information, travel tips and links related to web pages at the Slovak site (eunet.sk). Central Europe Online has plenty of links to Slovak servers (ceo.cz). Bratislava and other major Slovak cities are featured at Slovakia.com's web site (slovak.com) and Slovakia Online (savba.sk/logos), which provides reservations to upmarket hotels.

NEWSPAPERS & MAGAZINES

The Slovak Spectator (30 Sk), an English-language fortnightly paper published in Bratislava, includes the latest information on what is happening in the city. In Bratislava and most major tourist centres the main European and US newspapers and magazines are available.

RADIO & TV

BBC English-language programs are available 24 hours in Bratislava on FM 93.8 and in Košice on FM 103.2. TVs with satellite connections can receive English-language channels such as the news-oriented Super Channel, Eurosport or HBO.

TIME

The time in Slovakia is GMT/UTC plus one hour. At the end of March Slovakia goes on summer time and clocks are set forward an hour. At the end of October they're turned back an hour.

ELECTRICITY
The electric current is 220V, 50Hz.

WEIGHTS & MEASURES
The metric system is used in Slovakia.

HEALTH
Free first aid is provided to tourists who are involved in an accident. You must pay for any other hospital treatment unless your country has a reciprocal health-care agreement with Slovakia. For ambulance call ☎ 155 anywhere in the country, but don't expect the person who answers to be able to speak English. EU nationals receive free medical attention.

There are very few cases of AIDS in Slovakia, but naturally travellers should still use the usual precautions.

Water
Many Slovaks do not drink tap water because of its unpleasant taste – the result of heavy doses of chlorine. In some parts of the country the tap water can be polluted. Most visitors prefer bottled water.

Thermal Baths
Public thermal swimming pools are at Trenčianské Teplice and Komárno. Most of Slovakia's other spas are reserved for patients under medical supervision. Satur can only book stays at Piešťany, Lúčky and Dudince from about 2000 Sk per person, including accommodation, treatment and meals for one day. Slovthermae (☎ 36 21 80) at Radlinského 13, Bratislava, can only book stays at Dudince (from 2600 Sk all-inclusive). At other spa towns bookings are only possible directly with the spa hotel.

WOMEN TRAVELLERS
Sexual violence is low in comparison to Western countries and assaults on solo female travellers are rare. Nevertheless, caution is recommended; avoid deserted and unlit areas.

GAY & LESBIAN TRAVELLERS
Homosexuality has been legal since the 1960s and the age of consent is 16, but gay or lesbian partners do not have the same legal status as heterosexual partners.

The local gay organisation is Ganymedes (☎ 07-25 38 88), PO Box 4, Pošta 3, 83000 Bratislava. The organisation has a Trust Line (Linka dôvery; ☎ 07-211 54 61), available only on Monday between 6 and 8.30 pm. Lesbian organisation is Museion, Poste Restante 212, 820 12 Bratislava.

DISABLED TRAVELLERS
There are no facilities to speak of for disabled people. Transport is a major problem as buses and trams have no wheelchair access. KFC and McDonald's entrances and toilets are wheelchair friendly. Disabled people planning to travel with ČSA need to inform the airline of their needs when booking the ticket.

The only organisation in Slovakia is the Slovak Union for the Disabled (Slovenský zväz telesne postihnutých; ☎ 07-36 32 85/6).

DANGERS & ANNOYANCES
General emergency numbers for anywhere in Slovakia are: police ☎ 158, ambulance ☎ 155 and vehicle assistance ☎ 154. Crime is low compared with the west. Some Bratislava taxi drivers have been known to overcharge foreigners and in touristy places some waiters occasionally overcharge. Another problem is the increasing number of robberies that take place on international trains passing through the country. The victims are usually sleeping passengers, some of whom have been gassed to sleep in their compartments and then relieved of their valuables.

Confusingly, buildings on some streets have two sets of street numbers. The blue number is the actual street number while the red number is the old registration number. To make matters worse, the streets themselves are sometimes poorly labelled.

BUSINESS HOURS
On weekdays, shops open at around 8 or 9 am and close at 5 or 6 pm, although some major department stores stay open until 7 pm on Thursday and Friday. Only major department stores such as Tesco are open on weekends in major cities. Some bakeries and grocery stores open as early as 7 am. Many small

shops, particularly those in country areas, close for up to an hour for lunch between noon and 2 pm. Almost everything closes between 11 am and 1 pm on Saturday and all day Sunday. Some grocery stores open on weekends. Most restaurants are open every day but smaller ones in small towns and villages start running out of food after 7 pm and close their kitchens at 9 pm and Sunday evenings.

Most museums are closed on Monday and the day following a public holiday. Many gardens, castles and historic sites in Slovakia are closed from November to March and open on weekends only in April and October. Staff at some isolated sights take an hour off for lunch. In any sight where a guided tour is required, the ticket offices close an hour or so before the official closing time, depending on the length of the tour.

The main town museums stay open all year. Students usually get 50% off the entry price at museums, galleries, theatres, cinemas, fairs etc. Many churches remain closed except for services.

PUBLIC HOLIDAYS & SPECIAL EVENTS

Public holidays are New Year's & Independence Day (1 January), Three Kings Day (6 January), Good Friday and Easter Monday (March/April), Labour Day (1 May), Cyril and Methodius Day (5 July), SNP Day (29 August), Constitution Day (1 September), Our Lady of Sorrows Day (15 September), All Saints Day (1 November) and Christmas (24 to 26 December).

The Bratislava Lyre in May or June features rock concerts. During June or July folk dancers from all over Slovakia meet at the Východná Folklore Festival, 32km west of Poprad, and mid-June in Červený Kláštor. The Bratislava Jazz Days are held in September.

ACTIVITIES

Ice skating, fishing, horse riding, windsurfing and caving are popular in Slovakia. You can bungee jump in Štrbské Pleso (see the Vysoké Tatry section for more details).

Slovakia is one of eastern Europe's prime hiking areas. See the Malá Fatra, Vysoké Tatry and Slovenský raj sections for details.

There is of course excellent rock climbing in Vysoké Tatry. Paragliding is also becoming popular (Crystal ski (☎ 0849-914 60), Jasná, Nízke Tatry, charges from 650 Sk for two hours).

For information on rafting on the Dunajec River in Pieniny National Park, see the Dunajec Gorge section. Hiking is also good here. Some of Slovakia's major rivers such as Váh, Hron and Nitra also offer good canoeing and kayaking. T-Ski (☎ 0969-42 32 00), Starý Smokovec, Vysoké Tatry, can arrange rafting (about 700 Sk/person).

Slovakia has some of Europe's top-value ski resorts. The ski season runs from December to April in the Vysoké Tatry, Nízke Tatry and Malá Fatra. The best skiing is in Jasná, Nízke Tatry, and it's also good in Malá Fatra. The standard ski gear is available for hire at very competitive rates. The waits at ski lifts can be excruciatingly long during peak season. The runs are colour coded: black (difficult), red (moderate) and blue (easy).

Slovakia offers some of the best cycling terrain in central Europe, with uncrowded roads and beautiful scenery. East Slovakia especially is prime cycling territory. Mountain biking is excellent in Vysoké Tatry and Slovenský raj and mountain bikes can be rented at several places in the Vysoké Tatry, where they cost from 240 to 580 Sk for a day.

WORK

The unemployment rate in Slovakia is high and there are not many job opportunities for non-Slovak speakers. Your best bet is to find a job teaching English. The British Council has a teaching centre in Bratislava or try the Berlitz Language Centre (☎ 07-533 37 96), Na vŕšku 6, Bratislava.

ACCOMMODATION

Foreigners can often pay 30 to 100% more for accommodation than Slovaks. Unless otherwise stated, all prices quoted for rooms are for a single/double/triple/quad.

Camping

There are several hundred camping grounds, usually open from May to September. They're often accessible on public transport, but there's usually no hot water. Most have a small snack bar and many have small cabins for rent which are cheaper than a hotel room. Pitching your own tent in these camping grounds is definitely the least expensive form of accommodation. Camping on public land is prohibited.

Hostels

The Hostelling International (HI) handbook lists an impressive network of hostels, but you often find that they're either full or closed. There are only three Juniorhotels: Bratislava, Horný Smokovec (Vysoké Tatry) and Jasná pod Chopkom (Nízke Tatry). The last one is a normal hotel, but a hostel card should get you a discount. In July and August many student dormitories become temporary hostels. Satur and municipal information offices usually have information on hostels and can often make advance bookings.

The tourist hostels (*Turistické ubytovňy*) are not connected to the HI network. They provide very basic and cheap dormitory accommodation. Ask about tourist hostels at information offices and watch for the letters 'TU' on accommodation lists published in languages other than English.

Private Rooms & Pensions

Private rooms (look for signs reading '*privát*' or '*Zimmer frei*') are usually available in tourist centres, and AiCES tourist information offices and some travel agencies like Satur can book them. Some have a three-night minimum-stay requirement.

Many small pensions (often just glorified private rooms) exist, especially on Bratislava's outskirts and in touristy regions, and these offer more personalised service than the hotels and are cheaper.

Hotels

In Bratislava hotels are expensive, whereas those in smaller towns are usually cheaper.

There are five categories of hotels from one star (budget) to five star (luxury). The two star hotels are typically US$14/20, three star hotels are around US$38/59. There are very few one star hotels, and top end hotels are almost as expensive as in the West.

FOOD

The cheapest eateries are the self-service restaurants (*jedáleň*) or (*bistro*). These sometimes have really tasty dishes like barbecued chicken or hot German-style sausage. Train stations often have good cheap restaurants or buffets but the cheapest meals are to be had in busy beer halls. If the place is crowded with locals, is noisy and looks chaotic, chances are it will have great lunch specials at low prices. As a general rule a restaurant calling itself *reštaurácia* is usually cheaper than a 'restaurant'.

Hotel restaurants (up to three stars) are reasonable in dollar terms, though the atmosphere is often stuffy and formal. They will usually have menus in German and some in English with fish dishes available, and even vegetarians should be able to find something suitable. Hotel restaurants stay open later and don't close on weekends.

Lunches are generally bigger and cheaper than dinners in the less expensive places. Dinner is eaten early, between 6 and 7 pm. Don't expect to be served at any restaurant if you arrive within half an hour of closing time.

Always check the posted menu before entering a restaurant to get an idea of the price range. If no menu is displayed inside or out, insist on seeing one before ordering – the Slovak for menu is *Jedálny lístok*. It doesn't matter if it's only in Slovak (as is often the case). The main categories are *predjedlá* (starters), *polievky* (soups), *hotová jedlá* (ready-to-serve dishes), *jedlá na objednávku* (dishes prepared as they are ordered), *mäsité jedlá* (meat dishes), *ryby* (fish), *zelenina* (vegetables), *šaláty* (salads), *ovoce* (fruit), *zákusok* (dessert) and *nápoje* (drinks). Anything that comes with *knedle* (dumplings) will be a hearty meal.

Most beer halls have a system of marking everything you eat or drink on a small piece of paper which is left on your table.

Tipping is optional. If you were happy with the service, you could round up the bill to the next 5 Sk (or to the next 10 Sk if the bill is over 100 Sk).

There are great little pastry shops called *kaviáreň* or *cukráreň*. These offer cakes, puddings and coffee as good as anything you'll find in neighbouring Austria at a fraction of the price.

Local Specialities

Slovaks serve their meals with paprika and cuisine is strong on sauces and gravies and weak on fresh vegetables. Soup is normally the first course for lunch. Soups include *hovädzia polievka* (beef broth), *zemiaková polievka* (potato soup) and *zeleninová polievka* (vegetable soup). *Držková polievka* (tripe soup) is a treat not to be missed. Slovakis's traditional dish is *halušky* (small dumplings topped with grated cheese and bits of bacon). Meat dishes come with potatoes – either boiled, fried or as chips. Goulash or *segedín* (also known as koložárska kapusta – a beef goulash with sauerkraut in cream sauce) with knedle, flat circular bread dumplings. Carp (*kapor*) or trout (*pstruh*) can be crumbed and fried or baked. Vegetarian dishes include *vysmážaný syr* (fried cheese). Fruit dumplings *(ovocné knedle* or *guľky)*, with whole fruit inside, come with cottage cheese or crushed poppy seed and melted butter. A normal dessert is *palačinky so zavareninou* (jam pancakes). *Langoše*, a large, round fried doughnut brushed with oil and a variety of toppings, makes a great snack. You can get fairly good salads in Slovakia.

DRINKS

Slovak wine is good and cheap and there are some excellent sparkling wines. Well-known brands include Tokay from South Slovakia, and Kláštorné (a red) and Venušíno čáro (a white), both from the Carpathians north of Bratislava.

Pivo (beer) is also good, try Zlatý Bažant from Hurbanovo or Topvar from Topoľčany.

Special things to try are Demänovka (an exquisite bittersweet Slovak liqueur slightly sweetened with honey) and *slivovice* (plum brandy). *Grog* is rum with hot water and sugar – a great pick-me-up. *Limonáda* is a good nonalcoholic drink and the word is often used to refer to any soft drink, not just lemonade.

THINGS TO BUY

Good buys include china, Bohemian crystal, costume jewellery, folk ceramics, garnets, fancy leather goods, special textiles, lace, embroidery, shoes, colour-photography books, and souvenirs. Antiques and valuable-looking artworks are closely scrutinised by customs.

In most shops and supermarkets the number of people inside is controlled by the number of shopping carts or baskets available. Often it can be difficult to enter without one, so pick one up at the door or stand in line and wait for someone to leave. Shopping baskets are even required in some shoe shops!

Getting There & Away

AIR

Czech Airlines (ČSA) flies from Bratislava's Štefánik letisko (airport) to Prague (4180 Sk) several times a day with immediate connections to Montreal (twice a week), New York (four times a week) and Toronto (once a week). ČSA links Bratislava directly to Moscow twice a week.

Local carrier Tatra Air has three flights a day on working days and one on weekends from Bratislava to Košice (2603 Sk), and three a day to Prague (4600 Sk). This airline also flies daily to Zürich and from there it's possible to continue by Swiss Air and other airlines to almost anywhere in the world.

The new carrier Air Slovakia only flies from Bratislava to Tel Aviv, Larnaca and Kuwait.

LAND
Bus

Nine daily buses link Vienna (Mitte Busbahnhof) to Bratislava (64km, two hours, 120 Sk). For more information on international buses see Getting There & Away in the Bratislava section.

Eurolines has buses to major cities in Europe from Bratislava, including a weekly bus between Amsterdam and Bratislava (22 hours, 2850 Sk one way) via Brussels and Vienna (Czech transit visa not required). A 10% reduction is available to those aged under 26 or over 59.

Train

Western Europe Vienna (Südbahnhof) to Bratislava is a 64km hop done four times a day (1¼ hours, 260 Sk). All trains to/from Germany pass through Prague and a Czech transit visa is required by some nationals.

Eastern Europe Bratislava is linked to Budapest (215km, three hours, 380 Sk) by several daily express trains from Budapest-Keleti or Budapest-Nyugati, all via Štúrovo.

There are no direct trains from Bratislava to Poland; all connections are via the Czech Republic. Reservations are mandatory on all express trains passing through West Slovakia and you should avoid them if you don't have a Czech visa. Train express services from East Slovakia to Poland and Hungary avoid the Czech Republic and require reservations.

Unreserved local trains run three times a day between Muszyna, Poland, and Plaveč, Slovakia (16km, 20 minutes). In Plaveč there are train connections to/from Prešov (54km, 1½ hours) and Poprad (61km, two hours); from Muszyna trains run to Nowy Sącz (50km) and (less frequently) to Kraków (217km), in Poland. For unreserved local trains that connect Košice and Miskolc, Hungary, see the Košice section of this chapter.

The only daily train between Moscow and Bratislava is via Warsaw (1999km, 33 hours).

Car & Motorcycle

Some small road border crossings are open only to citizens of Slovakia, the Czech Republic, Hungary and Poland, though this could change. There is only one crossing to/from Austria, at Petržalka (in Bratislava) and Ukraine, but there are plenty of options to/from the Czech Republic, Hungary and Poland.

Walking

Walking in and out of Slovakia is cheap, easy and fun. By crossing on foot you avoid the hassle of buying an expensive international ticket (although this hassle is avoided at the Czech/Slovak border) and end up with a memorable experience.

Poland The most convenient place to cross is at Lysa Polana/Javorina between Starý Smokovec and Zakopane. See the Vysoké Tatry section of this chapter and Zakopane in the Poland chapter for details.

Hungary You can easily walk across the bridge over the Danube River between Komárno and Komárom. Frequent trains with low domestic fares run between these twin cities and Bratislava and Budapest, and it costs nothing to walk across the massive river bridge (1892).

The bus and train stations in Komárno are close to one another. To get to the border from the stations, walk due south on Petőfiho to the end of the street, then left a block and right at Azia Centrum Department Store. Continue south past Hotel Európa to the bridge, a 20-minute walk from the stations. Slovak and Hungarian customs are together on a peninsula in the middle of the river. For conditions on the Hungarian side, see the Komárom section in the Hungary chapter.

Eight buses a day run between Bratislava and Komárno (104km). Otherwise take one of the six local trains to/from Bratislava's Nové Mesto train station (94km, two hours). A bus to the Komárom train station across the river leaves from in front of the Komárno train station several times a day.

Austria You could hitch towards Vienna from Bratislava; see the Bratislava section.

RIVER

See Boat under Getting There & Away in the Bratislava section.

Getting Around

BUS

Buses are more expensive than trains, and on weekends bus services are more sharply reduced than rail services. Plan on doing most of your travel by train with side trips by bus. Bus tickets in Slovakia cost 15 Sk for 25km, 34 Sk for 50km, 60 Sk for 100km and 120 Sk for 200km.

Buses are known to leave a few minutes earlier than the given time on the timetable, so it is advisable to arrive at least 10 minutes prior to departure. Most bus stops still have old Czechoslovak ČSAD signs instead of the new SAD ones which only appear on buses.

When trying to decipher posted bus schedules beware of departure times bearing footnotes you don't completely understand as these buses often don't show up. Check the time at the information window whenever possible. It is helpful to know that *premáva* means 'it operates' and *nepremáva* means 'it doesn't operate'.

TRAIN

The Slovak Republic Railways or Železnice Slovenskej republiky (ŽSR) provides efficient service at low rates. Most of the places covered in this chapter are on or near the main railway line between Bratislava and Košice.

By express train from Bratislava it's 123km and 1¾ hours to Trenčín, 203km and three hours to Žilina, 344km and five hours to Poprad, 370km and 5½ hours to Spišská Nová Ves, and 445km and 6½ hours to Košice.

Most train stations in Slovakia have a left-luggage office (úschovňa) where you can leave your bag for 15 to 20 Sk, and/or lockers for 5 Sk.

CAR & MOTORCYCLE

The types of petrol available at almost all petrol stations around the whole country are special (91 octane), unleaded (95 octane), super (98 octane) and diesel. Unleaded petrol costs about 22 Sk per 1L. LPG gas is available in at least one location of each region – Bratislava only has one LPG outlet.

Road Rules

You can drive in Slovakia using your own license.

Speed limits are 40km/h to 50km/h in built-up areas, 90km/h on open roads and 130km/h on motorways; motorbikes are limited to 90km/h. At level crossings over railway lines the speed limit is 30km/h. Beware of speed traps on the autoroutes as the police can levy on-the-spot fines of up to 2000 Sk and foreigners are the preferred targets.

Tolls for unlimited use of the country's highways are 200 Sk for small cars, and 400 Sk for larger cars. You can be fined 5000 Sk if you do not have a sticker showing you have paid the toll charge. These are available from most petrol stations.

Rental

Europcar has rental offices in Bratislava and Košice, as well as at Bratislava airport (290 Sk service charge at this outlet). Its cheapest Škoda Felicias begin at 960 Sk a day plus 9.60 Sk a kilometre, or 11,800 Sk weekly with unlimited kilometres, 6% tax not included. A weekend rate of 3160 Sk runs from 3 pm Friday to 9 am Monday with unlimited kilometres. Add about 360 Sk daily for collision insurance and another 460 Sk for theft coverage. Europcar allows one-way rentals between Bratislava and Prague or Košice at no additional charge. Also check Avis, Hertz and other car rental agencies. In Bratislava, there are cheaper local companies (see Bratislava section and also ask the Bratislava Information Service for a list of local companies).

BICYCLE

Slovakia is small enough to be traversed by bicycle. Cyclists should be aware that roads are very narrow and potholed, and in towns the cobblestones and tram tracks can be a dangerous combination, especially when it has been raining. Theft is a problem in large cities, so a good long chain and lock are a must.

Many locals use bicycles, so it's fairly easy to transport them on trains. First purchase your train ticket and then take it with your bicycle to the railway luggage office. There you fill out a card which will be attached to your bike. You will be given a receipt that should list all your bike's accessories, such as lights and dynamo. The cost of transporting a bicycle is usually one-tenth of the train ticket. It is best to collect the bicycle from the goods carriage as soon as you arrive at your destination. You can also transport bicycles on most buses if they are not crowded.

HITCHING

Slovakia is no safer than other European countries when it comes to hitching: many hitchhikers are assaulted and/or raped, and each year a few are killed. Despite these dangers, many Slovaks, including young females, choose to hitch.

LOCAL TRANSPORT

Buses and trams within cities operate from around 4.30 am to 11.30 pm daily. Tickets sold at public transport offices and newsstands must be validated once you're aboard. Tickets are hard to find at night, on weekends and out in residential areas, so carry a good supply. Some cities have automatic ticket machines.

SLOVAKIA

RAILWAYS OF THE SLOVAK REPUBLIC (ŽSR)

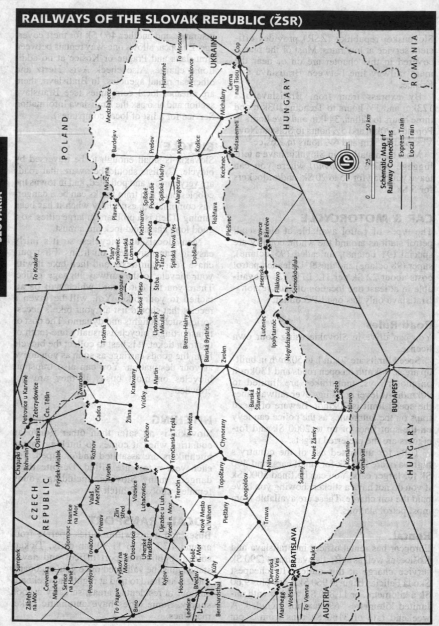

Schematic Map of
Railway Connections

—— Express Train
—— Local Train

0   25   50 km

Bratislava

☎ 07

Bratislava is Slovakia's largest city. Here the Carpathian Mountains, which begin at the Iron Gate of Romania, finally come to an end. As you arrive at the main train station, you'll see vineyards on the slopes of the Little Carpathian Mountains, where they meet the Danube River. The Austrian border is almost within sight of the city and Hungary is just 16km away.

Founded in 907 AD, Bratislava was already a large city in the 12th century. Commerce developed in the 14th and 15th centuries, and in 1467 the Hungarian Renaissance monarch Matthias Corvinus founded a university here, the Academia Istropolitana. The city became Hungary's capital in 1541, after the Turks captured Buda, and remained so from 1563 to 1830. In St Martin's Cathedral 11 Hungarian kings and seven queens were crowned. Bratislava flourished during the reign of Maria Teresa of Austria (1740-80) when some imposing baroque palaces were built. In 1918 the city was included in the newly formed Republic of Czechoslovakia, and in 1969 it became the state capital of a federal Slovak Republic but not until 1993 was it the capital of a fully independent country.

Many beautiful monuments survive in the old town to tell of its past under Hungarian rule, and Bratislava's numerous museums are surprisingly rich. Franz Liszt visited Bratislava 15 times, and the opera productions of the Slovak National Theatre rival anything in Europe. Bratislava isn't as swamped by western tourism as are Budapest and Prague (except on weekends when the Austrians invade).

Orientation

Hviezdoslavovo nám is a convenient reference point, with the old town to the north, the Danube to the south, Štúrova to the east and Bratislava Castle to the west.

Bratislava's main train station, Hlavná stanica, is several kilometres north of town. Tram No 1 runs from the lower level of this station to nám L Štúra near the centre. A few trains also use the Bratislava-Nové Mesto station, less conveniently located on the north-eastern side of the city.

The main bus station (autobusová stanica) is in a convenient modern building on Mlynské nivy, a little over 1km east of Štúrova.

The left-luggage office at the bus station is open weekdays from 5 am to 10 pm (there are two half-hour breaks) and weekends from 6 am to 6 pm. The left-luggage area at Hlavná stanica is open 24 hours.

Maps The most current map is Bratislava – Mapa mesta by BIS. If you are using public transport, Bratislava - Slovakia by Grznárik Štefan has public transport routes marked in the streets.

Maps of almost anywhere in Slovakia can be bought at Slovenská Kartografia, Pekná cesta 17 off Račianska (eastbound tram No 3, 5 or 11).

Information

General information about the city is supplied by the Bratislava Information Service, or BIS (☎ 533 37 15), Klobučnícka 2 (weekdays from 8 am to 7 pm, except from October to May when closing time is 4.30 pm, Saturday from 8.30 am to 1 pm). The staff sell an indexed city map and are very helpful. Kam v Bratislave (Where in Bratislava), available at BIS for 11.60 Sk, provides detailed information about what's on in town. There is a second, smaller BIS at the main train station.

Some newsstands and bookshops sell the English-language biweekly paper The Slovak Spectator, also a good source of information on what's happening in Bratislava.

Visa Extensions Visa or passport inquiries should be directed to the foreigners' police (Oddelenie cudzineckej polície), on the first floor to the left at Sasinkova 23 (open Monday, Wednesday and Friday from 7.30 am to noon and 1 to 3 pm, Wednesday until 5.30 pm and Friday until noon). To get there take tram No 5 from the corner of Obchodná and Poštová and get off at Americké nám.

Money The Všeobecná úverová banka has several offices around town. There is a poorly marked exchange office at Hlavná stanica open daily from 7.30 am to 6 pm, including an ATM. It's hidden to one side of the corridor, behind the 'Internationale Kasse' on the opposite side of the main hall from the left-luggage office. In the centre of town there is a branch on the corner of Poštová and Obchodná. They all change travellers cheques. The Poštová branch gives cash advances on Visa and MasterCard and has an ATM. Many other banks have ATMs and exchange offices around town.

There are 24-hour automatic currency-exchange machines (which convert the banknotes of 14 countries) outside the Slovenská štátna sporiteľňa, at Štúrova 11 near the ČSA office, and at nám SNP 18.

Post & Communications Mail addressed c/o poste restante, 81000 Bratislava 1, can be collected at window No 6 at the main post office, nám SNP 34 (open weekdays from 7 am to 8 pm, Saturday from 7 am to 6 pm). Letters from abroad are held for one month. To mail a parcel go to the office marked 'podaj a výdaj balíkov', through the next entrance, at nám SNP 35, but if it weighs more than 2kg and it is mailed outside the country than it has to be sent from the customs post office (colnica pošta) at Tomášikova 54. It is possible to make international telephone calls at Kolárska 12 and the main train station (both open 24 hours a day).

Cybercafes The Internet caffé (☎ 534 91 96; icaffe@tatrahome.sk), Muzejní, is at the rear of the Slovak National Museum and the entrance is through the museum cafe. It is open weekdays from 9 am to 9 pm and weekends from noon. One minute costs 1.50 Sk (minimum 15 minutes).

Travel Agencies Satur (☎ 542 22 05/6 68), Jesenského 5-9, can arrange air tickets, accommodation and tours in Slovakia, as well as international air, train and bus tickets.

The American Express representative in Bratislava is Tatratour (☎ 31 79 65), Mánesovo nám 3.

Bookshops The Big Ben Bookshop, Michalská 1, stocks a wide range of titles in English, as well as Lonely Planet guides. Knihy Slovenský spisovateľ, on the corner of Rybárska brána and Laurinská, sells useful hiking maps. You can find a vast selection of foreign news papers and magazines at Interpress Slovakia, on the corner of Michalská and Sedlárska.

Cultural Centres The British Council (☎ 53 11 85), Panská 17, is open Tuesday to Friday in the afternoons and Saturday morning. The US embassy has a Cultural and Information Section (USIS; ☎ 533 33 38), Hviezdoslavovo nám 4.

Laundry Improkom, Laurinská 16, offers one-day and cheaper, slower services. It's open weekdays from 8 am to 6 pm.

Medical & Emergency Services For medical emergencies call ☎ 49 49 49. The main outpatient clinic (☎ 39 61 51) is at Mýtna 5 and has a pharmacy. The 24-hour pharmacy (lekáreň) is at nám SNP 20.

The main police station (polícia) is at Sasinkova 23. For the foreigners' police, see the earlier Visa Extensions section.

Things to See

Begin your exploring at the **Slovak National Museum** (1928, free last Sunday of each month) opposite the hydrofoil terminal on the river. The museum features anthropology, archaeology, natural history and geology exhibits – notice the large relief map of Slovakia. (Unless otherwise noted, all of Bratislava's galleries and museums are closed on Monday and admission is typically around 20 Sk.)

A little further up the riverfront at Rázusovo nábrežie 2 is the ultramodern **Slovak National Gallery**, holding Bratislava's major art collection, with a good Gothic section. The gallery building daringly incorporates an 18th-century palace. The second building of the Slovak National Gallery is close by at nám L Štúra 4.

Backtrack slightly to nám L Štúra and on the corner with Mostová, you'll find the Art-Nouveau **Reduta Palace** (1914), which is now Bratislava's concert hall. Go north up Mostová to the neo-Baroque **Slovak National Theatre** (1886) on the right, with Ganymede's Fountain (1888) in front.

Crowded, narrow Rybárska brána penetrates the old town to Hlavné nám, at the centre of which is Roland's Fountain (1572).

SLOVAKIA

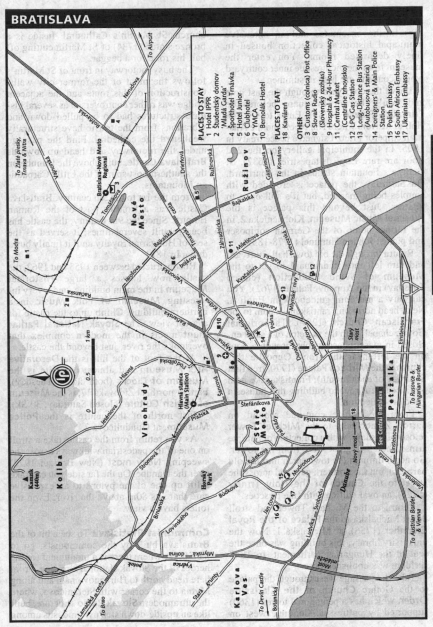

BRATISLAVA

PLACES TO STAY
1 Hotel IPPR
2 Studentský domov 'Mladá Garda'
4 Sporthotel Trnávka
5 Hotel Junior
6 Clubhotel
7 YMCA
10 Bernolák Hostel

PLACES TO EAT
18 Kaviáreň

OTHER
3 Customs (colnica) Post Office
8 Slovak Radio (Slovenský rozhlas)
9 Hospital & 24-Hour Pharmacy
11 Central Market (Centrálne trhovisko)
12 LPG Gas Station
13 Long-Distance Bus Station (Autobusová stanica)
14 Foreigners' & Main Police Station
15 Polish Embassy
16 South African Embassy
17 Ukrainian Embassy

To Airport
To Zlaté piesky, Trnava & Nitra
To Modra
Nenудоvа
Bratislava-Nové Mesto Regional
Nové Mesto
Tomášikova
Ружinov
Ružinovská
Dréřová
Bajkalská
Gagarinova
To Komárno
Vajnorská
Škultétyho
Záhradnícka
Miletičova
Prievozská
Košická
Karadžičova
Kvačalova
Mlynské nivy
Dulovo nám
Páričkova
Páľenisko
Mýtna
Dobrovičova
Dunajská
Starý most
Vinohrady
Hlavná
Podjavorinskej
Šancová
Hlavná stanica (Main Station)
Jeséniova
Pražská
Mudroňova
Štefánikova
Pražská
Staré Mesto
Panská
Pri vodárni
Nový most
Staromestská
Petržalka
Einsteinova
Einsteinova
Cesta
To Rusovce & Hungarian Border
See Central Bratislava
Koliba
Kamzík (440m)
Horský Park
Stromová
Brnianska
Búdková
Lovinského
Jána Stanislava
Ludvíka Svobodu
Mudroňova
To Austrian Border & Vienna
Vydrica
Mlynská dolina
potok
Karlova Ves
Devínska cesta
Lamačská cesta
Staré grunty
Botanická
Dúbravská
To Brno
To Devín Castle
Botanická
Danube
Most mládeže
0   0.5   1 km

To one side is the old town hall (1421), now the **Municipal Museum**, with torture chambers in the casemates and an extensive municipal historical collection housed in finely decorated rooms. You enter the museum from the picturesque inner courtyard where concerts are held in summer.

Leave the courtyard through the east gate and you'll be on a square before the **Primate's Palace** (1781). Enter to see the Hall of Mirrors where Napoleon and the Austrian emperor Franz I signed a peace treaty in 1805. In the municipal gallery on the 2nd floor are rare English tapestries (1632). St George's Fountain stands in the courtyard. On Saturday, the palace is crowded with couples being married, but it's still open to visitors. Just beyond this palace is the **Hummel Music Museum**, Klobučnícka 2, in the former home of the German composer and pianist Johann Hummel (1778-1837).

Return through the old town hall courtyard and turn left into Radničná 1 to get to the **Museum of Wine Production** (closed Tuesday) in the Apponyi Palace (1762). You can buy a museum guidebook in English. Next, head north on Františkánske nám to the **Franciscan Church** (1297). The original Gothic chapel, with the skeleton of a saint enclosed in glass, is accessible through a door on the left near the front. Opposite this church is the **Mirbach Palace** (1770, free first Saturday of each month), Františkánske nám 11, a beautiful rococo building that houses a good art collection.

From the palace continue around on narrow Zámočnícka to the **Michael Tower** (closed Tuesday), with a collection of antique arms. There's a great view from the tower. Go north through the tower arch into the old barbican, out the northern gate and across the street to the **Church of the Holy Trinity** (1725), an oval edifice with fine frescoes.

Return to the Michael Tower and stroll down Michalská to the **Palace of the Royal Chamber** (1756), at Michalská 1. Now the university library, this building was once the seat of the Hungarian parliament. In 1848 serfdom was abolished here.

Take the passage west through the palace to the Gothic **Church of the Clarissine Order**, which has a pentagonal tower (1360) supported by buttresses. Continue west on

Farská, then turn left into Kapitulská and go straight ahead to the 15th-century coronation church, **St Martin's Cathedral**. Inside is a bronze statue (1734) of St Martin cutting off half his robe for a beggar.

The busy motorway in front of St Martin's follows the moat of the former city walls. Construction of this route and the adjacent bridge was rather controversial as several historic structures had to be pulled down and vibrations from the traffic have structurally weakened the cathedral. Find the passage under the motorway and head up towards **Bratislava Castle**, built above the Danube on the southernmost spur of the Little Carpathian Mountains.

From the 1st to the 5th century, Bratislava Castle was a frontier post of the Roman Empire. Since the 9th century, the castle has been rebuilt several times; it served as the seat of Hungarian royalty until it finally burnt down in 1811.

Reconstructed between 1953 and 1962, the castle now houses a large **Historical Museum** in the main building, and a very interesting **Museum of Folk Music** in a northern building. Climb up to the castle for a great view. The **Slovak National Parliament** meets in the modern complex that overlooks the river, just beyond the castle.

At the foot of the hill is the **Decorative Arts Museum** and almost opposite is the **Museum of Clocks** (both closed Tuesday). Farther north, at Židovská 17, is the **Museum of Jewish Culture** (closed Saturday, 30 Sk).

Just north of the centre is the **Police Museum**, at Gunduličova 2.

As you return from the castle, take a stroll on one of the pedestrian walkways across the sweeping **Nový most** (New Bridge; 1972) over the Danube. On the far side you can take a lift up one of the pylons to an expensive café that sits 80m above the river. Even the toilets have a view.

Communist Bratislava To see a bit of the Bratislava built by the communists, go to nám SNP, where there is a monument for the heroes of the Slovak National Uprising. From here head north to Hurbanovo nám and along Mýtna to the corner with Štefaničova, where the ultramodern **Slovak Radio** structure, built like an upside-down step pyramid, sits among

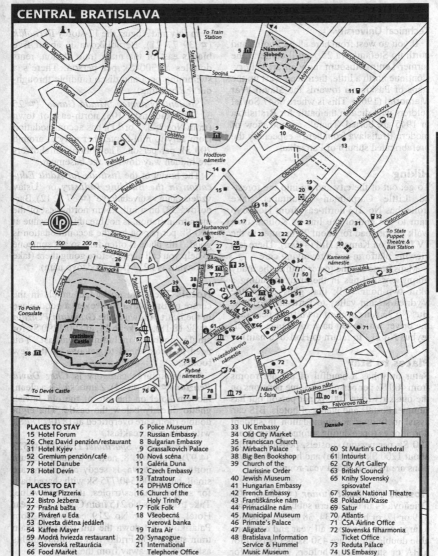

CENTRAL BRATISLAVA

PLACES TO STAY
15 Hotel Forum
26 Chez David penzión/restaurant
31 Hotel Kyjev
52 Gremium penzión/café
77 Hotel Danube
78 Hotel Devín

PLACES TO EAT
4 Umag Pizzeria
22 Bistro Jezbera
27 Prašná bašta
37 Piváreň u Eda
53 Divesta diétna jedáleň
54 Kaffee Mayer
59 Modrá hviezda restaurant
64 Slovenská reštaurácia
66 Food Market

OTHER
1 Slavín War Memorial
2 Romanian Embassy
3 Former Lenin Museum
5 Archbishop's Summer
   Palace

6 Police Museum
7 Russian Embassy
8 Bulgarian Embassy
9 Grassalkovich Palace
10 Nová scéna
11 Galéria Duna
12 Czech Embassy
13 Tatratour
14 DPHMB Office
16 Church of the
   Holy Trinity
17 Folk Folk
18 Všeobecná
   úverová banka
19 Tatra Air
20 Synagogue
21 International
   Telephone Office
23 Nám SNP & Monument
24 Keramika
25 Michael Tower
28 Main Post Office
29 Ufuv
30 Tesco
32 Charlie's Pub & Cinemas

33 UK Embassy
34 Old City Market
35 Franciscan Church
36 Mirbach Palace
38 Big Ben Bookshop
39 Church of the
   Clarissine Order
40 Jewish Museum
41 Hungarian Embassy
42 French Embassy
43 Františkánske nám
44 Primaciálne nám
46 Municipal Museum
47 Primate's Palace
48 Bratislava Information
   Service & Hummel
   Music Museum
49 Piano Bar
50 24 hour pharmacy
51 Improkom Laundrette
55 Hlavné nám
56 Museum of Clocks
57 Decorative Arts Museum
58 Slovak National Parliament

60 St Martin's Cathedral
61 Intourist
62 City Art Gallery
63 British Council
65 Knihy Slovenský
   spisovateľ
67 Slovak National Theatre
68 Pokladňa/Kasse
69 Satur
70 Atlantis
71 ČSA Airline Office
72 Slovenská filharmonia
   Ticket Office
73 Reduta Palace
74 US Embassy
75 17's Bar
76 Bus to Devín Castle
79 Slovak National Gallery
80 Slovak National
   Museum
81 Internet caffé
82 Hydrofoil Terminal

the housing estates. Some of the new buildings on nearby nám Slobody belong to the **Technical University**.

If you go west from here along Spojná and north up Štefánikova 25, you'll come to the former **Lenin Museum**, now an art gallery. Continue north a little, then head west up the steps of Puškinova towards the **Slavín War Memorial** (1965). This is where 6847 Soviet soldiers who died in the battle for Bratislava in 1945 are buried. There's a good view of modern Bratislava from here – especially the prefabricated suburb of Petržalka.

Hiking

To get out of the city and up into the forested Little Carpathian Mountains, take trolleybus No 213 north-east from Hodžovo nám to the end of the line at Koliba, then walk up the road for about 20 minutes to the **TV tower** on Kamzík Hill (440m). There is a viewing platform and a revolving café.

Maps posted at the tower outline the many hiking possibilities in the area, including a 6km two-hour walk that goes down the Vydrica stream valley to Partisan Meadow. Bus No 33 runs back to town from here (ask the driver where you have to change to trolleybus No 212 to return to Hodžovo nám).

Places to Stay

Satur only has a handful of private rooms from 400 Sk per person and some pensions on the outskirts from 700 Sk per person but has summer hostels and plenty of hotels. BIS can assist in finding accommodation in student dormitories (open during summer only – from 200 Sk per person), hostels, pensions (from about 1200 Sk a double) and hotels. Reservations are recommended year-round.

Hostels The *Hotel Junior* (☎ 23 43 40), Drieňová 14 in the eastern suburbs (tram Nos 8, 9 or 12, or bus Nos 34, 38 or 54) is beside a large pond. It's open all year and comfortable double rooms are 450 Sk per person for YHA or student card-holders (1100 Sk for others). This place is often full with groups.

The shabby but friendly *YMCA* (☎ 39 80 05), on the corner of Šancová and Karpatská, has 13 doubles, six triples and one five-bed room, all for 200 or 250 Sk per bed, but it's

often full. It's only an eight-minute downhill walk from the main train station.

In July and August the 12-storey *Bernolák* (☎ 39 77 21), Bernolákova 1, about five blocks east of the main train station, rents doubles at 300 Sk per person. There's a swimming pool and disco (audible throughout the building).

Študentský domov 'Mladá Garda' (☎ 25 31 36), Račianska 103, north-east of town (tram Nos 3, 5, 7 or 11), has accommodation from July to mid-September only at around 200 Sk per person. The communal showers are hidden way down in the basement.

The hostel of the *Institute for Adult Education in the Building Industry* or 'Ústav vzdelávania v stavebníctve' (☎ 37 52 12), Bardošová 33, on a hill 1.5km north-west of the main train station, is not breathtaking value at 390 Sk per person but the accommodation is good. This place is often full, so ask someone to help you call ahead before going there (take trolleybus No 212 from Hodžovo nám).

Hotels There are no budget hotels in the centre of Bratislava. However, a good place in the heart of town is the *Gremium Penzión* (☎ 32 18 18), Gorkého 11, at 890/1290 Sk for singles/doubles, including breakfast. You need to book ahead to get one of the few rooms.

In the splurge category is *Chez David Penzión* (☎ 531 38 24), Zámocká 13, a clean, modern hotel on the site of the old Jewish ghetto directly below the castle. The eight double rooms are overpriced at 1870/2977 Sk with bath and breakfast.

The two-storey *Športhotel Trnávka* (☎ 522 34 97), Nerudova 8, next to a small stadium north-east of town, is seedy and rooms are small, but at 406/540/775 Sk with shared bath for singles/doubles/triples, it's good value. Take trolleybus No 215 from Cintorínska near Hotel Kyjev, or No 219 eastbound from Palárikova just down the hill from the main train station. On Friday and Saturday nights ask for a room away from the disco.

Hotel IPPR (☎ 525 70 35), Nobelova 16, north-east of the centre, sometimes rents double rooms at 600 Sk per person, but you should call ahead as it's often full. *Clubhotel* (☎ 25 63 69), at Odbojárov 3, has rooms with shower (but shared toilet) which are good value at 510/880 Sk.

If you feel like spending up big, try the *Hotel Danube* (☎ 534 08 33), Rybné nám 1, where rooms with all the extras cost from 5072/5742 Sk.

Zlaté Piesky There are bungalows, a motel, a hotel and two camping grounds at Zlaté piesky (Golden Sands), which is near a clear blue lake 7km north-east of Bratislava. Tram Nos 2 (from the main train station) and 4 (from the city centre) terminate at Zlaté piesky. You can hire rowing boats and sailboards here in summer and there are also tennis courts.

As you cross the bridge from the tram stop you'll see *Hotel Flora* (☎ 25 79 88) on your left. Doubles here cost 620 Sk with shower or 480 Sk without (no singles) and the hotel restaurant is open daily until 10 pm. Next to the Flora is a lakeside *Zlaté piesky camping ground* (☎ 25 73 73) with 50 four-bed cottages without bath and 20 three-bed bungalows with private bath. Tent camping is possible and the facility is open from mid-April to mid-October. A poorer *camping ground* with run-down three-bed bungalows is nearby (but not on the lake). Camping is handled at reception but the bungalows are controlled by *Motel Evona Zlaté piesky* (☎ 25 73 65), a couple of minutes away. The motel's 35 double rooms with bath are open year-round but the bungalows are only available from mid-May to September.

Places to Eat
Restaurants – Budget There is a good supermarket in the basement of Tesco department store. One of the few places to get an early breakfast is *Bistro Jezbera*, nám SNP 11, which opens at 6.30 am from to 3 pm Monday to Friday. The stand-up buffet is in the basement, which you enter from around the corner.

The *food market*, on the corner of Hviezdoslavovo nám and Rybárska brána (open daily from 10.30 am to 10 pm), has a dozen cuisines at individual counters in the stand-up section or you can sit down and order spaghetti or pizza in the adjacent full-service restaurant.

The *Divesta dietná jedáleň*, Laurinská 8

(open weekdays from 10 am to 3 pm), is renovated, clean and provides low calorie food and a vegetarian menu.

Two good inexpensive pubs serving typical Slovak food for lunch and dinner are *Prašná bašta*, Zámočnícka 11, and *Piváreň u Eda*, Biela, that has a separate non-smoking room to eat in.

The pizzas served at *Umag pizzeria*, on the corner of nám Slobody and Žilinská, are good. A more central pizza place is the self-service *Little Caesar's pizza* on the ground floor in Tesco.

Restaurants – Mid-Range Worth trying is the wine restaurant *Vináreň Veľký františkáni*, Františkánske nám 10, in the old monastery beside the Mirbach Palace. Roma music is often played here.

The *Modrá hviezda restaurant*, Beblavého 14, on the way up to the castle, features local dishes such as cheese pie. The menu is in English. *Chez David kosher restaurant*, Zámocká 13, directly below the castle, is upmarket but not intolerably so. Carp served in the Jewish style is a speciality.

Restaurants – Top End The master chef in *Slovenská reštaurácia*, Hviezdoslavovo nám 20, prepares excellent versions of Slovak national dishes some of which he modifies to his taste. This does not come cheap but it's worth a splurge.

Cafés Excellent for coffee, cakes and ice cream is *Atlantis*, Štúrova 13 (daily until 9 pm). It has Bratislava's best ice cream; on Sunday afternoon the queue runs out the door and down the pavement.

The *Gremium art galerie café*, Gorkého 11, has a good atmosphere and is the place to sip a cup of Viennese coffee (Viedenská káva) without having to be too pretentious.

The Viennese-style and very classy *Kaffee Mayer*, Hlavné nám 4, has excellent but pricey coffee, cakes and light meals.

Entertainment
Opera and ballet are presented at the *Slovak National Theatre* (1886), on Hviezdoslavovo nám (often closed Sunday and during August). The local opera and ballet companies are outstanding.

Tickets are sold at the 'Pokladňa/Kasse' office (open weekdays from 8 am to 6 pm and Saturday from 9 am to 1 pm) on the corner of Jesenského and Komenského, behind the National Theatre.

An hour before the performance, ticket sales are at the theatre itself, but they're usually sold out (*vypredané*) by then, especially on weekends.

Nová scéna, Kollárovo nám 20, presents operettas, musicals and drama (the latter in Slovak). The ticket office is open weekdays from 12.30 to 7 pm and an hour before the performance but they're usually sold out.

The *Slovenská filharmonia* is based in the neo-rococo Reduta Palace (built in 1914) on the corner of nám L Štúra and Medená, across the park from the National Theatre. The ticket office (open weekdays from 1 to 5 pm) at Palackého 2 is inside the building.

The PKO Predpredaj vstupeniek, Hviezdoslavovo nám 24, has tickets for special events such as rock concerts.

The *Štátne Bábkové divadlo* (State Puppet Theatre), Dunajská 36, puts on puppet shows for kids, usually at 9 or 10 am and sometimes again at 1.30 or 2.30 pm. It's good fun.

There's often something happening at the *Dom kultúry* (House of Culture), nám SNP 12.

Clubs & Discos *Charlie's Pub*, Špitálska 4 (but enter from Rajská), has loud pop music, TVs all around and people dancing among the tables. There is a 30 Sk cover charge on weekends. It's one of the most popular meeting and drinking places for the city youth (open nightly from 6 pm to 4 am, until 6 am on Friday and Saturday).

Two bars that have live jazz bands several times a week are *17's Bar*, Hviezdoslavovo nám 17, and *Aligator*, Laurinská 7. They are also popular meeting places. A pleasant and quiet place for a drink is the *Piano Bar*, Laurinská 11.

The *Galéria Duna* at Radlinského 11 is a club that has rock bands, dance music or whatever the alternative scene has to offer.

Cinemas In the same complex as Charlie's Pub, Špitálska 4, are Bratislava's best art cinemas: *Marilyn, Charlie, Lumiere* and *Voskovec & Werich*. Other cinemas in the city centre include *Kino Mladosť*, Hviezdoslavovo nám 17 and *Kino Hviezda*, nám 1 mája 9.

Things to Buy
Keramika, on the corner of Hurbanovo and Župné nám, has a good selection of well-priced traditional folk ceramics. For other folk handicrafts head to the more expensive Uľuv at nám SNP, or Folk Folk at Obchodná 10.

Getting There & Away
Air Tatra Air (☎ 36 67 58), at Heydukova 29, has daily flights to/from Košice (2603 Sk one way). ČSA (☎ 36 10 38) at Štúrova 13 has daily flights to/from Prague. Satur and many other travel agents can book these flights.

Bus At Bratislava's main bus station (SAD/Eurolines information, ☎ 526 13 12), on Mlynské nivy in Nivy, you can usually buy your ticket from the driver if the bus is not full, but check first at the information counter. Advance tickets for the buses marked 'R' on the posted timetable may be purchased from the AMS counter. The footnotes on this timetable are in English.

Ten express buses a day run to Prague (4½ hours, 247 Sk, one hour faster than the train and about half the price) and there are seven buses a day to Komárno (104km, 66 Sk). Other buses leaving Bratislava daily include nine to Košice (7½ hours, 249 Sk), five to Bardejov (273 Sk), and one each to Banská Štiavnica and Tatranská Lomnica (200 Sk).

Eight buses a day connect Vienna (Mitte Busbahnhof) to Bratislava (1½ hours, 340 Sk). In Bratislava buy your ticket for this bus at the ticket window inside the bus station.

Other international buses leaving from the bus station go to Brussels (five a week), Budapest (daily, 400 Sk), Cologne (weekly), Frankfurt (twice weekly, 13 hours, 1600 Sk), Kraków (weekly), London (four times a week, 22½ hours, 4103 Sk), Munich (four times a week), Paris (twice a week, 2700 Sk), Sofia (five times a week) and Thessaloniki (weekly). Tickets may be purchased for crowns either at the international ticket window in the bus station or at the adjacent Eurolines office, depending on the destination. Beware of buses that transit the Czech Republic, as you could be 'kicked off' at the border if you don't have a visa.

Train All express trains between Budapest (2¾ hours, 380 Sk) and Prague (five hours, 528 Sk) call at Bratislava. Train services from Košice to Bratislava (via Poprad, Žilina and Trenčín; five hours, 210 Sk) are fairly frequent and couchettes are available on the night train.

There are four local trains a day between Vienna (Südbahnhof) and Bratislava's main train station (1¼ hours, 220 Sk). One nightly train departs for Moscow but there's no direct service to Poland. International train tickets are available at the station.

Two local trains a day run from Bratislava's Nové Mesto (regional) station to Győr, Hungary (two hours, 260 Sk), via Rajka. The ticket office at Nové Mesto will sell you a ticket only as far as the border (50 Sk) and you must pay the Hungarian conductor the balance. Otherwise buy a through ticket at the main train station or from Satur the day before.

Walking into Hungary or Austria If you don't want to bother getting an international train ticket, take a local train or bus to Komárno and walk across the bridge to Komárom in Hungary. See Train/Komárno in the Getting There & Away section for details.

The Austrian border is about 4km beyond Nový most along Viedenská cesta. Take bus No 47 from Hodžovo nám southbound across the bridge and get off at the next stop after high-rise Hotel Incheba. Walk 2km to the border and clear customs.

Boat A good day trip or an interesting way to arrive/leave Slovakia from May to mid-October, is with Raketa hydrofoils that ply the Danube between Bratislava and Vienna once a day, Wednesday to Sunday for 623 Sk one way (1¼ hours), 952 Sk return. Children aged 15 years and under and students pay half-price. Tickets and information are available at the hydrofoil terminal, Fajnorovo nábrežie 2. In late summer the service can be interrupted because of low water levels.

It's possible to travel between Bratislava and Budapest from mid-May to October, once a day (in July and August twice a day). The trip takes four hours and costs 1850 Sk one way, 2720 Sk return.

Getting Around

To/From the Airport The only way to get to Ivanka airport is on city bus No 24 from the train station (8km) or by taxi.

Tram & Bus Public transport in and around Bratislava is based on an extensive tram network complemented by bus and trolleybus. Orange automats at tram and trolleybus stops sell tickets (7 Sk per ride), but make sure that the green light is on before inserting coins.

Tourist tickets (*turistické cestovné lístky*) valid for 24 hours (35 Sk), 48 hours (65 Sk) or seven days (105 Sk) are sold at the DPHMB office in the underground passageway below Hodžovo nám (open weekdays from 6 am to 7 pm). These tickets are also sold at the window marked 'MHD' next to the taxi stand in front of the main train station. The validity of the ticket begins immediately upon purchase, so buy one only when you need it. If you are carrying luggage get a 3 Sk ticket for it otherwise inspectors mercilessly hand out 700 Sk fines.

Boat One hour boat sightseeing trips of Bratislava on the Danube leave from the hydrofoil terminal at Fajnorovo nábrežie for 50 Sk several times a day on the weekends from mid-April to mid-October. Another interesting trip is to Devín Castle twice a day (1¼ hours), except Saturday, from May to early October, and costs 50 Sk one way or 70 Sk for a return.

Taxi Bratislava's taxis all have meters and drivers are far less likely to try to overcharge you than those in Prague. Central Bratislava is small enough for you to be able to walk almost anywhere.

Car There are several inexpensive smaller local car rental companies (contact BIS or Satur for others) such as Favorit Car (☎ 28 41 52), Pri vinohradoch 275, that have a Škoda Felicie for 450 Sk/day plus 3 Sk/km. Europcar (☎ 524 51 66) is in the Hotel Devín, Riečna 4. Hertz has a desk in the lobby of Hotel Forum. Hertz and Europcar also have desks at Ivanka airport.

LPG gas is available only at Pristavná 1.

AROUND BRATISLAVA

From the 1st to the 5th century, **Devín Castle** was a frontier post of the Roman Empire, manned by the 14th Legion. In the 9th century the castle was a major stronghold of the Great Moravian Empire. The castle withstood the Turks but was blown up in 1809 by the French. Today it is regarded as a symbol of the Slovaks who maintained their identity despite a millennium of foreign rule. The Gothic ruins of Devín Castle (open from May to October, closed Monday) have an exhibit of artefacts.

Getting There & Away

Below the Bratislava end of Nový most is a city bus terminal where you can catch city bus No 29 (two every hour) west beside the Danube to the castle, on a hill where the Morava and Danube rivers meet. Stay on the bus to the end of the line and walk back to the castle. Austria is just across the rivers from Devín.

West Slovakia

TRENČÍN
☎ 0831

For centuries, where the Váh River valley begins to narrow between the White Carpathians and the Strážov Hills, Trenčín Castle guarded the south-west gateway to Slovakia and one of the routes from the Danube to the Baltic. Laugaricio, a Roman military post – the northernmost Roman camp in eastern Europe – was established here in the 2nd century AD. A rock inscription at Trenčín, dated 179 AD, mentions the stay of the Roman 2nd Legion and its victory over the Germanic Kvad tribes.

The mighty castle that now towers above the town was first mentioned in 1069 in a Viennese illustrated chronicle. In the 13th century the castle's master Matúš Čák held sway over much of Slovakia, and in 1412 Trenčín obtained the rights of a free royal city. The present castle dates from that period, and although both castle and town were destroyed by fire in 1790, much has been restored. Today Trenčín is a centre of the textile industry.

Orientation & Information

From the adjacent bus and train stations walk west through the city park and take the Tatra Passage under the highway to Mierové nám, the main square.

The well-informed staff at the AiCES municipal information centre (☎ 43 35 05), Štúrovo nám 10, can help you to find accommodation; in summer ask about student dorms.

Money The Všeobecná úverová banka, Mierové nám 48, changes travellers cheques, and another VÚB branch across the square at no 37 has a Visa/MasterCard ATM.

Post & Communications The telephone centre is in the main post office in Mierové nám.

Things to See

At the south-western end of Mierové nám are the baroque **Piarist Church** and the 16th-century **town gate** that plays old-fashioned tunes on the hour. The **art gallery** (closed Monday), in the former Piarist convent next to the church, features works by local artists, especially the realist painter MA Bazovský.

A covered stairway from the corner of the square opposite the Piarist Church leads up to the Gothic **parish church** and to the entrance to **Trenčín Castle** (open daily all year, 50 Sk). The highlight of the one-hour tour are the 18th century paintings of the ruling family. The so-called 'Well of Love' on the first terrace is a fantastic construction 70m deep. Above is the castle's great central tower, which provides a sweeping view of the area. At night the castle is illuminated with fairy-tale green and purple lights. A two hour show called Medieval Days, which includes sword fighting and ghosts is held from 9 pm every second Friday or Saturday from May to September.

The famous Roman inscription of 179 AD is behind Hotel Tatra and can only be seen through a window of the hotel's second floor – ask at the reception for permission to see it. The not so interesting **Trenčín Museum** (closed Monday) is at Mierové nám 46, next to Hotel Tatra.

Places to Stay

Camping The *Vodácky klub na ostrove camping ground* (☎ 53 40 13) is on Ostrov,

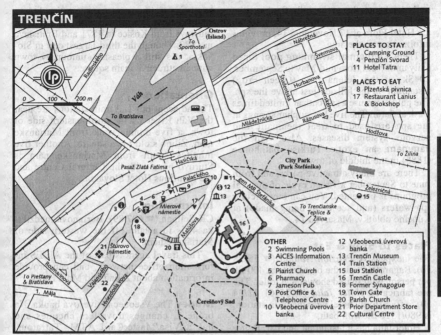

TRENČÍN

PLACES TO STAY
1 Camping Ground
4 Penzión Svorad
11 Hotel Tatra

PLACES TO EAT
8 Plzeňská pivnica
17 Restaurant Lanius & Bookshop

OTHER
2 Swimming Pools
3 AiCES Information Centre
5 Piarist Church
6 Pharmacy
7 Jameson Pub
9 Post Office & Telephone Centre
10 Všeobecná úverová banka
12 Všeobecná úverová banka
13 Trenčín Museum
14 Train Station
15 Bus Station
16 Trenčín Castle
18 Former Synagogue
19 Town Gate
20 Parish Church
21 Prior Department Store
22 Cultural Centre

SLOVAKIA

an island in the Váh River, opposite the large sports stadium near the city centre. Camping is 40 Sk per person, 55 Sk per tent, and nice little two and four-bed cabins are 100 Sk per person. Singles are accommodated for the same price aboard the ex-hydrofoil *Raketa*, now permanently moored at the camping ground. Though the rooms are often full, this place is well worth trying (both are only open from May to mid-September).

Hotels In the centre of town the only cheap accommodation is at *Penzión Svorad* (☎ 43 03 22), Palackého 4, where rooms with shared facilities cost 410/740 Sk. *Športhotel* (☎ 53 19 40) is in the middle of Ostrov Island, about a 20-minute walk from Mierové nám. Doubles with shower and toilet are 1000 Sk. The only central hotel is the top-of-the-line *Tatra* (☎ 50 61 11), gen MR Štefánika 2, where rooms including breakfast are 2400/3200 Sk.

Places to Eat

Plzeňská pivnica, in a damp basement in pasáž Zlatá Fatima, will serve a fairly hearty inexpensive Slovak meal. Better and pricier food is found in a pleasant atmosphere at *Restaurant Lanius*, Mierové nám 22. A popular bar is *Jameson Pub*, Mierové nám 13.

Getting There & Away

All express trains on the main railway line from Bratislava to Košice via Žilina stop here. If you are taking a train to Poland or Germany a Czech transit visa may be required. There are six buses a day to Bratislava, Žilina, Košice and several to go to Brno (134km), in the Czech Republic.

TRENČIANSKE TEPLICE
☎ 0831

Trenčianske Teplice is a spa town in a narrow valley 14km north-east of Trenčín. Hiking trails lead into the green hills flanking the resort. The Satur office (☎ 55 23 61), inside the Hotel Flora at 17 Novembra 14, provides information on the area.

There's a **thermal swimming pool** (open daily until 6 pm from mid-May to September, 20 Sk) at the Zelená žaba (Green Frog) restaurant on the hillside just above the spa. The public can use a spa bath at limited times – ask at Satur. The five hot sulphur springs at the spa are used to treat rheumatic and nervous system diseases. Also visit the **hammam**, an exotic Turkish bathhouse (1888) in the middle of town.

There are many attractive parks, and from June to September a varied cycle of musical programs is presented. You can buy circular spa wafers (and see them being made) at Kúpeľné oblátky, Masaryka 14.

Places to Stay & Eat
The inexpensive *Penzión Natália* (☎ 55 28 58), Bagarova 26, is the best value at 400 Sk per person with shared shower and toilet. The pre-fabricated *Hotel Jalta* (☎ 55 61 11/34 50), a five-storey hotel near the train station, is 980/1320 Sk with bath.

Hotel Jalta has a restaurant and bar. Better value is *R club reštaurácia* opposite the hotel on TG Masaryka. It has a good selection of Slovak dishes, including some vegetarian ones.

Getting There & Away
Trenčianske Teplice is accessible via a 6km branch line from Trenčianska Teplá on the main railway line between Trenčín and Žilina. Electric tram-type trains shuttle back and forth about once an hour. There are also some direct buses every half hour from Trenčín.

Central Slovakia

ŽILINA
☎ 089
Žilina, midway between Bratislava and Košice, at the junction of the Váh and Kysuca rivers, is the gateway to the Malá Fatra Mountains. Since its foundation in the 13th century at a crossing of medieval trade routes, Žilina

has been an important transportation hub, a status that was confirmed with the arrival of railways from Košice in 1871 and Bratislava in 1883. Though the third-largest city in Slovakia, it's still a pleasant, untouristy town with an attractive main square.

Orientation
The adjacent bus and train stations are near the Váh River on the north-eastern side of town, a five-minute walk from Mariánske nám, Žilina's old town square. Another five minutes south from Mariánske nám is Štúrovo nám, with the Cultural Centre and the luxurious Hotel Slovakia.

Information
CK Selinan (☎ 607 89), Burianova medzierka 4, is in a lane off the western side of Mariánské nám.

This travel agent is part of the AiCES information office network, and can provide information about Žilina and Malá Fatra.

Money The Všeobecná úverová banka, Na bráne 1, changes travellers cheques and has a Visa/MasterCard ATM. Tatratour, Mariánske nám 21, is the American Express representative.

Post & Communications The telephone centre is in the post office next to the train station.

Things to See
The recently renovated central square, with its picturesque church and covered walkway all around, could have been lifted straight out of Mexico. Other than this, the only sight worth seeking out is the naive art figures of metal and wire at the **Regional Museum** (closed Monday) in the Renaissance castle *(zámok)* across the river in Budatín, a 15-minute walk north-west from the train station. As you come out of the train station, turn right and go straight ahead for a few minutes, then go right under the train tracks and straight again till you reach the bridge over the river. The white castle tower is visible from there. **Považská galéria** at Hlinkovo nám has changing art exhibits.

Places to Stay

Hostels The *ubytovňa* at Nemocnica Slo-bodáreň (☎ 687 06 71), Na Hlinách, (take bus No 3 from the bus station) has basic rooms with shared facilities at 260 Sk per person.

Pensions These are the next best deal with *Pension GMK Centrum* (☎ 62 21 36), Mariánské nám 3, with smallish rooms from 650/800 Sk, including shower. Nicer is the *Penzión Majovey* (☎ 62 41 52/468 90), at Jána Milica 3, where doubles are 1000 Sk.

If these places are full, you can always resort to the comfortable *Hotel Slovan* (☎ 62 05 56), Kmetova 2, behind the Tesco department store, back towards the train station (1280/1480 Sk for a double/triple with bath, TV and breakfast).

Places to Eat

Gastro, Jána Milica 1, on the corner of Národní, is a good place for large sandwiches and inexpensive buffet food.

The trendier *Radničná vináreň*, Mariánské nám 28, is a new restaurant. Located in a cellar, it serves good, inexpensive meat dishes.

Campari Pizza, Zaymusova 4, on the north side of Štúrovo nám, has a nice back terrace where you can down pseudo-pizza and cheap red wine.

Getting There & Away

Žilina is on the main railway line from Bratislava to Košice via Trenčín and Poprad, and is served by fairly frequent express trains. Most trains between Prague and Košice also stop at Žilina. Express trains from Žilina take six hours to Prague (466km), 1½ hours to Trenčín (80km), three hours to Bratislava (203km), two hours to Poprad (141km) and three hours to Košice (242km).

For Poland, if you don't require a Czech visa, take a local train from Žilina to Český Těšín (69km) and walk across the border (see Walking in Getting There & Away section in the Czech Republic chapter). If you do need a separate Czech visa you will have to go via Poprad and the Javorina/Lysa Polana border crossing to Zakopane.

There are several buses a day to Brno (134km) and Prague.

THE MALÁ FATRA
☎ 089

The Malá Fatra (Little Fatra) Mountains stretch 50km across north-western Slovakia; Veľký Kriváň (1709m) is the highest peak. Two hundred sq km of this scenic range, north of the Váh River and east of Žilina, are included in Malá Fatra National Park. At the heart of the park is Vrátna, a beautiful mountain valley with forested slopes on all sides.

Noted for its rich flora, the Vrátna Valley has something for everyone. The hiking possibilities vary from easy tourist tracks through the forest to scenic ridge walks. There are plenty of places to stay and eat, though in midsummer and winter accommodation is tight. The valley is an easy day trip from Žilina. In winter Vrátna becomes a popular ski resort.

Information

The Mountain Rescue Service (Horská služba, ☎ 69 52 32), on the access road to Hotel Boboty, can provide detailed information on the park.

If you plan to hike, get the *Malá Fatra Vrátna turistická mapa* (1:50,000) by Vojenský kartografický ústav.

Familiarise yourself with the trail markers, as some foreign hikers have confused them with the slightly similar logging markers and become lost.

Things to See & Do

To explore this area, take the bus from Žilina that enters the Vrátna Valley just south of Terchová, where it runs through the **Tiesňavy Pass** which has rocky crags on both sides. One rock resembles a person praying (look back after you've gone through the pass).

Stay on the bus until **Chata Vrátna** (750m) where detailed maps of the area are posted. From just above Chata Vrátna, a two-seater chair lift climbs 770m to the Snilovské sedlo (1520m), a saddle midway between Chleb (1647m) and Veľký Kriváň. Take along a sweater or jacket as it will be a lot cooler on top. The chair lift only runs if at least 20 people are present – in summer there may be a queue. In rain the chair lift doesn't operate at all as there's no protection from the elements.

From Snilovské sedlo you can follow the red trail south-east along the mountain ridges

SLOVAKIA

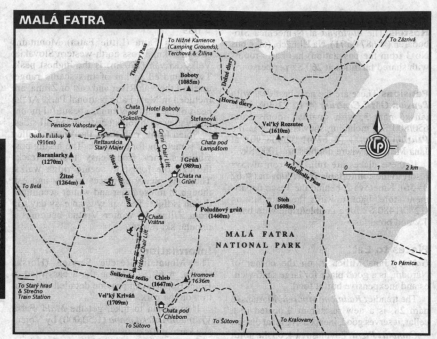

MALÁ FATRA

To Nižné Kamence
(Camping Grounds),
Terchová & Žilina

To Zázrivá

Thiessovy Pass

Dolné diery

Boboty
(1085m) ▲

Horné diery

Chata
pod
Sokolím

Hotel Boboty ■

Štefanová

Vel'ký Rozsutec
(1610m) ▲

Pension Vahostav ▲

Sedlo Príslop
(916m) ▲

Reštaurácia
Starý Majer

Grúni Chair Lift

Chata pod
Lampášom

Baraniarky ▲
(1270m)

Žitné
(1264m) ▲

Starå dolina Valley

Grúň
(989m) ▲

Chata na
Grúni

Medziholie Pass

0   1   2 km

To Belá

Stará dolina Valley

Chata
Vrátna

Poludňový grúň
(1460m)

Stoh
(1608m)

Vrátna Chair Lift

MALÁ FATRA
NATIONAL PARK

To Párnica

Snilovské sedlo

Chleb
(1647m)

Hromové
1636m

To Starý hrad
& Strečno
Train Station

Vel'ký Kriváň
(1709m)

Chata pod
Chlebom

To Šútovo

To Šútovo

To Kralovany

---

past Hromové (1636m), then north-east to Poludňový grúň (1460m) and Stoh (1608m) to the **Medziholie Pass** (1185m), right below the rocky summit of **Vel'ký Rozsutec** (1610m). An orange trail skirting the side of Stoh avoids a 200m climb.

From Medziholie it's easy to descend another green trail to **Štefanová**, a picturesque village of log houses with private rooms available (ask around). You can do the hike from Snilovské sedlo to Štefanová via Medziholie in about four hours. Other possible hikes from Snilovské sedlo are the blue trail to Starý Dvor via the ridges (three hours) and the red trail west to Strečno railway station via the Starý hrad ruins (6½ hours).

A good alternative if the chair lift isn't operating or you don't have much time, is to take the yellow trail from Chata Vrátna to **Chata na Grúni** at 970m (45 minutes). This mountain chalet has 30 beds and a restaurant but it's often closed or full. From Chata na Grúni the blue trail descends to Štefanová (45 minutes), where you can get buses back to Žilina.

Skiing There is good downhill skiing and snowboarding for all levels, with some 20 inexpensive lifts operating in the valley. Reasonable skis, boots and snowboards are generally available for hire. The best time is from late December to March.

Places to Stay & Eat

No camping is allowed in the Vrátna Valley. The nearest *camping grounds* are at Nižné Kamence, 3km west of Terchová, and at Varín, both on the way to/from Žilina.

The accommodation in some of the chalets can be booked through Slovakotour Terchová (☎ 69 52 22). *Chata Vrátna*, a large wooden chalet at 750m with 88 beds, is usually full with hikers in summer and skiers in winter. In spring and late autumn, groups of school children pack the dormitories. Regular hotel double/triple/quad rooms are 350 Sk per person, while the dormitory is 250 Sk per person and half-board is 200 Sk. A good *Restaurant Koliba* faces the bus stop below the hotel.

Chata pod Sokolím, on the hillside above Reštaurácia Starý Majer, has 60 beds (400 Sk per double) and a large restaurant. The view from here is great. If it's closed try *Pension Vahostav* (☎ 69 53 06) about 1km farther up the valley and costs 300 Sk per person.

Štefanová The *Chata pod Skalným mestom* (☎ 69 53 63), a few minutes up the green trail in Štefanová village, was being renovated at the time of writing. A few hundred metres beyond is the similar *Chata Pod Lampášom*, which charges 766 Sk per person for bed, breakfast and dinner. It's open year-round.

Reštaurácia Štefanová (☎ 69 53 25) rents cabins in the forest year-round, except in November. There are also several *privaty* around the village, look for the 'zimmer frei' signs.

The comfortable *Hotel Boboty* (☎ 69 52 28), a five-minute walk up from the bus stop near Štefanová, costs 700/1300 Sk with shower and breakfast is 110 Sk extra. The hotel has a sauna, a swimming pool and a restaurant.

Getting There & Away

A bus from Žilina to Chata Vrátna, 32km east, leaves from platform No 10 at Žilina bus station nine times a day taking about an hour. The bus travels via Krasňany, which has a natural history museum, and Terchová, where a folk festival is held in July.

If you come on a day trip, check the times of afternoon buses returning to Žilina from Štefanová at the information counter at Žilina bus station before setting out.

East Slovakia

East Slovakia is one of the most attractive touring areas in central Europe. In one compact region you can enjoy superb hiking in the High Tatra Mountains, rafting on the Dunajec River, historic towns such as Levoča and Bardejov, the great medieval castle at Spišské Podhradie, the charming spa of Bardejovské Kúpele and city life in Košice.

The proximity of Ukraine gives the region an exotic air. Getting around is easy, with frequent trains and buses to all these sights plus easy access to Poland and Hungary. In spite of all these advantages, exciting East Slovakia is still well off the beaten track.

THE VYSOKÉ TATRY
☎ 0969

The Vysoké Tatry (High Tatras) are the only truly alpine mountains in central Europe and one of the smallest high mountain ranges in the world. This 27km-long granite massif covers 260 sq km, forming the northernmost portion of the Carpathian Mountains. The narrow, rocky crests soar above wide glacial valleys with precipitous walls. At 2655m, Gerlachovský štít (Mt Gerlach) is the highest mountain in the entire 1200km Carpathian Mountains, and several dozen other peaks exceed 2500m.

Enhancing the natural beauty packed into this relatively small area are 30 valleys, almost 100 glacial lakes, and bubbling streams. The lower slopes are covered by dense coniferous forest. From 1500 to 1800m altitude, there's a belt of brushwood and knee pines, and above this are alpine flora and bare peaks.

Since 1949, most of the Slovak portion of this jagged range has been included in the Tatra National Park (TANAP), the first national park to be created in former Czechoslovakia, which complements a similar park in Poland. A network of 600km of hiking trails reaches all the alpine valleys and many peaks. The red-marked Tatranská magistrála trail follows the southern crest of the Vysoké Tatry for 65km through a striking variety of landscapes. Other routes are also colour-coded and easy to follow. Park regulations require you to keep to the marked trails and to refrain from picking flowers.

Climate & When to Go

When planning your trip, keep in mind the altitude. At 750m the camping grounds will be too cold for a tent from October to mid-May. There's snow by November (on some of the highest passes as early as September) and avalanches are a danger from November to June when the higher trails are closed (ask someone to translate the notices at the head of the trails for you). Beware of sudden thunderstorms, especially in the alpine areas where there's no protection, and always carry warm clothing. Remember that the assistance of the Mountain Rescue Service is not free. July and August are the warmest (and most crowded) months, and August and September are the best for high-altitude hiking. Hotel prices are at their lowest from April to mid-June, the months with the longest daylight hours.

The TANAP Mountain Rescue Service office next to Satur in Starý Smokovec can give you a weather report for the next day.

Orientation

The best centre for visitors is Starý Smokovec, a turn-of-the-century resort that is well connected to the rest of the country by road and rail. Tram-style electric trains run frequently between the three main tourist centres in the park: Štrbské Pleso (1320m), Starý Smokovec (990m) and Tatranská Lomnica (850m). At Poprad these trains link up with the national railway system. Buses also run frequently between the resorts. Cable cars, chair lifts and a funicular railway carry you up the slopes to hiking trails that soon lead you away from the throng. During winter, skiers flock to the area.

All three main train stations have left-luggage offices. Tatranská Lomnica's is open 24 hours a day, Starý Smokovec's from 5 am to 11 pm and Štrbské Pleso's on weekdays from 6.30 am to 6 pm and weekends from 7.30 am to 7.30 pm (it also has lockers).

Maps Our Vysoké Tatry map is intended for initial orientation only. Buy a proper *Vysoké Tatry* hiking map at a bookshop when you arrive in Slovakia. Good maps are also usually available at hotels or newsstands inside the park. When buying your Tatry hiking map, make sure you get one with summer hiking trails and not the winter ski routes.

Information

The main AiCES Tatry information centre (☎ 42 34 40) in Dom služieb, north-west of the Starý Smokovec train station, has plenty of information on the region. Another office (☎ 49 23 91) is next to Obchodný dom Toliar

(department store), opposite the Štrbské Pleso train station. During the summer/winter seasons they are open daily from 8.30 am to 6 pm, and during the off season they open weekdays from 9 am to 5 pm and Saturday from 9 to 11.30 am and noon to 2 pm. In Tatranská Lomnica the information service (☎ 46 79 51, ext 221) is in the museum building.

The helpful Satur office (☎ 42 24 17), just above the train station at Starý Smokovec, provides a guiding service, accommodation and tours. It's closed on Saturday afternoon and Sunday. Another Satur office is upstairs at Hotel Renomal, opposite the Tatranská Lomnica train station.

Money The Všeobecná úverová banka in the commercial centre above the bus station in Starý Smokovec changes travellers cheques and has a Visa/MasterCard ATM, as does the Poľhobanka, in Hotel Renomal opposite the Tatranská Lomnica railway station, and the Istrobanka in Štrbské Pleso.

Post & Communications The telephone centre is in the post office near Starý Smokovec train station (ask for directions to 'pošta').

Things to See & Do

Above Starý Smokovec From Starý Smokovec a funicular railway (at 1025m) carries you up to **Hrebienok** (1280m), a ski resort with a view of the Veľká Studená Valley. The funicular railway (built in 1908, 40 Sk one way) is closed in April and November, but if it's not running it takes less than an hour to walk up to Hrebienok (green trail). From Hrebienok the red Magistrála trail carries you down to several **waterfalls**, such as Vodopády Studeného potoka and Obrovský vodopád.

For great scenery follow the blue trail to Zbojnícka chata in the Veľká Studená Valley (three hours). Beyond Zbojnícka the blue trail climbs over a 2428m pass and descends to the Polish border.

The green trail leads north to Téryho chata in the Malá Studená Valley (three hours). The Zamkovského (formerly Nálepkova) chata is just off the Magistrála, only an hour from Hrebienok up the same trail. The round trip

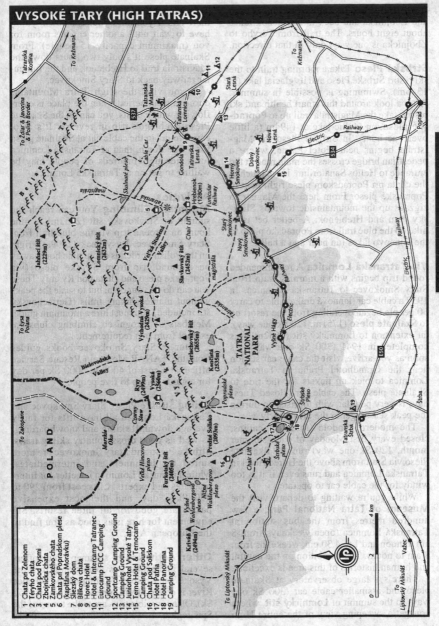

VYSOKÉ TARY (HIGH TATRAS)

SLOVAKIA

To Kežmarok

Tatranská Kotlina

To Ždiar & Javorina & Polish Border

To Žlar & Javorina & Polish Border

To Kežmarok

537

Tatranská Matliare

Tatranská Lomnica

Stará Lesná

Tatranská Lesná

Nová Lesná

Poprad

Electric Railway

Cable Car

Skalnaté pleso

Magistrála

Jahňací štít (2229m)

Lomnický štít (2632m)

Zamkovského chata

Dolný Smokovec

Horný Smokovec

Gondola

Bellanská

Tatry

Hrebienok (1280m)

Funicular Railway

Chair Lift

Veľká Studená Valley

Starý Smokovec

Nový Smokovec

Východná Vysoká (2425m)

Slavkovský štít (2452m)

To Lysá Polana

Bielovodská Valley

Gerlachovský štít (2655m)

Kôprová Valley

TATRA NATIONAL PARK

Končistá (2535m)

magistrála

Vyšné Hágy

Electric Railway

Štrba

To Zakopane

POLAND

Morské Oko

Rysy (2499m)

Vysoká (2560m)

Čierny Štav

Popradské pleso

Štrbské Pleso

Tatranská Štrba

E50

Veľká Hincovo pleso

Malé Hincovo pleso

Predná Solisko (2093m)

Štrbské pleso

Chair Lift

Furkotský štít (2405m)

Nižné Wahlenbergovo pleso

Vyšné Wahlenbergovo pleso

Kriváň (2494m)

To Liptovský Mikuláš

To Liptovský Mikuláš

Važec

1 Chata pri Zelenom
2 Teryho chata
3 Chata pod Rysmi
4 Zbojnícka chata
5 Zamkovského chata
6 Chata pri Popradskom plese
   (kapitána Morávku)
7 Sliezsky dom
8 Bilíkova chata
9 Horec Hotel
10 Hotel & Intercamp Tatranec
11 Eurocamp FICC Camping
   Ground
12 Sportcamp Camping Ground
13 Camping Ground
14 Juniorhotel Vysoké Tatry
15 Terno Hotel & Ternocamp
   Camping Ground
16 Chata pod Soliskom
17 Hotel Patria
18 Hotel Panoráma
19 Camping Ground

0   2   4 km

from Hrebienok to Zamkovského, Téryho and Zbojnícka and back to Hrebienok takes about eight hours. The trail from Téryho to Zbojnícka is one way, only in that direction.

Štrbské Pleso Take a morning train to the ski resort Štrbské Pleso and its glacial lake (at 1346m). Swimming is possible in summer. After a look around this smart health and ski resort, take the Magistrála trail up to **Popradské pleso**, an idyllic lake at 1494m (a little over one hour). In Štrbské Pleso the Magistrála begins near Hotel Patria, where a pedestrian bridge crosses the main road at the entrance to Helios Sanatorium. Have lunch at the chata pri Popradskom plese right next to Popradské pleso. From here the Magistrála zigzags up the mountainside towards Sliezsky dom and Hrebienok. A better bet is to hike up the blue trail from Popradské pleso to the Hincovo lakes (an hour and a half).

Via Tatranská Lomnica A recommended round trip begins with a morning train from Starý Smokovec to Tatranská Lomnica. In 1937 a cable car (lannová dráha) able to carry 30 people began operating from the resort up to **Skalnaté pleso** (1751m, 120 Sk one way); an extension to Lomnický štít (2632m) was completed in 1941 (300 Sk one way). As soon as you arrive, visit the cable car station near the Grandhotel Praha in Tatranská Lomnica to pick up tickets for the ride to Skalnaté pleso. The cable car (closed Tuesday) is very popular with tourists, so during the peak season get to the office early.

The modern gondola (four-seat cabins, closed every first Monday of each summer month, 120 Sk one way) runs to Skalnaté Pleso via Štart from above the Horec Hotel in Tatranská Lomnica and runs even if it is too windy for the cable car to operate.

While you're waiting to depart, visit the **Museum of Tatra National Park**, a few hundred metres from the bus station at Tatranská Lomnica (open weekdays from 8 am to noon and 1 to 4.30 pm, weekends from 8 am to noon). The exhibition on the natural and human histories of this area is excellent.

There's a large observatory at Skalnaté pleso and a smaller cable car (300 Sk one way) to the summit of **Lomnický štít**, where you get a sweeping view of the entire High Tatra range. You're only allowed 30 minutes there and if you miss your car down, you'll have to wait until another car has room for you (maximum capacity 15 people). From Skalnaté pleso it's only two hours down the Magistrála trail to Hrebienok and the funicular railway back to Starý Smokovec.

If you visit the High Tatra Mountains during a peak period when the place is overflowing with tourists, you can do the Skalnaté Pleso-Hrebienok trip in reverse. It's a lot easier to get in the cable car at Skalnaté pleso for a ride down, than at Tatranská Lomnica for a ride up. Hundreds of people may be waiting to get on at Tatranská Lomnica.

Activities
Mountain Climbing You can reach the summit of Slavkovský štít (2452m) in nine hours on a round trip via the blue trail from Starý Smokovec. Rysy Peak (2499m), right on the Polish border, is about nine hours away on a round trip from Štrbské pleso (via Popradské pleso and chata pod Rysmi). These you can do on your own, but to scale the peaks without marked hiking trails (Gerlachovský štít included) you must hire a mountain guide. Members of recognised climbing clubs are exempt from this requirement.

Satur in Starý Smokovec books guides from the TANAP Mountain Rescue Service office, at a cost of 4000 to 5000 Sk per day for a guide for up to five people.

Skiing Štrbské Pleso, Starý Smokovec and Tatranská Lomnica all have lifts for fairly average downhill skiing and snowboarding, as well as good cross-country skiing trails. Štrbské Pleso and Starý Smokovec are more suited for beginners and intermediates, while Tatranská Lomnica is better for intermediates and experts. Lifts cost from 290 to 490 Sk a day, and the most expensive passes are good for all three resorts. Ski equipment for hire is as good as you find in the European Alps.

Other Activities In summer, Satur offers several interesting bus excursions from the Vysoké Tatry resorts. Rafting on the Dunajec River is offered from June to September (550 Sk). Other possible trips are to the towns of the Spiš region, as well as to Zakopane (270 Sk) and Kraków (460 Sk), both in Poland. You can book at the Satur office in Starý Smokovec, but trips only take place if at least 30 people sign up.

There is bungee jumping in Štrbské Pleso, at Areál Snow, near the lift stations. A jump from a 50m tower costs 750 Sk on Friday and weekends.

Satur can also book scenic flights (from 30 minutes at 2420 Sk for up to three people).

Places to Stay

Camping No wild camping is permitted within the Tatra National Park. The nearest commercial camping ground to Starý Smokovec is the *Hotel Terno – camp* but it has been closed since 1997.

There are *camping grounds* at Tatranská Štrba and Stará Lesná (open from May to September) below Štrbské Pleso.

There are three camping grounds a couple of kilometres from Tatranská Lomnica (near the Tatranská Lomnica-Eurocamp train station on the line to Studený potok). The largest of these is the *Eurocamp FICC* (☎ 46 74 41), a five-minute walk from the train station, with 120 four-person luxury bungalows with private bath at 1760 Sk, plus regular hotel rooms with shared bath at 630 Sk a double (no singles). Camping is 100 Sk per person, 90 Sk per tent. The Eurocamp has restaurants (the good folkloric Koliba Restaurant), bars, shops, a supermarket, a swimming pool, tennis, sauna, disco, hot water and row upon row of parked caravans. This place is open all year.

An eight-minute walk south of the Eurocamp is the less expensive *Športcamp* (☎ 46 72 88) where apart from camping there are also four or five-person bungalows that need to be booked ahead in summer (open from June to September).

A ten-minute walk north of Eurocamp, towards Tatranská Lomnica, is the *Hotel & Intercamp Tatranec* (☎ 46 77 03). Hotel rooms are 600 Sk per person, four-person bungalows are 1600 Sk and camping is 80 Sk per person and 80 Sk per tent.

Chalets Up on the hiking trails are nine mountain chalets *(chaty)* but given their limited capacity and the popularity of the area, they may all be full in midsummer. Staff

at the AiCES or Satur offices in Starý Smokovec will be able to tell you if a certain chalet is open and may even telephone ahead to see if there's a place for you. Many of the chalets close for maintenance in November and May, while Chata pod Rysmi is only open from June to September. Although food is available at the chalets, you should take along some of your own supplies. A stay in a chata is one of the best mountain experiences the Tatry have to offer.

Satur in Starý Smokovec and Slovakoturist (☎ 42 20 31), just above the Pekná vyhliadka train station in Horný Smokovec, a 10-minute walk east from Satur in Starý Smokovec, can reserve beds at most of the chalets.

The following are the main chalets on the upper trails, from west to east:

Chata pod Soliskom – 1800m
Chata pri Popradskom plese – (also known as kpt Morávku); 1500m; costs 170/340/510 Sk per person in eight-bed, six-bed and double rooms; restaurant
Chata pod Rysmi – open June through October; highest of all at 2250m; dormitory-style at 140 Sk per person
Sliezsky dom – (☎ 42 52 61), 1670m; dorms are 310 Sk per person, doubles are 820 Sk and breakfast plus dinner are 160 Sk in this large prefabricated mountain hotel; restaurant and cafeteria
Zbojnícka chata – 1960m; dorms are 215 Sk with breakfast per person
Téryho chata – 2015m; dorms are 180 Sk plus 160 Sk for breakfast and dinner
Zamkovského chata (formerly *Nálepkova*) – 1475m; is 220 Sk per person in a dorm and 180 Sk for breakfast and dinner
Bilíkova chata – (☎ 42 22 66/7); 1220m; doubles in this attractive wooden chalet are 1190 Sk per double
Chata pri Zelenom plese (formerly *Brnčalova*); 1540m; dorms are 280 Sk

Private Rooms *Slovakoturist* (☎ 42 20 31) in Horný Smokovec has inexpensive private rooms.

Private rooms are advertised by 'Zimmer frei' signs outside numerous houses in *Ždiar* village, which is on the north side of the High Tatras and easily accessible from Poprad or Starý Smokovec on the Lysa Polana bus. Several small restaurants and pensions are

SLOVAKIA

also here. Ždiar is a pretty little village with sheep grazing in the fields and it makes a good base for exploring the High Tatras from this less frequented side.

Hotels Hotel prices almost double in the high seasons (mid-December to February and mid-June to September) compared with low seasons (March to mid-June and October to mid-December). Most prices quoted in this section are for high season.

Staff at the Satur office near the train station at Starý Smokovec will help you to find a room. Satur does not always know about last minute cancellations in hotels so if they can not direct you to any accommodation then tramp around to see what you can find. The staff can arrange rooms in all categories from low budget to deluxe.

Starý Smokovec The majestic turn-of-the-century three-star *Grandhotel* (☎ 46 79 41) has a certain elegance that the high-rise hotels lack but it's fading fast. Rooms cost 800/1200 Sk without bath, 1550/2300 Sk with bath. Breakfast and use of the indoor swimming pool are included. The nearby modern *Hotel Smokovec* (☎ 42 51 91; smokovec@pp.internet.sk) has spacious double and quad rooms at 1600/2800 Sk including bath and TV. It also has a swimming pool.

The 96-room *Park Hotel* (☎ 42 23 42), a circular five-storey hotel above the Nový Smokovec train station, is 875/1410 Sk with breakfast and private bath.

The *Hotel MS 70* (☎ 42 29 70), just west of the Park Hotel, is one of the least expensive at 940/1410 Sk for a double/triple with shared bath, or 1635 Sk for doubles with own bath.

One of the best deals at Starý Smokovec is *Pension Vesna* (☎ 42 27 74), a white two-storey building behind the large sanatorium opposite Nový Smokovec train station. Spacious doubles with shared bath and private balcony are 700 Sk and there's a kitchen where you can cook. You can take a short cut through the sanatorium grounds to get there (ask).

Another inexpensive hotel is the four-storey *Hotel Šport* (☎ 42 23 63/1) which costs 510/890 Sk with shared bath). A five-minute walk east from Starý Smokovec train station, it's popular with noisy youth groups.

Pension Poľana (☎ 42 25 18), across the street from the Sports Centrum at Pekná Vyhliadka train station, is 350 Sk per person with shared bath. The rooms are small but comfortable, each with a wash basin, and many also have a balcony. The cosy little bar downstairs serves a spicy bowl of tripe soup. The Poľana is often full.

The cheapest place to stay if you have a HI or ISIC card is the *Juniorhotel Vysoké Tatry* (☎ 42 26 61), just below the Horný Smokovec train station, for 210 Sk per person. The regular charge is about 330/620 Sk in small single/double rooms (with sink), breakfast 60 Sk extra. Guests are accommodated in half a dozen single-storey pavilions spread around the hotel grounds. The hotel is open all year, but it's often full of noisy school groups.

Tatranská Lomnica *Hotel Lomnica* was being renovated while this book was being updated.

The newer *Horec Hotel* (☎ 46 72 61), a five-minute walk up the hill from the train station, is 810 Sk for a double without bath, 910 Sk with bath, breakfast included.

One of Slovakia's most romantic hotels is the 91-room *Grandhotel Praha* (☎ 46 79 41), built in 1905, up the hill beside the cable car terminal. Rooms are 1760/2480 Sk, bath and breakfast included.

Štrbské Pleso The 11-storey *Hotel Panoráma* (☎ 49 21 11) next to the Obchodný dom Toliar department store, above the Štrbské Pleso train station, costs 1320/2070 Sk with bath, breakfast included.

The 150-room *Hotel Patria* (☎ 49 25 91), a huge A-frame hotel overlooking the lake, and a 10-minute walk uphill from the train station, costs from 1934 Sk for a double.

Hotel FIS (☎ 49 22 21), opposite the huge ski jumps five minutes beyond the Patria Hotel, costs from 1690/2180 Sk with shower. The sports hotel and the ski jumps were built for the 1970 International Ski Federation World Championships.

Places to Eat

Almost all the hotels and chalets in this region have their own restaurants. Just above the bus station at Starý Smokovec is *Fast*

Food Tatra but better is the self-service *bistro* in Hotel Smokovec. For typical Slovak food with a Roma band, head for the mid-range *Restaurant Koliba* just south-west of the train station. If you'd like to spend up, there's the elegant restaurant in the *Grand Hotel* (you're expected to dress up).

Restaurant Slalom, just east of the Tatranská Lomnica train station, has basic Slovak food. In Hotel Renomal is the pricier *Slovenská reštaurácia*, with national dishes.

There's a good self-service restaurant in *Obchodný dom Toliar* next to Štrbské Pleso train station (open daily from 8 am to 7 pm).

Entertainment
Starý Smokovec has the *Albas Laser disco* behind the town hall open daily from 9 pm to 4 am (50 Sk).

In Štrbské Pleso, there is a disco upstairs in Obchodný dom and opposite in the Slovenská reštaurácia.

Getting There & Away
Bus There are regular express buses from Bratislava to Tatranská Lomnica via Nitra, Banská Bystrica and Starý Smokovec.

From Starý Smokovec there are eight buses a day to Lysa Polana (one hour); hourly to Ždiar; six to Levoča (38km); two to Bardejov; four to Žilina; three to Trenčín; three to Bratislava; and one to Brno in the Czech Republic.

The Hungarian Volánbusz bus from Budapest to Tatranská Lomnica runs twice a week (seven hours).

Train To reach Vysoké Tatry, take one of the express trains running between Prague or Bratislava and Košice, and change at Poprad (couchettes are available). There are frequent narrow-gauge electric trains between Poprad and Starý Smokovec (13km, 7 Sk).

Alternatively, get off the express train at Tatranská Štrba, a station on the main line from Prague to Košice, and take the cog-wheel railway up to Štrbské Pleso (there are over 20 services daily), which climbs 430m over a distance of 5km. Also known as the 'rack railway', this service opened in 1896.

The booking offices in Starý Smokovec and

Tatranská Lomnica train stations can reserve sleepers and couchettes from Poprad to Prague, Karlovy Vary, Brno and Bratislava.

Poland For anyone interested in walking between Slovakia and Poland, there's a highway border crossing near Javorina, 30km from Tatranská Lomnica via Ždiar by bus. The Slovak bus between the border and Starý Smokovec is occasionally crowded and the bus stop is just 100m from the border (bus times posted). On the Polish side, buses can be full with people on excursions between Morskie Oko Lake and Zakopane, so this route is easier southbound than northbound.

You'll find a bank where you can change money at Lysa Polana on the Polish side, but there's no Slovak bank at Javorina. The rate offered at the border is about 10% worse than what you'll get in Zakopane. Southbound travellers should buy a few dollars worth of Slovak crowns at an exchange office in Poland to pay the onward bus fare to Starý Smokovec or Poprad, as this may not be possible at the border. Northbound, excess crowns are easily unloaded at exchange offices in Poland (at a loss). See the Tatra Mountains section in the Poland chapter for more details.

A bus direct from Poprad to Zakopane, Poland, leaves Starý Smokovec bus station on weekdays at 6.15 am (60km). This bus isn't listed on the posted schedule but Satur knows about it. Also ask Satur about its excursion buses to Zakopane and Kraków.

Getting Around
You can experience virtually every type of mountain transport here: funicular railway, cog-wheel or rack railway, narrow-gauge electric trains, cable cars, chair lifts and buses. Most popular are the electric trains that run from Poprad to Starý Smokovec (13km) and Štrbské Pleso (29km) about every half-hour. Trains also travel from Starý Smokovec to Tatranská Lomnica (6km) every 30 to 60 minutes. These trains make frequent stops along their routes; when there isn't a ticket window at the station, go immediately to the conductors upon boarding and buy your ticket from them.

SLOVAKIA

POPRAD
☎ 092

Poprad is a modern industrial city with little to interest visitors. However, it's an important transportation hub that you'll pass through at least once. The electric railway from here to Starý Smokovec was built in 1908 and was extended to Štrbské Pleso in 1912.

Information

Poprad AiCES information centre (☎ 72 17 00), nám Sv Egída 2950/114, covers the whole Tatry region. The staff speak English and provide accommodation lists.

Money You can change travellers cheques at the Ľudová banka, which is on the ná Sv Egída side of the Prior department store, and there is also a Visa/MasterCard ATM. The American Express representative is Tatratour (☎ 092-637 12) at nám Sv Egída 9.

Places to Stay & Eat

If you arrive late, you could stay at the rundown *Hotel Európa* (☎ 72 18 83) for 400/600 Sk (shared bath) just outside the Poprad train station. The hotel restaurant is not bad (the menu is in German).

Getting There & Away

Bus There are buses to almost everywhere in Slovakia from the large bus station next to the train station. Banská Bystrica (124km), Lysa Polana, Poland (via Starý Smokovec), Červený Kláštor, Levoča (26km), Spišské Podhradie (41km) and Bardejov (125km) are most easily reached by bus. Ask about buses to Zakopane, Poland.

Train Poprad is a major junction on the main railway line from Bratislava or Prague to Košice. Express trains run to Žilina (two hours) and Košice (1½ hours) every couple of hours. Electric trains climb 13km to Starý Smokovec, the main Vysoké Tatry resort, every hour or so. A feeder railway line runs north-east to Plaveč (two hours by local train), where you can get a connection to Muszyna, Poland, five times a day.

KEŽMAROK
☎ 0968

Over the centuries this fiercely independent town, whose north-western skyline is dominated by the mighty Vysoké Tatry range, was the second most important town in the region after Levoča. In the 13th century it was colonised by the Germans and was granted royal town status in 1380. The citizens of Kežmarok declared an independent republic in 1918 but almost immediately the town was incorporated into Czechoslovakia. Today it has a well preserved old centre with a castle and three interesting churches to admire.

If you can make it to Kežmarok on the second weekend in July, don't miss the festival of European Folk Crafts, with exhibits of craft making, folk dances and singing.

Orientation & Information

The bus and train stations are side by side across the river Poprad just north-west of the old town. To get into the old town walk south along Toporcerova until the New Evangelical Church where you turn left into Hviezdoslavova and the central Hlavné nám. If you arrive by bus it may drop you off at the bus stop 'Zlatý Bažant' on Toporcerova.

The AiCES information agency (☎ 40 47; infokk@kk.sinet.sk), Hlavné nám 46, can help with private rooms from 200 Sk per person. It also sells maps.

Things to See

The **New Evangelical Church** (1894) on the corner of Toporcerova and Hviezdoslavova is a huge reddish pseudo-Moorish structure with the mausoleum of Imre Thököly, who fought with Rákóczi against the Habsburg takeover of Hungary. Next door, the **Wooden Articulated Church** is more dignified. It was built in 1717 without a single nail and has an amazing cross shaped interior of carved and painted wood. Both are open daily between May and September from 11 am to noon and 2 to 5 pm.

North of Hlavné nám is the 15th century Gothic **Church of the Holy Cross**, nám Požárnikov, with beautifully carved wooden altars supposedly crafted by students of Master Pavol of Levoča.

The **Kežmarok Museum** has three local branches: temporary exhibits are at Dr

Alexandra; the home museum of Baroness Szimary is at Hradné nám; and the 15th century Kežmarok castle features an archaeology, history and period furniture exhibits (40 Sk). All are closed on Monday.

Places to Stay & Eat

The basic *Karpaty Camping* (☎ 52 24 90) is about 4km south-west of the town centre on the road to Poprad. Private rooms through AiCES are cheaper than hotels. *Hotel Štart* (☎ 52 29 15), a rustic place 10 minutes by foot north of the castle has doubles without/with bath for 350/450 Sk.

The Hungarian *Restaurant Thököly*, Hradné nám 5, is reasonable, or try *Pizza Bianca* at Hlavné nám 8 for pizza or pasta.

Getting There & Away

Buses are faster and more plentiful than trains from Vysoké Tatry – they are about hourly from Poprad, and there are eight daily ones from Starý Smokovec. There are also five daily buses to Červený Kláštor.

DUNAJEC GORGE
☎ 0964

Pieniny National Park (21 sq km), created in 1967, combines with a similar park in Poland to protect the 9km Dunajec River gorge between the Slovak village of Červený Kláštor and Szczawnica, Poland. The river here forms the international boundary between the two countries and the 500m limestone cliffs are impressive.

At the mouth of the gorge is a 14th-century fortified **Carthusian monastery**, now a park administrative centre and museum with a good collection of statuary and old prints of the area (open daily from May to September, closed Sunday and Monday from October to April, 25 Sk). Near the monastery from May to September is an **information centre** for the park.

From May to October, Dunajec raft trips depart from two locations at Červený Kláštor: a landing opposite the monastery and a second landing, with an office, 1km upriver west of the village. A raft will set out only when 12 passengers gather, and when business is slow you may have to wait. From the downriver terminus you can hike back to

the monastery in a little over an hour. The rafting operation on the Polish side is larger and better organised, so you might want to do your rafting there (see Dunajec Gorge in the Poland chapter for details). The raft trip in Slovakia is much shorter than the one in Poland.

Even if you don't go rafting, it's still worth coming to Červený Kláštor to hike along the riverside trail through the gorge on the Slovak side (no such trail exists on the Polish side).

Places to Stay

Just across a small stream from the monastery is a *camping ground* open from mid-June to mid-September. No bungalows are available. There are several pensions in the village, plus the new *Hotel Pldnik* (☎ 25 25) where a bed costs 400 Sk per person. It's usually booked out in summer.

One kilometre up the road to Veľký Lipník from the monastery is the *Hotel Dunajec*, with some inexpensive bungalows across the road.

Near Lesnica is the inexpensive *Pieniny chata* (☎ 0963-975 30) which is often full in summer. One of two doubles including breakfast is 430 Sk or a bed is 150 Sk per person.

Getting There & Away

Direct buses go to Červený Kláštor from Poprad. Although Poland is just across the river, there's no official border crossing here, so you must take a bus from Červený Kláštor to Stará Ľubovňa (25km), and then a train to Plaveč (16km), where a local train goes to Muszyna, Poland (16km) three times a day. From Muszyna there are Polish trains to Nowy Sącz (50km) and Kraków. Check connecting train times beforehand. There are also buses from Stará Ľubovňa to Bardejov, Prešov and Košice. Alternatively, use the Lysa Polana crossing to go directly to Zakopane.

SPIŠSKÁ NOVÁ VES
☎ 0965

Spišská Nová Ves, the administrative cen... of the Spiš region, is a modern city... history dating back to 1268. The... square is pleasant to walk... western part has been spoi... large apartment complexes bu...

SLOVAKIA

SPIŠSKÁ NOVÁ VES & SLOVENSKÝ RAJ

communist era. Spišská Nová Ves makes a good base from which to visit Levoča, Spišské Podhradie and the nearby Slovenský raj National Park.

Orientation & Information

The bus station is about 200m south-west of Spišská Nová Ves train station. A 24-hour left-luggage office is available at the train station. The helpful and knowledgeable staff at the AiCES information centre (☎ 42 82 92), nám MR Štefánika 10, can assist with accommodation and national park information.

Money You can change travellers cheques or use the 24-hour Visa/MasterCard ATM at the Slovenská sporiteľňa, nám MR Štefánika, opposite Hotel Metropol.

Post & Communications There's a telephone centre in the main post office, nám MR Štefánika 7 opposite Dom kultúry.

Things to See & Do

Just south-west of Spišská Nová Ves is Slovenský raj (the Slovak Paradise), a national park created in 1988 and featuring cliffs, caves, canyons, waterfalls and 1896 species of butterfly. This mountainous karst area is accessible via **Čingov**, 8km west of Spišská Nová Ves by bus. The closest train station to Slovenský raj is **Spišské Tomá-šovce**, less than an hour from Tomášovský výhľad on the green trail. Only local trains stop at this station.

From Čingov (elevation 494m) the blue trail leads up the Hornád River gorge, passing below Tomášovský výhľad, to Letanovský mlyn. The trail up the river is narrow and there are several ladders and ramps where hikers can only pass one by one. During peak periods hikers are allowed to travel only in an upstream direction from Čingov and return over the mountain (see hiking maps for more details on one-way routes).

One kilometre beyond Letanovský mlyn, a green trail leaves the river and climbs sharply

SPIŠSKÁ NOVÁ VES & SLOVENSKÝ RAJ

communist era. Spišská Nová Ves makes a good base from which to visit Levoča, Spišské Podhradie and the nearby Slovenský raj National Park.

Orientation & Information

The bus station is about 200m south-west of Spišská Nová Ves train station. A 24-hour left-luggage office is available at the train station. The helpful and knowledgeable staff at the AiCES information centre (☎ 42 82 92), nám MR Štefánika 10, can assist with accommodation and national park information.

Money You can change travellers cheques or use the 24-hour Visa/MasterCard ATM at the Slovenská sporiteľňa, nám MR Štefánika, opposite Hotel Metropol.

ost & Communications There's a tele-ne centre in the main post office, nám Štefánika 7 opposite Dom kultúry.

Things to See & Do

Just south-west of Spišská Nová Ves is Slovenský raj (the Slovak Paradise), a national park created in 1988 and featuring cliffs, caves, canyons, waterfalls and 1896 species of butterfly. This mountainous karst area is accessible via **Čingov**, 8km west of Spišská Nová Ves by bus. The closest train station to Slovenský raj is **Spišské Tomá-šovce**, less than an hour from Tomášovský výhľad on the green trail. Only local trains stop at this station.

From Čingov (elevation 494m) the blue trail leads up the Hornád River gorge, passing below Tomášovský výhľad, to Letanovský mlyn. The trail up the river is narrow and there are several ladders and ramps where hikers can only pass one by one. During peak periods hikers are allowed to travel only in an upstream direction from Čingov and return over the mountain (see hiking maps for more details on one-way routes).

One kilometre beyond Letanovský mlyn, a green trail leaves the river and climbs sharply

Alexandra; the home museum of Baroness Szimary is at Hradné nám; and the 15th century Kežmarok castle features an archaeology, history and period furniture exhibits (40 Sk). All are closed on Monday.

Places to Stay & Eat

The basic *Karpaty Camping* (☎ 52 24 90) is about 4km south-west of the town centre on the road to Poprad. Private rooms through AiCES are cheaper than hotels. *Hotel Štart* (☎ 52 29 15), a rustic place 10 minutes by foot north of the castle has doubles without/with bath for 350/450 Sk.

The Hungarian *Restaurant Thököly*, Hradné nám 5, is reasonable, or try *Pizza Bianca* at Hlavné nám 8 for pizza or pasta.

Getting There & Away

Buses are faster and more plentiful than trains from Vysoké Tatry – they are about hourly from Poprad, and there are eight daily ones from Starý Smokovec. There are also five daily buses to Červený Kláštor.

DUNAJEC GORGE
☎ 0964

Pieniny National Park (21 sq km), created in 1967, combines with a similar park in Poland to protect the 9km Dunajec River gorge between the Slovak village of Červený Kláštor and Szczawnica, Poland. The river here forms the international boundary between the two countries and the 500m limestone cliffs are impressive.

At the mouth of the gorge is a 14th-century fortified **Carthusian monastery**, now a park administrative centre and museum with a good collection of statuary and old prints of the area (open daily from May to September, closed Sunday and Monday from October to April, 25 Sk). Near the monastery from May to September is an **information centre** for the park.

From May to October, Dunajec raft trips depart from two locations at Červený Kláštor: a landing opposite the monastery and a second landing, with an office, 1km upriver west of the village. A raft will set out only when 12 passengers gather, and when business is slow you may have to wait. From the downriver terminus you can hike back to

the monastery in a little over an hour. The rafting operation on the Polish side is larger and better organised, so you might want to do your rafting there (see Dunajec Gorge in the Poland chapter for details). The raft trip in Slovakia is much shorter than the one in Poland.

Even if you don't go rafting, it's still worth coming to Červený Kláštor to hike along the riverside trail through the gorge on the Slovak side (no such trail exists on the Polish side).

Places to Stay

Just across a small stream from the monastery is a *camping ground* open from mid-June to mid-September. No bungalows are available. There are several pensions in the village, plus the new *Hotel Pldnik* (☎ 25 25) where a bed costs 400 Sk per person. It's usually booked out in summer.

One kilometre up the road to Veľký Lipník from the monastery is the *Hotel Dunajec*, with some inexpensive bungalows across the road.

Near Lesnica is the inexpensive *Pieniny chata* (☎ 0963-975 30) which is often full in summer. One of two doubles including breakfast is 430 Sk or a bed is 150 Sk per person.

Getting There & Away

Direct buses go to Červený Kláštor from Poprad. Although Poland is just across the river, there's no official border crossing here, so you must take a bus from Červený Kláštor to Stará Ľubovňa (25km), and then a train to Plaveč (16km), where a local train goes to Muszyna, Poland (16km) three times a day. From Muszyna there are Polish trains to Nowy Sącz (50km) and Kraków. Check connecting train times beforehand. There are also buses from Stará Ľubovňa to Bardejov, Prešov and Košice. Alternatively, use the Lysa Polana crossing to go directly to Zakopane.

SPIŠSKÁ NOVÁ VES
☎ 0965

Spišská Nová Ves, the administrative centre of the Spiš region, is a modern city with a history dating back to 1268. The long central square is pleasant to walk around, but its western part has been spoilt by the many large apartment complexes built during the

)km) every hour or so. All trains stop here.
feeder line runs 13km north to Levoča with
services every two or three hours.

Buses leave Spišská Nová Ves for Čingov
every couple of hours. There are morning
buses to Spišské Podhradie, Tatranská
Lomnica, Starý Smokovec and Štrbské Pleso.

LEVOČA
☎ 0966

Levoča is one of the country's most magnificent walled towns, and its main square is
full of beautiful Renaissance buildings. In the
13th century the king of Hungary invited
Saxon Germans to colonise the Spiš region
on the eastern borderlands of his kingdom, as
a protection against Tatar incursions and to
develop mining. One of the towns founded at
this time was Levoča, 26km east of Poprad.
Granted urban privileges in 1271, the merchants of Levoča grew very rich in the 14th
century.

To this day the medieval walls, street plan
and central square of Levoča have survived,
unspoiled by modern development. The town
is an easy stop on the way from Poprad to
either Prešov or Košice. A large Roma community resides here.

Orientation & Information
The train station is 1km south of town, down
the road beside the Hotel Faix. A left-luggage
service is available; ask at the station.

The AiCES information centre (☎ 51 37
63) at nám Majstra Pavla 58 provides town
and regional information, as well as accommodation assistance.

Money The Všeobecná úverová banka, nám
Majstra Pavla 28, changes travellers cheques,
and has a Visa/Mastercard ATM next to the
cinema on the Uholná side.

Post & Communications
centre Communications the telephone
Pavla 4, the post office m Majstra

Things t
Bastions and
eller arriving century walls gr
town begins ji at nám Slobody
the new Minorigh Košice Ga-
h (1750) on th

Nám Majstra Pavla, Levoča's central
square, is full of things to see. The 15th-
century **St James' Church** (closed Sunday,
admission 30 Sk) contains a gigantic Gothic
high altar (1517) by Master Pavol, one of the
largest and finest altars of its kind in Europe.
The Madonna on this altar appears on the
new 100 Sk banknote.

Next to St James' is the Gothic **town hall**,
enlivened by Renaissance arcades. Today it's
known as the **Museum of the Spiš Region**
(closed Monday) and its halls are more interesting than the exhibits. Beside the town hall
is a 16th-century **cage** where prisoners were
once exhibited.

There's a good **craft museum** (closed
Monday) in the 15th-century house at No 40.
While you're there have a peek in the courtyard of No 43. The **Evangelical church**
(1837), which once served the German community, is in the Empire style, as is the
former **district council** (1826), at No 59.
Thurzov dom (1532), No 7, now the **State
Archives**, is another fine building. At No 20
is the **Master Pavol Museum** (closed
Monday).

On a hill a couple of kilometres north of
town is the large neo-Gothic **Church of Mar-
iánska hora**, where the largest Catholic
pilgrimage in Slovakia is held early July.

Unless stated all museums are open
Tuesday to Sunday from 9 am to 5 pm,
between May to September and the rest of the
year from 8 am to 4 pm. Each one costs 15 Sk.

Places to Stay
Camping *Levočská Dolina Autocamp*
(☎ 51 27 05) is 5km north of nám Slobody
on the road to Závada. Bungalows are available
(open from mid-June to August only).

More convenient is *Autocamping Starý
mlyn* (☎ 51 36 51), with five or six-bed
deluxe bungalows at 240 Sk per person (no
camping) and a restaurant on the premises,
about 5km west of Levoča on the road to
Poprad.

Hotels The hostel-style *Hotel Texon* (☎ 51
44 93 or 0905-34 93 60), J Francisciho 45,
has basic double rooms for 200 Sk per
person. Take a bus to Obchodné centrum
Texon (shopping centre) from the bus station.

LEVOČA

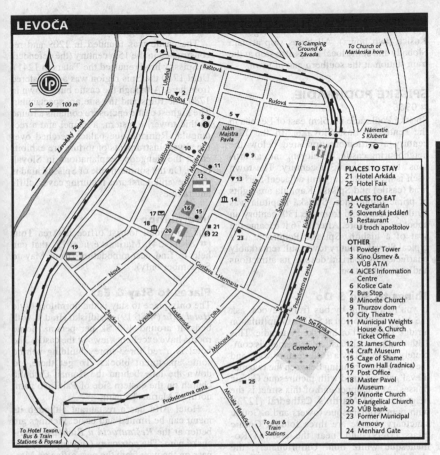

PLACES TO STAY
21 Hotel Arkáda
25 Hotel Faix

PLACES TO EAT
2 Vegetarián
5 Slovenská jedáleň
13 Restaurant
   U troch apoštolov

OTHER
1 Powder Tower
3 Kino Úsmev &
   VÚB ATM
4 AiCES Information
   Centre
6 Košice Gate
7 Bus Stop
8 Minorite Church
9 Thurzov dom
10 City Theatre
11 Municipal Weights
   House & Church
   Ticket Office
12 St James Church
14 Craft Museum
15 Cage of Shame
16 Town Hall (radnica)
17 Post Office
18 Master Pavol
   Museum
19 Minorite Church
20 Evangelical Church
22 VÚB bank
23 Former Municipal
   Armoury
24 Menhard Gate

SLOVAKIA

The 25-room *Hotel Faix* (☎ 51 23 35), Probstnerova cesta 22, between the train station and the old town, has basic doubles/triples for 680/920 Sk with shower/WC. The hotel restaurant is good.

Best value is the mid-range and modern *Hotel Arkáda* (☎ 51 23 73), nám Majstra Pavla 26. Large, bright rooms with TV, bathroom and toilet cost 940/1400 Sk.

Places to Eat

A basic bistro for an inexpensive meal is *Slovenská jedáleň*, nám Majstra Pavla 62.

Restaurant U troch apoštolov, upstairs at nám Majstra Pavla 11, is one of several good eateries on the square.

The popular *Vegetarián* is at Uholná 137, just off the north-west corner of the main square behind the cinema. It is open weekdays from 10 am to 3 pm.

Getting There & Away

Levoča is connected by 11 daily local trains to Spišská Nová Ves, which is 13km south on the main line from Bratislava to Prague and Košice. Bus travel is more practical as the are frequent services to Poprad (30 minutes), Spišské Podhradie (15km) and eight to Košice (two hours). All buses stop at nám Slobody and some local buses also stop at the train station at the southern end of town.

SPIŠSKÉ PODHRADIE
☎ 0966

Spišské Podhradie is 15km east of Levoča in the centre of East Slovakia. In the 12th century a settlement appeared below the neighbouring castle, developing into an artisans' town in the 13th century. The town itself is not outstanding but adjacent Spišský hrad (castle) and Spišská Kapitula are sights of prime importance. Spišská Kapitula was built by clergy and from the 13th century an abbot resided there. After 1776 it became the seat of a bishop. Spišské Podhradie is a typical Slovak country town, still remarkably unaffected by tourism despite its attractions and central location.

Things to See & Do
If you're arriving by bus from Levoča, ask the driver to drop you at **Spišská Kapitula**, on a ridge 1km west of Spišské Podhradie. This 13th-century ecclesiastical settlement is completely encircled by a 16th-century wall, and the single street running between the two medieval gates is lined with picturesque Gothic houses. At the upper end of this street is the magnificent **St Martin's Cathedral** (1273), with twin Romanesque towers and a Gothic sanctuary. Inside are three folding Gothic altars (1499) and, near the door, a Romanesque white lion. Unfortunately, the church is often closed. On opposite sides of the cathedral are the seminary and the Renaissance bishop's palace (1652).

Occupying a long ridge on the opposite side of Spišské Podhradie is the 180m-long **Spišský hrad**, the largest castle in Slovakia that in 1993 was added to the UNESCO's World Heritage List. The castle is directly above and east of the train station, 1km south of Spišské Podhradie's bus stop. Cross at the level crossing over the tracks near the station and follow the yellow markers up to the castle (closed Monday and from October to April, 40 Sk). The first gate is always locked, so carry on to the second one higher up. (If

you're driving or cycling, the access road is off the Prešov highway east of town.)

The castle was founded in 1209 and reconstructed in the 15th century (the defenders of Spišský hrad repulsed the Tatars in 1241). Until 1710 the Spiš region was administered from here. Although the castle burnt down in 1780, the ruins and the site are spectacular. The highest castle enclosure contains a round Gothic tower, a cistern, a chapel and a rectangular Romanesque palace perched over the abyss. Instruments of torture are exhibited in the dungeon (explanations in Slovak only). On the southern side of Spišský hrad is the Dreveník karst area featuring caves, cliffs and ravines.

Information
The unofficial tourist office is Area Tour (☎ 81 11 54), Marianské nám 22, that can help to find accommodation (from May to September only).

Places to Stay & Eat
The only place to stay is the dormitory-style *Hotel Alfa* (☎ 86 19) at sídlisko Hrad 1, with beds at around 400 Sk per person. Some rooms have excellent views of the castle. The hotel is a red three-storey building behind some apartment blocks. To get there, go down the lane behind the Roman Catholic church on the eastern side of Palešovo nám, north of Marianské nám.

Hotel Alfa has a restaurant although its menu can be limited and basic. Pickings are better at the *Reštaurácia u Richtára*, Marianské nám. The *potraviny* (supermarket) you pass on the way from the post office on Marianské nám to the train station has some basic supplies.

Getting There & Away
A secondary railway line connects Spišské Podhradie to Spišské Vlachy (9km), a station on the main line from Poprad to Košice. Departures are scheduled to connect with the Košice trains. You can leave your bags at the left-luggage office in the Spišské Podhradie train station (ask).

Buses from Levoča (15km), Spišská Nová Ves (25km) and Poprad (41km) are quite frequent.

BARDEJOV
☎ 0935

Bardejov received municipal privileges in 1320 and became a free royal town in 1376. Trade between Poland and Russia passed through the town and in the 15th century the Bardejov merchants grew rich. After an abortive 17th-century revolt against the Habsburgs, Bardejov's fortunes declined, but the medieval town survived. In late 1944 heavy fighting took place at the Dukla Pass into Poland, 54km north-east of Bardejov on the road to Rzeszów (the wrecks of a few tanks and planes can be seen from the road).

Since 1954 the town plan and the Gothic-Renaissance former houses of wealthy merchants lining the sloping central square have been carefully preserved. Much of the town walls, including the moat, towers and bastions, remain intact. The town holds several festivals, one of the liveliest being The Market (*jarmok*), when Radničné nám turns into one big market with lots of food, drink and good times included.

Orientation

The combined bus and train station (with a left-luggage office open every day from 7 am

BARDEJOV

PLACES TO STAY
1 Hotel Topľa
9 Hotel Republika

PLACES TO EAT
12 Hostinec Na hradbách
16 Cafe Amadeus
19 Maja sendvič

OTHER
2 Combined Train & Bus Station
3 Tesco Department Store
4 Post Office
5 Všeobecná úverová banka
6 Great Synagogue
7 Sports Centre Mier
8 Bastion (bašta)
10 Evangelical Church
11 Dolná Gate
13 Church of St Egídius
14 Statue of St Florián
15 Town Hall (radnica) & Museum
17 Investičná a rozvojová banka
18 Šariš Museum
20 AiCES Information Centre
21 Šariš Icon Museum
22 Natural History Museum
23 Franciscan Church
24 Ukranian Church
25 Prašná Gate
26 Horná Gate

To BAAL Športhotel
To Svidník & Bardejovské Kúpele
Dukelská
Topľa
Kúpeľná
Šibská Voda
Prerovská
Slovenská
České
Kellerova
Kačvinského
Nový sad
Lipy
Fučíkova
Hurbanova
Mlynská
TJ Partizán Stadium
To Stará Ľubovňa
Dlhý rad
Na hradbách
Krátky rad
Partizánská
Hviezdoslavova
Klášторská
Radničné námestie
Štóckova
Veterná
Komenského
Františkánov
Rhožňa
Jiráskova
Šancová
To Penzión Mihalov
To Prešov & Hospital
0   100   200 m

to 6.30 pm, except Sunday from 11 am to 8 pm) is a five-minute walk from Radničné nám, the town's main square.

Information

The very helpful AiCES information centre (☎ 72 60 72), at Radničné nám 21, can assist with guides, accommodation and guided tours.

Money The Investiční a rozvojová banka, Radničné nám 10, changes travellers cheques and has a Visa/MasterCard ATM.

Post & Communications The telephone centre is in the main post office at Dlhý rad 14.

Things to See

The 14th-century **Parish Church of St Egidius** is one of the most remarkable buildings in the country, with no less than 11 tall Gothic altarpieces, built from 1460 to 1510, all with their own original paintings and sculptures. The structural purity of the church and the 15th-century bronze baptismal font are striking.

Nearby is the **old town hall** (1509), the first Renaissance building in Slovakia, now a museum (closed Monday, 25 Sk) with more altarpieces and a historical collection. Two **museums** (closed Monday) face one another on Rhodyho at the southern end of the square. One has an excellent natural history exhibit, the other a collection of icons (both are 25 Sk). A fourth museum at Radničné nám 13 has temporary art exhibits.

Places to Stay

Penzión Mihalov (☎ 74 88 63), Mihalov 20, is good value – a bed is 165 Sk. It is in the south-western outskirts of town and bus No 8 goes there hourly.

The ageing *Hotel Republika* (☎ 72 27 21), right next to the parish church, has been renovated but was closed at the time of writing.

The smaller *Hotel Topľa* (☎ 72 26 36), Fučíkova 25, about six blocks west of the bus station, has rooms with bathroom at 426/530/636/742 Sk. The rooms are tolerable. There's a cheap beer hall downstairs.

The *BAAL Športhotel* (☎ 72 49 49), Kutuzovova 31, a modern two-storey hotel overlooking the Topľa River, has 20 double rooms with bath for 530 Sk per person.

Places to Eat

Apart for drab eating places at the hotels there is the beer hall at *Hostinec Na hradbách*, Stocklova 16, that is open weekdays until 10 pm but weekends only for lunch. A good lunch place is *Maja sendvič*, Radničné nám 15, that sells huge baguette sandwiches for 30 Sk. Popular cafes on and around the square include *Cafe Amadeus* at No 32. Among many *potraviny* (food shops) the supermarket *Centrum* at Slovenska 11 is the best.

Getting There & Away

Local trains run between Bardejov and Prešov (45km, 1¼ hours), but if you're coming from Košice, buses are faster. If you want to go to the Vysoké Tatry, look for a bus to Poprad (125km, 10 daily); there is one bus daily direct to Starý Smokovec, two to Bratislava (457km) and four to Žilina (278km).

To go to Poland, take a Stará Ľubovňa bus west to Plaveč (34km, 11 daily), where you can pick up a local train to Muszyna, Poland (five daily), from where there are Polish trains to Nowy Sącz and Kraków. There are buses from Bardejov direct to Krosno, Poland, via Svidník, once a day from Monday to Sunday.

BARDEJOVSKÉ KÚPELE

Just 6km north of Bardejov is Bardejovské Kúpele, one of Slovakia's most beautiful spas. From the late 18th century, Bardejovské Kúpele was one of the most popular spas in Hungary and was frequented by European high society. After WWII the communist authorities rebuilt the spa. Most of the hotels at the spa are reserved for patients undergoing medical treatment but there are two that do accept tourists, the Minerál and Mier.

Things to See & Do

Don't come to Bardejovské Kúpele expecting to enjoy a hot-spring bath, because it's impossible unless you've prebooked a program (contact a travel agent). Everyone is welcome to partake of the drinking cure, however, and crowds of locals constantly pace up and down the modern **colonnade** (1972), where an unending supply of hot mineral water streams from eight different springs (bring your own cup).

Near the colonnade is the Šarišské **Museum**, dedicated to local history and ethnography. Alongside this is one of Slovakia's best **skanzen**s, a fine collection of old farm buildings, rustic houses and wooden churches brought here from villages all over Slovakia. Both the museum and skanzen are open daily, except Monday, all year. A two-day Ruthenian/Šariš folk festival is held every year in July.

Cukráreň Domino, in the shopping mall opposite Hotel Minerál, sells *oplátky* (spa wafers), a local treat not to miss. Domino also dispenses *grog* (rum with hot water).

Getting There & Away

There's no train station, but Bardejovské Kúpele is connected to Bardejov by city bus Nos 1, 2, 3, 6, 7, 10, 11 and 15. Some long-distance buses for places as far away as Bratislava and Košice begin here.

KOŠICE
☎ 095

Košice is the second-largest city in Slovakia and capital of the eastern part of the country. Before WWI Košice had a Hungarian majority and the historic and ethnic influence of nearby Hungary remains strong. The Transylvanian prince Ferenc Rákóczi II had his headquarters at Košice during the Hungarian War of Independence against the Habsburgs (1703-11). The town became part of Czechoslovakia in 1918 but was again occupied by Hungary from 1938 to 1945. From 21 February to 21 April 1945, Košice served as the capital of liberated Czechoslovakia. On 5 April 1945 the Košice Government Programme was announced here, making communist dictatorship a virtual certainty.

Although now a major steel-making city with vast new residential districts built during communist rule, there is much in the re-vamped old town to be of interest to visitors. Churches and museums abound, and there's an active state theatre. The city is a good base for excursions to other East Slovak towns. Daily trains between Kraków and Budapest stop here, making Košice the perfect beginning or end to a visit to Slovakia.

Orientation
The adjacent bus and train stations are just east of the old town, a five-minute walk down Mlynská. Away from the stations, this street will bring you into Hlavné nám and nám Slobody, which become Hlavná both north and south of the squares. Much of your time in Košice will be spent on this colourful street. Large indexed city maps are posted at various locations around town.

The left-luggage office in the train station is open 24 hours, except for three 45-minute breaks.

Information
The AiCES information centre (☎ 186/622 69 37) at Hlavná 8 sells maps and guidebooks, books concert tickets and provides information about accommodation.

Visa Extensions The Úradovňa cudzineckej polície a pasovej služby (police and passport office), across the street from the huge Košice/Mestský municipal administration building on trieda Slovenského Národného Povstania, is the place to apply for visa extensions, complete police registration or report a lost passport or visa. Take bus No 19 west from the corner of Hlavná and Štúrova. It's open Monday and Wednesday from 10 am to noon and 12.30 to 6 pm; Tuesday, Thursday and Friday from 7 am to noon.

Money The Všeobecná úverová banka, Hlavná 112, changes travellers cheques and has a Visa/MasterCard ATM. There are many other banks with ecxhange counters and Visa/MasterCard ATMs in Košice.

Post & Communications There's a telephone centre in the main post office at Poštová 2.

Travel Agencies Satur (☎ 622 31 22), Hlavná 1 (in Hotel Slovan on the Rooseweltova side of the street), reserves sleepers and couchettes and sells international train tickets. (The several ticket windows marked 'medzinárodná pokladnica' in the train station also arranges these tickets.) Satur also has international bus tickets to many European cities, including Cologne, London, Munich, Rome and Zürich. Many of these buses actually leave from Bratislava and some transit the Czech Republic (check visa requirements). Satur also sells the various student and youth cards.

Tatratour (☎ 622 13 34), at Alžbetina 6, and CK Autotour at Továrenská 1, also sell international bus tickets.

For reduced student and under-26 train tickets to places outside Slovakia, try the 'Medzinárodná pokladnica' in the train station, and for bus and train tickets the travel agency Globus (☎ 622 05 77), Rooseweltova 3. The American Express representative is Tatratour.

Bookshops Petit, Hlavná 41, has a good selection of hiking maps and town plans.

Things to See

Košice's top sight is the **Cathedral of St Elizabeth** (1345-1508), a magnificent late-Gothic edifice five minutes walk west of the train station. In a crypt on the left side of the nave is the tomb of Ferenc Rákóczi. Duke Rákóczi was exiled to Turkey after the failed 18th-century Hungarian insurgency against Austria and only in 1905 was he officially pardoned and his remains reburied here.

Beside the cathedral is the 14th-century **Urban Tower**, now a kaváriéň. On the opposite side of the cathedral is the 14th-century **St Michael's Chapel** and the **Košice Programme House**, nám Slobody 27, where the 1945 National Front program was proclaimed. The building dates from 1779 and is now an art gallery (closed Monday) with a large collection by local painter Július Jakoby (1903-85).

Most of Košice's other historic sites are north along Hlavné nám and Hlavná. In the centre of the square is the ornate **State Theatre** (1899) with a musical fountain in front. Beside it at Hlavné nám 59 is the rococo former **town hall** (1780), now a cinema, and north of the theatre is a large **plague column** (1723). The Jesuit and Franciscan churches are also on the square. Further north at Hlavná 88 is the **Slovak Technical Museum** (closed Monday, 20 Sk).

The **East Slovak Museum** (1912, 20 Sk) is on nám Maratónu mieru at the northern end of Hlavná. The 1st and 2nd floors are dedicated to archaeology and prehistory. Don't miss the Košice Gold Treasure in the basement, a hoard of over 3000 gold coins dating from the 15th to the 18th centuries and discovered by chance in 1935. In the park behind the museum building is an old wooden church. Across the square at Hviezdoslavova 3 is the **Zoology Museum**.

Walk back along Hlavná to the State Theatre and take the narrow Univerzitná beside the Jesuit church east to **Mikluš Prison**, (closed Monday), Pri Miklušovej Väznici 10. This connected pair of 16th-century houses once served as a prison equipped with medieval torture chambers and cells. Tickets are available behind the nearby gate at Hrnčiarska 7. This is also the ticket office for the **Ferenc Rákóczi House Museum** and the new **Weapons Museum**; these are in the former Executioner's Katova Bastion, which was part of Košice's 15th-century fortifications. All three attractions can only been seen on a one hour tour for 30 Sk but a minimum of 10 visitors is required.

Most museums and galleries in Košice are closed on Sunday afternoon and on Monday.

Places to Stay

Camping South of the city is the *Autocamping Salaš Barca* (☎ 623 33 97). Take tram No 3 south along Južná trieda from the train station until the tram turns left at an underpass, then walk west on Alejová (the Rožňava Highway) for about 800m till you see the camping ground on the left. It is open from 15 April to 30 September and there are cabins (360/540 Sk for a double/triple) and tent space (50 Sk per person, 40 Sk per tent). The cabins are available year-round and there's a restaurant.

Hostels *Domov mládeže* (☎ 642 90 52), Medická 2, on the western side of town, is 130 Sk per person in two and three-bed rooms (student card not required).

Hotels The basic *Hotel Európa* (☎ 622 38 97), a grand old three-storey building just across the park from the train station, costs 370/610/810 Sk with shared showers/WC and singles with shower are 450 Sk.

The *TJ Metropol turistická ubytovňa* (☎ 625 59 48), Štúrova 32, is an attractive

KOŠICE

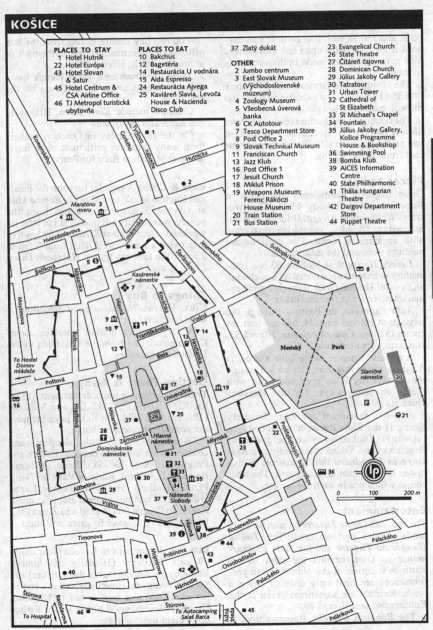

PLACES TO STAY
1 Hotel Hutník
22 Hotel Európa
43 Hotel Slovan & Satur
45 Hotel Centrum & ČSA Airline Office
46 TJ Metropol turistická ubytovňa

PLACES TO EAT
10 Bakchus
12 Bagetéria
14 Restaurácia U vodnára
15 Aida Espresso
24 Restaurácia Ajvega
25 Kaviáreň Slavia, Levoča House & Hacienda Disco Club

37 Zlatý dukát

OTHER
2 Jumbo centrum
3 East Slovak Museum (Východoslovenské múzeum)
4 Zoology Museum
5 Všeobecná úverová banka
6 CK Autotour
7 Tesco Department Store
8 Post Office 2
9 Slovak Technical Museum
11 Franciscan Church
13 Jazz Klub
16 Post Office 1
17 Jesuit Church
18 Mikluš Prison
19 Weapons Museum; Ferenc Rákóczi House Museum
20 Train Station
21 Bus Station

23 Evangelical Church
26 State Theatre
27 Čitáreň čajovna
28 Dominican Church
29 Július Jakoby Gallery
30 Tatratour
31 Urban Tower
32 Cathedral of St Elizabeth
33 St Michael's Chapel
34 Fountain
35 Július Jakoby Gallery, Košice Programme House & Bookshop
36 Swimming Pool
38 Bomba Klub
39 AiCES Information Centre
40 State Philharmonic
41 Thália Hungarian Theatre
42 Dargov Department Store
44 Puppet Theatre

SLOVAKIA

sports complex where cheerful rooms with shared bath are 280 Sk for a room with three beds, and 320 Sk with four beds. It's an easy walk from town but is often full with groups. You get a lot of tram noise in the very early morning.

The 12-storey pre-fabricated *Hotel Hutník* (☎ 635 11 15), Tyršovo nábrežie 6 (800/1260 Sk with bath), is a last resort.

The revamped and business oriented *Hotel Slovan* (☎ 623 27 16), Hlavná 1, is the best and priciest place to stay. The spotless rooms cost from 1950/2960 Sk.

Places to Eat

Great baguette sandwiches are made at *Bagetèria*, nám Slobody 40/74. The two-storey *Reštaurácia Ajvega*, Orlia 10, is an inexpensive, friendly, vegetarian restaurant with an English menu. The portions are medium sized and the meals are tasty.

Levoča House at ná Slobody 63 is a 16th-century warehouse renovated as a nightclub and a café. The *Kaviáreň Slavia* is a good up-market place for coffee and cakes.

Aida Espresso, on Poštová through the passage at Hlavné nám 74, has the best ice cream in town. *Čitáreň čajovna*, Hlavná 52, is a smoke-free teahouse.

A popular place to eat or have a drink is the inexpensive *Bakchus*, Hlavná 8. Through the passageway is an open courtyard with tables on sunny days. Try the Bakchus chicken.

A better restaurant for more leisurely dining is the *Zlatý ducat*, nám Slobody 16 (upstairs). Tucked away on the corner of Hrnčiarska and Vodná is the mid-range *Reštaurácia U vodnára* that specialises in fish dishes but has meat dishes as well. The trout comes with a pea in each eye socket.

Entertainment

The renovated *State Theatre* on nám Slobody holds regular performances. The *Thália Hungarian Theatre* and the *State Philharmonic* in Dom umenia are both in the south-west corner of the old town, but performances are held only once or twice a week. Recitals are sometimes given at the Konzervatórium, Hlavná 89.

The *Bábkové Divadlo*, Rooseweltova 1,

puts on puppet shows for children on weekday mornings and Sunday afternoon.

You can buy theatre tickets from the box office at the Information Centre, Hlavná 8, or at Štúdio SMER, Hlavná 76.

Jumbo centrum near Hotel Hutník has a theatre, cinema and a Laser Disco on the weekends.

Cinemas include *Kino Tatra*, Hlavná 8, and *Kino Slovan*, Hlavná 59.

On the first Sunday in October, runners from many countries participate in an International Marathon Race for Peace.

Bars & Clubs A popular bar with the locals and English speaking visitors is *Bomba klub* at Hlavná 5 down in a cellar from the passegeway, open until midnight but later on weekends. *Jazz klub* at Kováčská 39 has live jazz twice a week and is open from 5 pm to 2 am. Club fans can try the *Hacienda Disco Club*, Hlavná 65.

Things to Buy

Úľuv, Hlavná 76, has a good selection of local handicrafts.

A large street market operates along Cyrilometodejská from the Ukrainian to the Dominican churches.

Getting There & Away

Train Two evening trains depart from Košice for Kiev (1013km, 1542 Sk) and Moscow (1880km, 2423 Sk). The ticket price includes the compulsory sleeper charge.

Overnight trains with sleepers and couchettes are available between Košice and Prague (708km, 400 Sk), Brno (493km), Bratislava (445km), Karlovy Vary (897km), Plzeň (896km) and Františkovy Lázně (1081km). Daytime express trains connect Košice to Prague (via Poprad and Žilina) and Bratislava (via Banská Bystrica or Žilina).

Bus For shorter trips to Levoča (four daily, 99 km), Bardejov (10 daily, 1¾ hours), Bardejovské Kúpele (seven daily, 83km) and Spišské Podhradie (four daily, 64km), you're better off taking a bus. A bus to Užgorod, Ukraine (three hours, 130 Sk) leaves Košice up to eight times a day.

Car CK Autotour (☎ 622 40 66), Továrenská 1, represents Europcar. Tatratour or Satur may be able to help with cheaper vehicles.

Poland The daily *Cracovia* express train between Hungary and Kraków passes through Košice (reservations required). Northbound, the *Cracovia* travels early morning, and southbound overnight. A Košice-Kraków ticket costs 550 Sk. For information about unreserved local trains to Poland, see the Getting There & Away and Bardejov sections in this chapter.

There's a bus from Košice to Nowy Targ (135 Sk) early every Thursday and Saturday morning, and to Krosno (153 Sk) every Wednesday, Friday and Saturday. In both cases the fare is paid to the driver.

Hungary Local trains run the 88km from Košice to Miskolc, Hungary (2½ hours, 197 Sk) via Hidasnémeti every morning and afternoon. This is an easy way to cross the border as no reservations are required. If you take the morning train, get a ticket right through to Budapest (if you're going there), as you will have only five minutes to change trains at Miskolc and no time to change money and buy another ticket.

Alternatively, there are four unreserved local trains a day between Slovenské Nové Mesto, Slovakia, and Sátoraljaújhely, Hungary, with connections to/from Košice and Miskolc.

The *Rákóczi* express train links Košice to Budapest daily (4½ hours, 450 Sk), departing from Budapest-Keleti in the morning, Košice in the mid-afternoon (reservations optional).

There's a bus from Košice to Miskolc daily at 6.30 am (84km, 129 Sk). Book your ticket the day before at window No 1 in the bus station. On Tuesday and Thursday there is an early evening bus to Budapest (392 Sk) via Miskolc.

Getting Around
Bus and tram tickets cost 6 Sk and are available from tobacconists and newspaper stands.

Take the morning train, get a ticket (all the way) through to Budapest (if you're going there), as you will have only five minutes to change trains at Miskolc and no time to change money and buy another ticket.

Alternatively, there are local unreserved local trains to/in between Slovensko Nové Mesto, Slovakia, and Sátoraljaújhely, Hungary, with connections to/from Košice and Miskolc.

The Rákóczi express with links Budapest to Budapest daily (2½ hours, 1430 Sk) departing from Budapest Keleti the morning Košice in the mid-afternoon (reservations optional).

There's a bus from Košice to Miskolc daily at 6.30 am (2¾ hours, 129 Sk). Book your ticket the day before at window No 10 at the bus station. On Tuesday and Thursday there is an early evening bus to Budapest (422 Sk) via Miskolc.

Getting Around

Bus and tram tickets cost 6 Sk and are available from tobacconists and newspaper stands.

Car CV Sútour (☎ 622 40 63) Tovarenská 1, repair and European Transport or Satur, may be able to help with emergency vehicles.

Poland The daily Cracovia express runs between Hungary and Kraków, passing through Košice (reservations required). Northbound, the Cracovia arrives daily, morning, and southbound, overnight. A Košice-Kraków ticket costs 880 Sk. For information about unreserved local trains to Poland, see the Getting There & Away and Bardejov sections in this chapter.

There's a bus from Košice to Nowy Targ (275 Sk) early every Thursday and Saturday morning, and to Krosno (133 Sk) every Wednesday, Friday and Saturday. In both cases the fare is paid to the driver.

Hungary Local trains run the 88 km from Košice to Miskolc, Hungary (2¾ hours, 197 Sk) via Hidasnémeti every morning and afternoon. This is an easy way to cross the border as no reservations are required. If you

Slovenia

Little Slovenia (Slovenija) straddles Western and Eastern Europe. Many of its cities and towns bear the imprint of the Habsburg Empire and the Venetian Republic, while in the Julian Alps you'd think you were in Bavaria. The two-million Slovenes were economically the most well off among the peoples of what was once Yugoslavia, and the relative affluence and the orderliness of this nation is immediately apparent. Slovenia may be the gateway to the Balkans from Italy, Austria or Hungary, but it still has the feel of central Europe.

Slovenia is one Europe's most delightful surprises for travellers. Fairy-tale Bled Castle, breathtaking Lake Bohinj, scenic Postojna and Škocjan caves, the lush Soča Valley, Piran and Koper on the coast and thriving Ljubljana are great attractions, all accessible at much less than the cost of similar places in Western Europe. The amazing variety of settings packed into one small area makes this country truly a 'Europe in miniature'. An added bonus is that Slovenia is a nation of polyglots, and communicating with these friendly, helpful people is never difficult.

Facts about Slovenia

HISTORY

The early Slovenes settled in the river valleys of the Danube Basin and the eastern Alps in the 6th century. Slovenia was brought under Germanic rule in 748, first by the Frankish empire of the Carolingians, who converted the population to Christianity, and then as part of the Holy Roman Empire in the 9th century. The Austro-German monarchy took over in the early 14th century and continued to rule (as the Habsburg Empire from 1804) right up to the end of WWI in 1918 – with only one brief interruption. Over those six centuries, the upper classes became totally Germanised, though the peasantry retained their Slovenian identity. The Bible was trans-

AT A GLANCE

Capital	Ljubljana
Population	1.9 million
Area	20,256 sq km
Official Language	Slovenian
Currency	1 tolar (SIT) = 100 stotins
GDP	US$24 billion (1996)
Time	GMT/UTC+0100

lated into the vernacular during the Reformation in 1584, but Slovene did not come into common use as a written language until the early 19th century.

In 1809, in a bid to isolate the Habsburg Empire from the Adriatic, Napoleon established the so-called Illyrian Provinces (Slovenia, Dalmatia and part of Croatia) with Ljubljana as the capital. Though the Habsburgs returned in 1814, French reforms in education, law and public administration endured. The democratic revolution that swept Europe in 1848 also increased political and national consciousness among Slovenes,

SLOVENIA (SLOVENIJA)

and after WWI and the dissolution of the Austro-Hungarian Empire, Slovenia was included in the Kingdom of Serbs, Croats and Slovenes.

During WWII much of Slovenia was annexed by Germany, with Italy and Hungary taking smaller bits of territory. Slovenian Partisans fought courageously against the invaders from mountain bases, and Slovenia joined the Socialist Federal Republic of Yugoslavia in 1945.

Moves by Serbia in the late 1980s to assert its leading role culturally and economically among the Yugoslav republics was a big concern to Slovenes. When Belgrade abruptly ended the autonomy of Kosovo (where 90% of the population is ethnically Albanian) in late 1988, Slovenes feared the same could happen to them. For some years, Slovenia's interests had been shifting to the capitalist west and north; the Yugoslav connection, on the other hand, had become not only an economic burden but a political threat as well.

In the spring of 1990, Slovenia became the first Yugoslav republic to hold free elections and shed 45 years of communist rule; in December the electorate voted by 88% in favour of independence. The Slovenian government began stockpiling weapons, and on 25 June 1991 it pulled the republic out of the Yugoslav Federation. To dramatise their bid for independence, the Slovenian leaders deliberately provoked fighting with the federal army by attempting to take control of the border crossings, and a 10-day war ensued. But resistance from the Slovenian militia was determined and, as no territorial claims or minority issues were involved, the Yugoslav government agreed to a truce brokered by the EC. Slovenia got a new constitution in late December, and on 15 January 1992 the EC formally recognised the country. Slovenia was admitted to the United Nations in May 1992 and has now been invited to begin negotiations for full membership of the EU.

GEOGRAPHY & GEOLOGY

Slovenia is wedged between Austria and Croatia and shares much shorter borders with Italy and Hungary. Measuring just 20,256 sq km, Slovenia is the smallest country in eastern Europe, about the size of Wales or Israel. Much of the country is mountainous, culminating in the north-west with the Julian Alps and the nation's highest peak, Mt Triglav (2864m). From this jagged knot, the main Alpine chain continues east along the Austrian border, while the Dinaric range runs south-east along the coast into Croatia.

Below the limestone plateau of the Karst region between Ljubljana and Koper is Europe's most extensive network of karst caverns, which gave their name to other such caves around the world.

The coastal range forms a barrier isolating the Istrian Peninsula from Slovenia's corner of the Danube Basin. Much of the interior east of the Alps is drained by the rivers Sava and Drava, both of which empty into the Danube. The Soča flows through western Slovenia into the Adriatic.

CLIMATE

Slovenia is temperate with four distinct seasons, but the topography creates three individual climates. The north-west has an Alpine climate with strong influences from the Atlantic as well as abundant precipitation. Temperatures in the Alpine valleys are moderate in summer but cold in winter. The coast and western Slovenia as far north as the Soča Valley has a Mediterranean climate with mild, sunny weather much of the year, though the *burja*, a cold and dry north-easterly wind from the Adriatic, can be fierce at times. Most of eastern Slovenia has a continental climate with hot summers and cold winters.

Slovenia gets most of its rain in March and April and again in October and November. January is the coldest month with an average temperature of -2° C and July the warmest (21° C).

ECOLOGY & ENVIRONMENT

Slovenia is a very green country – more than half its total area is covered in forest – and is home to 2900 plant species; Triglav National Park is especially rich in indigenous flowering plants. Common European animals (deer, boar, chamois) live here in abundance, and rare species include *Proteus anguinus*, the unique 'human fish' that inhabits pools in karst caves.

GOVERNMENT & POLITICS

Slovenia's constitution provides for a parliamentary system of government. The National Assembly, which has exclusive jurisdiction over the passing of laws, consists of 90 deputies elected for four years by proportional representation. The 40 members of the Council of State, which performs an advisory role, are elected for five-year terms by regions and special-interest groups. The head of state, the president, is elected directly for a maximum of two five-year terms. Executive power is vested in the prime minister and the 15-member cabinet.

In the most recent parliamentary elections (November 1996), a centrist alliance of the Liberal Democrats, the People's Party and the Democratic Party of Pensioners of Slovenia garnered more than 55% of the vote, seating 49 MPs. LDS leader Janez Drnovšek, prime minister from the first elections in 1992, was again named head of government. In November 1997 President Milan Kučan was returned for his second term after winning nearly 56% of the popular vote.

ECONOMY

Slovenia has emerged as one of the strongest economies of the former socialist countries of Eastern Europe after a few tough years following independence. Inflation has dropped, employment is on the rise and per-capita GDP – currently 60% of the EU average – is expected to surpass that of Greece and Portugal by 2002.

But for many Slovenes, the economic picture remains unclear. Real wages continue to grow – but faster than inflation, which puts Slovenia's international competitiveness at a disadvantage. Inflation rocketed up to 200% after independence and has steadily decreased since; it is currently at about 9.5%. Unemployment continues to hover around 14.5%.

SLOVENIA

POPULATION & PEOPLE

Slovenia was the most homogeneous of all the Yugoslav republics; about 87% of the population (estimated at 1,991,000 in 1997) are Slovenes. There are just over 8500 ethnic Hungarians and some 2300 Roma (Gypsies) largely in the north-east as well as 3060 Italians on the coast. 'Others', accounting for 11.5% of the population, include Croats, Serbs, ethnic Albanians and those who identify themselves simply as 'Muslims'.

ARTS

Slovenia's best loved writer is the Romantic poet France Prešeren (1800-49), whose lyric poetry set new standards for Slovenian literature and helped to raise national consciousness. Disappointed in love, Prešeren wrote sensitive love poems but also satirical verse and epic poetry.

Many notable buildings, bridges and squares in Ljubljana and elsewhere in Slovenia were designed by the architect Jože Plečnik (1872-1957), who studied under Otto Wagner in Vienna.

Postmodernist painting and sculpture has been more or less dominated since the 1980s by the multimedia group Neue Slowenische Kunst (NSK) and the five-member artists' cooperative IRWIN. Avante-garde dance is best exemplified by Betontanc, an NSK dance company that mixes live music and theatrical elements (called 'physical theatre' here) with sharp political comment.

Since WWII, many Slovenian folk traditions have been lost, but compilations by the trio Trutamora Slovenica (available at music shops in Ljubljana) examine the roots of Slovenian folk music. Folk groups – both 'pure' and popular – to watch out for include the Avseniki, Ansambel Lojzeta Slaka, the Alpski Kvintet led by Oto Pestner, and the Roma band Šukar.

Popular music runs the gamut from Slovenian *chanson* (best exemplified by Vita Mavrič) and folk to jazz and techno, but it was punk music in the late 1970s and early 1980s, particularly the groups Pankrti, Borghesia and Laibach, that put Slovenia on the world stage.

LANGUAGE

Slovene is a South Slavic language written in the Roman alphabet and closely related to Croatian and Serbian. It is grammatically complex with lots of cases, genders and tenses and has something very rare in linguistics: the dual form. It's one *miza* (table) and three or more *mize* (tables) but two *mizi*.

Virtually everyone in Slovenia speaks at least one other language: Croatian, Serbian, German, English and/or Italian. English is definitely the preferred language of the young. See the Language Guide section at the end of the book for pronunciation guidelines and useful words and phrases. Lonely Planet's *Mediterranean Europe Phrasebook* contains a chapter on Slovene.

Facts for the Visitor

HIGHLIGHTS

Ljubljana, Piran and Koper have outstanding architecture; the hilltop castles at Bled and Ljubljana are impressive. The Škocjan Caves are among the foremost underground wonders of the world. The Soča Valley is indescribably beautiful in spring. The frescoed Church of St John the Baptist is in itself worth the trip to Lake Bohinj.

SUGGESTED ITINERARIES

Depending on the length of your stay, you might want to see and do the following in Slovenia:

Two days
    Visit Ljubljana
One week
    Visit Ljubljana, Bled, Bohinj, Škocjan Caves and Piran
Two weeks
    Visit all the places covered in this chapter

PLANNING
When to Go

Snow can linger in the mountains as late as June, but May and June are great months to be in the lowlands and valleys when everything is fresh and in blossom. (April can be a bit wet though.) In July and August, hotel rates are increased and there will be lots of tourists, especially on the coast. September is an excellent month to visit as the days are long and the weather still warm, and it's the best time for hiking and climbing. October and November can be rainy, and winter (December to March) is for skiers.

Maps

The Geodesic Institute of Slovenia (Geodetski Zavod Slovenije; GZS), the country's principal cartographic agency, produces national (1:300 000), regional (1:50 000) and topographical maps to the entire country (64 1:50 000-scale sheets) as well as city plans. The Alpine Association of Slovenia (Planinska Zveza Slovenije; PZS) has some 30 different hiking maps with scales as large as 1:25 000.

What to Bring

You don't have to remember any particular item of clothing – a warm sweater (even in summer) for the mountains at night, perhaps, and an umbrella in the spring or autumn – unless you plan to do some serious hiking or other sport.

TOURIST OFFICES

The Slovenian Tourist Board (Center za Promocijo Turizma Slovenije; CPTS; tel 061-189 1840; fax 061-189 1841; cpts@cpts.tradepoint.si) in Ljubljana's World Trade Centre at Dunajska cesta 160 is the umbrella organisation for tourist offices in Slovenia. It can handle requests for information in writing or you can check out its excellent Web site (see Internet Resources later).

The best office for face-to-face information in Slovenia – bar none – is the Ljubljana Tourist Information Centre. Most of the places described in this chapter have some form of tourist office but if the place you're visiting doesn't, seek assistance at a branch of one of the big travel agencies (eg Kompas, Emona Globtour or Slovenijaturist) or from hotel or museum staff.

Tourist Offices & Travel Agencies Abroad

The CPTS maintains tourist offices in the following eight countries:

Austria
(☎ 0222-715 4010; fax 0222-713 8177) Hilton Center, Landstrasser Hauptstrasse 2, 1030 Vienna
Germany
(☎ 089-2916 1202; fax 089-2916 1273) Maximilliansplatz 12a, 80333 Munich
Hungary
(☎ 1-156 8223; fax 1-156 2818) Gellérthegy utca 28, 1013 Budapest
Italy
(☎ 02-2951 1187; fax 02-2951 0997) Via Lazzaro Palazzi 2a/III, 20124 Milan
Netherlands & Belgium
(☎ 010-465 3003; fax 010-465 7514) Benthuizerstraat 29, 3036 CB Rotterdam
Switzerland
(☎ 01-212 6394; fax 01-212 5266) Löwenstrasse 54, 8001 Zurich
UK
(☎ 0171-287 7133; fax 0171-287 5476) 49 Conduit St, London W1R 9FB
USA
(☎ 212-358 9686; 212-358 9025) 345 East 12th St, New York, NY 10003

In addition, Kompas has representative offices in many cities worldwide, including:

Australia
(☎ 07-3831 4400) 323 Boundary St, Spring Hill, 4000 Queensland
Canada
(☎ 514-938 4041) 4060 Ste-Catherine St West, Suite 535, Montreal, Que H3Z 2Z3
France
(☎ 01 53 92 27 80) 14 Rue de la Source, 75016 Paris
South Africa
(☎ 011-884 8555) Norwich Towers, 3/F, 13 Fredman Drive, Santon

VISAS & EMBASSIES

Passport holders from Australia, Canada, Israel, Japan, New Zealand, Switzerland, USA and EU countries do not require visas for stays in Slovenia of up to 90 days; those from the EU as well as Switzerland can also enter on a national identity card for a stay of up to 30 days. Citizens of other countries requiring visas (including South Africans) can get them at any Slovenian embassy or consulate, at the border or Brnik airport. They cost the equivalent of £21/US$35 for single entry and £43/US$68 for multiple entry.

Slovenian Embassies Abroad

Australia
  (☎ 02-6243 4830) Advance Bank Centre, Level 6, 60 Marcus Clark St, Canberra, ACT 2601
Austria
  (☎ 0222-586 1307) Nibelungengasse 13, 1010 Vienna
Canada
  (☎ 613-565 5781) 150 Metcalfe St, Suite 2101, Ottawa, Ont K2P 1P1
Croatia
  (☎ 01-612 1503) Savska cesta 41/IX, 10000 Zagreb
Hungary
  (☎ 1-325 9202) Cseppkő utca 68, 1025 Budapest
Italy
  (☎ 06-808 1272) Via Ludovico Pisano 10, 00197 Rome
UK
  (☎ 0171-495 7775) Cavendish Court, Suite One, 11-15 Wigmore St, London W1H 9LA
USA
  (☎ 202-667 5363) 1525 New Hampshire Ave NW, Washington, DC 20036

Foreign Embassies in Slovenia

Selected countries with representation in Ljubljana appear below. Citizens of countries not listed here (eg South Africa) should contact their embassies in Vienna or Budapest.

Australia
  (☎ 061-125 4252; open weekdays 9 am to 1 pm) Trg Republike 3/XII
Canada
  (☎ 061-130 3570; open weekdays 9 am to 1 pm) Miklošičeva cesta 19
UK
  (☎ 061-125 7191; open weekdays 9 am till noon) Trg Republike 3/IV
USA
  (☎ 061-301 485; open Monday, Wednesday and Friday 9 am till noon) Pražakova ulica 4

CUSTOMS

Travellers can bring in the usual personal effects, a couple of cameras and electronic goods for their own use, 200 cigarettes, a generous 4L of spirits and 1L of wine.

MONEY

Currency

Slovenia's currency, the tolar, is abbreviated SIT. Prices in shops, at restaurants and train and bus fares are always in tolars, but some hotels, guesthouses and even camping grounds still use Deutschmarks (though the government has asked them not to) as the tolar is linked to it.

For that reason, some forms of accommodation listed in this chapter are quoted in DM – though you are never required to pay in the German currency.

There are coins of 50 stotin and one, two and five tolar and banknotes of 10, 20, 50, 100, 200, 500, 1000, 5000 and 10,000 tolars.

Exchange Rates

Australia	A$1	=	104 SIT
Canada	C$1	=	115 SIT
euro	€1	=	184 SIT
France	1FF	=	28 SIT
Germany	DM1	=	94 SIT
Japan	Y100	=	122 SIT
New Zealand	NZ$1	=	105 SIT
South Africa	Rand1	=	35 SIT
United Kingdom	UK£1	=	270 SIT
United States	US$1	=	166 SIT

Costs

Slovenia remains much cheaper than neighbouring Italy and Austria, but don't expect it to be a bargain basement like Hungary: everything costs about 50% more here.

If you stay in private rooms or at guesthouses, eat at medium-priced restaurants and travel 2nd class on the train or by bus, you should get by for under US$40 a day.

Those staying at hostels or college dormitories, eating takeaway for lunch and at self-service restaurants at night will cut costs considerably.

Travelling in a little more style and comfort – occasional restaurant splurges with bottles of wine, an active nightlife, staying at small hotels or guesthouses with 'character' – will cost about US$65 a day.

Cash & Travellers Cheques

It is very simple to change cash and travellers cheques at banks, travel agencies, any *menjalnica* (private exchange bureau) and certain post offices.

There's no black market, but exchange rates can vary, so it pays to keep your eyes open. Banks take a commission (*provizija*) of 1% or none at all, but tourist offices, travel agencies, exchange bureaus and hotels have ones of 3% to 5%.

Credit Cards & ATMs

Visa, MasterCard/Eurocard and American Express credit cards are widely accepted at upmarket restaurants, shops, hotels, car-rental firms and some travel agencies; Diners Club less so.

SKB Banka maintains more than 50 Cirrus-linked automated teller machines (ATMs) throughout the country; their locations are noted in the Information sections of the individual towns. At the time of writing, no other ATMs in Slovenia were open to foreign-account holders. Clients of Visa, however, can get cash advances in tolars from any A Banka branch, MasterCard and Eurocard holders from the Nova Ljubljanska Banka (☎ 061-125 0155) at Trg Republike 2 in Ljubljana and American Express customers from Atlas Express (☎ 061-133 2024 or ☎ 061-131 9020) at Trubarjeva cesta 50 in Ljubljana.

Taxes & Refunds

A 'circulation tax' (*prometni davek*) not unlike Value-Added Tax (VAT) covers the purchase of most goods and services here. Visitors can claim refunds on total purchases of 12,500 SIT or more (not including tobacco products or spirits) through Kompas MTS, which has offices at Brnik airport and some two dozen border crossings. Make sure you do the paperwork at the time of purchase.

Most towns and cities levy a 'tourist tax' on overnight visitors of between 150 and 300 SIT per person per night (less at camping grounds).

POST & COMMUNICATIONS
Post

Poste restante is sent to the main post office in a city or town (in the capital, it goes to the branch at Slovenska cesta 32, 1101 Ljubljana) where it is held for 30 days. American Express card holders can have their mail addressed c/o the Atlas Express, Trubarjeva cesta 50, 1000 Ljubljana.

Domestic mail costs 14 SIT for up to 20g

and 26 SIT for up to 100g. Postcards are 13 SIT. For international mail, the base rate is 90 SIT for 20g or less, 186 SIT for up to 100g and 70 to 90 SIT for a postcard, depending on the size. Then you have to add on the air-mail charge for every 10g: 16 SIT for Europe, 21 SIT for North America, 22 SIT for most of Asia and 28 SIT for Australasia. An aerogramme is 120 SIT.

Telephone

The easiest place to make long-distance calls as well as send faxes and telegrams is from a post office or telephone centre; the one at Trg Osvobodilne Fronte (Trg OF) near the train and bus stations in Ljubljana is open 24 hours a day.

Public telephones on the street do not accept coins; they require a phonecard (*telefonska kartica*) or phone tokens (*žetoni*), which are being used less and less these days. Both are available at all post offices and some newsstands.

Phonecards cost 600/900/1500/2600/3300/4000 SIT for 25/50/100/200/300/400 impulses. A local two-minute call absorbs one impulse, and a three-minute call from Slovenia will cost about 292 SIT to neighbouring countries, 357 SIT to Western Europe (including the UK) and 617 SIT to the USA or Australia. Rates are 25% cheaper between 7 pm and 7 am.

The international access code in Slovenia is 00. The international operator can be reached on ☎ 901 and international directory inquiries on ☎ 989. To call Slovenia from abroad, dial the international access code, ☎ 386 (Slovenia's country code), the area code (without the initial zero, eg 61 in Ljubljana) and the number.

INTERNET RESOURCES

The best single source of information on the Internet is the CPTS's SloWWWenia site: www.ijs.si:90/slo/. It has an interactive map where you can click on to more than two dozen cities, towns, ski resorts etc as well as information on culture, history, food and wine, getting to and from Slovenia and what's on.

See the Internet Resources section in the Ljubljana section for more sites.

BOOKS

Books are very expensive in Slovenia so try to buy whatever you can on the country before you arrive. Lonely Planet's *Slovenia* is the only complete and independent English-language guide to the country. *Discover Slovenia*, published annually by Cankarjeva Založba (3300 SIT), is a colourful and easy introduction.

NEWSPAPERS & MAGAZINES

Slovenia counts four daily newspapers, the most widely read being *Delo* (Work) and *Večer* (Evening). There are no English-language newspapers though the *International Herald Tribune*, the *Guardian International*, the *Financial Times* and *USA Today* are available on the day of publication in the afternoon at hotels and department stores in Ljubljana.

RADIO & TV

In July and August both Radio Slovenija 1 & 2 broadcast a report on the weather, including conditions on the sea and in the mountains, in English, German and Italian at 7.15 am. News, weather, traffic and tourist information in the same languages follows on Radio 1 at 9.35 am daily except Sunday. Also during this period Radio 2 broadcasts weekend traffic conditions after each news bulletin from Friday afternoon through Sunday evening. There's a nightly news bulletin at 10.30 pm throughout the year on Radio 1.

You can listen to radio 1 on MHz/FM frequencies 88.5, 90.0, 90.9, 91.8, 92.0, 92.9, 94.1 and 96.4 as well as AM 326.8. Radio 2 can be found on MHz/FM 87.8, 92.4, 93.5, 94.1, 95.3, 96.9, 97.6, 98.9 and 99.9.

PHOTOGRAPHY & VIDEO

Film and basic camera equipment are available throughout Slovenia, though the largest selection is in Ljubljana. Film prices vary but 24 exposures of 100 ASA Kodacolor II, Agfa or Fujifilm will cost about 650 SIT, 36 exposures 750 SIT. Ektachrome 100 (36 exposures) is 1110 SIT. Super 8 (P5-60) film costs about 1300 SIT while an EC45 video cassette is 1300 SIT. Developing print film costs about 2500 SIT for 36 prints. For 36 framed transparencies, expect to pay around 1200 SIT.

TIME

Slovenia is one hour ahead of GMT/UTC. The country goes onto summer time (GMT/UTC plus two hours) on the last Sunday in March when clocks are advanced by one hour. On the last Sunday in October they're turned back one hour.

ELECTRICITY

The electric voltage is 220V, 50 Hz, AC. Plugs are the standard European type with two round pins.

WEIGHTS & MEASURES

Slovenia uses the metric system.

LAUNDRY

Commercial laundrettes are pretty much nonexistent in Slovenia. The best places to look for do-it-yourself washers and dryers are hostels, college dormitories and camping grounds, and there are a couple of places in Ljubljana that will do your laundry reasonably quickly (see Laundry under Information in the Ljubljana section).

HEALTH

Foreigners are entitled to emergency medical aid at the very least; for subsequent treatment entitlement varies. Some EU countries (including the UK) have contractual agreements with Slovenia allowing their citizens free medical care while travelling in the country. This may require carrying a special form so check with your Ministry of Health or equivalent before setting out.

WOMEN TRAVELLERS

The Društvo Mesto Žensk (City of Women Association), part of the Government Office for Women's Affairs (☎ 061-125 112), is at Kersnikova ulica 4 in Ljubljana. It sponsors an international festival of contemporary arts called City of Women usually in October. In the event of an assault ring ☎ 080 124 or any of the following six numbers: ☎ 9780 to ☎ 9785.

GAY & LESBIAN TRAVELLERS

The gay association Roza Klub (☎ 061-130 4740), at Kersnikova ulica 4 in Ljubljana, publishes a quarterly newsletter called *Revolver* and organises a disco every Sunday night at the Klub K4 in Ljubljana. Magnus (☎ same as Rosa Klub) is the gay branch of the Student Cultural Centre (Študentski Kulturni Center; ŠKUC).

Lesbians can contact the ŠKUC-affiliated organisation LL (☎ 061-130 4740) at Metelkova ulica 6 in Ljubljana.

The GALfon (☎ 061-132 4089) is a hotline and source of general information for gays and lesbians. It operates daily from 7 to 10 pm. The Queer Resources Directory on the Internet (www.ljudmila.org/~siqrd) leaves no stone unturned.

DISABLED TRAVELLERS

A group that looks after the interests and special needs of physically challenged people is the Zveza Paraplegikov Republike Slovenije (ZPRS; ☎ 061-132 7138) at Štihova ulica 14 in Ljubljana.

SENIOR TRAVELLERS

Senior citizens may be entitled to discounts in Slovenia on things like transport (eg those over 60 years of age holding an international Rail Europe Seniors (RES) card get from 30% to 50% off on Slovenian Railways), museum admission fees etc, provided they show proof of age.

DANGERS & ANNOYANCES

Slovenia is hardly a violent or dangerous place. Police say that 90% of all crimes reported involve thefts so take the usual precautions. In the event of an emergency, the following numbers can be dialled nationwide:

Police ☎ 113
Fire/first aid/ambulance ☎ 112
Automobile assistance (AMZS) ☎ 987

LEGAL MATTERS

The permitted blood-alcohol level for motorists is 0.5g/kg (0.0g/kg for professional drivers) and the law is very strictly enforced. Anything over that could earn you a fine of 25,000 SIT and one to three points.

BUSINESS HOURS

Shops, groceries and department stores are open from 7.30 or 8 am to 7 pm on weekdays and to 1 pm on Saturday. Bank hours are generally from 8 am to 4.30 or 5 pm on weekdays (often with a lunchtime break) and till noon on Saturday. The main post office in any city or town is open from 7 am to 8 pm on weekdays, till 1 pm on Saturday and occasionally from 9 to 11 am on Sunday.

PUBLIC HOLIDAYS & SPECIAL EVENTS

Public holidays in Slovenia include two days at New Year (1 & 2 January), Prešeren Day (8 February), Easter Sunday & Monday (March/April), Insurrection Day (27 April), two days for Labour Day (1 & 2 May), National Day (25 June), Assumption Day (15 August), Reformation Day (31 October), All Saints' Day (1 November), Christmas (25 December) and Independence Day (26 December).

Though cultural events are scheduled year round, the highlights of Slovenia's summer season (July and August) are the International Summer Festival in Ljubljana; the Piran Musical Evenings; the Primorska Summer Festival at Piran, Koper, Izola and Portorož; and Summer in the Old Town in Ljubljana, with three or four cultural events a week taking place. The Cows' Ball (*Kravji Bal*) at Bohinj is a zany weekend of folk dance, music, eating and drinking in mid-September to mark the return of the cows to the valleys from their high pastures.

ACTIVITIES
Skiing

Skiing is by far the most popular sport in Slovenia, and every fourth Slovene is an active skier. The country has many well-equipped ski resorts in the Julian Alps, especially Vogel (skiing up to 1840m) above

Lake Bohinj, Kranjska Gora (1600m), Kanin (2300m) above Bovec, and Krvavec (1970m), east of Kranj. World Cup slalom and giant slalom events are held at Kranjska Gora in late December, and the current world ski-jumping record (200m) was set at nearby Planica in 1994.

All these resorts have multiple chair lifts, cable cars, ski schools, equipment rentals and large resort hotels.

Hiking

Hiking is almost as popular as skiing, and there are 7000km of marked trails and 165 mountain huts. You'll experience the full grandeur of the Julian Alps in Triglav National Park at Bohinj, and for the veteran mountaineer there's the Slovenian Alpine Trail, which crosses all the highest peaks in the country.

Kayaking, Canoeing & Rafting

The best white-water rafting is on the Soča, one of only half a dozen rivers in the European Alps whose upper waters are still unspoiled. The centre is at Bovec.

Fishing

Slovenia's rivers and Alpine lakes and streams are teeming with trout, grayling, pike and other fish. The best rivers for angling are the Soča, the Krka, the Kolpa and the Sava Bohinjka near Bohinj. Lake fishing is good at Bled and Bohinj.

Cycling

Mountain bikes are for hire at Bled and Bohinj. You can also rent bikes on the coast and in Ljubljana.

ACCOMMODATION
Camping

In summer, camping is the cheapest way to go, and there are conveniently located camping grounds all over the country. You don't always need a tent as some camping grounds have inexpensive bungalows or caravans, too. Two of the best camping grounds are Zlatorog on Lake Bohinj and Jezero Fiesa near Piran, though they can be very crowded in summer. It is forbidden to camp 'rough' in Slovenia.

Hostels & Student Dormitories

Slovenia has only a handful of 'official' hostels, including two in Ljubljana and one each in Bled and Koper, but not all of them are open year round. Some college dormitories accept travellers in the summer months.

Private Rooms & Apartments

Private rooms arranged by tourist offices and travel agencies can be inexpensive, but a surcharge of up to 50% is usually levied on stays of less than three nights. You can often bargain for rooms without the surcharge by going directly to any house with a sign reading 'sobe' (rooms).

Pensions & Guesthouses

A small guesthouse (called penzion or gostišče) can be good value, though in July and August you may be required to take at least one meal and the rates are higher then.

Farmhouses

The agricultural cooperatives of Slovenia have organised a unique program to accommodate visitors on working farms. Prices go from DM30 per person for a 2nd-category room with shared bath and breakfast in the low season (from September to about mid-December and mid-January to June) to around DM45 per person for a 1st-category room with private bath and all meals in the high season (July and August). Bookings can be made through ABC Farm & Countryside Holidays (☎ 061-576 127) at Ulica Jožeta Jame 16 in Ljubljana or at Brnik airport (☎ 064-261 684). Its British agent is Slovenija Pursuits (☎ 01763-852 646), 14 Hay St, Steeple Morden, Royston, Herts SG8 0PE.

Hotels

Hotel rates vary according to the season, with July and August being the peak season and May/June and September/October the shoulder seasons. In Ljubljana, prices are constant all year. Many resort hotels, particularly on the coast, close in winter.

FOOD

Slovenian cuisine is heavily influenced by the food of its neighbours. From Austria, it's klobasa (sausage), zavitek (strudel) and

Dunajski zrezek (Wiener schnitzel). *Njoki* (potato dumplings), *rižota* (risotto) and the ravioli-like *žlikrofi* are obviously Italian, and Hungary has contributed *golaž* (goulash), *paprikaš* (chicken or beef 'stew') and *palačinke* (thin pancakes filled with jam or nuts and topped with chocolate). And then there's that old Balkan standby, *burek*, a greasy, layered cheese, meat or even apple pie served at take-away places everywhere.

No Slovenian meal is complete without soup, be it the simple *goveja juha z rezanci* (beef broth with little egg noodles), *zelenjavna juha* (vegetable soup) or *gobova kremna juha* (creamed mushroom soup). There are many types of Slovenian dumplings; the cheese ones called *štruklji* are the most popular. Try also the baked delicacies, including *potica* (walnut roll) and *gibanica*, pastry filled with poppy seeds, walnuts, apple and/or sultanas and cheese and topped with cream. Traditional dishes are best tried at an inn (*gostilna* or *gostišče*).

DRINKS

The wine-growing regions of Slovenia are Podravje in the east, noted for such white wines as Renski Rizling (a true German Riesling), Beli Pinot (Pinot Blanc) and Traminec (Traminer); Posavje in the south-east (try the distinctly Slovenian light-red Cviček); and the area around the coast, which produces a hearty red called Teran made from Refošk grapes.

Žganje is a strong brandy or *eau de vie* distilled from a variety of fruits but most commonly plums. The finest brandy is Pleterska Hruška made from pears.

Getting There & Away

AIR

Slovenia's national airline, Adria Airways (JP; ☎ 061-133 4336 in Ljubljana, ☎ 064-223 555 at Brnik airport; www.kabi.si/~si21/aa), has nonstop flights to Ljubljana from 18 cities, including Amsterdam, Barcelona, Brussels, Copenhagen, Frankfurt, London (LHR), Manchester (May-September), Moscow, Munich, Ohrid (Macedonia), Paris

(CDG), Sarajevo, Skopje, Split, Tel Aviv, Tirana, Vienna and Zurich.

Other airlines that serve Ljubljana include Aeroflot (SU) from Moscow, Austrian Airlines (OS) from Vienna, Avioimpex (M4) from Skopje, British Airways (BA) from London, Lufthansa (LH) from Frankfurt and Swissair (SR) from Zurich.

LAND

Bus

Nova Gorica is the easiest exit/entry point between Slovenia and Italy as you can catch up to five buses a day to/from the Italian city of Gorizia or simply walk across the border at Rožna Dolina. Koper also has good connections with Italy: some 17 buses a day on weekdays go to/from Trieste, 21km to the north-east.

From Ljubljana you can catch a bus to Budapest three times a week and there's a weekly service to Lenti. Otherwise take one of up to five daily buses to Lendava; the Hungarian border is 5km to the north. The first Hungarian train station, Rédics, is only 2km beyond the border. From Rédics, there are up to 10 trains a day (1¼ hours) to Zalaegerszeg, from where there are three direct trains (3¾ hours) and five buses to Budapest.

For information about getting to/from other neighbouring countries and ones farther afield, see Getting There & Away in the Ljubljana section.

Train

The main train routes into Slovenia from Austria are Vienna to Maribor and Salzburg to Jesenice. Tickets cost 5615 SIT from Ljubljana to Salzburg (4½ hours) and 7906 SIT to Vienna (six hours). But it's cheaper to take a local train to Maribor (1011 SIT) and buy your ticket on to Vienna from there. Similarly, from Austria only buy a ticket as far as Jesenice or Maribor as domestic fares are much lower than international ones.

There are two trains a day between Munich and Ljubljana (seven hours, 9737 SIT) via Salzburg. The EuroCity *Mimara* travels by day, while the *Lisinski* express goes overnight (sleeping carriage available). A 258 SIT supplement is payable on the

SLOVENIA

Mimara. Seat reservations (160 SIT) are available on both.

Four trains a day run from Trieste to Ljubljana (three hours, 2464 SIT) via Divača and Sežana. From Croatia it's Zagreb to Ljubljana (2½ hours, 1513 SIT) via Zidani Most, or Rijeka to Ljubljana (2½ hours, 1460 SIT) via Pivka. Most services between Slovenia and Croatia require a change of trains at some point, but connections are immediate. The InterCity *Drava* and *Venezia Express* trains link Ljubljana with Budapest (7½ hours, 6747 SIT) via north-west Croatia and Zagreb respectively.

Car & Motorcycle
Slovenia maintains some 150 border crossings with Italy, Austria, Hungary and Croatia though not all are open to citizens of other countries.

SEA
Between early April and October on Friday, Saturday and Sunday the *Prince of Venice*, a 39m Australian-made catamaran seating some 330 passengers, sails between Portorož and Venice (2½ hours, 6860/9800 SIT one way/return) with an additional sailing on Tuesday from late June to early September. Another catamaran, the *Marconi*, links Trieste with Piran (35 minutes, 2000/4000 SIT return) on Wednesday, Friday and Sunday from mid-May to September.

LEAVING SLOVENIA
A departure tax of DM25/US$14 is levied on all passengers leaving Slovenia by air though this is almost always included in the ticket price.

Getting Around

BUS
Except for long journeys, the bus is preferable to the train in Slovenia and departures are frequent. In some cases you don't have much of a choice; travelling by bus is the only practical way to get to Bled and Bohinj, the Julian Alps and much of the coast from Ljubljana.

In Ljubljana you can buy your ticket with seat reservation (60 to 120 SIT, depending on the destination) the day before, but many people simply pay the driver on boarding. The one time you really might need a reservation is Friday afternoon, when many students travel from Ljubljana to their homes or people leave the city for the weekend.

Footnotes you might see on Slovenian bus schedules include: *vozi vsak dan* (runs daily); *vozi ob delavnikih* (runs on working days – Monday to Friday); *vozi ob sobotah* (runs on Saturday); and *vozi ob nedeljah in praznikih* (runs on Sunday and holidays).

TRAIN
Slovenske Železnice (SŽ; Slovenian Railways) operates on just over 1200km of track. The country's most scenic rail routes run along the Soča River from Jesenice to Nova Gorica via Bled (Bled Jezero station) and Bohinjska Bistrica (89km) and from Ljubljana to Zagreb (160km) along the Sava River.

On posted timetables in Slovenia, *odhod* or *odhodi vlakov* means 'departures' and *prihod* (or *prihodi vlakov*) is 'arrivals'. If you don't have time to buy a ticket, seek out the conductor who will sell you one for an extra charge of 200 SIT.

CAR & MOTORCYCLE
The use of seat belts in the front seats is compulsory in Slovenia, and a new law requires all vehicles to show their headlights throughout the day outside built-up areas. Speed limits for cars are 50km/h in built-up areas, 90km/h on secondary roads, 100km/h on main highways and 130km/h on motorways.

Tolls are payable on several motorways, but they're not terribly expensive; from Ljubljana to Postojna, for example, it costs 250 SIT for cars and motorcycles. Petrol remains relatively cheap: 100.40/103.50/119.80 SIT per litre for 91/95/98 octane. Diesel costs 100.50 SIT.

Slovenia's automobile club is the Avto Moto Zveza Slovenije (AMZS; tel 987)

Car Rental
Car rentals from international firms like National, Budget, Avis and Kompas Hertz vary widely in price, but expect to pay from about US$57/$287 a day/week with unlimited

mileage for a Renault 5 or Ford Fiesta. Optional collision insurance to reduce the excess/deductible is about US$8 a day extra, theft protection another US$8 and personal accident insurance US$2 to US$5. Smaller agencies like ABC Rent a Car and Avtoimpex in Ljubljana (see Getting Around in that section) have more competitive rates.

Some agencies have minimum-age rules (21 or 23 years) and/or require that you've had a valid licence for one or even two years.

HITCHING

Hitchhiking is legal everywhere except on motorways and some major highways and is generally easy; even young women do it. But hitching is never a totally safe way of getting around and, although we mention it as an option, we don't recommend it.

Ljubljana

☎ 061

Ljubljana (Laibach in German, population 270,000) is by far Slovenia's largest and most populous city. But in many ways the city, whose name almost means 'beloved' (ljubljena) in Slovene, does not feel like an industrious municipality of national importance but a pleasant, self-contented town with responsibilities only to itself and its citizens. The most beautiful parts of the city are the Old Town below the castle and the embankments designed by Plečnik along the narrow Ljubljanica River.

Ljubljana began as the Roman town of Emona, and legacies of the Roman presence can still be seen throughout the city. The Habsburgs took control of Ljubljana in the 14th century and later built many of the pale-coloured churches and mansions that earned the city the nickname 'White Ljubljana'. From 1809 to 1814, Ljubljana was the capital of the Illyrian Provinces, Napoleon's short-lived springboard to the Adriatic.

Despite the patina of imperial Austria, contemporary Ljubljana has a vibrant Slavic air all its own. It's like a little Prague without the hordes of tourists but with all the facilities you'll need. More than 25,000 students attend Ljubljana University's 14 faculties and three art academies so the city always feels young.

Orientation

The tiny bus station and renovated train station are opposite one another on Trg Osvobodilne Fronte (known as Trg OF) at the northern end of the centre (called Center). The 24-hour left-luggage office (*garderoba*; 160 SIT per piece) at the train station is on platform No 1. A smaller garderoba (open from 5.30 am to 8.30 pm) is inside the bus station.

Information

Tourist Offices The Tourist Information Centre (TIC; tel 133 0111; fax 133 0244; pcl.tic-lj@siol.net) is in the historical Kresija building south-east of Triple Bridge at Mačkova ulica 1. It's open weekdays from 8 am to 7 pm and on Saturday from 9 am to 5 pm. The branch office (☎ 133 9475) at the train station is open daily (including Sunday) June to September from 8 am to 9 pm (10 am to 6 pm the rest of the year). The TIC is well worth visiting to pick up free maps and brochures.

The Cultural Information Centre (☎ 214 025) next to Trg Francoske Revolucije 7 can answer questions about what's on in Ljubljana and has a free booklet listing all the city's museums, galleries and exhibitions.

The main office of the Alpine Association of Slovenia (☎ 134 3022; www.pzs.si) is at Dvoržakova ulica 9, a small house set back from the street.

Money The currency exchange office inside the train station is open daily from 6 am to 10 pm. It accepts travellers cheques, charges no commission and the rate is good. The best rate anywhere in Slovenia, though, is at Nova Ljubljanska Banka, Trg Republike 2 (open weekdays 8 am to 5 pm, on Saturday 9 am till noon). There's an A Banka branch at Slovenska cesta 50. The Hida exchange bureau in the Seminary building near the open-air market at Pogarčarjev trg 1 is open weekdays from 7 am to 7 pm and on Saturday to 2 pm. Another Hida branch at Čopova ulica 42 is open weekdays from 8 am to 8 pm and on Saturday to 1 pm.

SKB Banka Cirrus-linked ATMs are at Trg Ajdovščina 4, in the very centre of the big shopping mall; outside the Emona Globtour agency in the Maximarket passageway connecting Trg Republike with Plečnikov trg; and in the

Gledališka pasaža connecting Čopova ulica with Nazorjeva ulica. Next to the SKB Banka ATM on Trg Ajdovščina is a currency exchange machine that changes the banknotes of 18 countries into tolar.

Post & Communications Poste restante is held for 30 days at the post office at Slovenska cesta 32 (postal code 1101). It is open weekdays from 7 am to 8 pm and to 1 pm Saturday. You can make international telephone calls or send faxes from here or the main post office at Pražakova ulica 3, which keeps the same hours.

To mail a parcel you must go to the special customs post office at Trg OF 5 opposite the bus station and open round the clock. Make sure you bring your package open for inspection; the maximum weight is about 15kg, depending on the destination.

Internet Resources Useful Web sites for Ljubljana include:

www.ljubljana.si
   City of Ljubljana
www.uni-lj.si
   Ljubljana University (check out the Welcome chapter with practical information for foreign students)
www.sou.uni-lj/english.html
   Student Organisation of the University of Ljubljana (Študentska Organizacija Univerze Ljubljani; ŠOU)
www.ljudmila/org/
   Ljubljana Digital Media Lab (links with the multimedia group Neue Slowenische Kunst, the MOST-SIC volunteer work organisation etc)

There are two cybercafés with public-access Internet sites in Ljubljana: the Klub K4 Café (☎ 131 7010) at Kersnikova ulica 4 and Club Podhod (☎ 121 4100) in the underpass (subway) between Kongresni trg and Plečnikov trg.

Travel Agencies Backpackers and students should head for the Erazem travel office (☎ 133 1076) at Trubarjeva cesta 7. It can provide information, make bookings and it has a message board. It also sells ISIC cards (800 SIT) and, for those under 26 but not studying, FIYTO cards (700 SIT). Mladi Turist (☎ 125 8260), at Salendrova ulica 4

near the Municipal Museum, is the office of the Slovenian Youth Hostel Association. It sells hostel cards (800 to 1800 SIT, depending on your age), but you're supposed to have resided in the country for six months.

Slovenijaturist (☎ 131 5055), Slovenska cesta 58, sells BIJ international train tickets (one-third cheaper than regular fares) to those under 26 years of age.

The American Express representative is Atlas Express (☎ 133 2024 or tel 131 9020) at Trubarjeva cesta 50 in Ljubljana. It will hold clients' mail but doesn't cash travellers cheques.

Bookshops Ljubljana's largest bookshop is Mladinska Knjiga at Slovenska cesta 29. It also has a branch on Miklošičeva cesta 40, opposite the bus station. Another good chain with a shop at Slovenska cesta 37 is Cankarjeva Založba. Kod & Kam, Trg Francoske Revolucije 7, is excellent for travel guides and maps.

The best places for English and other foreign-language newspapers and magazines are the newsstand in the lobby of the Grand Hotel Union, Miklošičeva cesta 1, and the one in the basement of the Maximarket department store on Trg Republike.

Laundry A couple of the student dormitories, including Dijaški Dom Poljane about 1.5km east of the Old Town at Potočnikova ulica 3 and Dijaški Dom Kam (Building C) at Kardeljeva ploščad 14, north of the centre in Bežigrad, have washing machines and dryers that you can use, as does the Ježica camping ground. Alba at Wolfova ulica 12 near Prešernov trg is an old-style laundry and dry cleaner open weekdays from 8 am to 6 pm.

Medical Services You can see a doctor at the medical centre (*klinični center*; ☎ 133 6236 or ☎ 131 3123) at Zaloška cesta 7, which is in Tabor east of the Park hotel. The emergency unit (*urgenca*) is open 24 hours a day.

Things to See
The most picturesque sights of old Ljubljana are along both banks of the Ljubljanica, a tributary of the Sava that curves around the foot of Castle Hill.

Opposite the TIC in the Kresija building is the celebrated **Triple Bridge**. In 1931, Jože Plečnik added the side bridges to the original central span dating from 1842. On the northern side of the bridge is Prešernov trg with its pink **Franciscan church** (1660), a statue (1905) of poet France Prešeren and some lovely Art Nouveau buildings. A lively pedestrian street, Čopova ulica, runs to the north-west.

On the south side of the bridge in Mestni trg, the baroque **Robba Fountain** stands before the **town hall** (1718). Italian sculptor Francesco Robba designed this fountain in 1751 and modelled it after one in Rome. Enter the town hall to see the double Gothic courtyard. To the south of Mestni trg is **Stari trg**, atmospheric by day or night. North-east are the twin towers of the **Cathedral of St Nicholas** (1708), which contains impressive frescos. Behind the cathedral is Ljubljana's colourful open-air **produce market** (closed Sunday) and a lovely **colonnade** along the riverside designed by Plečnik.

Študentovska ulica, opposite the Vodnik statue in the market square, leads up to **Ljubljana Castle**. The castle has been under renovation for decades, but you can climb the 19th-century **Castle Tower** to the west (daily from 10 am to dusk; 200/100 SIT adults/children) and view the exhibits in a Gothic chapel and the **Pentagonal Tower** (closed Saturday and Monday). Reber ulica between Stari trg 17 & 19 also leads up to the castle.

There's another interesting area worth exploring on the west side of the Ljubljanica River. The **Municipal Museum**, Gosposka ulica 15 (open Tuesday to Saturday from 9 am to 7 pm, Sunday from 2 to 6 pm; 500/300 SIT for adults/seniors, students & children), is a good place to start. The museum has a well presented collection of Roman artefacts, plus a scale model of Roman Emona (Ljubljana). Upstairs rooms contain period furniture and household objects.

At Gosposka ulica 14 near the Municipal Museum is the **National & University Library** (1941) designed by Plečnik, and north on Gosposka ulica at Kongresni trg 12 is the main building of **Ljubljana University** (1902), formerly the regional parliament. The lovely **Philharmonic Hall** (Filharmonija), at No 10 on the south-east corner of the square,

is home to the Slovenian Philharmonic Orchestra. The **Ursuline Church of the Holy Trinity** (1726), with an altar by Robba, faces Kongresni trg to the west.

Walk west on Šubičeva ulica to several of the city's fine museums. The **National Museum**, Muzejska ulica 1 (open Tuesday to Sunday from 10 am to 6 pm, to 8 pm on Wednesday; 300/200 SIT), erected in 1885, has prehistory, natural history and ethnography collections. The highlight is a Celtic situla, a kind of pail, from the 6th century BC sporting a fascinating relief.

The **National Gallery**, Cankarjeva ulica 20, offers Slovenian portraits and landscapes from the 17th to 19th centuries, as well as copies of medieval frescos; the gallery's new wing to the north at Puharjeva ulica 9 (separate entrance) has a permanent collection of European paintings from the Middle Ages to the 20th century and is used for temporary exhibits. It is open Tuesday to Sunday from 10 am to 6 pm, and entry costs 500/300 SIT.

Diagonally opposite the National Gallery, at Cankarjeva ulica 15, is the **Museum of Modern Art**, where the International Biennial of Graphic Arts is held every other summer in odd-numbered years. It is open Tuesday to Saturday from 10 am to 6 pm and on Sunday to 1 pm. Admission costs 300/200 SIT for adults/seniors and children and it's free on Sunday. The Serbian Orthodox **Church of Sts Cyril & Methodius** opposite the Museum of Modern Art is worth entering to see the beautiful modern frescos (open Tuesday to Saturday from 3 to 6 pm). The subway from the Museum of Modern Art leads to Ljubljana's green lung, **Tivoli Park**.

If you have time (or the inclination) for another museum or two, head for the **Museum of Modern History**, Celovška cesta 23 just beyond the Tivoli Recreation Centre, which traces the history of Slovenia in the 20th century via multimedia, or the new **Slovenian Ethnographic Museum** at Metlikova ulica 2. Both are open Tuesday to Sunday from 10 am to 6 pm and cost 400/300 SIT.

Activities
The **Tivoli Recreation Centre**, in the Tivoli Park at Celovška cesta 25, has bowling alleys, tennis courts, an indoor swimming pool, a fitness centre and a roller-skating rink.

SLOVENIA

LJUBLJANA

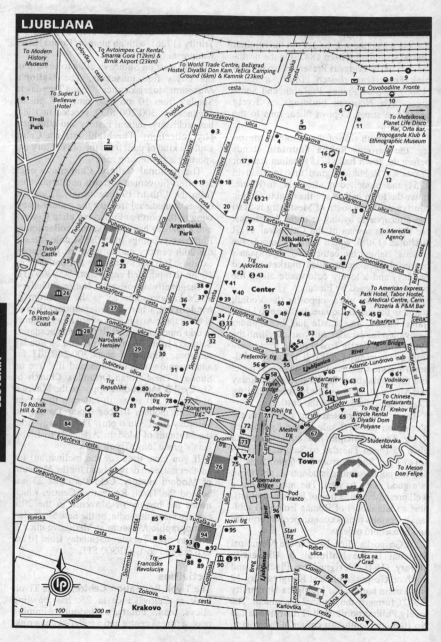

To Modern History Museum

Celovška cesta

To Avtoimpex Car Rental, Smarna Gora (12km) & Brnik Airport (23km)

To World Trade Centre, Bežigrad Hostel, Dijaški Don Kam, Ježica Camping Ground (6km) & Kamnik (23km)

Dunajska cesta

cesta

7

8 9

Trg Osvobodilne Fronte

10

To Super Li Bellevue Hotel

1

Tivoli Park

Tivolska

6

11

To Metelkova, Planet Life Disco Bar, Orto Bar, Propoganda Klub & Ethnographic Museum

cesta

5

Dvořakova ulica

Gosposvetska cesta

2

3

Pražakova

4

16

ulica

15

Kolodvorska

12

To Tivoli Castle

Tivolska

Puharjeva ul

Kersnikova ulica

Vošnjakova ulica

Slovenska cesta

17

Trdinova ulica

14

Cufarjeva

13

To Meredita Agency

19

18

21

Cigaletova ulica

Miklošičeva

20

Argentinski Park

Puharjeva ulica

Komenskega ulica

25

Prežihova ul

Stefanova ulica

23

24

24

22

Tavčarjeva

Miklošičev Park

Dalmatinova

44

Rešeljeva

To American Express, Park Hotel, Tabor Hostel, Medical Centre, Cerin Pizzeria & P&M Bar

26

Cankarjeva cesta

Županćićeva ulica

27

38

37

36

39

40

41

42

43

Trg Ajdovščina

Center

50

46

47

45

Prečna

To Postojna (53km) & Coast

Prešernova

28

Tomšičeva ulica

Beethovnova ulica

Nazorjeva ulica

34

33

51

49

48

Trubarjeva

cesta

To Tivoli Castle

29

Trg Narodnih Herojev

30

35

32

Slovenska cesta

Copova

52

54

53

River

Dragon Bridge

Kopitarjeva ul

Subiceva ulica

31

Prešernov trg

56

55

Ljubljanica

Adamič-Lundrovo nab

Trg Republike

80

Plečnikov trg

78

77

Kongresni

57

58

59

Triple Bridge

Wolfova ul

60

Pogaćarjev trg

63

61

Vodnikov trg

62

To Chinese Restaurants

To Rožnik Hill & Zoo

81

83

82

subway

64

65

Metodov

To Rog II Bicycle Rental & Dijaški Dom Polyane

84

79

Ribji trg

71

66

67

Mestni trg

Cankarjevo

Cirli

Studentovska ulica

Erjavčeva cesta

72

Dvorni trg

73

74

Old Town

68

70

69

To Meson Don Felipe

Gregorčičeva

76

75

Shoemaker Bridge

Vegova

ulica

Pod Tranćo

River

Igrisška ulica

Rimska

85

Tunjaška ul

Novi trg

95

Stari trg

96

Reber ulica

Ljubljanica

87

93

92

94

Ulica na Grad

86

88 89

90

91

Breg

Trg Francoske Revolucije

Gosposka

Gornji trg

Levstikov trg

97

98

99

Zoisova cesta

Rožna ul

Krakovo

Karlovška cesta

100

0   100   200 m

LJUBLJANA

PLACES TO STAY
- 34 Slon Hotel & Café
- 44 Turist Hotel & Klub Central Disco
- 50 Grand Hotel Union
- 86 Pri Mraku Guesthouse

PLACES TO EAT
- 12 Burek Stand
- 20 Evropa Café
- 22 Tavčarjev Hram
- 36 Daj-Dam
- 40 Skriti Kot
- 41 Šestica
- 42 Super 5 Food Stand
- 47 Napoli Pizzeria
- 60 Ribca Seafood Bar
- 65 Kolovrat
- 74 Ljubljanski Dvor
- 85 Foculus Pizzeria
- 96 Pizzeria Romeo
- 98 Sichuan
- 100 Špajza

OTHER
- 1 Tivoli Recreation Centre, Zlati Klub Sauna & Klub Manhattan Disco
- 2 Ilirija Swimming Pool
- 3 Alpine Association of Slovenia
- 4 Slovenijaturist Travel Agency & Burek Stand
- 5 Main Post Office
- 6 Canadian Embassy
- 7 Post Office (Customs)
- 8 City Airport Buses
- 9 Train Station & Tourist Office Branch
- 10 Bus Station
- 11 Kompas Cinema
- 13 Avis Car Rental
- 14 Kinoteka Cinema
- 15 Kompas Hertz Car Rental
- 16 US Embassy
- 17 City Bus Ticket Kiosks
- 18 Klub K4 & University Student Centre
- 19 Adria Airways Office
- 21 A Banka
- 23 National Car Rental
- 24 National Gallery
- 25 Serbian Orthodox Church
- 26 Museum of Modern Art
- 27 Opera House
- 28 National Museum
- 29 Parliament Building
- 30 Gajo Jazz Club
- 31 Mladinska Knjiga Bookshop
- 32 Post Office (Poste Restante)
- 33 Hida Exchange Bureau
- 35 Komuna Cinema
- 37 Cankarjeva Založba Bookshop
- 38 Skyscraper Building & Café
- 39 Kompas Travel Agency & Holidays' Pub
- 43 SKB Banka & ATM
- 45 TrueBar
- 46 Patrick's Irish Pub
- 48 Art Nouveau Bank Buildings
- 49 Union Cinema
- 51 Eldorado Disco
- 52 Franciscan Church
- 53 Erazem Travel Agency
- 54 Urbanc Building/ Centromerkur Department Store
- 55 Prešeren Monument
- 56 Ura Building
- 57 Alba Laundry
- 58 Horse's Tail Café Pub
- 59 Tourist Information Centre (TIC)
- 61 Produce Market
- 62 Cathedral of Saint Nicholas
- 63 Seminary/Hida Exchange Bureau
- 64 Bishop's Palace
- 66 Robba Fountain
- 67 Town Hall
- 68 Ljubljana Castle
- 69 Pentagonal Tower
- 70 Castle Tower
- 71 River Cruises
- 72 Delikatesa
- 73 Filharmonija
- 75 Burja Delicatessen
- 76 Ljubljana University
- 77 Club Podhod
- 78 Rock Café
- 79 Ursuline Church
- 80 Maximarket Shopping Arcade & Maxim Self-Service Restaurant
- 81 Emona Globtour Travel Agency
- 82 Nova Ljubljanska Banka
- 83 UK & Australian Embassy
- 84 Cankarjev Dom (Cultural Centre)
- 87 Ilirija Column
- 88 Križanke Ticket Office
- 89 Križanke/Summer Festival Theatre
- 90 Municipal Museum
- 91 Mladi Turist
- 92 Kod & Kam Bookshop
- 93 Cultural Information Centre
- 94 National & University Library
- 95 Academy of Arts & Sciences
- 97 Church of St James
- 99 Church of St Florian

There's even a popular sauna called **Zlati Klub** that has several saunas, a steam room, warm and cold splash pools and even a small outside pool surrounded by high walls so you can sunbathe in the nude (mixed sexes). Entry costs 1500 SIT at the weekend and 1200 SIT on weekdays and until 1 pm.

The outdoor **Ilirija pool** opposite the Tivoli hotel at Celovška cesta 3 is open in summer from 10 am to 7 pm on weekdays, 9 am to 8 pm at the weekend.

Organised Tours
From June to September, a two-hour guided tour in English (700/500 SIT adults/seniors, students & children) sponsored by the TIC departs daily at 5 pm from the town hall in Mestni trg. During the rest of the year there are tours at 11 am on Sunday only.

In summer a boat called the *Emona II* (☎ 448 112 or mobile ☎ 041-627 857) offers excursions on the Ljubljanica Tuesday to Sunday at 5 and 7 pm from the footbridge just west of Ribnji trg (500 SIT; children under 12 free).

Places to Stay

Camping Some 6km north of Center on the Sava at Dunajska cesta 270 (bus No 6 or 8) is *Camping Ježica* (☎ 168 3913), with a large, shady camping area (860 SIT per person plus 180 SIT for a caravan or tent) and three dozen cramped little bungalows for two costing 6600 SIT. The camping ground is open all year.

Hostels & Student Dormitories Four student dormitories (*dijaški dom*) open their doors to foreign travellers in July and August. The most central by far is the *Dijaški Dom Tabor* (☎ 321 067), opposite the Park hotel at Vidovdanska ulica 7 and affiliated with Hostelling International (HI). It charges 2880 SIT for a single room and 2200 SIT for a bed in a double or triple, including breakfast.

The *Dijaški Dom Bežigrad* (☎ 342 867), another HI member, is at Kardeljeva ploščad 28 in the Bežigrad district 2km north of the train and bus stations. It has doubles/triples with shower and toilet for 3600/4500 SIT and rooms with one to three beds with shared facilities for 1200 SIT per person. An HI card gets you about 10% off. The Bežigrad has 70 rooms available from late June to late August but only about 20 the rest of the year.

Private Rooms & Apartments The TIC has about 40 private rooms on its list, but just a handful are in Center. Most of the others would require a bus trip up to Bežigrad. Prices range from 2500 SIT for singles and 4000 SIT for doubles. It also has eight apartments and two studios – four of which are central – for one to four people costing from 8900 SIT to 16,700 SIT. Reception is at the Meredita agency (☎ 131 1102) in the Ledina shopping centre at Kotnikova ulica 5.

Guesthouse The closest thing to a pension in Ljubljana proper is the *Pri Mraku* pension (☎ 223 412; fax 301 197), west of Trg Francoske Revolucije at Rimska cesta 4, but its 30 rooms are small and quite expensive: 7050 SIT for a single with shower and breakfast and 9900 SIT for a double.

Hotels One of the best deals in town is the 15-room *Super Li Bellevue* hotel (☎ 133 4049) on the northern edge of Tivoli Park at Pod Gozdom 12. There are no rooms with private bath, but bright and airy singles with basins are 3050 SIT, doubles 6000 SIT.

The 122-room *Park* hotel (☎ 133 1306; fax 133 0546) at Tabor 9 is where most people usually end up as it's the city's only large budget hotel close to Center and the Old Town. It's pretty basic, but the price is right: 5500/7000 SIT for singles/doubles with breakfast and shared shower and 6800/8500 SIT with private shower. Students with cards get a 20% discount. The staff are very helpful and friendly.

Places to Eat

Restaurants The *Kolovrat* at Ciril-Metodov trg 14 opposite the cathedral is a renovated Slovenian gostilna with reasonably priced Slovenian meals (lunch menus at 750 and 1300 SIT) or you might try the *Tavčarjev Hram* at Tavčarjev ulica 4. The *Šestica* is a 200-year-old standby with a pleasant courtyard at Slovenska cesta 40. Main courses are in the 600-1200 SIT range and lunch menus are 900 and 1200 SIT. A much more upmarket (and expensive) alternative for Slovenian specialities is the attractive *Špajza* in the Old Town at Gornji trg 28.

The capital abounds in Italian restaurants and pizzerias. Among the best are the *Ljubljanski Dvor* at Dvorni trg 1 on the west bank of the Ljubljanica and *Foculus*, next to the Glej Theatre at Gregorčičeva ulica 3 (small/large pizzas 710/830 SIT, salad bar 390/560 SIT). Other pizza-pasta places include *Pizzeria Romeo* in the Old Town opposite the Café Julija at Stari trg 6, *Napoli* off Trubarjeva cesta at Prečna ulica 7 and the *Čerin* at the eastern end of Trubarjeva cesta at Znamenjska ulica 2.

Meson Don Felipe, south-east of Krekov trg at Streliška ulica 22, is Ljubljana's first – and only – tapas bar (300 to 1000 SIT).

If you've a yen for some Chinese food, the location of the *Sichuan* below the Church of St Florian at Gornji trg 23 is wonderful, but the food is much more authentic at the *Zlati Pav*, Zarnikova ulica 3 (enter from Poljanska cesta 20), and nearby *Shanghai* at Poljanska cesta 14.

Cafés For coffee and cakes you might try the truncated *Evropa* café at Gosposvetska cesta 2 on the corner of Slovenska cesta or the *Slon* café in the Slon hotel at Slovenska cesta 34. Better still (at least for the views) is the *Terasa Nebotičnik*, a café on the top (12th) floor of the Art Deco Skyscraper building at the corner of Slovenska cesta and Štefanova ulica.

Self-Service & Fast Food Among the two cheapest places for lunch are the *Maxim* self-service restaurant in the basement of the Maximarket shopping arcade on Trg Republike, and *Daj-Dam* at Cankarjeva ulica 4, which has a vegetarian menu (750 SIT). But don't expect Cordon Bleu food; it's real school cafeteria stuff. The best self-service restaurant in Ljubljana, according to cognoscenti, is *Skriti Kot*, very much a 'Hidden Corner' in the shopping arcade below Trg Ajdovščina. Hearty main courses go for 350 to 750 SIT.

For a quick and very tasty lunch, try the fried squid (650 to 850 SIT) or whitebait (300 to 450 SIT) at *Ribca*, a basement seafood bar below the Plečnik Colonnade in Pogarčarjev trg.

There are *burek stands* (about 250 SIT) at several locations in Ljubljana and among the best are the one on Pražakova ulica next to Slovenijaturist and the one at Kolodvorska ulica 20 (open 24 hours). If you want something more substantial, head for the outdoor *Super 5*, which faces Slovenska cesta from the shopping mall in Trg Ajdovščina. It serves cheap and cheerful Balkan grills like čevapčiči (700 SIT) and pljeskavica (440 to 540 SIT) as well as sausage (klobasa; 750 SIT) and is open 24 hours.

Self-Catering The *supermarket* in the basement of the Maximarket shopping arcade on Trg Republike has about the largest selection in town (open weekdays 9 am to 8 pm, Saturday 8 am to 3 pm). But the best places for picnic supplies are the city's many delicatessens including *Delikatesa* at Kongresni trg 9 and *Burja* at No 11 of the same square.

Entertainment

Ask the TIC for its monthly programme of events in English called *Where to? in Ljubljana*.

Cinema For first-run films, head for the *Komuna* cinema at Cankarjeva ulica 1 or the *Union* cinema at Nazorjeva ulica 2. They generally have three screenings a day. The *Kompas* cinema, Miklošičeva cesta 38, shows art and classic films as does the *Kinoteka* at No 28 of the same street. Cinema tickets generally cost 400 to 650 SIT, and discounts are usually available at the first performance on weekdays.

Clubs The most popular conventional clubs are *Eldorado* at Nazorjeva ulica 4 and *Klub Central* next to the Turist hotel at Dalmatinova ulica 15. The student *Klub K4* at Kersnikova ulica 4 has a disco on some nights. Other popular venues at present for Ljubljana's young bloods are *Planet Life* in the BTC shopping centre at Šmartinska cesta 152g north-east of the train station (bus Nos 2, 7 & 12) and the *Klub Manhattan* in the Tivoli Recreation Centre in Tivoli Park (Celovška cesta 25).

Gay & Lesbian Ljubljana A popular spot for both gays and lesbians alike on Sunday night is the *Roza Klub* at the Klub K4. It's open from 10 pm to 4 am. At the Metelkova squat, Ljubljana's version of Christiania in Copenhagen between Metelkova ulica and Maistrova ulica, there's a café-pub for gays (Thursday night is reserved for lesbians) called *Club Tiffany*. The *Propaganda Klub* at Grabloviěeva ulica 1 has a gay and lesbian night on Friday called 'Does Your Momma Know?'.

Classical Music, Opera & Dance Ljubljana is home to two orchestras. Concerts are held in various locations all over town, but the main venue – with up to 700 cultural events a year – is *Cankarjev Dom* on Trg Republike. The ticket office (☎ 222 815) in the basement of the nearby Maximarket mall is open weekdays from 10 am to 2 pm and 4.30 to 8 pm, Saturday from 10 am to 1 pm and an hour before performances. Tickets cost anywhere between 1500 and 2500 SIT with gala performances as much as 6000 SIT. Also check for concerts at the beautiful *Filharmonija* at Kongresni trg 10.

The ticket office (☎ 125 4840) of the *Opera House*, Župančičeva ulica 1, where ballets are also performed, is open Monday to Friday from 11 am to 1 pm and an hour before each performance.

For tickets to the Ljubljana Summer Festival and anything else staged at the *Križanke*, go to the booking office (☎ 126 4340 or ☎ 226 544) behind the Ilirija Column at Trg Francoske Revolucije 1-2. It is open weekdays from 10 am to 2 pm and from 6 to 8 pm, on Saturday from 10 am to 1 pm and on Sunday one hour before the performance.

Rock & Jazz Ljubljana has a number of excellent rock clubs with canned or live music including *Orto Bar* at Grablovičeva ulica 1 and the *Rock Café*, Plečnikov trg 1. For jazz, you can't beat the *Gajo Jazz Club* at Beethovnova ulica 8 near the Parliament building.

Pubs & Bars Pleasant and congenial places for a *pivo* or glass of *vino* include the outdoor *Konjski Rep* (Horse's Tail) café-pub in Prešernov trg during the warmer months; *TrueBar*, Trubarjeva cesta 53; *Patrick's Irish Pub*, Prečna ulica 6; *Holidays' Pub* next to the Kompas travel agency at Slovenska cesta 36; and *P&M Bar* just off Trubarjeva cesta at Znamenjska ulica 1.

Getting There & Away
Bus You can reach virtually anywhere in the country by bus from the capital. If you're heading for Bled or Bohinj, take the bus not the train. The train from Ljubljana to the former will leave you at the Lesce-Bled station, 4km south-east of the lake. The closest train station to Lake Bohinj is at Bohinjska Bistrica, 6km to the east, and it's on the branch line linking Nova Gorica with Jesenice.

The timetable in the shed-like bus station (☎ 134 3838 for information) on Trg OF lists all routings and times, but here are some sample frequencies and one-way fares: Bled (hourly, 790 SIT); Bohinj (hourly, 1190 SIT); Jesenice (hourly, 890 SIT); Koper (nine to 13 a day, 1650 SIT); Maribor (half-hourly, 1660

SIT); Murska Sobota (eight a day, 2430 SIT); Novo Mesto (up to 10 a day, 940 SIT); Piran (six to 10 a day, 1710 SIT); Postojna (half-hourly, 720 SIT).

Buses from Ljubljana serve a number of international destinations including: Belgrade (one daily, 5360 SIT); Berlin (Wednesday at 7.30 pm, 15,821 SIT); Budapest (Tuesday, Thursday and Friday at 10 pm, 4590 SIT); Frankfurt (Wednesday at 7.30 pm, 12,885 SIT); Klagenfurt (Wednesday at 6.15 am, 1310 SIT); Lenti (Thursday at 5.30 am, 3070 SIT); Munich (Tuesday to Thursday at 5.05 or 5.30 am, 5215 SIT); Novigrad (daily at 1.45 pm, 2300 SIT); Prague (Tuesday, Thursday and Saturday at 9 pm, 6940 SIT); Rijeka (daily at 7.40 pm, 1020 SIT); Rovinj (daily at 1.45 pm, 3200 SIT); Split (daily at 7.40 pm, 3620 SIT); Stuttgart (Wednesday and Thursday at 7.30 pm, 10,802 SIT); Trieste (Monday to Saturday at 6.25 am, 1460 SIT); Varaždin (Saturday and Sunday at 6.35 am, 2810 SIT); and Zagreb (four a day, 2030 SIT).

Train All domestic and international trains arrive at and depart from the station (☎ 316 768 for information) at Trg OF 6. Local trains leave Ljubljana regularly for Bled (51km, 486 SIT); Jesenice (64km, 590 SIT); Koper (153km, 1011 SIT); Maribor (156km, 1011 SIT); Murska Sobota (216km, 1356 SIT); Novo Mesto (75km, 651 SIT); and Ptuj (155km, 1011 SIT). Return fares are usually 20% cheaper than double the price, and there's a 160 SIT surcharge on the domestic InterCity train tickets.

For information on international trains to/from Ljubljana, see the introductory Getting There & Away section of this chapter.

Getting Around
To/From the Airport Bus No 28 (350 SIT) makes the run between Ljubljana and Brnik airport, 23km to the north-west, 15 or 16 times a day Monday to Friday and seven times daily at the weekend. A taxi will cost between 4000 and 4500 SIT.

Bus Ljubljana's bus system, run by LPP (☎ 159 4114 for information), is excellent and very user-friendly. There are 22 lines; five of them (Nos 1, 2, 3, 6 and 11) are considered main lines. These start at 3.15 am and run till midnight while the rest operate from 5 am to 10.30 pm. You can pay on board (120 SIT) or use tiny yellow plastic tokens (75 SIT) available at newsstands, tobacconists, post offices and the two kiosks on the pavement in front of Slovenska cesta 55.

Car & Motorcycle Three international car-rental chains are Kompas Hertz (☎ 311 241), Mikloši̇čeva ulica 11; National (☎ 126 3118), Štefanova ulica 13; and Avis (☎ 132 3395), Čufarjeva ulica 2. They also have counters at the airport. Two excellent smaller agencies are ABC Rent a Car (☎ 064-261 684) at Brnik airport and Avtoimpex (☎ 555 025), Celovška cesta 150.

Taxi You can call a taxi on one of 10 numbers: ☎ 9700 to 9709.

Bicycle Two places to rent bicycles are Rog (☎ 315 868), next to Rozmanova ulica 1 (1500 SIT per day; open weekdays 8 am to 7 pm, Saturday till noon) and Kos Damjan (☎ 553 606) at Tugomerjeva ulica 35 (1000 SIT).

Julian Alps

Slovenia shares the Julian Alps in the north-west corner of the country with Italy. Three-headed Mt Triglav (2864m), the country's highest peak, is climbed regularly by thousands of weekend warriors, but there are countless less ambitious hikes on offer in the region. Lakes Bled and Bohinj make ideal starting points – Bled with its comfortable resort facilities, Bohinj right beneath the rocky crags themselves. Most of this spectacular area falls within the boundaries of Triglav National Park, established in 1924.

BLED
☎ 064

Bled (population 5664), a fashionable resort at just over 501m, is set on an idyllic, 2km-long emerald-green lake with a little island and church in the centre and a dramatic castle towering overhead. Trout and carp proliferate in the clear water, which is surprisingly warm and a pleasure to swim in or go boating on. To the north-east, the highest peaks of the Kara-

vanke range form a natural boundary with Austria; the Julian Alps lie to the west. Bled has been a favourite destination for travellers for decades. All in all, it *is* beautiful but it can get very crowded – and pricey – in season.

Orientation
Bled village is at the north-eastern end of the lake below the castle. The bus station is also here on Cesta Svobode, but the main Lesce-Bled train station is about 4km to the south-east. In addition there's Bled Jezero, a branchline train station north-west of the lake, not far from the camping ground.

Information
Tourist Offices The tourist office (☎ 741 122; fax 741 555) is next to the Park hotel at Cesta Svobode 15. Ask for the useful English booklet *Bled Tourist Information*. From April to October the office is open Monday to Saturday from 8 am to 7 pm (to 10 pm in July and August) and from 10 am to 6 pm on Sunday (to 8 pm in July and August). From November to March the hours are 9 am to 5 pm Monday to Saturday and noon to 4 or 5 pm on Sunday. Kompas (☎ 741 515) in the Triglav shopping centre at Ljubljanska cesta 4 sells good hiking maps. The Triglav National Park office information centre (☎ 741 188) is at Kidričeva cesta 2 on the lake's northern shore (open from 8 am to 3 pm on weekdays only).

Money Gorenjska Banka in the Park hotel shopping complex and across from the casino on Cesta Svobode is open from 9 to 11.30 am and 2 to 5 pm on weekdays and 8 to 11 am on Saturday. SKB Banka has a branch with an ATM in the Triglav shopping centre.

Post & Communications The main post office, open weekdays from 7 am to 7 pm and on Saturday till noon, is at Ljubljanska cesta 10.

Things to See
There are several trails up to **Bled Castle** (open daily, 400/200 SIT for adults/children), the easiest being the one going south from behind the hostel at Grajska cesta 17. The castle was the seat of the Bishops of Brixen

(South Tyrol) for over 800 years; set atop a steep cliff 100m above the lake, it offers magnificent views in clear weather. The castle's **museum** presents the history of the area and allows a peep into a small 16th-century chapel.

Bled's other striking feature is tiny **Bled Island** at the western end of the lake. The tolling 'bell of wishes' echoes across the lake from the tall white belfry rising above the dense vegetation. It's said that all who ring it will get their wish; naturally it chimes constantly. Underneath the present baroque church are the foundations of what was a pre-Romanesque chapel, unique in Slovenia. Most people reach the island on a *pletna*, a large gondola hand-propelled by a boatman. The price (1000 to 1200 SIT per person, depending on the season) includes a half-hour visit to the island, church and belfry. If there are two or three of you it would be cheaper and more fun to hire a rowing boat (about 1000/1200 SIT an hour for three/five people) from the Castle Baths on the shore below the castle, in Mlino or at the large beach to the south-west.

You can ride **horses** at the Villa Viktorija, Cesta Svobode 27/a, for 2000 SIT per hour.

Vintgar Gorge An excellent half-day hike from Bled features a visit to this lovely gorge 4.5km to the north-west. Head north-west on Prešernova cesta then north on Partizanska cesta to Cesta v Vintgar. This will take you to Podhom, where signs point the way to the gorge entrance. Or take the bus or train (from Bled Jezero station) to Podhom, from where it's a 1.5km walk westward to the main entrance (open daily from May to October; 300/200 SIT). A wooden footbridge hugs the rock wall for 1600m along the Radovna River, crisscrossing the raging torrent four times over rapids, waterfalls and pools before reaching **Šum Waterfall**. From there a trail leads over Hom Hill (834m) eastward to the ancient pilgrimage **Church of St Catherine**. The trail then leads due south through Zasip and back to Bled. From late June to mid-September an Alpetour bus makes the run from Bled's bus station to Vintgar daily at 9.30 am and returns at about noon.

Places to Stay

Camping *Zaka* camp site (☎ 741 117) is in a quiet valley at the western end of the lake about 2.5km from the bus station. The location is good and there's even a beach, tennis courts, a large restaurant and a supermarket, but Zaka fills up very quickly in summer. The camping ground is open from April to October and costs from 765 to 1080 SIT per person.

Hostel The *Bledec* hostel (☎ 745 250), Grajska cesta 17, is open year round except in November, and has a total of 56 beds in 13 rooms and costs DM20 per person (or DM26 with breakfast). Check in is from 7 am to 10 pm.

Private Rooms Finding a private room in Bled is easy. The travel agencies have extensive lists, and there are lots of houses around the lake with '*sobe*' or '*Zimmer frei*' signs. Kompas has single/double rooms with shared shower from 1800/2600 SIT to 2000/3400 SIT, depending on the category and season, and singles/doubles with shower from 2200/3400 SIT to 3300/5600 SIT. Apartments for two range from 4200 to 6500. The rooms and apartments from Globtour Bled (☎ 741 821) at the Krim hotel, Ljubljanska cesta 7, and ATS (☎ 741 736), at the Vezenine mall at Kajuhova ulica 1, cost about the same.

Hotel Most of Bled's hotels are pretty expensive affairs. Among the cheapest is the 138-bed *Lovec* (☎ 741 500; fax 741 021), Ljubljanska cesta 6, with singles/doubles in the height of summer from 7125/10,450 SIT while the waterfront old-world *Grand Hotel Toplice* (☎ 7910; fax 741 841) at Cesta Svobode 12, charges from a budget-busting 11,500/17,500 SIT at the same time. An affordable (and romantic) alternative is the eight-room *Vila Viktorija* (☎/fax 742 485) at Cesta Svobode 27/a, with singles from 4000 to 5000 SIT and doubles 5000 to 7000 SIT, depending on the season.

Places to Eat

Bled's best choice for an affordable meal is the homy *Gostilna Pri Planincu* at Grajska cesta 8, a stone's throw from the bus station.

BLED

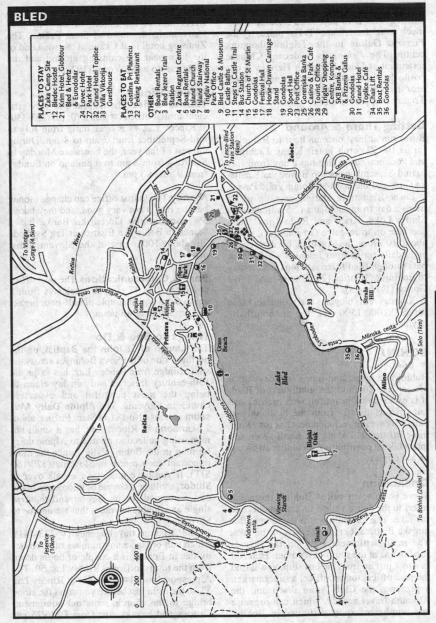

PLACES TO STAY
1 Zaka Camp Site
12 Bledec Hostel
21 Kredit Hotel Globtour
   Bled & Hertz
   & Eurodollar
24 Lovec Hotel
32 Park Hotel
32 Grand Hotel Toplice
33 Villa Viktorija
   Guesthouse

PLACES TO EAT
13 Gostilna Pri Planincu
22 Peking Restaurant

OTHER
2 Boat Rentals
3 Bled Jezero Train
   Station
4 Zaka Regatta Centre
5 Boat Rentals
6 Island Church
7 Island Stairway
8 Triglav National
   Park Office
9 Bled Castle & Museum
10 Castle Baths
11 Steps to Castle Trail
14 Bus Station
15 Church of St Martin
16 Gondolas
17 Festival Hall
18 Horse-Drawn Carriage
   Stand
19 Gondolas
20 Sport Hall
23 Post Office
25 Gorenjska Banka
26 Casino & Park Café
28 Tourist Office
29 Triglav Shopping
   Centre, Kompas,
   SKB Banka &
   & Pizzeria Gallus
30 Gondolas
31 Grand Hotel
   Toplice Café
34 Chair Lift
35 Boat Rentals
36 Gondolas

SLOVENIA

Excellent mushroom soup and grilled chicken with fries and salad shouldn't cost much more than 1800 SIT. For pizza, try the *Pizzeria Gallus* in the Triglav shopping centre. The *Peking* is a decent Chinese restaurant at Ulica Narodnih Herojev 3 opposite the Krim hotel. There's a small *market* near the bus station and a *supermarket* in the Triglav shopping centre.

Getting There & Around

Buses run at least once an hour to Bohinj as far as the Zlatorog hotel, Kranj, Ljubljana and Podhom-Zasip. One bus a day from July to mid-September goes to Bovec via Kranjska Gora and the heart-stopping Vršič Pass.

Lesce-Bled train station gets up to 15 trains a day from Ljubljana (55 minutes) via Škofja Loka, Kranj and Radovljica. They continue on to Jesenice (15 minutes), where about 10 cross the Austrian border. Up to eight daily trains from Jesenice via Podhom pass through Bled Jezero station on their way to Bohinjska Bistrica (20 minutes) and Nova Gorica (1¾ hours).

Kompas rents bicycles and mountain bikes for 500/1000/1500 SIT for an hour/half-day/day.

BOHINJ
☎ 064

Bohinj is a larger and much less developed glacial lake 26km to the south-west of Bled. It is exceedingly beautiful, with high mountains rising directly from the basin-shaped valley. There are secluded beaches for swimming off the trail along the north shore and many hiking possibilities, including an ascent of Mt Triglav.

Orientation

There is no town called Bohinj; the name refers to the entire valley, its settlements and the lake. The largest town in the area is Bohinjska Bistrica, 6km to the east of the lake. The main settlement right on the lake is Ribčev Laz at the south-east corner. Here, all in a row just up from the bus stop, you'll find the post office, tourist office, a supermarket, a pizzeria, the Club Amor disco and the Alpinum travel agency, which can organise any number of sport activities in Bohinj.

About 1km north across the Sava Bohinjka River and at the mouth of the Mostnica Canyon sits the town of Stara Fužina. The Zlatorog hotel is at Ukanc at the west end of the lake near the camping ground and the cable car up to Mt Vogel (1922m).

Information

Tourist Office The helpful and very efficient tourist office (☎ 723 370; fax 723 330) at Ribčev Laz 48 is open daily from July to mid-September from 7 am to 8 pm. During the rest of the year, the hours are Monday to Saturday from 8 am to 6 pm and on Sunday from 9 am to 3 pm.

Money The tourist office can change money but the rate is not very good, and they take a 3% commission. Gorenjska Banka has a branch in Bohinjska Bistrica at Trg Svobode 2b, about 100m east of the Slovenijaturist office.

Post & Communications The post office at Ribčev Laz 47 is open weekdays from 8 am to 6 pm with a couple of half-hour breaks and on Saturday till noon.

Things to See & Do

The **Church of St John the Baptist**, on the northern side of the Sava Bohinjka across the stone bridge from Ribčev Laz, has exquisite 15th-century frescoes and can lay claim to being the most beautiful and evocative church in Slovenia. The **Alpine Dairy Museum** at house No 181 in Stara Fužina, about 1.5km north of Ribčev Laz, has a small but interesting collection related to Alpine dairy farming in the Bohinj Valley, once the most important such centre in Slovenia (320/160 SIT). If you have time, take a walk over to **Studor**, a village a couple of kilometres to the east renowned for its *kozolci* and *toplarji*, single and double hayracks that are unique to Slovenia.

The Alpinum travel agency (☎ 723 441), which can organise any number of sport activities in Bohinj, is a couple of doors down from the tourist office at Ribčev Laz 50. The Alpinsport kiosk (☎ 723 486) at Ribčev Laz 53, to the right just before you cross the stone bridge to the church, rents out equipment. **Canoes** and **kayaks** cost from DM6/25 per hour/day. It also organises guided mountain tours and rafting trips on the Sava (DM35 to DM45) and 'canyoning' through the rapids of the Mostnica Gorge safely stuffed into a neoprene suit, life jacket and helmet for DM80.

The **Vogel cable car**, above the camping ground at the western end of Lake Bohinj about 5km from Ribčev Laz, will whisk you 1000m up into the mountains. It runs every half-hour year round except in November, from 7.30 am to 6 pm (till 8 pm in July and August). Adults/children pay 1000/700 SIT for a return ticket. From the upper station (1540m) you can scale **Mt Vogel** in a couple of hours for a sweeping view of the region.

Places to Stay
Camping The large and beautifully situated *Zlatorog* camping ground (☎ 723 441) on the lake near the Zlatorog hotel costs 900 to 1450 SIT per person, depending on the season; it's open from May to September.

Private Rooms The tourist office can arrange private singles/doubles with shower in Ribčev Laz, Stara Fužina and neighbouring villages for 1800/3000 SIT in the low season and up to 2300/3800 SIT in July and August (though there's always a 30% surcharge for stays of less than three days).

Places to Eat
The *MK*, a restaurant and pizzeria next to the Alpinum travel agency (Ribčev Laz 50), is very popular year round. If you've got wheels of any sort, head for *Gostišče Rupa* at house No 87 in Srednja Vas, about 5km north-east of Ribčev Laz. It has some of the best home-cooking in Slovenia. For a truly different lunch, try *Planšar* opposite the Alpine Dairy Museum at Stara Fužina 179. It specialises in homemade dairy products, and you can taste a number of local specialities for about 700 SIT. The *Mercator* supermarket at Ribčev Laz 49 is open weekdays from 7 am to 6.30 pm and to 5 pm on Saturday.

Getting There & Around
Bus services from Ribčev Laz to Ljubljana via Bled, Radovljica, Kranj and Bohinjska Bistrica are very frequent. There are also about six buses a day to Bohinjska Bistrica

via Stara Fužina, Studor and Srednja Vas. All of these buses stop near the post office on Triglavska cesta in Bohinjska Bistrica and in Ribčev Laz before carrying on to the Zlatorog hotel in Ukanc. The closest train station is at Bohinjska Bistrica on the Jesenice-Nova Gorica line.

Alpinum and Alpinsport rent bicycles and mountain bikes for DM7/30 per hour/day.

TREKKING MT TRIGLAV
The Julian Alps are among the finest hiking areas in central and eastern Europe. A mountain hut (*planinska koča* or *planinski dom*) is normally less than five hours' walk away. The huts in the higher regions are open from July to September, and in the lower regions from June to October. You'll never be turned away if the weather looks bad, but some huts on Triglav get very crowded at weekends, especially in August and September. A bed for the night should cost less than 1500 SIT per person. Meals are also available, so you don't need to carry a lot of gear. Leave most of your things below, but warm clothes, sturdy boots and good physical condition are indispensable.

The best months for hiking are August to October, though above 1500m you can encounter winter weather conditions at any time. Keep to the trails that are well marked with a red circle and a white centre, rest frequently and never *ever* try to trek alone. Before you set out, pick up a copy of the 1:20,000 *Triglav* map or the 1:50 000-scale *Julijske Alpe – Vzhodni Del (Julian Alps – Eastern Part)* published by the Alpine Association and available at bookshops and tourist offices.

The Route from Bohinj
An hour's hike west of the Zlatorog hotel at Ukanc is the **Savica Waterfall** (320/160 SIT), the source of the Sava River, which gushes from a limestone cave and falls 60m into a narrow gorge.

From the waterfall a path zigzags up the steep Komarča Crag. From the top of this cliff (1340m) there's an excellent view of Lake Bohinj. Further north, three to four hours from the falls, is the *Koča pri Triglavskih Jezerih* (mobile ☎ 0609-615 235; 1685m), a 104-bed hut at the southern end of the fantastic Triglav Lakes Valley where you'll spend the night. If you want a good overview of the valley and its seven permanent lakes (the others fill up in spring only), you can climb to Mt Tičarica (2091m) to the north-east in about one hour. An alternative – though longer – route from the waterfall to the Triglav Lakes Valley is via *Dom na Komni* (mobile ☎ 0609-611 221; 1520m) and the Komna Plateau.

On the second day, you hike up the valley, past the largest glacial lakes then north-east to the desert-like Hribarice Plateau (2358m). You descend to the Dolič Saddle (2164m) where the *Tržaška Koča na Doliču* (mobile ☎ 0609-614 780; 2152m) has 60 beds. You would have walked about four hours by now from the Koča pri Triglavskih Jezerih and could well carry on to *Dom Planika pod Triglavom* (mobile ☎ 0609-614 773; 2401m), about 1½ hours to the north-east, but this 80-bed hut fills up quickly.

From Dom Planika it's just over an hour to the summit of Triglav (2864m), a well trodden path indeed. Don't be surprised if you find yourself being turned over to have your bottom beaten with a birch switch. It's a long-established tradition for Triglav 'virgins'.

Soča Valley

BOVEC & KOBARID
☎ 065

The Soča Valley, defined by the bluer-than-blue Soča River, stretches from Triglav National Park to Nova Gorica and is one of the most beautiful and peaceful spots in Slovenia. Of course it wasn't always that way. During much of WWI, this was the site of the infamous Soča (or Isonzo) Front, which claimed the lives of an estimated one million people and was immortalised by the American writer Ernest Hemingway in his novel *A Farewell to Arms*. Today visitors flock to the town of **Kobarid** to relive these events at the award-winning **Kobarid Museum** (Gregorčičeva ulica 10; 500/400 SIT adults/students & children) or, more commonly, head for Bovec, 21km to the north, to take part in some of the best white-water rafting in Europe. The season lasts from April to October.

In Bovec, the people to see for the latter are Soča Rafting (☎ 196 200 or mobile ☎ 041-724 472) in the courtyard below the Alp hotel at Trg Golobarskih Žrtev 48 or Bovec Rafting Team (☎ 86 128) in the small kiosk further west on the same street opposite the Martinov Hram restaurant. Rafting trips on the Soča, taking between 1½ and 2½ hours with distances of from 10 to 21km, cost 4500 to 10,800 SIT (including neoprene long john, wind cheater, life jacket, helmet and paddle). A kayak costs from 2880 SIT for the day (3560 SIT with all equipment); a two-person canoe is 5570 SIT. There are kayaking courses on offer in summer (eg a two-day intensive course for beginners costs 9600 SIT).

In Kobarid, the tourist office in the Kobarid Museum (☎ 85 055) and, in Bovec, the Avrigo Tours agency (☎ 86 123) next to the Alp hotel at Trg Golobarskih Žrtev 47 can organise *private rooms* from 1700/3400 SIT for a single/double. There are four camping grounds in Bovec (*Polovnik*, ☎ 86 069, is the closest) and one in Kobarid (*Koren*, ☎ 85 312).

Getting There & Away
There are up to six buses a day between Kobarid and Bovec and to Tolmin. Other destinations include Ljubljana (two to five), Nova Gorica (four to six) and Cerkno (up to five). In July and August there's a daily bus to Ljubljana via the Vršič Pass and Kranjska Gora.

Karst Region

POSTOJNA
☎ 067

Vying with Bled as the top tourist spot in Slovenia, **Postojna Cave** continues to attract the hordes, but many travellers feel they've seen Disneyland after their visit – especially if they've first been to the more natural Škocjan Caves, 33km to the south-west. Visitors get to see about 5.7km of the cave's 27km on a 1½-hour tour in their own language; about 4km are covered by an electric train that will shuttle you through colourfully lit karst formations along the so-called Old Passage and the remaining 1700m is on foot. The tour ends with a viewing of a tank full of *Proteus anguinus*, the unique salamander-like beasties inhabiting Slovenia's karst caves. Dress warmly as the cave is a constant 8°C (with 95% humidity) all year.

From May to September, tours leave daily on the hour between 9 am and 6 pm. In March and April and again in October there are tours at 10 am, noon, 2 and 4 pm with an extra daily one at 5 pm in April and additional tours at the weekend in October at 11 am and 1, 3 and 5 pm. Between November and February, tours leave at 10 am and 2 pm on weekdays with extra ones added at noon and 4 pm at the weekend and on public holidays. Admission costs 1900/950 SIT for adults/ students & children.

If you have extra time, visit **Predjama Castle** (500/250 SIT), the awesome 16th-century fortress perched in the gaping mouth of a hilltop cavern 9km north-west of Postojna. As close as you'll get from Postojna by local bus (and during the school year only), though, is Bukovje, a village about 2km north-east of Predjama. A taxi from Postojna plus an hour's wait at the castle costs 5000 SIT.

Orientation & Information

The cave is about 2km north-west of Postojna's bus centre and bus station. The train station is a kilometre south-east of the centre. The unhelpful tourist office (☎ 24 477), Tržaška cesta 4, is open weekdays from 8 am to 6 pm (7 pm in summer) and till noon on Saturday. Kompas (☎ 24 281) at Titov trg 2a has *private rooms* from 2100 SIT per person.

Getting There & Away

Postojna is a day trip from Ljubljana or a stopover on the way to/from the coast or Croatian Istria; almost all buses between the capital and the coast stop there. There are direct trains to Postojna from Ljubljana (67km, one hour) and Koper (86km, 1½ hours).

ŠKOCJAN CAVES
☎ 067

These caves, near the village of Matavun 4km south-east of Divača (between Postojna and Koper), have been heavily promoted since 1986 when they were entered on UNESCO's World Heritage List. There are seven 1½-hour tours a day from June to September at 10 and 11.30 am and on the hour from 1 to 5 pm. In April, May and October

they leave at 10 am and at 1 and 3.30 pm. From November to March, there's a daily visit at 10 am and an extra one at 3 pm on Sunday and holidays. The entry fee is 1500 SIT for adults and 1000 SIT for children aged six to 12. These caves are in more natural surroundings – some consider a visit the highlight of their stay in Slovenia – than Postojna Cave but tough to reach without your own transport. From the train station at Divača (up to a dozen trains daily to/from Ljubljana), you can follow a path leading south-east through the village of Dolnje Ležeče to Matavun. The driver of any bus heading along the highway to/from the coast will let you off at the access road (there are huge signs announcing the caves) if you ask in advance. From there you can walk the remaining 1.5km to the caves' entrance.

The Coast

KOPER
☎ 066

Koper (population 24,400), only 21km south of Trieste, is the first of several quaint old coastal towns along the north side of the Istrian Peninsula. The town's Italian name, Capodistria, recalls its former status as capital of Istria under the Venetian Republic in the 15th and 16th centuries. After WWII, Koper's port was developed to provide Slovenia with an alternative to Italian Trieste and Croatian Rijeka. Once an island but now firmly connected to the mainland by a causeway, the Old Town's medieval flavour lingers despite the surrounding industry, container ports, high-rise buildings and motorways beyond its 'walls'. This administrative centre and largest town on the Slovene coast makes a good base for exploring the region.

Orientation

The bus and train stations are adjacent about a kilometre south-east of the Old Town at the end of Kolodvorska cesta.

Information

Tourist Office The tourist office (☎ 273 791), opposite the marina at Ukmarjev trg 7, is open June to September Monday to Saturday from 9 am to 10 pm and on Sunday from

10 am to 3 pm. During the rest of the year the hours are 9 am to 2 pm and 5 to 9 pm (till 1 pm on Sunday).

Money Nova Ljubljanska Banka, Pristaniška ulica 45, is open from 8.30 am till noon and from 3.30 to 6 pm on weekdays only. There are also a couple of private exchange offices on Pristaniška ulica, including Maki at No 13 and Feniks in the east wing of the large shopping complex and market across the street at No 2. Both are open from 7 or 7.30 am to 7 pm weekdays and to 1 pm on Saturday.

Post & Communications There's a post office at Muzejski trg 3 near the regional museum open weekdays from 8 am to 7 pm and on Saturday till 1 pm.

Things to See

From the stations you enter Prešernov trg through the **Muda Gate** (1516). Walk past the bridge-shaped **Da Ponte Fountain** (1666) and into Čevljarska ulica (Shoemaker's Street), a narrow pedestrian way that opens onto Titov trg, the medieval central square. Most of the things to see in Koper are clustered here.

The 36m-high **City Tower** (1480), which you can climb daily, stands next to the mostly 18th-century **Cathedral of St Nazarius**. The lower portion of the cathedral's façade is Gothic, the upper part Renaissance. To the north is the sublime **Loggia** (1463), now a café and gallery, and to the south the **Praetorian Palace** (1452), both good examples of the Venetian Gothic style. On the narrow lane behind the cathedral is a 12th-century Romanesque baptistry called the **Carmine Rotunda**. Trg Brolo to the east of the cathedral contains several more old Venetian buildings, including the **Brutti Palace**, now a library, at No 1 and the **Fontico**, a 14th-century granary, at No 4.

The **Koper Regional Museum**, open weekdays from 9 am to 1 pm (in summer also from 6 to 8 pm) and on Saturday till noon, is in the Belgramoni-Tacco Palace at Kidričeva ulica 19. It contains old maps and photos of the port and coast, 16th to 18th-century Italianate sculptures and paintings, and copies of medieval frescoes.

Places to Stay

The closest camping grounds are at Ankaran (*Adria*, ☎ 528 322), about 10km to the north by road, and at Izola (*Jadranka*, ☎ 61 202), 8km to the west.

Both the tourist office and Kompas (☎ 272 346) at Pristaniška ulica 17 opposite the vegetable market have *private rooms* for 1500 to 2260 SIT per person, depending on the category and season. Apartments for two are 4000 to 5170 SIT. Both levy a 30% surcharge if you stay less than three nights. Most of the rooms are in the new town beyond the train station.

In July and August *Dijaški Dom Koper* (☎ 273 252), an official hostel at Cankarjeva ulica 5 in the Old Town east of Trg Brolo, rents 380 beds in triple rooms at DM19 (DM15 after three nights) per person. With breakfast the rate is DM21. The rest of the year only about 10 beds are available. An HI card will get you a 10% discount.

The only hotel in the Old Town, the 80-room *Triglav* (☎ 272 001 or ☎ 274 094; fax 23 598) at Pristaniška ulica 3, is relatively affordable: singles with shower and breakfast are 4400 to 7410 SIT, depending on the season and room category, and doubles 6080 to 11,800 SIT. The 100-room *Žusterna* (☎ 284 385; fax 284 409), the Triglav's sister hotel about 1.5 km west on the main coastal road (Istrska cesta), charges from 4500/6400 SIT to 6200/8200 SIT for singles/doubles.

Places to Eat

For fried dough on the go head for the *burek shop* at Kidričeva ulica 8. The little *Bife Diana* at Čevljarska ulica 36 has čevapčiči, hamburgers and so on. A pizzeria called *Atrij* with a courtyard out the back at Triglavska ulica 2 is open most days till 10 pm.

One of the most colourful places in Koper for a meal is the *Istrska Klet* in an old palace at Župančičeva ulica 39. Main courses are 600 to 1000 SIT and this is a good place to try Teran, the hearty red (almost purple) wine from the Karst and coastal wine-growing areas. The *Taverna*, in a 15th-century salt warehouse at Pristaniška ulica 1 opposite the marina, has some decent fish dishes and lunch menus at 850 and 1000 SIT.

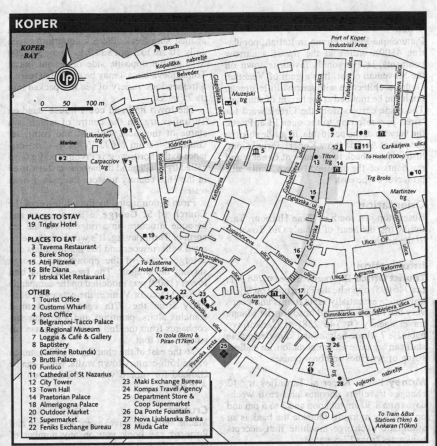

KOPER

KOPER BAY

Port of Koper Industrial Area

Beach

Kopališka nabrežje

Belveder

Muzejski trg

Glagoljaška ulica

Verdijeva ulica

Trubarjeva ulica

Dellavallejeva ulica

0   50   100 m

Ukmarjev trg

Ressljeva ulica

Kidričeva ulica

Kolodvorska

Cankarjeva ulica

To Hostel (100m)

Marina

Carpacciov trg

Kettejeva ulica

Gallusova

Martinžev trg

Trg Brolo

Župančičeva ulica

Triglavska ulica

Titov trg

Valvazojeva ulica

Cevljarska ulica

Tumova ulica

Ulica OF

Ulica Agrarne Reforme

To Žusterna Hotel (1.5km)

Pristaniška ulica

Gortanov trg

Dimnikarska ulica   Sabinjeva ulica

To Izola (8km) & Piran (17km)

Piranska cesta

Prešernov trg

Vojkovo nabrežje

To Train & Bus Stations (1km) & Ankaran (10km)

PLACES TO STAY
19 Triglav Hotel

PLACES TO EAT
3 Taverna Restaurant
6 Burek Shop
15 Atrij Pizzeria
16 Bife Diana
17 Istrska Klet Restaurant

OTHER
1 Tourist Office
2 Customs Wharf
4 Post Office
5 Belgramoni-Tacco Palace & Regional Museum
7 Loggia & Café & Gallery
8 Baptistery (Carmine Rotunda)
9 Brutti Palace
10 Fontico
11 Cathedral of St Nazarius
12 City Tower
13 Town Hall
14 Praetorian Palace
18 Almerigogna Palace
20 Outdoor Market
21 Supermarket
22 Feniks Exchange Bureau
23 Maki Exchange Bureau
24 Kompas Travel Agency
25 Department Store & Coop Supermarket
26 Da Ponte Fountain
27 Nova Ljubljanska Banka
28 Muda Gate

SLOVENIA

The large shopping centre and outdoor *market* (open most days from 7 am to 2 pm) on Pristaniška ulica also contains a *supermarket* and various *food shops*. The *Coop* supermarket in the big department store on Piranska cesta is open Monday to Saturday from 9 am to 7.30 pm.

Getting There & Away

There are buses almost every 20 minutes on weekdays to Piran (17km) and Portorož via Izola, and every 40 minutes at the weekend.

Buses also leave every hour or 90 minutes for Ljubljana via Divača and Postojna. You can also take the train to Ljubljana (2¼ hours), which is much more comfortable.

Up to 17 buses a day during the week depart for Trieste. The bus station in Trieste is immediately south-west of the train station in Piazza Libertà.

Destinations in Croatia include Buzet (three or four buses a day); Poreč (two or three); Pula (one or two); Rijeka (one); Rovinj (one); and Zagreb (two).

PIRAN
☎ 066

Picturesque Piran (Pirano in Italian; population 4800), sitting at the tip of a narrow peninsula, is everyone's favourite town on the Slovenian coast. It is a gem of Venetian Gothic architecture with narrow little streets, but it can be mobbed at the height of summer. The name derives from the Greek word for 'fire', *pyr*, referring to the ones lit at Punta, the very tip of the peninsula, to guide ships to the port at Aegida (now Koper). Piran's long history dates back to the ancient Greeks, and remnants of the medieval town walls still protect it to the east.

Orientation
Buses stop just south of Piran Harbour. Tartinijev trg, the heart of Piran's Old Town, is to the north.

Information
Tourist Office The tourist office (☎ 746 382; fax 746 095) opposite the Piran hotel on Stjenkova ulica essentially rents rooms and keeps very brief hours. Instead head for the Maona travel agency (☎ 746 228) at Cankarjevo nabrežje 7 whose helpful and knowledgeable staff can organise accommodation, an endless string of activities and boat cruises.

Money Banka Koper at Tartinijev trg 12 changes travellers cheques and cash weekdays from 8.30 am till noon and 3 to 5 pm and on Saturday morning. Outside the bank is an automatic exchange machine that accepts banknotes from 17 countries.

Post & Communications The post office at Cankarjevo nabrežje 5 is open weekdays from 8 am to 7 pm and till noon on Saturday.

Things to See
The **Maritime Museum**, in a 17th-century harbourside palace at Cankarjevo nabrežje 3, was under renovation at the time of writing. It has exhibits focusing on the three 'Ss' that have been so important to Piran's development over the centuries: the sea, sailing and salt-making (at Sečovlje south-east of Portorož). The museum's antique model ships are very fine; other rooms are filled with old figureheads, weapons and votive folk paintings placed in church for protection against shipwreck. Piran's **aquarium** (open daily 10 am to 1 pm and 2 to 7 pm; 300/200 SIT) on the opposite side of the marina at Tomažičeva ulica 4 may be small, but there's a tremendous variety of sea life packed into its 25 tanks.

The **town hall** and **court house** stand on Tartinijev trg, in the centre of which is a statue of the local violinist and composer Giuseppe Tartini (1692-1770). A short distance to the north-west is Prvomajski trg (also called trg Maja) and its baroque **cistern**, used in the 18th century to store the town's fresh water.

Piran is dominated by the tall tower of the **Church of St George**, a Renaissance and baroque structure on a ridge above the sea north of Tartinijev trg. It's wonderfully decorated with frescoes and has marble altars and a large statue of the eponymous George slaying the dragon. The free-standing **bell tower** (1609) was modelled on the campanile of San Marco in Venice; the octagonal **Baptistry** from the 17th century next to it contains altars, paintings and a Roman sarcophagus from the 2nd century later used as a baptismal font.

To the east of the church is a 200m stretch of the 15th-century **town walls**, which can be climbed for superb views of Piran and the Adriatic.

Cruises
Maona and other travel agencies in Piran and Portorož can book you on any number of cruises – from a loop that takes in the towns along the coast to day-long excursions to Venice, Trieste or Brioni National Park in Croatia.

From mid-May to October, the large catamaran *Marconi* goes down the Istrian coast in Croatia as far as the Brioni Islands and the national park there (two hours, 8500/8000 SIT return for adults/those over 60 and everyone on Wednesday), with a stop at Rovinj (1¼ hours, 4000/3500 SIT return). The boat leaves at 10 am and returns at about 6.45 pm except in September when it departs and returns 20 minutes earlier. At 8.35 pm (6.50 pm in September) on the same days the *Marconi* heads for Trieste (35 minutes,

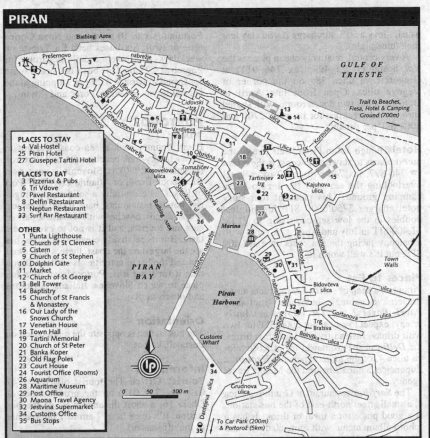

PIRAN

GULF OF TRIESTE

Trail to Beaches, Fiesa, Hotel & Camping Ground (700m)

PLACES TO STAY
4 Val Hostel
25 Piran Hotel
27 Giuseppe Tartini Hotel

PLACES TO EAT
3 Pizzerias & Pubs
6 Tri Vdove
7 Pavel Restaurant
8 Delfin Rzestaurant
31 Neptun Restaurant
33 Surf Bar Restaurant

OTHER
1 Punta Lighthouse
2 Church of St Clement
3 Cistern
9 Church of St Stephen
10 Dolphin Gate
11 Market
12 Church of St George
13 Bell Tower
14 Baptistry
15 Church of St Francis & Monastery
16 Our Lady of the Snows Church
17 Venetian House
18 Town Hall
19 Tartini Memorial
20 Church of St Peter
21 Banka Koper
22 Old Flag Poles
23 Court House
24 Tourist Office (Rooms)
26 Aquarium
28 Maritime Museum
29 Post Office
30 Maona Travel Agency
32 Jestvina Supermarket
34 Customs Office
35 Bus Stops

PIRAN BAY

Piran Harbour

Customs Wharf

To Car Park (200m) & Portorož (5km)

SLOVENIA

2000/4000 SIT one-way/return), returning the following morning.

The *Delfin* (mobile ☎ 0609-628 491) boat sails from Piran to the marina at Portorož via the Bernadin tourist complex (one hour, 800 to 1200 SIT) up to five times a day from April to October. In July and August the loop also takes in Fiesa and Strunjan.

Places to Stay
Camping The closest camping ground is *Camping Jezero Fiesa* (☎ 73 150) at Fiesa, 4km by road from Piran (but less than a kilo-

metre if you follow the coastal trail east of the Church of St George). It's in a quiet valley by two small, protected ponds, and close to the beach, but it gets very crowded in summer. It's open from June to September.

Private Rooms & Hostel The tourist offices in Piran and Portorož (☎ 747 015) and the Maona travel agency can arrange *private rooms* and *apartments* throughout the year, but the biggest choice is available in summer. Single rooms are 1880 to 2800 SIT, depending on the category and the season, while doubles are 2460 to 4700 SIT. Apartments for two are 4700 to 6110 SIT. They usually levy a 50% surcharge if you stay less then three nights.

A very central, relatively cheap place is the *Val* hostel (☎ 75 499; fax 746 911) at Gregorčičeva ulica 38a on the corner of Vegova ulica. Open from late April to October, it has two dozen rooms with shared shower and breakfast for between 2700 and 3000 SIT per person.

Hotel Though not in Piran itself one of the nicest places to stay on the coast is the *Fiesa* (☎ 746 897; fax 746 896), a 22-room hotel overlooking the sea near the Jezero Fiesa camping ground. This pleasant four-story hotel charges 3750/6000 SIT for singles/doubles in the low season, rising to 7125/11,400 SIT in July and August. A room with a balcony facing the sea costs an extra 400 SIT, but it's well worth it.

Places to Eat
Piran has a heap of seafood restaurants along Prešernovo nabrežje but most (including *Pavel*, *Pavel 2* and *Tri Vdove*) are fairly pricey; expect to pay about 5000 SIT for two with drinks. Instead try the local favourites: the *Delfin* near Prvomajski trg at Kosovelova ulica 4, or the more expensive *Neptun* at Župančičeva ulica 7 behind the Maona travel agency.

The *Surf Bar* restaurant at Grudnova ulica 1, a small street north-east of the bus station, is a good place for a meal or drink. It has a 'photo-album menu' with some 60 dishes and lots of pizzas. There are also several pizzerias along Prešernovo nabrežje near the Punta lighthouse/Church of St Clement, including *Palma* and *Zeko*. The *Jestvina* supermarket opposite Trg Bratstva 8 is open Monday to Saturday from 7 am to 8 pm.

Getting There & Away
The local bus company I&I (☎ 41 750 in Koper) links Piran with Portorož and Lucija (bus No 1); with Portorož and Fiesa (bus No 2; mid-April to August only); with Strunjan and Portorož (bus No 3); and with Portorož, Sečovlje and Padna (bus No 4). Schedules vary, but bus No 1 runs about every 10 to 15 minutes. The fare is 150 SIT.

Other destinations that can be reached from Piran include Ljubljana via Divača and Postojna (six to 10 a day) and Nova Gorica (one or two). Six buses head for Trieste on weekdays, and there's a daily departure for Zagreb at 4.25 am. One bus a day heads south for Croatian Istria at 4.25 pm, stopping at the coastal towns of Umag, Poreč and Rovinj.

PORTOROŽ
☎ 066

Every country with a sea coast has got to have a honky-tonk beach resort, and Portorož (population 2980) is Slovenia's very own Blackpool, Bondi or Atlantic City. The 'Port of Roses' is essentially a solid strip of high-rise hotels, restaurants, bars, travel agencies, shops, discos, beaches with turnstiles, parked cars and tourists, and it is not to everyone's taste. But its relatively clean, sandy beaches are the largest on the coast, there's a pleasant spa and the list of activities is endless. If you take it for what it is, Portorož can be a fun place to watch Slovenes, Italians, Austrians and others at play.

Orientation
The bus station is opposite the main beach on Postajališka pot.

Information
Tourist Office The tourist office (☎ 747 015; fax 747 013) on the ground floor of Obala 16, a short distance west of the bus station. It's open from 9 am to 7 pm (earlier in the off season).

Money Banka Koper below the Slovenija hotel at Obala 33 is open from 8.30 till noon and 3 to 5 pm on weekdays and on Saturday morning. It has an automatic exchange machine outside which accepts the banknotes of 18 countries. Feniks, a *bureau de change* next to the tourist office gives a good rate and does not charge commission. It's open from 9 am to 10 pm seven days a week. The SKB Banka at Obala 53 has a Cirrus-linked ATM.

Post & Communications The post office is at K Stari cesta 1 opposite the now empty Palace hotel (1891). It is open weekdays from 8 am to 7 pm and on Saturday till noon.

Activities

The beaches at Portorož, including the main one accommodating 6000 bodies, are 'managed' so you'll have to pay 350 SIT (250 SIT for children) to use them. They are open from 9 am to 7 pm in season. Umbrellas and deck chairs are available for 400 SIT.

The Terme Palace spa complex, just beyond the post office on K Stari cesta, is famous for thalassotherapy (treatment using sea water and its by-products). It is open Monday to Saturday from 7 am to 7 pm. The palatial indoor swimming pool here is open daily from 7 am to 9 pm. It costs 600/800 SIT for two/four hours on weekdays, 900/1200 SIT at the weekend, and 1000/1500 for the period from 1 to 9 pm on weekdays/at the weekend.

Places to Stay

The *Lucija* camping ground (☎ 771 027) has two locations. The 2nd-category site (1000 to 1200 SIT per person) is south-east of the marina at the end of Cesta Solinarjev less than 2km from the bus station, and the 1st-category site (1200 to 1400 SIT), 600km to

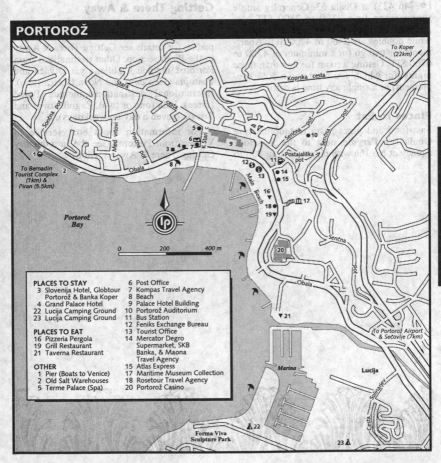

PORTOROŽ

Portorož Bay

To Bernadin
Tourist Complex
(1km) &
Piran (5.5km)

To Koper
(22km)

Koprska cesta

Postajališka pot

0   200   400 m

PLACES TO STAY
3 Slovenija Hotel, Globtour Portorož & Banka Koper
4 Grand Palace Hotel
22 Lucija Camping Ground
23 Lucija Camping Ground

PLACES TO EAT
16 Pizzeria Pergola
19 Grill Restaurant
21 Taverna Restaurant

OTHER
1 Pier (Boats to Venice)
2 Old Salt Warehouses
5 Terme Palace (Spa)

6 Post Office
7 Kompas Travel Agency
8 Beach
9 Palace Hotel Building
10 Portorož Auditorium
11 Bus Station
12 Feniks Exchange Bureau
13 Tourist Office
14 Mercator Degro Supermarket, SKB Banka, & Maona Travel Agency
15 Atlas Express
17 Maritime Museum Collection
18 Rosetour Travel Agency
20 Portorož Casino

To Portorož Airport
& Sečovlje (7km)

Marina

Lucija

Forma Viva
Sculpture Park

the west, is on the water. Both camps are open from May to September and get very crowded in summer.

The tourist office's accommodation service (☎ 746 199), on the mezzanine floor of Obala 16, has *private rooms* and *apartments* and is open daily from 9 am to 1 pm and 4 to 7 pm. You can also book them through Atlas Express (☎ 746 772) at Obala 55, just south of the bus station; Kompas (☎ 747 032), Obala 41; Globtour Portorož (☎ 73 356) in the Slovenija hotel at Obala 33; Rosetour (☎ 747 255) opposite the Maritime Museum Collection at Obala 16a; and Maona (☎ 746 423) at Obala 53. Generally single rooms range from 1800 to 2800 SIT, depending on the category and the season, while doubles are 2460 to 4700 SIT. Apartments for two go for a minimum of 4700 to 6700 SIT. Getting a room for less than three nights (for which you must pay a 50% supplement) or a single any time is difficult.

Places to Eat

Fast-food and pizza-pasta restaurants line Obala (eg *Pergola* next to the Rosetour agency at No 16a with pizzas costing 700 to 1000 SIT). But if you want a proper sit-down meal, the terrace at the *Taverna* in the sports field at Obala 22 looks out over the marina and the bay. The *Grill* restaurant, often with something large being roasted on a spit near the entrance, faces the main beach at Obala 20 and has an attractive covered terrace and a menu at 1100 SIT.

The *Mercator Degro* supermarket is a few steps away from the bus station. It is open weekdays from 7 am to 8 pm, Saturdays to 6 pm and Sunday from 8 am to 11 am.

Getting There & Away

Local I&I buses link Portorož with Piran, Strunjan, Fiesa, Lucija, Sečovlje and Podpadna; for details see Getting There & Away in the Piran section. Other destinations from Portorož include Ljubljana via Divača and Postojna (10 a day) and Nova Gorica (two). International destinations include Poreč (three), Pula (one or two), Zagreb (two) and Trieste (seven a day on weekdays).

For information about boat service to Venice from Portorož, see the introductory Getting There & Away section.

Yugoslavia (Југославија)

The new Federal Republic of Yugoslavia (SRJ), made up of Serbia and Montenegro, occupies the heart of the Balkan Peninsula astride the main road, rail and river routes from Western Europe to Asia Minor.

Since the withdrawal of Croatia, Slovenia, Bosnia-Hercegovina and Macedonia in 1991, Yugoslavia (Jugoslavija) seems to have become a mere 'Greater Serbia', with oppressed Hungarian, Slavic Muslim and Albanian minorities.

This tragic outcome and the continuing ethnic strife have cast a pall over a country still rich in mountains, rivers, seascapes, cultures, customs, cuisines and peoples. Now shorn of most of its coastal tourist resorts, rump Yugoslavia seems destined to be forgotten by the world of mass tourism. However, awaiting those visitors who do stray beyond the transit corridors to Turkey and Greece are the glorious gorges and beaches of Montenegro, the mystical Orthodox monasteries of southern Serbia and Kosovo, the imposing fortresses along the Danube, and hundreds of other tangible traces of a tumultuous history stretching back thousands of years.

United Nations (UN) sanctions have come and gone and seem to have barely dented Yugoslavia's pride, though the country's recent ventures against Kosovar Albanians have yet again tainted its reputation and brought renewed sanctions against the country.

Yugoslavia's tourist economy, though severely compromised as a result of internal upheavals and to a lesser degree by sanctions, is suffering and while the security of travellers in lesser volatile areas is guaranteed, travellers should avoid potential political and military hotspots and undertake travel in the country with a certain spirit of adventure.

Facts about Yugoslavia

HISTORY

The original inhabitants of this region were the Illyrians, followed by the Celts, who

AT A GLANCE

Capital	Belgrade
Population	11.3 million (Serbia 10.5 million Montenegro 680,000)
Area	102,350 sq km (Serbia 88,412 sq km Montenegro 13,938 sq km)
Official Language	Croatian/Serbian
Currency	1 Yugoslav Novi Dinar (DIN) = 100 paras
GDP	US$21 billion (1996)
Time	GMT/UTC+0100

arrived in the 4th century BC. The Roman conquest of Moesia Superior (Serbia) began in the 3rd century BC and under Augustus the empire extended to Singidunum (Belgrade) on the Danube. In 395 AD Theodosius I divided the empire and what is now Serbia passed to the Byzantine Empire, while Croatia remained part of the Western Roman Empire.

In the middle of the 6th century, Slavic tribes (Serbs, Croats and Slovenes) crossed

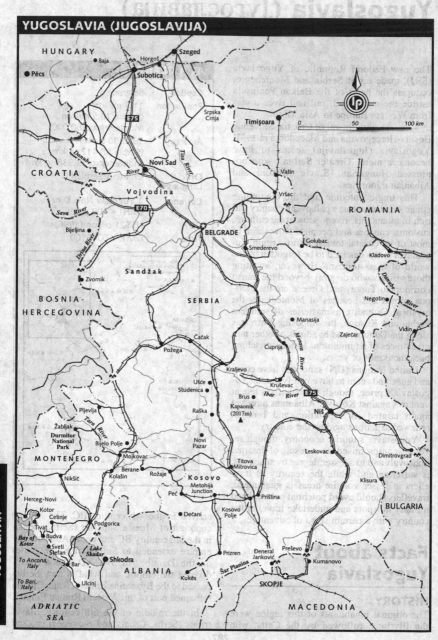

YUGOSLAVIA (JUGOSLAVIJA)

the Danube in the wake of the Great Migration of Nations and occupied much of the Balkan Peninsula. In 879 the Serbs were converted to the Orthodox Church by Sts Cyril and Methodius. In 969 Serbia broke free from Byzantium and established an independent state; however, Byzantium re-established its authority in the 11th century.

An independent Serbian kingdom returned in 1217 and during the reign of Stefan Dušan (1346-55) Serbia was a great power including much of present Albania and northern Greece within its boundaries. Numerous frescoed Orthodox monasteries were erected during this Serbian 'Golden Age'. After Stefan's death Serbia declined, and at the Battle of Kosovo on 28 June 1389 the Serbian army was defeated by the Ottoman Turks, ushering in 500 years of Islamic rule. The Serbs were pushed north as the Turks advanced into Bosnia in the 15th century and the city-state of Venice occupied the coast. By 1459 Serbia was a Turkish *pashalik* (province) and the inhabitants had become mere serfs. In 1526 the Turks defeated Hungary at the Battle of Mohács, expanding their realm north and west of the Danube.

The first centuries of Turkish rule brought stability to the Balkans but, as the power of the sultan declined, local Turkish officials and soldiers began to oppress the Slavs. After their defeat at Vienna in 1683, the Turks began a steady retreat.

By 1699 they had been driven out of Hungary and many Serbs moved north into Vojvodina, where they enjoyed Habsburg protection. Through diplomacy the sultan regained northern Serbia for another century, but a revolt in 1815 led to de facto Serbian independence in 1816.

Serbia's autonomy was recognised in 1829, the last Turkish troops departed in 1867, and in 1878, after Russia's defeat of Turkey in a war over Bulgaria, complete independence was achieved. Montenegro also declared itself independent of Turkey in 1878. Macedonia remained under Turkish rule into the 20th century.

The 20th Century

Tensions mounted after Austria's annexation of Bosnia-Hercegovina in 1908, with Russia backing Serbia. There was more overt trouble in Macedonia; in the First Balkan War (1912), Serbia, Greece and Bulgaria combined against Turkey for the liberation of Macedonia. The Second Balkan War (1913) saw Serbia and Greece join forces against Bulgaria, which had claimed all of Macedonia for itself. At about this time Serbia wrested control of Kosovo from Albania with the help of the Western powers.

WWI was an extension of these conflicts as Austria-Hungary used the assassination of Archduke Ferdinand by a Serb nationalist on 28 June 1914 as an excuse to invade Serbia. Russia and France came to Serbia's aid, while Germany backed Austria. Thus began 'the war to end all wars'. In the winter of 1915-16 a defeated Serbian army of 155,000 retreated across the mountains of Montenegro to the Adriatic from where it was evacuated to Corfu. In 1918 these troops fought their way back up into Serbia from Thessaloniki, Greece.

After WWI, Croatia, Slovenia and Vojvodina were united with Serbia, Montenegro and Macedonia to form the Kingdom of Serbs, Croats and Slovenes under the king of Serbia. In 1929 the name was changed to Yugoslavia. The Vidovdan constitution of 1921 created a centralised government dominated by Serbia. This was strongly opposed by the Croats and other minorities, forcing King Alexander to end the political turmoil by declaring a personal dictatorship in 1929. The 1934 assassination of the king by a Macedonian terrorist with links to Croat separatists brought to power a regent who continued the Serbian dictatorship. Corruption was rampant and the regent tilted towards friendship with Nazi Germany.

On 25 March 1941, Yugoslavia joined the Tripartite Alliance, a fascist military pact, after being promised Greek Macedonia and Thessaloniki by the Germans. This sparked mass protest demonstrations and a military coup that overthrew the profascist regency. Peter II was installed as king and Yugoslavia abruptly withdrew from the alliance. Livid, Hitler ordered an immediate invasion and the country was carved up between Germany, Italy, Hungary and Bulgaria. In Croatia, a fascist puppet state was set up which massacred hundreds of thousands of ethnic Serbs and Jews.

Almost immediately the Communist Party, under Josip Broz Tito, declared an armed uprising. There was also a monarchist resistance group, the Četniks, but they proved far less effective than Tito's partisans, and after 1943 the British gave full backing to the communists. A 1943 meeting of the Antifascist Council for the National Liberation of Yugoslavia (AVNOJ) at Jajce, in Bosnia, laid the basis for a future communist-led Yugoslavia.

The partisans played a major role in WWII by tying down huge Italian and German armies, but Yugoslavia suffered terrible losses, especially in Croatia and Bosnia-Hercegovina, where most of the fighting took place. According to the Serbian author Bogoljub Kočović some 487,000 Serbs, 207,000 Croats, 86,000 Muslims, 60,000 Jews, 50,000 Montenegrins, 32,000 Slovenes, 7000 Macedonians and 6000 Albanians died in the war. The resistance did, however, guarantee Yugoslavia's postwar independence.

Postwar Communism

In 1945 the Communist Party (which had been officially banned since 1920) won control of the national assembly, which in November abolished the monarchy and declared Yugoslavia a federal republic. Serbia's size was then greatly reduced when Bosnia-Hercegovina, Montenegro and Macedonia were granted republic status within this 'second' Yugoslavia. The Albanians of Kosovo and Hungarians of Vojvodina were denied republics of their own, however, on the pretext that they were not nations because their national homelands were outside the boundaries of Yugoslavia. Under Tito's slogan *bratstva i jedinstva* (brotherhood and unity), nationalist tendencies were suppressed.

Tito broke with Stalin in 1948 and, as a reward, received US$2 billion in economic and military aid from the USA and UK between 1950 and 1960. For the West this was a cheap way of protecting NATO's southern flank, but for Yugoslavia the Western subsidies alleviated the need for reform, contributing to the economic problems of today.

After the break with the USSR, Yugoslavia followed its own 'road to socialism' based on a federal system, self-management, personal

freedom and nonalignment. The decentralisation begun in 1951 was to lead to the eventual 'withering away of the state' of classical Marxism. Yugoslavia never became a member of either the Warsaw Pact or NATO, and in 1956 the country played a key role in the formation of the nonaligned movement.

The 1960s witnessed an economic boom in the north-west accompanied by liberalisation throughout the country, and in July 1966 Tito fired his hardline secret police chief Alexander Ranković. Growing regional inequalities led, however, to increased tension as Slovenia, Croatia and Kosovo demanded greater autonomy within the federation. In 1971 Tito responded with a 'return to Leninism', which included a purge of party reformers and a threat to use military force against Croatia.

With the most talented members of the leadership gone, Yugoslavia stagnated through the 1970s while borrowing billions of recycled petrodollars from the West. A 1970 constitutional amendment declared that the federal government would have control of foreign policy, defence, trade, the national economy and human rights, and all residual powers were vested in the six republics (Croatia, Bosnia-Hercegovina, Macedonia, Montenegro, Serbia and Slovenia) and two autonomous provinces of Serbia (Kosovo and Vojvodina). The 1974 constitution strengthened the powers of the autonomous provinces.

After Tito

Tito died in 1980 and the presidency then became a collective post rotated annually among nine members who were elected every four years by the national assembly, the six republics and the two autonomous provinces. This cumbersome system proved unable to solve either Yugoslavia's deepening economic problems or its festering regional and ethnic antagonisms.

In 1986 a working group of the Serbian Academy of Sciences prepared a memorandum calling on Serbia to reassert its hegemony in Yugoslavia. A year later Slobodan Milošević took over as party leader in Serbia by portraying himself as the champion of an allegedly persecuted Serbian minority in Kosovo. Milošević hoped to restore the flagging popularity of the League of Communists by inciting the Serbs' latent anti-Albanian sentiments. When moves by Serbia to limit Kosovo's autonomy led to massive protest demonstrations in the province in late 1988 and early 1989, the Serbian government unilaterally scrapped Kosovo's autonomy. Thousands of troops were sent to intimidate Kosovo's 90% Albanian majority, and in direct confrontations with the security forces dozens of civilians were shot dead.

Milošević's vision of a 'Greater Serbia' horrified residents of Slovenia and Croatia, who elected non-communist republican governments in the spring of 1990. These called for the creation of a loose Yugoslav 'confederation' which would allow Slovenia and Croatia to retain most of their wealth for themselves, and both republics threatened to secede from Yugoslavia if such reforms were not forthcoming. In the Serbian elections of December 1990, however, Milošević's policies paid off when the communists won 194 of 260 seats (the Albanians boycotted the election). In the other republics communists managed to hold on to Montenegro but lost Bosnia-Hercegovina and Macedonia.

In March 1991 Serbia's state-controlled media broadcast false reports of a massacre of ethnic Serbs in Croatia in an attempt to precipitate a crisis leading to a military takeover. This outraged prodemocratic Serbian students who, led by Serbian Renewal Movement leader Vuk Drašković, massed outside the TV studios in Belgrade demanding that those responsible be sacked.

Civil War

On 25 June 1991 Slovenia and Croatia declared themselves independent of Yugoslavia. This soon led to fighting as the federal army moved into Slovenia. Fearing a tidal wave of refugees, the European Community (EC), now known as the European Union (EU), rushed a delegation of foreign ministers to Yugoslavia to negotiate a truce, which soon broke down. In Belgrade, Milošević went on TV to reaffirm his support for Yugoslavia and the right of people to continue to live in it. He said the Yugoslav People's Army would intervene to defend Serbs wherever they lived.

On 7 July, federal and republican leaders met on Brijuni Island off Istria in the hope of preventing a full-scale civil war, while the EC imposed a weapons embargo on Yugoslavia and froze US$1 billion in aid and credits. It soon became clear that the matter would be decided in Croatia; on 18 July the Yugoslav government announced that all federal troops would be withdrawn from Slovenia within three months.

Intervention by the federal army on the side of Serb separatists in Croatia led to months of heavy fighting, with widespread property damage and thousands of casualties. The EC sent unarmed cease-fire monitors to the trouble areas in September and organised a peace conference in the Netherlands but this failed, and in November the EC applied economic sanctions against Serbia and Montenegro. On 20 December 1991 the federal prime minister, Ante Marković (a Croat), resigned after the army demanded 81% of the 1992 budget.

In December it was agreed that a UN peacekeeping force would be sent to Croatia and from 3 January 1992 a cease-fire generally held. On 15 January the EC recognised the independence of Croatia and Slovenia, whereupon both Macedonia and Bosnia-Hercegovina demanded recognition of their own independence. Montenegro alone voted to remain in Yugoslavia. The secession of Bosnia-Hercegovina, with its large Serb population, sparked bitter fighting as Serb militants with army backing again used force to seize territory, as they had done in Croatia.

The Third Yugoslavia

On 27 April 1992 a 'third' Yugoslav federation was declared by Serbia and Montenegro in a rushed attempt to escape blame for the bloodshed in Bosnia-Hercegovina. The rump state disclaimed responsibility for the federal army in Bosnia-Hercegovina and announced that all soldiers hailing from Serbia and Montenegro would be withdrawn.

In May 1992, with Sarajevo under siege and the world losing patience with what was seen as Serbian aggression, the UN Security Council passed a sweeping package of economic and diplomatic sanctions against Yugoslavia. In mid-July US and Western European warships began patrolling the Adriatic off Montenegro to monitor the embargo. Yugoslavia was denied its old seat at the UN in

September 1992 and in November a UN naval blockade was imposed. Sanctions against Yugoslavia were greatly strengthened in April 1993 after the Serb side rejected a peace plan for Bosnia-Hercegovina. Yet, despite severe economic hardship, the socialists won the December 1993 elections.

With the division of Bosnia into Serb and Croat-Muslim states in late 1995, the dream of a 'Greater Serbia' seemed close to reality, stained with the blood of tens of thousands of unfortunate people and soiled by the ashes of their burned homes.

Meanwhile, five years of hostile relations with Croatia officially ended in August 1996, with the signing of a landmark treaty which recognised national borders and normalised relations between the two countries.

In the winter of 1996/97 the Milošević government clumsily attempted to overturn local elections, leading to widespread and daily street marches fronted by a coalition grouping called *Zajedno* (Together). Zajedno ultimately hoped to topple the Milošević government, but after he backtracked and reinstated the election results the street marches fizzled out

The new constitution of rump Yugoslavia had made no mention of 'autonomous provinces', and the Albanian majority in Kosovo, long brutally repressed by Serbia, finally erupted in January 1998 with the Serb military and police machine moving in to systematically wipe out Albanian Kosovar resistance leaders in Kosovo, provoking a storm of protest from the West but no reaction other than a re-imposition of an arms embargo. By May 1998 the situation was volatile and still threatened to disrupt peace in the wider region. (See the Kosovo section later in this chapter for background information).

GEOGRAPHY

Mountains and plateaus account for the lower half of this 102,173-sq-km country (the size of the US state of Virginia), the remainder being the Pannonian Plain, which is drained by the Sava, Danube and Tisa rivers in the north-east. Yugoslavia's interior and southern mountains belong to the Balkan range, and the coastal range is an arm of the Alps. Most of the rivers flow north into the Danube, which runs through Yugoslavia for 588km. In the south many smaller rivers have cut deep canyons in the plateau, which make for memorable train rides.

When the country split up in 1991, most of the Adriatic coast went to Slovenia and Croatia, though the scenically superb 150km Montenegrin coast remains in Yugoslavia. The Bay of Kotor here is the only real fjord in southern Europe, and Montenegro's Durmitor National Park has ex-Yugoslavia's largest canyon. Between Ulcinj and Albania is one of the longest beaches on the eastern Adriatic.

GOVERNMENT & POLITICS

Yugoslavia has nominally at least a presidential parliamentarian system, with regular multi-party elections. Power, however, has remained firmly in the hands of Serb nationalist Slobodan Milošević, two-term president of Serbia and now president, in the largely ceremonial post, of Yugoslavia. Opposition parties are largely divided and fragmented, thus providing little opportunity for a change in political direction in the foreseeable future.

ECONOMY

After WWII, Yugoslavia was a war-torn land of peasants. From 1948 to 1951 a concentrated attempt was made to form agricultural cooperatives. This failed, however, and most of the land continued to be worked privately by small farmers. In 1953 individual private holdings were reduced to a maximum of 10 hectares.

During the 1950s, state property was handed over to the workers in a reaction against Stalinist state socialism. The economy was thus reorganised on the basis of 'self-management', and elected workers' councils began running the factories and businesses, with coordination from producers' councils on a regional level. State control was limited to the broadest economic planning.

This system soon led to inefficiencies and an expensive duplication of services without the full benefits of open competition. Since collectively owned property had no clear owner, it was impossible to enforce economic efficiency or to guarantee profits. Initiative was stifled and employees often used self-management to improve their own financial standing without feeling any responsibility towards their property. Income was spent on higher wages and, with little or no capital left for development, companies turned to the banks. The cycle of inefficiency and dependency deepened as companies borrowed with little hope of ever paying off the loans.

The crisis of 2000% inflation in 1989 shattered the self-management ideal and led reformers to believe that a return to private property was inevitable. At the beginning of 1990 the government attempted to halt inflation by stopping the printing presses of the Belgrade mint and declaring a wage freeze. Prices still jumped by 75% but by mid-1990 inflation had levelled off to 13% a year. However, in 1992 hyperinflation returned as the government again turned to printing money to finance government operations and the war in Bosnia-Hercegovina. UN economic sanctions did the rest.

In 1993 incomes were a tenth of what they had been three years previously, industrial output had dropped 40% from that of a year before and 60% of factory workers were unemployed. Over 80% of Yugoslav property is still collectively owned and if normal bankruptcy procedures were applied most firms would go broke. Many people get by on remittances from relatives overseas or by subsisting on their gardens and livestock.

The end of the Cold War has greatly reduced the strategic importance of the entire Balkan region and Western countries are unlikely to rush in with 1950s-style aid or 1970s-style loans, even assuming that peace and stability do somehow return. Yugoslavia owes foreign governments and banks about US$16 billion, most of it dating back to the 1970s.

After a period of relative currency stability with the novi dinar holding its own against the mighty deutschmark, Yugoslavia was finally forced, following the Kosovo débâcle, to devalue the dinar in April 1998 by about 45% bringing the value of the DM up to six dinars from the previous level of 3.3. While a boon for travellers, its effect on the long-suffering Yugoslav is bound to be negative.

POPULATION & PEOPLE

The 11 million people of the 'third' Yugoslavia include Serbs (62.3%), Albanians (16.6%), Montenegrins (5%), Hungarians (3.3%) and Slavic Muslims (3.1%), plus a smattering of Croats, Romas, Slovaks, Macedonians, Romanians, Bulgarians, Turks and Ukrainians. The Montenegrins are officially considered ethnic Serbs. In 1991 an estimated 170,000 Romas lived in Yugoslavia, 100,000 of them in Kosovo. There are about 500,000 war refugees from Croatia and Bosnia-Hercegovina in Serbia and another 64,000 in Montenegro.

Nearly a quarter of Vojvodina's population is Hungarian and 90% of Kosovars are Albanian. Around 200,000 Serbs also live in Kosovo and there are large Slavic Muslim and Albanian minorities in Montenegro. In total there are 1.8 million ethnic Albanians in present-day Yugoslavia, a large number considering that the population of Albania itself is only 3.2 million. Some 250,000 Slavic Muslims live in the Sandžak region of Serbia and Montenegro between Novi Pazar and Berane (part of Bosnia until 1918). The human rights of all minorities are challenged by an increasingly nationalistic Serbia.

Yugoslavia's largest cities are Belgrade (population 1.5 million), Novi Sad (250,000), Niš (230,000), Priština (210,000) and Subotica (160,000).

ARTS

The artistic group FIA (☎ 011-347 355), at Hilandarska 4, 11000 Belgrade, founded in 1989 by Stavislav Sharp and Nada Rajičić, uses art to explore Serbia's tumultuous present through 'Phobjects' – suggestive images juxtaposed against folk art, political symbols and provocative quotations.

At exhibitions, group members dress in black paramilitary uniforms and show videos of skits in which FIA 'conspiracies' are acted out. Their 1992 Belgrade exhibition was visited by over 50,000 people in two weeks before being suddenly closed by force.

Phobjects have been exhibited in the ruins of the railway station in Sarajevo and at the bombed-out zoo in Osijek (Croatia). Surrealist 'posters of conscience' bring the FIA message to the streets. Their works are often prophetic.

Film

The award-winning film *Underground*, by Sarajevo-born director Emil Kusturica, is worth seeing. Told in a chaotic, colourful style, the film deals with the history of former Yugoslavia over the last 50 years.

Literature

Nobel Prize winner Ivo Andrić is Serbia's most respected and most translated writer His novel *Na Drini Ćuprija* (Bridge over the Drina), which is about the gap between religions, accurately foresaw the disasters that befell the Balkans in the early 1990s. Respected writer Milorad Pavić's novel *Hazarski Rečnik* (Hazar Dictionary) is a historical narrative, interlaced with fact and fiction, which has also been translated into English.

An excellent source of rare and out-of-print books on Serbia is Eastern Books (☎/fax 0181-871 0880; info@easternbooks.com), 125a Astonville St, Southfields, London SW18 5AQ. View their web page at www.easternbooks.com.

Music

Serbia's vibrant dances are similar to those of neighbouring Bulgaria. Serbian folk musicians use the *caraba* (small bagpipes), *gajde* (larger bagpipes), *frula* (small flute), *duduk* (large flute) and the fiddle.

The gajde employed in much Balkan music probably dates back to 4th-century Celtic invasions; unlike Scottish sheepskin bagpipes, the gajde is made from goatskin. The music of the Albanians of Kosovo bears the deep imprint of five centuries of Turkish rule, with the high whine of an Arab *zorna* (flute) carrying the tune above the beat of a goatskin drum. The *kolo* (round dance) is often accompanied by Gypsy musicians.

Blehmuzika, or brass music, has become the national music of Serbia. Though documented as far back as 1335, blehmuzika evolved under the influence of Turkish and, later, Austrian military music.

For popular modern music check out Momčilo Bajagić, who often appears on CD together with his group Bajaga & Instruktori. His music fuses traditional elements with street poetry and jazz and he is very popular

with the younger generation. Đorđe Balašević, equally if not more popular, appeals to a wider listening audience, combining once again traditional folkloric elements with modern musical motifs.

SOCIETY & CONDUCT

The Serbs are a proud and hospitable people, despite their newly-tarnished reputation. Visitors are a source of pride and are made to feel welcome. As in Macedonia, respect for all religious establishments and customs should be shown; these should not be treated as tourist entertainment. Dress appropriately at all times – look at what locals are wearing. Learning some basic Serbian, Hungarian or Albanian will open doors and create smiles.

RELIGION

The Serbs and Montenegrins are Orthodox, the Hungarians are Roman Catholic and the Albanians are predominantly Muslim.

LANGUAGE

Ordinary Yugoslavs are most likely to know German as a second language, though educated people in Kosovo and Serbia can often speak French. Serbian is the common language, and Albanian is spoken in Kosovo.

Serbian and Croatian are almost the same language, although Serbian is written in Cyrillic and Croatian is written in Latin characters (see the Croatian & Serbian language section at the end of the book). Before the break-up of the Yugoslav Federation, the language was referred to as Serbo-Croatian, but this term is now obsolete. Serbs in Yugoslavia call their language Serbian.

The Latin alphabet is used by the Albanians in Kosovo and the Hungarians in Vojvodina. In Montenegro you'll encounter a mixture of Latin and Cyrillic, but in Serbia most things are written only in Cyrillic. It's advisable to spend an hour or two studying the Cyrillic alphabet if you want to be able to read street and travel destination signs. (See the Macedonian language section at the back of this book for an explanation of the alphabet.)

Facts for the Visitor

HIGHLIGHTS

Yugoslavia has a wealth of castles, such as Smederevo Castle on the Danube, which is Serbia's last medieval fortress. Petrovaradin Citadel at Novi Sad is one of Europe's great baroque fortresses and Belgrade's Kalemegdan Citadel must be mentioned for its historic importance. The old Montenegrin capital of Cetinje will please romantics. Of the beach resorts, Budva is chic but Ulcinj has more atmosphere and is much cheaper. Montenegro's Tara Canyon is good for nature lovers and river rafters and is on a par with any similar location in the world.

SUGGESTED ITINERARIES

Depending on the length of your stay, you might want to see and do the following things in Yugoslavia:

Two days
 Visit Novi Sad and Belgrade
One week
 Visit Novi Sad, Belgrade, Ulcinj, Budva and Cetinje
Two weeks
 Visit all areas covered in this chapter except Kosovo
One month
 Visit all areas covered in this chapter

PLANNING
Climate & When to Go

The interior has a more extreme continental climate than the Adriatic coast of Montenegro. Belgrade has average daily temperatures above 17°C from May to September, above 13°C in April and October and above 7°C in March and November. In winter a cold wind (koshava) often blows across Belgrade.

Books & Maps

Rebecca West's Black Lambs & Grey Falcons is a classic portrait of prewar Yugoslavia. Former partisan and leading dissident Milovan Djilas has written many fascinating books about history and politics in Yugoslavia, most of them published in English. Any good library will have a couple of them.

The disintegration of former Yugoslavia has produced a wealth of reading material. A highly recommended recent book (updated to July 1991) on the region's political upheaval is Remaking the Balkans by Christopher Čilić (Pinter Publishers). The precise background information contained in this slim volume offers a clear explanation of events. The Destruction of Yugoslavia by Branka Magaš (Verso Publishers) offers many insights into the period from the death of Tito in 1980 to the end of 1992. Other titles dealing with the turbulence of the 1990s include Yugoslavia: Death of a Nation by Laura Silber and Allan Little, based on the 1995 BBC documentary series of the same name, and Yugoslavia's Bloody Collapse, a 1996 publication by Christopher Bennett.

Current Hallwag or Baedeker maps of Yugoslavia are hard to find or non-existent. Older maps show the former borders. The Savezna Republika Jugoslavija Autokarta, showing the new borders and a few regional town maps, and the detailed Belgrade city map Plan Grada Beograd, are both available for 15 and 10 DIN respectively from the Tourist Organisation of Belgrade.

What to Bring

You should plan on bringing your own film and video requirements, to be on the safe side. Bring a universal bath plug, since hotels rarely supply them.

TOURIST OFFICES

All overseas offices of the Yugoslav National Tourist Office closed in 1991 but should gradually be reopening. Municipal tourist offices still exist in Belgrade, Novi Sad and Podgorica. Commercial travel agencies such as Montenegroturist and Putnik will often provide general information on their area.

VISAS & EMBASSIES

Most visitors require visas and these are issued at Yugoslav consulates for a set fee depending on your nationality. Australian passport holders are charged A$5 – UK passport holders as much as £30 for a double entry visa. You will most likely need a confirmed travel itinerary and an invitation from a Yugoslav citizen, or a confirmed hotel reservation before a visa will be issued.

Before the troubles of the early 90s you could get a Yugoslav visa at the border, but this is no longer possible; you *must* obtain your Yugoslav visa in advance at an embassy or consulate. As a result of the US-led re-imposition of sanctions on Yugoslavia in April 1998, US travellers in particular are being given a hard time obtaining a visa and may be subject to considerable questioning by consular authorities.

If you plan on entering Yugoslavia more than once, ask for a double or triple-entry visa, otherwise you'll have to apply for a visa again.

Yugoslav Embassies Abroad

In addition to those listed below, Yugoslav consulates or embassies are found in Bucharest, Budapest, Prague, Skopje, Sofia, Timişoara, Tirana and Warsaw. Try to avoid the chaotic Tirana consulate.

Australia
  (☎ 02-9362 3003; fax 02-9362 4555; yugcon@ rosebay.matra.com.au) 12 Trelawney St, Woollahra, NSW 2025
Canada
  (☎ 613-233 6289) 17 Blackburn Ave, Ottawa, Ontario, K1N 8A2
France
  (☎ 01 40 72 24 24; fax 01 40 72 24 10) 54 rue Faisanderie 16e, Paris
Greece
  (☎ 01-777 4344) Vasilisis Sofias 106, Athens
  (☎ 031-244 266) Komninon 4, Thessaloniki
Netherlands
  (☎ 070-363 2397) Groot Hertoginnelaan 30, 2517 EG, The Hague
UK
  (☎ 0171-370 6105; fax 0171-370 3836) 5 Lexham Gardens, London, W8 5JJ
USA
  (☎ 202-462 6566) 2410 California St NW, Washington DC, 20008

Foreign Embassies in Yugoslavia

Most consulates and embassies are on or near Belgrade's Kneza Miloša, a 10-minute walk south-east from the train station. Visas are payable in cash only, specifically US$ or DM, and vary in price considerably, depending on how long you are prepared to wait. Opening times may vary.

Albania
  (☎ 646 864; fax 642 941) Kneza Miloša 56 (weekdays, 9 to 11 am)
Australia
  (☎ 624 655; fax 628 189) Čika Ljubina 13 (8.30 am to 4.30 pm)
Bulgaria (Consulate)
  (☎ 646 422) Birčaninova 26 (weekdays, 8 am to 3 pm)
Canada
  (☎ 644 666; fax 641 343) Kneza Miloša 75 (weekdays, 8 am to noon and 1 to 4 pm)
Czech Republic (Consulate)
  (☎ 323 0133) Bulevar Revolucije 22 (Monday to Thursday from 9 to 11 am)
Hungary (Consulate)
  (☎ 444 0472) Ivana Milutinovića 75 (weekdays, 9 to 11 am)
Poland (Consulate)
  (☎ 644 866) Kneza Miloša 38 (weekdays, 10 am to noon)
Romania (Consulate)
  (☎ 646 071) Kneza Miloša 70 (weekdays, 8 am to 3 pm)
Slovakia (Consulate)
  (☎ 311 1052) Bulevar Umetnosti 18, Novi Beograd (weekdays except Wednesday, 8 to 11 am)
UK
  (☎ 645 055; fax 659 651) Generala Ždanova 46 (weekdays, 8.30 to 11 am)
USA
  (☎ 645 655; fax 644 053) Kneza Miloša 50 (weekdays, 8 to 11 am)

MONEY
Currency

Since 1991 the Yugoslav dinar has suffered repeated devaluations. In December 1993 Yugoslavia experienced the highest inflation in the history of Europe (higher even than the monthly 32,000% record set by Weimar Germany in 1923). To most of us, such a situation is inconceivable but the Yugoslavs are experienced at dealing with inflation.

In 1990 four zeros were knocked off the Yugoslav dinar, so 10,000 old dinars became one new dinar, and in mid-1993 another six zeros were dropped. When this currency in turn inflated into obsolescence, a 'super dinar' was issued in January 1994 with a value of one to 12 million old dinars. By mid-1996 a new currency, the 'novi dinar', was holding its own against harder currencies, but it, in turn, was devalued by 45% in April

1998. There are coins of five, 10 and 50 para and one novi dinar and notes of five, 10, 20, 50 and 100 dinars.

Note: Travellers are now *supposed* to fill in a currency declaration form listing all hard currency being brought into the country. This form should theoretically be provided at all entry points, but is more often than not ignored unless you ask for it. Beware: if you fail to produce a declaration form upon leaving the country, you *may* run the risk of having any hard currency in your possession confiscated. (see Leaving Yugoslavia in the Getting There & Away section of this chapter).

Exchange Rates

Australia	A$1	=	7.10 DIN
Canada	C$1	=	7.60 DIN
euro	€1	=	11.79 DIN
France	1FF	=	1.78 DIN
Germany	DM1	=	6.00 DIN
Switzerland	Sfr1	=	7.21 DIN
United Kingdom	UK£1	=	18.25 DIN
United States	US$1	=	0.90 DIN

Changing Money

All banks, travel agencies and hotels will change cash hard currency into Yugoslav dinars at the official rate; unlike in Western Europe, you won't be given a worse rate at the fancy hotels or on Sunday.

Bring cash, preferably Deutschmarks, as you can spend or change them almost anywhere. A few people in Yugoslavia still change money on the street and unlike Budapest, Bucharest and Prague, it's fairly straightforward to do so and you probably won't be ripped off (but still take care). It's technically illegal and in any case you would be better advised not to flash your cash out in the open.

Only change what you're sure you'll need, as it's difficult to change dinars back into hard currency. Conversion rates for major currencies in mid 1998 are listed below:

Tipping

It is common practice to round up restaurant bills to the nearest convenient figure and waiters may indeed assume that this is what you intend and keep the expected change anyway. Consequently, don't give the waiter more than you are prepared to part with as a tip. Taxi drivers will expect a round-up to the nearest convenient figure unless you have agreed on a fee beforehand.

POST & COMMUNICATIONS

Post

To mail a parcel from Yugoslavia, take it unwrapped to a main post office where the staff will inspect it before dispatch. Allow plenty of time to complete the transaction.

Mailing a letter to Europe will cost you 1.60 DIN and to Australia or the USA 2.30 DIN.

Receiving Mail You can receive mail addressed to poste restante in all towns for a small charge per letter.

Mail addressed c/o Poste Restante, 11101 Belgrade 1, Yugoslavia, will be held for one month at window No 2 in the main post office, Takovska 2.

Telephone

To place a long-distance phone call in Yugoslavia you usually go to the main post office. Avoid weekends as the office may be jammed with military personnel waiting to call home. International calls made from hotels are much more expensive. Calls from post offices go straight through and cost 19 DIN a minute to the USA and Australia, with no minimum.

Telephone cards purchased at post offices or news kiosks are an inexpensive, easy way of making international calls, but only in Belgrade as card phones are hard to find elsewhere. Cards can be bought in units of 100 (19 DIN), 200 (31 DIN), 300 (44 DIN) and 400 (56 DIN). The international access code for outgoing calls is ☎ 99. To call another town within Yugoslavia dial the area code with the initial zero and the number.

To call Yugoslavia from Western Europe dial the international access code, ☎ 381 (the country code for Yugoslavia), the area code (without the initial zero) and the number.

Fax

Faxes can be sent from the main post office in Belgrade, or from any large hotel.

INTERNET RESOURCES

A useful Web site for general information on Yugoslavia is www.yugoslavia.com. The Tourist Organisation of Belgrade has a Web site at www.beograd.com/belgrade–guide.

While Yugoslavia is connected to the Internet, access from within the country for the majority of Yugoslavs is fairly limited at present. See the Belgrade section for information on Internet cafes there.

NEWSPAPERS & MAGAZINES

There is a wide selection of Serbian newspapers and magazines, as will be obvious by the displays at street kiosks. Not so useful if you do not read Serbian. *Politika* is the main daily for serious reading.

Until publication was suspended in 1993 as a consequence of UN sanctions, the English-language *International Weekly* carried the best stories of the week from *Politika*. To date it has not made a reappearance.

Also before UN sanctions, many foreign-language publications were widely available in Yugoslavia. At the moment there is a healthy selection of foreign-language magazines, though not a very wide variety of foreign-language newspapers.

RADIO & TV

There are some 11 local TV stations in Belgrade, including two from Novi Sad. Satellite TV stations such as CNN, Eurosport and MTV are also available if the receiver is suitably equipped. There are fewer stations in regional areas. Many FM and AM radio stations cater to all tastes.

PHOTOGRAPHY & VIDEO

Bring all your own film, as that sold locally is expensive and may be unreliable outside Belgrade. Keep your camera stowed away while crossing the border and be careful about taking pictures of anything other than obvious tourist attractions, as you could arouse unwelcome curiosity. Taking photos from a train or bus is not advisable and photographing soldiers or military facilities will cause serious problems if you're caught. The funny little signs with a camera crossed out should be taken seriously.

Video paraphernalia – tapes and batteries – are available in Belgrade, but you are advised to bring your own since these things are generally more expensive in Yugoslavia.

TIME

Yugoslavia is one hour ahead of GMT/UTC. The country goes on summer time at the end of March when clocks are turned forward an hour. At the end of September they're turned back an hour.

ELECTRICITY

The current is 220V, 50Hz. Plugs are of the standard European two-pronged type.

WEIGHTS & MEASURES

Yugoslavia uses the metric system.

TOILETS

Public toilets outside Belgrade are probably better avoided as they tend to be unsanitary and smelly. Make full use of the facilities at restaurants and hotels. A 1 DIN charge is common for use of public toilets in Belgrade.

HEALTH

The cost of medical treatment in Yugoslavia is very low and if you're covered at home by a regular health insurance plan which includes treatment abroad, special travel medical insurance is unnecessary and a waste of money. Conditions, however, in state-run services may not be up to your expectations. Private clinics offer a more presentable level of service and will normally be covered by your travel insurance.

WOMEN TRAVELLERS

Women travellers should feel no particular concern about travel in Yugoslavia. Other than cursory interest shown by men towards solo women travellers, travel is hassle-free and easy. Dress more conservatively than usual in Albanian Muslim areas of Kosovo.

GAY & LESBIAN TRAVELLERS

Homosexuality has been legal in Yugoslavia since 1932. For more information, contact Arkadia, Brace Baruh 11, 11000 Belgrade.

YUGOSLAVIA

DISABLED TRAVELLERS

Few public buildings or streets have facilities for wheelchairs. Access could be problematic in Belgrade with its numerous inclines.

DANGERS & ANNOYANCES

Belgrade is a remarkably safe city, even late at night. Even around the seedy train station area there's no particular danger. Throughout Yugoslavia theft is rare.

Many Yugoslavs are chain-smokers who can't imagine that anyone might be inconvenienced by their habit, so choose your seat in trains, restaurants, bars and other public places carefully. Buses are supposed to be smoke-free and there are no-smoking sections on trains but this is sometimes ignored by other passengers.

If the subject turns to politics, it's best to listen to what Yugoslavs say rather than to tell them what you think, as nationalist passions can be unpredictable. It's striking the way Serbs who seem to be reasonable, amenable people suddenly become tense and defensive as soon as the subject of Kosovo comes up.

Don't give the police the impression you are anything but a tourist, otherwise you may be in for a searching interrogation. Avoid Kosovo for now unless you have a very good reason for going there.

BUSINESS HOURS

Banks in Yugoslavia keep long hours, often from 7 am to 7 pm weekdays and 7 am to noon on Saturday. On weekdays many shops close for lunch from noon to 4 pm but stay open until 8 pm. Department stores, supermarkets and self-service restaurants generally stay open throughout the day. On Saturday most government offices are closed, though shops stay open until 2 pm; many other businesses close at 3 pm.

PUBLIC HOLIDAYS & SPECIAL EVENTS

Public holidays include:

1 and 2 January
  New Year
6 and 7 January
  Orthodox Christmas

27 April
  Day of the FR of Yugoslavia
1 and 2 May
  International Labour Days
9 May
  Victory Day
29 and 30 November
  Republic Days

In addition, 28 March (Constitution Day) and 7 July (Uprising Day) are holidays in Serbia and 13 July is a holiday in Montenegro. If any of these should fall on a Sunday, then the following Monday or Tuesday is a holiday.

Orthodox Easter falls from anywhere between one and three weeks later than regular Easter. Most institutions close down at this time, so check the dates before you plan to visit Yugoslavia at Orthodox Easter time.

Belgrade hosts a film festival in February, an international theatre festival in mid-September, a festival of classical music in October and a jazz festival in November. The Novi Sad Agricultural Fair is in mid-May. Budva has a summer festival in July and August.

ACTIVITIES
Skiing

Serbia's largest ski centre is Kopaonik (2017m), south of Kraljevo, with 26 different runs covering a total of 54km. Get there from Belgrade by taking a bus to Brus (246km, five hours), then a local bus to the resort at Brzeče (18km). Otherwise take a bus from Belgrade to Kruševac (194km) and another from there to Brus (52km). Kopaonik has a 150-bed hostel (☎ 037-833 176) with three, four and five-bed rooms at 100 DIN per person, open year-round.

On the north side of the Šar Planina, which separates Kosovo from Macedonia, is Brezovica (1750m), Kosovo's major ski resort. Montenegro's main ski resort is at Žabljak. The ski season is from about December to March.

White-Water Rafting & Hiking

White-water rafting is offered on the Tara River in Montenegro's Durmitor National Park. See Travel Agencies in the Belgrade section for a contact address. For high-altitude lakes and one of the world's deepest canyons, Durmitor can't be beaten. This is also a popular hiking and skiing area.

LANGUAGE COURSES

Courses for linguists, or Slavists who wish to learn Serbian, are run in September each year by the International Slavic Centre (MSC) in Belgrade. For further details write to the MSC at Studenski trg 3, Belgrade.

ACCOMMODATION

You won't find any really inexpensive hotels in Yugoslavia, though the 1998 devaluation has had a beneficial levelling effect for travellers. Prices are often quoted in US dollars or DM, although payment in dinars is OK and hotel room prices are normally linked to the value of the dinar against these two foreign currencies. Be aware that the cost of accommodation may change considerably if the dinar slips further against the DM or the greenback. Foreigners still pay up to three times as much as locals at state-owned hotels – a legacy of the old socialist days when foreigners were supposed to be able to afford higher rates. Food prices are fortunately the same for everyone.

In summer you can camp along the Montenegrin coast; organised camping grounds are few and many of those that do exist are closed due to the absence of tourists. There's a hostel in Belgrade but it's far from the centre, overcrowded and overpriced. Other HI hostels exist at Kopaonik and Ulcinj (summer only). The hostel prices for foreigners are fixed in DM and thus staying in hostels could be more expensive and often less convenient than taking a private room.

Private rooms are usually available along the coast but seldom inland. They are hard to find in Belgrade and there are steep surcharges if you stay less than three nights. If you plan to stay that long, Budva and Bar make good central bases from which to make side trips to Cetinje and Ulcinj.

An overnight bus or train can sometimes get you out of an accommodation jam.

FOOD

The cheapest breakfast is Balkan *burek*, a greasy layered pie made with cheese (*sir*) or meat *(meso),* and it's available everywhere. *Krompirusa* is potato burek. Food is cheaper in

the interior than along the coast and meat dishes can be very cheap in Turkish-influenced areas.

Regional Dishes

Yugoslavia's regional cuisines range from spicy Hungarian goulash in Vojvodina to Turkish kebab in Serbia and Kosovo. A speciality of Vojvodina is *alaska čorba* (fiery riverfish stew). In Montenegro try the pastoral fare such as boiled lamb or *kajmak* (cream from boiled milk which is salted and turned into cheese).

Serbia is famous for grilled meats such as *čevapčići* (kebabs of spiced, minced meat, grilled), *pljeskavica* (a large, spicy hamburger steak) and *ražnjići* (a pork or veal shish kebab with onions and peppers). If you want to try them all at once, order *mešano meso* (a mixed grill of pork cutlet, liver, sausage, and minced meat patties with onions). Serbian *duveč* is grilled pork cutlets with spiced stewed peppers, zucchini and tomatoes in rice cooked in an oven – delicious.

Other popular dishes are *musaka* (aubergine and potato baked in layers with minced meat), *sarma* (cabbage stuffed with minced meat and rice), *kapama* (stewed lamb, onions and spinach served with yoghurt), *punjena tikvica* (zucchini stuffed with minced meat and rice), and peppers stuffed with minced meat, rice and spices, cooked in tomato sauce.

Most traditional Yugoslav dishes are based on meat so vegetarians will have problems, though every restaurant menu will include a Serbian salad *(Srpska salata)* of raw peppers, onions and tomatoes, seasoned with oil, vinegar and chilli. Also ask for *gibanica* (a layered cheese pie) and *zeljanica* (cheese pie with spinach). *Švopska salata* is also very popular, consisting of chopped tomatoes, cucumber and onion and topped with grated soft white cheese.

DRINKS

Beer (*pivo*) is always available. Nikšićko pivo brewed at Nikšić in Montenegro is terribly good when imbibed ice-cold at the beach on a hot summer day. Its taste has a smoky flavour in comparison with the Bip beer served around Belgrade, which tends to be on the flat side.

Yugoslav cognac (grape brandy) is called *vinjak*. Coffee is usually served Turkish-style, boiled in a small individual pot, 'black as hell, strong as death and sweet as love'. Hotel breakfast coffee is universally undrinkable. Drink tea instead. Superb espresso and capuccino, however, can be found at Belgrade's many cafés.

Getting There & Away

AIR

Since the lifting of UN sanctions in November 1995, JAT has recommenced services and provides for a limited but growing number of domestic and international destinations. As at mid-1998, services to the US and Australia had not resumed but that may change.

LAND

In mid-1991, all rail and road links between Croatia and Serbia were cut, making it necessary to do a loop through Hungary to travel from Zagreb to Belgrade. Five years later the border was reopened. The main vehicle and rail crossing is at Batrovci, near the town of Šid, on the main Belgrade-Zagreb *autoput*. Other border crossings at Bačka Palanka, Bogojevo and Bezdan were still under the control of UNPROFOR in mid-1998. The southern border between Croatia and Montenegro had not reopened as of mid-1998.

A couple of bus services use the main crossing instead of transiting through Hungary. You cross the border on foot and change to a Croatian/Serbian bus accordingly. At the time of going to press there were no train links between Yugoslavia and Croatia.

Private-vehicle crossings should be possible without too much difficulty.

Bus

Buses travelling to/from Slovenia and Macedonia can use the main Yugoslavia-Croatia border crossing instead of going through Hungary. Buses to/from Croatia require a change of bus at the border. Two agencies in Belgrade currently organise these itineraries.

In Belgrade, the travel agencies Basturist, Turist Biro Lasta and BS Tours all sell tickets for international buses (see Travel Agencies in the Belgrade section for addresses and contact numbers). Sample fares from Belgrade, payable in DM only, are:

Destination	Cost
Munich	DM107
Paris	DM155
Thessaloniki	DM22
Vienna	DM70
Zürich	DM174

Train

Only buy a ticket as far as your first stop in Yugoslavia, as domestic fares are much cheaper than international fares. Consider breaking your journey in Subotica, Niš or even Skopje for this purpose alone. A student card will get you a reduction on train fares from Yugoslavia to other Eastern European countries.

All the international 'name trains' mentioned here run daily all year unless otherwise stated.

Hungary & Beyond Since mid-1991, trains between Western Europe and Belgrade have run via Budapest, Subotica and Novi Sad. About six trains a day cover the 354km between Budapest and Belgrade (six hours, 410 DIN). The *Hunyadi* and the *Ivo Andrić* link just the two capitals. The *Hellas Express* runs between Thessaloniki (Solun) and Budapest, the *Balkan Express* between Istanbul and Budapest, and the *Avala* and *Beograd* express trains run between Belgrade and Vienna (Beč). Belgrade is 11 hours from Vienna (627km, 700 DIN) and 17 hours from Munich. Reservations are usually required on these trains.

An unreserved local train runs four times a day between Subotica and Szeged in Hungary (45km, 1¾ hours, 35 DIN).

Croatia You can take a direct train from Zagreb to Budapest then change to another train for Belgrade. Otherwise take the daily train from Zagreb to Pécs (Hungary), a bus from Pécs to Szeged and a train from Szeged across the border to Subotica in Vojvodina.

YUGOSLAVIA

You would have to spend at least one night somewhere along the way. (See the relevant chapters for ticket prices).

Romania From Romania the overnight *Bucureşti* express train runs between Bucharest and Beograd station (693km, 13 hours, 380 DIN) via Timişoara and there is also a day service, the *Banat* that departs Bucureşti at 10.55 am each day. Reservations are required on both trains. Two daily unreserved local trains on this route connect Timişoara to Vršac (76km).

Bulgaria & Turkey The most reliable service to/from Bulgaria and Turkey is the *Balkan Express* train, which connects Budapest with Istanbul and runs through Belgrade. From Istanbul the train goes via Sofia, Niš, Belgrade and Novi Sad. If bound for Bulgaria you can board this train in Novi Sad.

From Belgrade it's nine hours to Sofia (417km, 250 DIN) and 21½ hours to Istanbul (1051km, 560 DIN). The *Balkan Express* departs from Belgrade each morning at 10 am and reservations are required.

Greece The southern main line between Belgrade and Athens (1267km, 22 hours, 400 DIN) is through Skopje and Thessaloniki, with two trains a day. Reservations are recommended.

Car & Motorcycle
Following are the main highway entry/exit points around Yugoslavia (travelling clockwise), with the Yugoslav border post named.

Hungary There are crossings at Bački Breg (32km south of Baja), Kelebija (11km north-west of Subotica) and Horgoš (between Szeged and Subotica).

Romania You may cross at Sprska Crnja (45km west of Timişoara), Vatin (between Timişoara and Belgrade), Kaluđerovo (120km east of Belgrade) and Kladovo (10km west of Turnu Severin).

Bulgaria You have a choice of Negotin (29km north-west of Vidin), Zaječar (45km

south-west of Vidin), Gradina (at Dimitrovgrad between Sofia and Niš) and Klisura (66km west of Pernik).

Macedonia You can cross at Preševo (10km north of Kumanovo) and Đeneral Janković (between Uroševac and Skopje).

Albania There are crossings at Vrbnica (18km south-west of Prizren) and Božaj (24km south-east of Podgorica).

SEA
A ferry service operates between Bari or Ancona (Italy), and Bar in Montenegro. The Belgrade agent is Yugoagent at Kolarčeva 3. There are a couple of agents in Bar.

LEAVING YUGOSLAVIA
The airport departure tax on international flights is 90 DIN.

Travellers should be prepared to furnish the currency declaration that they were supposed to have completed upon entering the country. Failure to do so could mean confiscation of any hard currency you are carrying.

Getting Around

AIR
JAT domestic flights operate from Belgrade to Tivat (Montenegro) four to six times daily and to Podgorica (also in Montenegro) twice daily. Both fares cost about 500 DIN, plus 20 DIN domestic departure airport tax. These flights are heavily booked.

Only 15kg of checked baggage is allowed on domestic flights. JAT runs inexpensive buses between airports and city centres.

BUS
Though present-day Yugoslavia depends on railways far more than the other four countries of ex-Yugoslavia, there are also many buses. You'll depend on buses to travel along the Montenegrin coast from Bar to Budva and Ulcinj, to go from Montenegro to Kosovo and to get to Durmitor National Park. On long hauls, overnight buses can be exhausting but they do save you time and money.

TRAIN

The Jugoslovenske Železnice (JŽ) provides adequate railway services along the main interior line from Subotica to Novi Sad, Belgrade, Niš, Priština and Skopje and there's a highly scenic line from Belgrade down to the coast at Bar, especially between Kolašin and Bar. There are four classes of train: *ekspresni* (express), *poslovni* (rapid), *brzi* (fast) and *putnicki* (slow). Make sure you have the right sort of ticket for your train.

The train is cheaper than the bus and you don't have to pay for luggage. It is, however, slower and can get very crowded. The quality of the rolling stock varies enormously from OK to dilapidated and dirty. The international 'name' trains are usually of good quality. It's more reliable to make reservations in the train's originating station, unless reservations are mandatory from the in-between stations, in which case try to book the day before. Most trains have 'no smoking' compartments. Inter-Rail passes are valid in Yugoslavia, but Eurail passes are not.

All train stations (except in Kosovo) have left-luggage offices where you can dump your bag (passport required).

CAR & MOTORCYCLE

Yugoslavia's motorways *(autoput)* run southeast through Belgrade, Niš and Skopje towards Greece. Yugoslavs pay low tolls in dinars but foreign-registered vehicles pay much higher prices. Toll charges are posted at the motorway exit, not at the entrance. All other roads are free and, with a little time and planning, you can avoid the motorways.

Speed limits for private cars and motorcycles are 120km/h on motorways, 100km/h on 1st-class roads, 80km/h on 2nd-class roads and 60km/h in built-up areas.

Members of foreign automobile clubs get a reduced rate on towing services provided by the Automoto Savez Jugoslavije (AMSJ). It has branches in almost every town, with repair facilities available. Call ☎ 987 for AMSJ emergency assistance.

Petrol is available in regular (86 octane), super (98 octane) and unleaded or *bezolovni* (95 octane) varieties. In mid-1998 the cost was about 6 DIN for a litre of super.

Driving around Yugoslavia should present no particular problems these days. The hoards of transiting tourists have backed off and the roads are relatively untravelled and in good repair. All borders are open, including the one with Croatia (although at the time of writing, train and air routes had not been fully restored), and the large towns and the coast are quiet. The police are ever-vigilant and always on the lookout to fine unwary motorists on the spot for some minor infringement, so beware. Kosovo should be avoided because of the Serb-Albanian clashes and the continuing possibility of trouble. Take reasonable security precautions when parking – an alarm or steering wheel lock is a good idea.

HITCHING

While technically possible in Yugoslavia, you are more than likely to be hampered by drivers only covering short distances. By hitching you are also opening yourself up to unscrupulous opportunists and in any case, LP does not recommend hitching as a form of transport.

LOCAL TRANSPORT

Public transport strip tickets and tokens are available from newsstands in Belgrade. Punch your ticket as you board the vehicle.

ORGANISED TOURS

Day trips along the Danube and further afield are available. Check with the Tourist Organisation of Belgrade (☎ 011-324 8404) in the city centre for details. Ski Centar Durmitor organises one-week skiing packages and Putnik Tours in Belgrade has various tailored packages for visitors.

Belgrade (Београд)

☎ 011

The dominant role of Serbia (Srbija) in the former Yugoslav Federation was underlined by the inclusion within its boundaries of two formerly 'autonomous provinces', Vojvodina and Kosovo, and the national capital, Belgrade.

Belgrade (Beograd) is strategically situated on the southern edge of the Carpathian basin where the Sava River joins the Danube. Just east of the city is the Morava Valley, route of the famous 'Stamboul Road' from Turkey to Central Europe. At this major crossroads developed a city which has long been the flashpoint of the Balkans. It's an interesting place to look around for a few days, but accommodation is absurdly expensive.

Until WWI Belgrade was right on the border of Serbia and Austria-Hungary, and its citadel has seen many battles. Destroyed and rebuilt 40 times in its 2300-year history, Belgrade has never quite managed to pick up all the pieces. It is nonetheless a lively, vibrant city with fine restaurants and street cafés and a rhythm that reminds you more of northern Europe than the Balkans.

History

The Celtic settlement of Singidunum was founded in the 3rd century BC on a bluff overlooking the confluence of the Sava and Danube rivers. The Romans arrived in the 1st century AD and stayed till the 5th century. The present Slavic name Beograd (White City) first appeared in a papal letter dated 16 April 878.

Belgrade became the capital of Serbia in 1403, when the Serbs were pushed north by the Turks. In 1456 the Hungarians, under János Hunyadi, succeeded in defeating a Turkish northward advance, but in 1521 the Turks finally took Belgrade. In 1842 the city again became the capital of Serbia and in 1918, the capital of Yugoslavia. In April 1941, 17,000 lives were lost in a Nazi bombing raid on Belgrade. Soon after, on 4 July 1941, Tito and the Communist Party's central committee, meeting at Belgrade, decided to launch an armed uprising. Belgrade was liberated on 20 October 1944, and since then the population has grown six-fold to over 1.7 million.

Orientation

You'll probably arrive at the train station on the south side of the city centre or at one of the adjacent bus stations. The left-luggage office at the train station (open 24 hours) is just past the kiosks at the end of track No 9. Left luggage costs 5 DIN per piece. The left-luggage room at the main (BAS) bus station is open from 6 am to 10 pm and costs 6 DIN

per piece. A passport is required at both of these. Allow enough time to pick up your bag. For information on other facilities at the train station, see Getting There & Away at the end of the Belgrade section.

To walk into town from the train station, go east along Milovanovića for a block, then straight up Balkanska to Terazije, the heart of modern Belgrade. Kneza Mihaila, Belgrade's lively pedestrian boulevard, runs north-west through Stari Grad (the old town) from Terazije to Kalemegdan Park, where you'll find the citadel. The crowds are surprisingly chic, the cafés well patronised and the atmosphere bustling and businesslike.

Information

The friendly, helpful Tourist Organisation of Belgrade (☎ 635 622; fax 635 343; tob@beograd.com), open weekdays from 9 am to 8 pm and Saturday from 9 am to 4 pm, has an office in the underpass at the beginning of Terazije, on the corner of Kneza Mihaila. (Note the public toilets down there for future reference.) There's also a tourist office at the airport open daily from 8 am to 8 pm.

Information on HI hostels around Yugoslavia is available from Ferijalni Savez Beograd (☎ 324 8550; fax 322 0762), Makedonska 22, 2nd floor.

Motorists are assisted by the English-speaking staff at the special Informativni Centar (☎ 419 822) around the corner from the Automoto Savez Jugoslavije, Ruzveltova 16a, a little south-east of Tašmajdan Park.

Money The JIK Banka is across the park in front of the train station (open from 8 am to 8 pm weekdays and 8 am to 3 pm Saturday). The exchange window in the train station gives a slightly less favourable rate.

American Express travellers cheques can only be changed at the Karić Banka on the corner of Maršala Birjuzova and Pop Lukina, at the airport branch which is also open on weekends and at the Komercijalna Banka on trg Nikole Pašića. The Hyatt Regency and Inter Continental hotels accept credit cards and travellers cheques from guests. American Express is represented by Atlas Tours, Kosovska 8, 6th floor. Although the office is functioning they cannot yet provide any

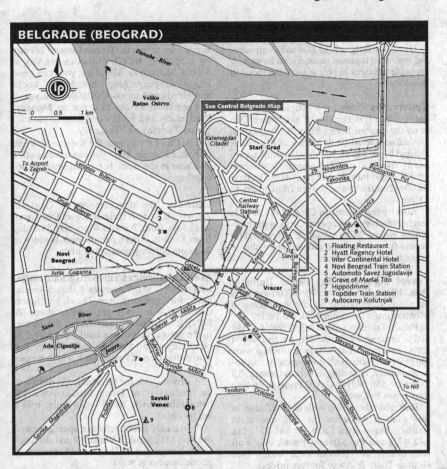

BELGRADE (BEOGRAD)

Danube River

Veliko
Ratno Ostrvo

0   0.5   1 km

Kalemegdan
Citadel

See Central Belgrade Map

Stari Grad

To Airport
& Zagreb

Leninov Bulevar

Druga Bulevar

Novi
Beograd

Jurija Gagarina

River

Sava

Ada Ciganlija

Jezero

Savska Magistrala

Poteska

Radnička

Vojvode Mišića

Bulevar Vojvode Mišića

Gazela

Central
Railway
Station

Nemanjina

Kneza Miloša

Savska

Bulevar Franše D'Epera

Trg
Slavija

Bulevar JNA

Vracar

Bulevar Mira

Teodora Draizera

Nemanjina Juriaha

Savski
Venac

Vojvode Stepe

Bulevar Stevana Prvovenčanog

29
Novembra

Takovska

Partizanski
Put

Nije Krovačevica

To Niš

1 Floating Restaurant
2 Hyatt Regency Hotel
3 Inter Continental Hotel
4 Novi Beograd Train Station
5 Automoto Savez Jugoslavije
6 Grave of Maršal Tito
7 Hippodrome
8 Topčider Train Station
9 Autocamp Košutnjak

American Express services nor cash travellers cheques.

There are a few private exchange offices in Belgrade. One very central office is VODR (open weekdays from 9 am to 7 pm and Saturday from 9 am to 3 pm). You may occasionally come across black marketeers angling for 'devize', but the difference between bank and black market rates nowadays is not great.

There are currently no ATM machines operating anywhere in Belgrade. Come prepared with cash.

Post & Communications The main post office, at Takovska 2, holds poste-restante mail (postcode 11101) at window No 2 for one month. International telephone calls can be placed here from 7 am to 10 pm daily. This is the only place in Belgrade where you can send a fax (one page to the USA or Australia costs 78 DIN, to Europe 60 DIN). A more convenient telephone centre (open 24 hours a day) is in the post office at Zmaj Jovina 17 in the centre of town.

The telephone centre in the large post office on the right (south) side of the train station opens weekdays from 7 am to midnight and weekends from 7 am to 10 pm.

Note that Belgrade is gradually introducing seven-digit phone numbers, so beware of probable changes to phone numbers listed in this section.

Cybercafés There are a couple of Internet cafés within five minutes of each other. One is on the ground floor of the *Bioskop Doma Omladine* cinema on the corner of Makedonska and Moše Pijade, but the six terminals are nearly always in use. The other is *Café Sezam* (☎ 322 7231; info@sezampro.yu) at Skadarska 40c (2nd floor) and is open from 10 am to 11 pm.

Also try the American Center (☎ 630 011; teachers@classroom.opennet.org) in the middle of Kneza Mihaila which offers public access from 10 am to 6 pm. All three charge around 15 DIN per hour.

Travel Agencies Ski Centar Durmitor (☎ 634 944), Kralja Petra 70, has information on white-water rafting, skiing and hiking in Montenegro's Durmitor National Park.

Putnik Travel Agency (☎ 330 669; fax 334 505), Terazije 27, is the largest and oldest travel agency in Yugoslavia. It offers a wide range of services both domestically and internationally, including tickets to Croatia. BS Tours (☎ 558 347) at Gavril Principa 46 also runs buses to Croatia.

Basturist (the office with the JAT sign in the window between the bus and train station), Turist Biro Lasta (☎ 641 251; fax 642 473) and the adjacent Putnik office all sell tickets for international buses (see Getting There & Away for fare prices).

Beograd Tours (☎ 641 258; fax 687 447) at Milovanovića 5, a block up the hill from the train station, will book couchettes and sleepers within Yugoslavia and tickets to other countries. The English-speaking staff provide reliable train information and sell tickets at the same prices charged in the station, but without the crowds.

Bookshops A good place to get your favourite magazine and possibly newspaper is at the Plato Bookshop, Vasina 17. Another option is at Jugoslovenska Knjiga above the Tourist Organisation of Belgrade office.

Libraries If you plan on spending any time in Belgrade, you can pay the 70 DIN membership fee to join the British Council Library (☎ 622 492; BCLib@britcoun.org.yu) at Kneza Mihailova 48. Here you can read English-language magazines, borrow books and videos and access CD-ROM archives. It is open from 11 am to 4 pm on Monday, Wednesday and Friday and from 2 pm to 7 pm on Tuesday and Thursday.

The City Library is at the Kalemegdan end of Kneza Mihaila. Here you can have a coffee or a beer in the snack bar, or do some photocopying.

Laundry The dry cleaners at Generala Ždanova 6, just off Bulevar Revolucije (open weekdays from 7 am to 8 pm and Saturday from 8 am to 3 pm), can do your laundry in 24 hours but they charge per item.

Medical Services The Boris Kidrič Hospital (☎ 683 755), Pasterova 1, has a special clinic for foreigners open Tuesday to Saturday from 7 am to 1 pm (consultations 20 DIN). It's also possible to consult the doctors in the regular clinic here until 7 pm daily. At other times go to the Klinički Centar just across the street at Pasterova 2, which is open 24 hours.

A dental clinic for foreigners (Stomatološka Služba) is at Ivana Milutinovića 15, behind the Slavija Hotel (open daily from 7 am to 7 pm).

Two handy pharmacies are open 24 hours: the Prvi Maj, Srpskih Vladara 9 and the Sveti Sava, Nemjanina 2. The first aid emergency phone number is ☎ 94.

Things to See

From the train station take tram No 1, 2 or 13 north-west to **Kalemegdan Citadel**, the strategic hill-top fortress at the junction of the Sava and Danube rivers. This area has been fortified since Celtic times and the Roman settlement of Singidunum was on the flood plain at the foot of the citadel. Much of what is seen today dates from the 17th century, including medieval gates, Orthodox churches, Muslim tombs and Turkish baths. Ivan Meštrović's *Monument of Gratitude to France* (1930) is at the citadel's entrance, and on the ramparts overlooking the rivers stands his 1928 statue *The Winner*. The large **Military Museum** on the battlements of the citadel presents a complete history of Yugoslavia in 53 rooms. The benches in the park around the citadel are relaxing and on summer evenings lots of people come strolling past.

Next to Kalemegdan Citadel is Stari Grad, the oldest part of Belgrade. The best museums are here, especially the **National Museum**, trg Republike, which has archaeological exhibits downstairs and paintings upstairs. The collection of European art is quite good. A few blocks away at Studentski trg 13 is the **Ethnographical Museum**, with an excellent collection of Serbian costumes and folk art. Detailed explanations are provided in English. Not far away, at Cara Uroša 20, is the **Gallery of Frescoes**, with full-size replicas of paintings from remote churches in Serbia and Macedonia. Belgrade's most memorable museum is the **Palace of Princess Ljubice**, on the corner of Svetozara Markovića and Kralija Petra, an authentic Balkan-style palace (1831) complete with period furnishings.

The **Skupština**, or Yugoslav parliament (built 1907-32), is at the beginning of Bulevar Revolucije, just before the main post office. East again, behind the main post office, is **Sveti Marko Serbian Orthodox Church** (built in 1932-39), with four tremendous pillars supporting a towering dome. There's a small Russian Orthodox church behind it.

If you'd like to visit the white marble **grave of Maršal Tito** (open from 9 am to 4 pm), it's within the grounds of his former residence on Bulevar Mira, a few kilometres south of the city centre (take trolleybus No 40 or 41 south from Kneza Miloša 64). The tomb and all of the museums are closed on Monday.

Escape the bustle of Belgrade on **Ada Ciganlija**, an island park in the Sava River just upstream from the city. In summer you can swim in the river (naturists walk 1km upstream from the others), rent a bicycle or just stroll among the trees. The many small cafés overlooking the beach sell cold beer at reasonable prices.

Places to Stay

Accommodation in Belgrade is generally expensive, compounded by the fact that foreigners can pay up to three times as much as Yugoslavs. Budget places are hard to come by and private rooms almost impossible to find. The 1998 devaluation of the dinar has in effect brought prices down, but how long the hotel prices will stay at the current level is anyone's guess. Prices listed here may change considerably.

A valuable tip which will save a day's travelling time, a night's hotel bill and a lot of aggravation, is to book a sleeper or couchette out of Belgrade. This is easily done and costs from 14 to 63 DIN extra. Just try getting a room for that! Don't forget that a train ticket is required in addition to the sleeper/couchette ticket.

If for some reason you can't get a sleeper or couchette, consider taking an overnight bus to your next destination. It's cheaper than the train and advance tickets are easily purchased at the bus station, but a bus trip is much more tiring.

Camping *Autocamp Košutnjak* (☎ 555 127), Kneza Višeslava 17, is about 8km south-west of the city centre. Camping is possible from May to September only, but there are expensive new bungalows open all year (180 DIN per person with private bath). The older, cheaper bungalows are permanently occupied by locals. Camping will cost about 60 DIN for two persons and a tent. It's a fairly pleasant wooded site with lots of shade, but pitch your tent far from the noisy restaurant. To get there take tram No 12 or 13 south from beside the train station to Kneza Višeslava, the next stop after you see the horse-racing track (hippodrome) on the left. From the tram stop it's 1km up the hill.

Private Rooms Private rooms have become more or less nonexistent in Belgrade. You will not be approached by anyone as you leave the bus or train station and finding one will be a challenge. It's better to opt for one of the cheaper hotels (if there is a room available), or fork out a bit extra for a room at a mid-range hotel in the centre.

CENTRAL BELGRADE

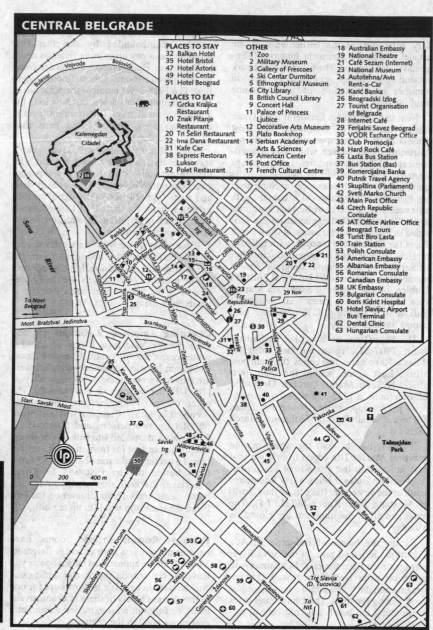

PLACES TO STAY
32 Balkan Hotel
35 Hotel Bristol
47 Hotel Astoria
49 Hotel Centar
51 Hotel Beograd

PLACES TO EAT
7 Grčka Kraljica Restaurant
10 Znak Pitanje Restaurant
20 Tri Šeširi Restaurant
22 Ima Dana Restaurant
31 Kafe Car
38 Express Restoran Luksor
52 Polet Restaurant

OTHER
1 Zoo
2 Military Museum
3 Gallery of Frescoes
4 Ski Centar Durmitor
5 Ethnographical Museum
6 City Library
8 British Council Library
9 Concert Hall
11 Palace of Princess Ljubice
12 Decorative Arts Museum
13 Plato Bookshop
14 Serbian Academy of Arts & Sciences
15 American Center
16 Post Office
17 French Cultural Centre
18 Australian Embassy
19 National Theatre
21 Café Sezam (Internet)
23 National Museum
24 Autotehna/Avis Rent-a-Car
25 Karić Banka
26 Beogradski Izlog
27 Tourist Organisation of Belgrade
28 Internet Café
29 Ferijalni Savez Beograd
30 VODR Exchange Office
33 Club Promocija
34 Hard Rock Café
36 Lasta Bus Station
37 Bus Station (Bas)
39 Komercijalna Banka
40 Putnik Travel Agency
41 Skupština (Parliament)
42 Sveti Marko Church
43 Main Post Office
44 Czech Republic Consulate
45 JAT Office Airline Office
46 Beograd Tours
47 Turist Biro Lasta
50 Train Station
53 Polish Consulate
54 American Embassy
55 Albanian Embassy
56 Romanian Consulate
57 Canadian Embassy
58 UK Embassy
59 Bulgarian Consulate
60 Boris Kidrič Hospital
61 Hotel Slavija; Airport Bus Terminal
62 Dental Clinic
63 Hungarian Consulate

Hotels Belgrade is full of state-owned B-category hotels charging 250/375 DIN and up for a single/double. The cheapest central place is *Hotel Centar* (☎ 644 055; fax 657 838), Savski trg 7, opposite the train station. It's 180 DIN for a basic single or 210 DIN for a single room with bath.

A reasonably cheap and handy state-run hotel is the *Hotel Bristol* (☎ 688 400; fax 637 453) at Karađorđeva 50, close to the bus stations. It's a bit run-down, but OK and the 180/260 DIN single/double rooms shouldn't be sneezed at.

If you are prepared to fork out more, the B-category *Hotel Beograd* (☎ 645 199; fax 643 746) at Nemanjina 6, visible from the main entrance to the train station, has time-worn singles/doubles for 220/310 DIN including breakfast. The *Hotel Astoria* (☎ 645 422; fax 686 437), nearby at M. Milovanovića 1, has singles/doubles with breakfast for 235/360 DIN.

The *Balkan Hotel* (☎ 687 466; fax 687 543) on the corner of Terazije and Prizrenska is very central and fine if you want that extra bit of comfort without going too overboard. A single/double will work out at around US$50/65.

For the record, and if you want to give your credit card a real workout, the *Inter Continental* (☎ 311 3333) and the *Hyatt Regency* (☎ 311 1234) over in dull Novi Beograd will charge you between US$150 and US$190 for the privilege of sleeping there.

Places to Eat

The *Expres Restoran Luksor*, at Balkanska 7, is the cheapest self-service place in town. Further up the street, the *Leskovac* takeaway window sells authentic Balkan-style hamburgers. A great place for breakfast burek near the train station is the *Burek i Pecivo* shop at Nemanjina 5, just below Hotel Beograd (open weekdays from 5 am to 1 pm and Saturday from 5 to 11 am). The *Kafe Car*, at Terazije 4 near the tourist office, is perfect for an espresso and a croissant.

For inexpensive seafood try the *Polet Restaurant*, Njegoševa 1. The attractive maritime décor is designed to resemble the interior of a large ship. The menu is only in Serbian but all prices are clearly listed. On weekdays between 1 and 6 pm there's a

special set menu of spicy fish soup (čorba), salad, bread and a main dish of fish and vegetables. The portions are large and the service is good.

The *Znak Pitanje* (Question Mark) restaurant, Kralja Petra 6 opposite the Orthodox church, is in an old Balkan inn serving traditional meat dishes, side salads and flat draught beer. You sit at low tables on low wooden stools. Look for the question-mark sign above the door. Prices are mid-range and the food is very good.

The *Grčka Kraljica*, at the Kalemegdan end of Kneza Mihaila, is a would-be Greek restaurant with vivid blue and white décor and Greek background muzak. The food is actually quite good, though heavy on the Serbian influence, and you can have Greek wine to accompany it. The location is particularly pleasant, situated as it is on a busy pedestrian mall. Prices are mid-range.

For local colour and if the budget is up to it, try the folkloric restaurants in the Bohemian quarter along Skadarska. In the evening, open-air folkloric, musical and theatrical performances are often staged here. There are a clutch of restaurants lining this atmospheric cobbled street among which the *Tri Šeširi* and *Ima Dana* stand out, but for more economical dining with all the atmosphere there are three good outdoor hamburger stands at the bottom end of Skadarska.

Finally, there are some even more atmospheric floating restaurants along the Danube river bank opposite the wooded island of Veliko Ratno Ostrovo, if you feel like a walk across the Brankov Most bridge towards Novi Beograd.

Entertainment

During the winter season, opera is performed at the elegant *National Theatre* (1869) on trg Republike. Their box office opens Tuesday to Sunday from 10 am to 1 pm, and from 3 pm on performance days. The Yugoslavs aren't pretentious about theatre dress – jeans are OK even at the opera.

Concerts are held at the concert hall of *Kolarčev University*, Studentski trg 5 (box office open daily from 10 am to noon and 6 to 8 pm). In October a festival of classical music is held here. The *Belgrade Philharmonia* is hidden at the end of the passageway at Studentski trg 11, directly across the street from the Ethnographical Museum.

Concerts also take place in the hall of the *Serbian Academy of Arts & Sciences*, Kneza Mihaila 35. The *French Cultural Centre*, Kneza Mihaila 31 (closed weekends), often shows free films and videos. In the evening throngs of street musicians play along Kneza Mihaila.

The British Council's Cultural Centre (☎ 323 2441; fax 324 9013; director.EΛ@britcoun.org.yu) has some captivating events each month from seminars to concerts and from talks to films. Contact the centre for details, or visit their Web site: www.britcoun.org/yugoslavia/yugeven.htm.

The Bilet Servis, trg Republike 5, has tickets to many events and the friendly English-speaking staff will search happily through their listings for something musical for you. Ask them about the *Teatar T*, Bulevard Revolucije 77a, which stages musicals several times a week (but is closed Wednesday and Thursday).

Belgrade has a growing number of discos, though most people do their socialising in the many fashionable cafés around trg Republike. One disco called *Club Promocija* is reached through a dark lane at Nušićeva 8 just off Terazije (open from 11 pm to 5 am daily except Sunday). If you really must add yet another HRC T-shirt to your collection, visit Belgrade's *Hard Rock Café* in a basement of an alleyway leading from Terazije. There is usually some live music on.

Things to Buy
There are thankfully – for the moment at least – few tacky tourist souvenirs on display to tempt you to part with your dollars or dinars. On trg Republike there is *Beogradski Izlog* (Belgrade Window), next to Bilet Servis, where you may find some tasteful local art and craftwork. Pottery features prominently, though you may also find souvenir sweaters and T-shirts emblazoned with 'Beograd' in Cyrillic.

Getting There & Away
Bus The two bus stations have computerised ticketing and there are overnight buses to many places around Yugoslavia. Buy your ticket as far ahead as you can to be assured of

a good seat. Posted destinations are in Cyrillic only. It is easier to buy your ticket from a ticket agency.

Train Belgrade is on the main railway lines from Istanbul and Athens to Western Europe. International trains on these routes are covered in the Getting There & Away section earlier in this chapter. Overnight domestic trains with couchettes or sleepers run from Belgrade to Bar (524km, 8½ hours), Peć (490km, 9½ hours) and Skopje (472km, nine hours). All trains depart from the main station on Savski trg.

Sample fares from Belgrade to Bar are as follows: 103 DIN in 2nd class in a three-bed compartment, 93 DIN in a four-bed compartment, 83 DIN in a six-bed compartment; 1st-class sleepers are 153 DIN. These prices are all-inclusive. Regular train tickets for the Belgrade-Bar journey (524km, 7½ hours) cost 69 DIN in 2nd class, or 90 DIN in 1st class.

Train Station At the main train station, the ticket counters are numbered 1 to 26. International tickets are sold at window Nos 3 and 4 and regular tickets at window Nos 7 to 20. Sleeper and couchette reservations are made in a separate office just off platform 1. Look for the blue and white 'bed' sign. Timetable and departure information is posted in Cyrillic only in the ticket hall. There is a currency-exchange window, a souvenir shop and Wasteels travel office in the smaller building facing the end of the tracks. Toilets and left luggage are next to platform 9.

Getting Around
To/From the Airport The JAT bus (15 DIN) departs from the street next to Hotel Slavija, trg Slavija (D. Tucovića), roughly every hour. This bus also picks up from the forecourt of the main train station. Surčin airport is 18km west of the city. If you're stuck at the airport waiting for a flight, visit the nearby Yugoslav Aviation Museum (closed Monday).

Public Transport Because Belgrade lacks a metro, the buses, trams and trolleybuses are tremendously overcrowded. Six-strip public transport tickets costing 8 DIN are sold at tobacco kiosks and you validate your own ticket by punching a strip once on board. If you pay a city bus or tram driver directly it will be about double the fare. Fold the top of the strip over each time you use it. Local bus riders usually have monthly passes, so don't be surprised if they do not seem to use tickets.

Taxi A motley bunch of old and new vehicles all in different colours, Belgrade's taxis are in plentiful supply. Flag fall is 4 DIN. A trip around the centre should cost between 10 and 20 DIN. Check that the taxi meter is running. If not, point it out to the driver.

Car Rental Autotehna/Avis (☎ 629 423), Obilićev Venac 25, and Putnik Hertz (☎ 641 566; fax 627 638) have cars from an expensive 915 DIN per day. A cash bond equivalent to US$500 must be paid in advance, or a credit card will suffice. Their cars are only for use within Yugoslavia.

Vojvodina (Војволина)

Vojvodina (21,506 sq km) was an autonomous province until 1990 when Serbia scrapped this arrangement and annexed Vojvodina to the Republic of Serbia. Slavs settled here in the 6th century, followed by Hungarians in the 10th century. Following their defeat at the hands of the Turks in 1389, many Serbs fled north but they and the Hungarians were later swamped by the 16th-century Turkish conquest. When the Habsburgs drove the Turks back across the Danube in the late 17th century the Vojvodina region again became a refuge for the Serbs, who had moved into this Hungarian-controlled area to escape unbroken Ottoman rule in the lands further south. The region remained a part of Hungary until 1918.

Today ethnic Serbs make up most of the population. Minorities include Hungarians (24%), Croats (8%), Slovaks (4%) and Romanians (3%). Some 170,000 ethnic Germans were expelled from Vojvodina after WWII and large numbers of Serbs immigrat-

ed here to occupy the areas the Germans formerly inhabited. As a result, the percentage of Serbs in the total population of Vojvodina increased from 37% in 1921 to 57.2% in 1991.

This low-lying land of many rivers merges imperceptibly into the Great Hungarian Plain and Romania's Banat. The Tisa River cuts southward through the middle of the region, joining the Danube midway between Novi Sad and Belgrade. The Sava and Danube rivers mark Vojvodina's southern boundary with Serbia; the Danube also separates Vojvodina from Croatia in the west. Numerous canals crisscross this fertile plain which provides much of Yugoslavia's wheat and corn. Most of Yugoslavia's crude oil comes from wells here.

NOVI SAD (НОВИ САД)
☎ 021

Novi Sad (Hungarian: Újvidék), capital of Vojvodina, is a friendly, modern city situated at a strategic bend of the Danube. The city developed in the 18th century when a powerful fortress was constructed on a hill-top overlooking the river to hold the area for the Habsburgs. Novi Sad remained part of the Austro-Hungarian empire until 1918 and it still has a Hungarian air about it today. The main sights can be covered in a couple of hours or you can make a leisurely day of it.

Novi Sad's attractions are simply wandering the pedestrian streets with their smart boutiques and outdoor cafés and visiting the Petrovaradin Citadel.

Orientation & Information
The adjacent train and bus stations are at the end of Bulevar Oslobođenja, on the northwest side of the city centre. There is a tourist agency to the right as you come out of the train station.

It's a brisk 40-minute walk from the train station to the city centre, otherwise catch bus No 4 (pay the conductor 3 DIN) from the station to Bulevar Mihajla Pupina, then ask directions to the tourist office at Dunavska 27, in a quaint old part of town. It has brochures and maps of Novi Sad.

The Automoto Klub Vojvodine is at Arse Teodorovića 15 off Pap Pavla.

YUGOSLAVIA

Post & Communications The telephone centre next to the main post office is open 24 hours. The postcode for Novi Sad is 21101.

Travel Agencies KSR Beograd Tours on Svetozara Miletića sells both domestic and international train tickets without the possible communication problems that you may have at the train station.

Things to See

There are two **museums** on Dunavska near the tourist office: both are part of the **Muzej Vojvodine**, one building is at No 35 and the other at No 39. The museums have exhibits on everything about Vojvodina and are worth a visit. They are open from Tuesday to Friday (9 am to 5 pm) and on weekends (9am to 2 pm). Entry is 3 DIN.

Walk across the old bridge to majestic **Petrovaradin Citadel** (built 1699-1780), the 'Gibraltar of the Danube', designed by French architect Vauban. The stairs beside the large church in the lower town lead up to the fortress. Today the citadel contains an expensive hotel, a restaurant and two small museums (closed Monday), but the chief

pleasure is simply to walk along the walls enjoying the splendid view of the city, river and surrounding countryside. There are up to 16km of underground galleries and halls below the citadel, but these can only be visited by groups.

Other sights in Novi Sad include three substantial **art galleries** (closed Monday and Tuesday) side by side on Vase Stajića, not far from trg Slobode, and the ultramodern **Serbian National Theatre** (1981).

Places to Stay

Camping There's a large *autocamp* (☎ 368 400) near the Danube at Ribarsko Ostrvo, with bungalows (158/163 DIN for a single/double) available all year. There is no free camping. Bus No 4 runs frequently from the train station to Liman via the city centre. From the end of the line walk towards the river. If you walk all the way from the centre of town, it will take about an hour.

Hotels The most appealing and oldest of Novi Sad's six hotels is *Hotel Vojvodina* (☎ 622 122; fax 615 445), right on trg Slobode. It has an attractive pastel façade and

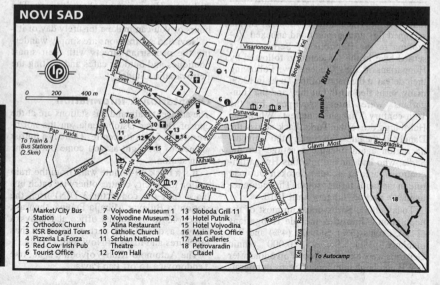

NOVI SAD

1 Market/City Bus Station	7 Vojvodine Museum 1	13 Sloboda Grill 11
2 Orthodox Church	8 Vojvodine Museum 2	14 Hotel Putnik
3 KSR Beograd Tours	9 Atina Restaurant	15 Hotel Vojvodina
4 Pizzeria La Forza	10 Catholic Church	16 Main Post Office
5 Red Cow Irish Pub	11 Serbian National Theatre	17 Art Galleries
6 Tourist Office	12 Town Hall	18 Petrovaradin Citadel

YUGOSLAVIA

is very conveniently located. The 62 rooms with private bath are 180/220 DIN for a single/double, breakfast included.

The even more pricey *Hotel Putnik* (☎ 615 555; fax 622 561), round the corner from the Vojvodina on Ilije Ognjanocića has singles/doubles for 480/600 DIN.

Places to Eat & Drink

The *Sloboda Grill 11*, on Modene in the centre, is cheap and unassuming. Take your pick and pay the cashier. The *Atina Restaurant*, next to the catholic church on trg Slobode, has a self-service section for a quick lunch and a full-service restaurant at the back. It's nothing special but at least there's a menu with prices clearly listed.

The *Pizzeria La Forza,* round the corner from the Atina at Katolička Porta 6, is a bright and cheery spot for a quick bite and if you really need a Big Mac, there's even a *McDonald's* cheek to jowl with the Town Hall.

The *Red Cow* Irish pub is a trendy spot for Guinness (cans only) and for an evening out. Enter via an arched alleyway off Zmaj Jovina or from an alleyway off Dunavska.

Getting There & Away

Novi Sad is on the main railway line between Budapest, Belgrade, Thessaloniki, Sofia and Istanbul. In the morning you can easily pick up the *Balkan Express* train to Istanbul (via Sofia; 1118km, 23 hours) or the *Hellas Express* to Thessaloniki (844km, 16 hours) in the afternoon. Trains to Subotica (99km, 1½ hours) and Belgrade (89km, 1½ hours) run every two hours. There are six trains daily to Budapest (274km, 6¼ hours) and one direct to Vienna (547 km, 9¼ hours).

SUBOTICA (СУБОТИЦА)
☎ 024

Subotica (Hungarian: Szabadka) is a large predominantly Hungarian-speaking city 10km from the Hungarian border at Kelebija. Over half the 180,000 inhabitants are of Hungarian origin and another quarter are Croats. Subotica is a useful transit point to/from Szeged (Hungary) and the train station is just a short walk from the centre of town.

The left-luggage office at the train station is open 24 hours (passport required). You pay when you collect your luggage later. The cost is 5 DIN per item.

Information

Putnik (☎ 525 400), Borisa Kidriča 4, is helpful with information and sells train tickets.

Money Vojvođanska Banka has a currency exchange office in the old town hall (open weekdays from 7.30 am to 7 pm and Saturday from 7.30 am to 1 pm). Other exchange offices are at the train station and at the Hotel Patria.

Things to See

The imposing Art Nouveau **town hall** (1910) contains an excellent **historical museum** (closed Sunday and Monday) on the 1st floor (captions in Serbian and Hungarian). Entry to the museum is through the rear entrance to the town hall. Check to see whether the exquisitely decorated council chambers on the same floor as the museum are open.

Palić, 8km east of Subotica on the railway line to Szeged, is the city's recreation centre, with a zoo, lake, sporting facilities, restaurants and pleasant walks. The attractive park was laid out in 1912 and the pointed water tower is visible from the train.

Places to Stay & Eat

The only hotel in Subotica is the seven-storey, B-category *Hotel Patria* (☎ 554 500; fax 551 762), on Đure Đakovića, three blocks left as you exit the train station. The Singles/doubles are 238/376 DIN with bath and breakfast.

There is a noticeable dearth of regular restaurants in the immediate town centre area, but the *Boss Pizzeria*, Engelsova 7 off Borisa Kidriča, is a relaxing spot for a decent pizza and a beer.

There are three hotels at Palić. The best is the *Park* near the train station. The *Jezero* is also near the station, while the less expensive *Sport* is close to the camping ground, about 10 minutes walk away. In winter only the Park is open. The train to/from Szeged stops near these hotels. You can also get there on bus No 6 from the main bus station near Hotel Patria in Subotica.

Getting There & Away

There are four local trains a day to/from Szeged, Hungary (45km, 1¾ hours, 35 DIN). Several daily buses also shuttle between Szeged and Subotica (DM4), but the train is more convenient. A daily bus links Subotica to Budapest (216km, DM25). Buses to Hungary must be paid for in either DM or Hungarian forints.

Subotica shares the same international train connections as Novi Sad with a 1½ hour time difference. (See Getting There & Away for Novi Sad).

Montenegro (Црна Гора)

The Republic of Montenegro (Crna Gora) occupies a corner of south-western Yugoslavia directly north of Albania, close to where the Dinaric Alps merge with the Balkan range. The republic's Adriatic coastline attracts masses of Serbian sunseekers, but there are also the spectacular Morača and Tara canyons in the interior.

Between Podgorica and Kolašin a scenic railway runs right up the Morača Canyon, with fantastic views between the countless tunnels. West of Mojkovac, the next station after Kolašin, is the 100km-long Tara Canyon, thought to be the second-largest in the world. Other striking features of this compact, 13,812-sq-km republic are the winding Bay of Kotor (the longest and deepest fjord in southern Europe) and Lake Skadar (the largest lake in the Balkans), which Montenegro shares with Albania. There are no major islands off the Montenegrin coast but the sandy beaches here are far longer than those further north in Croatia. Now cut off from northern Europe by the closed border with Croatia and the troubles in Bosnia-Hercegovina, Montenegro is a bit of a backwater these days.

History

Only tiny Montenegro kept its head above the Turkish tide which engulfed the Balkans for over four centuries. Medieval Montenegro was part of Serbia, and after the Serbian defeat at Kosovo Polje in 1389 the inhabitants of this mountainous region continued to resist the Turks. In 1482 Ivan Crnojević established an independent principality at Cetinje ruled by *vladike* (bishops) who were popularly elected after 1516. Beginning in 1697 the succession was limited to the Petrović Njegoš family (each bishop being succeeded by his nephew, who forged an alliance with Russia in 1711.

Intermittent wars with the Turks and Albanians continued until 1878, when the European portion of the Ottoman Empire largely collapsed and Montenegrin independence was recognised by the Congress of Berlin. Nicola I Petrović, Montenegro's ruler from 1860, declared himself king in 1910. In 1916 the Austrians evicted the bishop-king and in 1918 Montenegro was incorporated into Serbia. During WWII Montenegrins fought valiantly in Tito's partisan army and after the war the region was rewarded with republic status within Yugoslavia. In 1946 the administration shifted from Cetinje to Podgorica (known until 1991 as Titograd), a modern city with little to interest the visitor.

The history of Montenegro is hard to follow unless you remember that, like the Albanians, the Montenegrins were divided into tribes or clans, such as the Njegoš clan west of Cetinje and the Paštrović clan around Budva. While blind obedience to the clan leader helped Montenegrins resist foreign invasions, it has not made the transition to democracy easy.

Getting There & Away

In the past, most visitors to Montenegro arrived from Dubrovnik by car or bus. The 1991 fighting closed this route and until the situation normalises the easiest way to get there is by train from Belgrade to Bar. You can also fly directly to Tivat or Podgorica airports from Belgrade. Regular ferries also run from Bari and Ancona in Italy.

BAR (БАР)
☎ 085

Backed by a barren coastal range, Bar (Italian: Antivari) is a would-be modern city whose architects seemed to have graduated from the socialist cement school of thought. It is not a terribly attractive city, punctuated as it is with white apartment blocks surrounding a socialist kitsch commercial centre with its obligatory flying saucer-style buildings. It is however a strategically important city to Yugoslavia and is the terminus of the railway from Belgrade and Yugoslavia's only port.

The development of Bar as an Adriatic port for landlocked Serbia was first proposed in 1879, yet it was not until 1976 that the dream became a reality, with the opening of the train line. In Summer a daily ferry connects Bar with Bari and three times a week with Ancona in Italy. As long as the border between Croatia and Yugoslavia remains closed, Bar will probably be your gateway to Montenegro. Bar is a convenient transport centre and if you find a cheap private room it makes a good base for day trips to Ulcinj, Cetinje, Kotor and Budva.

Orientation
The ferry terminal in Bar is only a few hundred metres from the centre of town, but the bus and train stations are side by side about 2km south-east of the centre. The rather pebbly beach is north of the port.

Information
The tourist office next to Putnik near the port has a few brochures and the adjacent Montenegro Express office can answer questions in English.

Money There are a number of banks in the port area and you can change money at the post office. You may encounter touts asking to change your money illegally.

Places to Stay & Eat
Autocamp Susanj, 2km north of the ferry landing along the beach, is once again open for business during summer. However, it's a basic camp with fairly rundown facilities.

Putnik Turist Biro opposite the ferry terminal, open from 7 am to 9 or 10 pm in summer, arranges private rooms for around 60 DIN per person, depending on facilities. Putnik is normally open to meet boat arrivals and is the best bet for accommodation in Bar.

Hotel Topolica (☎ 11 244; fax 12 731), a crumbling four-story socialist relic on the beach a few hundred metres north of the port, is the only hotel as such in town. It offers hyperinflated singles/doubles for 432/960 DIN, including a paltry breakfast. Avoid it if you can.

The *Pizzeria Napoletana*, just up from the Putnik office, is handy if you are waiting for a ferry, and the *Grill Holiday*, between the bus and train stations, is convenient for a tasty hamburger if you are waiting for a bus or a train.

Getting There & Away
Four trains a day (two with couchettes) travel to/from Belgrade (524km, nine hours, 69 DIN). The left-luggage office at the train station is open from 7 am to 9 pm. There are buses to all destinations along the coast. In summer there is a daily ferry linking Bar to Bari (Italy) which leaves at either 9 or 10 pm, and another ferry to Ancona three times a week. Fares on most ferries must usually be paid for in hard currency. Out of season there are only three ferries a week to Bari. In midsummer all transport to/from Bar is very crowded as all of Serbia heads for the beach.

ULCINJ (УЛЦИЊ)
☎ 085
A broad highway tunnels through hills between olive groves for 26km from Bar to Ulcinj (Ulqin in Albanian, Dulcigno in Italian), near the Albanian border.

Founded by the Greeks, Ulcinj gained notoriety when it was used as a base by North African pirates from 1571 to 1878. There was even a slave market from which the few resident black families are descended.

The Turks held Bar and Ulcinj for over 300 years, and today there are many Muslim Albanians in Ulcinj. You'll notice the difference in people right away: the characteristic white headshawls of the women, the curious direct looks you get, the lively bazar atmosphere in the many small shops, and the sound of Albanian on the streets. Many older women in Ulcinj still wear traditional Islamic dress, especially on market day (Friday). It's a popular holiday resort for Serbs, who arrive en masse via the Belgrade-Bar train. In July and August it can get very crowded, although accommodation is always available.

Orientation

Ulcinj's bus station is about 2km south of Mala Plaža, the small beach below the old town. You will most likely be dropped off nearer the main drag, 26 Novembar, rather than at the bus station proper. Walk uphill along 26 Novembar to Mala Plaža and you'll pass several buildings with *sobe* and *zimmer* signs where you can rent a room.

Velika Plaža (Great Beach), Ulcinj's famous 12km stretch of unbroken sand, begins about 5km south-east of town (take the bus to Ada).

Information

Adriatours, at 26 Novembar 18, is about 500m from the bus station on the way into town on the right (see Places to Stay).

Money There are several banks in town. Room proprietors and restaurant owners will often change hard cash for you.

Post & Communications The telephone centre in the main post office, at the foot of 26 Novembar near the bus station, is open Monday to Saturday from 7 am to 9 pm and Sunday from 9 am to noon.

Things to See

The ancient **ramparts** of old Ulcinj overlook the sea, but most of the buildings inside were shattered by earthquakes in 1979 and later reconstructed. The **museum** (closed Monday) is by the upper gate. You can walk among the houses and along the wall for the view.

Places to Stay

Camping There are two camping grounds on Velika Plaža: *Milena* and *Neptun*. On Ada Island, just across the Bojana River from Albania, is *Camping Ada Bojana FKK*, a nudist camping ground accessible by bus (guests only).

Private Rooms *Adriatours* (☎ 52 057), 26 Novembar 18, is a private travel agency with helpful English-speaking staff who will find you a private room for about 60 DIN per

person a night. They're open all year. If you arrive outside business hours knock on the door of the adjacent house with the *zimmer frei* signs (owned by the same family) and if they can't accommodate you they'll suggest someone else who can.

If you continue into town towards Mala Plaža, you'll pass *Olcinium Travel Agency* (more private rooms) nearly opposite Kino Basta (Basta Cinema). Facing Mala Plaža itself is *Turist Biro 'Neptun' Montenegroturist*, with another selection of private rooms (60 DIN per person).

Hotels The cheapest hotel is the 240-room *Mediteran* (☎ 81 411), a pleasant modern hotel five minutes walk uphill from Mala Plaža. Singles/doubles with private bath and breakfast are 210/300 DIN and most have a balcony overlooking the sea. It's only open in the summer season.

Places to Eat

There are some chic eating places in the old town if your budget can stand a blowout. There are also numerous inexpensive restaurants around town offering cheap grilled meat or more expensive seafood. Try the *Dubrovnik Restaurant* next to the unfinished cultural centre on 26 Novembar.

Getting There & Away

Buses to/from Bar (26km, 10 DIN) run every couple of hours.

BUDVA (БУДВА)
☎ 086

Budva is Yugoslavia's top beach resort. A series of fine beaches punctuate the coastline all the way to Sveti Stefan, with the high coastal mountains forming a magnificent backdrop. Before the troubles, Budva used to cater mostly to people on package tours from northern Europe, but its main clientele these days is domestic. Although Budva is not cheap, you may find some good deals just outside the main tourist season of July and August. Though Bar is better positioned transport-wise as a base for making coastal day trips, Budva is far more beautiful and worth the extra effort and expense if you're not in a hurry.

Orientation & Information

The modern bus station is located in a new part of town about 1km from the old town. Upon exiting the bus station turn left, walk for about 150m before heading right until you hit the main road. Turn right and follow this road to the traffic lights. Turn left here and follow the road round until you come to the main square, trg Republike. There's no left-luggage office at Budva bus station.

The people at Montenegro Express on trg Republike near the old town are good about answering questions.

Money There are two banks on trg Republike: Montenegro Bank and Jugobank. Hotels will normally exchange cash without any problem.

Things to See

Budva's big tourist-puller is its old **walled town**. This was levelled by two earthquakes in 1979, after which the residents were permanently evacuated. Since then it has been completely rebuilt as a tourist attraction and the main square with its three churches, museum and fortress (there's a great view from the ramparts) is so picturesque it seems almost contrived. It's possible to walk three-quarters of the way around the top of the town wall. Start from near the north gate.

Budva's main beach is pebbly and fairly average. A better beach is **Mogren Beach**, reached by following a coastal path northwards for 500m or so. The path starts in front of the Grand Hotel Avala.

Only a few kilometres south-east of Budva is the former village of **Sveti Stefan**, an island now linked to the mainland. During the 1960s the entire village was converted into a luxury hotel but unlike Budva, which you may enter free, you will be charged to set foot on the hallowed soil of Sveti Stefan during the summer months. Settle for the long-range picture-postcard view and keep your money.

Places to Stay

Camping If you have a tent, try *Autocamp Avala* (☎ 51 205), behind Hotel Montenegro, 2km south-east along the shore (through a small tunnel). It's crowded with caravans, but at least it's near the beach. No bungalows are available but the manager may help you find

a private room nearby. Avala is open from June to September. Right next to Avala is *Autokamp Boreti*, which has less in the way of security (fences and gates especially).

Private Rooms *Maestral Tours* (☎ 52 250) at Mediteranska 23, just down from the post office, rents private rooms at around 60 to 70 DIN per person in July and August only. *Emona Globetour* nearby may also have private rooms, and a third place to try is *Montenegro Express* (☎ 51 443) on trg Republike, closer to the old town. You may be able to find your own room by looking for signs, but during the October to May low season finding a private room may take some searching out.

Hotels The easiest and most convenient option is the modern *Hotel Mogren* (☎ 51 780; fax 51 750) just outside the north gate of the old town. Rates are a fairly pricey 480/720 DIN for singles/doubles in July and August, but this place is open all year and prices out of season are 360/552 DIN.

Maestral Tours runs the *Hotel Mediteran* (☎ 51 423), about 2km south along the coast at Bečići. Prices here range from 280 to 375 DIN per person. Check with Maestral Tours for room availability first.

In the high season try asking for room-filler deals from the other resort hotels, but don't be too optimistic since room prices tend to be fixed by the government and demand is usually high.

Places to Eat

For a cheap feed without the frills, the *Restoran Centar* is upstairs beside the supermarket (above the vegetable market) just inland from the post office. At the bus station there is a reasonable *self-service restaurant* if you are in transit or waiting for a bus.

Budva has no shortage of expensive bars and restaurants along the seafront and in the old town. Unfortunately these bars and restaurants don't often display their prices outside, so always ask to see a menu before ordering. Locals tend to avoid these restaurants. Check out instead the *Restaurant Jadran* about 800m south along the waterfront. It is a popular local eating place and specialises in fish dishes at quite affordable prices.

Getting There & Away

There are almost hourly buses to Podgorica (74km) via Cetinje (31km) and 16 a day to Bar (38km). There are also buses to Belgrade and other parts of Yugoslavia.

If coming by train from Belgrade, get off at Podgorica and catch a bus from there to Budva. In the other direction it's probably best to take a bus from Budva to Bar and pick up the train to Belgrade there, since many people board the train at Podgorica.

If you choose to fly to Tivat, a JAT bus (15 DIN) will take you to Budva and drop you off at trg Republike.

Getting Around

From May to September a small tourist train shuttles up and down the beach from Budva to Bečići for 10 DIN a ride. Ask around the harbour for tourist boats to the little island of Sveti Stefan just across the bay.

CETINJE (ЦЕТИЊЕ)
☎ 086

Cetinje, perched on top of a high plateau between the Bay of Kotor and Skadar Lake, is the old capital of Montenegro, subject of songs and epic poems. The open, easily defended slopes help to explain Montenegro's independence, and much remains of old Cetinje, from museums to palaces, mansions and monasteries. At the turn of the century all the large states of Europe had embassies here. Short hikes can be made in the hills behind Cetinje Monastery. It's well worth spending the night here if you can find an inexpensive place to stay.

Orientation & Information

The bus station is 500m from the main square, Balšića Pazar. From the station turn left and the first right and you will find it easily. There is a big wall map in the square to help you get oriented with the main sights and reference points.

Things to See

The most imposing building in Cetinje is the State Museum, the former palace (1871) of Nicola I Petrović, the last king. Looted during WWII, only a portion of its original furnishings remain, but the many portraits

and period weapons give a representative picture of the times.

Nearly opposite is the older 1832 residence of the prince-bishop Petar II Petrović Njegoš, who ruled from 1830 to 1851. This building, now a museum, is also known as Biljarda Hall because of a billiard table installed in 1840.

Around the side of Biljarda Hall is a large glass-enclosed pavilion containing a fascinating relief map of Montenegro created by the Austrians in 1917 for tactical planning purposes. Ask one of the Biljarda Hall attendants to let you in.

Beyond the map is Cetinje Monastery, founded in 1484 but rebuilt in 1785. The monastery treasury contains a copy of the *Oktoih* or 'Octoechos' (Book of the Eight Voices) printed near here in 1494 – it's one of the oldest collections of liturgical songs in a Slavic language. Vladin Dom, the former Government House (1910) and now the National Gallery, is not far away.

Twenty km away at the summit of Mt Lovčen (1749m), the 'Black Mountain' which gave Montenegro its Italian name, is the mausoleum of Petar II Petrović Njegoš, a revered poet as well as ruler. The masterful statue of Njegoš inside is by Croatian sculptor Ivan Meštrović. There are no buses up Lovčen and taxis want 160 DIN return; the building is visible in the distance from Cetinje. From the parking lot you must climb 461 steps to the mausoleum and its sweeping view of the Bay of Kotor, mountains and coast. The whole of Mt Lovčen has been declared a national park.

Places to Stay & Eat

For a private room ask at *Intours* (☎ 21 157), the place marked 'Vincom Duty Free Shop' next to the post office. Chances are they'll send you to Petar Martinović, who lives a block away at Bajova Pivljanina 50, next to Belveder Mini Market.

If this fails you have a problem as the only hotel is the *Grand Hotel* (☎ 21 104), a modern so-called five-star hotel that would barely rate two stars anywhere else. Singles/doubles are 220/310 DIN with bath and breakfast. It's a five-minute walk from the centre.

There is not a glut of eating places in Cetinje. The *Restoran Cetinje* next to the post office and the *Mliječni Restoran* on the main square are usually closed out of season, but open in summer. Failing these two, you might opt for passable pasta or pizza at the *Spoleto* pizzeria further down from the post office.

Getting There & Away

There are 19 buses a day between Cetinje and Podgorica (45km), and a similar number back to Budva (31km).

You can easily make Cetinje a day trip from Bar by catching an early train to Podgorica, where you'll connect with a bus to Cetinje. An early afternoon bus down to Budva will give you some time at the beach and a chance to look around the reconstructed old town before taking a late afternoon bus back to Bar.

DURMITOR NATIONAL PARK

Montenegro's Durmitor National Park is a popular hiking and mountaineering area just west of **Žabljak**, a ski resort which is also the highest town in Yugoslavia (1450m). A chair lift from near Hotel Durmitor towards Mt Štuoc (1953m) operates in winter. Žabljak was a major partisan base during WWII, changing hands four times.

Some 18 mountain lakes dot the slopes of the Durmitor Range south-west of Žabljak. You can walk right around the largest lake, **Crno jezero** (Black Lake), 3km from Žabljak, in an hour or two, and swim in its waters in summer. The rounded mass of Međed (2287m) rises directly behind the lake, surrounded by a backdrop of other peaks, including Savin kuk (2313m). You can climb Savin kuk in eight hours there and back. The national park office next to Hotel Durmitor sells good maps of the park.

Durmitor's claim to fame is the 1067m-deep **Tara Canyon**, which cuts dramatically into the mountain slopes and plateau for about 100km. The edge of the Tara Canyon is about 12km north of Žabljak, a three-hour walk along a road beginning near Hotel Planinka. Yugoslav tourist brochures maintain that this is the second-largest canyon in the world after the Grand Canyon in the USA, a claim other countries such as Mexico and Namibia also make for their canyons, but any way you look at it, it's a top sight.

White-Water Tours

Travel agencies sometimes offer rubber-raft trips on the clean green water, over countless foaming rapids, down the steep forested Tara Gorge. These begin at Splavište near the Đurđevića Tara bridge. Three-day raft expeditions go right down the Tara River to the junction with the Piva River at Šćepan Polje (88km), near the border with Bosnia.

For advance information on white-water rafting on the Tara River contact Ski Centar Durmitor, (☎ 011-629 602; fax 011-634 944) Kralja Petra 70, Belgrade. At last report two-day, one-night raft trips departed from Žabljak every Monday from June to August; they cost about 500 DIN per person including transfers, meals and gear. There's a 10-person minimum to run a trip, so inquire well ahead. In winter the same Belgrade office will know all about ski facilities at Žabljak.

Places to Stay

The *tourist office* in the centre of Žabljak is not much help – it arranges expensive private rooms at 80 DIN for a single and hands out brochures written in Serbian.

Žabljak has four hotels owned by Montenegroturist. The *Planinka* (☎ 083-88 344) and *Jezera* (☎ 083-88 226) are modern ski hotels charging 132 DIN per person with half-board in summer. The *Hotel Žabljak* (☎ 083-88 300) right in the centre of town also offers rooms with half-board for 210 DIN per person.

The cheapest of the bunch is the old four-storey wooden *Hotel Durmitor* (☎ 083-88 278), past Hotel Jezera at the entrance to the national park, a 15-minute walk from town. Singles/doubles with shared bath here are 120 DIN, with half-board. Although the Durmitor seems to have the reputation of being run-down and unfit for foreigners, some of the rooms are quite pleasant, with balconies facing the mountains. Just be aware that there's no hot water or showers in the building.

On a hill-top five minutes' walk beyond the national park office is *Autocamp Ivan-do* which is little more than a fenced-off field. People around here rent *private rooms* at rates far lower than those charged in town and you'll get an additional discount if you have a sleeping bag and don't require sheets. Set right in the middle of the forest, Ivan-do is a perfect base for hikers.

Places to Eat

The *Restoran Sezam* next to the small market just below the Turist Biro bakes its own bread and is one of the only places apart from the hotels that serves meals.

Getting There & Away

The easiest way to get to Žabljak is to take a bus from Belgrade to Pljevlja (334km), then one of the two daily buses from Pljevlja to Žabljak (57km). On the return journey, these buses leave Žabljak for Pljevlja at 5 am and 5 pm, connecting for Mojkovac and Podgorica at Đurđevića Tara, where there's a spectacular bridge over the canyon. If you have to change buses at Pljevlja, hurry as they don't wait long.

As soon as you arrive at Žabljak inquire about onward buses to Belgrade, Pljevlja, Mojkovac and Podgorica at the red kiosk marked 'Turist Biro' beside the bus stop. Seats should be booked the day before.

Another jumping-off point is Mojkovac on the Belgrade-Podgorica line. About four trains daily run from Bar to Mojkovac (157km, two hours); catch the earliest one for the best connections. At Mojkovac you must walk 2km from the train station to the bus station, where you can pick up buses running from Podgorica to Pljevlja. They'll usually drop you at Đurđevića Tara and from there you may have to hitch the remaining 22km to Žabljak.

Coming from Bar, take a train to Podgorica and then take the afternoon bus from there direct to Žabljak.

Kosovo (Kocobo)

A visit to Kosovo (Kosova in Albanian) can be a traumatic experience, if it is at all possible. Probably nowhere in Europe are human rights as flagrantly and systematically violated as they are here. The people have an uninhibited friendliness and curiosity which sets them apart from other Yugoslavs and the direct looks you get are at first disconcerting. The region's poverty and backwardness are apparent, as is the watchful eye of the Serbian government. Police posts have taken the place of left-luggage facilities in the region's bus and train stations. Your presence may not be welcome.

Until recently an autonomous province, Kosovo is now an integral part of the Republic of Serbia. Just under two million people occupy Kosovo's 10,887 sq km, making it the most densely populated portion of Yugoslavia; it also has the highest birth rate. The Albanians adopted Islam after the Turkish conquest and today the region has a definite Muslim air, from the inhabitants' food and dress to the ubiquitous mosques. The capital, Priština, is a depressing, redeveloped city with showplace banks and hotels juxtaposed against squalor, but in the west the Metohija Valley between Peć and Prizren offers a useful transit route from the Adriatic to Macedonia, or Belgrade to Albania, plus a chance to see another side of this troubled land.

History

Isolated medieval Serbian monasteries tell of an early period which ended in 1389 with the Serbs' crushing defeat at the hands of the Turks at Kosovo Polje, just outside Priština (Prishtinë in Albanian). After this disaster the Serbs moved north, abandoning the region to the Albanians, descendants of the ancient Illyrians, who had inhabited this land for thousands of years.

In the late 19th century the ethnic Albanians, who make up 90% of the population today, struggled to free themselves of Ottoman rule. Yet in 1913, when the Turkish government finally pulled out, Kosovo was handed over to Serbia. Over half a million ethnic Albanians emigrated to Turkey and elsewhere to escape Serbian rule and by 1940 at least 18,000 Serb families had been settled on the vacated lands. During WWII, Kosovo was incorporated into Italian-controlled Albania and in October 1944 it was liberated by Albanian communist partisans to whom Tito had promised an autonomous republic within Yugoslavia. The area came under Tito's forces in early 1945, not without force.

After the war Tito wanted Albania itself included in the Yugoslav Federation as a seventh republic, with Kosovo united to it. This never came to pass and thus began two decades of pernicious neglect. Between 1954 and 1957 another 195,000 Albanians were coerced into emigrating to Turkey. After serious rioting in 1968 (and with the Soviet invasion of Czechoslovakia pushing Yugoslavia and Albania closer together), an autonomous province was created in 1974 and economic aid increased. Due to these concessions Kosovo is one of the only parts of ex-Yugoslavia where Tito is still warmly remembered. You see his portrait in restaurants and cafés everywhere and the main street in Peć is still named after him.

Yet the changes brought only cosmetic improvements and the standard of living in Kosovo (which has some of the most fertile land in the Balkans) remained a quarter the Yugoslav average. Kosovo was treated as a colony, its mines providing raw materials for industry in Serbia. In 1981, demonstrations calling for full republic status were put down by military force at a cost of over 300 lives. The 7000 young Albanians subsequently arrested were given jail terms of six years and up. This brutal denial of equality within the Yugoslav Federation sowed the seeds which led to the violent break-up of the country a decade later.

State of Emergency Trouble began anew in November 1988 as Albanian demonstrators protested against the sacking by Belgrade of local officials, including the provincial president Azem Vllasi, who was later arrested. A Kosovo coal miners' strike in February 1989 was followed by new limits imposed by Serbia on Kosovo's autonomy, a curfew and a state of emergency. This resulted in serious rioting, and 24 unarmed Albanian civilians were shot dead by the Yugoslav security forces.

On 5 July 1990 the Serbian parliament cancelled Kosovo's political autonomy and dissolved its assembly and government. The only Albanian-language daily newspaper, *Rilindja*, was banned and TV and radio broadcasts in Albanian ceased. In a process termed 'differentiation' some 115,000 Albanians suspected of having nationalist sympathies were fired from their jobs and Serbs installed in their places. At Priština University, 800 Albanian lecturers were sacked, effectively ending teaching in Albanian and forcing all but 500 of the 23,000 Albanian students to terminate their studies. Albanian secondary-school teachers were forced to work without salaries, otherwise the schools would have closed. All Albanians working in state hospitals were sacked, creating a growth industry in private clinics where most Albanian women now give birth. (This happened after rumours that the survival rate for male Albanian babies born in hospitals had suddenly dropped.)

Large numbers of Albanians went abroad after losing their jobs and a third of adult male Kosovars now work in Western Europe. Ironically, with Yugoslavia now in an economic tailspin, the families of the émigrés are fairly well off thanks to the hard currency their men send home, while the Serbs who took their government jobs are paid in supersoft Yugoslav dinars. The 20% of ethnic Albanians who do have jobs in Kosovo work almost exclusively in private businesses.

In September 1991, Serbian police and militia mobilised to block a referendum on independence for Kosovo, turning voters away and arresting election officials. The vote went ahead anyway and, with a 90% turnout, 98% voted in favour of independence from Serbia. In further elections on 24 May 1992, also declared illegal by Serbia, the writer Ibrahim Rugova was elected president of Kosovo. The unrecognised parliament of the Republic of Kosovo, elected at the same time as Mr Rugova, is attempting to create a parallel administration that can offer passive resistance to Serbia and has requested UN peacekeeping troops for Kosovo.

The Spectre of War An Albanian national uprising would certainly unleash the bloodiest of ex-Yugoslavia's latest series of civil wars and the Kosovars are intensely aware of the way Western countries stood by and tolerated ethnic genocide in Bosnia, so they have attempted to resist Serb aggression with non-violence. Yugoslavia stationed an estimated 40,000 troops and police in Kosovo and nobody doubted its readiness to use them. Serb nationalists are firmly convinced they have a historic right to Kosovo as part of a 'Greater Serbia' and a plan exists to colonise Kosovo with Serbs. In December 1992, Kosovo Serbs elected to parliament a thuggish militia leader named Arkan whose troops have been accused of murdering 3000 Muslims in northern Bosnia.

Early in 1998, however, the Serbian army clamped down on Albanians in Kosovo with a series of clinical attacks on so-called

YUGOSLAVIA

'Kosovar terrorists' principally in and around the village of Dečani near Peć. Officially only 40 or so Albanians were killed, including women and children, but the true number is likely to have been much higher. Condemned widely by most international governments, the Milošević regime ignored protests and continued the clampdown throughout the first half of 1998, attracting a US-led arms embargo on Serbia for its intransigence. A national referendum in Yugoslavia in April 1998 on whether foreign powers should be allowed to interfere in the internal matters of Yugoslavia was firmly rejected by the Serb majority and Yugoslavia's isolation from the international community was once again assured. As this chapter was being updated, arms were being covertly supplied to the Kosovars by Albanians in Albania and the Yugoslavia/Albania border region became one of high alert with the threat of all-out war between the two countries a strong possibility.

Warning As of mid-1998 it was almost impossible to visit Kosovo without a very good reason. Tourism was certainly not one of them. Tourist information on the area was only cursorily checked for this edition and may not be totally accurate should the situation ease and safe travel to the area be possible once more. Should you seek to cross into Kosovo you will almost certainly be stopped and questioned at the internal border. Whether you will be allowed into Kosovo will depend entirely on the prevailing political and military situation.

Getting There & Away
Getting to Kosovo from Serbia and Macedonia is technically easy as there are direct trains from Belgrade to Peć (490km, 9½ hours), and buses from Skopje to Prizren (117km).

Getting from the Adriatic coast to Kosovo, on the other hand, takes a full night or day. From Budva or Cetinje catch a bus to Podgorica and look for a direct bus to Peć from there. The buses usually go via Berane, though some may go via the 1849m Čakor pass. If you're leaving from Ulcinj, take an early bus to Bar, then a train to Podgorica.

Try to get as far as Peć or Prizren on the first day since accommodation between the coast and Kosovo is either nonexistent or dire. If you do get stuck, *Autocamp Berane* (☎ 084-61 822) is less than 1km from Berane bus station. If you are in a real bind, you could stop at Rožaje (32km from Berane) and spend the night at the truly dreadful *Rožaje Hotel* (☎ 0871-54 335), which charges 170 DIN for a dingy single. An early bus will carry you the 37km from Rožaje to Peć the next morning. There's nil to see or do in Rožaje. For the route to/from Albania, see the later Prizren section.

PEĆ (ПЕЋ)
☎ 039
Peć (Peja in Albanian), below high mountains between Podgorica and Priština, is a friendly, untouristed town of picturesque dwellings with some modern development. Ethnic Albanian men with their white felt skullcaps and women in traditional dress crowd the streets, especially on Saturday (market day). The horse wagons carrying goods around Peć share the streets with lots of beggars.

Orientation
The bus and train stations are about 500m apart, both in the east part of Peć about 1km from the centre. Neither station has a left-luggage room. Follow Rruga Maršal Tito west from the bus station into the centre of town.

Information
Try Kosmet Tours at Nemanjina 102; Putnik, Nemanjina 64; and Metohija Turist, Nemanjna 20.

Post & Communications The main post office and telephone centre is opposite the Hotel Metohija.

Things to See
There are eight well-preserved, functioning mosques in Peć, the most imposing of which is the 15th-century **Bajrakli Mosque**. Its high dome rises out of the colourful **bazar** (*čaršija*), giving Peć an authentic Oriental air.

By the river 2km west of Peć is the **Patrijaršija Monastery**, seat of the Serbian

Orthodox patriarchate in the 14th century, from 1557 to 1766 and again after 1920. The rebirth of the patriarchate in 1557 allowed the Serbs to maintain their identity during the darkest days of Ottoman domination, so this monastery is of deep significance to Serbs. Inside the high-walled compound are three mid-13th century churches, each of which has a high dome and glorious medieval frescoes. There is a detailed explanation in English in the common narthex (admission 20 DIN). Two km west of the monastery along the main highway is the **Rugovo Gorge**, an excellent hiking area.

Peć's most impressive sight, however, is 15km south and accessible by frequent local bus. The **Visoki Dečani Monastery** (1335), with its marvellous 14th-century frescoes, is a 2km walk from the bus stop in Dečani (Deçan in Albanian) through beautiful wooded countryside. This royal monastery, built under kings Dečanski and Dušan, survived the long Turkish period intact. From Dečani you can catch an onward bus to Prizren.

Places to Stay
Camping Over the bridge and 1km up the hill from the Metohija Hotel is the quiet and rather pleasant *Kamp Karagač* (☎ 22 358), with lots of shade. This camping ground has been privatised and its main business is now the restaurant. It doesn't really cater to campers any more, though this could change, so ask.

Hotels The B-category *Hotel Park* (☎ 21 864), just beyond Kamp Karagač, is your best bet. Prices here vary but it's not too expensive.

The A-category *Metohija Hotel* (☎ 22 611), Nemanjina 60, is a budget-breaker at 280/360 DIN for a single/double with private bath and breakfast. Also consider the private *Hotel Dypon* (☎ 31 593) which charges around 300 DIN for a single/double room.

None of the travel agencies in town offers private rooms.

Getting There & Away
Bus Services from Prizren (73km) and Skopje (190km) are good and there's a night bus to/from Belgrade (388km). In July and August buses run direct to Peć from Ulcinj (279km).

Train Express trains going between Belgrade and Peć stop at Kosovo Polje, a junction 8km west of Priština. From here, Peć is 91km away (two hours) while a separate line runs to Prizren (125km, three hours). There's an overnight train with couchettes to/from Belgrade.

PRIZREN (ПРИЗРЕН)
☎ 029
Prizren, which is the most Albanian-looking city in Yugoslavia, is midway between Peć and Skopje. The road from Shkodra reaches the Albanian border at Vrbnica, 18km west of Prizren.

Prizren was the medieval capital of 'Old Serbia' but much of what we see today is Turkish. Colourful houses climb up the hillside to the ruined citadel *(kalaja)*, from which the 15th-century Turkish bridge and 19 minarets are visible.

The Bistrica River emerges from a gorge behind the citadel and cuts Prizren in two on its way into Albania. East up this gorge is the Bistrica Pass (2640m), once the main route to Macedonia. Wednesday is market day, when the city really comes alive.

Orientation
The bus and train stations are adjacent on the west side of town, but there's no left-luggage facility in either. From the bus station follow Rruga Metohjska towards the mountains, then take Rruga Vidovdanska up the riverside into town.

Information
Try the Tourist Association of Prizren, Rruga Vidovdanska 51, or Putnik on trg Cara Dušana in the centre of town.

Post & Communications The main post office and telephone centre is adjacent to the Theranda Hotel.

Things to See
On your way into town from the bus station you'll see the huge white-marble Bankos Prizren building facing the river. On a backstreet behind the bank is the **Church of Bogorodica Ljeviška** (1307), which has an open bell tower above and frescoes inside. Nearby, a tall square tower rises above some

Turkish baths, now the **Archaeological Museum** (usually closed).

The **Sinan Pasha Mosque** (1561) beside the river in the centre is closed, as are the **Gazi Mehmed Pasha Baths** (1563) beyond the Theranda Hotel. A little back from these is the large dome of the beautifully appointed 16th-century **Bajrakli (Gazi Mehmed) Mosque**, which is still in use. Behind this mosque, on the side facing the river, is the **Museum of the Prizren League**, a popular movement which struggled for Albanian autonomy within the Ottoman Empire from 1878 to 1881. In 1881 Dervish Pasha suppressed the League, killing thousands of Albanians and exiling thousands more to Asia Minor.

The largest Orthodox church in Prizren is **Sveti Georgi** (1856) in the old town near the Sinan Pasha Mosque. Higher up on the way to the **citadel** is **Sveti Spas**, with the ruins of an Orthodox monastery.

Places to Stay & Eat

Unfortunately, no private rooms are available in Prizren. The B-category *Theranda Hotel* (☎ 22 292), by the river in the centre of town, charges 160/220 DIN for a single/double with private bath and breakfast.

Motel Putnik (☎ 43 107; fax 41 552), near the river three blocks from the bus station (ask directions), charges similar prices for foreigners and locals, which makes it relatively cheap (prices vary). The camping ground behind the motel has been officially closed for years but they'll probably let you pitch a tent there at no cost.

Several good *čevapčići* places lie between Sveti Georgi and Sinan Pasha.

Getting There & Away

Bus service is good from Priština (75km), Peć (73km) and Skopje (117km). Only slow local trains to Metohija junction (64km, 1½ hours) and Kosovo Polje (125km, three hours) leave from Prizren, so you're much better off coming and going by bus.

Buses to the Albanian border used to leave from the street beginning at Rruga Vidovdanska 77.

Appendix I – Climate Charts

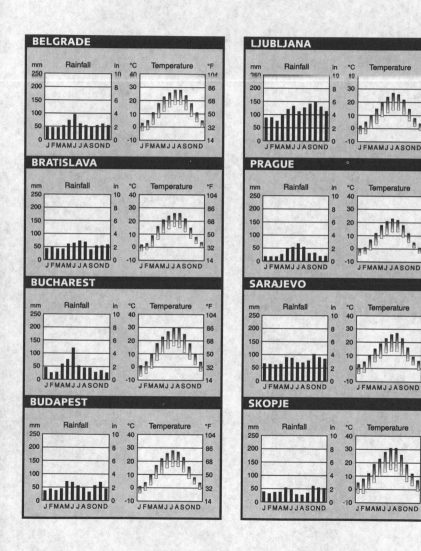

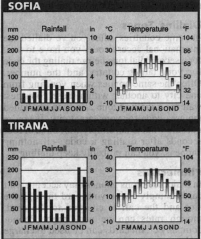

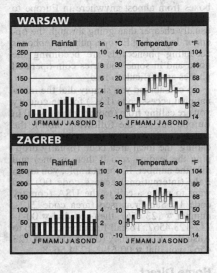

Appendix II – Telephones

Dial Direct

You can dial directly from public telephone boxes from almost anywhere in Europe to almost anywhere in the world. This is usually cheaper than going through the operator. In much of Europe, public telephones accepting phonecards are becoming the norm and in some countries coin-operated phones are difficult to find.

To call abroad you simply dial the international access code (IAC) for the country you are calling from (most commonly 00 in Europe but see the following table), the country code (CC) for the country you are calling, the local area code (usually dropping the leading zero if there is one) and then the number. If, for example, you are in Italy (international access code 00) and want to make a call to the USA (country code 1), San Francisco (area code 212), number ☎ 123 4567, then you dial ☎ 00-1-212-123 4567. To call from the UK (00) to Australia (61), Sydney (02), number ☎ 123 4567, you dial ☎ 00-61-2-1234 5678.

Home Direct

If you would rather have somebody else pay for the call, you can, from many countries, dial directly to your home country operator and then reverse charges; you can also charge the call to a phone company credit card. To do this, simply dial the relevant 'home direct' number to be connected to your own operator. For the USA there's a choice of AT&T, MCI or Sprint Global One home direct services. Home direct numbers vary from country to country – check with your telephone company before you leave, or with the international operator in the country you're ringing from. From phone boxes in some countries you may need a coin or local phonecard to be connected with the relevant home direct operator.

In some places (particularly airports), you may find dedicated home direct phones where you simply press the button labelled USA, Australia, Hong Kong or whatever for direct connection to the operator. Note that the home direct service does not operate to and from all countries, and that the call could be charged at operator rates, which makes it expensive for the person paying. Placing a call on your phone credit card is more expensive than paying the local tariff.

Dialling Tones

In some countries, after you've dialled the international access code, you have to wait for a second dial tone before dialing the code for your target country and the number. Often the same applies when you ring from one city to another within these countries: wait for a dialling tone after you've dialled the area code for your target city. If you're not sure what to do, simply wait three or four seconds after dialling a code – if nothing happens, you can probably keep dialling.

Phonecards

In major locations phones may accept credit cards: simply swipe your card through the slot and the call is charged to the card, though rates can be very high. Phone-company credit cards can be used to charge calls via your home country operator.

Stored-value phonecards are now almost standard all over Europe. You usually buy a card from a post office, telephone centre, newsstand or retail outlet and simply insert the card into the phone each time you make a call. The card solves the problem of finding the correct coins for calls (or lots of correct coins for international calls) and generally gives you a small discount.

Call Costs

The cost of international calls varies widely from one country to another: a US$1.20 call from Britain could cost you US$6 from Turkey. The countries in the table opposite are rated from * (cheap) to *** (expensive), but rates can vary depending on which country you are calling to (for example, from Italy it's relatively cheap to call North America, but more expensive to call Australia). Reduced rates are available at certain times, usually from mid-evening to early morning, though it varies from country to country – check the local phone book or ask the operator. Calling from hotel rooms can be very expensive.

Telephone Codes & Costs

	CC	cost (see text)	IAC	IO
Albania	355	***		
Andorra	376	**	00	821111
Austria	43	*	00	09
Belgium	32	**	00	1224 (private phone)
				1223 (public phone)
Bosnia	387	**	00	901
Bulgaria	359	***	00	
Croatia	385	**	99	901
Cyprus	357	***	00	
Cyprus (Turkish)	905		00	
Czech Republic	420	***	00	0149
Denmark	45	**	00	141
Estonia	372	***	8(w)00	007
Finland	358	**	990	020222
France	33	*	00(w)	12
Germany	49	*	00	00118
Gibraltar	350	***	00	100
Greece	30	*	00	161
Hungary	36	*	00(w)	09
Iceland	354	**	90	09
Ireland	353	*	00	114
Italy	39	**	00	15
Latvia	371	***	00	115
Liechtenstein	41 75	***	00	114
Lithuania	370	***	8(w)10 8(w)	194/195
Luxembourg	352	**	00	0010
Macedonia	389	***	99	
Malta	356	**	00	194
Morocco	212	***	00(w)	12
Netherlands	31	**	00	0800-0410
Norway	47	**	095	181
Poland	48	**	0(w)0	901
Portugal	351	*	00	099
Romania		***	40	071
Russia	7	***	8(w)10	
Slovakia	421	**	00	0149/0139
Slovenia	386	**	00	901
Spain	34	**	00(w)	025
Sweden	46	**	009(w)	0018
Switzerland	41	**	00	114
Tunisia	216	**	00	
Turkey	90	***	00	115
UK	44	*	00	155
Yugoslavia	381	***	99	901

CC – Country Code (to call *into* that country)
IAC – International Access Code (to call abroad *from* that country)
IO – International Operator (to make enquiries)
(w) – wait for dialling tone

Other country codes include: Australia 61, Canada 1, Hong Kong 852, India 91, Indonesia 62, Israel 972, Japan 81, Macau 853, Malaysia 60, New Zealand 64, Singapore 65, South Africa 27, Thailand 66, USA 1

Appendix III –
European Organisations

Membership of Political & Economic Organisations

	Council of Europe	EU	EFTA	NATO	Nordic Council	OECD	WEU
Albania	✓	–	–	–	–	–	–
Andorra	✓	–	–	–	–	–	–
Austria	✓	✓	–	–	–	✓	–
Belgium	✓	✓	–	✓	–	✓	✓
Bosnia-Hercegovina	•	–	–	–	–	–	–
Bulgaria	✓	–	–	–	–	–	–
Croatia	✓	–	–	–	–	–	–
Cyprus	✓	–	–	–	–	–	–
Czech Republic	✓	–	–	–	–	✓	–
Denmark	✓	✓	–	✓	✓	✓	–
Estonia	✓	–	–	–	–	–	–
Finland	✓	✓	–	–	✓	✓	–
France	✓	✓	–	✓	–	✓	✓
Germany	✓	✓	–	✓	–	✓	✓
Greece	✓	✓	–	✓	–	✓	✓
Hungary	✓	–	–	–	–	✓	–
Iceland	✓	–	✓	✓	✓	✓	–
Ireland	✓	✓	–	–	–	✓	–
Italy	✓	✓	–	✓	–	✓	✓
Latvia	✓	–	–	–	–	–	–
Lithuania	✓	–	–	–	–	–	–
Luxembourg	✓	✓	–	✓	–	✓	✓
Macedonia	✓	–	–	–	–	–	–
Malta	✓	–	–	–	–	–	–
Netherlands	✓	✓	–	✓	–	✓	✓
Norway	✓	–	✓	✓	✓	✓	–
Poland	✓	–	–	–	–	–	–
Portugal	✓	✓	–	✓	–	✓	✓
Romania	✓	–	–	–	–	–	–
Slovakia	✓	–	–	–	–	–	–
Slovenia	✓	–	–	–	–	–	–
Spain	✓	✓	–	✓	–	✓	✓
Sweden	✓	✓	–	–	✓	✓	–
Switzerland	✓	–	✓	–	–	✓	–
Turkey	✓	–	–	✓	–	✓	–
UK	✓	✓	–	✓	–	✓	✓
Yugoslavia	–	–	–	–	–	–	–

✓ full member   • special guest status

Council of Europe

Established in 1949, the Council of Europe is the oldest of Europe's political institutions. It aims to promote European unity, protect human rights and assist in the cultural, social and economic development of its member states, but its powers are purely advisory. Founding states were Belgium, Denmark, France, Ireland, Italy, Luxembourg, the Netherlands, Norway, Sweden and the UK. It now counts 40 members. Its headquarters are in Strasbourg.

European Union (EU)

Founded by the Treaty of Rome in 1957, the European Economic Community, or Common Market as it was once known, broadened its scope far beyond economic measures as it developed into the European Community (1967) and finally the European Union (1993). Its original aims were to develop and expand the economies of its member states by abolishing customs tariffs, coordinating transportation systems and general economic policies, establishing a common economic policy towards nonmember states, and promoting the free movement of labour and capital within its borders. Further measures included the abolishment of border controls and the linking of currency exchange rates. Since the 1991 Maastricht treaty, the EU is committed to establishing a common foreign and security policy and close cooperation in home affairs and the judiciary. A single European currency called the euro came into effect in January 1999.

The EEC's founding states were Belgium, France, West Germany, Italy, Luxembourg and the Netherlands – the Treaty of Rome was an extension of the European Coal and Steel Community (ECSC) founded by these six states in 1952. Denmark, Ireland and the UK joined in 1973, Greece in 1981, Spain and Portugal in 1986 and Austria, Finland and Sweden in 1995. Five more countries – Czech Republic, Estonia, Hungary, Poland and Slovenia – are expected to be granted full membership by 2002. The main EU organisations are the European Parliament (elected by direct universal suffrage, with growing powers), the European Commission (the daily government), the Council of Ministers (ministers of member states who make the important decisions) and the Court of Justice. The European Parliament meets in Strasbourg; Luxembourg is home to the Court of Justice. Other EU organisations are based in Brussels.

European Free Trade Association (EFTA)

Established in 1960 as a response to the creation of the European Economic Community, EFTA aims to eliminate trade tariffs on industrial products between member states, though each member retains the right to its own commercial policy towards nonmembers. Its four members (Iceland, Liechtenstein, Norway and Switzerland) cooperate with the EU through the European Economic Area agreement. Denmark and the UK left EFTA to join the EU in 1973 and others have since followed suit, leaving EFTA's future in doubt. Its headquarters are in Geneva.

North Atlantic Treaty Organisation (NATO)

The document creating this defence alliance was signed in 1949 by the USA, Canada and 10 European countries to safeguard their common political, social and economic systems against external threats (read: against the powerful Soviet military presence in Europe after WWII). An attack against any member state would be considered an attack against them all. Greece and Turkey joined in 1952, West Germany in 1955, and Spain in 1982; France withdrew from NATO's integrated military command in 1966 and Greece did likewise in 1974, though both remain members. NATO's Soviet counterpart, the Warsaw Pact founded in 1955, collapsed with the democratic revolutions of 1989 and the subsequent disintegration of the Soviet Union; most of its former members are now NATO associates. NATO's headquarters are in Brussels.

Nordic Council

Established in Copenhagen in 1952, the Nordic Council aims to promote economic, social and cultural cooperation among its member states (Denmark, Finland, Iceland, Norway and Sweden). Since 1971, the Council has acted as an advisory body to the Nordic Council of Ministers, a meeting of ministers from the member states responsible for the subject under discussion. Decisions taken by the Council of Ministers are usually binding, though member states retain full sovereignty. Environmental, tariff, labour and immigration policies are often coordinated.

Organisation for Economic Cooperation & Development (OECD)

The OECD was set up in 1961 to supersede the Organisation for European Economic Cooperation, which allocated US aid under the Marshall Plan and coordinated the reconstruction of postwar Europe. Sometimes seen as the club of the world's rich countries, the OECD aims to encourage economic growth and world trade. Its member states include most of Europe, as well as Australia, Canada, Japan, Mexico, New Zealand and the USA. Its headquarters are in Paris.

Western European Union (WEU)

Set up in 1955, the WEU was designed to coordinate the military defences between member states, to promote economic, social and cultural cooperation, and to encourage European integration. Social and cultural tasks were transferred to the Council of Europe in 1960, and these days the WEU is sometimes touted as a future, more 'European', alternative to NATO. It counts 10 full members and many more associate members and partners. Its headquarters are in Brussels.

Appendix IV – Alternative Place Names

The following abbreviations are used:

(A)	Albanian
(B)	Bulgarian
(C)	Czech
(Cr)	Croatian
(E)	English
(G)	German
(Gk)	Greek
(H)	Hungarian
(I)	Italian
(L)	Latin
(M)	Macedonian
(P)	Polish
(R)	Romanian
(Se)	Serbian
(Slk)	Slovak
(Sle)	Slovene
(T)	Turkish

ALBANIA
Shqipëri

Apollonia (Gk) – Pojan (A), Apolonia (L)
Berat (A) – Antipatria (L)
Butrint (A) – Buthroton (Gk)
Durrës (A) – Durazzo (I), Epidamnos (Gk), Dyrrhachium (L)
Elbasan (A) – Skampa (L), El Basan (T)
Gjirokastra, Gjirokastër (A) – Argyrokastron (Gk)
Korça, Korçë (A) – Koritsa (Gk)
Kruja (E) – Kruj (A)
Lezhë (A) – Alessio (I)
Saranda (E) – Sarandë (A), Onchesmos (Gk)
Tirana (E) – Tiranë (A)
Vlora (E) – Vlorë (A), Avlon (L)

BULGARIA
Bâlgariya

Bachkovo Monastery (E) – Bachkovski Manastir (B)
Balchik (B) – Krunoi (Gk), Dionysopolis (L)
Golden Sands (E) – Zlatni Pyasâtsi (B), Goldstrand (G)

Hisar (T) – Hisarya (B), Augusta (L)
Nesebâr (B) – Mesembria (Gk)
Plovdiv (B) – Philipopolis (Gk), Philibe (T)
Rila Monastery (E) – Rilski Manastir (B)
Ruse (B) – Rouschouk (T)
Shumen (B) – Chumla (T)
Sofia (E) – Sofiya (B), Serdica (L)
Sozopol (B) – Apollonia (Gk)
Stara Planina (B) – Balkan Mountains (E)
Sunny Beach (E) – Slânchev Bryag (B), Sonnenstrand (G)
Varna (B) – Odessos (Gk)
Vidin (B) – Bononia (L)

CROATIA
Hrvatska

Dalmatia (E) – Dalmacija (Cr)
Dubrovnik (Cr) – Ragusa (L)
Hvar (Island) (Cr) – Lesina (I)
Korčula (Cr) – Curzola (I)
Krk (Island) (Cr) – Veglia (I)
Kvarner (Gulf) (E) – Quarnero (I)
Lošinj (Island) (Cr) – Lussino (I)
Mljet (Island) (Cr) – Melita (I)
Osijek (Cr) – Eszék (H)
Plitvice Lakes (E) – Plitvicer Seen (G)
Poreč (Cr) – Parenzo (I), Parentium (L)
Pula (Cr) – Polensium (L)
Rab (Island) (Cr) – Arbe (G)
Rijeka (Cr) – Fiume (I), Reka (Sle)
Rovinj (Cr) – Rovigno (I)
Split (Cr) – Spalato (I)
Trogir (Cr) – Trau (G)
Zadar (Cr) – Zara (I), Iader (L)
Zagreb (Cr) – Agram (G)

CZECH REPUBLIC
Česká republika

Brno (C) – Brünn (G)
České Budějovice (C) – Budweis (G)
Český Krumlov (C) – Krumau (G)
Cheb (C) – Eger (G)
Danube (River) (E) – Dunáj (C)
Hluboká nad Vltavou (C) – Frauenberg (G)
Karlovy Vary (C) – Karlsbad (G)
Krkonoše (C) – Giant Mountains (E)

Krušné Hory (C) – Ore Mountains (E)
Labe (River) (C) – Elbe (G)
Mariánské Lázně (C) – Marienbad (G)
Plzeň (C) – Pilsen (G)
Prague (E) – Praha (C), Prag (G)
Telč (C) – Teltsch (G)
Vltava (River) (C) – Moldau (G)
Znojmo (C) – Znaim (G)

HUNGARY
Magyarország

(Lake) Balaton (H) – Plattensee (G)
Danube (E) – Duna (H), Donau (G)
Danube Bend (E) – Dunakanyar (H)
Debrecen (H) – Debrezin (G)
Eger (H) – Erlau (G)
Esztergom (H) – Gran (G)
Great Plain (E) – Nagyalföld (H)
Győr (H) – Raab (G)
Kisalföld (H) – Little Plain (E)
Kőszeg (H) – Guns (G)
Lendva (H) – Lendava (Sle)
Pécs (H) – Fünfkirchen (G)
Sopron (H) – Ödenburg (G)
Szeged (H) – Segedin (G)
Szombathely (H) – Steinamanger (G)
Transdanubia (E) – Dunántúl (H)
Vác (H) – Wartzen (G)
Vienna (E) – Bécs (H), Wien (G)

MACEDONIA
Makedonija

Ohrid (M) – Lihnidos (L)
Skopje (M) – Uskup (T), Scupi (L)

POLAND
Polska

Birkenau (G) – Brzezinka (P)
Bydgoszcz (P) – Bromberg (G)
Częstochowa (P) – Tschenstochau (G)
Gdańsk (P) – Danzig (G)
Gdynia (P) – Gdingen (G)
Gniezno (P) – Gnesen (G)
Kolobrzeg (P) – Kolberg (G)
Kętrzyn (P) – Rastenburg (G)
Kraków (P) – Krakau (G), Cracow (E)
Malbork (P) – Marienburg (G)
Malopolska (P) – Little Poland (Region) (E)
Nowy Sącz (P) – Neusandez (G)
Nysa (River) (P) – Neisse (G)
Odra (River) (P) – Oder (G)

Olsztyn (P) – Allenstein (G)
Opole (P) – Oppeln (G)
Oświęcim (P) – Auschwitz (G)
Poznań (P) – Posen (G)
Silesia (E) – Śląsk (P), Silesien (G)
Świnoujście (P) – Swinemünde (G)
Szczecin (P) – Stettin (G)
Sopot (P) – Zoppot (G)
Tannenberg (G) – Stębark (P)
Toruń (P) – Thorn (G)
Vistula (River) (E) – Wisla (P), Weichsel (G)
Warsaw (E) – Warszawa (P), Warschau (G)
Wielkopolska (P) – Great Poland (Region) (E)
Wroclaw (P) – Breslau (G)

ROMANIA
Romania

Alba Iulia (R) – Karlsburg/Weissenburg (G),
    Gyula Fehérvár (H), Apulum (L)
Baia Mare (R) – Nagybánya (H)
Braşov (R) – Kronstadt (G), Brassó (H)
Bucharest (E) – Bucureşti (R)
Cluj-Napoca (R) – Klausenburg (G), Kolozsvár
    (H), Napoca (L)
Constanţa (R) – Constantiana (L), Tomis (Gk),
    Küstendje (T)
Dobruja (E) – Dobrogea (R), Moesia Inferior (L)
Hunedoara (R) – Eisenmarkt (G)
Iaşi (R) – Jassy (G)
Mangalia (R) – Callatis (L)
Mediaş (R) – Mediasch (G)
Oradea (R) – Grosswardein (G), Nagyvárad (H)
Satu Mare (R) – Szatmárnémeti (H)
Sebeş (R) – Muhlbach (G)
Sibiu (R) – Hermannstadt (G), Cibinium (L),
    Nagyszében (H)
Sic (R) – Szék (H)
Sighişoara (R) – Schässburg (G), Szegesvár (H)
Suceava (R) – Soczow (P)
Timişoara (R) – Temeschburg (G), Temesvár (H)
Tirgu Mureş (R) – Marosvásárhely (H)
Transylvania (R) – Siebenbürgen (G), Erdély (H)

SLOVAKIA
Slovensko

Banská Bystrica (Slk) – Neusohl (G)
Bratislava (Slk) – Pressburg (G), Pozsony (H)
Dunaj (Slk) – Danube (E)
Gerlachovský štít (Slk) – Mt Gerlach (E)
Košice (Slk) – Kaschau (G), Kassa (H)
Levoča (Slk) – Leutschau (G)
Lučenec (Slk) – Losonc (H)
Malá Fatra (Slk) – Little Fatra (E)

Nízke Tatry (Slk) – Low Tatras (E)
Prešov (Slk) – Preschau (G)
Rožnava (Slk) – Rozsnyó (H)
Slovenské rudohorie (Slk) – Slovak Ore
  Mountains (E)
Slovenský raj (Slk) – Slovak Paradise (E)
Spišský hrad (Castle) (Slk) – Zipser Burg (G)
Trnava (Slk) – Nagyszombat (H)
Vysoké Tatry (Slk) – High Tatras (E)
Zlaté piesky (Slk) – Golden Sands (E)
Zvolen (Slk) – Altsohl (G)

SLOVENIA
Slovenija

Dolenjska (Sle) – Lower Carniola (E)
Gorenjska (Sle) – Upper Carniola (E)
Gorica (Sle) – Gorizia (I)
Gulf of Trieste (E) – Tržaški Zaliv (Sle),
  Golfo di Trieste (I)
Istria (E) – Istra (Sle)
Izola (Sle) – Isola (I)
Kobarid (Sle) – Caporetto (I)
Koper (Sle) – Capodistria (I)
Koroška (Sle) – Carinthia (E), Kärnten (G)
Kras (Sle) – Karst (E)

Ljubljana (Sle) – Laibach (G)
Notranjska (Sle) – Inner Carniola (E)
Piran (Sle) – Pirano (I)
Portorož (Sle) – Portorose (I)
Primorska (Sle) – Slovenian Littoral (E)
Soča (River) (Sle) – Isonzo (I)
Štajerska (Sle) – Styria (E), Steiermark (G)
Trieste (I) – Trst (Sle)
Venice (E) – Benetke (Sle), Venezia (I)
Vienna (E) – Dunaj (Sle), Wien (G)

YUGOSLAVIA
Jugoslavija

Bar (Se) – Antivari (I)
Belgrade (E) – Beograd (Se), Nándorfehérvár (H)
Kotor (Se) – Cattaro (I)
Montenegro (E) – Crna Gora (Se)
Novi Sad (Se) – Neusatz (G)
Peć (Se) – Pejë (A)
Priština (Se) – Prishtinë (A)
Senta (Se) – Zenta (H)
Serbia (E) – Srbija (Se)
Subotica (Se) – Szabadka (H)
Podgorica (Se) – Titograd (Se)
Ulcinj (Se) – Ulqin (A), Dulcigno (I)

Appendix V – International Country Abbreviations

The following is a list of official abbreviations that you may encounter on motor vehicles in Europe. Other abbreviations are likely to be unofficial ones, often referring to a particular region, province or even city. A vehicle entering a foreign country must carry a sticker identifying its country of registration, though this rule is not always enforced.

A	–	Austria
AL	–	Albania
AND	–	Andorra
B	–	Belgium
BG	–	Bulgaria
BIH	–	Bosnia-Hercegovina
BY	–	Belarus
CDN	–	Canada
CH	–	Switzerland
CY	–	Cyprus
CZ	–	Czech Republic
D	–	Germany
DK	–	Denmark
DZ	–	Algeria
E	–	Spain
EST	–	Estonia
ET	–	Egypt
F	–	France
FIN	–	Finland
FL	–	Liechtenstein
FR	–	Faroe Islands
GB	–	Great Britain
GE	–	Georgia
GR	–	Greece
H	–	Hungary
HKJ	–	Jordan
HR	–	Croatia
I	–	Italy
IL	–	Israel
IRL	–	Ireland
IS	–	Iceland
L	–	Luxembourg

LAR	–	Libya
LT	–	Lithuania
LV	–	Latvia
M	–	Malta
MA	–	Morocco
MC	–	Monaco
MD	–	Moldavia
MK	–	Macedonia
N	–	Norway
NL	–	Netherlands
NZ	–	New Zealand
P	–	Portugal
PL	–	Poland
RL	–	Lebanon
RO	–	Romania
RSM	–	San Marino
RUS	–	Russia
S	–	Sweden
SK	–	Slovakia
SLO	–	Slovenia
SYR	–	Syria
TN	–	Tunisia
TR	–	Turkey
UA	–	Ukraine
USA	–	United States of America
V	–	Vatican City
WAN	–	Nigeria
YU	–	Yugoslavia
ZA	–	South Africa

OTHER

CC	–	Consular Corps
CD	–	Diplomatic Corps
GBA	–	Alderney
GBG	–	Guernsey
GBJ	–	Jersey
GBM	–	Isle of Man
GBZ	–	Gibraltar

Language

This Language Guide contains pronunciation guidelines and basic vocabulary to help you get around Eastern Europe. For background information about the languages, see the Language sections under Facts for the Visitor in the relevant country chapters.

For more detailed coverage of the languages included here, see Lonely Planet's *Eastern Europe phrasebook* (for Bulgarian, Czech, Hungarian, Polish, Romanian and Slovak) and *Mediterranean Europe phrasebook* (for Albanian, Croatian and Serbian, Slovene and Macedonian).

Albanian

Pronunciation

Written Albanian is phonetically consistent and pronunciation shouldn't pose too many problems for English speakers. The Albanian 'rr' is trilled and each vowel in a diphthong is pronounced. However, Albanian possesses certain letters that are present in English but rendered differently. These include:

c	as the 'ts' in 'bits'
ç	as the 'ch' in 'church'
dh	as the 'th' in 'this'
gj	as the 'gy' in 'hogyard'
j	as the 'y' in 'yellow'
q	between 'ch' and 'ky', similar to the 'cu' in 'cure'
th	as the 'th' in 'thistle'
x	as the 'dz' in 'adze'
xh	as the 'j' in 'jewel'
zh	as the 's' in 'pleasure'

Basics

Hello.	*Tungjatjeta.*
Goodbye.	*Lamtumirë.*
	Mirupafshim. (informal)
Yes.	*Po.*
No.	*Jo.*
Please.	*Ju lutem.*
Thank you.	*Ju falem nderit.*
That's fine.	*Eshtë e mirë.*
You're welcome.	*S'ka përse.*
Excuse me.	*Me falni.*

Sorry. (excuse me, forgive me)	*Më vjen keq. (më falni, ju lutem)*
Do you speak English?	*A flisni anglisht?*
How much is it?	*Sa kushton?*
What's your name?	*Si quheni ju lutem?*
My name is ...	*Unë quhem ... /Mua më quajnë ...*

Getting Around

What time does the ... leave/arrive?	*Në ç'orë niset/ arrin ...?*
boat	*barka/lundra*
bus	*autobusi*
tram	*tramvaji*
train	*treni*

I'd like ...	*Dëshiroj ...*
a one-way ticket	*një biletë vajtje*
a return ticket	*një biletë vajtje-ardhje*

1st/2nd class	*klas i parë/i dytë*
timetable	*orar*
bus stop	*stacion autobusi*

Where is ...?	*Ku është ...?*
Go straight ahead.	*Shko drejt.*
Turn left.	*Kthehu majtas.*
Turn right.	*Kthehu djathtas.*
near	*afër*
far	*larg*

Signs

HYRJE	ENTRANCE
DALJE	EXIT
PLOTŚKA VENDE TË	FULL/NO VACANCIES
INFORMACION	INFORMATION
HAPUR/MBYLLUR	OPEN/CLOSED
E NDALUAR	PROHIBITED
POLICIA	POLICE
STACIONI I POLICISË	POLICE STATION
NEVOJTORJA	TOILETS
BURRA/GRA	MEN/WOMEN

Emergencies

Help!	Ndihmë!
Call a doctor!	Thirrni doktorin!
Call the police!	Thirrni policinë!
Go away!	Zhduku!/Largohuni!
I'm lost.	Kam humbur rrugën

Around Town

a bank	një bankë
chemist/pharmacy	farmaci
the ... embassy	... ambasadën
my hotel	hotelin tim
the market	pazarin
newsagency	agjensia e lajmeve
the post office	postën
the telephone exchange	centrali telefonik
the tourist office	zyra e informimeve turistike

What time does it open/close? — Në ç'ore hapet/mbyllet?

Accommodation

hotel	hotel
camping ground	vend kampimi

Do you have any rooms available? — A keni ndonjë dhomë të lirë?

a single room	një dhomë teke
a double room	një dhomë më dy krevatë

How much is it per night/per person? — Sa kushton një natë/për person?

Does it include breakfast? — A e përfshin edhe mëngjesin?

Time, Days & Numbers

What time is it?	Sa është ora?
today	sot
tomorrow	nesër
yesterday	dje
morning	mëngjes
afternoon	mbasdite

Monday	e hënë
Tuesday	e martë
Wednesday	e mërkurë
Thursday	e enjte
Friday	e premte
Saturday	e shtunë
Sunday	e diel

1	një	7	shtatë
2	dy	8	tetë
3	tre	9	nëntë
4	katër	10	dhjetë
5	pesë	100	njëqind
6	gjashtë	1000	njëmijë

one million	një milion

Bulgarian

Pronunciation

To a great extent the Bulgarians speak as they write, so Bulgarian spelling, unlike English, generally provides almost one-to-one representation of letter-sound correspondences. Most Bulgarian sounds occur in the English language as well, with some slight differences in the way sounds are produced. With a little practice you will have no problem making yourself understood.

Basics

Hello.	Zdraveyte.	Здравейте.
(informal)	Zdrasti.	Здрасти.
Goodbye.	Dovizhdane.	Довиждане.
(informal)	Chao.	Чао.
Yes.	Da.	Да.
No.	Ne.	Не.
Please.	Molya.	Моля.
Thank you.	Blagodarya.	Благодаря.
(informal)	Mersi.	Мерси.
I'm sorry.	Sâzhalyavam.	Съжалявам.
(forgive me)	(prostete)	(простете)
Excuse me.	Izvinete me.	Извинете ме.

I don't understand.
Az ne razbiram. — Аз не разбирам.
What's it called?
Kak se kazva tova? — Как се казва това?
How much is it?
Kolko struva? — Колко струва?

Getting Around

What time does the ... leave/arrive?
V kolko chasa zaminava/pristigha ...?
В колко часа заминава/пристига ...?

Bulgarian Cyrillic Alphabet

Vowels

Cyrillic	Roman	Pronunciation
а	ah	as the 'a' in 'father' (but shorter)
е	eh	as the 'e' in 'bet'
о	o	as in 'pot'
и	i	as in 'bit'
ъ	a	a characteristic Bulgarian neutral vowel sound; roughly resembles the 'a' in 'soda' or 'address'
у	u	as in 'put'

Consonants

Cyrillic	Roman	Pronunciation
Б б	b	as in 'boy'
В в	v	as 'v' in 'vice'
Г г	gh	as the 'g' in 'go'
Д д	d	as in 'door'
Ж ж	zh	as the 's' in 'pleasure'
З з	z	as in 'zoo'
Ј ј	y	as the 'y' in 'yes'
К к	k	as in 'king'
Л л	l	as in 'let'
М м	m	as in 'met'
Н н	n	as in 'net'
П п	p	as in 'pen'
Р р	r	as the trilled Scottish 'r'
С с	s	as in 'see'
Т т	t	as in 'tip'
Ф ф	f	as 'foot'
Х х	kh	as the 'ch' in Scottish loch
Ц ц	ts	as in 'lets'
Ч ч	ch	as in 'church'
Ш ш	sh	as in 'ship'
Щ щ	sht	as the '-shed' in 'pushed'
Ю ю	yu	as the word 'you' but shorter
Я я	ya	as in 'yard' but shorter

plane
samolehta самолетът
bus (city)
ghradskiya градският
avtobus автобус
bus (intercity)
mezhdughradskiya междуградският
avtobus автобус

train
vlakat влакът
tram
tramvayat трамваят

arrival	*pristigane*	пристигане
departure	*zaminavane*	заминаване
timetable	*razpisanie*	разписание

Where is the bus stop?
Kâde e avtobusnata spirka?
Къде е автобусната спирка?
Where is the train station?
Kâde e zhelezopâtnata gara?
Къде е железопътната гара?
Where is the left-luggage room?
Kâde e garderobât?
Къде е гардеробът?
Please show me on the map.
Molyu pokazhete mi na kartata.
Моля покажете ми на картата.

left	*lyavo*	ляво
right	*dyasno*	дясно
straight ahead	*napravo*	направо

Around Town

the bank	*bankata*	банката
the church	*tsarkvata*	църквата
the hospital	*bolnitsata*	олницата
the market	*pazara*	пазара
the museum	*muzeya*	музея
the post office	*poshtata*	пощата

the tourist information office
byuroto za turisticheska informatsiya
бюрото за туристическа информация

Signs

ВЙОД	ENTRANCE
ИЗЙОД	EXIT
ИНФОРМАЦИЯ	INFORMATION
ОТВОРЕНО	OPEN
ЗАТВОРЕНО	CLOSED
ЗАБРАНЕНО	PROHIBITED
ПОЛИЦЕЙСКО УПРАВЛЕНИЕ	POLICE STATION
ТОАЛЕТНИ	TOILETS
МЬЖЕ	MEN
ЖЕНИ	WOMEN

Accommodation

Do you have any rooms available?
Imateh li svobodni stai?
Имате ли свободни стаи?
How much is it?
Kolko struva?
Колко струва?
Does it include breakfast?
Zakuskata vklyuchena li e?
Закуската включена ли е?

hotel	*khotel*	хотел
guesthouse	*pansion*	пансион
private room	*stoya v chastna*	стоя в частна
	kvartira	квартира
single room	*edinichna*	единична
	staya	стая
double room	*dvoyna staya*	двойна стая

youth hostel
mladezhki hotel (hizha/obshtezhitie)
младежки хотел (хижа/общежитие)
camping ground
myasto za lageruvane/kâmpinguvane
място за лагеруване/къмпингуване

Time, Days & Numbers

What time is it?
Kolko e chasat?
Колко е часът?

today	*dnes*	днес
tonight	*dovechera*	довечера
tomorrow	*utre*	утре
yesterday	*vcherah*	вчера
in the morning	*sutrinta*	сутринта
in the evening	*vecherta*	вечерта

Monday	*ponedelnik*	понеделник
Tuesday	*vtornik*	вторник
Wednesday	*sryada*	сряда
Thursday	*chetvârtâk*	четвъртък
Friday	*petâk*	петък
Saturday	*sâbota*	събота
Sunday	*nedelya*	неделя

1	*edno*	едно
2	*dve*	две
3	*tri*	три
4	*chetiri*	четири
5	*pet*	пет
6	*shest*	шест
7	*sedem*	седем

Emergencies

Help!	*Pomosh!*	Помош!
Call a doctor!	*Povikayte lekar!*	Повикайте лекар!
Call the police!	*Povikayte politsiya!*	Повикайте полиция!
Go away!	*Mahayte se!*	Махайте се!
I'm lost.	*Zagubih se.*	Загубих се.

8	*osem*	осом
9	*devet*	девет
10	*deset*	десет
100	*sto*	сто
1000	*hilyada*	хиляда
one million	*edin milion*	един милион

Croatian, Serbian & Bosnian

Pronunciation

The writing systems of Bosnian, Croatian and Serbian are phonetically consistent: every letter is pronounced and its sound will not vary from word to word. With regard to the position of stress, only one rule can be given: the last syllable of a word is never stressed. In most cases the accent falls on the first vowel in the word.

Serbian uses the Cyrillic alphabet so it's worth familiarising yourself with it (see the Macedonian section in this chapter). Bosnian and Croatian use a Roman alphabet; many letters are pronounced as in English – the following are some specific pronunciations.

c	as the 'ts' in 'cats'
ć	as the 'cu' in 'cure'
č	as the 'ch' in 'chop'
đ	as the 'gu' in 'legume'
dž	as the 'j' in 'just'
j	as the 'y' in 'young'
lj	as the 'lli' in 'million'
nj	as the 'ny' in 'canyon'
š	as the 'sh' in 'hush'
ž	as the 's' in 'pleasure'

The principal difference between Serbian and Croatian is in the pronunciation of the vowel 'e' in certain words. A long 'e' in Serbian becomes 'ije' in Croatian (eg *reka/rijeka*, 'river'), and a short 'e' in Serbian becomes 'je' in Croatian (eg *pesma, pjesma*, 'song'). Sometimes, however, the vowel 'e' is the same in both languages, as in *selo*, 'village'. Bosnian shares some of its vocab with both Serbian and Croatian. There are also a number of variations in vocabulary. In the following phraselist these are indicated with 'B' for Bosnian, 'C' for Croatian and 'S' for Serbian.

Basics

Hello.
Zdravo. Здраво.
Goodbye.
Doviđenja. Довиђења.
Yes.
Da. Да.
No.
Ne. Не.
Please.
Molim. Молим.
Thank you.
Hvala. Хвала.
That's fine/
You're welcome.
U redu je/ У реду је/
Nema na čemu. Нема на чему.
Excuse me.
Oprostite. Опростите.
Sorry. (excuse me, forgive me)
Pardon. (izvinite) Пардон. (опростите извините)
Do you speak English?
Govorite li Говорите ли
engleski? енглески?
How much is it ...?
Koliko košta ...? Колико кошта ...?
What's your name?
Kako se zovete? Како се зовете?
My name is ...
Zovem se ... Зовем се ...

Getting Around

What time does the ... leave/arrive?
Kada ... Када ...
polazi/ полази/долази?
dolazi?

Signs

ENTRANCE/EXIT
УЛАЗ/ИЗЛАЗ
ULAZ/IZLAZ
FULL/NO VACANCIES
СВЕ ЈЕ ЗАУЗЕТО/НЕМА СЛОБОДНЕ СОБЕ
SVE JE ZAUZETO/ NEMA SLOBODNE SOBE
INFORMATION
ИНФОРМАЦИЈЕ
INFORMACIJE
OPEN/CLOSED
ОТВОРЕНО/ЗАТВОРЕНО
OTVORENO/ZATVORENO
POLICE
МИЛИЦИЈА
MILICIJA (S)/POLICIJA (B, C)
POLICE STATION
СТАНИЦА МИЛИЦИЈЕ
STANICA MILICIJE (S)/POLICIJA (B, C)
PROHIBITED
ЗАБРАЊЕНО
ZABRANJENO
ROOMS AVAILABLE
СЛОБОДНЕ СОБЕ
SLOBODNE SOBE
TOILETS
ТОАЛЕТИ
TOALETI (S, B)/ZAHODI (C)

boat
brod брод
bus (city)
autobus аутобус
(gradski) (градски)
bus (intercity)
autobus аутобус
(međugradski) (међуградски)
train
voz (S, B)/ воз
vlak (C)
tram
tramvaj трамвај

one-way ticket
kartu u jednom карту у једном
pravcu правцу
return ticket
povratnu kartu повратну карту

| 1st class | *prvu klasu* | прву класу |
| 2nd class | *drugu klasu* | другу класу |

Where is the bus/tram stop?
(Gde/Gdje) je autobuska/tramvajska stanica (S/B, C)/postaja (C)?
Гле је аутобуска/трамвајска станица?
Can you show me (on the map)?
Možete li mi pokazati (na karti)?
Можете ли ми показати (на карти)?
Go straight ahead.
Idite pravo napred (S)/naprijed (B, C)
Идите право напред.
Turn left.
Skrenite lijevo. (B, C)/Skrenite levo. (S)
Скрените лево.
Turn right.
Skrenite desno.
Скрените десно.
near/far
blizu/daleko
близу/далеку

Around Town

bank
banka банка
... embassy
... ambasada ... амбасада
my hotel
moj hotel мој хотел
market
tržnica (C)/ пијаца
pijaca (B, S)
post office
pošta пошта
telephone centre
telefonska телефонска централа
centrala
tourist office
turistički туристички
informativni biro информативни биро

Accommodation

hotel
hotel хотел
guesthouse
privatno приватно
prenoćište преноћиште
youth hostel
omladinsko омладинско
prenoćište преноћиште
camping ground
kamping кампинг

Do you have any rooms available?
Imate li slobodne sobe?
Имате ли слободне собе?
How much is it per night/per person?
Koliko košta za jednu noć/po osobi?
Колико кошта за једну ноћ/по особи?
Does it include breakfast?
Dali je u ceni (S)/cijeni (B, C)
uključen i doručak?
Дали је у цену укључен и доручак?

I'd like ...
Želim ...
Желим ...

a single room
sobu sa jednim krevetom
собу са једним креветом
a double room
sobu sa duplim krevetom
собу са дуплим креветом

Time, Days & Numbers

What time is it?
Koliko je sati? Колико је сати?
today
danas данас
tomorrow
sutra сутра
yesterday
juče (S, B) јуче
jučer (C)
in the morning
ujutro ујутро
in the afternoon
popodne поподне

Monday
ponedeljak понедељак
Tuesday
utorak уторак
Wednesday
sreda (S) среда
srijeda (B, C)
Thursday
četvrtak четвртак
Friday
petak петак
Saturday
subota субота
Sunday
nedelja (S) недеља
nedjelja (B, C)

Emergencies

Help!	
Upomoć!	
Упомоь!	
Call a doctor!	
Pozovite lekara! (B, S)	
Pozovite liječnika! (C)	
Позовите лекара!	
Call the police!	
Pozovite miliciju! (S)	
Pozovite policiju! (C)	
Позовите милицију!	
Go away!	
Idite!	
Идите!	
I'm lost.	
Izgubio sam se. (m)	
Izgubila sam se. (f)	
Изгубљен сам/Изгубљена сам.	

1	*jedan*	један
2	*dva*	два
3	*tri*	три
4	*četiri*	четири
5	*pet*	пет
6	*šest*	шест
7	*sedam*	седам
8	*osam*	осам
9	*devet*	девет
10	*deset*	десет
100	*sto*	сто
1000	*hiljada* (B, S)	иљада
	tisuća (C)	

one million	*jedan milion* (S)	један милион
	jedan milijun (B, C)	

Czech

Pronunciation

Many Czech letters are pronounced much the same way as their English counterparts. An accent lengthens a vowel and the stress is always on the first syllable. Words are pronounced as written, so if you follow the guidelines below you should have no trouble being understood. When consulting indexes on Czech maps, be aware that **ch** comes after **h**.

c	as the 'ts' in 'bits'
č	as the 'ch' in 'church'
ch	as in Scottish 'loch'
ď	as the 'd' in 'duty'
ě	as 'ye'
j	as the 'y' in 'yet'
ň	as the 'ni' in 'onion'
ř	as 'rzh'
š	as the 'sh' in 'ship'
ť	as the 'te' in 'stew'
ž	as the 's' in 'pleasure'

Basics

Hello.	*Ahoj, dobrý den.*
Goodbye.	*Na shledanou.*
Yes.	*Ano.*
No.	*Ne.*
Please.	*Prosím.*
Thank you.	*Děkuji.*
Sorry. (Forgive me)	*Promiňte.*

I don't understand.	*Nerozumím.*
What is it called?	*Jak se to jmenuje?*
How much is it?	*Kolik to stojí?*

Getting Around

What time does the ... leave/arrive?	*Kdy odjíždí/přijíždí ...?*
boat	*lod*
bus (city)	*(městský) autobus*
bus (intercity)	*(meziměstský) autobus*
train	*vlak*
tram	*tramvaj*

arrival	*příjezdy*
departure	*odjezdy*
timetable	*jízdní řád*

Where is the bus stop?	*Kde je autobusová zastávka ?*
Where is the station?	*Kde je nádraží?*
Where is the left-luggage room?	*Kde je úschovna zavazadel?*

Where is it?	*Kde je to?*
Please show me on the map.	*Prosím, ukážte mi to na mapě.*

left	*vlevo*
right	*vpravo*
straight ahead	*rovně*

Signs

VCHOD	ENTRANCE
VÝCHOD	EXIT
INFORMACE	INFORMATION
OTEVŘENO	OPEN
ZAVŘENO	CLOSED
ZAKÁZÁNO	PROHIBITED
POLICIE	POLICE STATION
TELEFON	TELEPHONE
ZÁCHODY/WC/	TOILETS
TOALETY	

Around Town

the bank	banka
the chemist	lékárna
the church	kostel
the market	tržiště
the museum	muzeum
the post office	pošta
the tourist	turistické informační
information office	centrum (středisko)
travel agency	cestovní kancelář

Accommodation

hotel	hotel
guesthouse	penzión
youth hostel	mládežnická noclehárna
camping ground	kemping
private room	privát
single room	jednol-kový pokoj
double room	dvoul-kový pokoj

Do you have any rooms available?	Máte volné pokoje?
How much is it?	Kolik to je?
Does it include breakfast?	Je v tom zahrnuta snídaně?

Emergencies

Help!	Pomoc!
Call a doctor/ ambulance/police!	Zavolejte doktora/ sanitku/policii!
Go away!	Běžte pryč!
I'm lost.	Zabloudil jsem. (m)
	Zabloudila jsem. (f)

Time, Days & Numbers

What time is it?	Kolik je hodin?
today	dnes
tonight	dnes večer
tomorrow	zítra
yesterday	včera
in the morning	ráno
in the evening	večer
Monday	pondělí
Tuesday	úterý
Wednesday	středa
Thursday	čtvrtek
Friday	pátek
Saturday	sobota
Sunday	neděle

1	jeden
2	dva
3	tři
4	čtyři
5	pět
6	šest
7	sedm
8	osm
9	devět
10	deset
100	sto
1000	tisíc
one million	milión

Hungarian

Pronunciation

It's a simplification, but Hungarian consonants are pronounced more or less as in English with about a dozen exceptions (listed below). Double consonants ll, tt and dd aren't pronounced as one letter as in English but lengthened so you can almost hear them as separate letters. Also, cs, zs, gy and sz (consonant clusters) are separate letters in Hungarian and appear that way in telephone books and other listings. For example, the word cukor, (sugar) appears in the dictionary before csak (only).

c	as the 'ts' in 'hats'
cs	as the 'ch' in 'church'
gy	as the 'j' in 'jury'
j	as the 'y' in 'yes'

ly	as the 'y' in 'yes'
ny	as the 'ni' in 'onion'
r	like a slightly trilled Scottish 'r'
s	as the 'sh' in 'ship'
sz	as the 's' in 'set'
ty	as the 'tu' in 'tube' in British English
w	as 'v' (found in foreign words only)
zs	as the 's' in 'pleasure'

Vowels are a bit trickier, and the semantic difference between **a**, **e** or **o** with and without an accent mark is great. For example, *hát* means 'back' while *hat* means 'six'.

a	as the 'o' in hot
á	as in 'father'
e	a short 'e' as in 'set'
é	as the 'a' in 'say' without the 'y' sound
i	as in 'hit' but shorter
í	as the 'ee' in 'feet'
o	as in 'open'
ó	a longer version of the above
ö	as the 'o' in 'worse'
ő	a longer version of ö
u	as in 'pull'
ú	as the 'ue' in 'blue'
ü	as the 'u' in French *vu* or *tu*; purse your lips tightly and say 'ee'
ű	a longer, breathier version of ü

Basics

Hello. (polite)	*Jó napot kívánok.*
Hello. (informal)	*Szia.*
Goodbye. (polite)	*Viszontlátásra.*
Goodbye. (informal)	*Viszlát.*
Yes.	*Igen.*
No.	*Nem.*
Please.	*Kérem.*
Thank you.	*Köszönöm.*
Sorry. (forgive me)	*Elnézést.*
Excuse me.	*Bocsánat.*
I don't understand.	*Nem értem.*
What is it called?	*Hogy hívják?*
How much is it?	*Mennyibe kerül?*

Getting Around

What time does the ... leave/arrive?	*Mikor indul/érkezik a ...?*
boat	*hajó*
bus (city)	*helyi autóbusz*
bus (intercity)	*távolsági autóbusz*
plane	*repülőgép*
train	*vonat*
tram	*villamos*

arrival	*érkezés*
departure	*indulás*
timetable	*menetrend*

Where is the bus stop?	*Hol van az autóbuszmegálló?*
Where is the station?	*Hol van a pályaudvar?*
Where is the left-luggage room?	*Hol van a csomagmegőrző?*
Please show me on the map.	*Kérem, mutassa meg a térképen.*

to the left	*balra*
to the right	*jobbra*
straight ahead	*egyenesen előre*

Around Town

Where is the ...?	*Hol van a ...?*
bank	*bank*
chemist	*gyógyszertár*
church	*templom*
market	*piac*
museum	*múzeum*
post office	*posta*
tourist office	*túrista információs iroda*

Accommodation

hotel	*szálloda*
guesthouse	*vendégház*
youth hostel	*ifjúsági szálló*
camping ground	*kemping*
private room	*fizetővendég szoba*

Signs

BEJÁRAT	ENTRANCE
KIJÁRAT	EXIT
INFORMÁCIÓ/ FELVILÁGOSÍTÁS	INFORMATION
NYITVA/ZÁRVA	OPEN/CLOSED
TILOS	PROHIBITED
RENDŐRŐR-KAPITÁNYSÁG	POLICE STATION
TELEFON	TELEPHONE
TOALETT/WC	TOILETS
FÉRFI	MEN
NŐI	WOMEN

Emergencies

Help!	Segítség!
Call a doctor!	Hívjon egy orvost!
Call an ambulance!	Hívjon mentőket!
Call the police!	Hívjon rendőrt!
Go away!	Menjen el!
I'm lost.	Eltévedtem.

Do you have rooms available?	Van szabad szobájuk?
How much is it?	Mibe kerül?
Does it include breakfast?	Az ár tartalmazza a reggelit?
single room	egyágyas szoba
double room	kétágyas szoba

Time, Days & Numbers

What time is it?	Hány óra?
today	ma
tonight	ma este
tomorrow	holnap
yesterday	tegnap
in the morning	reggel
in the evening	este
Monday	hétfő
Tuesday	kedd
Wednesday	szerda
Thursday	csütörtök
Friday	péntek
Saturday	szombat
Sunday	vasárnap

1	egy
2	kettő
3	három
4	négy
5	öt
6	hat
7	hét
8	nyolc
9	kilenc
10	tíz
100	száz
1000	ezer
one million	millió

Macedonian

Pronunciation

The spelling of Macedonian is more or less phonetic: almost every word is written exactly the way it's pronounced and every letter is pronounced. With regard to the position of word stress, only one rule can be given: the last syllable of a word is never stressed. There are 31 letters in the Cyrillic alphabet.

Basics

Hello.
Zdravo.   Здраво.
Goodbye.
Prijatno.   Пријатно.

The Cyrillic Alphabet

Cyrillic	Roman	Pronunciation
А а	a	as in 'rather'
Б б	b	as in 'be'
В в	v	as in 'vodka'
Г г	g	as in 'go'
Д д	d	as in 'do'
Ѓ ѓ	gj	as the 'gu' in 'legume'
Е е	e	as the 'e' in 'bear'
Ж ж	zh	as the 's' in 'pleasure'
З з	z	as in 'zero'
Ѕ ѕ	zj	as the 'ds' in suds
И и	i	as the 'i' in 'machine'
Ј ј	j	as the 'y' in 'young'
К к	k	as in 'keg'
Л л	l	as in 'let'
Љ љ	lj	as the 'lli' in 'million'
М м	m	as in 'map'
Н н	n	as in 'no'
Њ њ	nj	as the 'ny' in 'canyon'
О о	o	as the 'aw' in 'shawl'
П п	p	as in 'pop'
Р р	r	as in 'rock'
С с	s	as in 'safe'
Т т	t	as in 'too'
Ќ ќ	ć	as the 'cu' in 'cure'
У у	u	as the 'oo' in 'room'
Ф ф	f	as in 'fat'
Х х	h	as in 'hot'
Ц ц	c	as the 'ts' in 'cats'
Ч ч	č	as the 'ch' in 'chop'
Џ џ	dz	as the 'j' in 'judge'
Ш ш	š	as the 'sh' in 'shoe'

Yes/No.
Da/Ne. Да/Не.
Please.
Molam. Молам.
Thank you.
Blagodaram. Благодарам.
You're welcome.
Nema zošto/ Нема зошто/
Milo mi e. Мило ми е.
Excuse me.
Izvinete. Извинете.
Sorry. (forgive me)
Prostete ve Простете ве молам.
molam.

Do you speak
English?
Zboruvate li Зборувате ли
angliski? англиски?
What's your name?
Kako se vikate? Како се викате?
My name is ...
Jas se vikam ... Јас се викам ...
How much is it?
Kolku čini toa? Колку чини тоа?

Getting Around
What time does
the ... leave/arrive?
Koga zaminuva/ Кога заминува/
doagja ...? доаѓа ...?

boat
brod брод
bus (city)
avtobus (gradski) автобус (градски)
bus (intercity)
avtobus автобус
(megjugradski) (меѓуградски)
train
voz воз
tram
tramvaj трамвај

I'd like ...
Sakam ... Сакам ...
a one-way ticket
bilet vo eden билет во еден правец
pravec
a return ticket
povraten bilet повратен билет
1st/2nd class
prva/vtora klasa прва/втора класа

ENTRANCE
  ВЛЕЗ
  VLEZ
EXIT
  ИЗЛЕЗ
  IZLEZ
FULL/NO VACANCIES
  ПОЛНО/НЕМА МЕСТО
  POLNO/NEMA MESTO
INFORMATION
  ИНФОРМАЦИИ
  INFORMACII
OPEN/CLOSED
  ОТВОРЕНО/ЗАТВОРЕНО
  OTVORENO/ZATVORENO
POLICE
  ПОЛИЦИЈА
  POLICIJA
POLICE STATION
  ПОЛИЦИСКА СТАНИЦА
  POLICISKA STANICA
PROHIBITED
  ЗАБРАНЕТО
  ZABRANETO
ROOMS AVAILABLE
  СОБИ ЗА ИЗДАВАЊЕ
  SOBI ZA IZDAVANJE
TOILETS (MEN/WOMEN)
  КЛОЗЕТИ (МАШКИ/ЖЕНСКИ)
  KLOZETI (MAŠKI/ENSKI)

timetable
vozen red возен ред
bus stop
avtobuska stanica автобуска станица
train station
železnička stanica железничка станица

Where is ...?
Kade e ...? Каде е ...?
Go straight ahead.
Odete pravo Одете право напред.
napred.
Turn left/right.
Svrtete levo/desno. Свртете лево/десно.
near
blisku блиску
far
daleku далеку

I'd like to hire a car/bicycle.
Sakam da iznajmam kola/točak.
Сакам да изнајмам кола/точак.

Around Town
bank
  banka   банка
chemist/pharmacy
  apteka   аптека
the embassy
  ambasadata   амбасадата
my hotel
  mojot hotel   мојот хотел
the market
  pazarot   пазарот
newsagency/
stationers
  kiosk za vesnici/ киоск за весници/
  knižarnica   книжарница
the post office
  poštata   поштата
the telephone centre
  telefonskata   телефонската
  centrala   централа
the tourist office
  turističkoto biro туристичкото биро

What time does it
open/close?
  Koga se otvora/ Кога се отвора/
  zatvora?   затвора?

Accommodation
Do you have any rooms available?
  Dali imate slobodni sobi?
  Дали имате слободни соби?
How much is it per night/per person?
  Koja e cenata po noć/po osoba?
  Која е цената по нок/по особа?
Does it include breakfast?
  Dali e vključen pojadok?
  Дали е вкључен појадок?

a single room
  soba so eden krevet
  соба со еден кревет
a double room
  soba so bračen krevet
  соба со брачен кревет
for one/two nights
  za edna/dva večeri
  за една/два вечери

hotel
  hotel
  хотел
guesthouse
  privatno smestuvanje
  приватно сместување
youth hostel
  mladinsko prenokevalište
  младинско преноќевалиште
camping ground
  kamping
  кампинг

Time, Days & Numbers
What time is it?
  Kolku e časot?
  Колку е часот?

today	*denes*	денес
tomorrow	*utre*	утре
yesterday	*včera*	вчера
morning	*utro*	утро
afternoon	*popladne*	попладне
Monday	*ponedelnik*	понеделник
Tuesday	*vtornik*	вторник
Wednesday	*sreda*	среда
Thursday	*četvrtok*	четврток
Friday	*petok*	петок
Saturday	*sabota*	сабота
Sunday	*nedela*	недела
1	*eden*	еден
2	*dva*	два
3	*tri*	три
4	*četiri*	четири
5	*pet*	пет
6	*šest*	шест

Emergencies

Help!	
Pomoš!	Помош!
Call a doctor!	
Povikajte lekar!	Повикајте лекар!
Call the police!	
Viknete policija!	Викнете полиција!
Go away!	
Odete si!	Одете си!
I'm lost.	
Jas se zagubiv.	Јас се загубив.

7	*sedum*	седум
8	*osum*	осум
9	*devet*	девет
10	*deset*	десет
100	*sto*	сто
one million	*eden milion*	еден милион

Polish

Pronunciation

Written Polish is phonetically consistent, which means that the pronunciation of letters or clusters of letters doesn't vary from word to word. The stress almost always goes on the second-last syllable.

Vowels

a   as the 'u' in 'cut'
e   as in 'ten'
i   similar to the 'ee' in 'feet' but shorter
o   as in 'lot'
u   a bit shorter than the 'oo' in 'book'
y   similar to the 'i' in 'bit'

There are three vowels unique to Polish:

ą   a nasal vowel sound like the French *un*, similar to 'own' in 'sown'
ę   also nasalised, like the French *un*, but pronounced as **e** when word-final
ó   similar to Polish **u**

Consonants

In Polish, the consonants **b, d, f, k, l, m, n, p, t, v** and **z** are pronounced more or less as they are in English. The following consonants and clusters of consonants sound distinctly different to their English counterparts:

c   as the 'ts' in 'its'
ch   similar to the 'ch' in the Scottish *loch*
cz   as the 'ch' in 'church'
ć   much softer than Polish **c** (as 'tsi' before vowels)
dz   similar to the 'ds' in 'suds' but shorter
dź   as **dz** but softer (as 'dzi' before vowels)
dż   as the 'j' in 'jam'
g   as in 'get'
h   as **ch**

j   as the 'y' in 'yet'
ł   as the 'w' in 'wine'
ń   as the 'ny' in 'canyon' (as 'ni' before vowels)
r   always trilled
rz   as the 's' in 'pleasure'
s   as in 'set'
sz   as the 'sh' in 'show'
ś   as **s** but softer (as 'si' before vowels)
w   as the 'v' in 'van'
ź   softer version of **z** (as 'zi' before vowels)
ż   as **rz**

Basics

Hello. (informal)	*Cześć.*
Hello/	*Dzień dobry.*
Good morning.	
Goodbye.	*Do widzenia.*
Yes/No.	*Tak/Nie.*
Please.	*Proszę.*
Thank you.	*Dziękuję.*
Excuse me/	*Przepraszam.*
Forgive me.	
I don't understand.	*Nie rozumiem.*
What is it called?	*Jak to się nazywa?*
How much is it?	*Ile to kosztuje?*

Getting Around

What time does	*O której godzinie*
the ... leave/arrive?	*przychodzi/odchodzi ...?*
plane	*samolot*
boat	*statek*
bus	*autobus*
train	*pociąg*
tram	*tramwaj*

arrival	*przyjazd*
departure	*odjazd*
timetable	*rozkład jazdy*

Where is the	*Gdzie jest przystanek*
bus stop?	*autobusowy?*
Where is the	*Gdzie jest stacja*
station?	*kolejowa?*
Where is the left-	*Gdzie jest przecho-*
luggage room?	*walnia bagażu?*
Please show me	*Proszę pokazać mi*
on the map.	*to na mapie.*
left	*lewo*
right	*prawo*
straight ahead	*prosto*

LANGUAGE

Signs

WEJĄCIE	ENTRANCE
WYJĄCIE	EXIT
INFORMACJA	INFORMATION
OTWARTE	OPEN
ZAMKNIETE	CLOSED
WZBRONIONY	PROHIBITED
POSTERUNEK POLICJI	POLICE STATION
TOALETY	TOILETS
PANOWIE	MEN
PANIE	WOMEN

Around Town

the bank	bank
the chemist	apteka
the church	kościół
the city centre	centrum miasta
the market	targ/bazar
the museum	muzeum
the post office	poczta
the tourist office	informacja turystyczna

Accommodation

hotel	hotel
youth hostel	schronisko młodzieżowe
camping ground	kemping
private room	kwatera prywatna

Do you have any rooms available?	Czy są wolne pokoje?
How much is it?	Ile to kosztuje?
Does it include breakfast?	Czy śniadanie jest wliczone?

single room	pokój jednoosobowy
double room	pokój dwuosobowy

Emergencies

Help!	Pomocy!/Ratunku!
Call a doctor!	Proszę wezwać lekarza!
Call the police!	Proszę wezwać policję!
I'm lost.	Zgubiłem się. (m) Zgubiłam się. (f)

Time, Days & Numbers

What time is it?	Która jest godzina?
today	dzisiaj
tonight	dzisiaj wieczorem
tomorrow	jutro
yesterday	wczoraj
in the morning	rano
in the evening	wieczorem

Monday	poniedziałek
Tuesday	wtorek
Wednesday	środa
Thursday	czwartek
Friday	piątek
Saturday	sobota
Sunday	niedziela

1	jeden
2	dwa
3	trzy
4	cztery
5	pięć
6	sześć
7	siedem
8	osiem
9	dziewięć
10	dziesięć
20	dwadzieścia
100	sto
1000	tysiąc
one million	milion

Romanian

Pronunciation

Until the mid-19th century, Romanian was written in the Cyrillic script. Today Romanian employs 28 Latin letters, some of which bear accents. It's spelt phonetically, so once you learn a few simple rules you'll be able to read aloud the expressions that follow. Vowels without accents are pronounced as they are in Spanish or Italian. In Romanian there are no long and short vowels, but e, i, o and u can form a diphthong or triphthong with adjacent vowels. At the beginning of a word, e and i are pronounced 'ye' and 'yi', while at the end of a word i is almost silent. At the end of a word ii is pronounced 'ee'. The stress is usually on the penultimate syllable.

LANGUAGE

ă	as the 'a' in 'bare'
â	as the 'i' in 'river'
c	as 'k'
c	as 'ch' before 'e' and 'i'
ch	as 'k' before 'e' and 'i'
g	as in 'go'
g	as in 'gentle' before 'e' and 'i'
gh	as the 'g' in 'good'
î	as the 'i' in 'river'
ş	as 'sh'
ţ	as the 'tz' in 'tzar'

Basics

Hello.	Bună.
Goodbye.	La revedere.
Yes.	Da.
No.	Nu.
Please.	Vă rog.
Thank you.	Mulţumesc.
Sorry. (forgive me)	Iertaţi-mă.
Excuse me.	Scuzaţi-mă.
I don't understand.	Nu înţeleg.
What is it called?	Cum se cheamă?
How much is it?	Cît costă?

Getting Around

What time does	La ce oră
the ... leave/arrive?	pleacă/soseşte ...?
plane	avionul
boat	vaporul
bus (city/intercity)	autobusul
train	trenul
tram	tramvaiul
arrival	sosire
departure	plecare
timetable	mersul/orar

Signs

INTRARE	ENTRANCE
IEŞIRE	EXIT
INFORMAŢII	INFORMATION
DESCHIS	OPEN
ÎNCHIS	CLOSED
NU INTRAŢI	NO ENTRY
STAŢIE DE POLIŢIE	POLICE STATION
TOALETA	TOILETS

Where is the bus stop?	Unde este staţia de autobuz?
Where is the station?	Unde este gară?
Where is the left-luggage room?	Unde este biroul pentru bagaje de mînă?
Please show me on the map.	Vă rog arătaţi-mi pe hartă.

left	stînga
right	dreapta
straight ahead	drept înainte

Around Town

the bank	banca
the chemist	farmacistul
the church	biserica
the city centre	centrum oraşului
the ... embassy	ambasada ...
the market	piaţa
the museum	muzeu
the post office	poşta
the tourist office	birou de informatii turistice

Accommodation

hotel	hotel
guesthouse	casa de oaspeţi
youth hostel	camin studentesc
camping ground	camping
private room	cameră particulară
Do you have any rooms available?	Aveţi camere libere?
How much is it?	Cît costă?
Does it include breakfast?	Include micul dejun?
single room	o cameră pentru o persoană
double room	o cameră pentru două persoane

Time, Days & Numbers

What time is it?	Ce oră este?
today	azi
tonight	deseară
tomorrow	mîine
yesterday	ieri
in the morning	dimineaţa
in the evening	seară

Emergencies

Help!	Ajutor!
Call a doctor!	Chemaţi un doctor!
Call the police!	Chemaţi poliţia!
Go away!	Du-te!/Pleacă!
I'm lost.	Sînt pierdut.

Monday	luni
Tuesday	marţi
Wednesday	miercuri
Thursday	joi
Friday	vineri
Saturday	sîmbătă
Sunday	duminică

1	unu
2	doi
3	trei
4	patru
5	cinci
6	şase
7	şapte
8	opt
9	nouă
10	zece
100	o sută
1000	o mie
one million	milion

Slovak

Pronunciation

The 43 letters of the Slovak alphabet have similar pronunciation to those of Czech. In words of three syllables or less the stress falls on the first syllable. Longer words generally also have a secondary accent on the 3rd or 5th syllable. There are thirteen vowels (a, á, ä, e, é, i, í, o, ó, u, ú, y, ÿ), three semi-vowels (l, ľ, r) and five diphthongs (ia, ie, iu, ou, ô). Letters and diphthongs which may be unfamiliar to native English speakers include the following:

c	as the 'ts' in 'its'
č	as the 'ch' in 'church'
dz	as the 'ds' in 'suds'
dž	as the 'j' in 'judge'

ia	as the 'yo' in 'yonder'
ie	as the 'ye' in 'yes'
iu	as the word 'you'
j	as the 'y' in 'yet'
ň	as the 'ni' in 'onion'
ô	as the 'wo' in 'won't'
ou	as the 'ow' in 'know'
š	as the 'sh' in 'show'
y	as the 'i' in 'machine'
ž	as the 'z' in 'azure'

Basics

Hello.	Ahoj.
Goodbye.	Dovidenia.
Yes.	Áno.
No.	Nie.
Please.	Prosím.
Thank you.	D'akujem.
Excuse me/	Prepáčte mi/
Forgive me.	Odpuste mi.
I'm sorry.	Ospravedlňujem sa.

I don't understand.	Nerozumiem.
What is it called?	Ako sa do volá?
How much is it?	Koľko to stojí?

Getting Around

What time does the ... leave/arrive?	Kedy odchádza/ prichádza ...?
bus (city)	(mestský) autobus
bus (intercity)	(medzimestský) autobus
boat	loč
plane	lietadlo
train	vlak
tram	električka

Signs

VCHOD	ENTRANCE
VÝCHOD	EXIT
INFORMÁCIE	INFORMATION
OTVORENÉ	OPEN
ZATVORENÉ	CLOSED
ZAKÁZANÉ	PROHIBITED
POLÍCIA	POLICE STATION
TELEFÓN	TELEPHONE
ZÁCHODY/ WC/TOALETY	TOILETS

arrival	príchod
departure	odchod
timetable	cestovný poriadok
Where is the bus stop?	Kde je autobusová zastávka?
Where is the station?	Kde je vlaková stanica?
Where is the left-luggage room?	Kde je úschovňa batožín?
Please show me on the map.	Prosím, ukážte mi to na mape.
left	vľavo
right	vpravo
straight ahead	rovno

Around Town

the bank	banka
the chemist	lekárnik
the church	kostol
the city centre	stred (centrum) mesta
the market	trh
the museum	múzeum
the post office	pošta
the telephone centre	telefónnu centrálu
the tourist office	turistické informačné centrum

Accommodation

hotel	hotel
guesthouse	penzion
youth hostel	mládežnícka ubytovňa
camping ground	kemping
private room	privat
Do you have any rooms available?	Máte voľné izby?
How much is it?	Koľko to stojí?
Does it include breakfast?	Sú raňajky zahrnuté v cene?
single room	jednolôžková izba
double room	dvojlôžková izba

Time, Days & Numbers

What time is it?	Koľko je hodín?
today	dnes
tonight	dnes večer
tomorrow	zajtra
yesterday	včera
in the morning	ráno
in the evening	večer

Monday	pondelok
Tuesday	utorok
Wednesday	streda
Thursday	štvrtok
Friday	piatok
Saturday	sobota
Sunday	nedeľa

1	jeden
2	dva
3	tri
4	štyri
5	päť
6	sedem
8	osem
9	deväť
10	desať
100	sto
1000	tisíc
one million	milión

Slovene

Pronunciation

Slovene pronunciation isn't difficult. The alphabet consists of 25 letters, most of which are very similar to English. It doesn't have the letters 'q', 'w', 'x' and 'y', but the letters ê, é, ó, ò, č, š and ž are added. Each letter represents only one sound, with very few exceptions. The letters l and v are both pronounced like the English 'w' when they occur at the end of syllables and before vowels. Though words like trn (thorn) look unpronounceable, most Slovenes would add a short vowel before the 'r' to give a Scot's pronunciation of 'tern' or 'tarn'. Here is a list of letters specific to Slovene.

c   as the 'ts' in 'its'
č   as the 'ch' in 'church'
ê   as the 'a' in 'apple'
e   as the 'er' in 'opera' (when unstressed)
é   as the 'ay' in 'day'
j   as the 'y' in 'yellow'
ó   as the 'o' in 'more'
ò   as the 'o' in 'soft'
r   a rolled 'r' sound
š   as the 'sh' in 'ship'
u   as the 'oo' in 'good'
ž   as the 's' in 'treasure'

Basics

Hello.	Zdravo/Živio. (inf)
Good day.	Dober dan!
Goodbye.	Nasvidenje!
Yes/No.	Ja/Ne.
Please.	Prosim.
Thank you.	Hvala.
You're welcome.	Prosim/Ni za kaj!
Excuse me.	Oprostite.
My name is ...	Moje ime je ...
Where are you from?	Od kod ste?
I'm from ...	Sem iz ...

Getting Around

What time does ... leave/arrive?	Ob kateri uri ... odpelje/pripelge?
boat/ferry	ladja/trajekt
bus/tram	avtobus/tramvaj
train	vlak
one-way (ticket)	enosmerna (vozovnica)
return (ticket)	povratna (vozovnica)

Around Town

bank/exchange	banka/menjalnica
embassy	konzulat, ambasada

Emergencies

Help!	Na pomoč!
Call a doctor!	Pokličite zdravnika!
Call the police!	Pokličite policijo!
Go away!	Pojdite stran!

post office	pošta
telephone centre	telefonska centrala
tourist office	turistični informacijski urad

Accommodation

hotel	hotel
guesthouse	gostišče
camping ground	kamping

Do you have a ...?	Ali imate prosto ...?
bed	posteljo
cheap room	poceni sobo
single room	enoposteljno sobo
double room	dvoposteljno sobo

for one/two nights	za eno noč/za dve noči

How much is it per night/per person?	Koliko stane na noč/ na osebo?

Time, Days & Numbers

today	danes
tonight	danes zvečer
tomorrow	jutri
in the morning	zjutraj
in the evening	zvečer

Monday	ponedeljek
Tuesday	torek
Wednesday	sreda
Thursday	četrtek
Friday	petek
Saturday	sobota
Sunday	nedelja

1	ena	7	sedem
2	dve	8	osem
3	tri	9	devet
4	štiri	10	deset
5	pet	100	sto
6	šest	1000	tisoč

one million   milijon

LONELY PLANET

Phrasebooks

onely Planet phrasebooks are packed with essential words and phrases to help travellers communicate with the locals. With colour tabs for quick reference, an extensive vocabulary, use of script, these handy pocket-sized language guides cover day-to-day travel situations.

- handy pocket-sized books
- easy to understand Pronunciation chapter
- clear & comprehensive Grammar chapter
- romanisation alongside script to allow ease of pronunciation
- script throughout so users can point to phrases for every situations
- full of cultural information and tips for the traveller

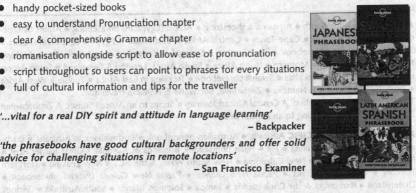

'...vital for a real DIY spirit and attitude in language learning'
– Backpacker

'the phrasebooks have good cultural backgrounders and offer solid advice for challenging situations in remote locations'
– San Francisco Examiner

Arabic (Egyptian) • Arabic (Moroccan) • Australia *(Australian English, Aboriginal and Torres Strait languages)* • Baltic States *(Estonian, Latvian, Lithuanian)* • Bengali • Brazilian • Burmese • Cantonese • Central Asia • Central Europe *(Czech, French, German, Hungarian, Italian and Slovak)* • Eastern Europe *(Bulgarian, Czech, Hungarian, Polish, Romanian and Slovak)* • Egyptian Arabic • Ethiopian (Amharic) • Fijian • French • German • Greek • Hill Tribes • Hindi/Urdu • Indonesian • Italian • Japanese • Korean • Lao • Malay • Mandarin • Mediterranean Europe *(Albanian, Croatian, Greek, Italian, Macedonian, Maltese, Serbian, Slovene)* • Mongolian • Nepali • Papua New Guinea • Pilipino (Tagalog) • Quechua • Russian • Scandinavian Europe *(Danish, Finnish, Icelandic, Norwegian and Swedish)* • South-East Asia *(Burmese, Indonesian, Khmer, Lao, Malay, Tagalog Pilipino, Thai and Vietnamese)* • Spanish (Castilian) *(Also includes Catalan, Galician and Basque)* • Spanish (Latin American) • Sri Lanka • Swahili • Thai • Tibetan • Turkish • Ukrainian • USA *(US English, Vernacular Talk, Native American languages and Hawaiian)* • Vietnamese • Western Europe *(Basque, Catalan, Dutch, French, German, Greek, Irish)*

LONELY PLANET

Guides by Region

Lonely Planet is known worldwide for publishing practical, reliable and no-nonsense travel information in our guides and on our web site. The Lonely Planet list covers just about every accessible part of the world. Currently there are nine series: travel guides, shoestring guides, walking guides, city guides, phrasebooks, audio packs, travel atlases, diving and snorkelling guides and travel literature.

AFRICA Africa – the South • Africa on a shoestring • Arabic (Egyptian) phrasebook • Arabic (Moroccan) phrasebook • Cairo • Cape Town • Central Africa • East Africa • Egypt • Egypt travel atlas • Ethiopian (Amharic) phrasebook • The Gambia & Senegal • Kenya • Kenya travel atlas • Malawi, Mozambique & Zambia • Morocco • North Africa • South Africa, Lesotho & Swaziland • South Africa, Lesotho & Swaziland travel atlas • Swahili phrasebook • Trekking in East Africa • Tunisia • West Africa • Zimbabwe, Botswana & Namibia • Zimbabwe, Botswana & Namibia travel atlas
Travel Literature: The Rainbird: A Central African Journey • Songs to an African Sunset: A Zimbabwean Story • Mali Blues: Travelling to an African Beat

AUSTRALIA & THE PACIFIC Australia • Australian phrasebook • Bushwalking in Australia • Bushwalking in Papua New Guinea • Fiji • Fijian phrasebook • Islands of Australia's Great Barrier Reef • Melbourne • Micronesia • New Caledonia • New South Wales & the ACT • New Zealand • Northern Territory • Outback Australia • Papua New Guinea • Papua New Guinea (Pidgin) phrasebook • Queensland • Rarotonga & the Cook Islands • Samoa • Solomon Islands • South Australia • Sydney • Tahiti & French Polynesia • Tasmania • Tonga • Tramping in New Zealand • Vanuatu • Victoria • Western Australia
Travel Literature: Islands in the Clouds • Sean & David's Long Drive

CENTRAL AMERICA & THE CARIBBEAN Bahamas and Turks & Caicos • Bermuda • Central America on a shoestring • Costa Rica • Cuba • Eastern Caribbean • Guatemala, Belize & Yucatan: La Ruta Maya • Jamaica • Mexico • Mexico City • Panama
Travel Literature: Green Dreams: Travels in Central America

EUROPE Amsterdam • Andalucia • Austria • Baltic States phrasebook • Berlin • Britain • Central Europe • Central Europe phrasebook • Czech & Slovak Republics • Denmark • Dublin • Eastern Europe • Eastern Europe phrasebook • Estonia, Latvia & Lithuania • Finland • France • French phrasebook • Germany • German phrasebook • Greece • Greek phrasebook • Hungary • Iceland, Greenland & the Faroe Islands • Ireland • Italian phrasebook • Italy • Lisbon • London • Mediterranean Europe • Mediterranean Europe phrasebook • Paris • Poland • Portugal • Portugal travel atlas • Prague • Romania & Moldova • Russia, Ukraine & Belarus • Russian phrasebook • Scandinavian & Baltic Europe • Scandinavian Europe phrasebook • Slovenia • Spain • Spanish phrasebook • St Petersburg • Switzerland • Trekking in Spain • Ukrainian phrasebook • Vienna • Walking in Britain • Walking in Italy • Walking in Switzerland • Western Europe • Western Europe phrasebook
Travel Literature: The Olive Grove: Travels in Greece

INDIAN SUBCONTINENT Bangladesh • Bengali phrasebook • Bhutan • Delhi • Goa • Hindi/Urdu phrasebook • India • India & Bangladesh travel atlas • Indian Himalaya • Karakoram Highway • Nepal • Nepali phrasebook • Pakistan • Rajasthan • South India • Sri Lanka • Sri Lanka phrasebook • Trekking in the Indian Himalaya • Trekking in the Karakoram & Hindukush • Trekking in the Nepal Himalaya
Travel Literature: In Rajasthan • Shopping for Buddhas

LONELY PLANET

Mail Order

Lonely Planet products are distributed worldwide. They are also available by mail order from Lonely Planet, so if you have difficulty finding a title please write to us. North and South American residents should write to Embarcadero West, 150 Linden St, Suite 251, Oakland CA 94607, USA; European and African residents should write to 10a Spring Place, London, NW5 3BH; and residents of other countries to PO Box 617, Hawthorn, Victoria 3122, Australia.

ISLANDS OF THE INDIAN OCEAN Madagascar & Comoros • Maldives • Mauritius, Reunion & Seychelles

MIDDLE EAST & CENTRAL ASIA Arab Gulf States • Central Asia • Iran • Israel & the Palestinian Territories • Israel & the Palestinian Territories travel atlas • Istanbul • Jerusalem • Jordan & Syria • Jordan, Syria & Lebanon travel atlas • Lebanon • Middle East on a shoestring • Turkey • Turkish phrasebook • Turkey travel atlas • Yemen
Travel Literature: The Gates of Damascus • Kingdom of the Film Stars: Journey into Jordan

NORTH AMERICA Alaska • Backpacking in Alaska • Baja California • California & Nevada • Canada • Florida • Hawaii • Honolulu • Los Angeles • Miami • New England USA • New Orleans • New York City • New York, New Jersey & Pennsylvania • Pacific Northwest USA • Rocky Mountain States • San Francisco • Seattle • Southwest USA • USA phrasebook • Washington, DC & the Capital Region
Travel Literature: Drive Thru America

NORTH-EAST ASIA Beijing • Cantonese phrasebook • China • Hong Kong • Hong Kong, Macau & Guangzhou • Japan • Japanese phrasebook • Japanese audio pack • Korea • Korean phrasebook • Kyoto • Mandarin phrasebook • Mongolia • Mongolian phrasebook • North-East Asia on a shoestring • Seoul • South West China • Taiwan • Tibet • Tibet phrasebook • Tokyo
Travel Literature: Lost Japan

SOUTH AMERICA Argentina, Uruguay & Paraguay • Bolivia • Brazil • Brazilian phrasebook • Buenos Aires • Chile & Easter Island • Chile & Easter Island travel atlas • Colombia • Ecuador & the Galapagos Islands • Latin American (Spanish) phrasebook • Peru • Quechua phrasebook • Rio de Janeiro • South America on a shoestring • Trekking in the Patagonian Andes • Venezuela
Travel Literature: Full Circle: A South American Journey

SOUTH-EAST ASIA Bali & Lombok • Bangkok • Burmese phrasebook • Cambodia • Ho Chi Minh City • Indonesia • Indonesian phrasebook • Indonesian audio pack • Jakarta • Java • Laos • Lao phrasebook • Laos travel atlas • Malay phrasebook • Malaysia, Singapore & Brunei • Myanmar (Burma) • Philippines • Pilipino (Tagalog) phrasebook • Singapore • South-East Asia on a shoestring • South-East Asia phrasebook • Thailand • Thailand's Islands & Beaches • Thailand travel atlas • Thai phrasebook • Thai audio pack • Thai Hill Tribes phrasebook • Vietnam • Vietnamese phrasebook • Vietnam travel atlas

ALSO AVAILABLE: Antarctica • Brief Encounters: Stories of Love, Sex & Travel • Chasing Rickshaws • Not the Only Planet: Travel Stories from Science Fiction • Travel with Children • Traveller's Tales

Index

Abbreviations

Bold indicates maps.

MAP LEGEND

BOUNDARIES

▬▪▬▪▬▪▬	International
▬▪▬▪▬▪▬	State
▬ ▬ ▬ ▬	Disputed

HYDROGRAPHY

	Coastline
	River, Creek
	Lake
	Intermittent Lake
	Salt Lake
	Canal
◎ ⤳	Spring, Rapids
⤳⧣	Waterfalls

✪	CAPITAL	National Capital
◉	CAPITAL	State Capital
●	CITY	City
●	Town	Town
●	Village	Village
○		Point of Interest
■		Place to Stay
▲		Camping Ground
⌂		Caravan Park
⌂		Hut or Chalet
▼		Place to Eat
▯		Pub or Bar

ROUTES & TRANSPORT

	Freeway
	Highway
	Major Road
	Minor Road
	Unsealed Road
	City Highway
	City Road
	City Street, Lane

	Pedestrian Mall
⇥═══┤	Tunnel
├─┼─●─	Train Route & Station
─●─Ⓜ─	Metro & Station
	Tramway
├─◆─┤	Cable Car or Chairlift
─ ─ ─ ─	Walking Track
─ ─ ─ ─	Ferry Route

AREA FEATURES

▨	Building	▨	Market
✿	Park, Gardens		Pedestrian Mall
+×+×+×	Cemetery	▬	Urban Area

MAP SYMBOLS

✈	Airport	⋔	Museum
⤳	Ancient or City Wall	←	One Way Street
∴	Archaeological Site	)(	Pass
⑤	Bank	★	Police Station
⚲	Beach	✉	Post Office
⚔	Border Crossing	◈	Shopping Centre
⛪	Castle or Fort	⛷	Ski field
⌒	Cave	⌂	Stately Home
⛪	Church	▭	Swimming Pool
⌒	Cliff or Escarpment	✡	Synagogue
⊘	Embassy	☎	Telephone
✛	Hospital	⛩	Temple
✳	Lookout	❶	Tourist Information
☪	Mosque	⊖	Transport
▲	Mountain or Hill	🐾	Zoo

Note: not all symbols displayed above appear in this book

LONELY PLANET OFFICES

Australia
PO Box 617, Hawthorn 3122, Victoria
tel: (03) 9819 1877 fax: (03) 9819 6459
e-mail: talk2us@lonelyplanet.com.au

USA
150 Linden St, Oakland, CA 94607
tel: (510) 893 8555 TOLL FREE: 800 275-8555
fax: (510) 893 8572
e-mail: info@lonelyplanet.com

UK
10a Spring Place, London, NW5 3BH
tel: (0171) 428 4800 fax: (0170) 428 4828
e-mail: go@lonelyplanet.co.uk

France
1 rue du Dahomey, 75011 Paris
tel: 01 55 25 33 00 fax: 01 55 25 33 01
e-mail: bip@lonelyplanet.fr

World Wide Web: www.lonelyplanet.com *or* **AOL keyword: lp**
Lonely Planet Images: lpi@lonelyplanet.com.au